A-Z HAMPS[HIRE]

C000178921

CONTENTS

Key to Map Pages	2-3
Large Scale Southampton	4
Large Scale Portsmouth	5
Map Pages	6-247
Large Scale W[inchester]	237
Large Scale Bournemouth	247
Index to Streets, Towns, Villages and selected Places of Interest	248-318
Index to Hospitals and Hospices	319-320

REFERENCE

Motorway	M27
A Road	A335
B Road	B3038
Dual Carriageway	
One-way Street Traffic flow on A Roads is indicated by a heavy line on the driver's left. Large Scale Pages Only	
Restricted Access	
Pedestrianized Road	
Track	
Footpath	
Residential Walkway	
Railway	Level Crossing, Station, Tunnel
Heritage Railway	Station
Built-up Area	HADRIAN WAY
Local Authority Boundary	
National Park Boundary	
Posttown Boundary	
Postcode Boundary Within Posttowns	

Map Continuation	16 · Small Scale Mapping 8 · Large Scale Mapping 4
Berth Number	101
Car Park Selected	P
Church or Chapel	†
Dock Gate Number	8
Fire Station	■
Hospital	H
House Numbers A & B Roads only	83 96
Information Centre	i
National Grid Reference	445
Police Station	▲
Post Office	★
Toilet With facilities for the Disabled	
Viewpoint	
Educational Establishment	
Hospital or Hospice	
Industrial Building	
Leisure or Recreational Facility	
Place of Interest	
Public Building	
Shopping Centre or Market	
Other Selected Buildings	

SCALES

Map Pages numbered in BLUE are 1:19,000
3⅓ inches to 1 mile

0 ¼ ½ ¾ 1 Mile
0 250 500 750 Metres 1 Kilometre
5.26 cm to 1 km — 8.47 cm to 1 Mile

Map Pages numbered in RED are 1:9,500
6⅔ inches to 1 mile

0 ⅛ ¼ Mile
0 250 500 Metres
10.52 cm to 1 km — 16.94 cm to 1 mile

Map Pages numbered in GREEN are 1:38,000
1⅔ inches to 1 mile

0 ¼ ½ ¾ 1 Mile
0 500 1 Kilometre
2.63 cm to 1 km — 4.23 cm to 1 mile

Head Office:
Fairfield Road, Borough Green, Sevenoaks, Kent TN15 8PP
Telephone: 01732 781000 (Enquiries & Trade Sales)
01732 783422 (Retail Sales)
www.a-zmaps.co.uk

Edition 1 2001 Edition 1b* 2004 (Part Revision)

KEY TO MAP PAGES

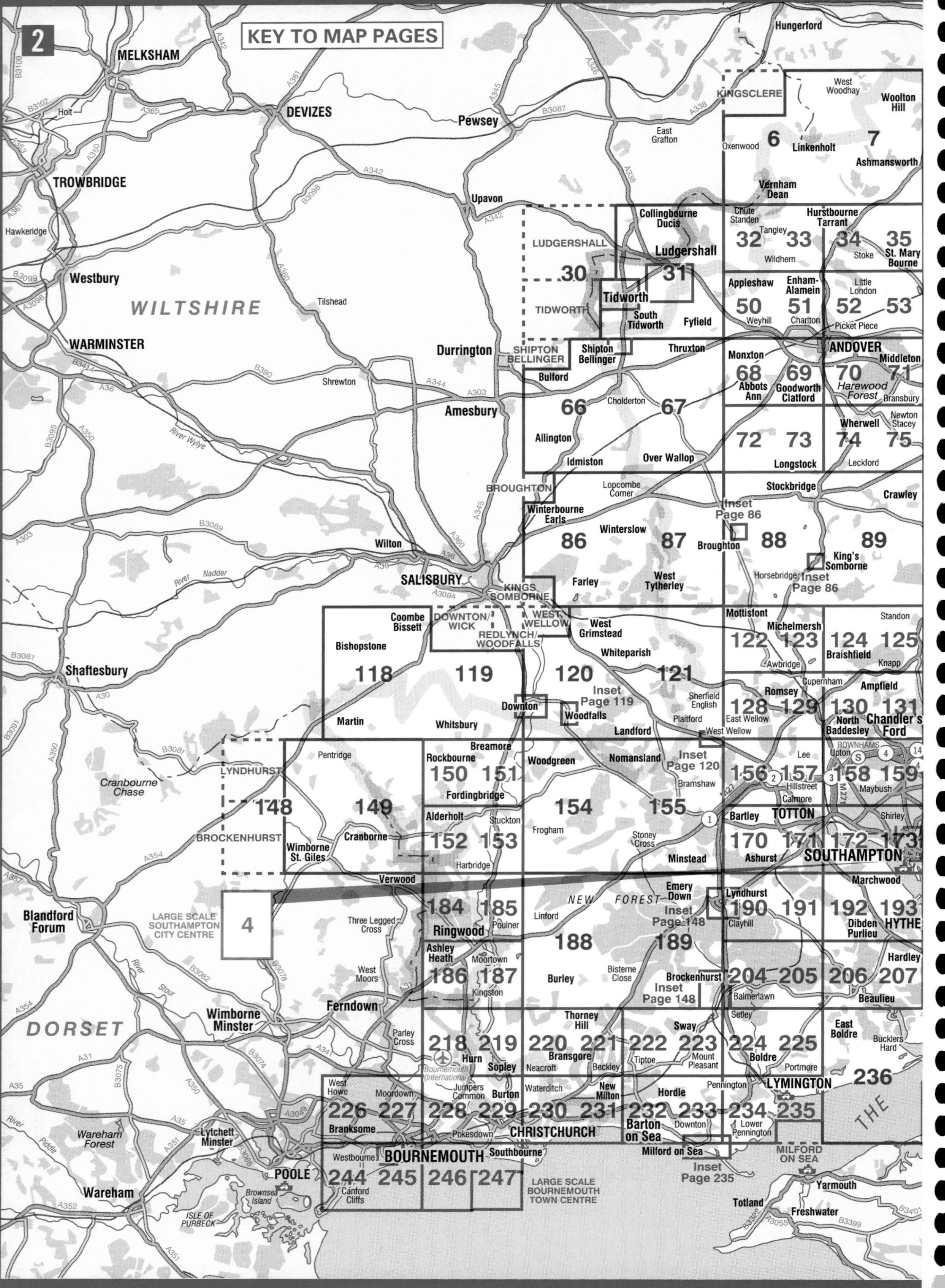

MELKSHAM
DEVIZES
Pewsey
Hungerford
TROWBRIDGE
Westbury
WILTSHIRE
WARMINSTER
Durrington
Amesbury
Wilton
SALISBURY
Shaftesbury
Cranbourne Chase
Blandford Forum
DORSET
Wimborne Minster
Ferndown
POOLE
Wareham
BOURNEMOUTH
CHRISTCHURCH
LYMINGTON
SOUTHAMPTON
ANDOVER
TOTTON
HYTHE
Ringwood
Tidworth
Ludgershall
Stockbridge
Romsey
Chandler's Ford
Lyndhurst
Brockenhurst
Fordingbridge
NEW FOREST
LARGE SCALE SOUTHAMPTON CITY CENTRE
LARGE SCALE BOURNEMOUTH TOWN CENTRE
Inset Page 86
Inset Page 119
Inset Page 120
Inset Page 148
Inset Page 235
Yarmouth
Freshwater
Totland
ISLE OF PURBECK
Brownsea Island

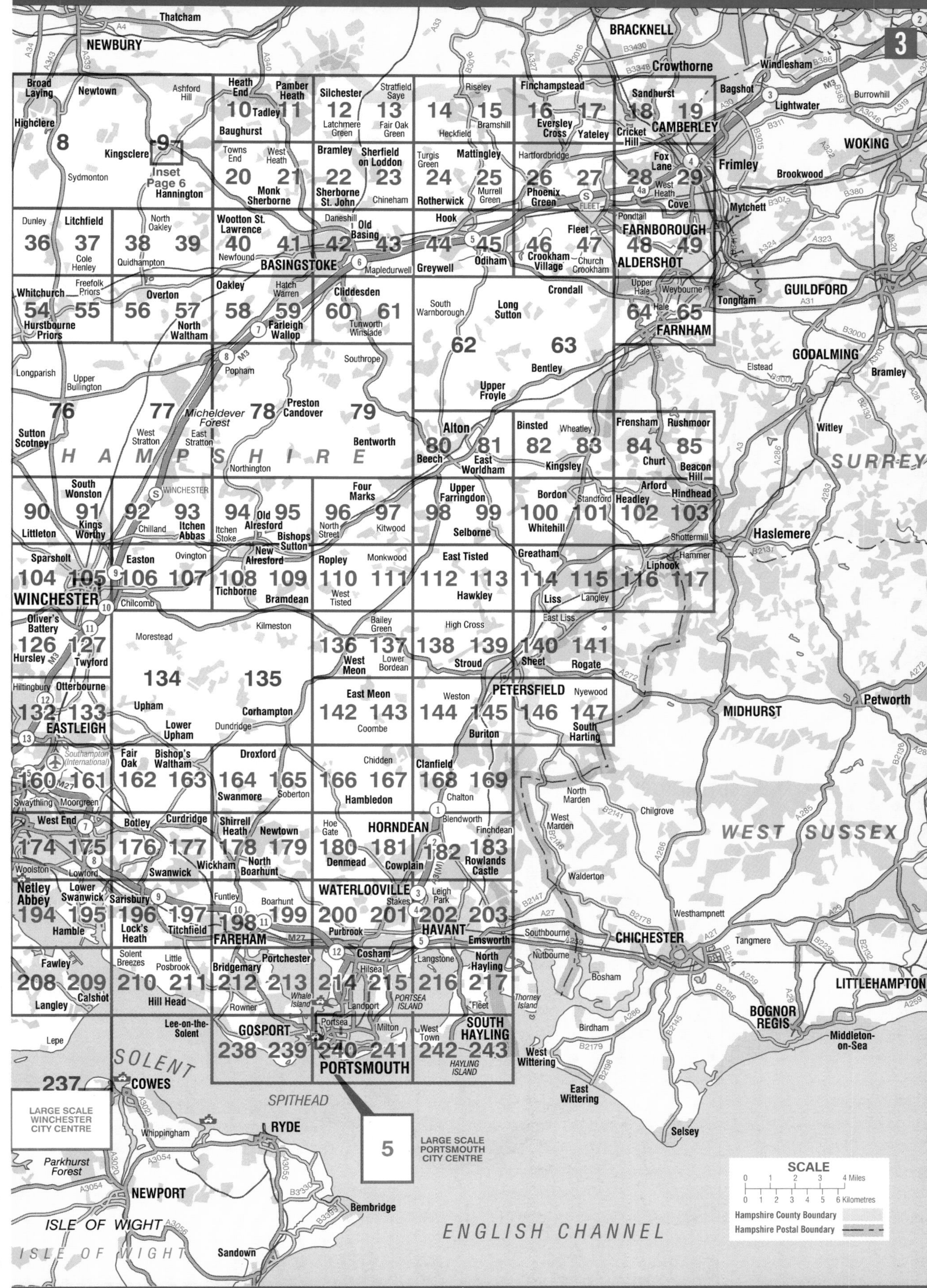

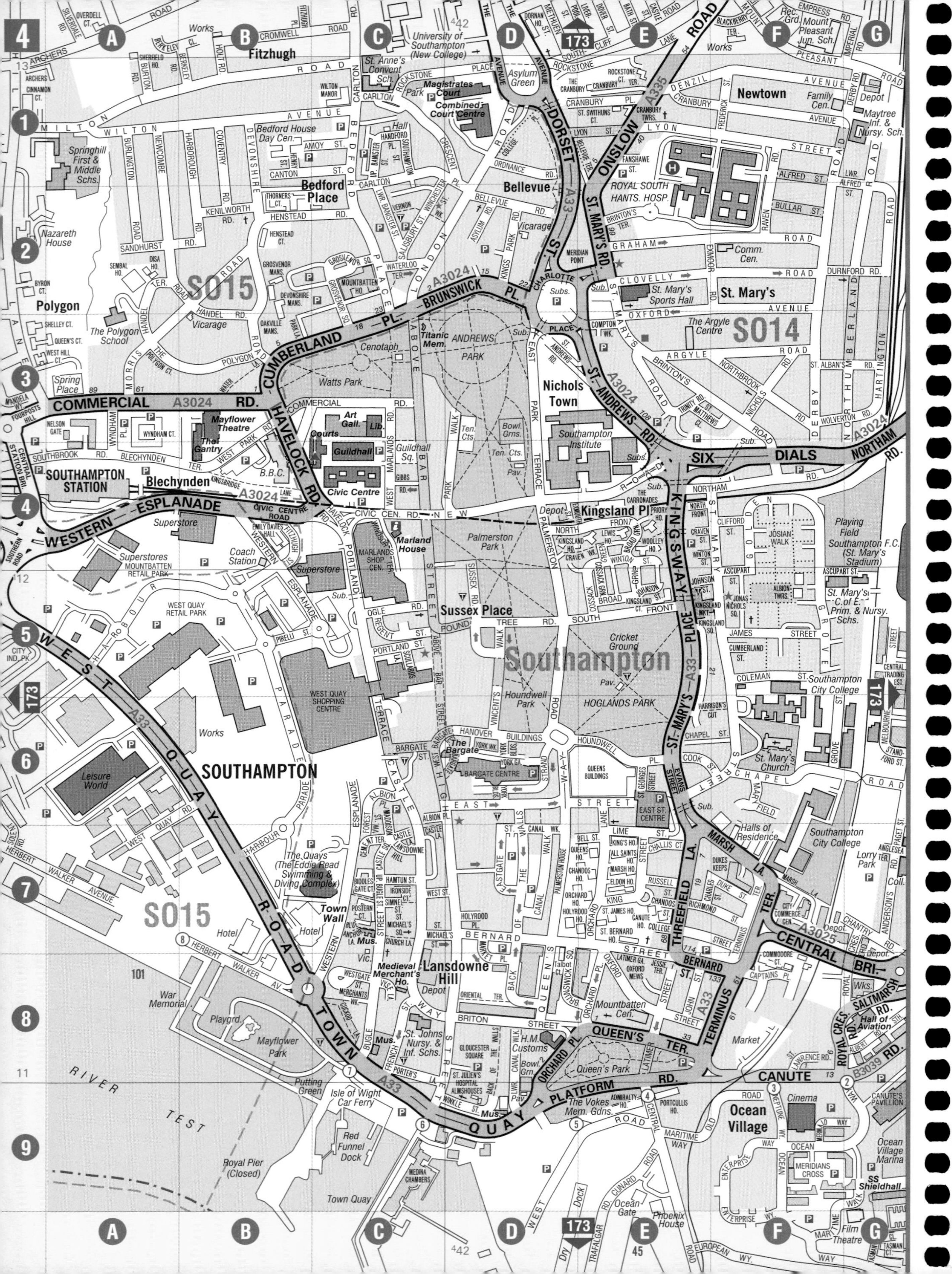

4
SOUTHAMPTON
Southampton
Polygon
Fitzhugh
Bedford Place
Bellevue
Newtown
St. Mary's
Nichols Town
Kingsland Pl.
Blechynden
Sussex Place
Lansdowne Hill
Ocean Village
SO15
SO14
University of Southampton (New College)
Royal South Hants. Hosp.
Southampton Station
Southampton Institute
Civic Centre
Guildhall
Art Gall.
Mayflower Theatre
Marlands Shop. Cen.
West Quay Shopping Centre
West Quay Retail Park
Leisure World
The Bargate
Bargate Centre
East St. Centre
Queens Buildings
Southampton City College
St. Mary's Church
Halls of Residence
Watts Park
Andrews Park
Palmerston Park
Houndwell Park
Hoglands Park
Queen's Park
Mayflower Park
Royal Pier (Closed)
Town Quay
Isle of Wight Car Ferry
Red Funnel Dock
Ocean Gate
Cinema
Canute's Pavilion
Ocean Village Marina
River Test
Commercial Rd.
Western Esplanade
West Quay Road
Town Quay
Platform Rd.
Canute Rd.
Central Bri.
Six Dials
Kingsway
St. Mary's Rd.
Dorset St.
Onslow Road
Cumberland Pl.
Havelock Rd.
Brunswick Pl.
St. Andrews Rd.
Terminus Ter.
Threefield La.
Above Bar Street
High Street
A3024
A33
A335
A3025
B3039
173
442
45

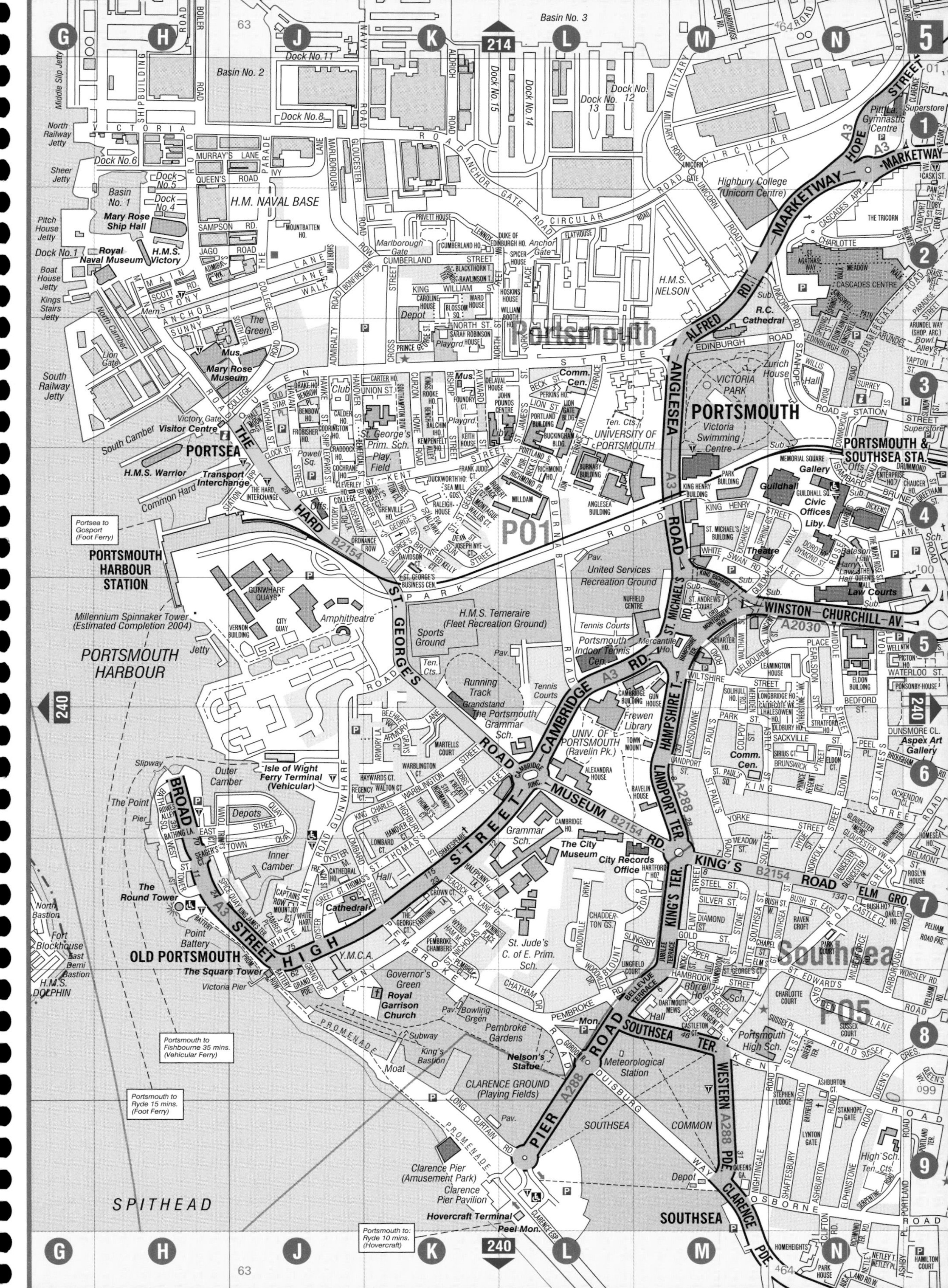

5
214
240
PORTSMOUTH HARBOUR
PORTSMOUTH HARBOUR STATION
PORTSEA
OLD PORTSMOUTH
PORTSMOUTH
Southsea
SOUTHSEA
SPITHEAD
H.M. NAVAL BASE
Mary Rose Ship Hall
Royal Naval Museum
H.M.S. Victory
Mary Rose Museum
H.M.S. Warrior
Visitor Centre
Transport Interchange
Gunwharf Quays
Millennium Spinnaker Tower (Estimated Completion 2004)
Isle of Wight Ferry Terminal (Vehicular)
Cathedral
The Round Tower
The Square Tower
Royal Garrison Church
Nelson's Statue
Hovercraft Terminal
Clarence Pier (Amusement Park)
Clarence Pier Pavilion
CLARENCE GROUND (Playing Fields)
Meteorological Station
The City Museum
City Records Office
UNIVERSITY OF PORTSMOUTH
Guildhall
Civic Offices
Law Courts
PORTSMOUTH & SOUTHSEA STA.
Cascades Centre
R.C. Cathedral
H.M.S. NELSON
Highbury College (Unicorn Centre)
United Services Recreation Ground
H.M.S. Temeraire (Fleet Recreation Ground)
Victoria Park
Aspex Art Gallery
Portsea to Gosport (Foot Ferry)
Portsmouth to Fishbourne 35 mins. (Vehicular Ferry)
Portsmouth to Ryde 15 mins. (Foot Ferry)
Portsmouth to: Ryde 10 mins. (Hovercraft)

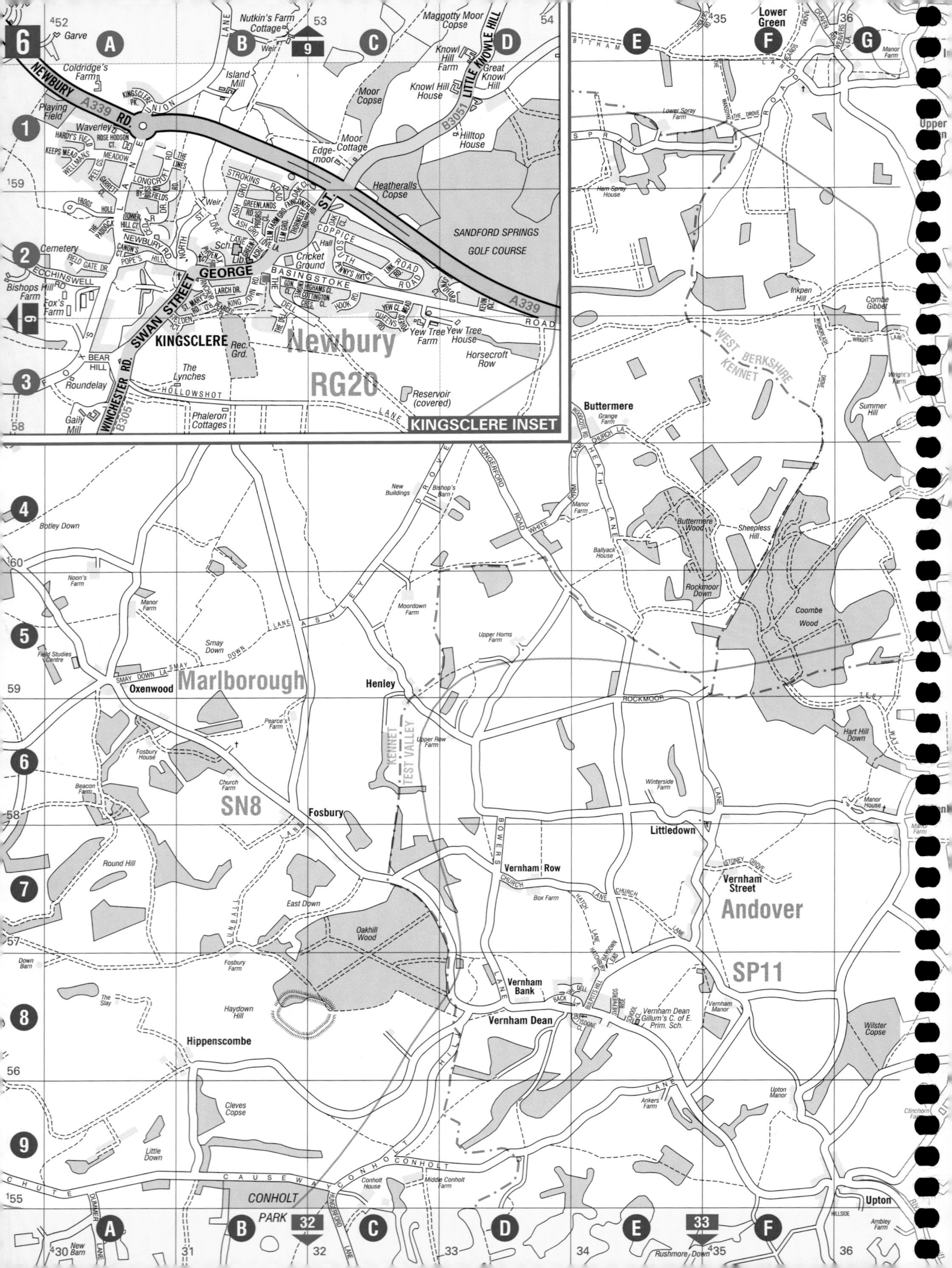
6
KINGSCLERE INSET
Kingsclere
Newbury
RG20
Sandford Springs
Golf Course
Heatheralls Copse
Moor Copse
Moor Cottage
Edgemoor
Island Mill
Nutkin's Farm Cottage
Maggotty Moor Copse
Knowl Hill Farm
Knowl Hill House
Great Knowl Hill
Hilltop House
Coldridge's Farm
Playing Field
Waverley
Cemetery
Bishops Hill Farm
Fox's Farm
Roundelay
Gaily Mill
The Lynches
Phaleron Cottages
Rec. Grd.
Cricket Ground
Yew Tree Farm
Yew Tree House
Horsecroft Row
Reservoir (covered)
Garve
Buttermere
Marlborough
SN8
Andover
SP11
Oxenwood
Henley
Fosbury
Vernham Row
Vernham Street
Littledown
Vernham Bank
Vernham Dean
Hippenscombe
Conholt Park
Upton
Lower Green
Botley Down
Noon's Farm
Manor Farm
Smay Down
Field Studies Centre
Pearce's Farm
Fosbury House
Church Farm
Beacon Farm
Round Hill
East Down
Oakhill Wood
Fosbury Farm
Down Barn
The Slay
Haydown Hill
Cleves Copse
Little Down
New Barn
Conholt House
Middle Conholt Farm
Rushmore Down
Ankers Farm
Upton Manor
Wilster Copse
Vernham Manor
Vernham Dean Gillum's C. of E. Prim. Sch.
Box Farm
Winterside Farm
Upper Row Farm
Upper Horns Farm
Moordown Farm
New Buildings
Bishop's Barn
Ballyack House
Buttermere Wood
Rockmoor Down
Sheepless Hill
Coombe Wood
Hart Hill Down
Manor House
Summer Hill
Wright's Farm
Combe Gibbet
Inkpen Hill
Lower Spray Farm
Ham Spray House
Grange Farm
Manor Farm
West Berkshire
Kennet
Test Valley
9
32
33

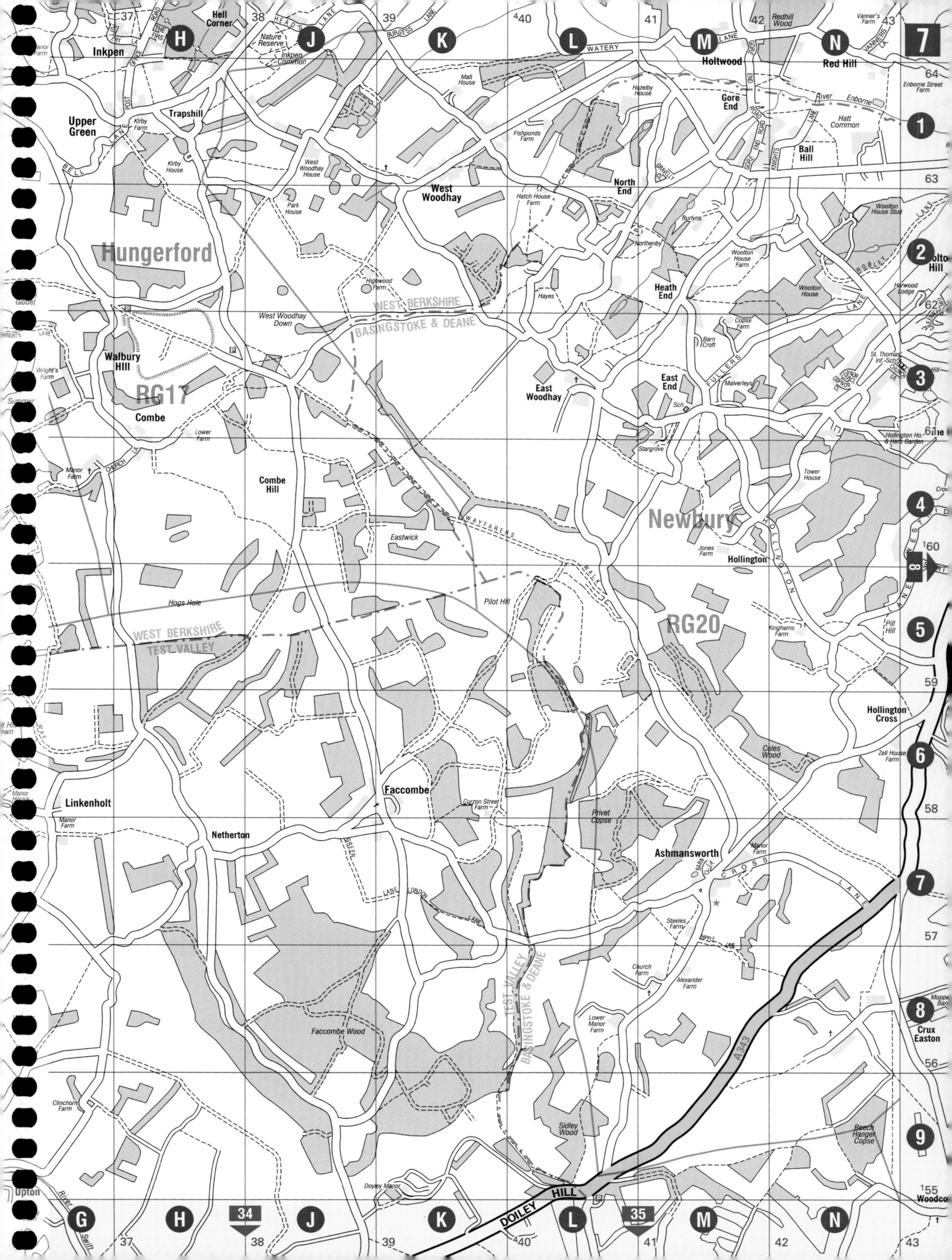
7
Inkpen
Hell Corner
Nature Reserve
Inkpen Common
Upper Green
Trapshill
Kirby Farm
Kirby House
West Woodhay House
West Woodhay
Park House
Hungerford
Malt House
Fishponds Farm
Hazelby House
Holtwood
Red Hill
Gore End
Hatt Common
Ball Hill
North End
Hatch House Farm
Northenby
Burlyns
Woolton House Stud
Woolton House Farm
Woolton House
Heath End
Harwood Lodge
Highwood Farm
Hayes
West Woodhay Down
WEST BERKSHIRE
BASINGSTOKE & DEANE
Walbury Hill
RG17
Combe
Lower Farm
Manor Farm
Wright's Farm
East Woodhay
East End
Copse Farm
Barn Croft
Malverleys
St. Thomas' Inf. Sch.
Stargrove
Hollington Ho. & Herb Garden
Combe Hill
Eastwick
Tower House
Newbury
Jones Farm
Hollington
WAYFARERS WALK
Hogs Hole
Pilot Hill
RG20
Kinghams Farm
Pill Hill
TEST VALLEY
Hollington Cross
Coles Wood
Zell House Farm
Linkenholt
Faccombe
Curzon Street Farm
Privet Copse
Netherton
Ashmansworth
Manor Farm
Steeles Farm
Church Farm
Alexander Farm
Lower Manor Farm
Faccombe Wood
A343
Crux Easton
Clinchorn Farm
Sidley Wood
Beech Hanger Copse
Doyley Manor
DOILEY HILL
Upton
River Swift
Woodcott
34
35
8

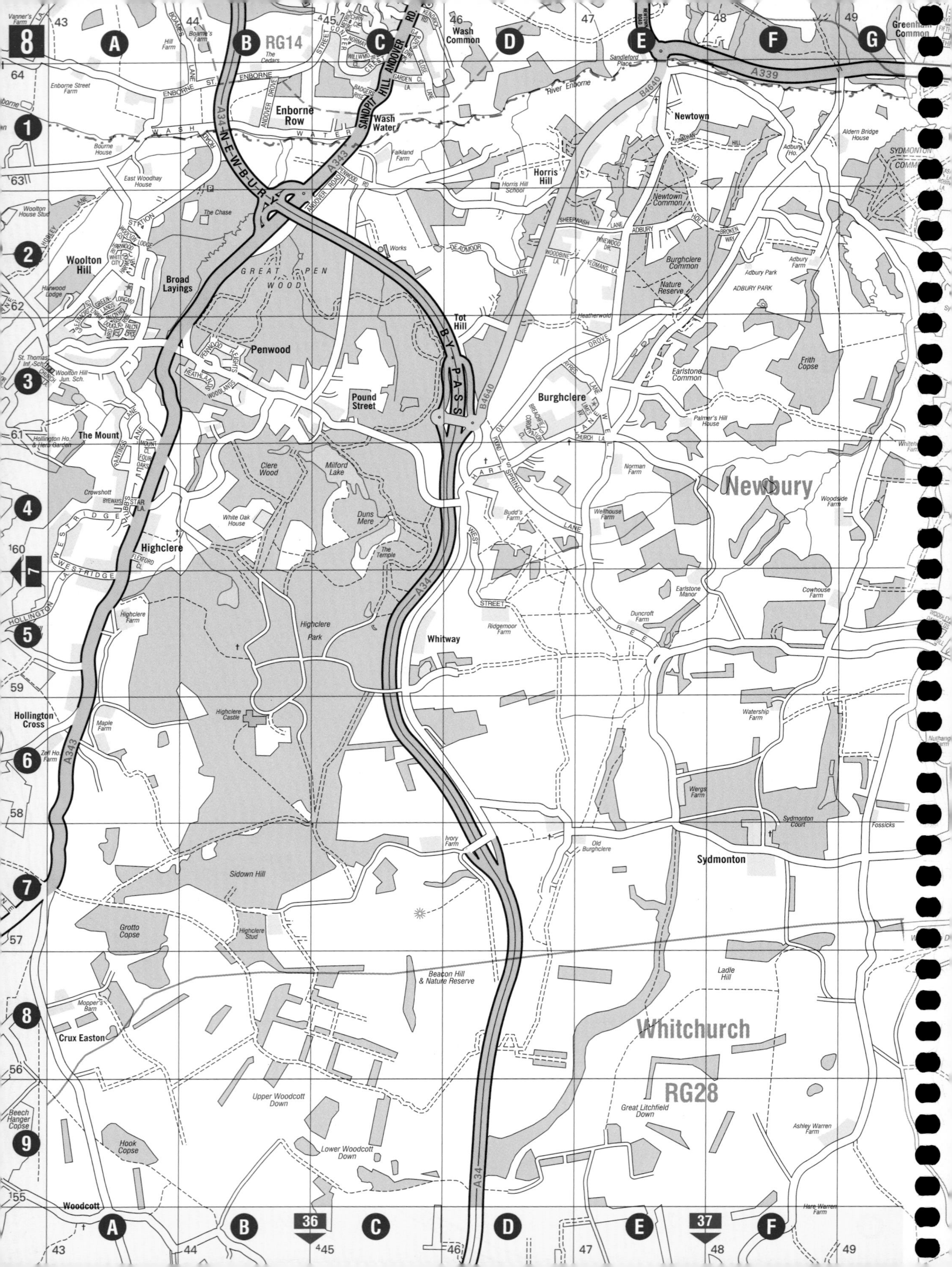

RG14
Wash Common
Enborne Row
Wash Water
Newtown
Sandleford Place
River Enborne
A339
Greenham Common
Woolton Hill
Broad Layings
Penwood
Pound Street
Tot Hill
Horris Hill
Burghclere
Newtown Common
Burghclere Common
Nature Reserve
Earlstone Common
Frith Copse
Adbury Park
Newbury
The Mount
Highclere
Clere Wood
Milford Lake
Duns Mere
The Temple
White Oak House
Highclere Park
Highclere Castle
Whitway
Hollington Cross
Highclere Farm
Maple Farm
Sidown Hill
Old Burghclere
Sydmonton
Sydmonton Court
Wergs Farm
Watership Farm
Grotto Copse
Highclere Stud
Beacon Hill & Nature Reserve
Ladle Hill
Whitchurch
RG28
Crux Easton
Mopper's Barn
Upper Woodcott Down
Lower Woodcott Down
Great Litchfield Down
Hook Copse
Beech Hanger Copse
Woodcott
Ashley Warren Farm
Hare Warren Farm
A34
A343
B4640
A34 NEWBURY BY-PASS
36
37
7

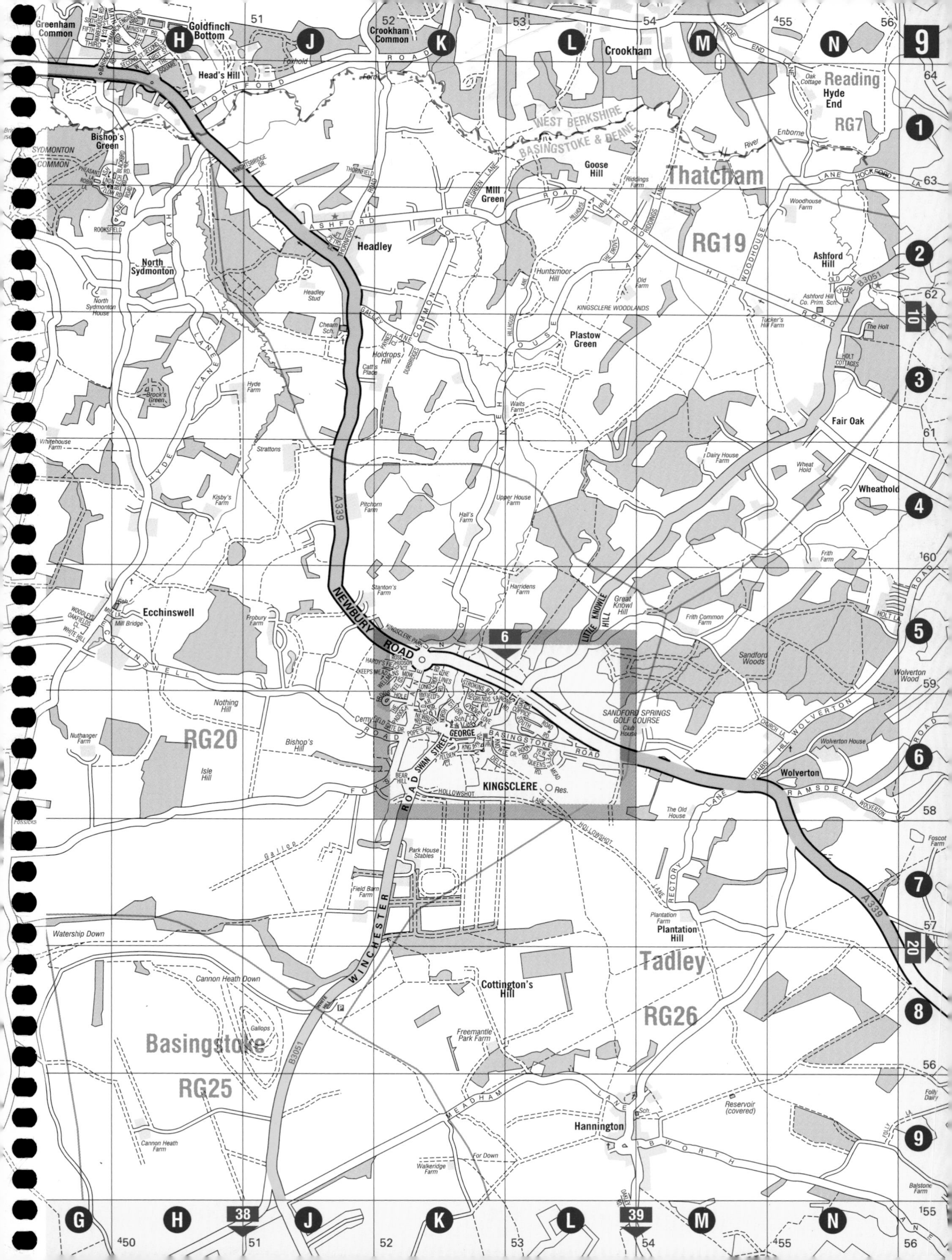
Greenham Common
Goldfinch Bottom
Crookham Common
Crookham
Head's Hill
Foxhold
THORNFORD ROAD
Reading
Oak Cottage
Hyde End
RG7
WEST BERKSHIRE
BASINGSTOKE & DEANE
River Enborne
Bishop's Green
SYDMONTON COMMON
Goose Hill
Thatcham
Mill Green
KNIGHTSBRIDGE DR.
ASHFORD HILL ROAD
Headley
RG19
North Sydmonton
ROOKSFIELD
Woodhouse Farm
Ashford Hill
B3051
Headley Stud
North Sydmonton House
Huntsmoor Hill
Old Farm
KINGSCLERE WOODLANDS
Ashford Hill Co. Prim. Sch.
Tucker's Hill Farm
The Holt
Cheam Sch.
Holdrops Hill
Catt's Place
Plastow Green
HOLT COTTAGES
Hyde Farm
Brock's Green
Waits Farm
Fair Oak
Whitehouse Farm
Strattons
Dairy House Farm
Wheat Hold
Wheathold
A339
Kisby's Farm
Pitchorn Farm
Upper House Farm
Hall's Farm
Frith Farm
Stanton's Farm
Harridens Farm
NEWBURY ROAD
LITTLE KNOWLE HILL
Great Knowl Hill
Ecchinswell
Frobury Farm
Frith Common Farm
HOLT LA.
Mill Bridge
ECCHINSWELL
Sandford Woods
Wolverton Wood
Nothing Hill
SANDFORD SPRINGS GOLF COURSE
Club House
CHURCH LA.
WOLVERTON ROAD
Wolverton House
Nuthanger Farm
RG20
Bishop's Hill
Isle Hill
GEORGE
SWAN STREET
BASINGSTOKE ROAD
KINGSCLERE
Res.
HOLLOWSHOT LANE
CRABS HILL
Wolverton
RAMSDELL ROAD
The Old House
Fossicks
Gallop
Park House Stables
RECTORY LANE
Foscot Farm
Field Barn Farm
Plantation Farm
Plantation Hill
Watership Down
WINCHESTER ROAD
Tadley
Cannon Heath Down
Cottington's Hill
RG26
WHITE HILL
Gallops
Basingstoke
Freemantle Park Farm
B3051
RG25
MEADHAM LANE
Reservoir (covered)
Folly Dairy
Hannington
Cannon Heath Farm
For Down
Walkeridge Farm
Balstone Farm
38
39
10
20
6

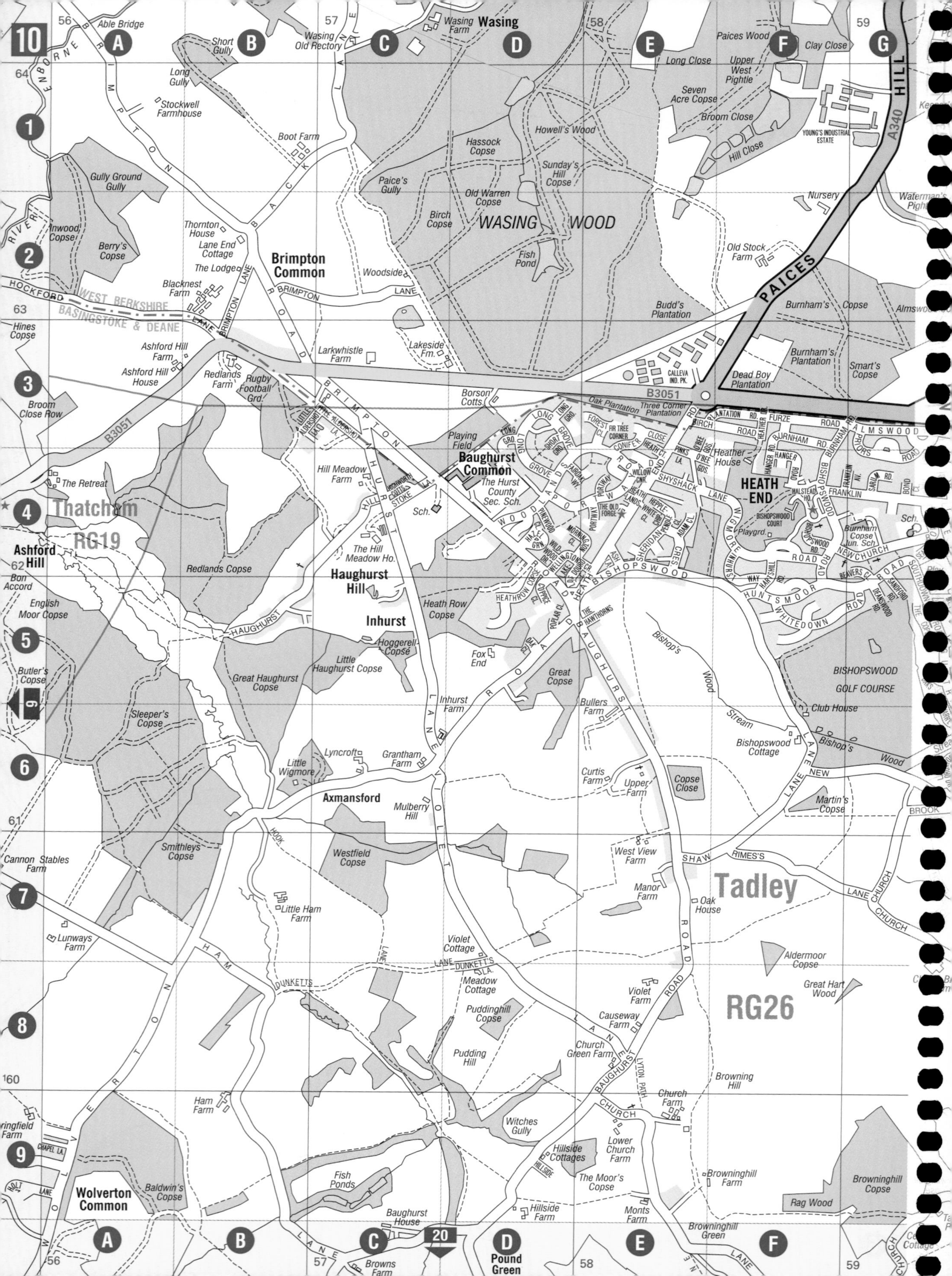

Able Bridge
Short Gully
Wasing Old Rectory
Wasing Farm
Wasing
Paices Wood
Clay Close
Long Close
Upper West Pightle
Long Gully
Stockwell Farmhouse
Seven Acre Copse
Broom Close
YOUNG'S INDUSTRIAL ESTATE
Hill Close
A340
HILL
Howell's Wood
Hassock Copse
Boot Farm
Gully Ground Gully
Paice's Gully
Sunday's Hill Copse
Old Warren Copse
Nursery
Waterman's Pightle
Inwood Copse
Berry's Copse
Birch Copse
WASING WOOD
Thornton House
Lane End Cottage
The Lodge
Brimpton Common
Fish Pond
Old Stock Farm
PAICES
Woodside
Blacknest Farm
HOCKFORD
WEST BERKSHIRE
BASINGSTOKE & DEANE
BRIMPTON LANE
Budd's Plantation
Burnham's Copse
Almswood
Hines Copse
Ashford Hill Farm
Ashford Hill House
Larkwhistle Farm
Lakeside Fm.
Redlands Farm
Rugby Football Grd.
CALLEVA IND. PK.
Burnham's Plantation
Smart's Copse
Dead Boy Plantation
Broom Close Row
Borson Cotts.
B3051
Oak Plantation
Three Corner Plantation
Playing Field
Baughurst Common
The Hurst County Sec. Sch.
Hill Meadow Farm
The Retreat
Thatcham
RG19
HEATH END
Heather House
BISHOPSWOOD COURT
Playgrd.
Burnham Copse Jun. Sch
Sch.
Ashford Hill
Bon Accord
English Moor Copse
Redlands Copse
The Hill Meadow Ho.
Haughurst Hill
Inhurst
Heath Row Copse
HAUGHURST
Butler's Copse
Great Haughurst Copse
Little Haughurst Copse
Hoggerell Copse
Fox End
Great Copse
Bishop's Wood Stream
BISHOPSWOOD GOLF COURSE
Club House
Sleeper's Copse
Inhurst Farm
Bullers Farm
Bishopswood Cottage
Lyncroft
Grantham Farm
Little Wigmore
Curtis Farm
Upper Farm
Copse Close
Martin's Copse
Axmansford
Mulberry Hill
Cannon Stables Farm
Smithleys Copse
Westfield Copse
West View Farm
Manor Farm
Oak House
Tadley
Little Ham Farm
Lunways Farm
Violet Cottage
Aldermoor Copse
Great Hart Wood
Meadow Cottage
Puddinghill Copse
Violet Farm
RG26
Causeway Farm
Pudding Hill
Church Green Farm
Browning Hill
Ham Farm
Church Farm
Witches Gully
Hillside Cottages
Lower Church Farm
The Moor's Copse
Fish Ponds
Browninghill Farm
Browninghill Copse
Rag Wood
Wolverton Common
Baldwin's Copse
Baughurst House
Hillside Farm
Monts Farm
Browninghill Green
Pound Green
Browns Farm
20
9
A
B
C
D
E
F
G
1
2
3
4
5
6
7
8
9
56
57
58
59
64
63
62
61
60

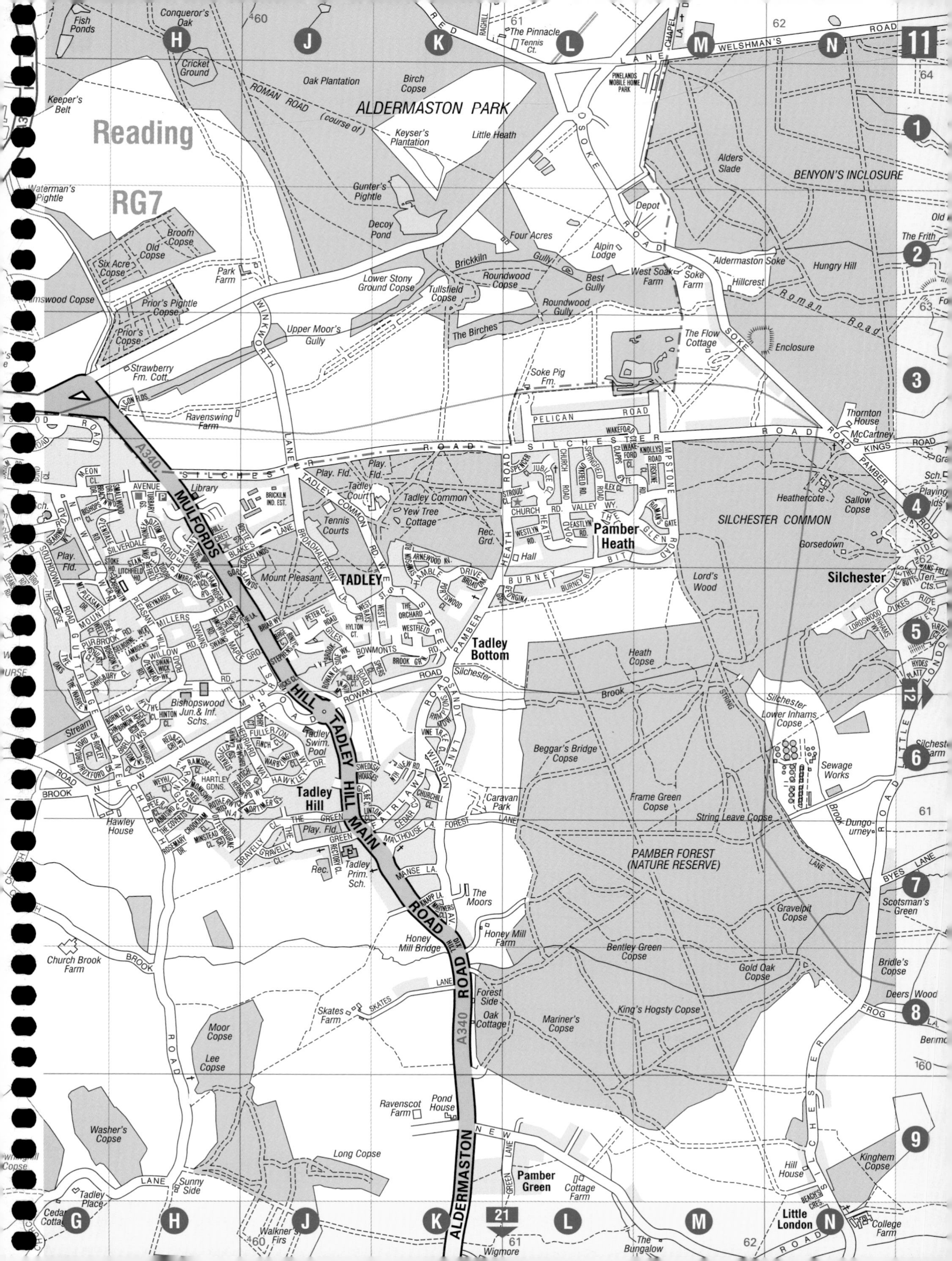

Reading
RG7
ALDERMASTON PARK
Oak Plantation
Birch Copse
Keyser's Plantation
Little Heath
ROMAN ROAD (course of)
Gunter's Pightle
Decoy Pond
Four Acres
Brickkiln Gully
Roundwood Copse
Best Gully
West Soak Farm
Soke Farm
Aldermaston Soke
Hungry Hill
Hillcrest
Alders Slade
BENYON'S INCLOSURE
Depot
Alpin Lodge
Lower Stony Ground Copse
Tullsfield Copse
Roundwood Gully
The Birches
Upper Moor's Gully
The Flow Cottage
Enclosure
Soke Pig Fm.
PELICAN ROAD
SILCHESTER ROAD
Thornton House
McCartney
KINGS ROAD
PAMBER ROAD
Heathercote
Sallow Copse
SILCHESTER COMMON
Gorsedown
Silchester
Lord's Wood
Pamber Heath
TADLEY
Mount Pleasant
Tadley Common
Yew Tree Cottage
Tadley Court
Tennis Courts
Rec. Grd.
Library
MULFORDS HILL
A340
Tadley Bottom
Heath Copse
Silchester Brook
Silchester Lower Inhams Copse
Sewage Works
Beggar's Bridge Copse
Frame Green Copse
String Leave Copse
PAMBER FOREST (NATURE RESERVE)
Caravan Park
Tadley Hill
TADLEY HILL MAIN ROAD
Bishopswood Jun.& Inf. Schs.
Tadley Swim. Pool
Hawley House
Tadley Prim. Sch.
The Moors
Honey Mill Bridge
Honey Mill Farm
Bentley Green Copse
Gravelpit Copse
Gold Oak Copse
Scotsman's Green
Bridle's Copse
Deers Wood
Church Brook Farm
Skates Farm
Forest Side
Oak Cottage
Mariner's Copse
King's Hogsty Copse
Moor Copse
Lee Copse
Ravenscot Farm
Pond House
Washer's Copse
Long Copse
Pamber Green
Cottage Farm
Hill House
Kinghem Copse
Little London
College Farm
Tadley Place
Sunny Side
Walkner's Firs
Wigmore
The Bungalow
ALDERMASTON ROAD
Strawberry Fm. Cott.
Ravenswing Farm
Park Farm
Prior's Pightle Copse
Prior's Copse
Six Acre Copse
Old Copse
Broom Copse
Waterman's Pightle
Keeper's Belt
Fish Ponds
Conqueror's Oak
Cricket Ground
The Pinnacle
PINELANDS MOBILE HOME PARK
WELSHMAN'S ROAD
Dungourney
Stream

12
21

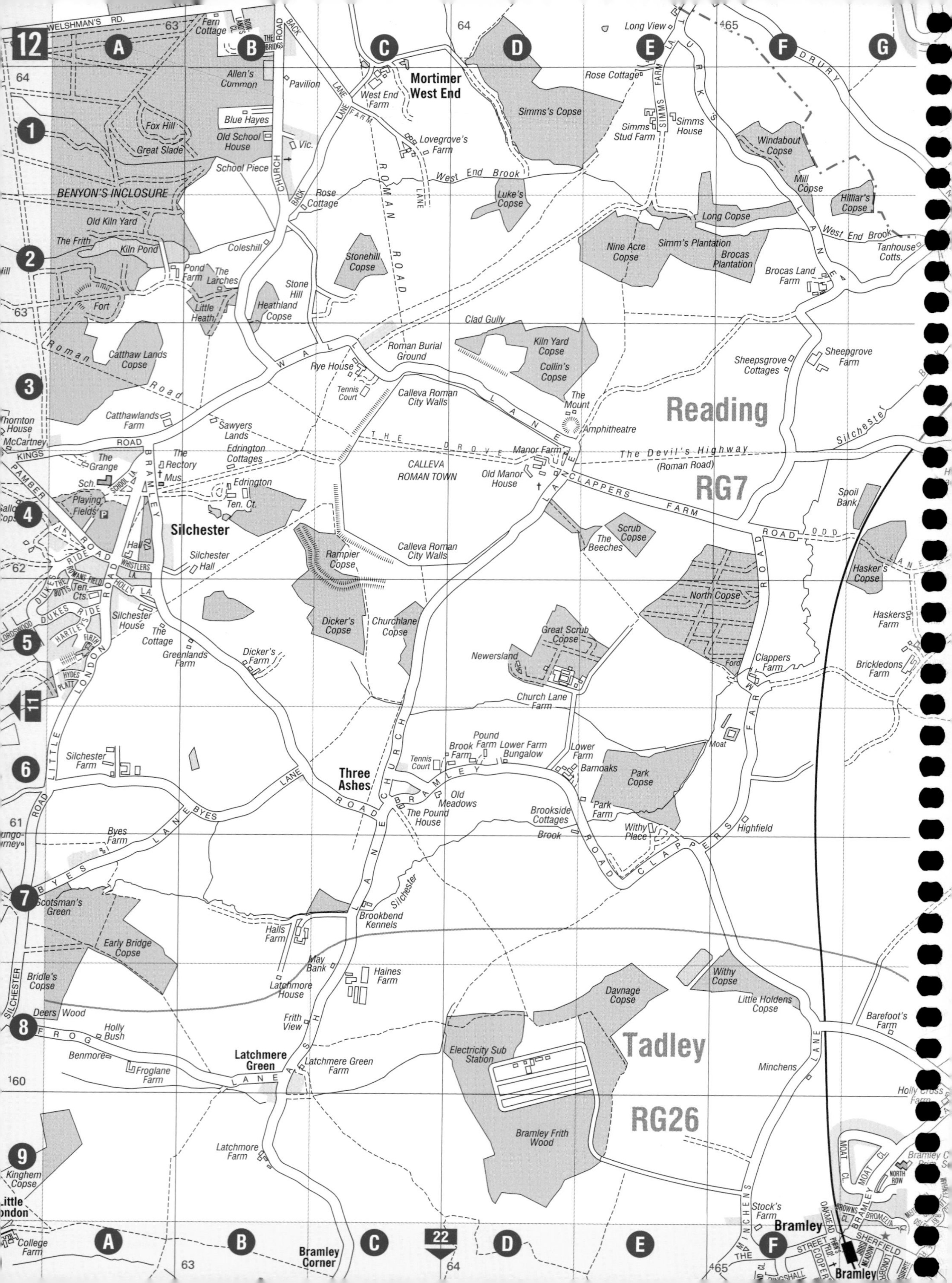

Mortimer West End
Silchester
Three Ashes
Latchmere Green
Bramley Corner
Bramley
Reading
RG7
Tadley
RG26
Benyon's Inclosure
Allen's Common
Fern Cottage
Blue Hayes
Old School House
Fox Hill
Great Slade
School Piece
Pavilion
West End Farm
Lovegrove's Farm
Simms's Copse
Simms Stud Farm
Simms House
Rose Cottage
Long View
Windabout Copse
Mill Copse
Hilliar's Copse
West End Brook
Luke's Copse
Long Copse
Nine Acre Copse
Simm's Plantation
Brocas Plantation
Brocas Land Farm
Tanhouse Cotts.
Old Kiln Yard
The Frith
Kiln Pond
Coleshill
Pond Farm
The Larches
Little Heath
Fort
Heathland Copse
Stone Hill
Stonehill Copse
Roman Road
Clad Gully
Kiln Yard Copse
Collin's Copse
Catthaw Lands Copse
Rye House
Roman Burial Ground
Sheepsgrove Cottages
Sheepgrove Farm
Calleva Roman City Walls
The Mount
Amphitheatre
Catthawlands Farm
Sawyers Lands
Edrington Cottages
The Drove
Manor Farm
The Devil's Highway (Roman Road)
Calleva Roman Town
Old Manor House
Clappers Farm Road
The Grange
The Rectory
Mus.
Edrington
Playing Fields
Ten. Ct.
Spoil Bank
Scrub Copse
The Beeches
Rampier Copse
Hasker's Copse
Silchester Hall
North Copse
Silchester House
The Cottage
Dicker's Copse
Churchlane Copse
Great Scrub Copse
Newersland
Haskers Farm
Greenlands Farm
Dicker's Farm
Clappers Farm
Ford
Brickledons Farm
Church Lane Farm
Moat
Silchester Farm
Pound Farm
Brook Farm
Lower Farm Bungalow
Lower Farm
Barnoaks
Park Copse
Old Meadows
The Pound House
Park Farm
Brookside Cottages
Withy Place
Highfield
Byes Farm
Scotsman's Green
Early Bridge Copse
Brookbend Kennels
Halls Farm
May Bank
Haines Farm
Latchmore House
Withy Copse
Davnage Copse
Little Holdens Copse
Barefoot's Farm
Bridle's Copse
Deers Wood
Holly Bush
Frith View
Benmore
Froglane Farm
Electricity Sub Station
Latchmere Green Farm
Minchens
Holly Cross Farm
Bramley Frith Wood
Latchmore Farm
Kinghem Copse
Little London
Stock's Farm
College Farm
Welshman's Rd.
Kings Road
Bramley Road
Byes Lane
Little London Road
Frog Lane
Church Lane
Drury Lane
Simms Farm Lane
Minchens Lane

11

22

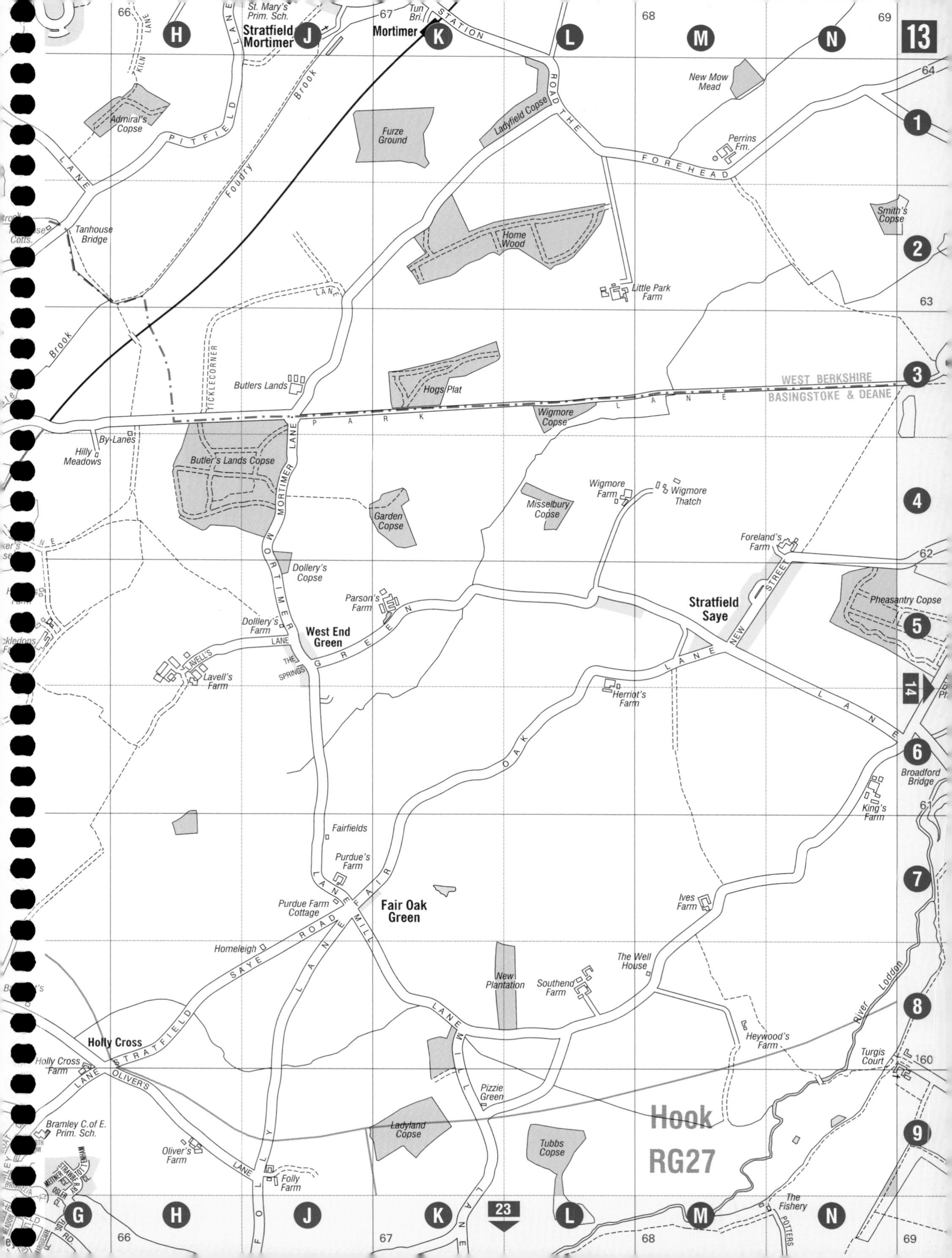
Stratfield Mortimer
St. Mary's Prim. Sch.
Mortimer
Tun Bri.
STATION ROAD
THE FOREHEAD
New Mow Mead
Perrins Fm.
Admiral's Copse
PITFIELD LANE
KILN LANE
Foudry Brook
Furze Ground
Ladyfield Copse
Smith's Copse
Tanhouse Bridge
Home Wood
Little Park Farm
TICKLECORNER LANE
Butlers Lands
Hogs Plat
WEST BERKSHIRE
BASINGSTOKE & DEANE
PARK LANE
Wigmore Copse
By-Lanes
Hilly Meadows
Butler's Lands Copse
MORTIMER LANE
Garden Copse
Misselbury Copse
Wigmore Farm
Wigmore Thatch
Foreland's Farm
NEW STREET
Dollery's Copse
Parson's Farm
Stratfield Saye
Pheasantry Copse
Dolllery's Farm
West End Green
GREEN LANE
LAVELL'S LANE
Lavell's Farm
THE SPRINGS
Herriot's Farm
OAK LANE
Broadford Bridge
King's Farm
Fairfields
Purdue's Farm
FAIR OAK LANE
Purdue Farm Cottage
Fair Oak Green
Ives Farm
Homeleigh
STRATFIELD SAYE ROAD
MILL LANE
FOLLY LANE
New Plantation
Southend Farm
The Well House
Heywood's Farm
River Loddon
Holly Cross
Holly Cross Farm
OLIVERS LANE
Turgis Court
Pizzie Green
Bramley C.of E. Prim. Sch.
Ladyland Copse
Tubbs Copse
Hook
RG27
Oliver's Farm
Folly Farm
The Fishery
POTTERS
RD
66
67
68
69
64
63
62
61
160
G
H
J
K
L
M
N
1
2
3
4
5
6
7
8
9

14
23

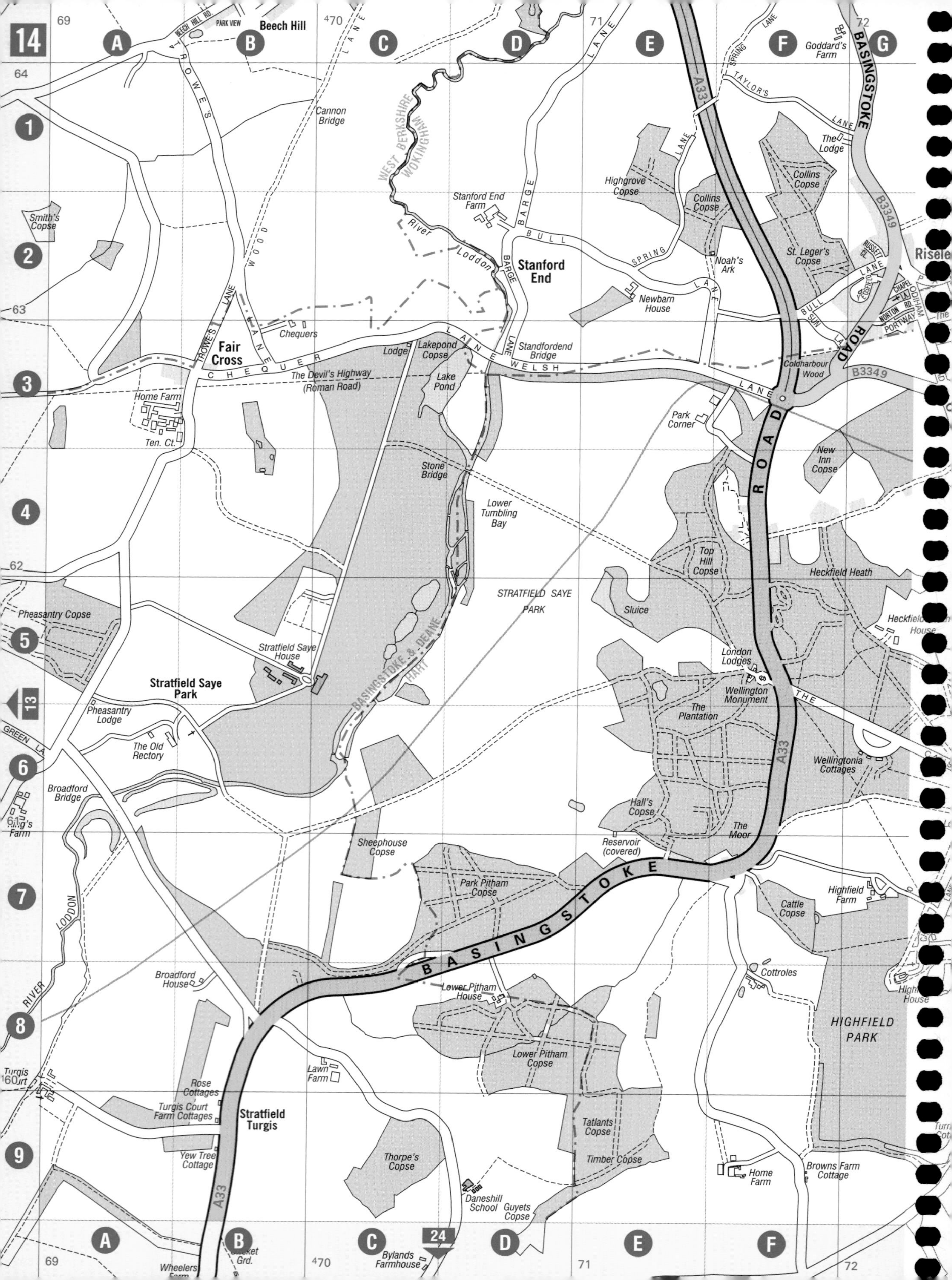

Beech Hill
Park View
Beech Hill Rd.
Rowe's
Cannon Bridge
West Berkshire
Wokingham
Smith's Copse
River Loddon
Stanford End Farm
Barge
Bull
Stanford End
Spring
Lane
Highgrove Copse
Collins Copse
Noah's Ark
Newbarn House
Wood Lane
Fair Cross
Chequers
Chequer Lane
Welsh Lane
Lodge
Lakepond Copse
Standfordend Bridge
Lake Pond
The Devil's Highway (Roman Road)
Home Farm
Ten. Ct.
Park Corner
Coldharbour Wood
B3349
Basingstoke Road
A33
Goddard's Farm
Taylor's Lane
The Lodge
Collins Copse
St. Leger's Copse
Russett
Bull Lane
Sun Lane
Chapel La.
Odiham Rd.
Norton Rd.
Portway
Riseley
New Inn Copse
Stone Bridge
Lower Tumbling Bay
Top Hill Copse
Heckfield Heath
Stratfield Saye Park
Sluice
Pheasantry Copse
Stratfield Saye House
Basingstoke & Deane
Hart
Stratfield Saye Park
Pheasantry Lodge
The Old Rectory
Green La.
Broadford Bridge
London Lodges
Wellington Monument
The Plantation
The
Wellingtonia Cottages
Heckfield House
Hall's Copse
The Moor
Reservoir (covered)
Sheephouse Copse
Park Pitham Copse
Highfield Farm
Cattle Copse
Loddon
River
Broadford House
Lower Pitham House
Cottroles
Highfield House
Highfield Park
Lawn Farm
Lower Pitham Copse
Turgis Court
Rose Cottages
Turgis Court Farm Cottages
Stratfield Turgis
Tatlants Copse
Yew Tree Cottage
Thorpe's Copse
Timber Copse
Home Farm
Browns Farm Cottage
Daneshill School
Guyets Copse
Cricket Grd.
Bylands Farmhouse
Wheelers Farm
13
24

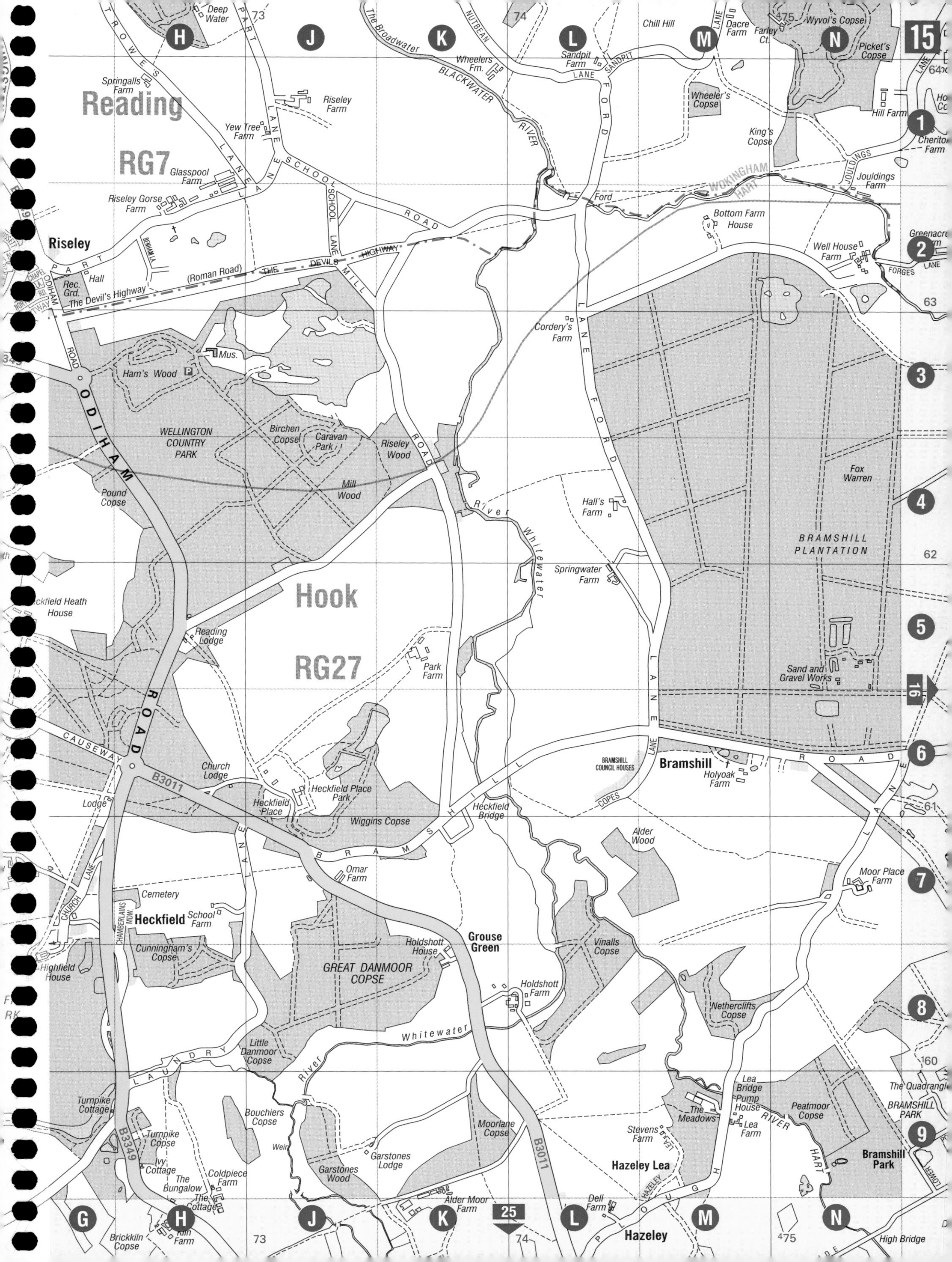

Reading
RG7
Riseley
Hook
RG27
Heckfield
Bramshill
Grouse Green
Hazeley Lea
Hazeley
WELLINGTON COUNTRY PARK
BRAMSHILL PLANTATION
GREAT DANMOOR COPSE
Springalls Farm
Riseley Farm
Yew Tree Farm
Glasspool Farm
Riseley Gorse Farm
Wheelers Fm.
Sandpit Farm
Chill Hill
Dacre Farm
Farley Ct.
Wyvol's Copse
Picket's Copse
Wheeler's Copse
King's Copse
Hill Farm
Jouldings Farm
Bottom Farm House
Well House Farm
Greenacre
Ford
Cordery's Farm
Ham's Wood
Mus.
Birchen Copse
Caravan Park
Riseley Wood
Mill Wood
Pound Copse
Fox Warren
Hall's Farm
Springwater Farm
Reading Lodge
Park Farm
Sand and Gravel Works
Church Lodge
Heckfield Place Park
Heckfield Place
Wiggins Copse
Heckfield Bridge
BRAMSHILL COUNCIL HOUSES
Holyoak Farm
Alder Wood
Moor Place Farm
Omar Farm
Cemetery
School Farm
Cunningham's Copse
Highfield House
Holdshott House
Holdshott Farm
Vinalls Copse
Netherclifts Copse
Little Danmoor Copse
Turnpike Cottage
Bouchiers Copse
Turnpike Copse
Ivy Cottage
The Bungalow
The Cottage
Coldpiece Farm
Garstones Wood
Garstones Lodge
Moorlane Copse
Alder Moor Farm
Stevens Farm
The Meadows
Lea Bridge
Pump House
Lea Farm
Peatmoor Copse
Bramshill Park
BRAMSHILL PARK
The Quadrangle
Dell Farm
Kiln Farm
Brickkiln Copse
High Bridge
Rec. Grd.
Hall
The Devil's Highway
(Roman Road)
THE DEVIL'S HIGHWAY
ODIHAM ROAD
SCHOOL ROAD
SCHOOL LANE
MILL ROAD
FORD LANE
SANDPIT LANE
NUTBEAN LANE
BLACKWATER RIVER
The Broadwater
River Whitewater
River Whitewater
WOKINGHAM
HART
RIVER HART
JOULDINGS LANE
FORGES LANE
BRAMSHILL ROAD
CAUSEWAY
B3011
B3349
CHURCH LANE
CHAMBERLAINS MDW.
LAUNDRY LANE
COPES
PLOUGH LANE
Weir
Lodge
16
25

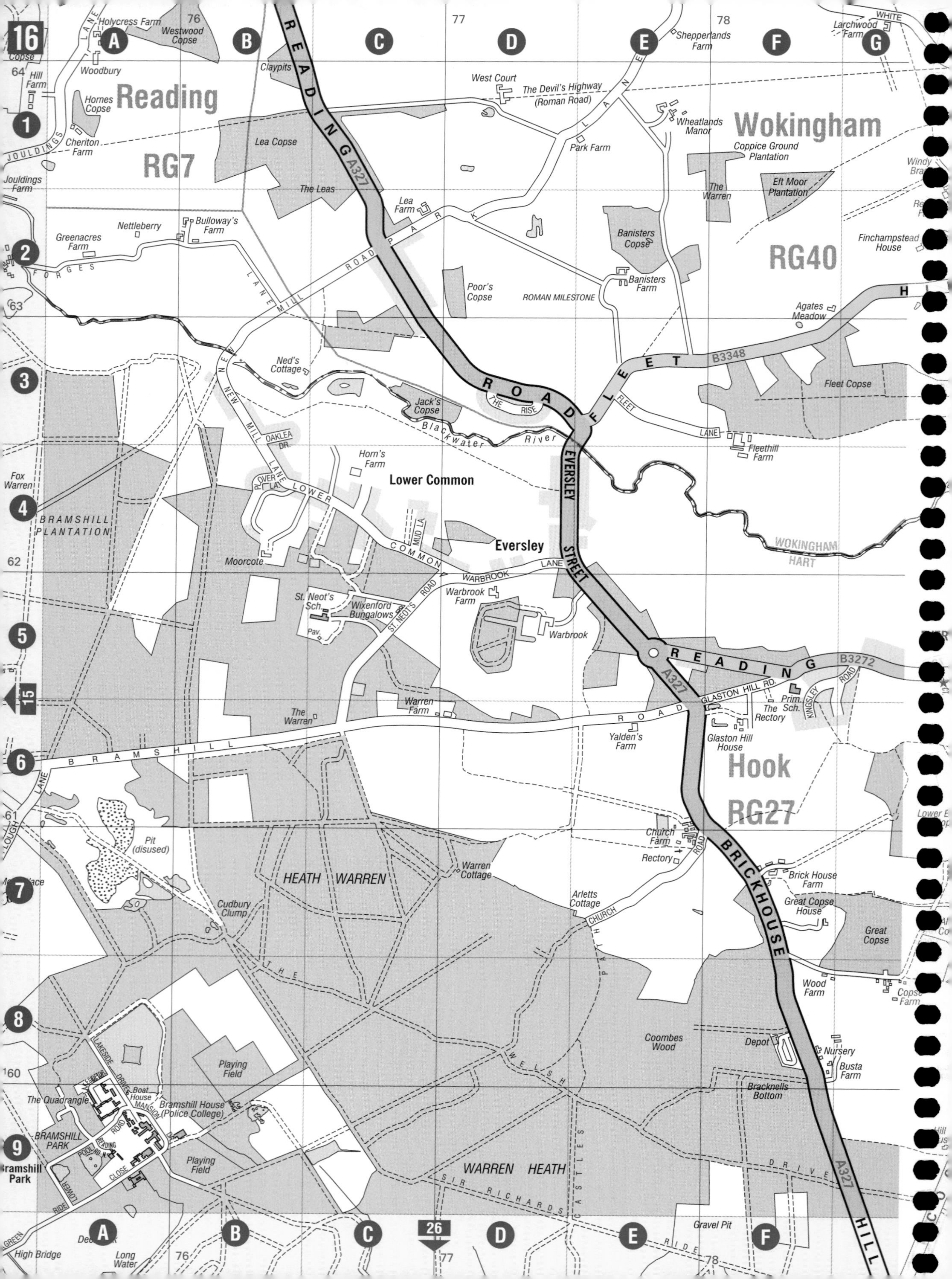

Reading
RG7
Wokingham
RG40
Hook
RG27
Holycress Farm
Westwood Copse
Woodbury
Hill Farm
Hornes Copse
Cheriton Farm
Jouldings Farm
Claypits
Lea Copse
The Leas
West Court
The Devil's Highway (Roman Road)
Shepperlands Farm
Wheatlands Manor
Park Farm
Larchwood Farm
Coppice Ground Plantation
Eft Moor Plantation
The Warren
Banisters Copse
Banisters Farm
Finchampstead House
Lea Farm
Nettleberry
Bulloway's Farm
Greenacres Farm
Poor's Copse
ROMAN MILESTONE
Agates Meadow
Ned's Cottage
Jack's Copse
Fleet Copse
Blackwater River
Fleethill Farm
Horn's Farm
Lower Common
Fox Warren
BRAMSHILL PLANTATION
Eversley
Moorcote
WOKINGHAM
HART
St. Neot's Sch.
Wixenford Bungalows
Pav.
Warbrook Farm
Warbrook
The Warren
Warren Farm
The Rectory
Prim. Sch.
Glaston Hill House
Yalden's Farm
Pit (disused)
HEATH WARREN
Warren Cottage
Church Farm
Rectory
Arletts Cottage
Brick House Farm
Great Copse House
Great Copse
Cudbury Clump
Wood Farm
Copse Farm
Coombes Wood
Depot
Nursery
Busta Farm
Playing Field
Bracknells Bottom
The Quadrangle
Boat House
Bramshill House (Police College)
BRAMSHILL PARK
Bramshill Park
WARREN HEATH
Gravel Pit
High Bridge
Long Water
READING ROAD
EVERSLEY STREET
BRICKHOUSE HILL
FLEET LANE
BRAMSHILL ROAD
GLASTON HILL RD.
A327
B3348
B3272

15
26

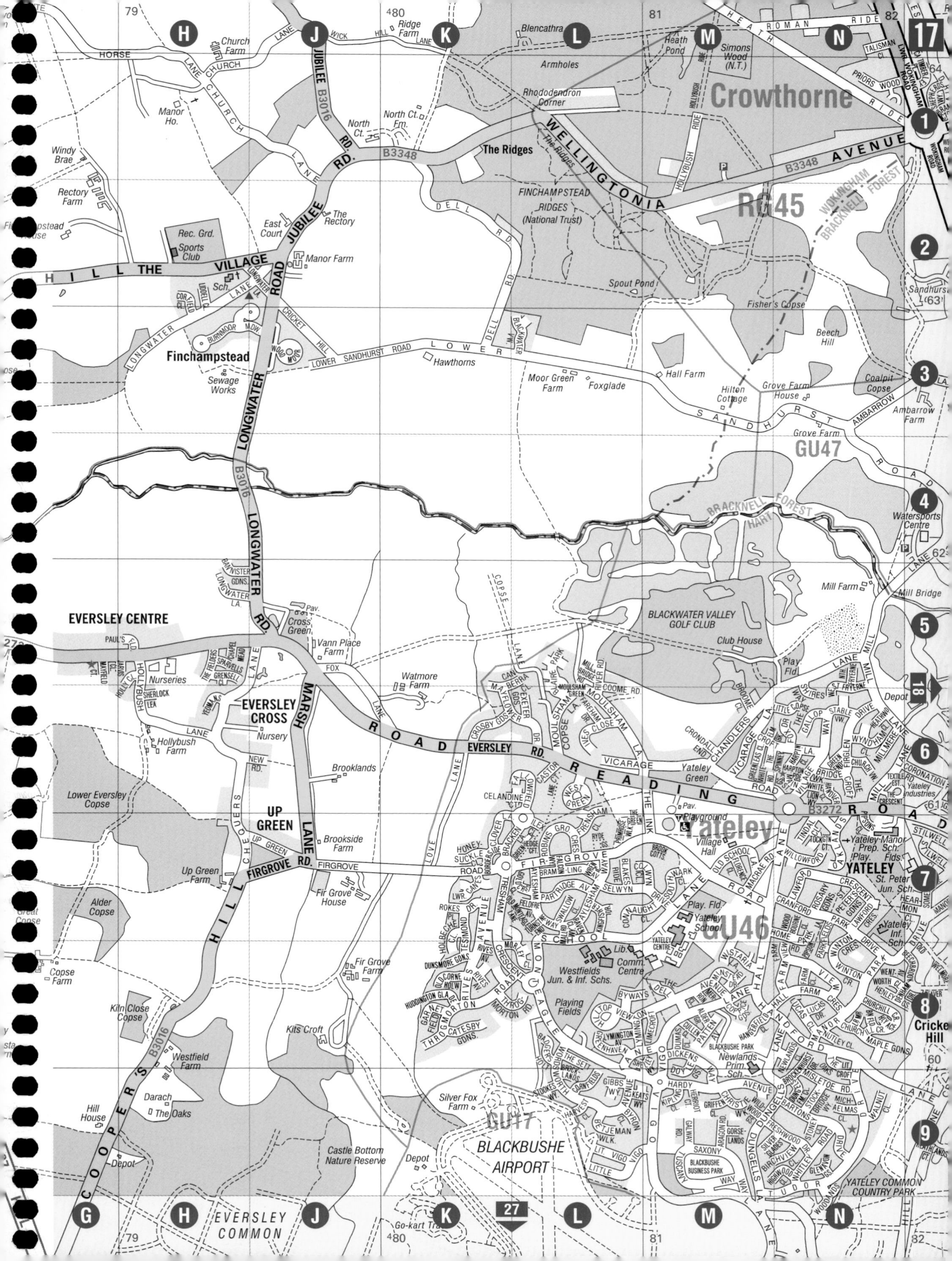
Crowthorne
RG45
GU47
GU46
GU17
Finchampstead
EVERSLEY CENTRE
EVERSLEY CROSS
UP GREEN
Yateley
YATELEY
BLACKBUSHE AIRPORT
EVERSLEY COMMON
BLACKWATER VALLEY GOLF CLUB
Club House
FINCHAMPSTEAD RIDGES (National Trust)
The Ridges
Rhododendron Corner
Armholes
Blencathra
Heath Pond
Simons Wood (N.T.)
Ridge Farm
Church Farm
Manor Ho.
Windy Brae
Rectory Farm
Rec. Grd.
Sports Club
Manor Farm
The Rectory
East Court
North Ct.
North Ct. Fm.
Sewage Works
Hawthorns
Moor Green Farm
Foxglade
Hall Farm
Hilton Cottage
Grove Farm House
Grove Farm
Coalpit Copse
Ambarrow Farm
Spout Pond
Fisher's Copse
Beech Hill
Sandhurst
Watersports Centre
Mill Farm
Mill Bridge
Vann Place Farm
Cross Green
Watmore Farm
Nurseries
Nursery
Hollybush Farm
Brooklands
Lower Eversley Copse
Brookside Farm
Up Green Farm
Alder Copse
Fir Grove House
Fir Grove Farm
Copse Farm
Kiln Close Copse
Kits Croft
Westfield Farm
Darach
The Oaks
Hill House
Depot
Castle Bottom Nature Reserve
Silver Fox Farm
Go-kart Track
Yateley Green
Village Hall
Playground
Play. Fld.
Yateley School
Westfields Jun. & Inf. Schs.
Playing Fields
Lib.
Comm. Centre
Yateley Manor Prep. Sch.
St. Peter Jun. Sch.
Yateley Inf. Sch.
Newlands Prim. Sch.
BLACKBUSHE BUSINESS PARK
Yateley Industries
YATELEY COMMON COUNTRY PARK
Cricket Hill
THE VILLAGE
HILL
JUBILEE RD.
LONGWATER ROAD
LONGWATER RD.
B3016
B3348
B3272
WELLINGTONIA AVENUE
LOWER SANDHURST ROAD
SANDHURST ROAD
READING ROAD
EVERSLEY RD.
MARSH LANE
FIRGROVE RD.
COOPER'S HILL
VICARAGE ROAD
SCHOOL LANE
MONTEAGLE LANE
VIGO LANE
HEATH RIDE
ROMAN RIDE
WICK HILL LANE
HORSE LANE
CHURCH LANE
DELL RD.
MILL LANE
BRACKNELL FOREST
HART
WOKINGHAM
G
H
J
K
L
M
N
1
2
3
4
5
6
7
8
9
18
27
79
480
81
82
64
63
62
61
60

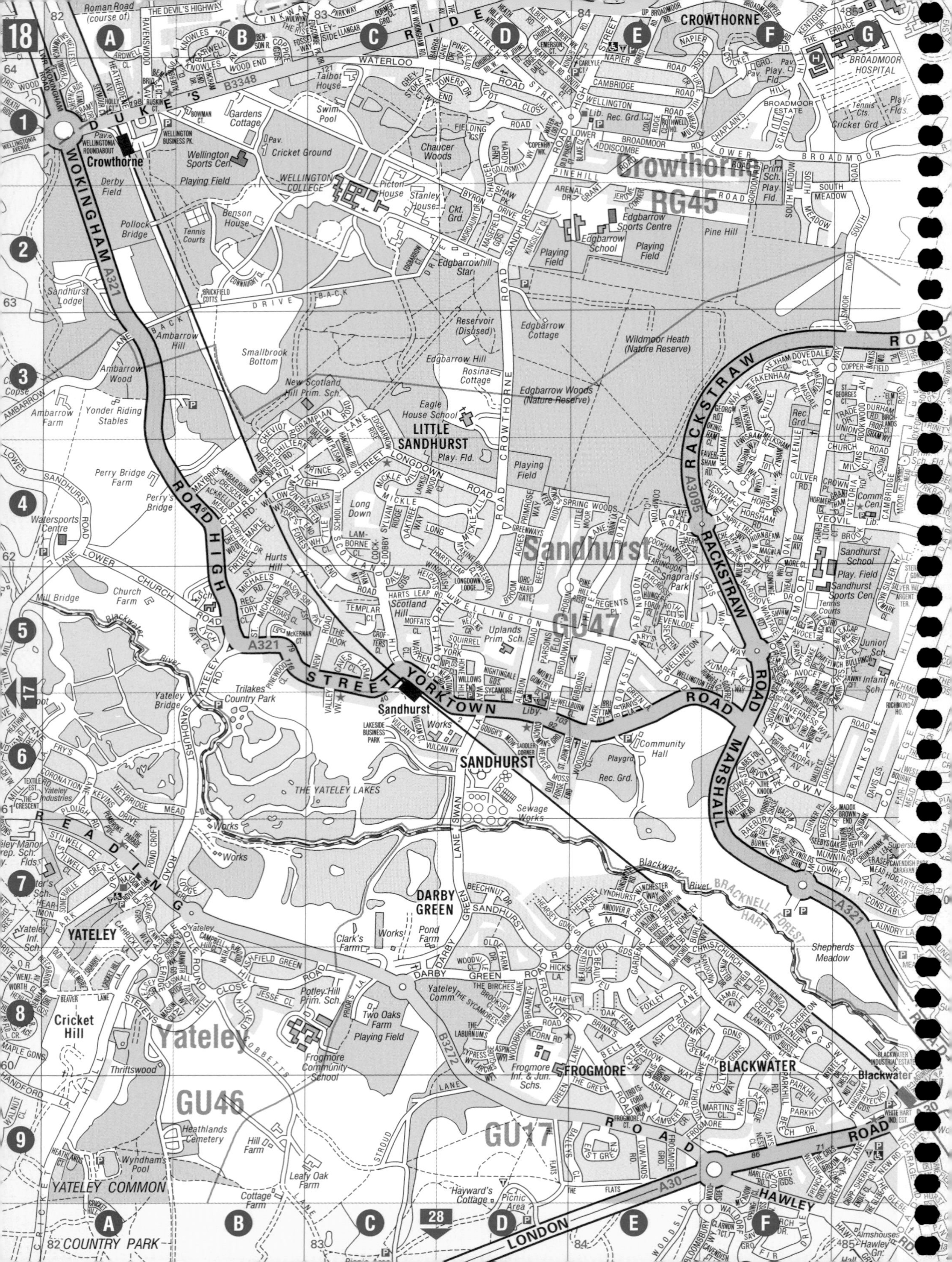
CROWTHORNE
Crowthorne
RG45
BROADMOOR HOSPITAL
WELLINGTON COLLEGE
Wellington Sports Cen.
Cricket Ground
Chaucer Woods
Edgbarrow Sports Centre
Edgbarrow School
Pine Hill
Wildmoor Heath (Nature Reserve)
Edgbarrow Woods (Nature Reserve)
Edgbarrow Hill
Eagle House School
LITTLE SANDHURST
New Scotland Hill Prim. Sch.
Smallbrook Bottom
Ambarrow Hill
Ambarrow Wood
Ambarrow Farm
Yonder Riding Stables
Sandhurst Lodge
Pollock Bridge
Perry Bridge Farm
Perry's Bridge
Watersports Centre
Church Farm
Mill Bridge
Blackwater River
Yateley Bridge
Trilakes Country Park
THE YATELEY LAKES
Sandhurst
GU47
Scotland Hill
Uplands Prim. Sch.
Snaprails Park
Sandhurst School
Sandhurst Sports Cen.
SANDHURST
Community Hall
Sewage Works
DARBY GREEN
Pond Farm
Clark's Farm
Two Oaks Farm
Playing Field
Potley Hill Prim. Sch.
Frogmore Community School
Frogmore Inf. & Jun. Schs.
FROGMORE
BLACKWATER
Blackwater
GU17
Yateley
YATELEY
GU46
Cricket Hill
Thriftswood
Heathlands Cemetery
Wyndham's Pool
YATELEY COMMON
COUNTRY PARK
Hill Farm
Leafy Oak Farm
Cottage Farm
Hayward's Cottage
Picnic Area
HAWLEY
Shepherds Meadow
BRACKNELL FOREST
HART
WOKINGHAM ROAD A321
DUKE'S RIDE
HIGH STREET
YORKTOWN ROAD
RACKSTRAW ROAD
MARSHALL ROAD
READING ROAD
LONDON ROAD A30
A3095
B3272
B3348
28
17

POPPY HILLS
DANGER AREA
BROADMOOR-BOTTOM
DANGER AREA
OWLSMOOR
COLLEGE
TOWN
ROYAL MILITARY
ACADEMY
CAMBERLEY
YORK
TOWN
CRAWLEY
HILL
GU15
Camberley
FORESTERS WAY
A3095
LONDON ROAD
A30
BLACKWATER VALLEY ROAD
A331
M3 MOTORWAY
Lower
Star Post
Windmill
Stem
Wishmoor
Cross
Deer Rock Hill
PASCHAL
WOOD
Saddleback Hill
OLDDEAN COMMON
Broadmoor Farm
Whortleberry
Hill
Reservoir
(Covered)
The Devil's Pound
Rifle Range
MEDICAL
RECEPTION
STATION
HOSPITAL
Wishton
Water Catchment
Area
Whitehill
Barossa Common
Playing Field
Bathing
Pool
Churchill
Hall
Victory
College
Alanbrooke
Hall
Staff
College
Upper Lake
Lower
Lake
Oak Grove
Sports
Ground
Government
House
American
Garden
Superstores
Blackwater
Tekels
Park
Sewage
Works
Filter
Beds
Krooner Park
(Football Grd)
Butter Hill
Butter
Bottom
Lorraine
Sch.
29

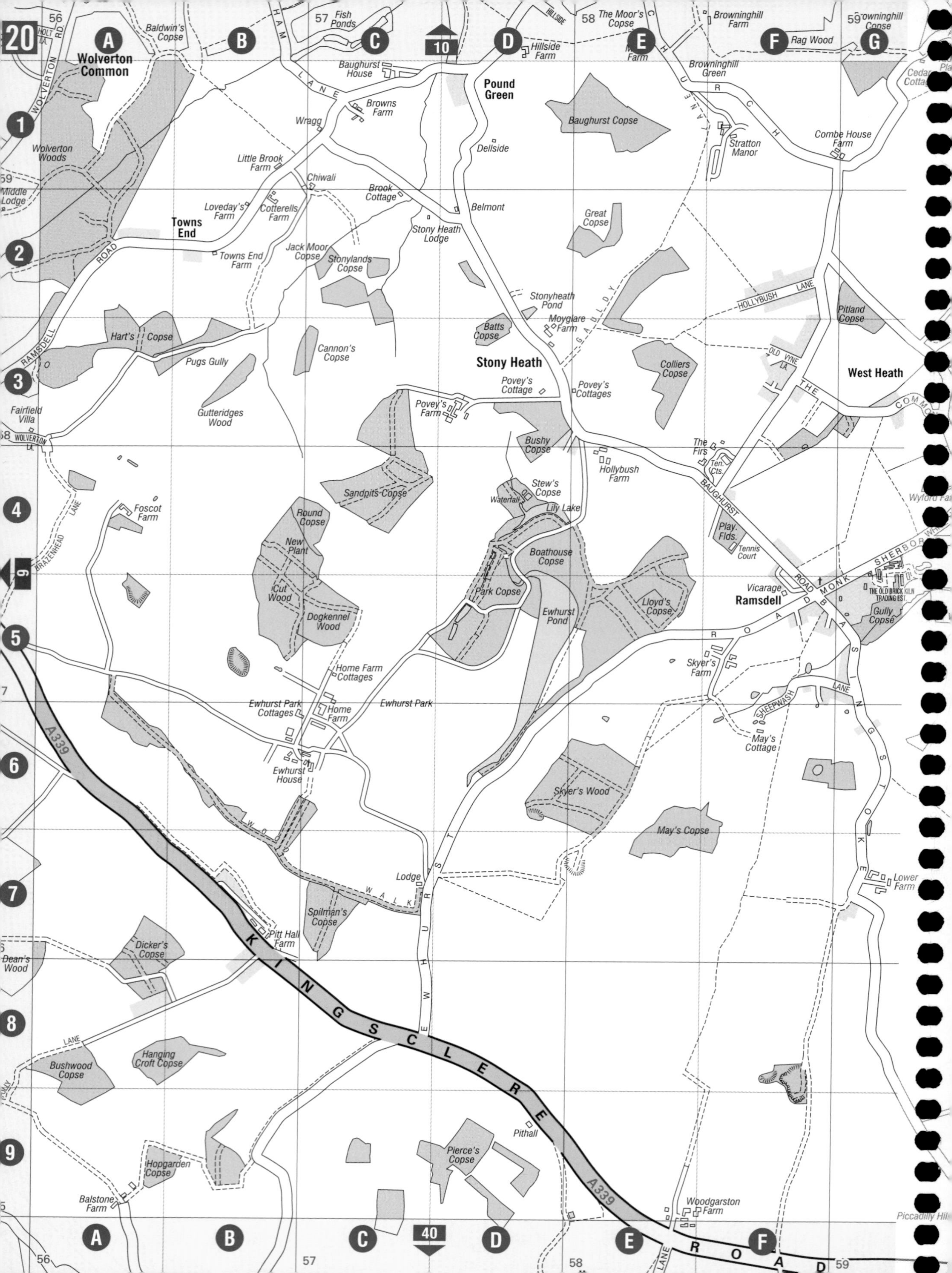
Wolverton Common
Baldwin's Copse
Fish Ponds
10
Hillside Farm
The Moor's Copse
Browninghill Farm
Rag Wood
Browninghill Green
Baughurst House
Pound Green
Browns Farm
Wragg
Baughurst Copse
Stratton Manor
Combe House Farm
Wolverton Woods
Little Brook Farm
Dellside
Chiwali
Middle Lodge
Brook Cottage
Loveday's Farm
Cotterells Farm
Belmont
Towns End
Stony Heath Lodge
Great Copse
Towns End Farm
Jack Moor Copse
Stonylands Copse
Hollybush Lane
Pitland Copse
Stonyheath Pond
Moyglare Farm
Batts Copse
Gaully
Hart's Copse
Cannon's Copse
Pugs Gully
Stony Heath
Colliers Copse
Old Vyne La.
West Heath
Povey's Cottage
Povey's Cottages
Fairfield Villa
Gutteridges Wood
Povey's Farm
The Common
Wolverton La.
Bushy Copse
The Firs
Ten. Cts.
Hollybush Farm
Stew's Copse
Waterfall
Lily Lake
Foscot Farm
Sandpits Copse
Brazenhead Lane
Round Copse
Baughurst Road
Play. Flds.
Tennis Court
New Plant
Boathouse Copse
Sherborne
Monk
9
Cut Wood
Park Copse
Vicarage
Ramsdell
The Old Brick Kiln Trading Est.
Lloyd's Copse
Gully Copse
Ewhurst Pond
Dogkennel Wood
Road
Skyer's Farm
Home Farm Cottages
Ewhurst Park Cottages
Home Farm
Ewhurst Park
Sheepwash Lane
May's Cottage
A339
Ewhurst House
Skyer's Wood
May's Copse
Wood Walk
Lodge
Lower Farm
Spilman's Copse
Pitt Hall Farm
Dicker's Copse
Dean's Wood
Ewhurst
Kingsclere Road
Lane
Hanging Croft Copse
Bushwood Copse
Pithall
Pierce's Copse
Hopgarden Copse
Balstone Farm
Woodgarston Farm
Piccadilly Hill
40
Lane
Road
56
57
58
59
A
B
C
D
E
F
G
1
2
3
4
5
6
7
8
9

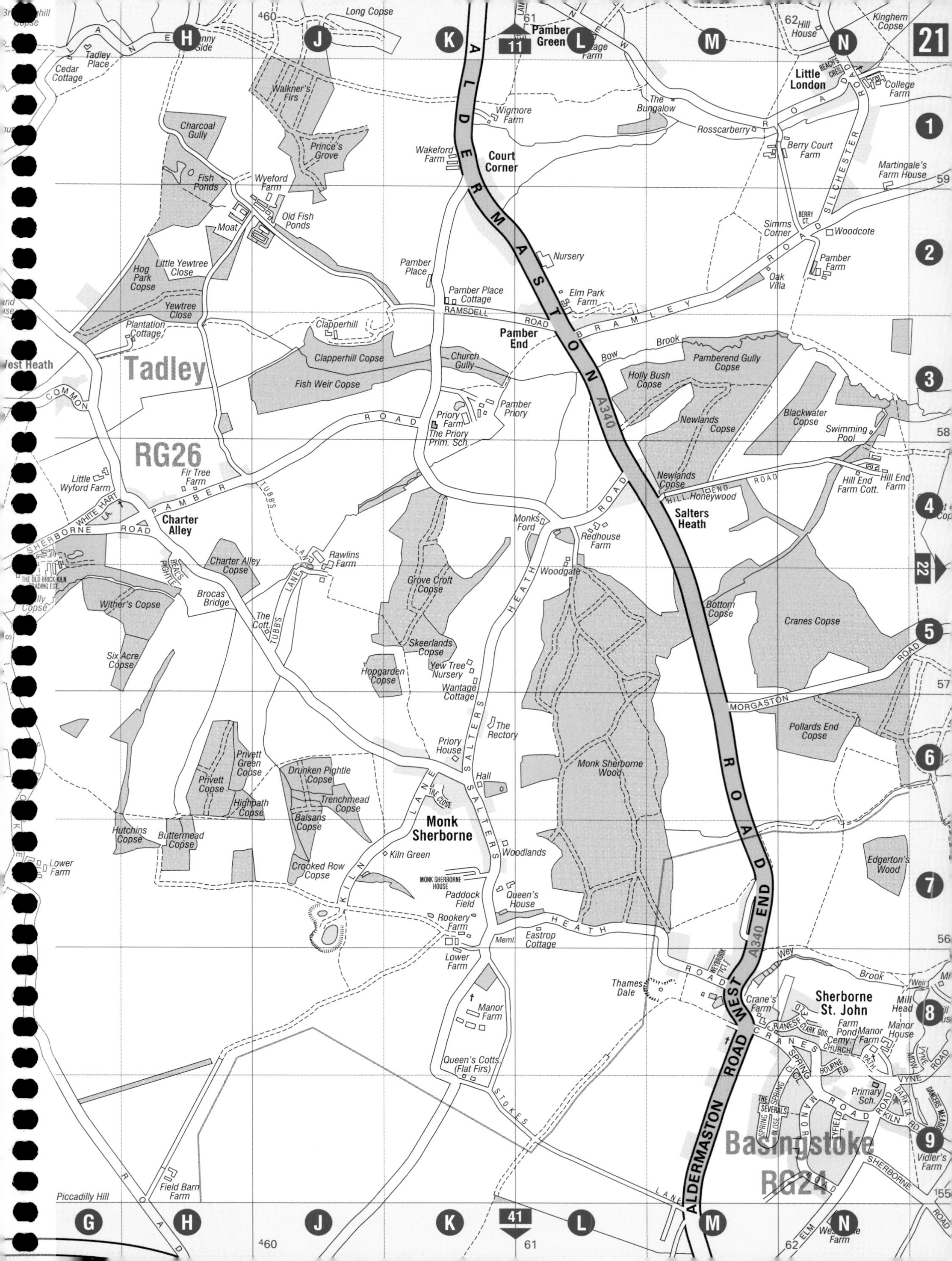
Tadley
RG26
Charter Alley
Monk Sherborne
Pamber End
Salters Heath
Court Corner
Little London
Sherborne St. John
Basingstoke
RG24
Pamber Green
ALDERMASTON ROAD
A340
ALDERMASTON ROAD WEST
A340 END
RAMSDELL ROAD
BRAMLEY ROAD
SILCHESTER ROAD
PAMBER ROAD
SHERBORNE ROAD
MORGASTON ROAD
HILL END ROAD
SALTERS HEATH
KILN LANE
STOKES LANE
Long Copse
Walkner's Firs
Prince's Grove
Charcoal Gully
Fish Ponds
Wyeford Farm
Old Fish Ponds
Moat
Hog Park Copse
Little Yewtree Close
Yewtree Close
Plantation Cottage
Clapperhill
Clapperhill Copse
Fish Weir Copse
Church Gully
Pamber Priory
Priory Farm
The Priory Prim. Sch.
Fir Tree Farm
Little Wyford Farm
Charter Alley Copse
Rawlins Farm
Brocas Bridge
Wither's Copse
Six Acre Copse
Grove Croft Copse
Skeerlands Copse
Hopgarden Copse
Yew Tree Nursery
Wantage Cottage
The Rectory
Priory House
Hall
Privett Green Copse
Privett Copse
Highpath Copse
Drunken Pightle Copse
Trenchmead Copse
Balsans Copse
Crooked Row Copse
Hutchins Copse
Buttermead Copse
Lower Farm
Kiln Green
Woodlands
Monk Sherborne House
Paddock Field
Queen's House
Rookery Farm
Eastrop Cottage
Lower Farm
Manor Farm
Queen's Cotts. (Flat Firs)
Field Barn Farm
Piccadilly Hill
Monk Sherborne Wood
Monks Ford
Redhouse Farm
Woodgate
Bottom Copse
Cranes Copse
Pollards End Copse
Edgerton's Wood
Newlands Copse
Honeywood
Holly Bush Copse
Pamberend Gully Copse
Newlands Copse
Blackwater Copse
Swimming Pool
Hill End Farm Cott.
Hill End Farm
Bow Brook
Nursery
Elm Park Farm
Pamber Place
Pamber Place Cottage
Wigmore Farm
Wakeford Farm
The Bungalow
Rosscarberry
Berry Court Farm
Martingale's Farm House
Simms Corner
Woodcote
Pamber Farm
Oak Villa
College Farm
Kinghem Copse
Hill House
Tadley Place
Cedar Cottage
Thames Dale
Crane's Farm
Farm Pond
Manor Farm
Manor House
Cemy.
Church
Mill Head
Primary Sch.
Vidler's Farm
Wey Brook
West Farm
The Old Brick Kiln Trading Est.
The Cott.
Tubb's Lane
White Hart La.
Common
Meml.
G H J K L M N
1 2 3 4 5 6 7 8 9
460 61 62
59 58 57 56 55
11
22
41

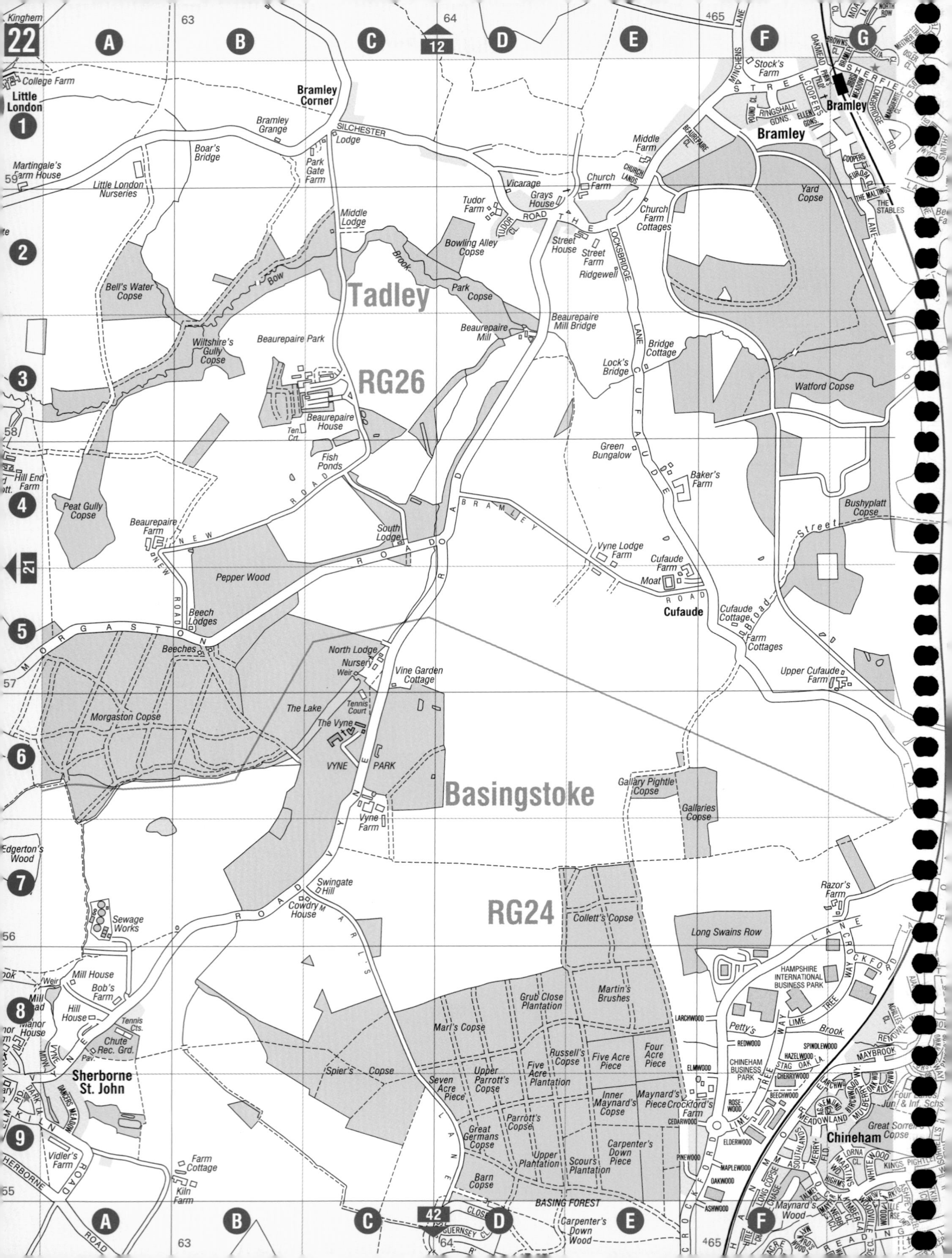
Kinghem
A
B
C
D
E
F
G
63
64
465
12
Little London
College Farm
Bramley Corner
Bramley Grange
Boar's Bridge
Martingale's Farm House
Little London Nurseries
Silchester
Lodge
Park Gate Farm
Middle Lodge
Vicarage
Grays House
Church Farm
Tudor Farm
Tudor Road
Middle Farm
Stock's Farm
Minchens Lane
Bramley
Sherfield Road
Ringshall Gdns.
Beaurepaire Cl.
Church Lands
Church Farm Cottages
Yard Copse
The Maltings
The Stables
Bowling Alley Copse
Street House
Street Farm
Ridgewell
Brook
Bow
Bell's Water Copse
Park Copse
Tadley
Beaurepaire Mill
Beaurepaire Mill Bridge
Wiltshire's Gully Copse
Beaurepaire Park
RG26
Lock's Bridge
Bridge Cottage
Watford Copse
Locksbridge Lane
Cufaude Lane
Beaurepaire House
Ten. Crt.
Fish Ponds
Green Bungalow
Baker's Farm
Hill End Farm
Peat Gully Copse
New Road
Bramley Road
Bushyplatt Copse
Beaurepaire Farm
South Lodge
Vyne Lodge Farm
Cufaude Farm
Moat
Street
21
Pepper Wood
Beech Lodges
Cufaude
Cufaude Road
Cufaude Cottage
Broad
Farm Cottages
Morgaston Road
Beeches
North Lodge
Nursery
Weir
Vine Garden Cottage
Upper Cufaude Farm
The Lake
Tennis Court
The Vyne
Morgaston Copse
Vyne
Park
Basingstoke
Gallary Pightle Copse
Gallaries Copse
Vyne Farm
Edgerton's Wood
Swingate Hill
Cowdry House
Vyne Road
Marl's
RG24
Collett's Copse
Razor's Farm
Sewage Works
Long Swains Row
Crockford Lane
Lime Tree Way
Hampshire International Business Park
Mill House
Bob's Farm
Hill House
Manor House
Tennis Cts.
Chute Rec. Grd.
Pav.
Grub Close Plantation
Martin's Brushes
Marl's Copse
Larchwood
Petty's Brook
Redwood
Spindlewood
Maybrook
Chineham Business Park
Hazelwood
Stag Oak La.
Cherrywood
Russell's Copse
Five Acre Piece
Four Acre Piece
Five Acre Plantation
Spier's Copse
Seven Acre Piece
Upper Parrott's Copse
Sherborne St. John
Inner Maynard's Copse
Maynard's Piece
Crockford's Farm
Elmwood
Rosewood
Beechwood
Meadowland
Cedarwood
Parrott's Copse
Great Germans Copse
Carpenter's Down Piece
Elderwood
Chineham
Great Sorrel Copse
Four Lanes Jun. & Inf. Schs.
Farm Cottage
Vidler's Farm
Upper Plantation
Scours Plantation
Pinewood
Maplewood
Oakwood
Ashwood
Kiln Farm
Barn Copse
Basing Forest
Long Copse Chase
Maynard's Wood
Carpenter's Down Wood
Guernsey Cl.
Kiln Road
Sherborne Road
42
465
1
2
3
4
5
6
7
8
9
59
58
57
56
55

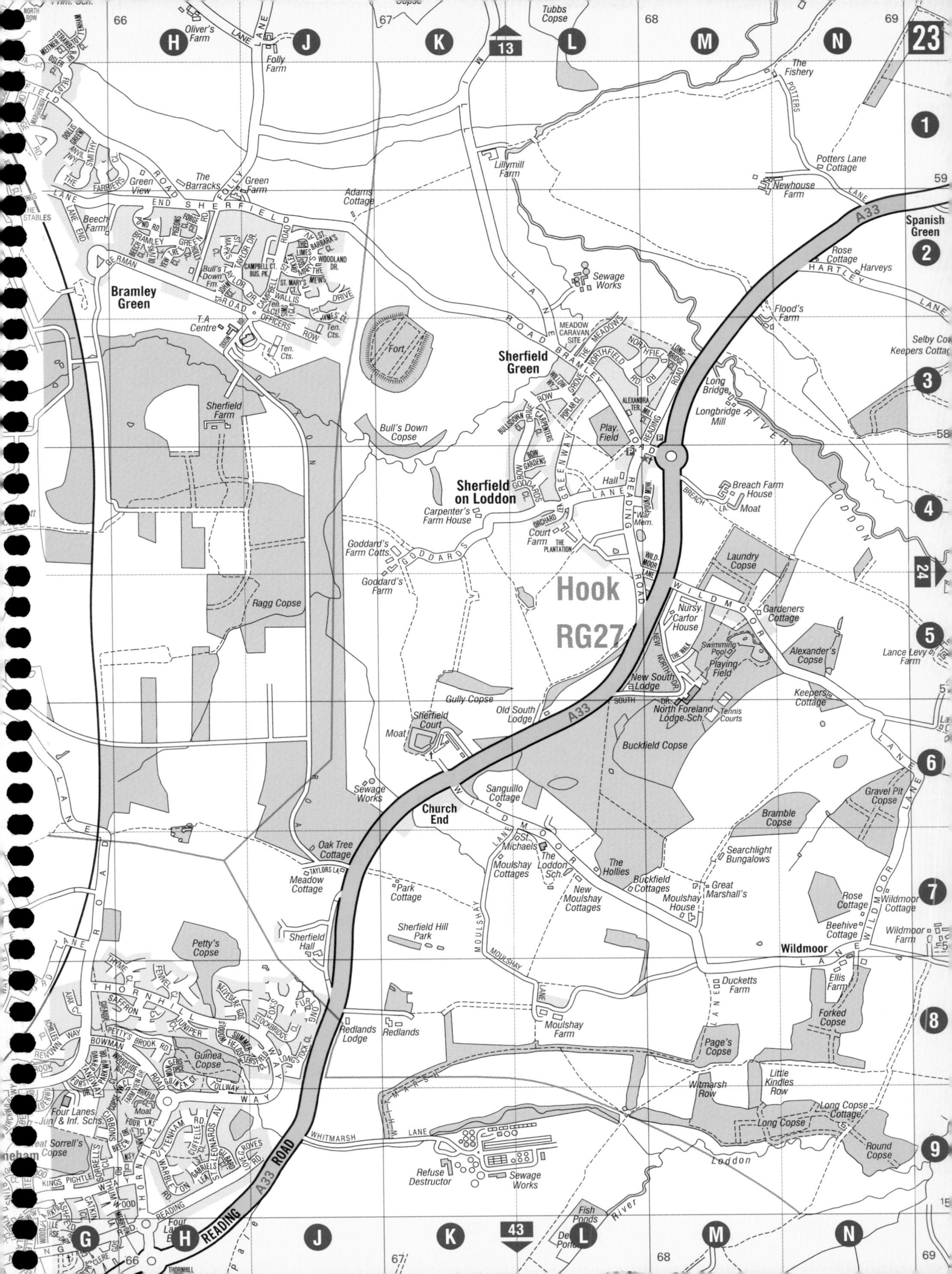

Bramley Green
Sherfield Green
Sherfield on Loddon
Hook
RG27
Church End
Wildmoor
Spanish Green
Lillymill Farm
Sewage Works
Fort
Bull's Down Copse
Sherfield Farm
Ragg Copse
Gully Copse
Sherfield Court
Petty's Copse
Guinea Copse
Laundry Copse
Buckfield Copse
Alexander's Copse
Bramble Copse
Gravel Pit Copse
Forked Copse
Page's Copse
Long Copse
Round Copse
Refuse Destructor
Longbridge Mill
River Loddon
A33
READING ROAD
WILDMOOR LANE
WHITMARSH LANE
MOULSHAY LANE
HARTLEY LANE
POTTERS LANE

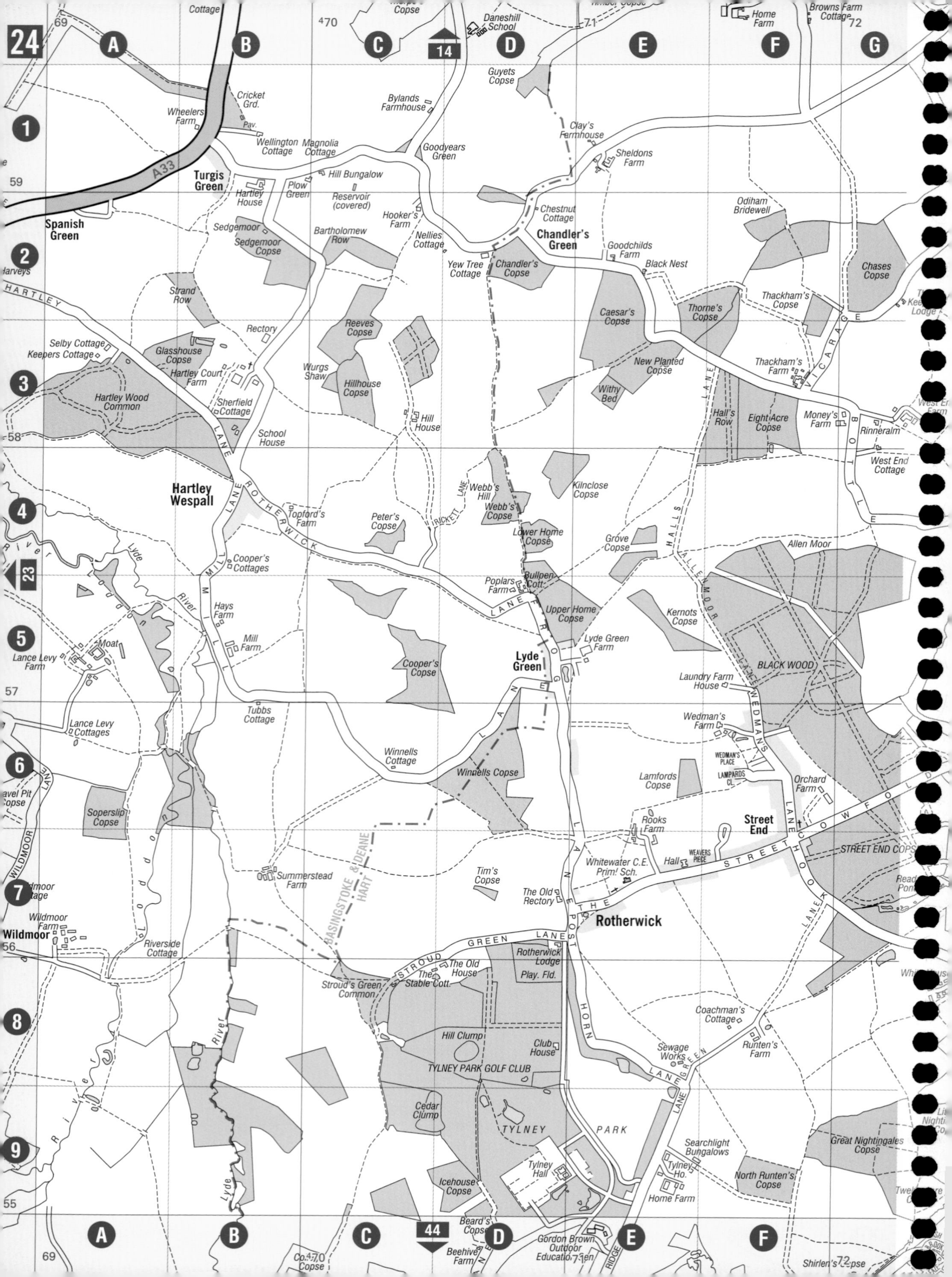
A
B
C
D
E
F
G
1
2
3
4
5
6
7
8
9
14
23
44
470
71
72
59
58
57
56
55
69
Cricket Grd.
Pav.
Wheelers Farm
Wellington Cottage
Magnolia Cottage
A33
Turgis Green
Spanish Green
Hartley House
Plow Green
Hill Bungalow
Reservoir (covered)
Daneshill School
Bylands Farmhouse
Goodyears Green
Guyets Copse
Clay's Farmhouse
Sheldons Farm
Home Farm
Browns Farm Cottage
Hooker's Farm
Nellies Cottage
Chestnut Cottage
Chandler's Green
Odiham Bridewell
Sedgemoor
Sedgemoor Copse
Bartholomew Row
Yew Tree Cottage
Chandler's Copse
Goodchilds Farm
Black Nest
Chases Copse
HARTLEY
Strand Row
Reeves Copse
Caesar's Copse
Thorne's Copse
Thackham's Copse
VICARAGE
Rectory
Selby Cottage
Keepers Cottage
Glasshouse Copse
Hartley Court Farm
Wurgs Shaw
Hillhouse Copse
New Planted Copse
Withy Bed
Thackham's Farm
Hartley Wood Common
Sherfield Cottage
Hill House
Hall's Row
Eight Acre Copse
Money's Farm
Rinneralm
School House
West End Cottage
BOTTLE
Hartley Wespall
ROTHERWICK
Webb's Hill
Webb's Copse
Kilnclose Copse
RICKETT LANE
Topford's Farm
Peter's Copse
Lower Home Copse
Grove Copse
HALLS
Allen Moor
ALLENMOOR
River Lodden
Lyde
Cooper's Cottages
Poplars Farm
Bullpen Cott.
Upper Home Copse
Kernots Copse
River
Hays Farm
MILL
LANE
Moat
Mill Farm
Lance Levy Farm
Cooper's Copse
Lyde Green
Lyde Green Farm
BLACK WOOD
Laundry Farm House
FROG
Tubbs Cottage
Lance Levy Cottages
Wedman's Farm
WEDMANS
WEDMAN'S PLACE
LAMPARDS CL.
Winnells Cottage
Winnells Copse
Lamfords Copse
Orchard Farm
Soperslip Copse
Rooks Farm
Street End
COWFOLD
STREET END COPSE
HOOK
WILDMOOR
LANE
Summerstead Farm
BASINGSTOKE & DEANE
HART
Whitewater C.E. Prim. Sch.
Hall
WEAVERS PIECE
THE STREET
Tim's Copse
The Old Rectory
Rotherwick
Wildmoor Farm
Wildmoor
Riverside Cottage
STROUD GREEN LANE
POST
Rotherwick Lodge
Play. Fld.
The Old House
The Stable Cott.
Stroud's Green Common
HORN
Coachman's Cottage
Hill Clump
Club House
Sewage Works
GREEN
Runten's Farm
TYLNEY PARK GOLF CLUB
Cedar Clump
TYLNEY
PARK
Searchlight Bungalows
Great Nightingales Copse
Tylney Hall
Tylney Ho.
North Runten's Copse
Icehouse Copse
Home Farm
Beard's Copse
Gordon Brown Outdoor Education Cen.
RIDGE
Beehive Farm
Shirlen's Copse

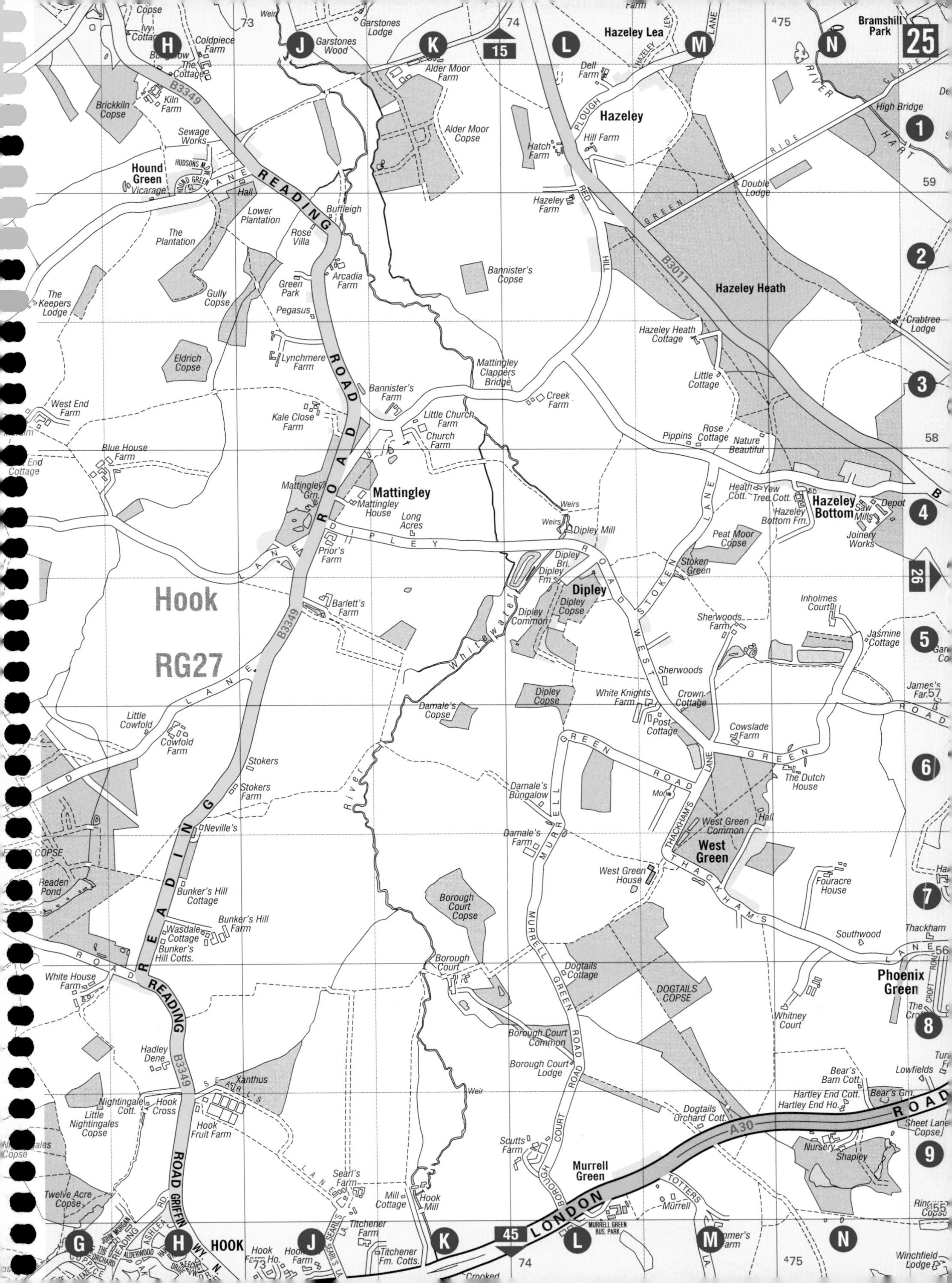
Hazeley Lea
Hazeley
Hazeley Heath
Hound Green
Mattingley
Hazeley Bottom
Dipley
Hook
RG27
West Green
Phoenix Green
Murrell Green
HOOK
Bramshill Park
Garstones Wood
Garstones Lodge
Alder Moor Farm
Alder Moor Copse
Brickkiln Copse
Kiln Farm
Coldpiece Farm
Sewage Works
Lower Plantation
The Plantation
Buffleigh
Rose Villa
Arcadia Farm
Green Park
Pegasus
Gully Copse
The Keepers Lodge
Eldrich Copse
Lynchmere Farm
Bannister's Farm
Bannister's Copse
Kale Close Farm
West End Farm
Blue House Farm
Little Church Farm
Church Farm
Mattingley Clappers Bridge
Creek Farm
Mattingley House
Long Acres
Prior's Farm
Barlett's Farm
Dipley Mill
Dipley Common
Dipley Copse
Hatch Farm
Hill Farm
Dell Farm
Hazeley Farm
Double Lodge
High Bridge
Crabtree Lodge
Hazeley Heath Cottage
Little Cottage
Pippins
Rose Cottage
Nature Beautiful
Heath Cott.
Yew Tree Cott.
Hazeley Bottom Fm.
Saw Mills
Depot
Joinery Works
Peat Moor Copse
Stoken Green
Inholmes Court
Sherwoods Farm
Jasmine Cottage
Sherwoods
White Knights Farm
Crown Cottage
Post Cottage
Cowslade Farm
The Dutch House
Damale's Copse
Damale's Bungalow
Damale's Farm
West Green Common
West Green House
Fouracre House
Southwood
Thackham
Little Cowfold
Cowfold Farm
Stokers
Stokers Farm
Neville's
Readen Pond
Bunker's Hill Cottage
Bunker's Hill Farm
Wasdale Cottage
Bunker's Hill Cotts.
White House Farm
Borough Court Copse
Borough Court
Dogtails Cottage
DOGTAILS COPSE
Whitney Court
Borough Court Common
Borough Court Lodge
Bear's Barn Cott.
Lowfields
Hartley End Cott.
Hartley End Ho.
Bear's Gn.
Dogtails Orchard Cott.
Sheet Lane Copse
Nursery
Shapley
Hadley Dene
Xanthus
Nightingale Cott.
Hook Cross
Little Nightingales Copse
Hook Fruit Farm
Scutts Farm
Twelve Acre Copse
Searl's Farm
Mill Cottage
Hook Mill
Murrell
MURRELL GREEN BUS. PARK
Titchener Farm
Titchener Fm. Cotts.
Hook Farm Ho.
Winchfield Lodge
READING ROAD
B3349
B3011
A30
LONDON ROAD
DIPLEY ROAD
WEST GREEN ROAD
MURRELL GREEN ROAD
BOROUGH COURT ROAD
THACKHAM'S LANE
STOKEN LANE
RED HILL
PLOUGH LANE
HAZELEY HEATH
GREEN RIDE
River Whitewater
River Hart
Weir
Weirs
15
26
45
73
74
475
59
58
57
56
55
1 2 3 4 5 6 7 8 9
G H J K L M N

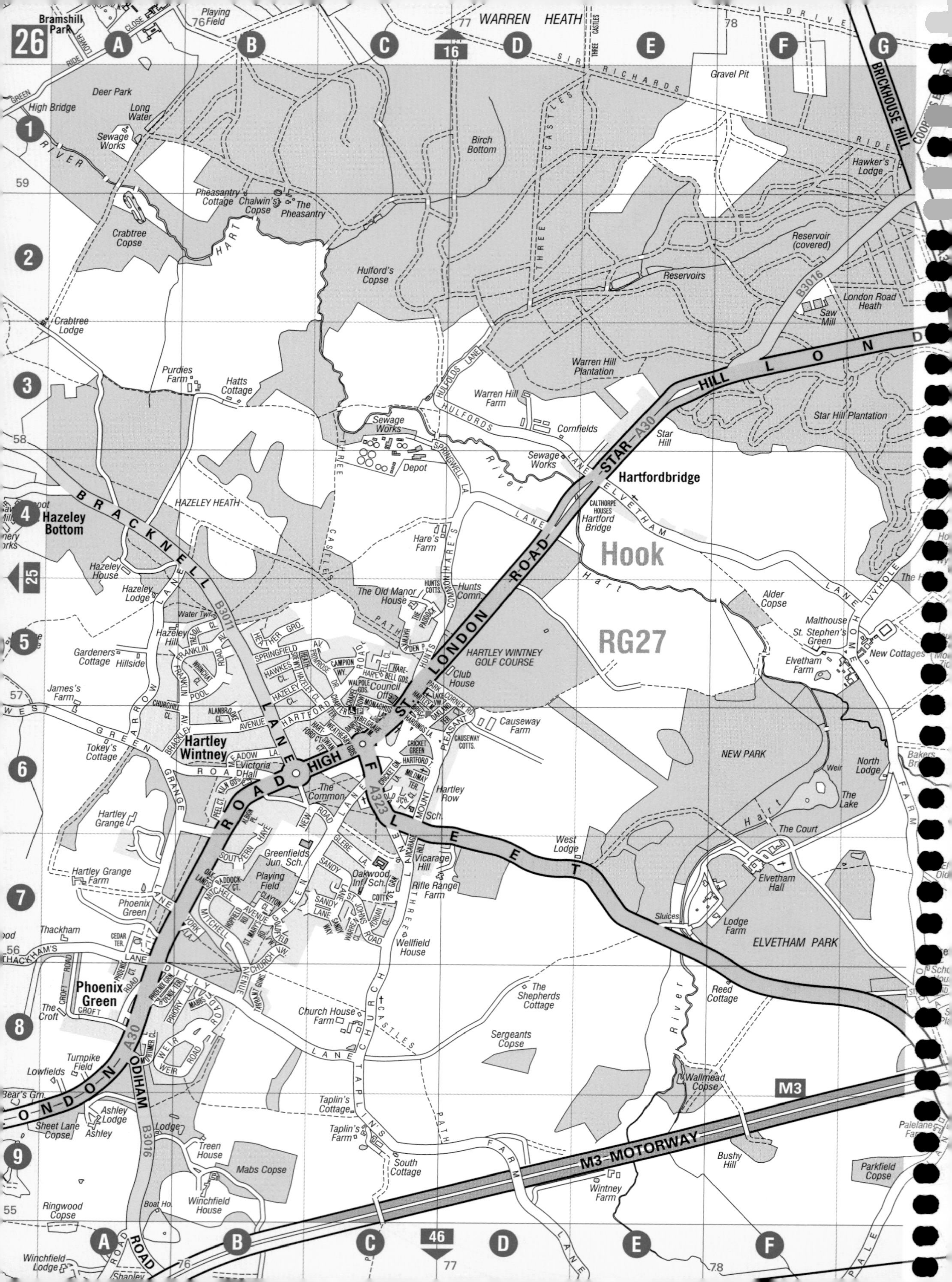

WARREN HEATH
Bramshill Park
Playing Field
Deer Park
High Bridge
Long Water
Sewage Works
Birch Bottom
Gravel Pit
SIR RICHARDS DRIVE
BRICKHOUSE HILL
Hawker's Lodge
Pheasantry's Cottage
Chalwin's Copse
The Pheasantry
Crabtree Copse
Hulford's Copse
Reservoir (covered)
Reservoirs
London Road Heath
Saw Mill
Crabtree Lodge
Purdies Farm
Hatts Cottage
Warren Hill Plantation
Warren Hill Farm
Cornfields
Star Hill Plantation
Star Hill
Depot
HAZELEY HEATH
Hazeley Bottom
Hartfordbridge
Hartford Bridge
Hook
Hare's Farm
Hazeley House
Hazeley Lodge
The Old Manor House
Hunts Comn.
Alder Copse
RG27
HARTLEY WINTNEY GOLF COURSE
Club House
Malthouse
St. Stephen's Green
Elvetham Farm
New Cottages
Gardeners Cottage
Hillside
Council Offs.
James's Farm
Hartley Wintney
Causeway Farm
Tokey's Cottage
Victoria Hall
The Common
NEW PARK
North Lodge
Hartley Row
Hartley Grange
The Lake
The Court
West Lodge
Greenfields Jun. Sch.
Playing Field
Oakwood Inf. Sch.
Vicarage Hill
Rifle Range Farm
Elvetham Hall
Hartley Grange Farm
Phoenix Green
Lodge Farm
ELVETHAM PARK
Thackham
Wellfield House
Phoenix Green
The Croft
The Shepherds Cottage
Reed Cottage
Church House Farm
Sergeants Copse
Turnpike Field
Lowfields
Wallmead Copse
Bear's Grn.
Ashley Lodge
Ashley
Taplin's Cottage
Taplin's Farm
Sheet Lane Copse
Treen House
Mabs Copse
South Cottage
Bushy Hill
Palelane Farm
Parkfield Copse
Winchfield House
Wintney Farm
Ringwood Copse
Winchfield Lodge
LONDON ROAD
STAR HILL
HIGH ST
BRACKNELL LANE
FLEET ROAD
ODIHAM ROAD
M3 MOTORWAY
M3
A30
A323
B3011
B3016
16
25
46

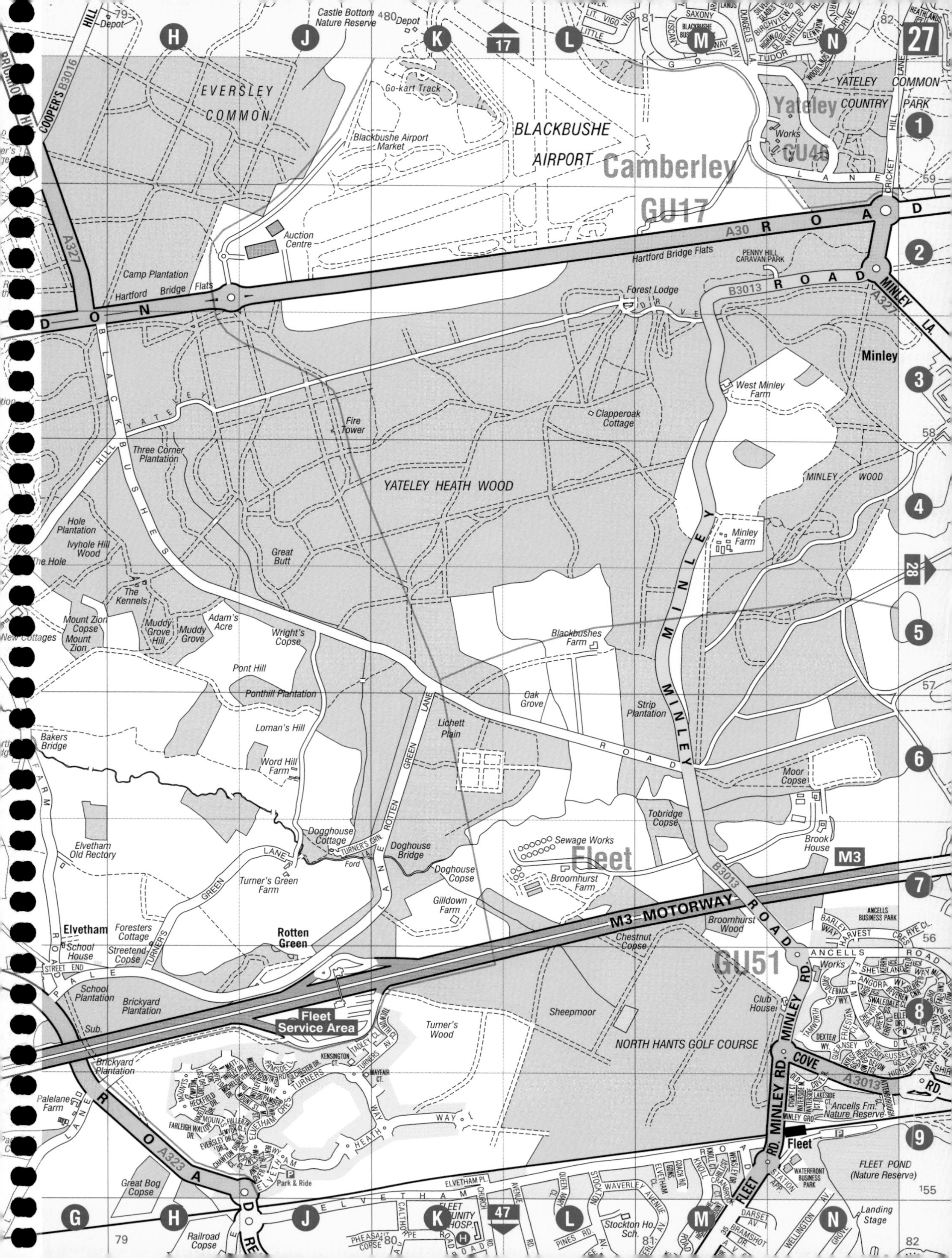

EVERSLEY COMMON
Castle Bottom Nature Reserve
Depot
Go-kart Track
Blackbushe Airport Market
BLACKBUSHE AIRPORT
Camberley
GU17
Yateley
Works
GU46
YATELEY COMMON COUNTRY PARK
Auction Centre
Camp Plantation
Hartford Bridge Flats
Forest Lodge
PENNY HILL CARAVAN PARK
Minley
West Minley Farm
Clapperoak Cottage
Fire Tower
Three Corner Plantation
YATELEY HEATH WOOD
MINLEY WOOD
Hole Plantation
Ivyhole Hill Wood
The Hole
Great Butt
Minley Farm
The Kennels
Mount Zion Copse
Mount Zion
New Cottages
Muddy Grove Hill
Muddy Grove
Adam's Acre
Wright's Copse
Blackbushes Farm
Pont Hill
Ponthill Plantation
Oak Grove
Strip Plantation
Loman's Hill
Lichett Plain
Bakers Bridge
Word Hill Farm
Moor Copse
Tobridge Copse
Brook House
Elvetham Old Rectory
Dogghouse Cottage
Doghouse Bridge
Sewage Works
Fleet
Turner's Green Farm
Ford
Doghouse Copse
Broomhurst Farm
Gilldown Farm
M3 MOTORWAY
Broomhurst Wood
ANCELLS BUSINESS PARK
Elvetham
Foresters Cottage
Rotten Green
Chestnut Copse
GU51
School House
Streetend Copse
Works
School Plantation
Brickyard Plantation
Club House
Sheepmoor
Fleet Service Area
Turner's Wood
NORTH HANTS GOLF COURSE
Sub.
Brickyard Plantation
Palelane Farm
Ancells Fm. Nature Reserve
Fleet
FLEET POND (Nature Reserve)
WATERFRONT BUSINESS PARK
Great Bog Copse
Park & Ride
FLEET COMMUNITY HOSP.
Stockton Ho. Sch.
Landing Stage
Railroad Copse
A30
B3013
A327
B3016
A323
A3013
M3
17
47
28

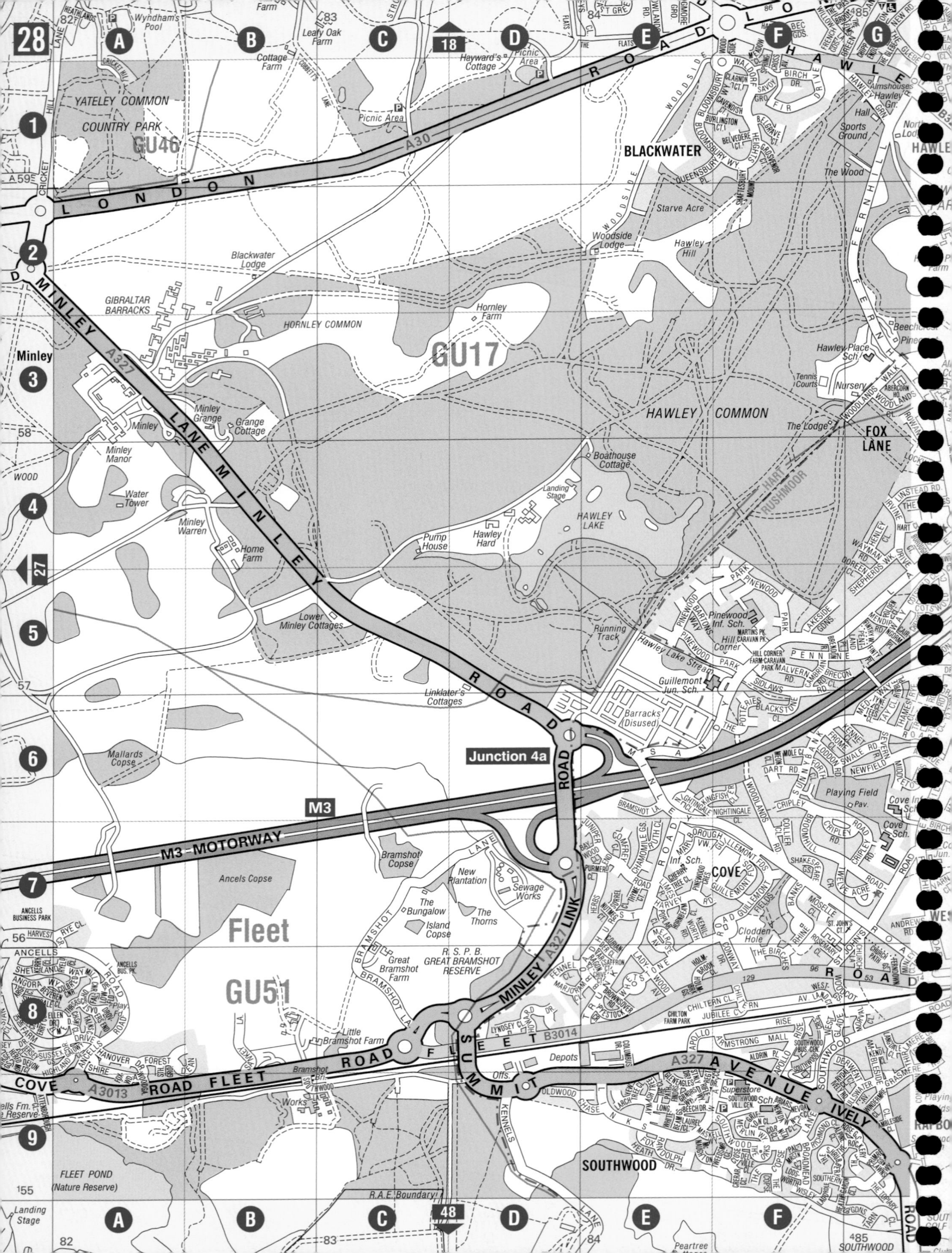
YATELEY COMMON
COUNTRY PARK
GU46
LONDON ROAD
A30
BLACKWATER
GIBRALTAR BARRACKS
HORNLEY COMMON
GU17
Minley
MINLEY LANE
MINLEY ROAD
A327
HAWLEY COMMON
HAWLEY LAKE
FOX LANE
Junction 4a
M3
M3 MOTORWAY
Fleet
GU51
COVE
SOUTHWOOD
FLEET POND (Nature Reserve)
R. S. P. B. GREAT BRAMSHOT RESERVE
MINLEY LINK
FLEET ROAD
B3014
A3013
SUMMIT AVENUE
IVELY ROAD
18
27
48

HAWLEY
HAWLEY PARK
Camberley
GU15
FRIMLEY
GU16
FRIMLEY GREEN
Farnborough
GU14
FARNBOROUGH GREEN
FARNBOROUGH STREET
NORTH FARNBOROUGH
FARNBOROUGH
FARNBOROUGH PARK
WEST HEATH
RAFBOROUGH
MYTCHETT
M3 MOTORWAY
Junc. 4
BLACKWATER VALLEY ROAD
A331
A325
FARNBOROUGH ROAD
PORTSMOUTH ROAD
FRIMLEY BY-PASS
Frimley
Farnborough North
Farnborough Main
Frimley Park Hospital
France Hill School
Farnborough Sixth Form Coll.
Farnborough Hill School
Oak Farm Community Sch.
St. Michael's Abbey
Rushmoor B.C. Offs.
Leisure Park
Cemetery
Lake
19
49

30

425 26 27 23

51

LUDGERSHALL INSET

A342 ANDOVER ROAD

TIDWORTH ROAD A3026

Castledown School

Sports Centre

Tidworth Down

Fowler Barracks

Busigny Barracks

Sprts. Grd.

Sports Ground

Newdrove Plantation

Ludgershall Business Park

Andover

SP11

Perham Down

Kemmel Rd.

Cambrai Barracks

Cachy Barracks

Sewage Works

Little Perham Copse

Great Perham Copse

Lamb Down

Sports Ground

Castle Farm

BUTT ST.

Warehouse

Pav. Playing Field

Crescent

Depot

LUDGERSHALL

Crawlboys Row

Marlins Farm

Poultry Houses

Castle Prim. Sch.

Rec. Grd.

Faberstown

Hazelberry Plantation

Hougoumont Farm

Sewage Works

Willis Wood

South Park

KENNET TEST VALLEY

Great Shoddesden

Meadow Copse

Shoddesden Grange

Barrow Plantation

A388

A342

COW LANE

31

TIDWORTH INSET

Sidbury Hill Plantation

Chalkpit Hill Plantation

Chalkpit Hill

Tank Obstacle Course

Chalkpit Wood

Playground

Clarendon Hill Plantation

Clarendon Hill

Reservoir

Miniature Range

Miniature Range

Football Ground

Tidworth Camp

Football Grd.

Highfield House (Nurses Home)

Playground

Aliwal Barracks

Mall Bazaar

Candahar Barracks

Delhi Barracks

Bellalabad Barracks

Mooltan Barracks

Lucknow Barracks

Sports Ground

Office

Cricket Grd. Pav.

Football Grd.

Zouch Prim. Sch.

Gason Hill

MILL PATH

Zouch Market

Works

Rec.

St. Andrews Rd.

PENNINGS ROAD A338

LUDGERSHALL ROAD A3026

North Tidworth

Manor Bridge

Tidworth

SP9

Clarendon Jun. & Inf. Schools

Playground

Military Workshops

Armoury Ct.

TIDWORTH

The Oval

Andover Plantation

Pickpit Hill

Plantation Rd.

Furze Hill Road

31

Ashdown

South Tidworth

30

PENNINGS

Zouch Prim. Sch.

Chalkpit Hill

North Tidworth

Clarendon Hill

Tidworth Camp

Golf Course

Club House

Home Farm

The Cross Belt

Tidworth

SP9

Sewage Works

A388 SALISBURY

148

49

150

49

31

31

30

31

66

BULFORD

22 23 24

31
Marlborough
Andover
SN8
SP11
Sunton
Cadley
Collingbourne Ducis
COLLINGBOURNE WOOD
Upper Chute
Chute Down
Mount Cowdown
Chantry
Limmer Copse
Limmer Pond
Rag Copse
Cow Down
Herridge Stud Farm
Lynden Down
Sunton Heath
Mount Orleans Farm
Wick Down
Shaw Hill
Widgerly Down
Blackmore Down
Sunnyhill Farm
Windmillhill Down
Castle (remains of)
Crawlboys Farm
Stert Copse
Coldridge Wood
Coldridge Down
Honey Bottom
Longbottom Farm
Biddesden Farm
Biddesden Ho.
Marlins Farm
Faberstown
Lambourne's Hill
LUDGERSHALL
Ludgershall Business Park
Castledown Sch.
Perham Down
Sewage Works
South Park
Great Shoddesden
Little Shoddesden
Littleton Copse
Redenham House
Pickpit Hill
TIDWORTH
South Tidworth
Ashdown Copse
Lamb Down
Newdown Copse
WARREN HILL
Kimpton Down Farm
Kimpton Wood
Kimpton
Gallop
Pickford Hill
Fyfield
Thruxton
THRUXTON AIRFIELD AND MOTOR RACING CIRCUIT
Kimpton C. of E. Prim Sch.
KENNET
TEST VALLEY
Dean Farm
Parsonage Farm
Manor Farm
New Barn
Bauks Hill
Forest House
MARLBOROUGH RD.
HIGH ST.
LUDGERSHALL RD.
TIDWORTH RD.
CHURCH RD.
TIDWORTH ROAD
ANDOVER ROAD
LUDGERSHALL ROAD
PARK RD
CHUTE CAUSEWAY
CHANTRY LANE
FOREST LANE
CRAWLBOYS ROAD
BIDDESDEN LANE
SHODDESDEN LANE
PRIVET LANE
DEACON ROAD
COW LANE
NODDINGTON
ROAD
A338
A346
A342
A3026
River Bourne
H
J
K
L
M
N
G
1
2
3
4
5
6
7
8
9
32
50
30
67
24
425
26
27
28
29
430
155
54
53
52
51
150
49
48
47
46

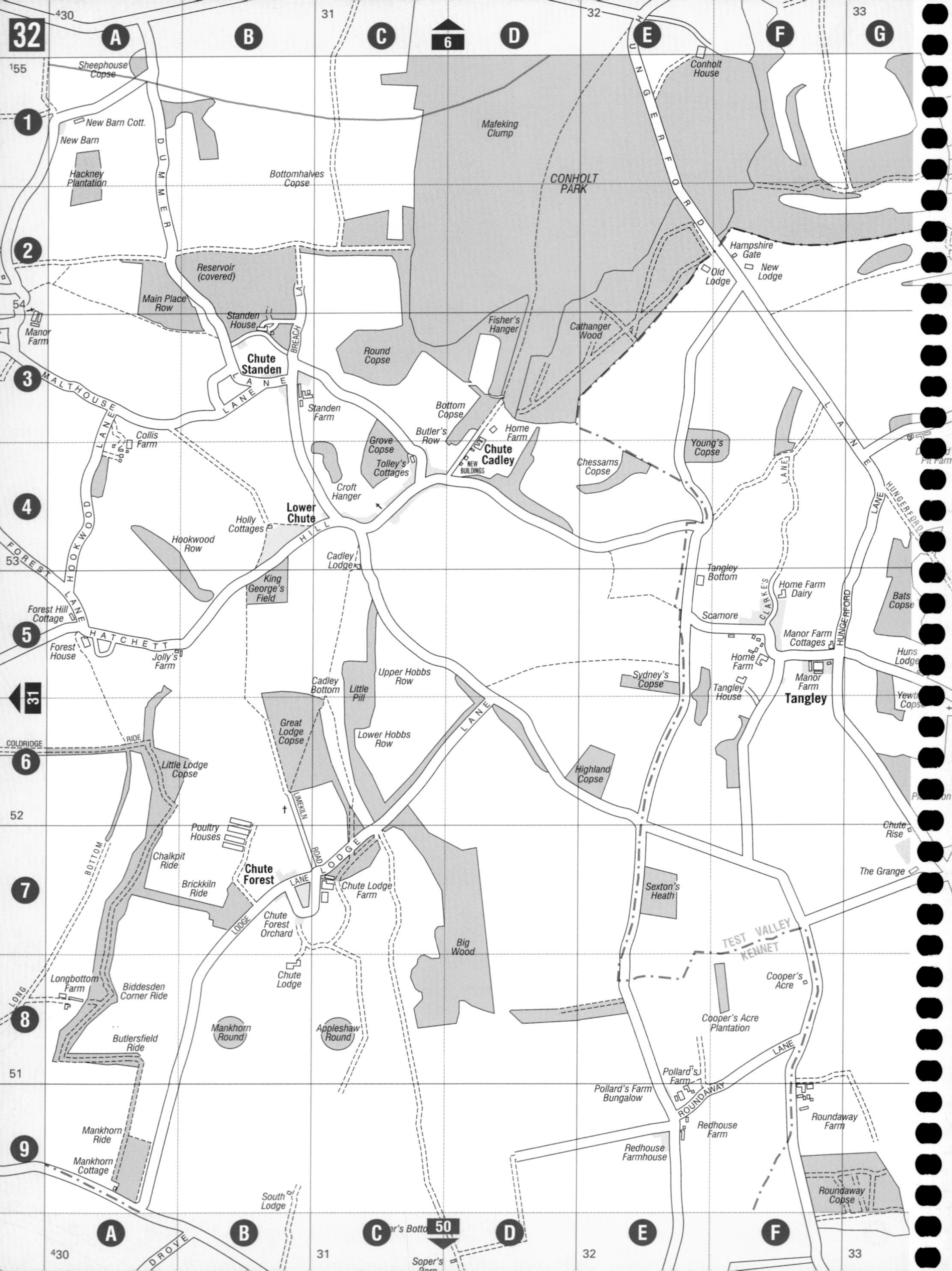
Sheephouse Copse
New Barn Cott.
New Barn
Hackney Plantation
DUMMER
Bottomhalves Copse
Mafeking Clump
CONHOLT PARK
HUNGERFORD
Conholt House
Hampshire Gate
New Lodge
Old Lodge
Reservoir (covered)
Main Place Row
Standen House
BREACH LA
Manor Farm
Chute Standen
MALTHOUSE LANE
Round Copse
Fisher's Hanger
Cathanger Wood
Standen Farm
Bottom Copse
Butler's Row
Home Farm
Chute Cadley
NEW BUILDINGS
Grove Copse
Tolley's Cottages
Collis Farm
Chessams Copse
Young's Copse
LANE
Croft Hanger
Lower Chute
Holly Cottages
Hookwood Row
HOOKWOOD LANE
HILL
FOREST LANE
Cadley Lodge
King George's Field
Tangley Bottom
CLARKE'S
Home Farm Dairy
HUNGERFORD LANE
Bats Copse
Forest Hill Cottage
Scamore
Manor Farm Cottages
Forest House
HATCHETT
Jolly's Farm
Upper Hobbs Row
Cadley Bottom
Little Pill
Sydney's Copse
Home Farm
Manor Farm
Tangley House
Tangley
Huns Lodge
Great Lodge Copse
Lower Hobbs Row
COLDRIDGE
RIDE
Little Lodge Copse
Highland Copse
LIMEKILN ROAD
Chute Rise
Poultry Houses
BOTTOM
Chalkpit Ride
Brickkiln Ride
Chute Forest
LODGE LANE
Chute Lodge Farm
Sexton's Heath
The Grange
Chute Forest Orchard
Big Wood
TEST VALLEY
KENNET
Chute Lodge
Longbottom Farm
Biddesden Corner Ride
LONG
Cooper's Acre
Cooper's Acre Plantation
Mankhorn Round
Appleshaw Round
Butlersfield Ride
Pollard's Farm
Pollard's Farm Bungalow
ROUNDAWAY LANE
Redhouse Farm
Roundaway Farm
Mankhorn Ride
Mankhorn Cottage
Redhouse Farmhouse
Roundaway Copse
South Lodge
DROVE
Soper's Barn

6
31
50

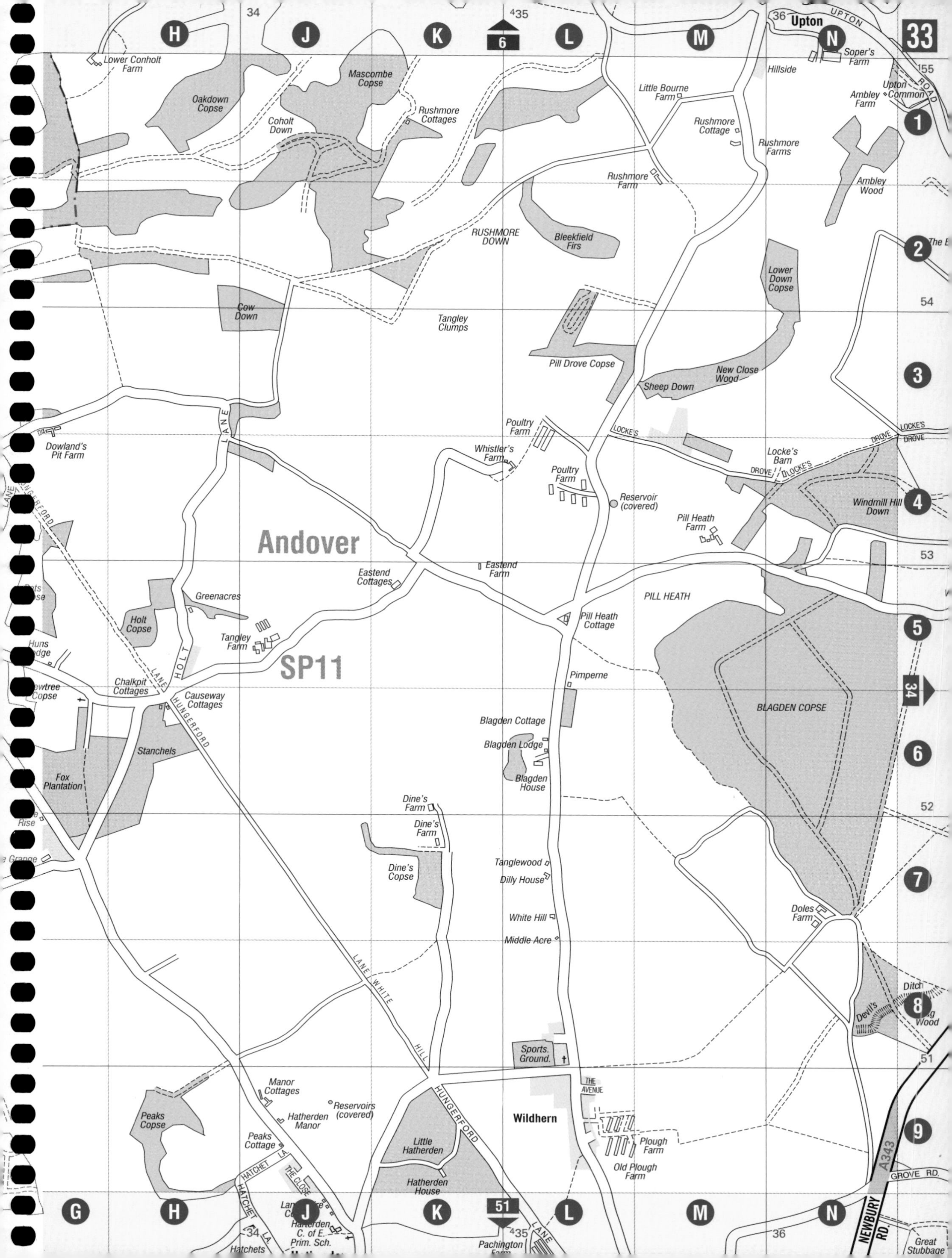
Upton
Soper's Farm
Hillside
Lower Conholt Farm
Mascombe Copse
Oakdown Copse
Coholt Down
Rushmore Cottages
Little Bourne Farm
Rushmore Cottage
Rushmore Farms
Rushmore Farm
Upton Common
Ambley Farm
Ambley Wood
RUSHMORE DOWN
Bleekfield Firs
Lower Down Copse
Cow Down
Tangley Clumps
Pill Drove Copse
New Close Wood
Sheep Down
Poultry Farm
Whistler's Farm
LOCKE'S DROVE
Locke's Barn
Reservoir (covered)
Windmill Hill Down
Pill Heath Farm
Dowland's Pit Farm
Andover
Eastend Cottages
Eastend Farm
PILL HEATH
Greenacres
Holt Copse
Tangley Farm
Pill Heath Cottage
SP11
HOLT LANE
Huns Lodge
Yewtree Copse
Chalkpit Cottages
Causeway Cottages
HUNGERFORD
Pimperne
BLAGDEN COPSE
Blagden Cottage
Blagden Lodge
Blagden House
Stanchels
Fox Plantation
Dine's Farm
Dine's Copse
Tanglewood
Dilly House
White Hill
Middle Acre
Doles Farm
WHITE HILL LANE
Devil's Ditch
Wood
Sports Ground
THE AVENUE
Manor Cottages
Reservoirs (covered)
Hatherden Manor
Wildhern
Peaks Copse
Peaks Cottage
Little Hatherden
Plough Farm
Old Plough Farm
Hatherden House
HATCHET LA.
THE CLOSE
Hatherden C. of E. Prim. Sch.
Hatchets
Pachington Farm
A343
NEWBURY RD.
GROVE RD.
Great Stubbage
UPTON ROAD
34
435
36
155
54
53
52
51
6
51
34

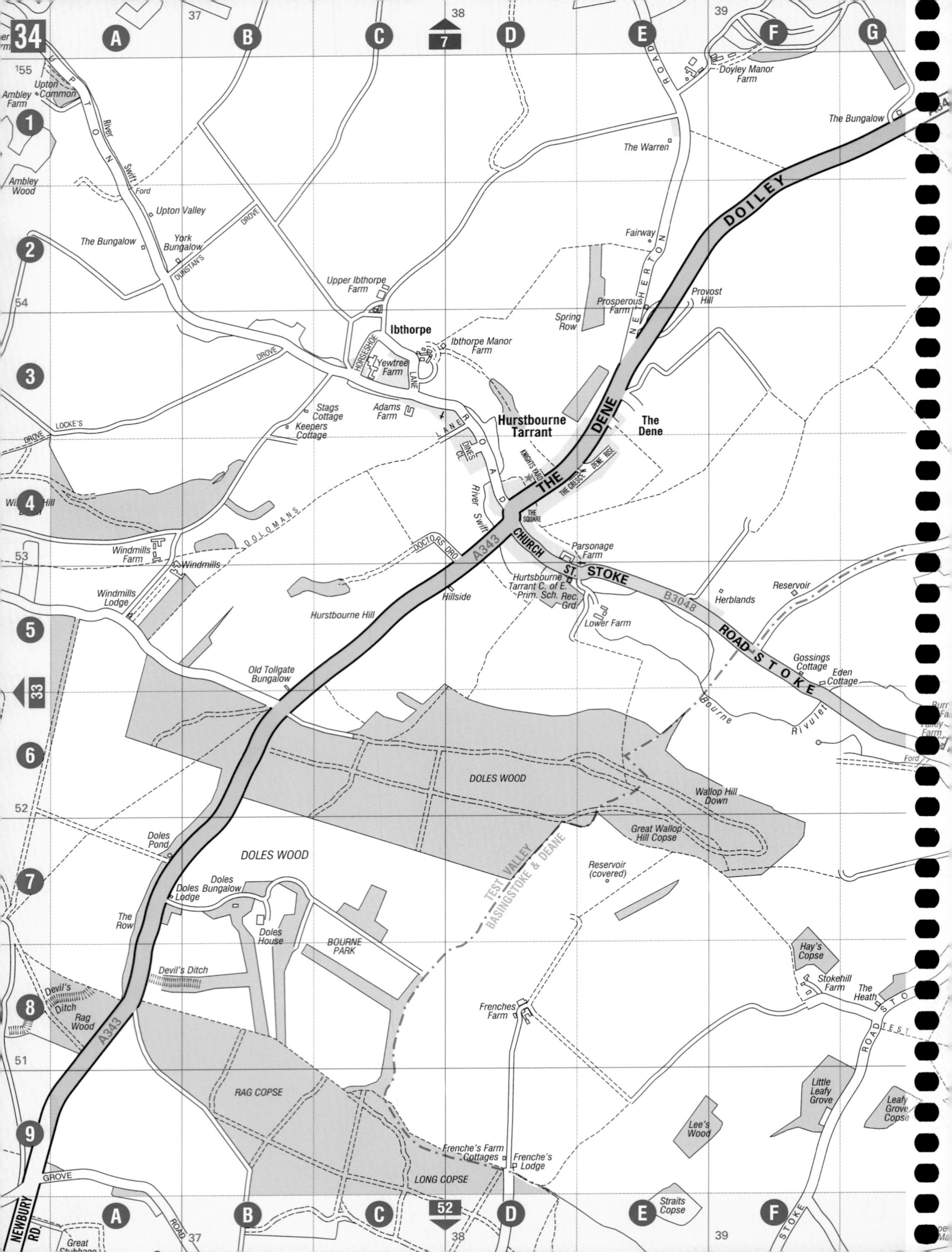

Upton Common
Ambley Farm
Ambley Wood
River Swift
Ford
Upton Valley
The Bungalow
York Bungalow
DUNSTAN'S
DROVE
Upper Ibthorpe Farm
Ibthorpe
Ibthorpe Manor Farm
HORSESHOE
Yewtree Farm
LANE
Stags Cottage
Keepers Cottage
Adams Farm
LOCKE'S
DROVE
Hurstbourne Tarrant
DINES CL.
KNIGHT'S YARD
THE SQUARE
River Swift
DOLOMANS
DOCTORS DRO.
Windmills Farm
Windmills
Windmills Lodge
Hurstbourne Hill
Hillside
A343
CHURCH ST.
STOKE ROAD
Parsonage Farm
Hurtsbourne Tarrant C. of E. Prim. Sch.
Rec. Grd.
Lower Farm
Old Tollgate Bungalow
Doyley Manor Farm
The Bungalow
The Warren
DOILEY
Fairway
NETHERTON ROAD
Prosperous Farm
Provost Hill
Spring Row
THE DENE
The Dene
THE CRESCENT
DENE RISE
B3048
STOKE
Reservoir
Herblands
Gossings Cottage
Eden Cottage
Bourne Rivulet
Ford
DOLES WOOD
Wallop Hill Down
Great Wallop Hill Copse
Doles Pond
DOLES WOOD
TEST VALLEY
BASINGSTOKE & DEANE
Reservoir (covered)
Doles Lodge
Doles Bungalow
The Row
Doles House
BOURNE PARK
Devil's Ditch
Devil's Ditch
Rag Wood
Hay's Copse
Stokehill Farm
The Heath
ROAD
TEST
Frenches Farm
RAG COPSE
Little Leafy Grove
Leafy Grove Copse
Lee's Wood
Frenche's Farm Cottages
Frenche's Lodge
LONG COPSE
GROVE
NEWBURY RD.
ROAD
Great Stubbage
Straits Copse
STOKE

7
33
52

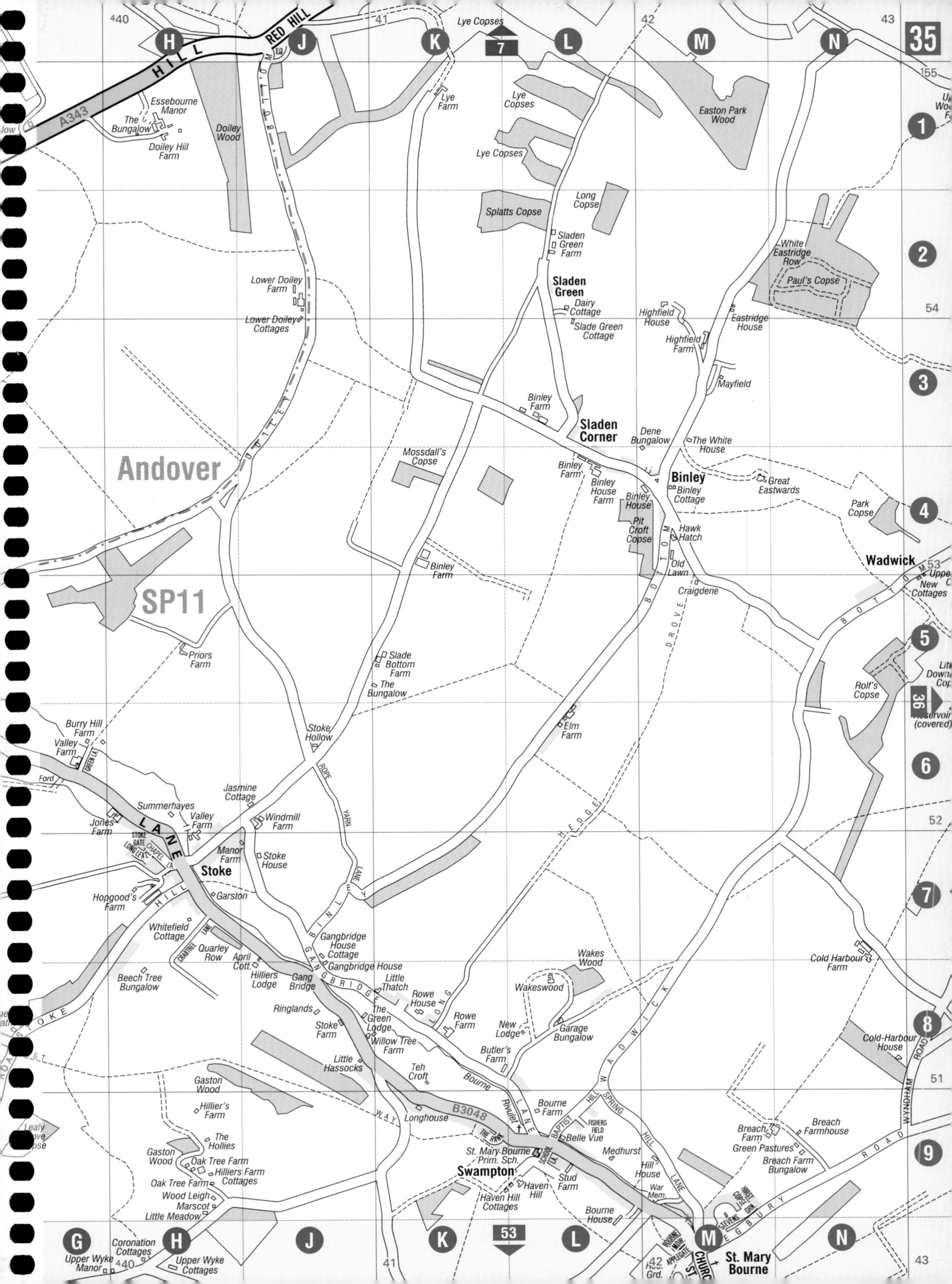
Andover
SP11
Red Hill
Hill
A343
Essebourne Manor
The Bungalow
Doiley Hill Farm
Doiley Wood
Lye Copses
Lye Farm
Easton Park Wood
Splatts Copse
Long Copse
Sladen Green Farm
Sladen Green
Dairy Cottage
Slade Green Cottage
White Eastridge Row
Paul's Copse
Eastridge House
Highfield House
Highfield Farm
Mayfield
Lower Doiley Farm
Lower Doiley Cottages
Binley Farm
Sladen Corner
Dene Bungalow
The White House
Binley
Binley Cottage
Great Eastwards
Binley House Farm
Binley House
Pit Croft Copse
Hawk Hatch
Old Lawn
Craigdene
Mossdall's Copse
Park Copse
Wadwick
Upper New Cottages
Rolf's Copse
Reservoir (covered)
Priors Farm
Slade Bottom Farm
The Bungalow
Stoke Hollow
Elm Farm
Burry Hill Farm
Valley Farm
Ford
Jasmine Cottage
Summerhayes
Valley Farm
Jones Farm
Windmill Farm
Manor Farm
Stoke House
Stoke
Garston
Hopgood's Farm
Whitefield Cottage
Quarley Row
April Cott.
Hilliers Lodge
Gang Bridge
Gangbridge House Cottage
Gangbridge House
Little Thatch
Rowe House
Rowe Farm
Beech Tree Bungalow
Ringlands
Stoke Farm
The Green Lodge
Willow Tree Farm
Little Hassocks
Teh Croft
Wakes Wood
Wakeswood
New Lodge
Garage Bungalow
Butler's Farm
Cold Harbour Farm
Cold-Harbour House
Gaston Wood
Hillier's Farm
The Hollies
Gaston Wood
Oak Tree Farm
Hilliers Farm Cottages
Oak Tree Farm
Wood Leigh
Marscot
Little Meadow
Longhouse
B3048
Bourne Rivulet
Bourne Farm
Belle Vue
Medhurst
Hill House
Breach Farm
Breach Farmhouse
Green Pastures
Breach Farm Bungalow
St. Mary Bourne Prim. Sch.
Swampton
Haven Hill
Haven Hill Cottages
Stud Farm
War Mem.
Bourne House
St. Mary Bourne
Coronation Cottages
Upper Wyke Manor
Upper Wyke Cottages
Long Lane
Binley Lane
Rope Yarn Lane
Gangbridge Lane
Bourne Lane
Wadwick Lane
Drove Hedge
Egbury Road
Wyndham Road
Spring Hill Lane
Bottom
Church St
Doiley Bottom
Stoke Hill
Green La.
Crabtree Lane
Chapel La.
Long Lea
Stoke Gate
School La.
Baptist Hill
Fishers Field
Hirst Copse
Stevens Grn.
Applegate
Bourne Mdw.
The Rank
Wakes Way
Leafy Grove Copse
7
36
53
440
41
42
43
155
54
53
52
51
H J K L M N
G H J K L M N
1 2 3 4 5 6 7 8 9

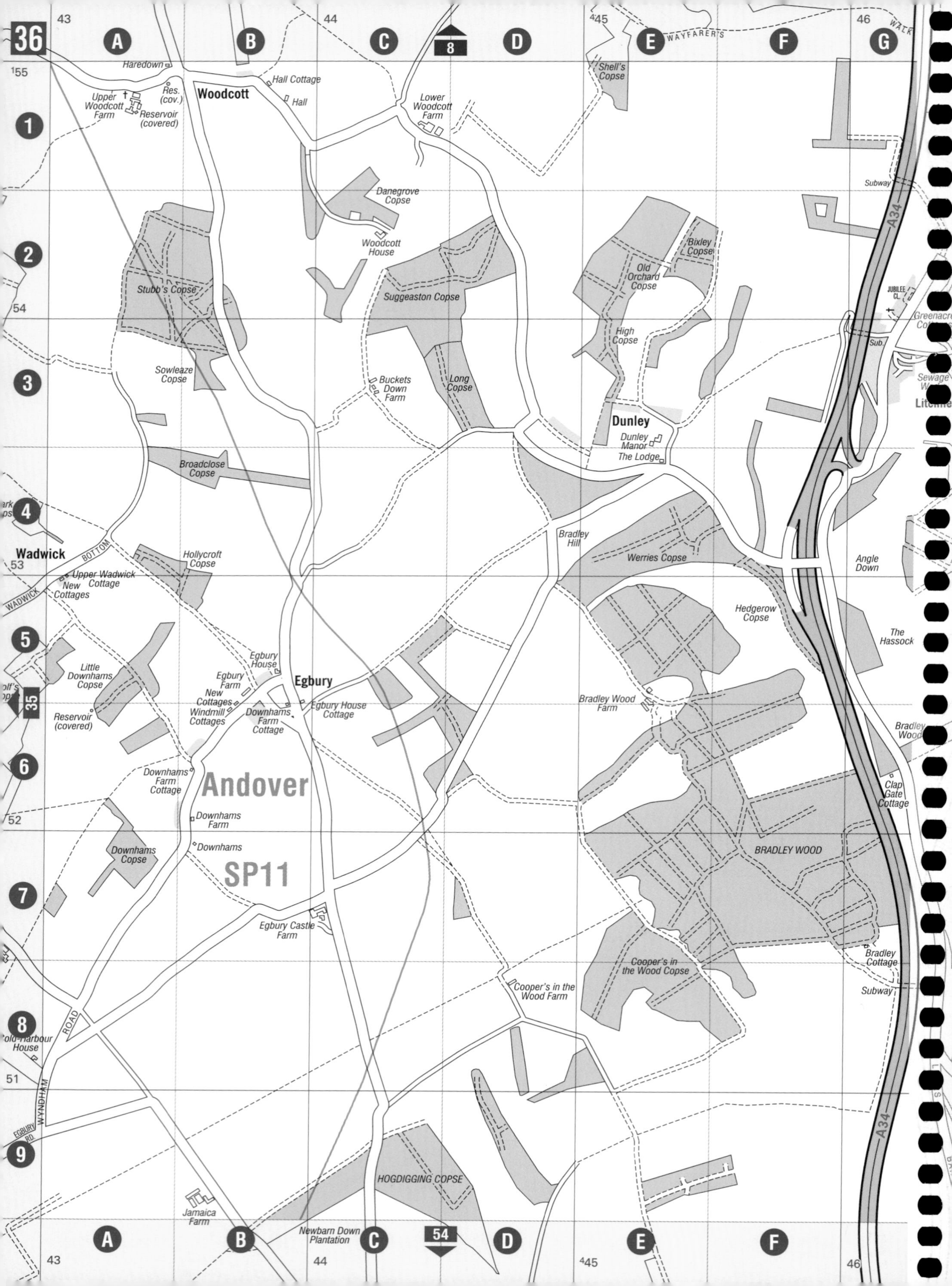

36
A
B
C
D
E
F
G
43
44
45
46
8
54
35
1
2
3
4
5
6
7
8
9
55
54
53
52
51
Haredown
Upper Woodcott Farm
Res. (cov.)
Reservoir (covered)
Woodcott
Hall Cottage
Hall
Lower Woodcott Farm
Shell's Copse
WAYFARER'S
WALK
Subway
Danegrove Copse
Woodcott House
Bixley Copse
Old Orchard Copse
A34
Stubb's Copse
Suggeaston Copse
JUBILEE CL.
Greenacre Cottages
Sub.
Sewage Works
Litchfield
High Copse
Sowleaze Copse
Buckets Down Farm
Long Copse
Dunley
Dunley Manor
The Lodge
Broadclose Copse
Bradley Hill
Wadwick
BOTTOM
WADWICK
Hollycroft Copse
Upper Wadwick Cottage
New Cottages
Werries Copse
Angle Down
Hedgerow Copse
The Hassock
Little Downhams Copse
Egbury House
Egbury Farm
New Cottages
Windmill Cottages
Egbury
Egbury House Cottage
Downhams Farm Cottage
Reservoir (covered)
Bradley Wood Farm
Bradley Wood
Downhams Farm Cottage
Andover
Clap Gate Cottage
Downhams Farm
Downhams
Downhams Copse
SP11
BRADLEY WOOD
Egbury Castle Farm
Cooper's in the Wood Copse
Bradley Cottage
Cooper's in the Wood Farm
Subway
Cold Harbour House
ROAD
WYNDHAM
EGBURY RD.
HOGDIGGING COPSE
Jamaica Farm
Newbarn Down Plantation

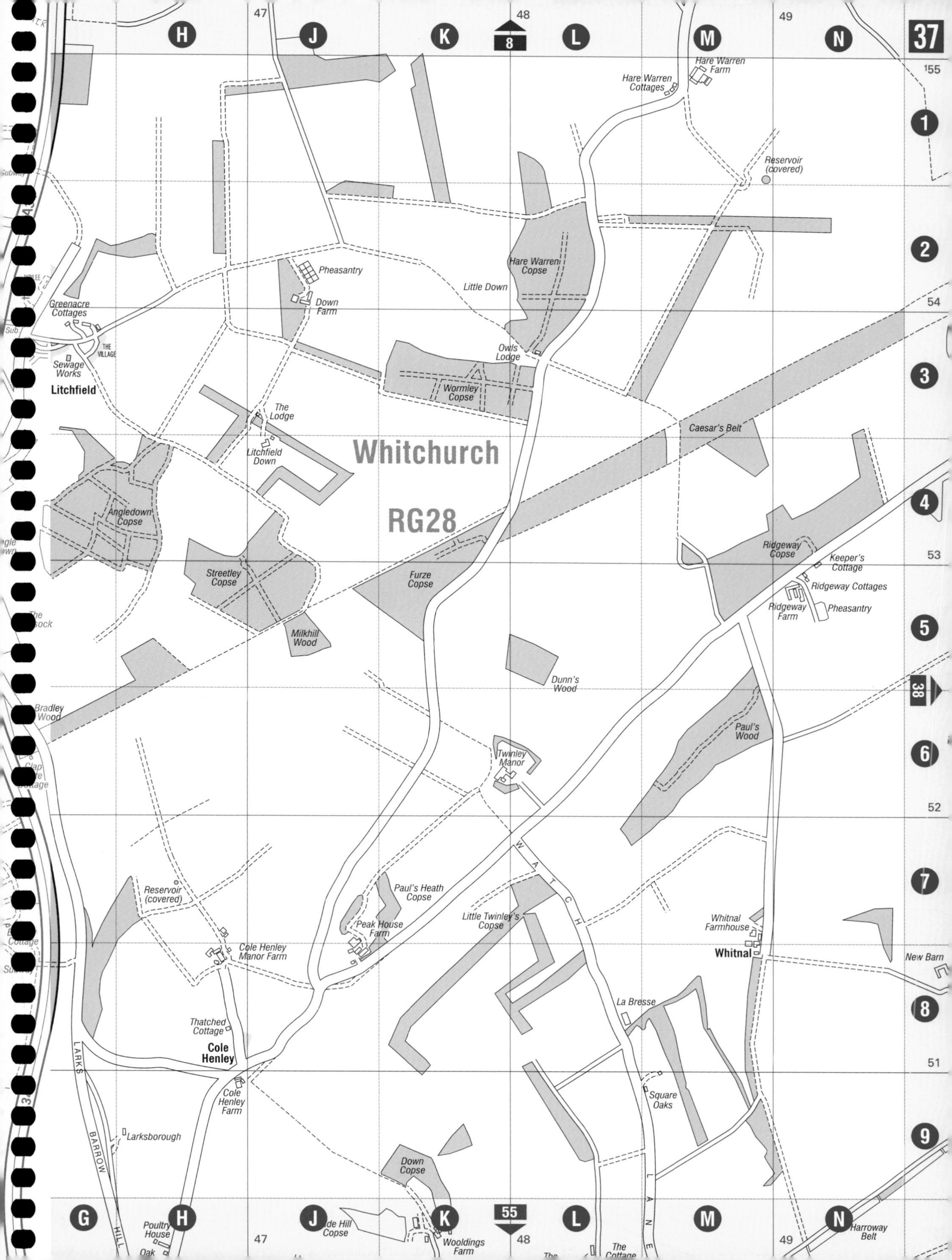
47
48
49
H
J
K
L
M
N
8
155
1
2
3
4
5
6
7
8
9
54
53
52
51
38
55
G
Hare Warren Farm
Hare Warren Cottages
Reservoir (covered)
Pheasantry
Down Farm
Hare Warren Copse
Little Down
Greenacre Cottages
THE VILLAGE
Sewage Works
Litchfield
Owls Lodge
Wormley Copse
The Lodge
Litchfield Down
Whitchurch
RG28
Caesar's Belt
Angledown Copse
Streetley Copse
Furze Copse
Milkhill Wood
Ridgeway Copse
Keeper's Cottage
Ridgeway Cottages
Ridgeway Farm
Pheasantry
Dunn's Wood
Bradley Wood
Paul's Wood
Twinley Manor
WATCH LANE
Reservoir (covered)
Paul's Heath Copse
Peak House Farm
Little Twinley's Copse
Whitnal Farmhouse
Whitnal
New Barn
Cole Henley Manor Farm
La Bresse
Thatched Cottage
Cole Henley
LARKS BARROW HILL
Cole Henley Farm
Square Oaks
Larksborough
Down Copse
Poultry House
Woodlings Farm
The Cottage
Harroway Belt

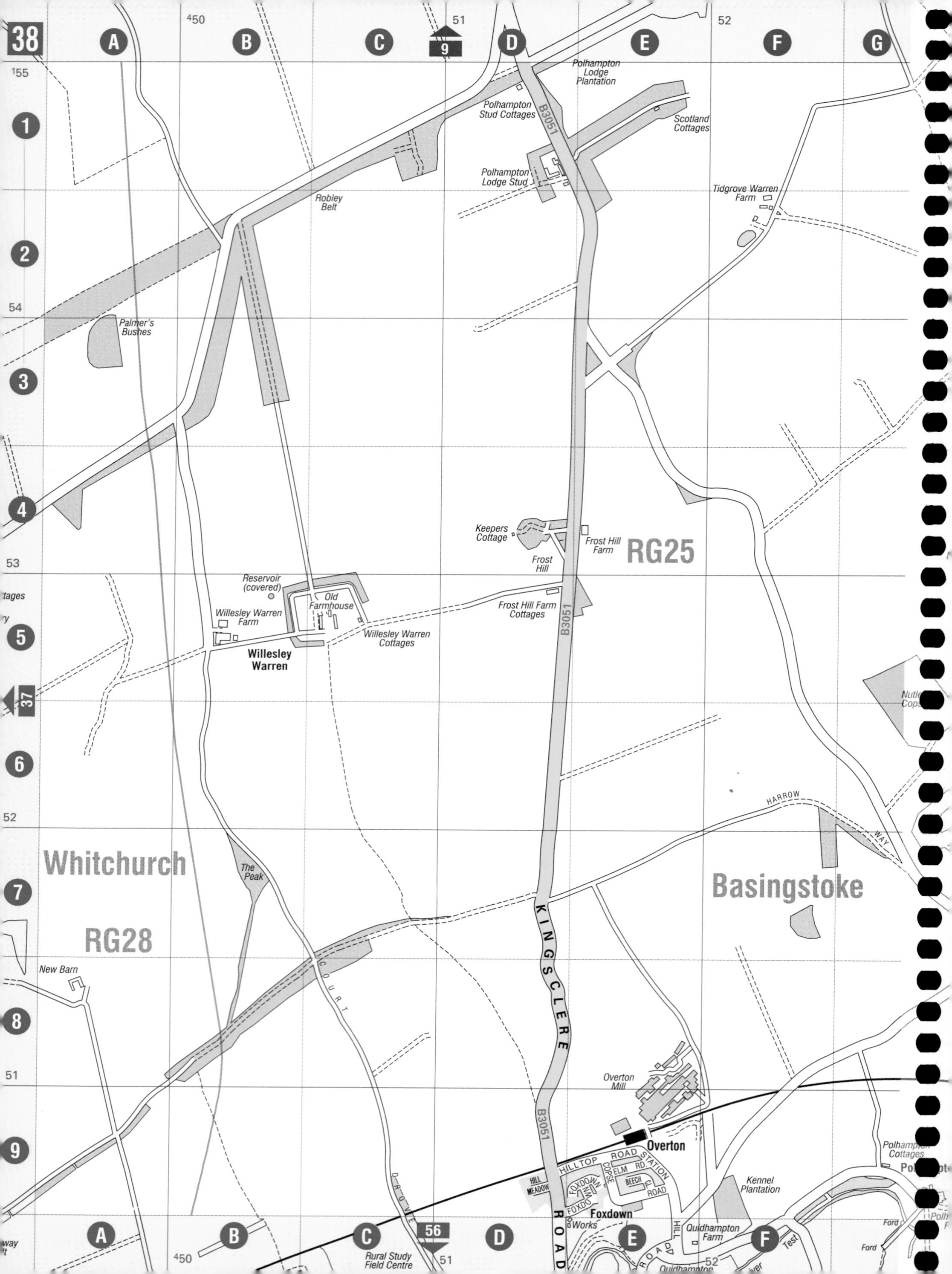

38

A   450   B   C   9   D   51   E   52   F   G

155

1

Polhampton Lodge Plantation

Polhampton Stud Cottages

Scotland Cottages

Robley Belt

2

Polhampton Lodge Stud

Tidgrove Warren Farm

54

Palmer's Bushes

3

4

Keepers Cottage

Frost Hill Farm

RG25

53

Frost Hill

Reservoir (covered)

Old Farmhouse

Frost Hill Farm Cottages

...tages

Willesley Warren Farm

5

Willesley Warren Cottages

ry

Willesley Warren

◀ **37**

Nutle... Cops...

6

52

HARROW

Whitchurch

The Peak

WAY

Basingstoke

7

RG28

K I N G S C L E R E

New Barn

8

C O U R T

51

Overton Mill

9

HILL MEADOW

B3051

Overton

Polhampton Cottages

Poll...

Kennel Plantation

HILL TOP ROAD
FOXDOWN COPPICE ELM RD
BEECH ROAD

Foxdown

...way...

Works

Quidhampton Farm

Ford

A   450   B   C   56   D   51   E   52   F

Rural Study Field Centre

Quidhampton

R O A D

Ford

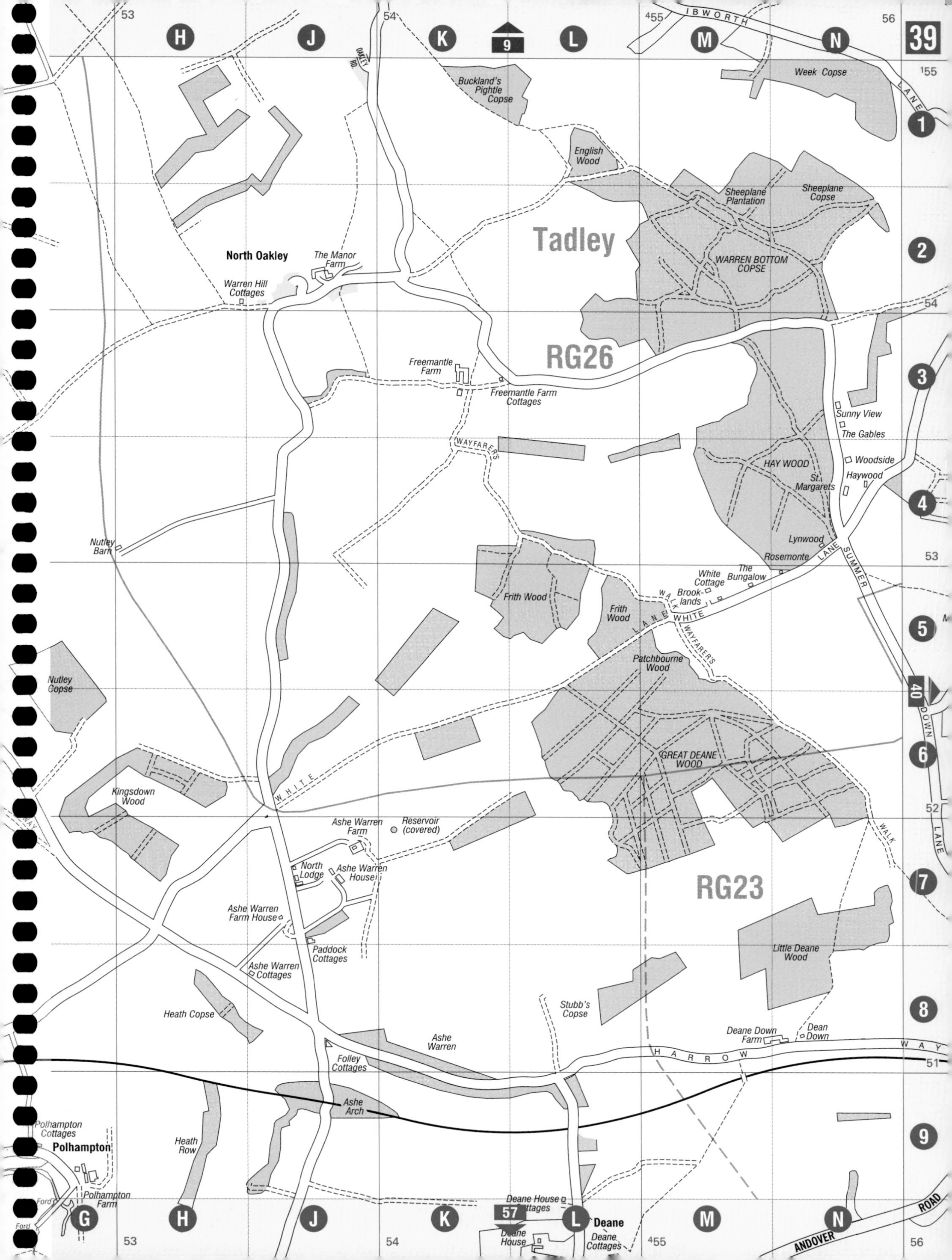

Tadley
RG26
RG23
North Oakley
The Manor Farm
Warren Hill Cottages
Buckland's Pightle Copse
English Wood
Week Copse
Sheeplane Plantation
Sheeplane Copse
WARREN BOTTOM COPSE
IBWORTH
LANE
OAKLEY RD.
Freemantle Farm
Freemantle Farm Cottages
WAYFARERS
Sunny View
The Gables
Woodside
Haywood
HAY WOOD
St. Margarets
Lynwood
Rosemonte
SUMMER LANE
Nutley Barn
Frith Wood
Frith Wood
White Cottage
The Bungalow
Brook-lands
WALK
LANE WHITE
WAYFARER'S
Patchbourne Wood
Nutley Copse
GREAT DEANE WOOD
DOWN LANE
Kingsdown Wood
WHITE
Ashe Warren Farm
Reservoir (covered)
North Lodge
Ashe Warren House
WALK
Ashe Warren Farm House
Paddock Cottages
Ashe Warren Cottages
Little Deane Wood
Stubb's Copse
Heath Copse
Ashe Warren
Deane Down Farm
Dean Down
HARROW WAY
Folley Cottages
Ashe Arch
Polhampton Cottages
Polhampton
Heath Row
Polhampton Farm
Ford
Ford
Deane House Cottages
Deane
Deane House
Deane Cottages
ANDOVER ROAD
9
40
57

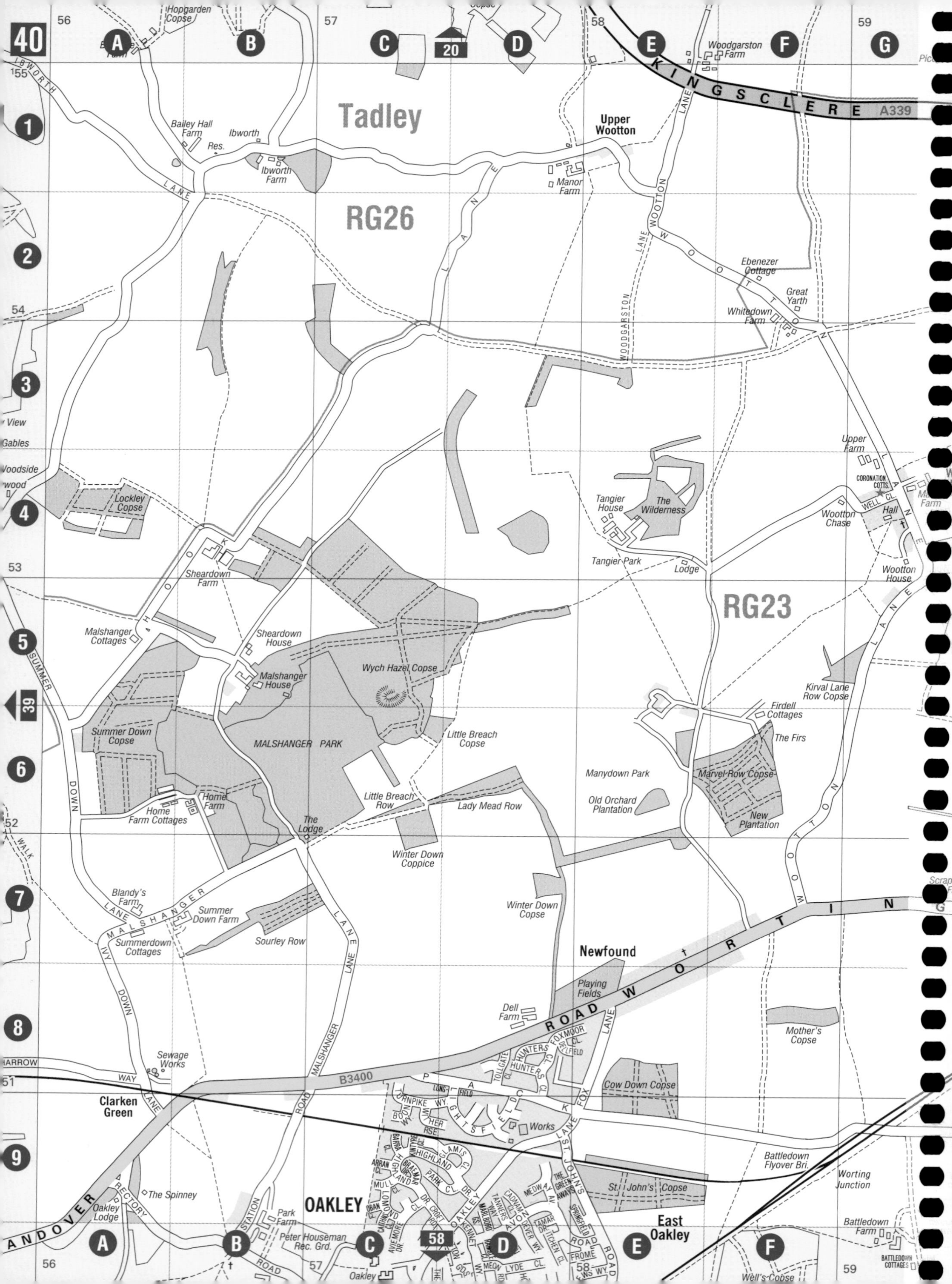
Tadley
RG26
RG23
Upper Wootton
Kingsclere
A339
Woodgarston Farm
Hopgarden Copse
Bailey Hall Farm
Ibworth
Res.
Ibworth Farm
Ibworth Lane
Manor Farm
Wootton Lane
Woodgarston Lane
Ebenezer Cottage
Great Yarth
Whitedown Farm
Upper Farm
Coronation Cotts.
Well Cl.
Hall
Wootton Chase
Wootton House
Tangier House
The Wilderness
Tangier Park
Lodge
Lockley Copse
Sheardown Farm
Hook Lane
Malshanger Cottages
Sheardown House
Malshanger House
Wych Hazel Copse
Summer Down Lane
Summer Down Copse
Malshanger Park
Little Breach Copse
Manydown Park
Kirval Lane Row Copse
Firdell Cottages
The Firs
Marvel Row Copse
New Plantation
Old Orchard Plantation
Home Farm
Home Farm Cottages
The Lodge
Little Breach Row
Lady Mead Row
Winter Down Coppice
Blandy's Farm
Malshanger Lane
Summer Down Farm
Summerdown Cottages
Sourley Row
Winter Down Copse
Newfound
Worting Road
Playing Fields
Dell Farm
Mother's Copse
Ivy Down Lane
Sewage Works
Harrow Way
B3400
Clarken Green
Foxmoor Cl.
Hunters Cl.
Tollgate Cl.
Cow Down Copse
Pardown
Turnpike Wy.
Longfield
Works
Highland
Park Cl.
Glamis Cl.
St. John's Copse
Battledown Flyover Bri.
Worting Junction
Andover Road
Rectory
The Spinney
Oakley Lodge
Station Road
Park Farm
Oakley
Peter Houseman Rec. Grd.
East Oakley
Battledown Farm
Battledown Cottages
Well's Copse
Medway Av.
The Green Aways
Springfield
Frome
Lyde Cl.
Itchen Cl.
Tamar Dr.
Avon
Oakley Lane
St. John's Lane
Fox Lane
20
39
58
56
57
58
59
55
54
53
52
51

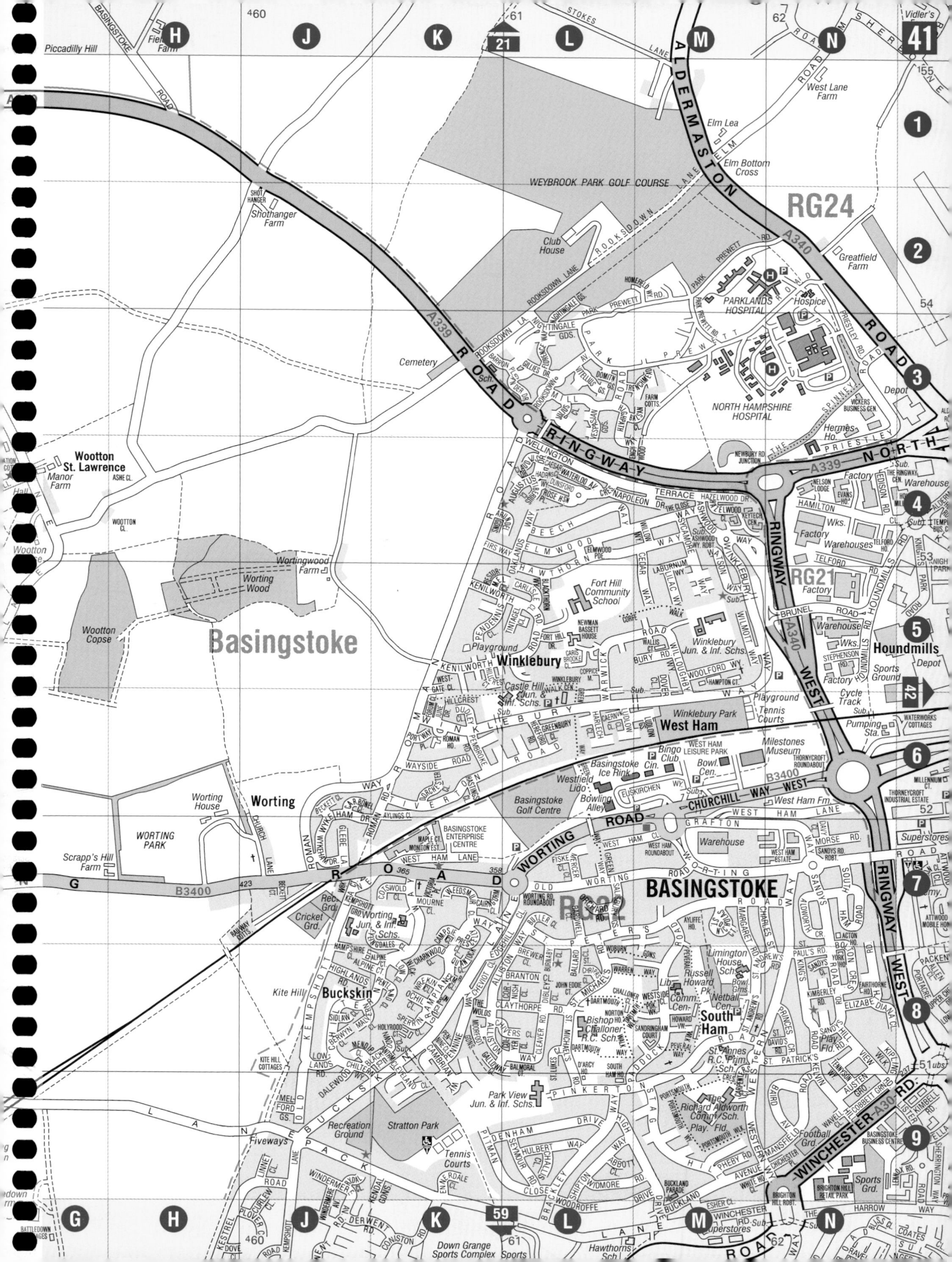

41
Basingstoke
BASINGSTOKE
Winklebury
Worting
Buckskin
South Ham
Houndmills
West Ham
Wootton St. Lawrence
RG24
RG21
RG22
WEYBROOK PARK GOLF COURSE
PARKLANDS HOSPITAL
NORTH HAMPSHIRE HOSPITAL
Fort Hill Community School
Winklebury Jun. & Inf. Schs.
Basingstoke Golf Centre
Stratton Park
Worting Park
Wootton Copse
Worting Wood
21
42
59

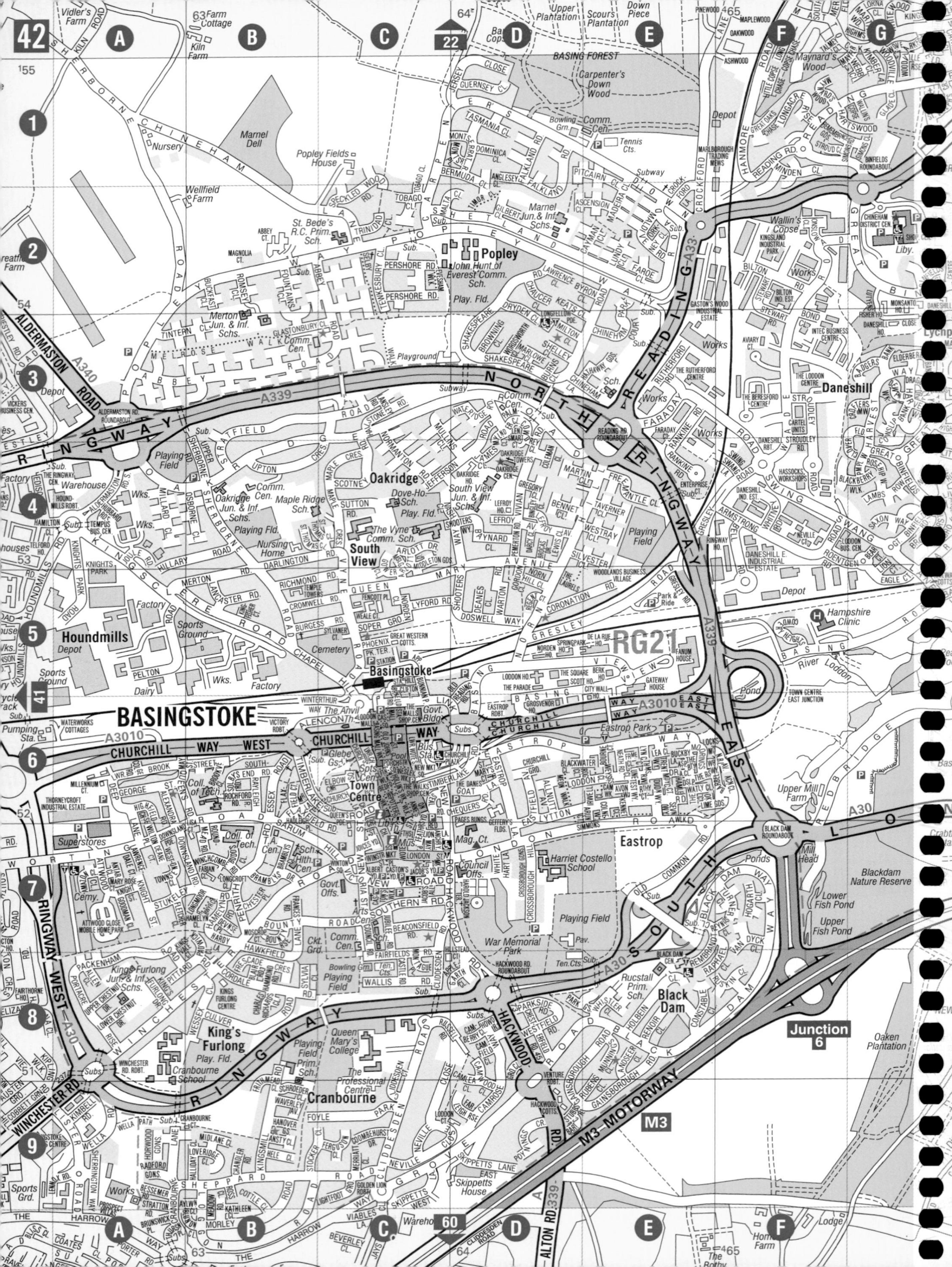

A
B
C
D
E
F
G
1
2
3
4
5
6
7
8
9
22
41
60
Vidler's Farm
Farm Cottage
Kiln Farm
Upper Plantation
Scours Plantation
Down Piece
BASING FOREST
Carpenter's Down Wood
Marnel Dell
Nursery
Popley Fields House
Wellfield Farm
Maynard's Wood
Popley
Oakridge
South View
Basingstoke
BASINGSTOKE
Houndmills
Daneshill
Eastrop
Town Centre
King's Furlong
Cranbourne
Black Dam
RG21
Hampshire Clinic
War Memorial Park
Harriet Costello School
Queen Mary's College
The Professional Centre
Cranbourne School
Blackdam Nature Reserve
Lower Fish Pond
Upper Fish Pond
Oaken Plantation
Upper Mill Farm
Mill Head
Junction 6
M3
M3 MOTORWAY
RINGWAY
NORTH RINGWAY
RINGWAY WEST
RINGWAY EAST
SOUTH RINGWAY
READING ROAD
CHURCHILL WAY
CHURCHILL WAY WEST
CHURCHILL WAY EAST
ALDERMASTON ROAD
CHINEHAM LANE
SHERBORNE ROAD
WORTING ROAD
WINCHESTER RD.
HACKWOOD RD.
ALTON RD.
A339
A340
A3010
A30
A33
Cemetery
Playing Field
Sports Ground
Superstores
Thorneycroft Industrial Estate
Daneshill E. Industrial Estate
Woodlands Business Village
Park & Ride
Skippetts House
Home Farm
Lodge

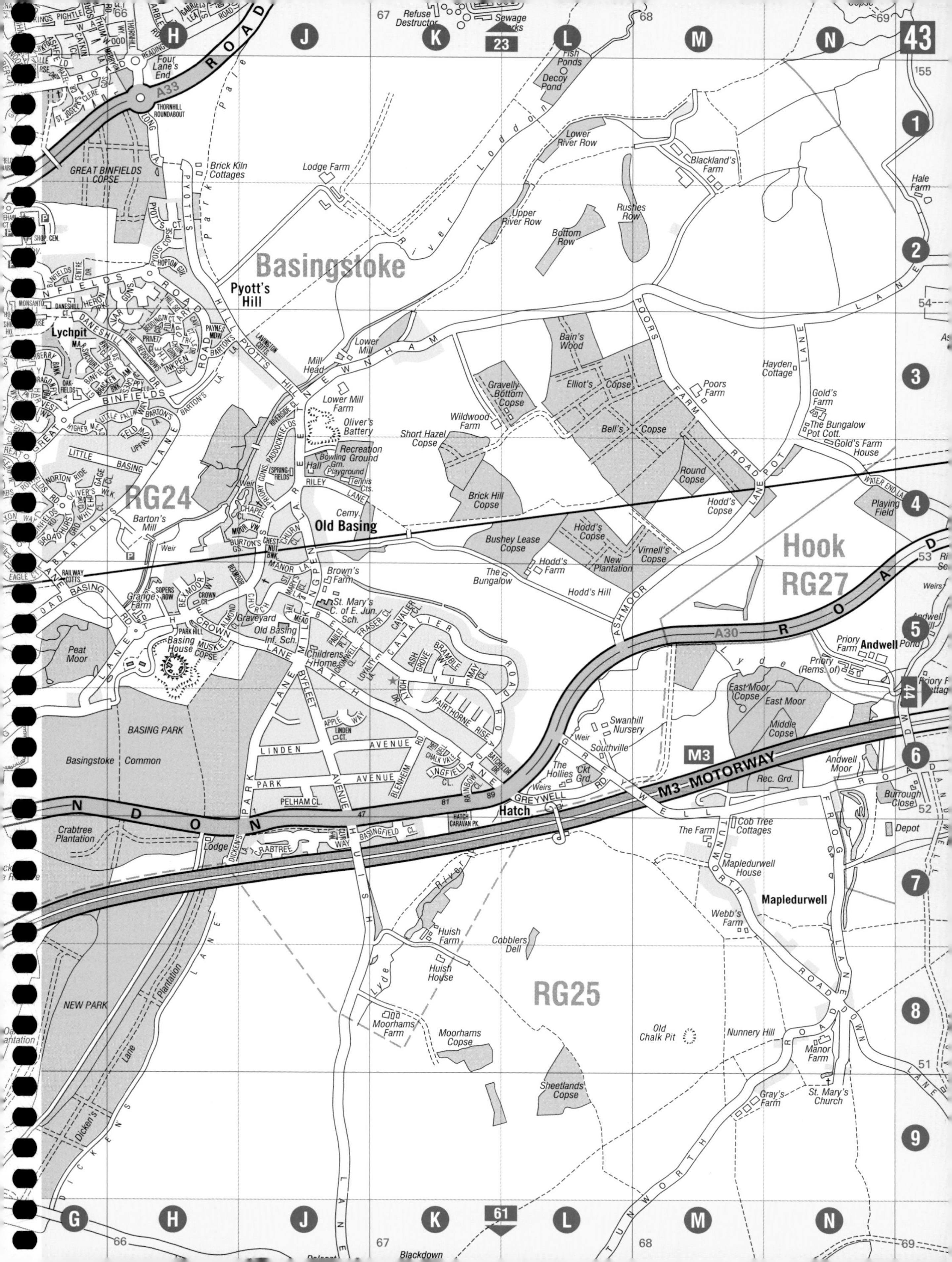

Basingstoke
Pyott's Hill
Lychpit
Old Basing
RG24
Hook
RG27
RG25
Hatch
Andwell
Mapledurwell
M3 MOTORWAY
A30
A33
Refuse Destructor
Sewage Works
Four Lane's End
Thornhill Roundabout
Great Binfields Copse
Brick Kiln Cottages
Lodge Farm
Fish Ponds
Decoy Pond
Lower River Row
Blackland's Farm
Hale Farm
Upper River Row
Bottom Row
Rushes Row
River Loddon
Lower Mill
Mill Head
Lower Mill Farm
Oliver's Battery
Recreation Ground
Bain's Wood
Elliot's Copse
Gravelly Bottom Copse
Hayden Cottage
Poors Farm
Gold's Farm
The Bungalow
Pot Cott.
Gold's Farm House
Wildwood Farm
Short Hazel Copse
Bell's Copse
Round Copse
Brick Hill Copse
Hodd's Copse
Playing Field
Barton's Mill
Cemy.
Bushey Lease Copse
Hodd's Farm
New Plantation
Virnell's Copse
Brown's Farm
The Bungalow
Hodd's Hill
Grange Farm
St. Mary's C. of E. Jun. Sch.
Graveyard
Old Basing Inf. Sch.
Childrens Home
Peat Moor
Basing House
Basing Park
Basingstoke Common
Priory Farm
Priory (Rems. of)
East Moor Copse
East Moor
Middle Copse
Swanhill Nursery
Southville
The Hollies
Ckt Grd.
Andwell Moor
Rec. Grd.
Burrough Close
Depot
Crabtree Plantation
Lodge
Hatch Caravan Pk.
The Farm
Cob Tree Cottages
Mapledurwell House
Webb's Farm
Huish Farm
Huish House
Cobblers Dell
New Park
Plantation Lane
Moorhams Farm
Moorhams Copse
Old Chalk Pit
Nunnery Hill
Manor Farm
Sheetlands Copse
Gray's Farm
St. Mary's Church
Dicken's Lane
Blackdown
23
61
44

RG27
RG25
Basingstoke
Newnham
Nately Scures
Water End
Andwell
Up Nately
Greywell
Hook Common
M3 MOTORWAY
LONDON ROAD
A30
A287
HART
BASINGSTOKE & DEANE
Gordon Brown Outdoor Education Cen.
College Copse
Compfield Copse
Webb's Copse
Hoggin's Copse
Hilly Copse
Ashmoor Copse
Mill Wood
Hang Wood
Butter Wood
Dark Wood
Carleton's Gorse
Shirlen's Copse
Hill Copse
Playing Field
Lyde Mill
Lyde Mill Bungalow
Deanlands Farm
Hale Farm
Manor Farm
Newnham Hill
Tithe Barn
Naishes Farm
Kings Bri.
The Barracks
Mushroom Farm
Hawksworth Cottage
Smokyhouse Copse
Nately Scures House
Upper Cakesbridge Copse
Lower Cakesbridge Copse
Wood Piddle Copse
Snipes Wood
The Rectory
Riding School
Crown Cottages
Scures Hill
Hilden
Bickmeads Copse
Beaumonts Copse
Withy Copse
Hurst Copse
Froghill Copse
Eastrop Farm Ho.
Plume House
Blae Grove House
Upper House Farm
White Hill
Greenacres
Picked Close
Hungry Lodge
Little Tunnel Bridge
Priory Farm Cottages
Black Kiln Bri.
Slades Bridge
Crossways
Greywell Hill
Greywell Hill Park
Dairy Cott.
Tunnel
Nap Pond
Little Bacon Copse
Forge Farm
Deptford Bri.
Old Pound Cottage
Mill Head
Manor Farm
River
Weir

24
43
62

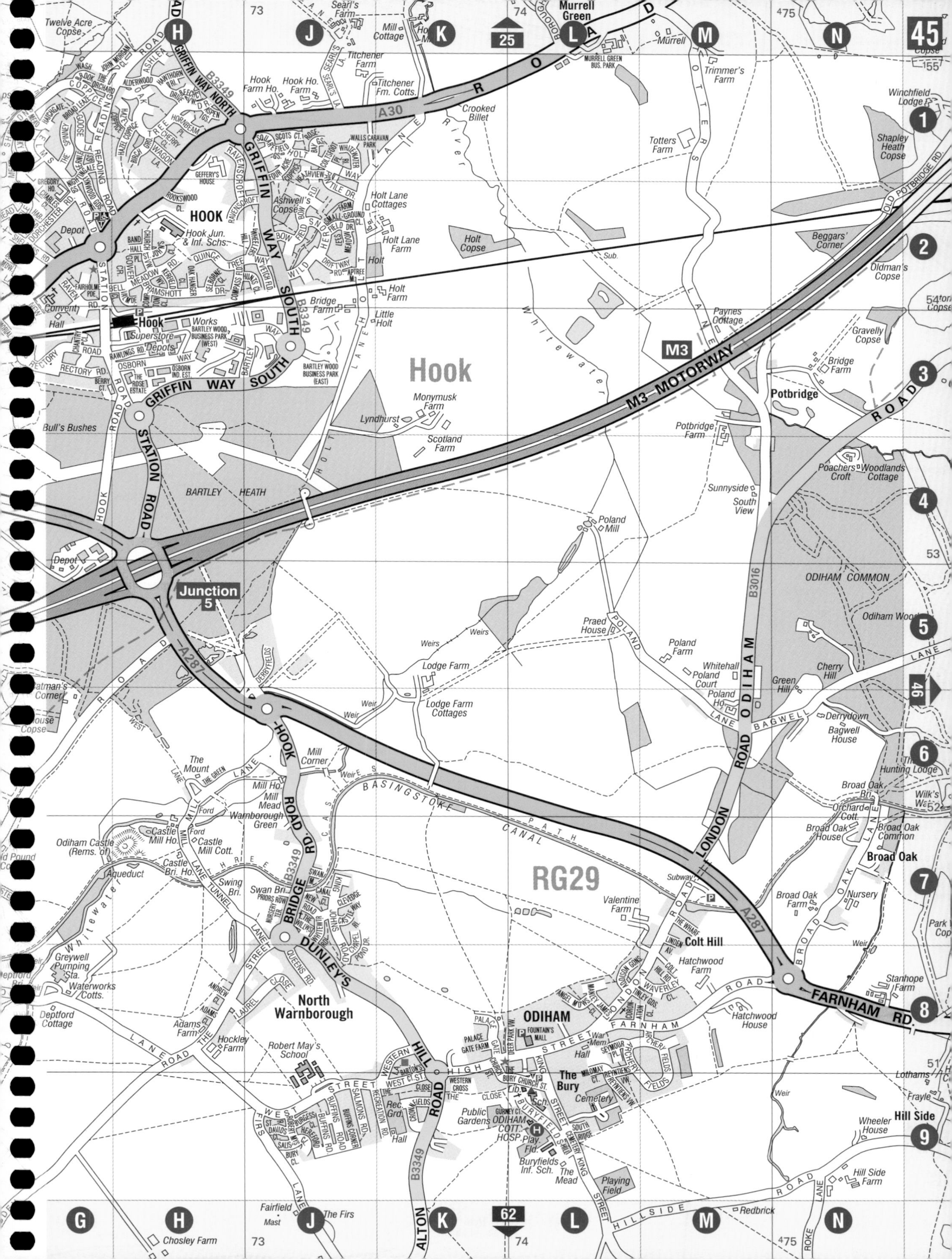
Hook
HOOK
Murrell Green
Potbridge
RG29
ODIHAM
North Warnborough
Colt Hill
Broad Oak
Hill Side
The Bury
M3 MOTORWAY
Junction 5
ODIHAM COMMON
BARTLEY HEATH
BASINGSTOKE CANAL
GRIFFIN WAY NORTH
GRIFFIN WAY SOUTH
STATION ROAD
HOOK ROAD
LONDON ROAD
FARNHAM RD.
ODIHAM ROAD
DUNLEY'S HILL
ALTON ROAD
HIGH ST.
HILLSIDE ROAD
Odiham Castle (Rems. of)
Hook Jun. & Inf. Schs.
Robert May's School
Lodge Farm
Lodge Farm Cottages
Poland Mill
Valentine Farm
Hatchwood Farm
Hatchwood House
Bartley Wood Business Park (West)
Bartley Wood Business Park (East)
Murrell Green Bus. Park

25
46
62

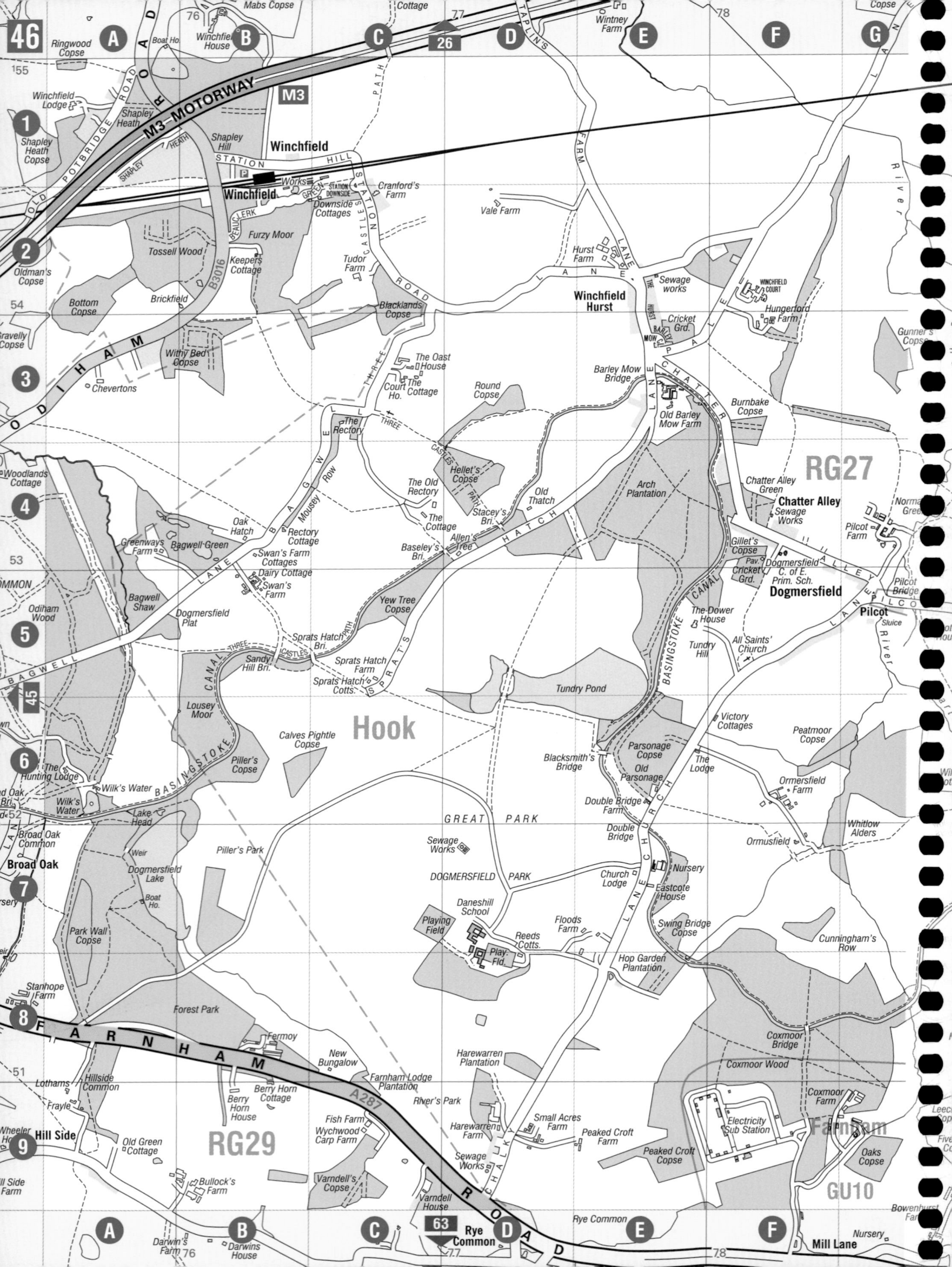
M3 MOTORWAY
Winchfield
Winchfield Hurst
Chatter Alley
Dogmersfield
Pilcot
Hook
RG27
RG29
GU10
Broad Oak
Hill Side
Rye Common
Mill Lane
Crondall
FARNHAM ROAD
A287
B3016
ODIHAM ROAD
BAGWELL LANE
HATCH LANE
CHATTER ALLEY
CHURCH LANE
BASINGSTOKE CANAL
GREAT PARK
DOGMERSFIELD PARK
Tundry Pond
Dogmersfield Lake
Tossell Wood
Furzy Moor
Cranford's Farm
Vale Farm
Hurst Farm
Sewage works
Cricket Grd.
Hungerford Farm
Barley Mow Bridge
Old Barley Mow Farm
Burnbake Copse
Round Copse
Arch Plantation
Hellet's Copse
The Old Rectory
Old Thatch
Swan's Farm
Dogmersfield Plat
Yew Tree Copse
Sprats Hatch Farm
Calves Pightle Copse
Piller's Copse
Lousey Moor
Wilk's Water
Blacksmith's Bridge
Parsonage Copse
Double Bridge Farm
Victory Cottages
Peatmoor Copse
Ormersfield Farm
Whitlow Alders
Cunningham's Row
Daneshill School
Reeds Cotts.
Floods Farm
Hop Garden Plantation
Coxmoor Wood
Coxmoor Farm
Electricity Sub Station
Peaked Croft Copse
Forest Park
Fermoy
New Bungalow
Farnham Lodge Plantation
River's Park
Harewarren Plantation
Harewarren Farm
Small Acres Farm
Peaked Croft Farm
Varndell's Copse
Varndell House
Berry Horn Cottage
Hillside Common
Lothams
Frayle
Old Green Cottage
Bullock's Farm
Darwins House
Park Wall Copse
Stanhope Farm
Oaks Copse
Bowenhurst Farm
26
45
63

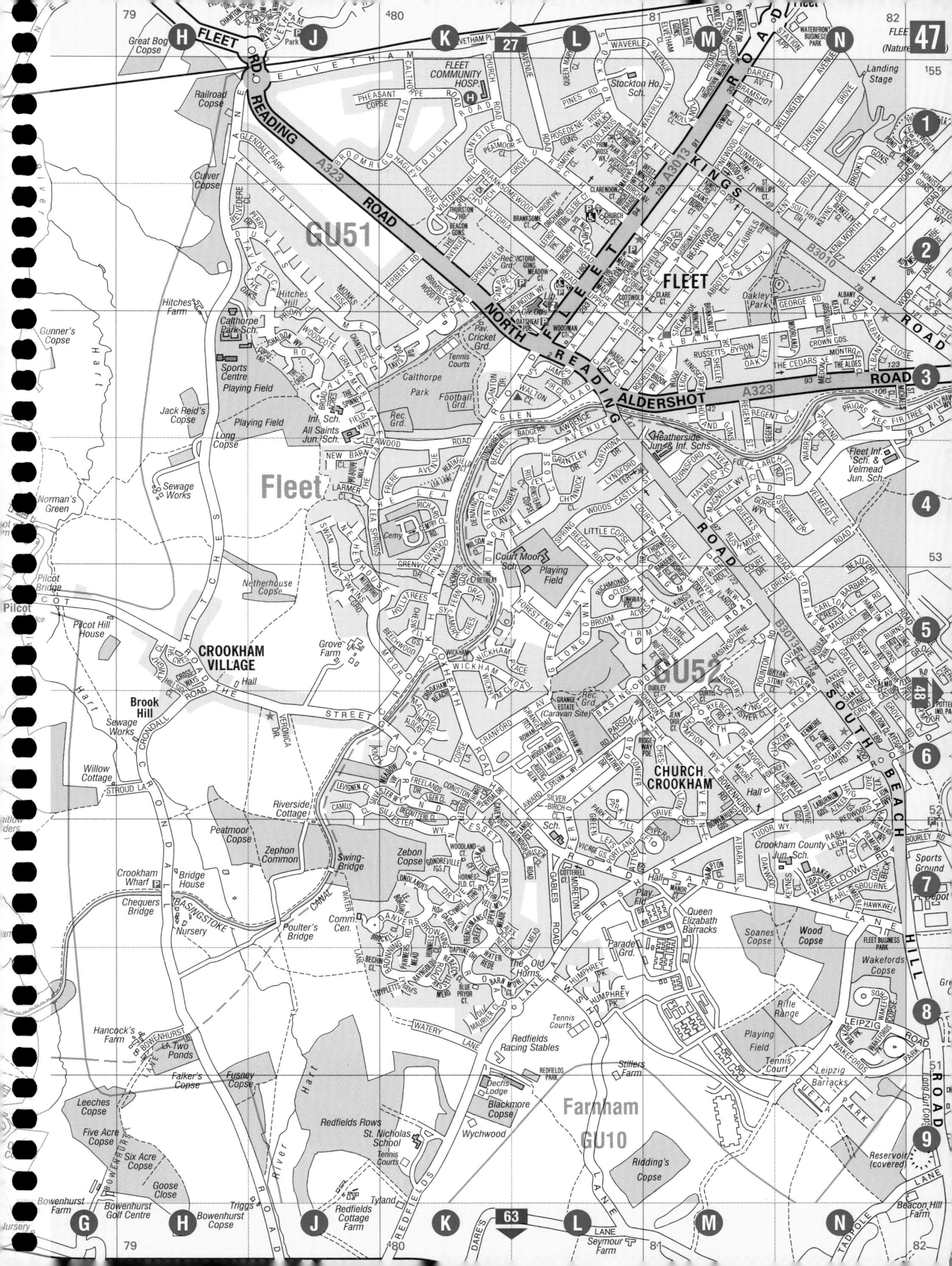

FLEET
GU51
GU52
Fleet
CROOKHAM VILLAGE
CHURCH CROOKHAM
Brook Hill
Farnham
GU10
READING ROAD
A323
NORTH
FLEET ROAD
A3013
KINGS ROAD
ALDERSHOT ROAD
B3010
B3013
SOUTH
BEACH
HILL
ROAD
ELVETHAM ROAD
CROOKHAM ROAD
HITCHES LANE
CRONDALL ROAD
BASINGSTOKE CANAL
Great Bog Copse
Railroad Copse
Culver Copse
Fleet Community Hosp.
Stockton Ho. Sch.
Calthorpe Park Sch.
Sports Centre
Playing Field
Calthorpe Park
Football Grd.
Cricket Grd.
Jack Reid's Copse
Long Copse
Hitches Farm
Gunner's Copse
Norman's Green
Sewage Works
Netherhouse Copse
Pilcot Bridge
Pilcot
Pilcot Hill House
Grove Farm
Court Moor Sch.
Heatherside Jun.& Inf. Schs.
Fleet Inf. Sch. & Velmead Jun. Sch.
Oakley Park
Landing Stage
Willow Cottage
Riverside Cottage
Peatmoor Copse
Zephon Common
Swing-Bridge
Zebon Copse
Crookham Wharf
Bridge House
Chequers Bridge
Nursery
Poulter's Bridge
Comm. Cen.
Crookham County Jun. Sch.
Queen Elizabeth Barracks
Parade Grd.
Soanes Copse
Wood Copse
Fleet Business Park
Wakefords Copse
Rifle Range
Leipzig Barracks
Redfields Racing Stables
Stillers Farm
Dechs Lodge
Blackmore Copse
Wychwood
Redfields Rows
St. Nicholas School
Ridding's Copse
Reservoir (covered)
Beacon Hill Farm
Hancock's Farm
Two Ponds
Falker's Copse
Fusney Copse
Leeches Copse
Five Acre Copse
Six Acre Copse
Goose Close
Bowenhurst Farm
Bowenhurst Golf Centre
Bowenhurst Copse
Triggs
Tyland
Redfields Cottage Farm
Seymour Farm
Sports Ground
27
63
48

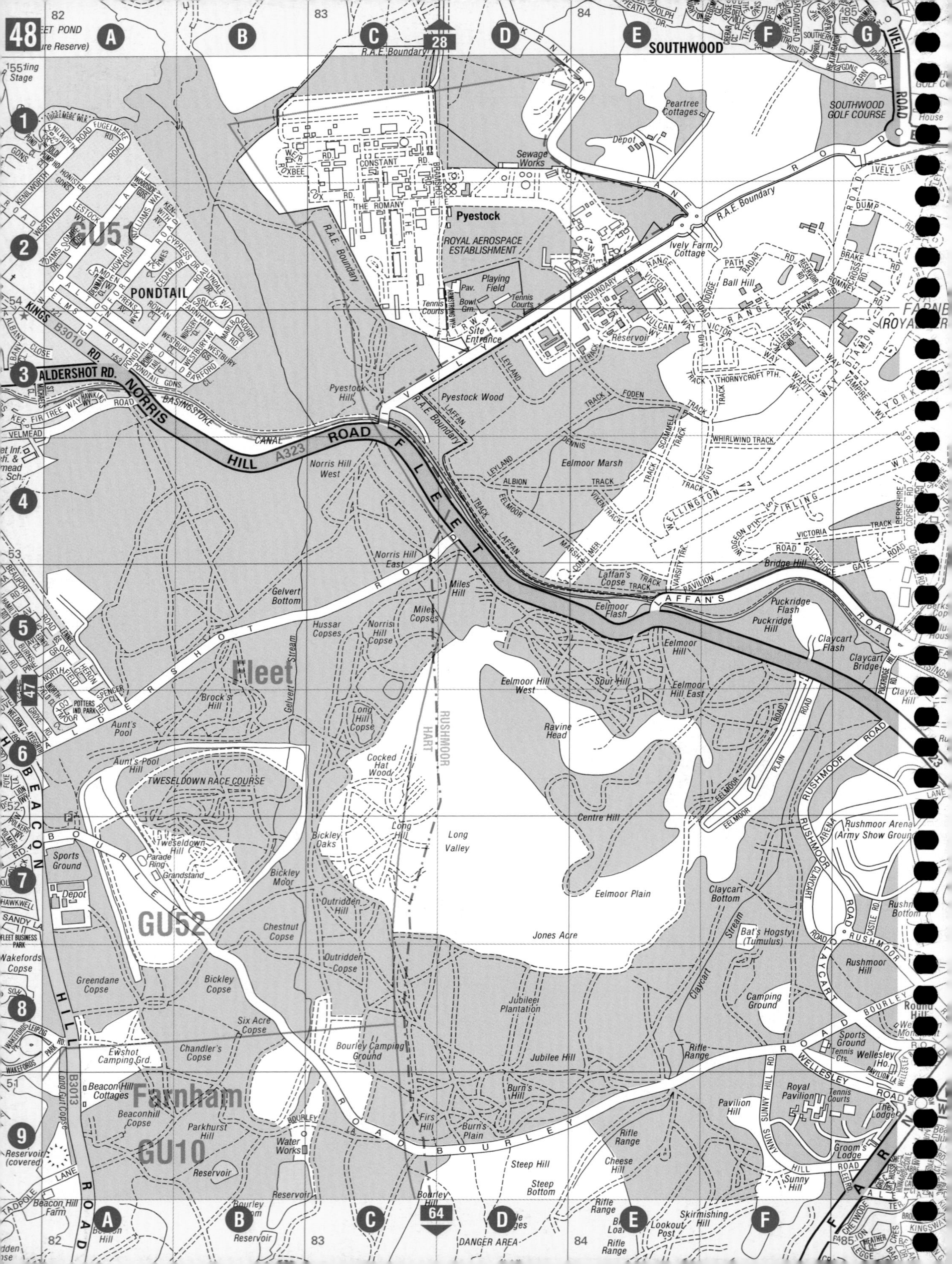
SOUTHWOOD
Pyestock
ROYAL AEROSPACE ESTABLISHMENT
PONDTAIL
GU51
Fleet
GU52
Farnham
GU10
TWESELDOWN RACE COURSE
SOUTHWOOD GOLF COURSE
Eelmoor Marsh
Eelmoor Plain
Long Valley
Jones Acre
Jubilee Plantation
Jubilee Hill
Rushmoor Arena (Army Show Ground)
NORRIS HILL ROAD
FLEET ROAD
ALDERSHOT RD.
BOURLEY ROAD
BEACON HILL ROAD
DANGER AREA
28
64
47

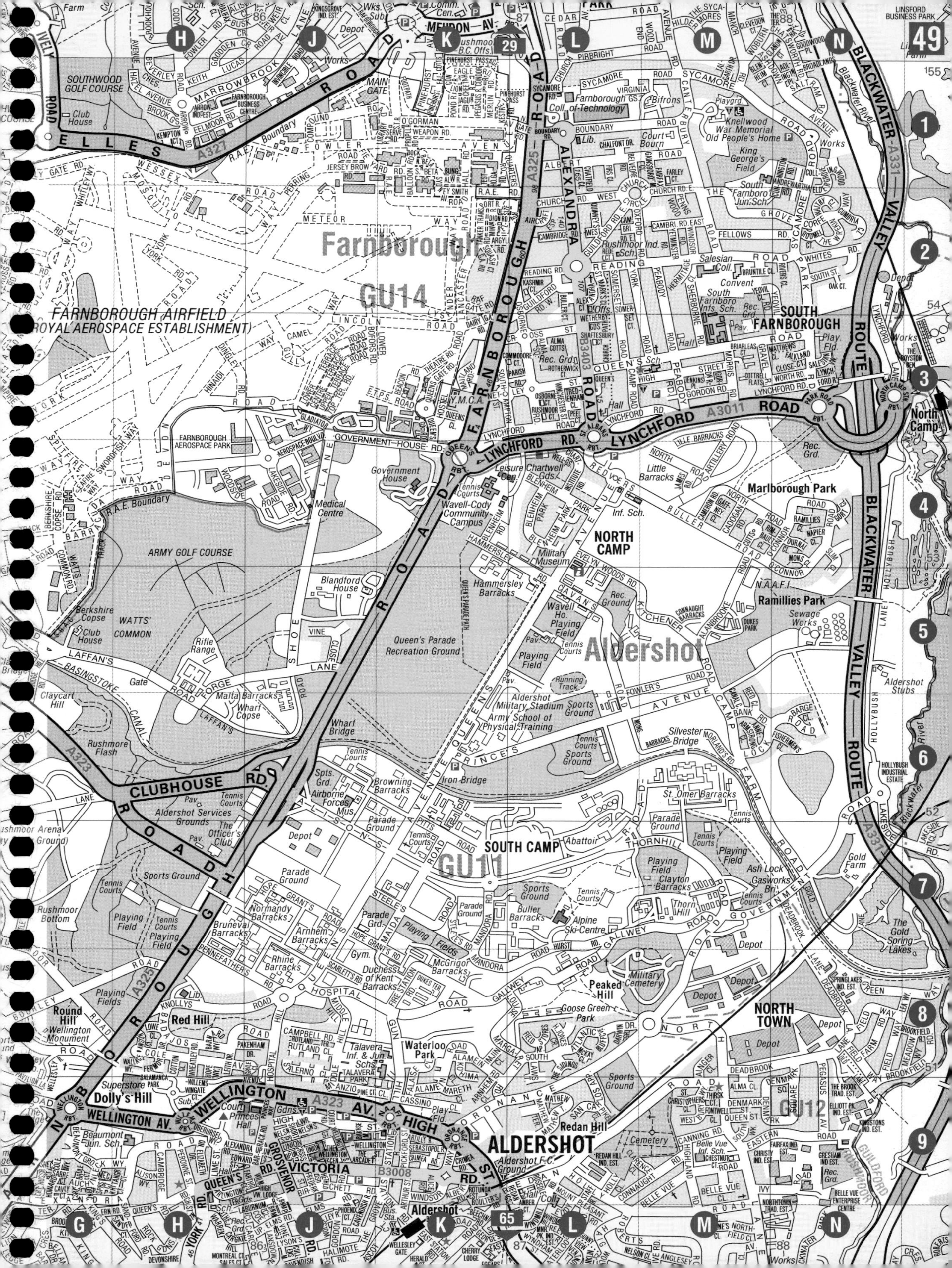
LINSFORD BUSINESS PARK
Farnborough
GU14
FARNBOROUGH AIRFIELD (ROYAL AEROSPACE ESTABLISHMENT)
SOUTHWOOD GOLF COURSE
Club House
ELLES ROAD
A327
FARNBOROUGH ROAD
A325
ALEXANDRA ROAD
LYNCHFORD ROAD
A3011
BLACKWATER VALLEY ROUTE
A331
Farnborough GS
Coll. of Technology
Knellwood War Memorial Old People's Home
King George's Field
South Farnboro Jun. Sch.
Salesian Coll.
Convent
South Farnboro Infs. Sch.
SOUTH FARNBOROUGH
North Camp
FARNBOROUGH AEROSPACE PARK
Government House
Medical Centre
Wavell-Cody Community Campus
Leisure Cen.
Chartwell Gds.
Little Barracks
Marlborough Park
NORTH CAMP
Military Museum
Hammersley Barracks
Blandford House
ARMY GOLF COURSE
Berkshire Copse
WATTS' COMMON
Rifle Range
Queen's Parade Recreation Ground
Ramillies Park
Sewage Works
Aldershot
Running Track
Aldershot Military Stadium
Army School of Physical Training
Sports Ground
Malta Barracks
Wharf Copse
Wharf Bridge
Claycart Hill
Rushmore Flash
BASINGSTOKE CANAL
A323
CLUBHOUSE RD.
Silvester Bridge
Aldershot Stubs
Iron Bridge
Browning Barracks
Airborne Forces Mus.
Aldershot Services Grounds
The Officer's Club
St. Omer Barracks
HOLLYBUSH INDUSTRIAL ESTATE
SOUTH CAMP
GU11
Abattoir
Playing Field
Clayton Barracks
Ash Lock
Gasworks Bri.
Gold Farm
The Gold Spring Lakes
Normandy Barracks
Bruneval Barracks
Arnhem Barracks
Rhine Barracks
Buller Barracks
Alpine Ski-Centre
McGrigor Barracks
Duchess of Kent Barracks
Peaked Hill
Military Cemetery
Rushmoor Bottom
Round Hill
Wellington Monument
Red Hill
Goose Green Park
NORTH TOWN
Waterloo Park
Talavera Inf. & Jun. Schs.
Dolly's Hill
Superstore
WELLINGTON AV.
Princes Hall
VICTORIA RD.
B3008
ALDERSHOT
Aldershot F.C. Ground
Redan Hill
Cemetery
GU12
Aldershot
Beaumont Jun. Sch.
29
65
G H J K L M N
1 2 3 4 5 6 7 8 9
86 87 88
155 54 53 52 51

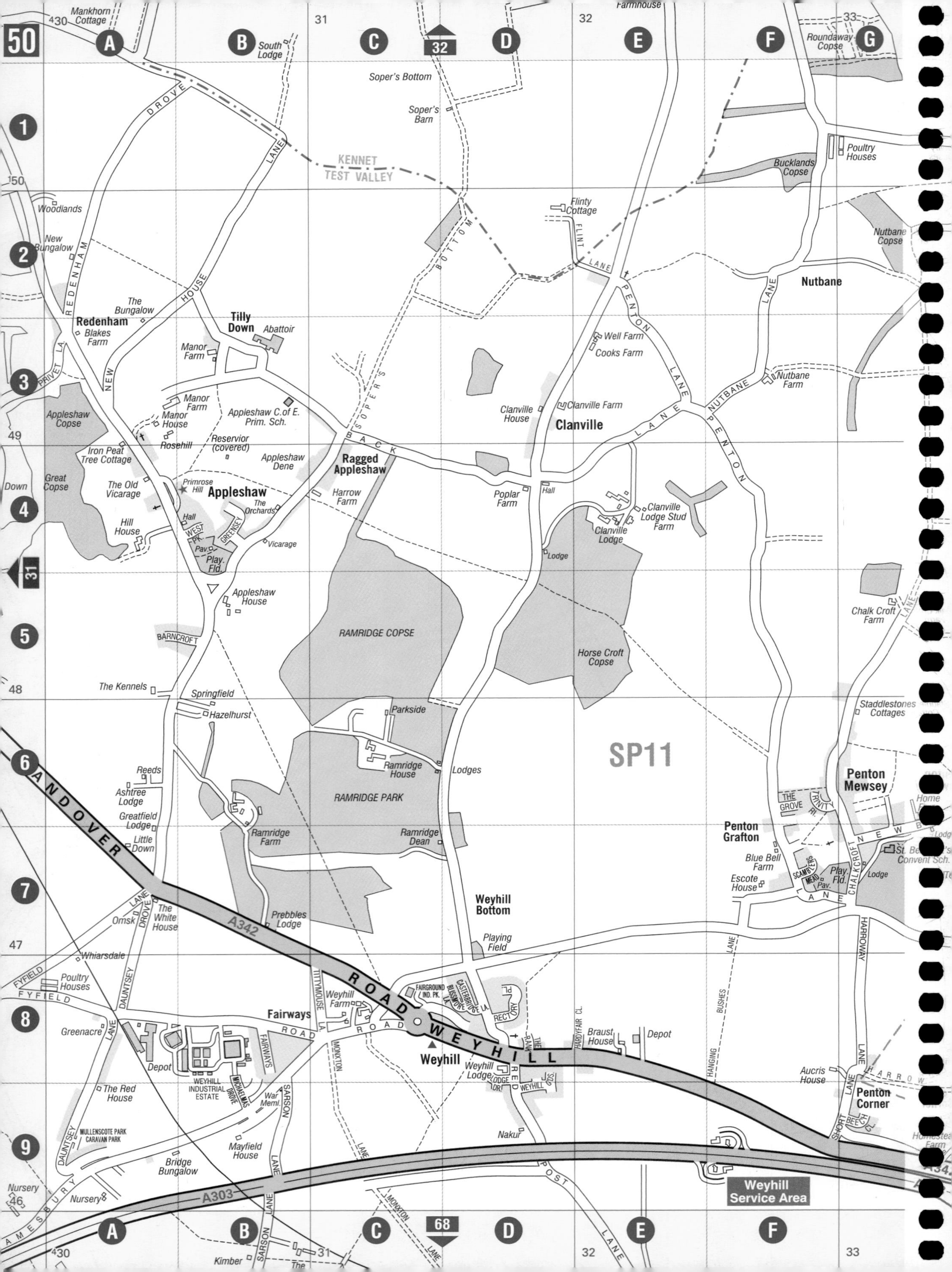
Mankhorn Cottage
South Lodge
Soper's Bottom
Soper's Barn
32
Farmhouse
Roundaway Copse
KENNET
TEST VALLEY
DROVE
HOUSE
LANE
Poultry Houses
Bucklands Copse
Woodlands
New Bungalow
REDENHAM
Flinty Cottage
FLINT
LANE
BOTTOM
Nutbane Copse
Nutbane
PENTON
The Bungalow
Redenham
Blakes Farm
Tilly Down
Abattoir
Manor Farm
Well Farm
Cooks Farm
PRIVET LA.
NEW
Nutbane Farm
NUTBANE
Manor Farm
Manor House
Appleshaw C.of E. Prim. Sch.
Clanville House
Clanville Farm
Clanville
Appleshaw Copse
Rosehill
Reservior (covered)
SOPER'S
BACK
Iron Peat Tree Cottage
Appleshaw Dene
Ragged Appleshaw
Great Copse
The Old Vicarage
Primrose Hill
Appleshaw
Harrow Farm
Poplar Farm
Hall
Down
The Orchards
Clanville Lodge Stud Farm
Hill House
Hall
WEST PK.
GREENSEY
Vicarage
Clanville Lodge
Pav.
Play. Fld.
Lodge
31
Appleshaw House
Chalk Croft Farm
BARNCROFT
RAMRIDGE COPSE
Horse Croft Copse
The Kennels
Springfield
Hazelhurst
Parkside
Staddlestones Cottages
SP11
Reeds
Ramridge House
Lodges
Ashtree Lodge
RAMRIDGE PARK
Penton Mewsey
THE GROVE
TRINITY RI.
Home
Greatfield Lodge
Ramridge Farm
Ramridge Dean
Penton Grafton
NEW
Little Down
ANDOVER
Blue Bell Farm
SCAMBLERS MEAD
Play. Fld.
Pav.
CHALKCROFT
Lodge
St. Be... Convent Sch.
Escote House
Weyhill Bottom
LANE
Omsk
DROVE
The White House
A342
Prebbles Lodge
Playing Field
HARROWAY
Whiarsdale
DAUNTSEY
FYFIELD
Poultry Houses
TITTYMOUSE LA.
ROAD
FAIRGROUND IND. PK.
CASTERBRIDGE
BUSSMORE LA.
LA.
PL.
RECTORY
HARDYFAIR CL.
BUSHES
Weyhill Farm
Fairways
Greenacre
LANE
ROAD
ROAD
WEYHILL
THE RANK
Braust House
Depot
FAIRWAYS
MONXTON
Weyhill
Weyhill Lodge
LODGE DR.
WEYHILL GDS.
HANGING
Aucris House
LANE
HARROW
Depot
The Red House
WEYHILL INDUSTRIAL ESTATE
MICHAELMAS DRIVE
War Meml.
SARSON
Penton Corner
SHORT LANE
BEECH CL.
DAUNTSEY
MULLENSCOTE PARK CARAVAN PARK
Nakur
Homestead Farm
Mayfield House
LANE
Bridge Bungalow
POST
A34
Weyhill Service Area
Nursery
A303
Nursery
AMESBURY
SARSON LANE
MONXTON
LANE
68
LANE
430
31
32
33
Kimber
The
50
49
48
47
46
A
B
C
D
E
F
G
1
2
3
4
5
6
7
8
9

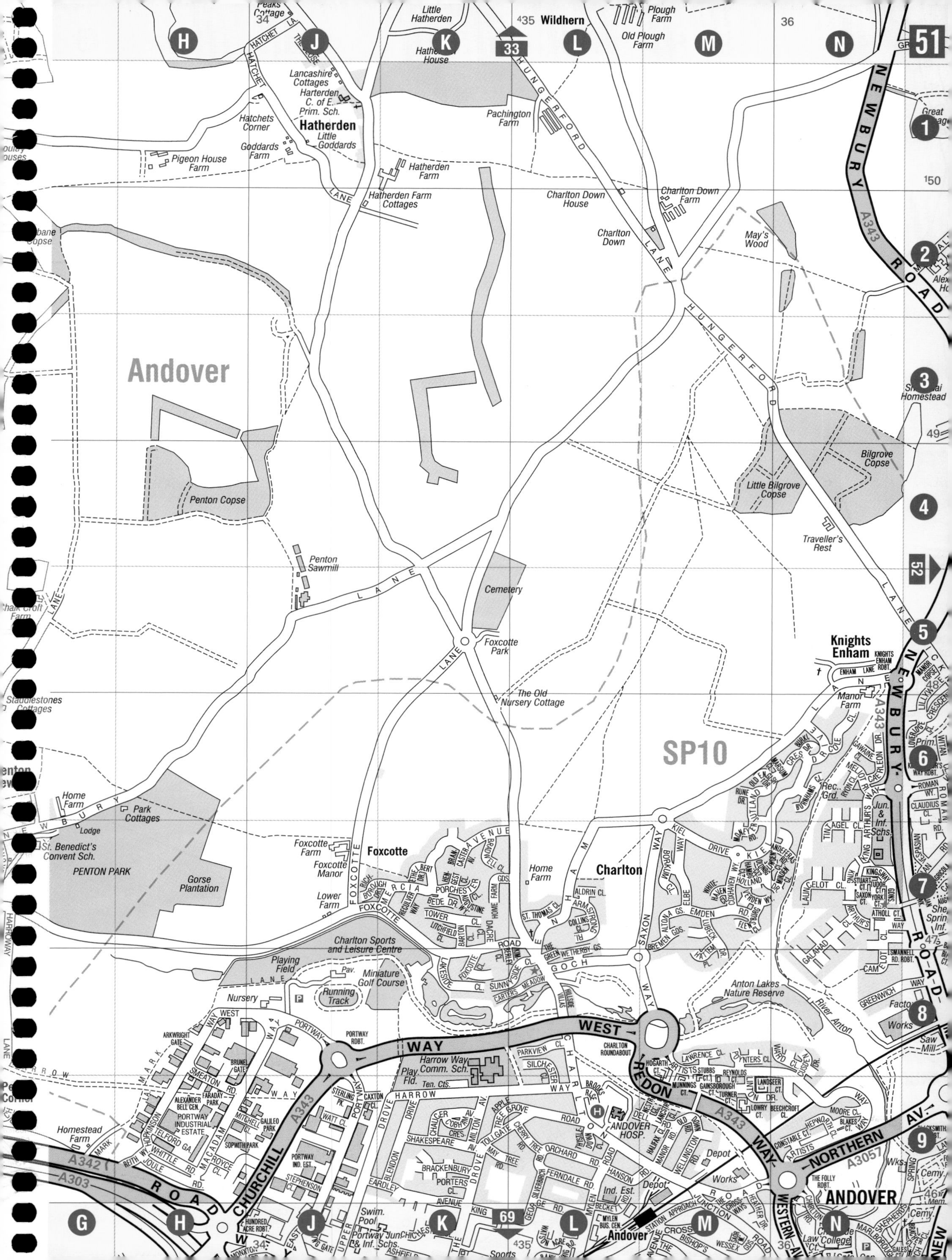
Andover
SP10
Hatherden
Wildhern
Knights Enham
Foxcotte
Charlton
ANDOVER
Little Hatherden
Hatherden House
Plough Farm
Old Plough Farm
Lancashire Cottages
Harterden C. of E. Prim. Sch.
Hatchets Corner
Little Goddards
Goddards Farm
Pigeon House Farm
Pachington Farm
Hatherden Farm
Hatherden Farm Cottages
Charlton Down House
Charlton Down Farm
Charlton Down
May's Wood
Penton Copse
Penton Sawmill
Cemetery
Foxcotte Park
The Old Nursery Cottage
Little Bilgrove Copse
Bilgrove Copse
Traveller's Rest
Manor Farm
Home Farm
Park Cottages
Lodge
St. Benedict's Convent Sch.
PENTON PARK
Gorse Plantation
Foxcotte Farm
Foxcotte Manor
Lower Farm
Charlton Sports and Leisure Centre
Playing Field
Miniature Golf Course
Running Track
Nursery
Anton Lakes Nature Reserve
River Anton
Harrow Way Comm. Sch.
PORTWAY INDUSTRIAL ESTATE
PORTWAY IND. EST.
ANDOVER HOSP.
Homestead Farm
Swim. Pool
Portway Jun. & Inf. Schs.
Andover
HUNGERFORD LANE
NEWBURY ROAD
A343
WEST WAY
PORTWAY ROBT.
CHARLTON ROUNDABOUT
REDON WAY
NORTHERN AV.
A3057
THE FOLLY RDBT.
WESTERN AV.
CHURCHILL WAY
A342
A303
HARROW WAY
KNIGHTS ENHAM RDBT.
ENHAM LANE
33
69
52
435
34
36
150
49
48
47
46

Andover
ANDOVER
SP10
Enham Alamein
Little London
Woodhouse
Smannell
East Anton
Picket Piece
Ridges Copse
Straits Copse
Mongomble Copse
Hackwood Copse
Great Stubbage
Camber's Copse
Postgrove Copse
Ashley Copse
Finkley House
Finkley Down Farm Park
Eastanton Farm
Eastanton Manor Farm
Red Cottages
Pond Cottages
Lapstone Farm
Melrose Farm
Sports Field
Walworth Industrial Estate
Harewood Farm
Harewood House
Convent Farm
Down House Farm
Trinley Buildings
Shanghai Homestead
Bilgrove Copse
Saw Mill
Norman Gate School Playing Fields
Vigo Jun. & Inf. Schs.
Shepherds Spring Jun. & Inf. Schs.
Icknield Sch.
A343
A3093
A3057
B3400
NEWBURY ROAD
CHURCHILL WAY
LONDON ROAD
SMANNELL ROAD
STOKE ROAD
MALTHOUSE LANE
ENHAM ARCH ROUNDABOUT
34
51
70

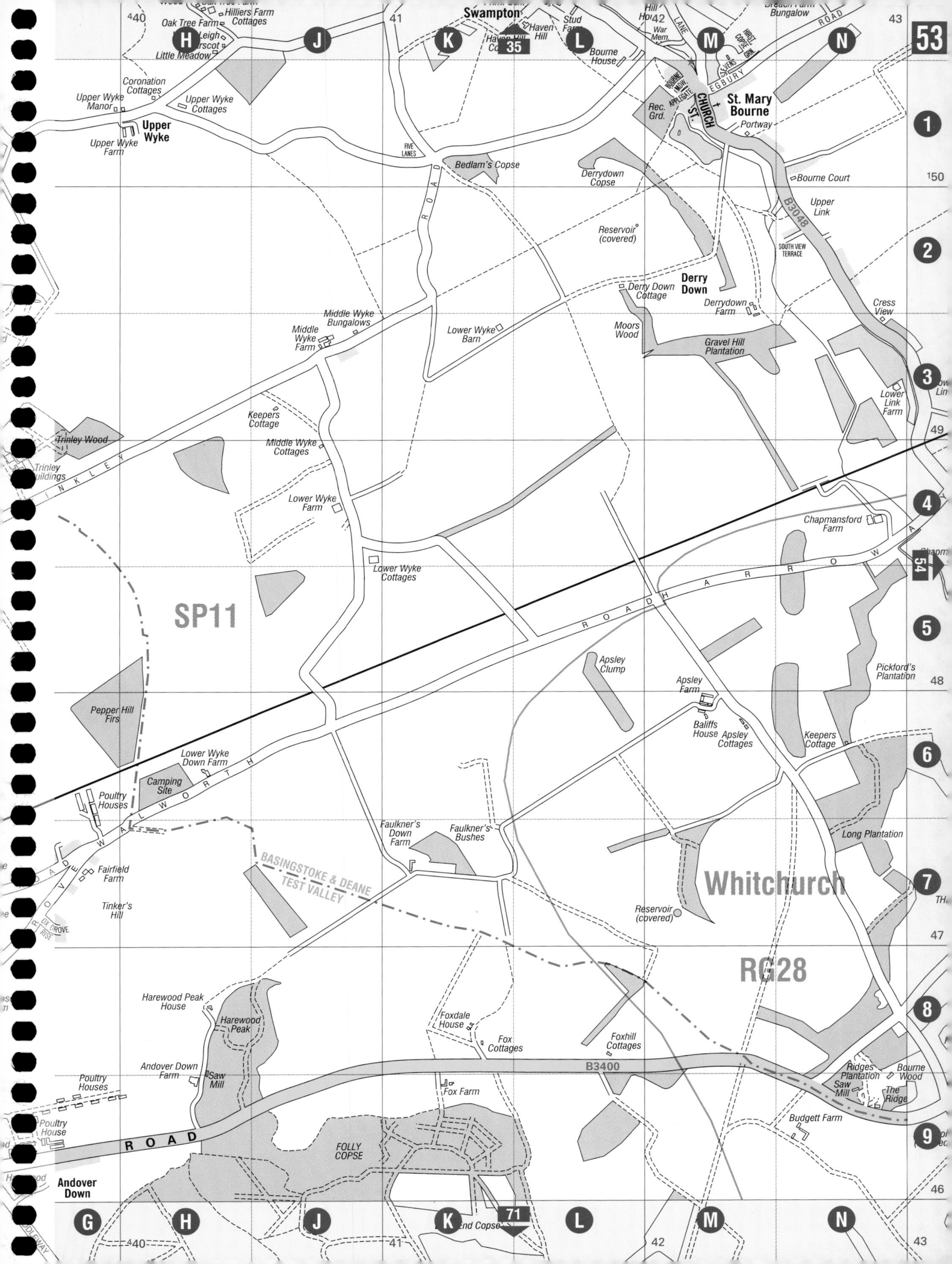

Swampton
Hilliers Farm Cottages
Oak Tree Farm
Haven Hill
Stud Farm
War Mem.
Bungalow
ROAD
Little Meadow
Bourne House
Coronation Cottages
Upper Wyke Manor
Upper Wyke Cottages
Rec. Grd.
CHURCH ST.
EGBURY
St. Mary Bourne
Portway
Upper Wyke
Upper Wyke Farm
FIVE LANES
Bedlam's Copse
Derrydown Copse
Bourne Court
ROAD
B3048
Upper Link
Reservoir (covered)
SOUTH VIEW TERRACE
Derry Down Cottage
Derry Down
Derrydown Farm
Cress View
Middle Wyke Bungalows
Middle Wyke Farm
Lower Wyke Barn
Moors Wood
Gravel Hill Plantation
Lower Link Farm
Keepers Cottage
Trinley Wood
Middle Wyke Cottages
Trinley Buildings
INKLEY
Lower Wyke Farm
Chapmansford Farm
Lower Wyke Cottages
HARROW
ROAD
SP11
Apsley Clump
Pickford's Plantation
Apsley Farm
Pepper Hill Firs
Baliffs House
Apsley Cottages
Keepers Cottage
Lower Wyke Down Farm
Camping Site
Poultry Houses
WALWORTH
Faulkner's Down Farm
Faulkner's Bushes
Long Plantation
BASINGSTOKE & DEANE
TEST VALLEY
Fairfield Farm
Whitchurch
Tinker's Hill
OX DROVE RISE
Reservoir (covered)
RG28
Harewood Peak House
Harewood Peak
Foxdale House
Fox Cottages
Foxhill Cottages
Andover Down Farm
Saw Mill
B3400
Ridges Plantation
Bourne Wood
Poultry Houses
Fox Farm
Saw Mill
The Ridge
Poultry House
Budgett Farm
ROAD
FOLLY COPSE
Andover Down
End Copse

35
54
71

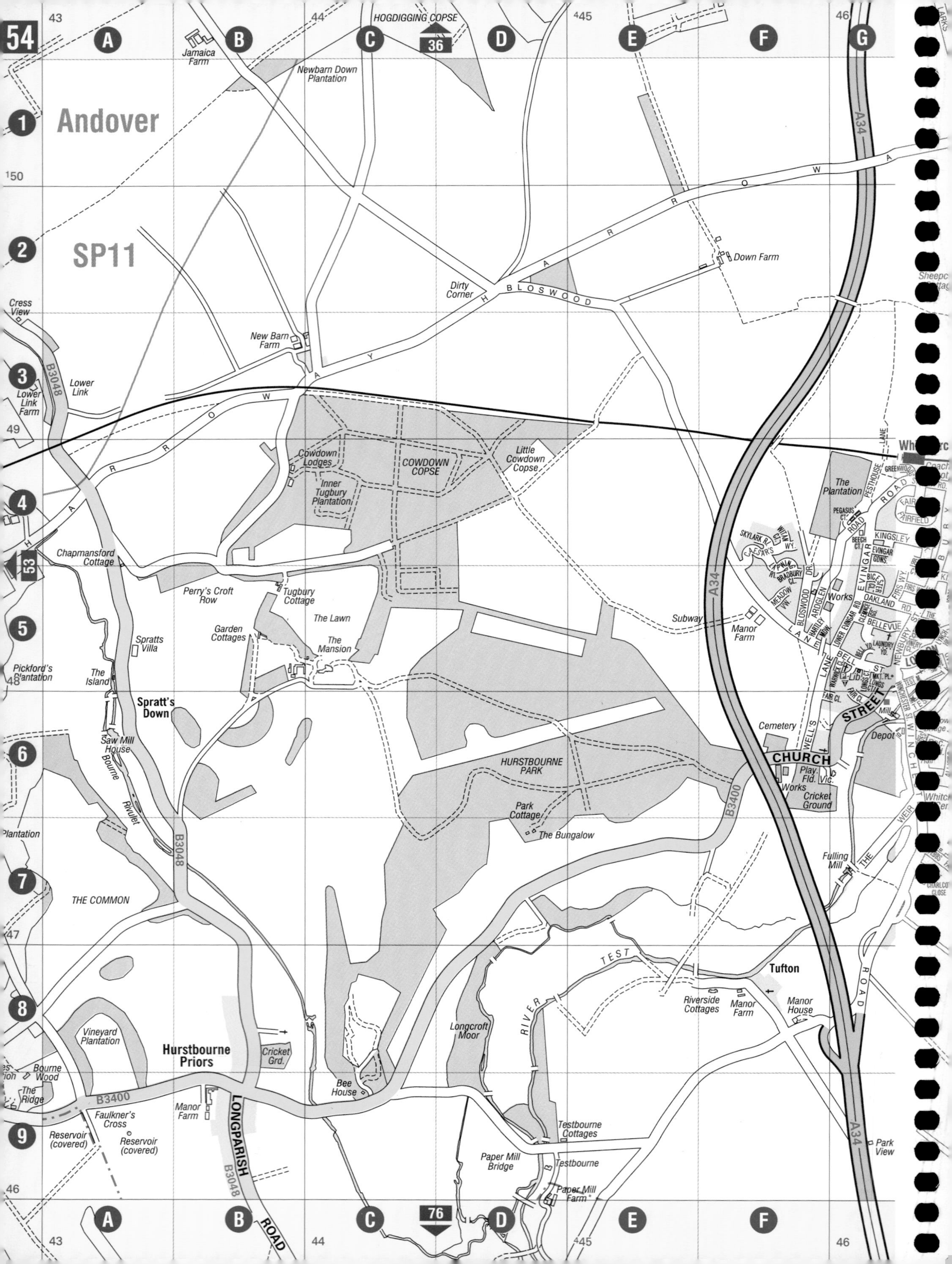
Andover
SP11
Jamaica Farm
Newbarn Down Plantation
HOGDIGGING COPSE
36
Down Farm
Dirty Corner
BLOSWOOD
HARROWAY
New Barn Farm
Cress View
Lower Link
Lower Link Farm
B3048
Cowdown Lodges
COWDOWN COPSE
Little Cowdown Copse
Inner Tugbury Plantation
The Plantation
Chapmansford Cottage
53
Perry's Croft Row
Tugbury Cottage
The Lawn
Garden Cottages
The Mansion
Spratts Villa
Pickford's Plantation
The Island
Spratt's Down
Saw Mill House
Bourne Rivulet
HURSTBOURNE PARK
Park Cottage
The Bungalow
Subway
Manor Farm
Cemetery
CHURCH STREET
Play. Fld.
Works
Cricket Ground
Fulling Mill
A34
B3400
THE COMMON
Plantation
Tufton
Riverside Cottages
Manor Farm
Manor House
RIVER TEST
Longcroft Moor
Vineyard Plantation
Hurstbourne Priors
Cricket Grd.
Bourne Wood
The Ridge
Faulkner's Cross
Reservoir (covered)
Manor Farm
Bee House
LONGPARISH ROAD
Testbourne Cottages
Paper Mill Bridge
Testbourne
Paper Mill Farm
76
Park View
WINCHESTER ROAD
THE WEIR
Depot
Mill
SKYLARK RI.
CAESAR'S
BRADBURY CL.
MEADOW VW.
BLOSWOOD DR.
ARDGLEN RD.
HARTLEY MDW.
EVINGAR RD.
EVINGAR GDNS.
KINGSLEY
PEGASUS CT.
BEECH CT.
PESTHOUSE LANE
OAKLAND RD.
BELLEVUE
BELL ST.
WELL'S LANE
LOWER EVINGAR RD.
LAUNDRY YD.
MKT. PL.
LONGS CT.
FAIR CL.
NEWBURY ST.
FAIRFIELD
FIRS WY.
A B C D E F G
1 2 3 4 5 6 7 8 9
43 44 445 46
150 49 48 47 46

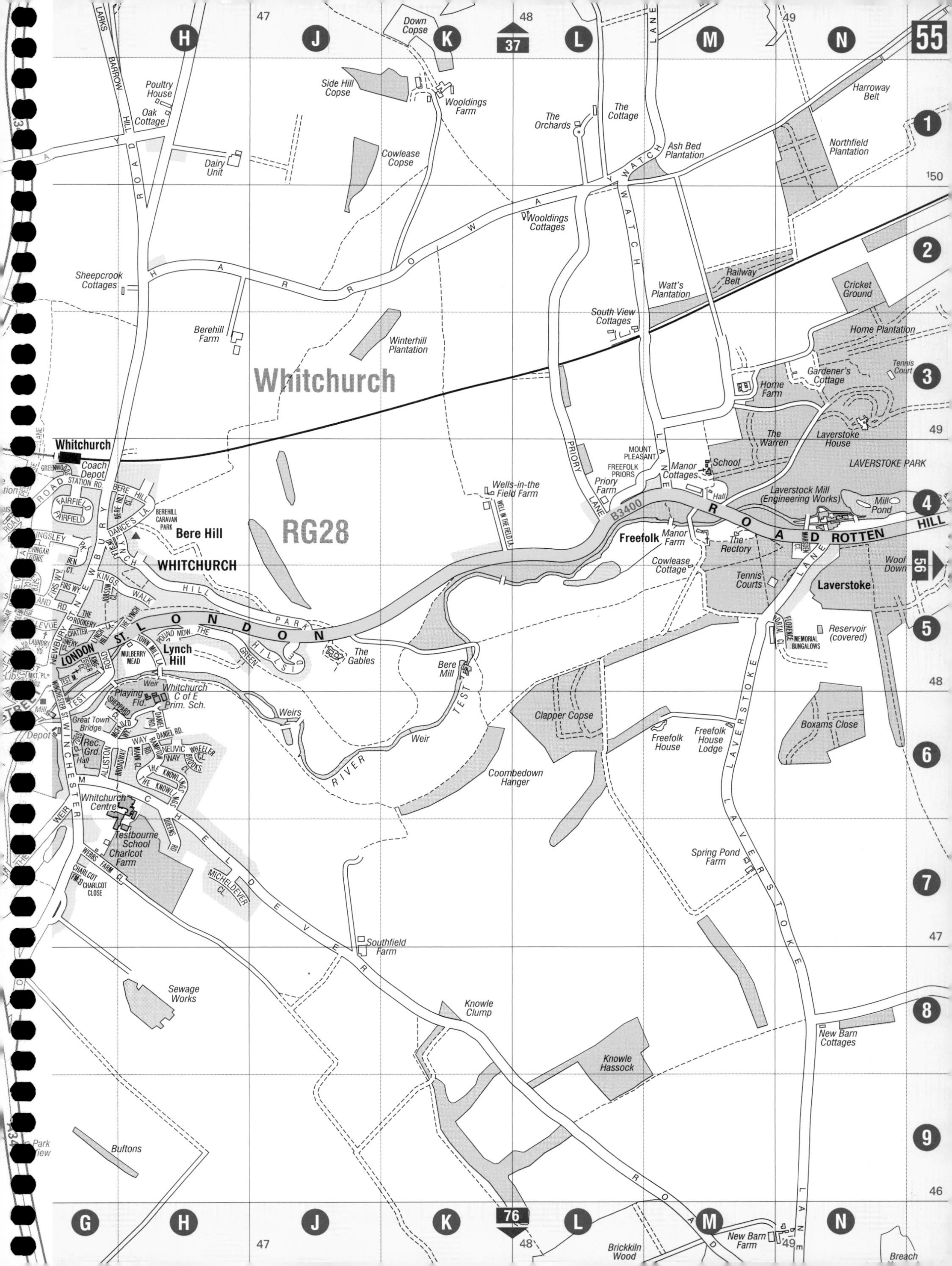

Whitchurch
RG28
WHITCHURCH
Bere Hill
Lynch Hill
Freefolk
Laverstoke
LAVERSTOKE PARK
Down Copse
Side Hill Copse
Wooldings Farm
Poultry House
Oak Cottage
Dairy Unit
Cowlease Copse
The Orchards
The Cottage
Ash Bed Plantation
Harroway Belt
Northfield Plantation
Wooldings Cottages
Sheepcrook Cottages
Berehill Farm
Winterhill Plantation
Watt's Plantation
Railway Belt
South View Cottages
Cricket Ground
Home Plantation
Gardener's Cottage
Tennis Court
Home Farm
The Warren
Laverstoke House
Mount Pleasant
Freefolk Priors
Priory Farm
Manor Cottages
School
Hall
Wells-in-the Field Farm
Laverstock Mill (Engineering Works)
Mill Pond
Manor Farm
The Rectory
Cowlease Cottage
Tennis Courts
Wool Down
Reservoir (covered)
Memorial Bungalows
Coach Depot
Berehill Caravan Park
The Gables
Bere Mill
Weirs
Weir
River Test
Clapper Copse
Freefolk House
Freefolk House Lodge
Boxams Close
Coombedown Hanger
Whitchurch C of E Prim. Sch.
Playing Fld.
Great Town Bridge
Rec. Grd.
Hall
Depot
Mill
Whitchurch Centre
Testbourne School
Charlcot Farm
Charlcot Close
Spring Pond Farm
Southfield Farm
Sewage Works
Knowle Clump
Knowle Hassock
New Barn Cottages
Buftons
Park View
Brickkiln Wood
New Barn Farm
Breach
HARROWAY
WATCH LANE
LARKS BARROW HILL
A34
PRIORY LANE
LAVERSTOKE LANE
LONDON ROAD
B3400
ROTTEN HILL
LONDON ST.
NEWBURY ST.
WINCHESTER ST.
MICHELDEVER ROAD
WEIR
BERE HILL
BERE HILL CL.
DANCE'S LA.
KINGS WALK
PARK HILL
THE HILLSIDE
THE GREEN
POUND MDW.
TOWN MILL LA.
MULBERRY MEAD
THE LYNCH
STATION RD.
GREENWOOD
FAIRFIELD
KINGSLEY PK.
FIRS WY.
BEN CT.
JOBSON CL.
THE ROOKERY
CHATTER
LAUNDRY YD.
MKT. PL.
SHEPPARD CL.
DANIEL RD.
ALLISTON WAY
BROADWAY
NEUVIC WAY
WHEELER CL.
BROOKS CL.
THE KNOWLINGS
QUEENS RD.
MICHELDEVER CL.
WEBBS FARM CL.
CHARLCOT FM.
MARSDEN CT.
PORTAL CL.
FLORENCE CL.
WELL IN THE FIELD LA.
LYNCH HILL
37
76
56
H J K L M N G
1 2 3 4 5 6 7 8 9
47 48 49 150 46

Foxdown
Quidhampton Farm
Quidhampton Pond
Quidhampton
Kennel Plantation
Rural Study Field Centre
Lordsfield Plantation
Northington Belt
Swimming Pool
Overton C. of E. Prim. School
Sewage Works
Court Farm
Lynch
Southington Mill
The Rectory
Sports Ground
Football Ground
Farm Cottages
Northington Farm
Southington
Parsonage Farm
Berrydown Court
Home Plantation
River Test
OVERTON
The Lodge
Berrydown Farm
South Berrydown
LAVERSTOKE PARK
Sports Ground
Basingstoke
ROTTEN HILL
Rotten Hill Copse
Jackson's Copse
Sapley Farm House
Turrill Hill Farm
Woodside
RG25
Reservoir (covered)
White Hill
Lower Whitehill Cottages
Keepers Cottage
Whitchurch
Pot Bottom Cottage
Southley Farm
Laverstoke Grange Farm
RG28
Quidhampton Southley Copse
Pilgrim's Copse
Copse Farm
Southley Copse
Upper Whitehill Farm
Pilgrim's Farm
LAVERSTOKE WOOD
Breach
Bramdown
B3400
B3051
KINGSCLERE ROAD
LONDON ROAD
HIGH ST.
WALTHAM ROAD

38
55
77

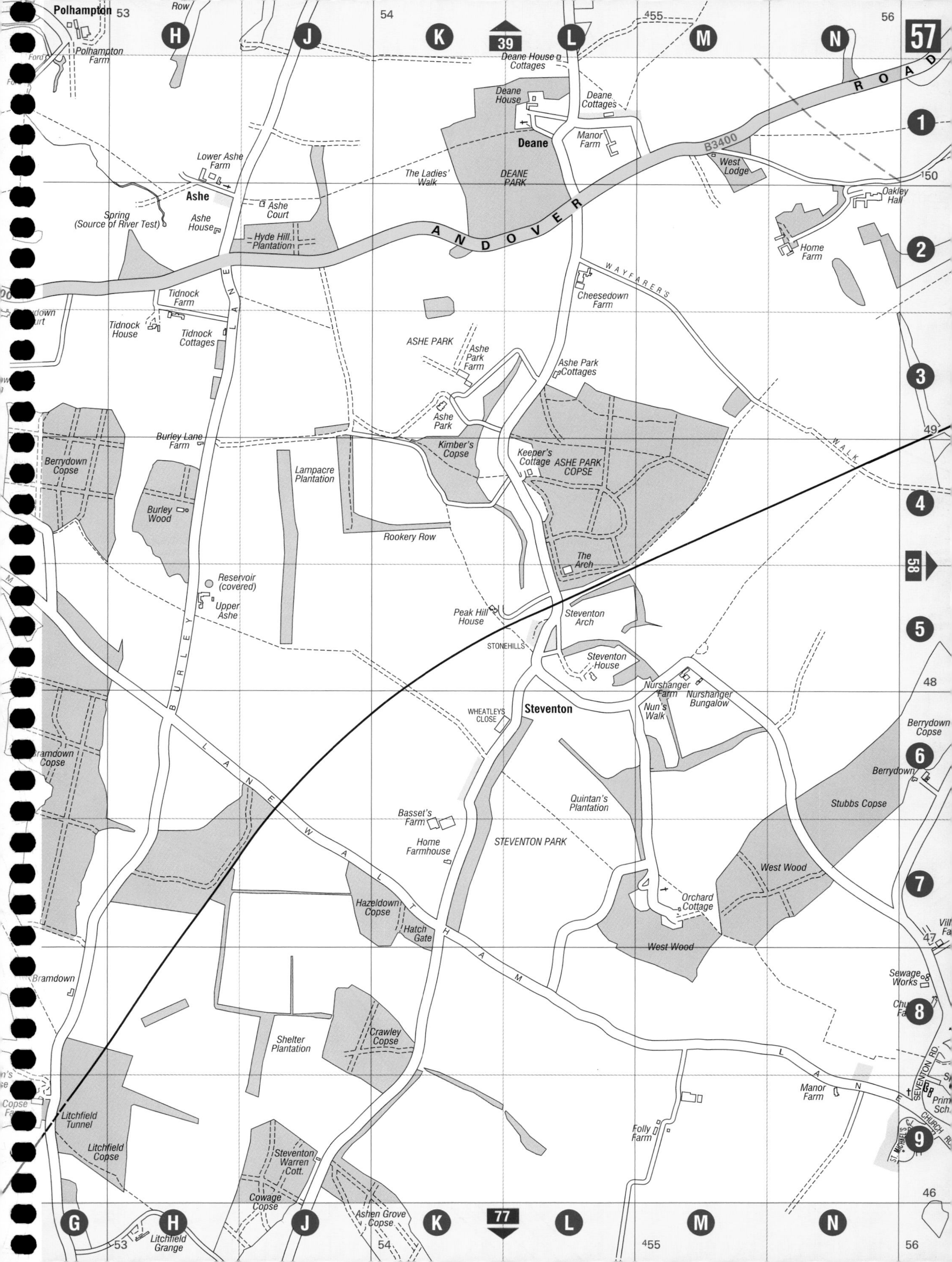
Polhampton
Polhampton Farm
Ford
Row
Deane House Cottages
Deane House
Deane Cottages
Deane
Manor Farm
ANDOVER ROAD
B3400
West Lodge
Oakley Hall
Home Farm
Lower Ashe Farm
Ashe
Ashe Court
Ashe House
Spring (Source of River Test)
Hyde Hill Plantation
The Ladies' Walk
DEANE PARK
Tidnock Farm
Tidnock House
Tidnock Cottages
WAYFARER'S WALK
Cheesedown Farm
ASHE PARK
Ashe Park Farm
Ashe Park Cottages
Ashe Park
Burley Lane Farm
Berrydown Copse
Lampacre Plantation
Kimber's Copse
Keeper's Cottage
ASHE PARK COPSE
Burley Wood
Rookery Row
The Arch
Reservoir (covered)
Upper Ashe
Peak Hill House
Steventon Arch
STONEHILLS
Steventon House
Nurshanger Farm
Nurshanger Bungalow
Nun's Walk
WHEATLEYS CLOSE
Steventon
BURLEY LANE
Bramdown Copse
Berrydown Copse
Berrydown
Stubbs Copse
Quintan's Plantation
Basset's Farm
Home Farmhouse
STEVENTON PARK
West Wood
Orchard Cottage
Hazeldown Copse
Hatch Gate
WALTHAM LANE
West Wood
Sewage Works
Bramdown
Shelter Plantation
Crawley Copse
LANE
Manor Farm
SEVENTON RD.
CHURCH RD.
ST. MICHAEL'S
Litchfield Tunnel
Litchfield Copse
Steventon Warren Cott.
Folly Farm
Cowage Copse
Ashen Grove Copse
Litchfield Grange
G H J K L M N
1 2 3 4 5 6 7 8 9
53 54 455 56
150 49 48 47 46
39 58 77

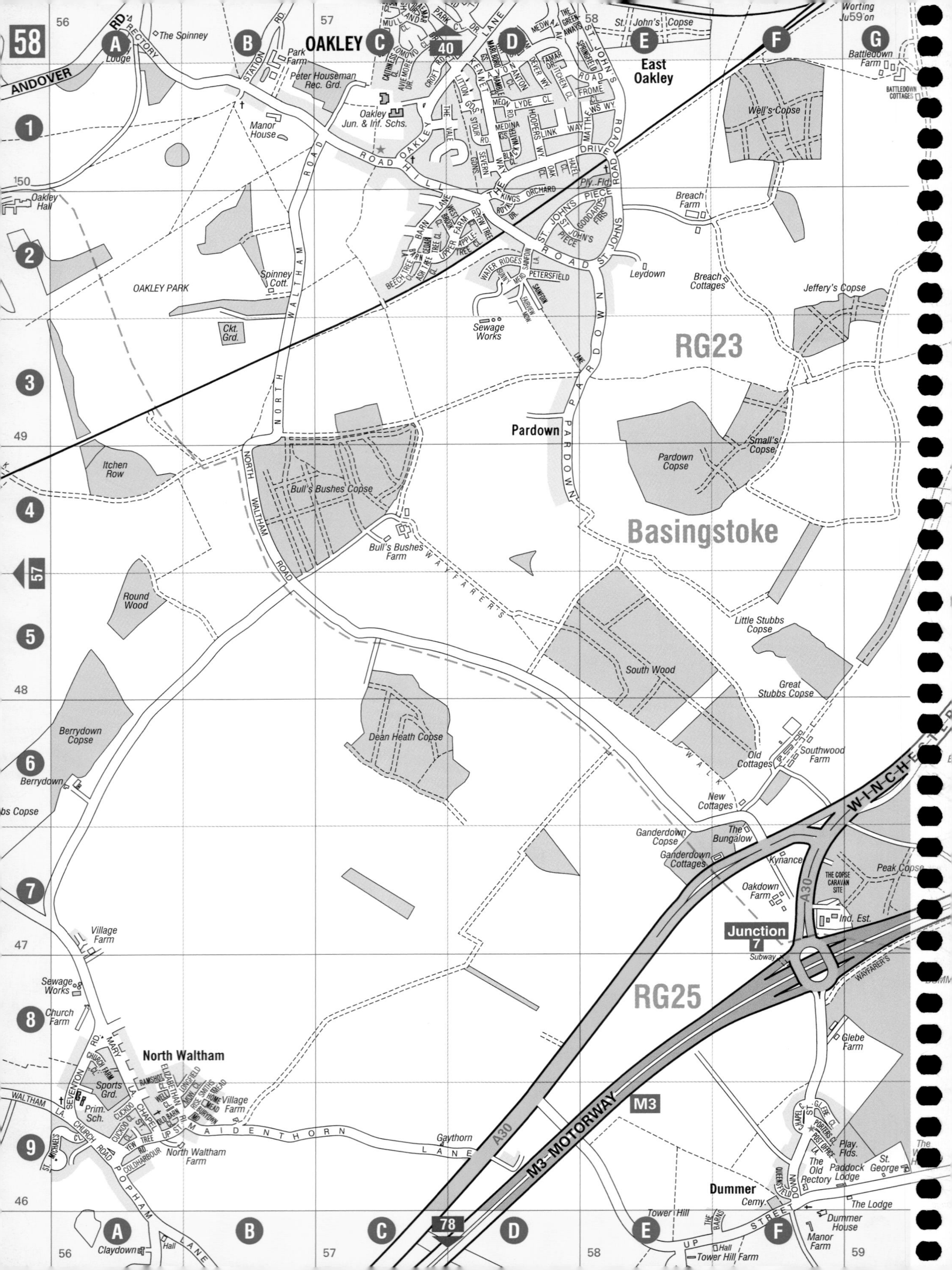

OAKLEY
East Oakley
Oakley Park
Pardown
Basingstoke
RG23
RG25
North Waltham
Dummer
Bull's Bushes Copse
Bull's Bushes Farm
South Wood
Dean Heath Copse
Pardown Copse
Small's Copse
Well's Copse
Jeffery's Copse
Little Stubbs Copse
Great Stubbs Copse
Itchen Row
Round Wood
Berrydown Copse
Berrydown
Ganderdown Copse
Ganderdown Cottages
The Bungalow
New Cottages
Old Cottages
Southwood Farm
Oakdown Farm
Kynance
Peak Copse
The Copse Caravan Site
Ind. Est.
Junction 7
Subway
Glebe Farm
Village Farm
Church Farm
Sewage Works
Sports Grd.
Prim. Sch.
North Waltham Farm
Gaythorn
Claydown
Tower Hill
Tower Hill Farm
The Old Rectory
Paddock Lodge
St. George
The Lodge
Dummer House
Manor Farm
Play. Flds.
Cemy.
Oakley Hall
Manor House
Spinney Cott.
Ckt. Grd.
Park Farm
Peter Houseman Rec. Grd.
Oakley Jun. & Inf. Schs.
The Spinney
Breach Farm
Breach Cottages
Leydown
Battledown Farm
Battledown Cottages
St. John's Copse
Sewage Works
NORTH WALTHAM ROAD
OAKLEY HILL
ST. JOHNS ROAD
PARDOWN
MAIDENTHORN LANE
POPHAM LANE
WAYFARERS WALK
M3 MOTORWAY
A30
WINCHESTER
ANDOVER
RECTORY RD.
STATION RD.
WALTHAM LA.
CHURCH ROAD
SEVENTON RD.
UP STREET

40
57
78

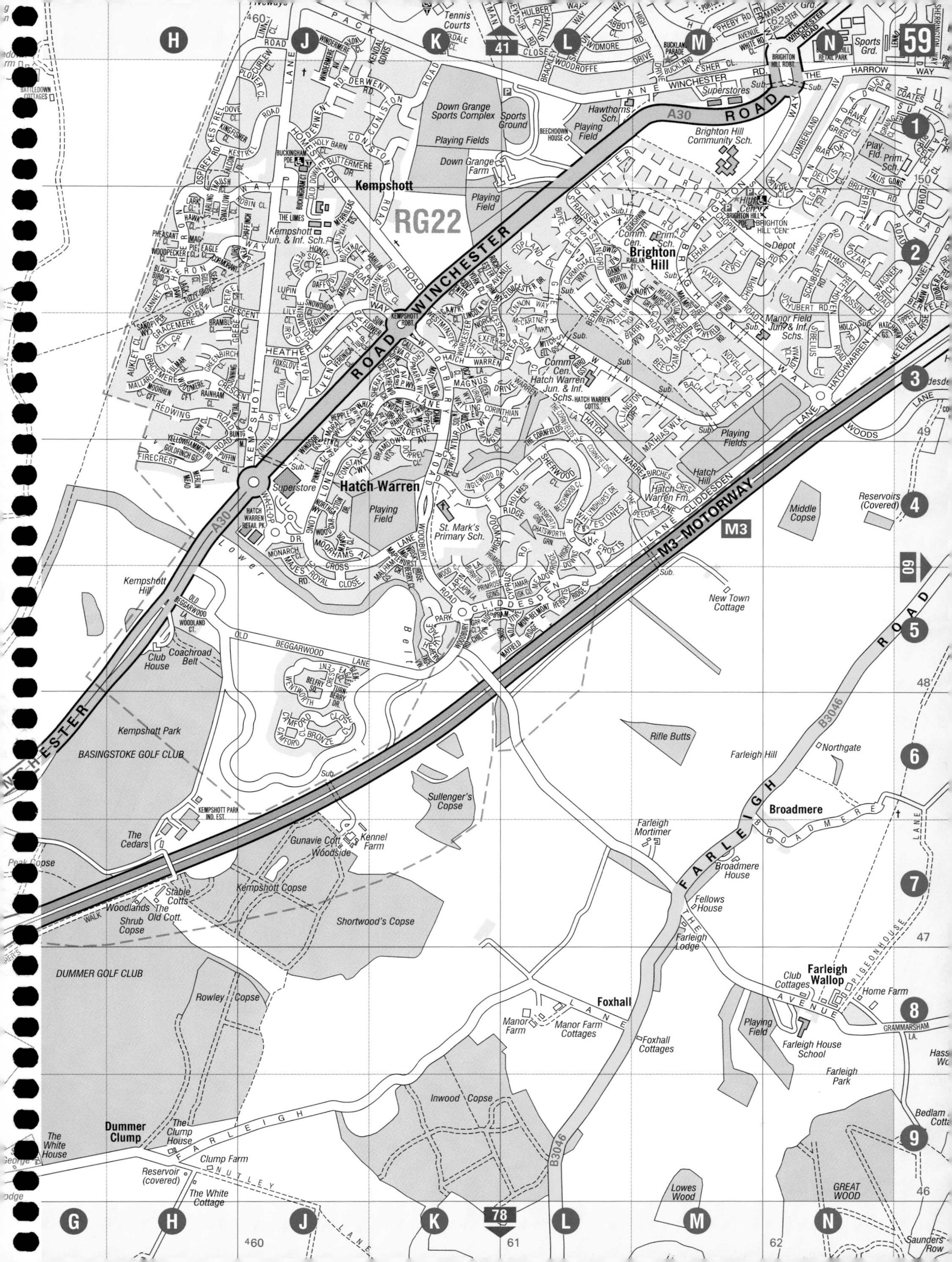

Kempshott
RG22
Brighton Hill
Hatch Warren
Down Grange Sports Complex
Playing Fields
Down Grange Farm
Sports Ground
Brighton Hill Community Sch.
Kempshott Jun. & Inf. Sch.
Superstore
Superstores
St. Mark's Primary Sch.
Hatch Warren Jun. & Inf. Schs.
Manor Field Jun. & Inf. Schs.
WINCHESTER ROAD
A30
M3 MOTORWAY
B3046
Kempshott Hill
Kempshott Park
BASINGSTOKE GOLF CLUB
DUMMER GOLF CLUB
Kempshott Copse
Shortwood's Copse
Sullenger's Copse
Rowley Copse
Inwood Copse
Rifle Butts
New Town Cottage
Middle Copse
Reservoirs (Covered)
Farleigh Hill
Northgate
Broadmere
Broadmere House
Farleigh Mortimer
Fellows House
Farleigh Lodge
Farleigh Wallop
Club Cottages
Home Farm
Farleigh House School
Farleigh Park
Foxhall
Foxhall Cottages
Manor Farm
Manor Farm Cottages
Dummer Clump
The Clump House
Clump Farm
The White House
The White Cottage
Reservoir (covered)
GREAT WOOD
Lowes Wood
Kennel Farm
Gunavie Cott.
Woodside
The Cedars
Stable Cotts
Woodlands
The Old Cott.
Shrub Copse
Peak Copse
Club House
Coachroad Belt
Hatch Warren Fm.
Hatch Hill
FARLEIGH ROAD
41
60
78

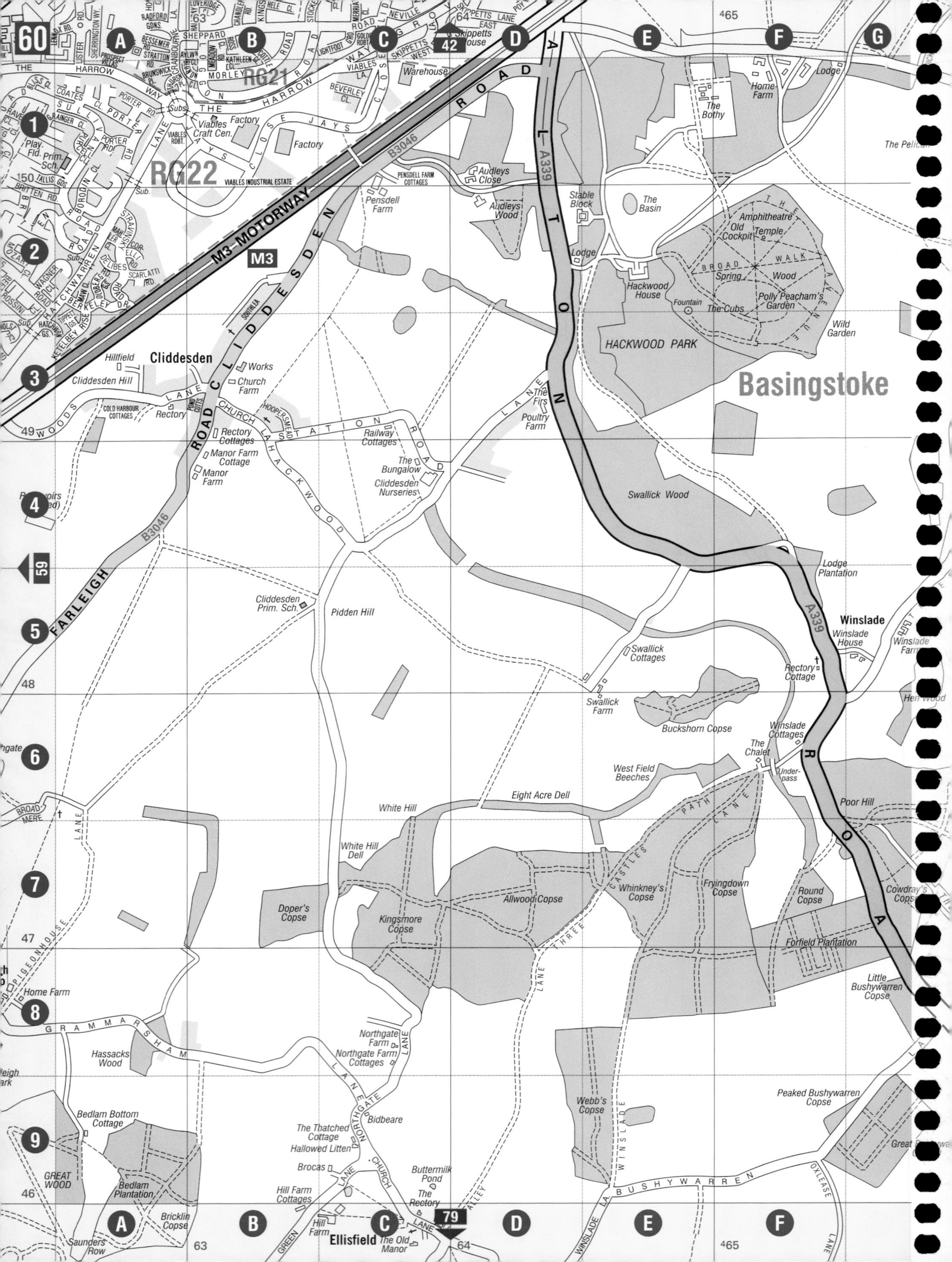

Cliddesden
Basingstoke
HACKWOOD PARK
Hackwood House
Winslade
Ellisfield
M3 MOTORWAY
RG21
RG22
Viables Industrial Estate
Viables Craft Cen.
Audleys Close
Audleys Wood
Pensdell Farm
The Basin
Stable Block
Lodge
Home Farm
The Bothy
Amphitheatre
Old Cockpit
Temple
Spring
Wood
Polly Peacham's Garden
The Cubs
Fountain
Wild Garden
Hillfield
Cliddesden Hill
Works
Church Farm
Rectory
Rectory Cottages
Manor Farm Cottage
Manor Farm
Railway Cottages
The Bungalow
Cliddesden Nurseries
The Firs
Poultry Farm
Swallick Wood
Lodge Plantation
Cliddesden Prim. Sch.
Pidden Hill
Winslade House
Swallick Cottages
Swallick Farm
Rectory Cottage
Buckshorn Copse
Winslade Cottages
The Chalet
Under-pass
West Field Beeches
Eight Acre Dell
White Hill
White Hill Dell
Poor Hill
Doper's Copse
Kingsmore Copse
Allwood Copse
Whinkney's Copse
Fryingdown Copse
Round Copse
Cowdray's Copse
Forfield Plantation
Little Bushywarren Copse
Home Farm
Hassacks Wood
Northgate Farm
Northgate Farm Cottages
Bedlam Bottom Cottage
Webb's Copse
Peaked Bushywarren Copse
Bidbeare
The Thatched Cottage
Hallowed Litten
Brocas
Buttermilk Pond
The Rectory
Hill Farm Cottages
Hill Farm
The Old Manor
GREAT WOOD
Bedlam Plantation
Bricklin Copse
Saunders Row
FARLEIGH ROAD
CLIDDESDEN ROAD
ALTON ROAD
A339
B3046
GRAMMARSHAM
NORTHGATE LANE
BUSHYWARREN
WINSLADE LANE
LANE THREE
CASTLES PATH LANE
OXLEASE LANE
STATION ROAD
HACKWOOD LANE
CHURCH LANE
WOODS LANE
PIGEONHOUSE
THE HARROW WAY
JAYS CLOSE
42
59
79

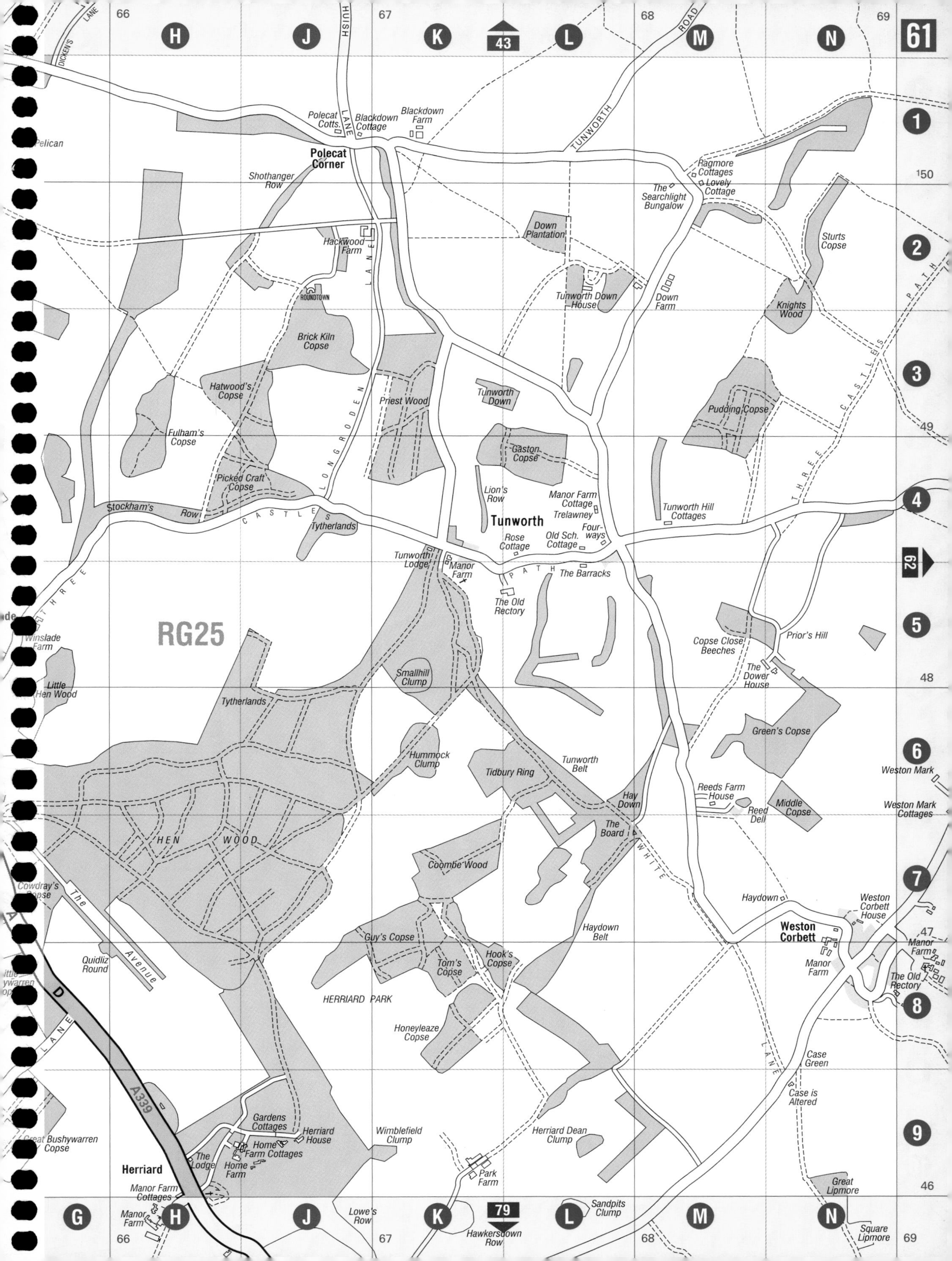

43
62
79
Polecat Corner
Polecat Cotts.
Blackdown Cottage
Blackdown Farm
Huish Lane
Dicken's Lane
Pelican
Shothanger Row
Tunworth Road
Ragmore Cottages
Lovely Cottage
The Searchlight Bungalow
Down Plantation
Hackwood Farm
Roundtown
Sturts Copse
Tunworth Down House
Down Farm
Knights Wood
Brick Kiln Copse
Priest Wood
Longroden Lane
Hatwood's Copse
Tunworth Down
Pudding Copse
Fulham's Copse
Gaston Copse
Picked Craft Copse
Lion's Row
Manor Farm Cottage
Trelawney
Tunworth Hill Cottages
Stockham's Row
Three Castles Path
Tytherlands
Tunworth
Rose Cottage
Old Sch. Cottage
Four-ways
Tunworth Lodge
Manor Farm
The Barracks
The Old Rectory
RG25
Winslade Farm
Little Hen Wood
Copse Close Beeches
Prior's Hill
The Dower House
Smallhill Clump
Tytherlands
Green's Copse
Hummock Clump
Tidbury Ring
Tunworth Belt
Weston Mark
Hay Down
Reeds Farm House
Reed Dell
Middle Copse
Weston Mark Cottages
Hen Wood
The Board
White Lane
Coombe Wood
Cowdray's Copse
The Avenue
Haydown
Weston Corbett House
Weston Corbett
Guy's Copse
Haydown Belt
Manor Farm
Tom's Copse
Hook's Copse
Quidliz Round
Herriard Park
The Old Rectory
Honeyleaze Copse
Case Green
Case is Altered
A339
Gardens Cottages
Herriard House
Wimblefield Clump
Herriard Dean Clump
Great Bushywarren Copse
Home Farm Cottages
The Lodge
Home Farm
Herriard
Park Farm
Great Lipmore
Manor Farm Cottages
Manor Farm
Lowe's Row
Hawkersdown Row
Sandpits Clump
Square Lipmore
66
67
68
69
150
49
48
47
46
G
H
J
K
L
M
N
1
2
3
4
5
6
7
8
9

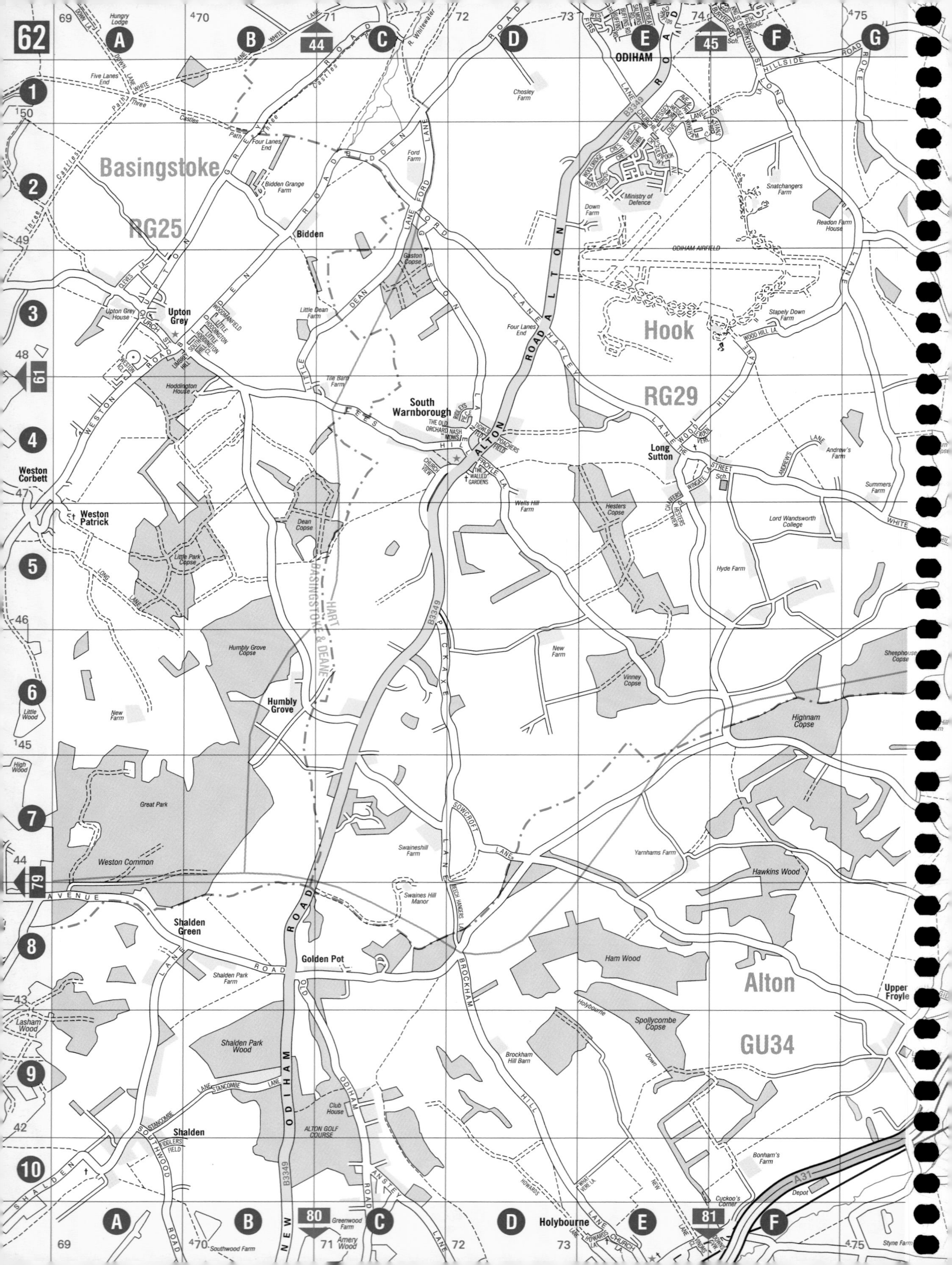

Hungry Lodge
Five Lanes End
Basingstoke
RG25
Four Lanes End
Bidden Grange Farm
Bidden
Ford Farm
Chosley Farm
ODIHAM
Ministry of Defence
Down Farm
Snatchangers Farm
Readon Farm House
ODIHAM AIRFIELD
Hook
Stapely Down Farm
Upton Grey
Upton Grey House
Little Dean Farm
Gaston Copse
Four Lanes End
Hoddington House
Tile Barn Farm
South Warnborough
THE WALLED GARDENS
RG29
Long Sutton
Andrew's Farm
Summers Farm
Lord Wandsworth College
Weston Corbett
Weston Patrick
Little Park Copse
Dean Copse
Wells Hill Farm
Hesters Copse
Hyde Farm
Humbly Grove Copse
HART
BASINGSTOKE & DEANE
New Farm
Vinney Copse
Sheephouse Copse
Little Wood
New Farm
Humbly Grove
Highnam Copse
High Wood
Great Park
Swaineshill Farm
Yarnhams Farm
Weston Common
Hawkins Wood
Swaines Hill Manor
Shalden Green
Golden Pot
Ham Wood
Shalden Park Farm
Alton
Upper Froyle
Lasham Wood
Spollycombe Copse
GU34
Shalden Park Wood
Brockham Hill Barn
Club House
ALTON GOLF COURSE
Shalden
Bonham's Farm
Depot
Cuckoo's Corner
Holybourne
Greenwood Farm
Amery Wood
Southwood Farm
Styne Farm
ALTON ROAD
ODIHAM ROAD
NEW ODIHAM ROAD
B3349
A31
PICKAXE LANE
SOWCROFT LANE
BROCKHAM HILL
SHALDEN LANE
SOUTHWOOD ROAD
STANCOMBE LANE
WESTON ROAD
HAYLEY LANE
GASTON LANE
BIDDEN ROAD
DEAN LANE
LEES HILL
WHITE LANE
HILLSIDE ROAD
LONG LANE
WOOD HILL LANE
THE STREET
ANSTEY LANE
ROKE LANE
44
45
61
79
80
81

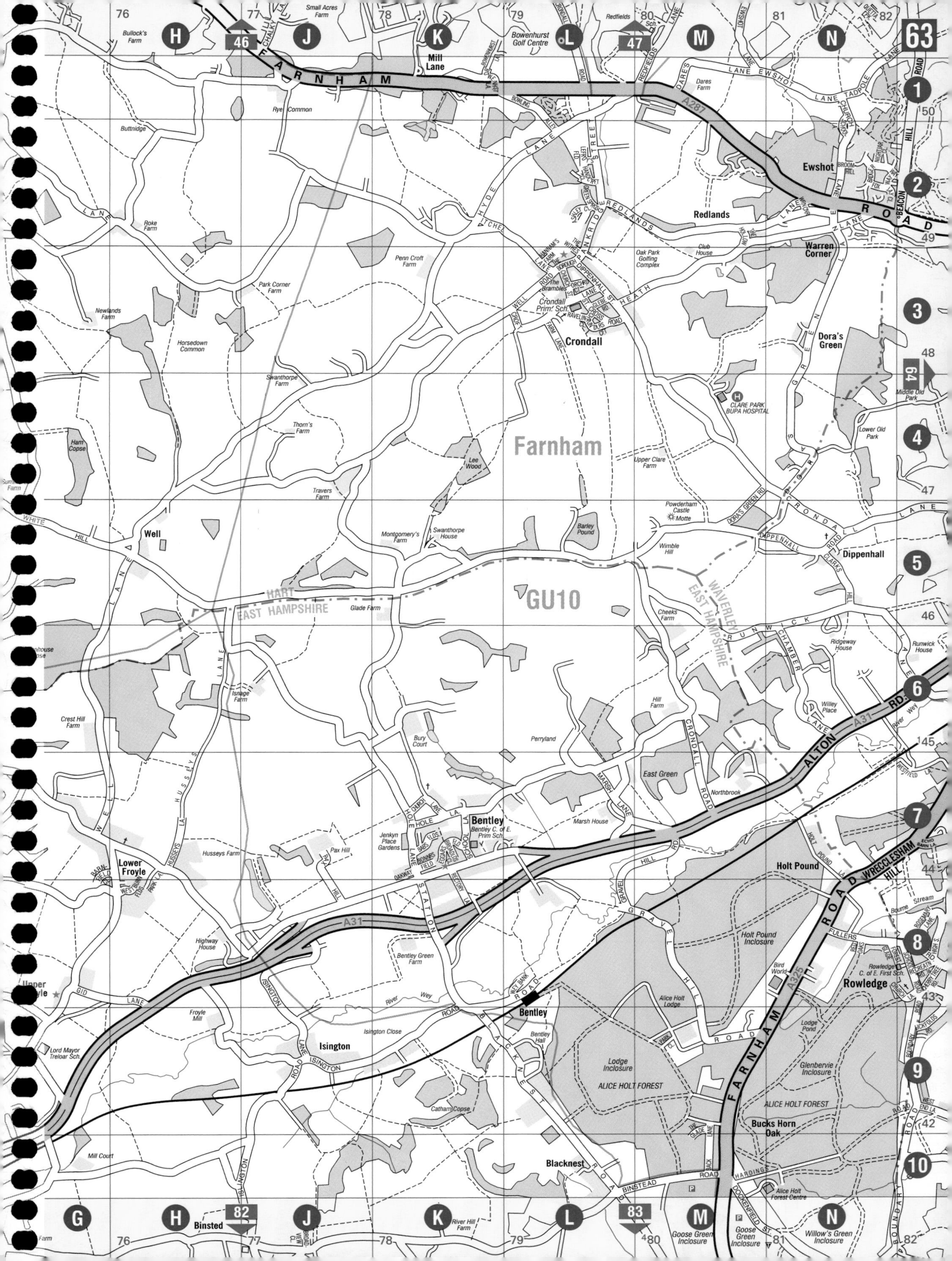

Farnham
GU10
Crondall
Ewshot
Redlands
Warren Corner
Dora's Green
Dippenhall
Well
Bentley
Lower Froyle
Upper Froyle
Isington
Blacknest
Holt Pound
Rowledge
Bucks Horn Oak
Mill Lane
FARNHAM ROAD
A287
A31
A325
ALTON RD.
HART
EAST HAMPSHIRE
WAVERLEY
ALICE HOLT FOREST
Lodge Inclosure
Holt Pound Inclosure
Glenbervie Inclosure
Alice Holt Lodge
Bird World
Lodge Pond
Alice Holt Forest Centre
Goose Green Inclosure
Willow's Green Inclosure
CLARE PARK BUPA HOSPITAL
Oak Park Golfing Complex
Club House
Bowenhurst Golf Centre
Powderham Castle Motte
Bullock's Farm
Small Acres Farm
Redfields
Rye Common
Buttnidge
Dares Farm
Roke Farm
Penn Croft Farm
Park Corner Farm
Newlands Farm
Horsedown Common
Swanthorpe Farm
Thorn's Farm
Ham Copse
Lee Wood
Upper Clare Farm
Travers Farm
Montgomery's Farm
Swanthorpe House
Barley Pound
Wimble Hill
Middle Old Park
Lower Old Park
Glade Farm
Cheeks Farm
Ridgeway House
Runwick House
Isnage Farm
Crest Hill Farm
Hill Farm
Willey Place
Perryland
Bury Court
East Green
Northbrook
Marsh House
Jenkyn Place Gardens
Pax Hill
Husseys Farm
Highway House
Bentley Green Farm
Froyle Mill
Lord Mayor Treloar Sch.
Isington Close
Catham Copse
Bentley Hall
Mill Court
River Hill Farm
Binsted
River Wey
Bourne Stream
Crondall Prim. Sch.
The Brambles
Bentley C. of E. Prim Sch.
Rowledge C. of E. First Sch.
H J K L M N G
46 47 64 82 83
76 77 78 79 80 81 82
1 2 3 4 5 6 7 8 9 10
50 49 48 47 46 145 44 43 42

48
63
GU10
GU9
EWSHOT
FARNHAM
HEATH END
UPPER HALE
HALE
HOG HATCH
CRANMORE
FARNHAM PARK
FARNHAM PARK (PUBLIC) GOLF COURSE
Farnham Castle
The Surrey Institute of Art & Design
Farnham Community Hospital
ROWHILL NATURE RESERVE
Caesar's Camp
Beacon Hill
Bricksbury Hill
Heath Hill
Upper Old Park
Knowle Farm
Middle Old Park
Claypit Wood
Old Park Farm
Ranger's House
Ravenswood House
Bushyreeds Copse
Bushy Coppice
Coxbridge Farm
Alderley Farm
Weydon Hill
DANGER AREA
ODIHAM ROAD
FARNHAM RD.
UPPER HALE RD.
FOLLY HILL
CASTLE HILL
CASTLE ST.
WEST STREET
EAST STREET
GUILDFORD RD.
FARNHAM BY-PASS
HALE ROAD
FARNBOROUGH ROAD
WAVERLEY LANE
FIRGROVE HILL
CRONDALL LANE

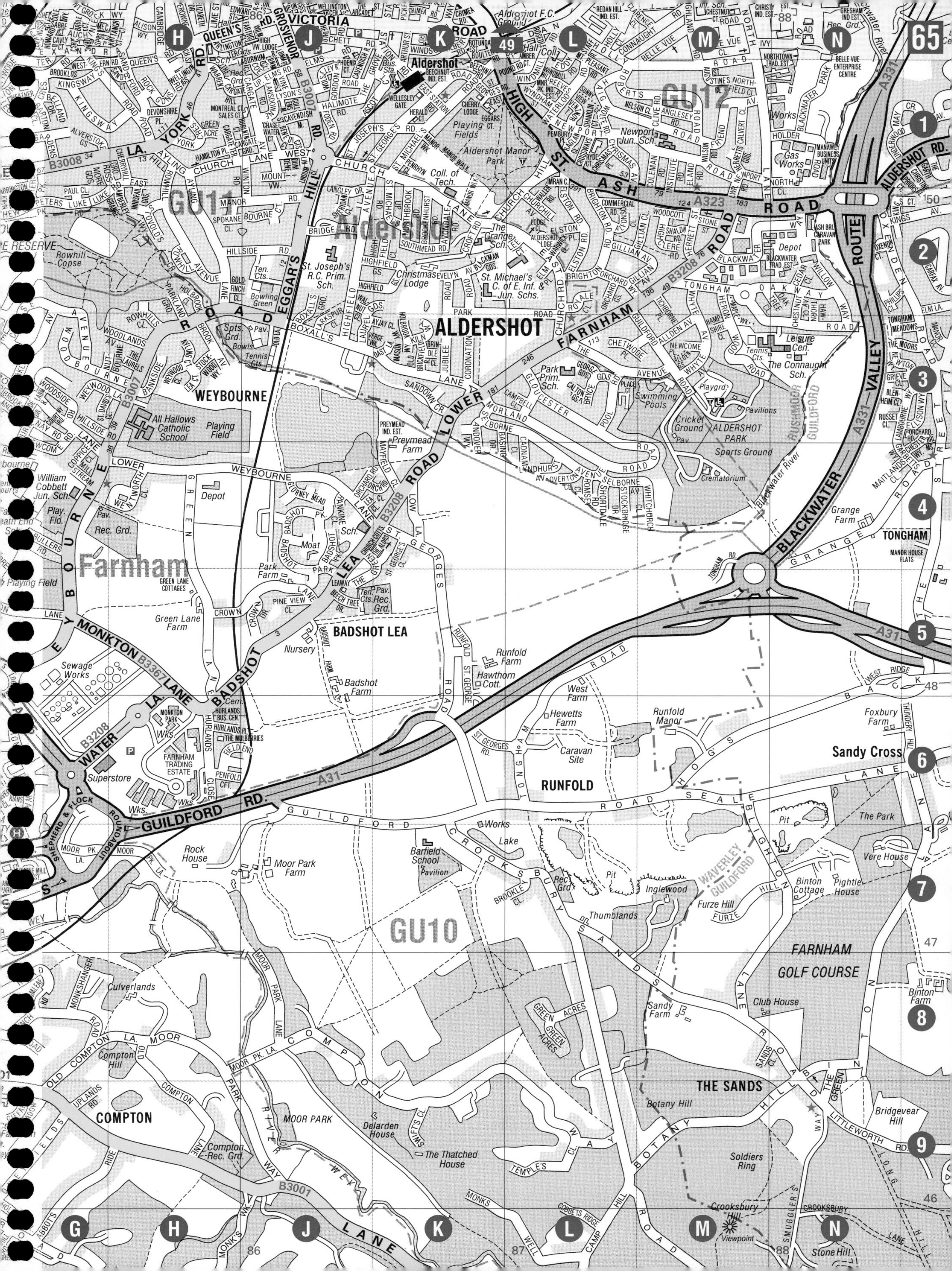

ALDERSHOT
Aldershot
GU11
GU12
GU10
Farnham
WEYBOURNE
BADSHOT LEA
RUNFOLD
THE SANDS
COMPTON
TONGHAM
Sandy Cross
MOOR PARK
FARNHAM GOLF COURSE
ALDERSHOT PARK
Sports Ground
Crematorium
Swimming Pools
Cricket Ground
The Connaught Sch.
Leisure Cen.
All Hallows Catholic School
Playing Field
St. Joseph's R.C. Prim. Sch.
St. Michael's C. of E. Inf. & Jun. Schs.
Christmas Lodge
Aldershot Manor Park
Coll. of Tech.
Newport Jun. Sch.
Park Prim. Sch.
William Cobbett Jun. Sch.
Superstore
FARNHAM TRADING ESTATE
Preymead Farm
Park Farm
Green Lane Farm
Badshot Farm
Runfold Farm
Hawthorn Cott.
West Farm
Hewetts Farm
Runfold Manor
Caravan Site
Foxbury Farm
Barfield School
Moor Park Farm
Rock House
Culverlands
Compton Hill
Compton Rec. Grd.
Delarden House
The Thatched House
Thumblands
Inglewood
Furze Hill
Binton Cottage
Pightle House
Vere House
The Park
Club House
Binton Farm
Sandy Farm
Botany Hill
Soldiers Ring
Bridgevear Hill
Crooksbury Hill
Viewpoint
Stone Hill
Grange Farm
Sewage Works
Depot
Nursery
GUILDFORD RD.
BLACKWATER VALLEY ROUTE
HIGH ST.
ASH ROAD
FARNHAM ROAD
LOWER WEYBOURNE LANE
WEYBOURNE ROAD
EGGAR'S HILL
BADSHOT LANE
MONKTON LANE
HOGS BACK
SEALE ROAD
CROOKSBURY ROAD
SANDS ROAD
BOTANY HILL
COMPTON WAY
MOOR PARK LANE
MONKS LANE
LITTLEWORTH RD.
WAVERLEY GUILDFORD
RUSHMOOR GUILDFORD
Blackwater River
A31
A331
A323
B3208
B3007
B3367
B3001
B3008

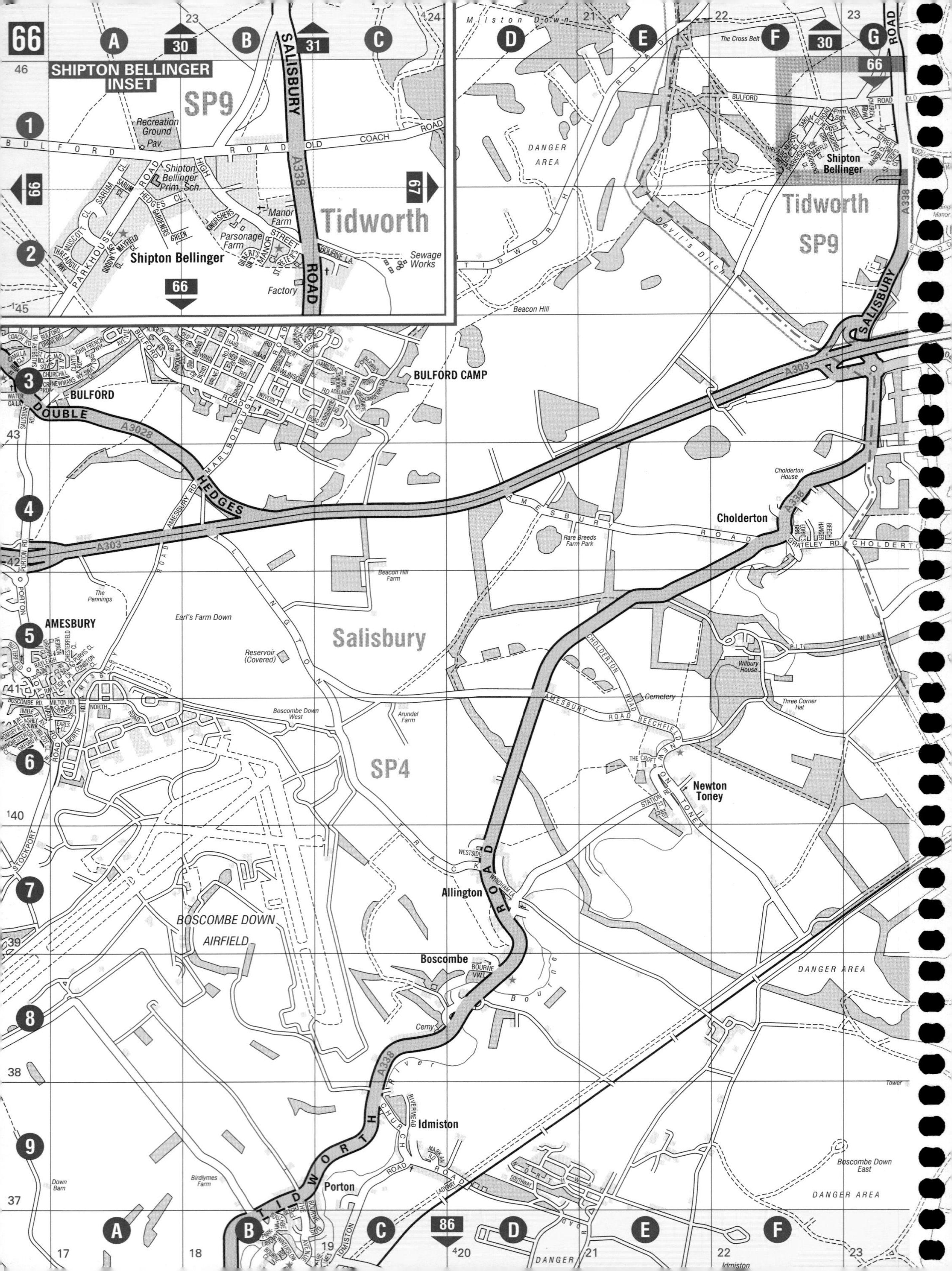

A   B   C   D   E   F   G

23   30   31   22   30   23

SHIPTON BELLINGER INSET

SP9

66

Tidworth

67

Shipton Bellinger

66

Shipton Bellinger

Tidworth

SP9

BULFORD CAMP

DANGER AREA

BULFORD

DOUBLE HEDGES

A303

Cholderton House

Cholderton

A338

Salisbury

Rare Breeds Farm Park

Beacon Hill Farm

The Pennings

AMESBURY

Earl's Farm Down

Reservoir (Covered)

Wilbury House

Three Corner Hat

Cemetery

SP4

Boscombe Down West

Arundel Farm

Newton Toney

THE CROFT

Allington

WESTSIDE

BOSCOMBE DOWN AIRFIELD

Boscombe

BOURNE VW

Cerny.

DANGER AREA

Down Barn

Birdlymes Farm

Idmiston

Porton

Boscombe Down East

DANGER AREA

Tower

A   B   C   D   E   F

17   18   19   86   20   21   22   23

DANGER

Idmiston

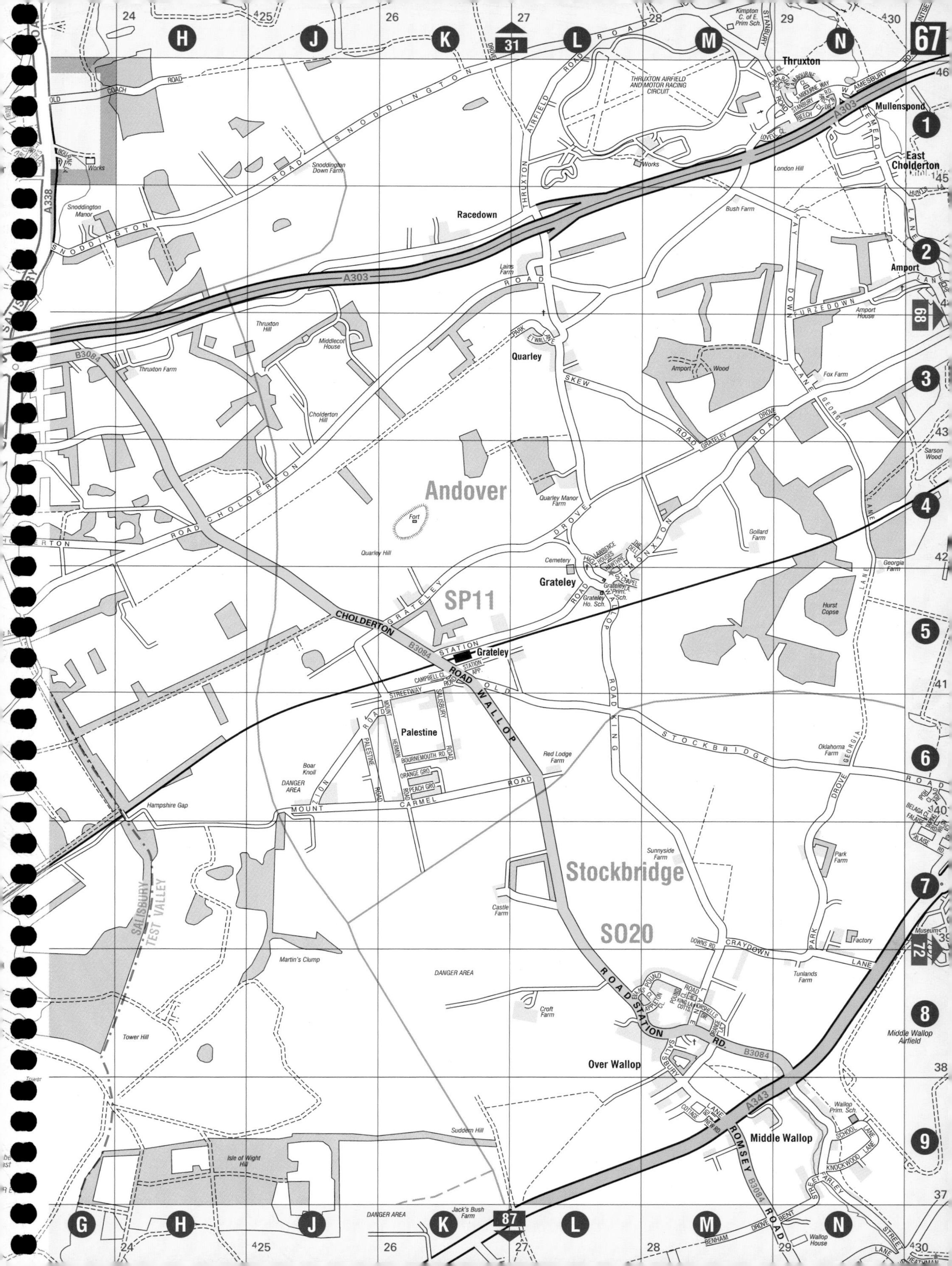

Andover
SP11
Stockbridge
SO20
Thruxton
Mullenspond
East Cholderton
Amport
Racedown
Quarley
Grateley
Palestine
Over Wallop
Middle Wallop
THRUXTON AIRFIELD AND MOTOR RACING CIRCUIT
A303
A338
A343
B3084
SNODDINGTON ROAD
CHOLDERTON ROAD
GRATELEY DROVE
WALLOP ROAD
STOCKBRIDGE ROAD
STATION ROAD
ROMSEY ROAD
MOUNT CARMEL ROAD
CRAYDOWN LANE
FURZEDOWN LANE
SKEW ROAD
KING LANE
GEORGIA LANE
Snoddington Manor
Snoddington Down Farm
Thruxton Hill
Thruxton Farm
Middlecot House
Cholderton Hill
Lains Farm
Quarley Manor Farm
Quarley Hill
Fort
Bush Farm
London Hill
Amport Wood
Amport House
Fox Farm
Sarson Wood
Gollard Farm
Georgia Farm
Hurst Copse
Oklahoma Farm
Red Lodge Farm
Boar Knoll
DANGER AREA
Hampshire Gap
Sunnyside Farm
Park Farm
Castle Farm
Martin's Clump
Factory
Tunlands Farm
Croft Farm
Tower Hill
Middle Wallop Airfield
Wallop Prim. Sch.
Suddern Hill
Isle of Wight Hill
Jack's Bush Farm
Wallop House
Kimpton C. of E. Prim Sch.
Grateley Prim. Sch.
Grateley Ho. Sch.
Cemetery
Works
SALISBURY
TEST VALLEY
31
68
72
87

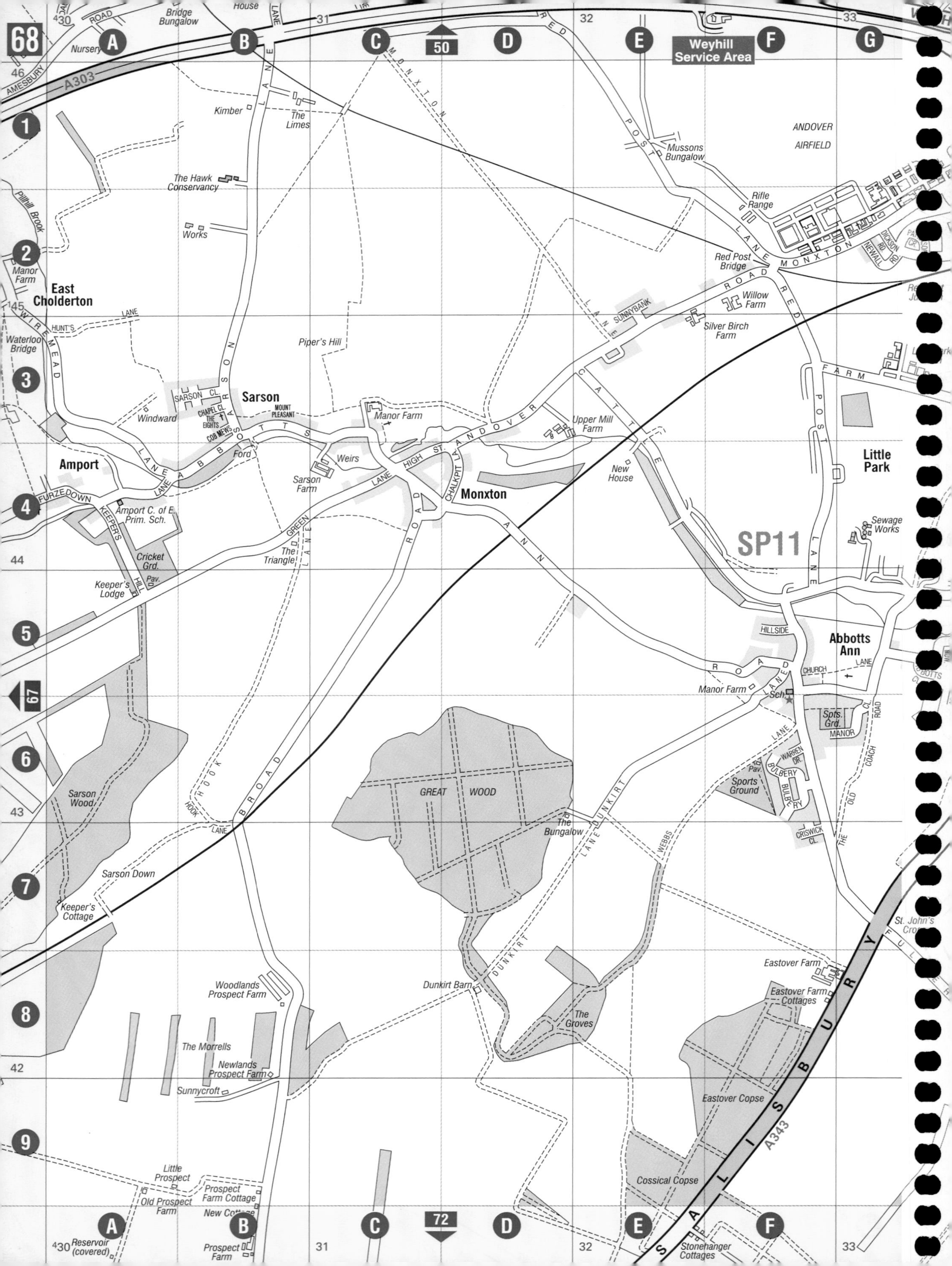
Weyhill Service Area
50
72
67
A303
Amesbury Road
Nursery
Bridge Bungalow
Kimber
The Limes
The Hawk Conservancy
Works
Manor Farm
East Cholderton
Waterloo Bridge
Wiremead
Hunt's Lane
Sarson Lane
Sarson
Sarson Cl.
Chapel Cl.
The Eights
Cob Mews
Mount Pleasant
Windward
Amport
Furzedown
Keepers Hill
Amport C. of E. Prim. Sch.
Cricket Grd.
Pav.
Keeper's Lodge
Abbotts Lane
Ford
Weirs
Sarson Farm
Manor Farm
Piper's Hill
Green Lane
The Triangle
Hook Lane
Broad Road
High St
Chalkpit La.
Monxton
Andover Road
Sunnybank
Upper Mill Farm
New House
Cattle Lane
Monxton Lane
Red Post Lane
Mussons Bungalow
Rifle Range
Red Post Bridge
Willow Farm
Silver Birch Farm
Andover Airfield
Dickson Rd.
Newall Rd.
Farm
Little Park
Post Lane
Sewage Works
SP11
Abbotts Ann
Hillside
Church Lane
Manor Farm
Sch.
Spts. Grd.
Manor
Warren Dr.
Bulbery
Sports Ground
Criswick Cl.
The Old Coach Road
Great Wood
The Bungalow
Dunkirt Lane
Webbs
Sarson Wood
Sarson Down
Keeper's Cottage
Dunkirt Barn
The Groves
Woodlands Prospect Farm
The Morrells
Newlands Prospect Farm
Sunnycroft
Eastover Farm
Eastover Farm Cottages
Eastover Copse
Cossical Copse
Salisbury Road
A343
St. John's Cross
Little Prospect
Prospect Farm Cottage
Old Prospect Farm
New Cottage
Reservoir (covered)
Prospect Farm
Stonehanger Cottages
430
31
32
33
46
45
44
43
42
A
B
C
D
E
F
G
1
2
3
4
5
6
7
8
9

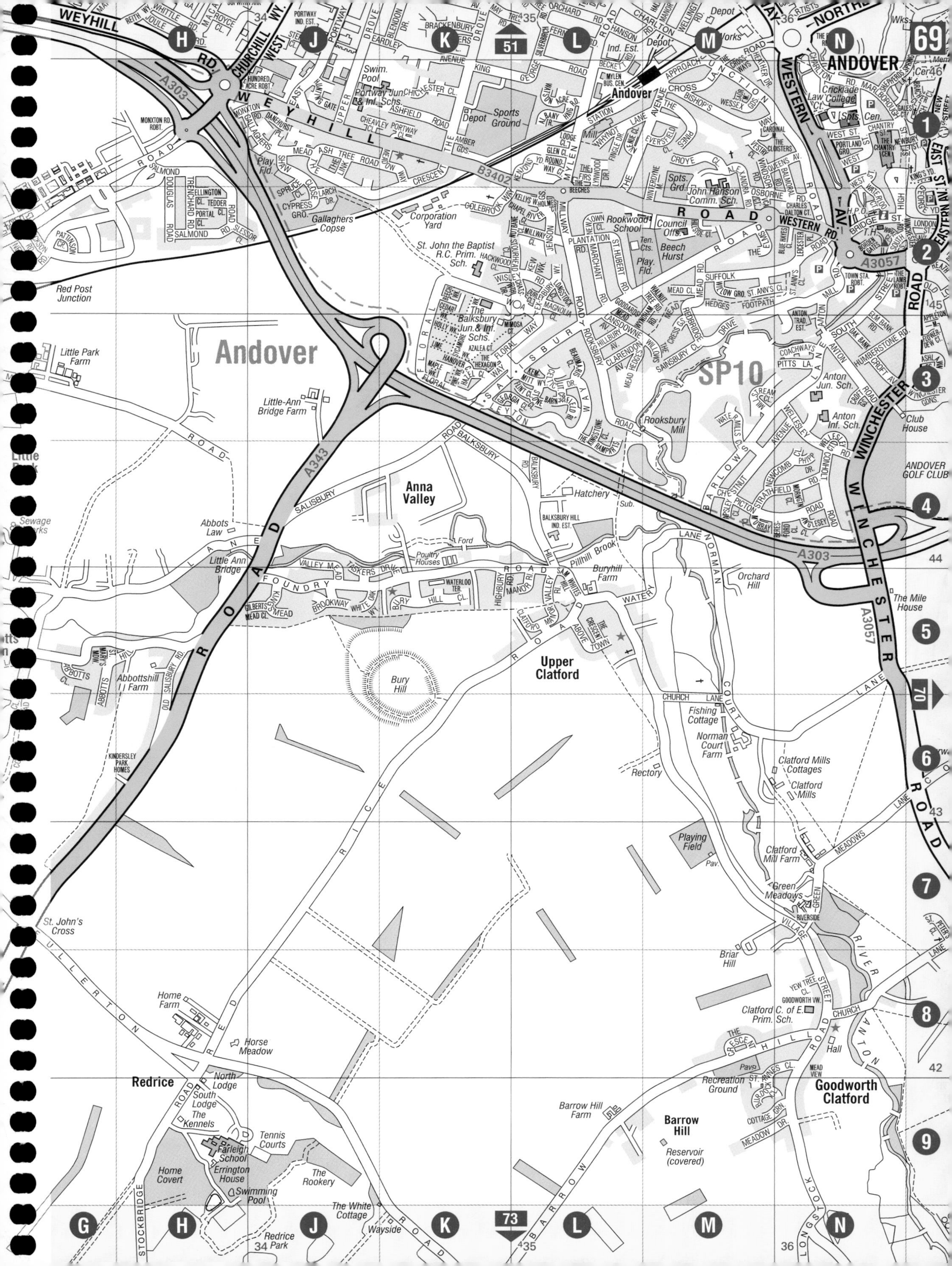

ANDOVER
Andover
SP10
Anna Valley
Upper Clatford
Goodworth Clatford
Redrice
Barrow Hill
Bury Hill
Little Park Farm
Little-Ann Bridge Farm
Red Post Junction
Gallaghers Copse
Corporation Yard
St. John the Baptist R.C. Prim. Sch.
The Balksbury Jun.& Inf. Schs.
Rooksbury Mill
Anton Jun. Sch.
Anton Inf. Sch.
ANDOVER GOLF CLUB
Club House
The Mile House
Hatchery
Buryhill Farm
Orchard Hill
Abbotts Law
Little Ann Bridge
Abbottshill Farm
Fishing Cottage
Norman Court Farm
Rectory
Clatford Mills Cottages
Clatford Mills
Playing Field
Clatford Mill Farm
Green Meadows
Briar Hill
Clatford C. of E. Prim. Sch.
Hall
Recreation Ground
Barrow Hill Farm
Reservoir (covered)
Home Farm
Horse Meadow
North Lodge
South Lodge
The Kennels
Tennis Courts
Farleigh School
Errington House
Swimming Pool
Home Covert
The Rookery
The White Cottage
Wayside
Redrice Park
St. John's Cross
Kindersley Park Homes
Swim. Pool
Portway Jun. & Inf. Schs.
Sports Ground
Depot
Spts. Grd.
John Hanson Comm. Sch.
Rookwood School
Council Offs.
Beech Hurst
Play. Fld.
Cricklade Law College
Spts. Cen.
WEYHILL ROAD
WESTERN ROAD
WINCHESTER ROAD
SALISBURY ROAD
RICE ROAD
BARROW ROAD
A303
A343
A3057
B3402
51
70
73

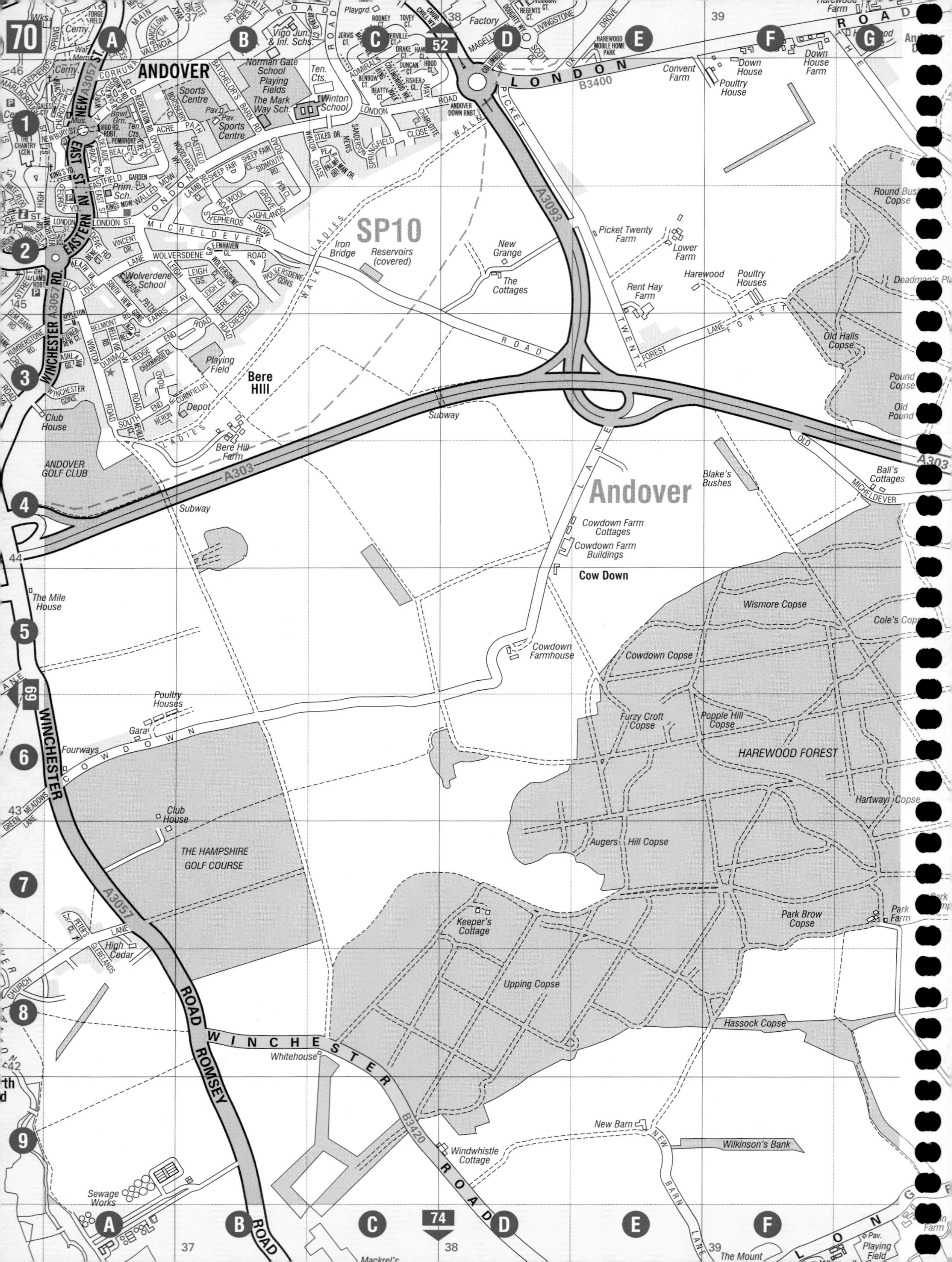
ANDOVER
SP10
Andover
Bere Hill
Cow Down
HAREWOOD FOREST
THE HAMPSHIRE GOLF COURSE
ANDOVER GOLF CLUB
LONDON ROAD
B3400
A303
A3093
A3057
B3420
WINCHESTER ROAD
ROMSEY ROAD
PICKET TWENTY
FOREST LANE
COWDOWN LANE
NEW BARN LANE
MICHELDEVER ROAD
LADIES WALK
Norman Gate School Playing Fields
The Mark Way Sch.
Winton School
Wolverdene School
Sports Centre
Reservoirs (covered)
Iron Bridge
New Grange
The Cottages
Picket Twenty Farm
Lower Farm
Harewood
Poultry Houses
Rent Hay Farm
Convent Farm
Down House
Poultry House
Down House Farm
Round Bush Copse
Old Halls Copse
Pound Copse
Old Pound
Ball's Cottages
Blake's Bushes
Cowdown Farm Cottages
Cowdown Farm Buildings
Wismore Copse
Cole's Copse
Cowdown Copse
Cowdown Farmhouse
Furzy Croft Copse
Popple Hill Copse
Hartway Copse
Augers Hill Copse
Park Brow Copse
Park Farm
Keeper's Cottage
Upping Copse
Hassock Copse
Whitehouse
New Barn
Wilkinson's Bank
Windwhistle Cottage
Sewage Works
High Cedar
Club House
Fourways
Poultry Houses
The Mile House
Bere Hill Farm
Depot
Playing Field
Subway
The Mount
Mackrel's
52
69
74
37
38
39
42
43
44
45
46

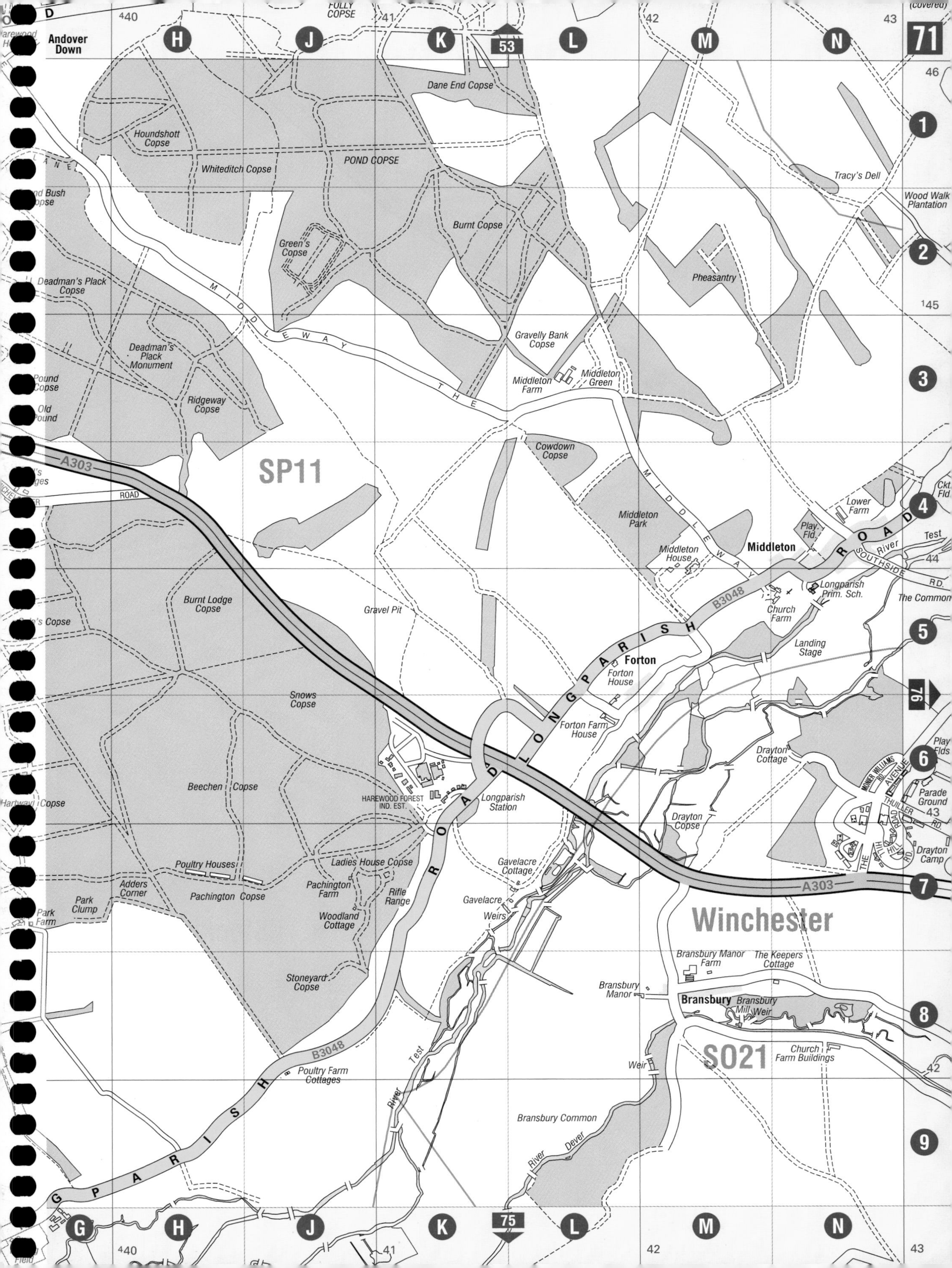

Andover Down
FULLY COPSE
53
H
J
K
L
M
N
Dane End Copse
Houndshott Copse
Whiteditch Copse
POND COPSE
Burnt Copse
Green's Copse
Tracy's Dell
Wood Walk Plantation
Pheasantry
Deadman's Plack Copse
Deadman's Plack Monument
THE MIDDLEWAY
Gravelly Bank Copse
Middleton Farm
Middleton Green
Ridgeway Copse
Old Pound
Pound Copse
Cowdown Copse
SP11
A303
ROAD
Middleton Park
Middleton House
Middleton
Lower Farm
Play Fld.
Ckt. Fld
River Test
SOUTHSIDE RD.
The Common
Longparish Prim. Sch.
Church Farm
LONGPARISH ROAD
B3048
Burnt Lodge Copse
Gravel Pit
Forton
Forton House
Landing Stage
Snows Copse
Forton Farm House
76
Drayton Cottage
Play Flds
Parade Ground
MONIER WILLIAMS RD.
AVENUE
THUILLIER RD.
THE HILL ROAD
HILL RD.
Drayton Camp
Beechen Copse
HAREWOOD FOREST IND. EST.
Longparish Station
Drayton Copse
Hartwell Copse
Poultry Houses
Ladies House Copse
Gavelacre Cottage
Adders Corner
Pachington Copse
Pachington Farm
Rifle Range
Park Clump
Park Farm
Gavelacre
Weirs
Woodland Cottage
Winchester
Bransbury Manor Farm
The Keepers Cottage
Stoneyard Copse
Bransbury Manor
Bransbury
Bransbury Mill Weir
SO21
Church Farm Buildings
Weir
Poultry Farm Cottages
River Test
Bransbury Common
River Dever
G
75
440
41
42
43
46
145
44
43
42
1
2
3
4
5
6
7
8
9

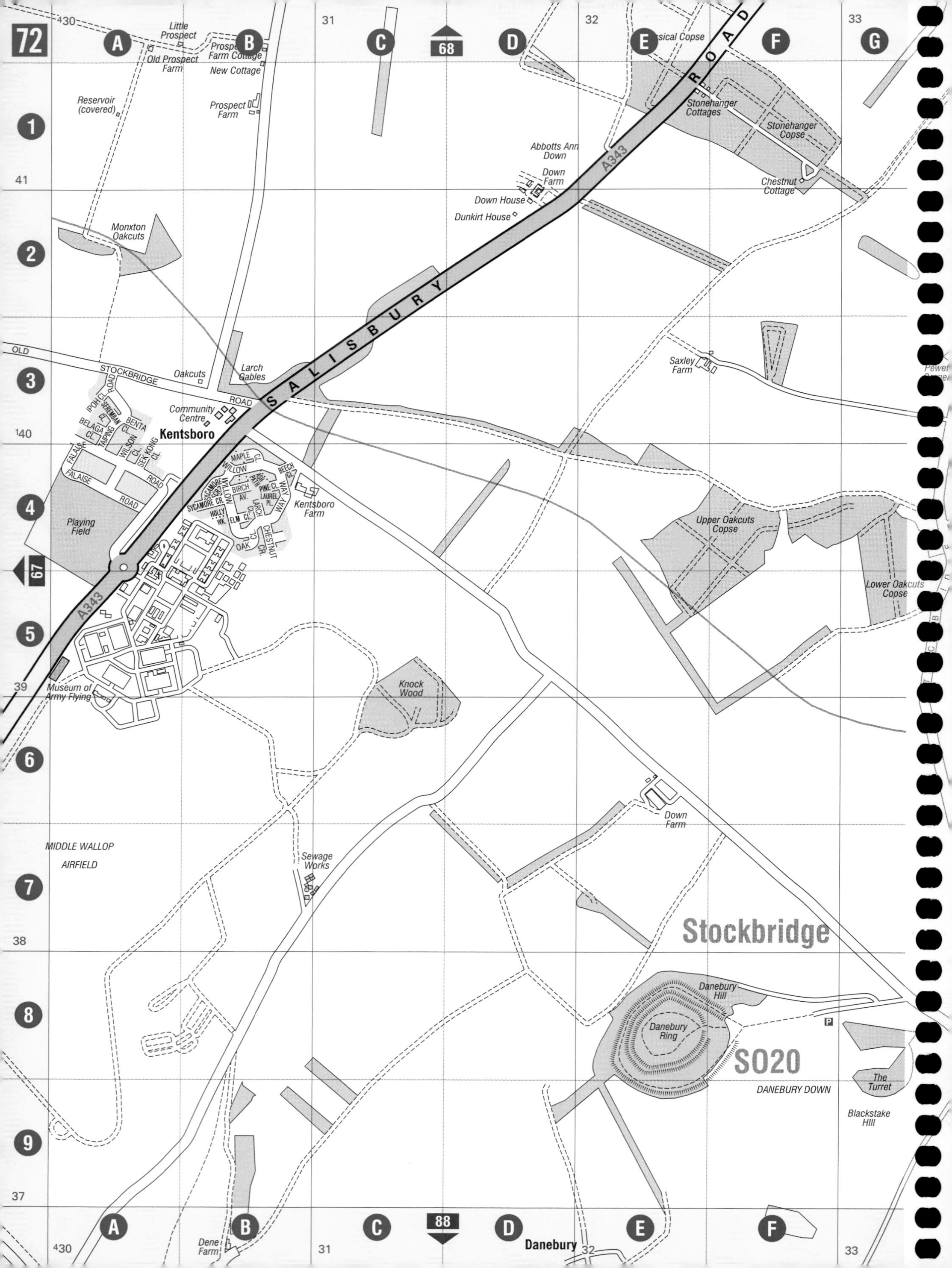

72

Little Prospect
Old Prospect Farm
Prospect Farm Cottage
New Cottage
Prospect Farm

Reservoir (covered)

Classical Copse
Stonehanger Cottages
Stonehanger Copse
Chestnut Cottage

Monxton Oakcuts

Abbotts Ann Down
Down Farm
Down House
Dunkirt House

SALISBURY   ROAD
A343

Saxley Farm

Pewet Copse

OLD
STOCKBRIDGE

Oakcuts
Larch Gables

ROAD

Community Centre

Kentsboro

140

IPOH RD
SEREMBAN CL
BENTA CL
BELAGA CL
TAIPING CL
WILSON CL
SEK KONG CL
FALLAK CL
FALAISE
ROAD
FALAISE
ROAD

MAPLE
WILLOW
WILLOW
BIRCH AV
SYCAMORE CR
HOLLY WK
ELM CL
LARCH CL
OAK
CHESTNUT CR
PINE CL
LAUREL PL
BEECH WAY WAY

Kentsboro Farm

Upper Oakcuts Copse

Lower Oakcuts Copse

Playing Field

67
A343

Museum of Army Flying

Knock Wood

Down Farm

MIDDLE WALLOP AIRFIELD

Sewage Works

Stockbridge

38

SO20

Danebury Hill
Danebury Ring

The Turret

DANEBURY DOWN

Blackstake Hill

37

430   31   68   32   33

Danebury

88

430   31   32   33

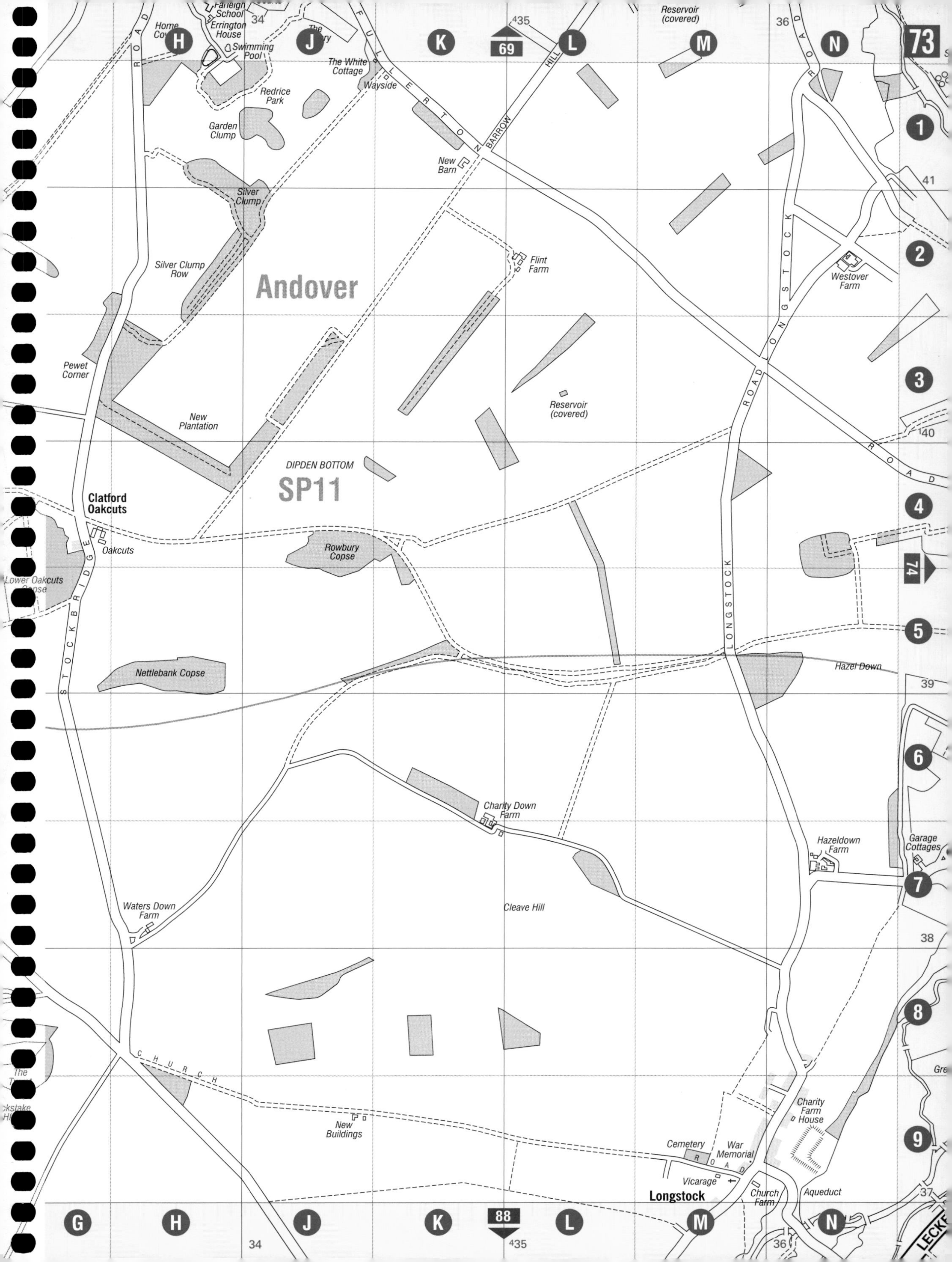
Andover
SP11
Clatford Oakcuts
Longstock
Farleigh School
Errington House
Swimming Pool
Home Co
The White Cottage
Wayside
Redrice Park
Garden Clump
Silver Clump
Silver Clump Row
FULLERTON ROAD
BARROW HILL
New Barn
Flint Farm
Reservoir (covered)
Westover Farm
LONGSTOCK ROAD
Pewet Corner
New Plantation
DIPDEN BOTTOM
Oakcuts
Rowbury Copse
Lower Oakcuts Copse
STOCKBRIDGE ROAD
Nettlebank Copse
Hazel Down
Charity Down Farm
Hazeldown Farm
Garage Cottages
Waters Down Farm
Cleave Hill
CHURCH
New Buildings
Cemetery
War Memorial
ROAD
Vicarage
Church Farm
Charity Farm House
Aqueduct
69
74
88
435
34
36
41
40
39
38
37
G
H
J
K
L
M
N
1
2
3
4
5
6
7
8
9

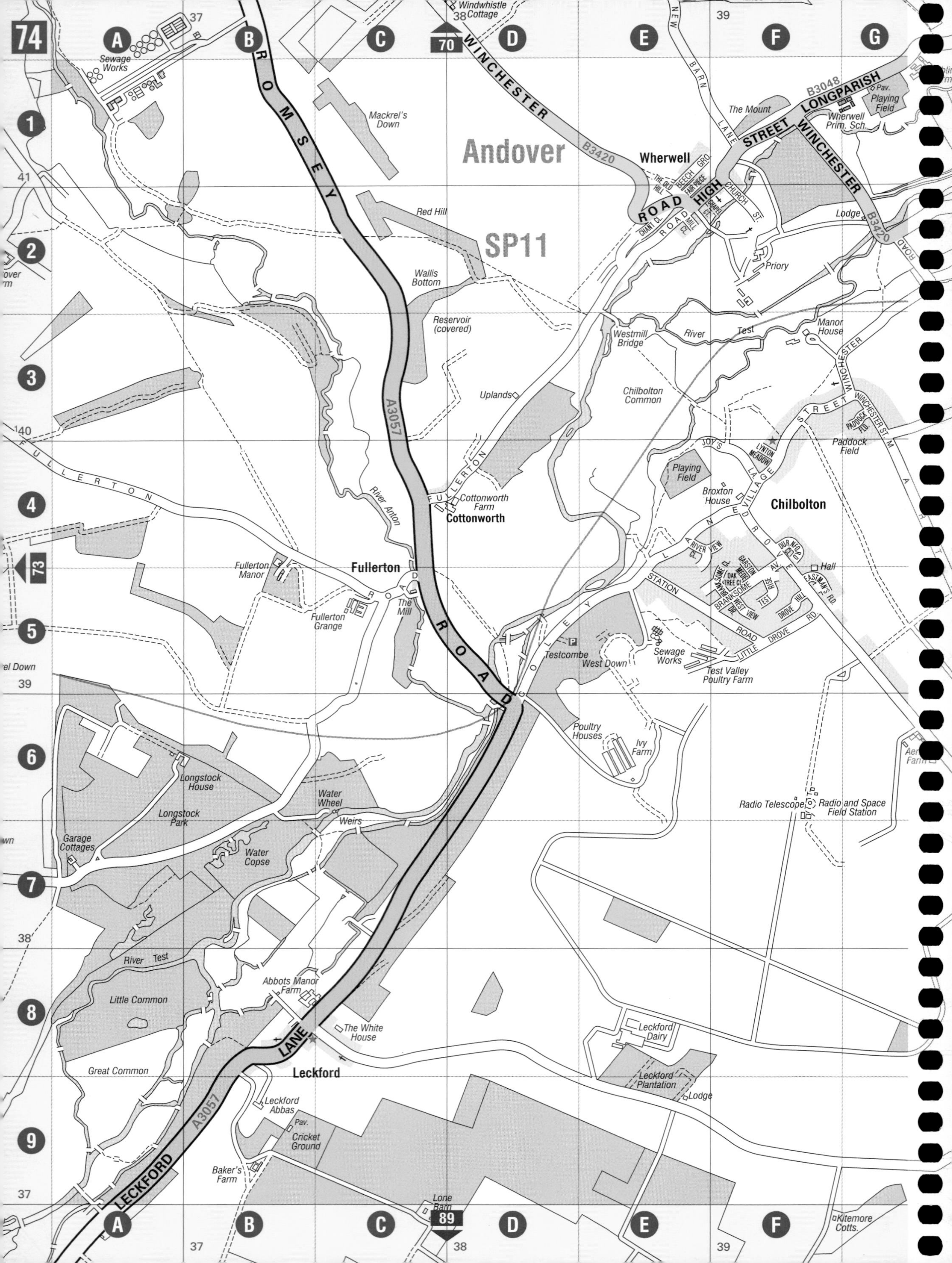

Andover
SP11
Wherwell
Chilbolton
Fullerton
Cottonworth
Leckford
ROMSEY ROAD
A3057
WINCHESTER
B3420
B3048
LONGPARISH
STREET
HIGH ROAD
NEW BARN LANE
Sewage Works
Mackrel's Down
Red Hill
Wallis Bottom
Reservoir (covered)
The Mount
Playing Field
Wherwell Prim. Sch.
Pav.
Lodge
Priory
River Test
Westmill Bridge
Manor House
Uplands
Chilbolton Common
Paddock Field
Broxton House
Cottonworth Farm
River Anton
Fullerton Manor
Fullerton Grange
The Mill
FULLERTON ROAD
Testcombe
West Down
Sewage Works
Test Valley Poultry Farm
Poultry Houses
Ivy Farm
Hall
STATION ROAD
LITTLE DROVE RD
VILLAGE LANE
JOY'S LANE
Longstock House
Longstock Park
Garage Cottages
Water Wheel
Weirs
Water Copse
Radio Telescope
Radio and Space Field Station
Little Common
Abbots Manor Farm
The White House
Great Common
Leckford Dairy
Leckford Plantation
Leckford Abbas
Cricket Ground
Baker's Farm
Lone Barn
Kitemore Cotts.
LECKFORD LANE
Windwhistle Cottage
70
73
89

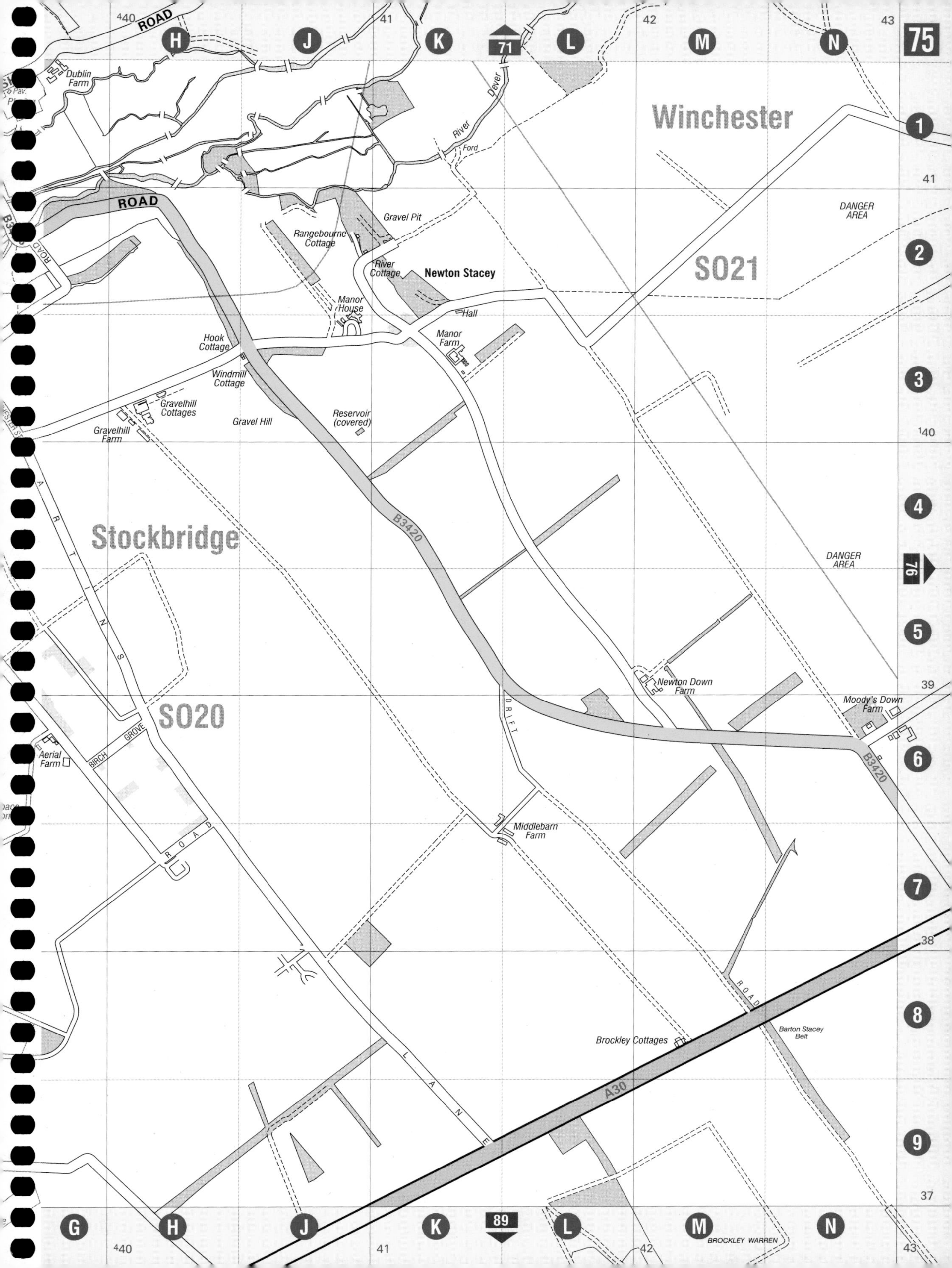

H J K 71 L M N

Winchester

SO21

1

41

DANGER AREA

2

Dublin Farm

ROAD

Gravel Pit

River Dever

Ford

ROAD

Rangebourne Cottage

River Cottage

Newton Stacey

Hall

Manor House

Hook Cottage

Manor Farm

Windmill Cottage

Gravelhill Cottages

Gravel Hill

Reservoir (covered)

Gravelhill Farm

Stockbridge

B3420

3

140

4

DANGER AREA

76

5

39

Newton Down Farm

Moody's Down Farm

SO20

Aerial Farm

BIRCH GROVE

DRIFT

B3420

6

ROAD

Middlebarn Farm

7

38

LANE

ROAD

8

Brockley Cottages

Barton Stacey Belt

A30

9

37

440 41 42 43

BROCKLEY WARREN

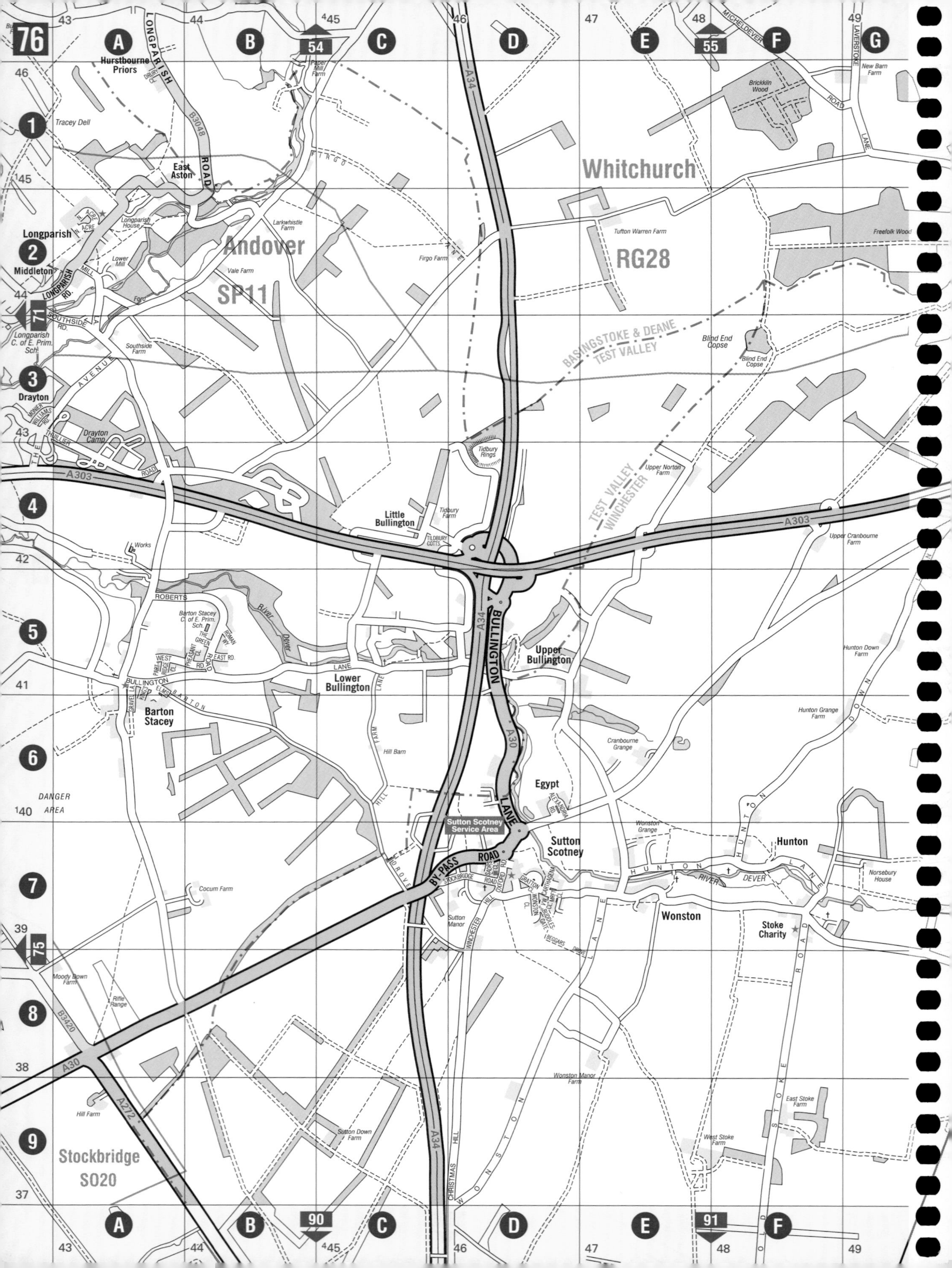
Hurstbourne Priors
LONGPARISH
Tracey Dell
East Aston
B3048
ROAD
Longparish
Middleton
Longparish House
Lower Mill
Larkwhistle Farm
Andover
SP11
Vale Farm
Ford
Southside Farm
Longparish C. of E. Prim. Sch.
Drayton
Drayton Camp
A303
Firgo Farm
FIRGO
Paper Mill Farm
A34
Whitchurch
Tufton Warren Farm
RG28
Brickkiln Wood
MICHELDEVER
LAVERSTOKE
New Barn Farm
Freefolk Wood
BASINGSTOKE & DEANE
TEST VALLEY
Blind End Copse
Tidbury Rings
Upper Norton Farm
TEST VALLEY
WINCHESTER
Little Bullington
Tidbury Farm
Upper Cranbourne Farm
Works
ROBERTS
Barton Stacey C. of E. Prim. Sch.
River Dever
BULLINGTON
Upper Bullington
Lower Bullington
Barton Stacey
Hunton Down Farm
Hunton Grange Farm
Cranbourne Grange
Hill Barn
Egypt
DANGER AREA
Sutton Scotney Service Area
LANE
Sutton Scotney
Wonston Grange
Hunton
BY-PASS ROAD
Norsebury House
Cocum Farm
Wonston
Stoke Charity
Sutton Manor
Moody Down Farm
Rifle Range
B3420
A30
A272
Hill Farm
Wonston Manor Farm
East Stoke Farm
Sutton Down Farm
West Stoke Farm
Stockbridge
SO20
CHRISTMAS HILL
WONSTON
OLD STOKE ROAD
54
55
71
75
90
91

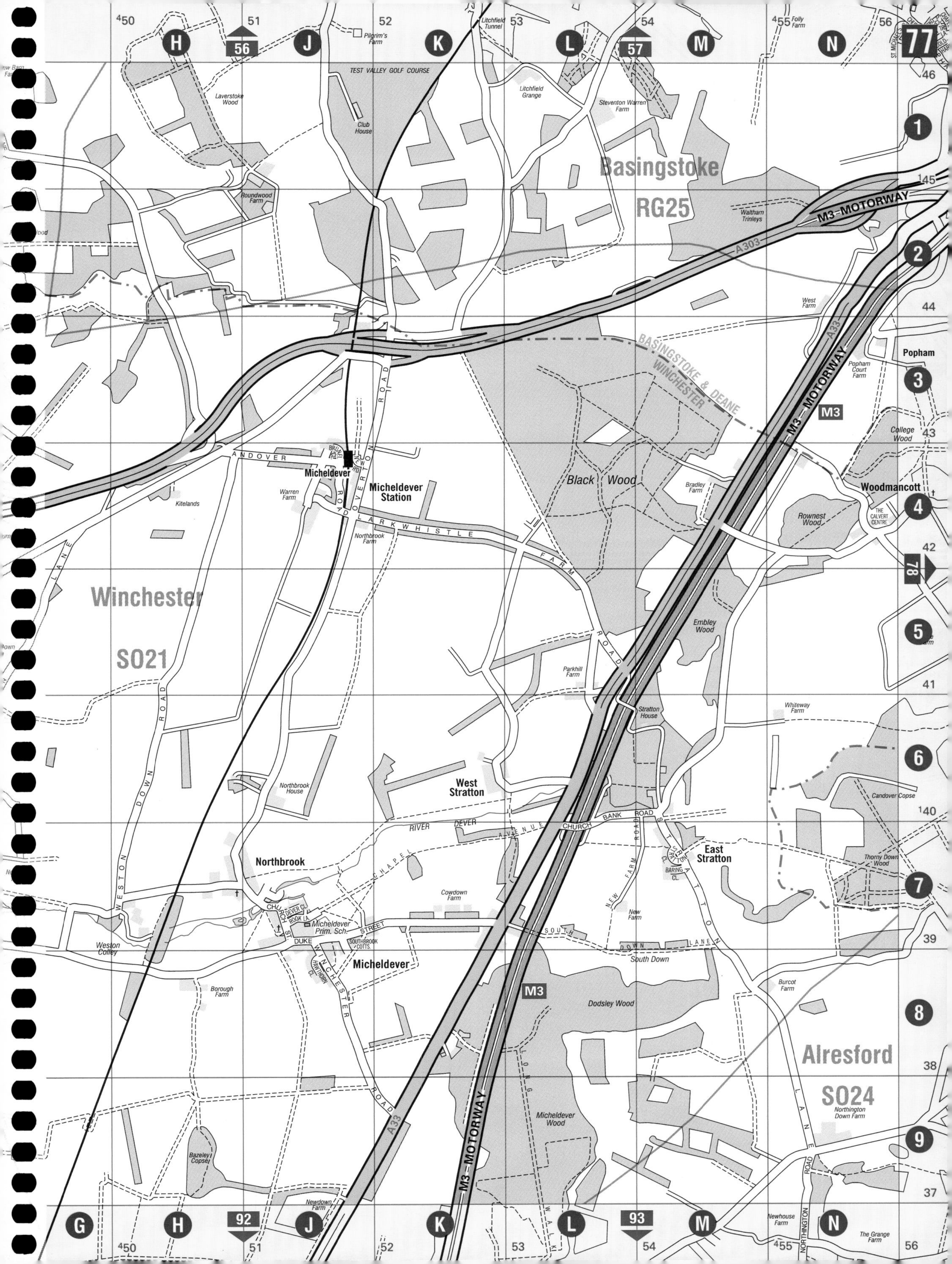
77
56
57
78
92
93
Basingstoke
RG25
Winchester
SO21
Alresford
SO24
M3 MOTORWAY
A303
A33
M3
BASINGSTOKE & DEANE
WINCHESTER
TEST VALLEY GOLF COURSE
Pilgrim's Farm
Litchfield Tunnel
Folly Farm
Laverstoke Wood
Club House
Litchfield Grange
Steventon Warren Farm
Roundwood Farm
Waltham Trinleys
West Farm
Popham
Popham Court Farm
College Wood
Woodmancott
THE CALVERT CENTRE
Rownest Wood
Bradley Farm
Black Wood
Micheldever
Micheldever Station
Warren Farm
Kitelands
ANDOVER
OVERTON ROAD
LARKWHISTLE FARM ROAD
Northbrook Farm
Embley Wood
Parkhill Farm
Stratton House
Whiteway Farm
WESTON DOWN ROAD
Northbrook House
West Stratton
Candover Copse
RIVER DEVER
AVENUE
CHURCH BANK ROAD
East Stratton
BARING CL.
NEW FARM ROAD
STRATTON LANE
Thorny Down Wood
Northbrook
CHAPEL
Cowdown Farm
New Farm
DEVER CL.
ROOK LA.
Micheldever Prim. Sch.
STREET
DUKE
SOUTHBROOK COTTS.
SOUTH
DOWN LANE
South Down
Weston Colley
Micheldever
WINCHESTER ROAD
Borough Farm
Burcot Farm
Dodsley Wood
LONG WALK
Micheldever Wood
Northington Down Farm
Bazeley Copse
Newdown Farm
Newhouse Farm
NORTHINGTON ROAD
The Grange Farm
G
H
J
K
L
M
N
1
2
3
4
5
6
7
8
9
450
51
52
53
54
455
56
146
145
44
43
42
41
140
39
38
37

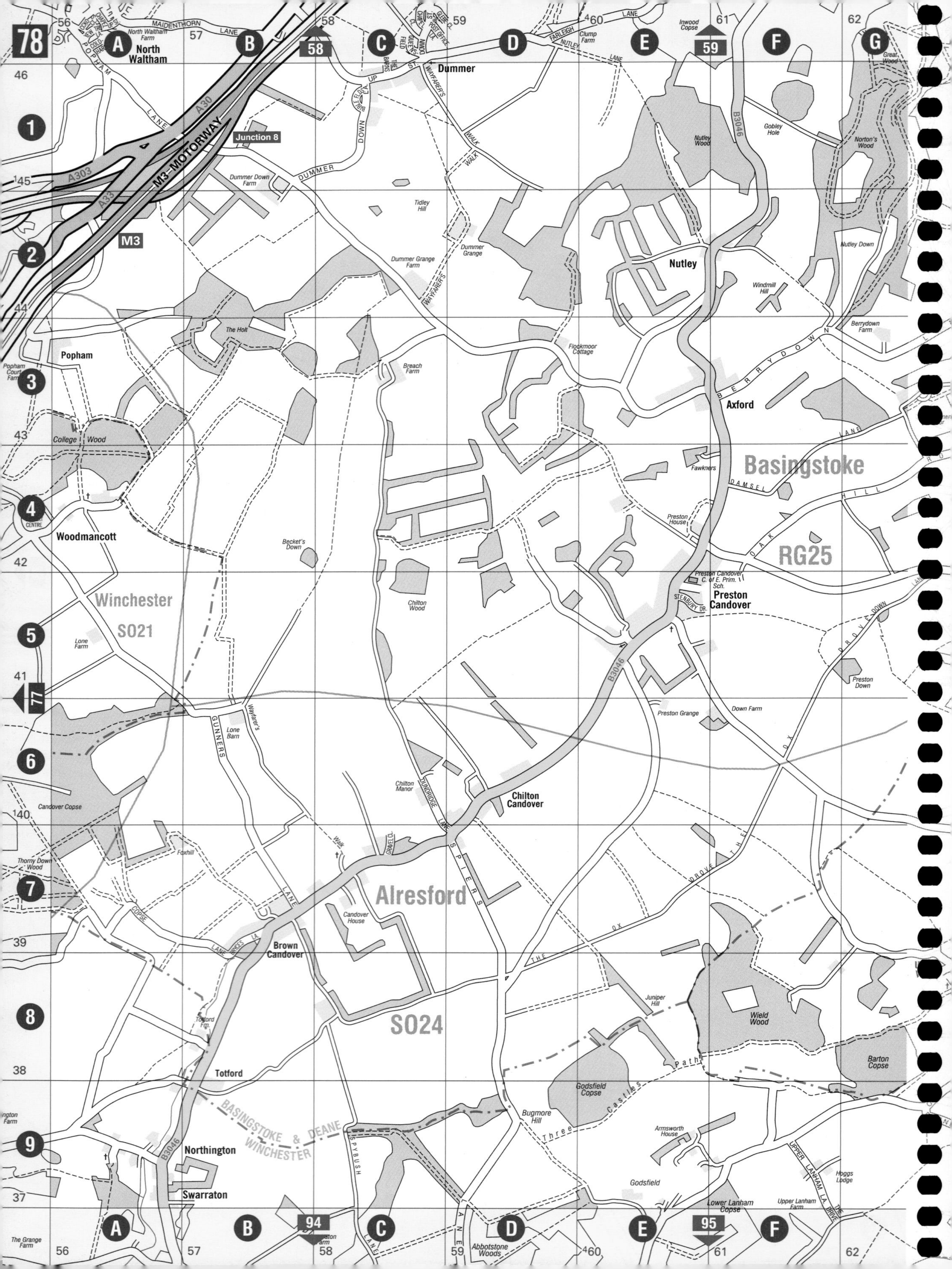
North Waltham
North Waltham Farm
MAIDENTHORN LANE
POPHAM LANE
58
59
Dummer
WAYFARER'S WALK
DUMMER DOWN LA
Farleigh
NUTLEY LANE
Clump Farm
Inwood Copse
Great Wood
A30
A303
A33
M3–MOTORWAY
M3
Junction 8
Dummer Down Farm
Tidley Hill
Dummer Grange
Dummer Grange Farm
Nutley Wood
B3046
Gobley Hole
Norton's Wood
Nutley
Nutley Down
Windmill Hill
Berrydown Farm
BERRYDOWN LA
The Holt
Flockmoor Cottage
Breach Farm
Popham
Popham Court Farm
Axford
College Wood
Basingstoke
Fawkners
DAMSEL LANE
HILL RD
Woodmancott
Becket's Down
Preston House
OAK
RG25
Preston Candover C. of E. Prim. Sch.
STENBURY DR.
Preston Candover
Winchester
SO21
Lone Farm
Chilton Wood
DROVE DOWN
Preston Down
77
Preston Grange
Down Farm
Lone Barn
GUNNERS LANE
Wayfarer's
Chilton Manor
DUNDRIDGE LANE
Chilton Candover
Candover Copse
Thorny Down Wood
Foxhill
Walk
GRAVEL CL.
SPIERS LANE
Alresford
COPSE LANE
Candover House
THE OX DROVE
Brown Candover
Juniper Hill
Wield Wood
Totford Fm.
SO24
Totford
Godsfield Copse
Three Castles Path
Barton Copse
BASINGSTOKE & DEANE
WINCHESTER
Bugmore Hill
SPYBUSH LANE
Armsworth House
Northington
Swarraton
Godsfield
UPPER LANHAM LA
Hoggs Lodge
Lower Lanham Copse
Upper Lanham Farm
THE DRIVE
94
95
Abbotstone Woods
The Grange Farm
A B C D E F G
1 2 3 4 5 6 7 8 9
56 57 58 59 60 61 62
46 45 44 43 42 41 140 39 38 37

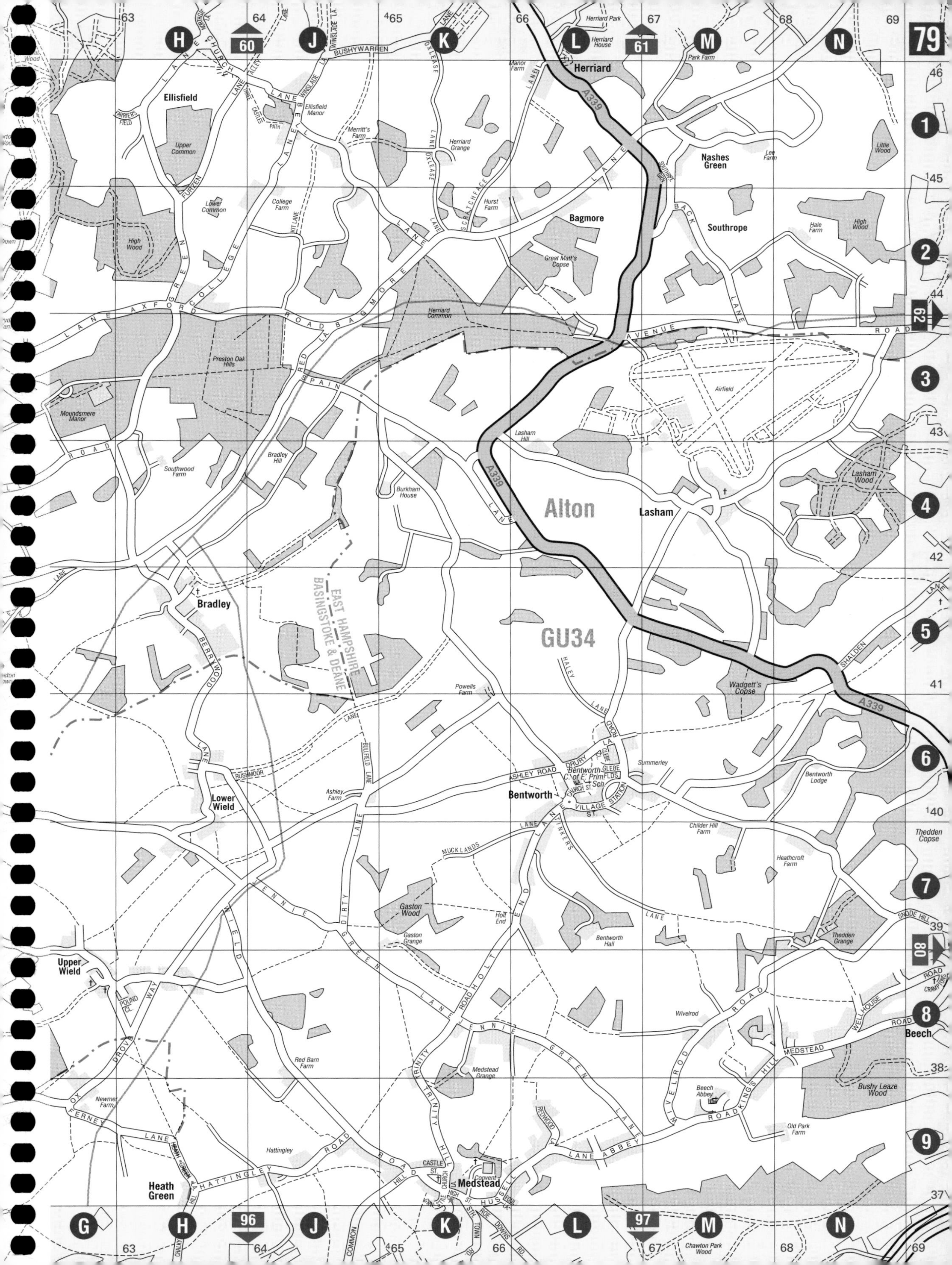

Herriard
Ellisfield
Upper Common
Lower Common
High Wood
Ellisfield Manor
Merritt's Farm
Herriard Grange
College Farm
Hurst Farm
Manor Farm
Herriard Park
Herriard House
Park Farm
Nashes Green
Lee Farm
Little Wood
Bagmore
Great Matt's Copse
Southrope
Hale Farm
High Wood
Herriard Common
Preston Oak Hills
Moundsmere Manor
Airfield
Lasham Hill
Bradley Hill
Southwood Farm
Burkham House
Alton
Lasham
Lasham Wood
Bradley
EAST HAMPSHIRE
BASINGSTOKE & DEANE
GU34
Powells Farm
Wadgett's Copse
Summerley
Bentworth C. of E. Prim. Sch.
Bentworth
Bentworth Lodge
Ashley Farm
Lower Wield
Childer Hill Farm
Heathcroft Farm
Thedden Copse
Gaston Wood
Holt End
Gaston Grange
Bentworth Hall
Thedden Grange
Upper Wield
Wivelrod
Beech
Red Barn Farm
Medstead Grange
Bushy Leaze Wood
Newmer Farm
Beech Abbey
Old Park Farm
Hattingley
Convent
Medstead
Heath Green
Chawton Park Wood
A339

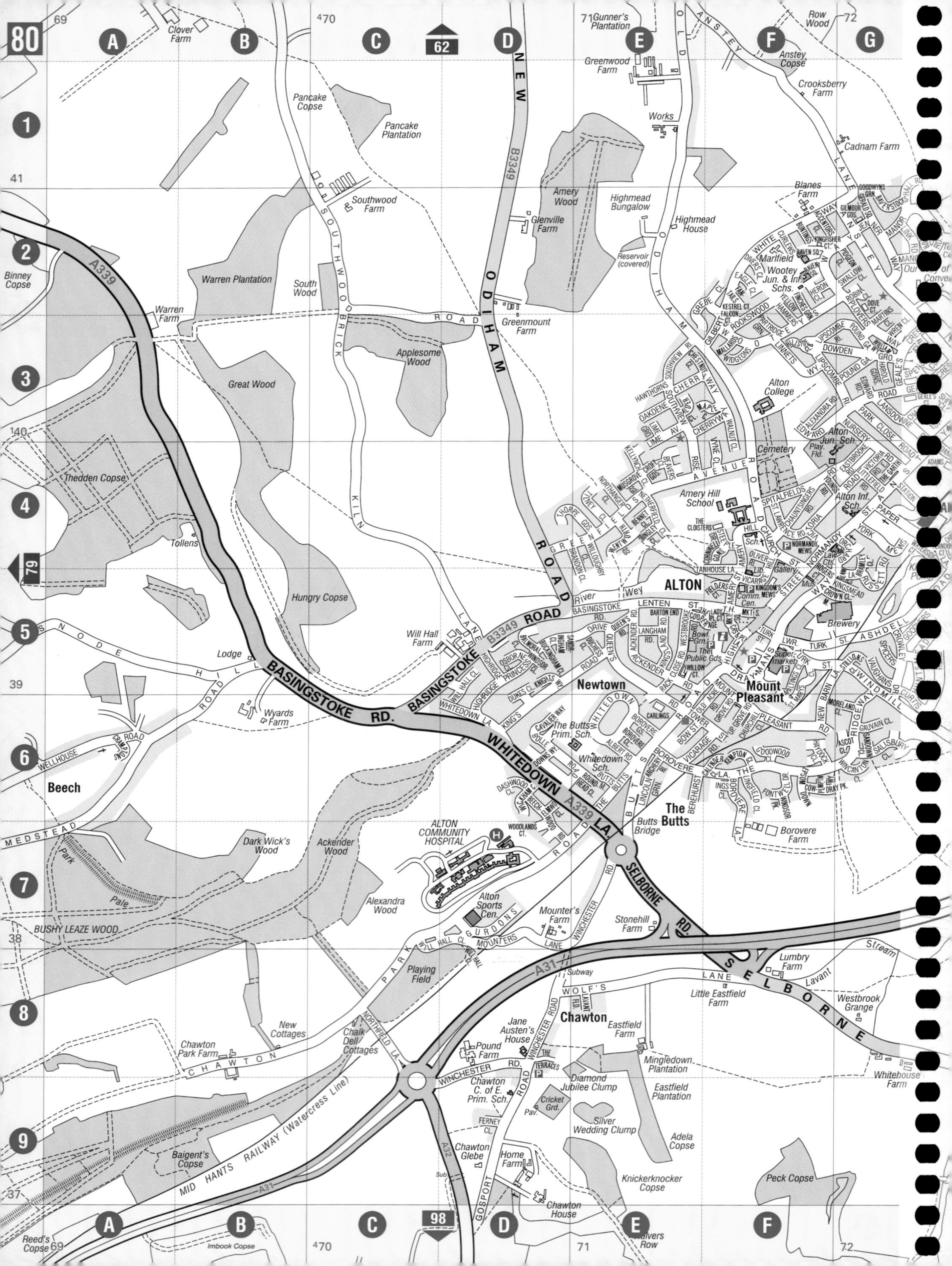
62
79
98
A
B
C
D
E
F
G
1
2
3
4
5
6
7
8
9
69
470
71
72
41
40
39
38
37
Clover Farm
Gunner's Plantation
Row Wood
Greenwood Farm
Anstey Copse
Crooksberry Farm
Pancake Copse
Pancake Plantation
Works
Cadnam Farm
Southwood Farm
Amery Wood
Highmead Bungalow
Glenville Farm
Highmead House
Blanes Farm
Binney Copse
Warren Plantation
South Wood
Reservoir (covered)
Marlfield
Wootey Jun. & Inf. Schs.
Warren Farm
Greenmount Farm
Applesome Wood
Great Wood
Alton College
Thedden Copse
Cemetery
Alton Jun. Sch.
Amery Hill School
Alton Inf. Sch.
Tollens
ALTON
Hungry Copse
Brewery
Will Hall Farm
Lodge
Newtown
Mount Pleasant
Wyards Farm
The Butts Prim. Sch.
Whitedown Sch.
Beech
The Butts
Butts Bridge
Borovere Farm
ALTON COMMUNITY HOSPITAL
Dark Wick's Wood
Ackender Wood
Alexandra Wood
Alton Sports Cen.
Mounter's Farm
Stonehill Farm
BUSHY LEAZE WOOD
Lumbry Farm
Playing Field
Little Eastfield Farm
Westbrook Grange
Chawton
Jane Austen's House
Eastfield Farm
New Cottages
Chawton Park Farm
Chalk Dell Cottages
Pound Farm
Mingledown Plantation
Whitehouse Farm
Chawton C. of E. Prim. Sch.
Diamond Jubilee Clump
Eastfield Plantation
Cricket Grd.
Silver Wedding Clump
Adela Copse
Baigent's Copse
Chawton Glebe
Home Farm
Knickerknocker Copse
Peck Copse
Chawton House
Reed's Copse
Imbook Copse
Walvers Row
A339
B3349
A31
A32
NEW ODIHAM ROAD
ODIHAM ROAD
BASINGSTOKE RD.
BASINGSTOKE ROAD
WHITEDOWN LA.
SELBORNE RD.
SELBORNE
SOUTHWOOD
BRICK KILN LANE
SNODE HILL ROAD
WELLHOUSE
MEDSTEAD ROAD
Park Pale
GURDONS
MOUNTERS LANE
WINCHESTER RD.
WINCHESTER ROAD
WOLF'S LANE
CHAWTON PARK ROAD
NORTHFIELD LA.
GOSPORT ROAD
MID HANTS RAILWAY (Watercress Line)
ANSTEY LANE
OLD ODIHAM ROAD
River Wey
LENTEN ST.
TURK ST.
ASHDELL
WINDMILL
PLEASANT
PAPER
Stream
Lavant
Subway

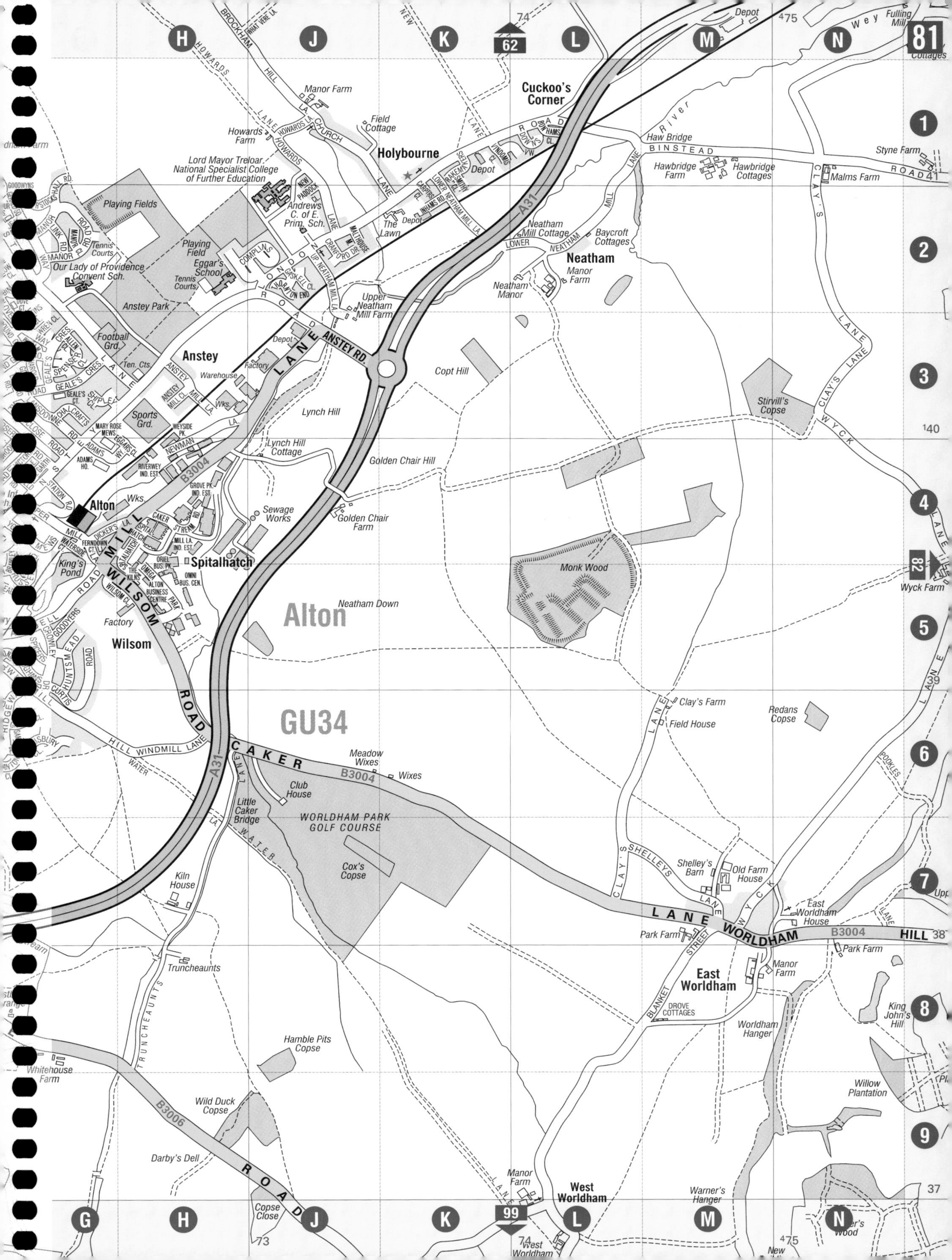
Alton
GU34
Holybourne
Cuckoo's Corner
Neatham
Anstey
Spitalhatch
Wilsom
East Worldham
West Worldham
Manor Farm
Field Cottage
Howards Farm
Lord Mayor Treloar National Specialist College of Further Education
Playing Fields
Playing Field
Eggar's School
Tennis Courts
Our Lady of Providence Convent Sch.
Anstey Park
Football Grd.
Sports Grd.
Andrews C. of E. Prim. Sch.
The Lawn
Depot
Neatham Mill Cottage
Baycroft Cottages
Neatham Manor
Upper Neatham Mill Farm
Haw Bridge
Hawbridge Farm
Hawbridge Cottages
Styne Farm
Malms Farm
Copt Hill
Lynch Hill
Lynch Hill Cottage
Golden Chair Hill
Golden Chair Farm
Sewage Works
Stirvill's Copse
Monk Wood
Wyck Farm
Neatham Down
King's Pond
Factory
Warehouse
Clay's Farm
Field House
Redans Copse
Meadow Wixes
Wixes
Club House
Little Caker Bridge
WORLDHAM PARK GOLF COURSE
Cox's Copse
Kiln House
Shelley's Barn
Old Farm House
East Worldham House
Park Farm
Manor Farm
Drove Cottages
Worldham Hanger
King John's Hill
Willow Plantation
Truncheaunts
Whitehouse Farm
Hamble Pits Copse
Wild Duck Copse
Darby's Dell
Copse Close
Warner's Hanger
Fulling Mill
A31
B3004
B3006
CAKER LANE
WORLDHAM HILL
BINSTEAD ROAD
WILSOM ROAD
MILL LANE
ANSTEY RD.
LONDON ROAD
WINDMILL HILL
CLAY'S LANE
WYCK LANE
BLANKET STREET
62
82
99

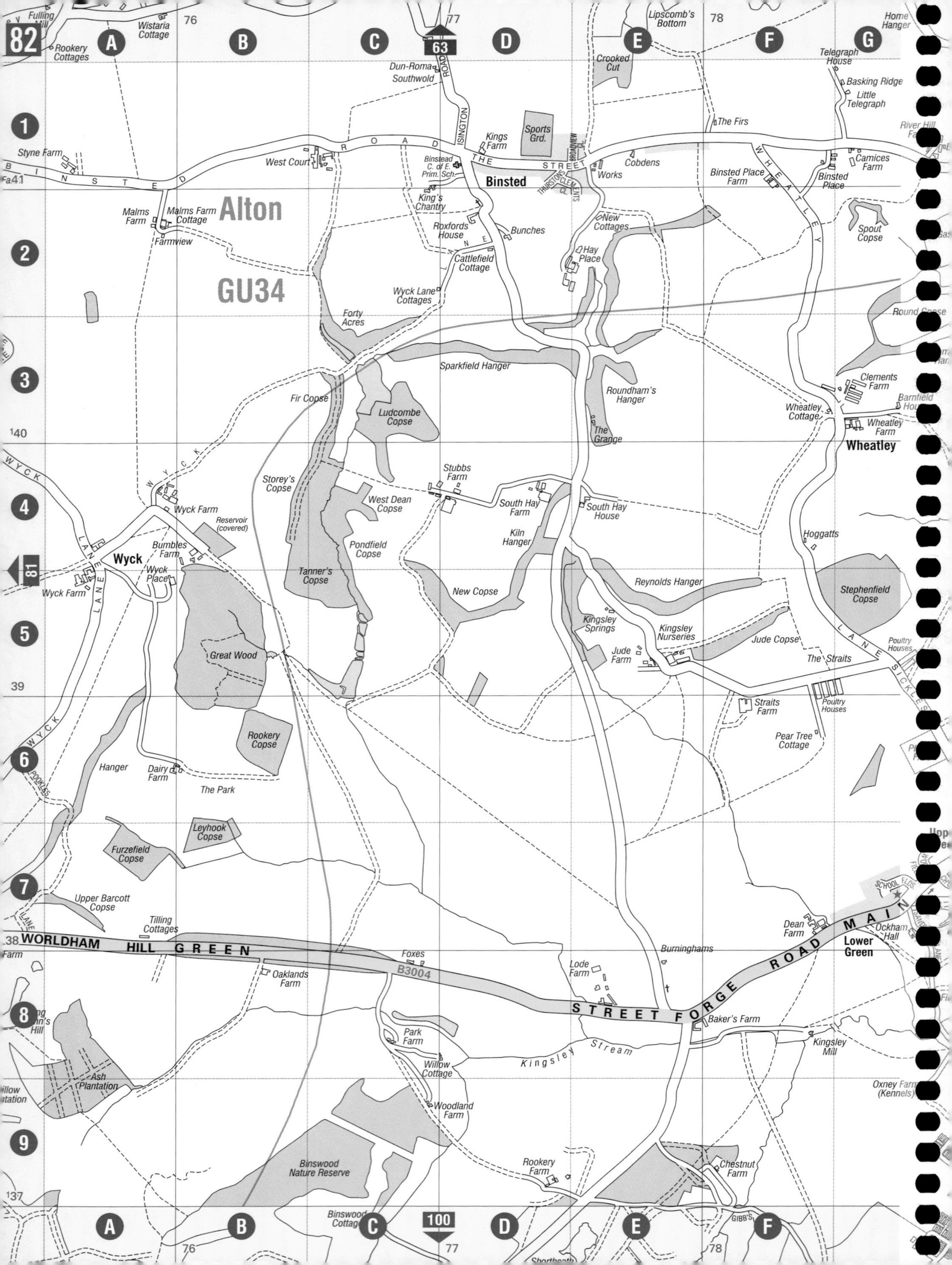
Alton
GU34
Binsted
Wheatley
Wyck
Lower Green
WORLDHAM HILL GREEN
STREET FORGE ROAD MAIN
B3004
BINSTED ROAD
THE STREET
ISINGTON ROAD
WHEATLEY LANE
WYCK LANE
SICKLE LANE
Wistaria Cottage
Rookery Cottages
Lipscomb's Bottom
Home Hanger
Crooked Cut
Telegraph House
Basking Ridge
Little Telegraph
Dun-Roma
Southwold
Styne Farm
West Court
Kings Farm
Sports Grd.
Binstead C. of E. Prim. Sch.
Cobdens
Works
The Firs
Binsted Place Farm
Binsted Place
Camices Farm
Malms Farm
Malms Farm Cottage
Farmview
King's Chantry
Roxfords House
Bunches
New Cottages
Spout Copse
Hay Place
Cattlefield Cottage
Wyck Lane Cottages
Forty Acres
Round Copse
Sparkfield Hanger
Roundham's Hanger
Clements Farm
Barnfield House
Fir Copse
Ludcombe Copse
Wheatley Cottage
Wheatley Farm
The Grange
Stubbs Farm
Storey's Copse
West Dean Copse
South Hay Farm
South Hay House
Wyck Farm
Reservoir (covered)
Kiln Hanger
Hoggatts
Bumbles Farm
Pondfield Copse
Wyck Place
Tanner's Copse
Reynolds Hanger
Stephenfield Copse
New Copse
Kingsley Springs
Kingsley Nurseries
Jude Copse
Poultry Houses
Great Wood
Jude Farm
The Straits
Straits Farm
Rookery Copse
Pear Tree Cottage
Hanger
Dairy Farm
The Park
Leyhook Copse
Furzefield Copse
Upper Barcott Copse
Tilling Cottages
School Flds
Dean Farm
Ockham Hall
Foxes
Burninghams
Oaklands Farm
Lode Farm
Baker's Farm
Park Farm
Kingsley Stream
Kingsley Mill
Willow Cottage
Ash Plantation
Oxney Farm (Kennels)
Woodland Farm
Binswood Nature Reserve
Rookery Farm
Chestnut Farm
Binswood Cottage
GIBB'S
Shortheath
POOKES LA.
63
81
100
76
77
78
140
39
138
137

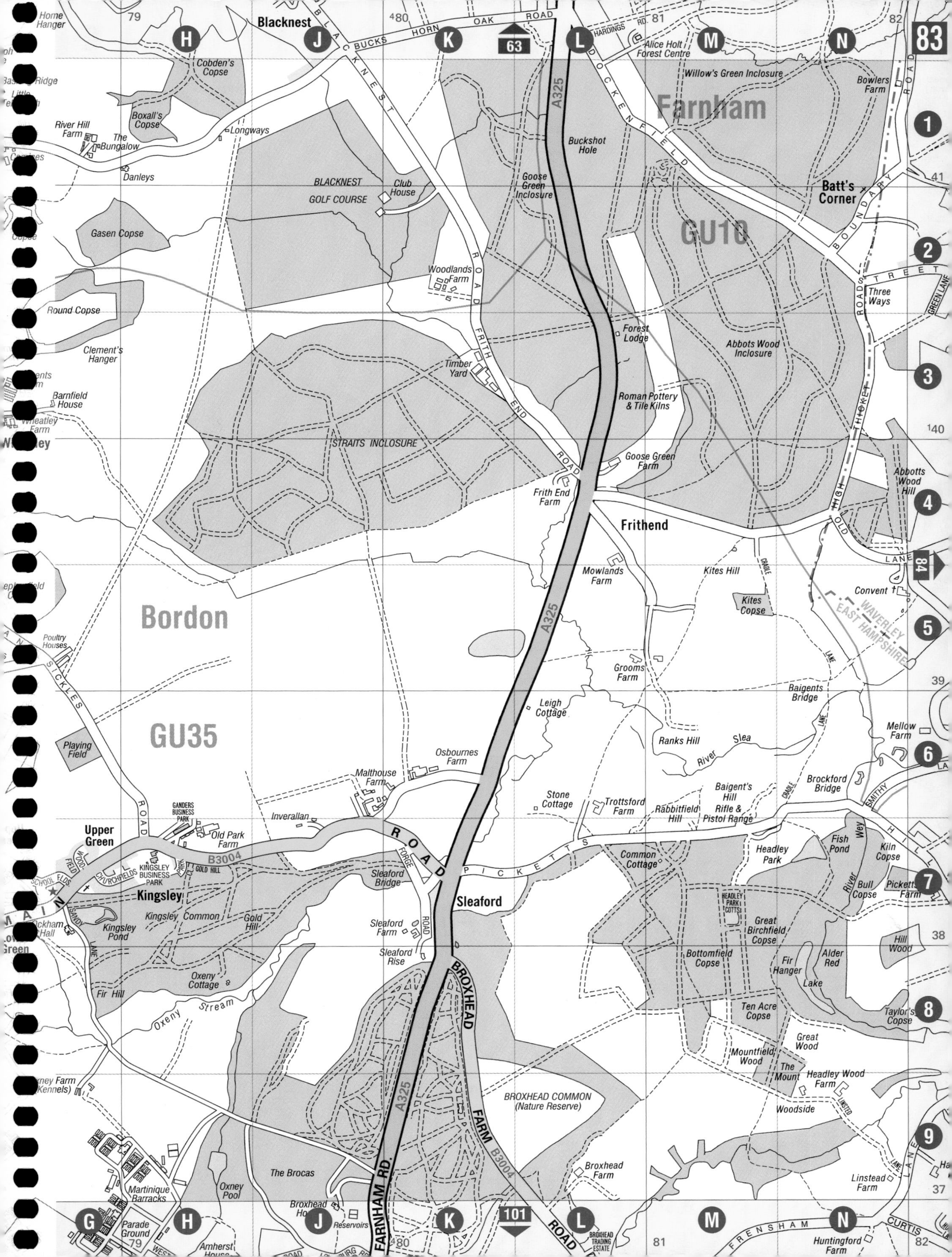

Blacknest
BLACKNEST
BUCKS HORN OAK ROAD
63
HARDINGS RD.
Alice Holt Forest Centre
DOCKENFIELD
Willow's Green Inclosure
Bowlers Farm
Farnham
Cobden's Copse
Boxall's Copse
River Hill Farm
The Bungalow
Longways
Danleys
A325
Buckshot Hole
Goose Green Inclosure
BLACKNEST GOLF COURSE
Club House
Batt's Corner
BOUNDARY ROAD
GU10
Gasen Copse
Woodlands Farm
FRITH END ROAD
STREET
Three Ways
GREEN LANE
Round Copse
Forest Lodge
Abbots Wood Inclosure
Clement's Hanger
Timber Yard
Barnfield House
Wheatley Farm
Roman Pottery & Tile Kilns
STRAITS INCLOSURE
HIGH THICKET ROAD
Goose Green Farm
Abbots Wood Hill
Frith End Farm
Frithend
OLD LANE
CRADLE
84
Mowlands Farm
Kites Hill
Convent
Kites Copse
Bordon
WAVERLEY
EAST HAMPSHIRE
Poultry Houses
SICKLES ROAD
Grooms Farm
LANE
Baigents Bridge
Leigh Cottage
Mellow Farm
GU35
Ranks Hill
River Slea
Playing Field
Osbournes Farm
Malthouse Farm
Stone Cottage
Trottsford Farm
Rabbitfield Hill
Baigent's Hill Rifle & Pistol Range
Brockford Bridge
SMITHY HILL
GANDERS BUSINESS PARK
Upper Green
Old Park Farm
Inverallan
ROAD
PICKETTS
B3004
Common Cottage
Headley Park
Fish Pond
Kiln Copse
Wey
KINGSLEY BUSINESS PARK
GOLD HILL
FORGE ROAD
Sleaford Bridge
River
Bull Copse
Picketts Farm
Kingsley
SCHOOL FLDS
CHURCHFIELDS
WOOD FIELD
MAIN
SANDY LANE
Sleaford
HEADLEY PARK COTTS
Great Birchfield Copse
Kingsley Common
Gold Hill
Kingsley Pond
Sleaford Farm
Hill Wood
Sleaford Rise
Bottomfield Copse
Fir Hanger
Alder Red
Lake
Oxeny Cottage
BROXHEAD
Fir Hill
Oxeny Stream
Ten Acre Copse
Taylor's Copse
Great Wood
Mountfield Wood
The Mount
Headley Wood Farm
BROXHEAD COMMON (Nature Reserve)
FARM
Woodside
LINSTED LANE
Broxhead Farm
The Brocas
FARNHAM RD.
Oxney Pool
Martinique Barracks
Linstead Farm
Parade Ground
Broxhead House
Reservoirs
101
BROXHEAD TRADING ESTATE
FRENSHAM
CURTIS
Huntingford Farm
Amherst House
WEST
G H J K L M N
79 480 81 82
1 2 3 4 5 6 7 8 9
41 140 39 38 37

Dockenfield
FRENSHAM
FRENSHAM COMMON
Frensham Great Pond
Frensham Country Park Interpretative Centre
Frensham Manor
Bordon
GU35
Hearn
ARFORD
Hindhead
GU26
WAVERLEY
EAST HAMPSHIRE
A287
River Wey
Wishanger Common
Smithfield
Dockenfield Farm
Dockenfield Manor
Manor Farm
Rock Barn Cottage
Heath Hill
Huntingford Bridge
Mellow Farm
Firs Close
Hoppery Hill
Pickets Hill House
Kiln Copse
Picketts Hill Farm
Horseshoe Farm
Hill Wood
Saunders Green
Taylor's Copse
Prospect Hill Farm
Bayfields Farm
Hartfield House
Headley Meadows
Brambletye
Hartfield Farm
The Oaks
Curtis Farm
Opax Farm
High Breck
Hearn House Farm
Hearn Copse
Hearn House
Little Hearn Copse
Meadow Cottage
Elliot's Farm
Plaster Hill Farm
Lower Coombe Farm
Coombe Farm
Hungry Coombe
Dalen Copse
Land of Nod Wood
Folly Plantation
Chintens Copse
Cain Farm
Land of Nod
Assisi
Park Copse
Park View Farm
Hills Copse
Stream Forest
Fish Pond
Stream Copse
Wishanger Lake
Wishanger Farm
Stream Farm
The Oasts
Wishanger Lodge
Gum Hill
New Farm
Kingsmead
Field House
Stud Farm
Symondstone Farm
Summer House Copse
Furze Hills Farm
Chinton Hanger
Barford Court
Barford Court Farm
Moreton House
Ford
Hales Copse
Furze Hill
Churt House
The Chase
Wayside Cottages
Buttermilk Hill
Harold's Hill
FRENSHAM COMMON COUNTRY PARK
The Hanger
Westhanger
Flat Copse
Three Ways
Bealeswood Common
Jeffrey's Copse
Middle Copse
Falkner's Copse
Grubb's Copse
Swan's Copse
Hallsgrove Copse
Ashbeds
Nash's Copse
The Ham
Rough Copse
Pitt Farm
Ham Ashbed
Pitt Hanger
Pitthanger
Lane End
St. Mary's School
Abbotts Wood Hill
Beech Field Copse
Stream Cottage
High Field Copse
Hoppery Copse
Ham Copse
Twelve Acre Copse
Dipping Tank Copse
The Cornered Copse
Furze Copse
Daniel's Copse
83
102

HANKLEY COMMON
Frensham Little Pond
Hillside Farm
Greenhills Farm
PRIORY LANE
GRANGE ROAD
RUSHMOOR
MELBRECK HOSPITAL
CARLISLE
WELLESLEY ROAD
LOWICKS ROAD
Mackenzies
Lowicks
Graywalls
SANDY LANE
Kettlebury Hill
Lowicks House
GLEBE LA.
The Flashes
Gold Hill
FRENSHAM COMMON COUNTRY PARK
Crosswater House
Harold's Hill
Crosswater Farm Gardens (Nursery)
Crosswater
Farnham
Stoneyside
The Devil's Jumps
Stony Jump
Lingwood
Churt Common
Barrow House
THURSLEY ROAD
Borrowstone
Tylosand
Sundial House
Coombe Ridge
Churt Place Farm
The Cedars
Silverbeck
Old Kiln Farm
Garden Cottage
Churt Lea
Bookhams
Churt Place Nursery
Silverbeck Farm
Sunward
Podmore
GU10
The Pack House
High Meadow
Hyde Copse
Hyde Farm
OLD KILN LANE
CRABTREE LANE
TILFORD ROAD
HOUSE LANE
OLD BARN LANE
Rec. Grd.
Hale Ho.
CHURT
Moreton House
Avalon Farm
Glenhead Farm
HYDE LANE
High Barn
Stock Farm
Marchants Farm
SILVER BIRCH COTTAGES
Fair View Farm
Green Cross Farm
Green Cross
St. John's C.of E. Inf. Sch.
Willow Farm
Green Farm
GREEN LANE
Chipstead
Barford Farm
Kitts Farm
Barford
Woodbury House
Oak Grove
Hyde Hill
HEATHER COTTAGES
Road Farm
Hill Lodge
Marchants Hill
Hindhead
Gravel Hanger
Churt Wynde Reservoir (covered)
A287
Hatch Hill House
GU26
HINDHEAD GOLF COURSE
Hindhead Playing Field
BEACON HILL
Linkside
103
The Central Deaconess House
Assisi
WHITMOOR VALE
Twizzletwig
Club
86
87
88
41
40
39
38
37

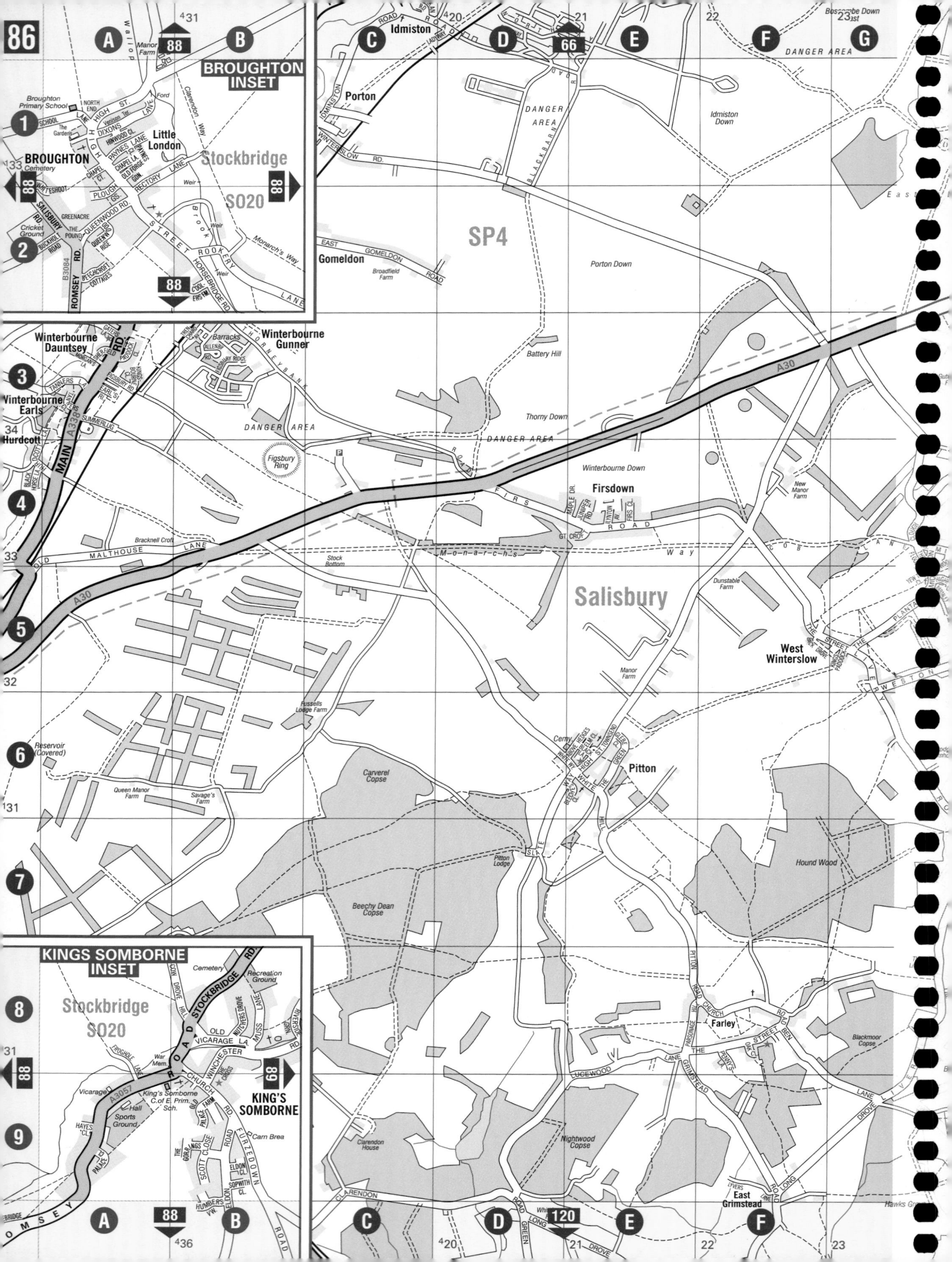
BROUGHTON INSET
Broughton Primary School
BROUGHTON
Little London
Stockbridge
SO20
Manor Farm
Clarendon Way
Monarch's Way
Cricket Ground
KINGS SOMBORNE INSET
KING'S SOMBORNE
King's Somborne C.of E. Prim. Sch.
Sports Ground
Recreation Ground
Cemetery
Carn Brea
Idmiston
Porton
Gomeldon
Broadfield Farm
DANGER AREA
Idmiston Down
Porton Down
Boscombe Down East
SP4
Winterbourne Dauntsey
Winterbourne Gunner
Winterbourne Earls
Hurdcott
Barracks
Figsbury Ring
Battery Hill
Thorny Down
Winterbourne Down
Firsdown
Bracknell Croft
Stock Bottom
Monarch's Way
Salisbury
New Manor Farm
Dunstable Farm
West Winterslow
Manor Farm
Fussells Lodge Farm
Reservoir (Covered)
Queen Manor Farm
Savage's Farm
Carverel Copse
Pitton
Pitton Lodge
Beechy Dean Copse
Hound Wood
Farley
Blackmoor Copse
Nightwood Copse
Clarendon House
East Grimstead
Hawks Grove
A30
A3057
B3084
A338
88
66
120

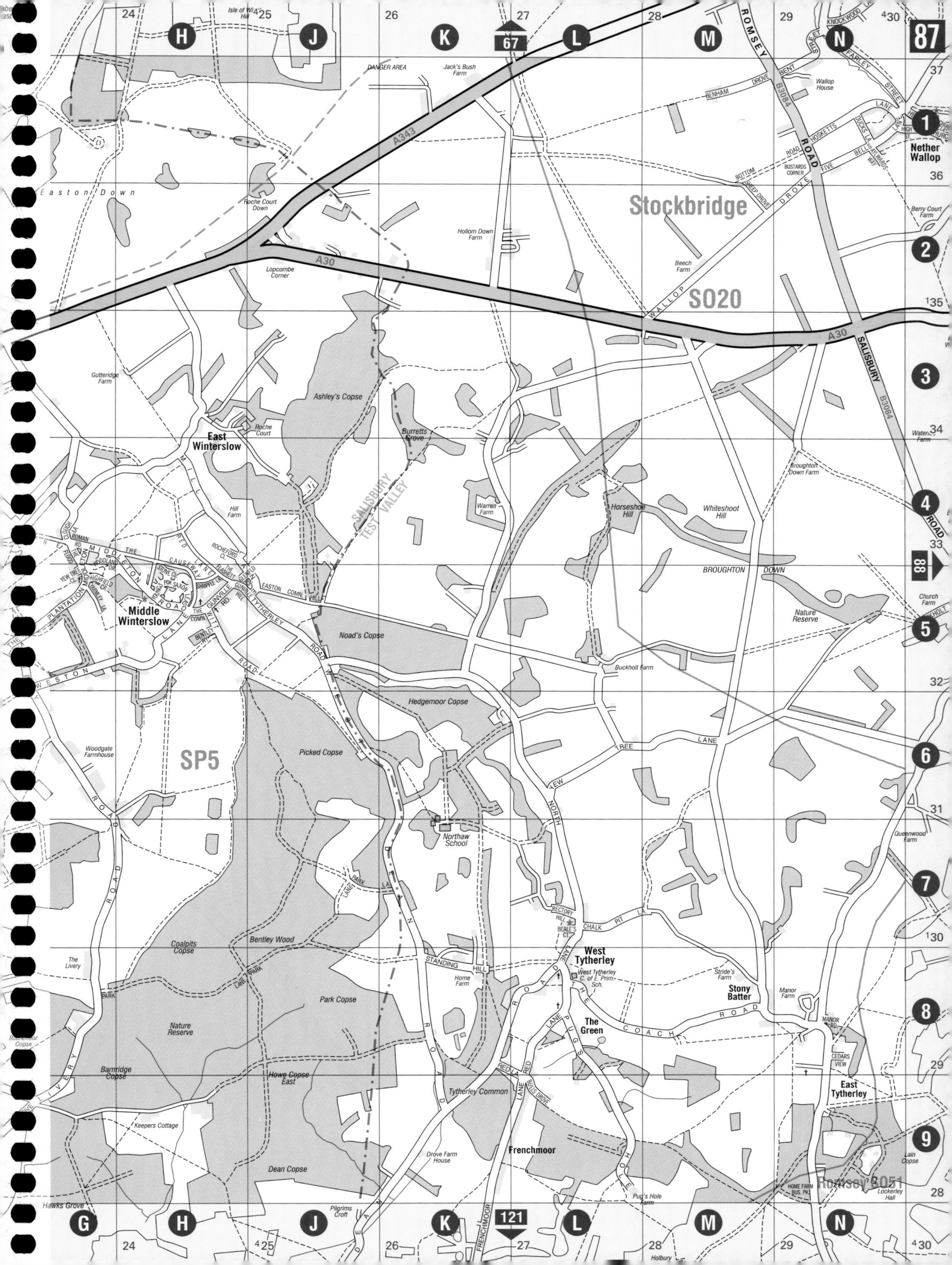

67
Stockbridge
SO20
SP5
Nether Wallop
East Winterslow
Middle Winterslow
West Tytherley
Stony Batter
The Green
East Tytherley
Frenchmoor
Tytherley Common
Easton Down
Roche Court Down
Lopcombe Corner
Hollom Down Farm
Beech Farm
Jack's Bush Farm
DANGER AREA
Wallop House
Berry Court Farm
Gutteridge Farm
Ashley's Copse
Roche Court
Burretts Grove
Hill Farm
Warren Farm
Horseshoe Hill
Whiteshoot Hill
Broughton Down Farm
BROUGHTON DOWN
Nature Reserve
Church Farm
Noad's Copse
Buckholt Farm
Hedgemoor Copse
Picked Copse
Woodgate Farmhouse
Northaw School
Queenwood Farm
Coalpits Copse
Bentley Wood
The Livery
Home Farm
Stride's Farm
Manor Farm
Park Copse
Barnridge Copse
Howe Copse East
Keepers Cottage
Drove Farm House
Dean Copse
Pilgrims Croft
Hawks Grove
Pug's Hole Farm
Lain Copse
Lockerley Hall
HOME FARM BUS. PK.
Romsey SO51
Holbury
SALISBURY TEST VALLEY
A343
A30
B3084
ROMSEY ROAD
SALISBURY ROAD
WALLOP DROVE
BENHAM DROVE
BOTTOM ROAD
FIVE BELLS LA.
HOSKETTS
DUCKS LA.
SHEEP DROVE
BUSTARDS CORNER
FARLEY STREET
KNOCKWOOD
BENT STREET
LANE
TREE LANE
NORTH LANE
MILL LANE
THE CAUSEWAY
MIDDLETON
ROMAN RD.
PLANTATION
EASTON COMM. HILL
TYTHERLEY ROAD
WEST DEAN ROAD
WESTON LANE
LIVERY ROAD
PARK LANE
STANDING HILL
RECTORY HILL
BEALE'S CT.
CHALK PIT LA.
West Tytherley C. of E. Prim. Sch.
THE COACH ROAD
PUGS HOLE
RED LA.
BULLS DROVE
FRENCHMOOR LANE
MANOR RD.
CEDARS VIEW
Isle of Wight Hill
G
H
J
K
L
M
N
1
2
3
4
5
6
7
8
9
24
25
26
27
28
29
30
28
29
31
32
33
34
35
36
37
121
88

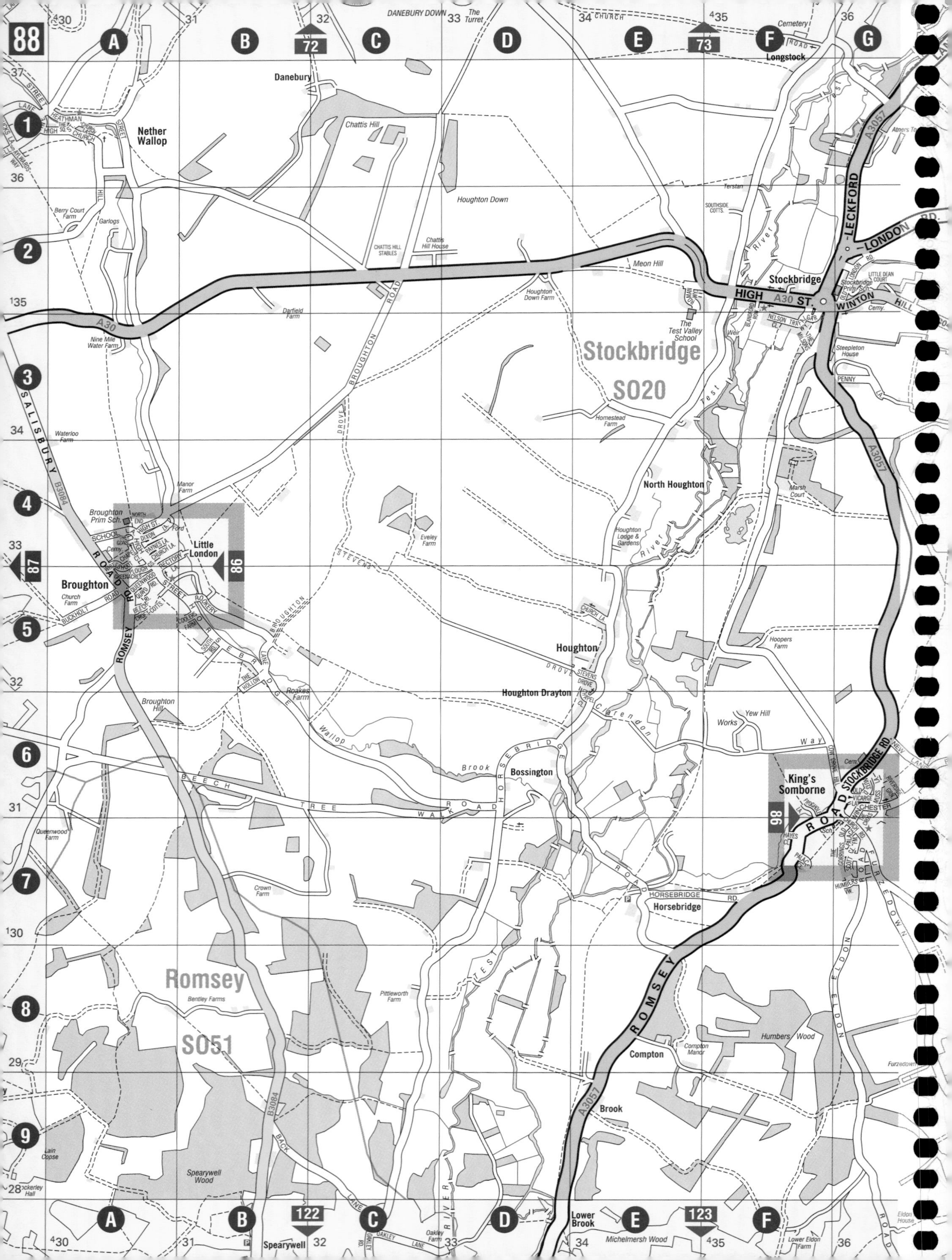

Danebury
Nether Wallop
Chattis Hill
Houghton Down
Longstock
Stockbridge
Stockbridge SO20
North Houghton
Broughton
Little London
Houghton
Houghton Drayton
Bossington
King's Somborne
Horsebridge
Romsey SO51
Compton
Brook
Lower Brook
Spearywell
A30
A3057
B3084
HIGH ST.
SALISBURY ROAD
ROMSEY RD.
ROMSEY ROAD
LECKFORD
LONDON RD.
WINTON HILL
STOCKBRIDGE RD.
BEECH TREE WALK ROAD
HORSEBRIDGE ROAD
HORSEBRIDGE RD.
BROUGHTON ROAD
Clarendon Way
Wallop Brook
River Test
Meon Hill
Houghton Down Farm
Darfield Farm
Nine Mile Water Farm
Berry Court Farm
Waterloo Farm
Manor Farm
Broughton Prim Sch.
Church Farm
Eveley Farm
Homestead Farm
Houghton Lodge & Gardens
The Test Valley School
Marsh Court
Hoopers Farm
Yew Hill
Works
Roakes Farm
Broughton Hill
Queenwood Farm
Crown Farm
Bentley Farms
Pittleworth Farm
Humbers Wood
Compton Manor
Spearywell Wood
Lain Copse
Michelmersh Wood
Oakley Farm
Lower Eldon Farm
Eldon House
Furzedown
Steepleton House
CHATTIS HILL STABLES
Chattis Hill House
SOUTHSIDE COTTS.
Terstan
Cemetery
DANEBURY DOWN
The Turret
72
73
86
87
98
122
123

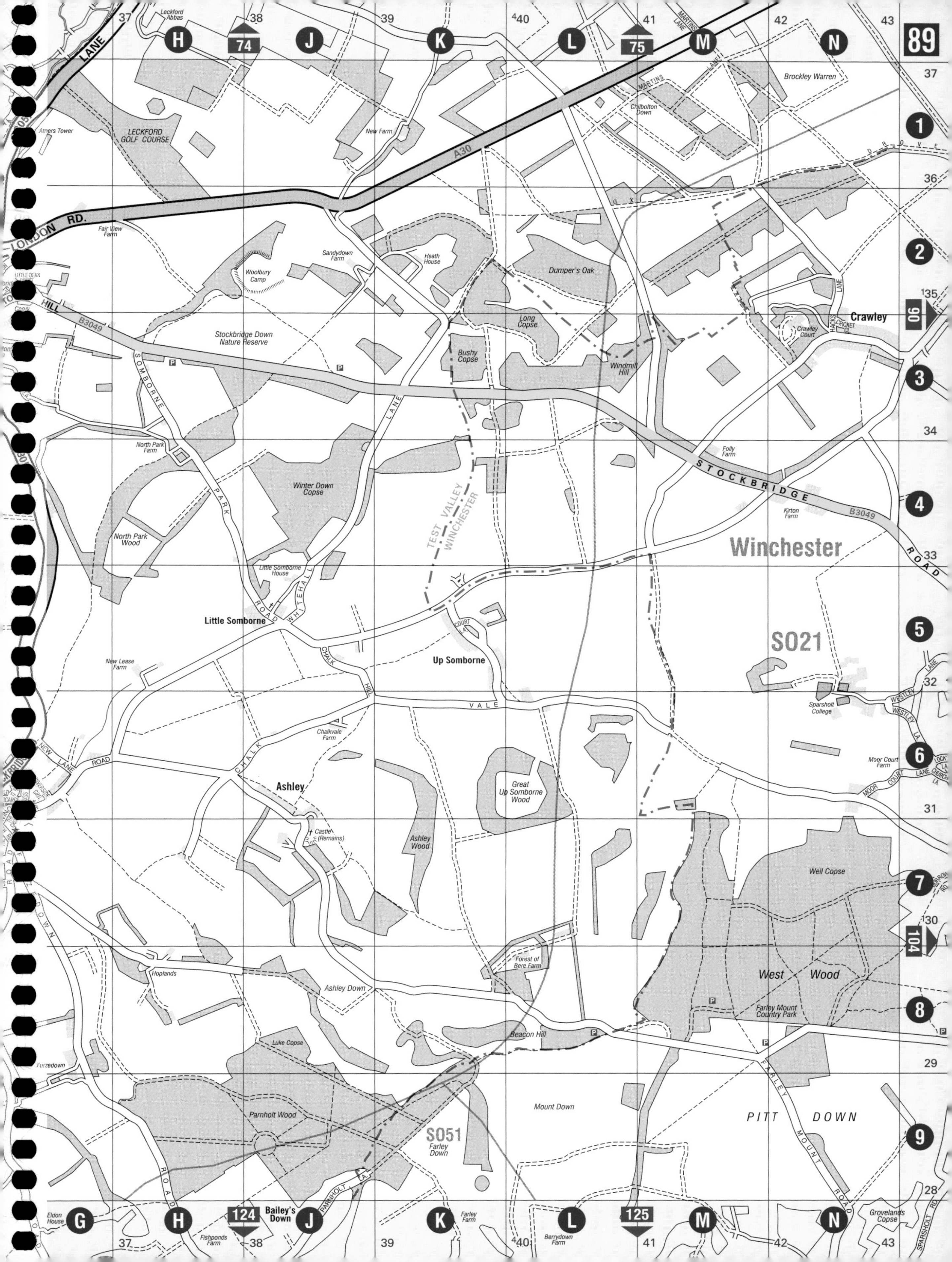

Leckford Abbas
LECKFORD GOLF COURSE
Atners Tower
New Farm
A30
LONDON RD.
Brockley Warren
Chilbolton Down
MARTINS LANE
Fair View Farm
Woolbury Camp
Sandydown Farm
Heath House
Dumper's Oak
Long Copse
Bushy Copse
Windmill Hill
Crawley
Crawley Court
Stockbridge Down Nature Reserve
B3049
SOMBORNE
North Park Farm
Winter Down Copse
North Park Wood
TEST VALLEY
WINCHESTER
Folly Farm
STOCKBRIDGE ROAD
Kirton Farm
Winchester
Little Somborne House
WHITEHALL
Little Somborne
Up Somborne
COURT LA
S021
New Lease Farm
CHALK HILL
VALE
Sparsholt College
WESTLEY LA.
Chalkvale Farm
Ashley
Great Up Somborne Wood
Moor Court Farm
MOOR COURT LANE
NEW LANE
ROAD
Castle (Remains)
Ashley Wood
Well Copse
Forest of Bere Farm
West Wood
Hoplands
Ashley Down
Farley Mount Country Park
Beacon Hill
Luke Copse
Furzedown
FARLEY MOUNT ROAD
Mount Down
PITT DOWN
Parnholt Wood
S051
Farley Down
PARNHOLT LA
Eldon House
Bailey's Down
Farley Farm
Fishponds Farm
Berrydown Farm
Grovelands Copse
SPARSHOLT RD

74 75 90 104 124 125

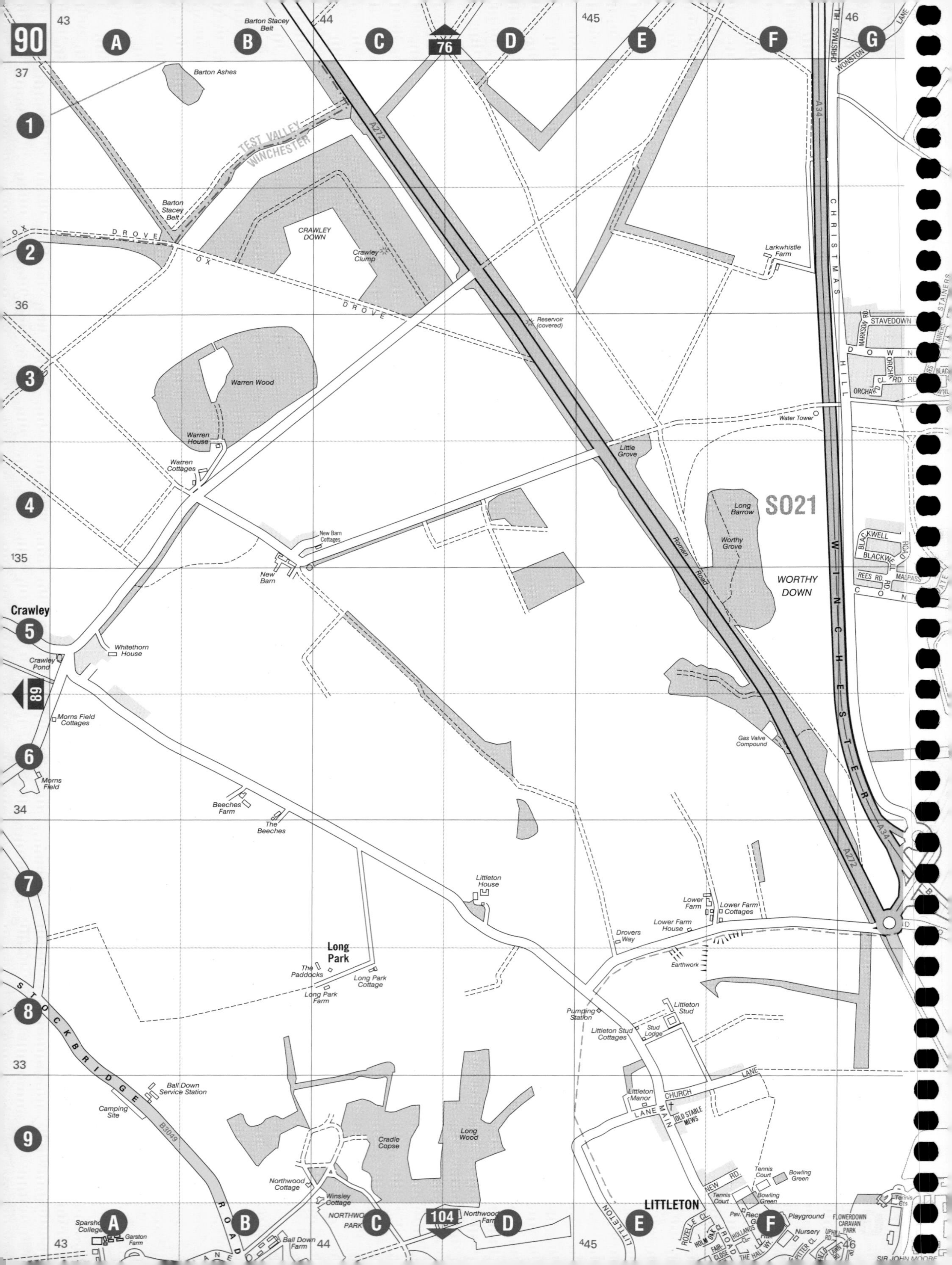
Barton Ashes
Barton Stacey Belt
TEST VALLEY
WINCHESTER
OX DROVE
CRAWLEY DOWN
Crawley Clump
Reservoir (covered)
Larkwhistle Farm
CHRISTMAS HILL
WONSTON LANE
A34
A272
STAVEDOWN RD
MARKSON RD
ORCHARD CL
DOWN
Water Tower
Warren Wood
Warren House
Warren Cottages
Little Grove
Long Barrow
Worthy Grove
SO21
WORTHY DOWN
Roman Road
BLACKWELL RD
REES RD
MALPASS
WINCHESTER ROAD
New Barn Cottages
New Barn
Crawley
Crawley Pond
Whitethorn House
Morns Field Cottages
Morns Field
Gas Valve Compound
Beeches Farm
The Beeches
Littleton House
Lower Farm
Lower Farm Cottages
Lower Farm House
Drovers Way
Earthwork
Long Park
The Paddocks
Long Park Cottage
Long Park Farm
Pumping Station
Littleton Stud
Stud Lodge
Littleton Stud Cottages
STOCKBRIDGE ROAD
B3049
Ball Down Service Station
Camping Site
Littleton Manor
CHURCH LANE
MAIN ROAD
OLD STABLE MEWS
Cradle Copse
Long Wood
Northwood Cottage
Winsley Cottage
NORTHWOOD PARK
Northwood Farm
Ball Down Farm
Sparsholt College
Garston Farm
LITTLETON
LITTLETON LANE
NEW RD
Tennis Court
Bowling Green
Playground
Nursery
FLOWERDOWN CARAVAN PARK
ROZELLE CL
HOLLANDS CL
THE HALL WY
SIR JOHN MOORE
Crawley

76
89
104

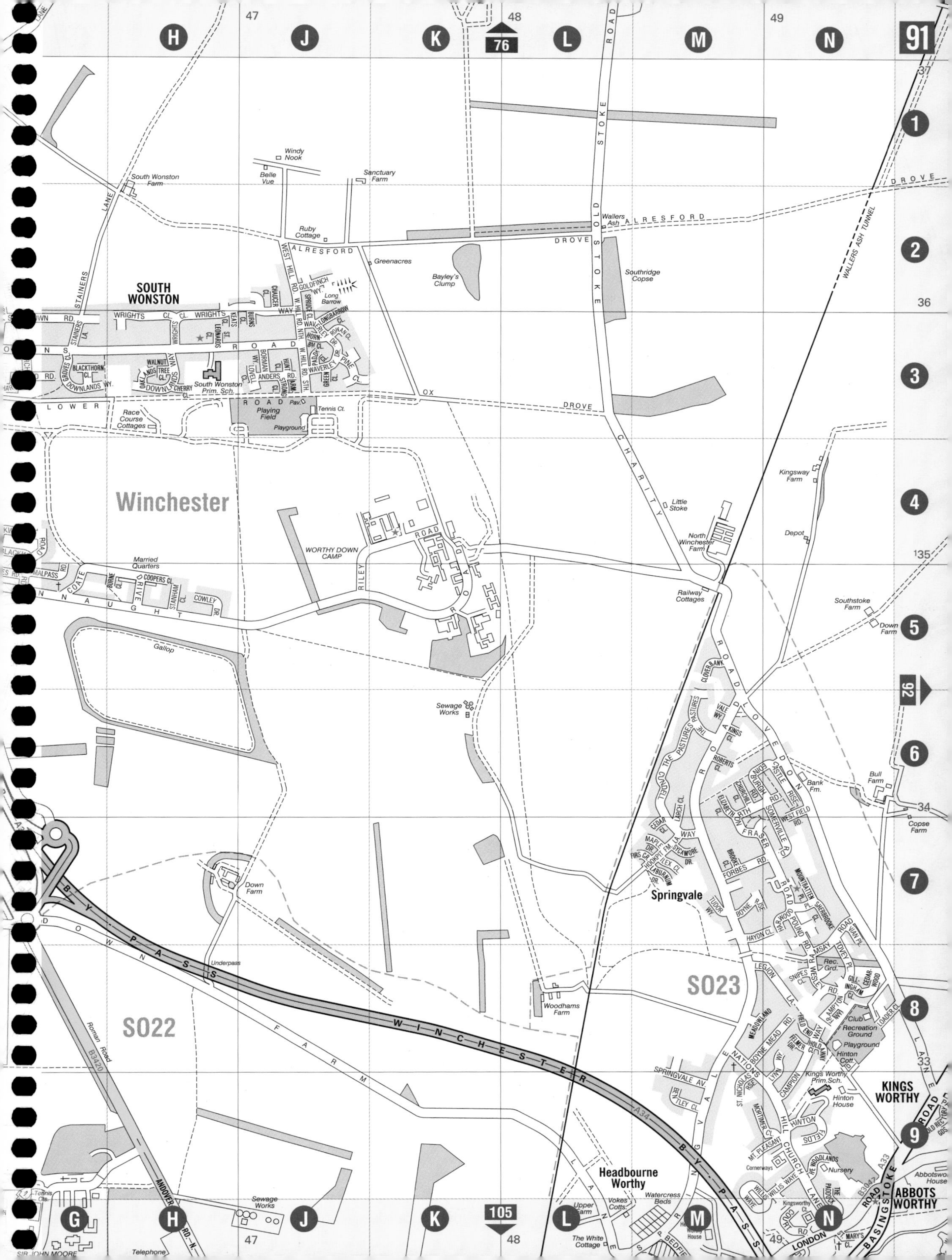
SOUTH WONSTON
Winchester
WORTHY DOWN CAMP
Springvale
SO23
SO22
KINGS WORTHY
ABBOTS WORTHY
Headbourne Worthy
South Wonston Farm
Windy Nook
Belle Vue
Sanctuary Farm
Ruby Cottage
Greenacres
Bayley's Clump
Southridge Copse
Wallers Ash
ALRESFORD DROVE
OX DROVE
WALLERS ASH TUNNEL
OLD STOKE ROAD
CHARITY
Long Barrow
South Wonston Prim. Sch.
Playing Field
Playground
Tennis Ct.
Race Course Cottages
Married Quarters
Gallop
Sewage Works
Down Farm
Underpass
Woodhams Farm
Little Stoke
North Winchester Farm
Railway Cottages
Kingsway Farm
Depot
Southstoke Farm
Down Farm
Bull Farm
Bank Fm.
Copse Farm
Rec. Grd.
Recreation Ground
Hinton Cott.
Kings Worthy Prim.Sch.
Hinton House
Nursery
Cornerways
Watercress Beds
Upper Farm
Vokes Cotts.
The White Cottage
Roman Road
WINCHESTER BY-PASS
A34
B3420
B3047
A33
DOWN FARM LANE
ANDOVER RD. N.
LOWER ROAD
STAINERS LANE
WRIGHTS CL.
RILEY ROAD
LONDON RD.
SPRINGVALE AV.
BASINGSTOKE ROAD
47
48
49
36
35
34
33
76
92
105

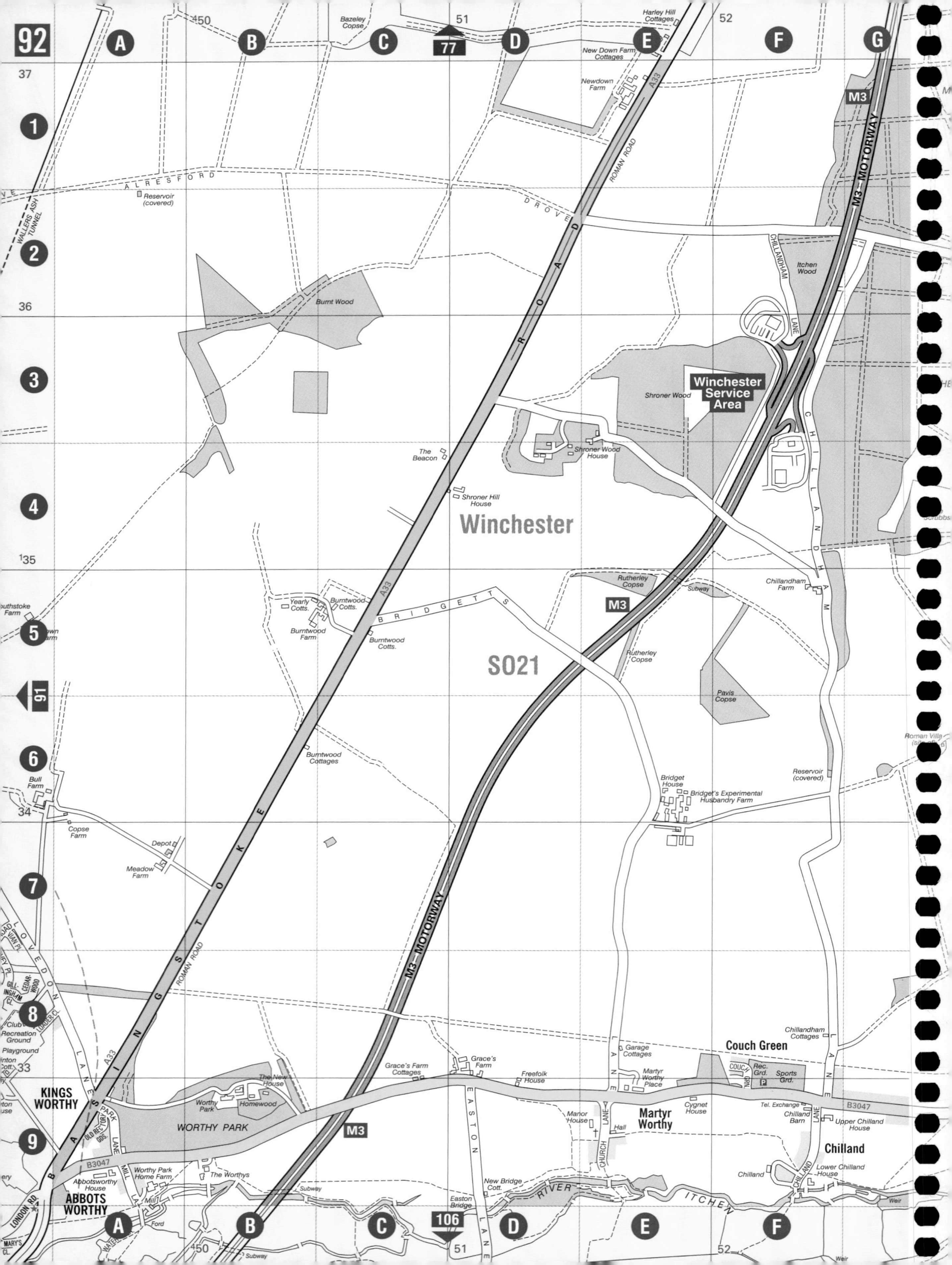

Bazeley Copse
Harley Hill Cottages
New Down Farm Cottages
Newdown Farm
ALRESFORD DROVE
Reservoir (covered)
WALLERS ASH TUNNEL
ROMAN ROAD
A33
Burnt Wood
CHILLANDHAM LANE
Itchen Wood
M3
M3 – MOTORWAY
Winchester Service Area
Shroner Wood
Shroner Wood House
The Beacon
Shroner Hill House
Winchester
Rutherley Copse
Subway
Chillandham Farm
Yearly Cotts.
Burntwood Cotts.
Burntwood Farm
BRIDGETTS
SO21
Rutherley Copse
Pavis Copse
Burntwood Cottages
Reservoir (covered)
Bridget House
Bridget's Experimental Husbandry Farm
Bull Farm
Copse Farm
Depot
Meadow Farm
BASINGSTOKE ROAD
LOVEDON LANE
Recreation Ground
Playground
Chillandham Cottages
Couch Green
Garage Cottages
Grace's Farm Cottages
Grace's Farm
Freefolk House
Martyr Worthy Place
Rec. Grd.
Sports Grd.
KINGS WORTHY
The New House
Worthy Park
Homewood
WORTHY PARK
PARK LANE
OLD RECTORY GDS.
B3047
Tel. Exchange
Chilland Barn
Upper Chilland House
Cygnet House
Manor House
Hall
CHURCH LANE
Martyr Worthy
Chilland
EASTON LANE
Worthy Park Home Farm
Abbotsworthy House
The Worthys
New Bridge Cott.
RIVER ITCHEN
Chilland
Lower Chilland House
Weir
ABBOTS WORTHY
Mill
Ford
Subway
Easton Bridge
LONDON RD.

77
91
106

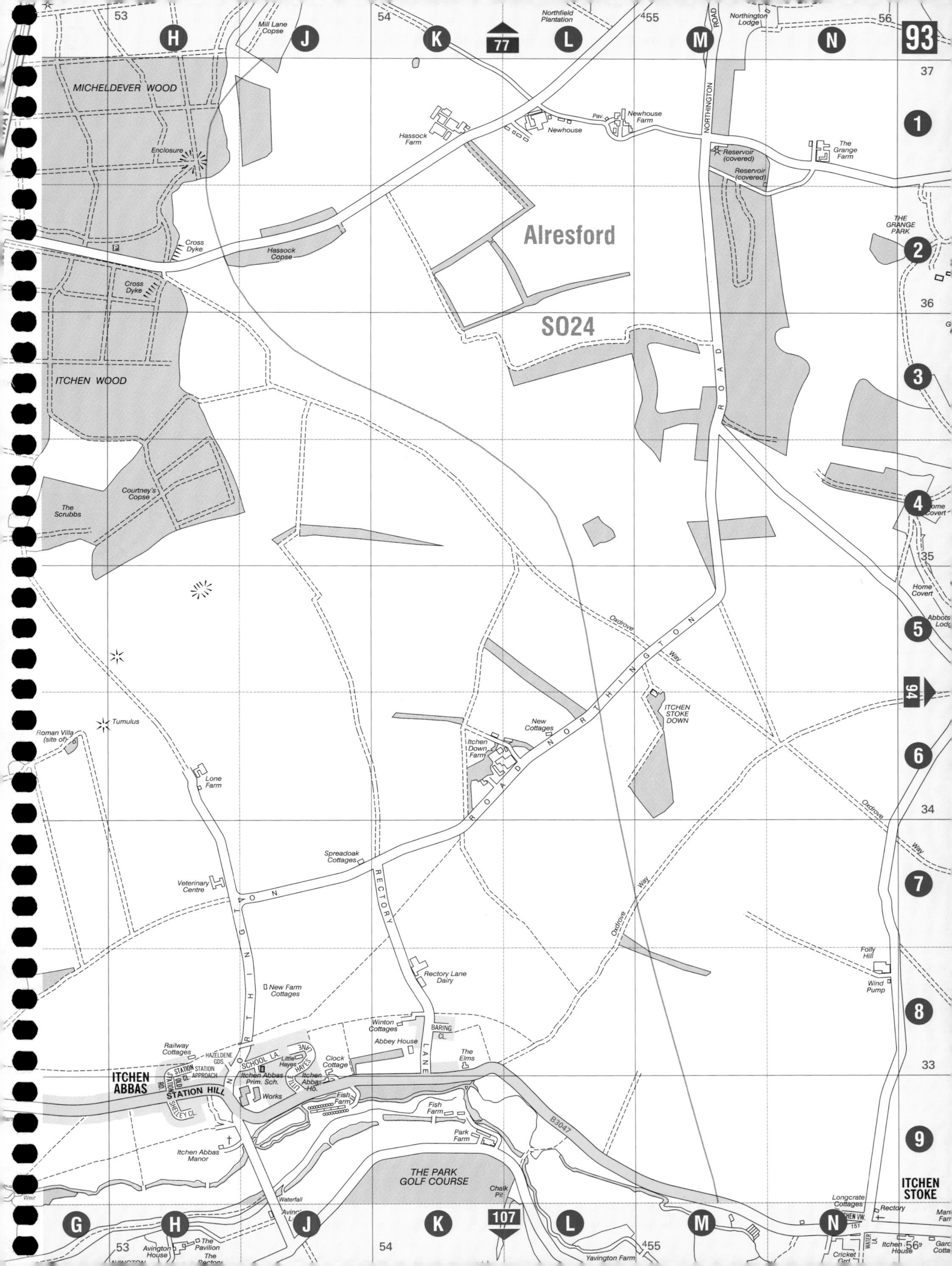

MICHELDEVER WOOD
Enclosure
Cross Dyke
Hassock Copse
Mill Lane Copse
Northfield Plantation
Hassock Farm
Newhouse
Newhouse Farm
Pav.
Northington Lodge
NORTHINGTON ROAD
Reservoir (covered)
The Grange Farm
THE GRANGE PARK
Alresford
SO24
ITCHEN WOOD
Courtney's Copse
The Scrubbs
Home Covert
Abbots Lodge
Oxdrove Way
ITCHEN STOKE DOWN
New Cottages
Itchen Down Farm
NORTHINGTON ROAD
Tumulus
Roman Villa (site of)
Lone Farm
Spreadoak Cottages
Veterinary Centre
RECTORY LANE
Rectory Lane Dairy
New Farm Cottages
Folly Hill
Wind Pump
Winton Cottages
Abbey House
BARING CL.
The Elms
Railway Cottages
HAZELDENE GDS.
STATION APPROACH
SCHOOL LA.
Little Hayes
HAYES
Clock Cottage
ITCHEN ABBAS
STATION HILL
Itchen Abbas Prim. Sch.
Itchen Abbas Ho.
Works
Fish Farm
Park Farm
B3047
Itchen Abbas Manor
THE PARK GOLF COURSE
Chalk Pit
Waterfall
Weir
ITCHEN STOKE
Longcrate Cottages
Rectory
Avington House
The Pavilion
The Rectory
Yavington Farm
Itchen House
Cricket Grd.

77
94
107

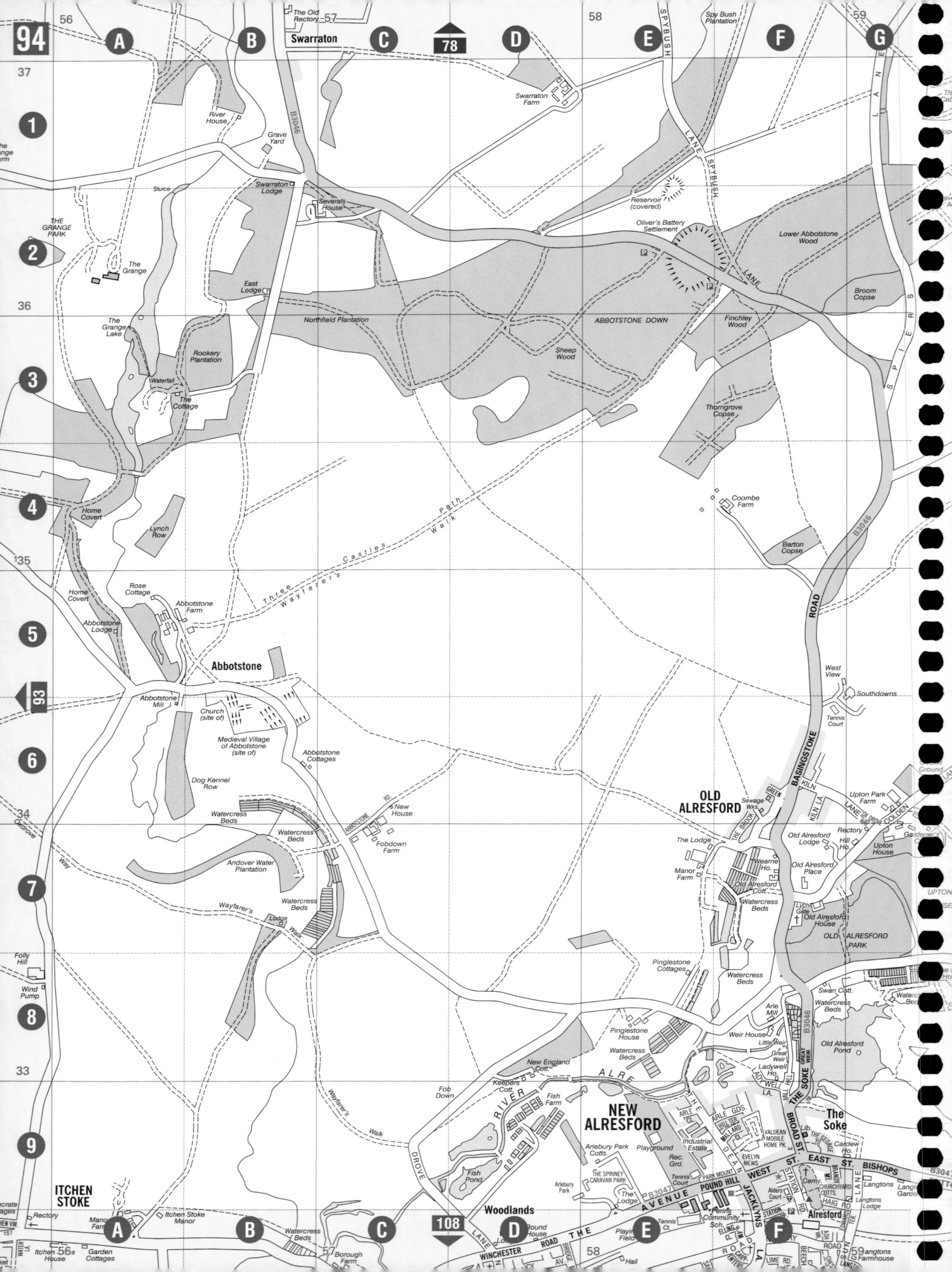
Swarraton
Swarraton Farm
River House
Grave Yard
Swarraton Lodge
Severals House
Sluice
THE GRANGE PARK
The Grange
East Lodge
The Grange Lake
Rookery Plantation
Northfield Plantation
Waterfall
The Cottage
Reservoir (covered)
Oliver's Battery Settlement
Lower Abbotstone Wood
ABBOTSTONE DOWN
Finchley Wood
Sheep Wood
Broom Copse
Thorngrove Copse
Home Covert
Lynch Row
Coombe Farm
Barton Copse
Three Castles Path
Wayfarer's Walk
Rose Cottage
Abbotstone Farm
Abbotstone Lodge
Abbotstone
Abbotstone Mill
Church (site of)
Medieval Village of Abbotstone (site of)
Abbotstone Cottages
Dog Kennel Row
Watercress Beds
Andover Water Plantation
Fobdown Farm
New House
West View
Southdowns
Tennis Court
OLD ALRESFORD
Sewage Wks.
The Lodge
Manor Farm
Upton Park Farm
Rectory
Old Alresford Lodge
Hill Ho.
Upton House
Old Alresford Place
Old Alresford House
OLD ALRESFORD PARK
Lych Gate
Pinglestone Cottages
Folly Hill
Wind Pump
Swan Cott.
Arle Mill
Weir House
Old Alresford Pond
Pinglestone House
New England Cott.
Keepers Cott.
Fob Down
Fish Farm
Fish Pond
NEW ALRESFORD
Arlebury Park Cotts.
Playground
Rec. Grd.
Industrial Estate
The Spinney Caravan Park
Arlebury Park
The Soke
ITCHEN STOKE
Rectory
Manor Farm
Itchen Stoke Manor
Itchen House
Garden Cottages
Borough Farm
Woodlands
Round House
Perins Community Sch.
Alresford
Langtons Lodge
Langtons Farmhouse
BASINGSTOKE ROAD
B3046
B3047
RIVER ALRE
THE AVENUE
WINCHESTER ROAD
POUND HILL
WEST ST.
EAST ST.
BROAD ST.
STATION RD.
JACKLYNS LA.
SPYBUSH LANE
SPIERS LANE
DROVE LANE
Oxdrove Way

78
93
108

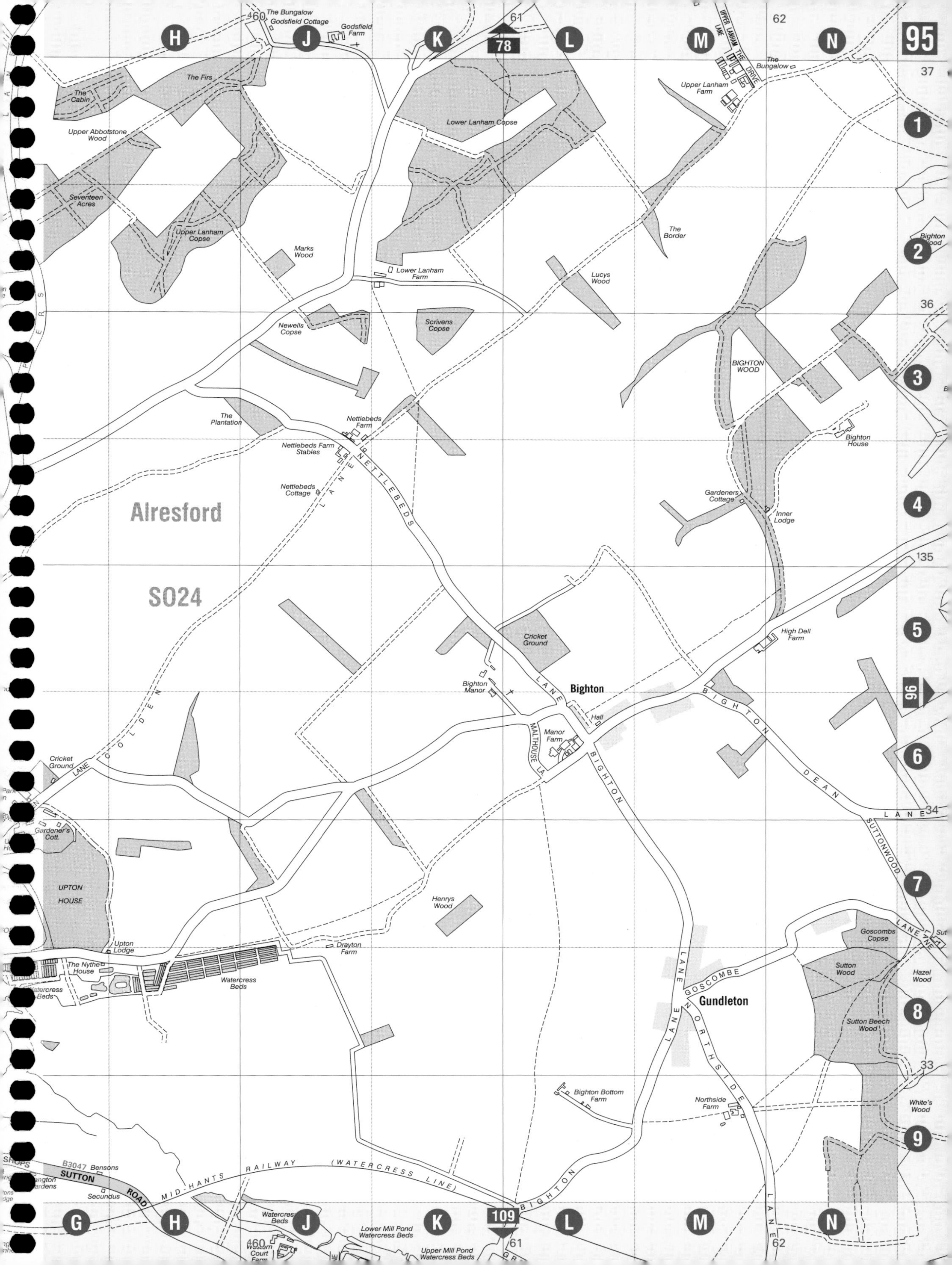

H J K L M N

37
1
Bighton Wood 2
36
3
4
135
5
96
6
34
7
8
33
9

The Bungalow
Godsfield Cottage
Godsfield Farm
460
Upper Lanham
The Drive
The Bungalow
Upper Lanham Farm

The Firs
The Cabin
Upper Abbotstone Wood

Seventeen Acres

Upper Lanham Copse

Marks Wood

Lower Lanham Copse

The Border

Lucys Wood

BIGHTON WOOD

Bighton House

Lower Lanham Farm

Newells Copse

Scrivens Copse

Gardeners Cottage

Inner Lodge

The Plantation
Nettlebeds Farm
Nettlebeds Farm Stables
Nettlebeds Cottage

Alresford

SO24

Cricket Ground

High Dell Farm

Bighton Manor

Bighton

Hall

Manor Farm

MALTHOUSE LA.

BIGHTON

BIGHTON DEAN LANE

SUTTONWOOD

Cricket Ground

Gardener's Cott.

UPTON HOUSE

Upton Lodge

The Nythe House

Watercress Beds

Watercress Beds

Henrys Wood

Drayton Farm

Goscombs Copse

Sutton Wood

Hazel Wood

Sutton Beech Wood

LANE GOSCOMBE

Gundleton

LANE NORTHSIDE

White's Wood

Bighton Bottom Farm

Northside Farm

SHOPS
B3047 Bensons
SUTTON ROAD
Secundus
460 Western Court Farm

MID HANTS RAILWAY (WATERCRESS LINE)

Watercress Beds

Lower Mill Pond Watercress Beds

Upper Mill Pond Watercress Beds

78
61
62

109
61
62

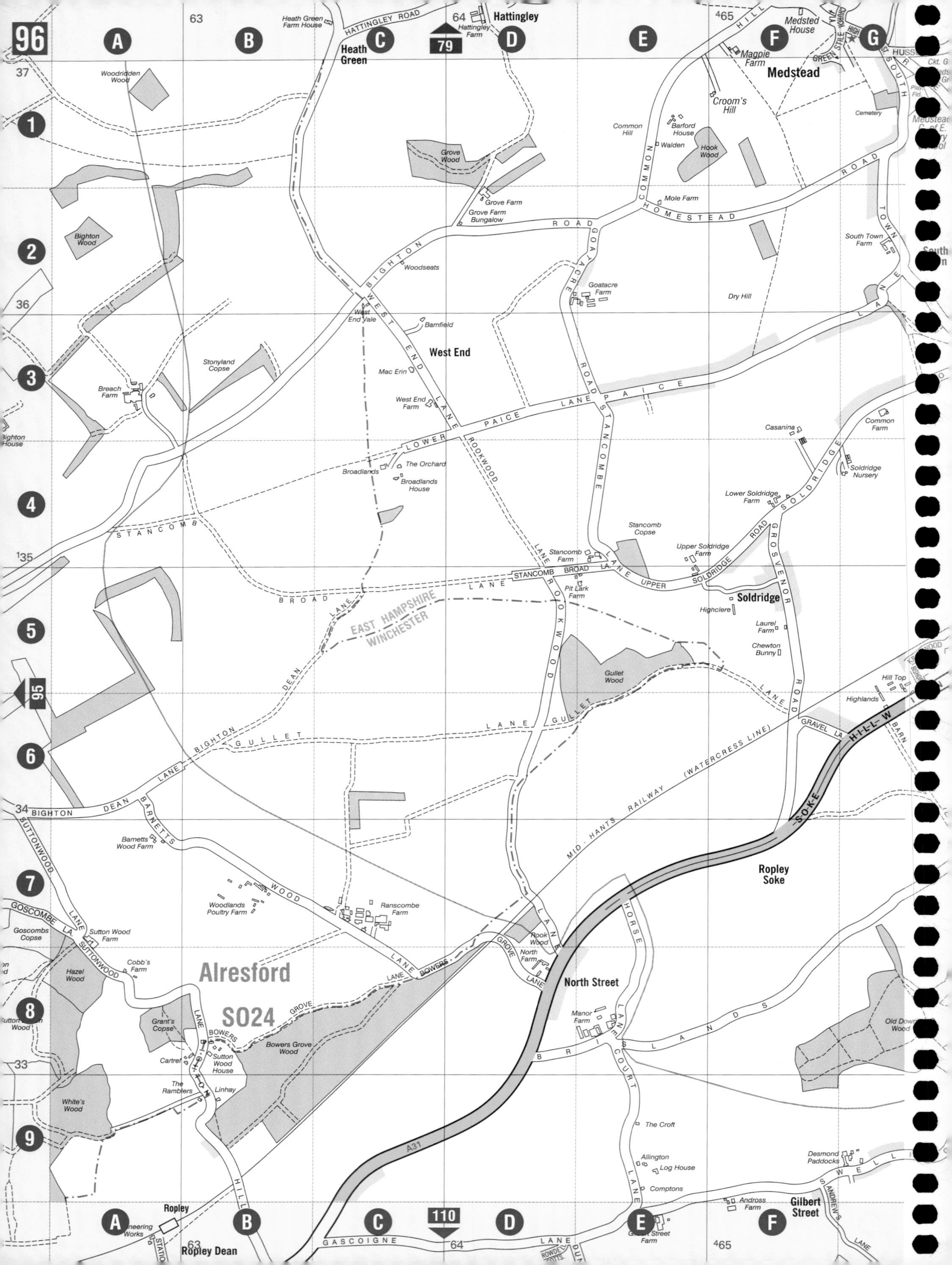

96
A
B
C
D
E
F
G
63
64
465
79
110
95
37
36
35
34
33
1
2
3
4
5
6
7
8
9
Heath Green Farm House
HATTINGLEY ROAD
Hattingley
Hattingley Farm
Heath Green
Medsted House
Magpie Farm
Medstead
Croom's Hill
Cemetery
Woodridden Wood
Grove Wood
Common Hill
Barford House
Walden
Hook Wood
Mole Farm
Grove Farm
Grove Farm Bungalow
HOMESTEAD ROAD
COMMON
Bighton Wood
South Town Farm
Woodseats
Goatacre Farm
Dry Hill
West End Vale
Barnfield
West End
Stonyland Copse
Breach Farm
Mac Erin
West End Farm
PAICE LANE
LOWER
Casanina
Common Farm
Bighton House
The Orchard
Broadlands
Broadlands House
ROOKWOOD
Soldridge Nursery
Lower Soldridge Farm
SOLDRIDGE
STANCOMB
Stancomb Copse
Upper Soldridge Farm
Stancomb Farm
STANCOMB BROAD LANE
UPPER SOLDRIDGE
GROSVENOR ROAD
Pit Lark Farm
Soldridge
BROAD LANE
Highclere
EAST HAMPSHIRE
WINCHESTER
Laurel Farm
Chewton Bunny
Gullet Wood
Hill Top
Highlands
DEAN LANE
GULLET LANE
GRAVEL LA
BARN
HILL
SOKE
MID - HANTS RAILWAY (WATERCRESS LINE)
BIGHTON DEAN LANE
SUTTONWOOD
BARNETTS
Barnetts Wood Farm
WOOD
Ropley Soke
Woodlands Poultry Farm
Ranscombe Farm
GOSCOMBE LA
Goscombs Copse
Sutton Wood Farm
Rook Wood
North Farm
HORSE
Hazel Wood
Cobb's Farm
BOWERS LANE
GROVE
North Street
Alresford
SO24
Manor Farm
Grant's Copse
BRISLANDS
COURT
Old Down Wood
Bowers Grove Wood
Cartref
Sutton Wood House
The Ramblers
Linhay
White's Wood
The Croft
A31
Allington
Log House
Desmond Paddocks
WELL
Comptons
Andross Farm
Gilbert Street
SANDREWS
Ropley
Engineering Works
GASCOIGNE LANE
Gilbert Street Farm
Ropley Dean

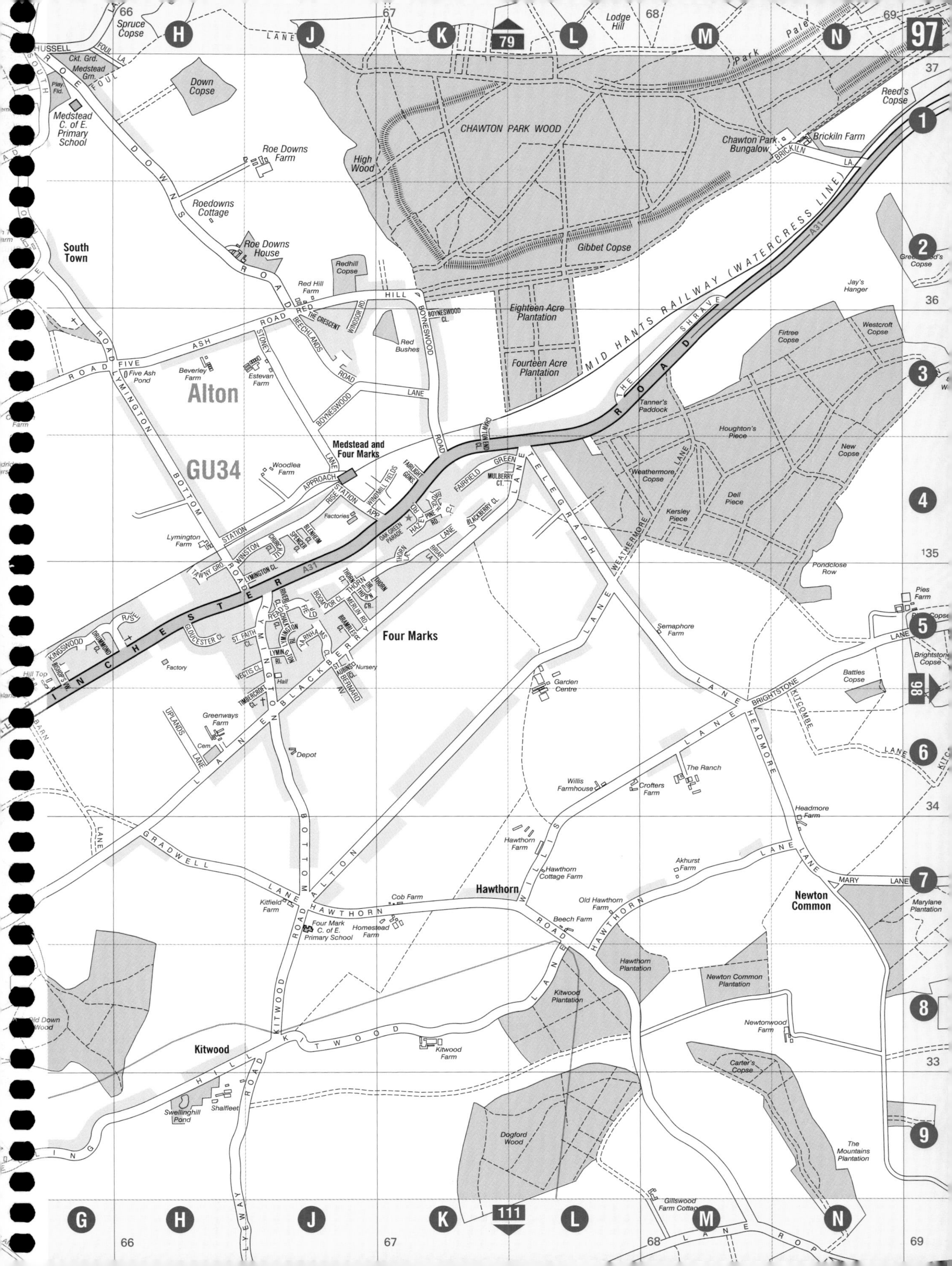
Spruce Copse
Lodge Hill
79
Down Copse
Medstead C. of E. Primary School
CHAWTON PARK WOOD
High Wood
Roe Downs Farm
Roedowns Cottage
Chawton Park Bungalow
Brickiln Farm
Reed's Copse
South Town
Roe Downs House
Gibbet Copse
Redhill Copse
Red Hill Farm
MID HANTS RAILWAY (WATERCRESS LINE)
Eighteen Acre Plantation
Fourteen Acre Plantation
Red Bushes
Jay's Hanger
Westcroft Copse
Firtree Copse
Five Ash Pond
Beverley Farm
Estevan Farm
Alton
GU34
Medstead and Four Marks
Woodlea Farm
Tanner's Paddock
Houghton's Piece
New Copse
Weathermore Copse
Dell Piece
Kersley Piece
Lymington Farm
Factories
Pondclose Row
Pies Farm
Semaphore Farm
Four Marks
Factory
Nursery
Hall
Garden Centre
Brightstone Copse
Battles Copse
98
Greenways Farm
Cem.
Depot
The Ranch
Willis Farmhouse
Crofters Farm
Headmore Farm
Hawthorn Farm
Hawthorn Cottage Farm
Akhurst Farm
Kitfield Farm
Cob Farm
Hawthorn
Newton Common
Marylane Plantation
Old Hawthorn Farm
Beech Farm
Four Mark C. of E. Primary School
Homestead Farm
Hawthorn Plantation
Newton Common Plantation
Kitwood Plantation
Old Down Wood
Newtonwood Farm
Kitwood
Kitwood Farm
Carter's Copse
Swellinghill Pond
Shalfleet
Dogford Wood
The Mountains Plantation
Gillswood Farm Cottage
111
A31
WINCHESTER ROAD
GRADWELL LANE
HAWTHORN ROAD
ALTON LANE
BLACKBERRY LANE
WEATHERMORE LANE
TELEGRAPH LANE
BRIGHTSTONE LANE
HEADMORE LANE
MARY LANE
KITWOOD ROAD
KITWOOD LANE
LYEWAY ROAD
BOTTOM ROAD
LYMINGTON BOTTOM
FIVE ASH ROAD
RED HILL
BOYNESWOOD ROAD
STATION APPROACH
THE SHRAVE
ROE DOWNS ROAD

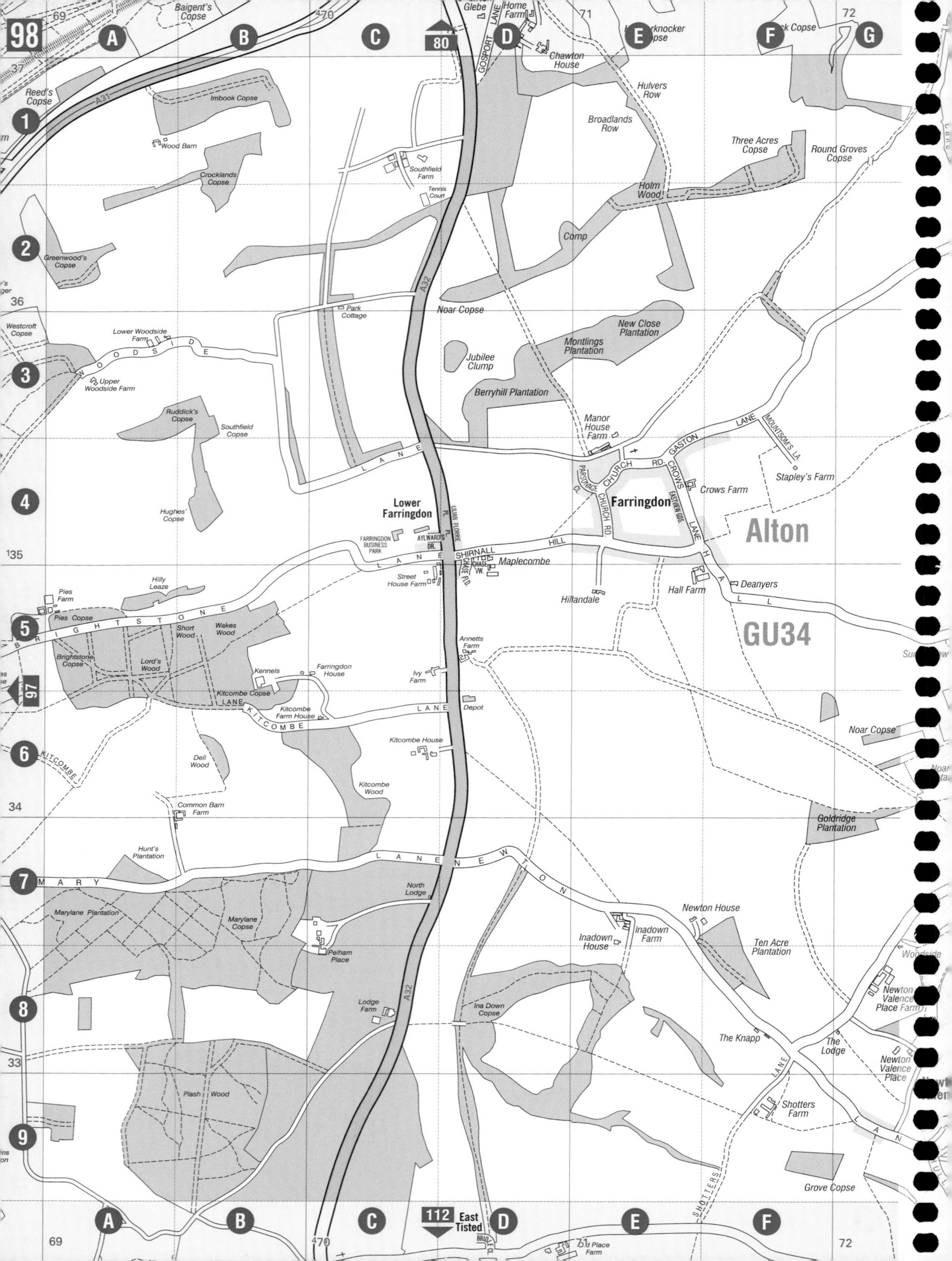

A
B
C
80
D
E
F
G
Baigent's Copse
Reed's Copse
A31
Imbook Copse
Wood Barn
Crocklands Copse
Greenwood's Copse
Southfield Farm
Tennis Court
Glebe
Home Farm
GOSPORT LANE
Chawton House
Hulvers Row
Broadlands Row
Three Acres Copse
Round Groves Copse
Holm Wood
Comp
A32
Noar Copse
New Close Plantation
Montlings Plantation
Jubilee Clump
Berryhill Plantation
Park Cottage
Westcroft Copse
Lower Woodside Farm
WOODSIDE
Upper Woodside Farm
Ruddick's Copse
Southfield Copse
Hughes' Copse
LANE
Manor House Farm
GASTON LANE
MOUNTSOM'S LA
Stapley's Farm
CHURCH RD
PARSONAGE CL
CROWS LANE
EASTVIEW GDS.
Crows Farm
Farringdon
CHURCH RD.
Alton
Lower Farringdon
FARRINGDON BUSINESS PARK
AYLWARD'S DR.
LILIAN PL.
FLORRIE PL.
SHIRNALL HILL
LANE
CHASE FLD.
CHASE VW.
Maplecombe
Street House Farm
Hillandale
Hall Farm
Deanyers
HALL
GU34
Hilly Leaze
Pies Farm
Pies Copse
BRIGHTSTONE
Short Wood
Wakes Wood
Brightstone Copse
Lord's Wood
Kennels
Farringdon House
Annetts Farm
Ivy Farm
Kitcombe Copse
LANE
Kitcombe Farm House
KITCOMBE LANE
Depot
97
KITCOMBE
Dell Wood
Kitcombe House
Kitcombe Wood
Noar Copse
Common Barn Farm
Goldridge Plantation
Hunt's Plantation
MARY LANE
NEWTON
North Lodge
Marylane Plantation
Marylane Copse
Pelham Place
Newton House
Inadown House
Inadown Farm
Ten Acre Plantation
Woodside
Newton Valence Place Farm
Lodge Farm
Ina Down Copse
The Knapp
The Lodge
Newton Valence Place
Plash Wood
LANE
Shotters Farm
SHOTTERS
Grove Copse
A
B
C
112 East Tisted
D
E
F
69
470
71
72
37
36
135
34
33
1
2
3
4
5
6
7
8
9
BRIDLE CL.
Old Place Farm

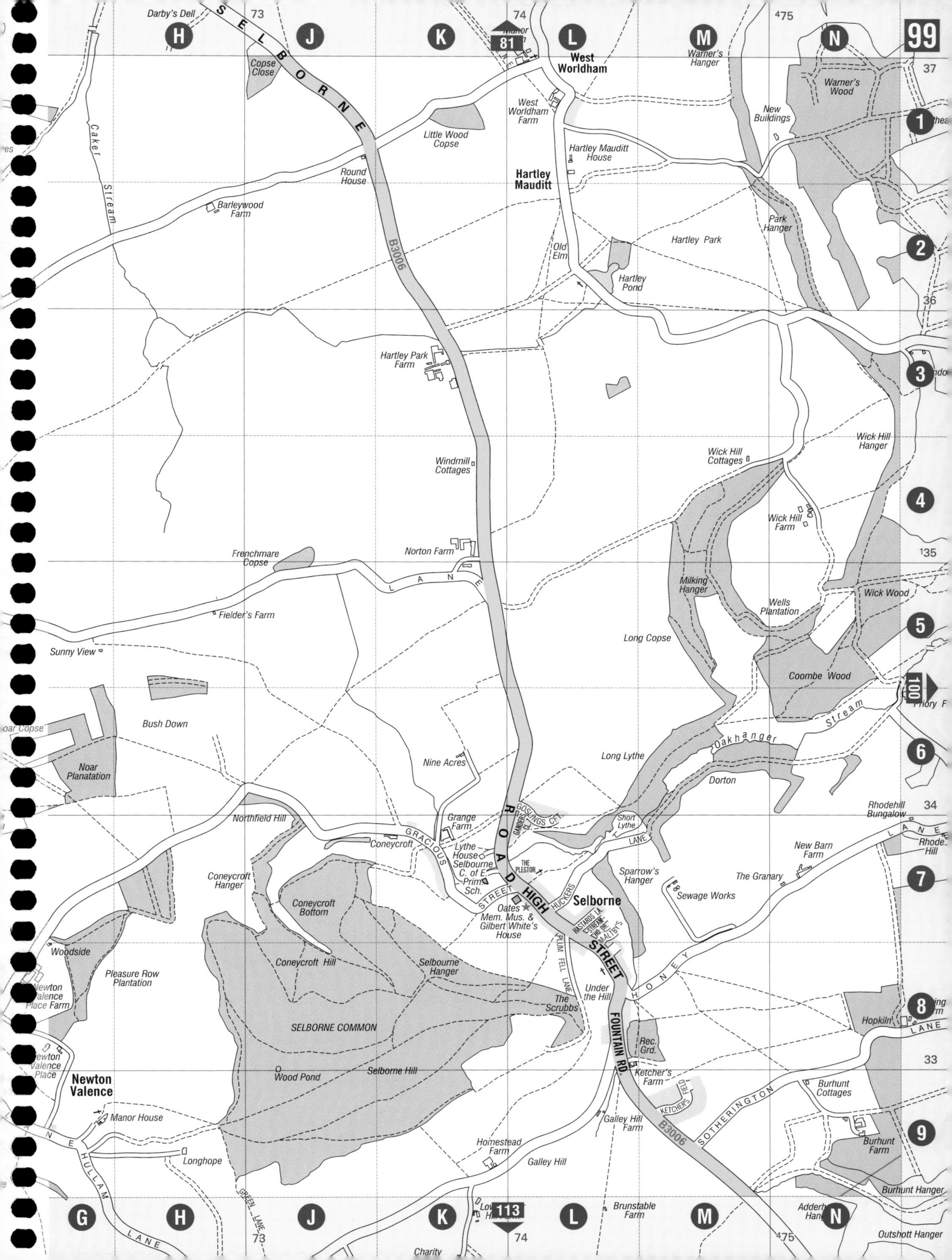
West Worldham
Hartley Mauditt
Selborne
Newton Valence
SELBORNE ROAD
B3006
HIGH STREET
FOUNTAIN RD.
SELBORNE COMMON
Selborne Hill
Wood Pond
Coneycroft Hill
Coneycroft Bottom
Coneycroft Hanger
Selbourne Hanger
The Scrubbs
Northfield Hill
Coneycroft
GRACIOUS STREET
Grange Farm
Lythe House
Selbourne C. of E. Prim. Sch.
Oates Mem. Mus. & Gilbert White's House
THE PLESTOR
HUCKERS
GOSLINGS CFT.
GANDERS CL.
PLUM FELL LANE
Under the Hill
Rec. Grd.
Ketcher's Farm
KETCHER'S FIELD
Galley Hill Farm
Galley Hill
Homestead Farm
SOTHERINGTON LANE
HONEY LANE
Sparrow's Hanger
Sewage Works
The Granary
New Barn Farm
Rhodehill Bungalow
Rhode Hill
Hopkiln
Burhunt Cottages
Burhunt Farm
Burhunt Hanger
Outshott Hanger
Brunstable Farm
Charity
Short Lythe
Long Lythe
Dorton
Oakhanger Stream
Coombe Wood
Wick Wood
Wells Plantation
Milking Hanger
Long Copse
Wick Hill Farm
Wick Hill Cottages
Wick Hill Hanger
Hartley Park
Hartley Pond
Old Elm
Park Hanger
Hartley Mauditt House
New Buildings
Warner's Wood
Warner's Hanger
West Worldham Farm
Little Wood Copse
Round House
Barleywood Farm
Caker Stream
Copse Close
Darby's Dell
Hartley Park Farm
Windmill Cottages
Norton Farm
Frenchmare Copse
LANE
Fielder's Farm
Sunny View
Bush Down
Noar Planatation
Nine Acres
Woodside
Pleasure Row Plantation
Newton Valence Place Farm
Newton Valence Place
Manor House
Longhope
HULLAM LANE
GREEN LANE
Priory F
H J K L M N G
1 2 3 4 5 6 7 8 9
73 74 475
37 36 135 34 33
81 100 113

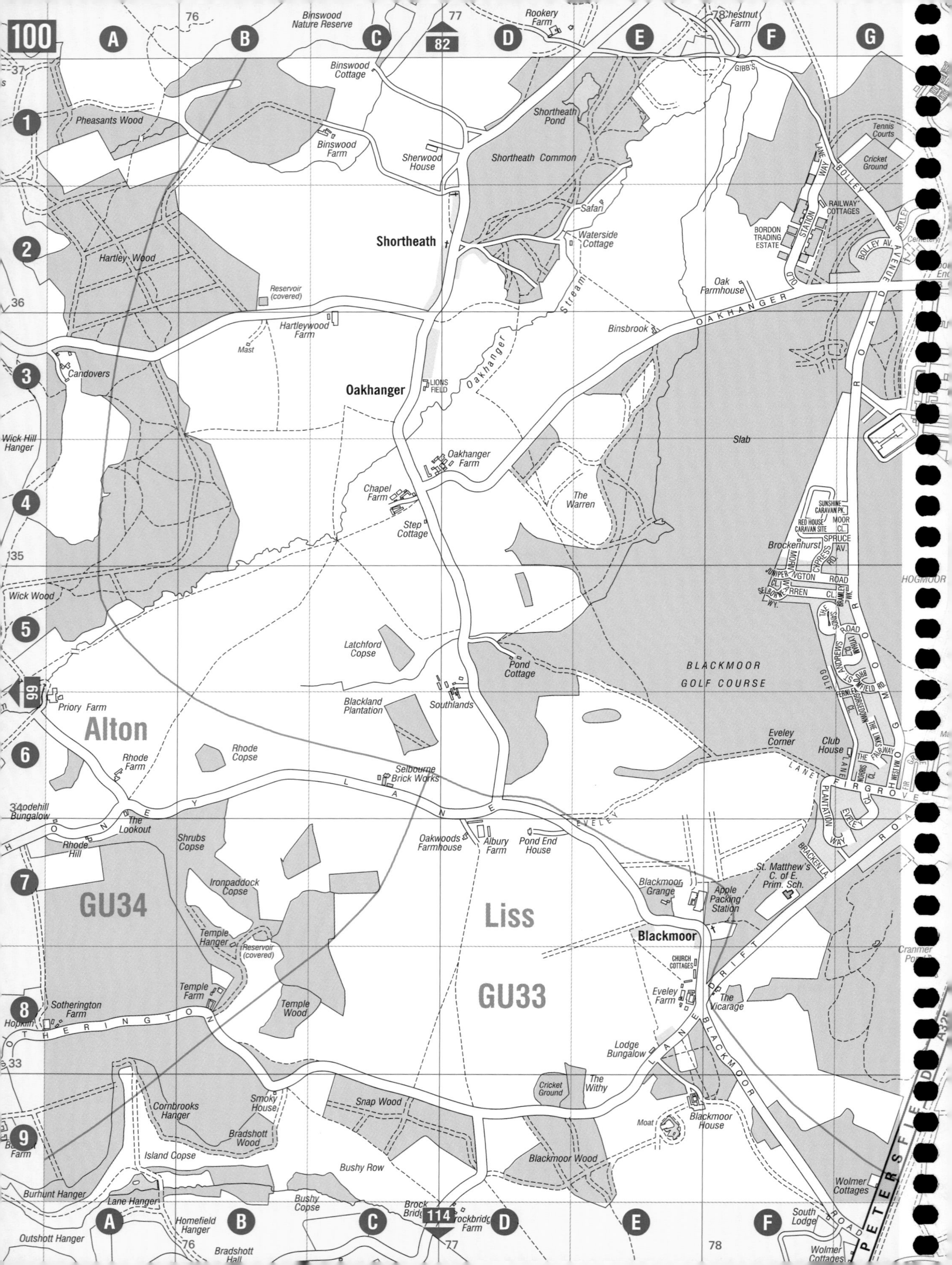

A
B
C
D
E
F
G
82
99
114
Binswood Nature Reserve
Rookery Farm
Chestnut Farm
Binswood Cottage
Pheasants Wood
Binswood Farm
Sherwood House
Shortheath Pond
Shortheath Common
Shortheath
Hartley Wood
Reservoir (covered)
Hartleywood Farm
Mast
Candovers
Oakhanger
Lions Field
Safari
Waterside Cottage
Oak Farmhouse
Binsbrook
Oakhanger Road
Bordon Trading Estate
Railway Cottages
Tennis Courts
Cricket Ground
Bolley Avenue
Wick Hill Hanger
Oakhanger Farm
Chapel Farm
Step Cottage
The Warren
Slab
Wick Wood
Latchford Copse
Pond Cottage
Blackmoor Golf Course
Priory Farm
Alton
Blackland Plantation
Southlands
Rhode Farm
Rhode Copse
Selbourne Brick Works
Eveley Corner
Club House
Hogmoor
Rhodehill Bungalow
The Lookout
Rhode Hill
Shrubs Copse
Oakwoods Farmhouse
Albury Farm
Pond End House
Ironpaddock Copse
GU34
Liss
Blackmoor Grange
Apple Packing Station
St. Matthew's C. of E. Prim. Sch.
Temple Hanger
Reservoir (covered)
Blackmoor
Church Cottages
Temple Farm
Temple Wood
GU33
Eveley Farm
The Vicarage
Sotherington Farm
Lodge Bungalow
Cricket Ground
The Withy
Cornbrooks Hanger
Smoky House
Snap Wood
Blackmoor House
Moat
Bradshott Wood
Island Copse
Bushy Row
Blackmoor Wood
Burhunt Hanger
Lane Hanger
Bushy Copse
Brockbridge Farm
Homefield Hanger
Wolmer Cottages
South Lodge
Outshott Hanger
Bradshott Hall
Petersfield Road
A325

Martinique Barracks
Oxney Pool
The Broca
Broxhead House
Reservoirs
Broxhead Farm
Instead Farm
Parade Ground
Amherst House
Bordon Camp
Louisburg Barbados Barracks
Wolfe Lodge
Sports Grd.
Lindford Bridge
Lindford Farm
St. Lucia House
Bordon Inclosure
Huntingford Farm
The Holme C. of E. Prim. Sch.
HEADLEY
Coolgreany Gardens
Hatch House Farm
The Triangle
Sewage Works
Weydown Farm
Chase Farm
Watermeadow Farm
Deadwater
LINDFORD
Headley Mill Farm
Headley Mill
Stream Farm
Reynolds House
The Meadow School
Mill Chase Community Sch.
Playing Field
Standford Grange Farm
The Oaks
Standford House
Standford Mill
Wey Valley Farm
Hatch Farm
Standford
Standford Grange
Sewage Works
PASSFIELD MILL BUSINESS PARK
Selbourne End
Cemetery
Playing Field
Bordon Jun. & Inf. Schools
Prince Philip Barracks
Bordon
GU35
Guadaloupe House
WOOLMER TRADING ESTATE
BORDON
Alexandra Park
TRENCHARD PARK
ST. LUCIA PARK
Weyford Jun. & Inf. Schs.
HOGMOOR INCLOSURE
Whitehill Chase
CHASE COMM. HOSP.
Comm. Cen.
Lib.
Eveley Wood
Whitehill
Forest Lodge
Woodlea Primary School
Earthwork
Hollywater Farm
Hollywater
The Firs
PASSFIELD COMMON
Tennis Court
Thornhill House
PASSFIELD ENTERPRISE CENTRE
Hollywater Green
WHITEHILL PARK
Mast
Round Hill
Hollywater Clump
Thorn Hill
Hollywater Pond
Lynchborough Wood
Lynchborough Lodge
Conford Moor
Cranmer Pond
Rifle Range
Fern Hill
Park Hill
Liphook
Keeper's Hill
Rifle Range
Horsebush Hill
Linchborough Park
Polecat Hill
GU30
Cranmer Bottom
WOOLMER FOREST
BRIMSTONE INCLOSURE
HIGH STREET CAMP ROAD
FARNHAM ROAD
A325
STATION ROAD
LINDFORD ROAD
B3002
BUDDS LANE
B3004
BROXHEAD FARM RD.
LIPHOOK ROAD
HEADLEY ROAD
STANDFORD LANE
MILL LANE
MILL CHASE ROAD
LIPHOOK ROAD
WALLDOWN ROAD
WHITEHILL ROAD
HOLLYWATER ROAD
FIELD
83
115
102
79
80
81
82
37
36
135
34
33
H J K L M N
G H J K L M N
1 2 3 4 5 6 7 8 9

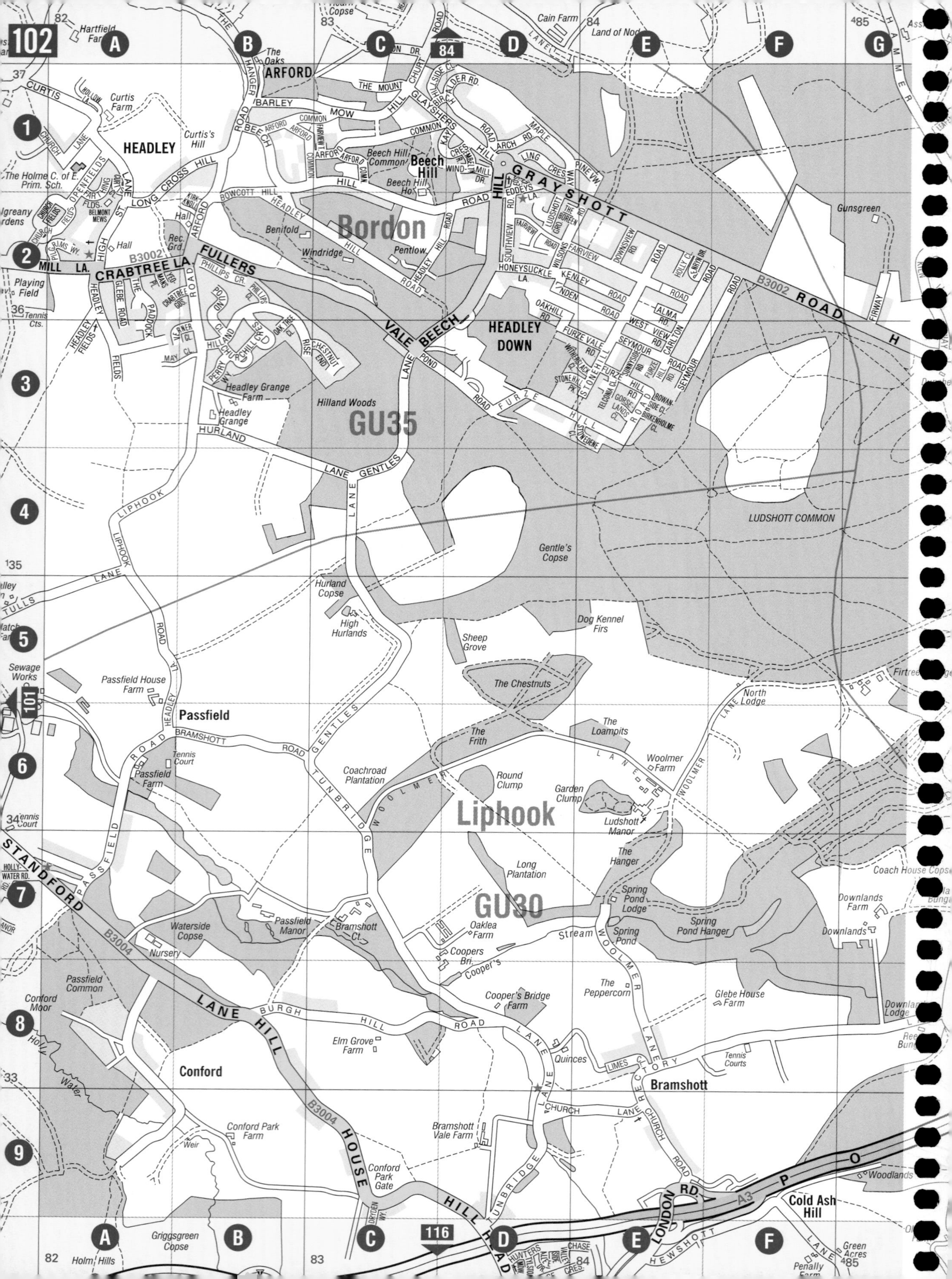

HEADLEY
ARFORD
Bordon
Beech Hill
GRAYSHOTT
HEADLEY DOWN
GU35
Passfield
Liphook
GU30
Conford
Bramshott
LUDSHOTT COMMON
Cold Ash Hill
Curtis Farm
Curtis's Hill
The Holme C. of E. Prim. Sch.
Beech Hill Common
Beech Hill Ho
Benifold
Windridge
Pentlow
Headley Grange Farm
Headley Grange
Hilland Woods
Gentle's Copse
Hurland Copse
High Hurlands
Sheep Grove
Dog Kennel Firs
The Chestnuts
The Frith
The Loampits
North Lodge
Woolmer Farm
Round Clump
Garden Clump
Ludshott Manor
The Hanger
Long Plantation
Coachroad Plantation
Passfield House Farm
Passfield Farm
Sewage Works
Tennis Court
Playing Field
Gunsgreen
Spring Pond Lodge
Spring Pond
Spring Pond Hanger
Downlands Farm
Downlands
Coach House Copse
Oaklea Farm
Coopers Bri.
Cooper's Bridge Farm
The Peppercorn
Glebe House Farm
Elm Grove Farm
Quinces
Tennis Courts
Waterside Copse
Passfield Manor
Bramshott Ct.
Nursery
Passfield Common
Conford Moor
Hollywater
Conford Park Farm
Weir
Conford Park Gate
Bramshott Vale Farm
Griggsgreen Copse
Holm Hills
Woodlands
Green Acres
Penally Farm
Cain Farm
Land of Nod
Hartfield Farm
The Oaks
CURTIS
CHURCH LANE
LONG CROSS HILL
MILL LA.
CRABTREE LA.
FULLERS
B3002
ROAD
HEADLEY FIELDS
GLEBE ROAD
PADDOCK
ARFORD ROAD
HEADLEY HILL ROAD
BOWCOTT HILL
BEECH HILL
VALE
BEECH
LANE
POND ROAD
FURZE HILL
HURLAND LANE
GENTLES LANE
LIPHOOK ROAD
TULLS LANE
HEADLEY ROAD
BRAMSHOTT ROAD
TUNBRIDGE LANE
WOOLMER LANE
PASSFIELD
STANDFORD LANE
B3004
BURGH HILL ROAD
HEADLEY DOWN
HOUSE HILL
LONDON RD.
A3
HEWSHOTT LANE
RECTORY LANE
CHURCH LANE
CHURCH ROAD
LIMES
GRAYSHOTT ROAD
B3002 ROAD
FIRWAY
HONEYSUCKLE LA.
WEST VIEW RD.
SEYMOUR ROAD
CARLTON
FURZE VALE RD.
OAKHILL RD.
STONEHILL
KENLEY ROAD
DENEN ROAD
ALMA RD.
HOLLY CL.
FAIRVIEW
DOWNSVIEW RD.
SOUTHVIEW RD.
LUDSHOTT GRO.
THE BOREEN
LING CRES
MAPLE
LARCH RD.
PINEVW
GLAYSHERS HILL
HILLSIDE CL.
ALDER RD.
THE MOUNT
BARLEY MOW HILL
COMMON
HANGER
Cooper's
Stream
84
116
101
A B C D E F G
1 2 3 4 5 6 7 8 9
82 83 84 85
37 36 35 34 33

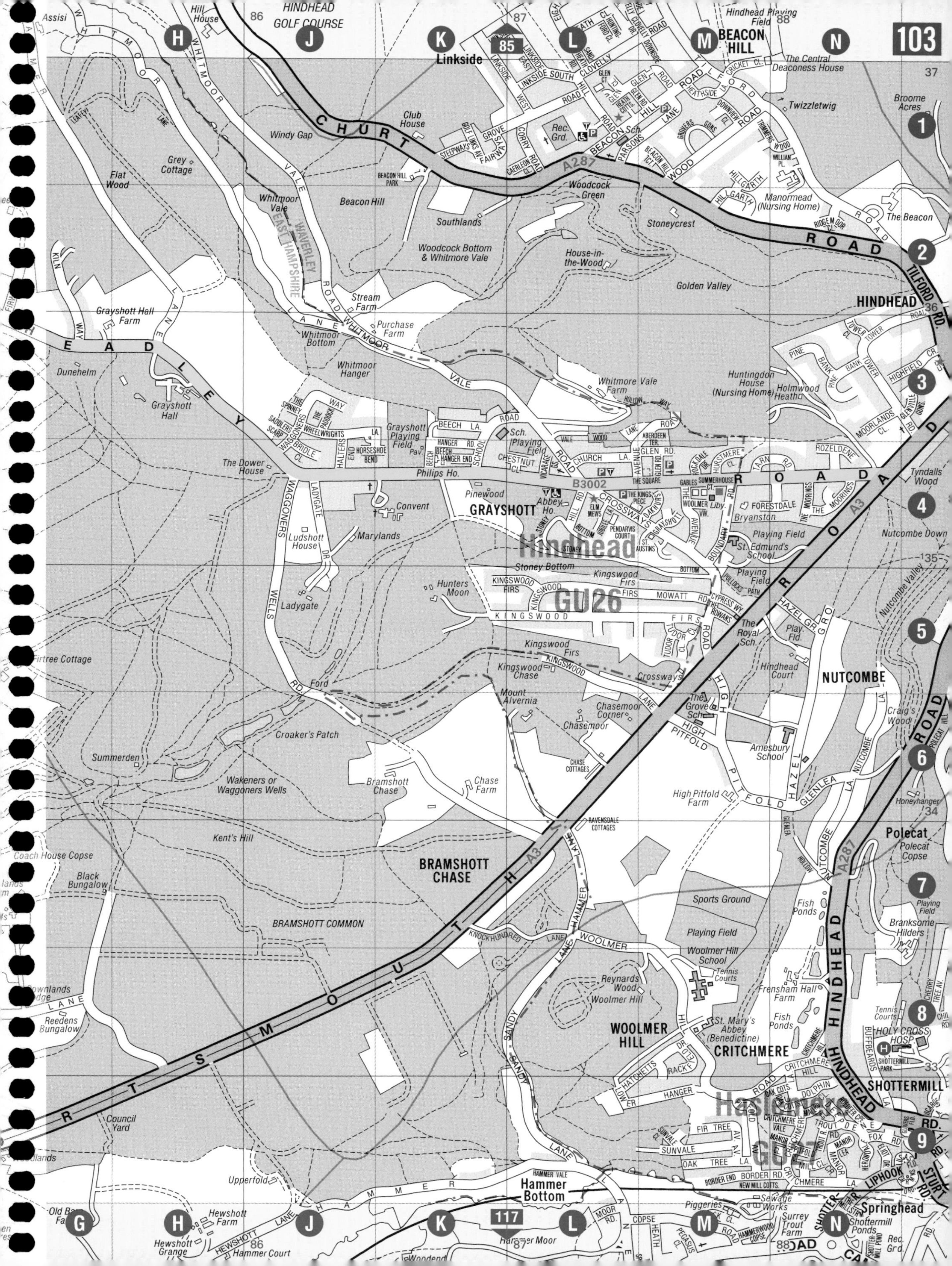
HINDHEAD GOLF COURSE
Linkside
BEACON HILL
Hindhead Playing Field
The Central Deaconess House
Broome Acres
Twizzletwig
CHURT ROAD
A287
Club House
Windy Gap
Grey Cottage
Flat Wood
Whitmoor Vale
Beacon Hill
Southlands
Woodcock Green
Stoneycrest
Manormead (Nursing Home)
The Beacon
Woodcock Bottom & Whitmore Vale
House-in-the-Wood
Golden Valley
HINDHEAD
EAST HAMPSHIRE
WAVERLEY
Stream Farm
Purchase Farm
Whitmoor Bottom
Grayshott Hall Farm
HEADLEY ROAD
Dunehelm
Grayshott Hall
Whitmoor Hanger
Whitmore Vale Farm
Huntingdon House (Nursing Home)
Holmwood Heath
Grayshott Playing Field
The Dower House
Philips Ho.
B3002
Pinewood
Convent
GRAYSHOTT
Abbey Ho.
Ludshott House
Marylands
Hindhead
GU26
Stoney Bottom
Kingswood Firs
Hunters Moon
Ladygate
Bryanston
Playing Field
St. Edmund's School
Tyndalls Wood
Nutcombe Down
Nutcombe Valley
The Royal Sch.
Firtree Cottage
Kingswood Chase
Crossways
Hindhead Court
NUTCOMBE
Mount Alvernia
Ford
Chasemoor Corner
Chasemoor
The Grove Sch.
Craig's Wood
Croaker's Patch
Amesbury School
Summerden
Bramshott Chase
Chase Farm
Wakeners or Waggoners Wells
High Pitfold Farm
Honeyhanger
Polecat
Polecat Copse
Kent's Hill
RAVENSDALE COTTAGES
Coach House Copse
BRAMSHOTT CHASE
Black Bungalow
Sports Ground
Fish Ponds
Branksome Hilders
BRAMSHOTT COMMON
Playing Field
Woolmer Hill School
Reynards Wood
Woolmer Hill
Frensham Hall Farm
Reedens Bungalow
PORTSMOUTH ROAD
A3
WOOLMER HILL
St. Mary's Abbey (Benedictine)
CRITCHMERE
HOLY CROSS HOSP
SHOTTERMILL
Haslemere
GU27
Council Yard
Upperfold
Hammer Bottom
Hewshott Farm
Hewshott Grange
Hammer Court
Hammer Moor
Piggeries
Sewage Works
Surrey Trout Farm
Springhead
Shottermill Ponds
HINDHEAD ROAD
85
117

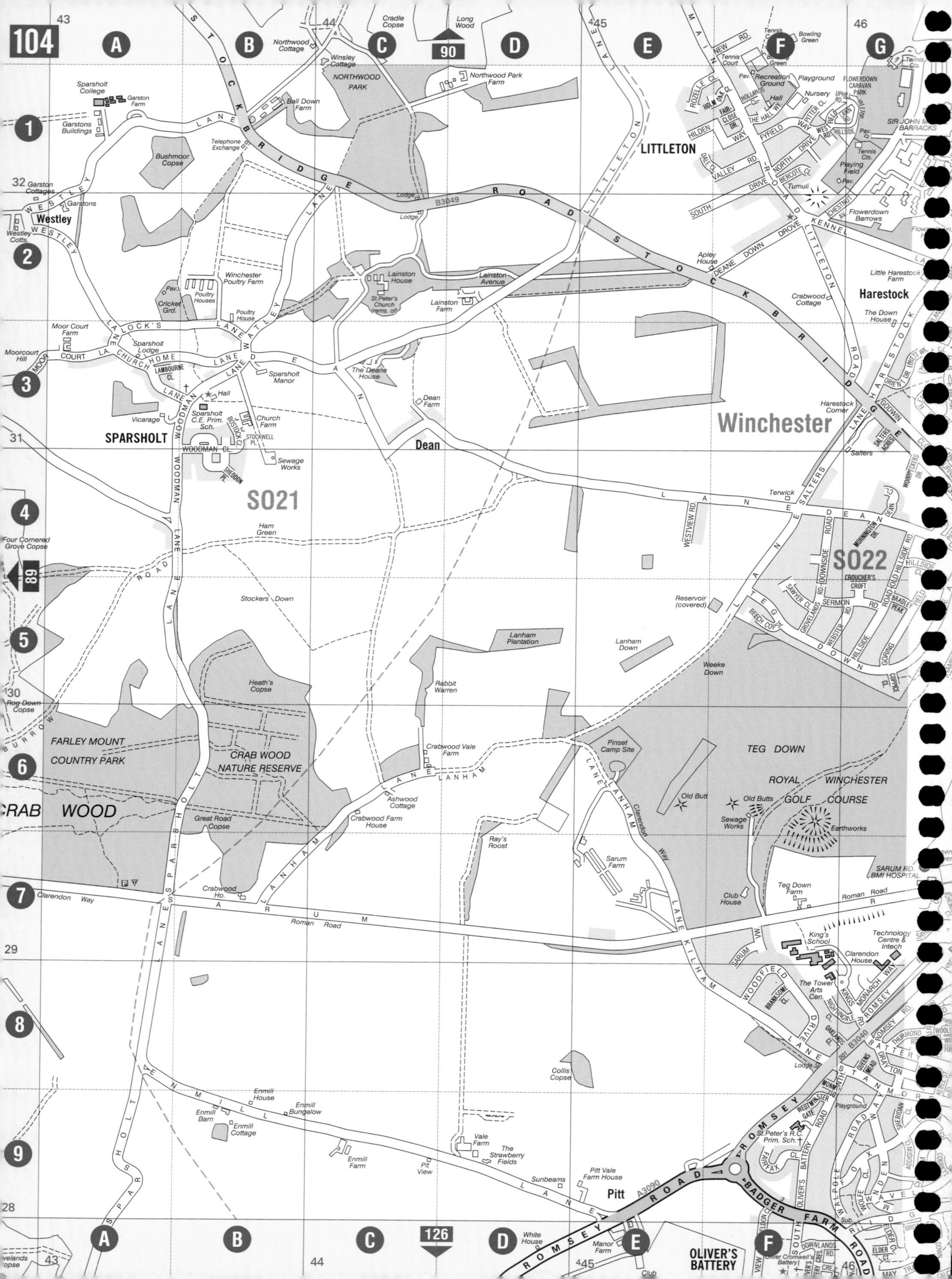

LITTLETON
Westley
Harestock
Winchester
SPARSHOLT
Dean
SO21
SO22
FARLEY MOUNT COUNTRY PARK
CRAB WOOD NATURE RESERVE
CRAB WOOD
TEG DOWN
ROYAL WINCHESTER GOLF COURSE
Pitt
OLIVER'S BATTERY
STOCKBRIDGE ROAD
ROMSEY ROAD
BADGER FARM ROAD
SARUM ROAD
Roman Road
Clarendon Way
KILHAM LANE
LANHAM LANE
SPARSHOLT LANE
WOODMAN LANE
ENMILL LANE
DEANE DOWN DROVE
Sparsholt College
Lainston House
Lanham Plantation
Weeke Down
Sir John Moore Barracks
King's School
Pinset Camp Site
Heath's Copse
Stockers Down
Ham Green
Enmill Farm
Vale Farm
Pitt Vale Farm House
Manor Farm
White House
90
89
126

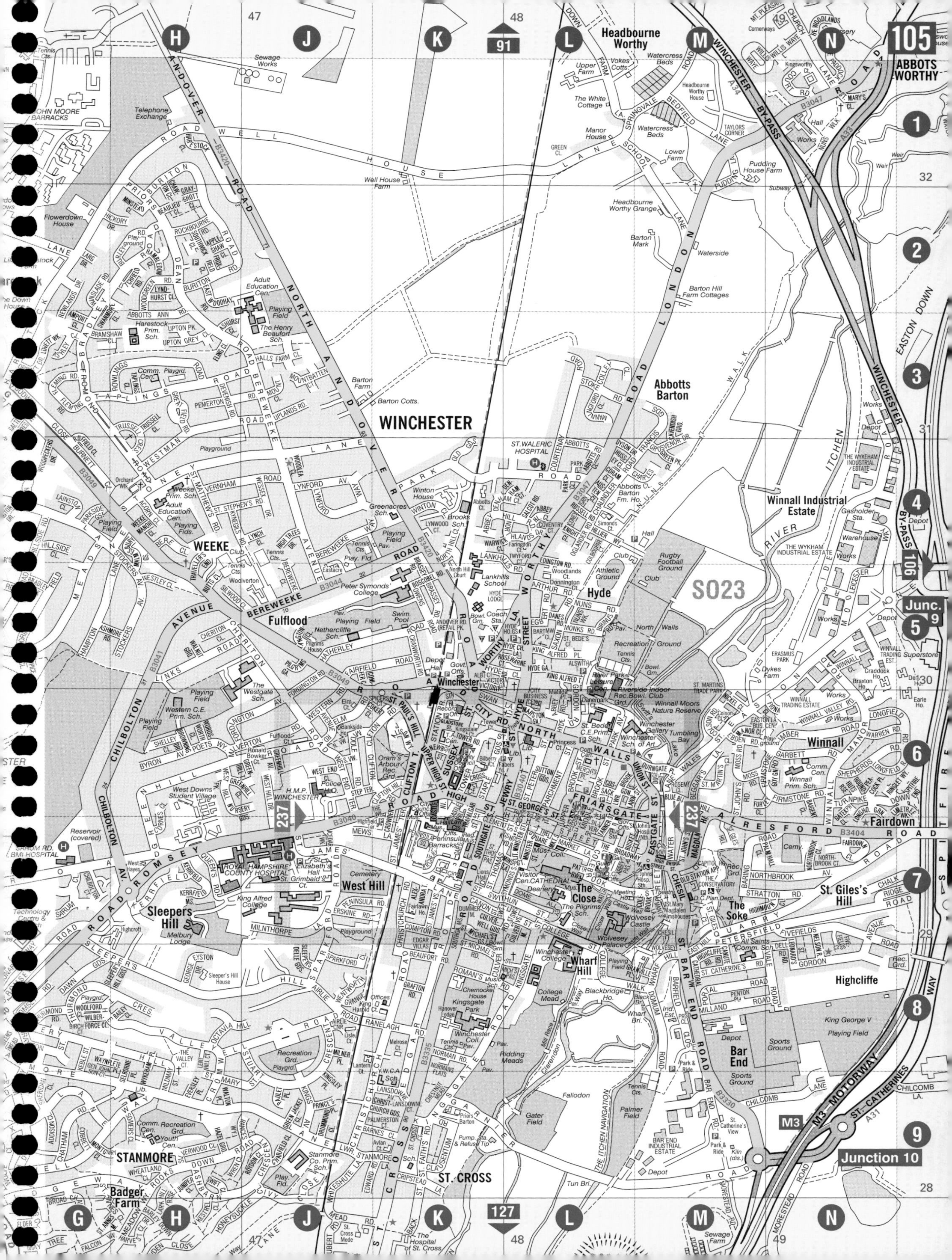
WINCHESTER
Headbourne Worthy
ABBOTS WORTHY
Abbotts Barton
Winnall Industrial Estate
WEEKE
Fulflood
Hyde
SO23
Winnall
Fairdown
St. Giles's Hill
The Soke
Highcliffe
Bar End
The Close
Wharf Hill
West Hill
Sleepers Hill
STANMORE
Badger Farm
ST. CROSS
WINCHESTER BY-PASS
M3 MOTORWAY
Junction 10
Junc. 9
ANDOVER ROAD
NORTH WALLS
HIGH ST.
ROMSEY ROAD
ALRESFORD ROAD
LONDON ROAD
KINGSGATE RD.
CHILBOLTON AVENUE
BEREWEEKE ROAD
ROYAL HAMPSHIRE COUNTY HOSPITAL
CATHEDRAL
Winchester College
Wolvesey Castle
H.M.P. WINCHESTER
King Alfred College
Peter Symonds' College
Recreation Ground
King George V Playing Field
Sports Ground
The Hospital of St. Cross
91
127
237
106

ABBOTS WORTHY
Abbotsworthy House
Worthy Park Home Farm
The Worthy
Mill
Ford
WATER LA.
Subway
M3
River Itchen
New Cott.
Easton Bridge
Chilland
Lower Chilland House
Weir
Pumping Station
The Old Rectory
CHURCH LANE
THE TERRACE
EASTON
Power House
Easton Lodge
Hall
St. Mary's Rectory
Sports Grd.
Chapel Field
Cocket's Mead
Earthwork
Beech Hill
Low Ground
EASTON DOWN
M3 MOTORWAY
Dairy Farm
Dairy Cottages
Lone Barn
EASTON LANE
Easton Manor Farm
CHAPEL LANE
DUKES
Winchester
Winnall Cottage Farm
White Hill Cott.
Shoulder of Mutton Farm
LONG WALK
Harfield Farm
Harley Hill
SO21
WINCHESTER BY-PASS
A33
Works
Depot
THE WYKEHAM INDUSTRIAL ESTATE
MOORSIDE ROAD
Junction 9
LINK
EASTON LANE
WINNALL TRADING EST.
Superstore
A272
Dennett Ho.
Earle Ho.
Craddock Ho.
LONGFIELD RD.
WINNALL MANOR RD.
Larkwhistle Farm
Pits Copse
Winnall Down Copse
Roseacre
Winnall Down Farm
Three Acres
Pits Farm
St. Swithun's School
Tennis Cts.
SPITFIRE
FAIR LANE
No Man's Land
Magdalen Hill Farm
Glencross
Narcunda
The Holding
Morn Hill Caravan Site
Green Pastures
Pits Farm House
Thornacre
Fairdown
ALRESFORD ROAD
B3404
ALRESFORD ROAD A31
Tumuli
MAGDALEN HILL DOWN
Works
Lodge
Magdalen Hill Cemetery
The Firs
QUARRY RD.
PETERSFIELD RD.
PETERSFIELD ROAD
A31
KINGS LANE
The Bungalow
M3 MOTORWAY
SPITFIRE WAY
Sports Ground
South Downs Way
Rec. Grd.
Highcliffe
Chilcomb Down
A272
Works
ST. CATHERINES
CHILCOMB
Range Cott.
The Manor House
Complyns
Chilcomb Manor
St. Kilda's
Hazeldown
Chilcomb
Hillacre
Tops and Bottoms Plantation
Velpins Bank Plantation
GYPSY LANE
Telegraph Hill
Telegraph Clump
Chilcomb Ranges
Rookery Cottages
Deacon View
Little Golders
92
105
134
A B C D E F G
1 2 3 4 5 6 7 8 9
450 51 52
32 31 130 29 28

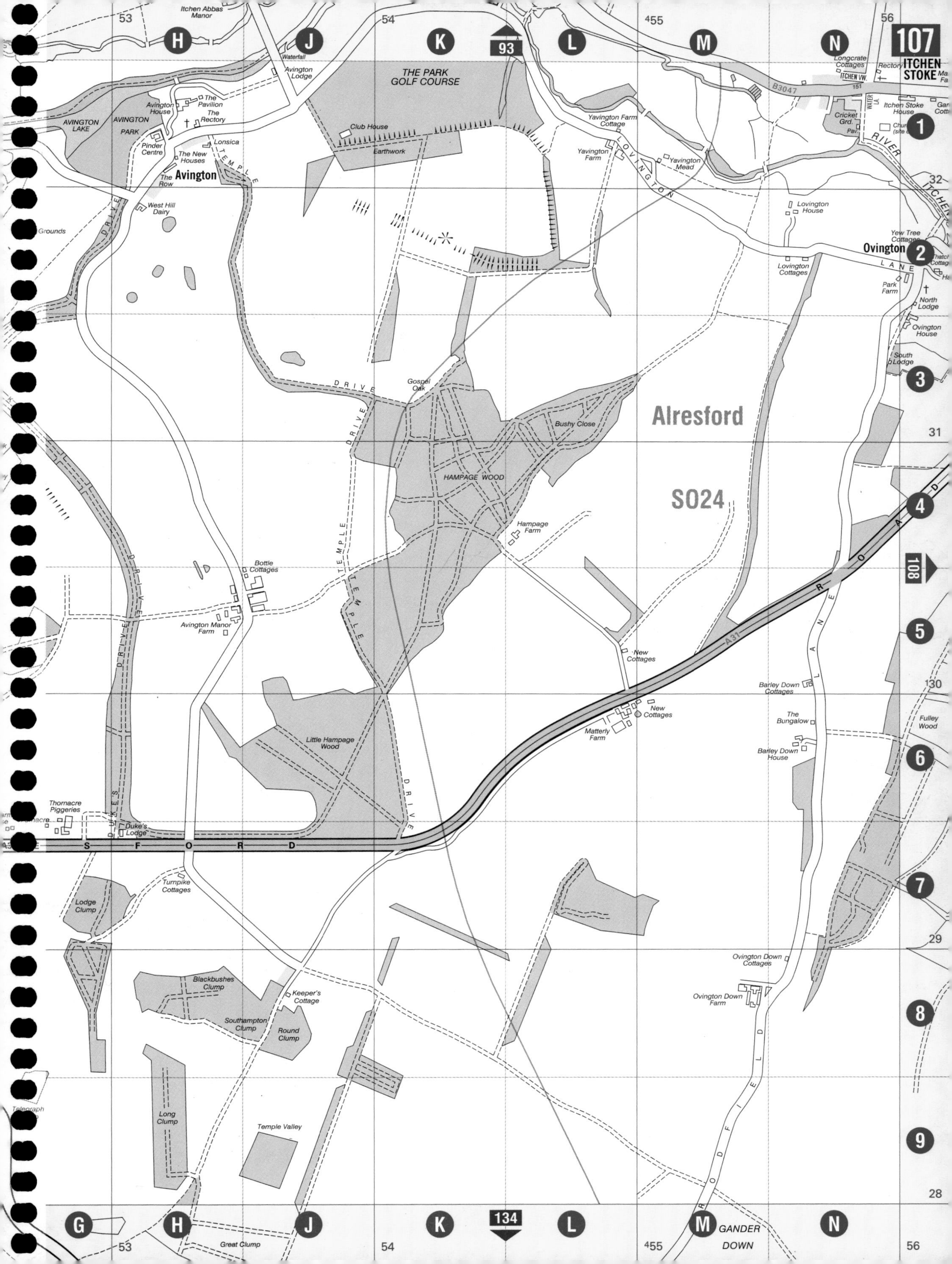
107
ITCHEN STOKE
Itchen Abbas Manor
Waterfall
Avington Lodge
THE PARK GOLF COURSE
Club House
Earthwork
Avington House
The Pavilion
The Rectory
AVINGTON LAKE
AVINGTON PARK
Pinder Centre
Lonsica
The New Houses
The Row
Avington
West Hill Dairy
Grounds
TEMPLE
DRIVE
Yavington Farm Cottage
Yavington Farm
Yavington Mead
LOVINGTON
LANE
Longcrate Cottages
Rectory
ITCHEN VW.
B3047
Itchen Stoke House
Cricket Grd.
WATER LA.
RIVER
ITCHEN
Lovington House
Lovington Cottages
Ovington
Yew Tree Cottage
Park Farm
North Lodge
Ovington House
South Lodge
Gospel Oak
Bushy Close
Alresford
HAMPAGE WOOD
SO24
Hampage Farm
Bottle Cottages
Avington Manor Farm
New Cottages
A31
ROAD
Barley Down Cottages
The Bungalow
Barley Down House
Fulley Wood
Matterly Farm
Little Hampage Wood
Thornacre Piggeries
DUKES
Duke's Lodge
SFORD
Turnpike Cottages
Lodge Clump
Blackbushes Clump
Keeper's Cottage
Southampton Clump
Round Clump
Ovington Down Cottages
Ovington Down Farm
Long Clump
Temple Valley
RODFIELD
Telegraph
GANDER DOWN
Great Clump
93
108
134
53
54
455
56
32
31
130
29
28
H J K L M N
G H J K L M N
1 2 3 4 5 6 7 8 9

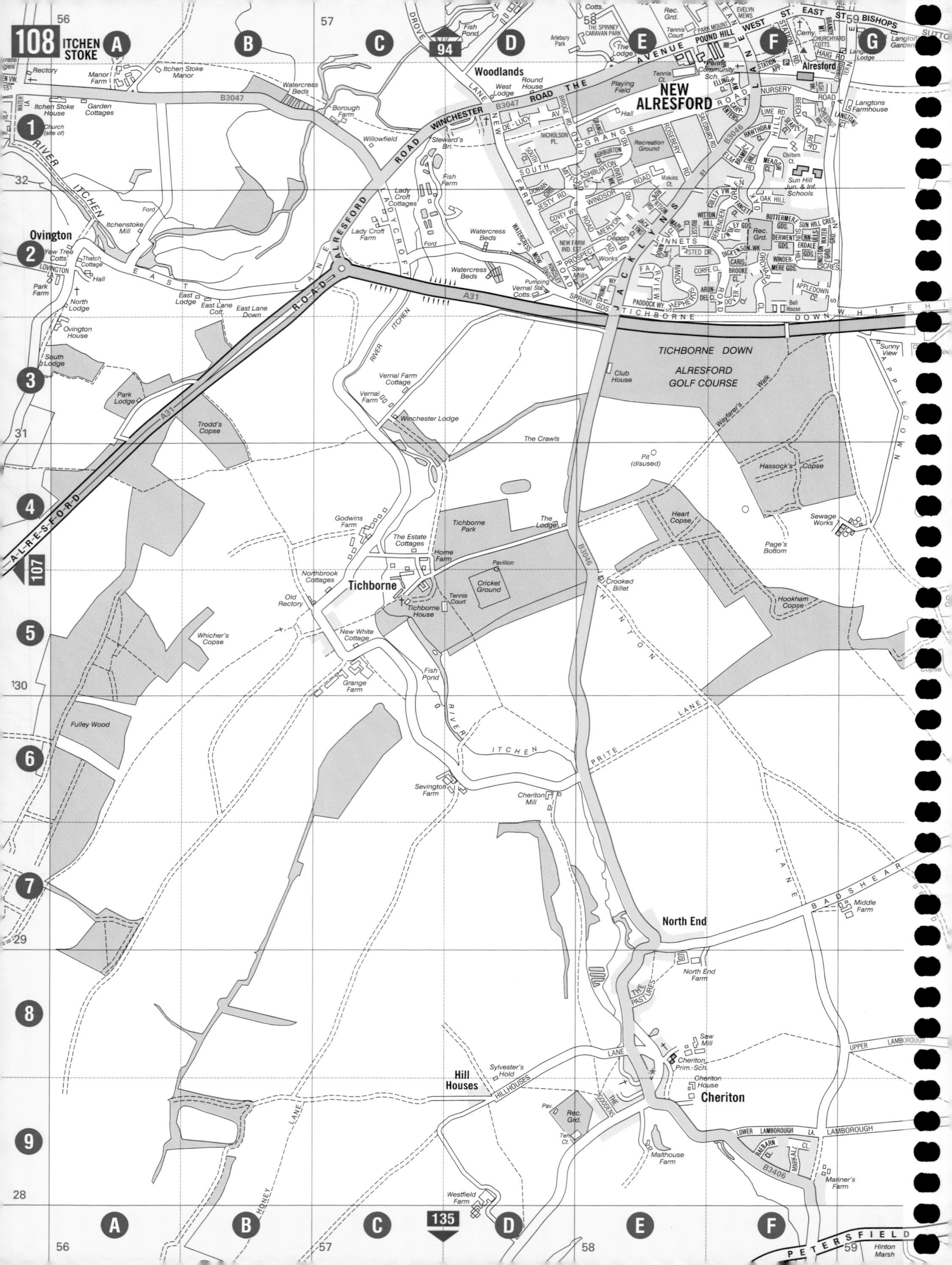
108
ITCHEN STOKE
A
B
C
D
E
F
G
56
57
58
59
94
107
135
Rectory
Manor Farm
Itchen Stoke Manor
Watercress Beds
B3047
Itchen Stoke House
Garden Cottages
Church (site of)
RIVER ITCHEN
Borough Farm
Willowfield
Woodlands
West Lodge
Round House
Fish Pond
Arlebury Park
THE SPINNEY CARAVAN PARK
The Lodge
Tennis Court
Rec. Grd.
EVELYN MEWS
PARK MOUNT
POUND HILL
WEST ST.
EAST ST.
BISHOPS
THE AVENUE
Parish Community Sch.
Tennis Ct.
Playing Field
Alresford
Cemy.
CHURCHYARD COTTS.
HAIG RD.
Langtons Lodge
NEW ALRESFORD
NURSERY
STATION RD.
STATION APP.
Langtons Farmhouse
LANGTONS CT.
WINCHESTER ROAD
Steward's Bri.
DE-LUCY AV.
Hall
GRANGE RD.
NICHOLSON PL.
Recreation Ground
ROSEBERY RD.
SALISBURY RD.
B3046
CARPENTERS
HAWTHORN CL.
LIME RD.
BEECH RD.
SOUTH RD.
SOUTH FARM
ASHBURTON CL.
ASHBURTON RD.
Makins Ct.
Chiltern Ct.
Sun Hill Jun. & Inf. Schools
Fish Farm
Lady Croft Cottages
LADYCROFT
DORIAN GRO.
JESTY RD.
WINDSOR RD.
ROAD
OAK HILL
COVEY WY.
MERYON RD.
JACKLYNS LANE
CULLEY VW.
WITTON HILL
BENENDEN
BUTTERMERE GDS.
SUN HILL CRES.
Lady Croft Farm
Watercress Beds
NEW FARM IND. EST.
PROSPECT RD.
Depots
LINNETS
Rec. Grd.
DERWENT GDS.
ERDALE
CONISTON
DICKENSON WK.
ASTED DR.
Ovington
Yew Tree Cotts.
Thatch Cottage
Hall
LOVINGTON
Itchenstoke Mill
Ford
Works
Saw Mill
Watercress Beds
Pumping Sta.
Vernal Cotts.
SPRING GDS.
FAIRVIEW
CORFE CL.
CARISBROOKE CL.
WINDERMERE GDS.
APPLEDOWN CL.
DOWN
PADDOCK WY.
SHEPHERDS
ARUNDEL CL.
ORCHARD CL.
Bell House
EAST LANE
ALRESFORD ROAD
A31
East Lodge
East Lane Cott.
East Lane Down
North Lodge
Park Farm
Ovington House
South Lodge
TICHBORNE DOWN
WHITE HILL
Sunny View
TICHBORNE DOWN
ALRESFORD GOLF COURSE
Club House
RIVER ITCHEN
Vernal Farm Cottage
Vernal Farm
Winchester Lodge
Park Lodge
Trodd's Copse
Wayfarer's Walk
The Crawls
Pit (disused)
Hassock's Copse
APPLEDOWN
Godwins Farm
Tichborne Park
The Lodge
Heart Copse
Sewage Works
The Estate Cottages
Home Farm
Page's Bottom
Pavilion
Cricket Ground
Northbrook Cottages
Tichborne
Old Rectory
Tennis Court
Tichborne House
Crooked Billet
HINTON
Hookham Copse
Whicher's Copse
New White Cottage
Fish Pond
Grange Farm
Fulley Wood
RIVER ITCHEN
PRITE LANE
Sevington Farm
Cheriton Mill
LANE
BADSHEAR
Middle Farm
North End
North End Farm
THE PASTURES
Saw Mill
UPPER LAMBOROUGH
Cheriton Prim. Sch.
Cheriton House
Hill Houses
Sylvester's Hold
HILLHOUSES LANE
Cheriton
THE GOODENS
Pav.
Rec. Grd.
Ten. Ct.
LOWER LAMBOROUGH LA.
LAMBOROUGH
RAEBARN CL.
MARKALL CL.
Malthouse Farm
B3406
Mariner's Farm
HONEY LANE
Westfield Farm
PETERSFIELD
Hinton Marsh
ALRESFORD ROAD
1
2
3
4
5
6
7
8
9
32
31
130
29
28

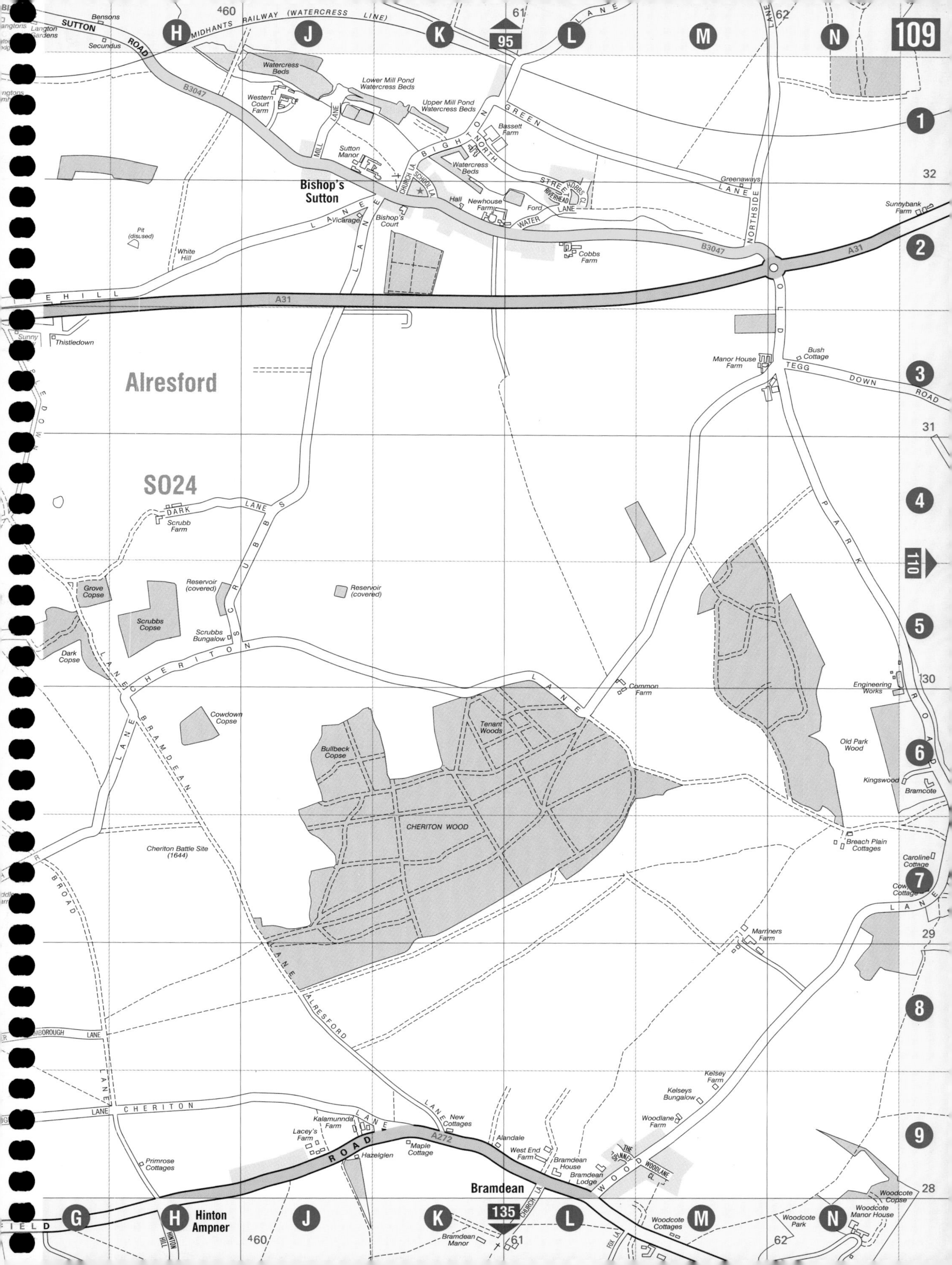
H
J
K
L
M
N
95
460
61
62
MIDHANTS RAILWAY (WATERCRESS LINE)
SUTTON ROAD
Bensons
Langton Gardens
Secundus
Watercress Beds
Lower Mill Pond Watercress Beds
Upper Mill Pond Watercress Beds
Western Court Farm
B3047
MILL LANE
Sutton Manor
Bishop's Sutton
BIGHTON
NORTH
GREEN
Bassett Farm
Watercress Beds
CHURCH LA.
SCHOOL LA.
Hall
Newhouse Farm
Ford
WATER LANE
STREET
HOBBS
RIVERHEAD
Greenaways
LANE
NORTHSIDE
Sunnybank Farm
Vicarage
Bishop's Court
Cobbs Farm
Pit (disused)
White Hill
A31
Thistledown
Alresford
SO24
OLD PARK ROAD
Manor House Farm
Bush Cottage
TEGG DOWN ROAD
DARK LANE
Scrubb Farm
SCRUBBS LANE
Grove Copse
Scrubbs Copse
Reservoir (covered)
Reservoir (covered)
Scrubbs Bungalow
Dark Copse
CHERITON LANE
Common Farm
Tenant Woods
Bullbeck Copse
Cowdown Copse
BRAMDEAN LANE
CHERITON WOOD
Old Park Wood
Engineering Works
Kingswood
Bramcote
Breach Plain Cottages
Caroline Cottage
Cheriton Battle Site (1644)
BROAD
Marriners Farm
ALRESFORD LANE
Kelsey Farm
Kelseys Bungalow
Woodlane Farm
CHERITON LANE
New Cottages
Kalamunnda Farm
Lacey's Farm
Hazelglen
Maple Cottage
A272
ROAD
Alandale
West End Farm
Bramdean House
Bramdean Lodge
THE SPINNEY
WOODLANE CL.
WOOD LANE
Bramdean
Primrose Cottages
Hinton Ampner
HINTON HILL
G
135
CHURCH LA.
Bramdean Manor
Woodcote Cottages
Woodcote Park
Woodcote Copse
Woodcote Manor House
FOX LA.
110
1
2
3
4
5
6
7
8
9
32
31
30
29
28

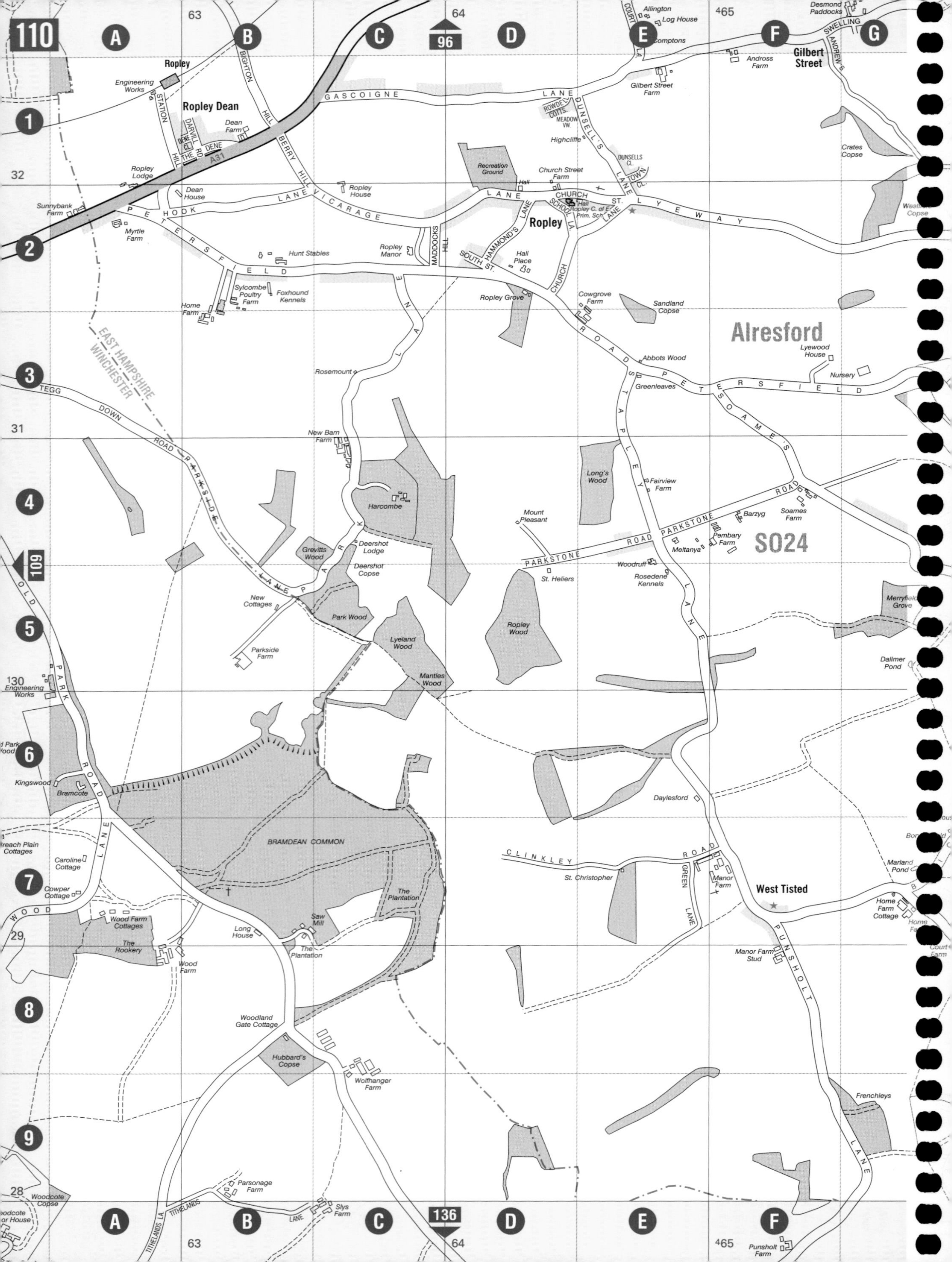
A
B
C
D
E
F
G
63
64
465
96
136
109
Ropley
Engineering Works
Ropley Dean
Dean Farm
Ropley Lodge
Dean House
Sunnybank Farm
Myrtle Farm
Hunt Stables
Ropley House
Ropley Manor
Sylcombe Poultry Farm
Foxhound Kennels
Home Farm
GASCOIGNE LANE
HOOK LANE
VICARAGE LANE
PETERSFIELD ROAD
A31
Recreation Ground
Church Street Farm
Hall
Highcliffe
Ropley
Hall Place
Ropley Grove
Cowgrove Farm
Sandland Copse
Allington
Log House
Comptons
Andross Farm
Gilbert Street
Gilbert Street Farm
Desmond Paddocks
SWELLING
Crates Copse
Alresford
Lyewood House
Nursery
Abbots Wood
Greenleaves
LYEWAY
STAPLEY LANE
SOAMES
PARKSTONE ROAD
Rosemount
New Barn Farm
Harcombe
Grevitts Wood
Deershot Lodge
Deershot Copse
New Cottages
Park Wood
Lyeland Wood
Mantles Wood
Parkside Farm
Long's Wood
Fairview Farm
Mount Pleasant
St. Heliers
Woodruff
Rosedene Kennels
Barzyg
Soames Farm
Pembary Farm
Meltanya
SO24
Ropley Wood
Merryfield Grove
Dallmer Pond
EAST HAMPSHIRE
WINCHESTER
TEGG DOWN ROAD
OLD PARK ROAD
Engineering Works
Kingswood
Bramcote
BRAMDEAN COMMON
Caroline Cottage
Cowper Cottage
Wood Farm Cottages
The Rookery
Wood Farm
Long House
Saw Mill
The Plantation
Daylesford
CLINKLEY ROAD
St. Christopher
GREEN LANE
Manor Farm
West Tisted
Home Farm Cottage
Marland Pond
Manor Farm Stud
PUNSHOLT LANE
Woodland Gate Cottage
Hubbard's Copse
Wolfhanger Farm
Frenchleys
Parsonage Farm
Slys Farm
TITHELANDS LANE
Woodcote Copse
Punsholt Farm
1
2
3
4
5
6
7
8
9
32
31
130
29
28

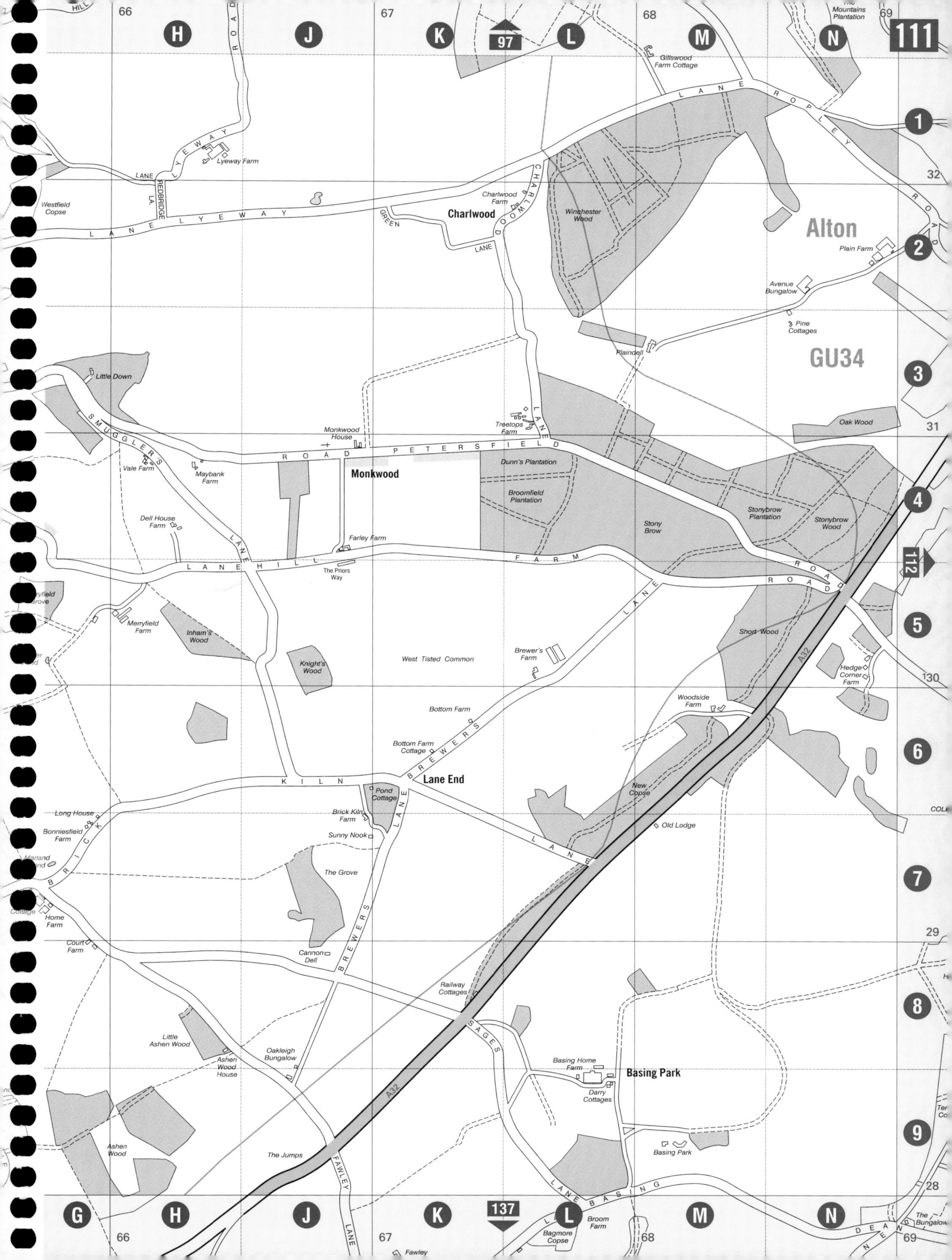

Charlwood
Monkwood
Lane End
Basing Park
Alton
GU34
Lyeway Farm
Westfield Copse
Charlwood Farm
Winchester Wood
Gilliswood Farm Cottage
Plain Farm
Avenue Bungalow
Pine Cottages
Plaindell
Little Down
Monkwood House
Treetops Farm
Oak Wood
Vale Farm
Maybank Farm
Dunn's Plantation
Broomfield Plantation
Stony Brow
Stonybrow Plantation
Stonybrow Wood
Dell House Farm
Farley Farm
The Priors Way
Merryfield Farm
Inham's Wood
Knight's Wood
West Tisted Common
Brewer's Farm
Short Wood
Hedge Corner Farm
Woodside Farm
Bottom Farm
Bottom Farm Cottage
New Copse
Old Lodge
Long House
Bonniesfield Farm
Pond Cottage
Brick Kiln Farm
Sunny Nook
The Grove
Home Farm
Court Farm
Cannon Dell
Railway Cottages
Little Ashen Wood
Ashen Wood House
Oakleigh Bungalow
Basing Home Farm
Darcy Cottages
Ashen Wood
The Jumps
Basing Park
Broom Farm
Bagmore Copse
Fawley
The Bungalow
Mountains Plantation
LYEWAY LANE
REDBRIDGE LA.
GREEN LANE
CHARLWOOD LANE
ROPLEY ROAD
PETERSFIELD ROAD
SMUGGLER'S LANE
HILL LANE
FARM ROAD
BREWERS LANE
KILN LANE
BRICK
SAGES
FAWLEY LANE
BASING LANE
DEAN
A32
97
112
137

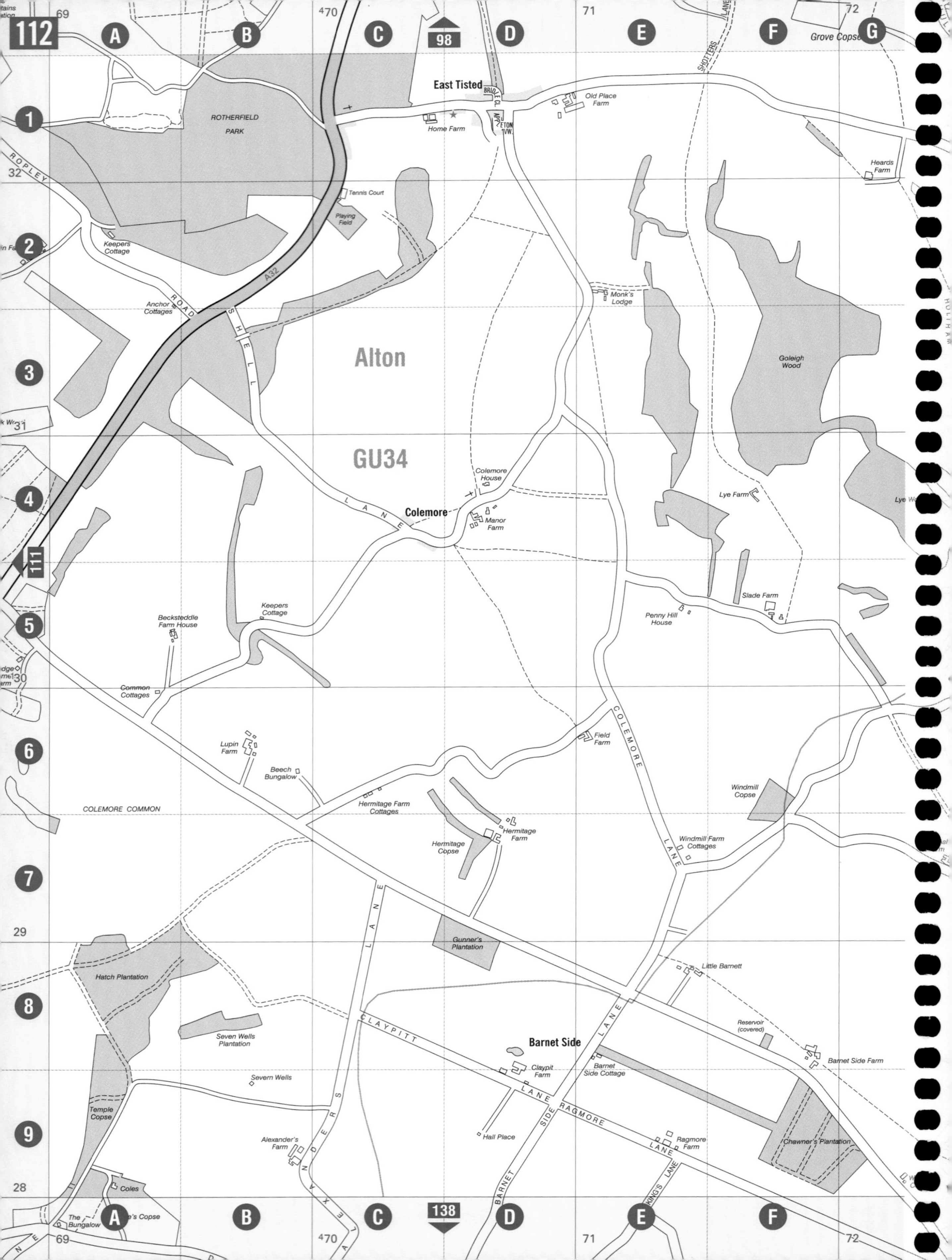
98
East Tisted
Old Place Farm
Home Farm
ROTHERFIELD PARK
Grove Copse
Heards Farm
ROPLEY ROAD
Tennis Court
Playing Field
Keepers Cottage
A32
Anchor Cottages
Monk's Lodge
SHELL LANE
Alton
GU34
Goleigh Wood
Colemore House
Colemore
Manor Farm
Lye Farm
111
Slade Farm
Penny Hill House
Keepers Cottage
Becksteddle Farm House
Common Cottages
COLEMORE LANE
Field Farm
Lupin Farm
Beech Bungalow
Windmill Copse
COLEMORE COMMON
Hermitage Farm Cottages
Hermitage Farm
Hermitage Copse
Windmill Farm Cottages
Gunner's Plantation
Little Barnett
Hatch Plantation
Seven Wells Plantation
Reservoir (covered)
Barnet Side
Barnet Side Farm
CLAYPITT LANE
Claypit Farm
Barnet Side Cottage
Severn Wells
Temple Copse
RAGMORE LANE
Hall Place
Alexander's Farm
ALEXANDERS LANE
Ragmore Farm
Chawner's Plantation
KING'S LANE
BARNET SIDE
Coles
The Bungalow
138

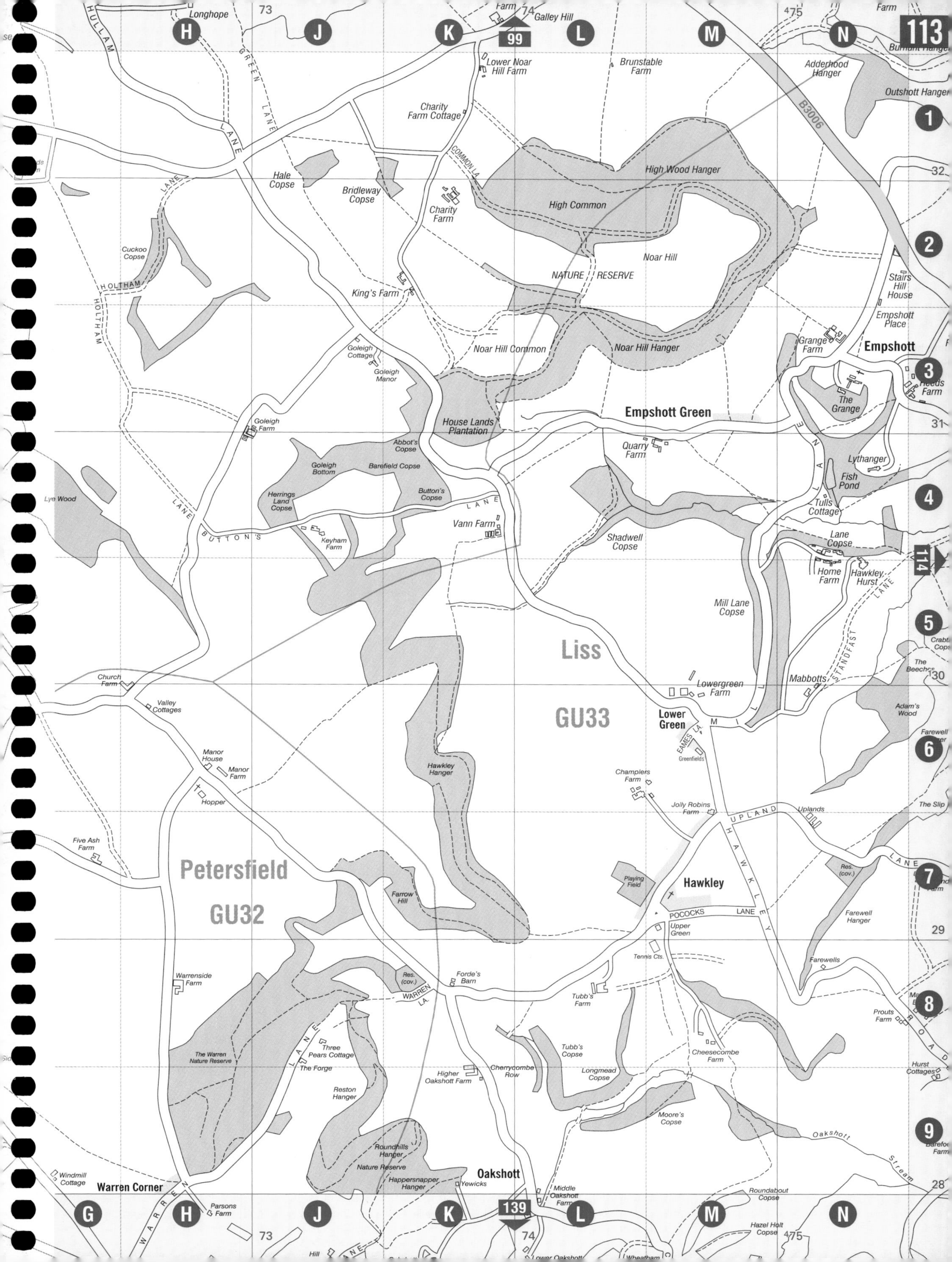

Longhope
Farm
Galley Hill
99
Lower Noar Hill Farm
Brunstable Farm
Adderhood Hanger
Outshott Hanger
B3006
Charity Farm Cottage
COMMON LA
High Wood Hanger
High Common
Hale Copse
Bridleway Copse
Charity Farm
Noar Hill
NATURE RESERVE
Cuckoo Copse
HOLTHAM
King's Farm
Stairs Hill House
Empshott Place
Grange Farm
Empshott
Noar Hill Common
Noar Hill Hanger
Goleigh Cottage
Goleigh Manor
Heeds Farm
The Grange
Empshott Green
House Lands Plantation
Goleigh Farm
Abbot's Copse
Quarry Farm
Lythanger
Goleigh Bottom
Barefield Copse
Fish Pond
Lye Wood
Herrings Land Copse
Button's Copse
Tulls Cottage
LANE
BUTTON'S
Vann Farm
Keyham Farm
Shadwell Copse
Lane Copse
Home Farm
Hawkley Hurst
114
Mill Lane Copse
Liss
STANDFAST
Crabtree Copse
The Beeches
Church Farm
Mabbotts
Lowergreen Farm
Adam's Wood
Valley Cottages
GU33
Lower Green
EAMES LA.
Greenfields
Farewell Hanger
Manor House
Manor Farm
Hawkley Hanger
Champlers Farm
Hopper
Jolly Robins Farm
Uplands
The Slip
UPLAND LANE
HAWKLEY
Five Ash Farm
Res. (cov.)
Petersfield
Playing Field
Hawkley
GU32
Farrow Hill
POCOCKS LANE
Upper Green
Farewell Hanger
Tennis Cts.
Farewells
Warrenside Farm
Res. (cov.)
Forde's Barn
WARREN LA.
Tubb's Farm
Prouts Farm
ROAD
The Warren Nature Reserve
Three Pears Cottage
The Forge
Tubb's Copse
Cheesecombe Farm
Higher Oakshott Farm
Cherrycombe Row
Longmead Copse
Hurst Cottages
Reston Hanger
Moore's Copse
Oakshott Stream
Roundhills Hanger
Nature Reserve
Windmill Cottage
Warren Corner
Happersnapper Hanger
Oakshott
Yewicks
Middle Oakshott Farm
Roundabout Copse
Parsons Farm
WARREN
139
Hazel Holt Copse
Lower Oakshott
Wheatham
Hill
G H J K L M N
73 74 475
1 2 3 4 5 6 7 8 9
32 31 30 29 28

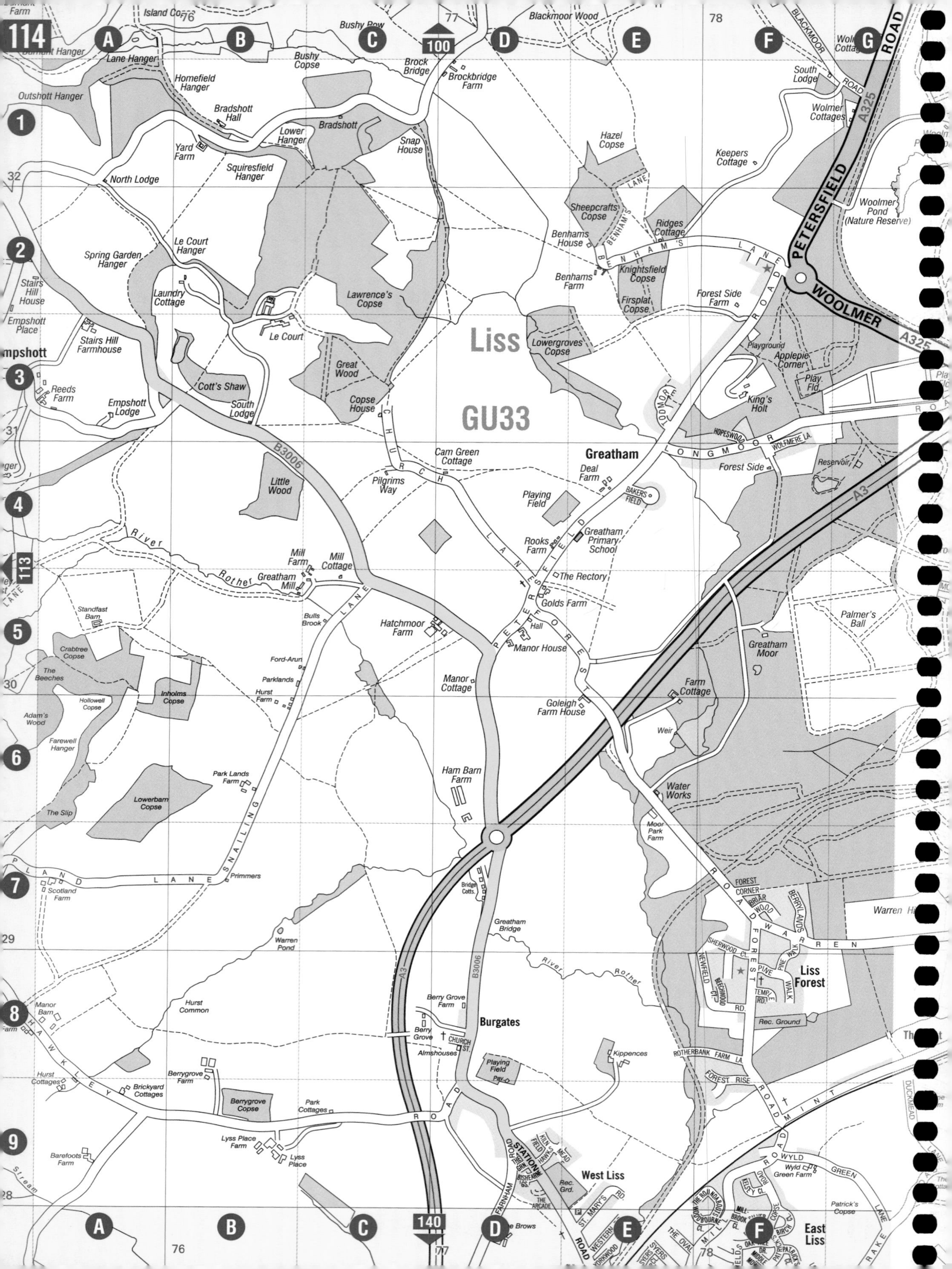

Liss
GU33
Greatham
Burgates
West Liss
Liss Forest
East Liss
Bushy Row
Blackmoor Wood
Island Copse
Lane Hanger
Bushy Copse
Brock Bridge
Brockbridge Farm
Homefield Hanger
Outshott Hanger
Bradshott Hall
Bradshott
Lower Hanger
Snap House
Yard Farm
North Lodge
Squiresfield Hanger
Hazel Copse
Keepers Cottage
South Lodge
Wolmer Cottages
Woolmer Pond (Nature Reserve)
Sheepcrafts Copse
Ridges Cottage
Benhams House
Benhams Farm
Knightsfield Copse
Firsplat Copse
Forest Side Farm
Le Court Hanger
Spring Garden Hanger
Laundry Cottage
Le Court
Lawrence's Copse
Stairs Hill House
Empshott Place
Stairs Hill Farmhouse
Great Wood
Lowergroves Copse
Playground
Applepie Corner
Play. Fld.
King's Holt
Reeds Farm
Cott's Shaw
South Lodge
Empshott Lodge
Copse House
Cam Green Cottage
Deal Farm
Forest Side
Reservoir
Pilgrims Way
Little Wood
Playing Field
Greatham Primary School
Rooks Farm
The Rectory
Mill Farm
Mill Cottage
Greatham Mill
River Rother
Standfast Barn
Bulls Brook
Golds Farm
Palmer's Ball
Hatchmoor Farm
Hall
Manor House
Greatham Moor
Crabtree Copse
The Beeches
Ford-Arun
Parklands
Hurst Farm
Inholms Copse
Hollowell Copse
Adam's Wood
Manor Cottage
Goleigh Farm House
Farm Cottage
Weir
Farewell Hanger
Park Lands Farm
Lowerbarn Copse
Ham Barn Farm
Water Works
The Slip
Moor Park Farm
Primmers
Scotland Farm
Bridge Cotts.
Forest Corner
Warren Pond
Greatham Bridge
Warren Hi
Rec. Ground
Manor Barn
Hurst Common
Berry Grove Farm
Berry Grove
Almshouses
Kippences
Hurst Cottages
Berrygrove Farm
Brickyard Cottages
Berrygrove Copse
Park Cottages
Playing Field
Pav.
Lyss Place Farm
Lyss Place
Barefoots Farm
Wyld Green Farm
Patrick's Copse
Rec. Grd.
The Arcade
The Brows
B3006
A3
A325
PETERSFIELD ROAD
WOOLMER
BLACKMOOR ROAD
BENHAM'S LANE
LONGMOOR ROAD
HOPESWOOD
WOLFMERE LA.
BAKERS FIELD
CHURCH LANE
PETERSFIELD ROAD
FOREST ROAD
SNAILING LANE
PLAND LANE
HAWKLEY ROAD
WARREN
STATION ROAD
FARNHAM ROAD
ST. MARY'S RD.
WESTERN ROAD
MINT ROAD
WYLD GREEN
ROTHERBANK FARM LA.
FOREST RISE
SHERWOOD CL.
NEWFIELD CT.
BEECHWOOD CT.
PINE WALK
TEMPLE RD.
BRIAR WOOD
BERRYLANDS
CHURCH ST.
HAWKS MEAD
DUCKMEAD
RAKE
100
140
113

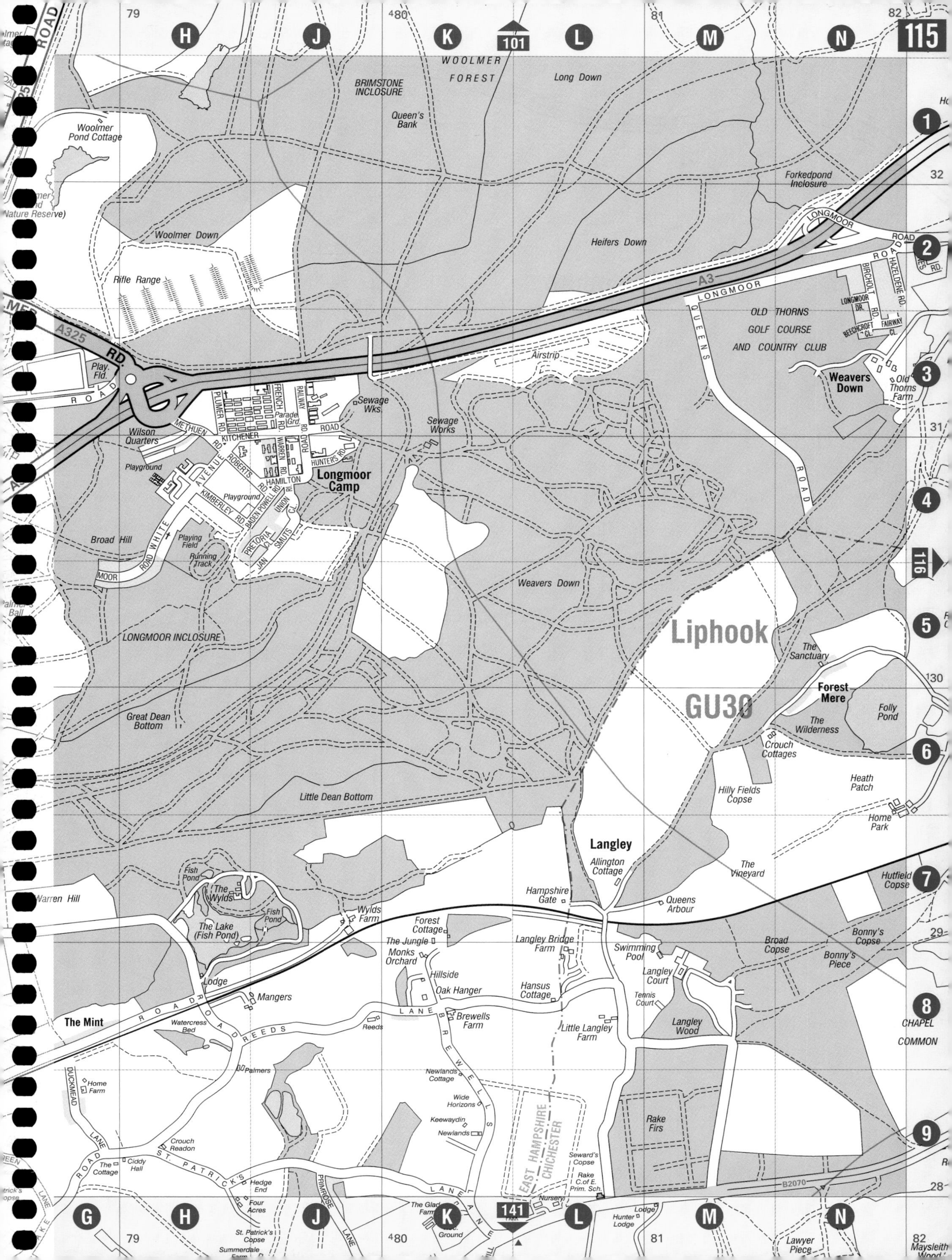

WOOLMER FOREST
BRIMSTONE INCLOSURE
Queen's Bank
Long Down
Woolmer Pond Cottage
Forkedpond Inclosure
Woolmer Down
Heifers Down
Rifle Range
A325
A3
LONGMOOR ROAD
OLD THORNS GOLF COURSE AND COUNTRY CLUB
Airstrip
Weavers Down
Old Thorns Farm
Play. Fld.
Sewage Wks.
Sewage Works
Wilson Quarters
Longmoor Camp
Playground
Broad Hill
Playing Field
Running Track
Weavers Down
LONGMOOR INCLOSURE
Liphook
GU30
The Sanctuary
Forest Mere
Folly Pond
The Wilderness
Crouch Cottages
Great Dean Bottom
Heath Patch
Hilly Fields Copse
Home Park
Little Dean Bottom
Langley
Allington Cottage
The Vineyard
Hutfield Copse
Fish Pond
The Wylds
Warren Hill
Hampshire Gate
Queens Arbour
The Lake (Fish Pond)
Wylds Farm
Forest Cottage
The Jungle
Monks Orchard
Langley Bridge Farm
Swimming Pool
Broad Copse
Bonny's Copse
Bonny's Piece
Langley Court
Lodge
Mangers
Hillside
Oak Hanger
Hansus Cottage
Tennis Court
The Mint
Watercress Bed
REEDS LANE
Reeds
Brewells Farm
Little Langley Farm
Langley Wood
CHAPEL COMMON
Palmers
Home Farm
Newlands Cottage
Wide Horizons
Keewaydin
Newlands
EAST HAMPSHIRE
CHICHESTER
Rake Firs
Crouch Readon
The Cottage
Ciddy Hall
ST. PATRICK'S LANE
Hedge End
Seward's Copse
Rake C.of E. Prim. Sch.
Nursery
B2070
Four Acres
The Glad Farm
Hunter Lodge
Lodge
St. Patrick's Copse
Lawyer Piece
Maysleith Wood
101
116
141

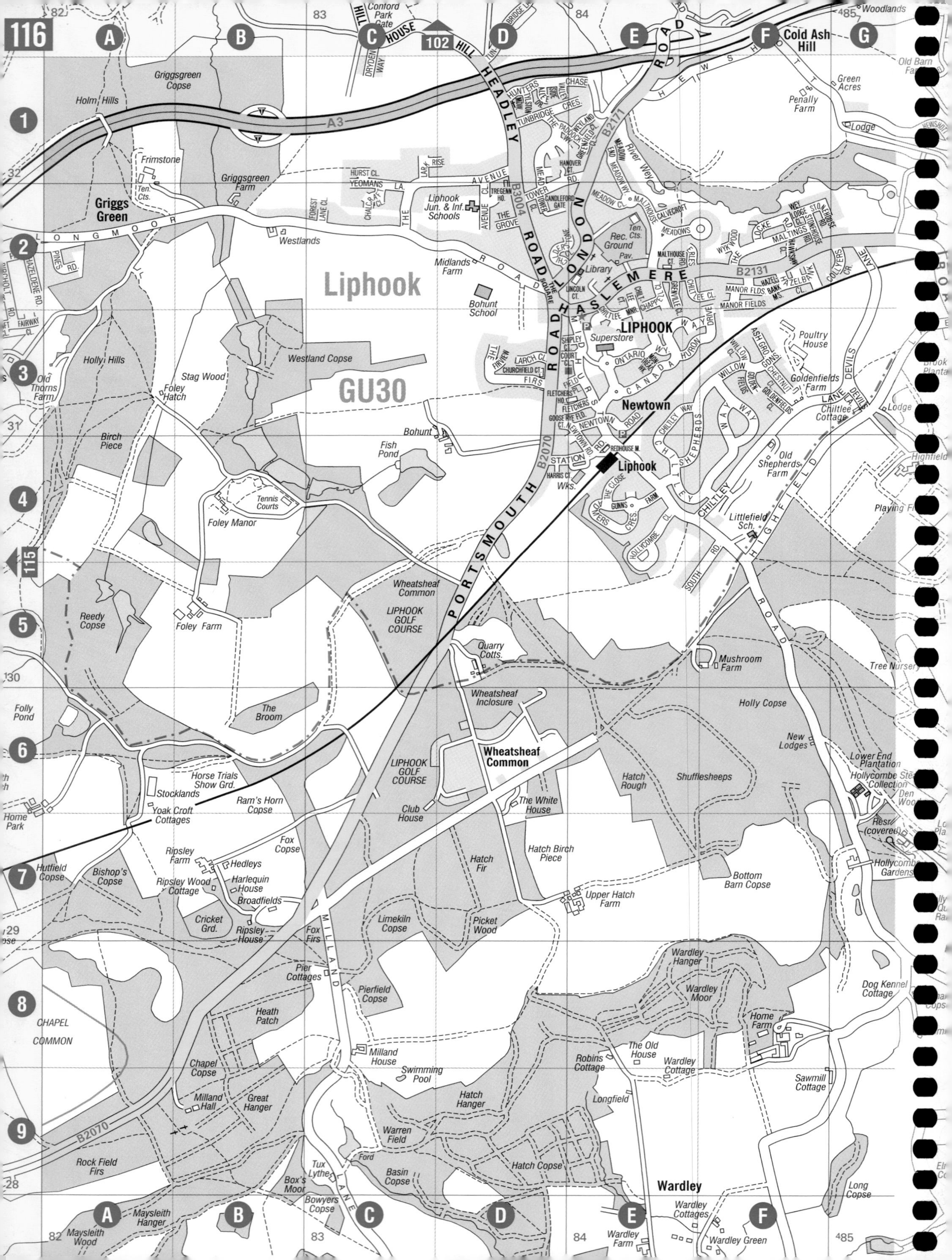

Liphook
GU30
LIPHOOK
Newtown
Griggs Green
Cold Ash Hill
Wheatsheaf Common
Wardley
Griggsgreen Copse
Holm Hills
Frimstone
Griggsgreen Farm
Westlands
Midlands Farm
Bohunt School
Liphook Jun. & Inf. Schools
Holly Hills
Old Thorns Farm
Stag Wood
Foley Hatch
Westland Copse
Birch Piece
Bohunt
Fish Pond
Foley Manor
Tennis Courts
Reedy Copse
Foley Farm
Wheatsheaf Common
LIPHOOK GOLF COURSE
Quarry Cotts.
Wheatsheaf Inclosure
The Broom
Folly Pond
Horse Trials Show Grd.
Stocklands
Yoak Croft Cottages
Ram's Horn Copse
Home Park
Club House
The White House
Hutfield Copse
Bishop's Copse
Ripsley Farm
Hedleys
Harlequin House
Ripsley Wood Cottage
Broadfields
Fox Copse
Hatch Fir
Hatch Birch Piece
Cricket Grd.
Ripsley House
Fox Firs
Limekiln Copse
Picket Wood
Upper Hatch Farm
Pier Cottages
Pierfield Copse
Heath Patch
CHAPEL COMMON
Chapel Copse
Milland House
Swimming Pool
Milland Hall
Great Hanger
Hatch Hanger
Warren Field
Rock Field Firs
Tux Lythe
Ford
Basin Copse
Hatch Copse
Box's Moor
Bowyers Copse
Maysleith Hanger
Maysleith Wood
Wardley Hanger
Wardley Moor
Home Farm
The Old House
Robins Cottage
Wardley Cottage
Longfield
Sawmill Cottage
Wardley Cottages
Wardley Farm
Wardley Green
Long Copse
Dog Kennel Cottage
Bottom Barn Copse
Hatch Rough
Shufflesheeps
Holly Copse
Mushroom Farm
Tree Nursery
New Lodges
Lower End Plantation
Hollycombe Steam Collection
Resr (covered)
Hollycombe Gardens
Littlefield Sch.
Old Shepherds Farm
Chiltlee Cottage
Goldenfields Farm
Poultry House
Lodge
Playing Fields
Penally Farm
Green Acres
Old Barn Farm
Woodlands
Superstore
Library
Rec. Ground
Pav.
Ten. Cts.
Station
Wks.
Liphook
A3
B2070
B3004
B2131
B2171
PORTSMOUTH ROAD
LONDON ROAD
HASLEMERE ROAD
HEADLEY ROAD
LONGMOOR ROAD
HEWSHOTT LANE
HIGHFIELD ROAD
MILLAND LANE
CHILTLEY LANE
DEVILS LANE
CONFORD PARK GATE
HOUSE HILL
102
115
A B C D E F G
1 2 3 4 5 6 7 8 9
82 83 84 485
32 31 130 29 28

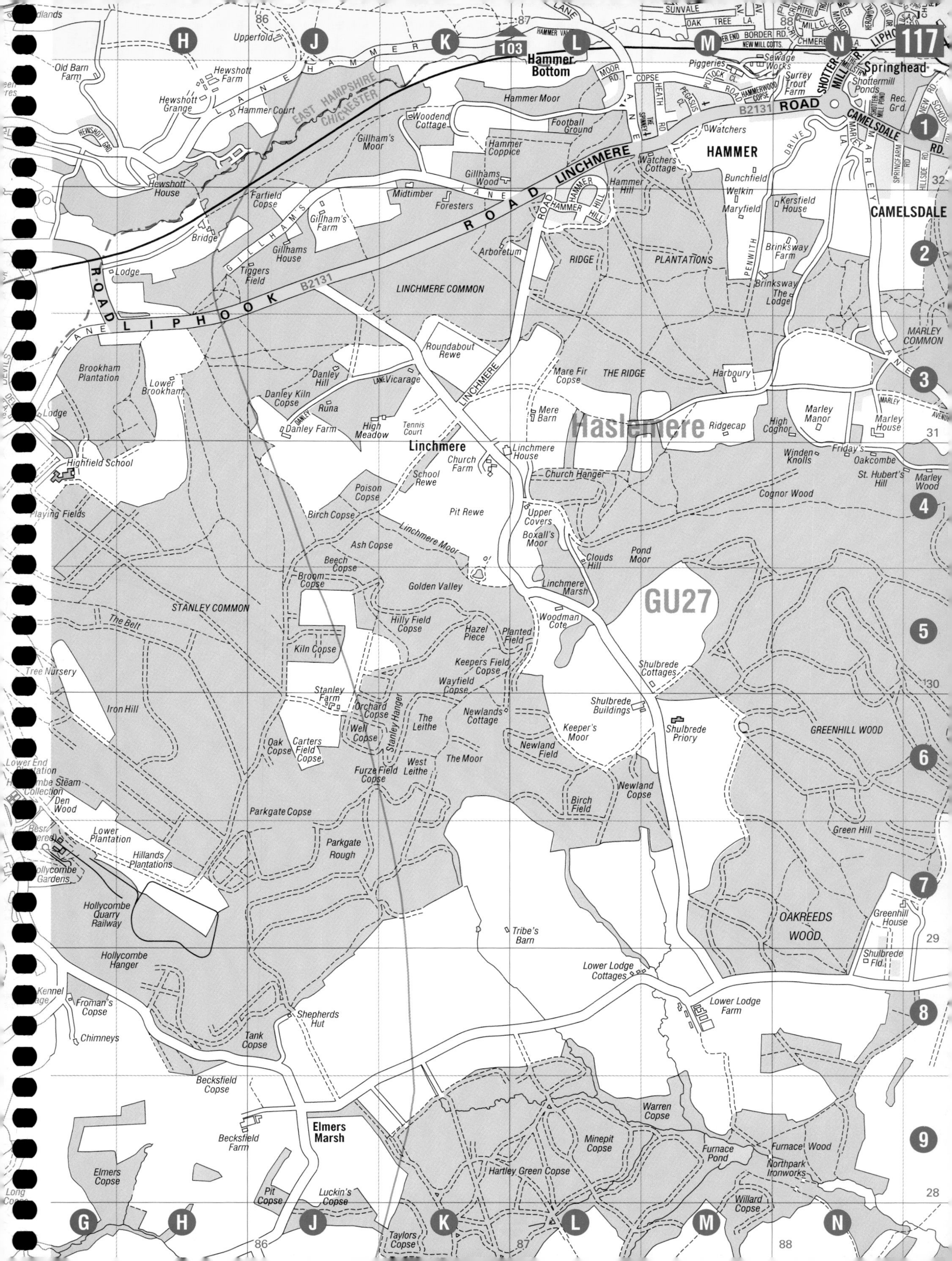
H
J
K
L
M
N
103
Hammer Bottom
Springhead
Upperfold
Old Barn Farm
Hewshott Farm
Hewshott Grange
Hammer Court
EAST HAMPSHIRE
CHICHESTER
Hammer Moor
HAMMER
CAMELSDALE
Woodend Cottage
Football Ground
Gillham's Moor
Hammer Coppice
Gillhams Wood
Hewshott House
Farfield Copse
Midtimber
Foresters
Gillham's Farm
Bridge
Gillhams House
Tiggers Field
Lodge
Arboretum
RIDGE
PLANTATIONS
LINCHMERE COMMON
LIPHOOK ROAD
LINCHMERE ROAD
B2131
Watchers
Watchers Cottage
Hammer Hill
Bunchfield
Welkin
Maryfield
Kersfield House
Brinksway Farm
Brinksway
The Lodge
Shottermill Ponds
Surrey Trout Farm
Piggeries
Sewage Works
MARLEY COMMON
Roundabout Rewe
Brookham Plantation
Lower Brookham
Danley Hill
Vicarage
Danley Kiln Copse
Runa
Danley Farm
High Meadow
Tennis Court
Mare Fir Copse
THE RIDGE
Harboury
Mere Barn
Haslemere
Ridgecap
High Cognor
Marley Manor
Marley House
Linchmere
Linchmere House
Church Farm
Highfield School
School Rewe
Church Hanger
Winden Knolls
Friday's
Oakcombe
St. Hubert's Hill
Marley Wood
Cognor Wood
Playing Fields
Poison Copse
Pit Rewe
Birch Copse
Upper Covers
Boxall's Moor
Linchmere Moor
Ash Copse
Clouds Hill
Pond Moor
Beech Copse
Broom Copse
Golden Valley
Linchmere Marsh
GU27
STANLEY COMMON
The Belt
Hilly Field Copse
Woodman Cote
Hazel Piece
Planted Field
Kiln Copse
Keepers Field Copse
Shulbrede Cottages
Tree Nursery
Wayfield Copse
Stanley Farm
Shulbrede Buildings
Iron Hill
Orchard Copse
The Leithe
Newlands Cottage
Keeper's Moor
Shulbrede Priory
GREENHILL WOOD
Well Copse
Stanley Hanger
Oak Copse
Carters Field Copse
Newland Field
The Moor
West Leithe
Furze Field Copse
Newland Copse
Birch Field
Lower End Plantation
Hollycombe Steam Collection
Den Wood
Parkgate Copse
Lower Plantation
Parkgate Rough
Green Hill
Hillands Plantations
Hollycombe Gardens
Hollycombe Quarry Railway
OAKREEDS WOOD
Greenhill House
Tribe's Barn
Hollycombe Hanger
Shulbrede Fld.
Lower Lodge Cottages
Lower Lodge Farm
Froman's Copse
Shepherds Hut
Chimneys
Tank Copse
Becksfield Copse
Warren Copse
Elmers Marsh
Becksfield Farm
Minepit Copse
Furnace Pond
Furnace Wood
Northpark Ironworks
Hartley Green Copse
Elmers Copse
Pit Copse
Luckin's Copse
Willard Copse
Taylors Copse
G
86
87
88
1
2
3
4
5
6
7
8
9
28
29
30
31
32

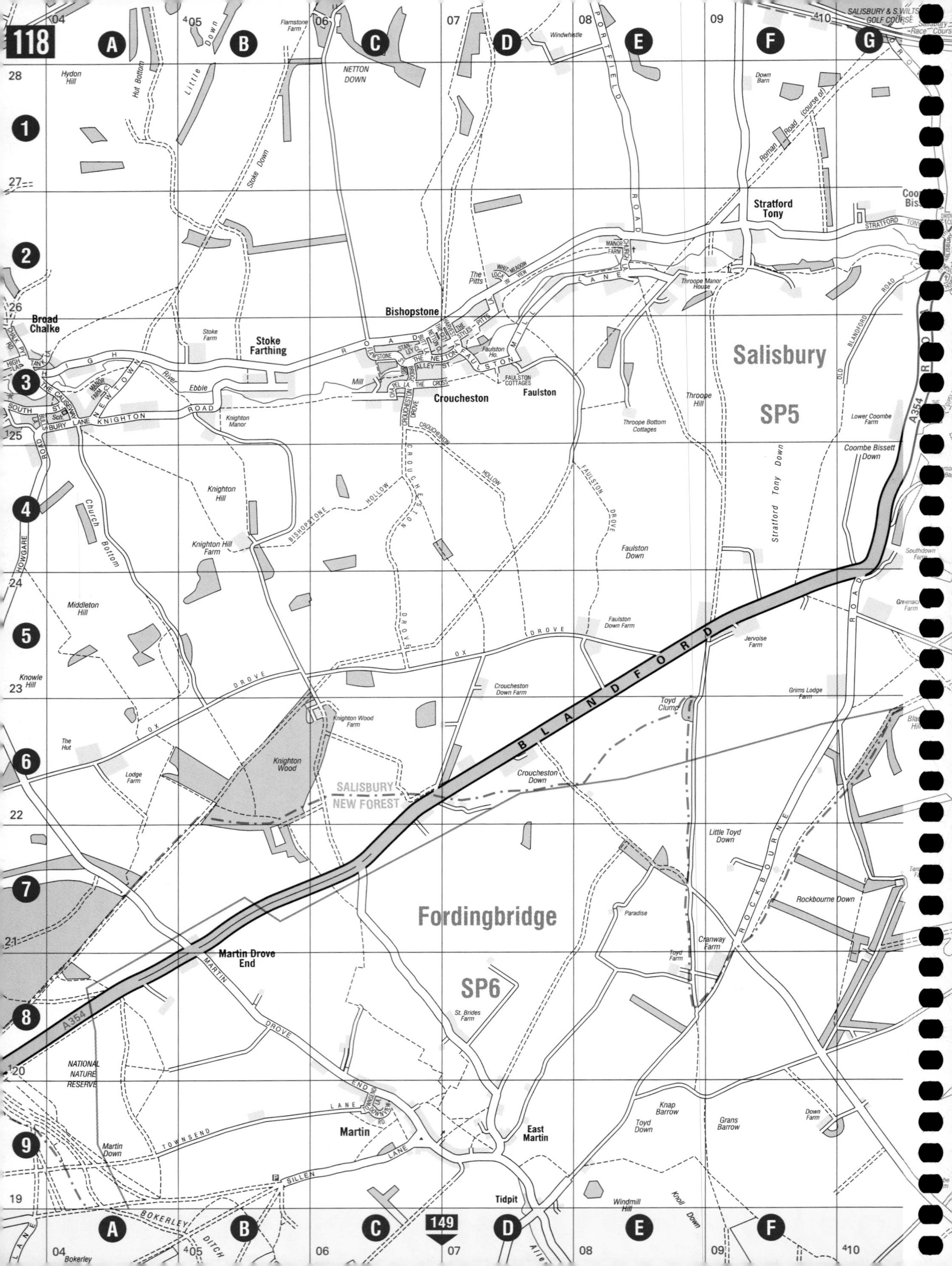

Hydon Hill
Hut Bottom
Little Down
Stoke Down
Flamstone Farm
NETTON DOWN
Windwhistle
PORTFIELD ROAD
Down Barn
Roman Road (course of)
Stratford Tony
Coombe Bissett
STRATFORD TONY
SALISBURY & S.WILTS GOLF COURSE
Salisbury Race Course
Manor Farm
CHURCH LA.
The Pitts
Lock
Throope Manor House
Bishopstone
Broad Chalke
Stoke Farm
Stoke Farthing
HIGH ROAD
River Ebble
Mill
Croucheston
Faulston
Faulston Ho.
FAULSTON COTTAGES
Salisbury
SP5
Throope Hill
Throope Bottom Cottages
OLD BLANDFORD ROAD
Lower Coombe Farm
Coombe Bissett Down
A354
Knighton Manor
KNIGHTON ROAD
BURY LANE
SOUTH ST.
THE CAUSEWAY
NEWTOWN
Knighton Hill
Knighton Hill Farm
Church Bottom
HOWGARE ROAD
BISHOPSTONE HOLLOW
CROUCHESTON DROVE
CROUCHESTON HOLLOW
FAULSTON DROVE
Faulston Down
Stratford Tony Down
Southdown Farm
Middleton Hill
Knowle Hill
Faulston Down Farm
OX DROVE
BLANDFORD ROAD
Jervoise Farm
Croucheston Down Farm
Toyd Clump
Grims Lodge Farm
Knighton Wood Farm
Knighton Wood
The Hut
Lodge Farm
Croucheston Down
SALISBURY
NEW FOREST
Little Toyd Down
ROCKBOURNE
Rockbourne Down
Fordingbridge
Paradise
Cranway Farm
Toyd Farm
Martin Drove End
MARTIN DROVE
SP6
St. Brides Farm
NATIONAL NATURE RESERVE
Martin Down
TOWNSEND LANE
SILLEN LANE
Martin
East Martin
Knap Barrow
Toyd Down
Grans Barrow
Down Farm
Tidpit
Windmill Hill
Knoll Down
BOKERLEY DITCH
Bokerley

149

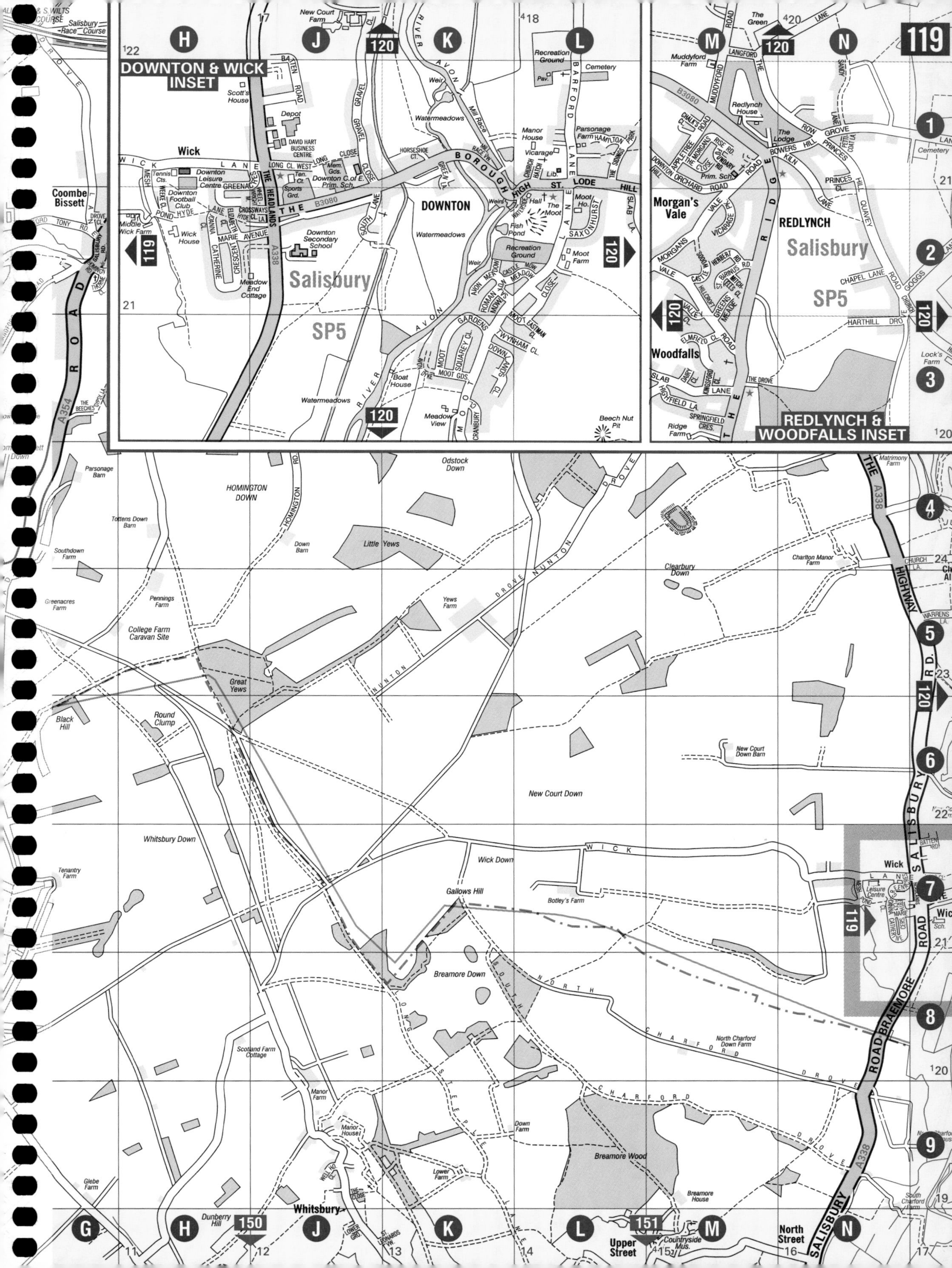
DOWNTON & WICK INSET
Wick
Downton Leisure Centre
Downton Football Club
Middle Wick Farm
Wick House
Scott's House
Depot
DAVID HART BUSINESS CENTRE
Downton C.of E. Prim. Sch.
Sports Grd.
Downton Secondary School
Meadow End Cottage
Salisbury
SP5
DOWNTON
Watermeadows
Weir
Mill Race
Recreation Ground
Cemetery
Manor House
Vicarage
Lib.
Parsonage Farm
Hall
The Moot
Fish Pond
Moot Ho.
Moot Farm
Boat House
Meadow View
Beech Nut Pit
New Court Farm
THE HEADLANDS
BOROUGH
HIGH ST.
LODE HILL
BARFORD LANE
SAXONHURST
B3080
A338
Coombe Bissett
Muddyford Farm
The Green
Redlynch House
The Lodge
Prim. Sch.
Morgan's Vale
REDLYNCH
Salisbury
SP5
Woodfalls
Ridge Farm
Lock's Farm
Cemetery
THE RIDGE
HARTHILL DRO.
CHAPEL LANE
REDLYNCH & WOODFALLS INSET
Parsonage Barn
HOMINGTON DOWN
Tottens Down Barn
Southdown Farm
Greenacres Farm
Pennings Farm
College Farm Caravan Site
Black Hill
Great Yews
Round Clump
Odstock Down
Down Barn
Little Yews
Yews Farm
NUNTON DRONE
Clearbury Down
Charlton Manor Farm
Matrimony Farm
New Court Down Barn
New Court Down
Whitsbury Down
Tenantry Farm
Wick Down
Gallows Hill
Botley's Farm
Breamore Down
North Charford Down Farm
Scotland Farm Cottage
Manor Farm
Manor House
Down Farm
Lower Farm
Breamore Wood
Breamore House
Glebe Farm
Dunberry Hill
Whitsbury
Upper Street
Countryside Mus.
North Street
SALISBURY ROAD
BREAMORE ROAD
A338
A354
CHARFORD DROVE
NORTH CHARFORD DROVE
SOUTH LONG STEEPLE LANE
WICK LANE
G H J K L M N
120 150 151

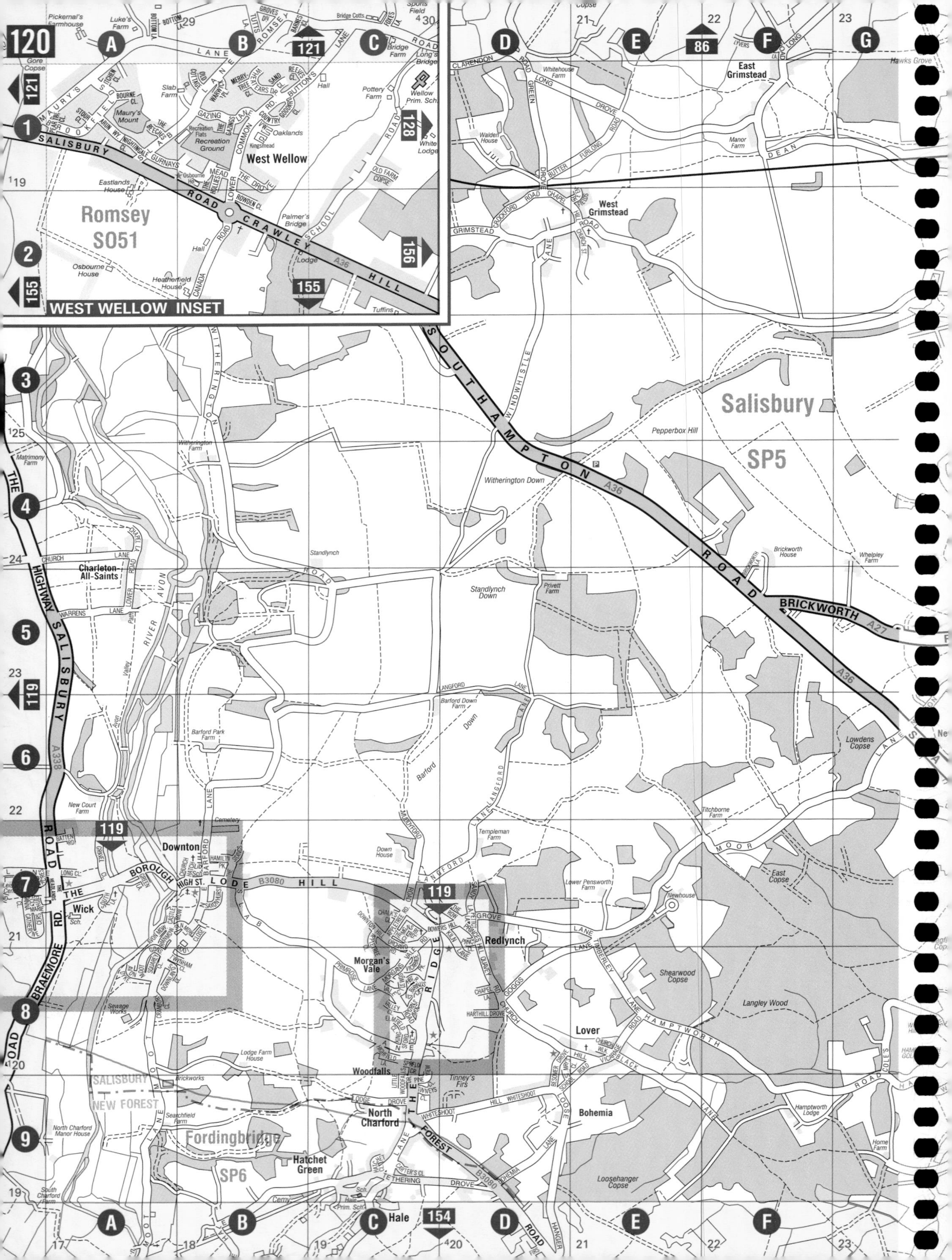
WEST WELLOW INSET
West Wellow
Romsey
SO51
Salisbury
SP5
Fordingbridge
SP6
East Grimstead
West Grimstead
Charleton-All-Saints
Downton
Wick
Redlynch
Morgan's Vale
Woodfalls
North Charford
Hatchet Green
Hale
Lover
Bohemia
SOUTHAMPTON ROAD
SALISBURY ROAD
CRAWLEY HILL
BRICKWORTH ROAD
HIGHWAY SALISBURY
BRAEMORE RD.
LODE HILL
THE RIDGE
Pepperbox Hill
Witherington Down
Standlynch Down
Langley Wood
Shearwood Copse
Loosehanger Copse
Lowdens Copse
Tinney's Firs
SALISBURY
NEW FOREST
121
155
156
128
86
119
154

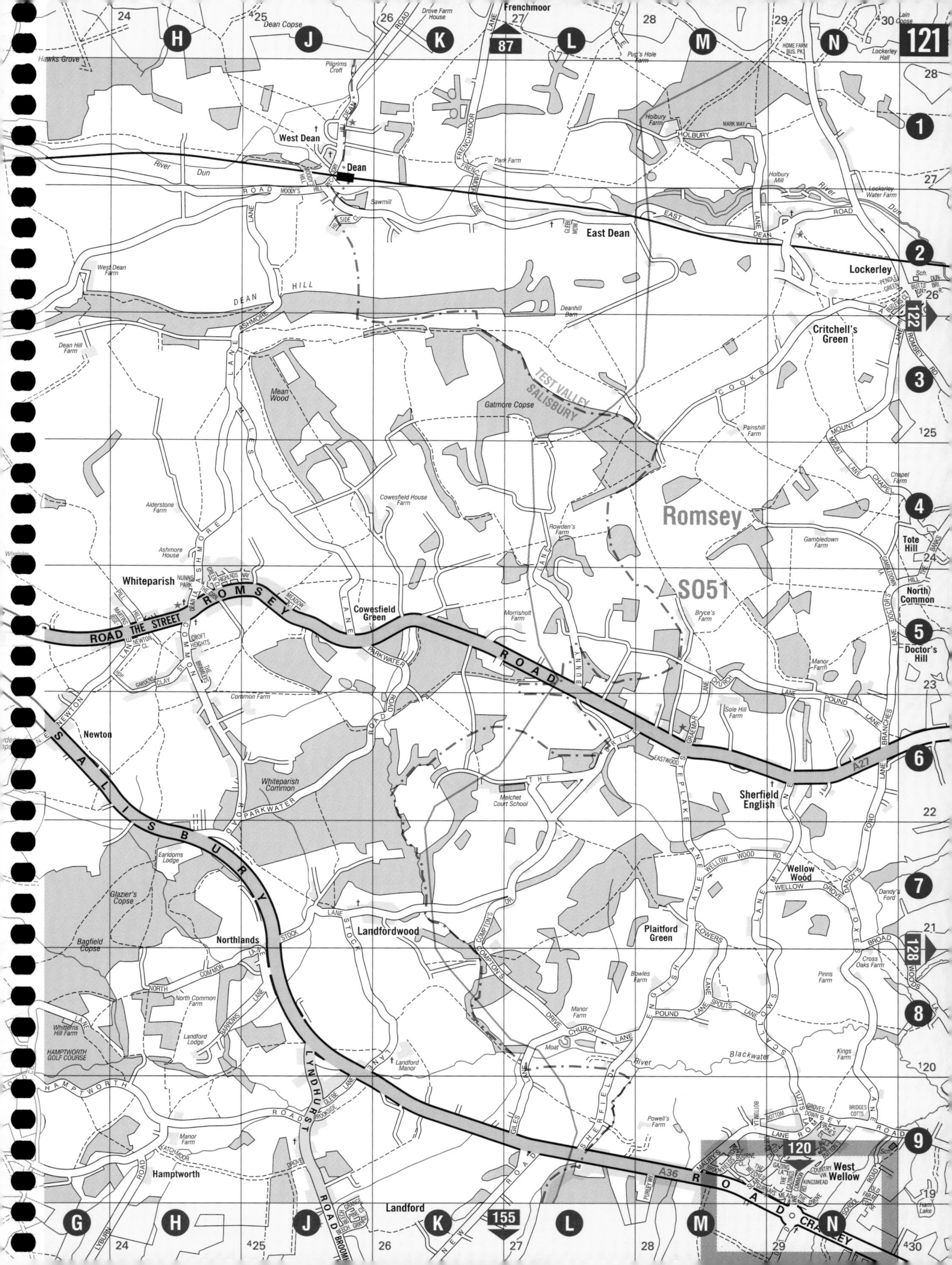
Frenchmoor
87
Dean Copse
Drove Farm House
Pilgrims Croft
Hawks Grove
Pug's Hole Farm
HOME FARM BUS. PK.
Lockerley Hall
Holbury Farm
MARK WAY
HOLBURY
West Dean
Dean
River Dun
MOODY'S ROAD
Park Farm
Holbury Mill
Lockerley Water Farm
Sawmill
East Dean
EAST DEAN ROAD
Lockerley
West Dean Farm
DEAN HILL
Deanhill Barn
Dean Hill Farm
122
Critchell's Green
COOKS LANE
ROMSEY RD
Mean Wood
Gatmore Copse
TEST VALLEY
SALISBURY
Painshill Farm
MOUNT LANE
Chapel Farm
Alderstone Farm
Cowesfield House Farm
Romsey
Rowden's Farm
Gambledown Farm
Tote Hill
Ashmore House
Whiteparish
SO51
North Common
Cowesfield Green
Morrisholt Farm
Bryce's Farm
ROAD THE STREET
ROMSEY ROAD
Doctor's Hill
Manor Farm
Common Farm
Sole Hill Farm
POUND LANE
Newton
A27
Sherfield English
Whiteparish Common
Melchet Court School
PARKWATER
Earldoms Lodge
WELLOW WOOD RD
Wellow Wood
WELLOW DROVE
Glazier's Copse
Dandy's Ford
Landfordwood
Plaitford Green
Bagfield Copse
Northlands
128
Cross Oaks Farm
Bowles Farm
Pinns Farm
North Common Farm
Manor Farm
Whitten's Hill Farm
Landford Lodge
HAMPTWORTH GOLF COURSE
Moat
Blackwater River
Kings Farm
Landford Manor
HAMPTWORTH ROAD
Powell's Farm
Manor Farm
SALISBURY
LYNDHURST ROAD
A36
120
Hamptworth
West Wellow
Landford
155
Ham Lake
CRAWLEY

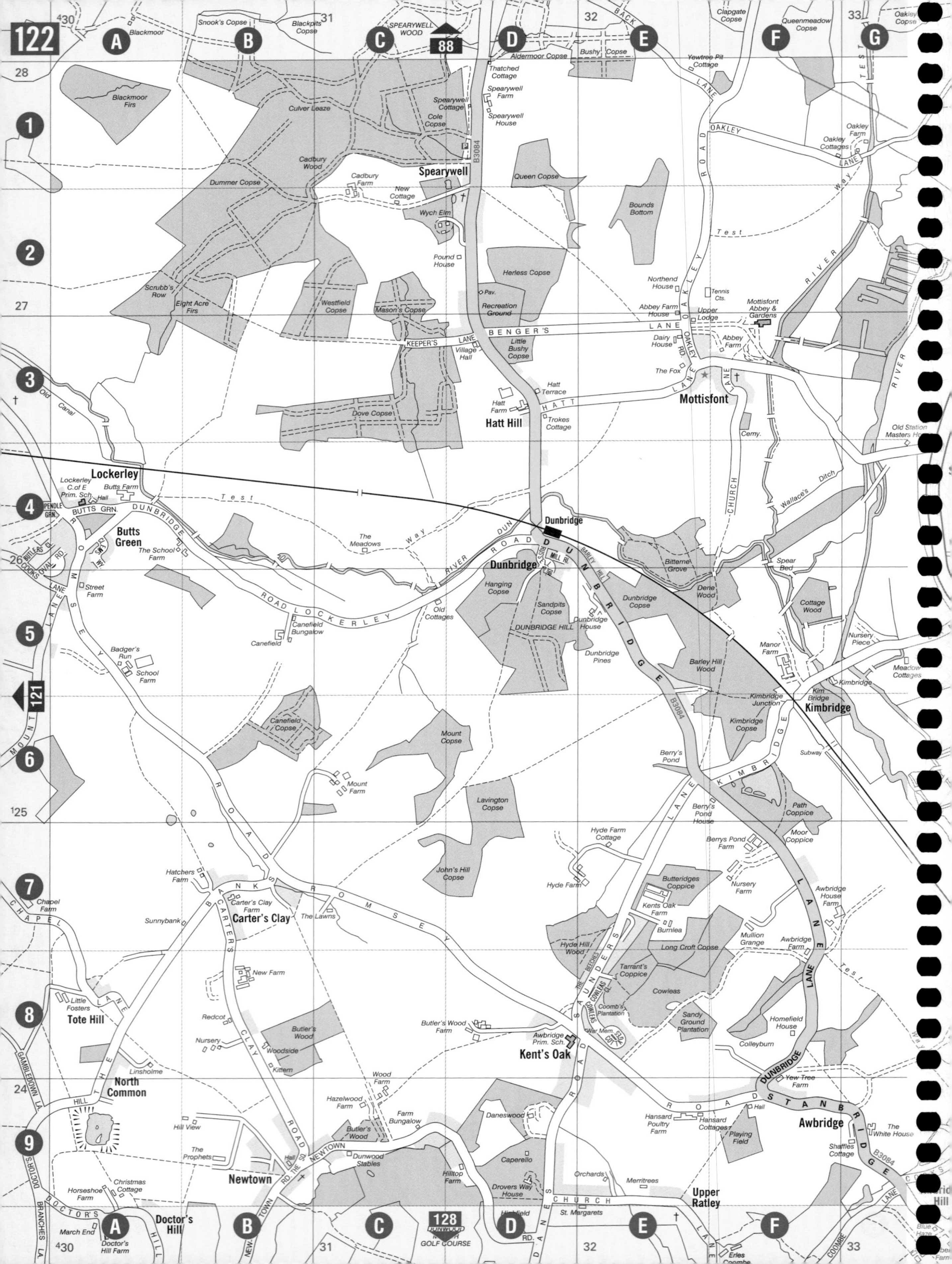
Spearywell
Hatt Hill
Mottisfont
Lockerley
Butts Green
Dunbridge
Kimbridge
Carter's Clay
Tote Hill
North Common
Kent's Oak
Newtown
Doctor's Hill
Upper Ratley
Awbridge
Blackmoor Firs
Culver Leaze
Dummer Copse
Cadbury Wood
Scrubb's Row
Eight Acre Firs
Westfield Copse
Mason's Copse
Dove Copse
Queen Copse
Bounds Bottom
Herless Copse
Recreation Ground
Little Bushy Copse
Mottisfont Abbey & Gardens
Dunbridge Copse
Barley Hill Wood
Kimbridge Copse
Canefield Copse
Mount Copse
Lavington Copse
John's Hill Copse
Butteridges Coppice
Long Croft Copse
Hyde Hill Wood
Tarrant's Coppice
Cowleas
Sandy Ground Plantation
Butler's Wood
Daneswood
Path Coppice
Moor Coppice
Cottage Wood
Bitterne Grove
Dene Wood
Hanging Copse
Sandpits Copse
DUNBRIDGE HILL
Dunbridge Pines
ROMSEY ROAD
LOCKERLEY ROAD
DUNBRIDGE LANE
KIMBRIDGE LANE
STANBRIDGE LANE
OAKLEY ROAD
BENGER'S LANE
KEEPER'S LANE
HATT LANE
CHURCH LANE
CARTERS CLAY
SAUNDERS LANE
CHAPEL LANE
THE HILL
DOCTOR'S HILL
NEWTOWN RD
DANES RD.
B3084
Test Way
RIVER TEST
Wallace's Ditch
Old Canal
88
121
128
DUNWOOD MANOR GOLF COURSE

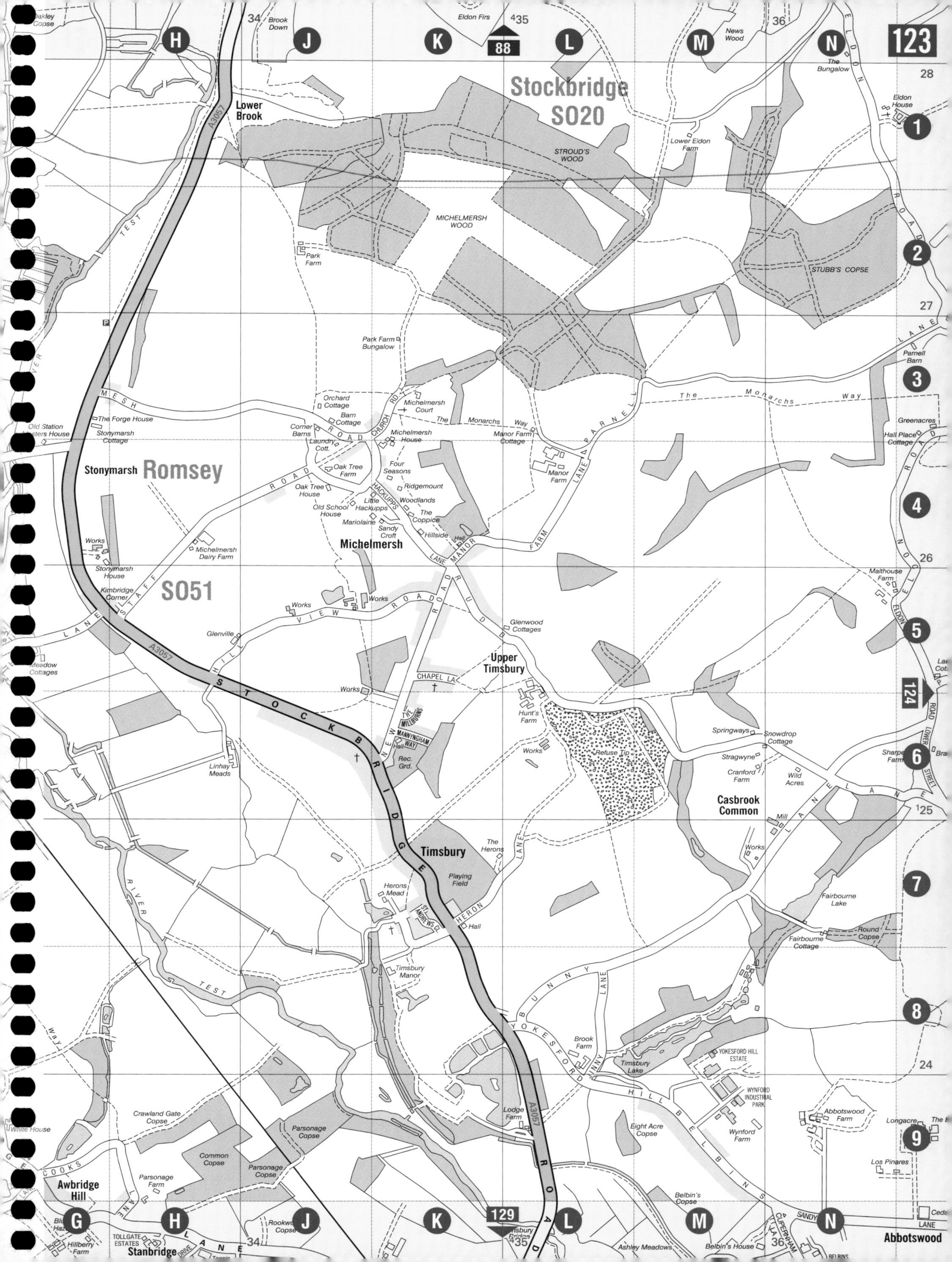

Stockbridge
SO20
Romsey
SO51
Lower Brook
Michelmersh
Upper Timsbury
Timsbury
Casbrook Common
Stonymarsh
Awbridge Hill
Stanbridge
Abbotswood
STROUD'S WOOD
MICHELMERSH WOOD
STUBB'S COPSE
Park Farm
Park Farm Bungalow
Lower Eldon Farm
Eldon House
The Bungalow
Eldon Firs
Brook Down
News Wood
Oakley Copse
Parnell Barn
The Monarchs Way
Greenacres
Hall Place Cottage
Orchard Cottage
Michelmersh Court
Barn Cottage
Corner Barns
Laundry Cott.
Michelmersh House
Manor Farm Cottage
Manor Farm
Oak Tree Farm
Oak Tree House
Four Seasons
Ridgemount
Old School House
Little Hackupps
Woodlands
The Coppice
Mariolaine
Sandy Croft
Hillside
Hall
The Forge House
Stonymarsh Cottage
Old Station
Stonymarsh House
Michelmersh Dairy Farm
Works
Kimbridge Corner
Glenville
Meadow Cottages
Glenwood Cottages
Malthouse Farm
Hunt's Farm
Refuse Tip
Springways
Snowdrop Cottage
Stragwyne
Cranford Farm
Wild Acres
Sharpe Farm
Linhay Meads
Rec. Grd.
Mill
The Herons
Playing Field
Herons Mead
Timsbury Manor
Fairbourne Lake
Round Copse
Fairbourne Cottage
Brook Farm
Timsbury Lake
YOKESFORD HILL ESTATE
WYNFORD INDUSTRIAL PARK
Wynford Farm
Eight Acre Copse
Abbotswood Farm
Longacre
Los Pinares
Lodge Farm
Crawland Gate Copse
White House
Parsonage Copse
Common Copse
Parsonage Farm
Belbin's Copse
Belbin's House
Ashley Meadows
Rookwood Copse
Hillberry Farm
TOLLGATE ESTATES
Cedar
A3057
STOCKBRIDGE ROAD
MESH ROAD
CHURCH RD
HACKUPPS
MANOR LANE
MANOR FARM
PARNELL LANE
STAFF ROAD
LANE
HILL VIEW ROAD
NEW ROAD
CHAPEL LA
YE MILLBURNS
MANNYNGHAM WAY
ST ANDREWS CL
HERON LANE
BUNNY LANE
YOKESFORD HILL
BELBINS
CUPERNHAM LA
SANDY LANE
ELDON ROAD
LOWER STREET
COOKS LANE
RIVER TEST
88
124
129

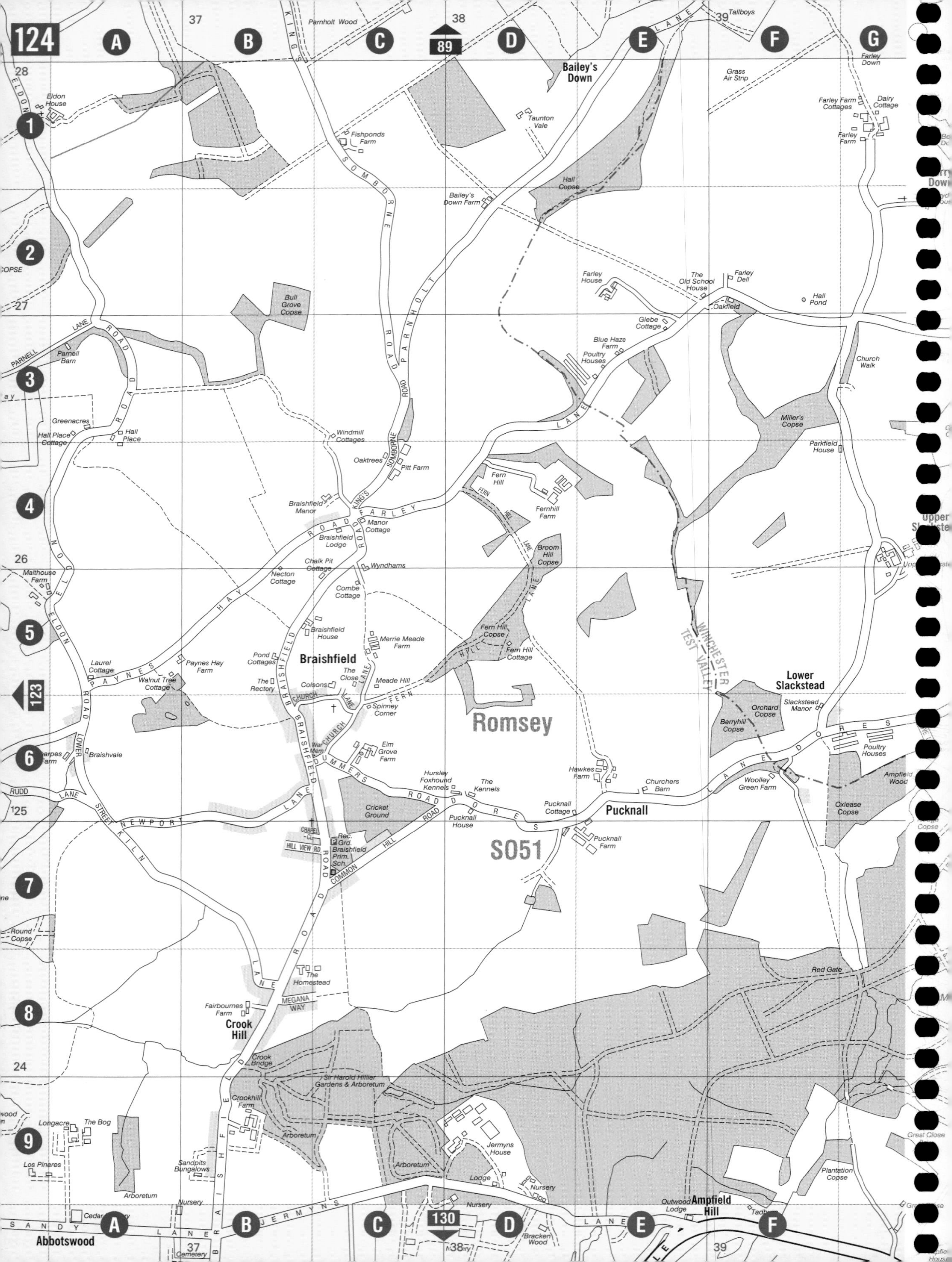
89
123
130
Bailey's Down
Braishfield
Romsey
SO51
Pucknall
Lower Slackstead
Crook Hill
Ampfield Hill
Abbotswood
Eldon House
Fishponds Farm
Taunton Vale
Grass Air Strip
Farley Down
Farley Farm Cottages
Dairy Cottage
Farley Farm
Parnholt Wood
Tallboys
Hall Copse
Bailey's Down Farm
Bull Grove Copse
Farley House
The Old School House
Farley Dell
Hall Pond
Oakfield
Glebe Cottage
Blue Haze Farm
Poultry Houses
Church Walk
Parnell Barn
Greenacres
Hall Place Cottage
Hall Place
Windmill Cottages
Oaktrees
Pitt Farm
Miller's Copse
Parkfield House
Fern Hill
Fernhill Farm
Braishfield Manor
Manor Cottage
Braishfield Lodge
Chalk Pit Cottage
Wyndhams
Broom Hill Copse
Malthouse Farm
Necton Cottage
Combe Cottage
Braishfield House
Merrie Meade Farm
Fern Hill Copse
Fern Hill Cottage
Laurel Cottage
Paynes Hay Farm
Pond Cottages
Walnut Tree Cottage
The Close
The Rectory
Colsons
Meade Hill
Spinney Corner
WINCHESTER
TEST VALLEY
Orchard Copse
Slackstead Manor
Berryhill Copse
Braishvale
War Mem
Elm Grove Farm
Hursley Foxhound Kennels
The Kennels
Hawkes Farm
Churchers Barn
Woolley Green Farm
Poultry Houses
Ampfield Wood
Cricket Ground
Pucknall House
Pucknall Cottage
Oxlease Copse
Pucknall Farm
Rec. Grd.
Braishfield Prim. Sch.
Round Copse
The Homestead
Red Gate
Fairbournes Farm
Crook Bridge
Sir Harold Hillier Gardens & Arboretum
Crookhill Farm
Longacre
The Bog
Arboretum
Jermyns House
Los Pinares
Sandpits Bungalows
Lodge
Nursery
Plantation Copse
Great Close
Outwood Lodge
Tadburn
Bracken Wood
Cemetery
ELDON ROAD
PARNELL LANE
PAYNES HAY ROAD
FARLEY LANE
KING'S SOMBORNE ROAD
PARNHOLT ROAD
FERN HILL LANE
BRAISHFIELD ROAD
CHURCH LANE
DUMMERS ROAD
DORES LANE
COMMON HILL ROAD
NEWPORT LANE
RUDD LANE
KILN LANE
LOWER STREET
MEGANA WAY
CHAPEL CL
HILL VIEW RD
JERMYNS LANE
SANDY LANE
BRAISHFIELD ROAD
28
27
26
25
24
37
38
39
1
2
3
4
5
6
7
8
9
A
B
C
D
E
F
G

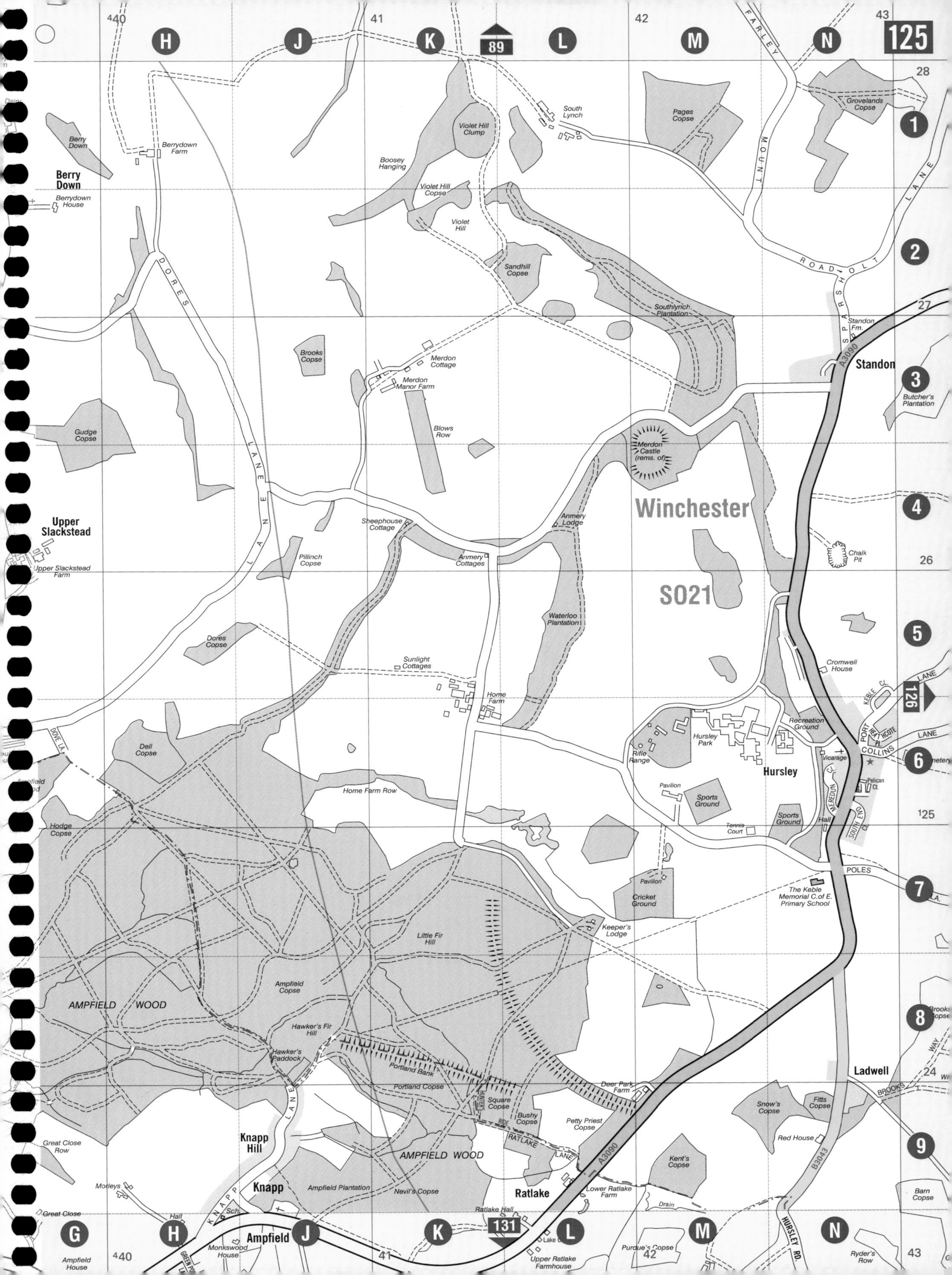

89
Winchester
SO21
Berry Down
Berrydown Farm
Berrydown House
Upper Slackstead
Upper Slackstead Farm
Gudge Copse
South Lynch
Pages Copse
Grovelands Copse
Violet Hill Clump
Boosey Hanging
Violet Hill Copse
Violet Hill
Sandhill Copse
Southlynch Plantation
Brooks Copse
Merdon Cottage
Merdon Manor Farm
Blows Row
Merdon Castle (rems. of)
Standon
Standon Fm.
Butcher's Plantation
Anmery Lodge
Sheephouse Cottage
Anmery Cottages
Pillinch Copse
Chalk Pit
Waterloo Plantation
Dores Copse
Sunlight Cottages
Home Farm
Cromwell House
Recreation Ground
Hursley Park
Hursley
Rifle Range
Vicarage
Pavilion
Sports Ground
Tennis Court
Hall
Dell Copse
Home Farm Row
Hodge Copse
Cricket Ground
The Keble Memorial C.of E. Primary School
Keeper's Lodge
Little Fir Hill
Ampfield Copse
AMPFIELD WOOD
Hawker's Fir Hill
Hawker's Paddock
Portland Bank
Portland Copse
Square Copse
Bushy Copse
Deer Park Farm
Petty Priest Copse
Ladwell
Snow's Copse
Fitts Copse
Red House
Great Close Row
Knapp Hill
Knapp
Ampfield Plantation
Nevil's Copse
Ratlake
Lower Ratlake Farm
Kent's Copse
Drain
Barn Copse
Morleys
Great Close
Hall
Sch
Ratlake Hall
Ampfield
Ampfield House
Monkswood House
Upper Ratlake Farmhouse
Purdue's Copse
Ryder's Row
DORES LANE
LANE
FARLEY MOUNT ROAD
HOLT LANE
SPARSHOLT
A3090
B3043
HURSLEY RD.
POLES LA.
COLLINS LANE
KEBLE CL.
HEATHCOTE PL.
PORT LANE
MEREDUN CL.
SOUTH END CL.
Pelican Ct.
BROOKS
WAY
DOVE LA.
KNAPP LANE
RATLAKE LANE
HUNTERS RIDE
126
131
440
41
42
43
28
27
26
125
24
H
J
K
L
M
N
G
1
2
3
4
5
6
7
8
9

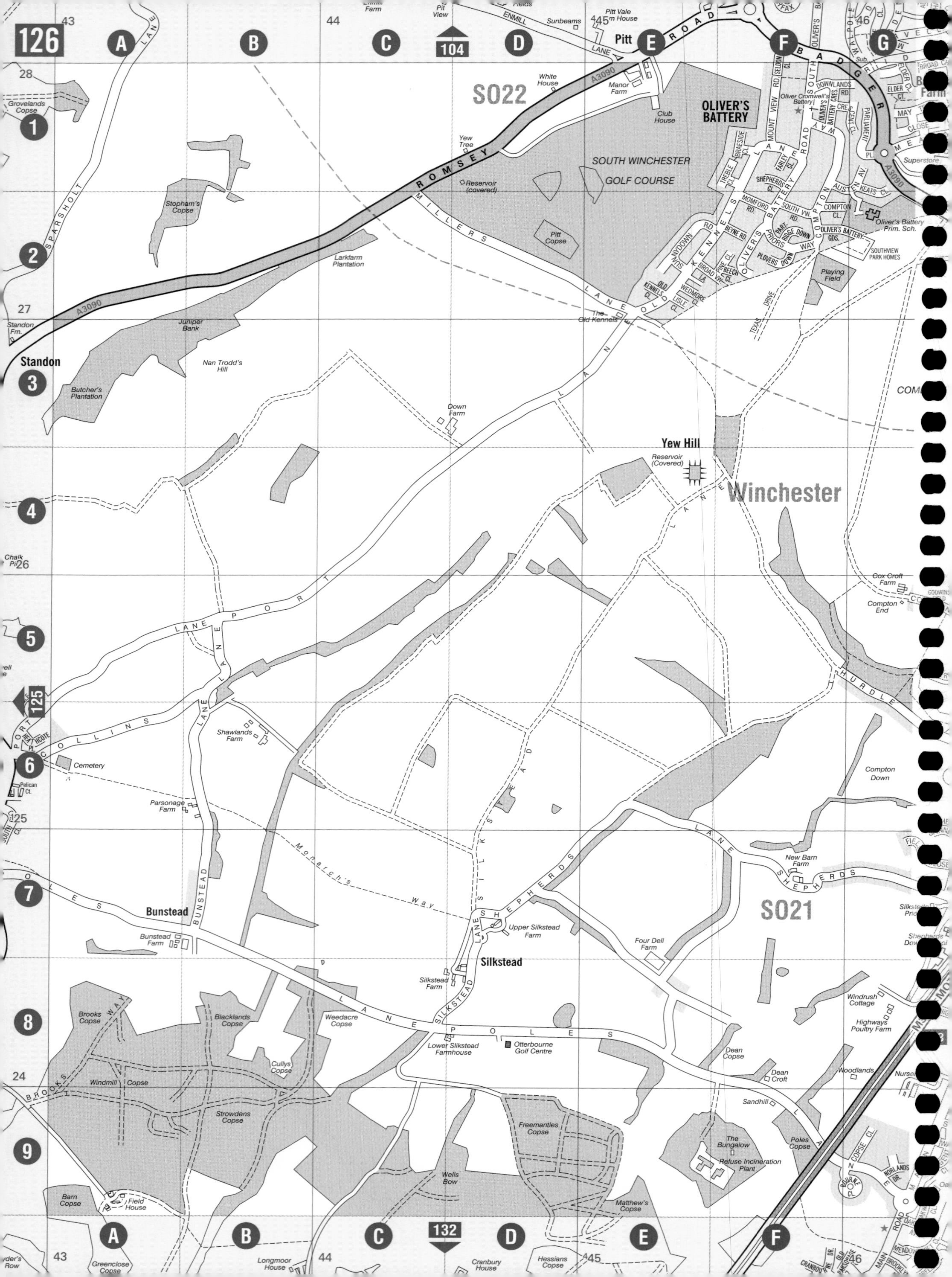
SO22
OLIVER'S BATTERY
SOUTH WINCHESTER GOLF COURSE
Pitt
Standon
Stopham's Copse
Larkfarm Plantation
Juniper Bank
Butcher's Plantation
Nan Trodd's Hill
Down Farm
Yew Hill
Reservoir (Covered)
Winchester
Cox Croft Farm
Compton End
Compton Down
Shawlands Farm
Cemetery
Parsonage Farm
Monarch's Way
Bunstead
Bunstead Farm
New Barn Farm
SO21
Upper Silkstead Farm
Silkstead
Silkstead Farm
Four Dell Farm
Brooks Copse
Blacklands Copse
Weedacre Copse
Windrush Cottage
Highways Poultry Farm
Lower Silkstead Farmhouse
Otterbourne Golf Centre
Cullys Copse
Dean Copse
Dean Croft
Woodlands
Windmill Copse
Strowdens Copse
Sandhill
Freemantles Copse
The Bungalow
Refuse Incineration Plant
Poles Copse
Wells Bow
Barn Copse
Field House
Matthew's Copse
Greenclose Copse
Longmoor House
Cranbury House
Hessians Copse
ROMSEY ROAD
A3090
SPARSHOLT LANE
MILLERS LANE
OLD KENNELS LANE
PORT LANE
COLLINS LANE
BUNSTEAD LANE
POLES LANE
SILKSTEAD LANE
SHEPHERDS LANE
HURDLE WAY
BROOKS WAY
BADGER
South Winchester Golf Course
Club House
Manor Farm
White House
Yew Tree
Reservoir (covered)
Pitt Copse
The Old Kennels
Oliver Cromwell's Battery
Oliver's Battery Prim. Sch.
Playing Field
Southview Park Homes
Superstore
Sunbeams
Pitt Vale House
ENMILL LANE
Chalk Pit
Pelican Ct.
104
132
125

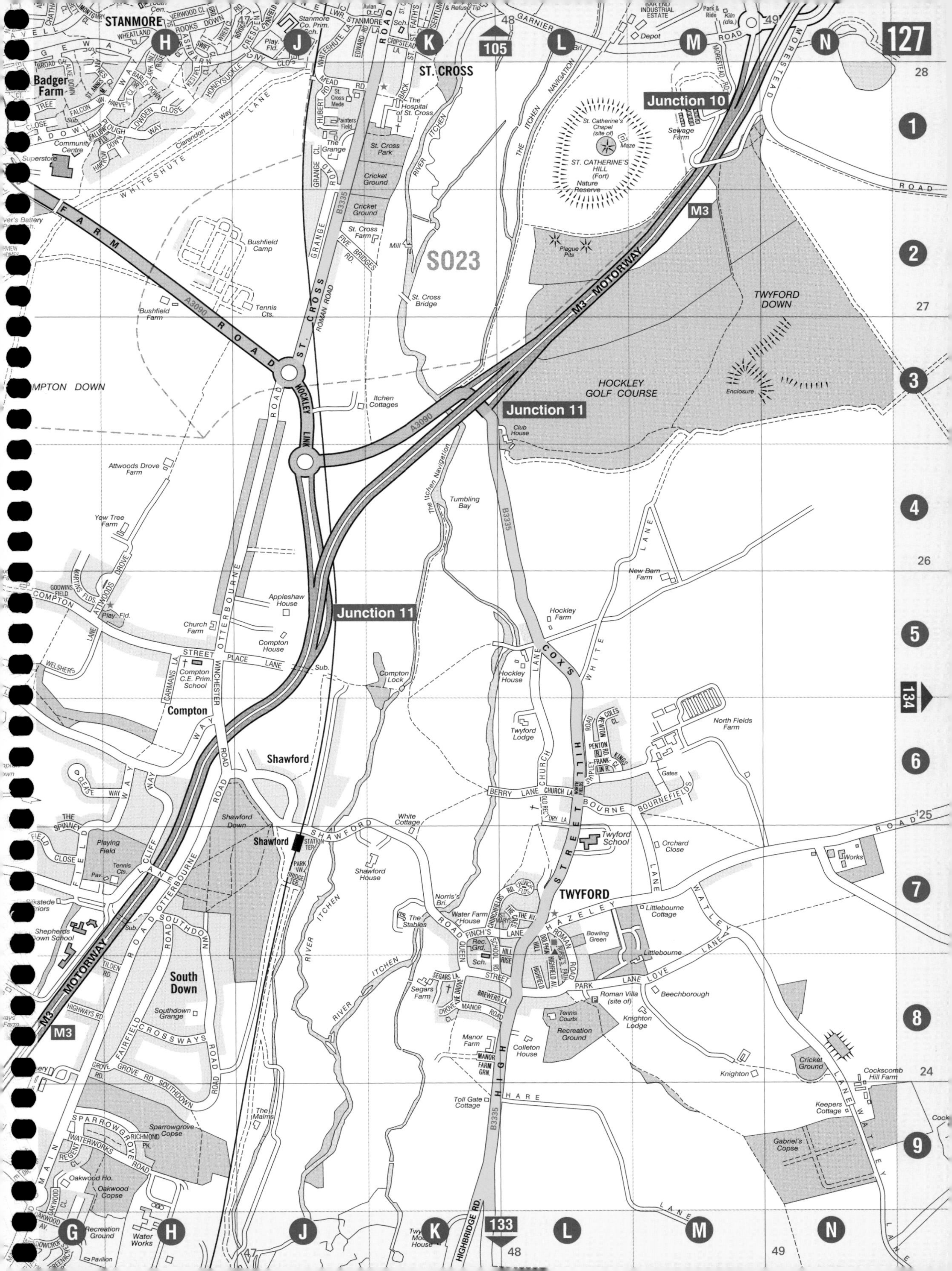
STANMORE
Badger Farm
ST. CROSS
Junction 10
St. Catherine's Chapel (site of)
Maze
ST. CATHERINE'S HILL (Fort)
Nature Reserve
Sewage Farm
M3
Plague Pits
SO23
TWYFORD DOWN
M3 MOTORWAY
HOCKLEY GOLF COURSE
Enclosure
Junction 11
Club House
St. Cross Park
Cricket Ground
St. Cross Farm
Mill
St. Cross Bridge
The Hospital of St. Cross
The Grange
Painters Field
St. Cross Mede
Community Centre
Superstore
FARM ROAD
A3090
Bushfield Camp
Bushfield Farm
Tennis Cts.
MPTON DOWN
HOCKLEY LINK
Itchen Cottages
RIVER ITCHEN
THE ITCHEN NAVIGATION
The Itchen Navigation
Tumbling Bay
B3335
Attwoods Drove Farm
Yew Tree Farm
New Barn Farm
Hockley Farm
Appleshaw House
Church Farm
Compton House
COMPTON STREET
Compton C.E. Prim. School
Compton
Sub.
Compton Lock
Hockley House
COX'S HILL
Twyford Lodge
North Fields Farm
Gates
Shawford
Shawford Down
WHITE LANE
BERRY LANE
CHURCH LANE
BOURNE
BOURNEFIELDS
White Cottage
Twyford School
Orchard Close
Works
Shawford House
Playing Field
Tennis Cts.
Pav.
Norris's Bri.
TWYFORD
Littlebourne Cottage
Water Farm House
The Stables
Bowling Green
Littlebourne
HAZELEY ROAD
Rec. Grd.
Sch.
Segars Farm
Roman Villa (site of)
Beechborough
Tennis Courts
Recreation Ground
Knighton Lodge
Manor Farm
Colleton House
Knighton
Cricket Ground
Cockscomb Hill Farm
Keepers Cottage
Gabriel's Copse
Toll Gate Cottage
HARE LANE
HIGH STREET
WATLEY LANE
Silkstede Priors
Shepherds Down School
South Down
Southdown Grange
M3 MOTORWAY
CROSSWAYS ROAD
OTTERBOURNE ROAD
SOUTHDOWN ROAD
Sparrowgrove Copse
WATERWORKS ROAD
Oakwood Ho.
Oakwood Copse
The Malms
Recreation Ground
Water Works
Pavilion
HIGHBRIDGE RD.
105
133
134
H J K L M N
G H J K L M N
1 2 3 4 5 6 7 8 9
28 27 26 125 24
47 48 49

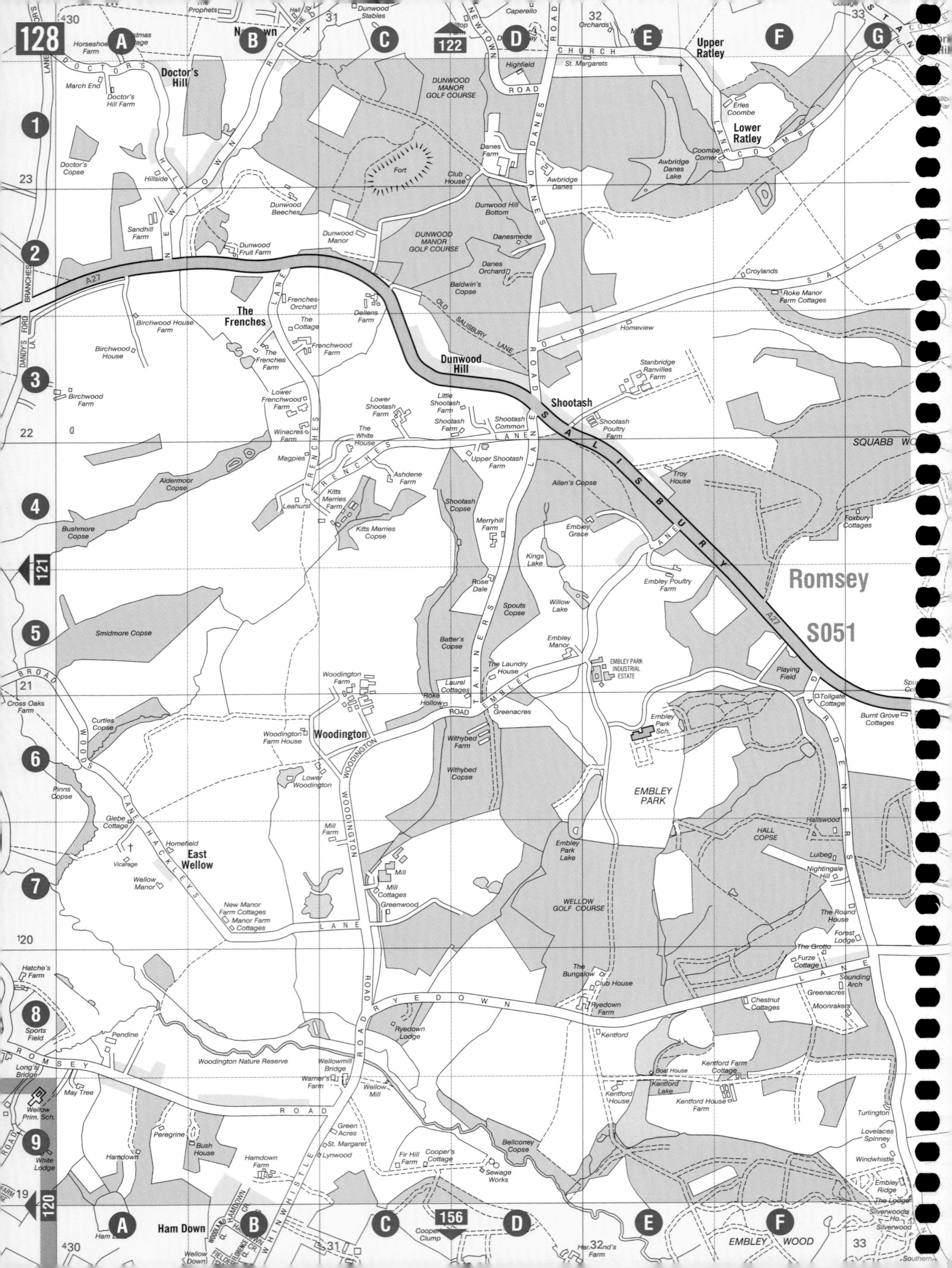
Doctor's Hill
Newtown
Upper Ratley
Lower Ratley
DUNWOOD MANOR GOLF COURSE
The Frenches
Dunwood Hill
Shootash
Romsey
S051
Woodington
East Wellow
EMBLEY PARK
WELLOW GOLF COURSE
Ham Down
EMBLEY WOOD
SQUABB WOOD
A27
Horseshoe Farm
March End
Doctor's Hill Farm
Doctor's Copse
Hillside
Sandhill Farm
Dunwood Beeches
Dunwood Fruit Farm
Dunwood Manor
Fort
Danes Farm
Club House
Awbridge Danes
Dunwood Hill Bottom
Danesmede
Danes Orchard
Baldwin's Copse
Highfield
St. Margarets
Erles Coombe
Coombe Corner
Awbridge Danes Lake
Croylands
Roke Manor Farm Cottages
Homeview
Stanbridge Ranvilles Farm
Birchwood House Farm
Birchwood House
Birchwood Farm
Frenches Orchard
The Cottage
Dellens Farm
Frenchwood Farm
The Frenches Farm
Lower Frenchwood Farm
Winacres Farm
Lower Shootash Farm
Little Shootash Farm
Shootash Farm
Shootash Common
Shootash Poultry Farm
The White House
Magpies
Upper Shootash Farm
Ashdene Farm
Kitts Merries Farm
Kitts Merries Copse
Leahurst
Aldermoor Copse
Bushmore Copse
Allen's Copse
Troy House
Foxbury Cottages
Shootash Copse
Merryhill Farm
Embley Grace
Kings Lake
Embley Poultry Farm
Rose Dale
Spouts Copse
Willow Lake
Smidmore Copse
Batter's Copse
Embley Manor
EMBLEY PARK INDUSTRIAL ESTATE
The Laundry House
Laurel Cottages
Roke Hollow
Greenacres
Playing Field
Tollgate Cottage
Burnt Grove Cottages
Embley Park Sch.
Woodington Farm
Woodington Farm House
Withybed Farm
Withybed Copse
Lower Woodington
Cross Oaks Farm
Curtles Copse
Pinns Copse
Glebe Cottage
Vicarage
Homefield
Wellow Manor
Mill Farm
Mill
Mill Cottages
Greenwood
New Manor Farm Cottages
Manor Farm Cottages
Embley Park Lake
HALL COPSE
Hallswood
Luibeg
Nightingale Hill
The Round House
Forest Lodge
The Grotto
Furze Cottage
Sounding Arch
Greenacres
Moonrakers
Chestnut Cottages
The Bungalow
Club House
Ryedown Farm
Kentford
Hatche's Farm
Sports Field
Pendine
Ryedown Lodge
Woodington Nature Reserve
Wellowmill Bridge
Warner's Farm
Wellow Mill
Long's Bridge
May Tree
Wellow Prim. Sch.
White Lodge
Peregrine
Bush House
Hamdown
Hamdown Farm
Green Acres
St. Margaret
Lynwood
Fir Hill Farm
Cooper's Cottage
Bellconey Copse
Sewage Works
Boat House
Kentford Farm Cottage
Kentford House
Kentford Lake
Kentford House Farm
Turlington
Lovelaces Spinney
Windwhistle
Embley Ridge
The Lodge
Silverwoods
Silverwood
Cooper Clump
Ham Lea
Wellow Down
DOCTOR'S LANE
NEWTOWN ROAD
HILL
CHURCH ROAD
DANES ROAD
COOMBE LANE
STANBRIDGE LANE
OLD SALISBURY LANE
SALISBURY ROAD
FRENCHES LANE
SHOOTASH LANE
TANNERS LANE
EMBLEY ROAD
WOODINGTON ROAD
GARDENERS LANE
BROAD ROAD
WOODS LANE
HACKLEYS LANE
RYEDOWN LANE
ROMSEY ROAD
WHINWHISTLE ROAD
DANDY'S FORD LA.
BRANCHES LANE
HAMDOWN CR.
WOODLAND CL.
FLORENCE CL.
FIELDER CL.
A B C D E F G
1 2 3 4 5 6 7 8 9
23 22 21 120 19
430 31 32 33
121 120 122 156

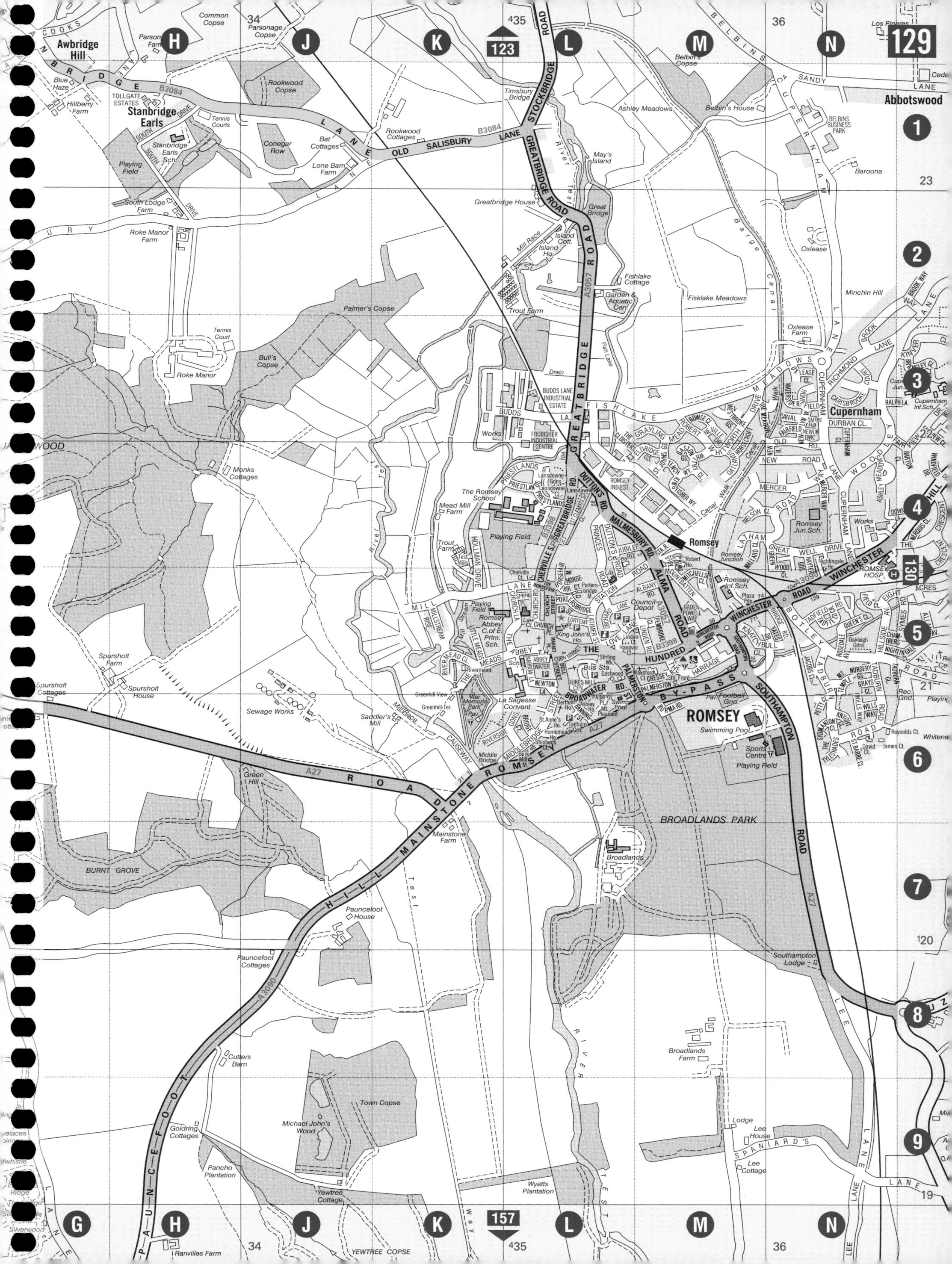

Awbridge Hill
Stanbridge Earls
Abbotswood
Cupernham
ROMSEY
Romsey
BROADLANDS PARK
Broadlands
Common Copse
Parsonage Copse
Rookwood Copse
Conegar Row
Palmer's Copse
Bull's Copse
Roke Manor
Roke Manor Farm
South Lodge Farm
Monks Cottages
Spursholt Farm
Spursholt House
Spursholt Cottages
Sewage Works
Saddler's Mill
Green Hill
BURNT GROVE
Mainstone Farm
Pauncefoot House
Pauncefoot Cottages
Cutters Barn
Town Copse
Michael John's Wood
Goldring Cottages
Pancho Plantation
Yewtree Cottage
Wyatts Plantation
YEWTREE COPSE
Ranvilles Farm
Broadlands Farm
Southampton Lodge
Lee House
Lee Cottage
Belbin's Copse
Belbin's House
Ashley Meadows
Fishlake Meadows
Fishlake Cottage
Greatbridge House
Great Bridge
Timsbury Bridge
Trout Farm
Oxlease
Oxlease Farm
Minchin Hill
Baroona
BELBINS BUSINESS PARK
BUDDS LANE INDUSTRIAL ESTATE
FROBISHER INDUSTRIAL CENTRE
ROMSEY IND. EST.
The Romsey School
Mead Mill Farm
Playing Field
Romsey Abbey C. of E. Prim. Sch.
La Sagesse Convent
War Memorial Park
Swimming Pool
Sports Centre
Romsey Jun. Sch.
Romsey Inf. Sch.
ROMSEY HOSP.
Council Depot
King John's Ho.
Bus Sta.
Middle Bridge
STOCKBRIDGE ROAD
GREATBRIDGE ROAD
OLD SALISBURY LANE
A3057
B3084
A27
A3090
B3398
MAINSTONE
HILL
PAUNCEFOOT
SOUTHAMPTON ROAD
WINCHESTER ROAD
PALMERSTON ST.
THE HUNDRED
BY-PASS
MALMESBURY RD.
ALMA ROAD
FISHLAKE MEADOWS
CUPERNHAM LANE
SPANIARD'S LANE
LEE LANE
BELBINS
SANDY LANE
River Test
Barge Canal
123
130
157
435
34
36
23
22
21
20
19
1
2
3
4
5
6
7
8
9
G
H
J
K
L
M
N

A
B
C
D
E
F
G
124
129
158
1
2
3
4
5
6
7
8
9
37
38
39
23
22
20
19
Abbotswood
Arboretum
Cedar Nursery
Sandy Lane
Jermyns Lane
Cemetery
Abbotswood House
Baroona
Nursery
Lodge
Ampfield Hill
Outwood Lodge
Tadburn
Plantation Copse
Great Close
A3090
Bracken Wood
Fishery and Fish Farm
Ganger Farm
Woodley Close Flats
Woodley Cl.
South Holmes Copse
Lower Farm
Gosport Farm
Gosport
The Straight Mile
Minchin Hill
Woodley
Woodlands
Bramble Cottages
Green Lane Farm
Oxlease Copse
Ganger Wood
Crampmoor Farm
Romsey
Crampmoor
Cupernham
Cupernham Jun. Sch.
Cupernham Inf. Sch.
Winchester Hill
Winchester Road
Crampmoor Lane
SO51
Halterworth Crossing
Highwood (The Stroud School)
Swimming Pool
Tadburn Lake
Harefield
Halterworth Farm
Highwood Lane
Playing Fields
Green Lane
Halterworth Lodge
Romsey Hosp.
Playing Field
Emer Bog
Highwood Cottage
Halterworth
Baddesley Common
Highwood Farmhouse
Warren Farm
Luzborough View
Romsey Cemetery
Halterworth County Primary School
Montfort College
Lights Copse
Playing Field
Whitenap
Botley Road
Romsey
Whitenap Farm
Reynolds Ct.
Depot
Luzborough Farm
Brooklyn
A27
Scrag Hill
Depot
Test Valley Business Park
Alpine Lodge
The Mountbatten School
Abbey Park Ind. Est.
The Quadrangle
The Premier Centre
The Triton Centre
Park Court
Depots
Works
Abbey Enterprise Centre
Beggarspath Wood
Nutburn
North Baddesley
Luzborough Plantation
Luzborough Lane
Keepers Cottage
Ashfield Lodge
Parker's Moor
Lower Ashfield Farm
Mountbatten Park
Ashfield
A3057
Hoe Cottage
Hoe Farm
Hatchet Cottage
Mill
Hoe Copse
Ashfield Copse
Malthouse Cottage
Spaniards Lane
Upper Ashfield Farm
Hoe Lane
Rownhams Lane
Bracken Lane
Driving Range
Calveslease Copse
Chilworth

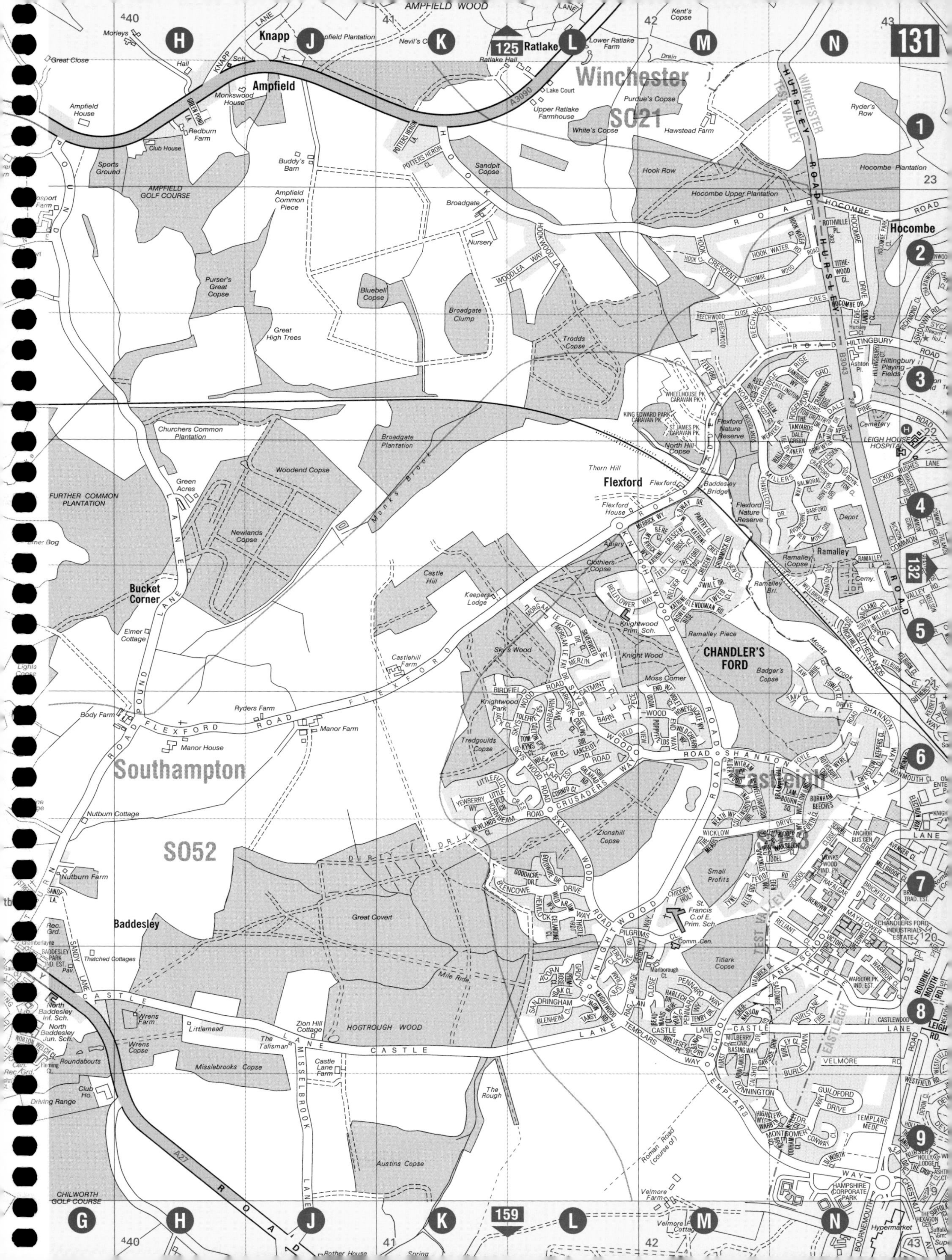

Knapp
Ampfield
Ratlake
125
Winchester
SO21
Hocombe
Flexford
Bucket Corner
CHANDLER'S FORD
Southampton
SO52
Eastleigh
SO53
Baddesley
Ampfield Golf Course
Chilworth Golf Course
Hiltingbury
Ramalley
132
159
Knightwood Prim. Sch.
St. Francis C.of E. Prim. Sch.
Chandlers Ford Industrial Estate
Hampshire Corporate Park
Hypermarket

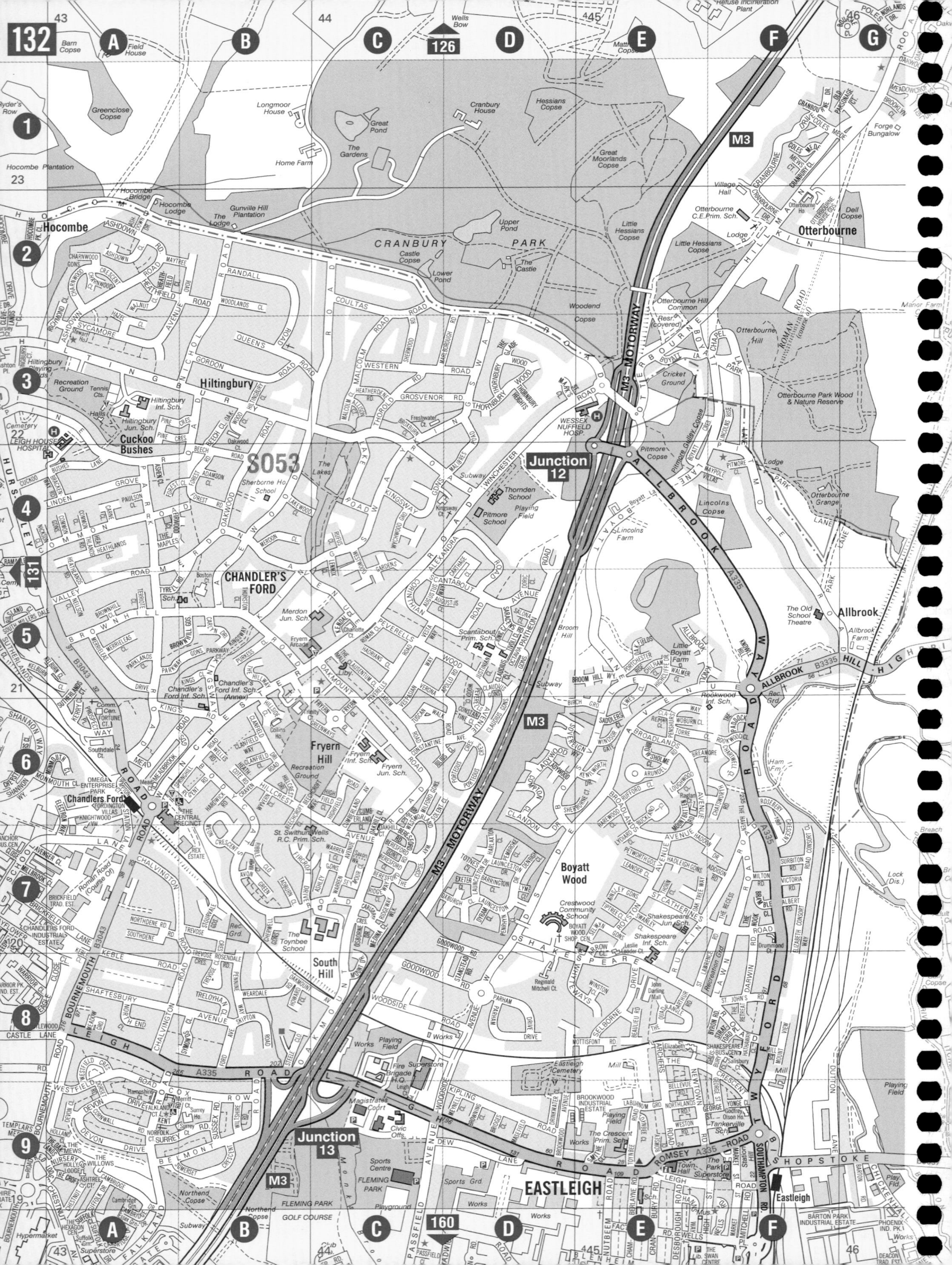

126
131
160
Hocombe
Hiltingbury
Cuckoo Bushes
S053
CHANDLER'S FORD
Chandlers Ford
Fryern Hill
South Hill
Boyatt Wood
Otterbourne
Allbrook
EASTLEIGH
Eastleigh
CRANBURY PARK
Cranbury House
Great Pond
The Gardens
Home Farm
Longmoor House
Greenclose Copse
Barn Copse
Field House
Hessians Copse
Great Moorlands Copse
Little Hessians Copse
Upper Pond
Lower Pond
The Castle
Castle Copse
Gunville Hill Plantation
Hocombe Plantation
Hocombe Bridge
Hocombe Lodge
The Lodge
Woodend Copse
Otterbourne Hill Common
Otterbourne Hill
Otterbourne Park Wood & Nature Reserve
Cricket Ground
Pitmore Copse
Lincolns Copse
Lincolns Farm
Otterbourne Grange
The Old School Theatre
Allbrook Farm
Broom Hill
Little Boyatt Farm
Wessex Nuffield Hosp.
Junction 12
Junction 13
M3
M3 MOTORWAY
A335
B3335
B3043
Thornden School
Pitmore School
Sherborne Ho School
Merdon Jun. Sch.
Fryern Arcade
Fryern Inf. Sch.
Fryern Jun. Sch.
Recreation Ground
Scantabout Prim. Sch.
Hiltingbury Inf. Sch.
Hiltingbury Jun. Sch.
Leigh House Hospital
Chandler's Ford Inf. Sch.
Rookwood Inf. Sch.
Crestwood Community School
Shakespeare Jun. Sch.
Shakespeare Inf. Sch.
St. Swithun Wells R.C. Prim. Sch.
The Toynbee School
Fire Brigade H.Q.
Superstore
Magistrates Court
Civic Offs.
Sports Centre
FLEMING PARK
FLEMING PARK GOLF COURSE
Eastleigh Cemetery
Brookwood Industrial Estate
The Crescent Prim. Sch.
Town Hall
Tankerville Sch.
Barton Park Industrial Estate
Chandlers Ford Industrial Estate
Brickfield Trad. Est.
Omega Enterprise Park
The Central Precinct
Northend Copse
Refuse Incineration Plant
Wells Bow
Mattock Copse
Village Hall
Otterbourne C.E.Prim. Sch.
Dell Copse
Little Hessians Copse
Ham Fm.
Lock (Dis.)
Playing Field

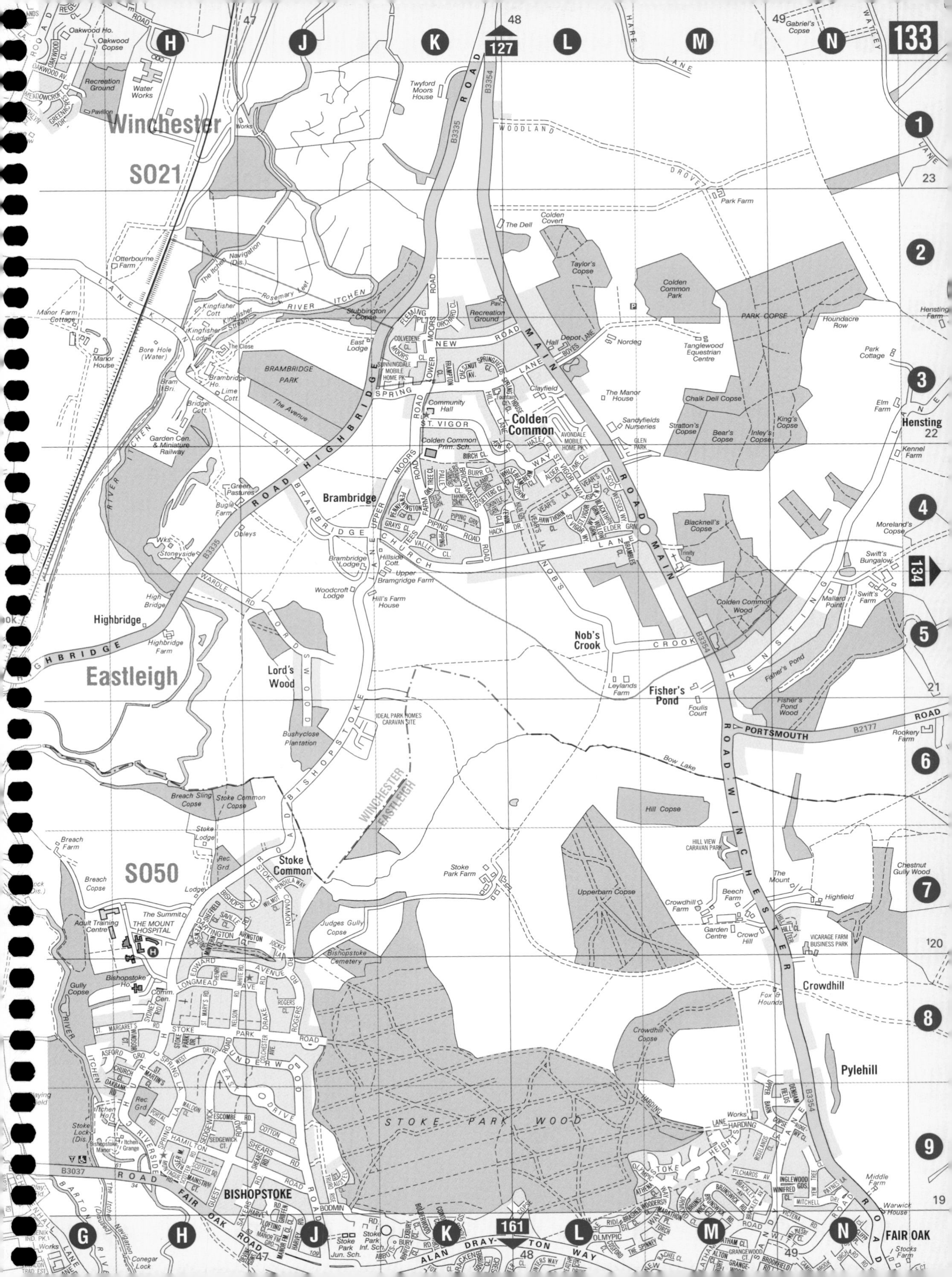

Winchester
SO21
Eastleigh
SO50
Colden Common
Brambridge
Highbridge
Lord's Wood
Nob's Crook
Fisher's Pond
Stoke Common
Hensting
Crowdhill
Pylehill
BISHOPSTOKE
FAIR OAK
127
161
134
H
J
K
L
M
N
G
1
2
3
4
5
6
7
8
9
47
48
49
23
22
21
20
19
Oakwood Ho.
Oakwood Copse
Recreation Ground
Water Works
Pavilion
Twyford Moors House
Gabriel's Copse
HARE LANE
WOODLAND DROVE
Park Farm
Otterbourne Farm
Manor Farm Cottage
Manor House
Bore Hole (Water)
Kingfisher Cott
Kingfisher Lodge
Kingfisher Stream
The Itchen Navigation (Dis.)
Rosemary Leet
RIVER ITCHEN
Stubbington Copse
BRAMBRIDGE PARK
The Avenue
Brambridge Ho.
Lime Cott.
Bridge Cott.
Bram Bri.
The Close
Garden Cen. & Miniature Railway
Green Pastures
Bugle Farm
Obleys
Stoneyside
High Bridge
Highbridge Farm
HIGHBRIDGE ROAD
B3335
B3354
MAIN ROAD
WINCHESTER ROAD
The Dell
Colden Covert
Taylor's Copse
Colden Common Park
PARK COPSE
Houndacre Row
Hensting Farm
Recreation Ground
East Lodge
Depot
Hall
Nordeg
Tanglewood Equestrian Centre
Park Cottage
Clayfield
The Manor House
Sandyfields Nurseries
Chalk Dell Copse
Stratton's Copse
Bear's Copse
Inley's Copse
King's Copse
Elm Farm
Kennel Farm
Community Hall
Colden Common Prim. Sch.
ST. VIGOR WAY
SPRING LANE
NEW ROAD
BOYES LANE
AVONDALE MOBILE HOME PK
GLEN PARK
SONNINGDALE MOBILE HOME PK
Blacknell's Copse
Moreland's Copse
Swift's Bungalow
Swift's Farm
Mallard Point
Colden Common Wood
CHURCH LANE
BRAMBRIDGE
Brambridge Lodge
Hillside Cott.
Upper Bramgridge Farm
Hill's Farm House
Woodcroft Lodge
WARDLE RD
LORDS WOOD
NOBS CROOK
HENSTING LANE
Leylands Farm
Foulis Court
Fisher's Pond
Fisher's Pond Wood
PORTSMOUTH ROAD
B2177
Rookery Farm
Bow Lake
Hill Copse
IDEAL PARK HOMES CARAVAN SITE
Bushyclose Plantation
BISHOPSTOKE ROAD
WINCHESTER
EASTLEIGH
Breach Sling Copse
Stoke Common Copse
Stoke Lodge
Breach Farm
Breach Copse
Rec. Grd.
HILL VIEW CARAVAN PARK
Stoke Park Farm
Upperbarn Copse
The Mount
Chestnut Gully Wood
Beech Farm
Highfield
Crowdhill Farm
Garden Centre
Crowd Hill
VICARAGE FARM BUSINESS PARK
Fox & Hounds
Crowdhill Copse
Judges Gully Copse
Bishopstoke Cemetery
The Summit
Adult Training Centre
THE MOUNT HOSPITAL
Gully Copse
Bishopstoke Ho.
Comm. Cen.
STOKE COMMON ROAD
LONGMEAD AVE
STOKE PARK ROAD
UNDERWOOD ROAD
SPRING LA.
RIVERSIDE
HAMILTON
Itchen Ho.
Stoke Lock (Dis.)
Bishopstoke Manor
Itchen Grange
RIVER ITCHEN
STOKE PARK WOOD
HARDING LANE
Works
Middle Farm
Warwick House
Stocks Farm
B3037
FAIR OAK ROAD
ALAN DRAYTON WAY
Stoke Park Jun. Sch.
Stoke Park Inf. Sch.
BARTON
Conegar Lock
The Itchen Navigation (Disused)

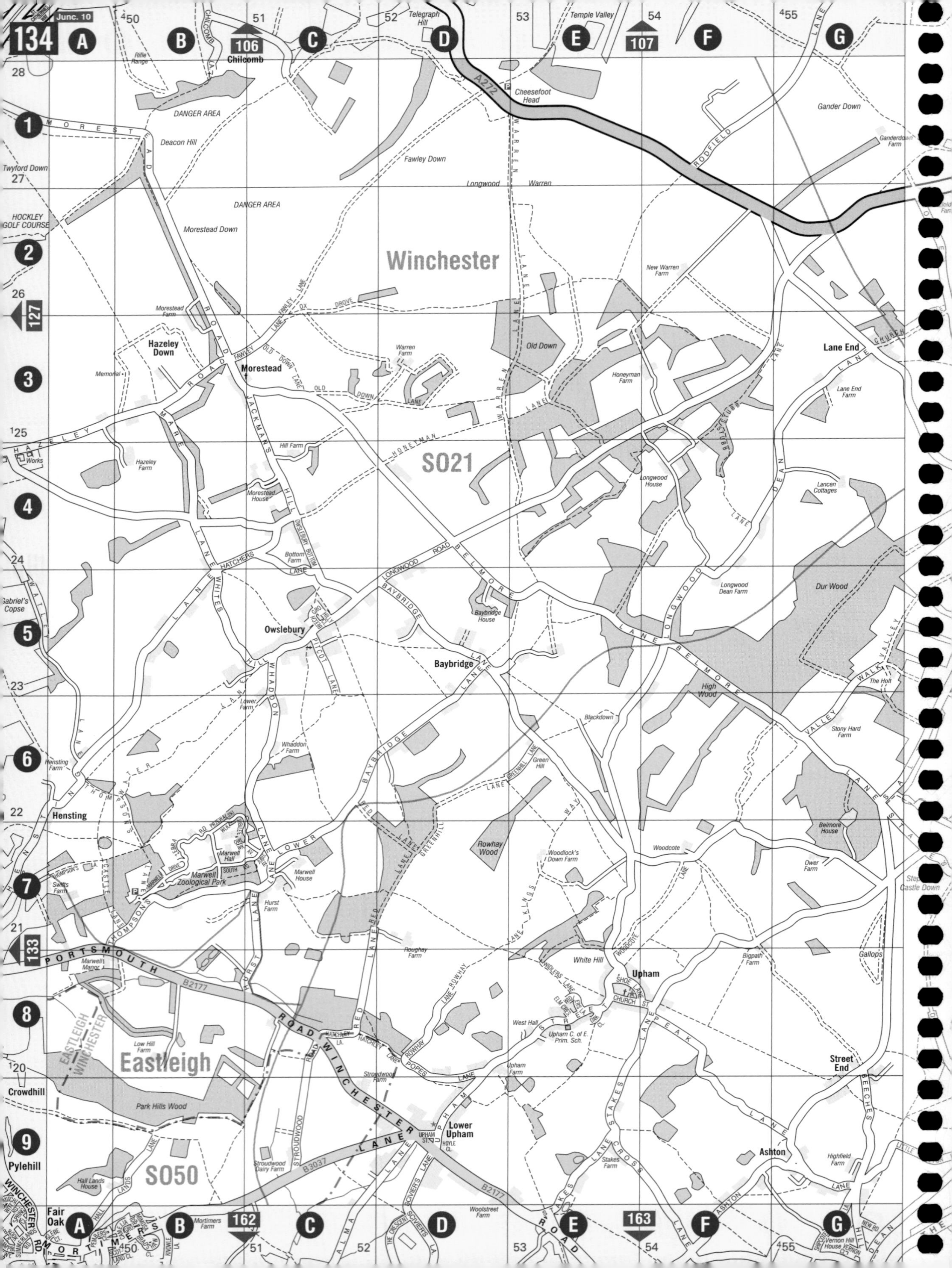
Winchester
SO21
SO50
Eastleigh
Morestead
Owslebury
Baybridge
Upham
Lower Upham
Hensting
Lane End
Street End
Ashton
Chilcomb
Hazeley Down
Marwell Zoological Park
Park Hills Wood
Dur Wood
Old Down
Fawley Down
Morestead Down
Deacon Hill
DANGER AREA
Cheesefoot Head
Temple Valley
Telegraph Hill
Gander Down
Twyford Down
HOCKLEY GOLF COURSE
Crowdhill
Pylehill
Fair Oak
Gabriel's Copse
Rowhay Wood
High Wood
White Hill
Green Hill
Blackdown
Woodcote
Longwood Warren
PORTSMOUTH ROAD
WINCHESTER ROAD
B2177
B3037
A272
106
107
127
133
162
163

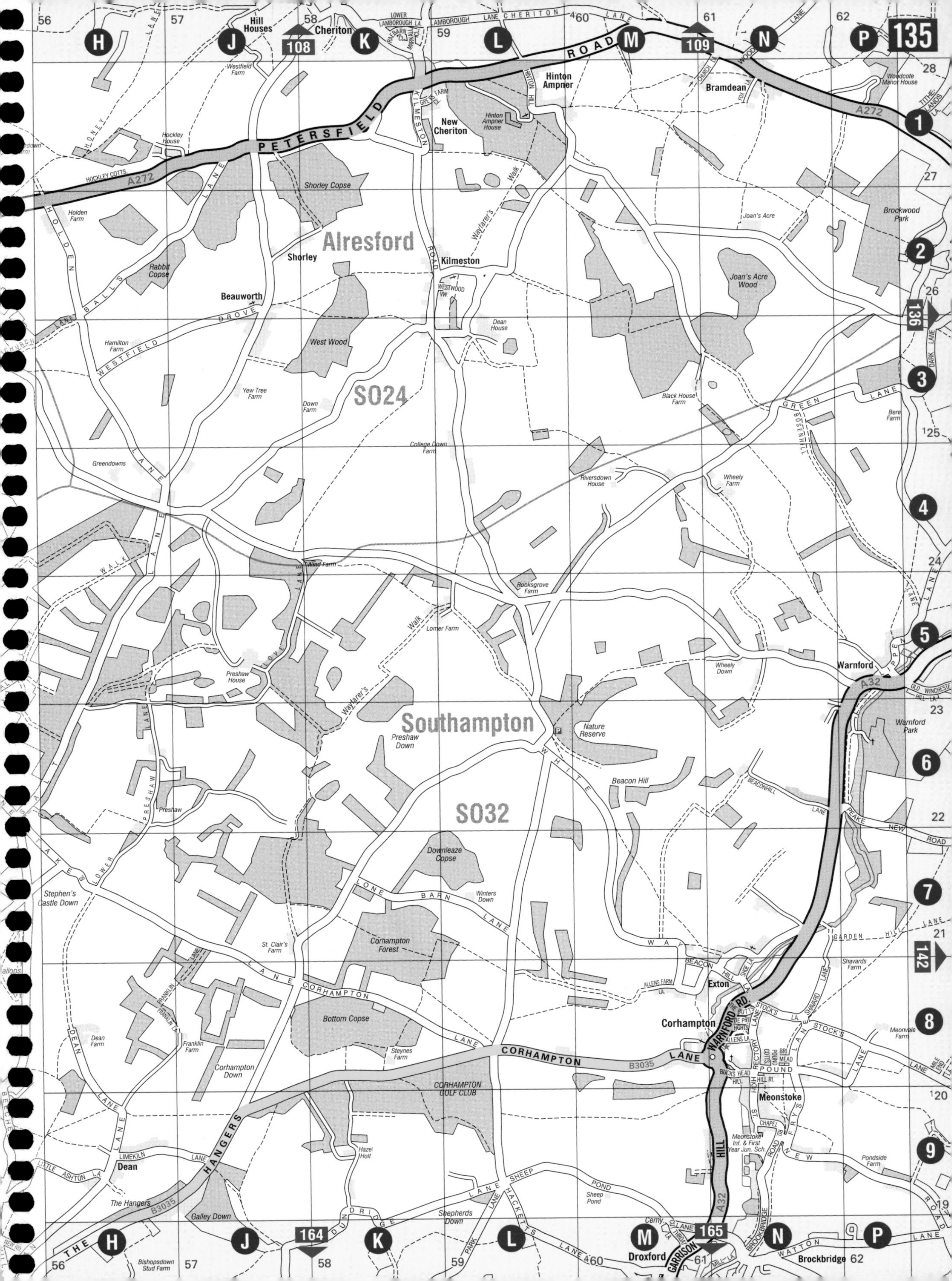
Hill Houses
Cheriton
108
109
Westfield Farm
Hinton Ampner
Bramdean
Woodcote Manor House
Hinton Ampner House
New Cheriton
Hockley House
PETERSFIELD ROAD
A272
HOCKLEY COTTS.
Shorley Copse
Holden Farm
Brockwood Park
Joan's Acre
Alresford
Shorley
Kilmeston
Rabbit Copse
Beauworth
Joan's Acre Wood
WESTWOOD VW.
Dean House
136
Hamilton Farm
WESTFIELD DROVE
West Wood
Yew Tree Farm
Down Farm
SO24
Black House Farm
GREEN LANE
Bere Farm
College Down Farm
Greendowns
Riversdown House
Wheely Farm
Wind Farm
Rooksgrove Farm
Lomer Farm
Preshaw House
Wheely Down
Warnford
A32
Warnford Park
Southampton
Nature Reserve
Preshaw Down
Beacon Hill
Preshaw
SO32
Downleaze Copse
Stephen's Castle Down
LONE BARN LANE
Winters Down
St. Clair's Farm
Corhampton Forest
Shavards Farm
142
Exton
Corhampton
Bottom Copse
Dean Farm
Franklin Farm
Steynes Farm
CORHAMPTON LANE
B3035
Meonvale Farm
Corhampton Down
CORHAMPTON GOLF CLUB
Meonstoke
Meonstoke Inf. & First Year Jun. Sch.
Hazel Holt
Dean
LIMEKILN LANE
LITTLE ASHTON LA
HANGERS
Pondside Farm
Sheep Pond
The Hangers
Galley Down
Shepherds Down
164
165
Droxford
Brockbridge
Bishopsdown Stud Farm

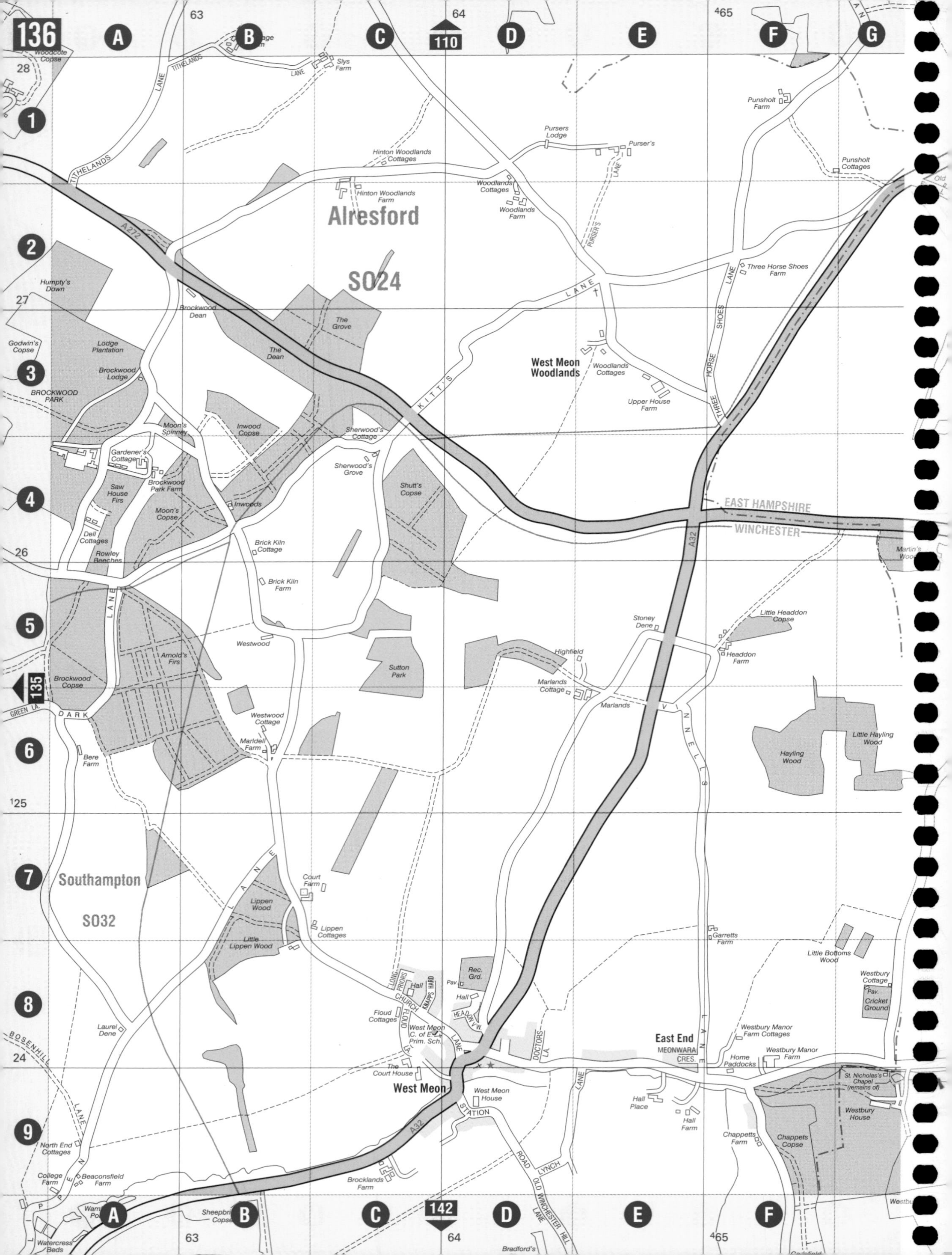
Alresford
SO24
West Meon Woodlands
Southampton
SO32
West Meon
East End
EAST HAMPSHIRE
WINCHESTER
A272
A32
Slys Farm
Punsholt Farm
Pursers Lodge
Purser's
Hinton Woodlands Cottages
Hinton Woodlands Farm
Woodlands Cottages
Woodlands Farm
Punsholt Cottages
Three Horse Shoes Farm
Humpty's Down
Brockwood Dean
The Grove
Godwin's Copse
Lodge Plantation
The Dean
Brockwood Lodge
BROCKWOOD PARK
Woodlands Cottages
Upper House Farm
Moon's Spinney
Inwood Copse
Sherwood's Cottage
Gardener's Cottage
Sherwood's Grove
Shutt's Copse
Saw House Firs
Brockwood Park Farm
Inwoods
Moon's Copse
Dell Cottages
Brick Kiln Cottage
Rowley Beeches
Brick Kiln Farm
Martin's Wood
Stoney Dene
Little Headdon Copse
Westwood
Highfield
Headdon Farm
Arnold's Firs
Sutton Park
Brockwood Copse
Marlands Cottage
Marlands
Westwood Cottage
Marldell Farm
Bere Farm
Hayling Wood
Little Hayling Wood
Court Farm
Lippen Wood
Lippen Cottages
Little Lippen Wood
Garretts Farm
Little Bottoms Wood
Rec. Grd.
Westbury Cottage
Cricket Ground
Hall
Pav.
Floud Cottages
Laurel Dene
West Meon C. of E. Prim. Sch.
Westbury Manor Farm Cottages
Westbury Manor Farm
MEONWARA CRES.
Home Paddocks
The Court House
St. Nicholas's Chapel (remains of)
West Meon House
Hall Place
Hall Farm
Westbury House
Chappetts Farm
Chappets Copse
North End Cottages
College Farm
Beaconsfield Farm
Brocklands Farm
Watercress Beds
TITHELANDS LANE
KITT'S LANE
PURSER'S LANE
THREE HORSE SHOES LANE
DARK LANE
GREEN LA
BOSENHILL LANE
LONG PRIORS
CHURCH LANE
KNAPPS HARD
FLOUD LA
HEADON VW.
DOCTORS LA
STATION ROAD
LYNCH LANE
OLD WINCHESTER HILL LANE
VANNELLS LANE
135
110
142

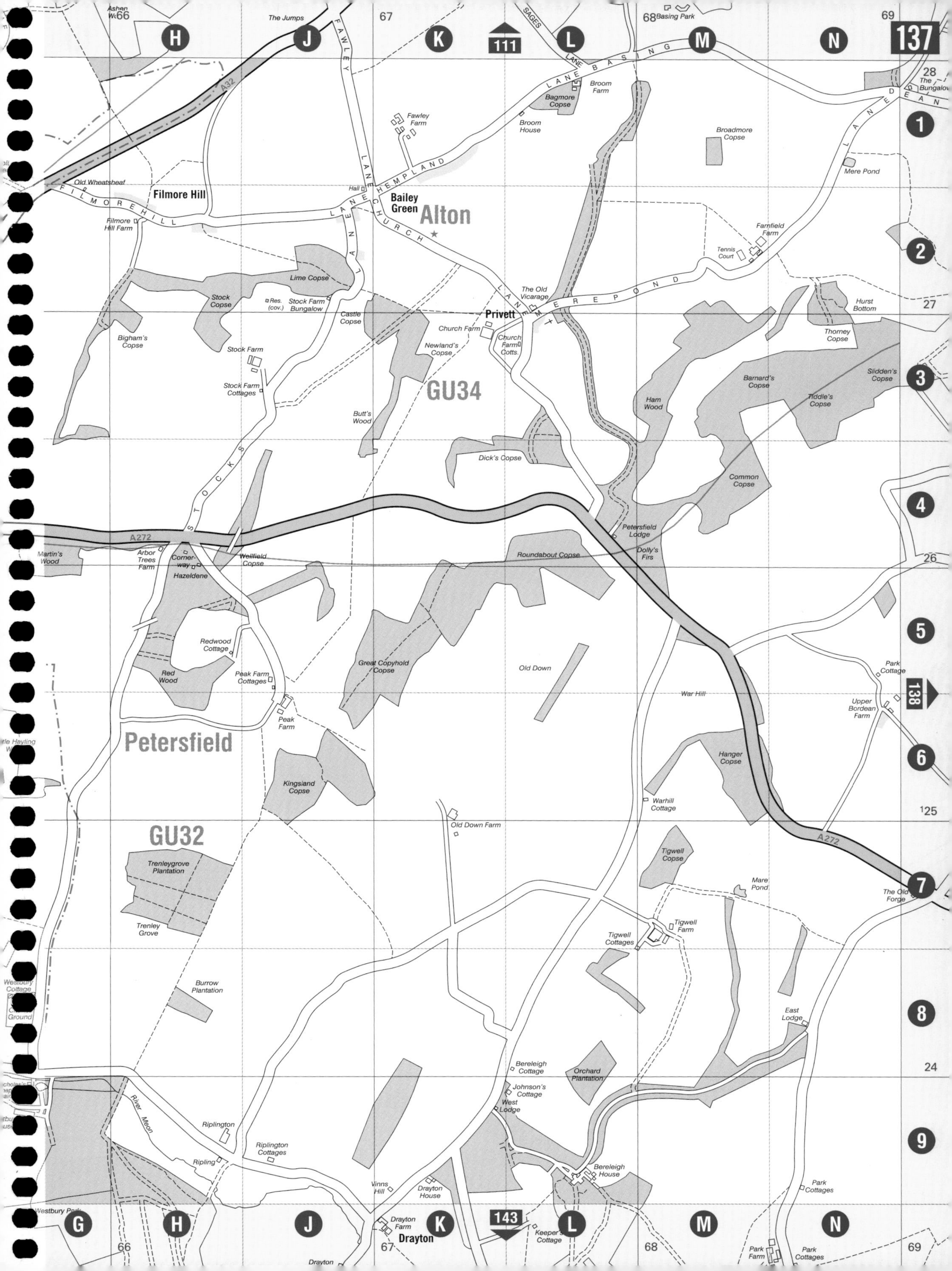
111
143
138
Alton
Petersfield
GU34
GU32
Filmore Hill
Bailey Green
Privett
Drayton
A32
A272
Ashen Wd
The Jumps
Basing Park
FAWLEY LANE
SAGES LANE
BASING LANE
DEAN LANE
HEMPLAND LANE
FILMORE HILL
CHURCH LANE
MERE POND
STOCKS
Fawley Farm
Broom Farm
Bagmore Copse
Broom House
Broadmore Copse
Mere Pond
The Bungalow
Old Wheatsheaf
Filmore Hill Farm
Hall
Farnfield Farm
Tennis Court
Hurst Bottom
Thorney Copse
Lime Copse
Stock Copse
Res. (cov.)
Stock Farm Bungalow
Castle Copse
The Old Vicarage
Church Farm
Church Farm Cotts.
Newland's Copse
Bigham's Copse
Stock Farm
Stock Farm Cottages
Butt's Wood
Ham Wood
Barnard's Copse
Slidden's Copse
Tiddle's Copse
Common Copse
Dick's Copse
Petersfield Lodge
Dolly's Firs
Martin's Wood
Arbor Trees Farm
Cornerway
Hazeldene
Wellfield Copse
Roundabout Copse
Redwood Cottage
Red Wood
Peak Farm Cottages
Peak Farm
Great Copyhold Copse
Old Down
War Hill
Park Cottage
Upper Bordean Farm
Hanger Copse
Kingsland Copse
Warhill Cottage
Old Down Farm
Trenleygrove Plantation
Trenley Grove
Tigwell Copse
Mare Pond
The Old Forge
Tigwell Farm
Tigwell Cottages
Burrow Plantation
Westbury Cottage
Ground
East Lodge
Bereleigh Cottage
Orchard Plantation
Johnson's Cottage
West Lodge
River Meon
Riplington
Riplington Cottages
Ripling
Bereleigh House
Vinns Hill
Drayton House
Park Cottages
Westbury Park
Drayton Farm
Keeper's Cottage
Park Farm
Park Cottages
Drayton
G
H
J
K
L
M
N
1
2
3
4
5
6
7
8
9
66
67
68
69
24
25
26
27
28

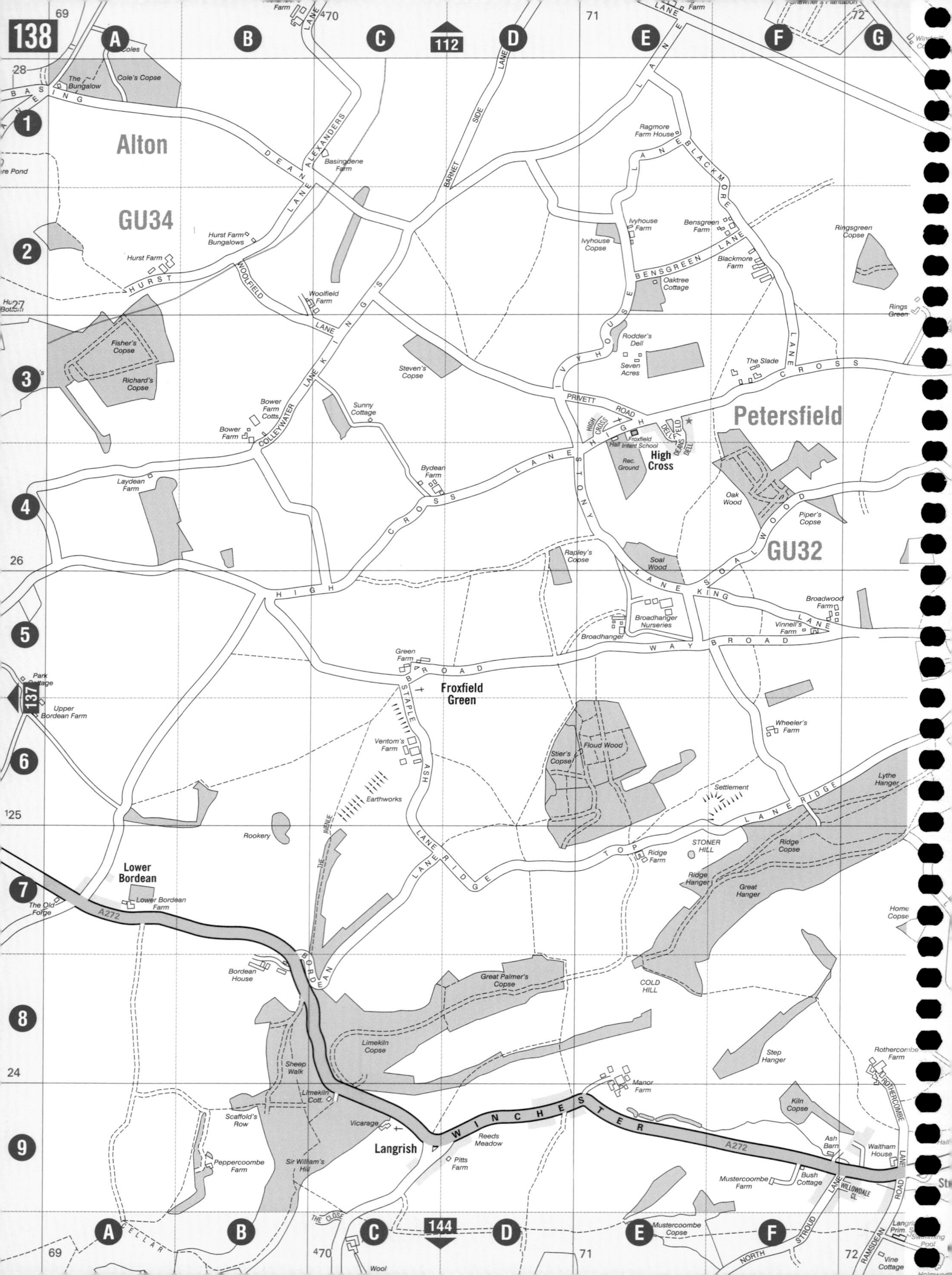
112
144
137
Alton
GU34
Petersfield
GU32
High Cross
Froxfield Green
Lower Bordean
Langrish
The Bungalow
Cole's Copse
Coles
Basingdene Farm
Hurst Farm Bungalows
Hurst Farm
Woolfield Farm
Fisher's Copse
Richard's Copse
Steven's Copse
Sunny Cottage
Bower Farm Cotts
Bower Farm
Laydean Farm
Bydean Farm
Ragmore Farm House
Ivyhouse Farm
Ivyhouse Copse
Bensgreen Farm
Blackmore Farm
Oaktree Cottage
Ringsgreen Copse
Rings Green
Rodder's Dell
Seven Acres
The Slade
Froxfield Infant School
Hall
Rec. Ground
Oak Wood
Piper's Copse
Rapley's Copse
Soal Wood
Broadwood Farm
Broadhanger Nurseries
Broadhanger
Vinnell's Farm
Green Farm
Park Cottage
Upper Bordean Farm
Ventom's Farm
Earthworks
Wheeler's Farm
Stier's Copse
Floud Wood
Settlement
Lythe Hanger
Rookery
Stoner Hill
Ridge Farm
Ridge Copse
Ridge Hanger
Great Hanger
The Old Forge
Lower Bordean Farm
Home Copse
Bordean House
Great Palmer's Copse
Cold Hill
Limekiln Copse
Sheep Walk
Step Hanger
Rothercombe Farm
Manor Farm
Limekiln Cott.
Kiln Copse
Scaffold's Row
Vicarage
Reeds Meadow
Ash Barn
Waltham House
Peppercoombe Farm
Sir William's Hill
Pitts Farm
Mustercoombe Farm
Bush Cottage
Mustercoombe Copse
Vine Cottage
Wool
Basing Lane
Dean Lane
Alexanders Lane
Barnet Side Lane
Hurst Lane
Woolfield Lane
Kings Lane
Colleywater Lane
Blackmore Lane
Bensgreen Lane
Ivyhouse Lane
Privett Road
High Cross
Deans Dell
Delfield
High Cross Lane
Stony Lane
Soalwood Lane
King Lane
Broadway Road
High Lane
Broad Road
Staple Ash Lane
The Avenue
Ridge Lane
Top Lane
Bordean Lane
Winchester Road
A272
The Close
Cellar
North Stroud Lane
Willowdale Cl.
Ramsdean Road
Rothercombe Lane
69
470
71
72
28
27
26
25
24
A
B
C
D
E
F
G
1
2
3
4
5
6
7
8
9

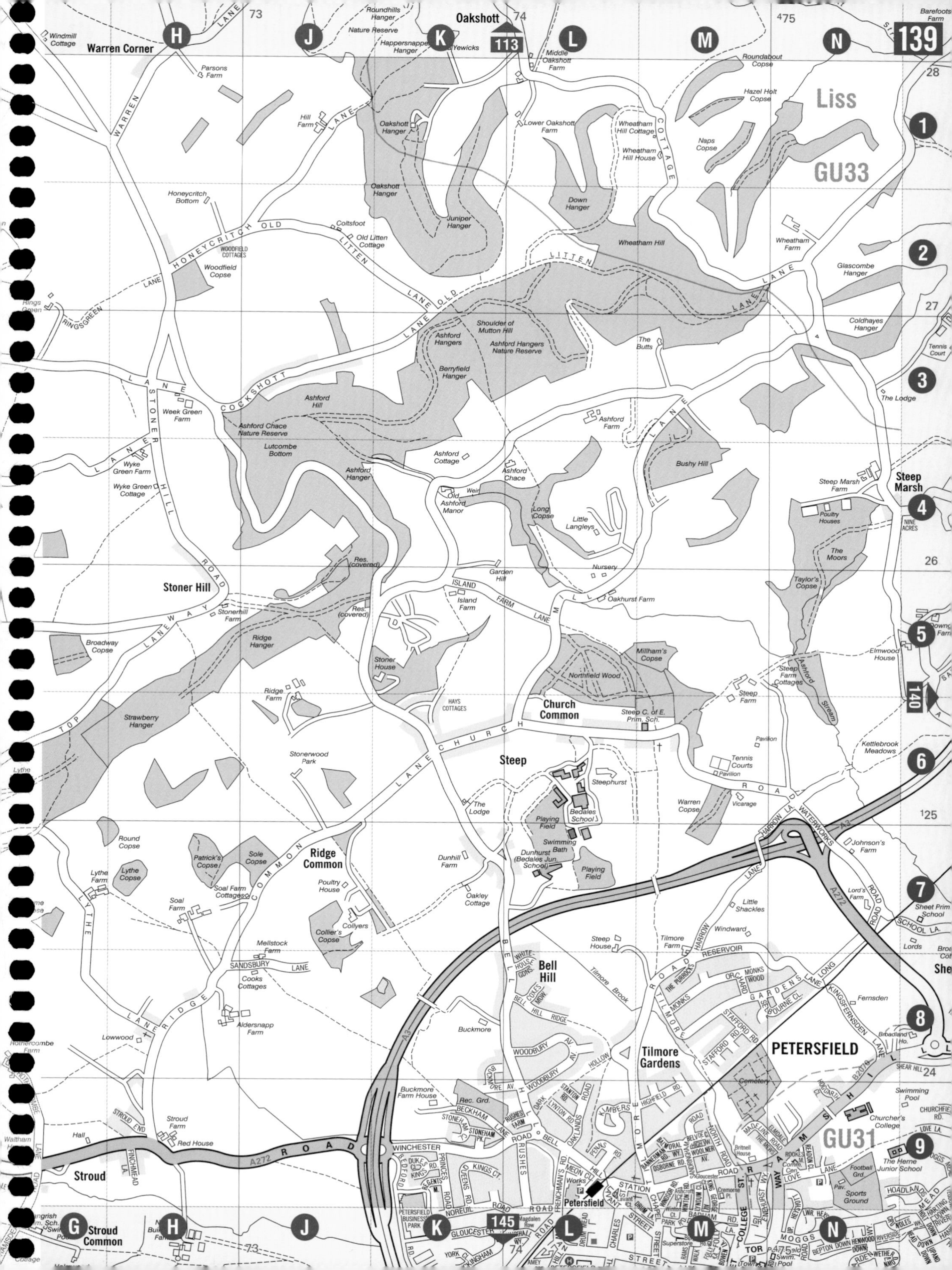
Oakshott
113
Warren Corner
Windmill Cottage
Roundhills Hanger
Nature Reserve
Happersnapper Hanger
Yewicks
Middle Oakshott Farm
Barefoots Farm
Roundabout Copse
Hazel Holt Copse
Liss
GU33
Parsons Farm
Hill Farm
Oakshott Hanger
Lower Oakshott Farm
Wheatham Hill Cottage
Wheatham Hill House
Naps Copse
Honeycritch Bottom
Down Hanger
Juniper Hanger
Coltsfoot
Old Litten Cottage
Wheatham Hill
Wheatham Farm
Woodfield Cottages
Woodfield Copse
Glascombe Hanger
Coldhayes Hanger
Rings Green
Shoulder of Mutton Hill
Ashford Hangers
Ashford Hangers Nature Reserve
The Butts
Tennis Court
Berryfield Hanger
The Lodge
Ashford Hill
Week Green Farm
Ashford Farm
Ashford Chace Nature Reserve
Lutcombe Bottom
Bushy Hill
Wyke Green Farm
Wyke Green Cottage
Ashford Cottage
Ashford Chace
Ashford Hanger
Steep Marsh Farm
Steep Marsh
Old Ashford Manor
Weir
Long Copse
Little Langleys
Poultry Houses
Nine Acres
The Moors
Res. (covered)
Garden Hill
Nursery
Taylor's Copse
Stoner Hill
Island Farm
Oakhurst Farm
Stonerhill Farm
Broadway Copse
Ridge Hanger
Stoner House
Millham's Copse
Northfield Wood
Elmwood House
Steep Farm Cottages
Ashford Stream
Ridge Farm
Hays Cottages
Church Common
Steep C. of E. Prim. Sch.
Steep Farm
140
Strawberry Hanger
Pavilion
Kettlebrook Meadows
Stonerwood Park
Steep
Steephurst
Tennis Courts
The Lodge
Bedales School
Warren Copse
Vicarage
Playing Field
Swimming Bath
Round Copse
Patrick's Copse
Sole Copse
Ridge Common
Dunhill Farm
Dunhurst (Bedales Jun. School)
Johnson's Farm
Lythe Farm
Lythe Copse
Soal Farm Cottages
Poultry House
Oakley Cottage
Lord's Farm
Little Shackles
Sheet Prim School
Soal Farm
Collyers
Collier's Copse
Windward
Lords
Mellstock Farm
Steep House
Tilmore Farm
Bell Hill
Cooks Cottages
Tilmore Brook
Fernsden
Aldersnapp Farm
Buckmore
Broadland Ho.
Lowwood
Rothercombe Farm
Tilmore Gardens
PETERSFIELD
Cemetery
Swimming Pool
Buckmore Farm House
Rec. Grd.
Churcher's College
Stroud Farm
Red House
GU31
Hall
Britnell House
The Herne Junior School
Football Grd.
Stroud
Sports Ground
Petersfield
Petersfield Business Park
145
Magdalen Row
Superstore
Stroud Common
73
74
475
28
27
26
25
24
A272
A3
B2070
WARREN
LANE
HONEYCRITCH OLD LANE
LITTEN LANE
COCKSHOTT LANE
OLD LITTEN LANE
COTTAGE
RINGSGREEN
STONER HILL ROAD
TOP LANEWAY
ISLAND FARM LANE
CHURCH LANE
ROAD
WATERWORKS
HARROW LA.
LYTHE
RIDGE COMMON
SANDSBURY LANE
RIDGE LANE
BELL HILL
RESERVOIR ROAD
MONKS ORCHARD
TILMORE GARDENS
STAFFORD RD
KINGSFERNSDEN LANE
LONG LANE
SHEAR HILL
SCHOOL LA.
WOODBURY AV.
HOLLOW
HIGHFIELD RD
WINCHESTER ROAD
RUSHES ROAD
BELL ROAD
NOREUIL ROAD
GLOUCESTER
STATION
CHAPEL
BARHAM RD.
COLLEGE
DRAGON
LOVE LANE
MOGGS
HOADLANDS
FINCHMEAD LA.
STROUD END

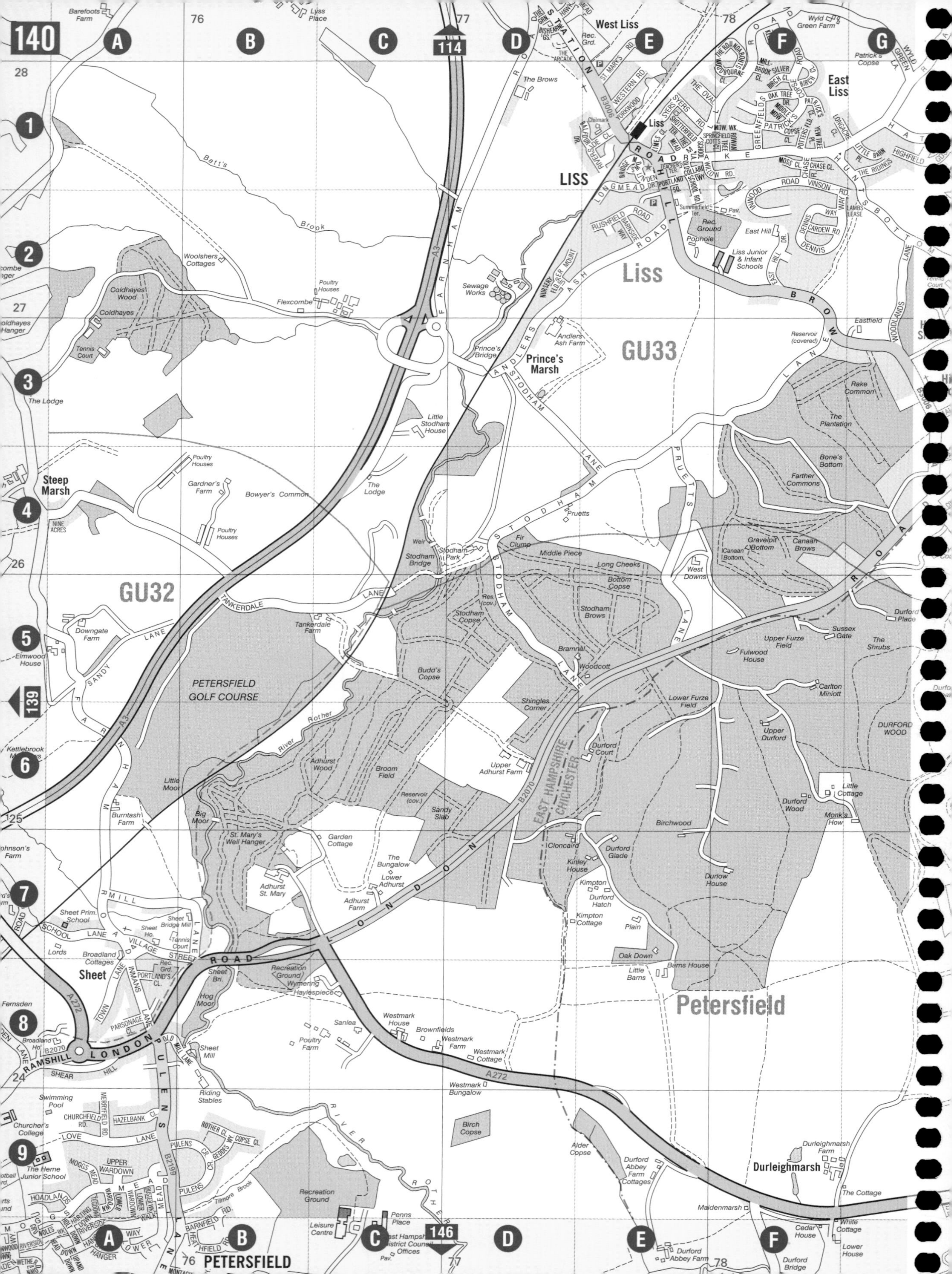

Barefoots Farm
Lyss Place
West Liss
East Liss
Liss
LISS
Prince's Marsh
GU33
GU32
Steep Marsh
Coldhayes Wood
Coldhayes
Flexcombe
Woolshers Cottages
Poultry Houses
Sewage Works
Batt's Brook
The Brows
Little Stodham House
Gardner's Farm
Bowyer's Common
The Lodge
Andlers Ash Farm
Rec. Ground
Pophole
East Hill
Liss Junior & Infant Schools
Eastfield
Rake Common
The Plantation
Bone's Bottom
Farther Commons
Pruetts
Gravelpit Bottom
Canaan Brows
Canaan Bottom
West Downs
Fir Clump
Middle Piece
Long Cheeks
Bottom Copse
Stodham Brows
Stodham Bridge
Stodham Park
Stodham Copse
Tankerdale Farm
Downgate Farm
Elmwood House
PETERSFIELD GOLF COURSE
Budd's Copse
Bramnal
Woodcott
Shingles Corner
Durford Place
Sussex Gate
The Shrubs
Upper Furze Field
Fulwood House
Carlton Miniott
Lower Furze Field
Upper Durford
DURFORD WOOD
Durford Court
EAST HAMPSHIRE
CHICHESTER
Upper Adhurst Farm
Adhurst Wood
Broom Field
Sandy Slab
Little Moor
Big Moor
Burntash Farm
St. Mary's Well Hanger
Garden Cottage
The Bungalow
Lower Adhurst
Adhurst St. Mary
Adhurst Farm
Little Cottage
Durford Wood
Monk's How
Birchwood
Cloncaird
Kinley House
Durford Glade
Durlow House
Kimpton Durford Hatch
Kimpton Cottage
Plain
Oak Down
Barns House
Little Barns
Petersfield
Sheet
Sheet Prim. School
Lords
Broadland Cottages
Sheet Bridge Mill
Rec. Grd.
Recreation Ground
Wymering
Haylespiece
Hog Moor
Sheet Mill
Riding Stables
Poultry Farm
Sanlea
Westmark House
Brownfields
Westmark Farm
Westmark Cottage
Westmark Bungalow
Birch Copse
Alder Copse
Durford Abbey Farm Cottages
Durleighmarsh Farm
Durleighmarsh
The Cottage
Maidenmarsh
White Cottage
Cedar House
Lower House
Durford Bridge
Durford Abbey Farm
Swimming Pool
Churcher's College
The Herne Junior School
UPPER WARDOWN
Recreation Ground
Leisure Centre
Penns Place
East Hampshire District Council Offices
PETERSFIELD
A3
A272
B2070
B3006
B2199
FARNHAM ROAD
LONDON ROAD
STODHAM LANE
TANKERDALE LANE
SANDY LANE
RAKE ROAD
HILL BROW
River Rother
114
146
139

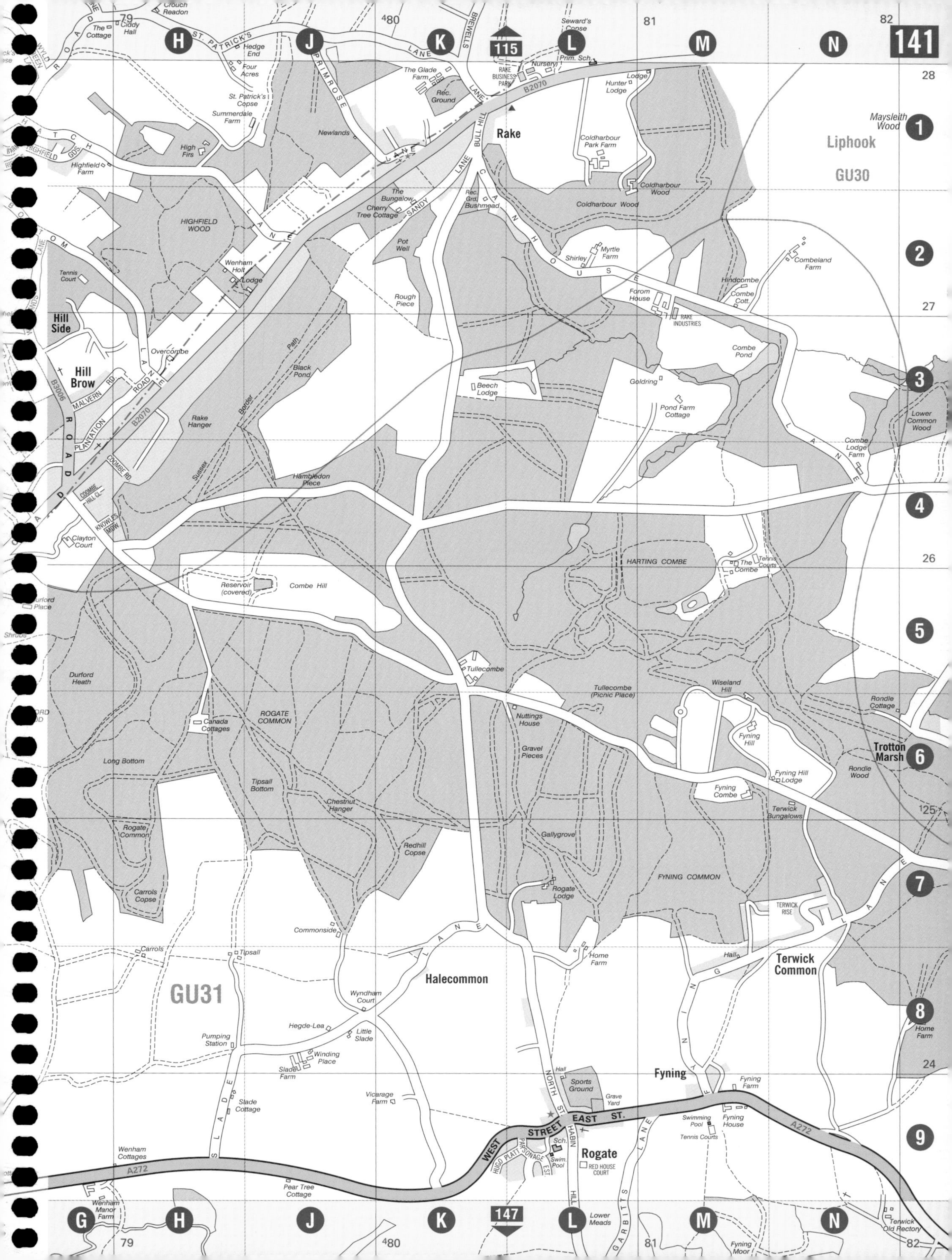
141
115
147
H
J
K
L
M
N
G
79
480
81
82
28
27
26
125
24
1
2
3
4
5
6
7
8
9
Crouch Readon
The Cottage
Ciddy Hall
ST. PATRICK'S LANE
Hedge End
Four Acres
St. Patrick's Copse
Summerdale Farm
PRIMROSE
BREWELLS
Seward's Copse
Prim. Sch.
Nursery
The Glade Farm
Rec. Ground
RAKE BUSINESS PARK
B2070
Hunter Lodge
Lodge
Maysleith Wood
Liphook
GU30
Rake
BULL HILL
Newlands
High Firs
HATCH LANE
HIGHFIELD GDS
Highfield Farm
Coldharbour Park Farm
Coldharbour Wood
SANDY LANE
The Bungalow
Cherry Tree Cottage
Rec. Grd.
Bushmead
HIGHFIELD WOOD
Pot Well
Myrtle Farm
Shirley
COMBE HOUSE LANE
Combeland Farm
Hindcombe
Combe Cott.
Farom House
RAKE INDUSTRIES
Tennis Court
Wenham Holt
Lodge
Rough Piece
Hill Side
Combe Pond
Black Pond
Path
Overcombe
Hill Brow
MALVERN RD.
B3006
ROAD
PLANTATION ROAD
B2070
Goldring
Beech Lodge
Pond Farm Cottage
Border
Rake Hanger
Sussex
Lower Common Wood
Combe Lodge Farm
COOMBE RD
COOMBE HILL CL.
Hambledon Piece
KNOWLES MDW
Clayton Court
HARTING COMBE
The Combe
Tennis Courts
Reservoir (covered)
Combe Hill
Durford Place
Shrubs
Durford Heath
Tullecombe
Tullecombe (Picnic Place)
Wiseland Hill
Nuttings House
Rondle Cottage
Canada Cottages
ROGATE COMMON
Fyning Hill
Trotton Marsh
Gravel Pieces
Long Bottom
Fyning Hill Lodge
Rondle Wood
Tipsall Bottom
Fyning Combe
Chestnut Hanger
Terwick Bungalows
Rogate Common
Gallygrove
Redhill Copse
FYNING COMMON
Carrols Copse
Rogate Lodge
TERWICK RISE
Commonside
Home Farm
Hall
Terwick Common
Carrols
Tipsall
Halecommon
GU31
Wyndham Court
Hegde-Lea
Little Slade
Pumping Station
Winding Place
Slade Farm
Fyning
Home Farm
Hall
Sports Ground
Grave Yard
Fyning Farm
Slade Cottage
Vicarage Farm
SLADE LANE
NORTH ST
EAST ST.
Swimming Pool
Fyning House
Tennis Courts
A272
WEST STREET
Sch.
Swim. Pool
Rogate
RED HOUSE COURT
HUGO PLATT
PARSONAGE EST
HABIN HILL
GARBITTS LANE
Wenham Cottages
Pear Tree Cottage
Wenham Manor Farm
Lower Meads
Fyning Moor
Terwick Old Rectory

North End Cottages
River Meon
Brocklands Farm
136
Warnford Pond
Sheepbridge Copse
A32
Watercress Beds
Bradford's Clump
Gadsfield
OLD WINCHESTER HILL
Manor Farm Dairy
Hayden House
Hayden Barn
WARNFORD PARK
St. John's House (remains of)
STATION RD
LYNCH LA
OLD WINCHESTER HILL LANE
Lower Peake Cottage
PEAKE NEW ROAD
Bullshead Copse
Henwood Copse
Whitewool Pond
Peake Farm
Peake Wood
Southampton
Whitewool Lodge
Whitewool Farm
135
Roll's Copse
GARDEN HILL LANE
SO32
EAST HAMPSHIRE
WINCHESTER
Old Winchester Hill Nature Reserve
Old Winchester Hill
Old Winchester Hill Fort
The Seven Wells
Castle Cottages
END LANE
Harvestgate
MILE
STOCKS LANE
Harvestgate Farm
Stocks Cottage
Stocks Farm
Shogden Wood
Shady Grove
Waterlooville
Teglease Down
Little West End Farm
Teglease Copse
NEW ROAD
PO7
166
Westend Down
WATTON LANE

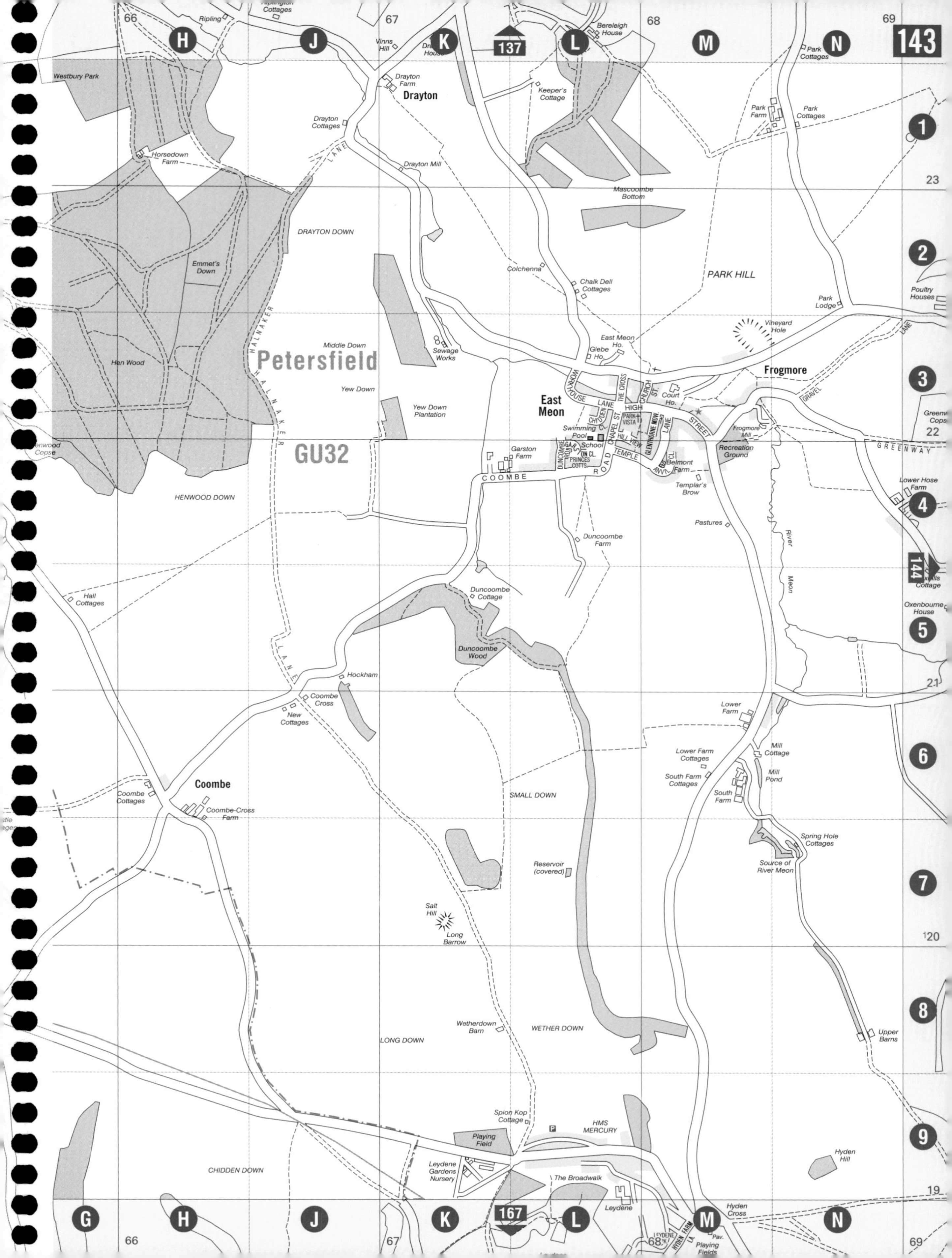
Petersfield
GU32
East
Meon
Drayton
Frogmore
Coombe
DRAYTON DOWN
HENWOOD DOWN
PARK HILL
SMALL DOWN
WETHER DOWN
LONG DOWN
CHIDDEN DOWN
Westbury Park
Horsedown Farm
Emmet's Down
Hen Wood
Middle Down
Yew Down
Yew Down Plantation
Sewage Works
Drayton Mill
Drayton Cottages
Drayton Farm
Keeper's Cottage
Mascoombe Bottom
Colchenna
Chalk Dell Cottages
East Meon Ho.
Glebe Ho.
Vineyard Hole
Park Lodge
Park Farm
Park Cottages
Poultry Houses
Court Ho.
Swimming Pool
School
Garston Farm
Belmont Farm
Templar's Brow
Recreation Ground
Frogmore Mill
Lower Hose Farm
Pastures
Duncoombe Farm
Duncoombe Cottage
Duncoombe Wood
Hall Cottages
Hockham
Coombe Cross
New Cottages
Coombe Cottages
Coombe-Cross Farm
Lower Farm
Lower Farm Cottages
South Farm Cottages
South Farm
Mill Cottage
Mill Pond
Spring Hole Cottages
Source of River Meon
River Meon
Oxenbourne House
Reservoir (covered)
Salt Hill
Long Barrow
Wetherdown Barn
Upper Barns
Spion Kop Cottage
Playing Field
HMS MERCURY
Leydene Gardens Nursery
The Broadwalk
Leydene
Hyden Cross
Hyden Hill
Playing Fields
WORKHOUSE LANE
HIGH STREET
CHURCH ST.
THE CROSS
CHAPEL ST.
HILL VIEW
TEMPLE
COOMBE ROAD
GREENWAY
GRAVEL LANE
HALNAKER LANE
137
144
167
G H J K L M N
1 2 3 4 5 6 7 8 9
66 67 68 69
23 22 21 120 19

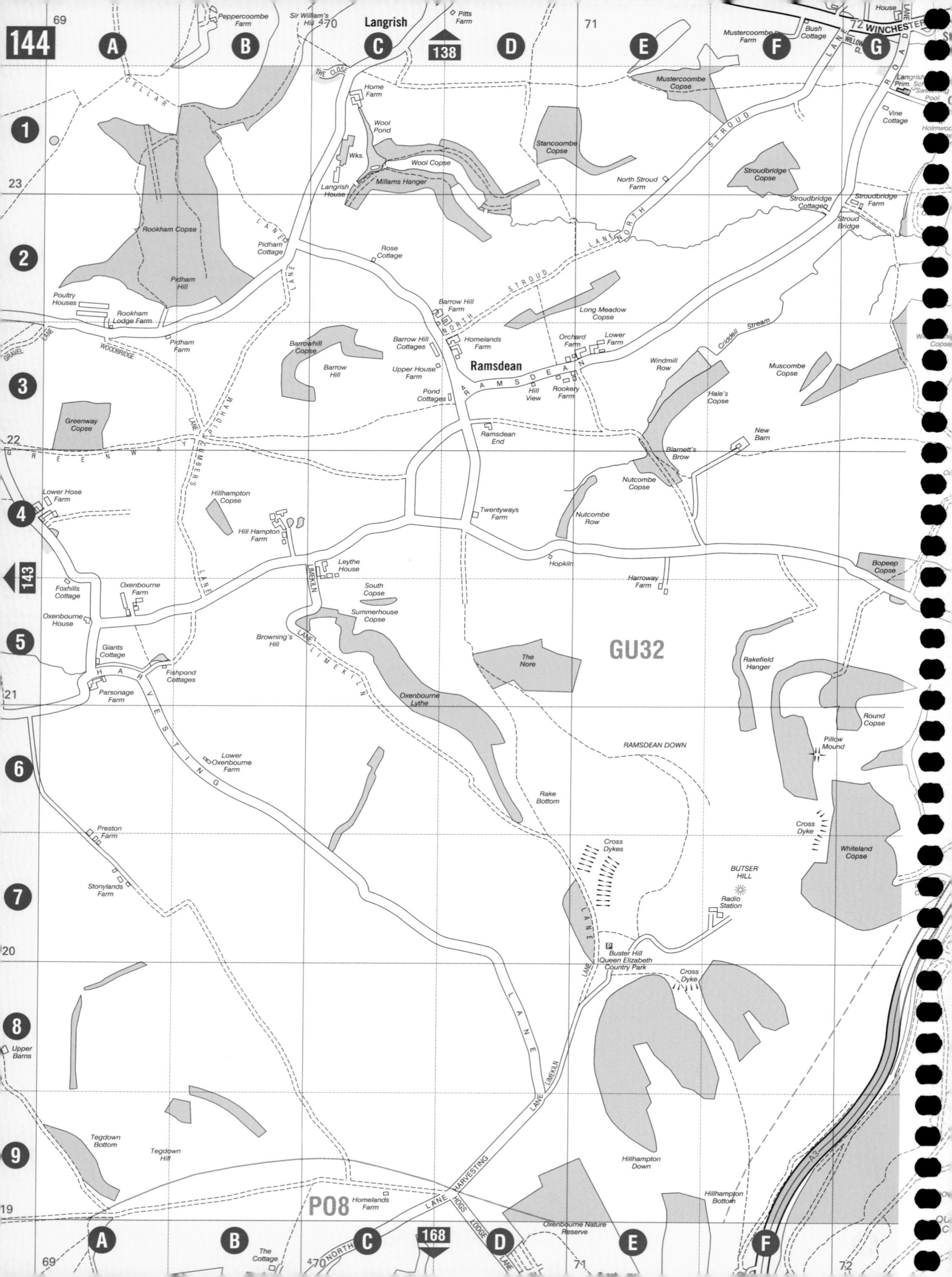

A B C D E F G

69 70 71 72

Peppercoombe Farm
Sir William's Hill 470
Langrish
Pitts Farm
House
WINCHESTER
Mustercoombe Farm
Bush Cottage
Langrish Prim. Sch.
Swimming Pool

1

23

THE CLOSE
Home Farm
Wool Pond
Wks.
Langrish House
Millams Hanger
Wool Copse
Stancoombe Copse
Mustercoombe Copse
North Stroud Farm
Stroudbridge Copse
Vine Cottage
Holmwood

Rookham Copse
LANE
STROUD
Stroudbridge Cottage
Stroud Bridge
Stroudbridge Farm

2

Pidham Cottage
Pidham Hill
Rose Cottage
LANE NORTH
STROUD
Long Meadow Copse
Crisdell Stream
Copse

Poultry Houses
Rookham Lodge Farm
Pidham Farm
GRAVEL LANE
WOODBRIDGE
Barrowhill Copse
Barrow Hill Farm
Barrow Hill Cottages
Homelands Farm
Orchard Farm
Lower Farm
Windmill Row
Muscombe Copse

3

22

Greenway Copse
GREENWAY
Barrow Hill
Upper House Farm
Pond Cottages
Ramsdean End
RAMSDEAN
Hill View
Rookery Farm
Hale's Copse
New Barn

LANE PIDHAM
Hillhampton Copse
Twentyways Farm
Nutcombe Copse
Blarnett's Brow

4

143
Lower Hose Farm
Foxhills Cottage
Oxenbourne House
Oxenbourne Farm
Hill Hampton Farm
LIMEKILN
Leythe House
South Copse
Hopkiln
Nutcombe Row
Harroway Farm
Bopeep Copse

5

21

Giants Cottage
Fishpond Cottages
Parsonage Farm
HARVESTING LANE
Browning's Hill
Summerhouse Copse
LANE LIMEKILN
Oxenbourne Lythe
The Nore
GU32
Rakefield Hanger
Round Copse
Pillow Mound

6

Lower Oxenbourne Farm
RAMSDEAN DOWN
Rake Bottom
Cross Dyke
Whiteland Copse

7

20

Preston Farm
Stonylands Farm
Cross Dykes
BUTSER HILL
Radio Station
LANE LIMEKILN

8

Upper Barns
P
Buster Hill
Queen Elizabeth Country Park
Cross Dyke

9

19

Tegdown Bottom
Tegdown Hill
Homelands Farm
Oxenbourne Nature Reserve
Hillhampton Down
Hillhampton Bottom
A3

P08
NORTH LANE
168
HOGS LODGE LANE
HARVESTING LANE

A B C D E F

69 470 70 71 72

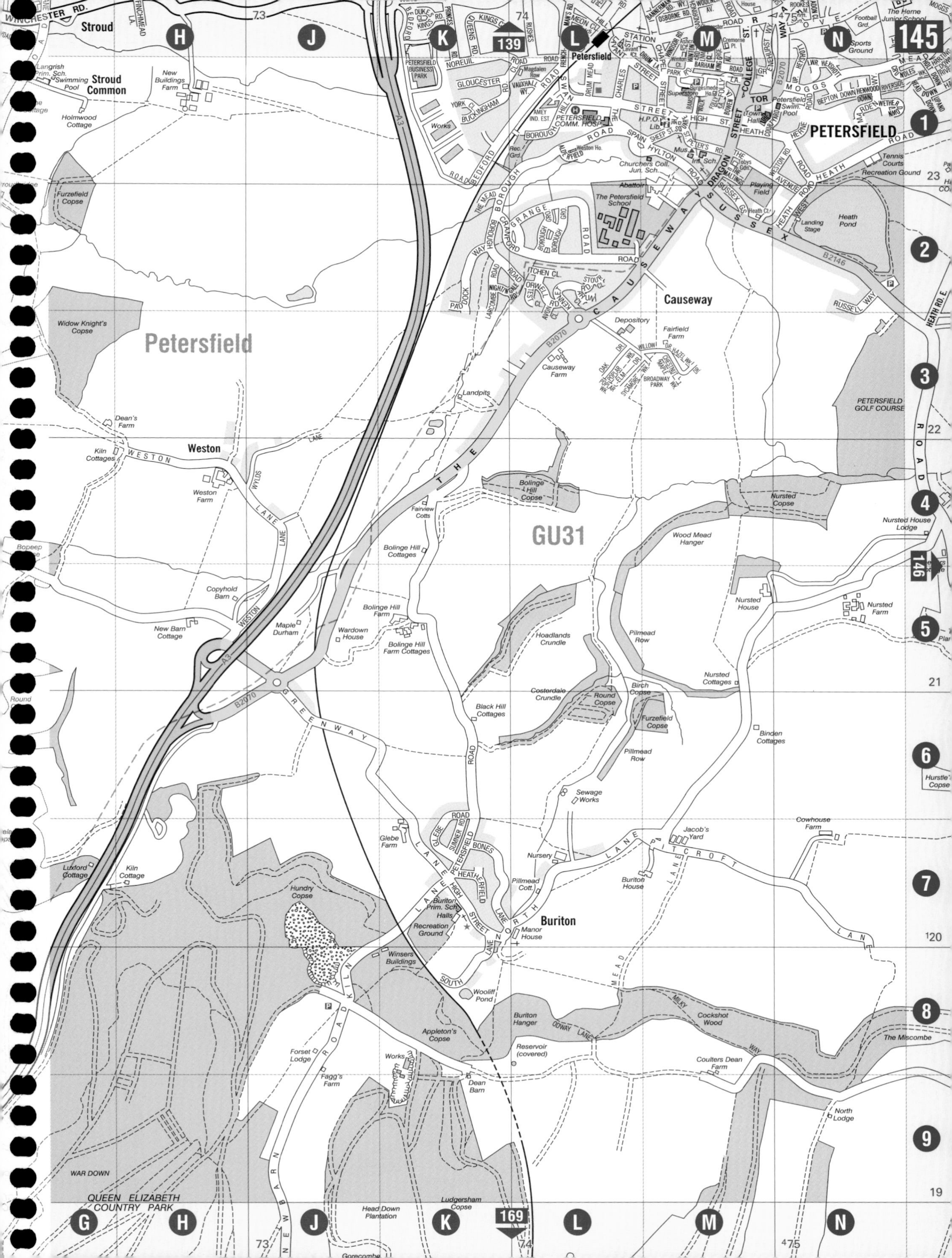

Stroud
Stroud Common
Petersfield
PETERSFIELD
Causeway
Weston
GU31
Buriton
The Petersfield School
Petersfield Comm. Hosp.
Widow Knight's Copse
Furzefield Copse
Holmwood Cottage
New Buildings Farm
Dean's Farm
Kiln Cottages
Weston Farm
Copyhold Barn
New Barn Cottage
Maple Durham
Wardown House
Bolinge Hill Farm
Bolinge Hill Farm Cottages
Bolinge Hill Cottages
Bolinge Hill Copse
Fairview Cotts
Landpits
Causeway Farm
Fairfield Farm
Depository
Broadway Park
Heath Pond
Landing Stage
Petersfield Golf Course
Nursted Copse
Nursted House Lodge
Nursted House
Nursted Farm
Wood Mead Hanger
Hoadlands Crundle
Pilmead Row
Nursted Cottages
Costerdale Crundle
Round Copse
Birch Copse
Furzefield Copse
Black Hill Cottages
Binden Cottages
Pillmead Row
Sewage Works
Glebe Farm
Nursery
Jacob's Yard
Cowhouse Farm
Buriton House
Pillmead Cott.
Manor House
Buriton Prim. Sch.
Recreation Ground
Winsers Buildings
Hundry Copse
Kiln Cottage
Luxford Cottage
Wooliff Pond
Buriton Hanger
Cockshot Wood
The Miscombe
Appleton's Copse
Reservoir (covered)
Coulters Dean Farm
Forset Lodge
Fagg's Farm
Works
Dean Barn
North Lodge
War Down
Queen Elizabeth Country Park
Head Down Plantation
Ludgersham Copse
B2070
B2146
A3
139
146
169

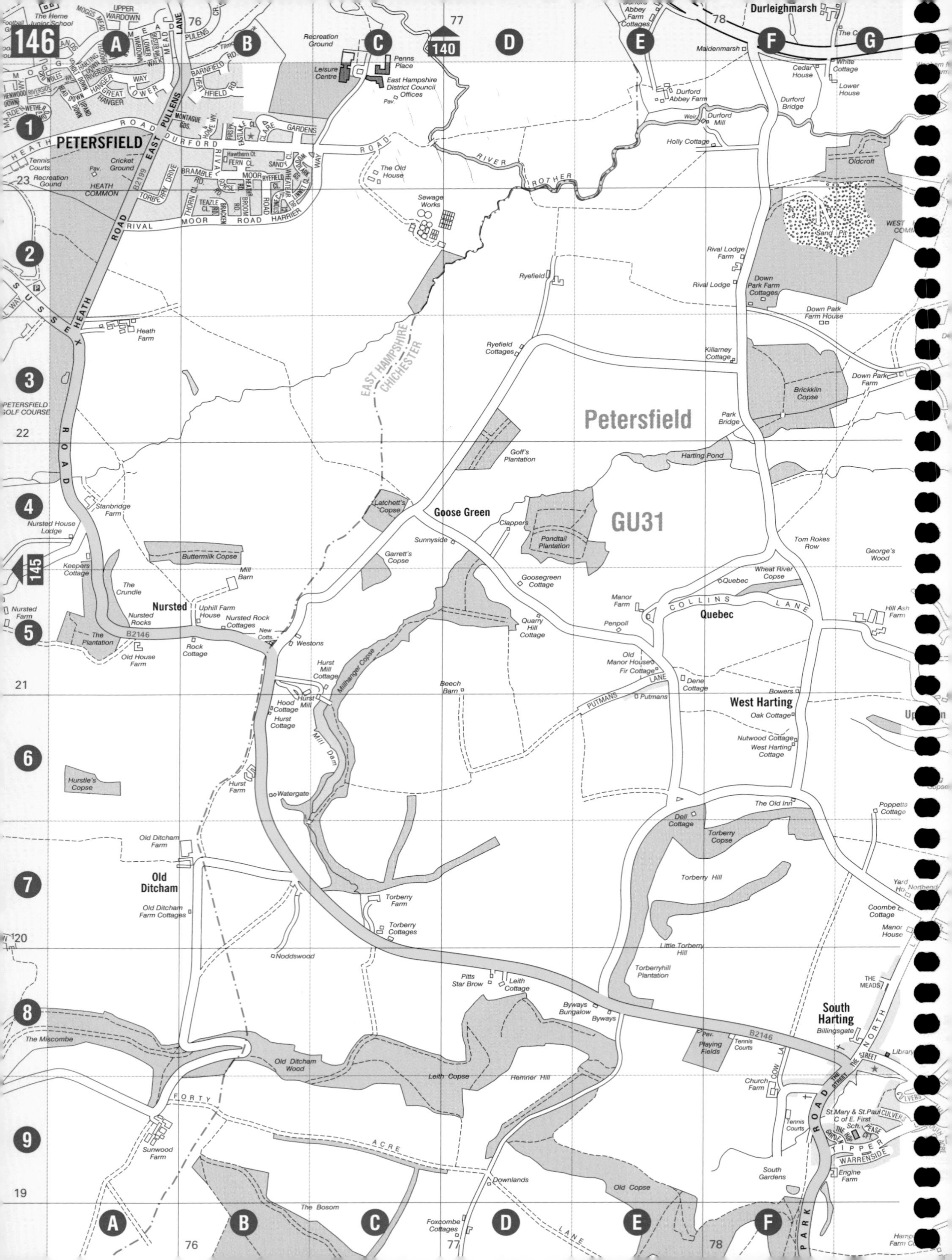

146
A
B
C
D
E
F
G
1
2
3
4
5
6
7
8
9
23
22
21
20
19
76
77
78
140
145
PETERSFIELD
Petersfield
GU31
Durleighmarsh
The Herne Junior School
UPPER WARDOWN
Recreation Ground
Leisure Centre
Penns Place
East Hampshire District Council Offices
Maidenmarsh
White Cottage
Cedar House
Lower House
Durford Abbey Farm
Durford Bridge
Weir
Durford Mill
Holly Cottage
Oldcroft
Tennis Courts
Cricket Ground
Recreation Ground
HEATH COMMON
The Old House
RIVER ROTHER
Sewage Works
Sand Pit
WEST COMMON
Rival Lodge Farm
Rival Lodge
Down Park Farm Cottages
Down Park Farm House
Ryefield
Heath Farm
Ryefield Cottages
Killarney Cottage
Down Park Farm
Brickkiln Copse
EAST HAMPSHIRE
CHICHESTER
PETERSFIELD GOLF COURSE
Park Bridge
Goff's Plantation
Harting Pond
Stanbridge Farm
Nursted House Lodge
Latchett's Copse
Goose Green
Clappers
Sunnyside
Pondtail Plantation
Tom Rokes Row
George's Wood
Buttermilk Copse
Keepers Cottage
Garrett's Copse
Mill Barn
The Crundle
Goosegreen Cottage
Wheat River Copse
Quebec
Nursted
Uphill Farm House
Nursted Rock Cottages
Manor Farm
COLLINS LANE
Quebec
Hill Ash Farm
Nursted Farm
Nursted Rocks
New Cotts.
Quarry Hill Cottage
Penpoll
The Plantation
B2146
Weston
Rock Cottage
Old House Farm
Hurst Mill Cottage
Old Manor House
Fir Cottage
Dene Cottage
Millhanger Copse
Beech Barn
PUTMANS LANE
Putmans
Bowers
Hood Cottage
Hurst Mill
West Harting
Hurst Cottage
Oak Cottage
Mill Dam
Nutwood Cottage
West Harting Cottage
Hurstle's Copse
Hurst Farm
Watergate
The Old Inn
Poppetts Cottage
Dell Cottage
Torberry Copse
Old Ditcham Farm
Old Ditcham
Torberry Hill
Torberry Farm
Old Ditcham Farm Cottages
Torberry Cottages
Coombe Cottage
Manor House
Noddswood
Little Torberry Hill
Torberryhill Plantation
Pitts Star Brow
Leith Cottage
THE MEADS
Byways Bungalow
Byways
South Harting
Billingsgate
The Miscombe
Pav.
Playing Fields
Tennis Courts
Old Ditcham Wood
Leith Copse
Hemner Hill
Church Farm
FORTY ACRE
St.Mary & St.Paul C of E. First Sch.
Sunwood Farm
Tennis Courts
WARRENSIDE
Engine Farm
Downlands
South Gardens
Old Copse
The Bosom
Foxcombe Cottages
LANE
PARK ROAD
SUSSEX ROAD
HEATH ROAD
EAST PULLENS LANE
B2199
DURFORD ROAD
HEATH ROAD
RIVAL MOOR ROAD
HARRIER

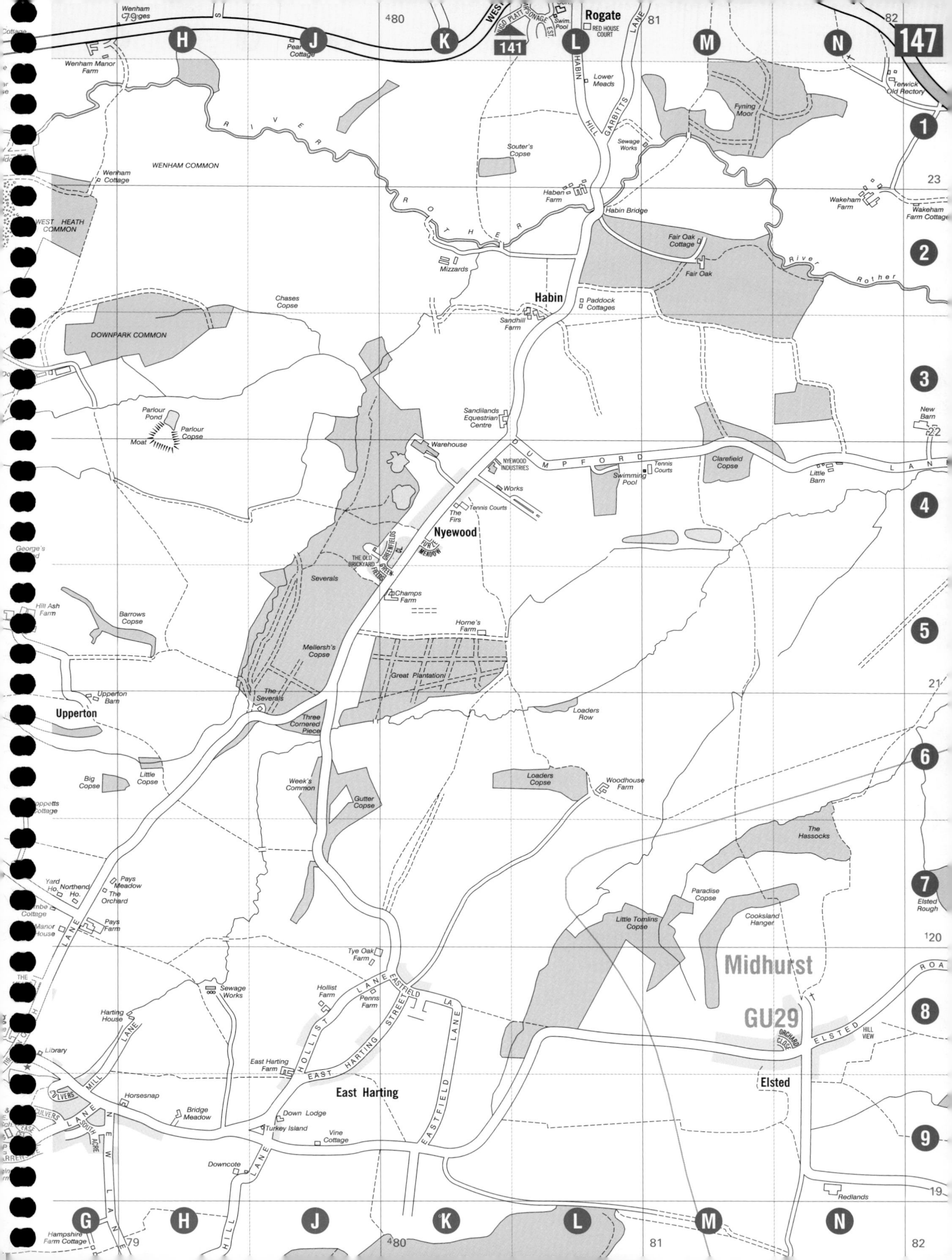

Rogate
Habin
Nyewood
Upperton
East Harting
Elsted
Midhurst
GU29
WENHAM COMMON
DOWNPARK COMMON
WEST HEATH COMMON
River Rother
Wenham Manor Farm
Wenham Cottage
Pear Cottage
Lower Meads
Souter's Copse
Sewage Works
Haben Farm
Habin Bridge
Fyning Moor
Terwick Old Rectory
Wakeham Farm
Wakeham Farm Cottage
Fair Oak Cottage
Fair Oak
Mizzards
Chases Copse
Paddock Cottages
Sandhill Farm
Parlour Pond
Parlour Copse
Moat
Sandilands Equestrian Centre
Warehouse
NYEWOOD INDUSTRIES
Works
Tennis Courts
Swimming Pool
Clarefield Copse
Little Barn
New Barn
DUMPFORD LANE
The Firs
THE OLD BRICKYARD
GREENFIELDS CL
FURZE MEADOW
GREEN FIELDS
Severals
Champs Farm
Hill Ash Farm
Barrows Copse
Horne's Farm
Mellersh's Copse
Great Plantation
The Severals
Upperton Barn
Three Cornered Piece
Loaders Row
Big Copse
Little Copse
Week's Common
Gutter Copse
Loaders Copse
Woodhouse Farm
The Hassocks
Paradise Copse
Cooksland Hanger
Little Tomlins Copse
Elsted Rough
Yard Ho.
Northend Ho.
Pays Meadow
The Orchard
Pays Farm
Tye Oak Farm
Sewage Works
Hollist Farm
Penns Farm
Harting House
Library
East Harting Farm
Horsesnap
Bridge Meadow
Down Lodge
Turkey Island
Vine Cottage
Downcote
Redlands
Hampshire Farm Cottage
HABIN HILL
GARBITTS LANE
HOLLIST LANE
EAST HARTING STREET
EASTFIELD LANE
EASTFIELD LA
MILL LANE
NEW LANE
HILL LANE
ELSTED ROAD
ORCHARD CLOSE
HILL VIEW
SOUTH ACRE
CULVERS
RED HOUSE COURT
PARSONAGE EST.
Swim. Pool
141
H J K L M N
G H J K L M N
1 2 3 4 5 6 7 8 9
479 480 81 82
23 22 21 120 19

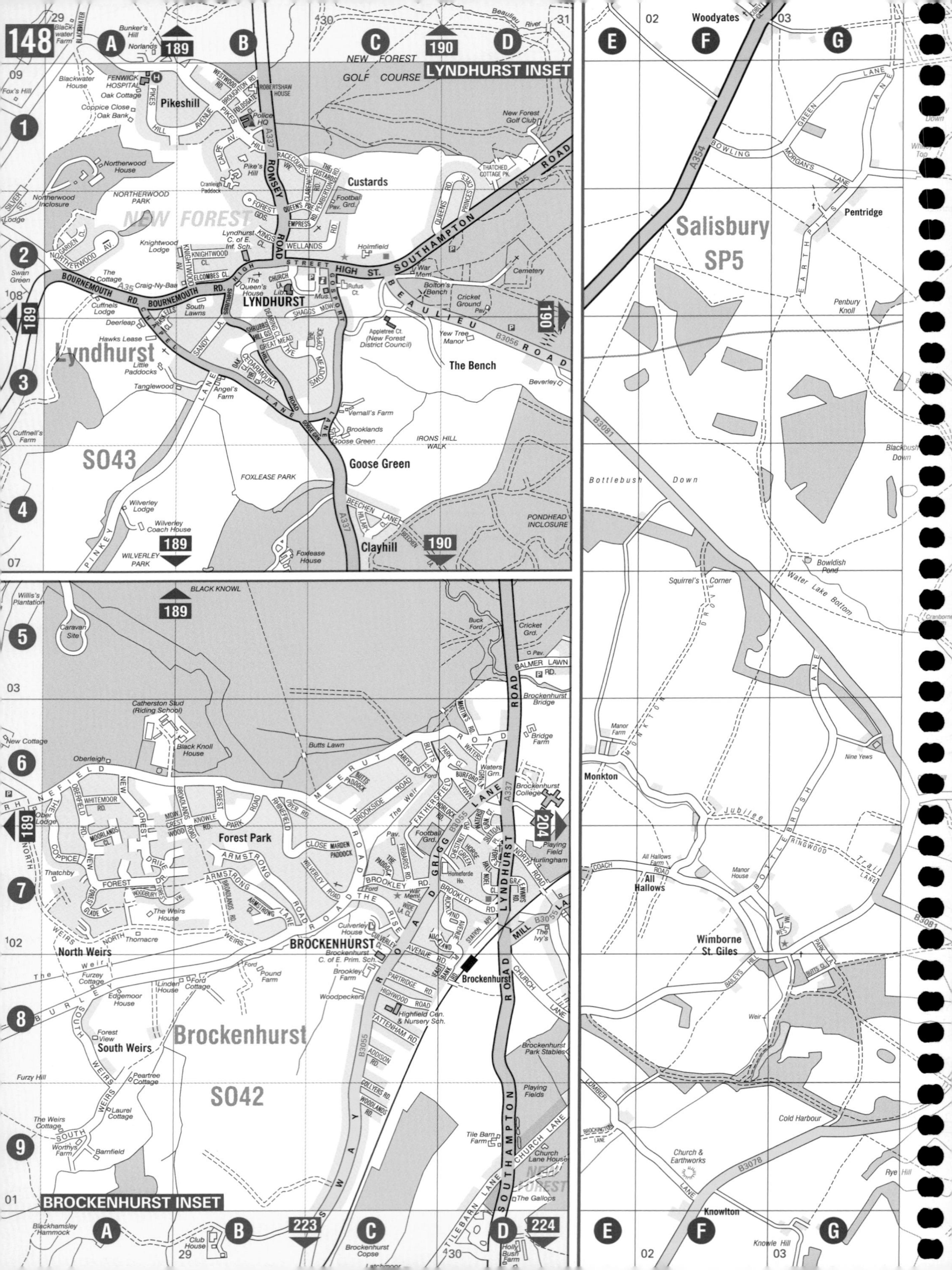
LYNDHURST INSET
Pikeshill
Fenwick Hospital
Police HQ
Custards
New Forest Golf Course
New Forest
Northerwood House
Northerwood Park
Lyndhurst
Lyndhurst
Bournemouth Rd.
High St.
Southampton Road
Romsey Road
Beaulieu Road
The Bench
Goose Green
Foxlease Park
Irons Hill Walk
Clayhill
Pondhead Inclosure
Wilverley Park
SO43
BROCKENHURST INSET
Black Knowl
Caravan Site
Catherston Stud (Riding School)
Black Knoll House
Butts Lawn
Forest Park
Rhinefield Road
Brockenhurst
Brockenhurst
Brookley Rd.
Lyndhurst Road
Brockenhurst College
North Weirs
South Weirs
Burley Road
Southampton Road
Sway Road
Playing Fields
Tile Barn Farm
SO42
Woodyates
Salisbury
SP5
Pentridge
Bowling Green Lane
Penbury Knoll
Bottlebush Down
Squirrel's Corner
Bowldish Pond
Water Lake Bottom
Monkton
Manor Farm
Nine Yews
Jubilee Trail
All Hallows
Wimborne St. Giles
Cold Harbour
Church & Earthworks
Knowlton
Knowle Hill
Rye Hill

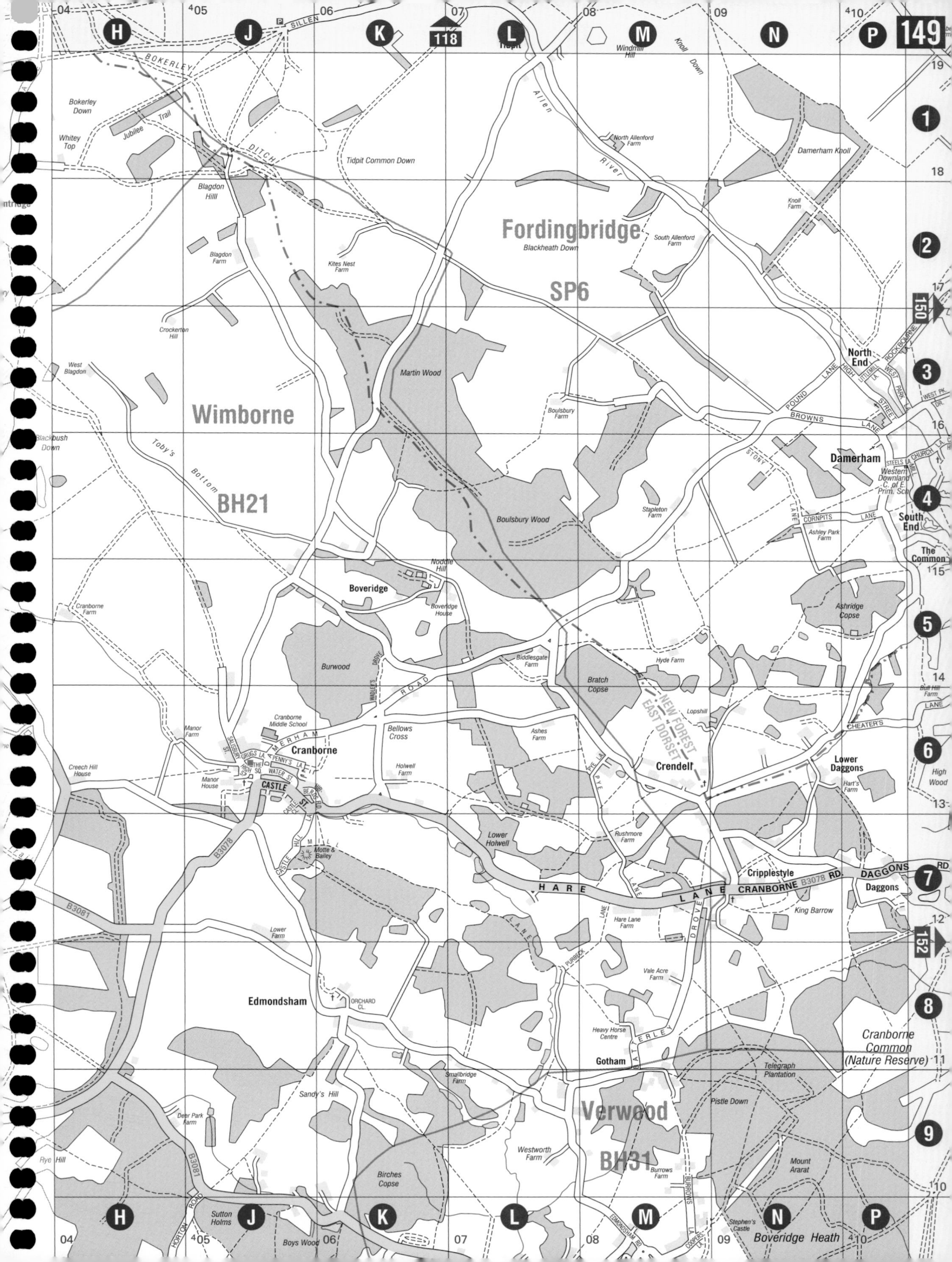
Fordingbridge
SP6
Wimborne
BH21
Verwood
BH31
Cranborne
Boveridge
Damerham
North End
South End
The Common
Cripplestyle
Daggons
Lower Daggons
Crendell
Gotham
Edmondsham
Martin Wood
Boulsbury Wood
Burwood
Bratch Copse
Ashridge Copse
Tidpit Common Down
Blackheath Down
Damerham Knoll
Bokerley Down
Whitey Top
Blagdon Hill
Cranborne Common (Nature Reserve)
Telegraph Plantation
Pistle Down
Mount Ararat
Boveridge Heath
Birches Copse
Sandy's Hill
Sutton Holms
Boys Wood
Rye Hill
HARE LANE
CRANBORNE RD.
DAGGONS RD
NEW FOREST
EAST DORSET
B3078
B3081

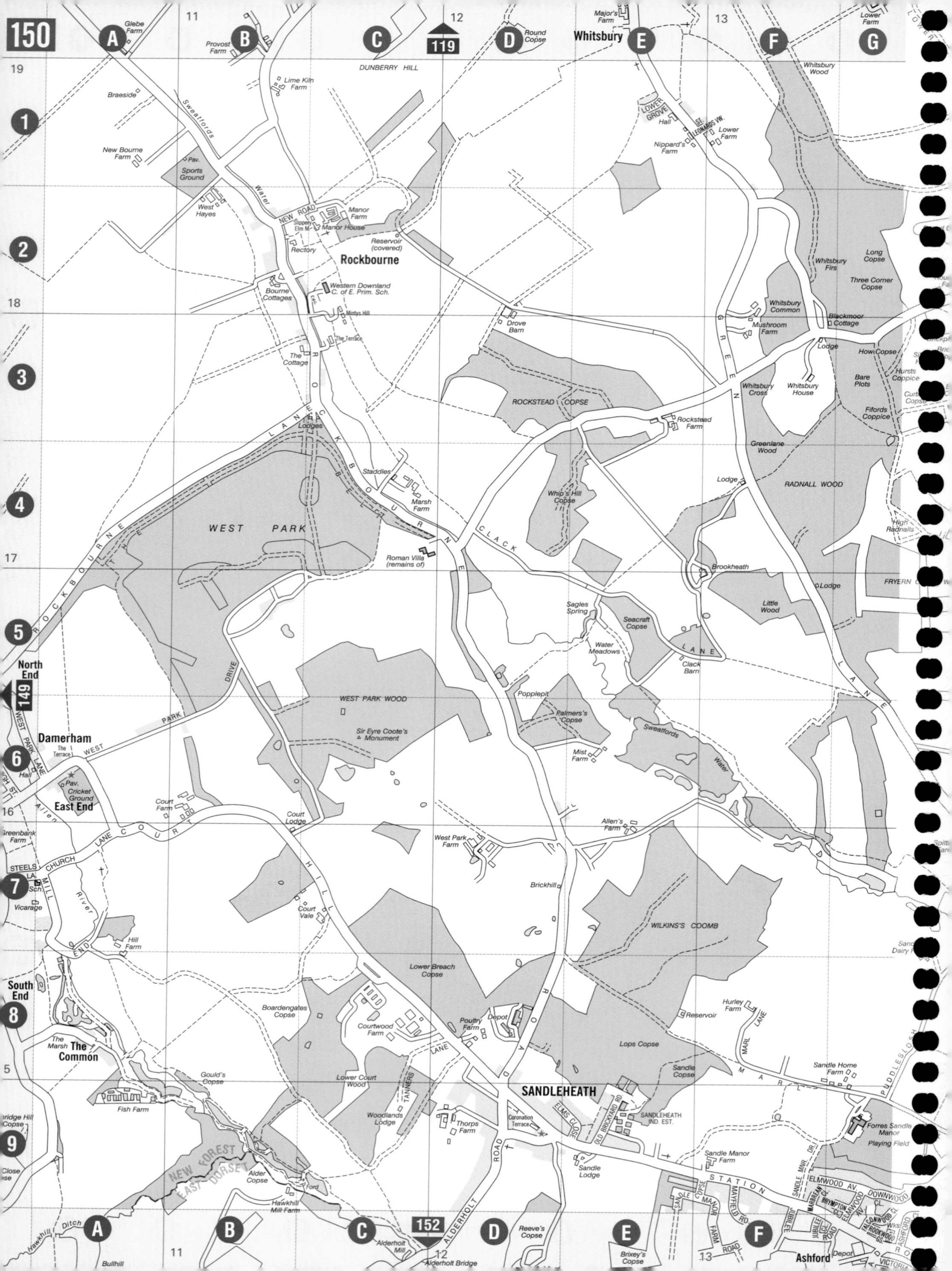

119
152
149
Whitsbury
Rockbourne
Damerham
North End
East End
South End
The Common
SANDLEHEATH
Ashford
Glebe Farm
Provost Farm
DUNBERRY HILL
Round Copse
Major's Farm
Lower Farm
Whitsbury Wood
Braeside
Sweatfords
Lime Kiln Farm
New Bourne Farm
Pav.
Sports Ground
West Hayes
Water
NEW ROAD
Manor Farm
Manor House
Slippery Elm M.
Rectory
Reservoir (covered)
Bourne Cottages
Western Downland C. of E. Prim. Sch.
Mintys Hill
The Terrace
The Cottage
LOWER GROVE
Hall
ST. LEONARDS VW.
Lower Farm
Nippard's Farm
Long Copse
Whitsbury Firs
Three Corner Copse
Whitsbury Common
Blackmoor Cottage
Mushroom Farm
Lodge
How Copse
Drove Barn
Whitsbury Cross
Whitsbury House
Bare Plots
Hursts Coppice
Fifords Coppice
ROCKSTEAD COPSE
Rockstead Farm
GREEN LANE
Greenlane Wood
Lodges
ROCKBOURNE LANE
Staddles
Marsh Farm
Lodge
RADNALL WOOD
Whip's Hill Copse
WEST PARK
High Radnalls
CLACK LANE
Roman Villa (remains of)
Brookheath
Lodge
FRYERN
Little Wood
Sagles Spring
Seacraft Copse
Water Meadows
Clack Barn
DRIVE
WEST PARK WOOD
Popplepit
Palmers's Copse
Sir Eyre Coote's Monument
Sweatfords Water
Mist Farm
WEST PARK LANE
The Terrace
WEST PARK
Hall
Pav.
Cricket Ground
Court Farm
Court Lodge
Allen's Farm
Greenbank Farm
COURT LANE
West Park Farm
STEELS LA.
CHURCH
MILL
Sch.
Vicarage
River Allen
Brickhill
Court Vale
HILL
WILKINS'S COOMB
Hill Farm
END
Sandle Dairy Farm
Lower Breach Copse
Boardengates Copse
Hurley Farm
Reservoir
Poultry Farm
Depot
Courtwood Farm
MARL LANE
Lops Copse
The Marsh
LANE
Sandle Copse
Sandle Home Farm
Gould's Copse
Lower Court Wood
TANNERS
PUDDLESLOSH
Fish Farm
Woodlands Lodge
Thorps Farm
Coronation Terrace
ELMS CLOSE
OLD BRICKYARD RD.
SANDLEHEATH IND. EST.
Forres Sandle Manor
Playing Field
Bridge Hill Copse
NEW FOREST
EAST DORSET
Alder Copse
ALDERHOLT ROAD
Sandle Lodge
Sandle Manor Farm
STATION
SANDLE MNR. DR.
ELMWOOD AV.
DOWNWOOD
Ford
Hawkhill Mill Farm
SANDLE COPSE
MANOR FARM ROAD
MAYFIELD RD.
JUBILEE
Hawkhill Ditch
Reeve's Copse
Alderholt Mill
Alderholt Bridge
Brixey's Copse
Bullhill
Depot
VICTORIA

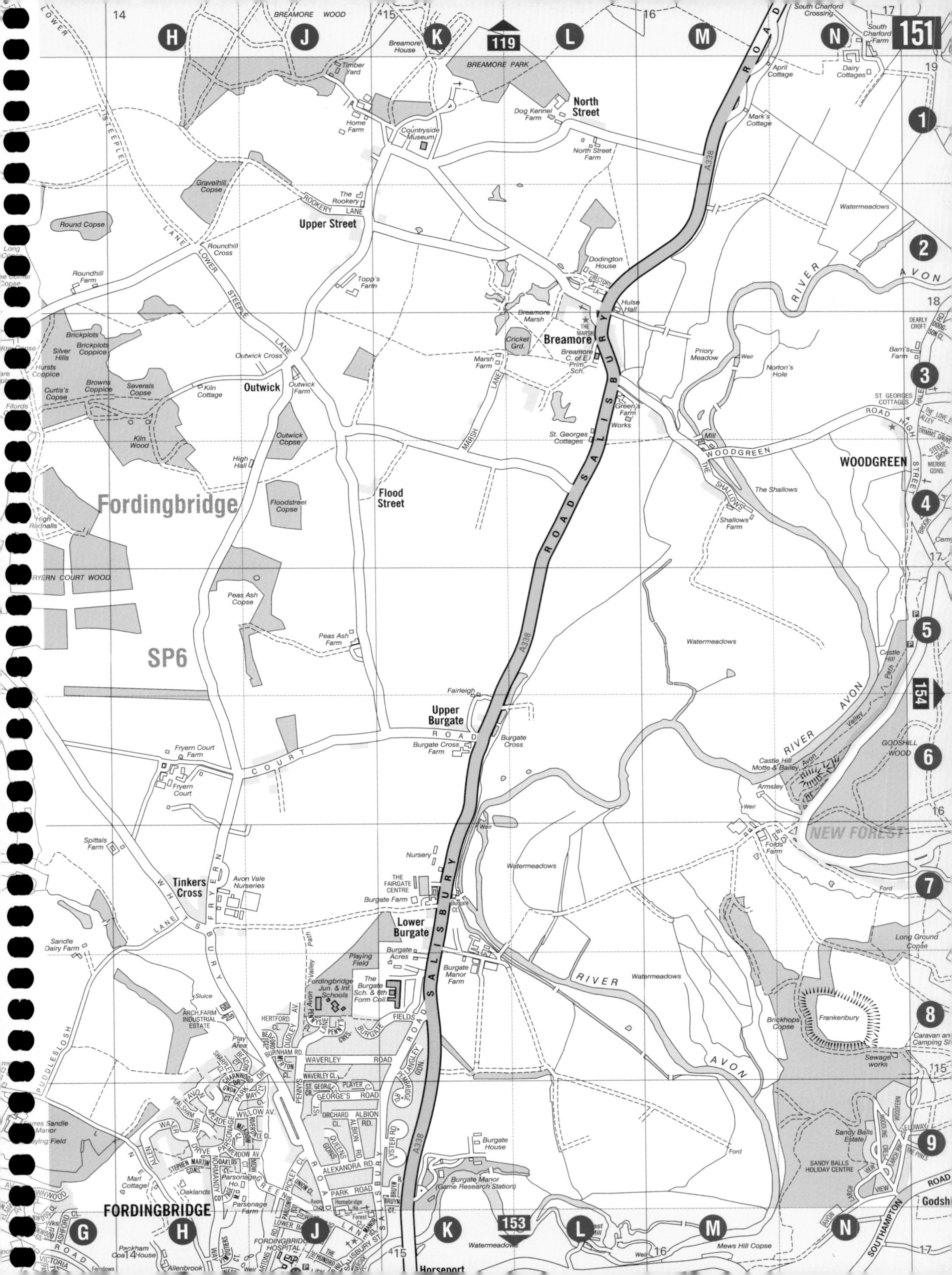

BREAMORE WOOD
BREAMORE PARK
Breamore House
Timber Yard
Home Farm
Countryside Museum
North Street
Dog Kennel Farm
North Street Farm
South Charford Crossing
South Charford Farm
April Cottage
Dairy Cottages
Mark's Cottage
Watermeadows
Gravelhill Copse
The Rookery
ROOKERY LANE
Upper Street
Round Copse
Roundhill Cross
Roundhill Farm
LOWER STEEPLE LANE
Dodington House
RECTORY LA.
Topp's Farm
Hulse Hall
Breamore Marsh
THE MARSH
Breamore
Cricket Grd.
Breamore C. of E. Prim. Sch.
Marsh Farm
MARSH LANE
Priory Meadow
Weir
Norton's Hole
RIVER AVON
DEARLY CROFT
DODGSON CL.
Barn's Farm
ST. GEORGES COTTAGES
HALE
HIGH STREET
Brickplots
Silver Hills
Brickplots Coppice
Hursts Coppice
Browns Coppice
Severals Copse
Curtis's Copse
Kiln Cottage
Kiln Wood
Outwick Cross
Outwick
Outwick Farm
Outwick Copse
Green's Farm
Works
St. Georges Cottages
Mill
WOODGREEN ROAD
THE SHALLOWS
The Shallows
WOODGREEN
MERRIE GDNS.
High Hall
Flood Street
Fordingbridge
Floodstreet Copse
ROAD SALISBURY
A338
Shallows Farm
High Radnalls
FRYERN COURT WOOD
Peas Ash Copse
Peas Ash Farm
SP6
Watermeadows
Castle Hill
Valley Path
154
Fairleigh
Upper Burgate
ROAD
Burgate Cross
Burgate Cross Farm
Fryern Court Farm
COURT
Fryern Court
Castle Hill Motte & Bailey
Armsley
GODSHILL WOOD
Weir
NEW FOREST
Spittals Farm
Folds Farm
Nursery
Watermeadows
Tinkers Cross
Avon Vale Nurseries
THE FAIRGATE CENTRE
Burgate Farm
Burgate Cl.
Ford
Lower Burgate
Long Ground Copse
Sandle Dairy Farm
WHITSBURY LANE
FRYERN
Playing Field
Valley Path
Burgate Acres
Burgate Manor Farm
RIVER AVON
Watermeadows
Fordingbridge Jun. & Inf. Schools
The Burgate Sch. & 6th Form Coll.
Sluice
ARCH FARM INDUSTRIAL ESTATE
HERTFORD CL.
BURGATE FIELDS
Brickhops Copse
Frankenbury
Caravan and Camping Si
Sewage works
PUDDLESLOSH
Play Area
BURNHAM RD.
WAVERLEY ROAD
WAVERLEY CL.
PLAYER CL.
LANGLEY GDN.
PEMBRIDGE RD.
ST. GEORGE'S ROAD
ORCHARD CL.
ALBION RD.
WILLOW AV.
Sandy Balls Estate
SANDY BALLS HOLIDAY CENTRE
Burgate House
ALEXANDRA RD.
PARK ROAD
LYSTER RD.
QUEENS GDNS.
Burgate Manor (Game Research Station)
Marl Cottage
Oaklands
Parsonage Ho.
Parsonage Farm
STEPHEN MARTIN GDNS.
NORMANDY
FORDINGBRIDGE
FORDINGBRIDGE HOSPITAL
SALISBURY ST.
LOWER BANK RD.
Horseport
Watermeadows
Mews Hill Copse
SOUTHAMPTON ROAD
Godsh
Peckham House
Allenbrook
VICTORIA ROAD

119
153

150
149
184
Alder Copse
Hawkhill Mill Farm
Ford
Sandle Lodge
Hawkhill Ditch
Bullhill Copse
Andrew's Copse
Reeve's Copse
Brixey's Copse
Alderholt Mill
ALDERHOLT ROAD
Alderholt Bridge
Alderholt Mill Farm
Avon Farm
Ashford Water
Perry Copse
Ashford
THE OLD VINERIES
ASHFORD WORKS INDUSTRIAL ESTATE
Fish Farm
Ashford House
Poultry House
Perry Farm House
Bowerwood Cottages
The Embers
Edge Hill
Depot
SANDLE COPSE
MANOR FARM ROAD
MAYFIELD RD.
JUBILEE
ELMWOOD
Garett's Copse
Lower Bullhill Farm
North Lodge
Old Manor House
Higher Bullhill Farm
CHEATER'S LA.
Pond Close
Hill Farm
Hill Copse
DORSET
HAMPSHIRE
BOWERWOOD ROAD
Bowerwood House
Landlubbers Cottage
Manor Farm Bungalow
Home Farm
Chapel Lodge
East Lodge
Old Vicarage
Manor Farm
Pippin Cottage
Alderholt Park
Hill Cottage Farm
Hill Cottage
New Farm
Berrylands
MIDGHAM ROAD
Hart's Copse
Park Farm
The Rookery
FORDINGBRIDGE ROAD
Wolvercroft Farm
Highwood Cottage
Salisbury Arms Farm
Shalotte House
Midgham Wood
Cross Farm
Presseys Corner
Wolvercrate Copse
Highfield Farm
Bonfire Hill
DOWN LODGE CL.
WINDSOR WAY
HILLBURY ROAD
Camel Green
Hilbury Wood
Saw Mill
Midgham Farm
ALDERHOLT
Daggons
Vicarage Farm
Church Cottages
Birch Hill
The Piggery
Strouds Firs
COOPERS CL.
CAMEL GREEN
HAYTERS WAY
St. James C. of E. First School
Hillbury Farm
DAGGONS ROAD
STATION ROAD
B3078
The Grange
HIGHWOOD CL.
STATION YD.
OLD FORGE CL.
LIME TREE CL.
PEAR TREE CL.
ALDER DRIVE
PARK LANE
ANTELLS WAY
SOUTH HILL
FIR TREE
SILVER TREE
Holmwood
The Bungalow
Pug's Plantation
CHURCHILL CL.
GROVE
APPLE TREE
BRAMBLE CL.
ASH CL.
TUDOR CL.
HILLBURY PARK (MOBILE HOME PARK)
KESTREL WY
EARLSWOOD DRIVE
BIRCHWOOD DRIVE
BLACKWATER
ATTWOOD CL.
Charing Cross
PINE RD
OAK ROAD
RINGWOOD ROAD
BROOMFIELD DR.
BEECH CL.
FERN CL.
HAZEL CL.
SAXON WAY
EAST DORSET
NEW FOREST
Thornes Piece
Maryfield
Nurseries
Recreation Ground
Ringwood Forest
Five Acres
Marsh Lands
St. Annes
Sleepbrook Farm
Oak Tree Farm
Poultry Houses
Drove End Farm
Cross Roads Plantation
Rifle Range
NORTH LANE
Stanford Point
Warren Park Farm
ALDERHOLT COMMON
Lomer Copse
Bottom
Bleakhill Farm
LOMER
CRANBORNE COMMON (Nature Reserve)
Braemoor
The Bungalow
Bleak Hill
Whitefield
SLEEP BOTTOM
Daffodil Cottage
Christmas Rose Cottage
Primrose Cottage
Decoy Pond
Sleep Brook
Verwood
Ford
Hill Crest
DROVE
KENT
Sand Point
North Plumley Drove
North Plumley Farmhouse
BH31
Hamer Copse
Hamer
Hamer Brook
Kent Hill
Fire Tower
North Plumley Cottages
Cootman's Copse
BOVERIDGE HEATH
PLUMLEY WOOD
Kent Hill Plantation

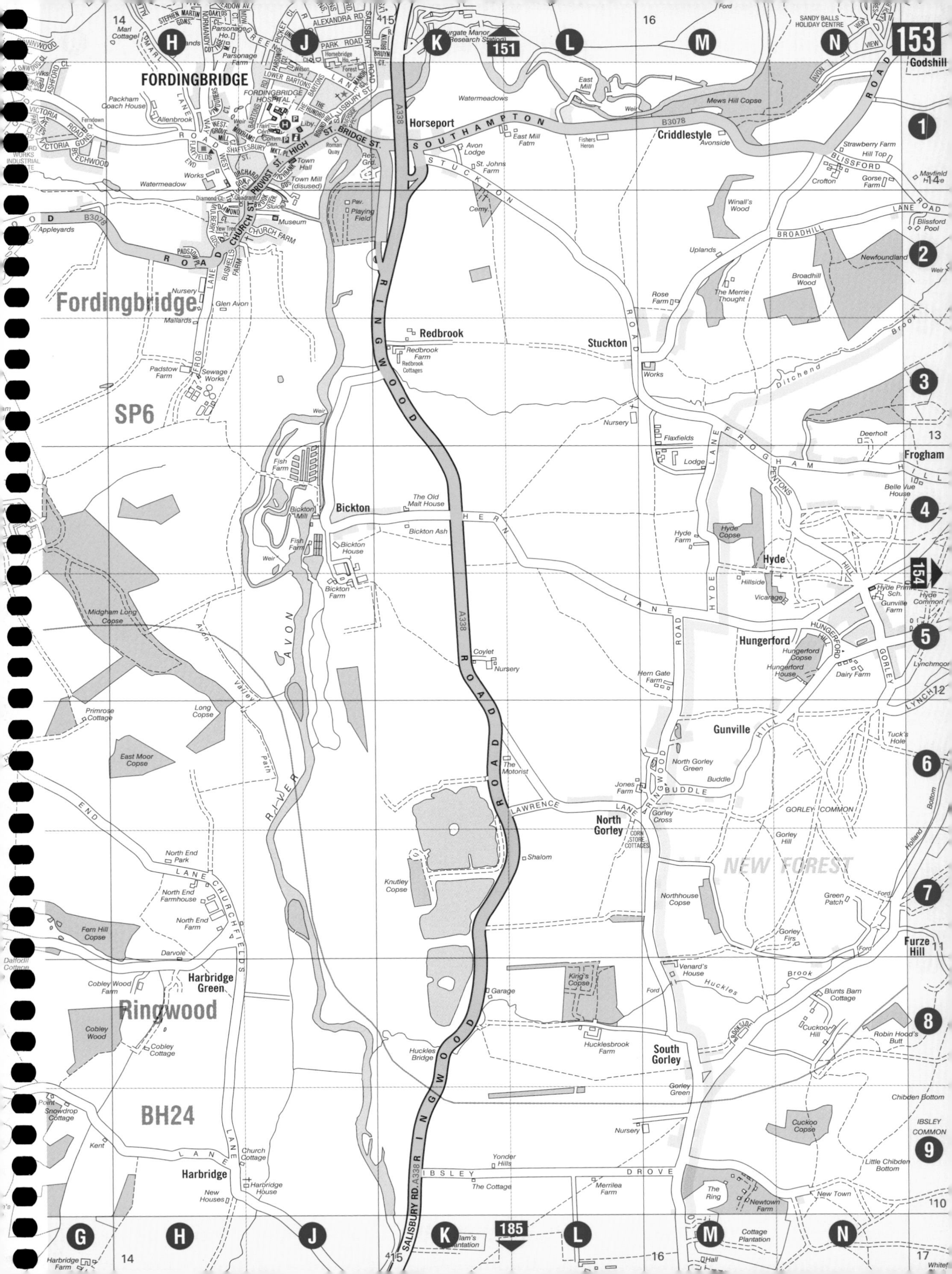
FORDINGBRIDGE
Fordingbridge
Horseport
Criddlestyle
Godshill
SANDY BALLS HOLIDAY CENTRE
Burgate Manor Research Station
East Mill
Watermeadows
Mews Hill Copse
SOUTHAMPTON
B3078
Avon Lodge
St. Johns Farm
East Mill Farm
Fishers Heron
Strawberry Farm
Hill Top
BLISSFORD
Crofton
Gorse Farm
Mayfield House
Blissford Pool
BROADHILL LANE ROAD
Winall's Wood
Uplands
Newfoundland
Broadhill Wood
The Merrie Thought
Rose Farm
Stuckton
STUCKTON ROAD
Cemy.
Redbrook
Redbrook Farm
Redbrook Cottages
Works
Ditchend Brook
Nursery
Flaxfields
Lodge
FROGHAM HILL
Frogham
Deerholt
Belle Vue House
PENTONS
Hyde Copse
Hyde Farm
Hyde
Hillside
Vicarage
Hyde Prim. Sch.
Hyde Common
Gunville Farm
HYDE LANE
Hungerford
Hungerford Copse
Hungerford House
HUNGERFORD HILL
Dairy Farm
GORLEY
Lynchmoor
LYNCH
Hern Gate Farm
Gunville
North Gorley Green
Buddle
Tuck's Hole
Jones Farm
BUDDLE LANE
Gorley Cross
GORLEY COMMON
North Gorley
CORN STORE COTTAGES
Gorley Hill
NEW FOREST
Northhouse Copse
Green Patch
Ford
Gorley Firs
Furze Hill
Venard's House
Huckles Brook
Blunts Barn Cottage
Cuckoo Hill
Robin Hood's Butt
Hucklesbrook Farm
South Gorley
Gorley Green
Chibden Bottom
IBSLEY COMMON
Cuckoo Copse
Little Chibden Bottom
Nursery
New Town
The Ring
Newtown Farm
Cottage Plantation
Hall
IBSLEY DROVE
Merrilea Farm
Yonder Hills
The Cottage
SALISBURY RD. A338
RINGWOOD ROAD
A338
Packham Coach House
Allenbrook
FORDINGBRIDGE HOSPITAL
Watermeadow
Town Hall
Town Mill (disused)
Roman Quay
Rec. Grd.
Pav.
Playing Field
Museum
CHURCH FARM
Appleyards
PADSTOW ROAD
B3078
Nursery
Glen Avon
Mallards
Padstow Farm
Sewage Works
FROG LANE
SP6
Weir
Fish Farm
Bickton Mill
Bickton
The Old Malt House
Bickton Ash
HERN LANE
Bickton House
Bickton Farm
Midgham Long Copse
Avon Valley Path
RIVER AVON
Coylet
Nursery
Primrose Cottage
Long Copse
East Moor Copse
The Motorist
LAWRENCE LANE
Shalom
Knutley Copse
North End Park
END LANE
North End Farmhouse
North End Farm
CHURCHFIELDS
Fern Hill Copse
Darvole
Harbridge Green
Cobley Wood Farm
Ringwood
Cobley Wood
Cobley Cottage
Garage
King's Copse
Huckles Bridge
BH24
Snowdrop Cottage
Kent
Church Cottage
Harbridge
Harbridge House
New Houses
Harbridge Farm
Plantation
151
154
185
G H J K L M N
1 2 3 4 5 6 7 8 9
14 15 16 17
10 11 12 13 14

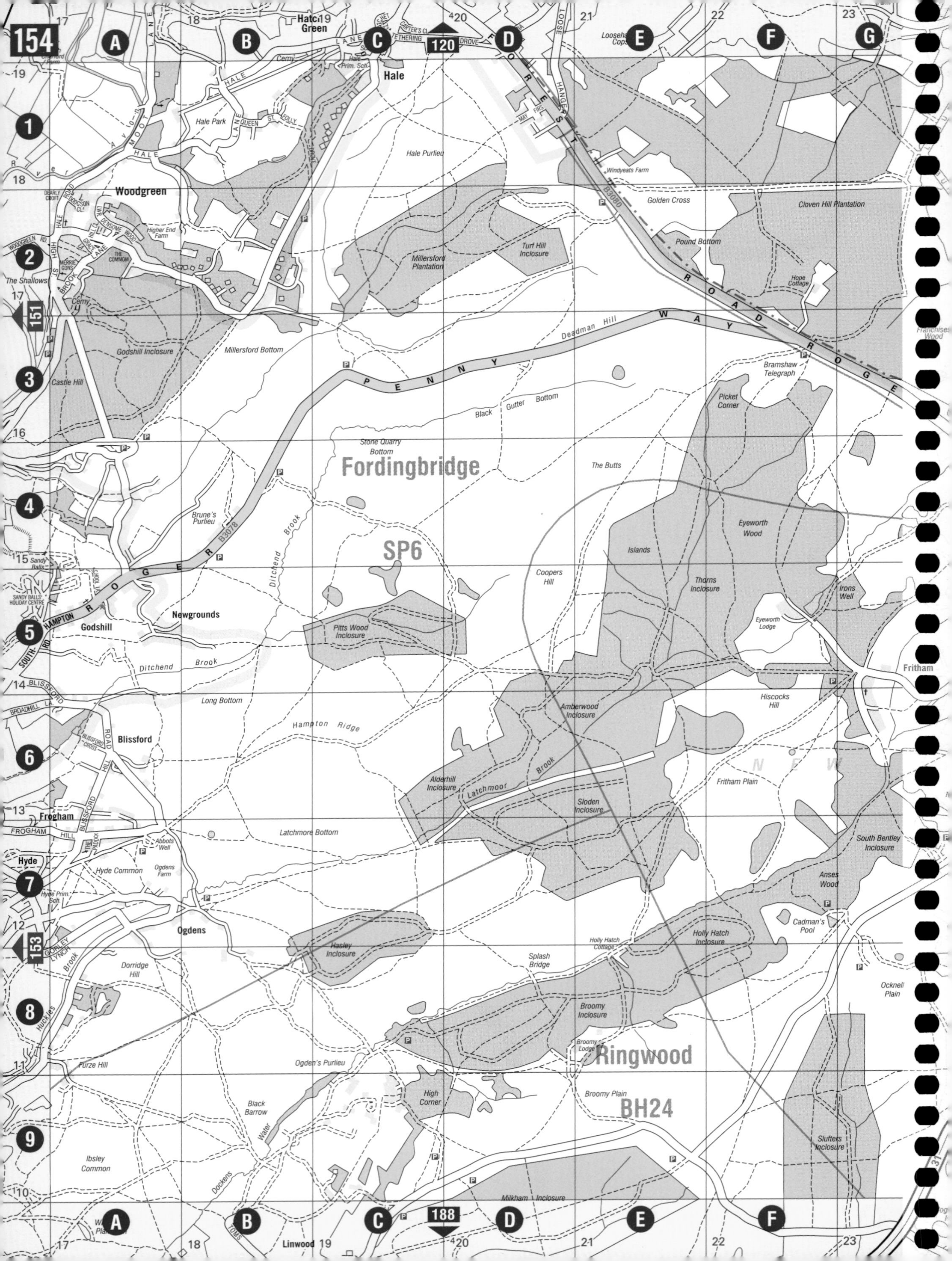
Hatch Green
Hale
Cemy
Hale Park
Hale Purlieu
Woodgreen
Higher End Farm
The Common
The Shallows
Godshill Inclosure
Castle Hill
Millersford Bottom
Millersford Plantation
Turf Hill Inclosure
Windyeats Farm
Golden Cross
Cloven Hill Plantation
Pound Bottom
Hope Cottage
Deadman Hill
PENNY WAY
ROGER ROAD
Bramshaw Telegraph
Picket Corner
Black Gutter Bottom
Stone Quarry Bottom
Fordingbridge
The Butts
Brune's Purlieu
Ditchend Brook
SP6
Islands
Eyeworth Wood
Coopers Hill
Thorns Inclosure
Irons Well
Eyeworth Lodge
Sandy Balls
Sandy Balls Holiday Centre
Newgrounds
Godshill
Pitts Wood Inclosure
Fritham
Long Bottom
Amberwood Inclosure
Hiscocks Hill
Blissford
Hampton Ridge
Alderhill Inclosure
Latchmoor Brook
Fritham Plain
Sloden Inclosure
Frogham
Abbots Well
Latchmore Bottom
South Bentley Inclosure
Hyde
Hyde Common
Ogdens Farm
Anses Wood
Cadman's Pool
Ogdens
Holly Hatch Cottage
Holly Hatch Inclosure
Hasley Inclosure
Dorridge Hill
Splash Bridge
Ocknell Plain
Broomy Inclosure
Broomy Lodge
Ringwood
Furze Hill
Ogden's Purlieu
High Corner
Broomy Plain
Black Barrow
BH24
Ibsley Common
Slufters Inclosure
Milkham Inclosure
Linwood
NEW

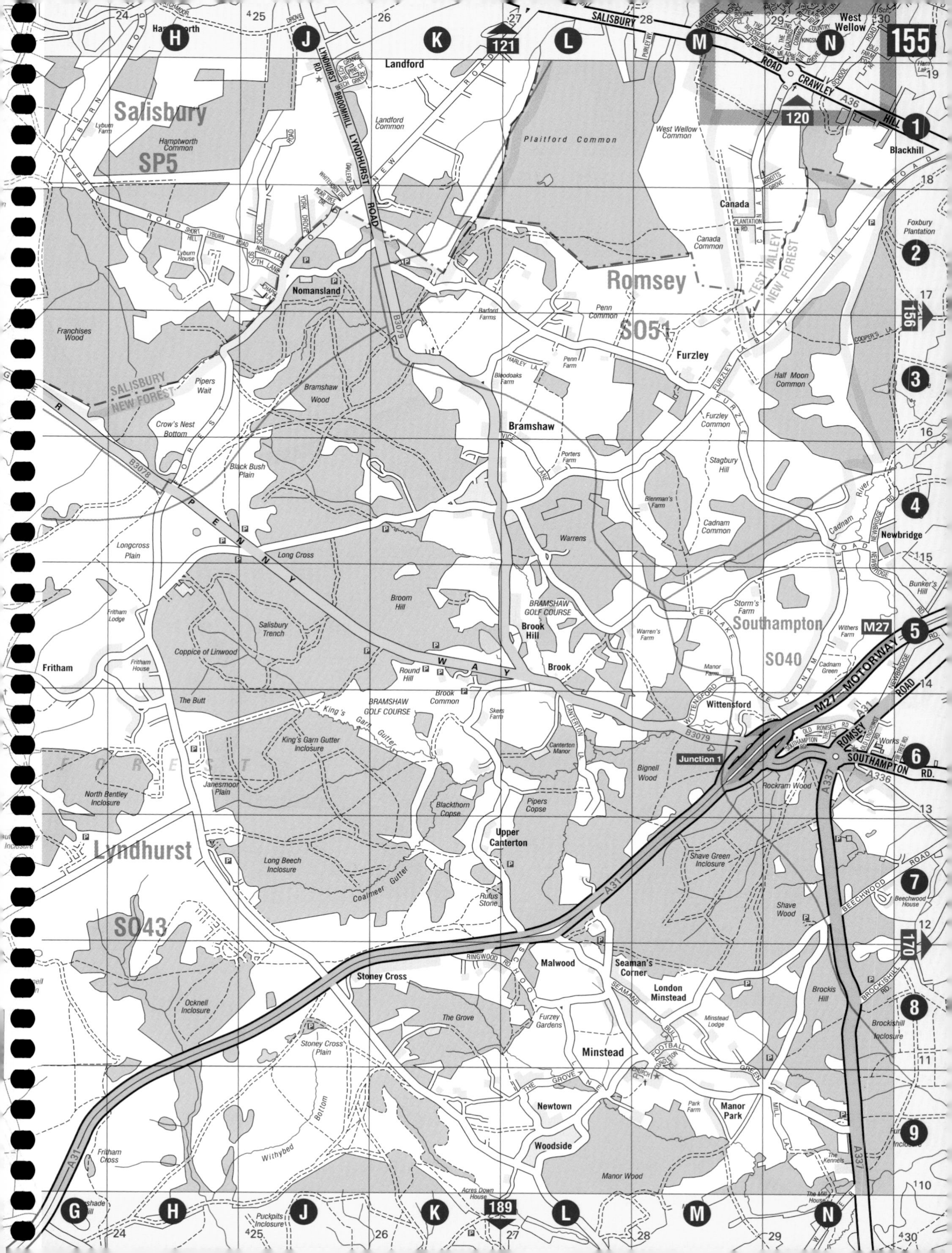

Landford
Salisbury
SP5
Hamptworth Common
Lyburn Farm
Landford Common
Plaitford Common
West Wellow Common
West Wellow
Blackhill
Canada
Canada Common
Romsey
SO51
Nomansland
Penn Common
Furzley
Franchises Wood
Pipers Wait
Bramshaw Wood
Bramshaw
Half Moon Common
Foxbury Plantation
Crow's Nest Bottom
Furzley Common
Stagbury Hill
Black Bush Plain
Blenman's Farm
Cadnam Common
Warrens
Newbridge
Longcross Plain
Long Cross
Broom Hill
BRAMSHAW GOLF COURSE
Storm's Farm
Southampton
SO40
Salisbury Trench
Brook Hill
Fritham Lodge
Coppice of Linwood
Fritham
Brook
Wittensford
Junction 1
Bignell Wood
Rockram Wood
King's Garn Gutter Inclosure
North Bentley Inclosure
Janesmoor Plain
Blackthorn Copse
Pipers Copse
Upper Canterton
Lyndhurst
Long Beech Inclosure
Shave Green Inclosure
Shave Wood
SO43
Rufus Stone
Malwood
Seaman's Corner
London Minstead
Stoney Cross
Ocknell Inclosure
The Grove
Furzey Gardens
Minstead
Brockis Hill
Stoney Cross Plain
Newtown
Manor Park
Woodside
Fritham Cross
Withybed
Manor Wood
M27 MOTORWAY
A31
A337
B3078
B3079
120
121
156
170
189

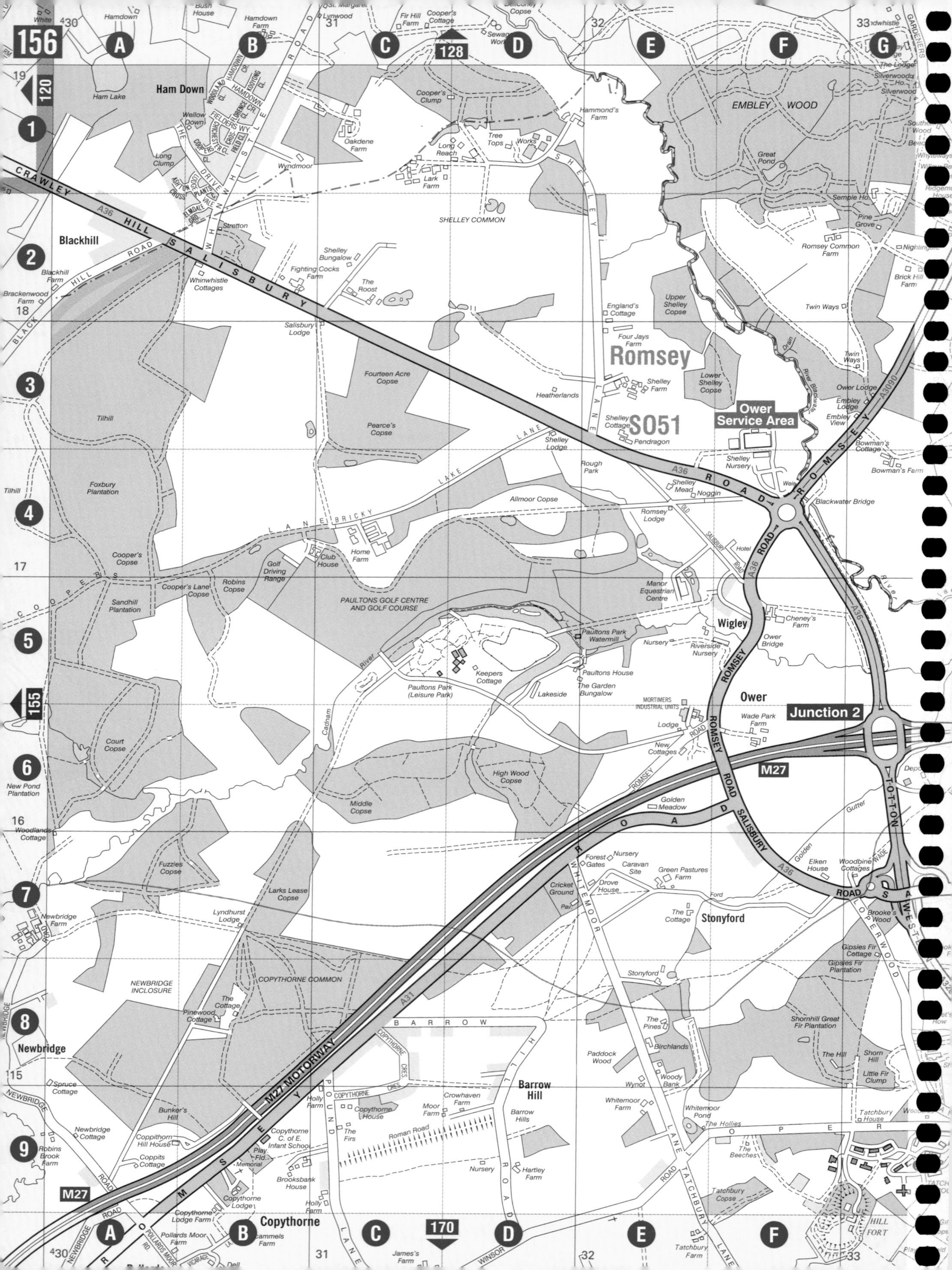
156
128
120
155
170
A
B
C
D
E
F
G
1
2
3
4
5
6
7
8
9
19
18
17
16
15
430
31
32
33
Ham Down
Ham Lake
Hamdown
Hamdown Farm
Bush House
Lynwood
Fir Hill Farm
Cooper's Cottage
Sewage Works
Cooper's Clump
Oakdene Farm
Long Reach
Tree Tops
Works
Lark Farm
Hammond's Farm
Wellow Down
Long Clump
Wyndmoor
Stretton
WHINWHISTLE ROAD
SHELLEY LANE
SHELLEY COMMON
EMBLEY WOOD
Great Pond
Semple Ho.
Pine Grove
Romsey Common Farm
Brick Hill Farm
Twin Ways
Silverwood Ho.
The Lodge
CRAWLEY HILL
SALISBURY ROAD
A36
Blackhill
Blackhill Farm
Brackenwood Farm
BLACK HILL ROAD
Whinwhistle Cottages
Shelley Bungalow
Fighting Cocks Farm
The Roost
Salisbury Lodge
England's Cottage
Upper Shelley Copse
Four Jays Farm
Romsey
Shelley Farm
Lower Shelley Copse
Heatherlands
Shelley Cottage
SO51
Pendragon
Ower Service Area
Shelley Nursery
Twin Ways
Ower Lodge
Embley Lodge
Embley View
Bowman's Cottage
Bowman's Farm
River Blackwater
Drain
A3090
ROMSEY ROAD
Fourteen Acre Copse
Pearce's Copse
Tilhill
Foxbury Plantation
Shelley Lodge
Rough Park
Shelley Mead
Noggin
Blackwater Bridge
BRICKY LANE
LAKE LANE
Allmoor Copse
Romsey Lodge
Hotel
Cooper's Copse
Golf Driving Range
Club House
Home Farm
COOPERS
Cooper's Lane Copse
Robins Copse
Sandhill Plantation
PAULTONS GOLF CENTRE AND GOLF COURSE
Manor Equestrian Centre
Wigley
Cheney's Farm
Ower Bridge
Paultons Park Watermill
Nursery
Riverside Nursery
Paultons House
The Garden Bungalow
Keepers Cottage
Paultons Park (Leisure Park)
Lakeside
River
Cadnam
Ower
MORTIMERS INDUSTRIAL UNITS
Lodge
Wade Park Farm
Junction 2
New Cottages
Court Copse
New Pond Plantation
High Wood Copse
Middle Copse
M27
Golden Meadow
Gutter
TOTTON
Woodlands Cottage
Fuzzies Copse
Forest Gates
Nursery
Caravan Site
Green Pastures Farm
Elken House
Woodbine Cottages
Larks Lease Copse
Cricket Ground
Drove House
Ford
Pav
Newbridge Farm
Lyndhurst Lodge
The Cottage
Stonyford
Brooke's Wood
WHITEMOOR
Gipsies Fir Cottage
Gipsies Fir Plantation
LOPERWOOD
NEWBRIDGE INCLOSURE
COPYTHORNE COMMON
Stonyford
The Cottage
Pinewood Cottage
Newbridge
A31
BARROW HILL
The Pines
Shornhill Great Fir Plantation
Birchlands
Paddock Wood
The Hill
Shorn Hill
Little Fir Clump
M27 MOTORWAY
Spruce Cottage
NEWBRIDGE
Bunker's Hill
Holly Farm
COPYTHORNE CRES
Copythorne House
Crowhaven Farm
Moor Farm
Barrow Hill
Barrow Hills
Woody Bank
Wynot
Whitemoor Farm
Whitemoor Pond
The Hollies
Tatchbury House
Newbridge Cottage
Coppithorn Hill House
Coppits Cottage
Copythorne C. of E. Infant School
Play. Fld.
Memorial
The Firs
Roman Road
Robins Brook Farm
Brooksbank House
Nursery
Hartley Farm
The Beeches
COPER
POUND LANE
TATCHBURY LANE
Tatchbury Copse
HILL FORT
Copythorne Lodge
Copythorne Lodge Farm
Holly Farm
Copythorne
Pollards Moor Farm
Cammels Farm
POLLARDS MOOR RD.
VICARAGE
James's Farm
WINSOR ROAD
Tatchbury Farm
NEWBRIDGE ROAD

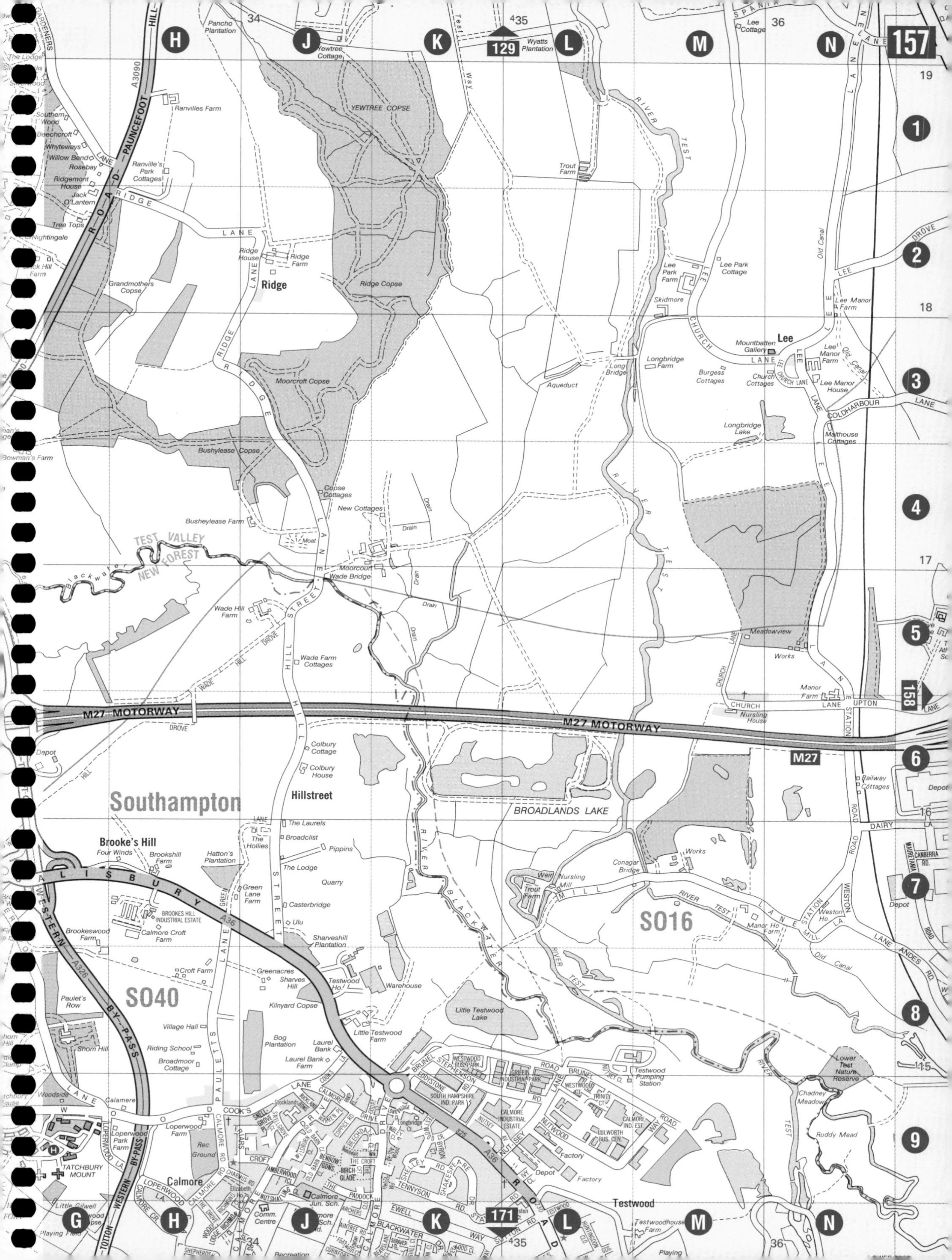
H
J
K
L
M
N
G
1
2
3
4
5
6
7
8
9
34
435
36
19
18
17
16
115
129
158
171
Pancho Plantation
Yewtree Cottage
Wyatts Plantation
Lee Cottage
SPANIARDS LANE
LEE LANE
A3090
PAUNCEFOOT HILL ROAD
GARDENERS
Ranvilles Farm
YEWTREE COPSE
RIVER TEST
TEST WAY
Trout Farm
The Lodge
Southern Wood
Beechcroft
Whyteways
Willow Bend
Rosebay
Ridgemont House
Jack O'Lantern
Tree Tops
Nightingale
Ranville's Park Cottages
RIDGE LANE
Ridge House
Ridge Farm
Ridge
Grandmothers Copse
Ridge Copse
Lee Park Farm
Lee Park Cottage
Skidmore
Old Canal
LEE DROVE
Lee Manor Farm
Lee
Mountbatten Gallery
CHURCH LANE
Longbridge Farm
Long Bridge
Burgess Cottages
Church Cottages
Lee Manor House
Aqueduct
Moorcroft Copse
COLDHARBOUR LANE
Malthouse Cottages
Longbridge Lake
Bowman's Farm
Bushylease Copse
Copse Cottages
New Cottages
Drain
Busheylease Farm
Moat
TEST VALLEY
NEW FOREST
Blackwater
Moorcourt
Wade Bridge
Wade Hill Farm
WADE HILL DROVE
HILL STREET
Meadowview
Works
Wade Farm Cottages
Manor Farm
UPTON LANE
STATION ROAD
Nursling House
M27 MOTORWAY
M27
Depot
Colbury Cottage
Colbury House
Railway Cottages
Southampton
Hillstreet
BROADLANDS LAKE
DAIRY LA.
The Laurels
Broadclist
The Hollies
Pippins
Brooke's Hill
Four Winds
Brookshill Farm
Hatton's Plantation
The Lodge
Quarry
Works
Conagar Bridge
Weir
Nursling Mill
Trout Farm
MILL LANE
CANBERRA RD.
SALISBURY ROAD
A36
WESTERN
Green Lane Farm
Casterbridge
BROOKES HILL INDUSTRIAL ESTATE
Calmore Croft Farm
Ulu
SO16
RIVER TEST
Weston Ho
Manor Ho Farm
Brookeswood Farm
Sharveshill Plantation
A326
BY-PASS
Croft Farm
Greenacres
Sharves Hill
Testwood Ho
Warehouse
Old Canal
ANDES RD.
Paulet's Row
SO40
Kilnyard Copse
Little Testwood Lake
RIVER BLACKWATER
Shorn Hill
Village Hall
Bog Plantation
Little Testwood Farm
Riding School
Laurel Bank
Laurel Bank Farm
Broadmoor Cottage
PAULETTS LANE
WESTWOOD BUS. PARK
GRIFFIN INDUSTRIAL PARK
Testwood Pumping Station
Lower Test Nature Reserve
SOUTH HAMPSHIRE IND. PARK
CALMORE INDUSTRIAL ESTATE
CALMORE IND. EST.
LULWORTH BUS. CEN.
Chadney Meadow
Woodside
Calamere
COOK'S LANE
CALMORE RD
Loperwood Farm
Loperwood Park Farm
Rec. Ground
Ruddy Mead
TATCHBURY MOUNT
Calmore
CROFT
Factory
Depot
TENNYSON RD
Calmore Jun. Sch.
Testwood
Little Gilwell
Comm. Centre
Testwoodhouse Farm
TOTTON WESTERN BY-PASS
LOPERWOOD LA.
EWELL WAY
BLACKWATER DR.
Playing Field
Recreation
Playing

158
130
172
157
Romsey
SO51
SO52
SO16
Southampton
Toothill
Telegraph Wood Camp
TOOT HILL
Upper Toothill
Lower Toothill
Thatched Cottage
The Yews
Middle Farm
Packridge
Kiln Farm Riding Sch.
Kiln Farm House
Rownhams Plantation
Home Copse
Long Copse
CALVESLEASE COPSE
Upper Ashfield Farm
Malthouse Cottage
SPANIARDS LA.
HOE LANE
LEE DROVE
TOOTHILL ROAD
PACKRIDGE LANE
ROWNHAMS LANE
UPPER TOOTHILL ROAD
NIGHTINGALE WOOD
Greenhill Copse
Greenhill Cottage
Greenhill
COLDHARBOUR LANE
Grove Farm
ROMSEY GOLF COURSE
Club Ho.
ROMSEY ROAD
A3057
M27
M271
M271 MOTORWAY
M27 MOTORWAY
Rownhams Service Area
Subway
ROWNHAMS PARK
Austrey Wood
Routs Copse
Aldermoor Copse
DYMER'S WOOD
Tanner's Brook
Parkers Farm
ROWNHAMS
Clams Copse
LORDS WOOD
White Lodge
Fields Cottage
TEST VALLEY
EASTLEIGH
Grove Lodge Farm
Fir Copse
Lymers Copse
UPTON CRESCENT
Upton
LYMER LA.
Lymer Villas
UPTON LANE
Playing Field
Grove Place
The Atherley School
Junction 3
Play. Fld. Rownhams C.of E. Prim. Sch.
Fish Pond
ROWNHAMS HOUSE
St. Johns Home
Comm. Cen.
NURSLING STREET
Bridgers Farm
Nursling
Nursling C. of E. Prim. Sch.
Recreation Ground
Halls
MILL ESTATE YARD
Belmont House
Rosebank Lodge
Sinclair Jun. & Inf. Schs.
Play. Fld.
Oaklands Community School
Oakland Swimming Pool
LORDS HILL DISTRICT CENTRE
Lib.
Fairisle Jun. & Inf. Schs.
Elm Villa
The Cedar Sch.
BMX Track
Pav.
Railway Cottages
Depot
DAIRY LANE
CANBERRA ROAD
MAURETANIA ROAD
ORIANA WAY
NURSLING INDUSTRIAL ESTATE
HOME COVERT
Adanac Farm
Lordshill Outdoor Recreation Centre
Hillyfields
Yewtree Farm
FROGMORE LANE
Europa Tennis Centre
Bargain Farm
Works
Superstore
Junction 1
BROWNHILL WAY
WESTON LA.
ANDES ROAD
TEST LANE
TEST VALLEY SMALL BUSINESS CENTRE
YEOMAN INDUSTRIAL PARK
REDBRIDGE LANE
LOWER REDBRIDGE ROAD
Club House
LOWER TEST NATURE RESERVE
Lord's Hill
Aldermoor
Aldermoor Bridge
Nursling Plantation
Comm. Cen.
Adventure Playground
Coxford Copse
PRINCESS ANNE HOSP.
Millbrook Community School
ORDNANCE SURVEY OFFICES
Maybush
Coxford
Shirley Warren
Old Shirley
Holy Family R.C. Primary School
Mansel Junior & Infant Schools
Playing Field
Millbrook Towers
MANSEL PARK
WINDERMERE AVENUE
BROWNHILL ROAD
Shirley Warren Prim. Sch.
Newlands Jun. & Inf.
A
B
C
D
E
F
G
1
2
3
4
5
6
7
8
9
37
38
39
19
18
17
16
115

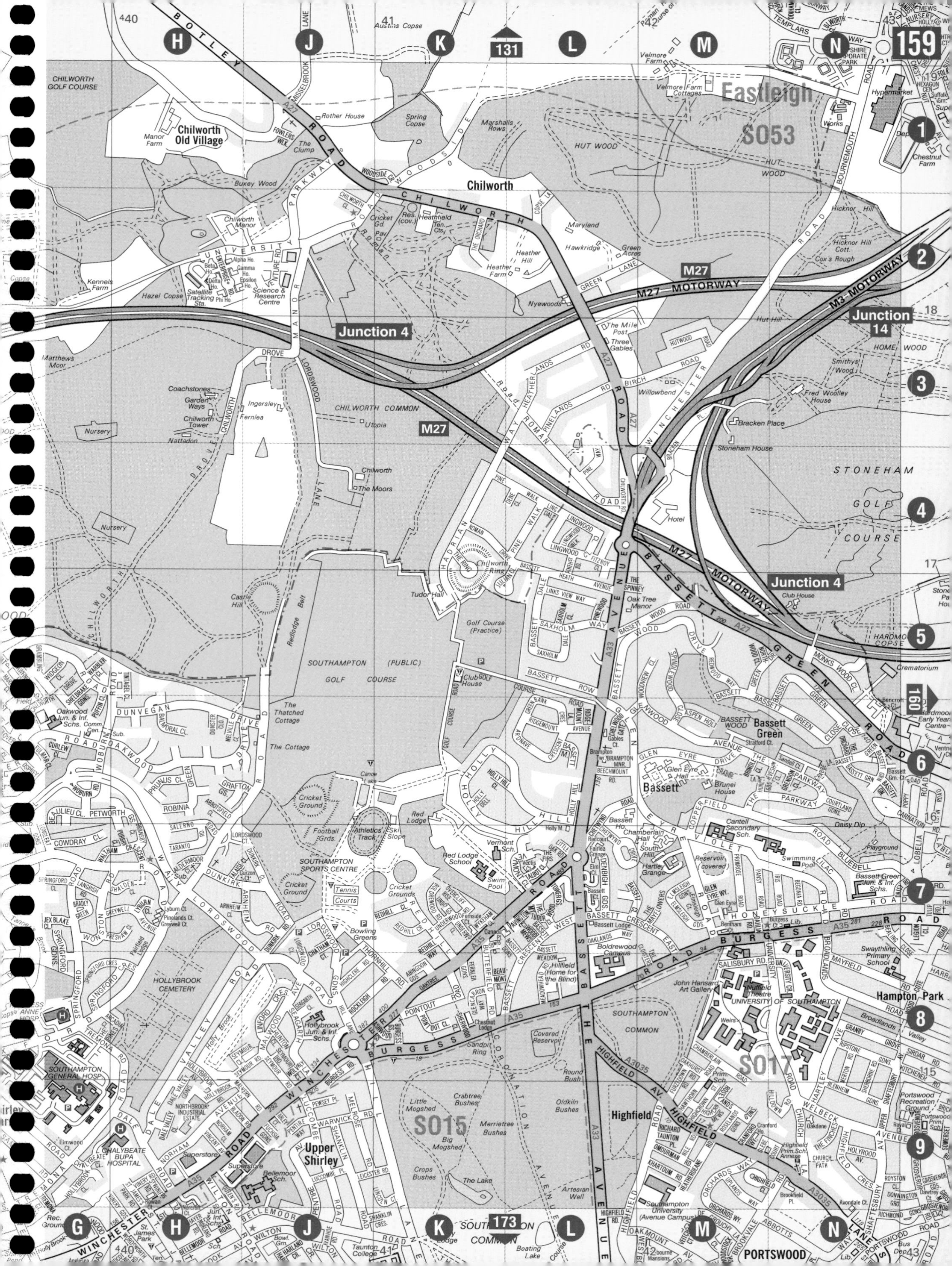
Chilworth Old Village
Chilworth
Eastleigh
SO53
HUT WOOD
Junction 4
M27
M27 MOTORWAY
M3 MOTORWAY
Junction 14
CHILWORTH COMMON
STONEHAM GOLF COURSE
SOUTHAMPTON (PUBLIC) GOLF COURSE
SOUTHAMPTON SPORTS CENTRE
Bassett Green
Bassett
SOUTHAMPTON COMMON
SO15
SO17
Upper Shirley
Highfield
Hampton Park
PORTSWOOD
BURGESS ROAD
WINCHESTER ROAD
BASSETT AVENUE
THE AVENUE
HIGHFIELD AV.
UNIVERSITY OF SOUTHAMPTON
SOUTHAMPTON GENERAL HOSP.
HOLLYBROOK CEMETERY
131
173
160

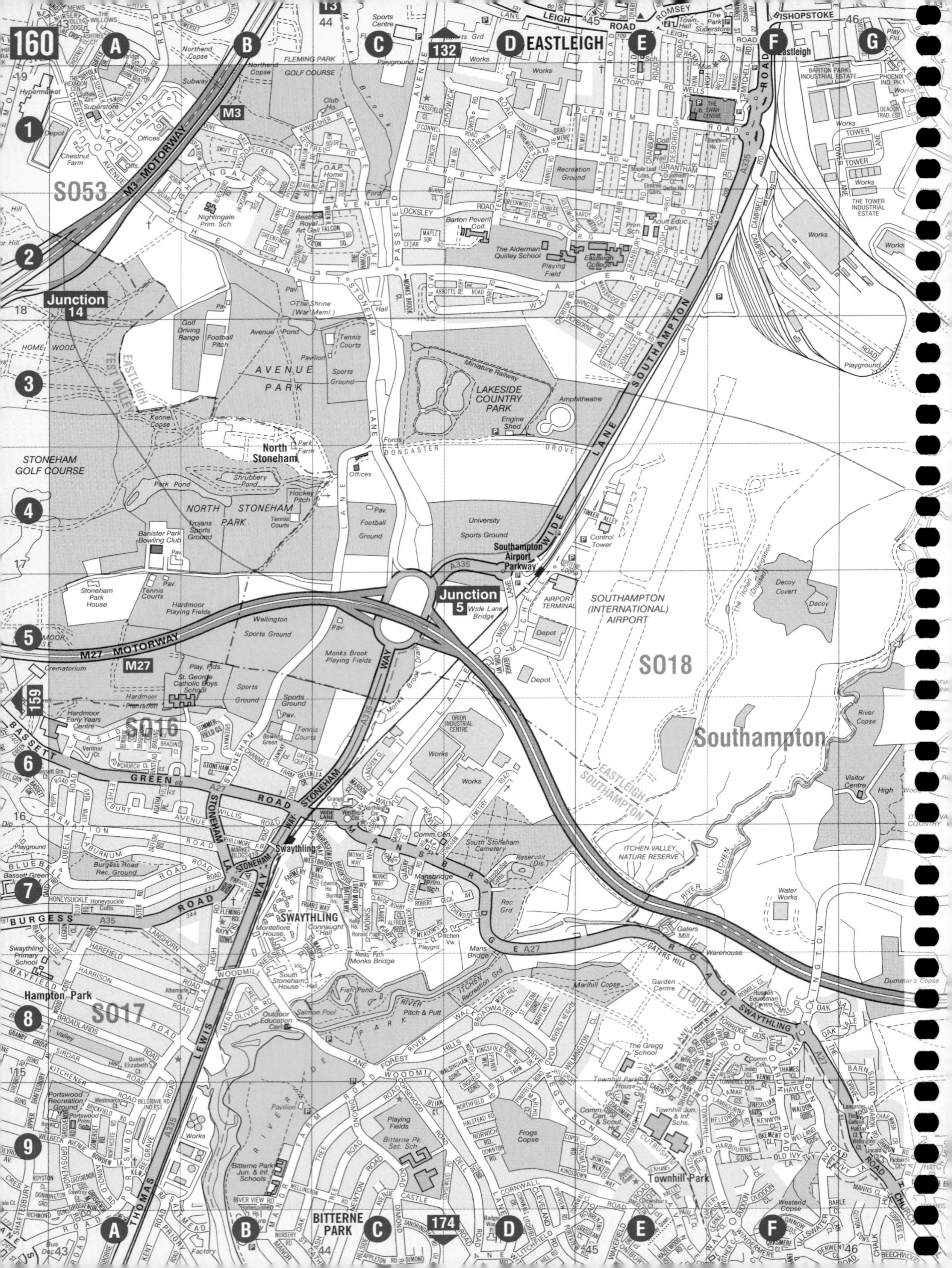
160
A
B
C
D
E
F
G
1
2
3
4
5
6
7
8
9
13
132
159
174
EASTLEIGH
Eastleigh
BISHOPSTOKE
LEIGH ROAD
ROMSEY ROAD
FLEMING PARK GOLF COURSE
Sports Centre
Northend Copse
Subway
M3
M3 MOTORWAY
S053
Hypermarket
Superstore
Depot
Offices
Chestnut Farm
Nightingale Prim. Sch.
Beatrice Royal Art Gall.
Barton Peveril Coll.
The Alderman Quilley School
Eastleigh College
Playing Field
Recreation Ground
BLENHEIM ROAD
GRANTHAM AVENUE
CHERBOURG ROAD
DERBY ROAD
FACTORY ROAD
WELLS PLACE
THE SWAN CENTRE
Adult Educ. Cen.
BARTON PARK INDUSTRIAL ESTATE
PHOENIX IND. PK.
DEACON TRAD. EST.
TOWER LANE
THE TOWER INDUSTRIAL ESTATE
Works
Playground
CHESTNUT AVENUE
PASSFIELD AVENUE
MONKS WAY
STONEHAM LANE
Junction 14
The Shrine (War Meml.)
Golf Driving Range
Football Pitch
Avenue Pond
Tennis Courts
Pavilion
Sports Ground
AVENUE PARK
HOME WOOD
TEST VALLEY
EASTLEIGH
Kennel Copse
LAKESIDE COUNTRY PARK
Miniature Railway
Amphitheatre
Engine Shed
DONCASTER DROVE
North Stoneham
Park Farm
Shrubbery Pond
Park Pond
STONEHAM GOLF COURSE
NORTH STONEHAM PARK
Hockey Pitch
Trojans Sports Ground
Banister Park Bowling Club
Football Ground
University Sports Ground
SOUTHAMPTON
WIDE LANE
Southampton Airport Parkway
Control Tower
AIRPORT TERMINAL
SOUTHAMPTON (INTERNATIONAL) AIRPORT
Junction 5
Wide Lane Bridge
Stoneham Park House
Hardmoor Playing Fields
Wellington Sports Ground
M27 MOTORWAY
M27
Crematorium
St. George Catholic Boys School
Hardmoor Plantation
Hardmoor Early Years Centre
Monks Brook Playing Fields
S016
S018
Depot
ORION INDUSTRIAL CENTRE
Decoy Covert
Decoy
River Copse
Southampton
Visitor Centre
EASTLEIGH SOUTHAMPTON
ITCHEN VALLEY NATURE RESERVE
BASSETT GREEN ROAD
STONEHAM WAY
Swaythling
South Stoneham Cemetery
Reservoir (Dis.)
MANSBRIDGE ROAD
Mansbridge Prim. Sch.
Burgess Road Rec. Ground
Bassett Green
BURGESS ROAD
SWAYTHLING
Connaught Hall
Montefiore House
Monks Path Monks Bridge
Mans Bridge
Gaters Mill
GATERS HILL
Warehouse
Water Works
Dummer's Copse
Marlhill Copse
Garden Centre
Russell Equestrian Centre
SWAYTHLING ROAD
Swaythling Primary School
Hampton Park
S017
Outdoor Education Cen.
Salmon Pool
South Stoneham House
Fish Pond
ITCHEN Recreation Grd
RIVER WALK
Pitch & Putt
RIVERSIDE PARK
FOREST HILLS DRIVE
WOODMILL LANE
The Gregg School
Townhill Park House
Townhill Jun. & Inf. Schs.
Frogs Copse
Playing Fields
Bitterne Pk. Sec. Sch.
Bitterne Park Jun. & Inf. Schools
Townhill Park
Westend Copse
Portswood Recreation Ground
Queen Elizabeth Ct.
THOMAS LEWIS WAY
A335
A27
A35
BITTERNE PARK
CHURCH HILL
Factory
43
44
45
46
16
17
18
19

BISHOPSTOKE
FAIR OAK
Eastleigh
Stoke Park
SO50
SO30
Hatch Bottom
WEST END
Moorgreen
MOORGREEN HOSPITAL
Hedge End
133
162
175
47
48
49
H
J
K
L
M
N
G
1
2
3
4
5
6
7
8
9
19
18
17
16
15
ROAD
FAIR OAK ROAD
ALAN DRAYTON WAY
OAKGROVE RD.
HAIG ROAD
ORCHARD AV.
TEMPLECOMBE ROAD
SANDY LANE
EASTLEIGH ROAD
BOTLEY ROAD
WINCHESTER ROAD
ALLINGTON LANE
FIRTREE LANE
HOGWOOD LANE
QUOB LANE
BURNETTS LANE
BUBB LANE
BLIND LANE
TOLLBAR WAY
HIGH STREET
BOTLEY ROAD
M27 MOTORWAY
M27
B3037
B3354
B3342
B3035
River Itchen
Itchen Navigation
Conegar Lock
Fish House Bay
Chicken Hall Farm
Works
Viaduct
Stoke Park Jun. Sch.
Stoke Park Inf. Sch.
West Horton Farm
Playground
Upper House Cottages
Factory
The Kings Sch.
The Wyvern Comm. Sch.
Fair Oak Inf. Sch.
Fair Oak Jun. Sch.
Playing Field
Cemy.
Rec. Grd.
Quobleigh Pond
Lake Farm
Lapstone Farm
Hammerley Farm
Firtree Farm
Allington Manor Farm Cottages
ALLINGTON MANOR FARM BUS. CEN.
Allington Manor School
Allston
Foxholes Farm
Woodlands
Comm. Cen.
Hog Wood
Willow Farm
Hearts Row
Hearts Copse
Milkmead Copse
Railway Cottage
Chalcroft Farm
Vocus Copse
High Hill Row
Paynes Row
Sunnyhills Copse
High Hill
West Point
WHITE HARMONY ACRES IND. EST.
Downs Copse
Round Copse
CHALCROFT DISTRIBUTION PARK
The Bungalow
Hill Crest
Reservoir
Wood
ITCHEN VALLEY COUNTRY PARK
Bushy Copse
Withybed Covert
Oaklands
Square Covert
Holly Rise
Animal Welfare Centre
Ridgeway Copse
OAKTREE CARAVAN PARK
South Lodge
Home Covert
Moorgreen Farm
Salems Cottages
Jacksons Farm
Little Moorgreen Farm
Newlands
Dummer's Copse
Langholm
Berrywood Farm
Public Open Space
The King's Prim. Sch.
MOORGREEN PARK CARAVAN SITE
St. James' C. of E. Prim. Sch.
Playing Field
Moorgreen Dairy Farm
Moorgreen Rec. Grd.
Hospice
Hatch Grange (Recreation Ground)
Lib.
Dowd's Farm
Moorlands
Mus.
Comm. Cen.
Depot
Hampshire Tennis & Health Club
Westwood Copse
WELLINGTON PK.
CENTRE 27 RETAIL PK.
NELSON INDUSTRIAL PARK
Bridge Cottage
Middle Farm
Warwick House
Stocks Farm

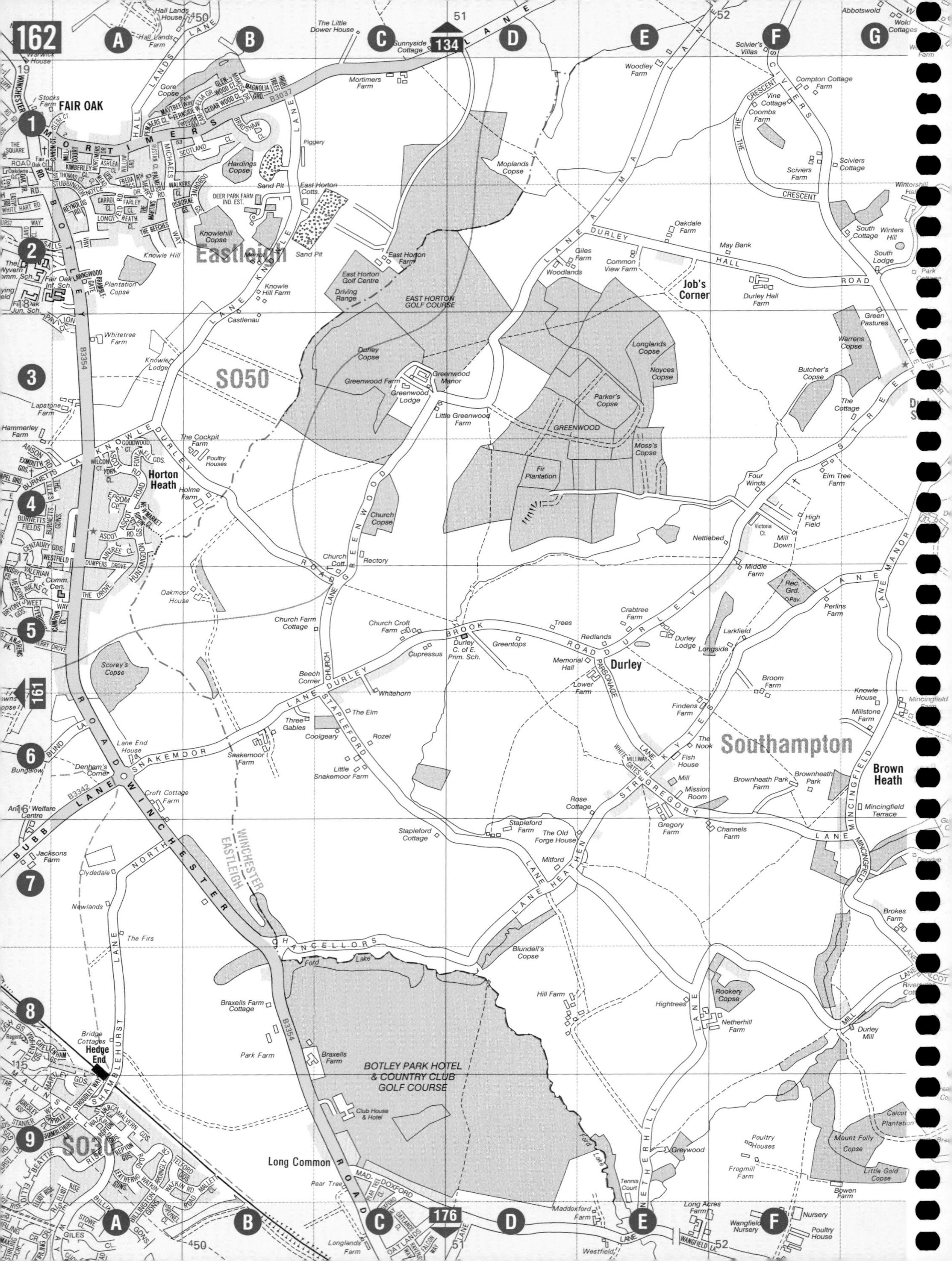

Fair Oak
Eastleigh
SO50
Horton Heath
Durley
Job's Corner
Southampton
Brown Heath
Hedge End
SO30
Long Common
East Horton Golf Course
Botley Park Hotel & Country Club Golf Course
Mortimers Lane
Durley Hall Road
Durley Street
Durley Brook Road
Snakemoor Lane
Chancellors Lane
Heathen Lane
Netherhill Lane
Mincingfield Lane
Manor Lane
Sciviers Lane
Church Lane
Greenwood Lane
Knowle Lane
Botley Road
Winchester Road
Bubb Lane
North Lane
Shamblehurst Lane
Stapleford Lane
Gregory Lane
Kytes Lane
Parsonage Lane
Wangfield La.
Greenwood Manor
Greenwood Farm
Little Greenwood Farm
Durley Copse
Church Copse
Longlands Copse
Noyces Copse
Parker's Copse
Moss's Copse
Fir Plantation
Scorey's Copse
Blundell's Copse
Rookery Copse
Mount Folly Copse
Little Gold Copse
Calcot Plantation
Warrens Copse
Butcher's Copse
Knowlehill Copse
Hardings Copse
Mopland Copse
Durley Mill
Netherhill Farm
Braxells Farm
Park Farm
Mortimers Farm
Woodley Farm
Oakdale Farm
Durley Hall Farm
Sciviers Farm
Compton Cottage Farm
Middle Farm
Crabtree Farm
Broom Farm
Findens Farm
Gregory Farm
Channels Farm
Brownheath Park Farm
Millstone Farm
Perlins Farm
Brokes Farm
Snakemoor Farm
Little Snakemoor Farm
Stapleford Farm
Horton Heath
Jacksons Farm
Maddoxford Farm
Long Acres Farm
Bowen Farm
Frogmill Farm
Westfield
Greywood
Hill Farm
Hightrees
Clydedale
Newlands
The Firs
Lane End House
Denham's Corner
Croft Cottage Farm
Durley C. of E. Prim. Sch.
Memorial Hall
Club House & Hotel
B3354
B3037
B3342
134
176
161

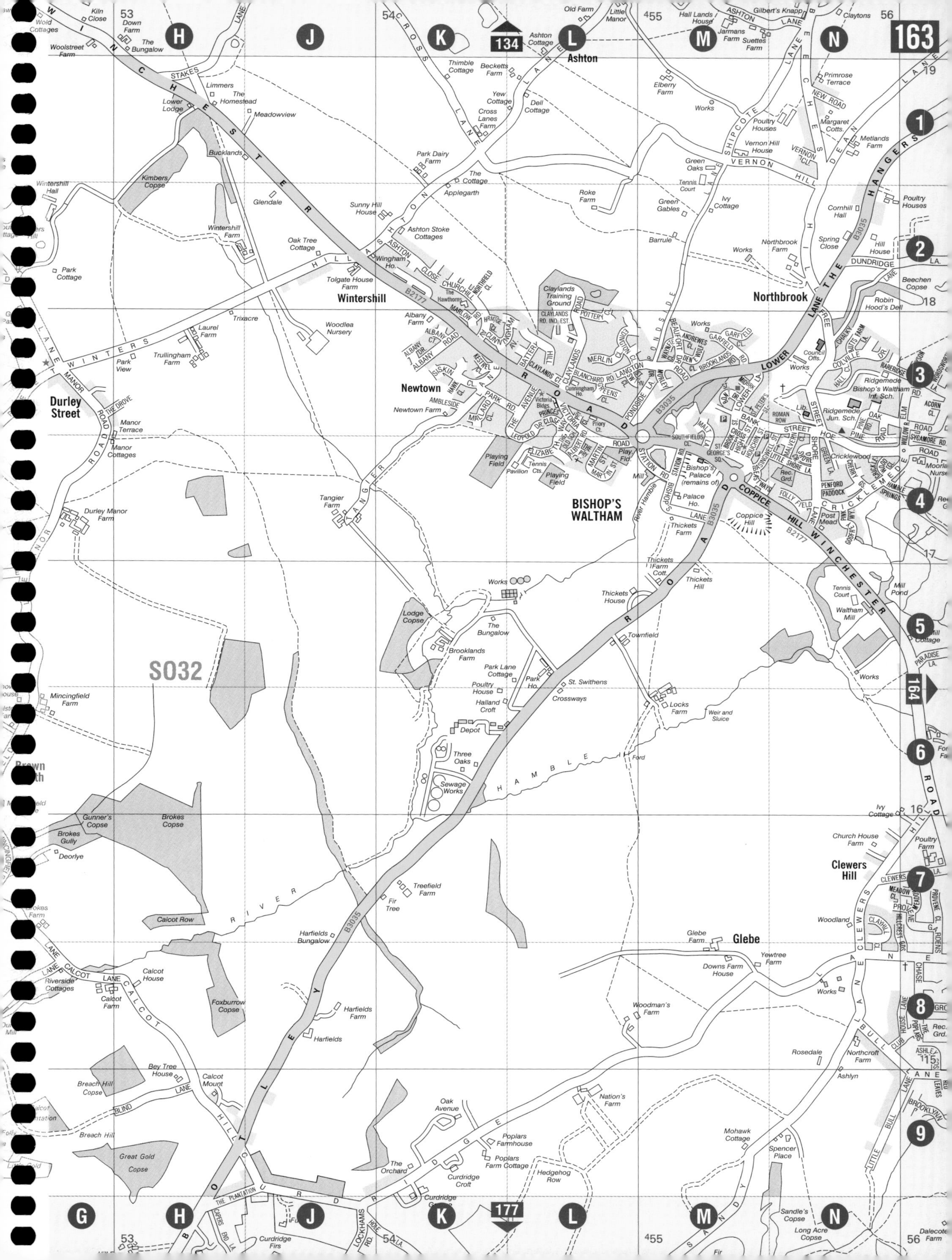
Ashton
Wintershill
Newtown
Durley Street
Northbrook
BISHOP'S WALTHAM
Clewers Hill
Glebe
SO32
WINCHESTER ROAD
BOTLEY ROAD
CURDRIDGE LANE
HAMBLE RIVER
Ashton Cottage
Becketts Farm
Thimble Cottage
Yew Cottage
Cross Lanes Farm
Dell Cottage
Park Dairy Farm
The Cottage
Applegarth
Sunny Hill House
Ashton Stoke Cottages
Oak Tree Cottage
Wingham Ho.
Tolgate House Farm
Albany Farm
Woodlea Nursery
Trixacre
Laurel Farm
Trullingham Farm
Park View
Wintershill Farm
Wintershill Hall
Glendale
Kimbers Copse
Bucklands
Meadowview
The Homestead
Limmers
Lower Lodge
Woolstreet Farm
Kiln Close
Wold Cottages
Down Farm
The Bungalow
Park Cottage
Manor Terrace
Manor Cottages
Durley Manor Farm
Newtown Farm
Tangier Farm
Playing Field
Pavilion
Tennis Cts.
Claylands Training Ground
Works
Lodge Copse
The Bungalow
Brooklands Farm
Park Lane Cottage
Park Ho.
Poultry House
Halland Croft
Depot
Three Oaks
Sewage Works
St. Swithens
Crossways
Townfield
Thickets House
Thickets Farm Cott.
Thickets Hill
Thickets Farm
Locks Farm
Weir and Sluice
Ford
Coppice Hill
Bishop's Palace (remains of)
Palace Ho.
Mill
River Hamble
Old Farm
Little Manor
Hall Lands House
Jarmans Farm
Suettes Farm
Gilbert's Knapp
Claytons
Elberry Farm
Primrose Terrace
Margaret Cotts.
Poultry Houses
Vernon Hill House
Metlands Farm
Green Oaks
Tennis Court
Roke Farm
Green Gables
Ivy Cottage
Barrule
Northbrook Farm
Cornhill Hall
Spring Close
Hill House
Beechen Copse
Robin Hood's Dell
Council Offs.
Ridgemede
Bishop's Waltham Inf. Sch.
Ridgemede Jun. Sch.
Cricklewood
Rec. Grd.
Post Mead
Tennis Court
Waltham Mill
Mill Pond
Paradise La.
Ivy Cottage
Church House Farm
Poultry Farm
Woodland
Glebe Farm
Downs Farm House
Yewtree Farm
Woodman's Farm
Rosedale
Northcroft Farm
Ashlyn
Nation's Farm
Mohawk Cottage
Spencer Place
Sandle's Copse
Long Acre Copse
Dalecote Farm
Oak Avenue
Poplars Farmhouse
Poplars Farm Cottage
Hedgehog Row
The Orchard
Curdridge Croft
Curdridge Firs
Harfields Farm
Harfields
Harfields Bungalow
Treefield Farm
Fir Tree
Calcot Row
Gunner's Copse
Brokes Copse
Brokes Gully
Deorlye
Mincingfield Farm
Calcot House
Calcot Farm
Riverside Cottages
Foxburrow Copse
Bey Tree House
Calcot Mount
Breach Hill Copse
Breach Hill
Great Gold Copse
Blind Lane
Calcot Lane
The Plantation
Lockhams Rd.
134
164
177
53
54
55
56
19
18
17
16
15

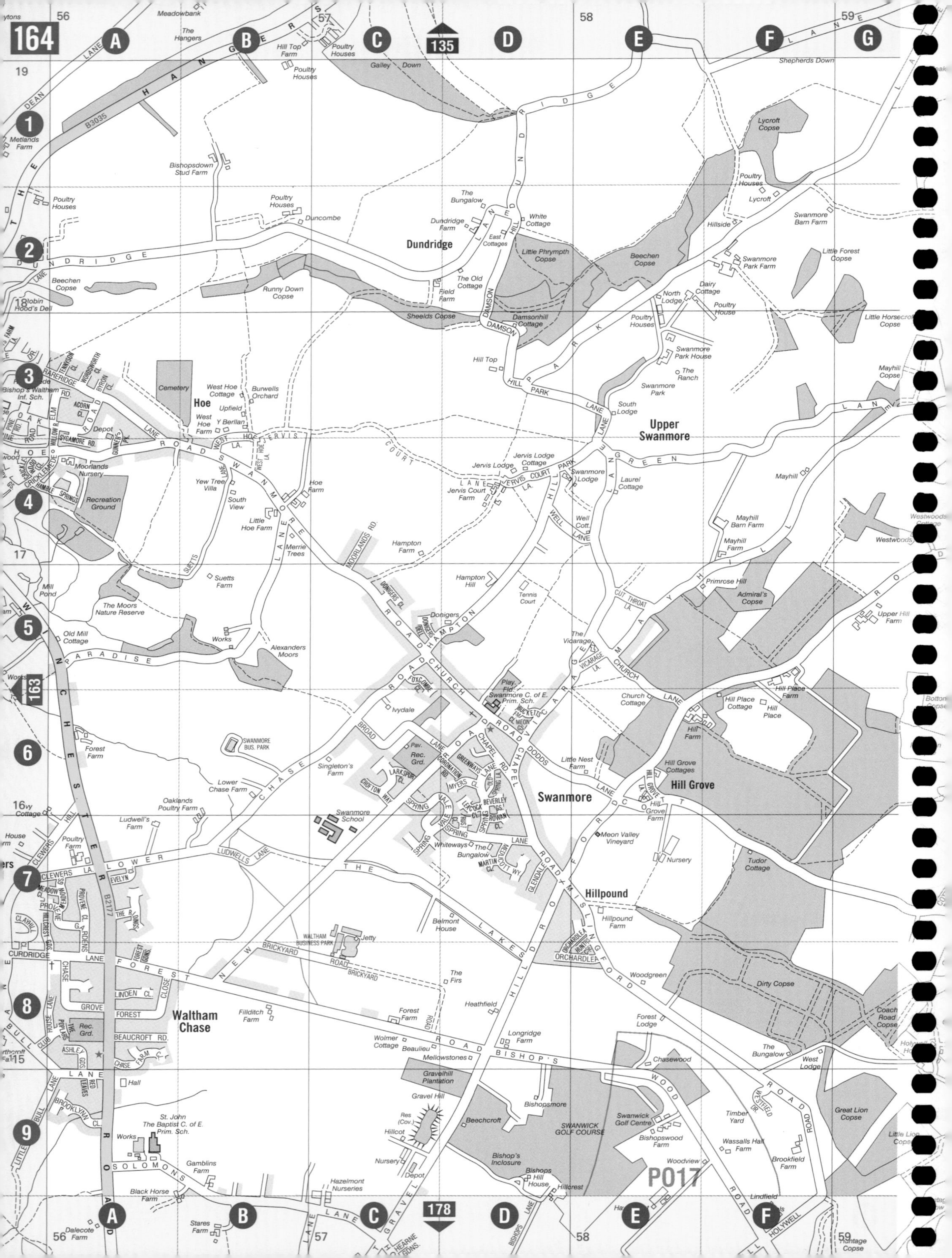

56
57
58
59
A
B
C
D
E
F
G
135
178
163
19
17
16
15
1
2
3
4
5
6
7
8
9
Meadowbank
The Hangers
Hill Top Farm
Poultry Houses
Galley Down
Shepherds Down
HANGERS
B3035
DEAN LANE
Metlands Farm
Bishopsdown Stud Farm
Poultry Houses
Duncombe
DUNDRIDGE
DUNDRIDGE LANE
Dundridge
The Bungalow
Dundridge Farm
White Cottage
East Cottages
Little Phrymph Copse
The Old Cottage
Field Farm
Beechen Copse
Runny Down Copse
Robin Hood's Dell
Sheelds Copse
Damsonhill Cottage
DAMSON HILL
Lycroft Copse
Poultry Houses
Lycroft
Swanmore Barn Farm
Hillside
Beechen Copse
Swanmore Park Farm
Little Forest Copse
Dairy Cottage
North Lodge
Poultry House
Poultry Houses
Little Horsecroft Copse
Swanmore Park House
The Ranch
Swanmore Park
Mayhill Copse
Hill Top
PARK LANE
South Lodge
Upper Swanmore
Cemetery
Hoe
West Hoe Cottage
Burwells Orchard
Upfield
Y Berllan
West Hoe Farm
Bishop's Waltham Inf. Sch.
Depot
HOE ROAD
Moorlands Nursery
Recreation Ground
Yew Tree Villa
South View
Hoe Farm
Little Hoe Farm
Merrie Trees
SWANMORE LANE
JERVIS COURT LANE
Jervis Lodge
Jervis Lodge Cottage
Jervis Court Farm
Swanmore Lodge
Laurel Cottage
GREEN LANE
Mayhill
Mayhill Barn Farm
Mayhill Farm
Westwoods
Well Cott.
WELL LANE
Hampton Farm
MOORLANDS RD.
Suetts Farm
Mill Pond
The Moors Nature Reserve
Hampton Hill
Tennis Court
Primrose Hill
Admiral's Copse
CUT THROAT LA.
Upper Hill Farm
Old Mill Cottage
Works
Alexanders Moors
PARADISE
Donigers
HAMPTON
The Vicarage
VICARAGE LA.
CHURCH LANE
MAYHILL
Play. Fld.
Swanmore C. of E. Prim. Sch.
Church Cottage
Hill Place Cottage
Hill Place
Hill Place Farm
Ivydale
SWANMORE BUS. PARK
Forest Farm
Pav.
Rec. Grd.
Singleton's Farm
Little Nest Farm
Hill Farm
Hill Grove Cottages
Hill Grove
Swanmore
Lower Chase Farm
Oaklands Poultry Farm
Ludwell's Farm
Swanmore School
CHASE
Hill Grove Farm
Meon Valley Vineyard
Nursery
Tudor Cottage
Poultry Farm
LOWER CHASE ROAD
LUDWELLS LANE
Whiteways
The Bungalow
Hillpound
Hillpound Farm
MISLINGFORD ROAD
CLEWERS LA.
B2177
WINCHESTER ROAD
Belmont House
THE LAKES
WALTHAM BUSINESS PARK
Jetty
CURDRIDGE
NEW BRICKYARD ROAD
ORCHARDLEA
Woodgreen
Dirty Copse
Coach Road Copse
FOREST LANE
The Firs
Heathfield
Forest Farm
Forest Lodge
Waltham Chase
Filldich Farm
Rec. Grd.
BEAUCROFT RD.
Longridge Farm
Wolmer Cottage
Beaulieu
Mellowstones
BISHOP'S WOOD ROAD
The Bungalow
West Lodge
Chasewood
Gravelhill Plantation
Gravel Hill
Hall
Bishopsmore
Beechcroft
SWANWICK GOLF COURSE
Swanwick Golf Centre
Timber Yard
Great Lion Copse
St. John The Baptist C. of E. Prim. Sch.
Works
Res (Cov.)
Hillcot
Bishopswood Farm
Wassalls Hall Farm
Little Lion Copse
Nursery
Depot
Bishop's Inclosure
Woodview
Brookfield Farm
SOLOMONS LANE
Gamblins Farm
Bishops Hill House
Hillcrest
PO17
Black Horse Farm
Hazelmont Nurseries
Lindfield
Stares Farm
Dalecote Farm
GRAVEL HILL
HOLYWELL
HEARNE GDNS.
BISHOPS LANE
Heritage Copse

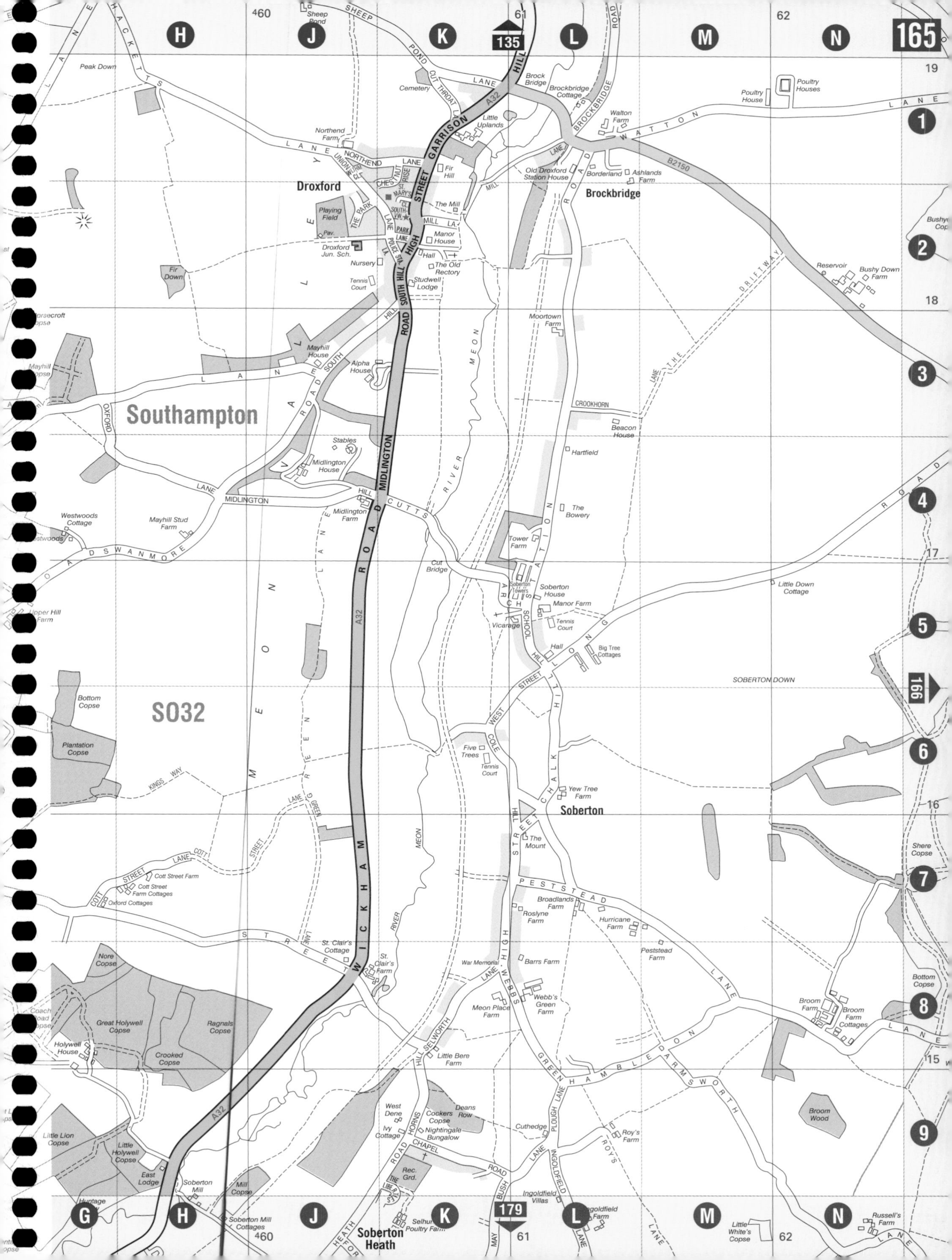

H
J
K
L
M
N
460
61
62
135
179
166
Droxford
Brockbridge
Southampton
SO32
Soberton
Soberton Heath
Peak Down
Sheep Pond
Cemetery
Northend Farm
Brock Bridge
Brockbridge Cottage
Little Uplands
Poultry House
Poultry Houses
Walton Farm
Fir Hill
Old Droxford Station House
Borderland
Ashlands Farm
Playing Field
The Mill
Manor House
Droxford Jun. Sch.
Nursery
Hall
The Old Rectory
Tennis Court
Studwell Lodge
Fir Down
Reservoir
Bushy Down Farm
Moortown Farm
Mayhill House
Alpha House
Beacon House
Hartfield
Stables
Midlington House
Midlington Farm
The Bowery
Westwoods Cottage
Mayhill Stud Farm
Tower Farm
Cut Bridge
Soberton House
Manor Farm
Vicarage
Little Down Cottage
Upper Hill Farm
Big Tree Cottages
SOBERTON DOWN
Bottom Copse
Plantation Copse
Five Trees
Yew Tree Farm
The Mount
Cott Street Farm
Cott Street Farm Cottages
Oxford Cottages
Broadlands Farm
Roslyne Farm
Hurricane Farm
Peststead Farm
St. Clair's Cottage
St. Clair's Farm
War Memorial
Barrs Farm
Nore Copse
Great Holywell Copse
Ragnals Copse
Meon Place Farm
Webb's Green Farm
Broom Farm
Broom Farm Cottages
Bottom Copse
Shere Copse
Holywell House
Crooked Copse
Little Bere Farm
West Dene
Cockers Copse
Deans Row
Ivy Cottage
Nightingale Bungalow
Cuthedge
Roy's Farm
Broom Wood
Little Lion Copse
Little Holywell Copse
East Lodge
Soberton Mill
Mill Copse
Rec. Grd.
Soberton Mill Cottages
Ingoldfield Villas
Ingoldfield Farm
Little White's Copse
Russell's Farm
RIVER MEON
A32
B2150
WICKHAM ROAD
MIDLINGTON ROAD
HIGH STREET
GARRISON HILL
SOUTH HILL
WATTON LANE
NORTHEND LANE
STATION ROAD
CROOKHORN LANE
THE DRIFTWAY
SWANMORE ROAD
HAMBLEDON LANE
PESTSTEAD LANE
CHALK HILL
WEBBS GREEN
CHAPEL ROAD
PLOUGH LANE
INGOLDFIELD LANE
KINGS WAY

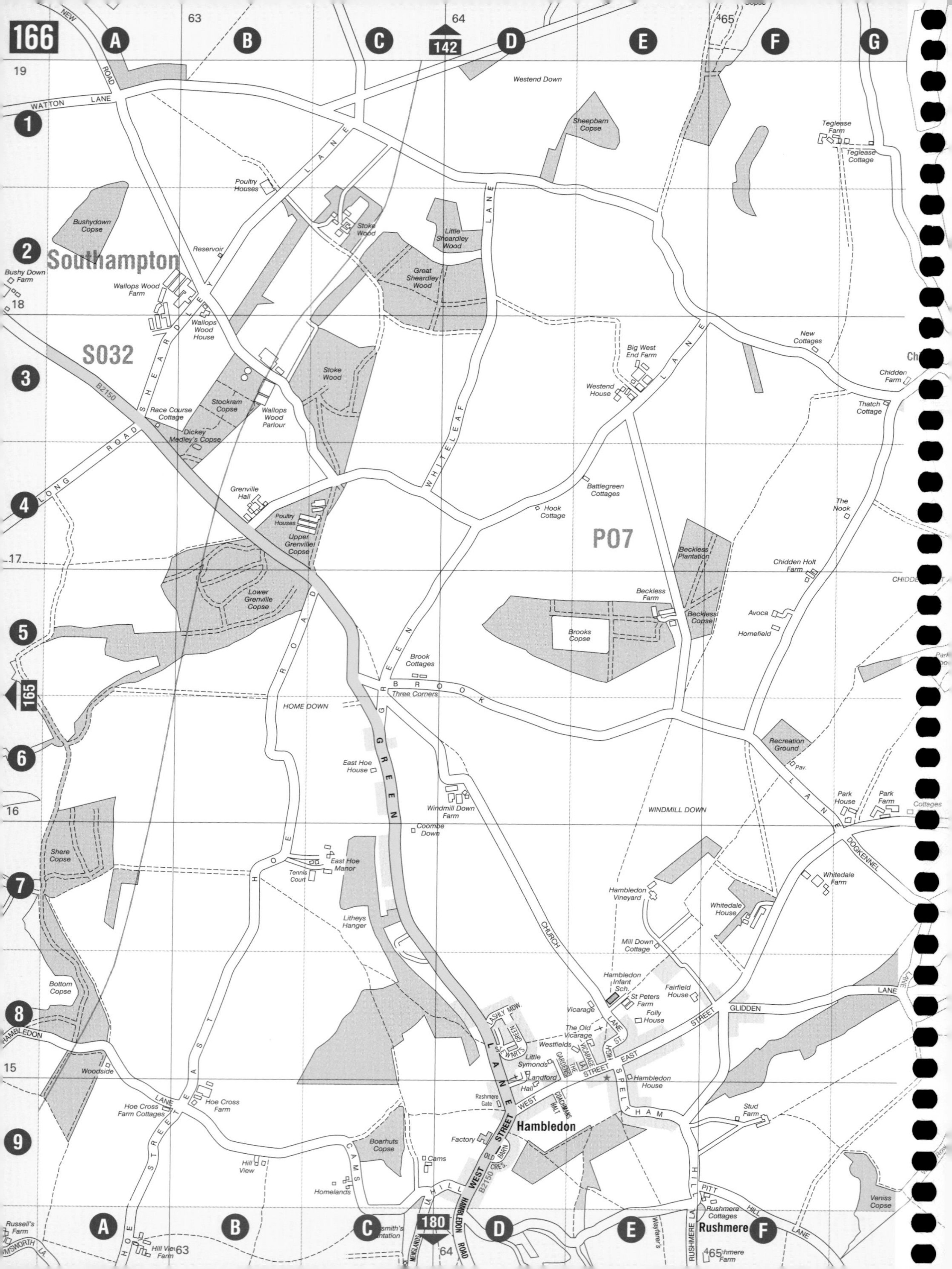

Southampton
SO32
PO7
Watton Lane
New Road
Westend Down
Sheepbarn Copse
Teglease Farm
Teglease Cottage
Poultry Houses
Bushydown Copse
Reservoir
Stoke Wood
Little Sheardley Wood
Great Sheardley Wood
Bushy Down Farm
Wallops Wood Farm
Wallops Wood House
Sheardley Lane
Whiteleaf Lane
Big West End Farm
Westend House
New Cottages
Chidden Farm
Thatch Cottage
Race Course Cottage
Stockram Copse
Wallops Wood Parlour
Dickey Medley's Copse
Long Road
B2150
Grenville Hall
Upper Grenville Copse
Battlegreen Cottages
Hook Cottage
The Nook
Beckless Plantation
Chidden Holt Farm
Lower Grenville Copse
Beckless Farm
Brooks Copse
Beckless Copse
Avoca
Homefield
Brook Cottages
Brook Lane
Three Corners
Home Down
Green Lane
Recreation Ground
Pav.
East Hoe House
Windmill Down Farm
Coombe Down
Windmill Down
Park House
Park Farm
Cottages
Shere Copse
Hoe Road
East Hoe Manor
Tennis Court
Dogkennel Lane
Whitedale Farm
Hambledon Vineyard
Whitedale House
Litheys Hanger
Church Lane
Mill Down Cottage
Bottom Copse
Hambledon Infant Sch.
St Peters Farm
Fairfield House
Glidden Lane
Vicarage
Folly House
Lashly Mdw.
Stewarts Green
The Old Vicarage
Westfields
Little Symonds
Landford
Hall
East Street
High St.
Speltham
Hambledon House
Hambledon Lane
Woodside
Hoe Cross Farm Cottages
Hoe Cross Farm
East Street
Rashmere Gate
West Street
Hambledon
Stud Farm
Factory
Old Barn Cres.
Boarhuts Copse
Cams
Cams Hill
Hill View
Homelands
Hambledon Road
Pitt Hill Lane
Rushmere Cottages
Veniss Copse
Russell's Farm
Hill View Farm
Menslands La.
Wayfarer's
Rushmere La.
Rushmere
Rushmere Farm

142
165
180

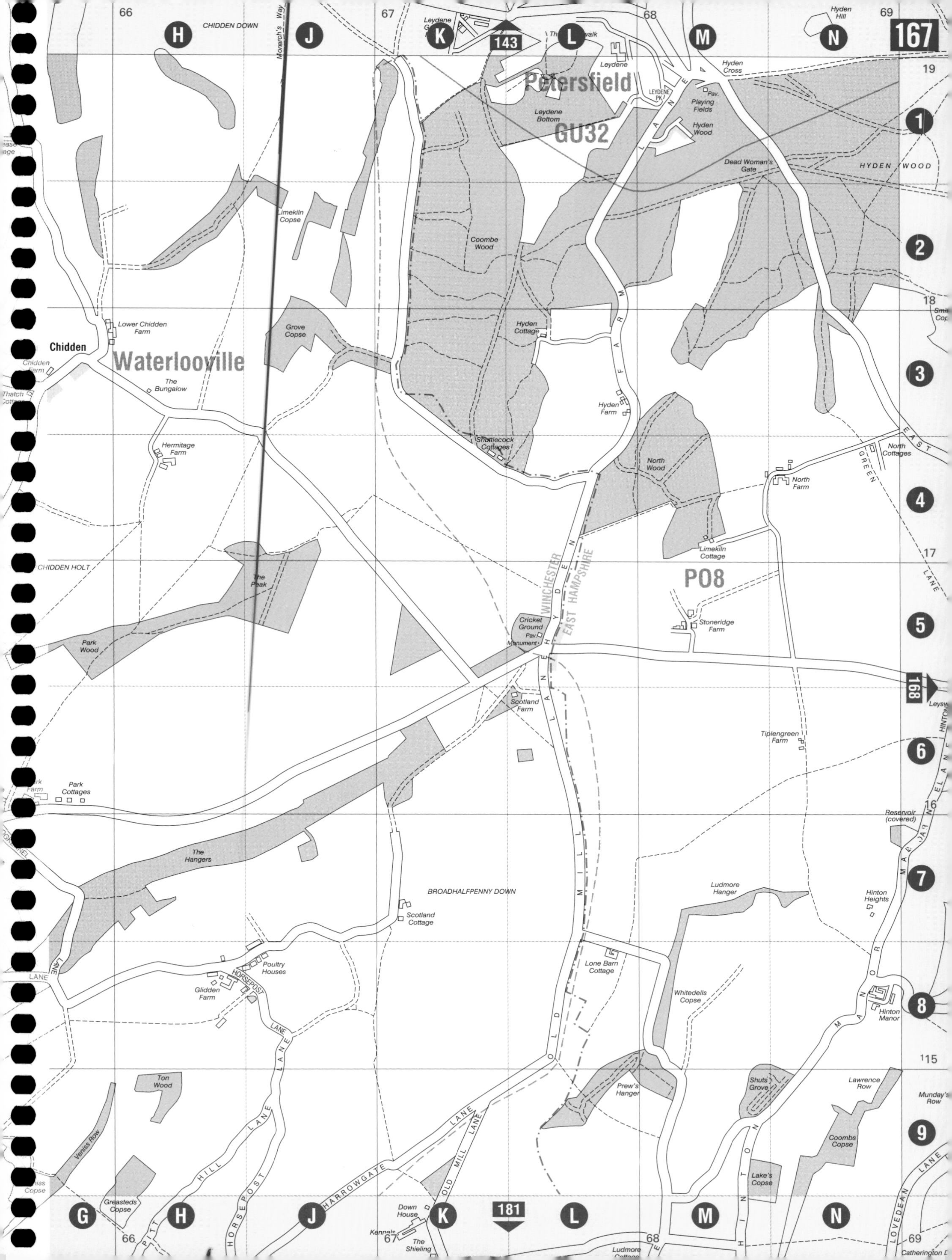
CHIDDEN DOWN
Monarch's Way
Leydene
143
Petersfield
Leydene Bottom
GU32
Hyden Cross
Playing Fields
Hyden Wood
Dead Woman's Gate
HYDEN WOOD
Hyden Hill
Limekiln Copse
Coombe Wood
Lower Chidden Farm
Chidden
Waterlooville
Grove Copse
Hyden Cottage
The Bungalow
Hyden Farm
Hermitage Farm
Shuttlecock Cottages
North Wood
North Cottages
North Farm
EAST
GREEN
FARM LANE
CHIDDEN HOLT
Limekiln Cottage
PO8
The Peak
WINCHESTER
EAST HAMPSHIRE
HYDEN LANE
Cricket Ground
Pav.
Monument
Stoneridge Farm
Park Wood
168
Scotland Farm
Tiplengreen Farm
Park Cottages
Reservoir (covered)
The Hangers
BROADHALFPENNY DOWN
Ludmore Hanger
Hinton Heights
Scotland Cottage
Lone Barn Cottage
Poultry Houses
Glidden Farm
HORSEPOST LANE
Whitedells Copse
Hinton Manor
MANOR LANE
OLD MILL LANE
Ton Wood
Prew's Hanger
Shuts Grove
Lawrence Row
Munday's Row
Veniss Row
Coombs Copse
HARROWGATE LANE
HILL LANE
Lake's Copse
Greasteds Copse
Down House
Kennels
The Shieling
181
HINTON
LOVEDEAN LANE
Ludmore Cottage
Catherington
66
67
68
69
19
18
17
16
115

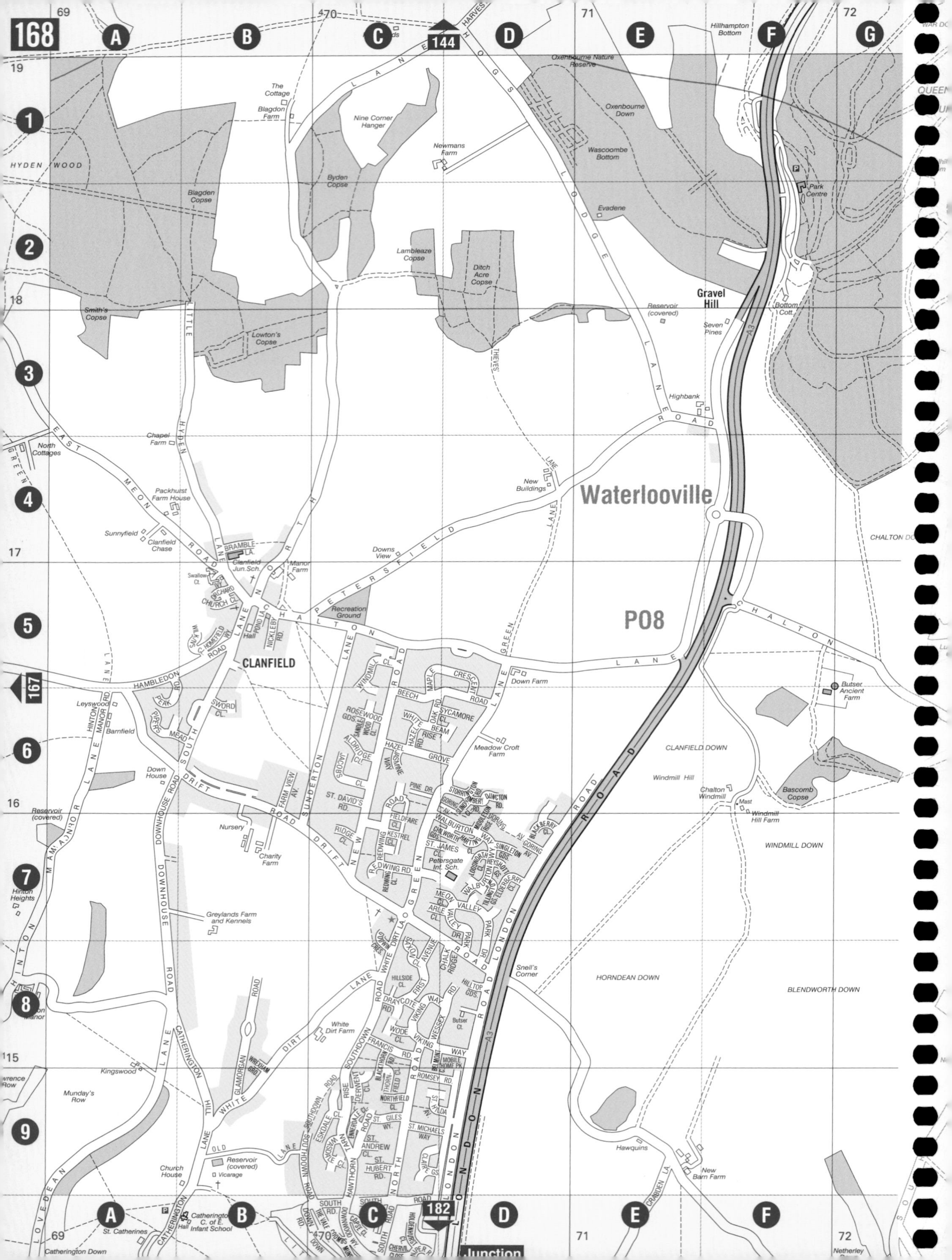
144
167
182
Waterlooville
PO8
CLANFIELD
Gravel Hill
HYDEN WOOD
Oxenbourne Nature Reserve
Oxenbourne Down
Wascoombe Bottom
Hillhampton Bottom
Park Centre
Evadene
Nine Corner Hanger
Newmans Farm
The Cottage
Blagdon Farm
Blagden Copse
Byden Copse
Lambleaze Copse
Ditch Acre Copse
Smith's Copse
Lowton's Copse
Reservoir (covered)
Seven Pines
Bottom Cott.
Highbank
Chapel Farm
North Cottages
Packhurst Farm House
Sunnyfield
Clanfield Chase
Clanfield Jun.Sch.
Manor Farm
Downs View
New Buildings
Recreation Ground
Down Farm
Butser Ancient Farm
CHALTON DOWN
CLANFIELD DOWN
Windmill Hill
Chalton Windmill
Mast
Windmill Hill Farm
WINDMILL DOWN
Bascomb Copse
Meadow Croft Farm
Leyswood
Barnfield
Down House
Nursery
Charity Farm
Petersgate Int. Sch.
Greylands Farm and Kennels
Hinton Heights
Snell's Corner
HORNDEAN DOWN
BLENDWORTH DOWN
White Dirt Farm
Kingswood
Munday's Row
Hawquins
New Barn Farm
Church House
Vicarage
Catherington C. of E. Infant School
St. Catherines
Catherington Down
Netherley
Junction
EAST MEON ROAD
HAMBLEDON ROAD
CHALTON LANE
PETERSFIELD ROAD
LONDON ROAD
HOGS LODGE LANE
NORTH LANE
HYDEN LANE
LITTLE
SOUTH LANE
DOWNHOUSE ROAD
DRIFT ROAD
HINTON MANOR LANE
CATHERINGTON LANE
WHITE DIRT LANE
OLD LANE
LOVEDEAN LANE
CRABDEN LA.
A3
69
70
71
72
19
18
17
16
15

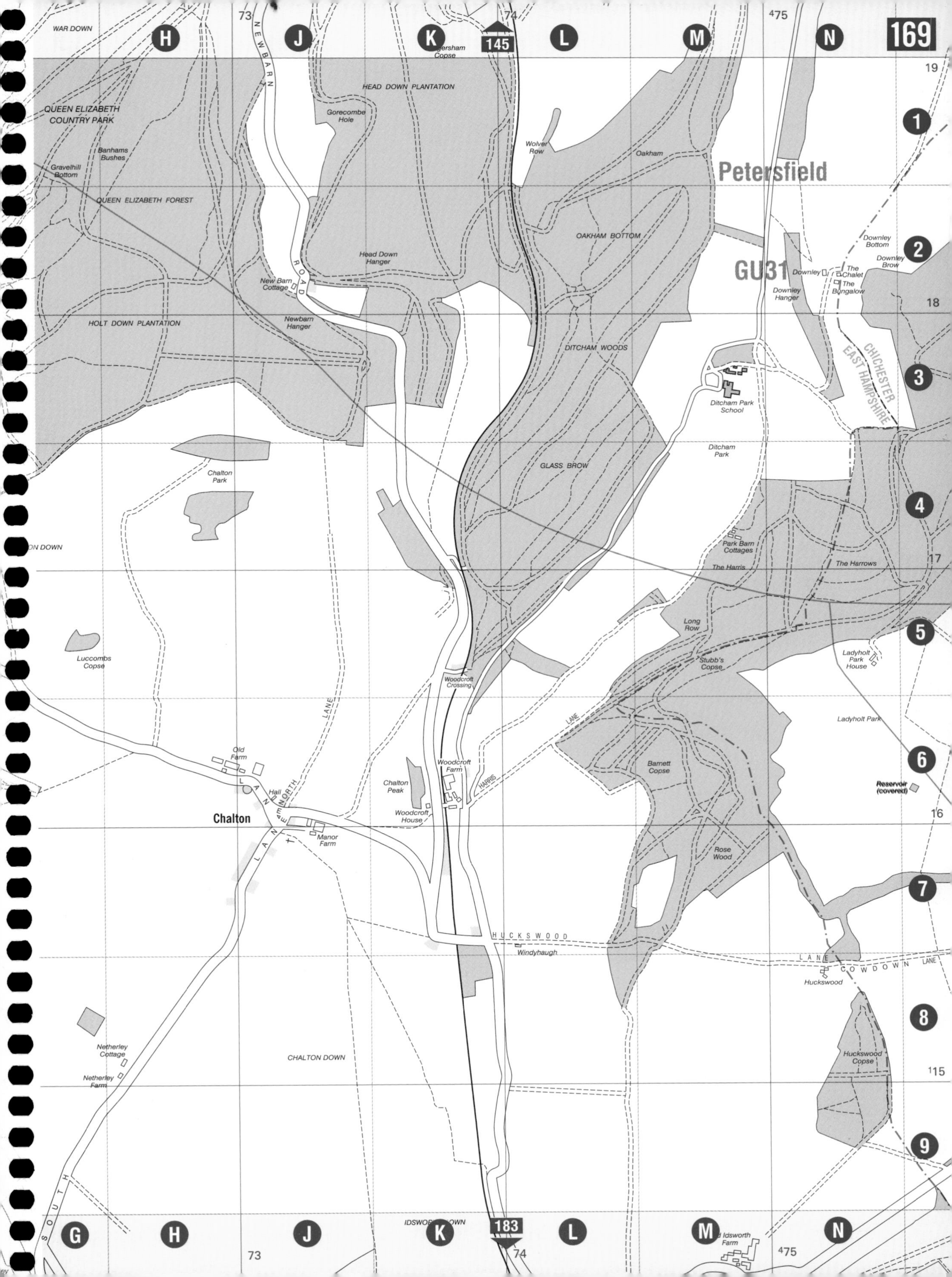
WAR DOWN
H
J
K
L
M
N
73
74
475
145
19
18
17
16
115
1
2
3
4
5
6
7
8
9
HEAD DOWN PLANTATION
Gorecombe Hole
QUEEN ELIZABETH COUNTRY PARK
Banhams Bushes
Gravelhill Bottom
QUEEN ELIZABETH FOREST
Wolver Row
Oakham
Petersfield
OAKHAM BOTTOM
Head Down Hanger
NEWBARN ROAD
New Barn Cottage
Newbarn Hanger
HOLT DOWN PLANTATION
GU31
Downley Bottom
Downley Brow
Downley
The Chalet
The Bungalow
Downley Hanger
DITCHAM WOODS
CHICHESTER
EAST HAMPSHIRE
Ditcham Park School
Ditcham Park
Chalton Park
GLASS BROW
Park Barn Cottages
The Harris
The Harrows
Long Row
Stubb's Copse
Ladyholt Park House
Luccombs Copse
Woodcroft Crossing
Ladyholt Park
LANE
Old Farm
NORTH LANE
Hall
Chalton
Manor Farm
Woodcroft Farm
HARRIS
Chalton Peak
Woodcroft House
Barnett Copse
Reservoir (covered)
Rose Wood
HUCKSWOOD
Windyhaugh
LANE
COWDOWN LANE
Huckswood
Netherley Cottage
Netherley Farm
CHALTON DOWN
Huckswood Copse
SOUTH LANE
G
IDSWORTH DOWN
183
Idsworth Farm

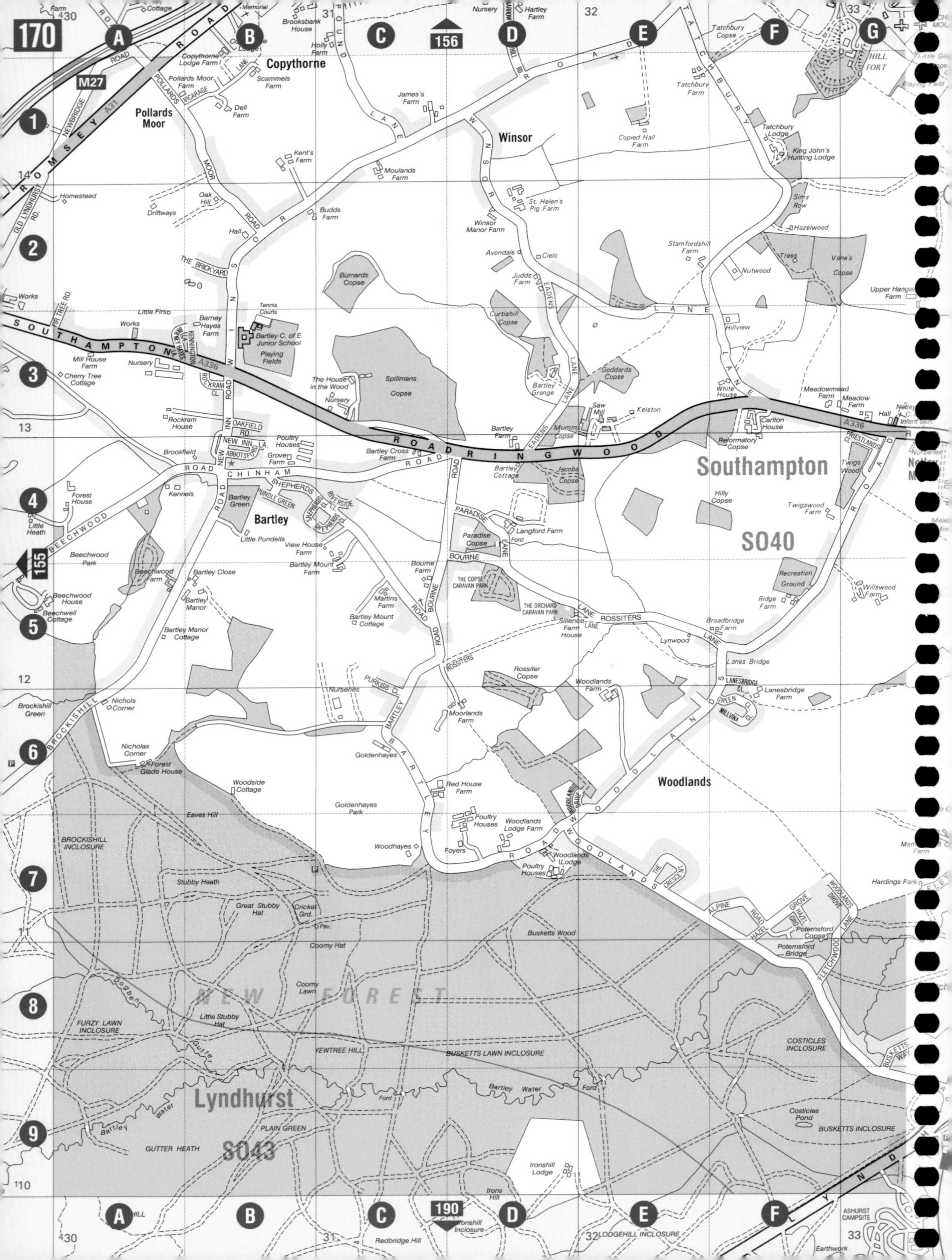
Copythorne
Pollards Moor
Winsor
Bartley
Southampton
SO40
Woodlands
NEW FOREST
Lyndhurst
SO43
M27
A31
A336
ROMSEY ROAD
SOUTHAMPTON ROAD
RINGWOOD ROAD
CHINHAM ROAD
BEECHWOOD
BROCKISHILL
Copythorne Lodge Farm
Pollards Moor Farm
Scammells Farm
Dell Farm
Brooksbank House
Holly Farm
James's Farm
Kent's Farm
Moulands Farm
Budds Farm
Tatchbury Copse
Tatchbury Farm
Tatchbury Lodge
King John's Hunting Lodge
Copied Hall Farm
St. Helen's Pig Farm
Winsor Manor Farm
Homestead
Driftways
Oak Hill
Burnards Copse
Spillmans Copse
Bartley C. of E. Junior School
Playing Fields
Tennis Courts
Barney Hayes Farm
Mill House Farm
Cherry Tree Cottage
Rockram House
Poultry Houses
Grove Farm
Bartley Cross Farm
Bartley Green
Forest House
Little Heath
Kennels
Beechwood Park
Beechwood Farm
Beechwood House
Beechwell Cottage
Bartley Close
Bartley Manor
Bartley Manor Cottage
Little Pundells
View House Farm
Bartley Mount Farm
Martins Farm
Bartley Mount Cottage
Bourne Farm
Paradise Copse
Langford Farm
THE COPSE CARAVAN PARK
THE ORCHARD CARAVAN PARK
Sillence Farm House
Rossiter Copse
Woodlands Farm
Moorlands Farm
Lynwood
Broadbridge Farm
Lanes Bridge
Lanesbridge Farm
Ridge Farm
Recreation Ground
Willswood Farm
Twigswood Farm
Hilly Copse
Twigs Wood
Carlton House
Reformatory Copse
Meadowmead Farm
Meadow Farm
Hazelwood
Vane's Copse
Upper Hanger Farm
Nutwood
Hillview
Stamfordshill Farm
Sims Row
Goddards Copse
Curtishill Copse
Bartley Grange
Judds Farm
Avondale
Cielo
Saw Mill
Kelston
Mumms Copse
Jacobs Copse
Bartley Farm
Bartley Cottage
The House in the Wood
Nursery
Nurseries
Nicholas Corner
Nichols Corner
Brockishill Green
Forest Glade House
Woodside Cottage
Goldenhayes
Goldenhayes Park
Red House Farm
Woodlands Lodge Farm
Woodhayes
Foyers
Woodlands Lodge
Eaves Hill
BROCKISHILL INCLOSURE
Stubby Heath
Great Stubby Hat
Cricket Grd.
Pav.
Coomy Hat
Coomy Lawn
Little Stubby Hat
FURZY LAWN INCLOSURE
YEWTREE HILL
BUSKETTS LAWN INCLOSURE
Busketts Wood
Bartley Water
Ford
PLAIN GREEN
GUTTER HEATH
Ironshill Lodge
Irons Hill
Ironshill Inclosure
Redbridge Hill
LODGEHILL INCLOSURE
COSTICLES INCLOSURE
Costicles Pond
BUSKETTS INCLOSURE
Potternsford Copse
Potternsford Bridge
Hardings Park
ASHURST CAMPSITE
Earthwork
HILL FORT
Dogben Gutter
156
155
190
A B C D E F G
1 2 3 4 5 6 7 8 9
430 31 32 33
14 13 12 11 110

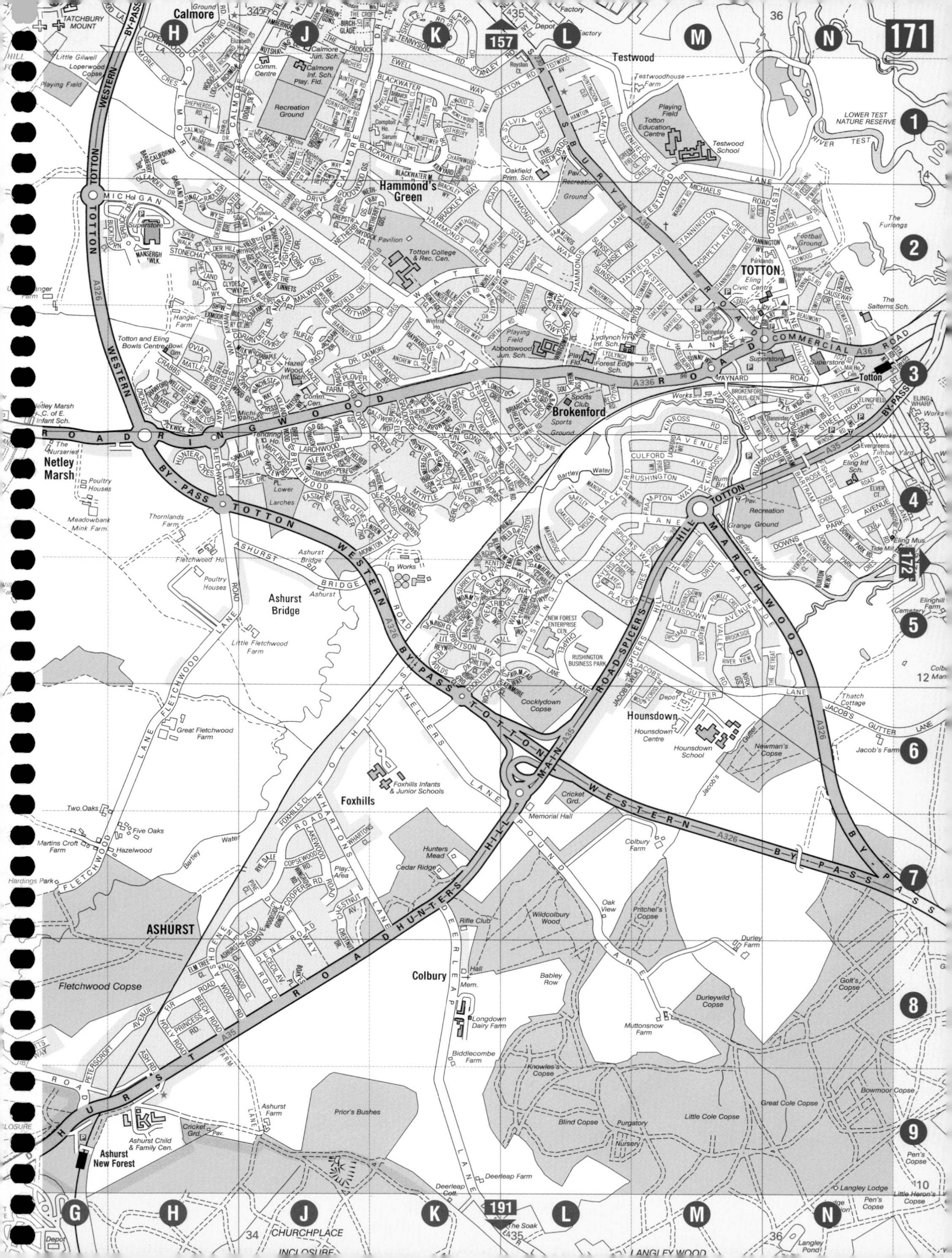
Calmore
Testwood
LOWER TEST NATURE RESERVE
RIVER TEST
Testwood School
Totton Education Centre
Hammond's Green
Totton College & Rec. Cen.
TOTTON
COMMERCIAL ROAD
Brokenford
Sports Ground
Netley Marsh
TOTTON WESTERN BY-PASS
RINGWOOD ROAD
Ashurst Bridge
Hounsdown
Hounsdown School
Foxhills
Foxhills Infants & Junior Schools
Colbury
ASHURST
Fletchwood Copse
Ashurst New Forest
Prior's Bushes
Little Cole Copse
Great Cole Copse
Blind Copse
Purgatory
Durleywild Copse
Wildcolbury Wood
Cocklydown Copse
RUSHINGTON BUSINESS PARK
NEW FOREST ENTERPRISE CEN.
Eling Mus.
Tide Mill
The Saltems Sch.
CHURCHPLACE INCLOSURE
LANGLEY WOOD
157
172
191

172
158
192
171
A
B
C
D
E
F
G
1
2
3
4
5
6
7
8
9
37
38
39
14
12
11
110
M271
SO16
SO40
LOWER TEST NATURE RESERVE
The Furlongs
The Salterns Sch.
Redbridge
Redbridge Wharf
REDBRIDGE CHANNEL
REDBRIDGE VEHICLE TERMINAL
Eling Great Marsh
Eling Channel
Eling
Eling Hill
Eling Wharf
Timber Yard
Elinghill Farm
Cemetery
Colbury Manor
Cole's Farm
Boat Pound
RIVER TEST
SOUTHAMPTON DOCKS
PRINCE CHARLES CONTAINER TERMINAL
MARITIME FREIGHTLINER TERMINAL
Customs and Excise Office
Jubilee House (Customs and Excise)
King George V Dry Dock
Imperial House
Warehouses
Travelling Crane
Sewage Works
Tanner's Creek
Luggy Creek
Depot
Police Post
MILLBROOK
Millbrook Recreation Ground
MILLBROOK TRADING ESTATE
MILLBROOK FLYOVER
REDBRIDGE FLYOVER
REDBRIDGE CAUSEWAY
TOTTON BY-PASS
COMMERCIAL RD.
TEBOURBA WAY
MILLBROOK ROAD
WINCHESTER ROAD
REDBRIDGE HILL
Wimpson
Mansel Park
Newlands Jun. & Inf. Schools
Test Playing Field
Green Park
Tennis Courts
Redbridge Comm. Sch.
Redbridge Prim. Sch.
Mason Moor Prim. Sch.
Western Comm. Hosp.
Fire Brigade H.Q.
Regents Pk. Sec. Sch.
Old Shirley
Shirley Warren Prim. Sch.
Pleasure Cycle Track
Shirley Pond
Govt. Resettlement Cen.
T.A. Centre
Solent Bus. Cen.
BURY BRICKFIELD PARK CARAVAN SITE
Bury Copse
The Kennels
Bury Farm
Bury Marsh
Slowhill Copse
Holly Cottage
Trotts
Trotts Farm
Sparrow's Copse
East Veugles Copse
Great Orchard Copse
Fatroak Copse
Little Orchard Copse
Gregory Cooper's Copse
Spragg's Copse
Pooksgreen
Coffin's Farm
Kites Copse
Bowmoor Copse
Pen's Copse
Great Heron's Copse
Heron's Hill
Little Heron's Copse
Dumper's Farm
Great Dumper's Copse
Little Staplewood Farm
Hammer's Copse
Park's Farm
Playing Field
Cork's Farm
Refuse Incineration Plant
Cork Field Rec. Grd.
BMX Track
Tavell's Farm
Recreation Ground
MARCHWOOD
Marchwood Jun. Sch.
Marchwood Yacht Club
Jetty
MARCHWOOD INDUSTRIAL ESTATE
Laboratory
Southampton Institute of Higher Education Marine Operations Centre
Byam's House
Fifteen Acre Copse
McMullen Barracks
Marchwood Military Port
Crookedhays Copse
Horseclose Copse
Pumpfield
Withybeds
MARCHWOOD BY-PASS
A35
A36
A33
A326
A3057
JACOB'S GUTTER LANE
MARCHWOOD ROAD
BURY ROAD
POOKSGREEN
STAPLEWOOD LANE
TAVELLS LANE
LONG LANE
HYTHE ROAD
MAIN ROAD
CRACKNORE HARD LANE
ADMIRALTY WAY
MAGAZINE LANE
WESTERN AVENUE
WEST BAY RD.
HERBERT WALKER AVENUE
MILLBROOK POINT RD.
FIRST AVENUE
SECOND AVENUE
THIRD AVENUE
OAKLEY ROAD
STANTON ROAD
KING GEORGE'S AVENUE
PRINCE OF WALES AVE
REGENT'S PARK ROAD
WIMPSON LANE
TEST LANE
GOVER ROAD
REDBRIDGE LANE

159
SOUTHAMPTON COMMON
Southampton
SHIRLEY
PORTSWOOD
SO17
Westwood Park
Portswood Park
Bevois Mount
Bevois Town
Bevois Valley
Banister Park
Fitzhugh
SO15
Freemantle
Hill
Polygon
Bedford Place
Bellevue
Newtown
NORTHAM
St. Mary's
Nichols Town
Fourposts
Millbrook
Blechynden
SOUTHAMPTON
WESTERN DOCKS
Sussex Place
SO14
Chapel
Crosshouse
Lansdowne Hill
Ocean Village
MAYFLOWER PARK
ROYAL PIER (Closed)
TOWN QUAY
RIVER TEST
SOUTHAMPTON NEW FOREST
Southampton to E. Cowes 60mins.
Southampton to: Cowes 22mins. (Fast Ferry) Hythe 12mins. (Passenger Ferry)
EASTERN DOCKS
Empress Dock
Ocean Dock
Marchwood Military Port
Ship Repair Yard
Sports Ground
174
193
G H J K L M N
1 2 3 4 5 6 7 8 9
440 41 42 43

A
B
C
D
E
F
G
160
1
2
3
4
5
6
7
8
9
173
194
43
44
45
46
SO17
SO18
SO14
SO19
BITTERNE PARK
Townhill Park
Midanbury
ST. DENYS
St. Denys
Bevois Valley
BITTERNE
Bitterne
Southampton
NORTHAM
Millbank
Merry Oak
Belvidere
Chapel
Crosshouse
ITCHEN
Woolston
Sholing
Sholing Common
Pleasant View
Botany Bay
Peartree Green
Ocean Village
Newtown
WOOLSTON
Weston
EASTERN DOCKS
WESTON POINT
MAYFIELD PARK
Mayfield Park
Riverside Park
Freemantle Common
Donkey Common
Millers Pond Open Space
Jurd's Lake
RIVER ITCHEN
THE A3025 ITCHEN BRIDGE
COBDEN BRIDGE
NORTHAM BRIDGE
PORTSMOUTH ROAD
BITTERNE ROAD
WEST END ROAD
ST. DENYS ROAD
THOMAS LEWIS WAY
BELVIDERE PARADE
Itchen College
St. Mary's College
Centurion Industrial Park
Belgrave Industrial Estate
Willments Industrial Estate
Woolston Sec. Sch.
Weston Park Jun. & Inf. Schs.
Chamberlayne Leisure Cen.
Weston Park Boys Secondary School
Veracity Recreation Ground
Sholing Girls Sec. Sch.
Harefield Jun. & Inf. Schs.
Deep Dene Rec. Grd.
Recreation Ground
Cemetery
Refuse Tip

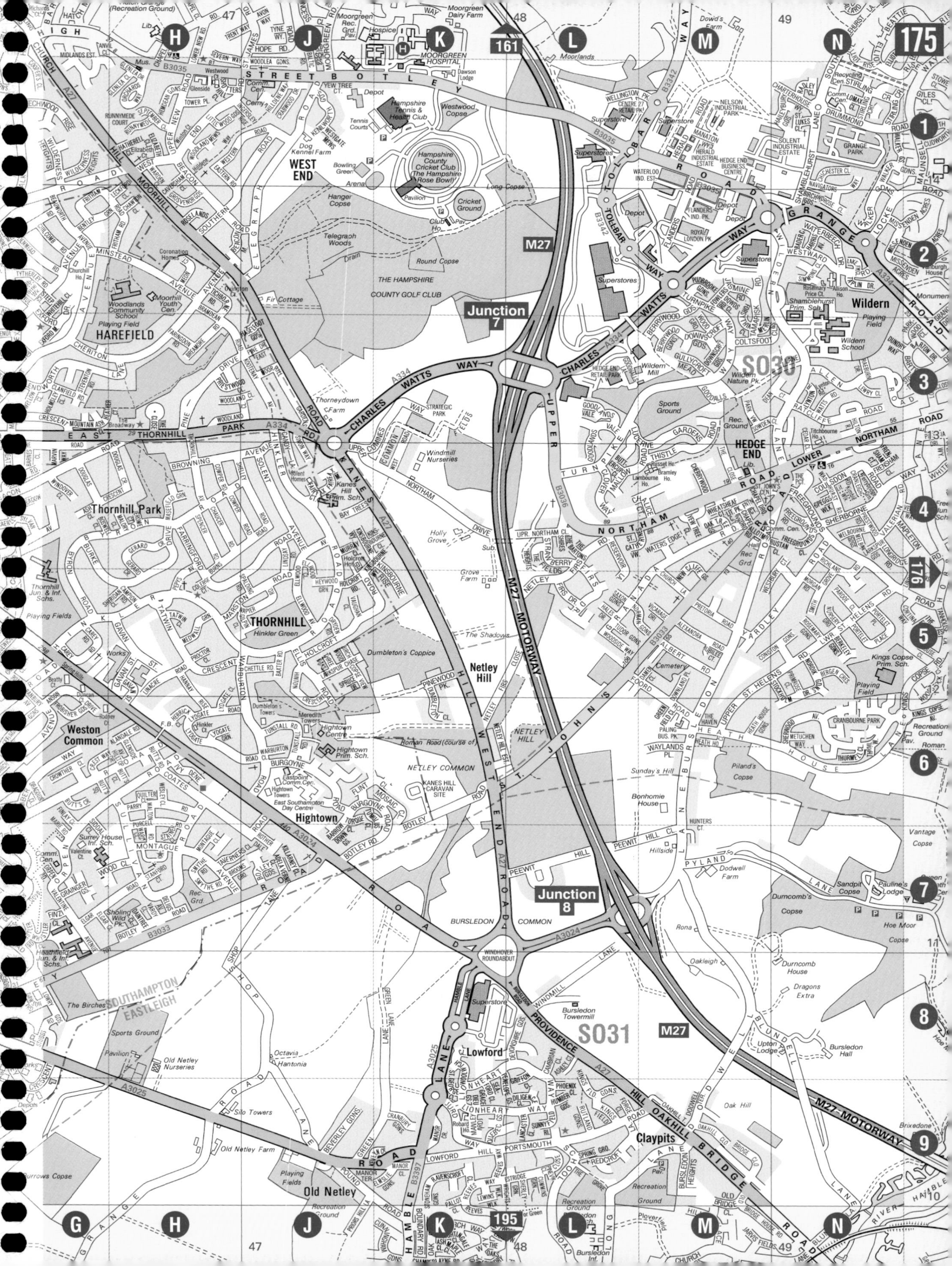
175
161
176
195
47
48
49
WEST END
HAREFIELD
Thornhill Park
THORNHILL
Hinkler Green
Weston Common
Hightown
Netley Hill
HEDGE END
Wildern
Lowford
Claypits
Old Netley
SO30
SO31
M27
M27 MOTORWAY
Junction 7
Junction 8
Hampshire County Cricket Club (The Hampshire Rose Bowl)
THE HAMPSHIRE COUNTY GOLF CLUB
Telegraph Woods
Hanger Copse
Long Copse
Round Copse
Westwood Copse
Dumbleton's Coppice
NETLEY COMMON
BURSLEDON COMMON
WINDHOVER ROUNDABOUT
Bursledon Towermill
Sports Ground
Old Netley Nurseries
Old Netley Farm
Burrows Copse
Silo Towers
Octavia
Hantonia
The Birches
SOUTHAMPTON
EASTLEIGH
Moorgreen Hospital
Moorgreen Dairy Farm
Moorlands
Dowd's Farm
Nelson Industrial Park
Solent Industrial Estate
Grange Park
Hedge End Business Centre
Waterloo Ind. Est.
Royal London Pk.
Flanders Ind. Pk.
Wildern School
Wildern Mill
Wildern Nature Pk.
Hedge End Retail Park
Strategic Park
Windmill Nurseries
Holly Grove
Grove Farm
The Shadows
Kanes Hill Caravan Site
Woodlands Community School
Moorhill Youth Cen.
Thornhill Jun. & Inf. Schs.
Kanes Hill Prim. Sch.
Hightown Prim. Sch.
Kings Copse Prim. Sch.
Cemetery
Sunday's Hill
Piland's Copse
Bonhomie House
Vantage Copse
Dodwell Farm
Durncomb's Copse
Sandpit Copse
Pauline's Lodge
Hoe Moor Copse
Durncomb House
Dragons Extra
Upton Lodge
Bursledon Hall
Oak Hill
Brixedone
RIVER HAMBLE
CHARLES WATTS WAY
THORNHILL PARK RD.
KANES HILL
WEST END ROAD
BOTLEY ROAD
PROVIDENCE HILL
OAKHILL
BURSLEDON BRIDGE
GRANGE ROAD
TOLLBAR WAY
UPPER NORTHAM ROAD
LOWER NORTHAM ROAD
ST. JOHNS ROAD
HAMBLE LANE
PORTSMOUTH ROAD
MOORHILL ROAD
STREET BOTLEY

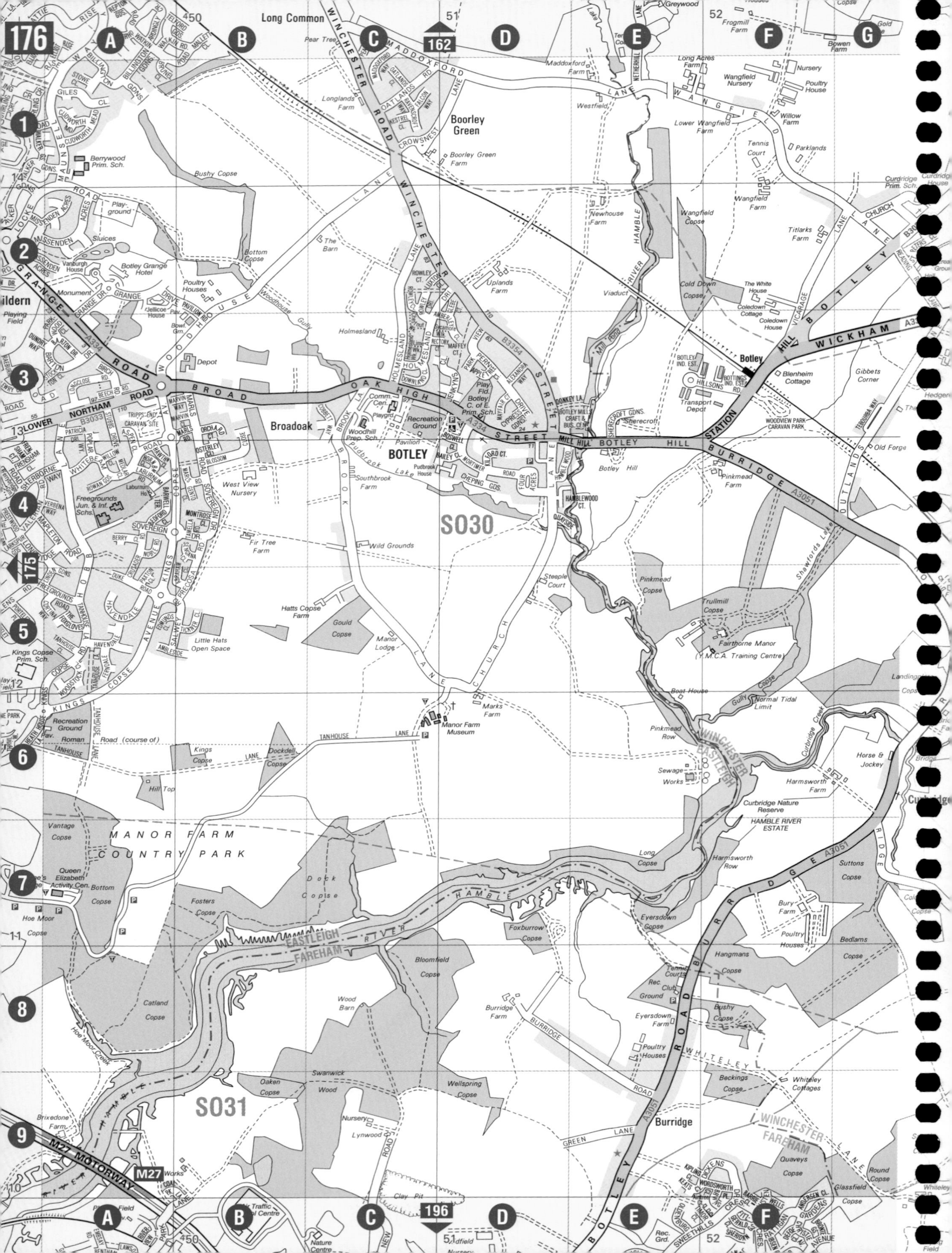

Long Common
Pear Tree
Boorley Green
Boorley Green Farm
Longlands Farm
Maddoxford Farm
Westfield
Long Acres Farm
Frogmill Farm
Bowen Farm
Wangfield Nursery
Nursery
Poultry House
Lower Wangfield Farm
Willow Farm
Tennis Court
Parklands
Berrywood Prim. Sch.
Bushy Copse
Play-ground
Sluices
Botley Grange Hotel
Vanburgh House
Monument
Playing Field
Bottom Copse
The Barn
Poultry Houses
Jellicoe House
Woodhouse Gully
Newhouse Farm
Uplands Farm
Viaduct
Wangfield Copse
Wangfield Farm
Curdridge Prim. Sch.
Titlarks Farm
Cold Down Copse
The White House
Coledown Cottage
Coledown House
Holmesland
Depot
Botley
Botley Ind. Est.
Bottings Ind. Est.
Blenheim Cottage
Gibbets Corner
Transport Depot
Woodview Park Caravan Park
Broadoak
Comm. Cen.
Playgrd
Recreation Ground
Woodhill Prep. Sch.
Pavilion
Play. Fld.
Botley C. of E. Prim. Sch.
Botley Mills Craft & Bus. Cen.
Sherecroft
Botley Hill
Old Forge
BOTLEY
Pudbrook House
Pudbrook Lake
Southbrook Farm
West View Nursery
Laburnum Ho.
Freegrounds Jun. & Inf. Schs.
Pinkmead Farm
SO30
Fir Tree Farm
Wild Grounds
Steeple Court
Pinkmead Copse
Trullmill Copse
Shawfords Lake
Hatts Copse Farm
Gould Copse
Manor Lodge
Little Hats Open Space
Fairthorne Manor (Y.M.C.A. Training Centre)
Kings Copse Prim. Sch.
Boat House
Gully Copse
Normal Tidal Limit
Landing Copse
Marks Farm
Manor Farm Museum
Recreation Ground
Pav.
Roman Road (course of)
Kings Copse
Dockdell Copse
Hill Top
Pinkmead Row
Sewage Works
WINCHESTER
EASTLEIGH
Curbridge Creek
Horse & Jockey
Harmsworth Farm
Curbridge Nature Reserve
HAMBLE RIVER ESTATE
Vantage Copse
MANOR FARM COUNTRY PARK
Queen Elizabeth Activity Cen.
Bottom Copse
Hoe Moor
Copse
Dock Copse
Fosters Copse
Long Copse
Harmsworth Row
Suttons Copse
Eyersdown Copse
Bury Farm
Poultry Houses
Bedlams Copse
Foxburrow Copse
EASTLEIGH
FAREHAM
Bloomfield Copse
Hangmans Copse
Tennis Courts
Rec. Ground
Club
Bushy Copse
Eyersdown Farm
Catland Copse
Wood Barn
Burridge Farm
Hoe Moor Creek
Poultry Houses
Oaken Copse
Swanwick Wood
Wellspring Copse
Beckings Copse
Whiteley Cottages
SO31
Brixedone Farm
Nursery
Lynwood
Burridge
WINCHESTER
FAREHAM
Quaveys Copse
Round Copse
Glassfield Copse
M27 MOTORWAY
Works
Clay Pit
Air Traffic Control Centre
Rec. Grd.
Nature Centre
HAMBLE RIVER
WINCHESTER ROAD
MADDOXFORD LANE
WANGFIELD LANE
GRANGE ROAD
BROAD OAK
HIGH STREET
MILL HILL
BOTLEY HILL
STATION HILL
WICKHAM ROAD
BURRIDGE ROAD
LOWER NORTHAM ROAD
CHURCH LANE
TANHOUSE LANE
BROOK LANE
KINGS COPSE AVENUE
OUTLANDS LANE
BURRIDGE ROAD
WHITELEY LANE
GREEN LANE
BOTLEY ROAD
A334
A3051
B3354
B3033
162
175
196
450
51
52

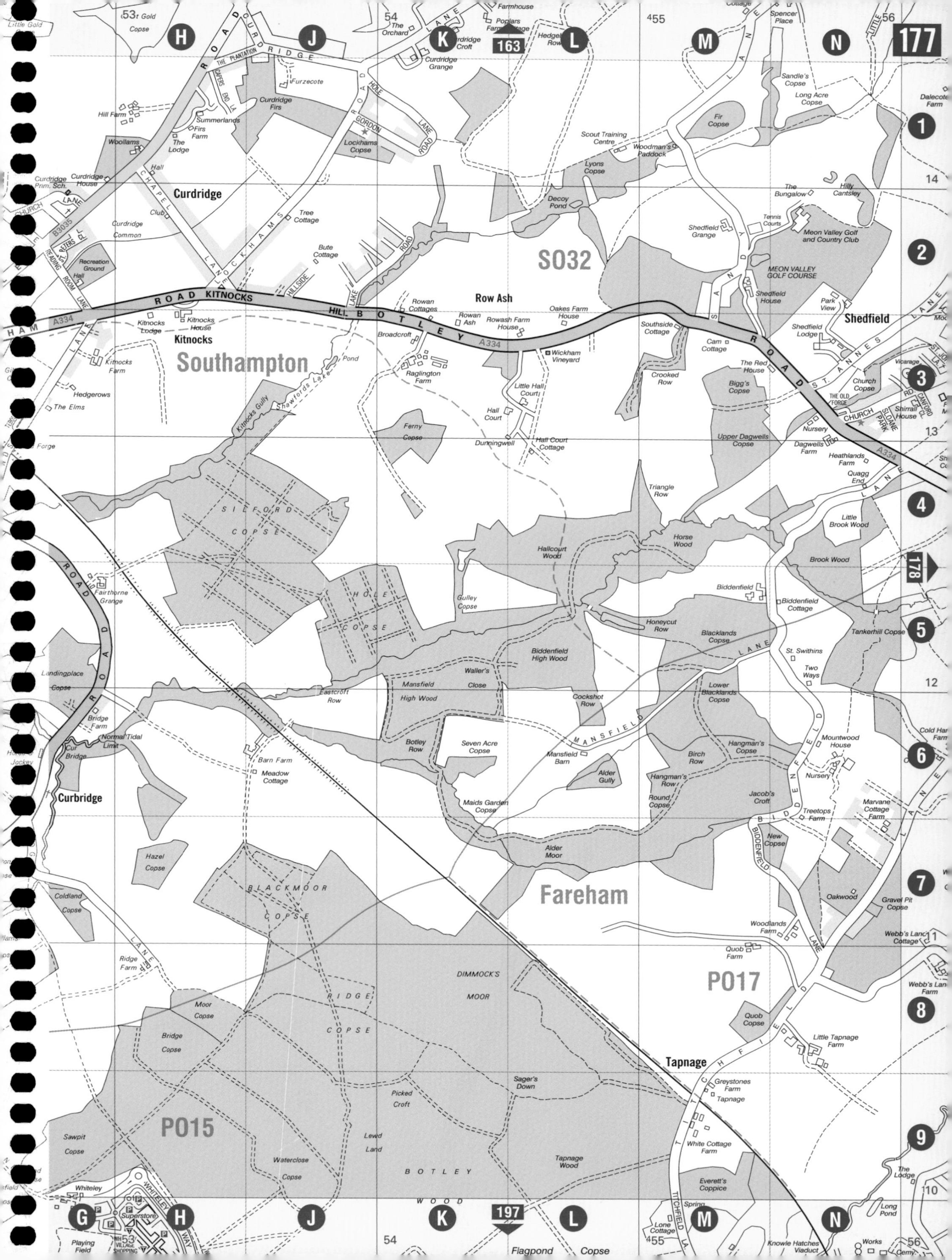
Curdridge
Row Ash
Shedfield
Kitnocks
Southampton
SO32
Fareham
PO17
PO15
Curbridge
Tapnage
Whiteley
BOTLEY ROAD A334
KITNOCKS HILL
Meon Valley Golf and Country Club
MEON VALLEY GOLF COURSE
SILFORD COPSE
HOLE COPSE
Hallcourt Wood
Biddenfield High Wood
Mansfield High Wood
BLACKMOOR COPSE
DIMMOCK'S MOOR
RIDGE COPSE
BOTLEY WOOD
Tapnage Wood
Brook Wood
Tankerhill Copse
Wickham Vineyard
163
178
197

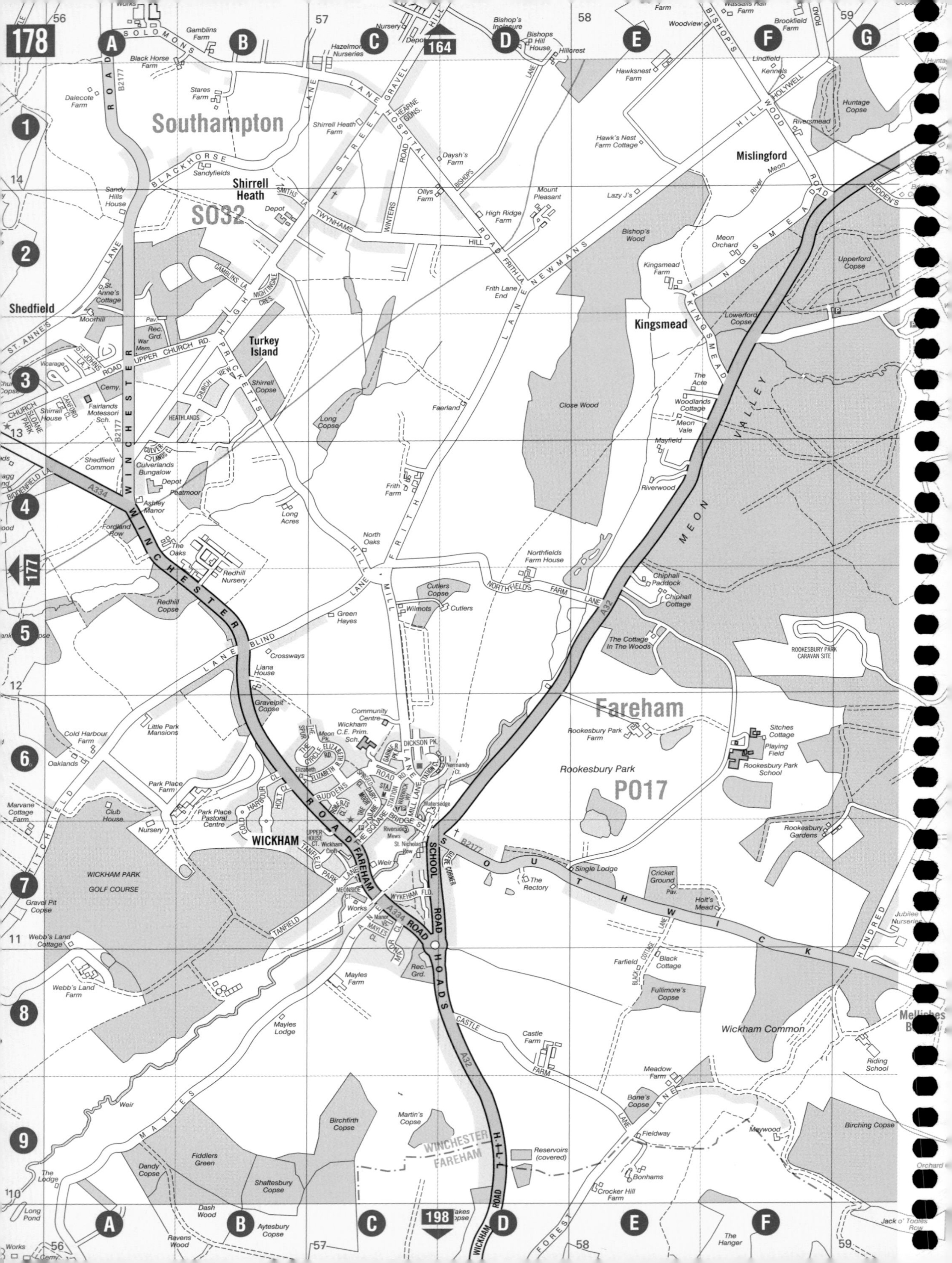
Southampton
SO32
Shirrell Heath
Shedfield
Turkey Island
Mislingford
Kingsmead
Fareham
PO17
WICKHAM
Rookesbury Park
Wickham Common
Close Wood
Bishop's Wood
WICKHAM PARK GOLF COURSE
WINCHESTER
FAREHAM
MEON VALLEY
164
177
198

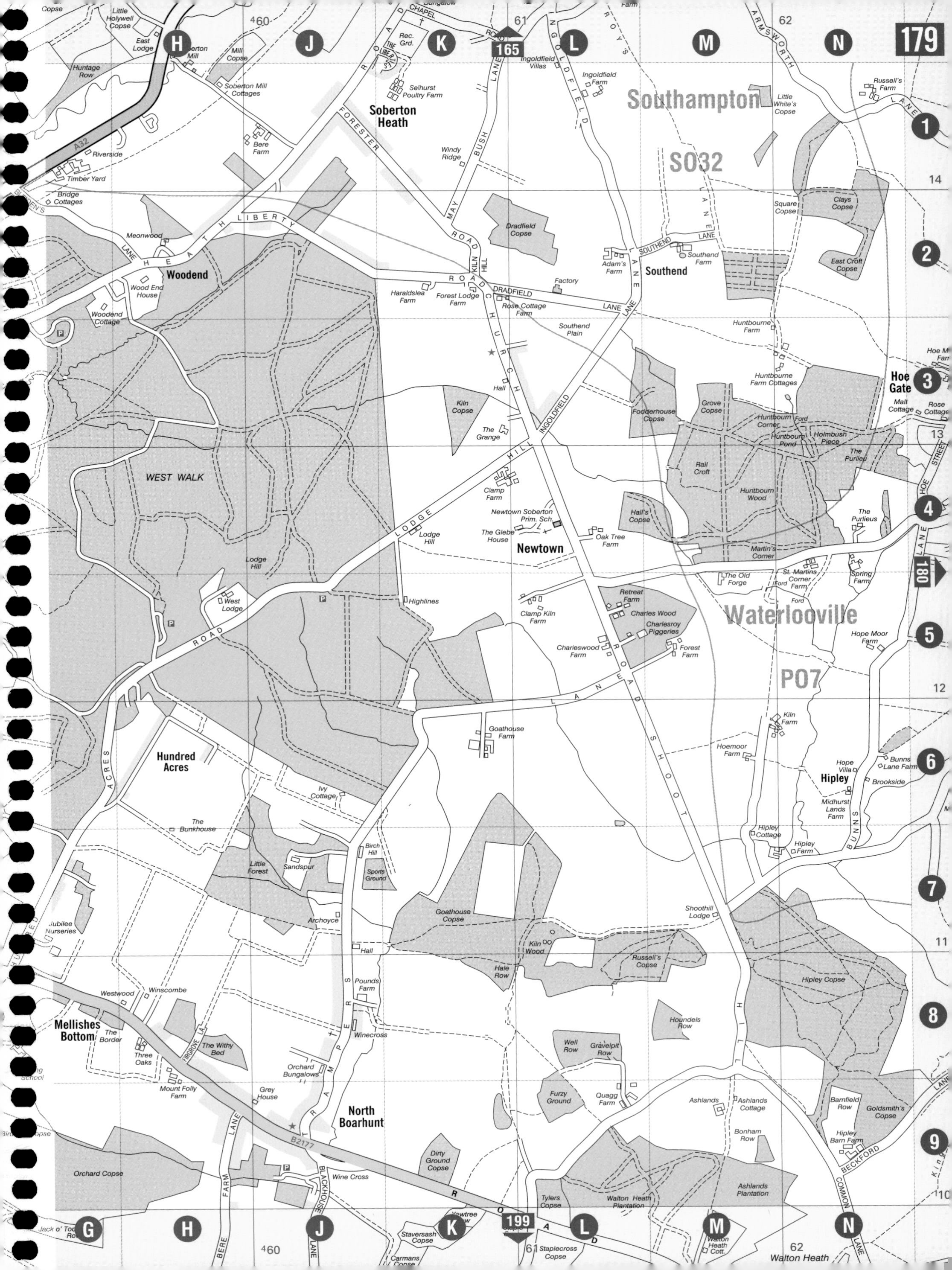
Southampton
SO32
Waterlooville
PO7
Soberton Heath
Woodend
Southend
Newtown
Hoe Gate
Hipley
Hundred Acres
Mellishes Bottom
North Boarhunt
WEST WALK
Little Holywell Copse
Huntage Row
East Lodge
Soberton Mill
Mill Copse
Soberton Mill Cottages
Riverside
Timber Yard
Bridge Cottages
Bere Farm
Rec. Grd.
Selhurst Poultry Farm
Windy Ridge
Ingoldfield Villas
Ingoldfield Farm
Little White's Copse
Russell's Farm
Square Copse
Clays Copse
East Croft Copse
Dradfield Copse
Adam's Farm
Southend Farm
Meonwood
Wood End House
Woodend Cottage
Haraldslea Farm
Forest Lodge Farm
Rose Cottage Farm
Factory
Southend Plain
Huntbourne Farm
Huntbourne Farm Cottages
Kiln Copse
Hall
The Grange
Fodderhouse Copse
Grove Copse
Huntbourn Corner
Huntbourn Pond
Holmbush Piece
The Purlieu
Malt Cottage
Rose Cottage
Rail Croft
Huntbourn Wood
Clamp Farm
Newtown Soberton Prim. Sch.
The Glebe House
Hall's Copse
Oak Tree Farm
Lodge Hill
Martin's Corner
The Purlieus
The Old Forge
St. Martins Corner Farm
Spring Farm
West Lodge
Highlines
Retreat Farm
Charles Wood
Charlesroy Piggeries
Clamp Kiln Farm
Charleswood Farm
Forest Farm
Hope Moor Farm
Goathouse Farm
Kiln Farm
Hoemoor Farm
Hope Villa
Bunns Lane Farm
Brookside
Midhurst Lands Farm
Ivy Cottage
The Bunkhouse
Hipley Cottage
Hipley Farm
Birch Hill
Little Forest
Sandspur
Sports Ground
Goathouse Copse
Archoyce
Shoothill Lodge
Jubilee Nurseries
Kiln Wood
Hall
Russell's Copse
Hale Row
Hipley Copse
Westwood
Winscombe
Pounds Farm
Houndels Row
The Border
Three Oaks
The Withy Bed
Winecross
Well Row
Gravelpit Row
Orchard Bungalows
Mount Folly Farm
Grey House
Furzy Ground
Quagg Farm
Ashlands
Ashlands Cottage
Barnfield Row
Goldsmith's Copse
Hipley Barn Farm
Bonham Row
Orchard Copse
Dirty Ground Copse
Wine Cross
Ashlands Plantation
Tylers Copse
Walton Heath Plantation
Staversash Copse
Staplecross Copse
Walton Heath Cott.
Walton Heath
Carmans Copse
CHAPEL ROAD
LIBERTY
FORESTER ROAD
MAY BUSH LANE
KILN HILL
INGOLDFIELD LANE
ROY'S LANE
ARMSWORTH LANE
HEATH LANE
CHURCH ROAD
DRADFIELD LANE
SOUTHEND LANE
LODGE HILL
LODGE ROAD
HOE STREET
BUNNS LANE
ACRES
LANE END
SHOOT ROAD
HILL
RAMPERS
BERE FARM LANE
FIRGROVE LA
BLACKHOUSE LANE
B2177
BECKFORD
COMMON LANE
A32
165
180
199
G H J K L M N
1 2 3 4 5 6 7 8 9
14 13 12 11 10
460 61 62

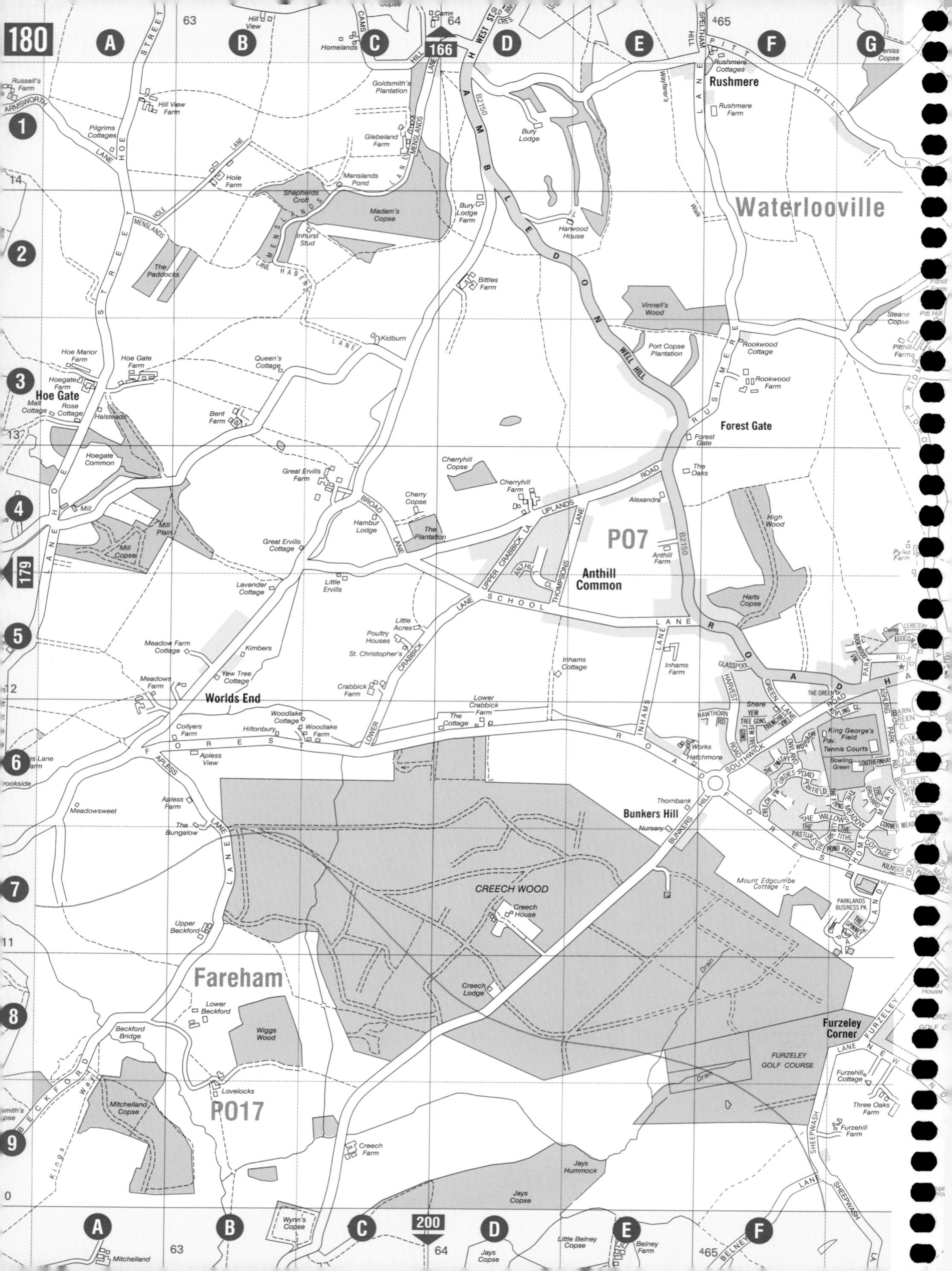
A
B
C
D
E
F
G
63
64
465
166
179
200
1
2
3
4
5
6
7
8
9
Waterlooville
Rushmere
Hoe Gate
Forest Gate
Anthill Common
Worlds End
Bunkers Hill
Furzeley Corner
Fareham
PO7
PO17
CREECH WOOD
Russell's Farm
Pilgrims Cottages
Hill View Farm
Hill View
Homelands
Goldsmith's Plantation
Glebeland Farm
Menslands Pond
Shepherds Croft
Madam's Copse
Inhurst Stud
The Paddocks
Hole Farm
Bury Lodge
Bury Lodge Farm
Harwood House
Bittles Farm
Rushmere Cottages
Rushmere Farm
Vinnell's Wood
Port Copse Plantation
Rookwood Cottage
Rookwood Farm
Steane Copse
Kidburn
Hoe Manor Farm
Hoe Gate Farm
Hoegate Farm
Malt Cottage
Rose Cottage
Halsteads
Queen's Cottage
Bent Farm
Hoegate Common
Mill
Mill Plain
Mill Copse
Great Ervills Farm
Great Ervills Cottage
Cherryhill Copse
Cherryhill Farm
Cherry Copse
Hambur Lodge
The Plantation
Alexandra
The Oaks
High Wood
Anthill Farm
Harts Copse
Little Ervills
Lavender Cottage
Little Acres
Poultry Houses
St. Christopher's
Meadow Farm Cottage
Kimbers
Meadows Farm
Yew Tree Cottage
Crabbick Farm
Lower Crabbick Farm
The Cottage
Woodlake Cottage
Woodlake Farm
Hiltonbury
Collyers Farm
Aples View
Inhams Cottage
Inhams Farm
Works
Hatchmore
Thornbank
Nursery
King George's Field
Pav.
Tennis Courts
Bowling Green
Apless Farm
Meadowsweet
The Bungalow
Upper Beckford
Creech House
Creech Lodge
Mount Edgcumbe Cottage
PARKLANDS BUSINESS PK.
Lower Beckford
Wiggs Wood
Beckford Bridge
Lovelocks
Mitchelland Copse
Creech Farm
FURZELEY GOLF COURSE
Furzehill Cottage
Three Oaks Farm
Furzehill Farm
Jays Hummock
Jays Copse
Wynn's Copse
Little Belney Copse
Belney Farm
Mitchelland
Drain
ARMSWORTH LANE
HOE STREET
HOE LANE
HOLE LANE
MENSLANDS LANE
HAMBLEDON ROAD
B2150
WEST ST.
SPELTHAM HILL
PITT HILL LANE
WELL HILL
RUSHMERE LANE
UPLANDS ROAD
BROAD LANE
UPPER CRABBICK LA.
ANTHILL CL.
THOMPSONS LANE
SCHOOL LANE
CRABBICK LANE
LOWER CRABBICK LANE
FOREST ROAD
INHAMS LANE
SOUTHWICK ROAD
BUNKERS HILL
FOREST LANE
APLESS LANE
BECKFORD LANE
Kings Way
SHEEPWASH LANE
FURZELEY ROAD
NEW ROAD
BELNEY LANE
Wayfarer's Walk
GLASSPOOL
GREEN LANE
HARVEST ROAD
HAWTHORN RD.
THE GREEN
ASHLING PARK RD.
KIDMORE LANE

167
H
J
K
L
M
N
66
67
68
69
Greasteds Copse
Down House
Kennels
The Shieling
Old Mill House
Ludmore Cottage
Lake's Copse
The Ranch
Poultry Houses
Old Mill
The Haven
Hillcrest
Mill Copse
Hinton Daubnay
Old Lodge
New Lodge
Rabbit Copse
Strip Lychets
Pithill Ho.
Pithill Cottage
Pithill Farm
Steane Copse
Pitt Hill
Pitthill Farm
HARROWGATE LANE
PITT LANE
HORSEPOST LANE
SAWYER'S HILL
OLD MILL LANE
MANOR LANE
LOVEDEAN LANE
WINCHESTER
EAST HAMPSHIRE
Crabdens Row
Lovedean Electricity Sub Station
Crabdens Copse
Stoneacre Copse
Millfield Farm
The Warren
Reservoir (covered)
CROUCH LANE
Coldhill Farm
COLDHILL LA.
Lovedean Farm
Coldhill Copse
DAY LANE
Broadway Cottages
Broadway Farm House
BROADWAY LANE
The Crossways
Kimberley House
Denmead Farm
KIDMORE LANE
WHITE HORSE LANE
DENMEAD LANE
Little Denmead Farm
Denmead Farm
Broadway Cottage
Arrow
Pyles Farm
Blackhouse
Eastland Gate Cottages
Eastland Gate
NEW ROAD
Yoells Copse
Lovedean
YOELLS' LANE
OLD BARN GDS.
James's Copse
PO8
EAST HAMPSHIRE
HAVANT
Meadowlands Jun. Sch.
Meadowlands Inf. Sch.
Rec. Grd.
TANNERS LANE
Merrett's Farm
CEMETERY LA.
LUDCOMBE
Kidmore Farm
Shrover
Woodcroft Farm
Woodcroft
Wecock
Wecock Village Centre
DENMEAD
HAMBLEDON ROAD
ANMORE ROAD
Denmead Caravan Pk.
Shafters Farm
Anmore Dell
Kings Pond
Anmore
Clarendon Farm
Denmead Infant Sch.
Denmead Jun. Sch.
White Wings Ho.
Mill Cross
MILL ROAD
MAPLE DR.
Rachel Madocks School
Woodlands Prim. Sch.
Wecock Common
HART PLAIN AV.
MILTON ROAD
COWPLAIN
Soake Copse
Soake
Soake House
SOAKE ROAD
B2150
MEAD END ROAD
Mead End
Borrows Recreation Ground
BYNGS BUSINESS PARK
Soake Lodge
SILVERDALE DRIVE
SUTTON ROAD
OAKLANDS GROVE
DURLEY AVENUE
KINGS GROVE
LINDA GROVE
The Glenwood School
HART PLAIN AVENUE
Cowplain Comp. Sch.
South Downs College
Hart Plain Inf. Sch.
Hart Plain Jun. Sch.
Playing Fields
THE QUEEN'S INCLOSURE
A3
Club House
FURZELEY GOLF COURSE
Piper's Hill Wood
NEWLANDS
CLOSEWOOD ROAD
HAVANT
WINCHESTER
HAMBLEDON ROAD
Old Park Farm
Closewood Farm
Closewood House
WATERLOOVILLE
THE BRAMBLES ENTERPRISE CENTRE
Works
Swim. Pool
Playground
Bowling Grn.
Waterlooville Rec. Grd.
Pav.
Tennis Courts
Park Wood
Bull's Lodge
WALLIS ROAD
HIGHFIELD ROAD
LONDON ROAD
Weir
201
BRAMBLES FARM INDUSTRIAL ESTATE
PIPERS WOOD INDUSTRIAL ESTATE
JUBILEE BUS. CEN.
St. Peters R.C. Prim. Sch.
182
1
2
3
4
5
6
7
8
9
10
11
12
13
14
G

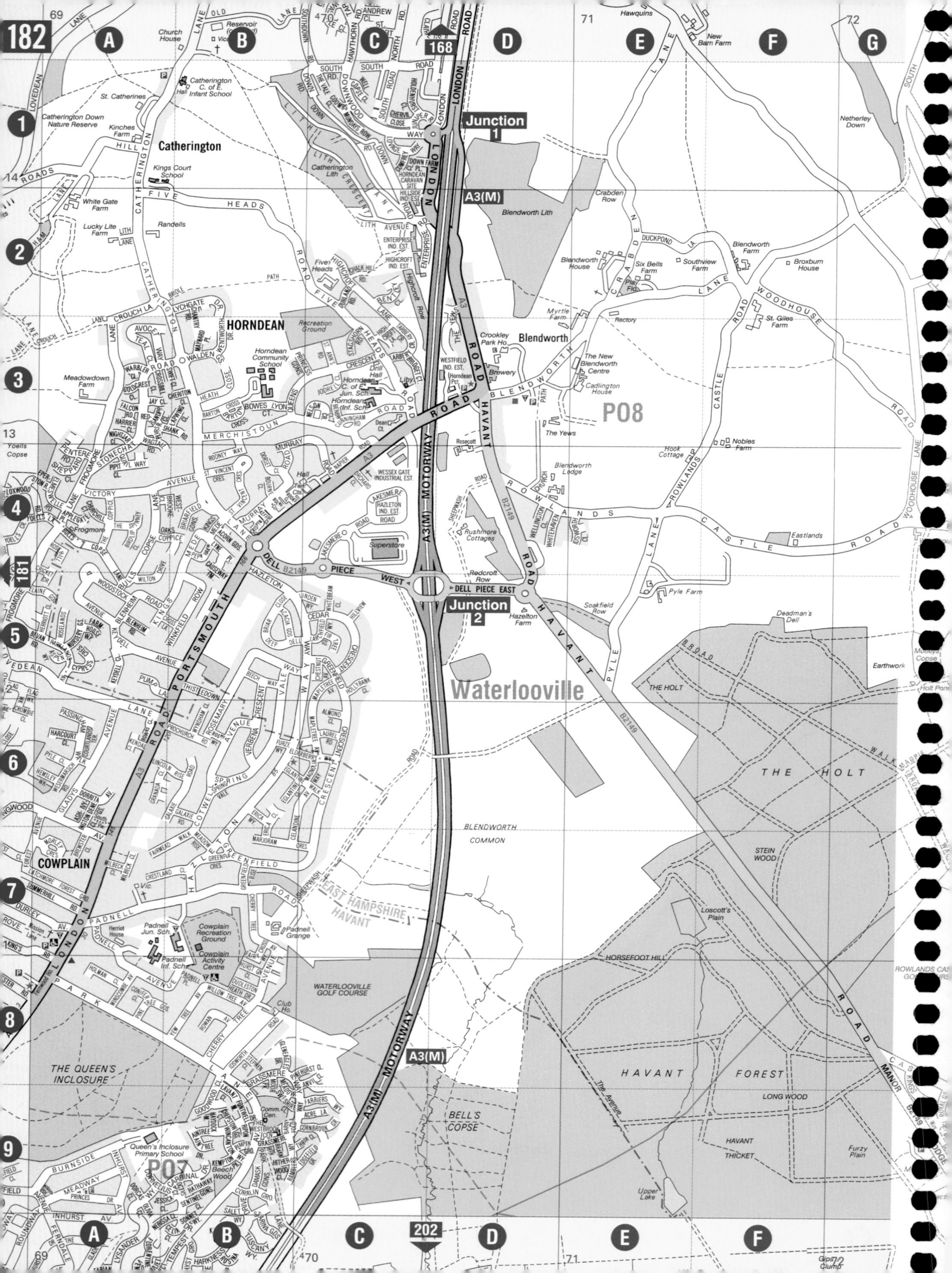
Catherington
HORNDEAN
Blendworth
Waterlooville
COWPLAIN
PO8
PO7
Junction 1
Junction 2
A3(M)
168
181
202
THE HOLT
HAVANT FOREST
THE QUEEN'S INCLOSURE
WATERLOOVILLE GOLF COURSE
BLENDWORTH COMMON
EAST HAMPSHIRE
HAVANT
Catherington Down Nature Reserve
Blendworth Lith
Catherington Lith
Horndean Community School
Recreation Ground
Cowplain Recreation Ground
Cowplain Activity Centre
Queen's Inclosure Primary School
WESSEX GATE INDUSTRIAL EST.
HAZLETON IND. EST.
WESTFIELD IND. EST.
ENTERPRISE IND. EST.
HIGHCROFT IND. EST.
HILLSIDE IND. EST.
Superstore
BELL'S COPSE
STEIN WOOD
LONG WOOD
HAVANT THICKET
Loscott's Plain
Furzy Plain
Upper Lake
Netherley Down
Hawquins
New Barn Farm
Blendworth Farm
Broxburn House
Southview Farm
Six Bells Farm
Crabden Row
St. Giles Farm
Nobles Farm
Hook Cottage
Eastlands
Pyle Farm
Deadman's Dell
Earthwork
Soakfield Row
Hazelton Farm
Redcroft Row
Rushmore Cottages
Blendworth Lodge
The Yews
Cadlington House
The New Blendworth Centre
Crookley Park Ho.
Brewery
Meadowdown Farm
White Gate Farm
Lucky Lite Farm
Randells
Kinches Farm
Kings Court School
Catherington C. of E. Infant School
St. Catherines
Church House
Reservoir
Yoells Copse
Padnell Grange
Padnell Jun. Sch.
Padnell Inf. Sch.
Herriot House
Club Ho.
LONDON ROAD
PORTSMOUTH ROAD
A3(M) MOTORWAY
HAVANT ROAD
B2149
DELL PIECE WEST
DELL PIECE EAST
CASTLE ROAD
ROWLANDS CASTLE ROAD
WOODHOUSE LANE
BLENDWORTH LANE
FIVE HEADS ROAD
CATHERINGTON LANE
HORSEFOOT HILL
MANOR ROAD
PARK LANE
PADNELL ROAD
HAZLETON WAY
LOVEDEAN LANE
69
470
71
72
14
13
A
B
C
D
E
F
G
1
2
3
4
5
6
7
8
9

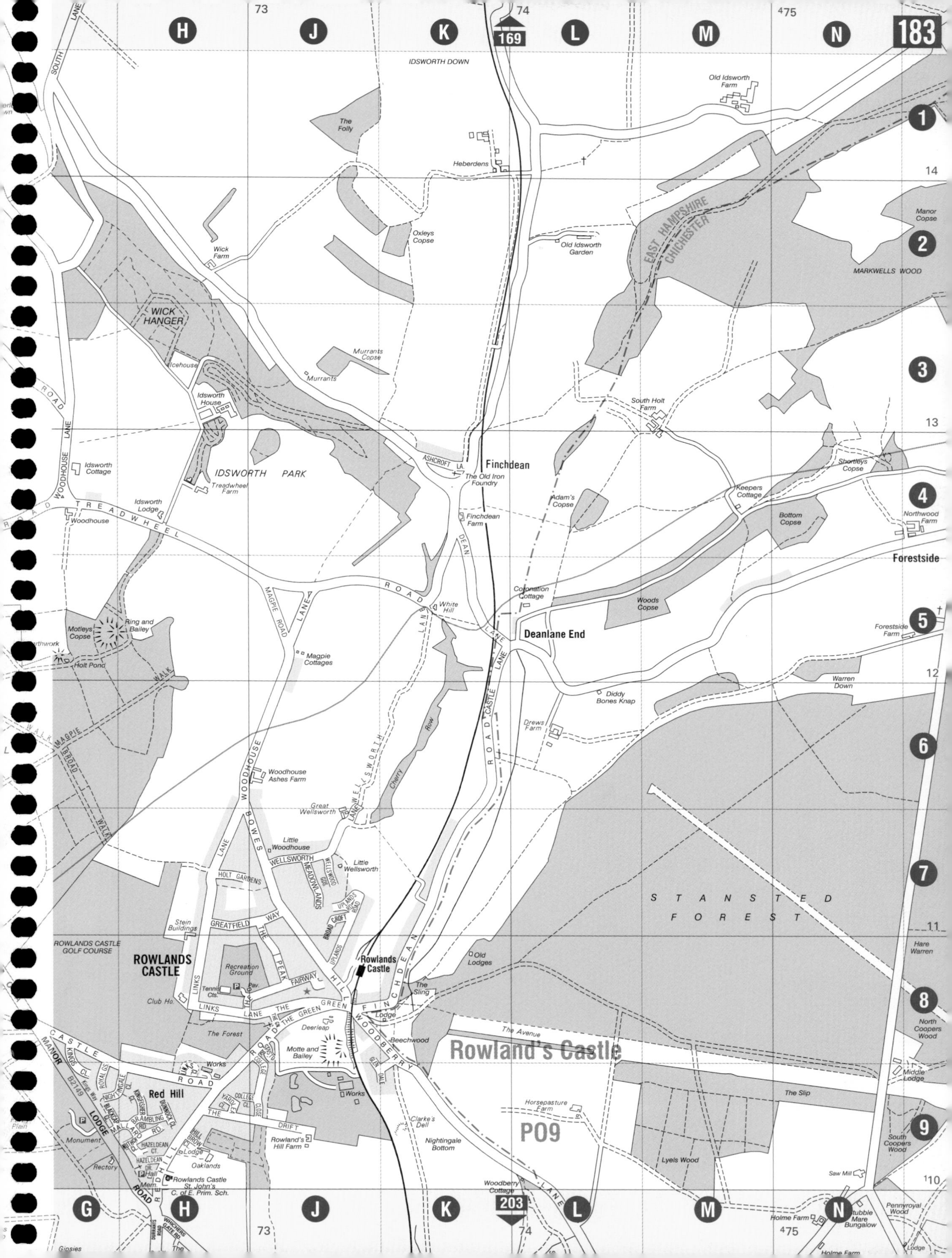
IDSWORTH DOWN
The Folly
Heberdens
Old Idsworth Farm
Oxleys Copse
Wick Farm
Old Idsworth Garden
EAST HAMPSHIRE
CHICHESTER
Manor Copse
MARKWELLS WOOD
WICK HANGER
Murrants Copse
Murrants
Icehouse
Idsworth House
South Holt Farm
Finchdean
The Old Iron Foundry
IDSWORTH PARK
Idsworth Cottage
Treadwheel Farm
Shortleys Copse
Keepers Cottage
Adam's Copse
Idsworth Lodge
Woodhouse
Finchdean Farm
Bottom Copse
Northwood Farm
Forestside
Coronation Cottage
Woods Copse
White Hill
Motleys Copse
Ring and Bailey
Deanlane End
Forestside Farm
Holt Pond
Magpie Cottages
Warren Down
Diddy Bones Knap
Drews Farm
Woodhouse Ashes Farm
Cherry Row
Great Wellsworth
Little Woodhouse
Little Wellsworth
STANSTED FOREST
Stein Buildings
ROWLANDS CASTLE GOLF COURSE
ROWLANDS CASTLE
Recreation Ground
Rowlands Castle
Old Lodges
Hare Warren
The Sling
Club Ho.
Lodge
The Forest
Deerleap
Motte and Bailey
Beechwood
The Avenue
North Coopers Wood
Rowland's Castle
Works
Red Hill
Middle Lodge
The Slip
Horsepasture Farm
Clarke's Dell
PO9
Monument
Rowland's Hill Farm
Nightingale Bottom
South Coopers Wood
Rectory
Oaklands
Lyels Wood
Rowlands Castle St. John's C. of E. Prim. Sch.
Saw Mill
Woodberry Cottage
Holme Farm
Stubble Mare Bungalow
Pennyroyal Wood
Gipsies
169
203

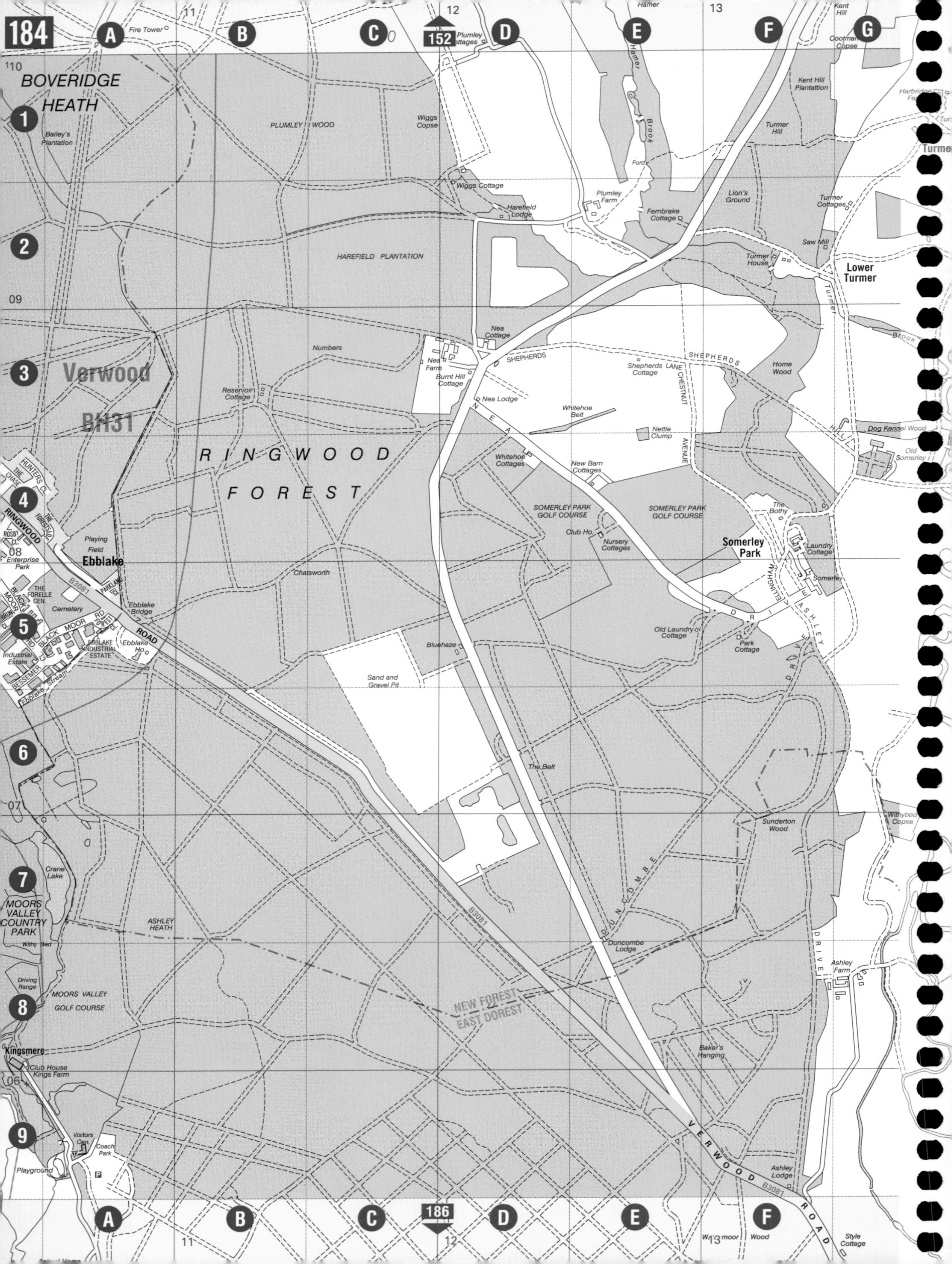

BOVERIDGE HEATH
Fire Tower
Bailey's Plantation
PLUMLEY WOOD
Wiggs Copse
Plumley Cottages
Hamer
Hamer Brook
Kent Hill
Cootman Copse
Kent Hill Plantation
Turmer Hill
Ford
Wiggs Cottage
Harefield Lodge
Plumley Farm
Fernbrake Cottage
Lion's Ground
Turmer Cottages
Saw Mill
Turmer House
Lower Turmer
HAREFIELD PLANTATION
Verwood
BH31
Numbers
Nea Cottage
Nea Farm
Burnt Hill Cottage
SHEPHERDS
Shepherds Cottage
LANE
CHESTNUT AVENUE
Home Wood
Reservoir Cottage
Nea Lodge
Whitehoe Belt
Nettle Clump
Dog Kennel Wood
Old Somerley
RINGWOOD FOREST
Whitehoe Cottages
New Barn Cottages
SOMERLEY PARK GOLF COURSE
Club Ho.
Nursery Cottages
The Bothy
Somerley Park
Laundry Cottage
Somerley
ELLINGHAM DRIVE
ASHLEY DRIVE
Old Laundry Cottage
Park Cottage
HUNTERS CL
THE CHASE
RINGWOOD
ROSBY CL
Playing Field
Ebblake
Enterprise Park
B3081
PARKLAND
THE FORELLE CEN.
Cemetery
BLACK MOOR RD
Ebblake Bridge
ROAD
Industrial Estate
EBBLAKE INDUSTRIAL ESTATE
Ebblake Ho.
BESSEMER
Ebblake Stream
Chatsworth
Bluehaze
Sand and Gravel Pit
The Belt
Sunderton Wood
Withybed Copse
Crane Lake
MOORS VALLEY COUNTRY PARK
ASHLEY HEATH
Withy Bed
DUNCOMBE
Duncombe Lodge
Driving Range
MOORS VALLEY GOLF COURSE
NEW FOREST
EAST DORSET
Ashley Farm
Kingsmere
Club House
Kings Farm
Baker's Hanging
Visitors Cen.
Coach Park
Playground
VERWOOD ROAD
Ashley Lodge
Style Cottage
Wood

152
186

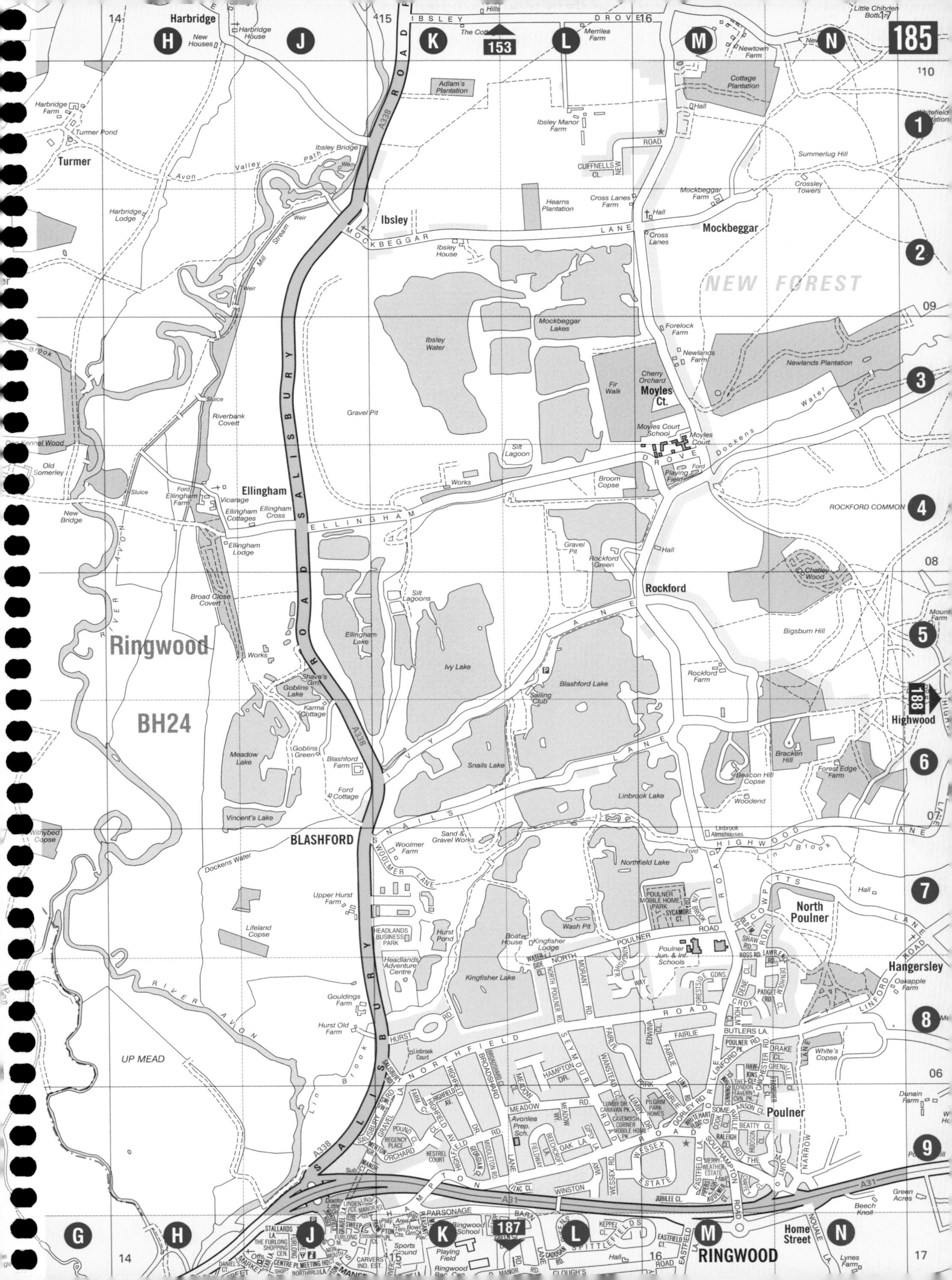
Harbridge
Ibsley
Mockbeggar
Turmer
NEW FOREST
Ellingham
Moyles Ct.
Rockford
Ringwood
BH24
Blashford
North Poulner
Hangersley
Poulner
Highwood
Home Street
RINGWOOD
SALISBURY ROAD
A338
A31
Ibsley Water
Mockbeggar Lakes
Ivy Lake
Blashford Lake
Snails Lake
Linbrook Lake
Northfield Lake
Kingfisher Lake
Ellingham Lake
Meadow Lake
Vincent's Lake
Goblins Lake
Newlands Plantation
Cottage Plantation
Adlam's Plantation
Hearns Plantation
Summerlug Hill
Bigsburn Hill
Rockford Common
Up Mead
River Avon
Dockens Water
153
187
188

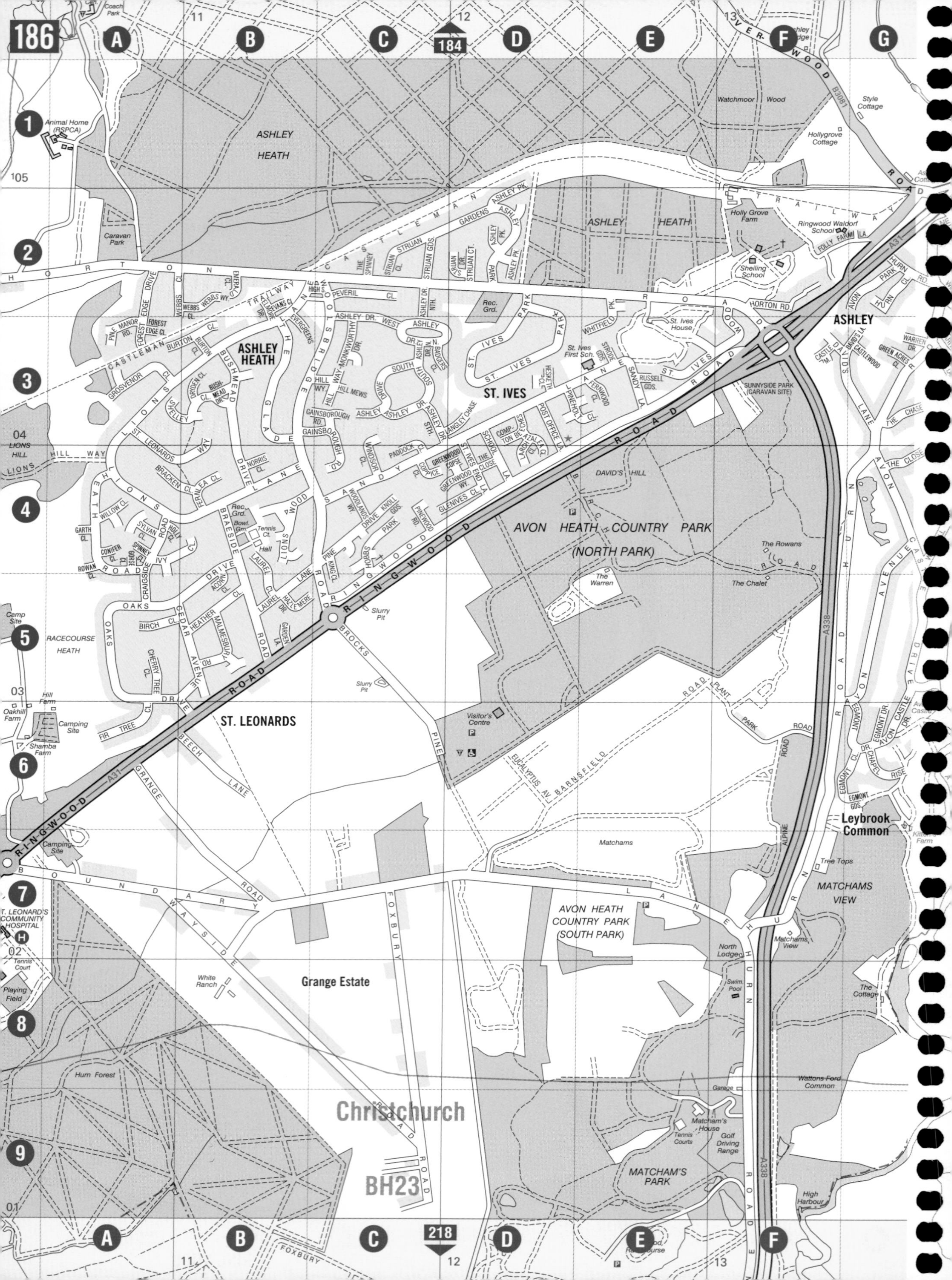

184
218
ASHLEY HEATH
ST. IVES
ST. LEONARDS
ASHLEY
AVON HEATH COUNTRY PARK (NORTH PARK)
AVON HEATH COUNTRY PARK (SOUTH PARK)
Grange Estate
Christchurch
BH23
MATCHAM'S PARK
MATCHAMS VIEW
Leybrook Common
RACECOURSE HEATH
LIONS HILL
Hurn Forest
Watchmoor Wood
Animal Home (RSPCA)
Caravan Park
Holly Grove Farm
Ringwood Waldorf School
Sheiling School
St. Ives House
St. Ives First Sch.
SUNNYSIDE PARK (CARAVAN SITE)
DAVID'S HILL
The Rowans
The Chalet
The Warren
Visitor's Centre
Slurry Pit
Matchams
Tree Tops
North Lodge
Swim. Pool
Matcham's House
Tennis Courts
Golf Driving Range
High Harbour
Wattons Ford Common
The Cottage
White Ranch
Camping Site
Hill Farm
Oakhill Farm
Shamba Farm
Camp Site
T. LEONARD'S COMMUNITY HOSPITAL
Playing Field
Style Cottage
Hollygrove Cottage
HORTON ROAD
RINGWOOD ROAD
BOUNDARY LANE
VERWOOD ROAD
HURN ROAD
BROCKS PINE
WAYSIDE ROAD
FOXBURY ROAD
PLANT PARK ROAD
EUCALYPTUS AV
BARNSFIELD
BEECH LANE
GRANGE
A31
A338
B3081

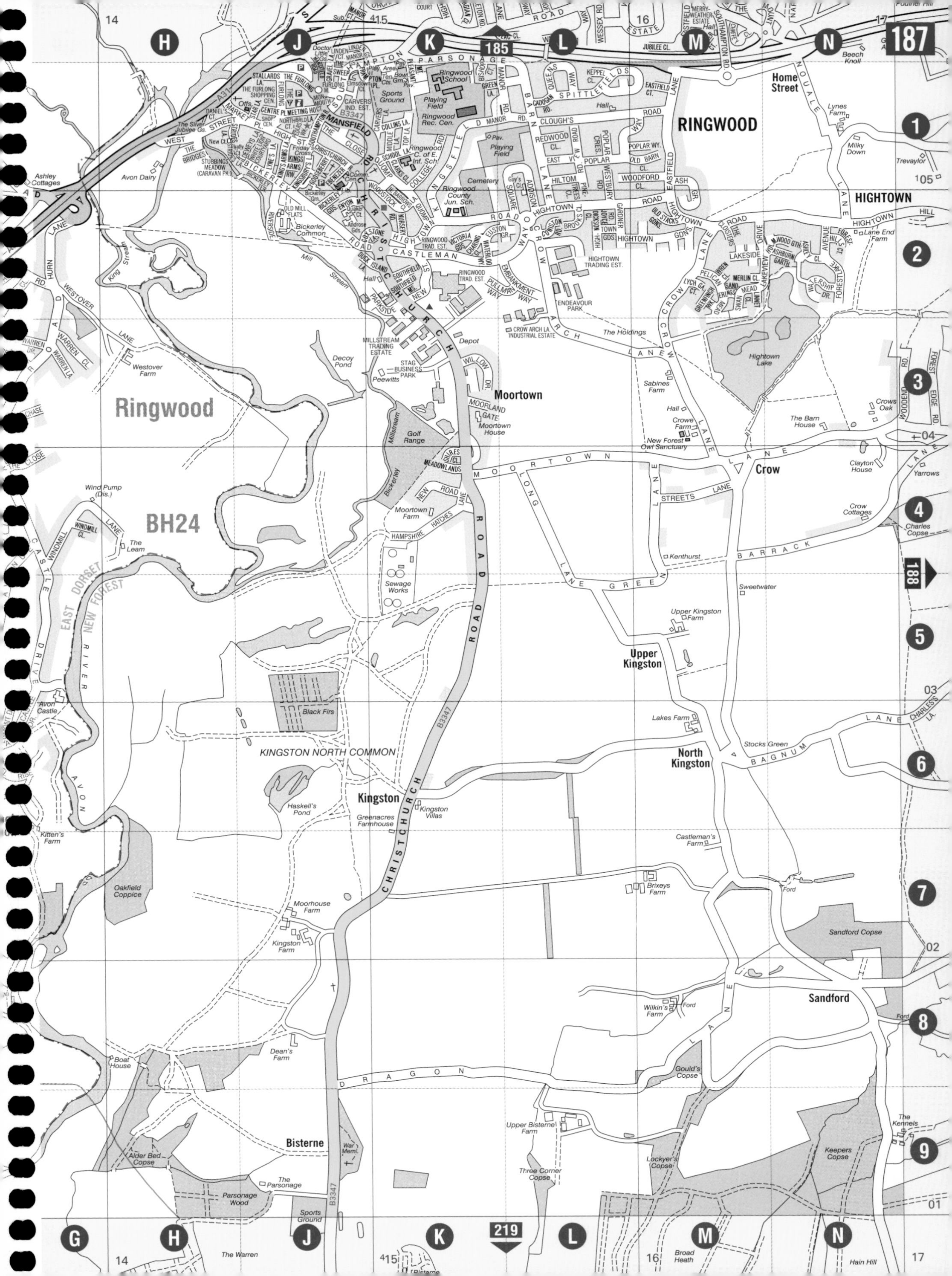
RINGWOOD
Ringwood
BH24
HIGHTOWN
Home Street
Moortown
Crow
Upper Kingston
North Kingston
Kingston
Sandford
Bisterne
KINGSTON NORTH COMMON
Ringwood School
Playing Field
Ringwood Rec. Cen.
Sports Ground
Cemetery
Ringwood County Jun. Sch.
Bickerley Common
Hightown Lake
Golf Range
Sewage Works
Black Firs
Haskell's Pond
Oakfield Coppice
Sandford Copse
Keepers Copse
Lockyer's Copse
Three Corner Copse
Gould's Copse
Parsonage Wood
Alder Bed Copse
Westover Farm
Wind Pump (Dis.)
The Leam
Avon Castle
Kitten's Farm
Moorhouse Farm
Kingston Farm
Dean's Farm
Boat House
The Parsonage
Upper Bisterne Farm
Wilkin's Farm
Brixeys Farm
Castleman's Farm
Lakes Farm
Upper Kingston Farm
Sweetwater
Kenthurst
Crow Cottages
Charles Copse
Clayton House
Yarrows
The Barn House
Crows Oak
Sabines Farm
Crowe Farm
New Forest Owl Sanctuary
Moortown Farm
Moortown House
Decoy Pond
Peewitts
Lynes Farm
Milky Down
Trevaylor
Beech Knoll
Lane End Farm
Stocks Green
Greenacres Farmhouse
Kingston Villas
The Kennels
Hain Hill
Broad Heath
The Warren
Avon Dairy
Ashley Cottages
CHRISTCHURCH ROAD
B3347
MOORTOWN LANE
BARRACK
BAGNUM LANE
DRAGON
LONG LANE
GREEN LANE
CROW LANE
CROW ARCH LANE
HIGHTOWN ROAD
CASTLEMAN WAY
RIVER AVON
EAST DORSET
NEW FOREST
HIGHTOWN TRADING EST.
ENDEAVOUR PARK
RINGWOOD TRAD. EST.
MILLSTREAM TRADING ESTATE
STAG BUSINESS PARK
CROW ARCH LA. INDUSTRIAL ESTATE
The Holdings
185
188
219
H J K L M N G
1 2 3 4 5 6 7 8 9
14 415 16 17
105 04 03 02 01

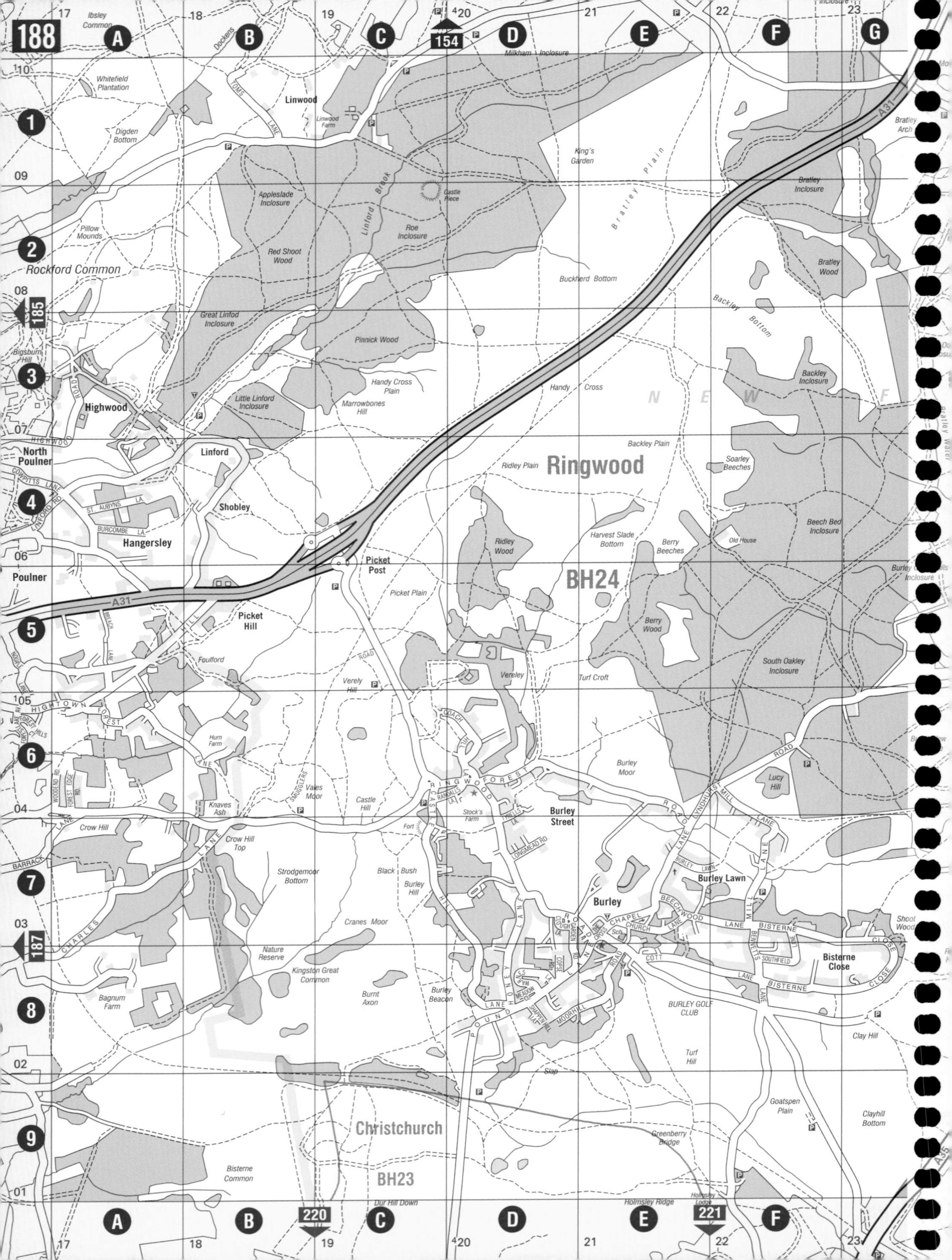

Ibsley Common
Dockens
Milkham Inclosure
Whitefield Plantation
Linwood
Linwood Farm
Digden Bottom
King's Garden
Bratley Plain
Bratley Arch
Appleslade Inclosure
Castle Piece
Linford Brook
Bratley Inclosure
Pillow Mounds
Roe Inclosure
Red Shoot Wood
Rockford Common
Buckherd Bottom
Bratley Wood
Backley Bottom
Great Linfod Inclosure
Pinnick Wood
Bigsburn Hill
Handy Cross Plain
Marrowbones Hill
Handy Cross
Backley Inclosure
Highwood
Little Linford Inclosure
NEW F
North Poulner
Linford
Backley Plain
Ridley Plain
Ringwood
Soarley Beeches
Shobley
Hangersley
Harvest Slade Bottom
Berry Beeches
Old House
Beech Bed Inclosure
Ridley Wood
Picket Post
Poulner
Picket Plain
BH24
A31
Picket Hill
Berry Wood
Foulford
Verely Hill
Vereley
Turf Croft
South Oakley Inclosure
Hurn Farm
Burley Moor
Lucy Hill
Vales Moor
Castle Hill
Knaves Ash
Stock's Farm
Burley Street
Crow Hill
Crow Hill Top
Fort
Strodgemoor Bottom
Black Bush
Burley Hill
Burley Lawn
Burley
Cranes Moor
Shoot Wood
Nature Reserve
Kingston Great Common
Bisterne Close
Bagnum Farm
Burnt Axon
Burley Beacon
BURLEY GOLF CLUB
Clay Hill
Turf Hill
Slap
Goatspen Plain
Clayhill Bottom
Christchurch
Greenberry Bridge
Bisterne Common
BH23
Dur Hill Down
Holmsley Ridge
Holmsley Lodge
HIGHWOOD ROAD
COMPITTS LANE
LINFORD RD
ST AUBYNS LA
BURCOMBE LA
TOMS LANE
HIGHTOWN
FOREST LANE
CHARLES
BARRACK
RINGWOOD FOREST ROAD
COACH HILL
SMUGGLERS
CHAPEL LANE
BEECHWOOD LANE
BISTERNE CLOSE
LYNDHURST ROAD
MILL LANE
POUND LANE
HONEY LANE
MOORHILL
LONGMEAD RD
BURLEY LAWN
SOUTHFIELD
BENNETTS LANE

154
185
187
220
221

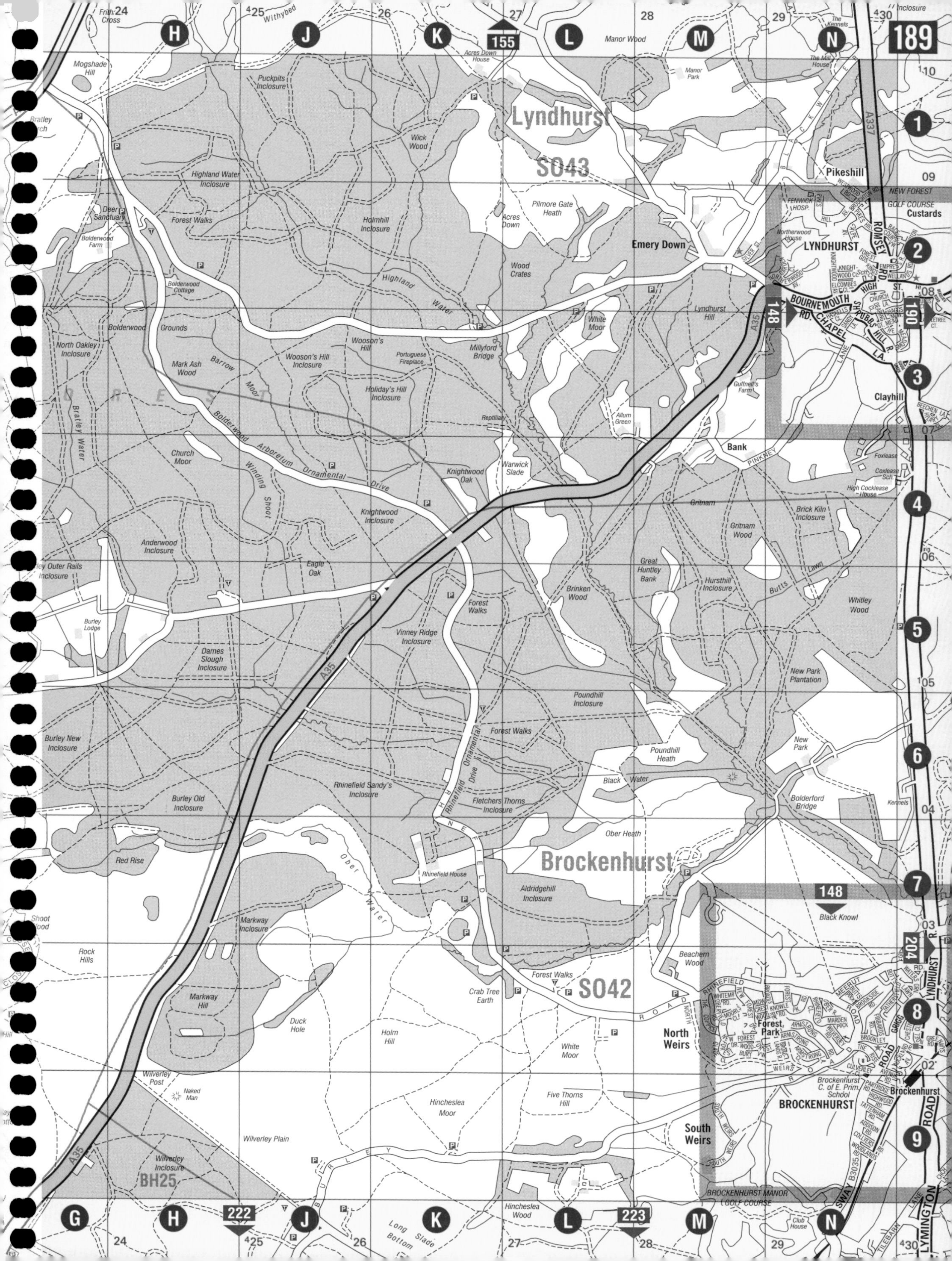
Lyndhurst
SO43
Emery Down
LYNDHURST
Pikeshill
Custards
Clayhill
Bank
Brockenhurst
BROCKENHURST
SO42
North Weirs
South Weirs
Forest Park
BH25
Mogshade Hill
Puckpits Inclosure
Wick Wood
Highland Water Inclosure
Holmhill Inclosure
Acres Down
Pilmore Gate Heath
Wood Crates
Deer Sanctuary
Bolderwood Farm
Bolderwood Cottage
Bolderwood
Grounds
North Oakley Inclosure
Mark Ash Wood
Barrow Moor
Wooson's Hill Inclosure
Holiday's Hill Inclosure
Millyford Bridge
White Moor
Lyndhurst Hill
Church Moor
Knightwood Oak
Warwick Slade
Knightwood Inclosure
Anderwood Inclosure
Eagle Oak
Burley Lodge
Forest Walks
Vinney Ridge Inclosure
Dames Slough Inclosure
Brinken Wood
Great Huntley Bank
Hursthill Inclosure
Gritnam Wood
Brick Kiln Inclosure
Whitley Wood
New Park Plantation
Poundhill Inclosure
Burley New Inclosure
Burley Old Inclosure
Rhinefield Sandy's Inclosure
Fletchers Thorns Inclosure
Poundhill Heath
Black Water
New Park
Bolderford Bridge
Ober Heath
Red Rise
Rhinefield House
Aldridgehill Inclosure
Black Knowl
Markway Inclosure
Rock Hills
Beachern Wood
Crab Tree Earth
Markway Hill
Duck Hole
Holm Hill
White Moor
Wilverley Post
Naked Man
Hincheslea Moor
Five Thorns Hill
Brockenhurst C. of E. Prim. School
Wilverley Plain
Wilverley Inclosure
Hincheslea Wood
Long Slade Bottom
BROCKENHURST MANOR GOLF COURSE
NEW FOREST GOLF COURSE
A35
A337
B3035
Bolderwood Arboretum Ornamental Drive
Rhinefield Ornamental Drive
Highland Water
Ober Water
Bratley Water
Manor Wood
Manor Park
Withybed
Frith Cross
Inclosure
Butts Lawn
Gritnam
Pinkney
BOURNEMOUTH RD.
ROMSEY RD.
HIGH ST.
LYMINGTON ROAD
LYNDHURST RD.
RHINEFIELD ROAD
GRIGG
SWAY
155
148
190
204
222
223
H J K L M N G
24 25 26 27 28 29 30
1 2 3 4 5 6 7 8 9

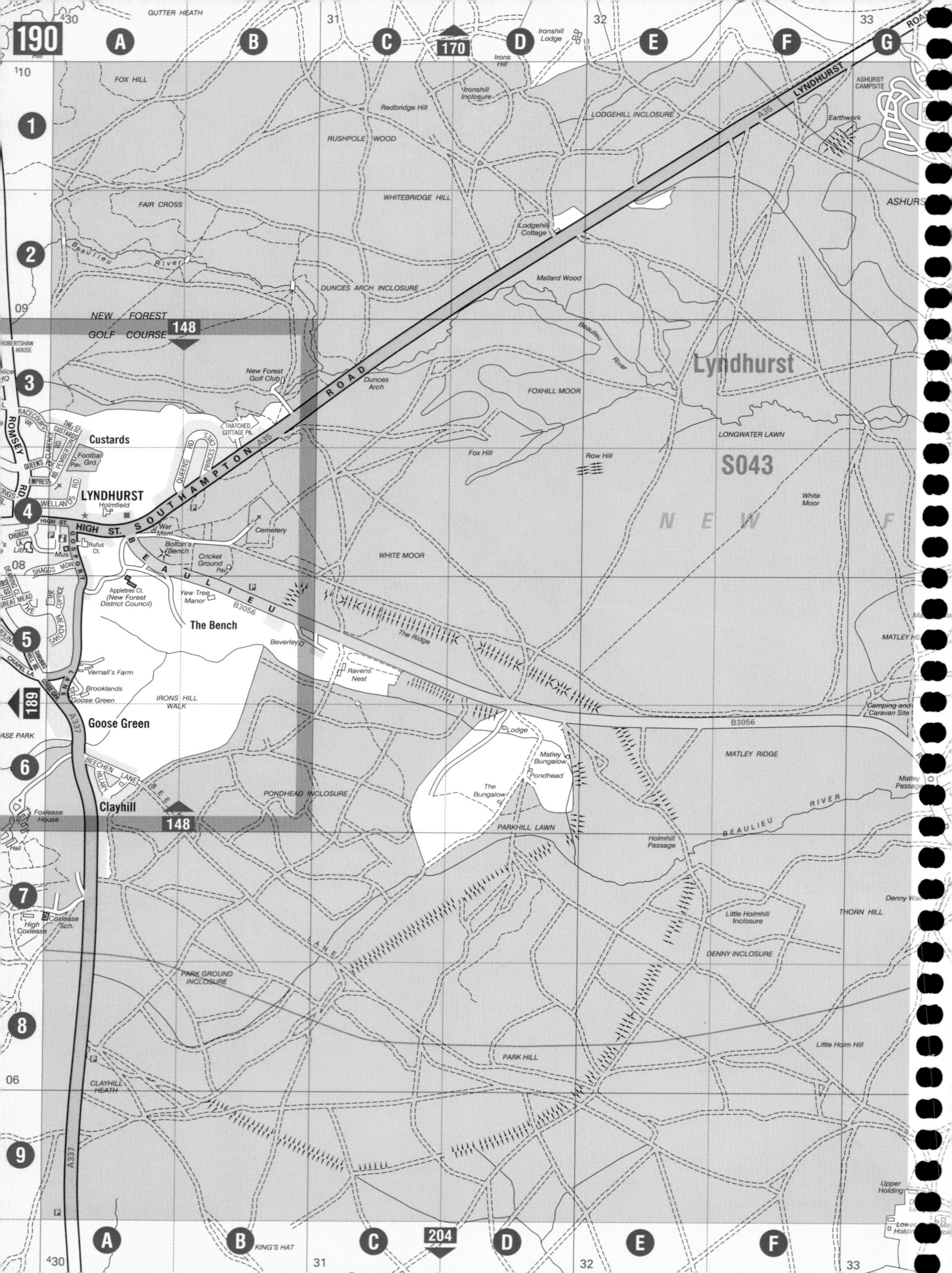
GUTTER HEATH
FOX HILL
Ironshill Lodge
Irons Hill
Ironshill Inclosure
Redbridge Hill
RUSHPOLE WOOD
LODGEHILL INCLOSURE
ASHURST CAMPSITE
Earthwork
LYNDHURST ROAD
A35
FAIR CROSS
WHITEBRIDGE HILL
Lodgehill Cottage
ASHURST
Beaulieu River
Mallard Wood
DUNCES ARCH INCLOSURE
NEW FOREST GOLF COURSE
148
ROBERTSHAW HOUSE
New Forest Golf Club
Dunces Arch
SOUTHAMPTON ROAD
Lyndhurst
FOXHILL MOOR
THATCHED COTTAGE PK.
Custards
LONGWATER LAWN
Football Grd.
Fox Hill
Row Hill
S043
LYNDHURST
Holmfield
White Moor
HIGH ST.
NEW F
War Mem.
Cemetery
Rufus Ct.
Bolton's Bench
Cricket Ground
WHITE MOOR
SHAGGS MDW
GOSPORT
BEAULIEU
B3056
Appletree Ct. (New Forest District Council)
Yew Tree Manor
The Ridge
The Bench
Beverley
MATLEY HEATH
Ravens Nest
Vernall's Farm
Brooklands
Goose Green
IRONS HILL WALK
Camping and Caravan Site
189
Goose Green
Lodge
MATLEY RIDGE
Matley Bungalow
Pondhead
BEECHEN LANE
HILLARY
PONDHEAD INCLOSURE
The Bungalow
Matley Passage
Foxlease House
Clayhill
PARKHILL LAWN
BEAULIEU RIVER
Holmhill Passage
A337
Denny Wait
Coxlease Sch.
High Coxlease
Little Holmhill Inclosure
THORN HILL
LANE
DENNY INCLOSURE
PARK GROUND INCLOSURE
Little Holm Hill
PARK HILL
CLAYHILL HEATH
Upper Holding
Lower Holding
KING'S HAT
204
170
A B C D E F G
1 2 3 4 5 6 7 8 9
430 31 32 33
110 09 08 06

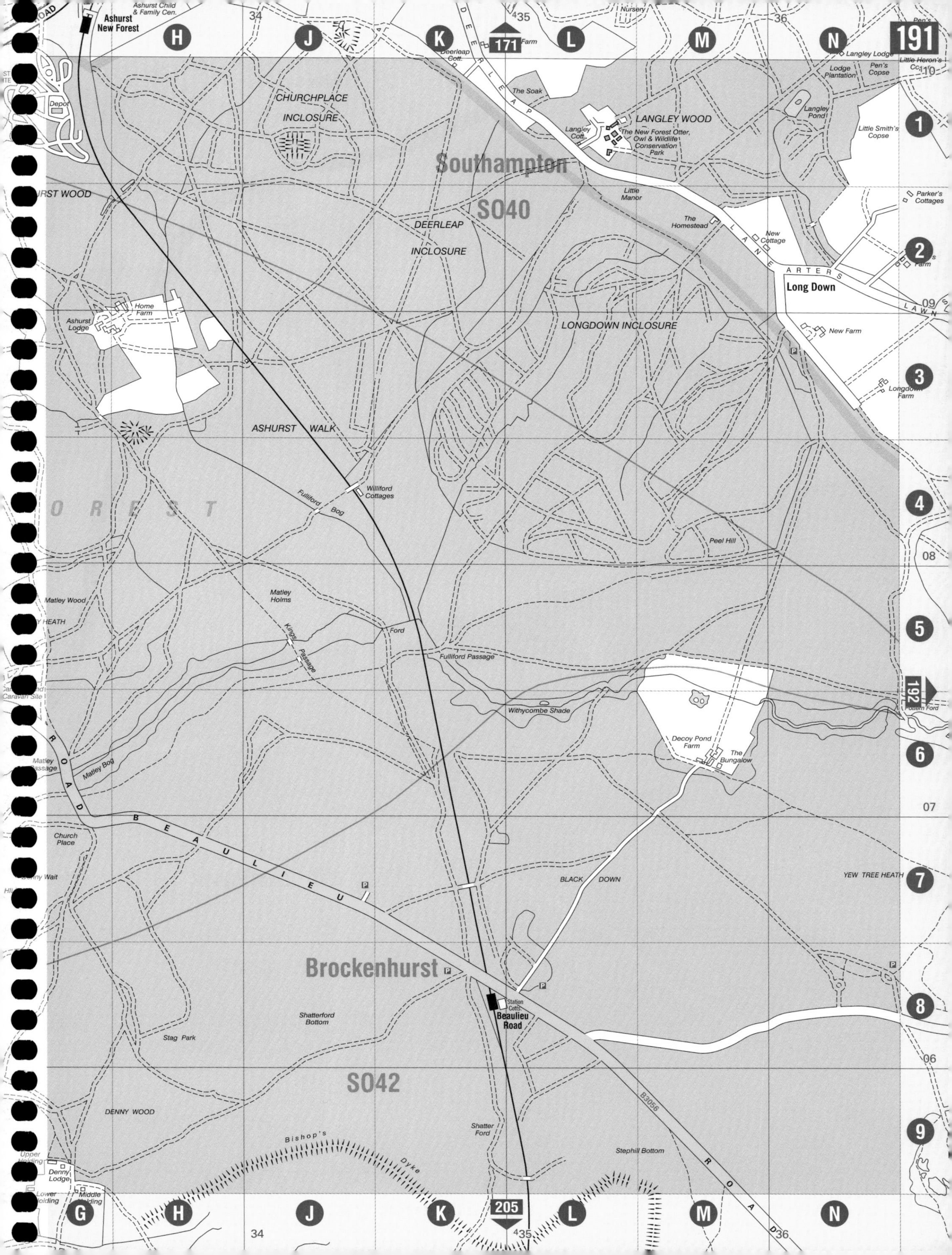
Ashurst
New Forest
Ashurst Child & Family Cen.
CHURCHPLACE
INCLOSURE
Depot
Deerleap Cott.
The Soak
LANGLEY WOOD
Langley Cott.
The New Forest Otter, Owl & Wildlife Conservation Park
Langley Lodge
Lodge Plantation
Pen's Copse
Little Heron's
Langley Pond
Little Smith's Copse
Southampton
SO40
DEERLEAP
INCLOSURE
Little Manor
The Homestead
New Cottage
Parker's Cottages
Long Down
LONGDOWN INCLOSURE
New Farm
Longdown Farm
Home Farm
Ashurst Lodge
ASHURST WALK
Williford Cottages
Fulliford Bog
Peel Hill
Matley Wood
Matley Holms
Kings Passage
Ford
Fulliford Passage
Withycombe Shade
Decoy Pond Farm
The Bungalow
Pottern Ford
Matley Passage
Matley Bog
Church Place
BLACK DOWN
YEW TREE HEATH
Denny Wait
BEAULIEU ROAD
Brockenhurst
Station Cotts.
Beaulieu Road
Shatterford Bottom
Stag Park
SO42
DENNY WOOD
B3056
Shatter Ford
Stephill Bottom
Bishop's Dyke
Upper Holding
Denny Lodge
Lower Holding
Middle Holding
DEERLEAP LANE
ARTERS LAWN
H J K L M N G
1 2 3 4 5 6 7 8 9
34 435 36
110 09 08 07 06

171
192
205

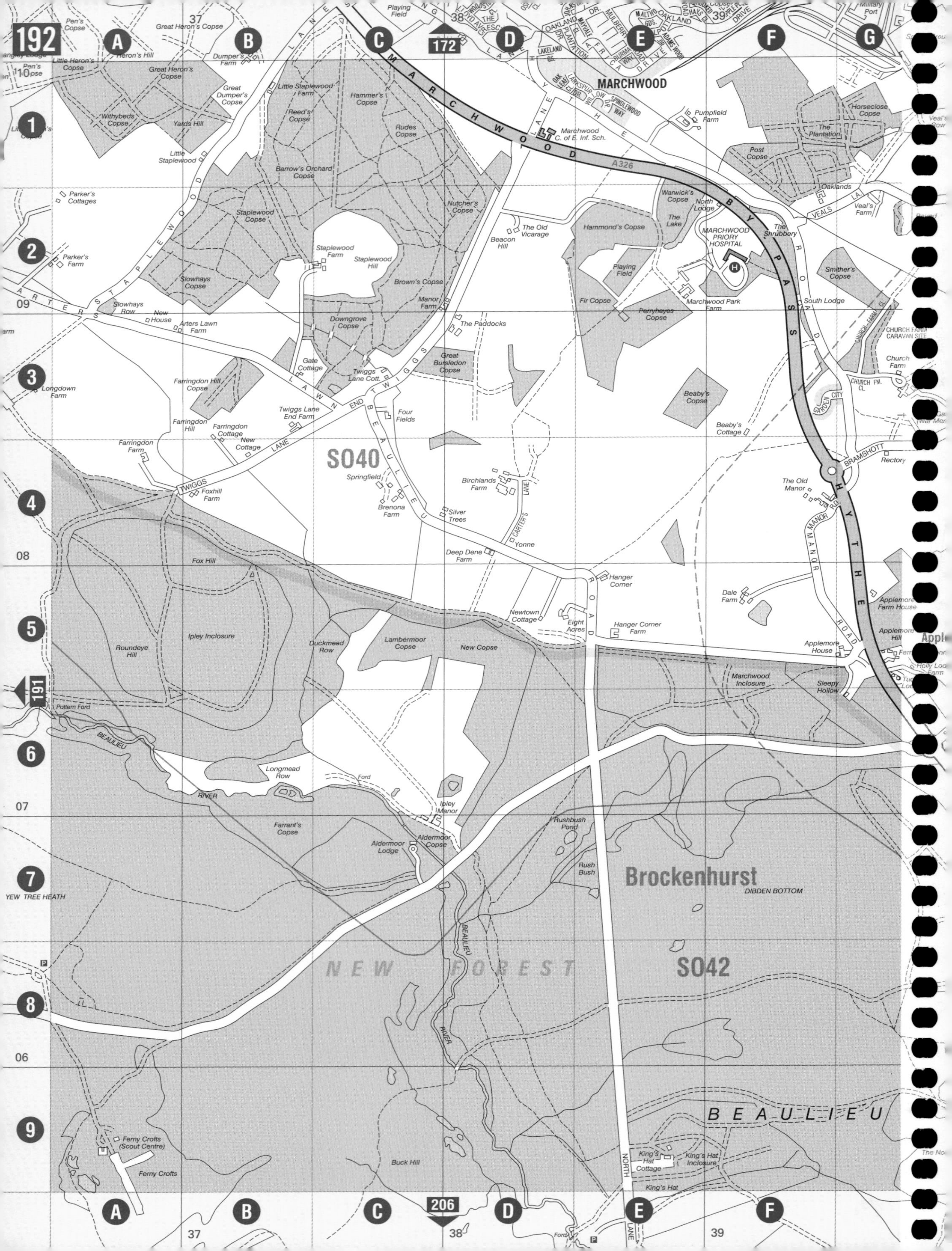

MARCHWOOD
MARCHWOOD BY-PASS
A326
Marchwood C. of E. Inf. Sch.
MARCHWOOD PRIORY HOSPITAL
SO40
SO42
Brockenhurst
NEW FOREST
BEAULIEU
DIBDEN BOTTOM
YEW TREE HEATH
Pen's Copse
Great Heron's Copse
Heron's Hill
Little Heron's Copse
Great Heron's Copse
Dumper's Farm
Great Dumper's Copse
Withybeds Copse
Yards Hill
Little Staplewood
Little Staplewood Farm
Reed's Copse
Hammer's Copse
Rudes Copse
Barrow's Orchard Copse
Parker's Cottages
Parker's Farm
Staplewood Copse
Staplewood Farm
Staplewood Hill
Brown's Copse
Nutcher's Copse
Slowhays Copse
Slowhays Row
New House
Arters Lawn Farm
Manor Farm
Downgrove Copse
The Paddocks
Great Bursledon Copse
Gate Cottage
Twiggs Lane Cott.
Longdown Farm
Farringdon Hill Copse
Farringdon Hill
Farringdon Cottage
New Cottage
Twiggs Lane End Farm
Farringdon Farm
Foxhill Farm
Four Fields
Springfield
Brenona Farm
Silver Trees
Birchlands Farm
Yonne
Deep Dene Farm
Hanger Corner
Newtown Cottage
Eight Acres
Hanger Corner Farm
Beacon Hill
The Old Vicarage
Hammond's Copse
Playing Field
Fir Copse
Perryhayes Copse
Warwick's Copse
North Lodge
The Lake
The Shrubbery
Marchwood Park Farm
Beaby's Copse
Beaby's Cottage
Pumpfield Farm
Post Copse
Horseclose Copse
The Plantation
Oaklands
Veal's Farm
Smither's Copse
South Lodge
CHURCH FARM CARAVAN SITE
Church Farm
Rectory
The Old Manor
Dale Farm
Applemore Farm House
Applemore Hill
Applemore House
Sleepy Hollow
Marchwood Inclosure
Fox Hill
Ipley Inclosure
Roundeye Hill
Duckmead Row
Lambermoor Copse
New Copse
Pottern Ford
Longmead Row
Ford
Ipley Manor
Farrant's Copse
Aldermoor Lodge
Aldermoor Copse
Rushbush Pond
Rush Bush
Ferny Crofts (Scout Centre)
Ferny Crofts
Buck Hill
King's Hat Cottage
King's Hat Inclosure
King's Hat
RIVER
BEAULIEU RIVER
ARTERS LAWN
STAPLEWOOD LANE
TWIGGS LANE
TWIGGS LANE END
BEAULIEU ROAD
CARTER'S LANE
HANGER ROAD
NORTH LANE
HYTHE ROAD
HYTHE BY-PASS
MANOR ROAD
VEALS LA.
BRAMSHOTT
CHURCH FM. CL.
GARDEN CITY
MARCHWOOD ROAD
OAKLAND DR.
LAKELAND GG.
Playing Field
Military Port
172
206
191
37
38
39
10
09
08
07
06
A
B
C
D
E
F
G
1
2
3
4
5
6
7
8
9

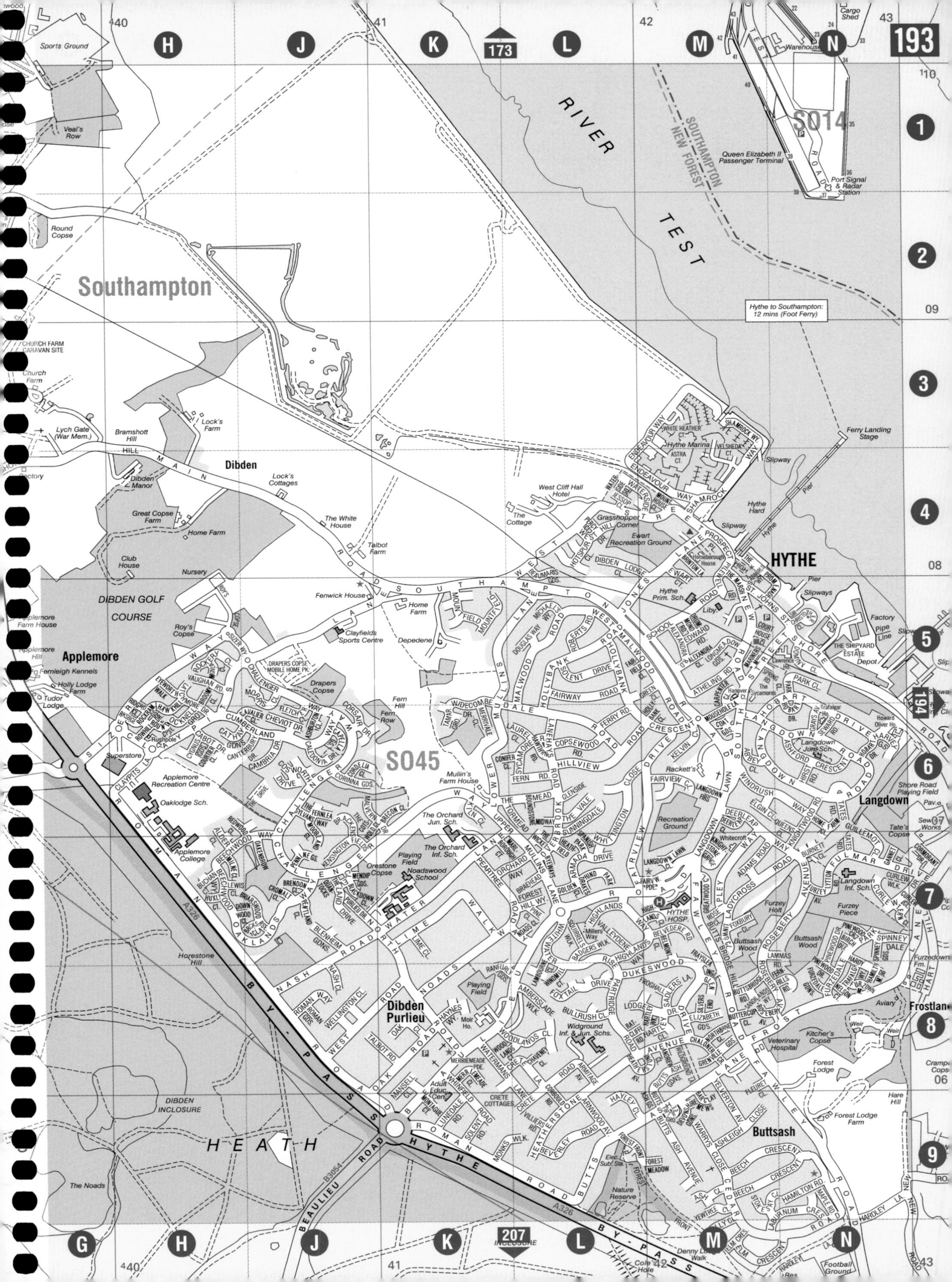193
173
207
H
J
K
L
M
N
G
1
2
3
4
5
6
7
8
9
440
41
42
43
09
08
07
06
RIVER TEST
SOUTHAMPTON
NEW FOREST
S014
S045
Queen Elizabeth II Passenger Terminal
Port Signal & Radar Station
Cargo Shed
Warehouse
TEST ROAD
Hythe to Southampton: 12 mins (Foot Ferry)
Ferry Landing Stage
Slipway
Hythe Hard
Hythe Pier
Pier
Slipways
Factory
Pipe Line
THE SHIPYARD ESTATE
Depot
HYTHE
Hythe Marina
SHAMROCK WAY
ENDEAVOUR WAY
West Cliff Hall Hotel
The Cottage
Grasshopper Corner
Ewart Recreation Ground
Hythe Prim. Sch.
Liby.
Homeborough House
Southampton
Sports Ground
Veal's Row
Round Copse
CHURCH FARM CARAVAN SITE
Church Farm
Lych Gate (War Mem.)
Bramshott Hill
Lock's Farm
Dibden
Dibden Manor
Rectory
Lock's Cottages
Great Copse Farm
Home Farm
The White House
Talbot Farm
Club House
Nursery
DIBDEN GOLF COURSE
Applemore Farm House
Applemore Hill
Applemore
Fernleigh Kennels
Holly Lodge Farm
Tudor Lodge
Roy's Copse
Fenwick House
Home Farm
Depedene
Clayfields Sports Centre
DRAPERS COPSE MOBILE HOME PK.
Drapers Copse
Fern Hill
Fern Row
Superstore
Rushpole Ct.
Applemore Recreation Centre
Oaklodge Sch.
Applemore College
Mullin's Farm House
The Orchard Jun. Sch.
The Orchard Inf. Sch.
Playing Field
Orestone Copse
Noadswood School
Recreation Ground
Rackett's
Langdown Lawn
Whitecroft
Hythe Hosp.
Langdown
Langdown Jun. Sch.
Langdown Inf. Sch.
Shore Road Playing Field
Tate's Copse
Furzey Holt
Furzey Piece
Buttsash Wood
Veterinary Hospital
Kitcher's Copse
Forest Lodge
Forest Lodge Farm
Hare Hill
Frostlane
Aviary
Weir
Buttsash
Widground Inf. & Jun. Schs.
Dibden Purlieu
Moir Ho.
Adult Educ. Cen.
CRETE COTTAGES
Elec. Sub. Sta.
Nature Reserve
Horestone Hill
DIBDEN INCLOSURE
HEATH
The Noads
Denny Lodge Walk
Cole Hole
Football Ground
A326
B3054
BEAULIEU ROAD
HYTHE ROAD
BY-PASS
ROMAN WAY
CLAYPITS LA.
CHALLENGER WAY
SOUTHAMPTON ROAD
MAIN ROAD
WEST STREET
JONES LANE
PROSPECT PL.
HIGH ST.
ST. JOHNS ST.
SHORE ROAD
SOUTH STREET
LANGDOWN ROAD
FAWLEY ROAD
FROST LANE
BUTTS ASH LANE
LONG LANE
NORTH WATER ROAD
NOADS WAY
WEST ROAD
LOWER MULLINS LANE
UPPER MULLINS LANE
BECHWOOD WAY
DUKESWOOD DRIVE
HIGHLANDS WAY
FAIRVIEW DRIVE
ARMADA DRIVE
LADYCROSS
ROSEBERY AVENUE
HOBART DRIVE
FULMAR DRIVE
WINDRUSH WAY
DEERLEAP WAY
ADAMS ROAD
HEATHERSTONE AV.
BULLRUSH CL.
NASH ROAD
LIME WALK
OAK ROAD
HARDLEY LA.
NEW ROAD

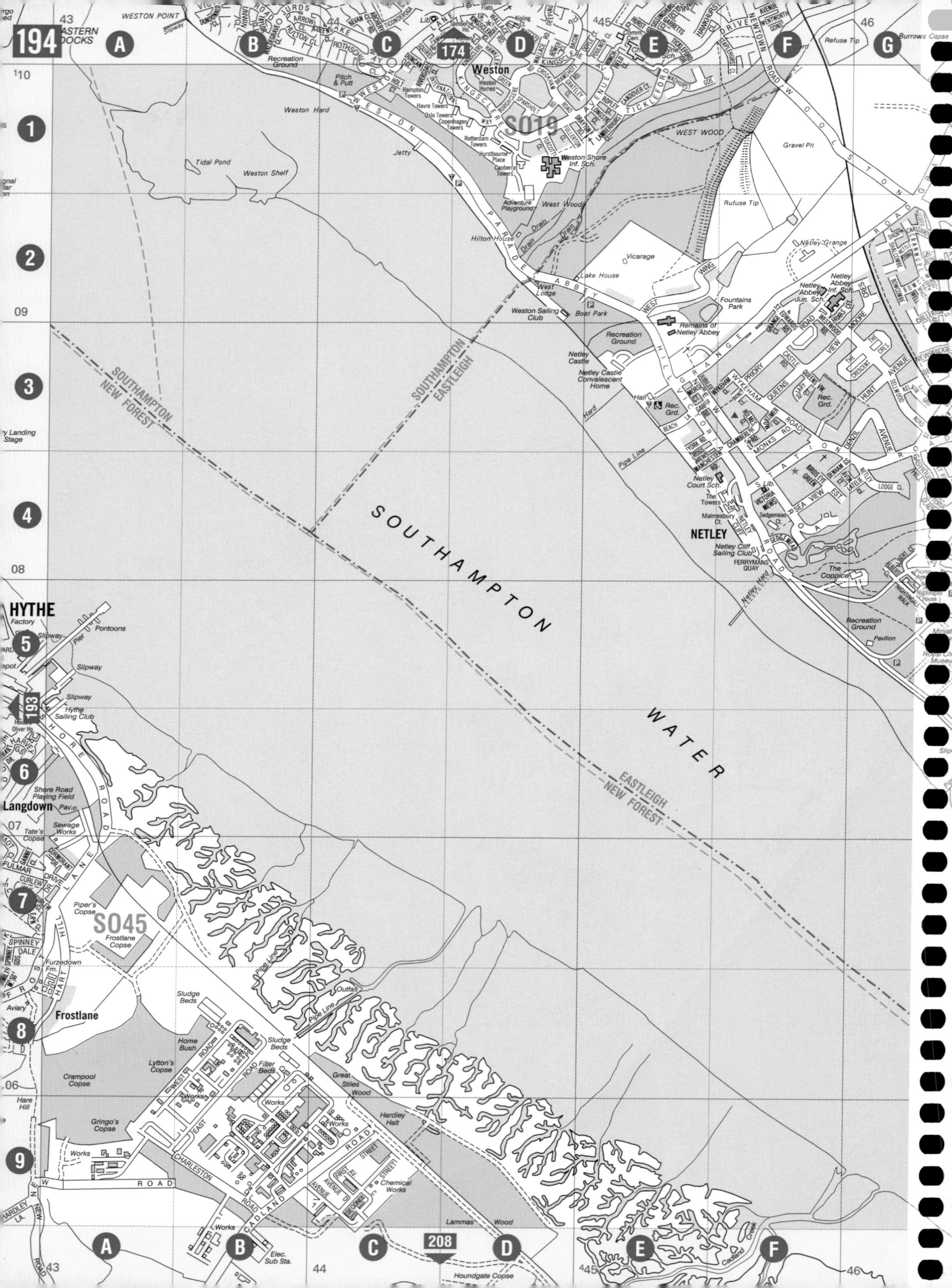
SOUTHAMPTON WATER
Weston
Netley
HYTHE
Langdown
Frostlane
SO19
SO45
Weston Shore Inf. Sch.
Weston Hard
Tidal Pond
Weston Shelf
Jetty
West Wood
Gravel Pit
Refuse Tip
Rufuse Tip
Vicarage
Lake House
Fountains Park
Remains of Netley Abbey
Netley Castle
Netley Castle Convalescent Home
Weston Sailing Club
Boat Park
Recreation Ground
Netley Abbey Inf. Sch.
Netley Abbey Jun. Sch.
Netley Grange
Netley Court Sch.
Netley Cliff Sailing Club
Ferrymans Quay
The Coppice
Pavilion
Netley Hard
Pipe Line
SOUTHAMPTON NEW FOREST
SOUTHAMPTON EASTLEIGH
EASTLEIGH NEW FOREST
Pontoons
Pier
Slipway
Hythe Sailing Club
Shore Road Playing Field
Sewage Works
Tate's Copse
Piper's Copse
Frostlane Copse
Furzedown Fm.
Sludge Beds
Home Bush
Lytton's Copse
Filter Beds
Crampool Copse
Hare Hill
Gringo's Copse
Works
Chemical Works
Great Stiles Wood
Hardley Halt
Lammas Wood
Elec. Sub Sta.
Houndgate Copse
Cadland Creek
Outfall
Burrows Copse
Weston Point
Eastern Docks
174
193
208
43
44
45
46
06
07
08
09
10

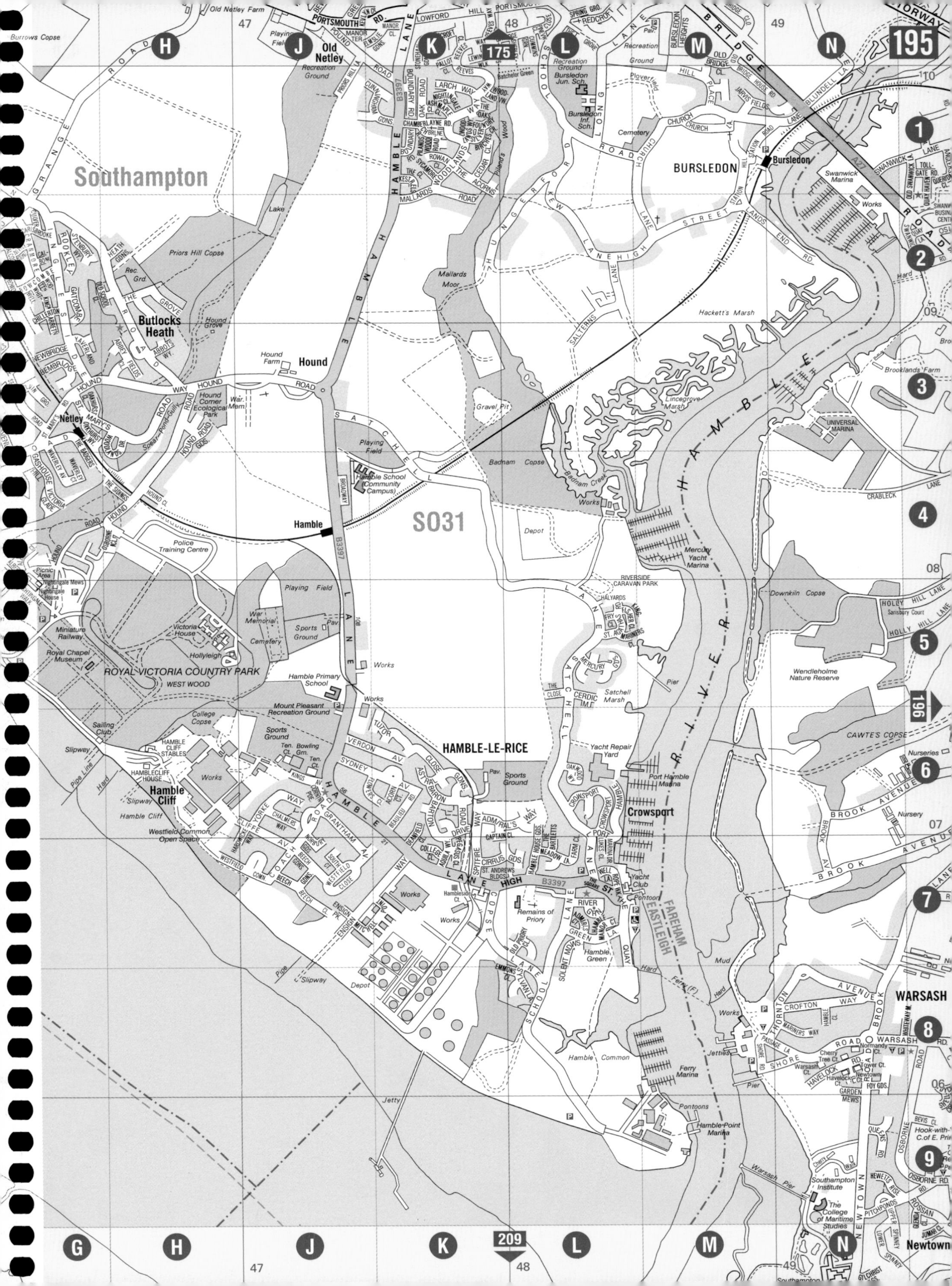

Southampton
Old Netley
Old Netley Farm
Burrows Copse
Playing Field
Recreation Ground
PORTSMOUTH RD.
LOWFORD
HILL
175
Batchelor Green
Bursledon Jun. Sch.
Bursledon Inf. Sch.
Recreation Ground
BURSLEDON HEIGHTS
OLD BRIDGE CL.
BRIDGE RD.
BLUNDELL LA.
Ploverfield
Cemetery
CHURCH RD.
BURSLEDON
Bursledon
Swanwick Marina
Works
HIGH STREET
LANDS END RD.
HUNGERFORD
LONG LANE
HAMBLE LANE
B3397
MALLARDS ROAD
Lake
Priors Hill Copse
Rec. Grd.
Butlocks Heath
Hound Grove
Mallards Moor
SALTERNS LANE
Hackett's Marsh
Hard
Brooklands Farm
Hound Farm
Hound
HOUND ROAD
HOUND WAY
Hound Corner Ecological Park
War Mem.
Gravel Pit
Lincegrove Marsh
UNIVERSAL MARINA
Netley
ST. MARY'S ROAD
SATCHELL LANE
Playing Field
Hamble School (Community Campus)
Badnam Copse
Badnam Creek
RIVER HAMBLE
CRABLECK LANE
Works
Hamble
SO31
Depot
Mercury Yacht Marina
Police Training Centre
RIVERSIDE CARAVAN PARK
Downkiln Copse
HOLLY HILL LANE
Sarisbury Court
Picnic Area
Nightingale Mews
Miniature Railway
Royal Chapel Museum
Victoria House
War Memorial
Playing Field
Sports Ground
Cemetery
Hollyleigh
ROYAL VICTORIA COUNTRY PARK
WEST WOOD
Works
Hamble Primary School
Wendleholme Nature Reserve
Pier
Satchell Marsh
Mount Pleasant Recreation Ground
Sailing Club
College Copse
Sports Ground
HAMBLE CLIFF STABLES
Ten. Bowling Grn.
HAMBLE-LE-RICE
Yacht Repair Yard
CAWTE'S COPSE
Nurseries
196
Slipway
Pipe Line
Hard
HAMBLECLIFF HOUSE
Works
Hamble Cliff
Hamble Cliff
Sports Ground
Port Hamble Marina
BROOK AVENUE
Nursery
Westfield Common Open Space
Crowsport
HIGH STREET
B3397
Yacht Club
Pontoon
Works
Remains of Priory
FAREHAM
EASTLEIGH
Works
Hamble Green
Mud
Pipe
Slipway
Depot
Ferry (F)
Hard
Works
CROFTON WAY
WARSASH
Jetties
Hamble Common
Ferry Marina
Pier
WARSASH RD.
Jetty
Pontoons
Hamble Point Marina
Warsash Pier
Southampton Institute
The College of Maritime Studies
NEWTOWN RD.
Newtown
G
H
J
K
L
M
N
1
2
3
4
5
6
7
8
9
47
48
49
06
07
08
09
10
209

176
210
195
A
B
C
D
E
F
G
1
2
3
4
5
6
7
8
9
450
51
52
10
09
08
07
06
M27 MOTORWAY
M27
Air Traffic Control Centre
Playing Field
Clay Pit
Nature Centre
Brick Works
Works
Midfield Nursery
Hillcrest Nursery
Nursery
Glen House
Friend's Farm
Rookery Farm
Quaveys Copse
Glassfield Copse
Gull Coppice
Rec. Grd.
Whiteley
Whiteley Prim. Sch.
Swanwick
Lower Swanwick
Swanwick Business Centre
BOTLEY ROAD
BRIDGE ROAD
A27
A3051
Brooklands
Brooklands Farm
Hard
Sarisbury Comm. Cen.
Sarisbury Green
SARISBURY
Beacon Bottom
PARK GATE BUS. CEN.
Holmleigh
Swanwick Hill
SEGENSWORTH WEST IND. EST.
PARK GATE
Bridge View
Depot
Playground
Sarisbury C. of E. Jun School
Rivendale
Pond
Swanwick House
Beresford Lodge
Summervale House
The Meadows
Drill Hall
Park Gate Prim. Sch.
Lord Wilson School
Southampton
SO31
Cemetery
Holly Hill Woodland Park
WINNARD'S COPSE
Holly Hill Mans.
Sarisbury Inf. Sch.
Brookfield Community School
CAWTE'S COPSE
Nurseries
Nursery
Lock's Wood
Playground
LOCKS HEATH
Comm. Cen.
Superstores
Woodlands
Course Park
Roxburgh Ho.
Comm. Hall
Play Area
St. Michael's Road Open Space
Danehurst
Rec. Grd.
WARSASH
Locks Heath Jun. & Inf. Schs.
Fleetend
Dibles Park Caravan Site
Hamble Park Caravan Site
Hook-with-Warsash C. of E. Prim. Sch.
Dibles Bottom
Football Ground
Hook Lake
Mallows
Hook Lane Rec. Ground
Sand & Gravel Pit
Great Abshot Farm
Abshot
Little Abshot Farm
Little Abshot Farm Cottages
Abshot Manor Country Club
Twelve Acre Farm
PO14
Recreation Ground
The Wilderness
Titchfield Common
Hopes Charity
St. Anthony's R.C. Prim. Sch.
Hookhead Coppice
Hookgate Coppice
Newtown
Hook
(PROPOSED)

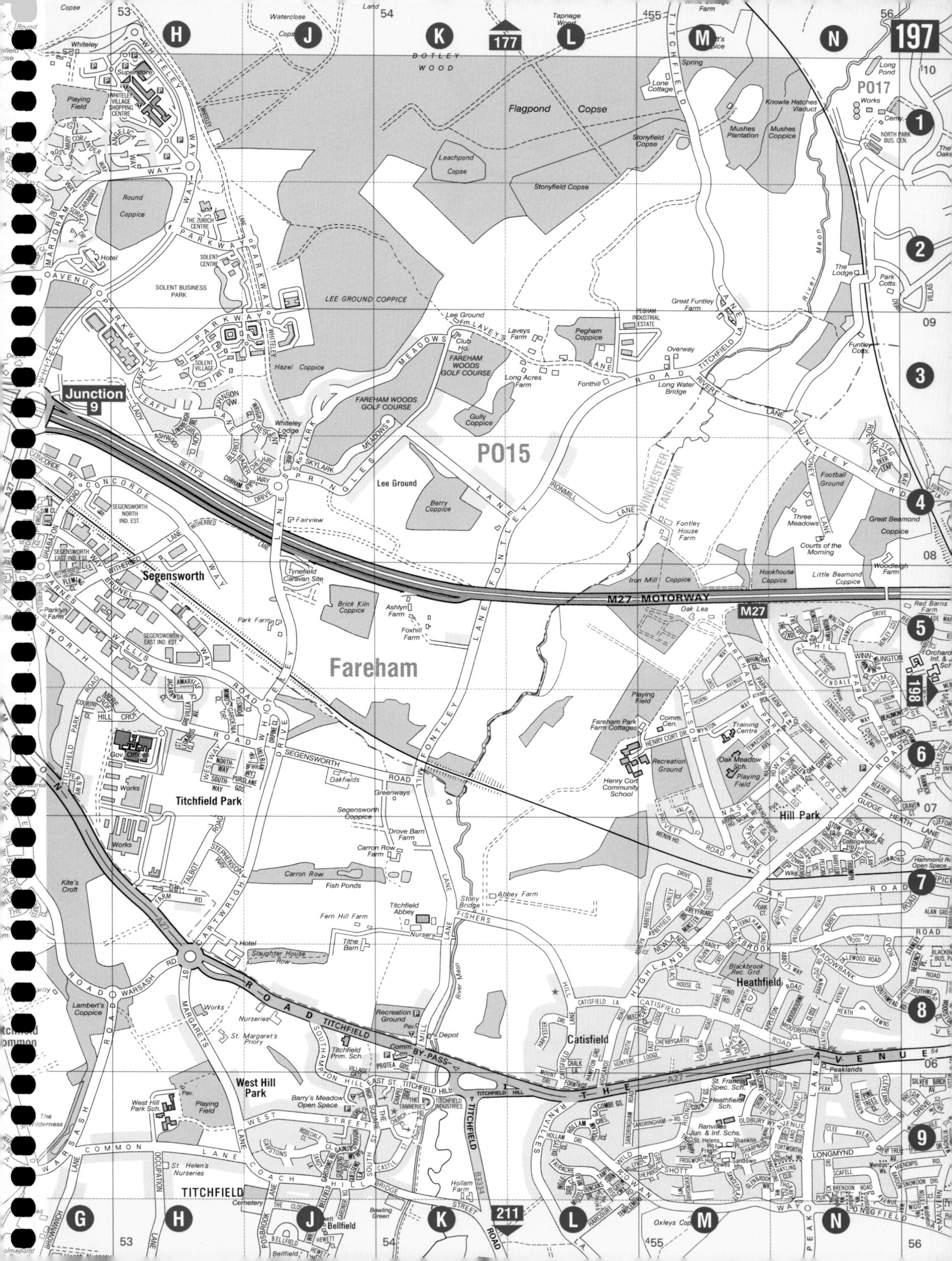

177
211
198
Junction 9
M27 MOTORWAY
M27
PO15
PO17
Fareham
Segensworth
Titchfield Park
TITCHFIELD
West Hill Park
Catisfield
Heathfield
Hill Park
Bellfield
BOTLEY WOOD
Flagpond Copse
Leachpond Copse
Stonyfield Copse
Stonyfield Copse
LEE GROUND COPPICE
Hazel Coppice
Round Coppice
Lee Ground
Berry Coppice
Brick Kiln Coppice
Iron Mill Coppice
Hookhouse Coppice
Little Beamond Coppice
Great Beamond Coppice
Gully Coppice
Pegham Coppice
Mushes Plantation
Mushes Coppice
Knowle Hatches Viaduct
Lone Cottage
Great Funtley Farm
PEGHAM INDUSTRIAL ESTATE
Overway
Fonthill
Long Water Bridge
Funtley Cotts.
The Lodge
Park Cotts.
Football Ground
Three Meadows
Courts of the Morning
Woodleigh Farm
Red Barns Farm
FAREHAM WOODS GOLF COURSE
Club Ho.
Laveys Farm
Long Acres Farm
Lee Ground Fm.
Whiteley Lodge
Superstore
WHITELEY VILLAGE SHOPPING CENTRE
Playing Field
THE ZURICH CENTRE
SOLENT CENTRE
SOLENT BUSINESS PARK
SOLENT VILLAGE
Hotel
SEGENSWORTH NORTH IND. EST.
SEGENSWORTH EAST IND. EST.
Parklyn Farm
Park Farm
Fairview
Tynefield Caravan Site
Ashlyn Farm
Foxhill Farm
Oak Lea
Fontley House Farm
Fareham Park Farm Cottages
Comm. Cen.
Training Centre
Henry Cort Community School
Recreation Ground
Oak Meadow Sch.
Gov. Offices
Works
Oakfields
Greenways
Segensworth Coppice
Drove Barn Farm
Carron Row Farm
Carron Row
Fish Ponds
Kite's Croft
Titchfield Abbey
Fern Hill Farm
Tithe Barn
Nursery
Stony Bridge
Abbey Farm
Slaughter House Row
Lambert's Coppice
Nurseries
St. Margaret's Priory
Recreation Ground
Pav.
Depot
Titchfield Prim. Sch.
Comm. Cen.
Barry's Meadow Open Space
TITCHFIELD INDUSTRIES
West Hill Park Sch.
St. Helen's Nurseries
Cemetery
Bowling Green
Hollam Farm
Blackbrook Rec. Grd.
St. Francis Spec. Sch.
Heathfield Sch.
Ranvilles Jun. & Inf. Schs.
Peaklands
Hammond Rd Open Space
Oxleys Copse
Whiteley
Long Pond
Works
Cemy.
NORTH PARK BUS. CEN.
WHITELEY WAY
PARKWAY
AVENUE
SKYLARK
MEADOWS
SPRINGLES LANE
FONTLEY LANE
FONTLEY ROAD
TITCHFIELD LANE
FUNTLEY ROAD
RIVER LANE
IRONMILL LANE
WINCHESTER FAREHAM
CONCORDE WAY
BARNES WAY
SEGENSWORTH ROAD
WITHERBED LANE
BRUNEL WAY
WALLIS ROAD
CARTWRIGHT DRIVE
TITCHFIELD ROAD
TITCHFIELD BY-PASS
A27
B3334
WARSASH ROAD
ST. MARGARETS LANE
COMMON LANE
COACH HILL
WEST STREET
SOUTH ST.
THE SQUARE
EAST ST.
BRIDGE STREET
CATISFIELD LA.
HIGHLANDS ROAD
THE AVENUE
OAK ROAD
GUDGE HEATH LANE
HILLSON DRIVE
FAREHAM PARK ROAD
HENRY CORT DR.
PRIVETT ROAD
RANVILLES LANE
LONGFIELD AVENUE
PEAK LANE
River Meon
G
H
J
K
L
M
N
1
2
3
4
5
6
7
8
9
53
54
455
56
10
09
08
07
06

198
178
212
197
A
B
C
D
E
F
G
1
2
3
4
5
6
7
8
9
56
57
58
59
Dandy Copse
Fiddlers Green
Shaftesbury Copse
Reservoirs (covered)
Long Pond
Dash Wood
Aytesbury Copse
Blakes Copse
Crocker Farm
Jack o' Row
Ravens Wood
Works
Cemy.
RAVENSWOOD HOUSE
NORTH PARK BUS. CEN.
The Oaks
Playing Field
The Tors
Knowle Cotts.
Park Cotts.
VILLAS
Heytesbury Farm Cotts.
Heytesbury Farm
Saw Mill
Crockerhill
WICKHAM ROAD
FOREST LANE
The Hanger
Carpenters Copse
Chancellors Copse
Homerhill Copse
Pigeonhouse Copse
Old Vine Cottage
Chalk Pit Cottages
CHALK LANE
ALBANY BUSINESS CENTRE
Albany Farm
Charity Farm
WINCHESTER
FAREHAM
WALLINGTON
Whitedell Farm
Whitedell Cottages
Recreation Ground
Playing Field
Boundary Oak School
Funtley
FUNTLEY LA.
LAKESIDE ROAD
Cressey Cottages
Great Beamond Coppice
Woodleigh Farm
Drake Cottages
Kneller Court
DEAN FARM ESTATE
Dean Farm
Dean Farm Cottages
Hellyers Farm
The Lodge
Junction 10
M27
M27 MOTORWAY
North Fareham
Spurlings Farm Cottages
Park View Cottages
North Fareham Farm
Spurlings Farm
NINE ELMS LANE
SPURLINGS ROAD
WHITEDELL LANE
Red Barns Farm
Fareham Common
Pond
Furze Hall
Furzehall Farm
Orchard Lea Inf. & Jun. Schs.
KNELLER COURT
KILN ROAD
Uplands
THE MALLARDS
Uplands Old Peoples Home
Uplands Prim. Sch.
Play. Fld.
Cemetery
Works
Warehouse
KILN ACRE (IND. SITE)
Park Vw. Ho.
Downbarn Farm
Spurlings Yard
BOARHUNT ROAD
STANDARD WAY
FAREHAM INDUSTRIAL PARK
BRIDGE INDUSTRIES
Wallington River
North Wallington
Wallington Orchard
WALLINGTON CT.
FAREHAM HTS.
Depot
HIGHLANDS
FROSTHOLE
Stirling Ct.
INVERNESS
ARGYLE CRES.
HEATHER GDS.
CRAVEN
GUDGE HEATH
GIFFORD CL.
PO15
Depot
Hammond Road Open Space
OXFORD CLO.
DENBIGH
Leisure Cen.
Bowling Green
Park Lane Recreation Ground
WILLIAM PRICE GDS.
SERPENTINE
TURNPIKE
ST. CHRISTOPHER'S HOSPITAL
OLD TURNPIKE BUSINESS PARK
Superstore
Harrison Prim. Sch.
Old Manor Ho.
Adult Educ. Cen.
WALLINGTON WAY
Wallington
Wallington House
FORT WALLINGTON IND. EST.
MILITARY ROAD
PARADISE
SPICEWOOD
OAK ROAD
BLACKBROOK
BLACKBROOK BUS. PARK
Fareham Junction
Beechwood Lodge
Elmwood Lodge
SOUTHAMPTON ROAD
NORTHWOOD SQUARE
OSBORN ROAD
Civ. Cen.
Lib.
FAREHAM SHOPPING CEN.
LYSSES PATH
Ind. Est.
Wykeham Ho. Sch.
CAMS HILL
Blackbrook House Maternity Home
THE AVENUE
A27
Fareham
Depot
Western Ct.
Magistrates Ct.
WEST STREET
Market
Police H.Q.
Bus Stn.
EAST STREET
Madison Ct.
Cams Hill School
NORTH PARK
St. Jude's R.C. Prim. Sch.
Bishopswood
Fareham College
WESTERN WAY
EASTERN WAY
BELVOIR
FAREHAM
The Gillies
The Gillies Open Space
ELMHURST CLOSE
Recreation Ground
Swan Quay
Bath Lane Cottages
Upper Quay
Town Quay
Home Farm Office Village
Cams Hall
Wallisdean Inf. Sch.
Wallisdean Jun. Sch.
PO14
Playing Field
Neville Lovett Comm. Sch.
BROADLAW WALK SHOPPING PRECINCT
West End
Play. Fld.
THE BOATYARD IND. EST.
The Ropewalk
QUAY SIDE COMMERCE CENTRE
GOSPORT ROAD
Fareham Lake
Club House
Wilderness
SOUTH PARK
Cunigre Pond
Football Ground
Cam Alders Sports Centre
CAMS HALL GOLF COURSE

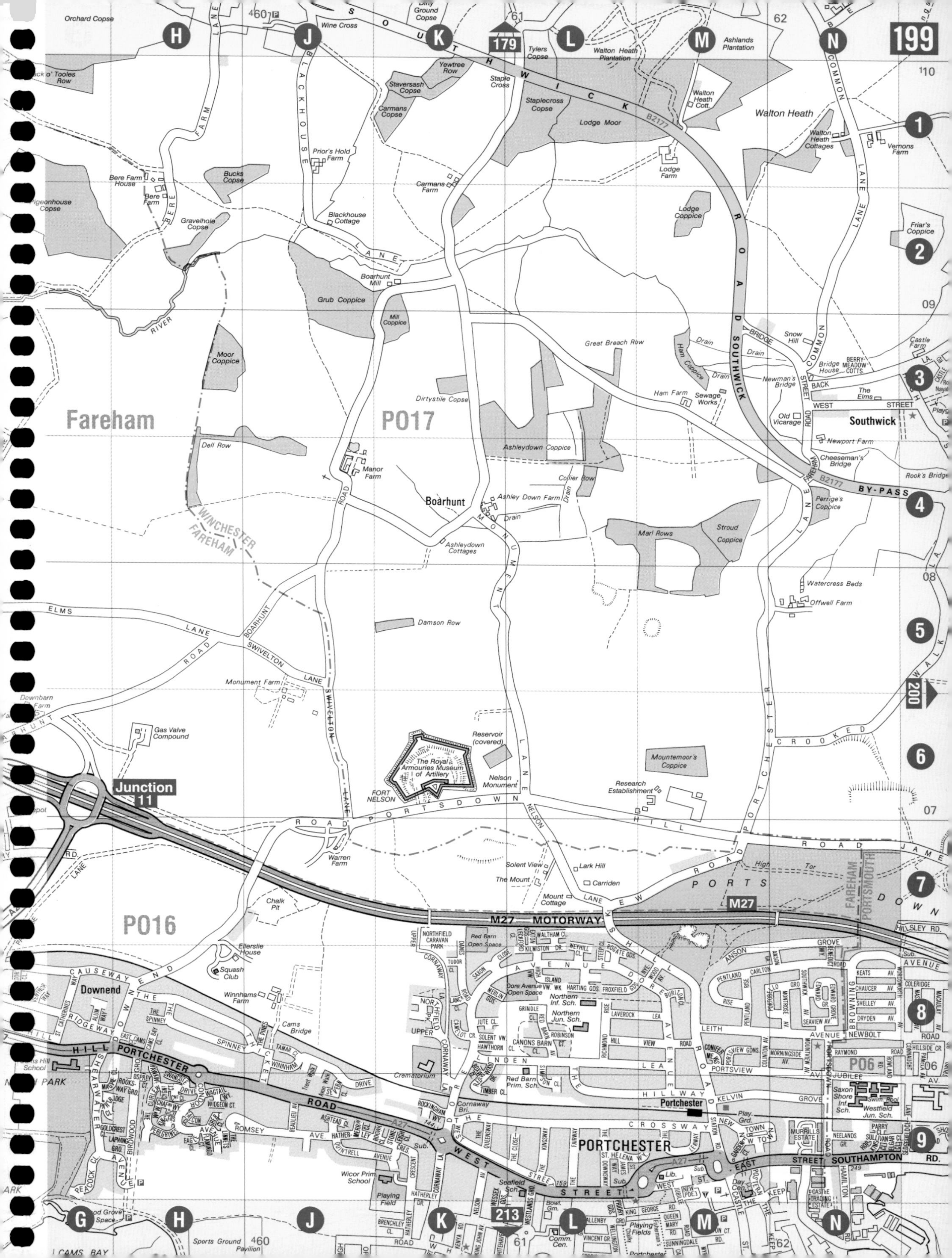

Fareham
PO17
PO16
PO6
Southwick
Boarhunt
Portchester
PORTCHESTER
Downend
Walton Heath
Junction 11
M27 MOTORWAY
SOUTHWICK ROAD
B2177
BY-PASS
PORTSDOWN HILL ROAD
MONUMENT LANE
SWIVELTON LANE
BOARHUNT ROAD
ELMS LANE
BLACKHOUSE LANE
BERE FARM LANE
COMMON LANE
PORTCHESTER LANE
CROOKED WALK LANE
WEST STREET
EAST STREET
SOUTHAMPTON RD.
PORTCHESTER ROAD
CAUSEWAY
DOWNEND ROAD
NELSON LANE
Orchard Copse
Wine Cross
Dirty Ground Copse
Tylers Copse
Walton Heath Plantation
Ashlands Plantation
Yewtree Row
Staversash Copse
Carmans Copse
Staple Cross
Staplecross Copse
Lodge Moor
Walton Heath Cott.
Walton Heath Cottages
Vernons Farm
Prior's Hold Farm
Bucks Copse
Bere Farm House
Bere Farm
Pigeonhouse Copse
Gravelhole Copse
Carmans Farm
Blackhouse Cottage
Lodge Farm
Lodge Coppice
Friar's Coppice
Boarhunt Mill
Grub Coppice
Mill Coppice
RIVER
Moor Coppice
Great Breach Row
Ham Coppice
Drain
Snow Hill
Castle Farm
Bridge House
BERRY-MEADOW COTTS
Newman's Bridge
Ham Farm
Sewage Works
The Elms
Old Vicarage
Dirtystile Copse
Dell Row
Ashleydown Coppice
Newport Farm
Cheeseman's Bridge
Rook's Bridge
Manor Farm
Collier Row
Ashley Down Farm
Perrige's Coppice
WINCHESTER FAREHAM
Ashleydown Cottages
Marl Rows
Stroud Coppice
Watercress Beds
Offwell Farm
Damson Row
Monument Farm
Downbarn Farm
Gas Valve Compound
Reservoir (covered)
The Royal Armouries Museum of Artillery
FORT NELSON
Nelson Monument
Mountemoor's Coppice
Research Establishment
Warren Farm
Solent View
The Mount
Lark Hill
Carriden
Mount Cottage
High Tor
FAREHAM PORTSMOUTH
Chalk Pit
Ellerslie House
Squash Club
Winnhams Farm
Cams Bridge
Crematorium
NORTHFIELD CARAVAN PARK
Red Barn Open Space
Dore Avenue Open Space
Northern Inf. Sch.
Northern Jun. Sch.
Red Barn Prim. Sch.
Cornaway Bri.
Saxon Shore Inf. Sch.
Westfield Jun. Sch.
Play. Grd.
MURRILLS ESTATE
CASTLE TRADING ESTATE
Wicor Prim. School
Playing Field
Seafield Sch.
Bowl. Grn.
Comm. Cen.
Lib.
Playing Fields
Day Cen.
Sports Ground Pavilion
Cams Hill School
CAMS BAY
179
200
213
110
09
08
07
06
460
61
62
249

180
214
199
Place Wood
Southwick
H.M.S. Dryad
Southwick Park Golf Course
Fareham
PO17
Lye Heath
Wymering
Paulsgrove
Portsdown Hill
Fort Southwick
Winchester
Portsmouth
Southampton Road
M27 Motorway
Southwick Road
B2177
Pigeon House Lane
Belney Lane
Crookhorn Walk
Queen Alexandra Hosp.
King Richard School
Sheepwash Farms
Roman Road (Course of)
Pitymoor Coppice
Sawyer's Wood
Potwell Farm
Pigeon House Farm
Moat & Bailey
Ring Work & Bailey Castle
Defence Research Agency
Paulsgrove Chalk Pit

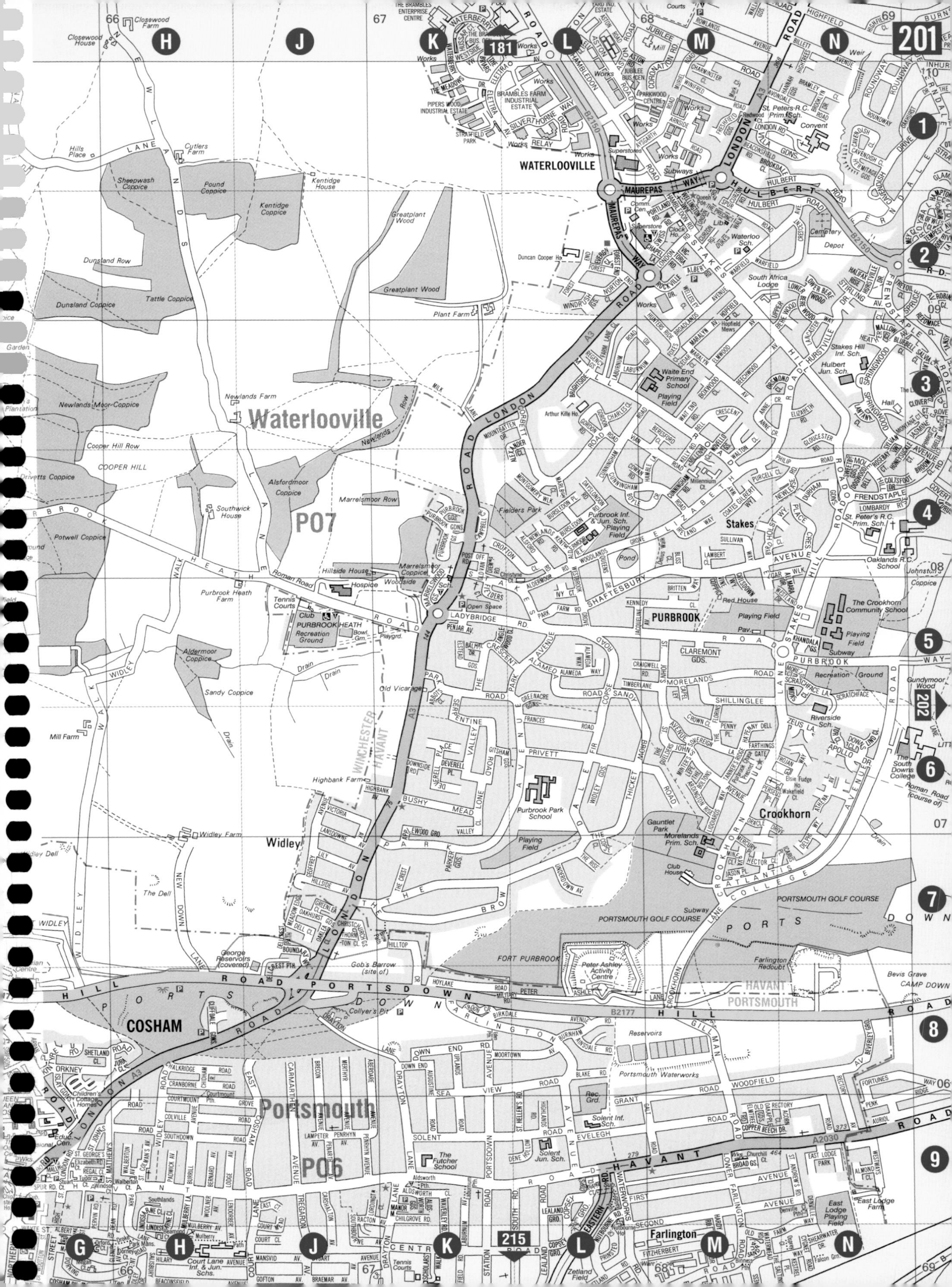

66
67
68
69
H
J
K
L
M
N
181
202
215
G
1
2
3
4
5
6
7
8
9
10
09
08
07
06
Closewood Farm
Closewood House
Hills Place
Cutlers Farm
Sheepwash Coppice
Pound Coppice
Kentidge House
Kentidge Coppice
Greatplant Wood
Dunsland Row
Dunsland Coppice
Tattle Coppice
Plant Farm
Newlands Farm
Newlands Moor Coppice
Waterlooville
Cooper Hill Row
COOPER HILL
Drivetts Coppice
Alsfordmoor Coppice
Marrelsmoor Row
Southwick House
PO7
Potwell Coppice
Purbrook Heath Farm
Hillside House
Hospice
Marrelsmoor Coppice
Tennis Courts
Club
PURBROOK HEATH
Recreation Ground
Aldermoor Coppice
Sandy Coppice
Mill Farm
Old Vicarage
Highbank Farm
Widley Farm
Widley
The Dell
George Reservoirs (covered)
Gob's Barrow (site of)
Collyer's Pit
COSHAM
Portsmouth
PO6
Waterlooville
WATERLOOVILLE
BRAMBLES FARM INDUSTRIAL ESTATE
PIPERS WOOD INDUSTRIAL ESTATE
Superstores
Superstore
Waterloo Sch.
South Africa Lodge
Duncan Cooper Ho.
Waite End Primary School
Playing Field
Arthur Kille Ho.
Millennium Ct.
Fielders Park
Purbrook Inf. & Jun. Sch. Playing Field
Pond
Stakes
PURBROOK
Red House
Playing Field
The Crookhorn Community School
Stakes Hill Inf. Sch.
Hulbert Jun. Sch.
St. Peter's R.C. Prim. Sch.
Oaklands R.C. School
Johnston's Coppice
Recreation Ground
Gundymoor Wood
Riverside Sch.
The South Downs College
Roman Road (course of)
Crookhorn
Gauntlet Park
Morelands Prim. Sch.
Purbrook Park School
Playing Field
PORTSMOUTH GOLF COURSE
PORTS DOWN
FORT PURBROOK
Peter Ashley Activity Centre
Farlington Redoubt
Bevis Grave
CAMP DOWN
HAVANT
PORTSMOUTH
WINCHESTER
HAVANT
PORTSDOWN HILL ROAD
B2177
Reservoirs
Portsmouth Waterworks
Rec. Grd.
Solent Inf. Sch.
Solent Jun. Sch.
The Futcher School
HAVANT ROAD
A2030
East Lodge Playing Field
East Lodge Farm
Farlington
Court Lane Inf. & Jun. Schs.
Children's Cottage Homes
LONDON ROAD
A3
MAUREPAS WAY
HULBERT ROAD
B2150
STAKES HILL ROAD
LADYBRIDGE RD.
SHAFTESBURY AVENUE
PURBROOK WAY
PARK AVENUE
PRIVETT
THE BROW
HEATH ROAD
WIDLEY WALK
NEW DOWN LANE
NEWLANDS LANE
HAMBLEDON ROAD
CROOKHORN LANE
COLLEGE
EASTERN RD.
FARLINGTON AVENUE
WOODFIELD
SEA VIEW
SOLENT ROAD
DRAYTON LANE
PORTSDOWN
EAST COSHAM ROAD
CARMARTHEN AVENUE

182
216
201
A
B
C
D
E
F
G
1
2
3
4
5
6
7
8
9
HAVANT
FOREST
SIR GEORGE STAUNTON
COUNTRY PARK
George Canning
Monument
Deerslaughter
Plain
Middle
Clearing
Thicket
Bottom
Gipsies
Clump
Cabbagefield
Row
Thicket Lawn
Bondfields
Plain
Gammon's
Hill
Hammick
Copse
The
Lake
The Avenue
LEIGH
PARK
LEIGH PARK
Leigh Park
Gardens
High Lawn
Visitor
Centre
Leigh Park
Gardens
STAUNTON
COUNTRY
PARK
Ornamental
Farm
Warren
Park
Mary Rose
House
Cherrytree
Row
Busby
Lease
Park House
Prim. Sch.
Park
Community School
Playing Fld.
Warren Park
Prim.Sch.
Riders
Jun. & Inf.
Schools
Playground
Works
Warehouse
Great
Copse
Front Lawn
Jun. Sch.
Front Lawn
Inf. Sch.
Front Lawn
Rec. Grd.
Stockheath
Stockheath
Common
Havant
PO9
Battin's
Copse
Open
Space
Hermitage
Stream
Barncroft
Inf. Sch.
Barncroft
Jun. Sch.
Bedhampton
Trosnant
Jun. & Inf.
Schs.
Playing Fields
Havant
College
Civic
Offices
Leisure Cen.
& Swimming
Pool
Magistrates
Ct.
Adult
Education
Centre
Hook's Lane
Recreation
Ground
St. Thomas More's
R.C. Prim. Sch.
Rugby
Ground
Bidbury
Jun. Sch.
Bidbury
Mead
Rec. Grd.
S.E. Hants
Drama
Centre
Bedhampton
Training
Cen.
Hermitage
Bridge
HAVANT
WAR MEMORIAL
HOSPITAL
Havant
MERIDIAN
CENTRE
Fairfield
Inf. Sch.
Glenhurst
Sch.
Water
Works
THE TANNERIES
INDUSTRIAL ESTATE
Brockhampton
Old Mill
House
Bosmere
Jun. Sch.
Superstore
Council
Depot
Incinerator
HAVANT BUSINESS
CENTRE
Sewage
Works
Recreation
Ground
Forty Acre Farm
Wade
Court
Southbrook
Simond's
Hill
Oaklands R.C.
School
Johnston's
Coppice
Superstore
Hypermarket
LITTLEPARK
WOOD
The
South Downs
College
Roman Villa
(Site of)
Roman Road (course of)
Gundymoor
Wood
Littlepark House
Rec. Grd.
PORTS DOWN
Bevis Grave
CAMP DOWN
Belmont
Castle
HAVANT
RETAIL
PARK
Bowling
Alley
Old Manor
Farm
Waterlooville
PO7
A3(M)
Junction 3
Junc. 4
Junction 5
A3(M) MOTORWAY
HULBERT ROAD
PURBROOK WAY
MIDDLE PARK WAY
PETERSFIELD ROAD
NEW ROAD
BEDHAMPTON ROAD
HAVANT BY-PASS
HARTS FARM WAY
SOLENT ROAD
BEDHAMPTON HILL
PARK ROAD NORTH
PARK ROAD SOUTH
LANGSTONE ROAD
B2150
B2149
B2177
A2030
A27
A3023
69
470
71
72
10
09
08
07
06

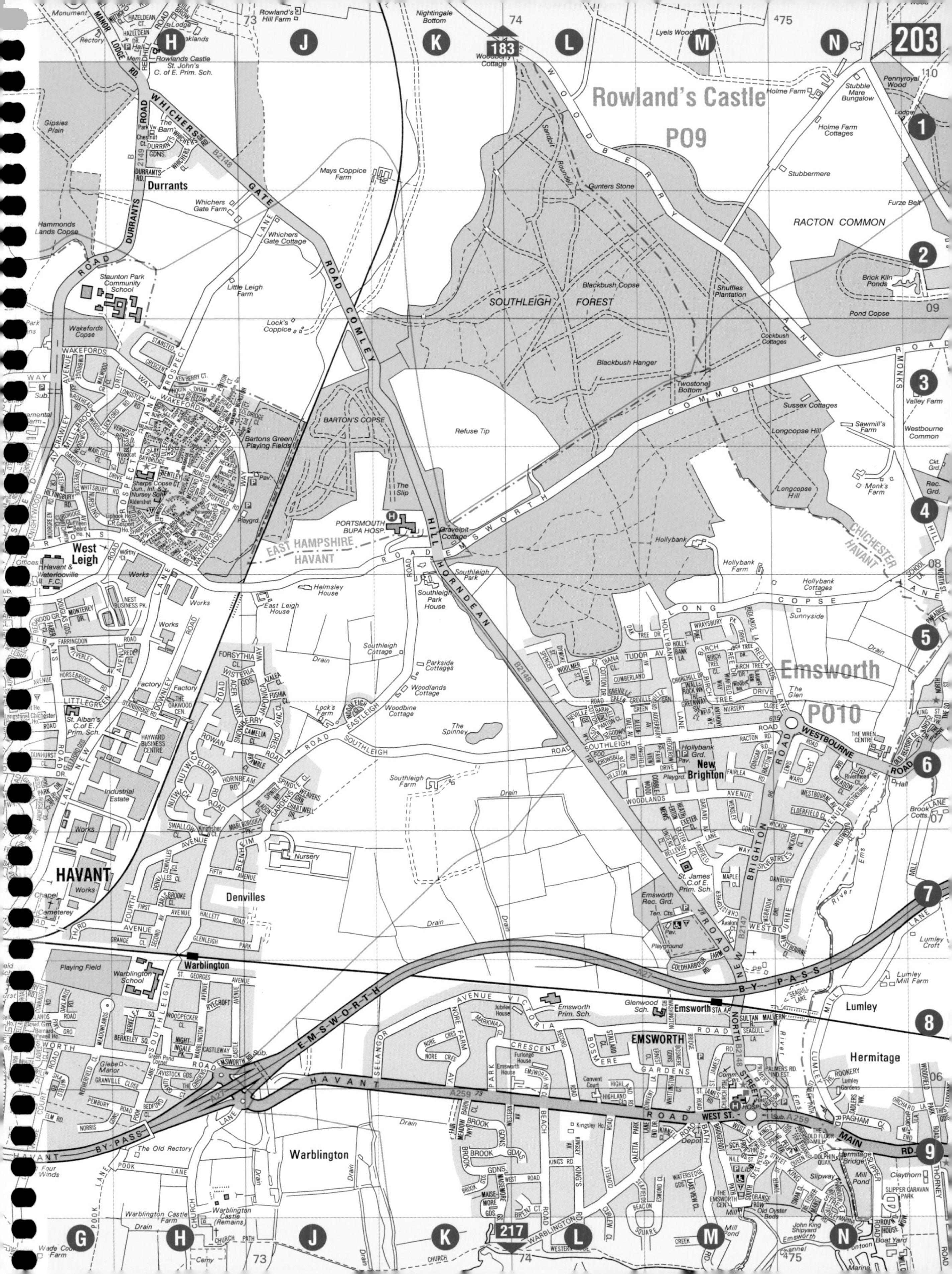
Rowland's Castle
PO9
Emsworth
PO10
HAVANT
West Leigh
Durrants
Denvilles
New Brighton
EMSWORTH
Warblington
Hermitage
Lumley
SOUTHLEIGH FOREST
RACTON COMMON
EAST HAMPSHIRE
HAVANT
CHICHESTER
HAVANT
PORTSMOUTH BUPA HOSP.
Staunton Park Community School
Warblington School
Emsworth Prim. Sch.
St. James' C.of E. Prim. Sch.
St. Alban's C.of E. Prim. Sch.
Refuse Tip
Industrial Estate
HAYWARD BUSINESS CENTRE
Warblington Castle (Remains)
Blackbush Copse
Blackbush Hanger
Gunters Stone
Barton's Copse
Bartons Green Playing Fields
Emsworth Rec. Grd.
Hollybank
Longcopse Hill
Sussex Cottages
Monk's Farm
Pond Copse
Brick Kiln Ponds
183
217
G
H
J
K
L
M
N
1
2
3
4
5
6
7
8
9

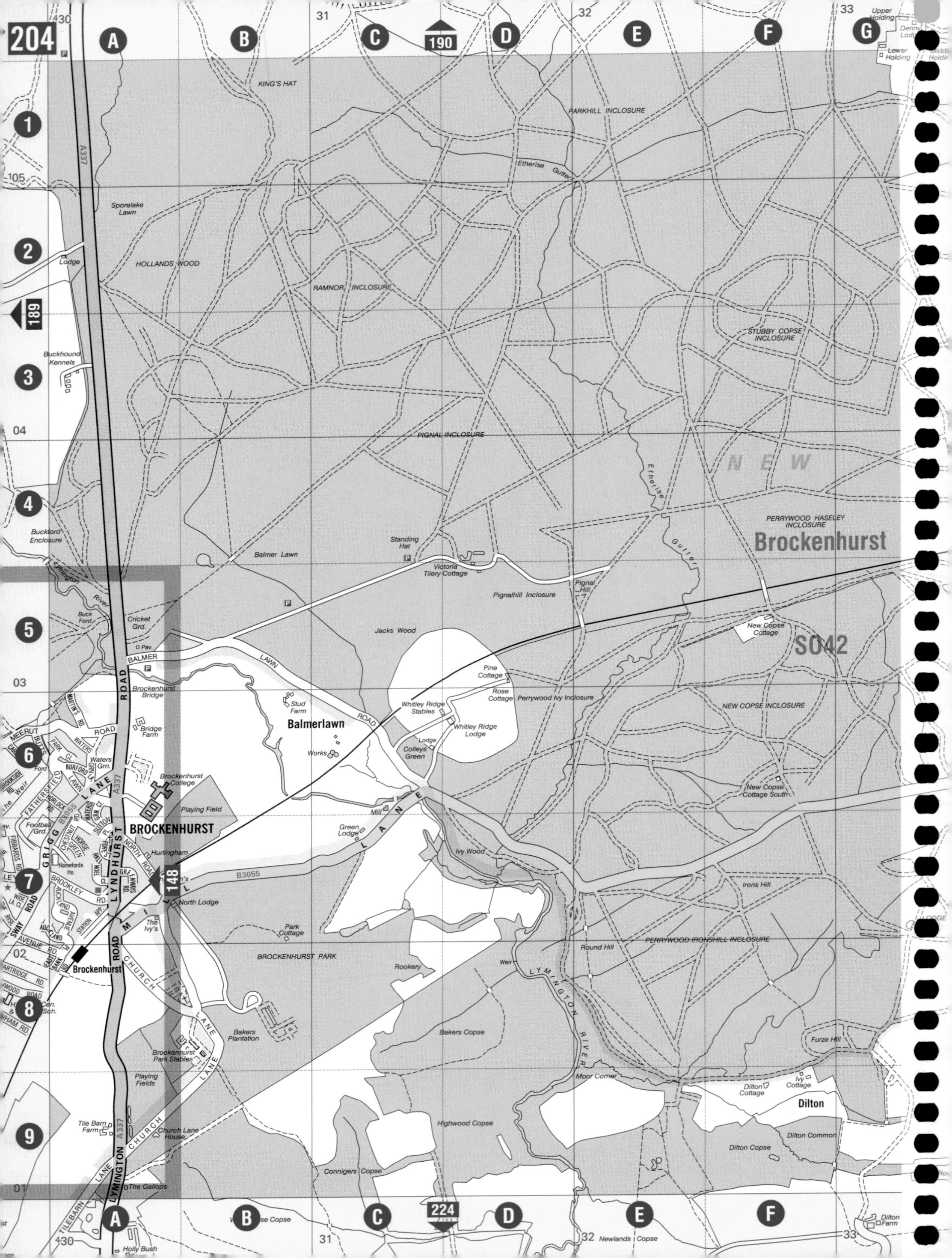
KING'S HAT
PARKHILL INCLOSURE
Etherise Gutter
Sporelake Lawn
HOLLANDS WOOD
RAMNOR INCLOSURE
Lodge
Buckhound Kennels
STUBBY COPSE INCLOSURE
PIGNAL INCLOSURE
NEW
PERRYWOOD HASELEY INCLOSURE
Brockenhurst
Buckford Enclosure
Standing Hat
Balmer Lawn
Victoria Tilery Cottage
Pignal Hill
Pignalhill Inclosure
Lymington River
Buck Ford
Cricket Grd.
Jacks Wood
New Copse Cottage
SO42
Pine Cottage
Rose Cottage
Perrywood Ivy Inclosure
BALMER LAWN ROAD
Brockenhurst Bridge
Stud Farm
Balmerlawn
Whitley Ridge Stables
Whitley Ridge Lodge
NEW COPSE INCLOSURE
Bridge Farm
Waters Grn.
Works
Lodge
Colleys Green
Brockenhurst College
New Copse Cottage South
Playing Field
BROCKENHURST
Mill
Green Lodge
MILL LANE
Ivy Wood
Hurlingham
Homeforde Ho.
B3055
LYNDHURST ROAD
NORTH ROAD
Irons Hill
North Lodge
The Ivy's
Park Cottage
Round Hill
PERRYWOOD IRONSHILL INCLOSURE
Brockenhurst
BROCKENHURST PARK
Rookery
Weir
LYMINGTON RIVER
CHURCH LANE
Bakers Plantation
Bakers Copse
Furze Hill
Brockenhurst Park Stables
Moor Corner
Dilton Cottage
Ivy Cottage
Playing Fields
Dilton
Tile Barn Farm
Church Lane House
Highwood Copse
Dilton Common
Dilton Copse
Connigers Copse
The Gallops
LYMINGTON ROAD
A337
TILEBARN LANE
Newlands Copse
Dilton Farm
Holly Bush
Upper Holding
Lower Holding
MEERUT ROAD
BUTTS
GRIGG LANE
SWAY ROAD
BROOKLEY RD.
Football Grd.
Partridge Rd.
190
189
148
224

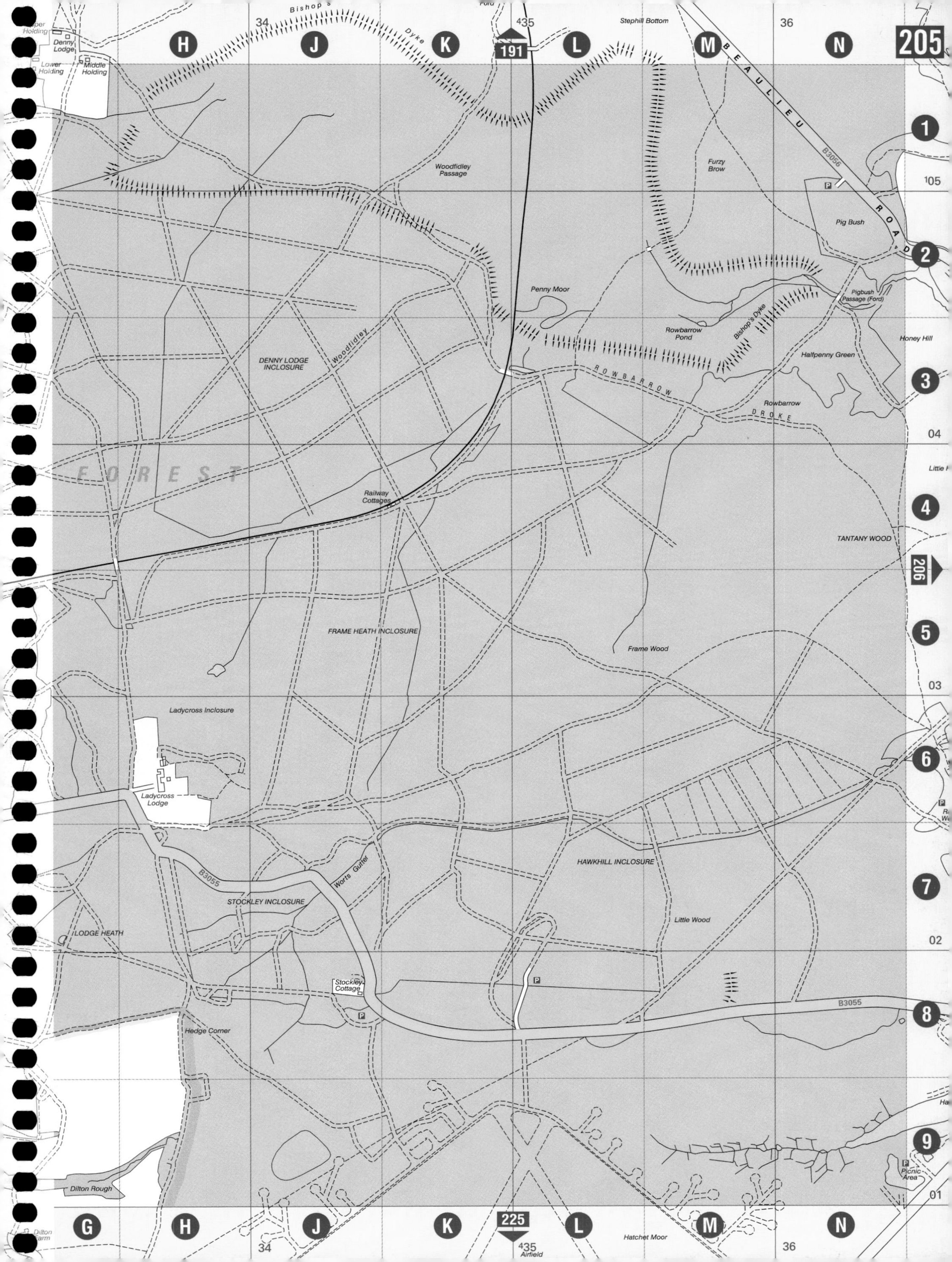

Bishop's Dyke
Denny Lodge
Lower Holding
Middle Holding
Stephill Bottom
BEAULIEU ROAD
B3056
Woodfidley Passage
Furzy Brow
Pig Bush
Penny Moor
Pigbush Passage (Ford)
Rowbarrow Pond
Bishop's Dyke
Honey Hill
Halfpenny Green
DENNY LODGE INCLOSURE
Woodfidley
ROWBARROW
Rowbarrow
DROKE
FOREST
Railway Cottages
TANTANY WOOD
FRAME HEATH INCLOSURE
Frame Wood
Ladycross Inclosure
Ladycross Lodge
HAWKHILL INCLOSURE
B3055
Worts Gutter
STOCKLEY INCLOSURE
LODGE HEATH
Little Wood
Stockley Cottage
B3055
Hedge Corner
Picnic Area
Dilton Rough
Hatchet Moor
Airfield

191
206
225

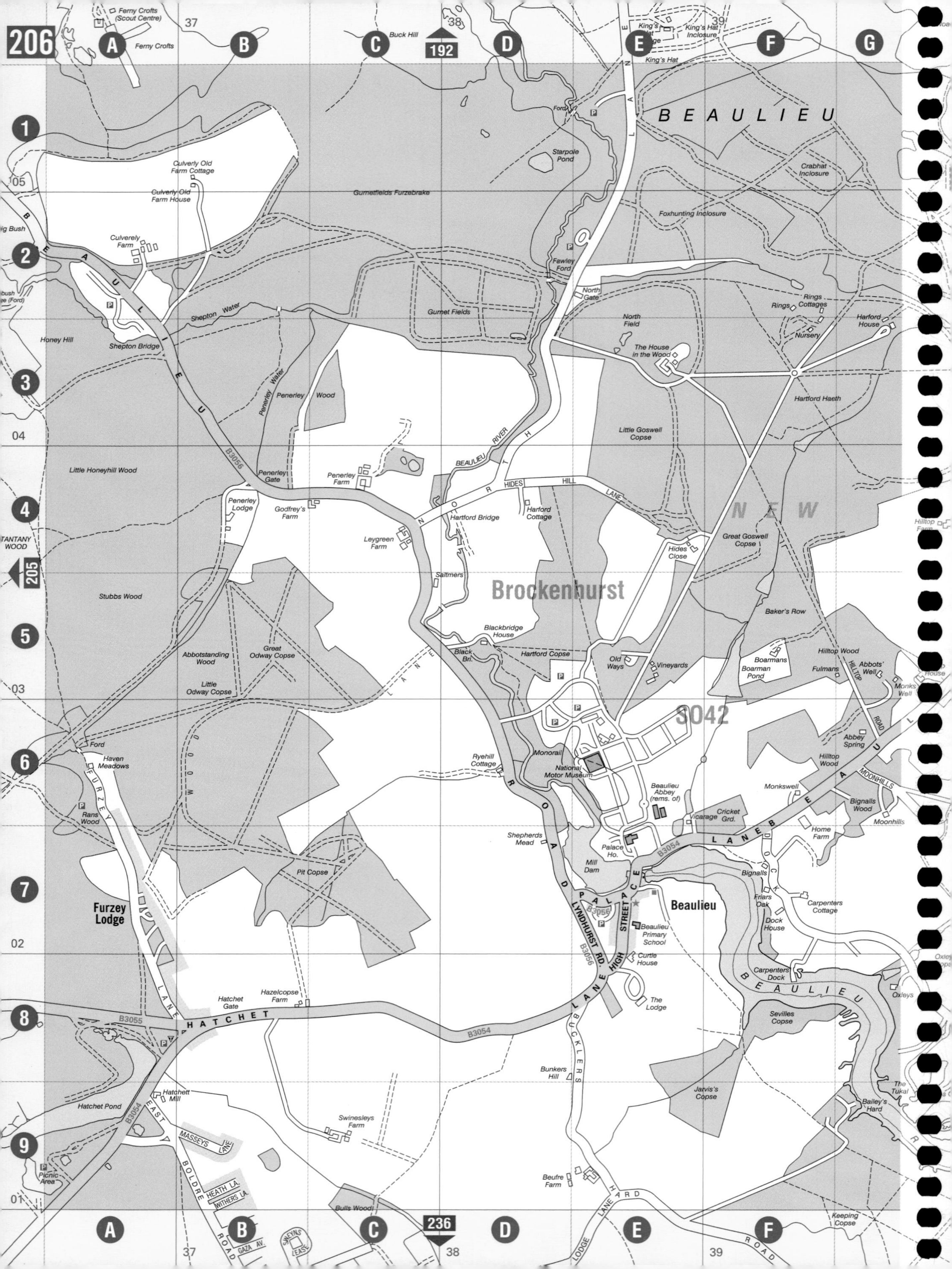

A
B
C
D
E
F
G
192
205
236
37
38
39
05
04
03
02
01
1
2
3
4
5
6
7
8
9
Ferny Crofts (Scout Centre)
Ferny Crofts
Buck Hill
King's Hat Inclosure
King's Hat
BEAULIEU
Culverly Old Farm Cottage
Culverly Old Farm House
Gurnetfields Furzebrake
Starpole Pond
Crabhat Inclosure
Foxhunting Inclosure
Culverely Farm
Honey Hill
Shepton Water
Shepton Bridge
Fawley Ford
North Gate
Gurnet Fields
North Field
The House in the Wood
Rings
Rings Cottages
Nursery
Harford House
Hartford Haeth
Penerley Wood
Penerley Water
B3056
Little Goswell Copse
Little Honeyhill Wood
Penerley Gate
Penerley Farm
BEAULIEU RIVER
HIDES HILL LANE
NORTH
Penerley Lodge
Godfrey's Farm
Hartford Bridge
Harford Cottage
NEW
Great Goswell Copse
Leygreen Farm
Hides Close
Saltmers
Brockenhurst
Stubbs Wood
Baker's Row
Blackbridge House
Abbotstanding Wood
Great Odway Copse
Black Bri.
Hartford Copse
Old Ways
Vineyards
Boarmans
Boarman Pond
Hilltop Wood
Fulmans
Abbots' Well
Monks Well
Little Odway Copse
SO42
Ford
Haven Meadows
FURZEY
Rans Wood
Ryehill Cottage
Monorail
National Motor Museum
Beaulieu Abbey (rems. of)
Abbey Spring
Hilltop Wood
Monkswell
Bignalls Wood
Moonhills
Vicarage
Cricket Grd.
Home Farm
Shepherds Mead
Palace Ho.
B3054
Mill Dam
Pit Copse
Bignalls
Friars Oak
Carpenters Cottage
Furzey Lodge
Beaulieu
Dock House
Beaulieu Primary School
Curtle House
Carpenters Dock
The Lodge
LYNDHURST RD.
HIGH STREET
PALACE
LANE
Hatchet Gate
Hazelcopse Farm
Sevilles Copse
Oxleys
HATCHET
B3055
Bunkers Hill
BUCKLERS
Jarvis's Copse
The Tukal
Bailey's Hard
Hatchett Mill
Hatchet Pond
EAST BOLDRE ROAD
MASSEYS LANE
Swinesleys Farm
Picnic Area
HEATH LA.
WITHERS LA.
Beufre Farm
HARD
LODGE LANE
Bulls Wood
Keeping Copse
GAZA AV.
ROAD
TANTANY WOOD

HEATH
FOREST
FAWLEY INCLOSURE
HYTHE ROAD
HYTHE BY-PASS
A326
B3054
Cole's Hole
Denny Lodge Walk
Nature Reserve
Sports Ground
Football Ground
Club
Res. (Cov.)
Oil Depot
CADLAND RD.
Hardley
HARDLEY INDUSTRIAL ESTATE
CHEVRON BUSINESS PARK
Gravel Pit
Hardley Bridge (Ford)
Depot
LIME KILN LANE ESTATE
LITTLE HOLBURY PARK HOMES
Little Holbury Farmhouse
Little Holbury
Mill Pond
Stonyford Pond
HOLBURY PURLIEU
Pitts Copse Farm
The Warren
Pitts Copse
Dark Water
Heather Hill
Holbury Manor
HOLBURY
Holbury Manor Park
Southampton
SO45
Stonyford Hill Farm
Mount Pleasant Farmhouse
Warren Copse
Ipers Bridge
Ipers Bridge Farm
ROLLESTONE ROAD
Rollestone Farm
Rollestone Copse
GREEN LANE
Green Rollestone Copse
Hilltop Farm
Hilltop Gate
Hill Top
Hilltop House
Monks Well
LEPE ROAD
EXBURY ROAD
Moonhills Gate
Moonhills Copse
Cowleys Heath (Nursery)
Stock Water
Cowleys Copse
Stock Copse
Otterwood Gate
Otterwood
Otterwood Farm
Oxleys Copse
THE HUMMICKS
Oxleys
KINGS COPSE INCLOSURE
East Stock Copse
Stock Bungalow
Cuckoo Pens
Stock Cottages
South Stock Copse
Spearbed Copse
Tarks Reach
Braces Quay
Landing Stage
Landing Stages
The Tukal
RIVER
Sims Wood
Steerleys Copse
Magazine Fields (Nursery)
Meadow Close Copse
Butney Row
Yard Wood
SUMMER LANE
COWLEYS LANE
The Noads
193
236
208
H J K L M N G
1 2 3 4 5 6 7 8 9
440 41 42 43
05 04 03 02 01

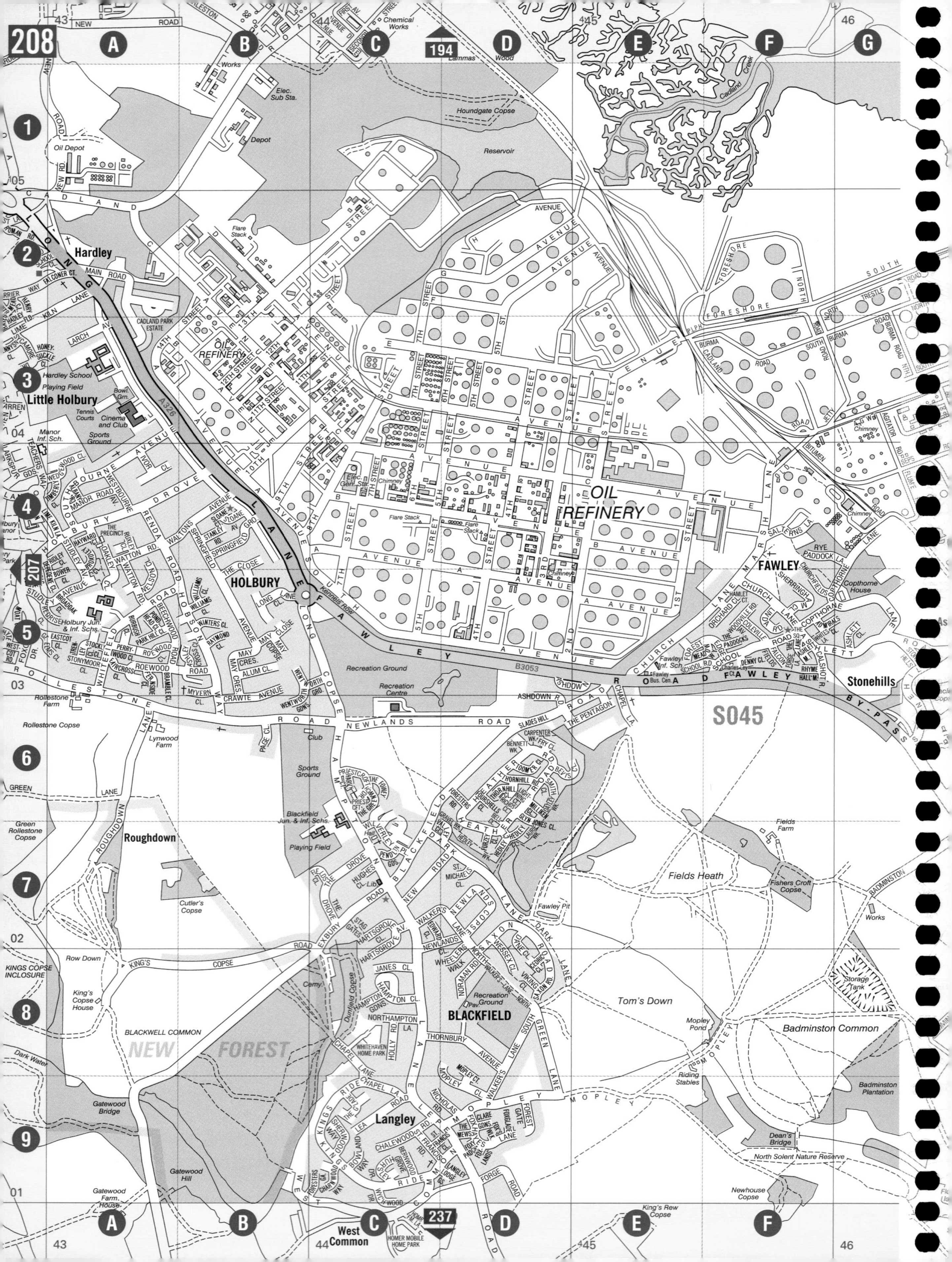

194
207
237
Hardley
Little Holbury
HOLBURY
OIL REFINERY
FAWLEY
Stonehills
S045
Roughdown
BLACKFIELD
Langley
West Common
NEW FOREST
Chemical Works
Works
Elec. Sub Sta.
Lammas Wood
Houndgate Copse
Reservoir
Depot
Oil Depot
Flare Stack
Cadland Creek
CADLAND PARK ESTATE
Hardley School
Playing Field
Tennis Courts
Cinema and Club
Bowl. Grn.
Sports Ground
Manor Inf. Sch.
Holbury Jun. & Inf. Schs.
Recreation Ground
Recreation Centre
Kennels Row
Rollestone Farm
Rollestone Copse
Lynwood Farm
Green Rollestone Copse
Club
Blackfield Jun. & Inf. Schs.
Playing Field
Cutler's Copse
Row Down
KINGS COPSE INCLOSURE
King's Copse House
BLACKWELL COMMON
Dark Water
Gatewood Bridge
Gatewood Hill
Gatewood Farm House
Cemy.
Dunfield Copse
WHITEHAVEN HOME PARK
HOMER MOBILE HOME PARK
Recreation Ground
Fawley Pit
Fields Heath
Fields Farm
Fishers Croft Copse
Works
Tom's Down
Storage Tank
Mopley Pond
Badminston Common
Riding Stables
Badminston Plantation
Dean's Bridge
North Solent Nature Reserve
Newhouse Copse
King's Rew Copse
Copthorne House
Fawley Inf. Sch.
Fawley Bus. Cen.
Chimney
Elec. Gen. Sta.
NEW ROAD
CADLAND ROAD
LONG LANE
A326
FAWLEY ROAD
B3053
FAWLEY BY-PASS
ROLLESTONE ROAD
NEWLANDS ROAD
ASHDOWN ROAD
HAMPTON LANE
BLACKFIELD ROAD
KING'S COPSE ROAD
EXBURY ROAD
LEPE ROAD
MOPLEY
DARK LANE
SOUTH STREET
FORESHORE
BURMA ROAD
MARSH LANE
CHURCH LANE
SCHOOL ROAD
CALSHOT ROAD
DROVE
MAIN ROAD
KILN LANE
LARCH AV.
BOURNE ROAD
RENDA ROAD
SOUTH AVENUE
THE CLOSE
GREEN LANE
ROUGHDOWN LANE
FORGE ROAD
FOREST GATE
CHAPEL LANE
KINGS RIDE
COMMON RIDE
THORNBURY AVENUE
NORTHAMPTON LA.
WALKER'S LANE
NEWLANDS COPSE
43
44
45
46
05
04
03
02
01
A
B
C
D
E
F
G
1
2
3
4
5
6
7
8
9

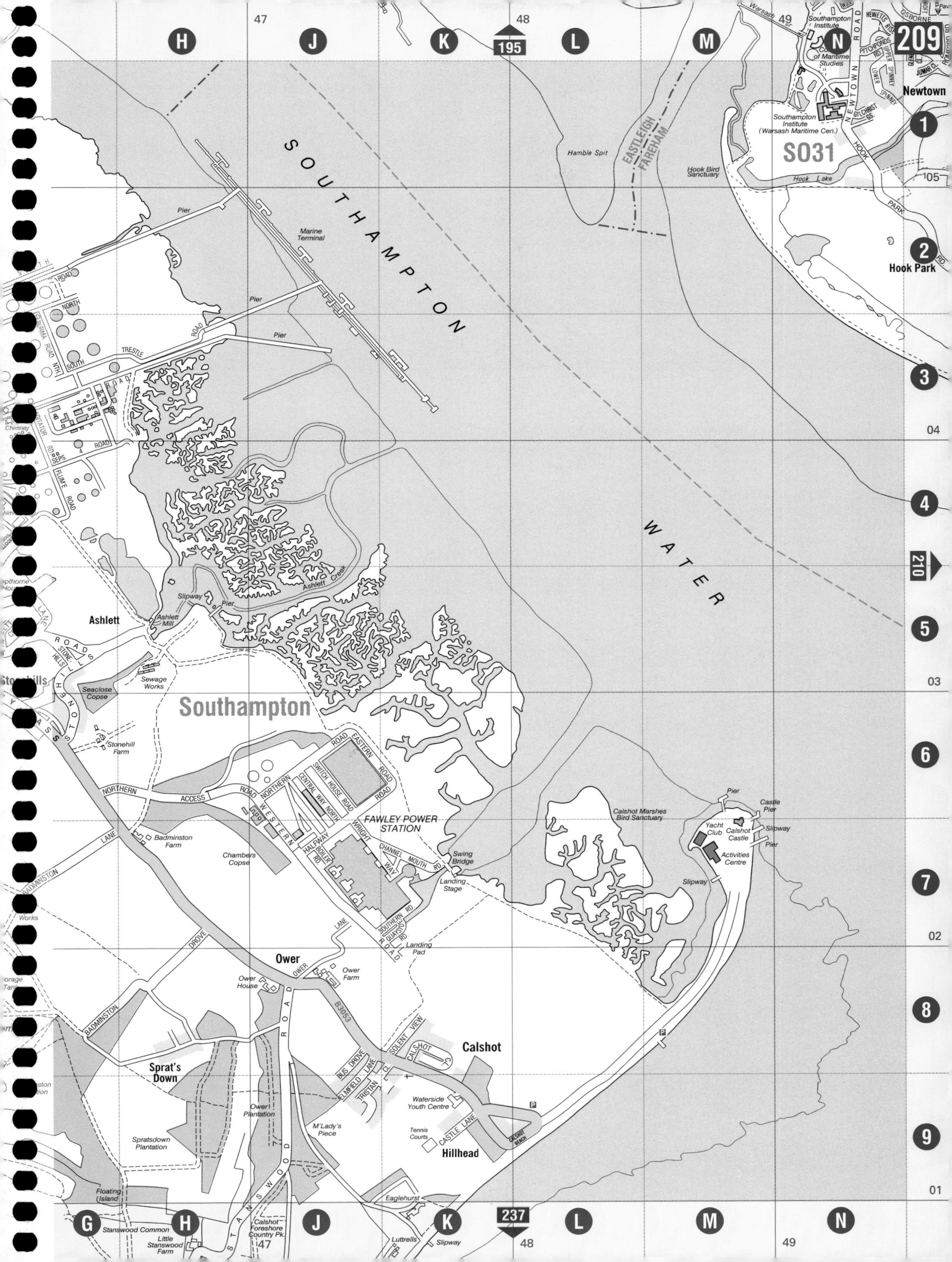

KILN

H 47 **J** **K** 48 195 **L** **M** 49 **N**

Newtown

SOUTHAMPTON

Southampton Institute of Maritime Studies

Southampton Institute (Warsash Maritime Cen.)

SO31

1

Hook Bird Sanctuary

Hamble Spit

EASTLEIGH FAREHAM

Hook Lake

Marine Terminal

Pier

Pier

Pier

2
Hook Park

105

ROAD

3

04

W A T E R

4

210

5

03

Ashlett Creek

Slipway

Pier

Ashlett

Ashlett Mill

Sewage Works

Southampton

Seaclose Copse

Stonehill

Stonehill Farm

ROADS STONE HILLS

NORTHERN ACCESS

NORTHERN ROAD

WESTERN ROAD

EASTERN ROAD

ROAD

SWITCH HOUSE ROAD

CENTRAL WALK NORTH

WRIGHT

FAWLEY POWER STATION

HALFWAY WAY

CHANNEL MOUTH RD.

Swing Bridge

Landing Stage

Calshot Marshes Bird Sanctuary

Pier

Castle Pier

Yacht Club

Calshot Castle

Slipway

Pier

Activities Centre

Slipway

6

02

7

Badminston Farm

Chambers Copse

SOUTHERN LANE

QUAYSIDE RD.

Landing Pad

Ower

Ower Farm

8

BADMINSTON

DROVE

Ower House

ROAD

OWER

B3053

Sprat's Down

Ower Plantation

Spratsdown Plantation

M'Lady's Piece

SOLENT VIEW

CALSHOT

BUS DRIVE

ELMFIELD LANE

TRISTAN

Calshot

Waterside Youth Centre

Tennis Courts

CASTLE LANE

CALSHOT ROAD

9

Floating Island

Stanswood Common

Little Stanswood Farm

STANSWOOD ROAD

Calshot Foreshore Country Pk.

Eaglehurst

Luttrells

Slipway

Hillhead

01

G Stanswood Common **H** 47 **J** **K** 237 48 **L** **M** 49 **N**

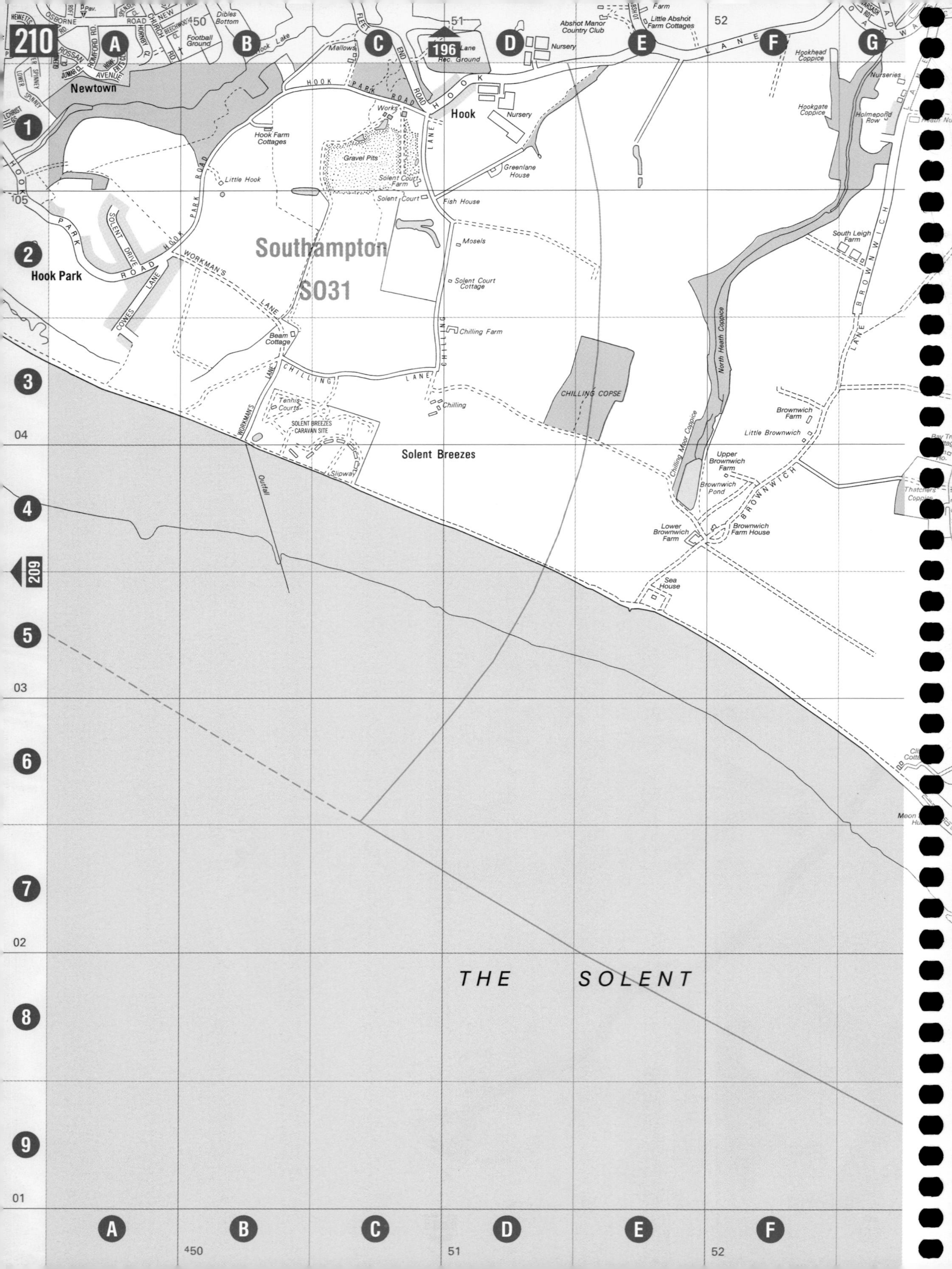

Newtown
Hook Park
Hook
Southampton
SO31
Solent Breezes
THE SOLENT
Hook Lake
Dibles Bottom
Football Ground
Mallows
Works
Gravel Pits
Hook Farm Cottages
Little Hook
Solent Court Farm
Solent Court
Fish House
Mosels
Solent Court Cottage
Chilling Farm
Chilling
Beam Cottage
Tennis Courts
SOLENT BREEZES CARAVAN SITE
Slipway
Outfall
Nursery
Greenlane House
Abshot Manor Country Club
Little Abshot Farm Cottages
Farm
Lane Rec. Ground
CHILLING COPSE
North Heath Coppice
Chilling Moor Coppice
Hookhead Coppice
Hookgate Coppice
Holmepond Row
Nurseries
South Leigh Farm
Brownwich Farm
Little Brownwich
Upper Brownwich Farm
Brownwich Pond
Lower Brownwich Farm
Brownwich Farm House
Sea House
Thatchers Coppice
HOOK PARK ROAD
HOOK LANE
WORKMAN'S LANE
CHILLING LANE
SOLENT DRIVE
COWES LANE
FLEET END ROAD
BROWNWICH LANE
OSBORNE ROAD
ROMFORD RD.
AVENUE
NEW
CHURCH RD.
HORNBY CL.
BEECHWOOD CL.
ROSSAN
JUMAR CL.
LOWER SPINNEY
196
209
450
51
52
105
04
03
02
01
A
B
C
D
E
F
G
1
2
3
4
5
6
7
8
9

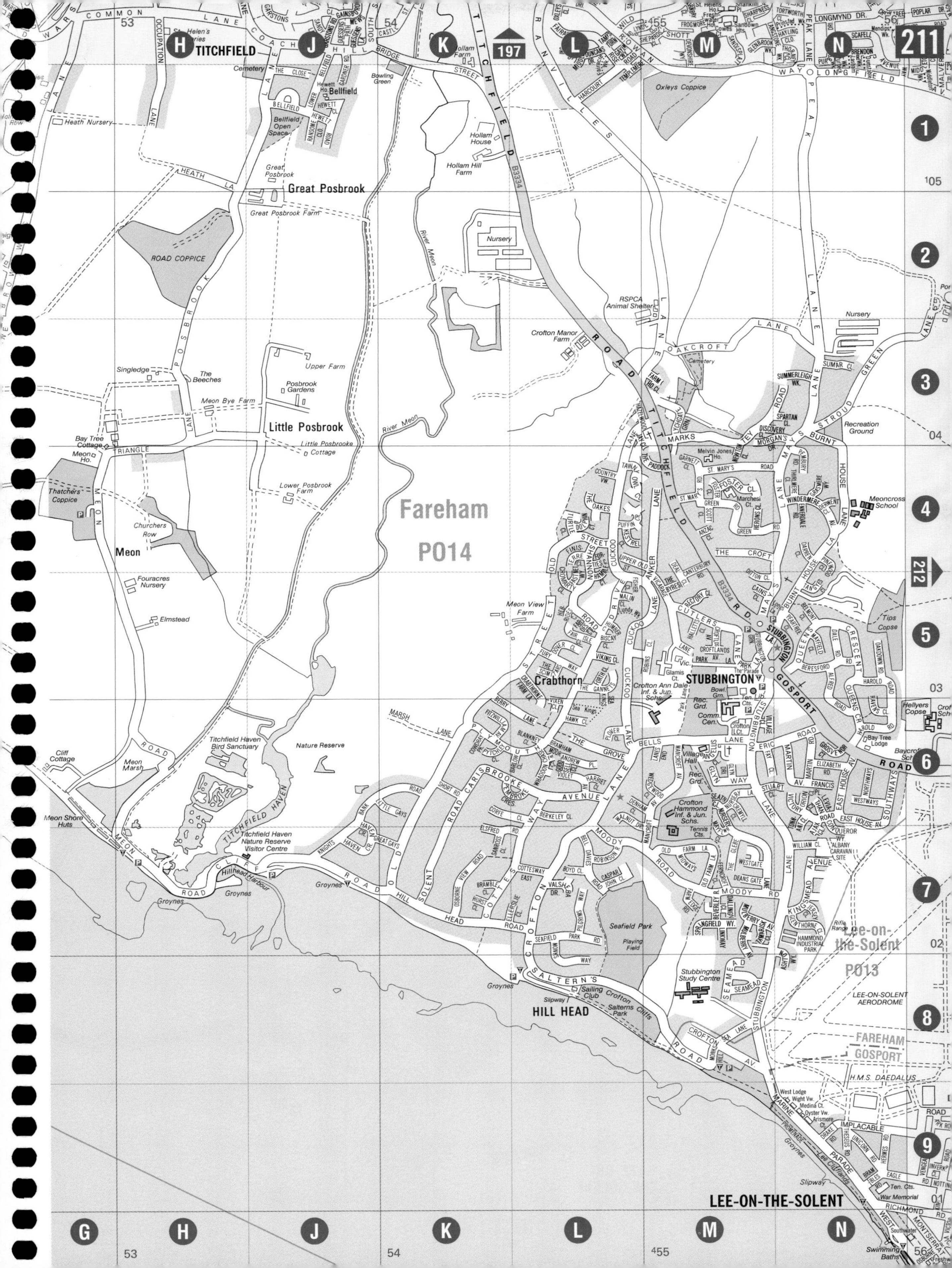

TITCHFIELD
Great Posbrook
Little Posbrook
Meon
Fareham
PO14
Crabthorn
STUBBINGTON
HILL HEAD
LEE-ON-THE-SOLENT
Lee-on-the-Solent
PO13
LEE-ON-SOLENT AERODROME
FAREHAM
GOSPORT
H.M.S. DAEDALUS
ROAD COPPICE
Oxleys Coppice
Titchfield Haven Bird Sanctuary
Nature Reserve
Titchfield Haven Nature Reserve Visitor Centre
Seafield Park
Crofton Cliffs Saltern Park
Stubbington Study Centre
Meoncross School
Recreation Ground
Tips Copse
Hellyers Copse
RSPCA Animal Shelter
Crofton Manor Farm
Holam Hill Farm
Hollam House
Nursery
Upper Farm
Posbrook Gardens
Meon Bye Farm
Great Posbrook Farm
Lower Posbrook Farm
Little Posbrooke Cottage
Thatchers Coppice
Churchers Row
Fouracres Nursery
Elmstead
Meon View Farm
Cliff Cottage
Meon Marsh
Meon Shore Huts
Heath Nursery
Bellfield
Crofton Ann Dale Inf. & Jun. Schs.
Crofton Hammond Inf. & Jun. Schs.
Hammond Industrial Park
Rifle Range
Albany Caravan Site
Sailing Club
Hillhead Harbour
Groynes
Slipway
River Meon
B3334
197
212
G H J K L M N
1 2 3 4 5 6 7 8 9
53 54 455 56
105 04 03 02 01

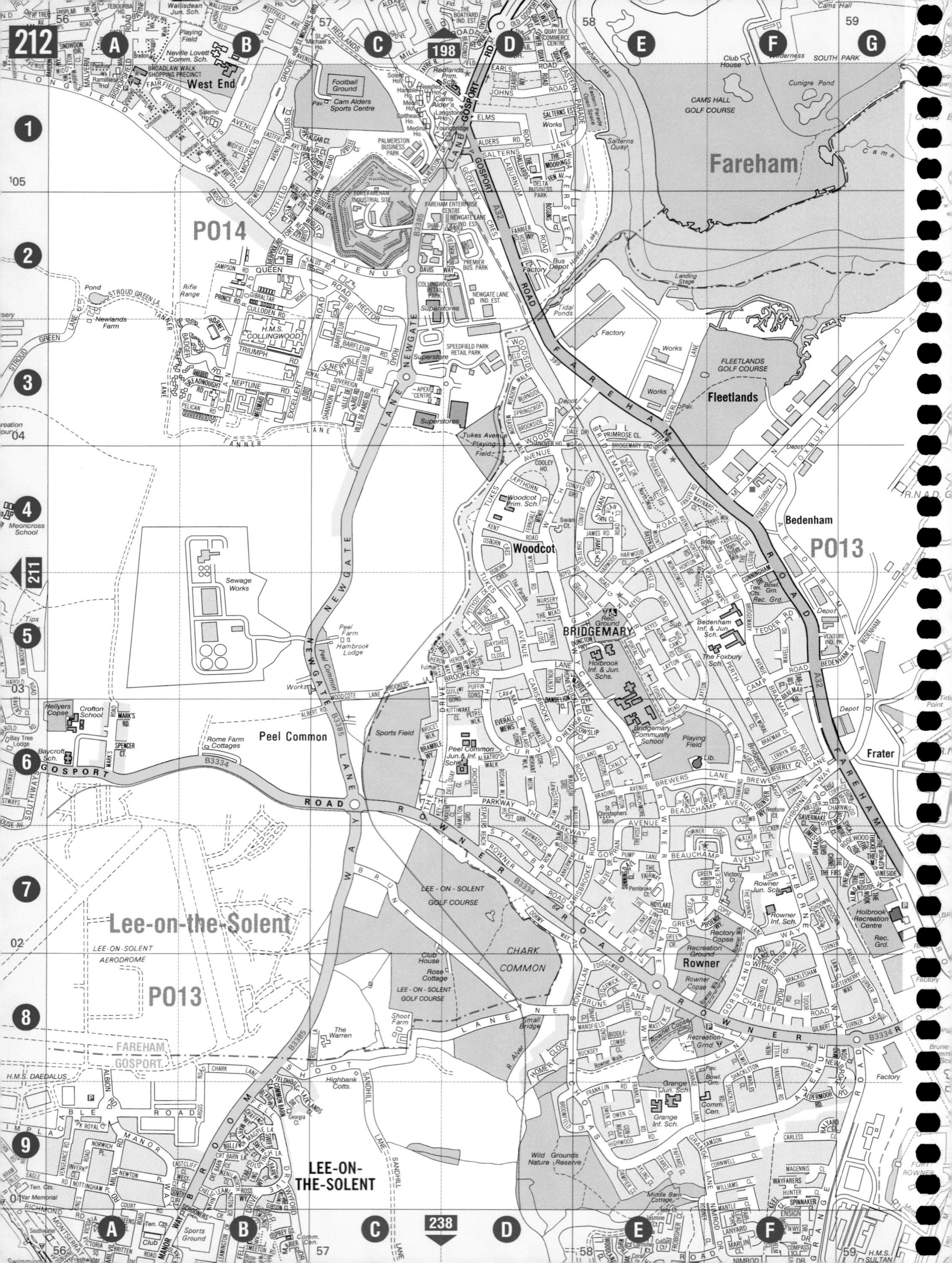
212
198
238
211
Fareham
Fleetlands
Bedenham
Frater
Woodcot
BRIDGEMARY
Rowner
Peel Common
Lee-on-the-Solent
LEE-ON-
THE-SOLENT
West End
PO14
PO13
PO13
CAMS HALL
GOLF COURSE
Cams Hall
SOUTH PARK
Cunigre Pond
Fareham Lake
FLEETLANDS
GOLF COURSE
LEE - ON - SOLENT
GOLF COURSE
CHARK
COMMON
LEE-ON-SOLENT
AERODROME
FAREHAM
GOSPORT
H.M.S. DAEDALUS
H.M.S.
COLLINGWOOD
Sewage
Works
Wild Grounds
Nature Reserve
FORT FAREHAM
INDUSTRIAL SITE
Cam Alders
Sports Centre
Football
Ground
NEWGATE
LANE
GOSPORT
ROAD
FAREHAM
ROAD
ROWNER
ROAD
A32
B3385
B3334
TANNER
LANE
STROUD GREEN LA
Newlands
Farm
Peel
Farm
Hambrook
Lodge
Tukes Avenue
Playing
Field
Woodcot
Prim. Sch.
Holbrook
Inf. & Jun.
Schs.
Bridgemary
Community
School
Bedenham
Inf. & Jun.
Sch.
The Foxbury
Sch.
Peel Common
Jun. & Inf.
Schs.
Rowner
Jun. Sch.
Rowner
Inf. Sch.
Holbrook
Recreation
Centre
Grange
Jun. Sch.
Grange
Inf. Sch.
Crofton
School
Baycroft
Sch.
Superstores
Superstore
Superstores
SPEEDFIELD PARK
RETAIL PARK
COLLINGWOOD
RETAIL
PARK
NEWGATE LANE
IND. EST.
PREMIER
BUS. PARK
PALMERSTON
BUSINESS
PARK
FAREHAM ENTERPRISE
CENTRE
Rifle
Range
Pond
Club
House
Rose
Cottage
Shoot
Farm
The
Warren
Highbank
Cotts.
Rome Farm
Cottages
Sports Field
Recreation
Ground
Rectory
Copse
Rowner
Copse
Factory
Works
Depot
56
57
58
59

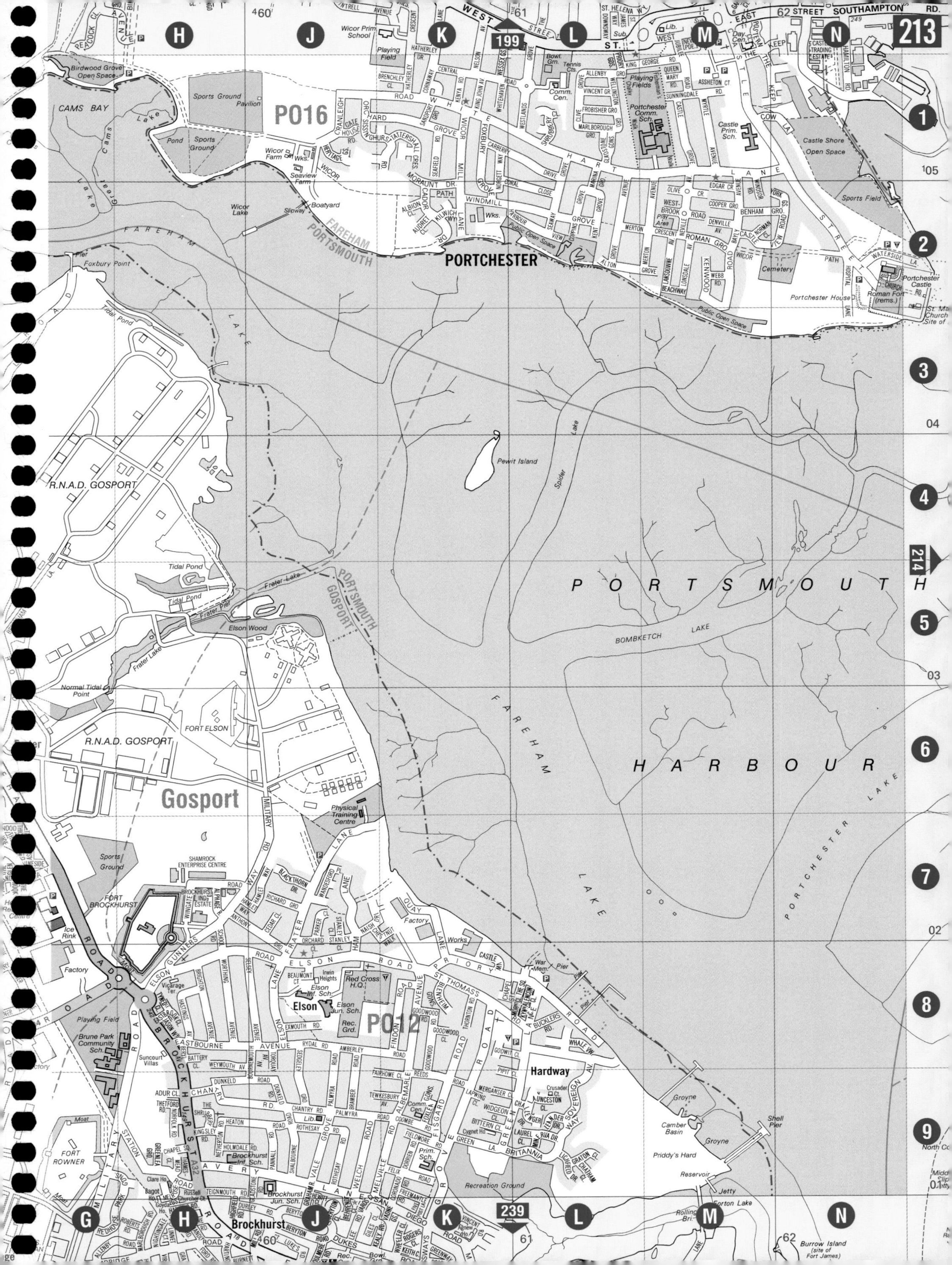
H
J
K
L
M
N
199
WEST STREET
EAST STREET
SOUTHAMPTON RD.
Wicor Prim. School
Playing Field
Birdwood Grove Open Space
CAMS BAY
Sports Ground Pavilion
PO16
Pond
Sports Ground
Wicor Farm
Seaview Farm
Wicor Lake
Slipway
Boatyard
FAREHAM
PORTSMOUTH
PORTCHESTER
Playing Fields
Portchester Comm. Sch.
Castle Prim. Sch.
Castle Shore Open Space
Sports Field
Cemetery
Public Open Space
Portchester House
Portchester Castle
Roman Fort (rems.)
Foxbury Point
Pier
Tidal Pond
R.N.A.D. GOSPORT
Pewit Island
Spider Lake
PORTSMOUTH
HARBOUR
BOMBKETCH LAKE
FAREHAM LAKE
PORTCHESTER LAKE
Frater Lake
Frater Pier
Elson Wood
Normal Tidal Point
FORT ELSON
Gosport
GOSPORT
Physical Training Centre
Sports Ground
SHAMROCK ENTERPRISE CENTRE
FORT BROCKHURST
Ice Rink
Factory
Playing Field
Brune Park Community Sch.
Suncourt Villas
Red Cross H.Q.
Elson
Elson Inf. Sch.
Elson Jun. Sch.
Rec. Grd.
PO12
Hardway
War Mem.
Pier
Groyne
Camber Basin
Priddy's Hard
Reservoir
Jetty
Shell Pier
Recreation Ground
FORT ROWNER
Brockhurst Inf. Sch.
Brockhurst Jun. Sch.
Brockhurst
Forton Lake
Burrow Island (site of Fort James)
239
214
G
1
2
3
4
5
6
7
8
9
105
04
03
02
60
61
62

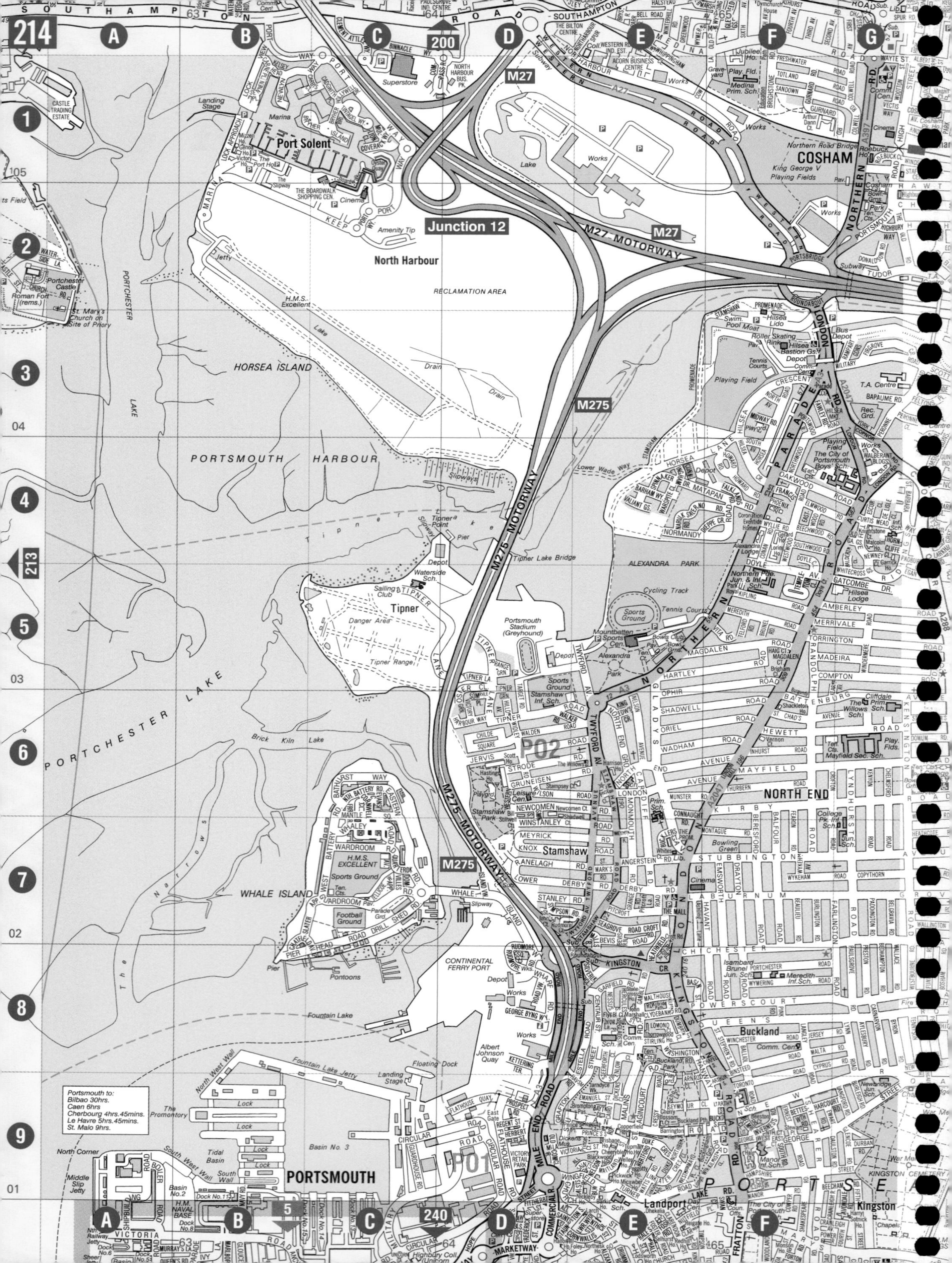
214
SOUTHAMPTON ROAD
200
213
Port Solent
Marina
Landing Stage
THE BOARDWALK SHOPPING CEN.
Junction 12
M27
M27 MOTORWAY
North Harbour
NORTH HARBOUR BUS. PK.
Superstore
Amenity Tip
RECLAMATION AREA
H.M.S. Excellent
COSHAM
King George V Playing Fields
Northern Road Bridge
Portchester Castle
Roman Fort (rems.)
St. Mary's Church on Site of Priory
CASTLE TRADING ESTATE
PORTCHESTER LAKE
HORSEA ISLAND
PORTSMOUTH HARBOUR
Tipner Lake
Tipner Point
Tipner
Tipner Range
Danger Area
Sailing Club
Waterside Sch.
Tipner Lake Bridge
M275
M275 MOTORWAY
Hilsea Lido
Hilsea Bastion
ALEXANDRA PARK
Cycling Track
Sports Ground
Portsmouth Stadium (Greyhound)
Mountbatten Sports Cen.
Alexandra Park
PO2
Stamshaw
Stamshaw Park
NORTH END
Brick Kiln Lake
The Narrows
WHALE ISLAND
H.M.S. EXCELLENT
Sports Ground
Football Ground
CONTINENTAL FERRY PORT
Pontoons
Fountain Lake
Fountain Lake Jetty
Albert Johnson Quay
Floating Dock
Landing Stage
Basin No. 3
Tidal Basin
The Promontory
North Corner
PORTSMOUTH
H.M. NAVAL BASE
PO1
Buckland
Landport
Kingston
PORTSEA
Portsmouth to:
Bilbao 30hrs.
Caen 6hrs
Cherbourg 4hrs.45mins.
Le Havre 5hrs.45mins.
St. Malo 9hrs.
5
240

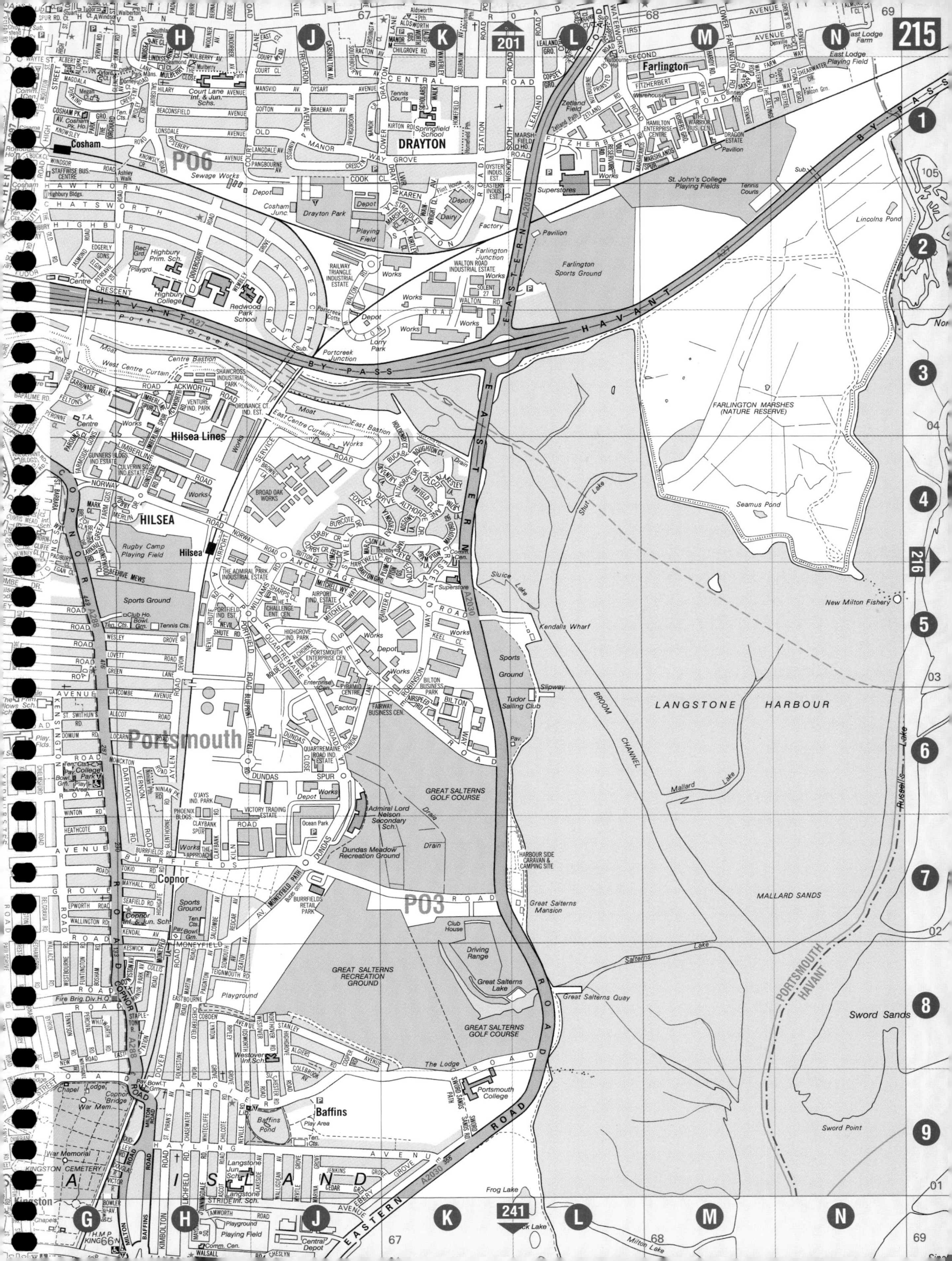

201
241
216
H
J
K
L
M
N
G
1
2
3
4
5
6
7
8
9
66
67
68
69
105
04
03
02
01
Cosham
DRAYTON
Farlington
P06
P03
HILSEA
Hilsea
Hilsea Lines
Copnor
Baffins
Portsmouth
Kingston
HAVANT BY PASS
A27
A2030
A288
EASTERN ROAD
Port Creek
Moat
West Centre Curtain
Centre Bastion
East Centre Curtain
East Bastion
Drayton Park
Playing Field
Sewage Works
Cosham Junc.
Farlington Junction
Portcreek Junction
Railway Triangle Industrial Estate
Walton Road Industrial Estate
Lorry Park
Highbury Prim. Sch.
Highbury College
Redwood Park School
Court Lane Inf. & Jun. Schs.
Springfield School
Zetland Field
Superstores
St. John's College Playing Fields
Farlington Sports Ground
Pavilion
Farlington Marshes (Nature Reserve)
Lincolns Pond
Seamus Pond
New Milton Fishery
East Lodge Farm
East Lodge Playing Field
Hamilton Enterprise Centre
The Warrior Bus. Cen.
Dragon Estate
Shawcross Industrial Park
Venture Ind. Park
Broad Oak Works
Rugby Camp Playing Field
Sports Ground
The Admiral Park Industrial Estate
Airport Ind. Estate
The Challenge Ent. Cen.
Highgrove Ind. Park
Portsmouth Enterprise Cen.
Bilton Business Park
Fairway Business Cen.
Pyramid Centre
Quartremaine Road Ind. Estate
Kendalls Wharf
Tudor Sailing Club
Slipway
LANGSTONE HARBOUR
BROOM CHANNEL
Mallard Lake
Mallard Sands
Great Salterns Golf Course
Admiral Lord Nelson Secondary Sch.
Ocean Park
Victory Trading Estate
O'Jays Ind. Park
Phoenix Bldgs.
Dundas Meadow Recreation Ground
Burrfields Retail Park
Harbour Side Caravan & Camping Site
Great Salterns Mansion
Club House
Driving Range
Great Salterns Recreation Ground
Great Salterns Lake
Great Salterns Quay
Salterns Lake
Russell's Lake
PORTSMOUTH HAVANT
Sword Sands
Sword Point
Playground
Westover Inf. Sch.
The Lodge
Portsmouth College
Baffins Pond
Play Area
Copnor Inf. & Jun. Sch.
Fire Brig. Div. H.Q.
College Park
War Mem.
War Memorial
Kingston Cemetery
Langstone Jun. Sch.
Langstone Inf. Sch.
Playing Field
Central Depot
Frog Lake
Milton Lake
HAYLING ISLAND AVENUE

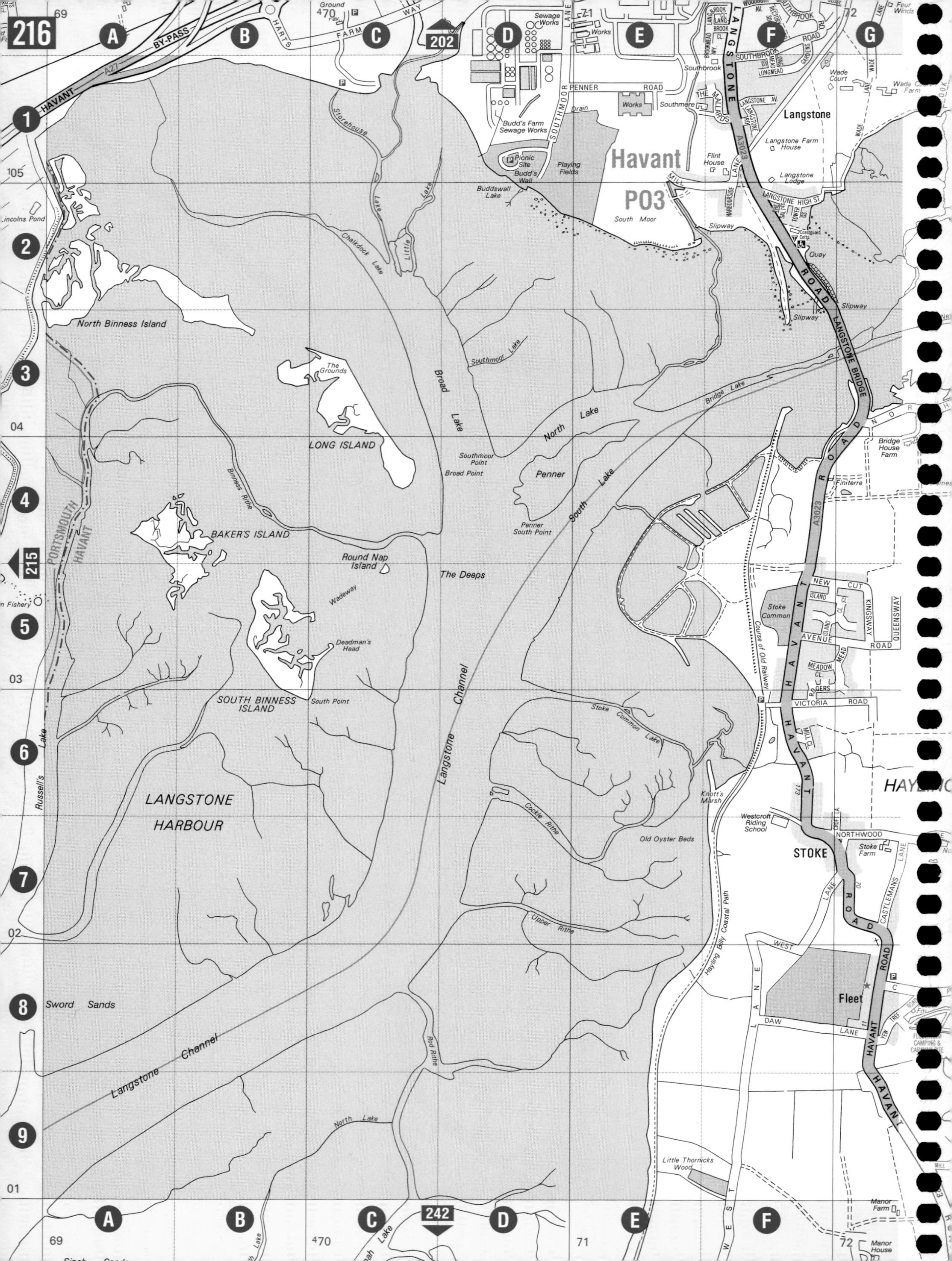

HAVANT BY-PASS
A27
HARTS FARM WAY
Sewage Works
Works
Budd's Farm Sewage Works
SOUTHMOOR LANE
PENNER ROAD
Works
Southbrook
Southmere
Havant
PO3
South Moor
Playing Fields
Picnic Site
Budd's Wall
Buddswall Lake
LANGSTONE
A3023
Langstone
Langstone Farm House
Flint House
Langstone Lodge
LANGSTONE HIGH ST.
Slipway
Quay
LANGSTONE BRIDGE
Wade Court
North Binness Island
Storehouse Lake
Chalkdock Lake
Little Lake
Broad Lake
Southmoor Lake
North Lake
Bridge Lake
The Grounds
LONG ISLAND
Southmoor Point
Broad Point
Penner
Penner South Point
South Lake
Binness Rithe
BAKER'S ISLAND
Round Nap Island
The Deeps
Wadeway
Deadman's Head
SOUTH BINNESS ISLAND
South Point
PORTSMOUTH
HAVANT
Russell's Lake
LANGSTONE HARBOUR
Langstone Channel
Stoke Common Lake
Cockle Rithe
Upper Rithe
Old Oyster Beds
Knott's Marsh
Course of Old Railway
Hayling Billy Coastal Path
Bridge House Farm
Finiterre
Stoke Common
NEW CUT
ISLAND
AVENUE
KINGSWAY
QUEENSWAY
ROAD
MEADOW CL.
VICTORIA ROAD
HAVANT ROAD
Westcroft Riding School
NORTHWOOD
STOKE
Stoke Farm
CASTLEMANS LANE
WEST LANE
Fleet
DAW LANE
Sword Sands
Rod Rithe
North Lake
Little Thornicks Wood
Manor Farm
Manor House
HAYLING
Lincolns Pond
A B C D E F G
1 2 3 4 5 6 7 8 9
69 470 71 72
105 04 03 02 01

202
215
242

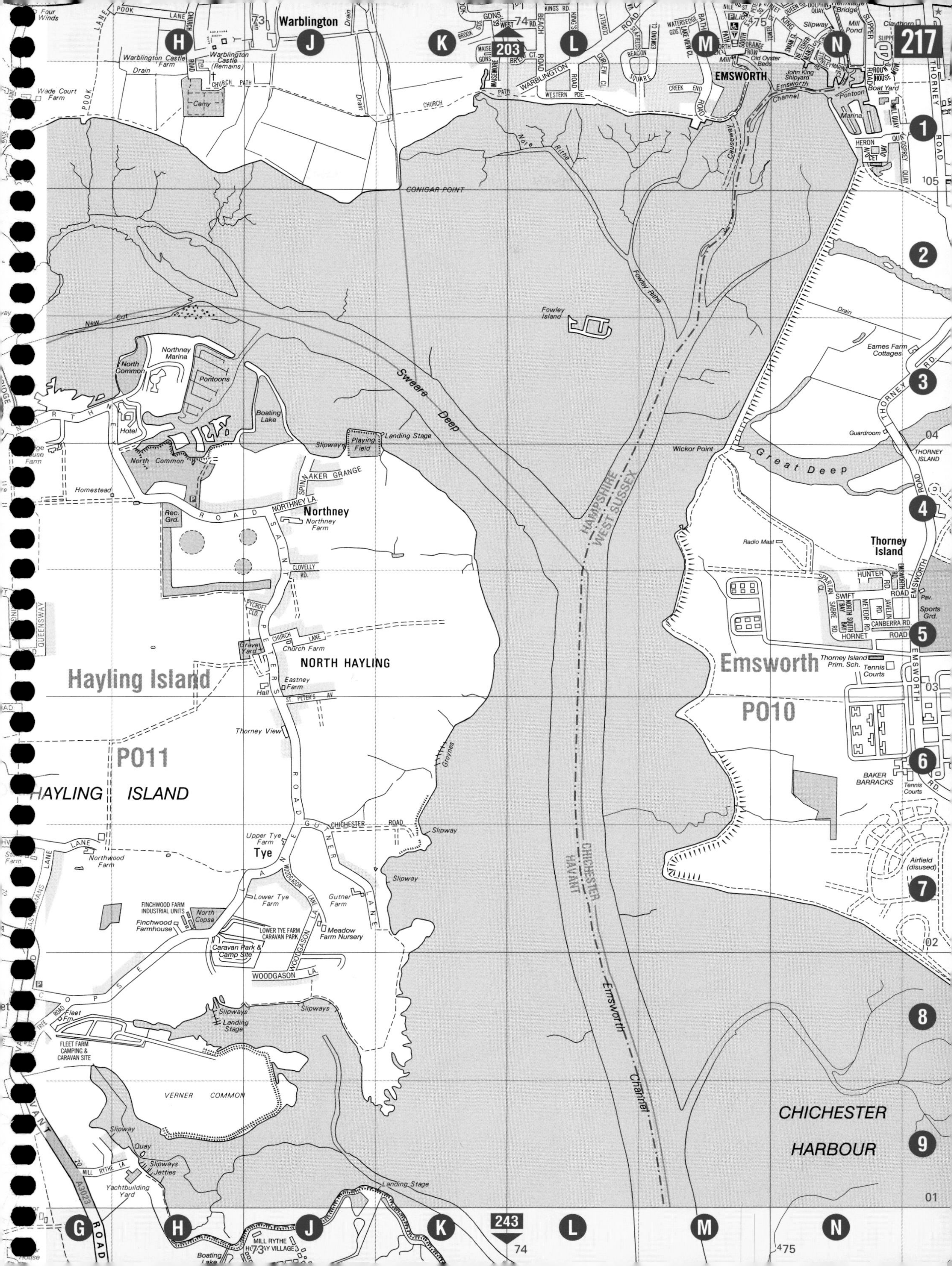

Warblington

Emsworth

Thorney
Island

Emsworth

PO10

Hayling Island

PO11

HAYLING ISLAND

Tye

North Hayling

Northney

CHICHESTER

HARBOUR

MATCHAM'S PARK
High Harbour
Ringwood Racecourse
FOXBURY ROAD
Test Track
Foxbury Hill
Pumping Station
Week Wood
BARNSFIELD HEATH
HEATH ROAD
WEST HEATH ROAD
WATERMAIN ROAD
HURN FOREST
Fir Grove Farm
Week Farm
EAST DORSET
CHRISTCHURCH
Christchurch
Week Common
BH23
Longfield
Caravan Site
Bostwick Farm
Fir Grove Copse
Keys Copse
Moors River
Barnfield Heath
Ebley
Caravan Site
Christchurch Ski Centre
Kellsacre
PLANTATION
EAST
HORNS ROAD
A338
HGV Training Centre
PORT VIEW CARAVAN PARK
Tory's Fire
Fillybrook
Avon Common
Ventura
The Mount
MOUNT PLEASANT CAMPING PARK
ENTERPRISE WAY
Works
Tank
Rifle Range
NORTH EAST INDUSTRIAL AREA
AVIATION PARK
Flying Club
Causeway
NORTH WEST INDUSTRIAL AREA
AVIATION PARK WEST
Pithouse Copse
Refuse Plant
Sewage Works
BOURNEMOUTH INTERNATIONAL AIRPORT
Bournemouth Aviation Mus.
SOUTH EAST SECTOR
East Parley
Control Tower
Troublefield Cottage
Troublefield Copse
Government Offices
PITHOUSE LANE
Airport Terminal
PUSSEX
Sopley Common
(Nature Reserve)
CAUSEWAY
Dudmoor Farm
PARLEY LANE
B3073
PARLEY GOLF COURSE & DRIVING RANGE
Alice in Wonderland Family Park
College of Air Traffic Control
MERRITOWN LA.
Merritown Farm
Merritown
MOORS CLOSE
MATCHAMS LANE
Hurn
Club House
Bounds Farm
Merritown Copse
DALES LANE
Dales House
HURN COURT LANE
Humbridge Farm
Sewage Works
Hurn Br.
AVON
Football Pitch
Hurn Bridge Sports Club
Cricket Grd.
Brickfield Cottage
Bournemouth
BH8
Hillside Cotts
West Hurn
MILL LANE
CHRISTCHURCH ROAD
Berry Hill Purification Works
Hurn Court Farm
Mill Copse
Home Farm
Ramsdown Plantation
Rams Down
Berry Hill
HURN COURT LANE
Park Cottages
Berry Hill

186
228

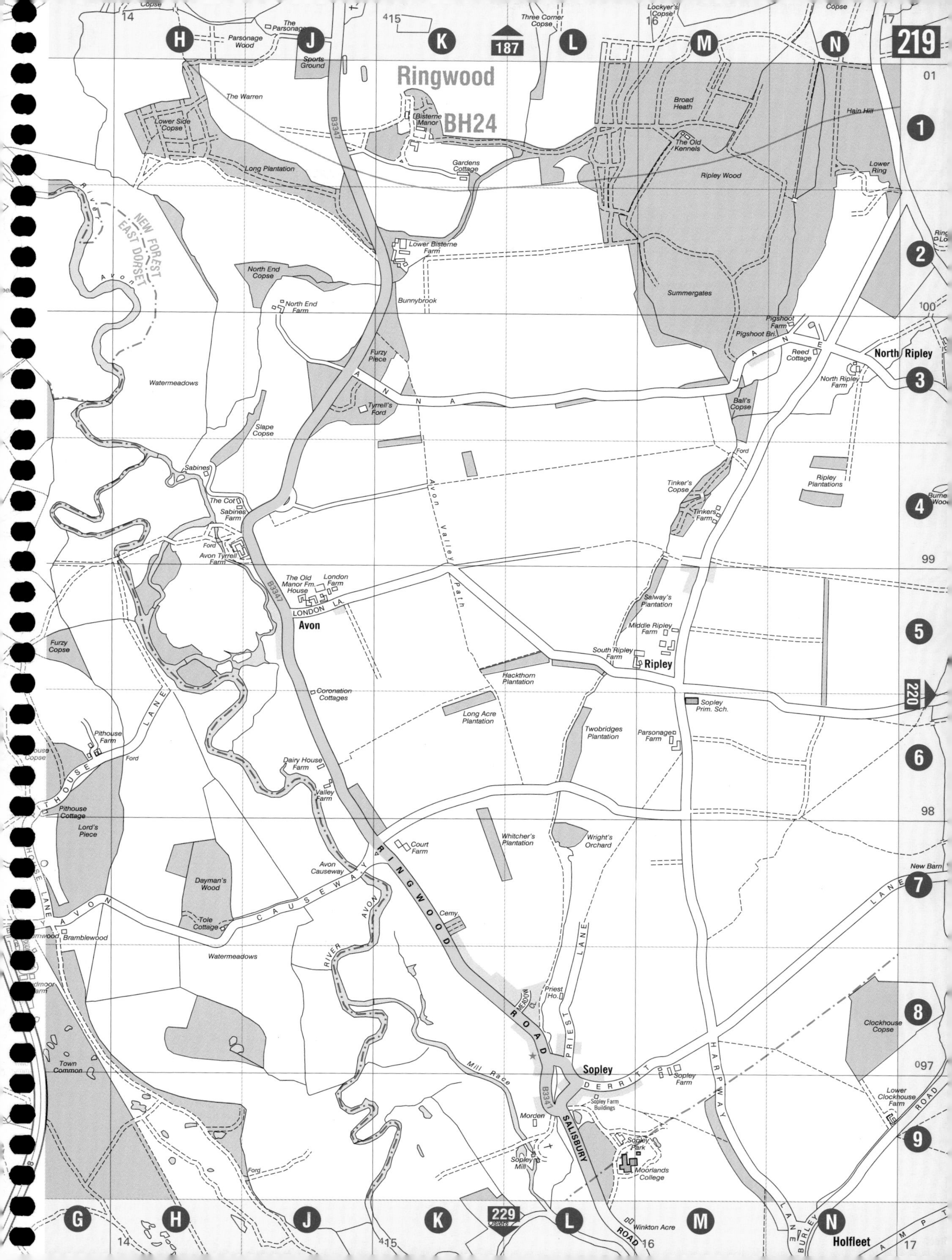
Ringwood
BH24
The Parsonage
Parsonage Wood
Sports Ground
Three Corner Copse
Lockyer's Copse
187
The Warren
Lower Side Copse
Bisterne Manor
Broad Heath
Hain Hill
The Old Kennels
Long Plantation
Gardens Cottage
Ripley Wood
Lower Ring
NEW FOREST
EAST DORSET
River Avon
Lower Bisterne Farm
North End Copse
Bunnybrook
Summergates
North End Farm
Pigshoot Farm
Pigshoot Bri.
Furzy Piece
Reed Cottage
North Ripley
North Ripley Farm
Watermeadows
Tyrrell's Ford
Ball's Copse
Slape Copse
Ford
Ripley Plantations
Sabines
Tinker's Copse
The Cot
Sabines Farm
Tinkers Farm
Avon Valley Path
Avon Tyrrell Farm
The Old Manor Fm. House
London Farm
B3347
LONDON LA.
Salway's Plantation
Avon
Middle Ripley Farm
Furzy Copse
South Ripley Farm
Ripley
Hackthorn Plantation
Coronation Cottages
Sopley Prim. Sch.
220
Long Acre Plantation
Pithouse Farm
Twobridges Plantation
Parsonage Farm
Dairy House Farm
Valley Farm
Pithouse Cottage
Lord's Piece
Court Farm
Whitcher's Plantation
Wright's Orchard
Avon Causeway
Dayman's Wood
New Barn
Cemy.
Tole Cottage
Bramblewood
Watermeadows
RINGWOOD ROAD
AVON CAUSEWAY
PRIEST LANE
Priest Ho.
MEADOW
Clockhouse Copse
Town Common
Mill Race
Sopley
DERRITT LANE
Sopley Farm
HARPWAY
Lower Clockhouse Farm
Sopley Farm Buildings
Morden
SALISBURY ROAD
Sopley Park
Sopley Mill
Moorlands College
Ford
229
Osiers
Winkton Acre
Holfleet
BURLEY LANE
G H J K L M N
14
415
16
17
01
100
99
98
097
1 2 3 4 5 6 7 8 9

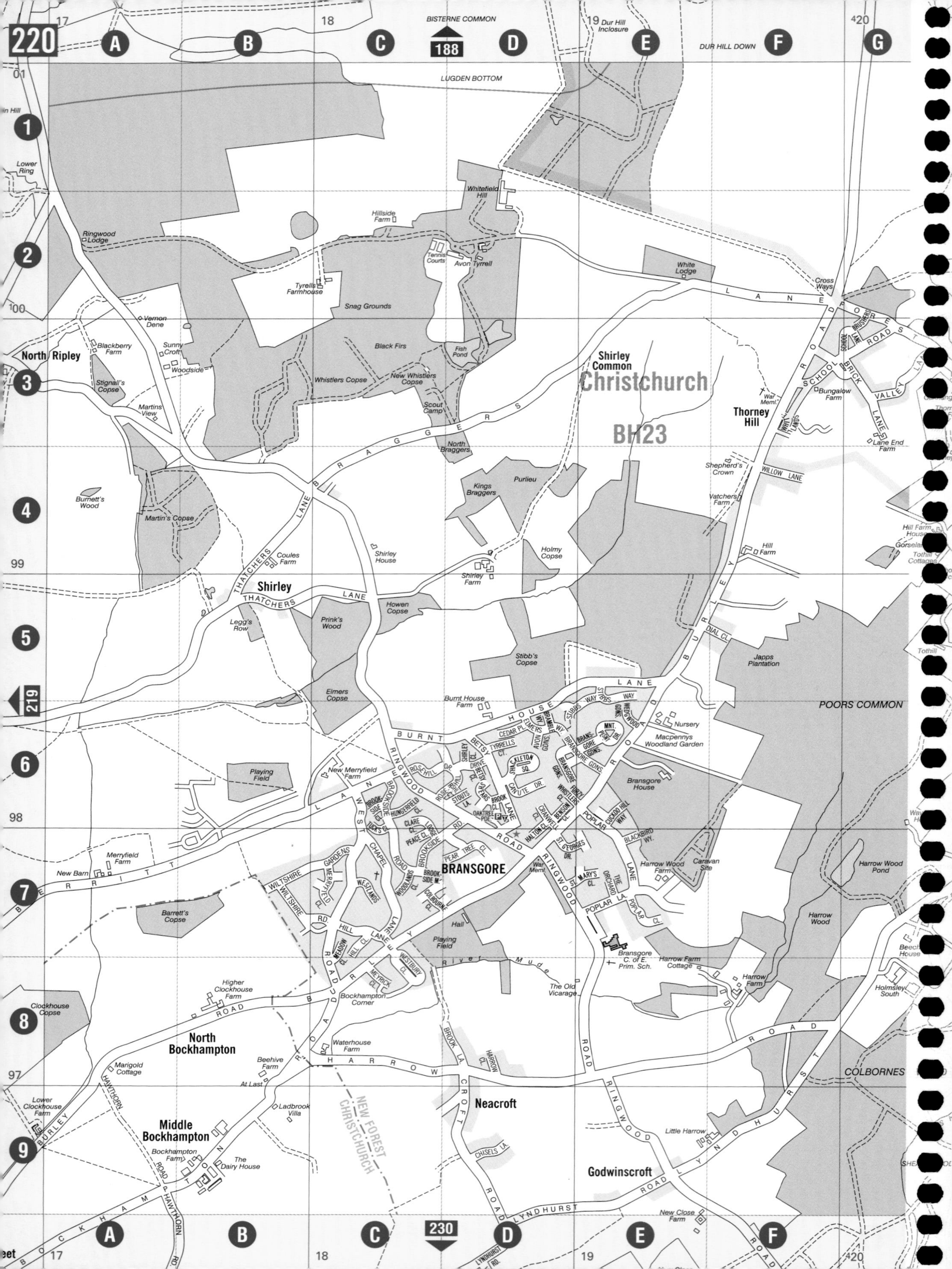
BISTERNE COMMON
188
Dur Hill Inclosure
DUR HILL DOWN
LUGDEN BOTTOM
Lower Ring
Whitefield Hill
Hillside Farm
Ringwood Lodge
Tennis Courts
Avon Tyrrell
White Lodge
Cross Ways
Tyrells Farmhouse
Snag Grounds
Vernon Dene
Blackberry Farm
Sunny Croft
Woodside
Black Firs
Fish Pond
North Ripley
Stignall's Copse
Whistlers Copse
New Whistlers Copse
Scout Camp
Shirley Common
Christchurch
BH23
Bungalow Farm
Thorney Hill
War Meml.
Martins View
North Braggers
Lane End Farm
Shepherd's Crown
Kings Braggers
Purlieu
Burnett's Wood
Martin's Copse
Vatchers Farm
Hill Farm House
Holmy Copse
Shirley House
Coules Farm
Hill Farm
Shirley Farm
Shirley
Howen Copse
Legg's Row
Prink's Wood
Stibb's Copse
Japps Plantation
Elmers Copse
219
Burnt House Farm
POORS COMMON
Nursery
Macpennys Woodland Garden
Playing Field
New Merryfield Farm
Bransgore House
Merryfield Farm
New Barn
BRANSGORE
War Meml.
Harrow Wood Farm
Caravan Site
Harrow Wood Pond
Barrett's Copse
Harrow Wood
Hall
Playing Field
River Mude
Bransgore C. of E. Prim. Sch.
Harrow Farm Cottage
Harrow Farm
The Old Vicarage
Higher Clockhouse Farm
Bockhampton Corner
Clockhouse Copse
Holmsley South
North Bockhampton
Waterhouse Farm
Beehive Farm
Marigold Cottage
At Last
COLBORNES
Lower Clockhouse Farm
Ladbrook Villa
Neacroft
NEW FOREST
CHRISTCHURCH
Middle Bockhampton
Little Harrow
Bockhampton Farm
The Dairy House
Godwinscroft
New Close Farm
230

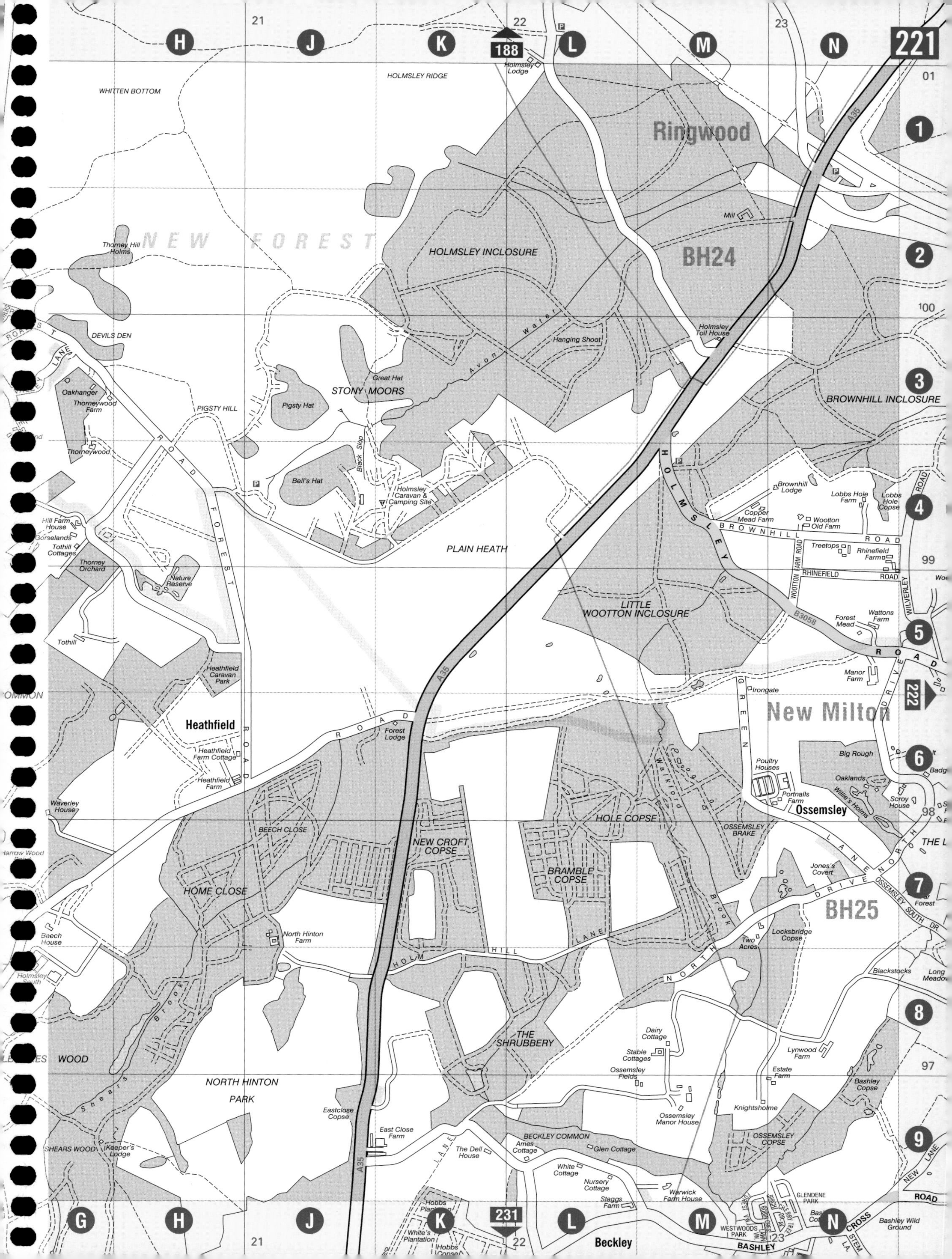
Ringwood
BH24
NEW FOREST
HOLMSLEY INCLOSURE
HOLMSLEY RIDGE
WHITTEN BOTTOM
Holmsley Lodge
Thorney Hill Holms
DEVILS DEN
Oakhanger
Thorneywood Farm
Thorneywood
PIGSTY HILL
Pigsty Hat
STONY MOORS
Great Hat
Bell's Hat
Black Slop
Holmsley Caravan & Camping Site
Avon Water
Hanging Shoot
Mill
Holmsley Toll House
BROWNHILL INCLOSURE
Brownhill Lodge
Copper Mead Farm
Wootton Old Farm
Lobbs Hole Farm
Lobbs Hole Copse
BROWNHILL ROAD
Treetops
Rhinefield Farm
RHINEFIELD ROAD
WOOTTON FARM ROAD
WILVERLEY ROAD
HOLMSLEY ROAD
B3058
PLAIN HEATH
LITTLE WOOTTON INCLOSURE
Forest Mead
Wattons Farm
Manor Farm
Irongate
New Milton
Hill Farm House
Gorselands
Tothill Cottages
Thorney Orchard
Nature Reserve
FOREST ROAD
Tothill
Heathfield Caravan Park
Heathfield
Heathfield Farm Cottage
Heathfield Farm
Forest Lodge
A35
Waverley House
Big Rough
Oaklands
Scroy House
Willie's Holms
Poultry Houses
Portnalls Farm
Ossemsley
OSSEMSLEY BRAKE
HOLE COPSE
Walkford Brook
GREEN LANE
NEW CROFT COPSE
BRAMBLE COPSE
BEECH CLOSE
HOME CLOSE
Jones's Covert
OSSEMSLEY NORTH DRIVE
OSSEMSLEY SOUTH DR
BH25
Beech House
North Hinton Farm
HOLM HILL LANE
NORTH LANE
Two Acres
Locksbridge Copse
Holmsley South
Blackstocks
Long Meadow
THE SHRUBBERY
Dairy Cottage
Stable Cottages
Ossemsley Fields
Estate Farm
Lynwood Farm
Bashley Copse
WOOD
NORTH HINTON PARK
Shears Brook
SHEARS WOOD
Keeper's Lodge
Eastclose Copse
East Close Farm
BECKLEY COMMON
Ames Cottage
The Dell House
Glen Cottage
Knightsholme
Ossemsley Manor House
OSSEMSLEY COPSE
White Cottage
Nursery Cottage
Staggs Farm
Warwick Farm House
GLENDENE PARK
Hobbs Plantation
White's Plantation
Hobbs Copse
Beckley
WESTWOODS PARK
BASHLEY
BASHLEY CROSS ROAD
Bashley Wild Ground
NEW LANE
188
231
222
H J K L M N G
21 22 23
01 100 99 98 97
1 2 3 4 5 6 7 8 9

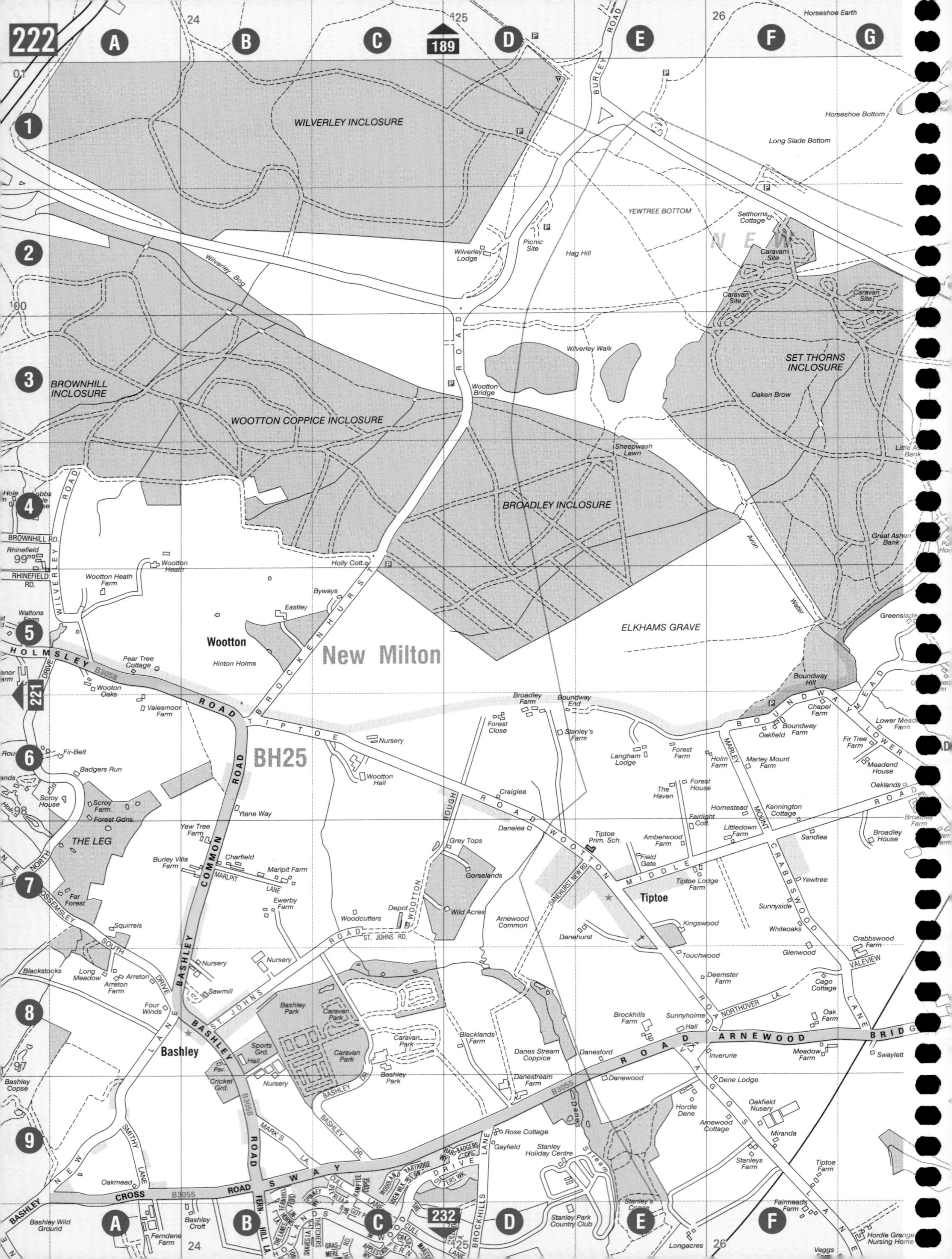
A
B
C
D
E
F
G
189
24
425
26
01
100
99
98
97
1
2
3
4
5
6
7
8
9
221
232
25
Horseshoe Earth
Horseshoe Bottom
Long Slade Bottom
BURLEY ROAD
WILVERLEY INCLOSURE
YEWTREE BOTTOM
Setthorns Cottage
Caravan Site
Wilverley Lodge
Picnic Site
Hag Hill
Wilverley Bog
ROAD
Wilverley Walk
SET THORNS INCLOSURE
Oaken Brow
BROWNHILL INCLOSURE
Wootton Bridge
WOOTTON COPPICE INCLOSURE
Sheepwash Lawn
BROADLEY INCLOSURE
Great Ashen Bank
Avon Water
BROWNHILL RD.
Rhinefield
RHINEFIELD RD.
WILVERLEY ROAD
Wootton Heath
Wootton Heath Farm
Holly Cott.
Byways
Eastley
BROCKENHURST
ELKHAMS GRAVE
Greenslade
Wattons Farm
Wootton
Hinton Holms
New Milton
HOLMSLEY DRIVE
Pear Tree Cottage
B3058
Wooton Oaks
Valesmoor Farm
ROAD
TIPTOE
Boundway Hill
Broadley Farm
Boundway End
Forest Close
Stanley's Farm
BOUNDWAY
Chapel Farm
Boundway Farm
Oakfield
Fir Tree Farm
Lower Mead Farm
LOWER MEAD
Nursery
BH25
Fir-Belt
Badgers Run
Scroy House
Scroy Farm
Forest Gdns.
THE LEG
Wootton Hall
Langham Lodge
Forest Farm
Holm Farm
MARLEY
Marley Mount Farm
Meadend House
Oaklands
Craiglea
The Haven
Forest House
Homestead
Kennington Cottage
ROAD
Fairlight Cott.
Ytene Way
Yew Tree Farm
Danelea
Tiptoe Prim. Sch.
Amberwood Farm
Littledown Farm
Sandlea
Broadley House
Grey Tops
Burley Villa Farm
Charfield
Marlpit Farm
MARLPIT LANE
COMMON
ROUGH
Gorselands
WOOTTON
DANEHURST NEW RD
Field Gate
MIDDLE
Tiptoe Lodge Farm
MOUNT
CRABBSWOOD
Yewtree
NORTH
Far Forest
Ewerby Farm
Depot
Woodcutters
Wild Acres
Arnewood Common
Tiptoe
Sunnyside
Kingswood
Whiteoaks
OSSEMSLEY SOUTH
Squirrels
ST. JOHNS RD.
Danehurst
Crabbswood Farm
Touchwood
Glenwood
VALEVIEW
Blackstocks
Long Meadow
Arreton
Arreton Farm
Nursery
Nursery
BASHLEY
Sawmill
ST. JOHNS
Deemster Farm
Cago Cottage
DRIVE
Four Winds
LANE
Bashley Park
Caravan Park
Brockhills Farm
Sunnyholme
Hall
NORTHOVER LA.
Oak Farm
Bashley
Sports Grd.
Hall
Blacklands Farm
ARNEWOOD
BRIDGE
Caravan Park
Caravan Park
Danes Stream Coppice
Danesford
Inverurie
Meadow Farm
Swaylett
Pav.
Cricket Grd.
Nursery
Bashley Park
Danestream Farm
Danewood
Bashley Copse
B3058
BASHLEY DR.
B3055
Dene Lodge
Oakfield Nusery
Hordle Dene
Arnewood Cottage
SMITHY LANE
MARK'S LA.
BASHLEY DR.
Rose Cottage
Gayfield
Stanley Holiday Centre
Danes Stream
Miranda
NEW
Oakmead
SWAY
Stanleys Farm
Tiptoe Farm
BASHLEY
CROSS
B3055
ROAD
FERN HILL LA.
Stanley's Copse
Fairmeads Farm
Bashley Wild Ground
Ferndene Farm
Bashley Croft
Stanley Park Country Club
Longacres
Hordle Grange Nursing Home
Vaggs
BROCKHILLS
LANE
HOLLANDS

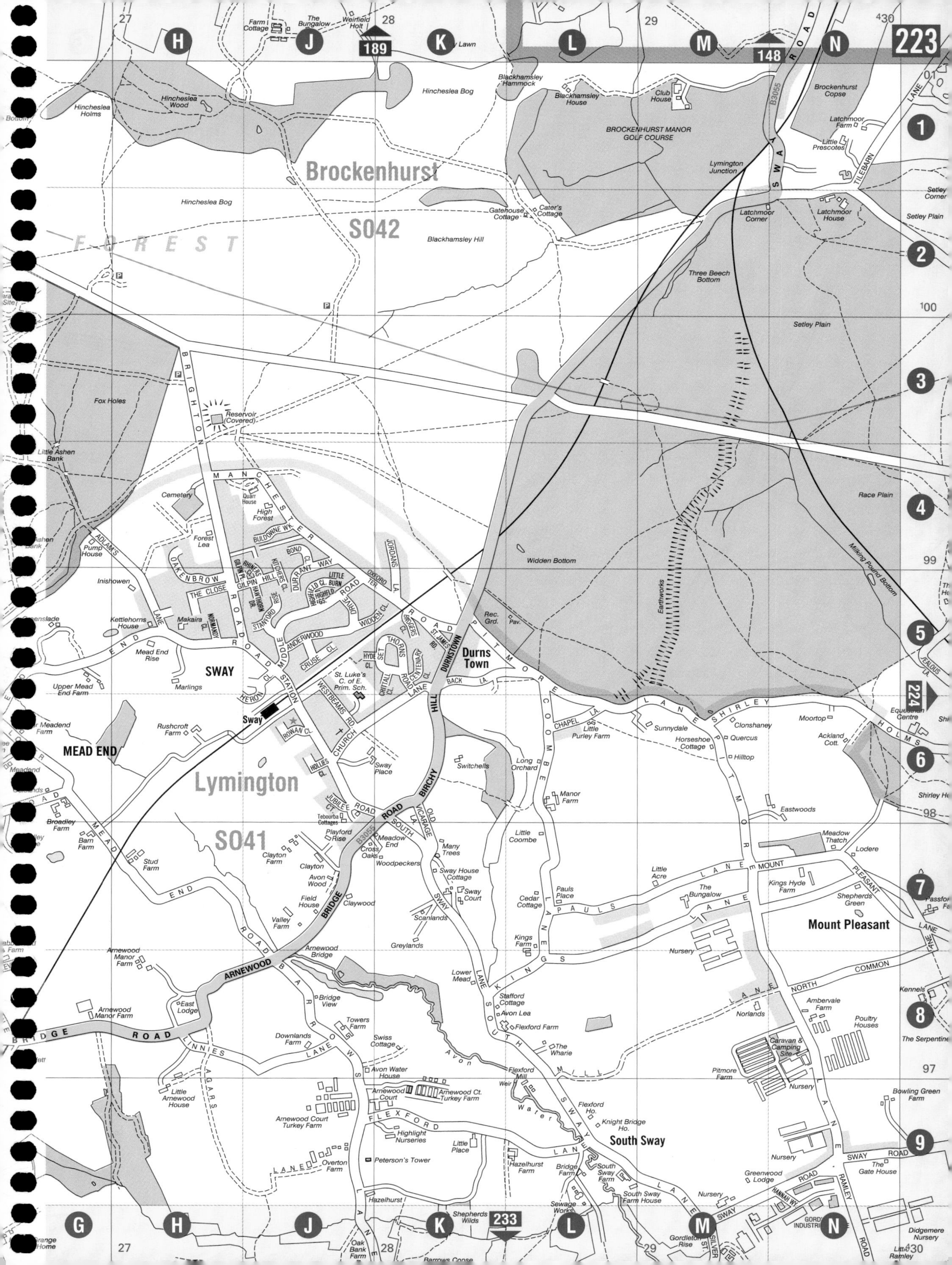

H
J
K
L
M
N
189
148
27
28
29
430
Farm Cottage
The Bungalow
Weirfield Holt
ROAD
Hincheslea Holms
Hincheslea Wood
Hincheslea Bog
Blackhamsley Hammock
Blackhamsley House
Club House
B3055
Brockenhurst Copse
Latchmoor Farm
Little Prescotes
BROCKENHURST MANOR GOLF COURSE
Lymington Junction
SWAY
TILEBARN
LANE
Brockenhurst
Hincheslea Bog
Gatehouse Cottage
Cater's Cottage
Latchmoor Corner
Latchmoor House
Setley Corner
Setley Plain
S042
FOREST
Blackhamsley Hill
Three Beech Bottom
100
Setley Plain
BRIGHTON
Fox Holes
Reservoir (Covered)
Little Ashen Bank
Race Plain
MANCHESTER
Cemetery
Quarr House
High Forest
Forest Lea
BULDOWNE WK.
BOND
DURRANT WAY
KITCHERS CL.
JORDANS LA.
OXFORD TER.
Widden Bottom
Earthworks
Milking Pound Bottom
99
ADLAM'S
Pump House
OAKENBROW
GILPIN HILL
LITTLE BURN
HIGHFIELD CL.
DRIVE
Inishowen
THE CLOSE
STATION ROAD
STANFORD RISE
WIDDEN CL.
Rec. Grd.
Pav.
Kettlehorns House
LANE
Makaira
NORMANDY CL.
ANDERWOOD
THORNS
ROAD
ST. JAMES RD.
DURNSTOWN
Durns Town
PITMORE
END
Mead End Rise
SWAY
MIDDLE
CRUSE CL.
HYDE CL.
SET
CENTENARY
CRITTALL CL.
BACK LA.
Upper Mead End Farm
Marlings
HERON CL.
St. Luke's C. of E. Prim. Sch.
WESTBEAMS
LANE
HILL
SHIRLEY
224
Meadend Farm
Rushcroft Farm
Sway
ROWAN CL.
RD.
CHAPEL LA.
Little Purley Farm
COOMBE
Sunnydale
Horseshoe Cottage
Clonshaney
Quercus
Hilltop
Moortop
Ackland Cott.
HOLMS
Equestrian Centre
MEAD END
CHURCH
Sway Place
Switchells
Long Orchard
Lymington
HOLLIES CL.
BIRCHY
Manor Farm
Eastwoods
Shirley Holms
Broadley Farm
MEAD
JUBILEE CT.
ROAD
Tebourba Cottages
SOUTH
VICARAGE
OLD
98
Barn Farm
S041
Playford Rise
B3055
Meadow End
Little Coombe
Meadow Thatch
Lodere
Stud Farm
Clayton Farm
Cross Oaks
Many Trees
Woodpeckers
MOUNT
LANE
Clayton
Avon Wood
Sway House Cottage
Little Acre
Kings Hyde Farm
PLEASANT
END
BRIDGE
Sway Court
Cedar Cottage
Pauls Place
The Bungalow
Shepherds Green
Field House
Claywood
PAULS
LANE
Mount Pleasant
Scanlands
Valley Farm
SWAY
Kings Farm
LANE
ROAD
Greylands
Nursery
Arnewood Manor Farm
Arnewood Bridge
KINGS
ARNEWOOD
Lower Mead
COMMON
NORTH
Kennels
LANE
Ambervale Farm
East Lodge
Bridge View
Stafford Cottage
Norlands
Poultry Houses
Arnewood Manor Farm
Avon Lea
Flexford Farm
BRIDGE
ROAD
Towers Farm
SOUTH
Caravan & Camping Site
The Serpentine
Downlands Farm
Swiss Cottage
The Wharie
LINNIES
LANE
Avon
MILL
97
Avon Water House
Flexford Mill
Pitmore Farm
Little Arnewood House
Weir
AGARS
Arnewood Court
Arnewood Ct. Turkey Farm
Nursery
Bowling Green Farm
Water
Flexford Ho.
Arnewood Court Turkey Farm
FLEXFORD
Highlight Nurseries
Knight Bridge Ho.
South Sway
Little Place
LANE
SWAY ROAD
Overton Farm
Peterson's Tower
Hazelhurst Farm
Bridge Farm
South Sway Farm
Nursery
The Gate House
Greenwood Lodge
ROAD
RAMLEY
South Sway Farm House
Nursery
HANNAH WY.
Hazelhurst
Sewage Works
Shepherds Wilds
233
G
SWAY
Didgemere Nursery
Gordleton Rise
SILVER ST.
Oak Bank Farm
Barrows Copse
Little Ramley

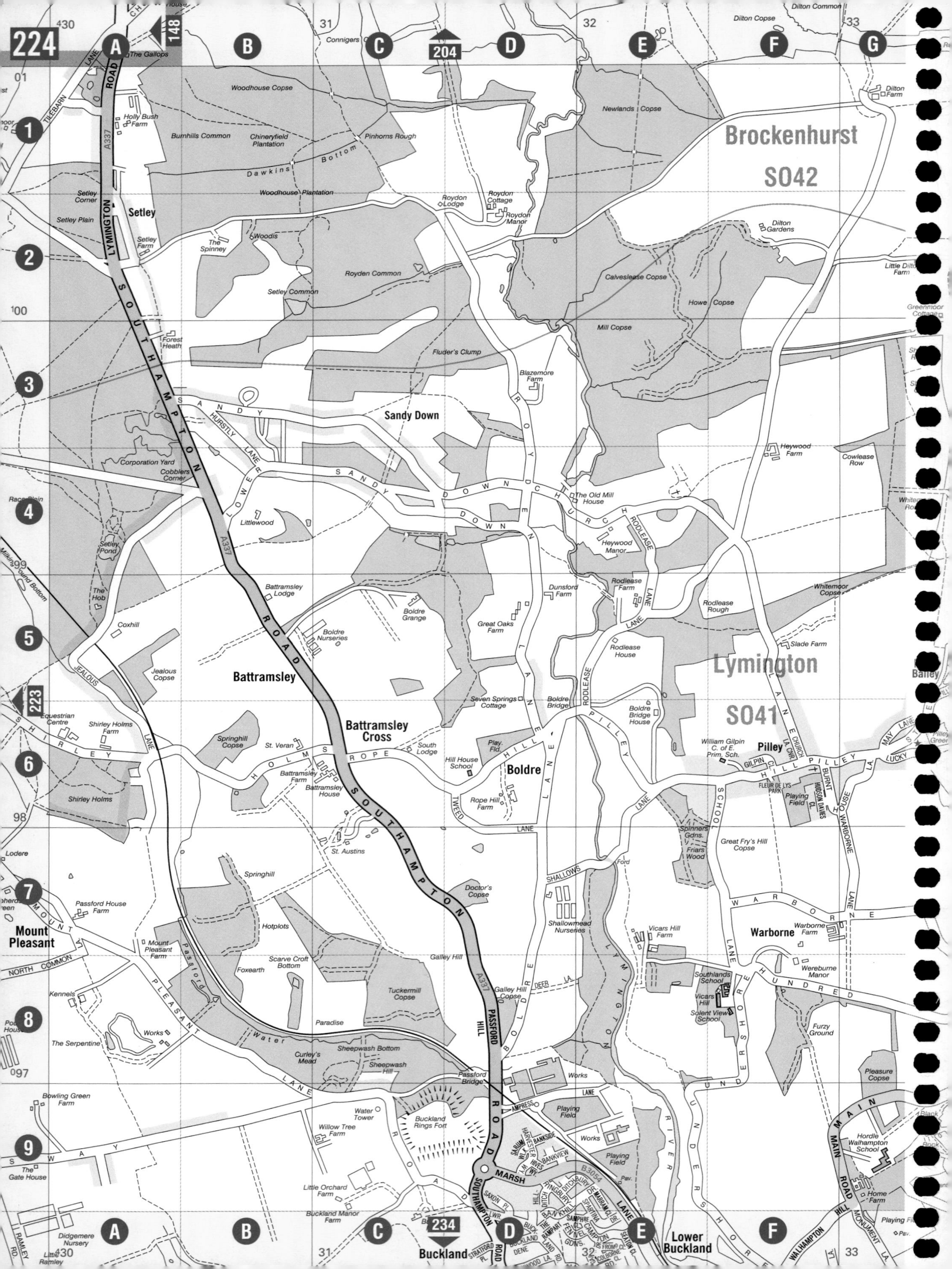

148
204
234
223
Brockenhurst
SO42
Lymington
SO41
Setley
Sandy Down
Battramsley
Battramsley Cross
Boldre
Pilley
Warborne
Mount Pleasant
Lower Buckland
Buckland
The Gallops
Woodhouse Copse
Holly Bush Farm
Burnhills Common
Chineryfield Plantation
Pinhorns Rough
Dawkins Bottom
Woodhouse Plantation
Setley Corner
Setley Plain
Setley Farm
The Spinney
Woodis
Royden Common
Setley Common
Roydon Lodge
Roydon Cottage
Roydon Manor
Newlands Copse
Dilton Copse
Dilton Common
Dilton Farm
Dilton Gardens
Little Dilton Farm
Calveslease Copse
Howe Copse
Mill Copse
Fluder's Clump
Forest Heath
Blazemore Farm
Corporation Yard
Cobblers Corner
Race Plain
Littlewood
Setley Pond
The Hob
Coxhill
Jealous Copse
Battramsley Lodge
Boldre Grange
Boldre Nurseries
Great Oaks Farm
Dunsford Farm
The Old Mill House
Heywood Manor
Heywood Farm
Cowlease Row
Rodlease Farm
Rodlease Rough
Rodlease House
Whitemoor Copse
Slade Farm
Seven Springs Cottage
Boldre Bridge
Boldre Bridge House
Equestrian Centre
Shirley Holms Farm
Shirley Holms
Springhill Copse
St. Veran
South Lodge
Hill House School
Play. Fld.
William Gilpin C. of E. Prim. Sch.
Fleur de Lys Park
Playing Field
Battramsley Farm
Battramsley House
Rope Hill Farm
St. Austins
Spinners Gdns.
Friars Wood
Great Fry's Hill Copse
Lodere
Springhill
Doctor's Copse
Passford House Farm
Shallowmead Nurseries
Hotplots
Vicars Hill Farm
Warborne Farm
Mount Pleasant Farm
Scarve Croft Bottom
Foxearth
Galley Hill
Wereburne Manor
Kennels
Tuckermill Copse
Galley Hill Copse
Southlands School
Vicars Hill
Solent View School
Furzy Ground
Works
The Serpentine
Paradise
Curley's Mead
Sheepwash Bottom
Sheepwash Hill
Passford Bridge
Pleasure Copse
Bowling Green Farm
Water Tower
Buckland Rings Fort
Willow Tree Farm
Hordle Walhampton School
The Gate House
Little Orchard Farm
Buckland Manor Farm
Home Farm
Didgemere Nursery
Little Ramley
Ford
Pav.
LYMINGTON ROAD
SOUTHAMPTON ROAD
A337
TILEBARN LANE
SANDY DOWN
HURSTLY
LOWER LANE
ROYDON LANE
CHURCH LANE
RODLEASE LANE
JEALOUS LANE
SHIRLEY HOLMS
ROPE HILL
TWEED LANE
BOLDRE LANE
PILLEY HILL
PILLEY LANE
SCHOOL LANE
GILPIN CL.
BURNT HOUSE LA.
HUDSON DAVIES CL.
WARBORNE LANE
LUCKY LA.
MAY LANE
SHALLOWS LANE
LYMINGTON RIVER
PASSFORD HILL
Passford Water LANE
DEER LA.
SHOREPLACE
HUNDRED LANE
UNDERSHORE
MOUNT PLEASANT
NORTH COMMON
PLEASANT LANE
SWAY ROAD
MAIN ROAD
MARSH LANE
B3054
WALHAMPTON HILL
MONUMENT LA.
RAMLEY RD.
STRATFORD PL.
430
31
32
33
01
100
99
98
097

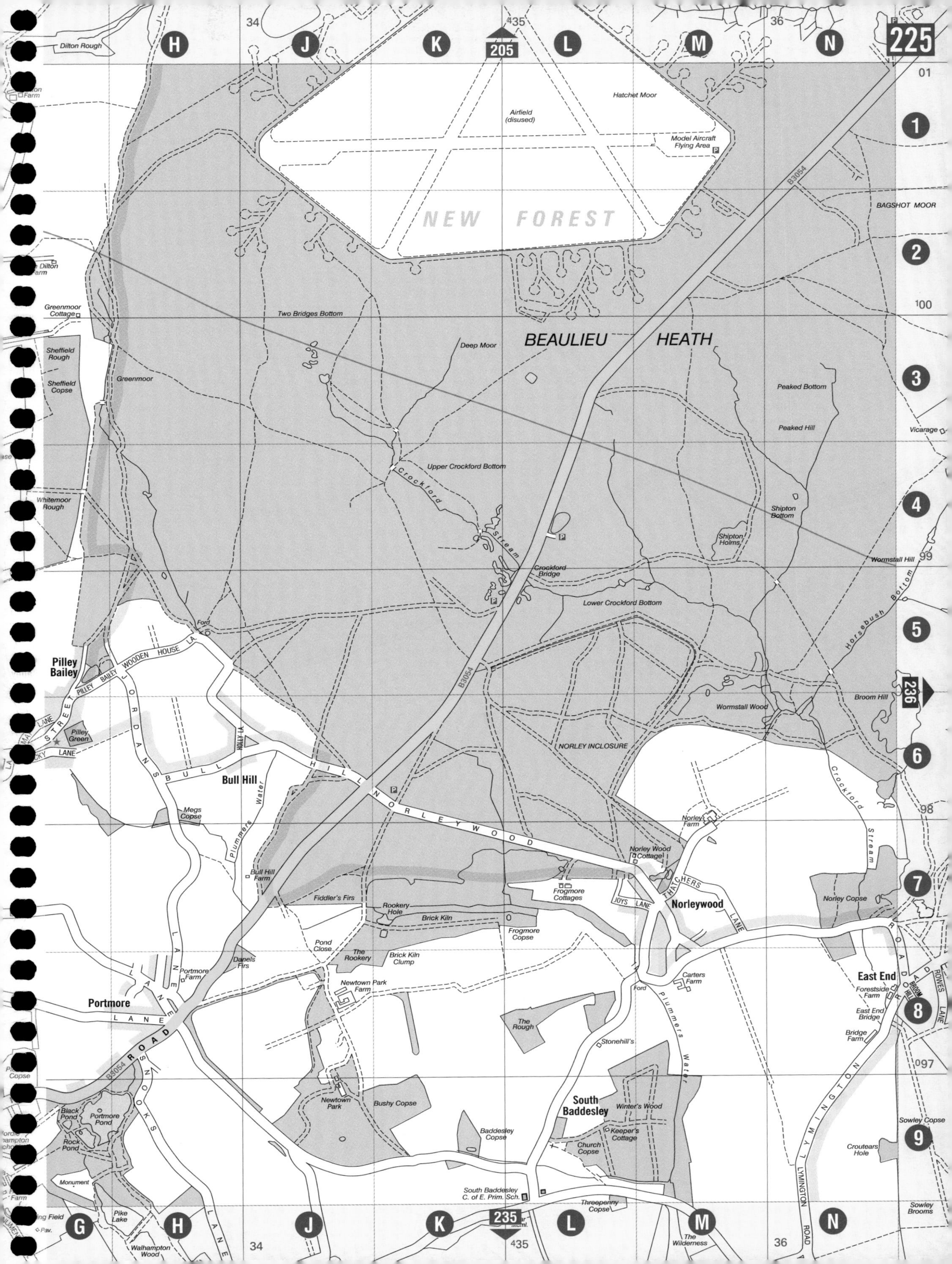

Map labels

NEW FOREST

BEAULIEU HEATH

BAGSHOT MOOR

Hatchet Moor

Model Aircraft Flying Area

Airfield (disused)

Deep Moor

Two Bridges Bottom

Peaked Bottom

Peaked Hill

Vicarage

Upper Crockford Bottom

Shipton Holms

Shipton Bottom

Wormstall Hill

Crockford Bridge

Lower Crockford Bottom

Broom Hill

HorseBush Bottom

Wormstall Wood

NORLEY INCLOSURE

Crockford Stream

Greenmoor Cottage

Sheffield Rough

Sheffield Copse

Greenmoor

Whitemoor Rough

Dilton Rough

Dilton Farm

Ford

Pilley Bailey

Pilley Green

Pilley

Bull Hill

Megs Copse

Bull Hill Farm

Norley Farm

Norley Wood Cottage

Norley Copse

Norleywood

Fiddler's Firs

Rookery Hole

Brick Kiln

Frogmore Cottages

Frogmore Copse

JOYS LANE

HATCHERS LANE

Carters Farm

East End

Forestside Farm

East End Bridge

Bridge Farm

Brick Kiln Clump

The Rookery

Pond Close

Portmore Farm

Danels Firs

Newtown Park Farm

Portmore

Newtown Park

Bushy Copse

The Rough

Ford

Stonehill's

South Baddesley

Winter's Wood

Sowley Copse

Croutears Hole

Black Pond

Portmore Pond

Rock Pond

Monument

Pike Lake

Walhampton Wood

Baddesley Copse

Church Copse

Keeper's Cottage

South Baddesley C. of E. Prim. Sch.

Threepenny Copse

The Wilderness

Sowley Brooms

Plumpers Water

Plummers Water

BULL LANE

JORDANS LANE

WOODEN HOUSE LA.

HOLLY LA.

HILL

NORLEYWOOD

SNOOKS LANE

LYMINGTON ROAD

ROAD

LANE

B3054

STREET

MAIN LANE

RORY LANE

Crockford Stream

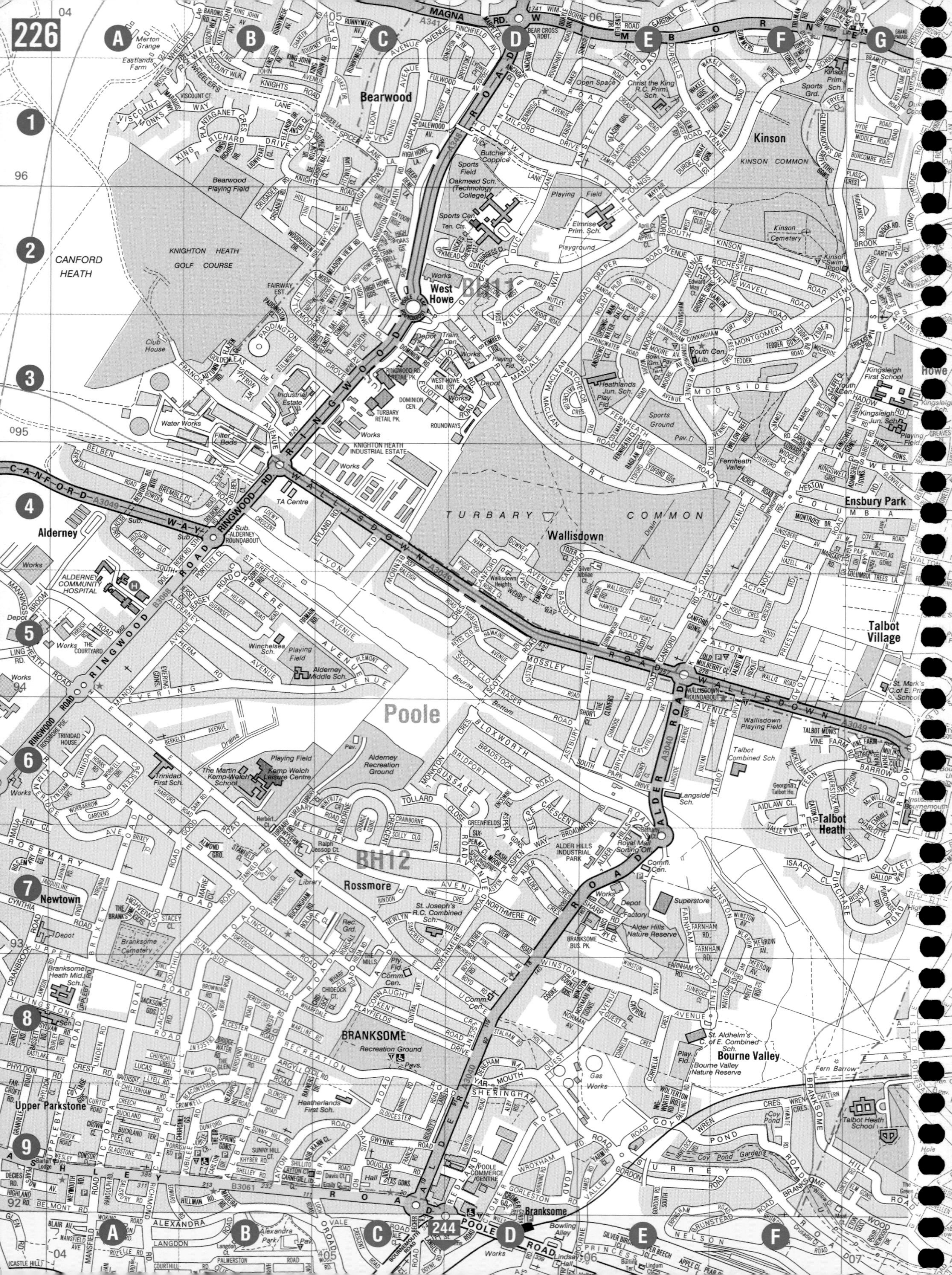
Bearwood
Kinson
KINSON COMMON
CANFORD HEATH
KNIGHTON HEATH GOLF COURSE
Bearwood Playing Field
West Howe
BH11
Alderney
ALDERNEY COMMUNITY HOSPITAL
TURBARY COMMON
Wallisdown
Ensbury Park
Talbot Village
Poole
Alderney Recreation Ground
Talbot Heath
BH12
Rossmore
Newtown
Branksome Cemetery
Upper Parkstone
BRANKSOME
Recreation Ground
Bourne Valley
Bourne Valley Nature Reserve
Alder Hills Nature Reserve
Coy Pond Gardens
Talbot Heath School
Branksome
244

H
J
K
L
M
N
G
1
2
3
4
5
6
7
8
9
08
09
410
96
95
94
93
92
BH22
BH23
BH10
BH9
BH8
BH3
BH4
BH2
BH1
Ensbury
Christchurch
Northbourne
Muscliff
Red Hill
East Howe
Moordown
Charminster
Bournemouth
Winton
Talbot Woods
Student Village
Springbourne
BOURNEMOUTH
NORTHBOURNE MEADOWS
NORTHBOURNE ROUNDABOUT
Sewage Works
Vernold's Coppice
MUSCLIFF ARBORETUM
The Wilderness
Muscliff Park
Redhill Park
Hillview Prim. Sch.
Winton Prim. Sch.
Bournemouth School for Girls
Bournemouth School
Summerbee First & Jun. Schs.
North Cemetery
Crematorium
Strouden Park Playing Fields
Bournemouth University (Talbot Campus)
The Arts Institute at Bournemouth
UNIVERSITY ROUNDABOUT
BOUNDARY ROUNDABOUT
TALBOT ROUNDABOUT
EAST AVENUE ROUNDABOUT
Victoria Park
Slades Farm Sch.
Glenmoor Sch.
Winton Sch.
Recreation Ground
Playing Fields
Winton Rec. Grd.
Linwood Sch.
Swim. Pool
Mortuary Chapel
CEMETERY
MEYRICK PARK GOLF COURSE
MEYRICK PARK
Dean Park Cricket Ground
BOURNEMOUTH NUFFIELD HOSP.
Bus Sta.
PARKWAY RETAIL PK
BOURNEMOUTH CENTRAL BUS. PK
WIMBORNE ROAD
CASTLE LANE
CHARMINSTER ROAD
RICHMOND PARK ROAD
TALBOT AVENUE
WESSEX WAY
LANSDOWNE ROAD
228
245

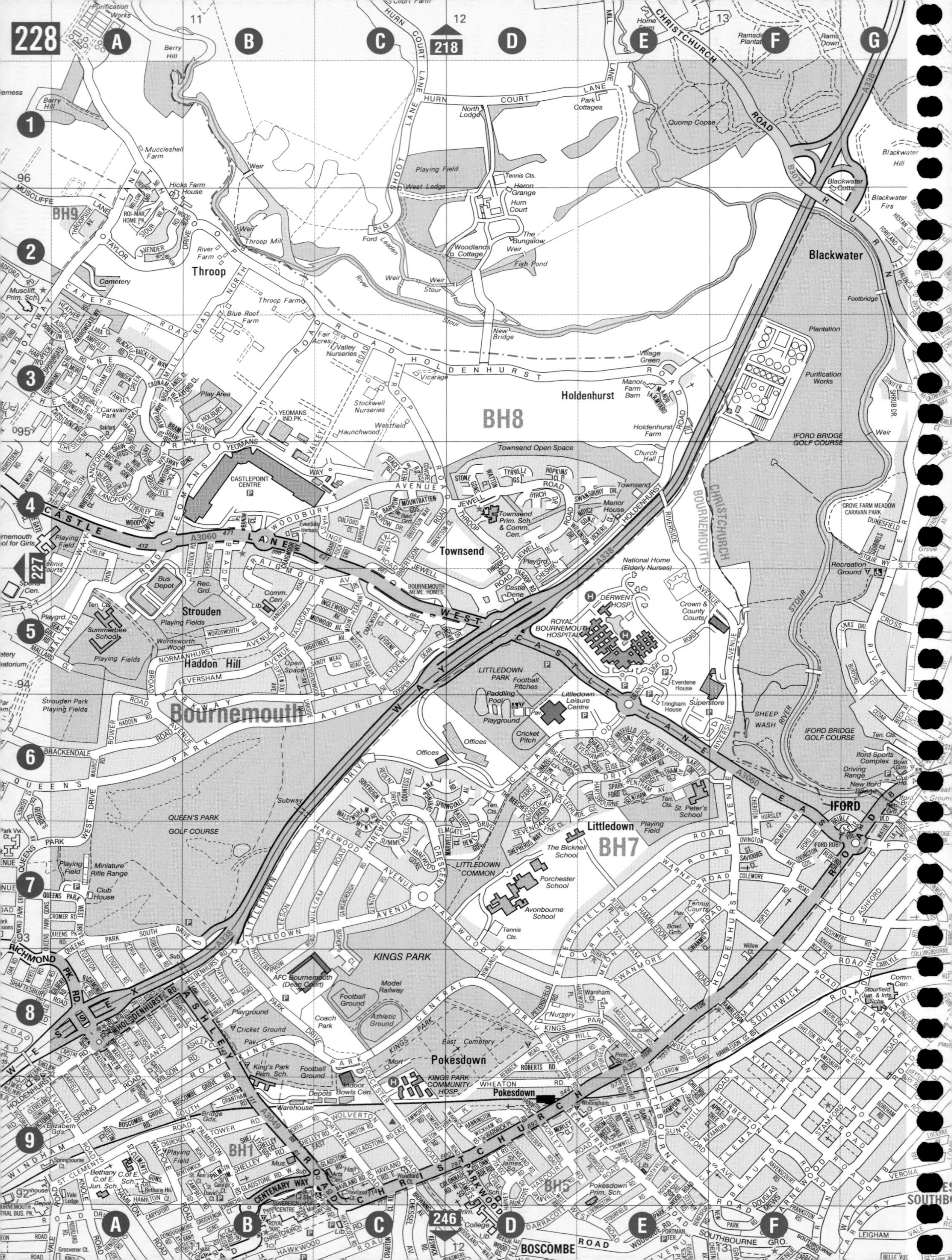

218
227
246
Throop
Holdenhurst
BH8
Townsend
Blackwater
Strouden
Haddon Hill
Bournemouth
Littledown
BH7
IFORD
Pokesdown
KINGS PARK
QUEEN'S PARK GOLF COURSE
IFORD BRIDGE GOLF COURSE
CASTLEPOINT CENTRE
ROYAL BOURNEMOUTH HOSPITAL
BH9
BH1
BH5
BOSCOMBE
CHRISTCHURCH
BOURNEMOUTH
Queen's Park
Springbourne

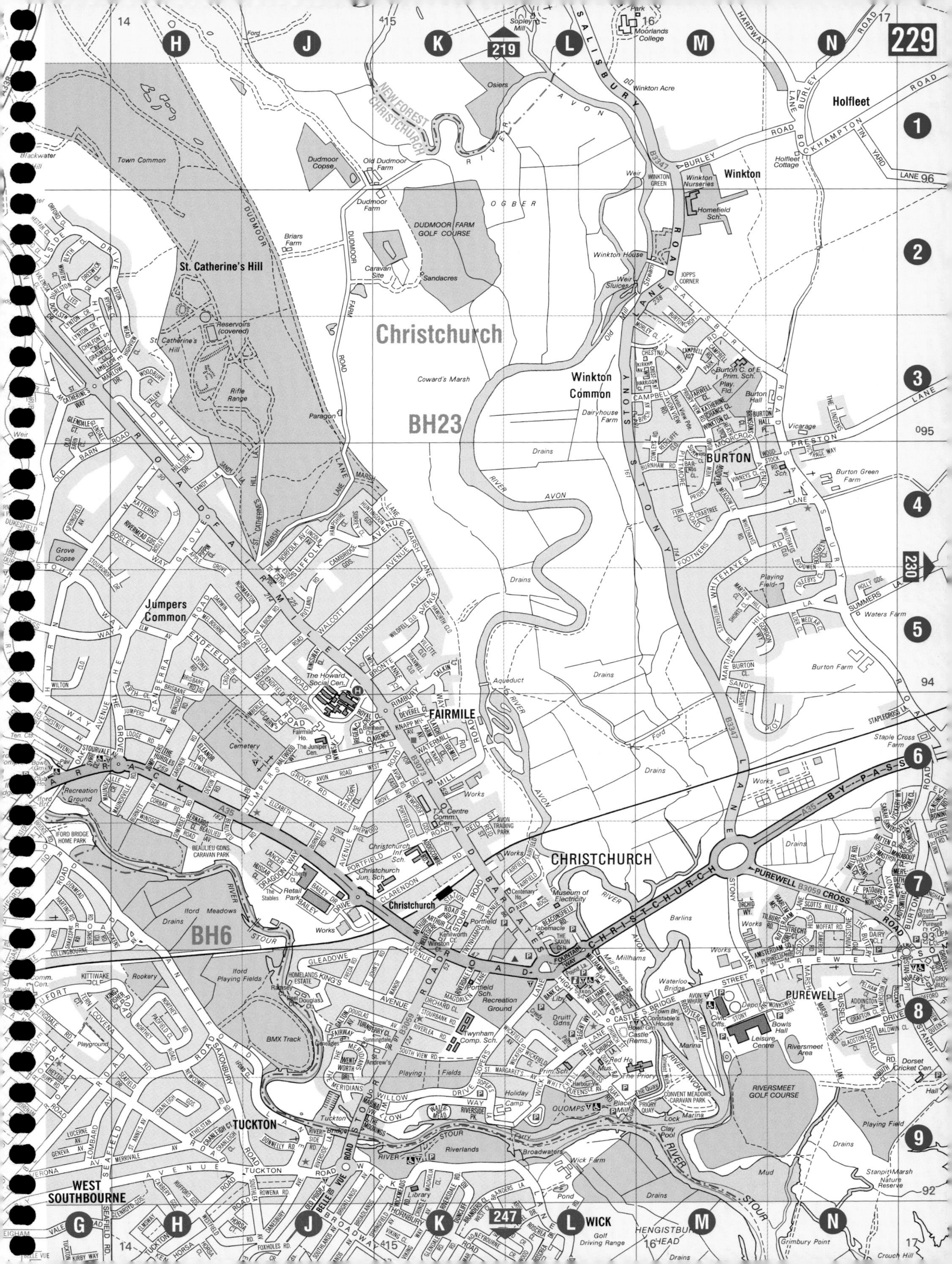

229
219
230
247
Christchurch
BH23
BH6
CHRISTCHURCH
Holfleet
Winkton
Winkton Common
BURTON
FAIRMILE
PUREWELL
TUCKTON
WEST SOUTHBOURNE
WICK
St. Catherine's Hill
Town Common
Jumpers Common
Dudmoor Copse
Dudmoor Farm
Old Dudmoor Farm
DUDMOOR FARM GOLF COURSE
Coward's Marsh
Iford Meadows
Iford Playing Fields
Rookery
BMX Track
Riverlands
Broadwaters
Wick Farm
RIVERSMEET GOLF COURSE
Riversmeet Area
Stanpit Marsh Nature Reserve
Playing Field
Burton Farm
Waters Farm
Burton Green Farm
Staple Cross Farm
Moorlands College
Winkton Nurseries
Homefield Sch.
Osiers
Sopley Mill
NEW FOREST
CHRISTCHURCH
RIVER AVON
RIVER STOUR
SALISBURY ROAD
STONY LANE
CHRISTCHURCH BY-PASS
BARRACK ROAD
FAIRMILE ROAD
BARGATES
PUREWELL CROSS ROAD
Christchurch
Museum of Electricity
The Priory
Castle (Rems.)
Red Ho. Mus.
Leisure Centre
Civic Offs.
Twynham Comp. Sch.
Portfield Sch.
Recreation Ground
Cemetery
Grove Copse
Hengistbury Head
Golf Driving Range
Grimbury Point
Crouch Hill
Mud
Drains

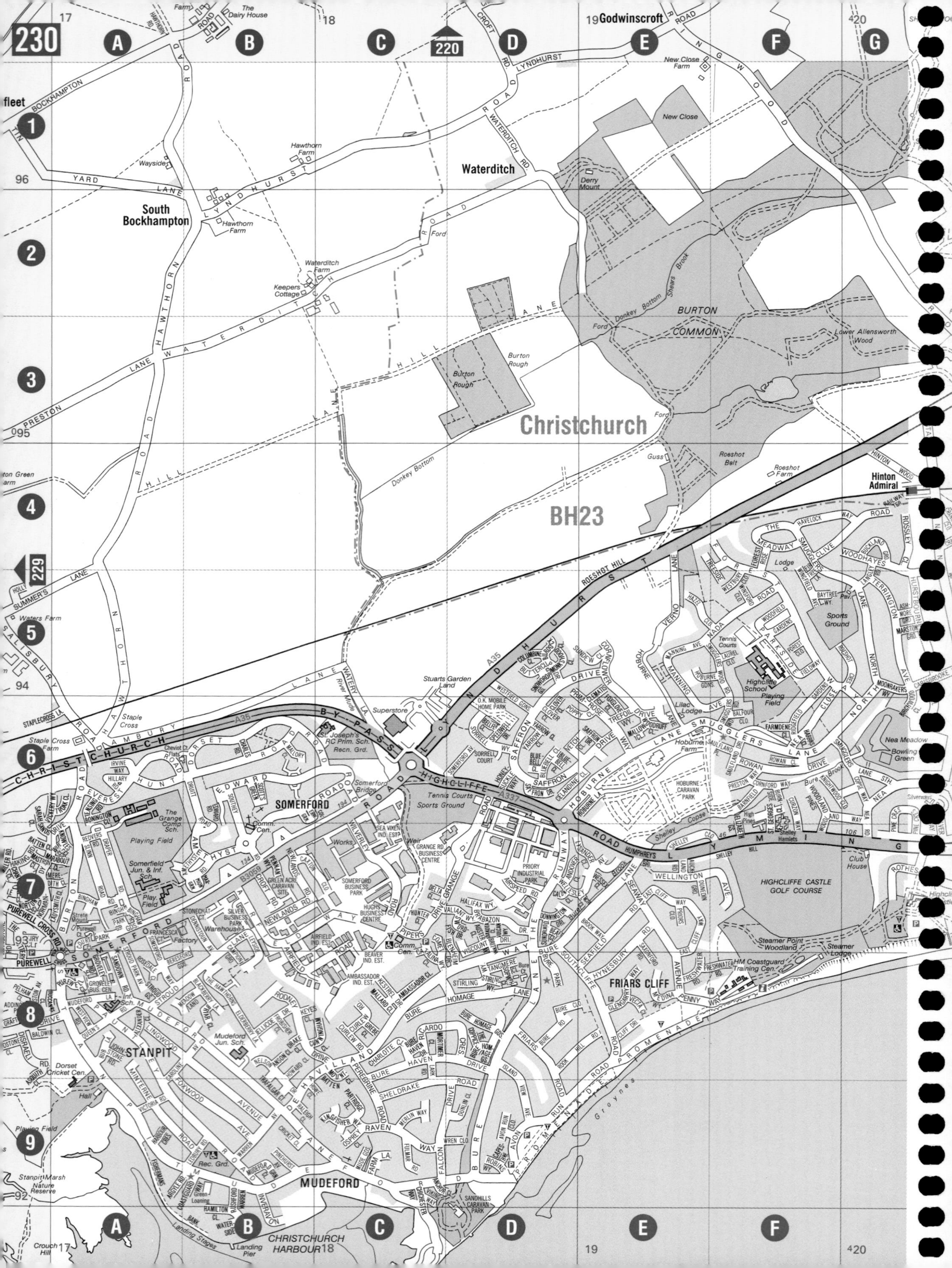

230
220
229
Godwinscroft
South Bockhampton
Waterditch
Hawthorn Farm
Waterditch Farm
Keepers Cottage
New Close Farm
New Close
Derry Mount
Burton Common
Burton Rough
Lower Allensworth Wood
Christchurch
BH23
Roeshot Belt
Roeshot Farm
Hinton Admiral
Donkey Bottom
Shears Brook
Staple Cross
Staple Cross Farm
Waters Farm
Superstore
Stuarts Garden Land
St. Joseph's RC Prim. Sch.
Recn. Grd.
O.K. Mobile Home Park
Somerford
The Grange Comp. Sch.
Playing Field
Somerfield Jun. & Inf. Sch.
Tennis Courts
Sports Ground
Priory Industrial Park
Somerford Business Park
Hughes Business Centre
Grange Rd Business Centre
Airfield Ind. Est.
Beaver Ind. Est.
Ambassador Ind. Est.
Hoburne Farm
Hoburne Caravan Park
Highcliffe School
Lilac Lodge
Nea Meadow
Bowling Green
Shelley Hamlets
Highcliffe Castle Golf Course
Club House
Steamer Point Woodland
Steamer Lodge
HM Coastguard Training Cen.
Friars Cliff
Stanpit
Mudeford Jun. Sch.
Dorset Cricket Cen.
Purewell
Mudeford
Sandhills Caravan Park
Christchurch Harbour
Landing Pier
Landing Stages
Stanpit Marsh Nature Reserve
Crouch Hill
Groynes
Christchurch By-Pass
Lyndhurst Road
Highcliffe Road
Humphrey's Bri.
Lymington Road
Smugglers Lane
Bure Lane
Mudeford Lane
Stanpit
Promenade
A35
A337
B3059

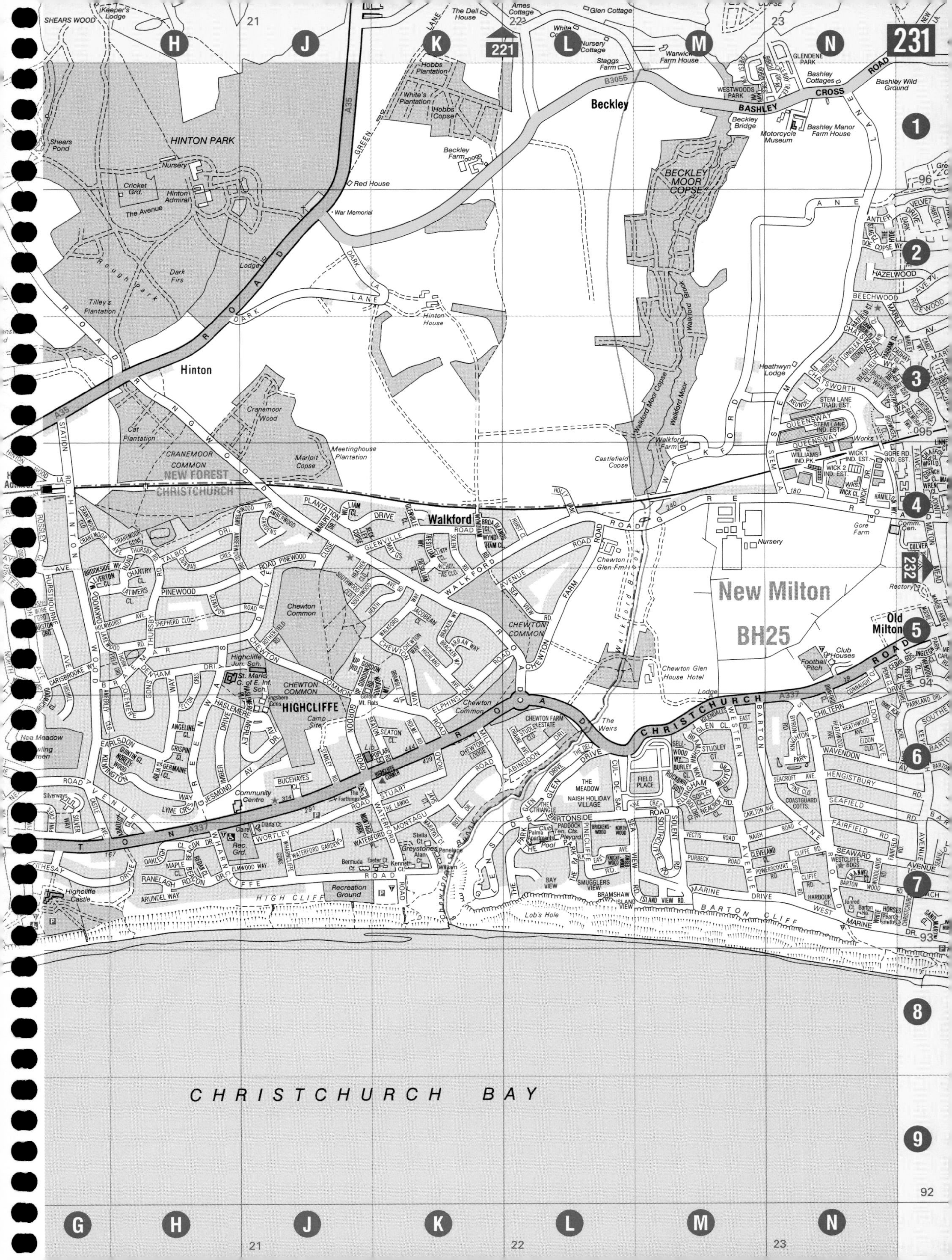
Hinton Park
Beckley
Walkford
Highcliffe
New Milton
BH25
Old Milton
Hinton
Christchurch Bay
New Forest
Christchurch

NEW MILTON
New Milton
BH25
ASHLEY
Golden Hill
Old Milton
BARTON ON SEA
CHRISTCHURCH BAY
BARTON-ON-SEA GOLF COURSE
BARTON COMMON
Ballard School
Ballard Prep. Sch.
Playing Field
Great Ballard Lodge
Pond Copse
Great Wear Copse
Bashley Wild Ground
Bashley Croft
Ferndene Farm
Stanley Holiday Centre
Stanley Park Country Club
Stanley's Copse
Stanleys Farm
Tiptoe Farm
Fairmeads Farm
Hordle Grange Nursing Home
Vaggs Farm
Longacres
Vernalls Farm
Rec. Grd.
Ivy Holme
Ashley Inf. Sch.
Lavender Farm
North End Lodge
Syringa
Noah's Ark Farm
Sports Ground
Play. Fld.
Ashley Jun. Sch.
Peter's Farm
White Croft
Breakhill Copse
Works
Sand and Gravel Pits
Superstore
Tennis Club
Hooper's Hill Farm
Hooper's Hill
Ashley Manor Farm
Lodge
The Lodge
Home Farm
Furzy Mount
Ashley Clinton
Ashley Bri.
Angels Cottage
Becton Farm
Keepers Cottage
Honeylake Wood
Dane Stream
Island Copse
Hordle Manor
Beckton Bunny
Groynes
Club House
Durlston Court School
Ten. Cts.
Nursery
New Milton Rec. Cent.
The Arnewood School
Cemetery
Gore Farm
Gore Grange
New Milton Jun. Sch.
New Milton Inf. Sch.
Forest Arts Cen.
KING GEORGE MOBILE HOME PARK
THE MEADOWS CARAVAN SITE
Rec. Ground
Bowling Grns.
Comm. Cen.
Liby.
The Fernmount Centre
Lakeside Pines
Station
Rectory
LYMINGTON ROAD
CHRISTCHURCH ROAD
MILFORD ROAD
STATION ROAD
FERNHILL LANE
MANOR ROAD
ASHLEY ROAD
ANGEL LANE
BARTON COMMON ROAD
MARINE DRIVE
CROOKED LANE
A337
B3058
B3055
A
B
C
D
E
F
G
1
2
3
4
5
6
7
8
9
24
425
26
96
95
94
93
92
222
231

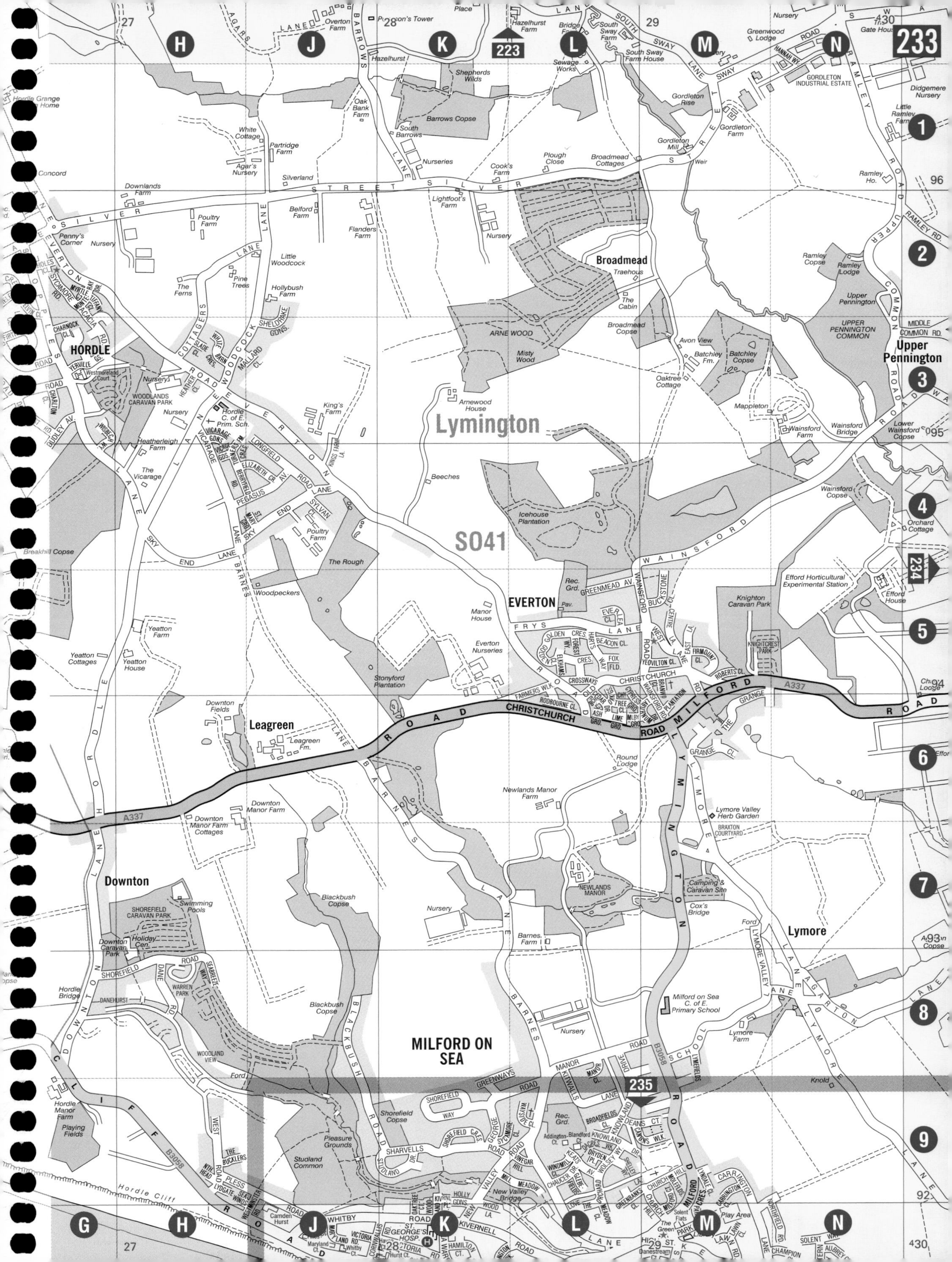

233
223
234
235
H
J
K
L
M
N
G
27
28
29
430
96
95
94
93
92
1
2
3
4
5
6
7
8
9
Lymington
SO41
HORDLE
EVERTON
MILFORD ON SEA
Broadmead
Upper Pennington
Leagreen
Downton
Lymore
Hazelhurst Farm
Hazelhurst
Shepherds Wilds
Barrows Copse
South Barrows
Oak Bank Farm
Overton Farm
South Sway Farm
South Sway Farm House
Sewage Works
Greenwood Lodge
GORDLETON INDUSTRIAL ESTATE
Didgemere Nursery
Little Ramley Farm
Gordleton Rise
Gordleton Farm
Gordleton Mill
Weir
Ramley Ho.
Hordle Grange Home
Concord
White Cottage
Partridge Farm
Agar's Nursery
Silverland
Nurseries
Cook's Farm
Plough Close
Broadmead Cottages
Downlands Farm
SILVER STREET
Poultry Farm
Belford Farm
Lightfoot's Farm
Flanders Farm
Nursery
Penny's Corner
Little Woodcock
Pine Trees
The Ferns
Hollybush Farm
Traehous
The Cabin
Broadmead Copse
ARNE WOOD
Misty Wood
Avon View
Batchley Fm.
Batchley Copse
Oaktree Cottage
Ramley Copse
Ramley Lodge
Upper Pennington
UPPER PENNINGTON COMMON
MIDDLE COMMON RD.
UPPER RAMLEY RD.
COMMON ROAD
Westmoreland Court
WOODLANDS CARAVAN PARK
Hordle C. of E. Prim. Sch.
King's Farm
Arnewood House
Mappleton
Wainsford Farm
Wainsford Bridge
Lower Wainsford Copse
Heatherleigh Farm
The Vicarage
Beeches
Icehouse Plantation
Wainsford Copse
Orchard Cottage
Breakhill Copse
Poultry Farm
The Rough
SKY END LANE
WAINSFORD ROAD
Woodpeckers
Rec. Grd.
Pav.
Manor House
Efford Horticultural Experimental Station
Efford House
Knighton Caravan Park
KNIGHTCREST PARK
Yeatton Farm
Yeatton Cottages
Yeatton House
Everton Nurseries
FRYS LANE
Stonyford Plantation
Downton Fields
Leagreen Fm.
CHRISTCHURCH ROAD
MILFORD ROAD
A337
Round Lodge
Newlands Manor Farm
Lymore Valley Herb Garden
BRAXTON COURTYARD
Downton Manor Farm
Downton Manor Farm Cottages
NEWLANDS MANOR
Camping & Caravan Site
Cox's Bridge
Ford
Blackbush Copse
Nursery
Barnes Farm
SHOREFIELD CARAVAN PARK
Swimming Pools
Downton Caravan Park
Holiday Cen.
WARREN PARK
Hordle Bridge
Milford on Sea C. of E. Primary School
Lymore Farm
LYMINGTON ROAD
B3058
Knold
Hordle Manor Farm
Playing Fields
Shorefield Copse
Pleasure Grounds
Studland Common
Rec. Grd.
Hordle Cliff
CLIFF ROAD
New Valley Bridge
Camden Hurst
St. George's Hosp.
Solent Flats
The Green
Play Area
Danestream

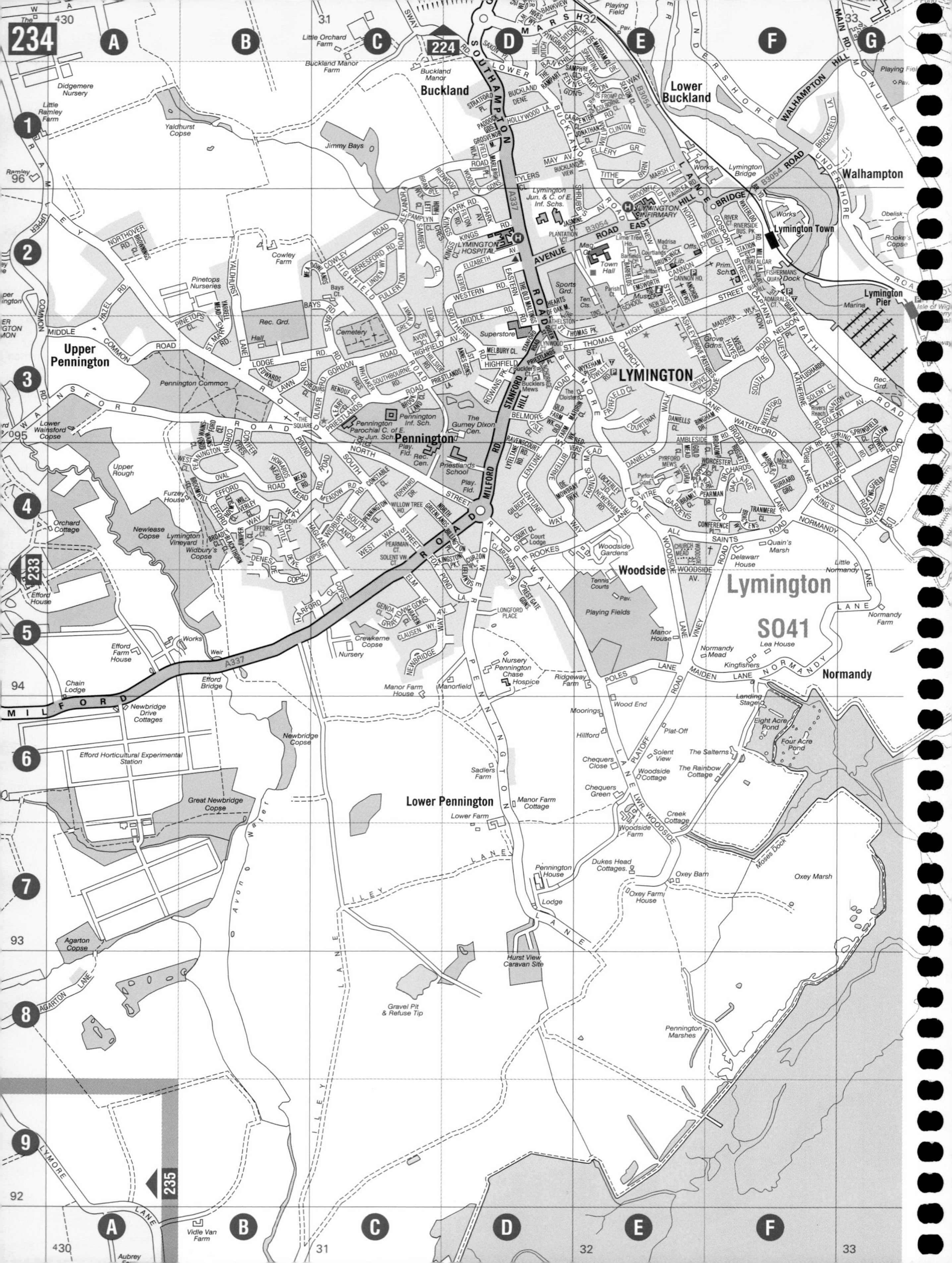

234
224
233
235
Buckland
Lower Buckland
Walhampton
Lymington Pier
Lymington Town
Lymington Bridge
LYMINGTON
Upper Pennington
Pennington
Woodside
Lymington
SO41
Normandy
Lower Pennington
Southampton Road
Milford Road
Pennington Common
Efford Horticultural Experimental Station
Great Newbridge Copse
Newbridge Copse
Oxey Marsh
Pennington Marshes
Gravel Pit & Refuse Tip
Hurst View Caravan Site
Playing Fields
Lymington Infirmary
Lymington Hospital
Town Hall
Priestlands School
The Gurney Dixon Cen.
Pennington Inf. Sch.
Yaldhurst Copse
Jimmy Bays
Didgemere Nursery
Little Ramley Farm
Upper Rough
Newlease Copse
Lymington Vineyard
Agarton Copse
Avon Water
Ridgeway Farm
Moses Dock
Eight Acre Pond
Four Acre Pond
Marina

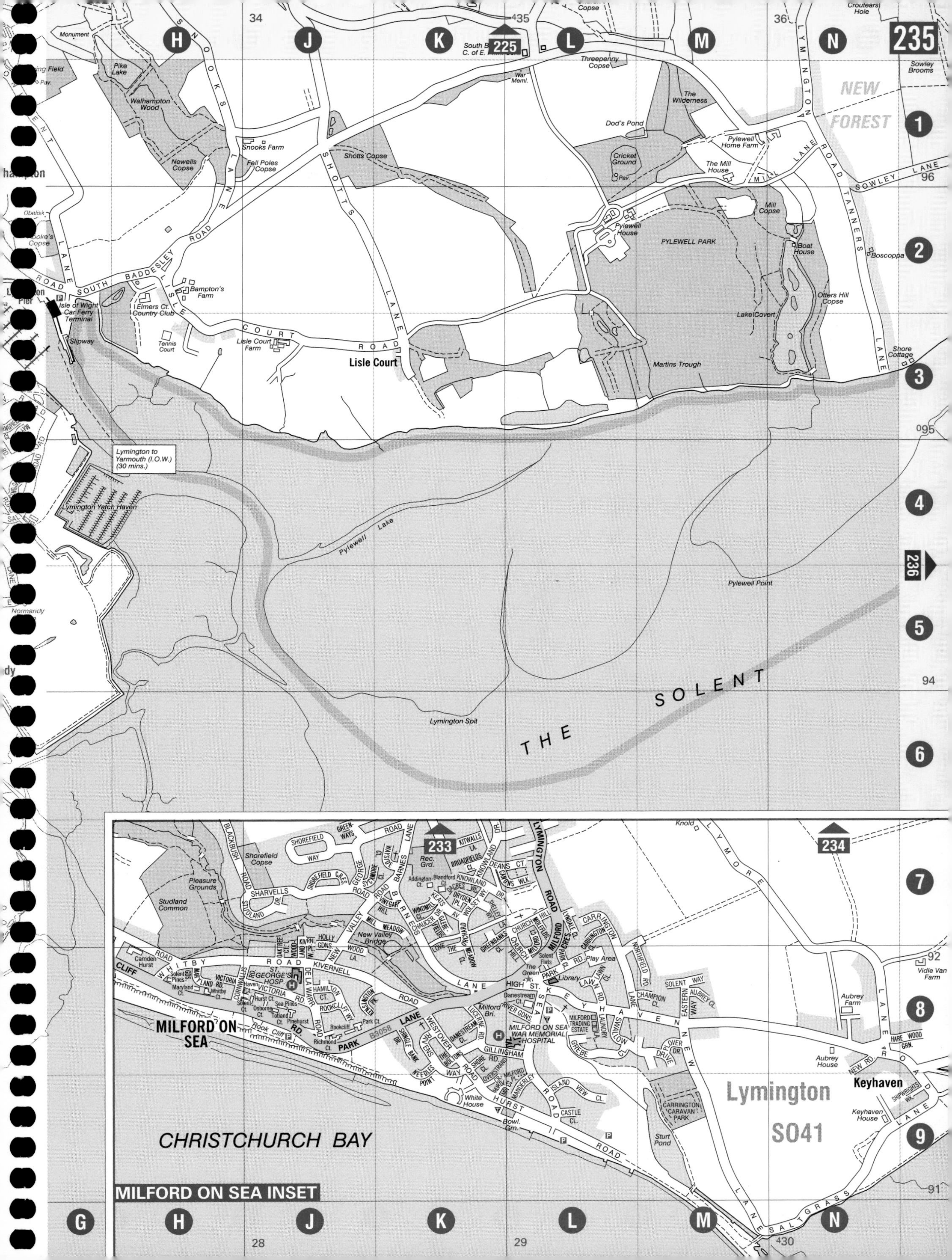

NEW FOREST

THE SOLENT

Lisle Court

Pylewell Lake

Lymington Spit

Pylewell Point

Lymington to Yarmouth (I.O.W.) (30 mins.)

Lymington Yacht Haven

Isle of Wight Car Ferry Terminal

Slipway

PYLEWELL PARK

Martins Trough

Lake Covert

Otters Hill Copse

Shore Cottage

Boscoppa

Boat House

Mill Copse

The Mill House

Pylewell Home Farm

Pylewell House

Cricket Ground

Dod's Pond

The Wilderness

Threepenny Copse

War Meml.

South Bdln. C. of E.

Monument

Pike Lake

Walhampton Wood

Snooks Farm

Shotts Copse

Fell Poles Copse

Newells Copse

South Baddesley Road

Shotts Lane

Snooks Lane

Lisle Court Road

Bampton's Farm

Elmers Ct. Country Club

Tennis Court

Lisle Court Farm

Sowley Brooms

Sowley Lane

Tanners Lane

Lymington Road

Crouters Hole

Copse

Normandy

Obelisk

Cooke's Copse

225

236

CHRISTCHURCH BAY

MILFORD ON SEA

MILFORD ON SEA INSET

Lymington

SO41

Keyhaven

Shorefield Copse

Pleasure Grounds

Studland Common

Camden Hurst

CLIFF

Solent Pines

Victoria Rd

Maryland Rd

Whitby

Osborne Ct.

Sea Pines

Totland Rd.

Richmond

Rookcliff

Pinehurst

Park Ct.

Rookcliff Way

ST. GEORGE'S HOSP.

Milford Bri.

River Gdns.

Danestream

Gillingham

White House

Bowl. Grn.

New Valley Bridge

Windmill Ct.

Greenbanks

The Green

Play Area

MILFORD ON SEA WAR MEMORIAL HOSPITAL

Milford Trading Estate

Solent Flats

Library

Park

Sturt Pond

Carrington Caravan Park

Aubrey House

Aubrey Farm

Vidle Van Farm

Hare Wood Grn.

New Rd.

Keyhaven House

Knold

Shorefield Way

Greenways

Kitwalls La.

Broadfields

Rec. Grd.

Barnes La.

Knowland

Blandford

Addington

Deans Ct.

Carrington La.

Lymington Road

Lymore Lane

Saltgrass Lane

Shippers Wk.

233

234

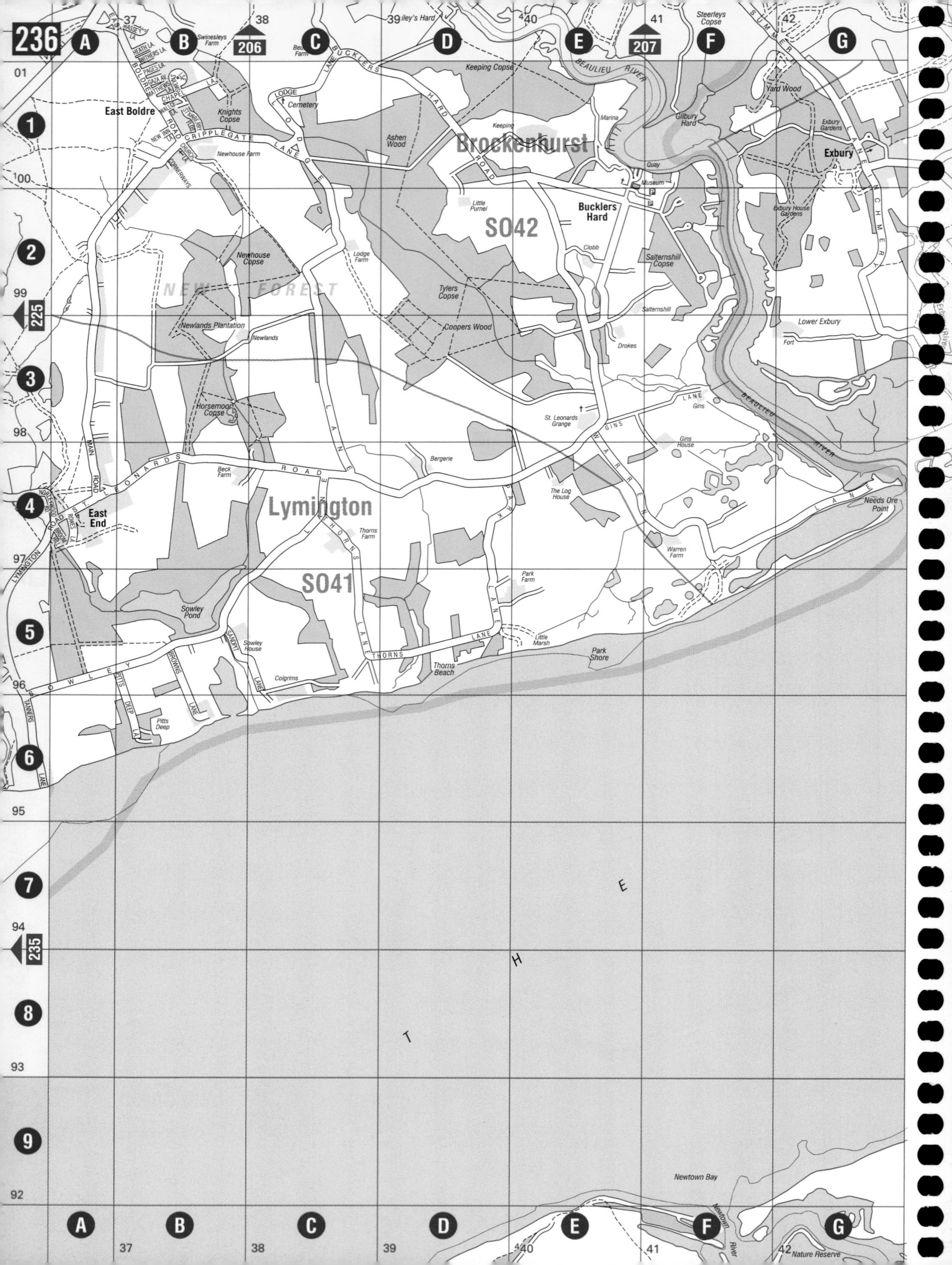
East Boldre
Swinesleys Farm
Knights Copse
Newhouse Farm
Cemetery
Keeping Copse
Ashen Wood
Brockenhurst
Beaulieu River
Marina
Gilbury Hard
Steerleys Copse
Yard Wood
Exbury Gardens
Exbury
Quay
Museum
Bucklers Hard
Little Purnel
SO42
Clobb
Saltemshill Copse
Lodge Farm
Newhouse Copse
NEW FOREST
Tylers Copse
Saltemshill
Newlands Plantation
Newlands
Coopers Wood
Drokes
Lower Exbury
Fort
Horsemoor Copse
St. Leonards Grange
Gins
Gins House
Bergerie
Beck Farm
ST. LEONARDS ROAD
MAIN ROAD
Lymington
The Log House
East End
Needs Ore Point
Thorns Farm
Warren Farm
SO41
Park Farm
Sowley Pond
Sowley House
Little Marsh
Park Shore
Colgrims
Thorns Beach
SOWLEY
Pitts Deep
T H E
Newtown Bay
Newtown River
Nature Reserve
A B C D E F G
1 2 3 4 5 6 7 8 9
206
207
225
235

Calshot
Hillhead
Eaglehurst
Sprat's Down
208
209
Langley
West Common
Dark Water
Whitefield Farm
Stanswood Farm
Southampton
SO45
Nelson's Place
STANSWOOD BAY
Cadland House
East Hill Farm
Lepe Farm
Stone Farm
STANSWOOD ROAD
Exbury River
LANE
Inchmerry House
Lepe
Lepe Country Park
Stone Point
Stansore Point
THE SOLENT
COWES ROADS
Cowes to Southampton 20 mins (Fast Ferry)
Egypt Point
Cowes
PO31
QUEEN'S ROAD
ESPLANADE
Cowes Castle
Cowes High Sch.
COWES
Sir Max Aitken Mus.
Winnall Moors Nature Reserve
Swift's Lake
Tumbling Bay
ST. WINCHESTER STATION
105
County Record Office
GLADSTONE ST.
CITY RD.
HYDE ST.
NORTH WALLS
Theatre Royal
Ref. Lib.
T.A. Cen.
Ashburton Ct.
County Council Offs.
Elizabeth II Ct.
Oram's Arbour Recreation Grd.
Winchester
St. Bede C.E. Prim. Sch.
Gallery
Winchester Sch. of Art
Comm. Cen.
UPPER HIGH ST.
CLIFTON TER.
ST. PAUL'S HILL
SUSSEX ST.
JEWRY ST.
B3040
ST. GEORGE'S ST.
FRIARSGATE
EASTGATE ST.
Police H.Q.
H.M.P. WINCHESTER
ROMSEY ROAD
HIGH STREET
West-gate
The Castle
Gt. Hall
Law Courts
Mus.
Museums
Royal Hampshire Reg. Mus.
Peninsula Barracks
The Brooks Experience
H.P.O.
Gov. Offs.
Bus Sta.
City Mus.
Morleys Coll.
Guildhall Gallery
City Mill
Y.H.A.
King Alfred's Statue
SO22
ROYAL HAMPSHIRE COUNTY HOSPITAL
Marfield Ho.
St. James' Hall
St. Elizabeth's Hall
St. Grimbalds Ct.
West Hill
Cemetery
The Screen Cinema
St. Thomas Cen.
SOUTHGATE ST.
WINCHESTER CATHEDRAL
Cathedral Visitor Cen.
SO23
Triforium Gallery
Deanery
The Close
Friends Meeting House
D.C. Offs.
Abbey Grounds
Chesil Theatre
Wolvesey Castle
Wolvesey Palace
Playing Field
The Pilgrims Sch.
Priory Ga.
Kings Ga.
J.Austen Plaque
COLLEGE STREET
CANON STREET
ST. SWITHUN STREET
ST. CROSS ROAD
B3335
Dummer Mews
Alwyn Hall
King Alfred's College
Playground
Winchester College
Medecroft
Milnthorpe
St. Mary's College
War Meml.
Play. Fld.
Wharf Hill
Millers Ho.

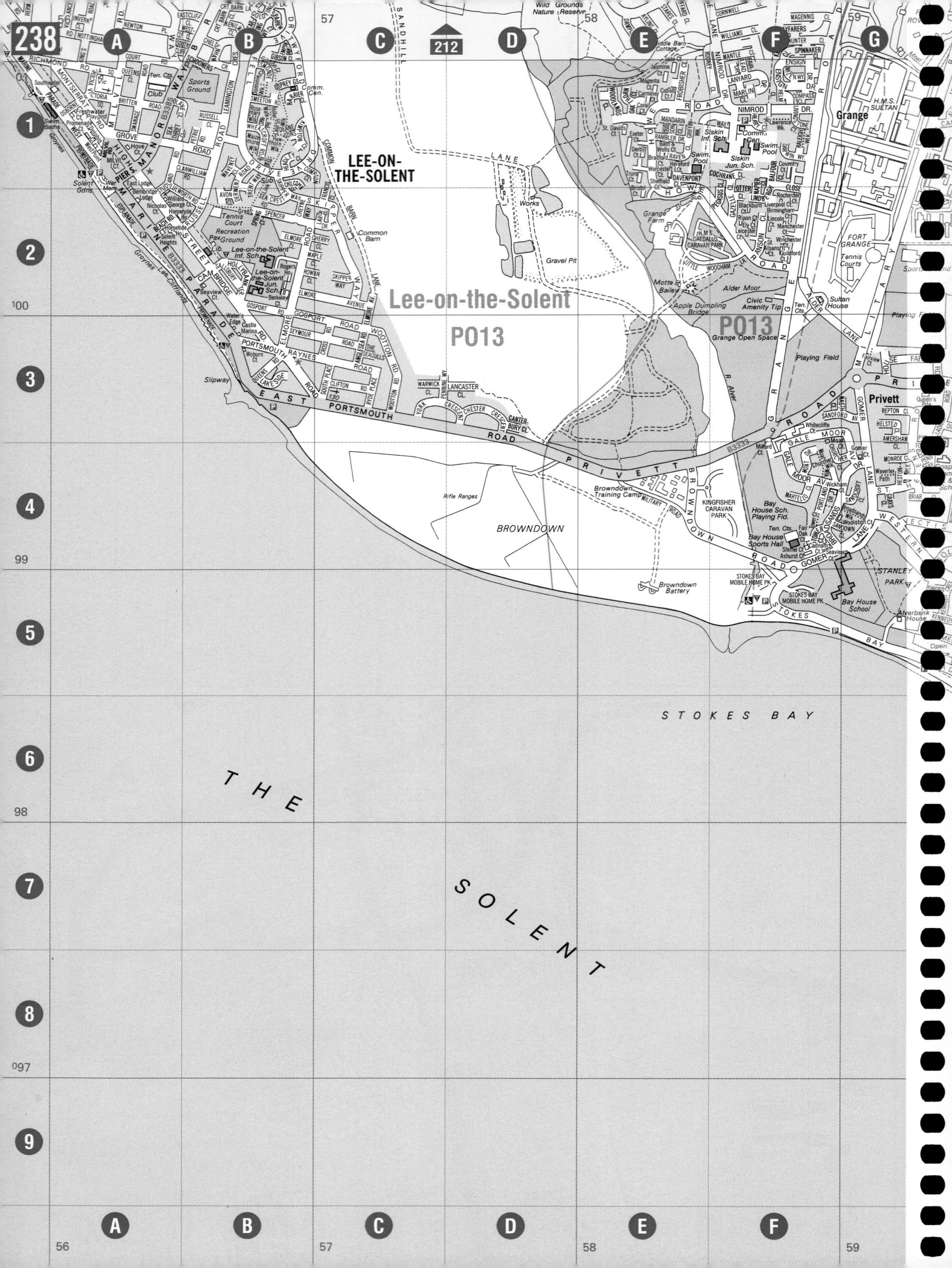

LEE-ON-THE-SOLENT
Lee-on-the-Solent
PO13
Grange
Privett
STOKES BAY
THE SOLENT
BROWNDOWN
Browndown Battery
Rifle Ranges
Gravel Pit
Common Barn
Alder Moor
Grange Open Space
Playing Field
Bay House School
H.M.S. SULTAN
FORT GRANGE
EAST PORTSMOUTH ROAD
PRIVETT ROAD
MARINE PARADE
212

H
J
K
L
M
N
G
213
240
460
61
62
01
100
99
98
097
1
2
3
4
5
6
7
8
9
PORTSMOUTH HARBOUR
Burrow Island (site of Fort James)
Royal Clarence Yard
Landing Stage
Weevil Lake
Jetty
Priddy's Hard
Forton Lake
Rolling Bri.
PORTSMOUTH
GOSPORT
Yacht Marina
King Charles's Fort
Esplanade Gdns.
Portsea to Gosport (Foot Ferry)
South Wharf
Landing Stage
Slipways
North Bastion
West Demi Bastion
H.M.S. DOLPHIN
Haslar Jetty
Submarine Mus.
H.M. Sub. Holland 1
Recreation Ground
ROYAL HOSPITAL HASLAR
Haslar Royal Naval Cemetery
H.M.P. HASLAR
Defence Research Agency
Haslar Bridge
Seafield
Workhouse Lake
Stoke Lake
GOSPORT PARK
The Dell
Ewer Common
Clayhall
Anglesey
Alverstoke
ALVERSTOKE
Newtown
Forton
Brockhurst
Camdentown
Gosport
GOSPORT
Ann's Hill
Ann's Hill Cemetery
PRIVETT PARK
Privett
PO12
Sports Ground
Playing Field
H.M.S. Sultan
FORT ROWNER
St. Vincent Leisure Cen.
St. Vincent College
St. Georges Barracks
St. George Barracks
Walpole Park
Boating Pond
Cockle Pond
Superstore
Gas Works
GOSPORT WAR MEM. HOSP.
Thorngate Hall
Leesland Park
Leesland C. of E. Jun. Sch.
Alverstoke Jun. Sch.
Tennis & Squash Club
Northcott House
Alverbank House
Stokes Bay Open Space
Sailing Club
Moncton House
Royal Naval Physiological Laboratory
GOSPORT & STOKES BAY GOLF COURSE
FORT MONCKTON
Club House
FORT GILKICKER
Gilkicker Point
Groynes
SPITHEAD
PROMENADE
STOKES BAY ROAD
MILITARY ROAD
FORT ROAD
CLAYHALL ROAD
HASLAR ROAD
DOLPHIN WAY
SEA WALL
ADMIRALTY
FOSTER ROAD
BURY ROAD
PRIVETT ROAD
FORTON ROAD
MUMBY ROAD
SOUTH STREET
HIGH STREET
BROCKHURST RD.
JELLICOE AVENUE
ANGLESEY ROAD
SOLENT WAY
VILLAGE ROAD
A32
B3333

A
B
C
D
E
F
G
214
239
5
01
100
99
98
97
63
64
65
1
2
3
4
5
6
7
8
9
PORTSMOUTH
Portsmouth
PORTSMOUTH & SOUTHSEA
Portsea
PORTSMOUTH HARBOUR
Old Portsmouth
Landport
Fratton
Somers Town
Southsea
SOUTHSEA
GREETHAM
Kingston
PO1
PO5
H.M. NAVAL BASE
Millennium Spinnaker Tower (Est. Comp. 2004)
Portsea to Gosport (Foot Ferry)
Portsmouth to Ryde 15mins. (Foot Ferry)
Portsmouth to Fishbourne 35mins. (Fast Ferry)
Portsmouth to Ryde 10mins. (Hovercraft) (Foot Ferry)
I.O.W. Hovercraft Terminal
SOUTHSEA COMMON
South Parade Pier
Southsea Castle Mus.
Sea Life Centre
D-Day Mus.
The Pyramids Leisure Cen.
The Rock Gardens
Canoe Lake
Model Village
Proposed Development Portsmouth F.C. & Retail Park
SPITHEAD
ENGLISH

215
242
LANGSTONE HARBOUR
CHANNEL
P03
P04
MILTON
Eastney
Eastney Sports Ground
FORT CUMBERLAND
Fraser Range (Defence Research Agency)
Southsea Caravan Activity Park
Danger Area
West Winner
Langstone Channel
PORTSMOUTH
HAVANT
Langstone Marina
Lock Gates
Lock Lake
Eastney Lake
Milton Lake
Milton Locks
Locks Sailing Club
Milton Piece
Towpath Mead
Duck Lake
Swan Lake
Frog Lake
University of Portsmouth Langstone Campus
Queen Elizabeth The Queen Mother Hall (Hall of Residence)
Langstone Campus
ST. JAMES HOSPITAL
ST. MARY'S HOSPITAL (East Wing)
ST. MARY'S HOSPITAL (West Wing)
Milton Cemetery
Highland Road Cemetery
H.M.P. KINGSTON
KINGSTON CEMETERY
War Memorial
PORTSMOUTH F.C. (Fratton Park)
FRATTON IND. EST.
ST. GEORGE'S IND. CENTRE
SOUTHSEA WORKS IND. EST.
CLUSTER IND. EST.
Proposed Development of Portsmouth F.C. & Retail Park
Recreation Ground
Playing Field
Central Depot
East Shore Sch.
Langstone Jun. Sch.
Langstone Inf. Sch.
Cricket Ground
Fair Oak Ho.
Cheriton Ho.
Waterside Sch.
Hamble Ho.
Woodlands
King Villa
Light Villa
Devine Villa
Tennis Courts
University of Portsmouth Milton Campus
BRANSBURY PARK
Playing Fields
Miniature Railway
Eastney Pumping Station Mus.
HENDERSON PARK MOBILE HOMES
Royal Marines Mus.
Eastney Fort East
Eastney Fort West
Swim. Baths
St. Helen's Playing Field
Miniature Golf Course
Rose Garden
Lumps Fort
Putting Green
Inshore Rescue Boat Station
University of Portsmouth Marine Lab.
THE KENCH
FERRY
Landing Stages
Landing Stage
Ferry (Foot)
Slipway
Sewage Works
Sewage Outfall
Pipe Lines
Groynes
Pipes
Gunner Point
SINAH
EASTERN ROAD
MILTON ROAD
VELDER AV.
EASTNEY ROAD
LANGSTONE ROAD
HENDERSON ROAD
HIGHLAND ROAD
FERRY ROAD
FORT CUMBERLAND ROAD
ROYAL GATE
ESPLANADE
EASTNEY ESPLANADE
EASTERN PARADE
BRANSBURY ROAD
DRIFTWOOD GDNS.
ST. GEORGES RD.
CROMWELL RD.
DEVONSHIRE AVENUE
EASTFIELD AVENUE
A288
A2030
B2154
G H J K L M N
1 2 3 4 5 6 7 8 9
66 67 68 69
01 100 99 98 97

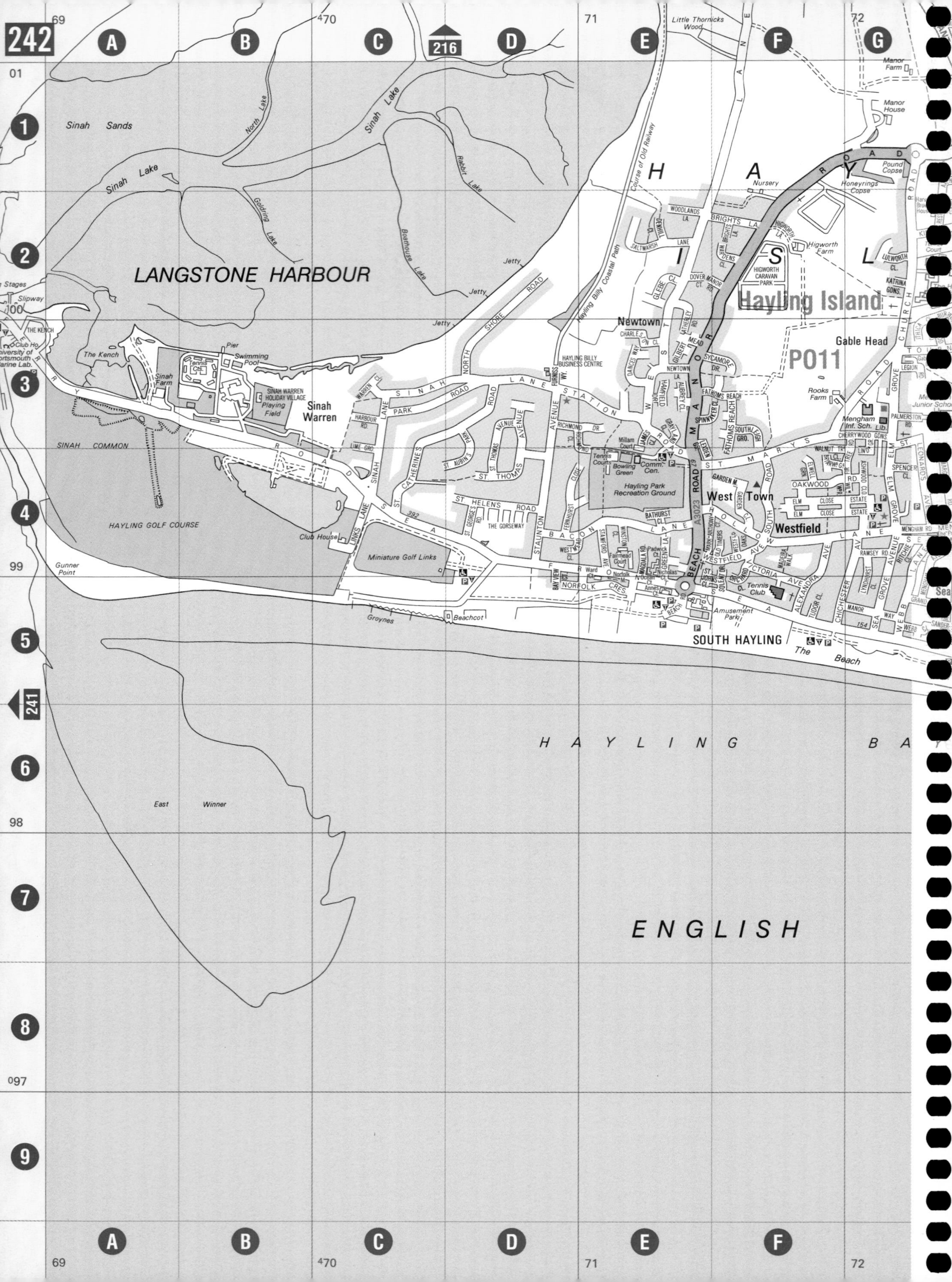
LANGSTONE HARBOUR
Sinah Sands
Sinah Lake
North Lake
Golding Lake
Rabbit Lake
Boathouse Lake
Jetty
The Kench
Pier
Swimming Pool
Sinah Farm
SINAH WARREN HOLIDAY VILLAGE
Playing Field
Sinah Warren
SINAH COMMON
HAYLING GOLF COURSE
Club House
Miniature Golf Links
Gunner Point
Groynes
Beachcot
East Winner
HAYLING BAY
ENGLISH
H A Y L I N G I S L A N D
Hayling Island
PO11
Newtown
West Town
Westfield
SOUTH HAYLING
The Beach
Amusement Park
Tennis Club
Hayling Park Recreation Ground
Bowling Green
Comm. Cen.
Millam Court
HAYLING BILLY BUSINESS CENTRE
Hayling Billy Coastal Path
Course of Old Railway
HIGWORTH CARAVAN PARK
Higworth Farm
Nursery
Honeyrings Copse
Pound Copse
Manor House
Manor Farm
Little Thornicks Wood
Gable Head
Rooks Farm
Mengham Inf. Sch.
Lib.
Junior School
SINAH LANE
STATION ROAD
MANOR ROAD
BEACH ROAD
SEA FRONT
ST MARYS ROAD
BACON LANE
NORTH SHORE ROAD
ST HELENS ROAD
ST THOMAS AVENUE
ST CATHERINES ROAD
LINKS LANE
ELM GROVE
CHURCH ROAD
WESTFIELD AVENUE
THE GORSEWAY
NORFOLK CRES.
A3023
216
241

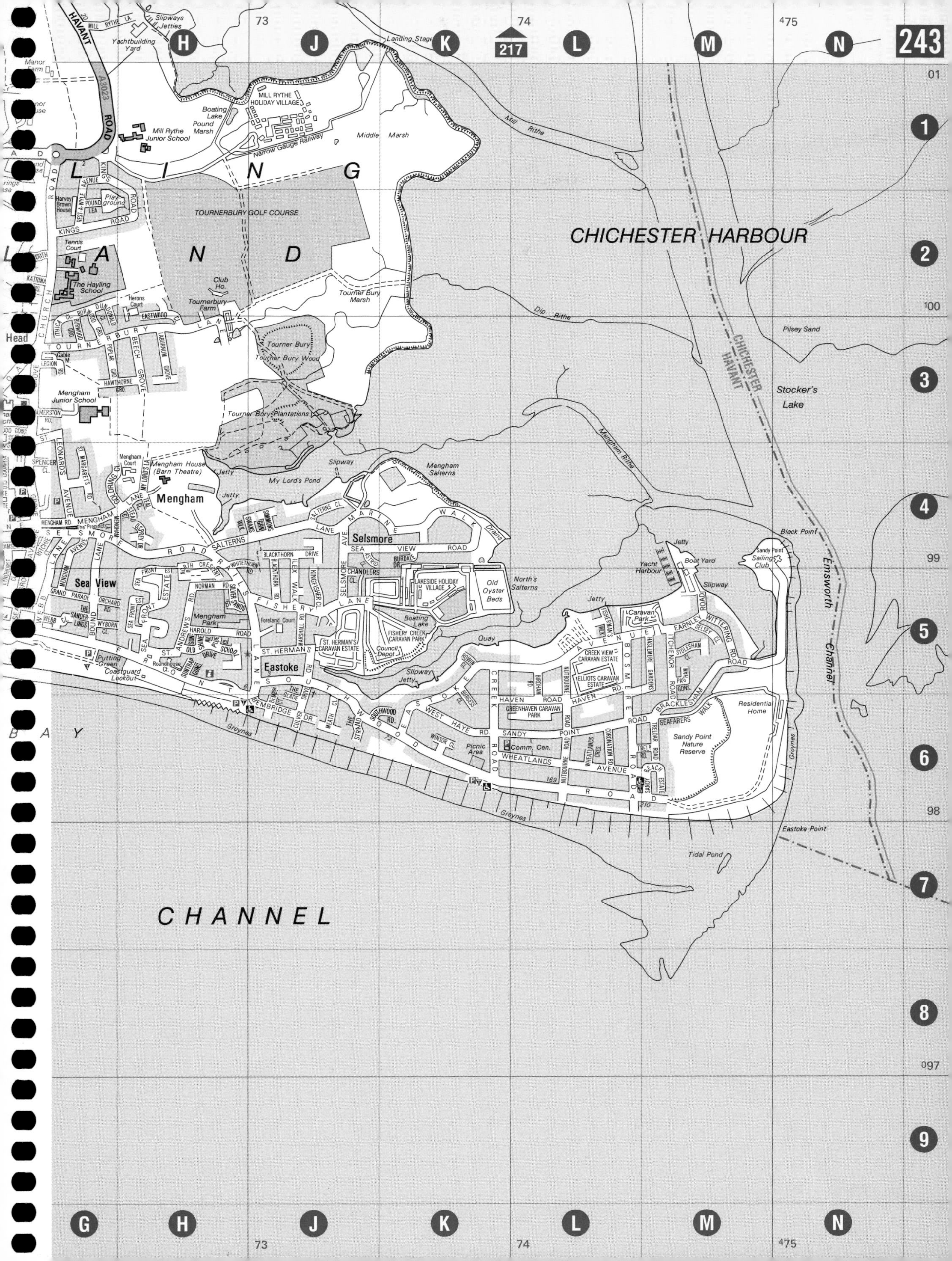
CHICHESTER HARBOUR
CHANNEL
B A Y
Mengham
Eastoke
Selsmore
Sea View
TOURNERBURY GOLF COURSE
Mill Rythe Junior School
MILL RYTHE HOLIDAY VILLAGE
The Hayling School
Mengham Junior School
Mengham House (Barn Theatre)
Tourner Bury Wood
Tourner Bury Marsh
Middle Marsh
Mengham Salterns
Mengham Rithe
Dip Rithe
Mill Rithe
Pilsey Sand
Stocker's Lake
Emsworth Channel
Black Point
Sandy Point Sailing Club
Sandy Point Nature Reserve
Yacht Harbour
Boat Yard
Eastoke Point
Tidal Pond
Groynes
LAKESIDE HOLIDAY VILLAGE
FISHERY CREEK CARAVAN PARK
ST. HERMAN'S CARAVAN ESTATE
CREEK VIEW CARAVAN ESTATE
ELLIOTS CARAVAN ESTATE
GREENHAVEN CARAVAN PARK
Old Oyster Beds
North's Salterns
My Lord's Pond
Coastguard Lookout
Putting Green
Residential Home
CHICHESTER
HAVANT
217
73
74
475
100
99
98
097
01
G H J K L M N
1 2 3 4 5 6 7 8 9

A
B
C
D
E
F
G
1
2
3
4
5
6
7
8
9
04
05
06
07
405
92
91
90
89
88
226
ASHLEY
ALEXANDRA RD.
ALDER RD.
POOLE COMMERCE CENTRE
Branksome
BRANKSOME
BH12
POOLE
BOURNEMOUTH
BOURNEMOUTH ROAD
A35
NORTH LODGE RD.
PARKSTONE
PARKSTONE AVENUE
Courthill First Sch.
Alexandra Park
Bowling Alley
Lindsay Hall
Superstore
The Victoria Sch.
Convent
Monastery
WESSEX
Uplands School
Poole
CLIFTON ROAD
Branksome Park
BH13
BH14
Canford Cliffs
PARKSTONE GOLF COURSE
Club House
Overlinks Viewpoint
Ponds
Luscombe Valley
Lilliput
Lilliput C. of E. First Sch.
HARBOUR PROSPECT
LILLIPUT ROAD
Compton Acres
Branksome Park Wood
Pleasure Gardens
Berkeley Towers
Branksome Chine
HERBERT HOSPITAL
Library
King's College Chislehurst Flats
WESTERN ROAD
CANFORD CLIFFS ROAD
PINECLIFF ROAD
B3065
B3369
Hospice
Minterne Grange
Evening Hill
Harbour Watch
Lanscombe Valley Nature Reserve
East Dorset Sailing Club
Pigeon Bottom
Cliffs Chine Gardens
Canford Cliffs
ST. ANN'S HOSPITAL
Little Fosters
Waters Edge
SHORE ROAD
POOLE HARBOUR
Groynes
PROMENADE
Sandbanks Pav.
Putt. Grn.
Jetty
Boat House
PANORAMA ROAD
BANKS ROAD
SANDBANKS
The Towans
Landing Stage

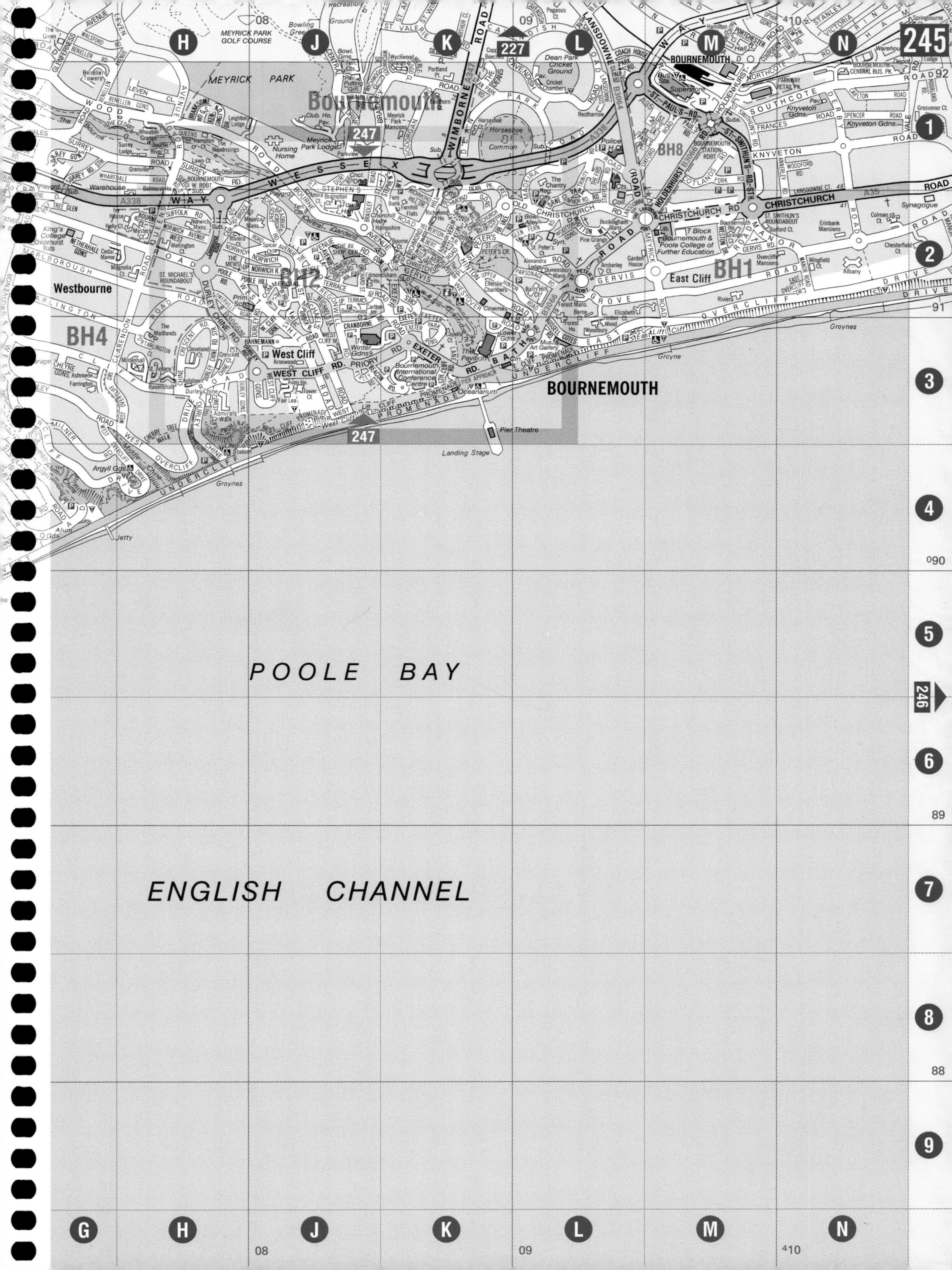
POOLE BAY
ENGLISH CHANNEL
BOURNEMOUTH
Westbourne
West Cliff
East Cliff
BH1
BH2
BH4
BH8
MEYRICK PARK
MEYRICK PARK GOLF COURSE
Dean Park Cricket Ground
Pier Theatre
Landing Stage
227
247
246

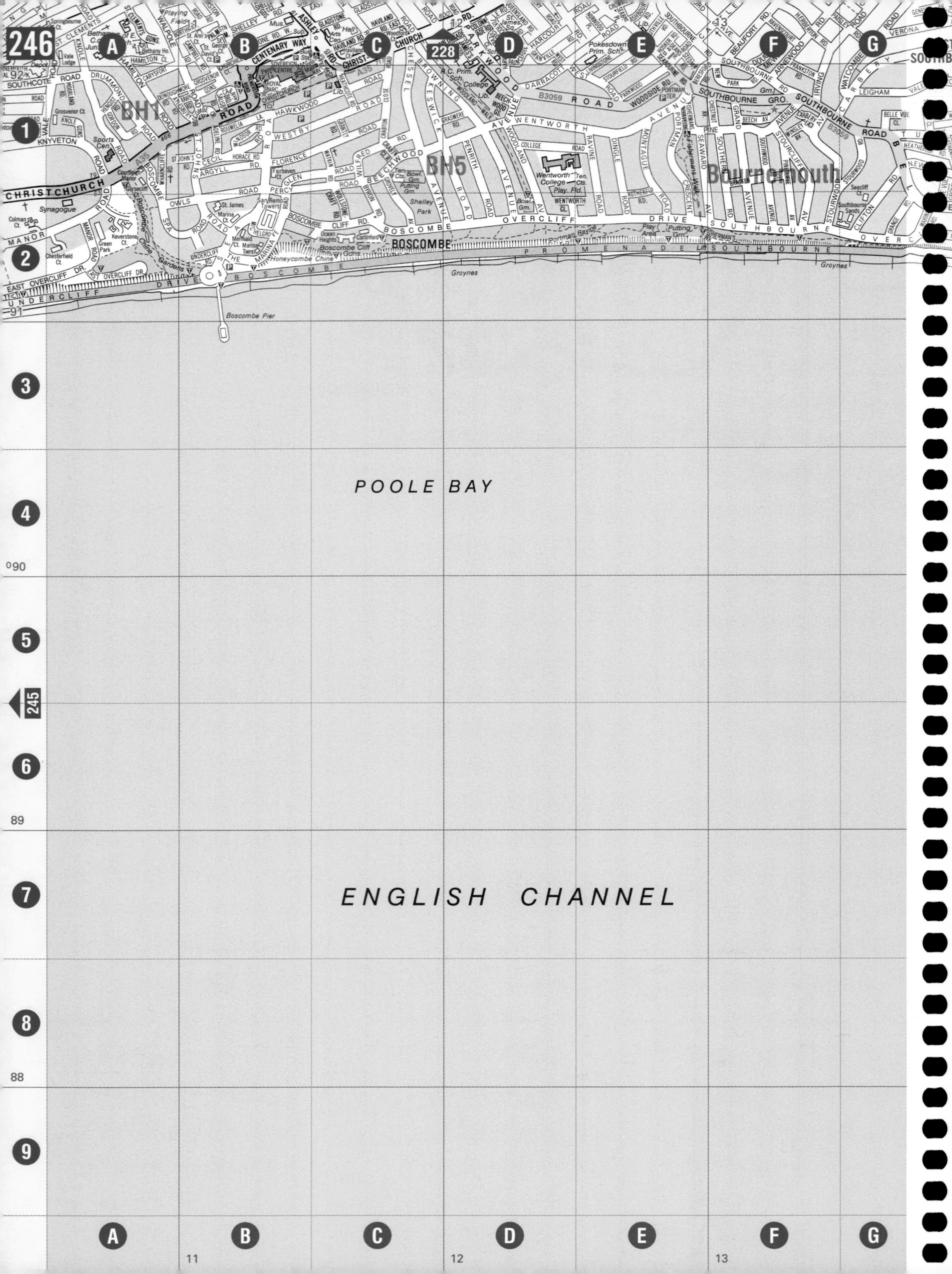
A
B
C
D
E
F
G
1
2
3
4
5
6
7
8
9
228
245
BH1
BH5
Bournemouth
POOLE BAY
ENGLISH CHANNEL
CHRISTCHURCH ROAD
CENTENARY WAY
SOUTHBOURNE GRO.
WENTWORTH AV.
OVERCLIFF DRIVE
BOSCOMBE
PROMENADE
SOUTHBOURNE
UNDERCLIFF DRIVE
EAST OVERCLIFF DR.
Boscombe Pier
Groynes
Boscombe Chine Gardens
Honeycombe Chine
Boscombe Cliff Gdns.
Wentworth College
Shelley Park
Sports Cen.
Synagogue
Pokesdown Prim. Sch.
R.C. Prim. Sch.
Southbourne Sands
Seacliff Ct.
Fisherman's Walk
B3059
A35
92
91
90
89
88
11
12
13

WEST SOUTHBOURNE
H
J
K
L
M
N
229
WICK
HENGISTBURY HEAD
Christchurch
BH23
Grimbury Marsh
Crouch Hill
BH6
CHRISTCHURCH BOURNEMOUTH
SOLENT MEADS GOLF COURSE
SOLENT MEADS
Wick Hams
SOUTHBOURNE
PROMENADE
BROADWAY
Groynes
White Pits
HENGISTBURY HEAD
Coastguard Lookout Station
1
2
3
4
245
WESSEX WAY
A338
WIMBORNE RD.
A347
Meyrick Park Lodge
Horseshoe Common
Council Offices
Town Hall
Churchill Hall
Central Gardens
Bournemouth
BH1
BH2
BH4
Upper Gardens
Lower Gardens
The Avenue Shopping Centre
Bournemouth Register Office
Synagogue
Cinemas
The Pavilion
The Winter Gardens
Bournemouth International Centre
East Cliff
Russell Cotes Art Gallery & Mus.
IMAX Cinema
Oceanarium
West Cliff
BOURNEMOUTH
POOLE BAY
Pier Theatre
Bournemouth Pier
Landing Stage
DURLEY CHINE RD.
WEST CLIFF RD.
PRIORY ROAD
EXETER ROAD
BATH ROAD
B3066
UNDERCLIFF DRIVE
Lifeguard Station
5
6
7
8
9
G
H
J
K
L
M
N
245

INDEX

Including Streets, Places & Areas, Industrial Estates, Selected Subsidiary Addresses
and Selected Places of Interest.

HOW TO USE THIS INDEX

1. Each street name is followed by its Posttown or Postal Locality and then by its map reference; e.g. Abbeydore Rd. *Ports* . . . .8D **200** is in the Portsmouth Posttown and is to be found in square 8D on page **200**. The page number being shown in bold type.
   A strict alphabetical order is followed in which Av., Rd., St., etc. (though abbreviated) are read in full and as part of the street name; e.g. Abbeyfield Dri. appears after Abbey Enterprise Cen. but before Abbey Fields Clo.

2. Streets and a selection of Subsidiary names not shown on the Maps, appear in the index in *Italics* with the thoroughfare to which it is connected shown in brackets; e.g. *Abbey Wlk. Roms* . . . .5L *129 (off Church St.)*

3. Places and areas are shown in the index in **blue type**, the map reference referring to the actual map square in which the town or area is located and not to the place name; e.g. **Abbotswood.** **1N 129**

4. An example of a selected place of interest is Action Stations Exhibition Mus. 2B 240 (3J 5)

5. Map references shown in brackets; e.g. *Abbey Pas. Win* . . . .7L **105** (9N **237**) refer to entries that also appear on the large scale pages **4-5**, **237** and **247**.

GENERAL ABBREVIATIONS

All : Alley	Cir : Circus	Gt : Great	M : Mews	Sq : Square
App : Approach	Clo : Close	Grn : Green	Mt : Mount	Sta : Station
Arc : Arcade	Comn : Common	Gro : Grove	Mus : Museum	St : Street
Av : Avenue	Cotts : Cottages	Ho : House	N : North	Ter : Terrace
Bk : Back	Ct : Court	Ind : Industrial	Pal : Palace	Trad : Trading
Boulevd : Boulevard	Cres : Crescent	Info : Information	Pde : Parade	Up : Upper
Bri : Bridge	Cft : Croft	Junct : Junction	Pk : Park	Va : Vale
B'way : Broadway	Dri : Drive	La : Lane	Pas : Passage	Vw : View
Bldgs : Buildings	E : East	Lit : Little	Pl : Place	Vs : Villas
Bus : Business	Embkmt : Embankment	Lwr : Lower	Quad : Quadrant	Vis : Visitors
Cvn : Caravan	Est : Estate	Mc : Mac	Res : Residential	Wlk : Walk
Cen : Centre	Fld : Field	Mnr : Manor	Ri : Rise	W : West
Chu : Church	Gdns : Gardens	Mans : Mansions	Rd : Road	Yd : Yard
Chyd : Churchyard	Gth : Garth	Mkt : Market	Shop : Shopping	
Circ : Circle	Ga : Gate	Mdw : Meadow	S : South	

POSTTOWN AND POSTAL LOCALITY ABBREVIATIONS

Abb W : Abbots Worthy	*Bord* : Bordon	*Chil C* : Chilton Candover	*E End* : East End	*Frog* : Frogham
Abb A : Abbotts Ann	*Bosc* : Boscombe	*Chine* : Chineham	*E Dock* : Eastern Docks	*F'mre* : Frogmore
Ald : Aldbourne	*Bot* : Botley	*Chol* : Cholderton	*E Graf* : East Grafton	*Frox* : Froxfield
Alder : Alderbury	*Bourn* : Bournemouth	*Christ* : Christchurch	*E Grim* : East Grimstead	*Froy* : Froyle
A'hlt : Alderholt	*Brfld* : Braishfield	*Chu C* : Church Crookham	*E Har* : East Harting	*Fy'd* : Fyfield
A'mstn : Aldermaston	*Bram* : Brambridge	*Churt* : Churt	*Eastl* : Eastleigh	*Gods* : Godshill
A'sht : Aldershot	*Bramd* : Bramdean	*Chut C* : Chute Cadley	*E Meon* : East Meon	*Gom* : Gomeldon
All : Allington	*Braml* : Bramley	*Chut F* : Chute Forest	*Estn* : Easton	*Good C* : Goodworth Clatford
Alr : Alresford	*B'shaw* : Bramshaw	*Chut S* : Chute Standen	*E Stra* : East Stratton	*Gor L* : Gorley Lynch
Alt : Alton	*B'shtt* : Bramshott	*Clan* : Clanfield	*E Tis* : East Tisted	*Gos* : Gosport
Ame : Amesbury	*B'shtt C* : Bramshott Chase	*Cla* : Clanville	*E Tyth* : East Tytherley	*Grat* : Grateley
A'prt : Amport	*Brams* : Bramshill	*Clid* : Cliddesden	*E Wel* : East Wellow	*Gray* : Grayshott
Amp : Ampfield	*Brnk* : Branksome	*Col C* : Colden Common	*E Woody* : East Woodyates	*Gthm* : Greatham
And : Andover	*Brnk P* : Branksome Park	*Colem* : Colemore	*E Wor* : East Worldham	*Gt Shod* : Great Shoddesden
And D : Andover Down	*Brans* : Bransgore	*Coll T* : College Town	*Ecc* : Ecchinswell	*Green* : Greenham
Anna V : Anna Valley	*Brea* : Breamore	*Coll D* : Collingbourne Ducis	*Edm* : Edmondsham	*Grey* : Greywell
App : Appleshaw	*Brim* : Brimpton	*Coll K* : Collingbourne Kingston	*Ellis* : Ellisfield	*Gund* : Gundleton
Ash : Ash	*Brim C* : Brimpton Common	*Combe* : Combe	*E'std* : Elsted	*Hale* : Hale
Ashe : Ashe	*Brit* : Britford	*Comp* : Compton	*Elve* : Elvetham	*Hamb* : Hamble
Ash H : Ashford Hill	*Bro Ch* : Broad Chalke	*C'hlt* : Conholt	*Ems* : Emsworth	*Hmbdn* : Hambledon
Ashy : Ashley	*Broc* : Brockenhurst	*Coom B* : Coombe Bissett	*Enb* : Enborne	*Hang* : Hangersley
Ashy H : Ashley Heath	*B'ton* : Brockington	*Copy* : Copythorne	*Enh A* : Enham Alamein	*Hann* : Hannington
A'wrth : Ashmansworth	*Brook* : Brook	*Cptn* : Corhampton	*E'sly* : Eversley	*Harb* : Harbridge
Asht : Ashurst	*Bro'tn* : Broughton	*Cosh* : Cosham	*E Cen* : Eversley Centre	*H Wes* : Hartley Wespall
Ash V : Ash Vale	*Bro C* : Brown Candover	*Cot* : Cottonworth	*E'sly C* : Eversley Cross	*H Win* : Hartley Wintney
Avtn : Avington	*Bucks H* : Bucks Horn Oak	*Cowes* : Cowes	*Evtn* : Everton	*H'way* : Hardway
Avon : Avon	*Bulf* : Bulford	*Cowp* : Cowplain	*Ews* : Ewshot	*Hasl* : Haslemere
Awb : Awbridge	*Bulf B* : Bulford Barracks	*Cram* : Crampmoor	*Exby* : Exbury	*Hat W* : Hatch Warren
Bad L : Badshot Lea	*Bull H* : Bull Hill	*Cran* : Cranborne	*Ext* : Exton	*Hath* : Hatherden
Ball : Ball Hill	*Bton* : Buriton	*Craw* : Crawley	*Fac* : Faccombe	*Hav* : Havant
Bart : Bartley	*Burg* : Burgate	*Crip* : Cripplestyle	*F Oak* : Fair Oak	*Hawk* : Hawkley
Bart S : Barton on Sea	*Burgh* : Burghclere	*Cron* : Crondall	*Fare* : Fareham	*Hay I* : Hayling Island
Bar S : Barton Stacey	*Burl* : Burley	*Crook V* : Crookham Village	*Far W* : Farleigh Wallop	*Haz H* : Hazeley Heath
Bas : Basingstoke	*Bur* : Burridge	*Crow* : Crow	*Far H* : Farley Hill	*Head* : Headley (Bordon)
Baug : Baughurst	*Burs* : Bursledon	*C'then* : Crowthorne	*Farl* : Farlington	*H'ly* : Headley (Thatcham)
Beau : Beaulieu	*Burt* : Burton	*Curd* : Curdridge	*Farn* : Farnborough	*Head D* : Headley Down
Bea : Beauworth	*Butt* : Buttermere	*Dam* : Damerham	*F'ham* : Farnham	*Heck* : Heckfield
Bed : Bedhampton	*Cad* : Cadnam	*Dea* : Deane	*Farr* : Farringdon	*H End* : Hedge End
Bch : Beech	*Cal* : Calmore	*Den* : Denmead	*Fawl* : Fawley	*Navy* : H M Naval Base
B Hill : Beech Hill	*Cals* : Calshot	*Dib* : Dibden	*Fern* : Ferndown	*H'rd* : Herriard
Bent : Bentley	*Cam* : Camberley	*Dib P* : Dibden Purlieu	*Finch* : Finchampstead	*Highb* : Highbridge
Bentw : Bentworth	*Can C* : Canford Cliffs	*Dipp* : Dippenhall	*Firs* : Firsdown	*High* : Highclere
Bigh : Bighton	*Cath* : Catherington	*Dock* : Dockenfield	*Fish P* : Fishers Pond	*Highc* : Highcliffe
B'std : Binsted	*Chal* : Chalton	*Dogm* : Dogmersfield	*Fle* : Fleet	*Hight* : Hightown
Bish G : Bishops Green	*Chan F* : Chandler's Ford	*Down* : Downton (Lymington)	*Fobd* : Fobdown	*Hill B* : Hill Brow
B'stne : Bishopstone	*Charl* : Charlton	*D'ton* : Downton (Salisbury)	*Fordb* : Fordingbridge	*Hils* : Hilsea
Bish S : Bishops Sutton	*Charl S* : Charlton All Saints	*Dray* : Drayton	*Fordl* : Ford	*Hind* : Hindhead
Bish W : Bishops Waltham	*Char D* : Charlton Down	*Drox* : Droxford	*F'bri* : Fordingbridge	*Hint* : Hinton
Black : Blackfield	*Char A* : Charter Alley	*Dum* : Dummer	*Fort* : Forton	*Hint A* : Hinton Ampner
Blkmr : Blackmoor	*Chat* : Chattis Hill	*Dun* : Dunbridge	*F'bry* : Fosbury	*Holb* : Holbury
B'wtr : Blackwater	*Chaw* : Chawton	*Durl* : Durley	*Four M* : Four Marks	*Holt P* : Holt Pound
Blash : Blashford	*Cher* : Cheriton	*Durr* : Durrington	*Free* : Freefolk	*Holyb* : Holybourne
Bliss : Blissford	*Chlbn* : Chilbolton	*E Bol* : East Boldre	*Fren* : Frensham	*Hom* : Homington
Bock : Bockhampton	*Chilc* : Chilcomb	*E Chol* : East Cholderton	*Frim* : Frimley	*Hook* : Hook
Bold : Boldre	*Chilw* : Chilworth	*E Dean* : East Dean	*Frim G* : Frimley Green	*Hook C* : Hook Common

Hord : Hordle
Horn : Horndean
H Hth : Horton Heath
Houtn : Houghton
Hnd G : Hound Green
Hung : Hungerford (Berkshire)
Hun : Hungerford (Fordingbridge)
Hurs : Hursley
Hur P : Hurstbourne Priors
Hur T : Hurstbourne Tarrant
Hurn : Hurn
Hyde : Hyde
Hythe : Hythe
Ibly : Ibsley
Ibt : Ibthorpe
Idm : Idmiston
Ids : Idsworth
Ink : Inkpen
Ink C : Inkpen Common
Is'ton : Isington
It Ab : Itchen Abbas
It Sto : Itchen Stoke
Kemp : Kempshott
Key : Keyhaven
Kilm : Kilmeston
Kim : Kimbridge
Kimp : Kimpton
Kimp D : Kimpton Down
K're : Kingsclere
Kingsl : Kingsley
King S : Kings Somborne
King W : Kings Worthy
Kint H : Kintbury Holt
Know : Knowle
Land : Landford
Langr : Langrish
Lang : Langstone
Lash : Lasham
Lave : Laverstoke
Lcky : Lockerley
Lee : Lee
Lee S : Lee-on-the-Solent
L'mre : Linchmere
Lind : Lindford
Linw : Linwood
Lip : Liphook
Liss : Liss
Lit L : Little London
L Pk : Little Park
Lit S : Little Sandhurst
Lit Sh : Little Shoddesden
Lit Som : Little Somborne
L Hth : Locks Heath
Lngmr : Longmoor
Longp : Longparish
Longs : Longstock
Long S : Long Sutton
Love : Lovedean
Lover : Lover
Lwr C : Lower Chute
Lwr F : Lower Farringdon
Lwr Fr : Lower Froyle
Lwr S : Lower Swanwick
Lwr Wd : Lower Wield
Lud : Ludgershall
Lych : Lychpit
L'ton : Lymington
Lyn : Lyndhurst
Map : Mapledurwell
March : Marchwood
M'tin : Martin
Mart W : Martyr Worthy
Matt : Mattingley
Meds : Medstead
Meon : Meonstoke
Mich : Micheldever
Mich S : Micheldever Station
Michm : Michelmersh
Mid W : Middle Wallop
Mid Wy : Middle Wyke
Mil S : Milford on Sea
Min : Minstead
Mis : Mislingford
Mock : Mockbeggar
Monk S : Monk Sherborne
Mnkwd : Monkwood
Monx : Monxton
Mort : Mortimer
Mort C : Mortimer Common
Mort W : Mortimer West End
Mott : Mottisfont
Myt : Mytchett
Nat S : Nately Scures
Navy : H M Naval Base
Nea : Neacroft
Neth W : Nether Wallop
Net A : Netley Abbey
N'bry : Newbury
New M : New Milton
Newn : Newnham
Newt T : Newton Toney
Newt V : Newton Valence
Newt : Newtown (Fareham)
New : Newtown (Newbury)
New C : Newtown Common
Nom : Nomansland
Nor W : Norley Wood
N Bad : North Baddesley
N Boar : North Boarhunt
N'brne : Northbourne
N End : North End
N Gor : North Gorley
N'ton D : Northington Down
N Lit : North Litchfield
N Wal : North Waltham
N War : North Warnborough
Nun : Nunton
Nurs : Nursling
Nye : Nyewood
Oakh : Oakhanger
Okly : Oakley
Ocn V : Ocean Village
Odi : Odiham
Old Al : Old Alresford
Old B : Old Basing
Oss : Ossemsley
Ott : Otterbourne
Over : Overton
Ovr W : Over Wallop
Ower : Ower
Owl : Owlsmoor
Ows : Owslebury
Oxen : Oxenwood
Pad C : Padworth Common
Pale : Palestine
P End : Pamber End
P Grn : Pamber Green
P Hth : Pamber Heath
Park G : Park Gate
Park : Parkstone
Parl : Parley
Pass : Passfield
Penn : Pennington
P Cnr : Penton Corner
Pen G : Penton Grafton
Pen H : Penton Harroway
Pen M : Penton Mewsey
Pent : Pentridge
Per D : Perham Down
Ptsfld : Petersfield
Pic P : Picket Piece
P Twen : Picket Twenty
Pill : Pilley
Pitt : Pitton
Plait : Plaitford
Poole : Poole
Portc : Portchester
P'mre : Portmore
Port : Porton
Port D : Porton Down
Ports : Portsmouth
Port S : Port Solent
Poul : Poulner
P Can : Preston Candover
Prior D : Priors Dean
Priv : Privett
Pur : Purbrook
Quar : Quarley
Rag A : Ragged Appleshaw
Rake : Rake
R'dll : Ramsdell
R'hm : Redenham
Redl : Redlynch
Red P : Red Post Bridge
Ring : Ringwood
Rise : Riseley
Rockb : Rockbourne
Rock : Rockford
Rog : Rogate
Roms : Romsey
Ropl : Ropley
Roth : Rotherwick
Row : Rowledge
Row C : Rowland's Castle
Rown : Rownhams
R'fld : Runfold
St I : St Ives
St L : St Leonards
St M : St Mary Bourne
S'hrst : Sandhurst
S'th : Sandleheath
Sar G : Sarisbury Green
Seale : Seale
Seg W : Segensworth West
Selb : Selborne
Shald : Shalden
Shaw : Shaw
Shed : Shedfield
Sher : Sherborne St John
Sher E : Sherfield English
Sher L : Sherfield-on-Loddon
Ship B : Shipton Bellinger
Shir H : Shirrell Heath
Shoot : Shootash
Shot : Shottermill
Sil : Silchester
Slea : Sleaford
Sman : Smannell
Sob : Soberton
Sotn : Southampton
Sotn I : Southampton International Airport
South : Southbourne
S G'ly : South Gorley
S Hart : South Harting
S'sea : Southsea
S Warn : South Warnborough
S'wick : Southwick
S Won : South Wonston
S'wd B : Southwood Bus. Pk.
Spar : Sparsholt
Spen W : Spencers Wood
S'frd : Standford
Steep : Steep
Steep M : Steep Marsh
Stev : Steventon
Stockb : Stockbridge
Stoke : Stoke
Sto C : Stoke Charity
Ston C : Stoney Cross
Str S : Stratfield Saye
Str T : Stratfield Turgis
Strd : Stroud
Stub : Stubbington
Sut S : Sutton Scotney
S'fld : Swallowfield
Swanm : Swanmore
Swanw : Swanwick
Sway : Sway
T'ley : Tadley
Tang : Tangley
Thor I : Thorney Island
Thru : Thruxton
Thur : Thursley
Tichb : Tichborne
Tidw : Tidworth
Tilf : Tilford
Tims : Timsbury
Tip : Tiptoe
Titch : Titchfield
Tong : Tongham
Tot : Totton
Tuft : Tufton
Tun : Tunworth
Twy : Twyford
Up Ch : Upper Chute
Up Cl : Upper Clatford
Up Farr : Upper Farringdon
Up Fro : Upper Froyle
Up Wld : Upper Wield
Up Wn : Upper Wootton
Uphm : Upham
Up N : Up Nately
Up Som : Up Somborne
Upt G : Upton Grey
Ver D : Vernham Dean
Ver : Verwood
Wal : Walhampton
Walk : Walkford
Wal C : Waltham Chase
Wal I : Walworth Ind. Est.
W'frd : Warnford
Wars : Warsash
Wash W : Wash Water
Water : Waterlooville
Well C : Wellington College
Westb : Westbourne
W Dean : West Dean
W End : West End
W Dock : Western Docks
W Gri : West Grimstead
W Har : West Harting
W Meon : West Meon
West : Weston
Wes C : Weston Corbett
W Tis : West Tisted
W Tyth : West Tytherley
W Wel : West Wellow
W'hll : Weyhill
Wey : Weymouth
Wher : Wherwell
Whitc : Whitchurch
W'hill : Whitehill
White : Whiteley
W'ish : Whiteparish
W'bry : Whitsbury
Wick : Wickham
Wid : Widley
Wim : Wimborne
Wim G : Wimborne St Giles
Win : Winchester
W'fld : Winchfield
Wink : Winkton
Wins : Winsor
Wint D : Winterbourne Dauntsey
Wint E : Winterbourne Earls
Wint G : Winterbourne Gunner
W'slw : Winterslow
Wok : Wokingham
Wolv : Wolverton
Wolv C : Wolverton Common
W'flls : Woodfalls
W'grn : Woodgreen
W'lnds : Woodlands (Southampton)
Wood : Woodlands (Wimborne)
W'cott : Woodmancott
Wool H : Woolton Hill
Woot L : Wootton St Lawrence
Wor D : Worthy Down
Wort : Worting
Wrec : Wrecclesham
Yate : Yateley

A

Aaron Ct. *March* 8E **172**
A Avenue. *Hythe* 3A **208** (in two parts)
Abbas Grn. *Hav* 2D **202**
Abbatt Clo. *Lud* 1F **30**
Abbetts La. *Cam* 1K **29**
Abbey Clo. *Hythe* 6M **193**
Abbey Ct. *Bas* 2B **42**
Abbey Ct. *Cam* 8M **19**
Abbey Ct. *F'ham* 8E **64**
Abbey Ct. *Sotn* 3L **173**
Abbeydore Rd. *Ports* 8D **200**
Abbey Enterprise Cen. *Roms* 7C **130**
Abbeyfield Dri. *Fare* 7M **197**
Abbey Fields Clo. *Net A* 3H **195**
Abbey Hill. *Net A* 2D **194**
Abbey Hill Clo. *Win* 4L **105**
Abbey Hill Rd. *Win* 4K **105**
Abbey Pk. Ind. Est. *Roms* 6C **130**
Abbey Pas. *Win* 7L **105** (9N **237**)
Abbey Rd. *Bas* 2B **42**
Abbey Rd. *Bch & Meds* 9L **79**
Abbey Rd. *Fare* 7N **197**
Abbey St. *F'ham* 8E **64**
Abbey, The. *Roms* 5L **129**
Abbey Wlk. *Roms* 5L **129** (off Church St.)
Abbey Water. *Roms* 5L **129**
Abbey Way. *Farn* 8L **29**
Abbotsbury Rd. *Eastl* 1K **161**
Abbots Clo. *Fle* 2M **47**
Abbots Clo. *Highc* 7H **231**
Abbots Clo. *Water* 5K **201**
Abbotsfield. *Tot* 3L **171**
Abbotsfield Clo. *Sotn* 6H **159**
Abbotsford. *Bart* 4B **170**
Abbot's Ride. *F'ham* 9G **64**
Abbotstone Av. *Hav* 5G **202**
Abbotstone Rd. *Fobd* 7C **94**
Abbots Way. *Fare* 8N **197**
Abbots Way. *Net A* 3H **195**
Abbotswood. 1N **129**
Abbotswood Clo. *Roms* 3B **130**
Abbotswood Clo. *T'ley* 6H **11**
Abbott Clo. *Bas* 9L **41**
Abbott Clo. *Bourn* 6L **227**
Abbott Rd. *Bourn* 6L **227**
Abbotts Ann. 5G **68**
Abbotts Ann Rd. *A'prt* 4B **68**
Abbotts Ann Rd. *Win* 3H **105**
Abbotts Clo. *Abb A* 5G **69**
Abbotts Clo. *Tidw* 7C **30**
Abbotts Clo. *Win* 4L **105**
Abbotts Cotts. *Dock* 3A **84**
Abbotts Ct. *Win* 4K **105**
Abbotts Drove. *W Wel* 1N **155**
Abbotts Hill. *Abb A* 6G **69**
Abbotts Rd. *Eastl* 2C **160**
Abbotts Rd. *Tidw* 7C **30**
Abbotts Rd. *Win* 4L **105**
Abbotts Way. *Sotn* 1N **173**
A'Becket Ct. *Ports* 3B **240** (6K **5**)
Abercorn Ho. *B'wtr* 3G **28**
Abercrombie Gdns. *Sotn* 7F **158**
Aberdare Av. *Ports* 8J **201**
Aberdare Rd. *Bourn* 3J **227**
Aberdeen Clo. *Fare* 6A **198**
Aberdeen Rd. *Sotn* 1A **174**
Aberdeen Ter. *Gray* 3M **103**
Aberdour Clo. *Sotn* 2F **174**
Abingdon Clo. *Gos* 3K **239**
Abingdon Dri. *Highc* 6L **231**
Abingdon Gdns. *Sotn* 8K **159**
Abingdon Rd. *S'hrst* 5E **18**
Abinger Rd. *Bourn* 8D **228**
Abney Rd. *Bourn* 3H **227**
Above Bar St. *Sotn* 5L **173** (3C **4**)
Above Hedges. *Pitt* 6E **86**
Above Town. *Up Cl* 5L **69**
Abraham Clo. *Bot* 5B **176**
Abshot Clo. *Fare* 8E **196**
Abshot Rd. *Fare* 8E **196**
Acacia Av. *Owl* 4F **18**
Acacia Gdns. *Water* 5B **182**
Acacia Rd. *Hord* 2G **233**
Acacia Rd. *Sotn* 5D **174**
Academy Clo. *Cam* 5N **19**
Accentors Clo. *Alt* 2F **80**
Acer Way. *Hav* 5H **203**
Achilles Clo. *Chine* 8G **22**
Ackender Rd. *Alt* 5E **80**
Ackrells Mead. *S'hrst* 4B **18**
Ackworth Rd. *Ports* 3H **215**
Acland Rd. *Bourn* 6M **227**
Acorn Bus. Cen. *Ports* 1E **214**
Acorn Clo. *Bas* 6F **42**
Acorn Clo. *Christ* 6J **229**
Acorn Clo. *Gos* 7F **212**
Acorn Clo. *March* 9F **172**
Acorn Clo. *New M* 2D **232**
Acorn Clo. *Ports* 9N **201**
Acorn Clo. *St L* 5B **186**
Acorn Clo. *Win* 4H **105**
Acorn Ct. *Hamb* 6K **195**
Acorn Dri. *Rown* 4D **158**
Acorn Gdns. *Water* 4B **182**
Acorn Gro. *Chan F* 8L **131**
Acorn Keep. *F'ham* 2F **64**
Acorn M. *Farn* 5J **29**
Acorn Rd. *B'wtr* 8D **18**
Acorns, The. *Burs* 1K **195**
Acorn Workshops. *Sotn* 3N **173**
Acre Ct. *And* 1A **70**
Acre La. *Water* 9C **182**
Acre Path. *And* 1A **70**
Acres Rd. *Bourn* 4F **226**
Action Stations Exhibition Mus. 2B **240** (3J **5**)
Acton Ho. *Bas* 7N **41**
Acton Rd. *Bourn* 5F **226**
Adair Rd. *S'sea* 5H **241**
Adam Clo. *Baug* 4E **10**
Adames Rd. *Ports* 1F **240**
Adampur Rd. *Tidw* 8F **30**
Adams Clo. *Farn* 6H **29**
Adams Clo. *H End* 8M **161**
Adams Clo. *N War* 8H **45**
Adam's Clo. *Per D* 5B **30**
Adams Dri. *Fle* 2A **48**
Adamsfield Gdns. *Bourn* 4G **226**
Adams Ho. *Alt* 4G **81**
Adamson Clo. *Chan F* 4B **132**
Adams Pk. Rd. *F'ham* 6F **64**
Adams Rd. *Hythe* 7M **193**
Adams Way. *Alt* 4G **81**
Adams Way. *Fare* 4F **196**
Adams Wood Dri. *March* 9E **172**
Adbury Holt. *New* 2E **8**
Adcock Ct. *Sotn* 4D **158**
Addenbroke. Gos *3L 239* (off Willis Rd.)
Adderbury Av. *Ems* 6M **203**
Addington Ct. *Mil S* 7K **235**
Addington Pl. *Christ* 8N **229**

Addiscombe Rd.—Ampfield Clo.

Addiscombe Rd. Christ. 7K 229
Addiscombe Rd. C'then 1E 18
Addison Clo. Roms. 3A 130
Addison Clo. Win 9G 105
Addison Gdns. Odi 8L 45
Addison Rd. Broc 8C 148
Addison Rd. Eastl 7F 132
Addison Rd. Frim 4N 29
Addison Rd. Sar G 3C 196
Addison Rd. S'sea 4F 240
Addison Sq. Ring 1L 187
Addis Sq. Sotn 1N 173 (in two parts)
Adelaide Clo. Bulf B 3C 66
Adelaide Clo. Christ. 6J 229
Adelaide Clo. Per D. 4B 30
Adelaide La. Bourn 2K 245 (6M 247)
Adelaide Pl. Fare. 8E 198
Adelaide Rd. And 1A 70
Adelaide Rd. Sotn. 2A 174
Adela Verne Clo. Sotn 7J 175
Adeline Rd. Bourn 1B 246
Adey Clo. Sotn 8F 174
Adhurst Rd. Hav. 5G 202
Adlam's La. Sway 4G 223
Adlington Pl. Farn. 1N 49
Admers Cres. Lip 4E 116
Admiral Pk. Ind. Est., The. Ports 5H 215
Admirals Clo. Fawl 5F 208
Admiral's Corner. S'sea. 5E 240
Admirals Ct. Hamb 7L 195
Admirals Ct. L'ton 2F 234
Admirals Ct. S'sea 5D 240
Admiral's Rd. L Hth 5E 196
Admirals Wlk. Bourn 3H 245 (9H 247)
Admirals Wlk. Gos 4H 239
Admiral's Wlk. Ports 1A 240 (2H 5)
Admirals Way. And. 1C 70
Admiral's Way. Hamb 6K 195
Admirals Way. Hythe 4M 193
Admiralty Ho. Sotn 8M 173 (9E 4)
Admiralty Rd. Bourn 2J 247
Admiralty Rd. Gos 5N 239
Admiralty Rd. Ports 2B 240 (3J 5)
Admiralty Way. Cam. 9H 19
Admiralty Way. March 7E 172
Adrian Clo. H Win. 7C 26
Adsdean Clo. Hav 5E 202
Adstone La. Ports 4K 215
Adur Clo. Gos. 9H 213
Adur Clo. W End 1F 174
Aerial Rd. S'wick 7C 200
Aerodrome Rd. Gos 4F 212
Aerospace Boulevd. Farn 4J 49
Africa Dri. March 9E 172
Agars La. Hord 9H 223
Agarton La. Mil S 8N 233
Aghemund Clo. Chine 9F 22
Agincourt Rd. Ports 9E 214
Agitator Rd. Hythe 3G 208
Agnew Ho. Gos. 1K 239
Agnew Rd. Gos. 5E 212
Agra Rd. Tidw. 8F 30
Agricola Wlk. And. 7A 52
Agwi Rd. Hythe 3G 208
Aikman La. Tot. 3H 171
Ailsa La. Sotn 6B 174
Ainger Clo. A'sht 8M 49
Ainsdale Rd. Ports 8L 201
Ainsley Gdns. Eastl 7E 132
Aintree Clo. H Hth. 4A 162
Aintree Ct. White. 1E 196
Aintree Dri. Water. 9B 182
Aintree Rd. Cal 1J 171
Airborne Forces Mus. 6J 49
Aircraft Esplanade. Farn 2L 49
Aird Clo. Wool H. 3A 8
Airfield Ind. Est. Christ 7C 230
Airfield Rd. Christ. 7B 230
Airfield Way. Christ. 7B 230
Airlie Corner. Win 8J 105
Airlie Rd. Win 8J 105
Airport Ind. Est. Ports. 5J 215
Airport Service Rd. Ports 4H 215
Airspeed Rd. Christ 7D 230
Airspeed Rd. Ports. 6K 215
Ajax Clo. Chine. 8G 23
Ajax Clo. Fare. 7N 211
Akeshill Clo. New M 1C 232
Alameda Rd. Water. 5L 201
Alameda Way. Water. 5L 201
Alamein Rd. A'sht 9K 49
Alamein Rd. Enh A 3A 52
Alanbrooke Clo. H Win 6B 26
Alanbrooke Rd. A'sht 5M 49
Alan Ct. Christ 7K 231
Alandale Rd. Sotn. 6H 175
Alan Drayton Way. Eastl 1K 161
Alan Gro. Fare. 7A 198
Albacore Av. Wars 8B 196
Albany. Bourn. 2N 245
Albany Bus. Cen. Fare 2D 198
Albany Cvn. Site. Fare 7N 211
Albany Clo. Bart S 5A 232
Albany Clo. Fle 3N 47
Albany Ct. Bish W. 3K 163
Albany Ct. Cam. 3L 29
Albany Ct. Fle 2N 47
Albany Ct. Gos 3K 239
Albany Dri. Bish W. 3K 163
Albany Pk. Cam 3K 29
Albany Pk. Ct. Sotn. 2L 173
Albany Pk. Ind. Est. Cam 3L 29
Albany Rd. And. 1L 69
Albany Rd. Bish W 3K 163
Albany Rd. Fle 3M 47
Albany Rd. Holb 4A 208
Albany Rd. Roms. 5M 129
Albany Rd. Sotn. 4H 173
Albany Rd. S'sea. 4E 240
Albatross Wlk. Gos. 6D 212
Albemarle Av. Gos 9K 213
Albemarle Ct. Sotn 8A 160
Albemarle Rd. Bourn 7K 227
Alberta Gdns. Bulf B. 3A 66
Albert Clo. Net A. 4G 194 (in two parts)
Albert Ct. Win. 5K 105
Albert Gro. S'sea. 4E 240
Albert Rd. A'sht. 9K 49
Albert Rd. Alt 6E 80
Albert Rd. Bish W. 4L 163
Albert Rd. Bourn 2K 245 (6L 247)
Albert Rd. Cosh 1G 215
Albert Rd. C'then 1D 18
Albert Rd. Eastl. 7F 132
Albert Rd. Fare 6B 212
Albert Rd. Farn 1L 49
Albert Rd. H End 5M 175
Albert Rd. New M. 3A 232
Albert Rd. Poole 9B 226
Albert Rd. S'sea 4E 240
Albert Rd. Water 2M 201
Albert Rd. N. Sotn 7N 173
Albert Rd. S. Sotn 7N 173 (8G 4)
Albert St. Fle. 3L 47
Albert St. Gos. 2L 239
Albert Wlk. C'then 1D 18
Albert Yd. Bas. 7C 42
Albion Clo. Fare 2K 213
Albion Pl. H Win. 6B 26
Albion Pl. Sotn. 6L 173 (6C 4) (in two parts)
Albion Rd. Christ. 5J 229
Albion Rd. F'bri 9J 151
Albion Rd. Lee S. 8A 212
Albion Rd. S'hrst 6D 18
Albion Towers. Sotn 6N 173 (5F 4)
Albretia Av. Water. 7L 181
Albury Pl. Chan F. 3N 131
Alby Rd. Poole 9D 226
Alcantara Cres. Sotn. 7A 174
Alcester Rd. Poole 8B 226
Alchorne Pl. Ports. 5J 215
Alcot Clo. C'then. 1D 18
Aldbury Ct. New M 7B 232
Alderbrook Clo. C'then 1A 18
Alder Clo. Alt. 3E 80
Alder Clo. Burt 5N 229
Alder Clo. Col C 4L 133
Alder Clo. Dib P 6H 193
Alder Clo. March. 8E 172
Alder Clo. Roms. 6C 130
Alder Cres. Poole 7D 226
Alder Dri. A'hlt 5C 152
Alderfield. Ptsfld. 1L 145
Alder Gro. Yate 8M 17
Alder Hill Dri. Tot 2H 171
Alder Hills. Poole 7E 226
Alder Hills Ind. Pk. Poole 7D 226
Alderholt. 5C 152
Alderholt Mill. 1C 152 (Industrial Monument)
Alderholt Rd. S'hth. 1D 152
Alder La. Gos 2F 238
Alderley Rd. Bourn. 2H 227
Aldermaston Rd. Monk S & Sher 1K 21
Aldermaston Rd. Sher & Bas 9M 21
Aldermaston Rd. T'ley & P Grn 8K 11
Aldermaston Rd. Roundabout. Bas 3A 42
Aldermaston Rd. S. Bas. 4A 42
Aldermoor. 7F 158
Aldermoor Av. Sotn. 7F 158
Aldermoor Clo. Sotn. 7H 159
Aldermoor Rd. Gos. 9F 212
Aldermoor Rd. Sotn 7F 158
Aldermoor Rd. Water 5L 201
Aldermoor Rd. E. Water 4L 201
Alderney. 4A 226
Alderney Av. Bas. 3K 59
Alderney Av. Poole 5A 226
Alderney Clo. Sotn 7D 158
Alderney Roundabout. Poole 4B 226
Alder Rd. Head D 1D 102
Alder Rd. Poole 9C 226
Alder Rd. Sotn 7E 158
Alders Clo. Bas 6E 42
Alders Ct. Alr. 9F 94
Aldershot. 9M 49
Aldershot F.C. 9L 49
Aldershot Ho. Hav 4H 203
Aldershot Lodge. A'sht 2L 65
Aldershot Military Mus. 4L 49
Aldershot Rd. Ash 1N 65
Aldershot Rd. Chu C. 7L 47
Aldershot Rd. Fle. 3M 47
Alders Rd. Fare. 1D 212
Alders, The. Bad L 4K 65
Alders, The. Chu C 6K 47
Alderwood. Chine. 9G 22
Alderwood Av. Chan F 6M 131
Alderwood Clo. Hav 6B 202
Alderwood Dri. Hook 1H 45
Aldrich Rd. Navy 1B 240 (1K 5)
Aldridge Clo. Water 6C 168
Aldridge Rd. Bourn. 2G 227
Aldrin Clo. Charl 7L 51
Aldrin Pl. Farn. 8F 28
Aldroke St. Ports 1G 215
Aldsworth Clo. Ports 9K 201
Aldsworth Gdns. Ports 9K 201
Aldsworth Path. Ports 9K 201
Aldwell St. S'sea. 3E 240
Aldwick Clo. Farn 6J 29
Aldworth Cres. Bas. 7N 41
Alec Rose Ho. Gos 3L 239
Alec Rose La. Ports 2D 240 (4N 5)
Alecto Rd. Gos 4K 239
Alencon Clo. Gos 8L 213
Alencon Link. Bas. 6B 42
Alexander Bell Cen. And. 9H 51
Alexander Clo. Christ 8A 230
Alexander Clo. Tot 2K 171
Alexander Clo. Water 3L 201
Alexander Ct. Sotn 4J 173
Alexander Gro. Fare 9C 198
Alexander Rd. Over. 3E 56
Alexanders La. Priv. 1C 138
Alexandra Av. Cam 8J 19
Alexandra Av. Hay I. 5F 242
Alexandra Clo. Hythe 5M 193
Alexandra Ct. Bord 4K 101
Alexandra Ct. Farn 2L 49
Alexandra Ho. Ports 3C 240 (6L 5)
Alexandra Lodge. Bourn 2L 245 (7N 247)
Alexandra Rd. A'sht 9G 48 (in two parts)
Alexandra Rd. Alt 3F 80
Alexandra Rd. And. 1M 69
Alexandra Rd. Bas 6A 42
Alexandra Rd. Bourn. 9F 228
Alexandra Rd. Chan F. 4C 132
Alexandra Rd. Farn. 1L 49
Alexandra Rd. F'bri 9J 151
Alexandra Rd. H End 5M 175
Alexandra Rd. Hythe 5M 193
Alexandra Rd. L'ton 2C 234
Alexandra Rd. Poole. 1A 244
Alexandra Rd. Ports 1E 240
Alexandra Rd. Sotn. 4J 173
Alexandra St. Gos. 1J 239
Alexandra Ter. N War 7J 45 (off Bridge Rd.)
Alexandra Ter. Sher L 3L 23
Alexandra Ter. Win 7K 105 (9K 237)
Alexandra Way. Bot 3D 176
Alexandria Rd. Sut S 6D 76
Alfonso Clo. A'sht 2L 65
Alford Rd. Bourn 7H 227
Alfred Clo. Tot. 2J 171
Alfred Rd. Fare. 5N 211
Alfred Rd. F'ham. 9E 64
Alfred Rd. Ports 2C 240 (3M 5)
Alfred Rose Ct. Sotn. 7C 160
Alfred St. Sotn. 4N 173 (1F 4)
Alfriston Gdns. Sotn 6F 174
Algiers Rd. Ports. 8J 215
Alhambra Rd. S'sea. 6F 240
Alice Holt Forest Cen. 10M 63
Alice in Wonderland Maze. 8B 218
Alice Rd. A'sht 9K 49
Alington Clo. Poole 6A 244
Alington Rd. Bourn 8L 227
Alington Rd. Poole. 6A 244
Alipore Clo. Poole 2B 244
Alison Clo. Farn. 9H 29
Alison's Rd. A'sht. 6J 49
Alison Way. A'sht. 9H 49
Alison Way. Win 6K 105 (6K 237)
Allan Gro. Roms 5A 130
Allaway Av. Ports. 9A 200
Allbrook. 5F 132
Allbrook Ct. Hav 3D 202
Allbrook Hill. Eastl 5F 132
Allbrook Knoll. Eastl. 5E 132
Allbrook Way. Eastl 4E 132
Allcot Rd. Ports. 6G 215
Allden Av. A'sht. 3M 65
Allden Gdns. A'sht. 3M 65
Allee Dri. Lip 1D 116
Allenby Gro. Fare 1L 213
Allenby Rd. Cam 7J 19
Allenby Rd. Gos. 1G 239
Allenby Rd. Wint G 3B 86
Allen Clo. Alt 3G 81
Allen Clo. Bas 8A 42
Allendale Av. Ems. 6L 203
Allendale Clo. S'hrst 3C 18
Allenmoor La. Roth 4E 24
Allen Rd. H End. 3N 175
Allens Farm La. Ext. 8M 135
Allens La. Meon. 8N 135
Allen's Rd. S'sea. 5F 240
Allen Water Dri. F'bri. 9H 151
Allerton Clo. Tot. 1K 171
Alley La. Ellis 1J 79
Alley, The. B'stne 3C 118
Alley, The. W'grn 2A 154 (off High St.)
All Hallows. 7F 148
Alliance Clo. Gos 7F 212
Allington. 7D 66
Allington La. W End & F Oak 8F 160
Allington Mnr. Farm Bus. Cen. F Oak 4J 161
Allington Rd. Sotn. 3C 172
Allington Track. All. 4B 66
Allington Way. Ame 6A 66
Allison Ho. H End 2N 175
Alliston Way. Bas. 8K 41
Alliston Way. Whitc 6G 55
Allmara Dri. Water. 5N 201
Allnutt Av. Bas 6D 42
Allotment Rd. H End. 4M 175
Allotment Rd. Sar G. 4B 196
All Saints Cres. Farn 4G 29
All Saints Ho. Sotn. 7E 4
All Saints Rd. L'ton 4E 234
All Saints St. Ports 1D 240
Alma Clo. A'sht 9M 49
Alma Cotts. Farn 3L 49
Alma La. F'ham 3D 64
Alma La. Uphm 2E 162
Alma Rd. Bord 4K 101
Alma Rd. Bourn. 7K 227
Alma Rd. Head D. 2E 102
Alma Rd. Roms 5M 129
Alma Rd. Sotn 2M 173
Alma Sq. Farn 3L 49
Alma St. Gos 1J 239
Almatade Rd. Sotn. 3E 174
Alma Ter. S'sea 4H 241
Alma Way. F'ham 3F 64
Almond Clo. Farn. 5J 29
Almond Clo. Hav 9N 201
Almond Clo. Old B. 5H 43
Almond Clo. Water. 6C 182
Almond Ct. Chu C 5N 47
Almond Ct. Sotn 4H 173
Almond Gro. Poole 7B 226
Almond Rd. Sotn. 4H 173
Almondsbury Rd. Ports. 7A 200
Almondside. Gos. 7G 212
Almswood Rd. T'ley 3G 10
Aloes, The. Fle. 3N 47
Alphage Rd. Gos 7H 213
Alpha Ho. Sotn 2H 159
Alphington Av. Frim. 3N 29
Alphington Grn. Frim. 3N 29
Alpine Clo. Farn 9F 28
Alpine Clo. Sotn. 2F 174
Alpine Ct. Bas. 8J 41
Alpine Rd. Asht 7F 170
Alpine Rd. Ring 7F 186
Alpine Rd. W'hill 6J 101
Alpine Ski Cen. 7L 49
Alresford Drove. S Won 2J 91
Alresford La. Bramd 8J 109
Alresford Rd. Hav. 5E 202
Alresford Rd. Win 7M 105
Alresford Rd. Win & Alr 7F 106
Alsace Wlk. Cam 3K 29
Alsford Rd. Water. 4L 201
Alswitha Ter. Win 5L 105
Alten Rd. Water 8K 181
Althorpe Dri. Ports 4K 215
Alton. 5F 80
Altona Gdns. And 7M 51
Alton Bus. Cen. Alt. 5H 81
Alton Clo. F Oak. 1M 161
Alton Ct. Win 4L 105 (off Northlands Dri.)
Alton Golf Course. 9C 62
Alton Gro. Fare. 2L 213
Alton La. Four M. 7J 97
Alton Ride. B'wtr 7E 18
Alton Rd. Bourn 5F 226
Alton Rd. Clid & H'rd 9D 42
Alton Rd. F'ham. 7N 63 & 9B 64
Alton Rd. Fle. 2A 48
Alton Rd. S Warn & Odi 4D 62
Alton Rd. E. Poole 3B 244
Alton Sports Cen. 7D 80
Alum Chine Rd. Bourn 2F 244
Alum Clo. Holb. 5B 208
Alumdale Rd. Bourn 3F 244
Alumhurst Rd. Bourn 2F 244
Alum Way. Fare 8G 199
Alum Way. Sotn 3F 174
Alvandi Gdns. New M. 3C 232
Alvara Rd. Gos 5J 239
Alver Bri. Vw. Gos 4K 239
Alvercliffe Dri. Gos. 5H 239
Alver Quay. Gos 4K 239
Alver Rd. Gos. 3K 239
Alver Rd. Ports. 1F 240
Alverstoke. 4J 239
Alverstoke Gdns. A'sht 1G 65
Alverstone Rd. S'sea 2H 241
Alveston Av. Fare 9N 197
Alwin Pl. F'ham 3D 64
Alyne Ho. Sotn 2L 173
Alyth Rd. Bourn 8G 226
Amarylis Clo. Fare 5H 197
Amazon Clo. Bas 7A 42
Ambarrow Cres. S'hrst. 4B 18
Ambarrow La. S'hrst 3N 17
Ambassador Clo. Christ 8C 230
Ambassador Ind. Est. Christ 8C 230
Amber Clo. Bord. 5K 101
Amber Ct. A'sht. 9L 49
Amber Gdns. And. 1K 69
Amberley Clo. Bot 3D 176
Amberley Clo. Highc 6G 231
Amberley Clo. N Bad 7D 130
Amberley Ct. Bourn 2L 245 (7N 247)
Amberley Ct. Tot. 5L 171
Amberley Grange. A'sht 2H 65
Amberley Rd. Clan. 6D 168
Amberley Rd. Gos. 8J 213
Amberley Rd. Ports 5G 214
Amberslade Wlk. Dib P. 8L 193
Amberwood. New M. 7L 231
Amberwood Clo. Cal. 9J 157
Amberwood Dri. Cam 6N 19
Amberwood Dri. Walk 4H 231
Amberwood Gdns. Walk. 4J 231
Ambledale. Sar G 5B 196
Ambleside. Bish W. 3K 163
Ambleside. Bot. 5A 176
Ambleside. Christ. 3G 229
Ambleside Clo. Farn. 8G 28
Ambleside Ct. Gos 6J 239
Ambleside Cres. F'ham. 4C 64
Ambleside Gdns. Sotn 7E 174
Ambleside Rd. L'ton 3E 234
Ambrose Rd. T'ley 5H 11
Ambury La. Christ 6A 230
Amersham Clo. Gos. 3G 238
Amery Hill. Alt 4F 80
Amery St. Alt 5F 80
Amesbury. 5A 66
Amesbury Rd. Ame 5A 66 (in two parts)
Amesbury Rd. Bourn 8F 228
Amesbury Rd. Chol 4D 66
Amesbury Rd. Newt T 6D 66
Amesbury Rd. Wey 1N 67
Amethyst Gro. Water 1B 202
Amethyst Rd. Christ. 7B 230
Amey Ind. Est. Ptsfld 1L 145
Amherst Rd. Bord 1H 101
Amira Ct. Bourn 2J 245 (6J 247)
Amity Way. Cam. 8N 19
Amoy St. Sotn. 4L 173 (1B 4)
Ampfield. 1H 131
Ampfield Clo. Hav. 5B 202

Ampfield Golf Course 1H 131
Ampfield Hill 9E 124
Ampfield Rd. *Bourn* 3A 228
Amport 2N 67
Amport Clo. *Lych* 3H 43
Amport Clo. *Win* 3G 105
Amport Ct. *Hav* 3D 202
Ampress La. *L'ton* 9D 224
Ampthill Rd. *Sotn* 3G 172
Amsterdam Sq. *Christ* 8M 229
Amyas Ct. *S'sea* 3K 241
Ancasta Rd. *Sotn* 3N 173
Ancells Bus. Pk. *Fle* 8A 28 (Ancells Rd.)
Ancells Bus. Pk. *Fle* 7N 27 (Harvest Cres.)
Ancells Farm Nature Reserve 9N 27
Ancells Rd. *Fle* 8N 27
Anchorage Rd. *Ports* 5J 215
Anchorage, The. *Gos* 3L 239
Anchorage Way. *L'ton* 3D 234
Anchor Bus. Cen. *Chan F* 7N 131
Anchor Clo. *Bourn* 1D 226
Anchor Clo. *Christ* 9C 230
Anchor Ga. *Ports* 1C 240 (2L 5)
Anchor Ga. Rd. *Navy* 1B 240 (1K 5)
Anchor La. *Ports* 2A 240 (3H 5)
Anchor Mdw. *Farn* 8H 29
Anchor M. *L'ton* 2E 234
Anchor Rd. *Bourn* 1D 226
Anchor Rd. *K're* 2B 6
Anchor Yd. *Bas* 7C 42
Ancrum Lodge. *Poole* 2F 244
Andalusian Gdns. *White* 1E 196
Andbourne Ct. *Bourn* 2J 247
Andeferas Rd. *And* 7N 51
Anderby Rd. *Sotn* 9C 158
Andersen Clo. *White* 1F 196
Anderson Clo. *Hav* 6G 202
Anderson Clo. *Roms* 2B 130
Anderson's Rd. *Sotn* 7N 173 (7G 4)
Anders Rd. *S Won* 3J 91
Anderwood Dri. *Sway* 5J 223
Andes Clo. *Sotn* 7A 174
Andes Rd. *Nurs* 8A 158
Andlers Ash Rd. *Liss* 3D 140
Andover 1M 69
Andover Clo. *Christ* 7D 230
Andover Down 9G 52
Andover Down Roundabout. *And* 1D 70
Andover Dri. *Elve* 9J 27
Andover Drove. *Wash W* 1B 8
Andover Golf Club 3N 69
Andover Ho. *Hav* 4G 202
Andover La. *Gt Shod* 4E 30
Andover Mus. 1A 70
Andover Rd. *B'wtr* 7E 18
Andover Rd. *Dea* 2K 57
Andover Rd. *Lud* 1C 30
Andover Rd. *Mich S* 4J 77
Andover Rd. *Monx* 3D 68
Andover Rd. *N'bry* 1C 8
Andover Rd. *Okly* 8B 40
Andover Rd. *Sotn* 4J 173
Andover Rd. *S'sea* 5G 241
Andover Rd. *Wash W* 2C 8
Andover Rd. *Win* 3J 105 (6L 237)
Andover Rd. N. *Win* 1H 105
Andover Rd. Retail Pk. *Win* 5K 105
Andover Way. *A'sht* 3K 65
Andrewartha Rd. *Farn* 1N 49
Andrew Bell St. *Ports* 1D 240
Andrew Clo. *Dib P* 8M 193
Andrew Clo. *N War* 8H 45
Andrew Clo. *Ports* 1G 241
Andrew Clo. *Tot* 3K 171
Andrew Cres. *Water* 8L 181
Andrewes Clo. *Bish W* 3M 163
Andrew La. *New M* 4E 232
Andrew Pl. *Fare* 6L 211
Andrews Clo. *Bourn* 3E 226
Andrews Clo. *Chu C* 5M 47
Andrew's La. *Long S* 4F 62
Andrew's La. *Ropl* 9F 96
Andrews Rd. *Farn* 7G 28
Andromeda Rd. *Sotn* 7D 158
Androse Gdns. *Ring* 2J 187
Andwell Drove. *And & Map* 6A 44
Andwell La. *And* 6A 44
Anfield Clo. *F Oak* 2N 161
Anfield Ct. *F Oak* 2M 161
Angel Cres. *Sotn* 4D 174
Angelica Ct. *Water* 3A 202
Angelica Gdns. *H Hth* 4N 161
Angelica Way. *White* 1H 197
Angeline Clo. *Highc* 6H 231
Angel La. *New M* 7D 232
Angel Meadows. *Odi* 8L 45
Angelo Clo. *Water* 1A 202
Angelus Clo. *Fare* 6M 211
Angerstein Rd. *Ports* 7E 214
Anglers Pl. *Bas* 6E 42
Anglers Way. *Lwr S* 1A 196
Anglesea Building. *Ports* 2C 240 (4L 5)
Anglesea Ct. *Sotn* 1G 173
Anglesea Rd. *Lee S* 3C 238
Anglesea Rd. *Ports* 2C 240 (3M 5)
Anglesea Rd. *Sotn* 1G 173
Anglesea Ter. *Sotn* 7N 173 (7G 4)
Anglesey 5J 239
Anglesey Arms Rd. *Gos* 5J 239
Anglesey Av. *Farn* 5H 29
Anglesey Clo. *And* 4N 69
Anglesey Clo. *Bas* 1D 42
Anglesey Rd. *A'sht* 1M 65
Anglesey Rd. *Gos* 6J 239
Anglesey Vw. *Gos* 4K 239
Anglia Ct. *Bourn* 7J 247
Angmering Ho. *Ports* 2D 240
Angora Way. *Fle* 8N 27
Angus Clo. *Fare* 6A 198
Anjou Clo. *Bourn* 1B 226
Anjou Cres. *Fare* 7N 197
Anker La. *Fare* 4M 211
Ankerwyke. *Gos* 7D 212
Anmore 6J 181
Anmore Clo. *Hav* 5D 202
Anmore Dri. *Water* 8L 181
Anmore La. *Water* 6J 181
Anmore Rd. *Water* 5H 181
Anna La. *Brans* 3J 219
Anna Valley 5K 69
Anne Armstrong Clo. *A'sht* 6M 49
Anne Clo. *Christ* 5K 229
Anne Cres. *Water* 3M 201
Annerley Rd. *Bourn* 1N 245
Annes Ct. *Hay I* 5E 242
Annes Way. *Chu C* 5N 47
Annettes Cft. *Chu C* 7K 47
Ann's Hill 2H 239
Ann's Hill Rd. *Gos* 1J 239
Ansell Rd. *Frim* 4N 29
Anson Clo. *A'sht* 8H 49
Anson Clo. *Christ* 8B 230
Anson Clo. *Gos* 2F 238
Anson Clo. *Ring* 9M 185
Anson Dri. *Sotn* 6G 175
Anson Gro. *Fare* 8M 199
Anson Rd. *H Hth* 4N 161
Anson Rd. *S'sea* 2H 241
Anstey 3H 81
Anstey Clo. *Bas* 9B 42
Anstey Clo. *Bourn* 1E 226
Anstey La. *Alt* 10C 62
Anstey Mill Clo. *Alt* 3H 81
Anstey Mill La. *Alt* 3H 81
Anstey Rd. *Alt* 4G 80
Anstey Rd. *Bourn* 1E 226
Anstey Rd. *Roms* 3A 130
Antar Clo. *Bas* 7A 42
Antell's Way. *A'hlt* 4D 152
Anthill Clo. *Water* 4D 180
Anthill Common 4D 180
Anthony Gro. *Gos* 7H 213
Anthony's Av. *Poole* 5A 244
Anthony Way. *Ems* 6M 203
Antler Dri. *New M* 2N 231
Anton Clo. *Okly* 1D 58
Anton Clo. *Roms* 5B 130
Anton La. *Enh A* 4A 52
Anton Mill Rd. *And* 3N 69
Anton Rd. *And* 3N 69
Anton Trad. Est. *And* 2N 69
Antrim Clo. *Bas* 8K 41
Anvil Clo. *E Meon* 4M 143
Anvil Clo. *Water* 8C 182
Anvil Clo. *W End* 9G 161
Anvil Ct. *S'sea* 3J 241
Anvil Theatre 6C 42
Anvil Way. *Braml* 1G 23
Anzac Clo. *Fare* 4M 211
Anzio Clo. *A'sht* 9J 49
Apex Cen. *Fare* 3C 212
Apex Dri. *Frim* 3M 29
Apless La. *Den* 6A 180
Apollo Clo. *Poole* 7B 226
Apollo Ct. *S'sea* 3E 240
Apollo Dri. *Bord* 5K 101
Apollo Dri. *Water* 6N 201
Apollo Pl. *Sotn* 2E 174
Apollo Ri. *S'wd B* 8E 28
Apollo Rd. *Chan F* 5D 132
Apple Clo. *Poole* 1E 244
Appledore M. *Farn* 5J 29
Appledown Clo. *Alr* 2F 108
Appledown La. *Alr* 3G 108
Applegarth Clo. *Bas* 8C 42
Applegate. *St M* 1M 53
Applegate Pl. *Water* 4A 182
Apple Gro. *Christ* 4H 229
Apple Ind. Est. *Fare* 4F 196
Applemore 6H 193
Applemore Recreation Cen. 6H 193
Appleshaw 4B 50
Appleshaw Clo. *T'ley* 6H 11
Appleshaw Clo. *Win* 2H 105
Appleshaw Grn. *Hav* 5C 202
Appleshaw Way. *Per D* 5B 30
Appleslade Way. *New M* 1C 232
Appleton Clo. *Ovr W* 8M 67
Appleton M. *And* 3A 70
Appleton Rd. *Fare* 8M 197
Appleton Rd. *Sotn* 1C 174
Appleton Vw. *E Tis* 1D 112
Appletree Clo. *Bourn* 9F 228
Appletree Clo. *Cal* 1J 171 (in two parts)
Appletree Clo. *New M* 5B 232
Appletree Clo. *Okly* 2D 58
Appletree Clo. *Redl* 7C 120
Appletree Ct. *Bot* 3D 176
Appletree Ct. *Lyn* 3C 148
Apple Tree Gro. *And* 9K 51
Appletree Mead. *Hook* 2J 45
Apple Tree Rd. *A'hlt* 5C 152
Appletree Rd. *Redl* 1M 119
Apple Tree Way. *Owl* 4F 18
Apple Way. *Old B* 6J 43
Applewood. *Park G* 4D 196
Applewood Gdns. *Sotn* 7E 174
Applewood Gro. *Water* 6K 201
Applewood Pl. *Tot* 4J 171
Applewood Rd. *Hav* 6C 202
Appley Ct. *Cam* 8K 19
Appley Dri. *Cam* 7K 19
Approach Rd. *F'ham* 9E 64
Approach, The. *Ports* 7H 215
April Clo. *Bourn* 2E 226
April Clo. *Cam* 2L 29
April Clo. *Sotn* 3F 174
April Ct. *Bourn* 2E 226
April Gro. *Sar G* 6B 196
April Sq. *Ports* 1E 240
Apsley Clo. *And* 4M 69
Apsley Pl. *Chan F* 3N 131
Apsley Rd. *S'sea* 3H 241
Aquila Way. *Hamb* 7K 195
Aquitania Ho. *Sotn* 5A 174
Arabian Gdns. *White* 2F 196
Aragon Rd. *Yate* 9M 17
Aragon Way. *Bourn* 1M 227
Arbour Ct. *Win* 7K 237
Arcade, The. *A'sht* 9J 49
Arcade, The. *Bourn* 2K 245 (7M 247)
Arcade, The. *Liss* 9D 114
Arcadia Av. *Bourn* 7M 227
Arcadia Clo. *Sotn* 8H 159
Arcadia Rd. *Christ* 5J 229
Archdale Clo. *Bourn* 4H 227
Archer Ho. *Gos* 6L 239
Archers. *Sotn* 4K 173 (1A 4)
Archers Clo. *Cal* 1J 171
Archers Rd. *Eastl* 8E 132
Archers Rd. *Sotn* 3K 173 (1A 4)
Archery Fields. *Odi* 8M 45
Archery Gdns. *Sotn* 8D 174
Archery Gro. *Sotn* 8C 174
Archery La. *Fare* 7E 198
Archery La. *Win* 7K 105 (8K 237)
Archery Ri. *Alt* 6E 80
Archery Rd. *Sotn* 9C 174
Arch Farm Ind. Est. *F'bri* 8H 151
Archway Rd. *Poole* 1C 244
Arcot Rd. *Tidw* 8F 30
Arc, The. *Cowes* 5P 237
Arden Clo. *Gos* 3H 239
Arden Clo. *Sotn* 1F 174
Arden Rd. *Bourn* 3K 227
Arden Wlk. *New M* 4C 232
Ardglen Rd. *Whitc* 5F 54
Ardingly Cres. *H End* 9A 162
Ardington Ri. *Water* 6M 201
Ardnave Cres. *Sotn* 6L 159
Ardwell Clo. *C'then* 1A 18
Arena La. *A'sht* 7F 48
Arenal Dri. *C'then* 2D 18
Arena Leisure Cen. 7L 19
Arford 1B 102
Arford Comn. *Head* 1B 102
Arford Rd. *Head* 2B 102
Argente Clo. *Fle* 8N 27
Argent Ter. *Coll T* 5G 18
Argosy Clo. *Wars* 8C 196
Argus Rd. *Lee S* 9B 212
Argyle Clo. *W'hill* 5J 101
Argyle Cres. *Fare* 7A 198
Argyle Rd. *Christ* 9A 230
Argyle Rd. *Sotn* 5M 173 (3E 4)
Argyll Rd. *Bourn* 1B 246
Argyll Rd. *Poole* 8B 226
Ariel Clo. *Bourn* 1L 247
Ariel Dri. *Bourn* 1L 247
Ariel Rd. *Ports* 2F 240
Arismore Ct. *Lee S* 9N 211
Ark Royal Cres. *Lee S* 9A 212
Arkwright Clo. High 4A 8 (off Tubb's La.)
Arkwright Ga. *And* 8H 51
Arlebury Pk. *Alr* 9D 94
Arle Clo. *Alr* 9E 94
Arle Clo. *Water* 7C 168
Arle Gdns. *Alr* 9F 94
Arlesford Golf Course 3E 108
Arlington Ct. *New M* 6C 232
Arlington Pl. *Win* 6M 237
Arlington Ter. *A'sht* 9H 49
Arliss Rd. *Sotn* 1F 172
Arlott Ct. *Sotn* 2K 173
Arlott Dri. *Bas* 4C 42
Armada Clo. *Rown* 4D 158
Armada Dri. *Hythe* 7L 193
Armadale Ho. Sotn 4A 174 (off Kent St.)
Arminers Clo. *Gos* 6K 239
Armitage Av. *Dib P* 8L 193
Armory La. *Ports* 3B 240 (6K 5)
Armstrong Clo. *Broc* 7B 148
Armstrong Clo. *S Won* 3J 91
Armstrong Clo. *Water* 8L 181
Armstrong Ct. *Sotn* 6E 158
Armstrong La. *Broc* 7B 148
Armstrong Mall. *S'wd B* 8F 28
Armstrong Ri. *Charl* 7L 51
Armstrong Rd. *Bas* 4F 42
Armstrong Rd. *Broc* 7B 148
Armstrong Way. *Farn* 2D 48
Armsworth La. *Sob & Hmbdn* 8M 165
Army Golf Course 5G 49
Army Physical Training Corps Mus. 6K 49 (off Queen's Av.)
Arnaud Clo. *Ports* 9E 214
Arne Av. *Poole* 7C 226
Arne Clo. *Bas* 3M 59
Arne Cres. *Poole* 7C 226
Arnewood Av. *T'ley* 4K 11
Arnewood Bri. Rd. *Sway* 8F 222
Arnewood Ct. *Bourn* 3J 245 (8J 247)
Arnewood Rd. *Bourn* 1F 246
Arnheim Clo. *Sotn* 7H 159
Arnheim Rd. *Sotn* 7J 159
Arnhem Clo. *A'sht* 9K 49
Arnold Rd. *Eastl* 3E 160
Arnold Rd. *Sotn* 9A 160
Arnolds Clo. *Bart S* 6A 232
Arnside Rd. *Water* 1M 201
Arnwood Av. *Dib P* 9L 193
Arragon Ct. *Water* 1A 202
Arran Clo. *Okly* 9C 40
Arran Clo. *Ports* 8G 200
Arran Way. *Walk* 5K 231
Arras Ho. *Fare* 7M 197
Arreton. *Net A* 2G 195
Arreton Ct. *Gos* 2J 239
Arrow Clo. *Eastl* 7E 132
Arrow Clo. *Sotn* 9B 174
Arrow Ind. Est. *Farn* 1H 49
Arrow La. *H Win* 6A 26
Arrow Rd. *Farn* 1H 49
Arters Lawn. *March* 2N 191
Arthur Clo. *Bourn* 9K 227
Arthur Clo. *F'ham* 9D 64
Arthur Dann Ct. *Ports* 1F 214
Arthur Kille Ho. *Water* 3L 201
Arthur La. *Christ* 7K 229
Arthur Pope Ho. *S'sea* 3E 240
Arthur Rd. *Christ* 7K 229
Arthur Rd. *Eastl* 8E 132
Arthur Rd. *F'ham* 9D 64 (in two parts)
Arthur Rd. *Sotn* 3J 173
Arthur Rd. *Win* 5L 105
Arthurs Gdns. *H End* 8M 161
Arthur St. *A'sht* 9K 49
Arthur St. *Ports* 9F 214
Artillery Clo. *Ports* 8D 200
Artillery Rd. *A'sht* 9K 49 (High St.)
Artillery Rd. *A'sht* 4M 49 (North Rd.)
Artists Way. *And* 8M 51
Art Sculpture Pk. 3J 87
Arun Clo. *Ptsfld* 2L 145
Arun Ct. *Bas* 6E 42
Arundel Clo. *Alr* 2E 108
Arundel Clo. *Fle* 3N 47
Arundel Clo. *New M* 3N 231
Arundel Clo. *Pass* 7N 101
Arundel Dri. *Fare* 7C 198
Arundel Gdns. *Bas* 4L 41
Arundel Ho. *Sotn* (SO14) 4A 174
Arundel Ho. *Sotn* (SO15) 2L 173
Arundel Pl. *F'ham* 8D 64
Arundel Rd. *Eastl* 6E 132
Arundel Rd. *Gos* 2H 239
Arundel Rd. *Tot* 2H 171
Arundel St. *Ports* 2D 240 (3N 5)
Arundel Way. *Highc* 7H 231
Arundel Way. *Ports* 2D 240 (3N 5)
Arun Rd. *W End* 8F 160
Arun Way. *W Wel* 1A 120
Ascension Clo. *Bas* 2D 42
Ascham Rd. *Bourn* 9M 227
Ascot Clo. *Alt* 6G 80
Ascot Clo. *Fare* 7F 196
Ascot Ct. *A'sht* 1J 65
Ascot Rd. *H Hth* 4A 162
Ascot Rd. *Ports* 9H 215
Ascupart St. *Sotn* 6N 173 (5F 4) (in two parts)
Asford Gro. *Eastl* 8G 133
Ashbarn Cres. *Win* 9H 105
Ashbourne Ct. *Bourn* 6N 247
Ashbourne Rd. *Bourn* 9E 228
Ash Bri. Cvn. Pk. *Ash* 2N 65
Ashbridge Ri. *Chan F* 3M 131
Ashburn Gth. *Hight* 2N 187
Ashburnham Clo. *Sotn* 5B 174
Ashburton Clo. *Alr* 1E 108
Ashburton Clo. *Dib* 6J 193
Ashburton Ct. *S'sea* 8N 5
Ashburton Gdns. *Bourn* 5H 227
Ashburton Rd. *Alr* 1E 108
Ashburton Rd. *Gos* 5H 239
Ashburton Rd. *S'sea* 5D 240 (9N 5)
Ashbury Dri. *B'wtr* 3J 29
Ashbury Rd. *Bord* 5J 101
Ashby Cres. *Tot* 3K 171
Ashby Pl. *Gos* 3M 239
Ashby Pl. *S'sea* 5D 240 (9N 5)
Ashby Rd. *Sotn* 7F 174
Ashby Rd. *Tot* 3K 171
Ash Clo. *A'hlt* 5D 152
Ash Clo. *B'wtr* 8E 18
Ash Clo. *Burs* 1K 195
Ash Clo. *Col C* 3K 133
Ash Clo. *Fare* 9A 198
Ash Clo. *Gos* 3K 239
Ash Clo. *Hythe* 9M 193
Ash Clo. *N Bad* 7E 130
Ash Clo. *Roms* 6B 130
Ash Clo. *Sotn* 4G 175
Ash Clo. *Tidw* 7E 30
Ash Clo. *Water* 7M 181
Ash Copse. *Water* 5N 181
Ash Ct. *Sotn* 7D 174
Ashcroft Ct. *Ptsfld* 9M 139
Ashcroft La. *Water* 4K 183
Ashdell Rd. *Alt* 5G 80
Ashdene. *Sotn* 2G 172
Ashdene Rd. *Asht* 8H 171
Ashdown. *Bourn* 3H 245 (9H 247)
Ashdown. *Fawl* 5D 208
Ashdown. *Gos* 7F 212
Ashdown Av. *Farn* 9M 29
Ashdown Clo. *Chan F* 2A 132
Ashdown Dri. *Chan F* 2A 132
Ashdown Rd. *Chan F* 2A 132
Ashdown Rd. *Fawl* 6D 208
Ashdown Ter. *Tidw* 9D 30
Ashdown Wlk. *New M* 4D 232
Ashdown Way. *Roms* 5A 130
Ashe 2H 57
Ashe Clo. *Woot L* 4H 41
Ashen Clo. *Chan F* 4A 132
Ashe Rd. *Hav* 4H 203
Ashfield 8A 130
Ashfield. *Chine* 9G 23
Ashfield Grn. *Yate* 8B 18
Ashfield Rd. *And* 1K 69
Ashford 1G 152
Ashford Chace Nature Reserve 3J 139
Ashford Clo. *F'bri* 1G 153
Ashford Clo. *Ports* 8F 200
Ashford Cres. *Hythe* 6N 193
Ashford Hangers Nature Reserve 3K 139

Ashford Hill—Baileys Clo.

Ashford Hill 2N 9
Ashford Hill Rd. H'ly & Ash H 2J 9
Ashford Rd. Bourn 7G 228
Ashford Rd. F'bri 2F 152
Ashford Works Ind. Est. F'bri 1G 152
Ash Gro. Asht 7J 171
Ash Gro. Evtn 6L 233
Ash Gro. K're 2B 6
Ash Gro. Lip 3F 116
Ash Gro. Old B 5K 43
Ash Gro. Ring 1M 187
Ashington Clo. Water 6A 182
Ashington Pk. New M 5D 232
Ash La. Baug 4E 10
Ash La. Lit L & Sil 8B 12
Ashlawn Gdns. And 3A 70
Ashlea. Hook 1H 45
Ashlea Clo. F Oak 1A 162
Ashleigh Clo. Hythe 9M 193
Ashleigh Ri. Bourn 4H 227
Ashlet Gdns. New M 2E 232
Ashlett 5G 209
Ashlett Clo. Fawl 5G 208
Ashlett Lawn. Hav 3D 202
Ashlett M. Fawl 5F 208
Ashlett Rd. Fawl 5F 208
Ashley 3E 232 (New Milton)
Ashley 3F 186 (Ringwood)
Ashley 7J 89 (Stockbridge)
Ashley Arnwood Ct. New M 4C 232
Ashley Castle 7J 89
Ashley Clo. Bourn 8B 228
Ashley Clo. Cron 2L 63
Ashley Clo. Hav 5D 202
Ashley Clo. Ring 2N 187
Ashley Clo. Swanw 2E 196
Ashley Clo. Water 5N 181
Ashley Clo. Win 3G 105
Ashley Comn. Rd. New M 1D 232
Ashley Ct. Burs 8L 175
Ashley Ct. Gos 2J 239
Ashley Cres. Sotn 8G 174
Ashley Cross Clo. Holb 5B 208
Ashley Dri. B'wtr 9E 18
Ashley Dri. Blash 5F 184
Ashley Dri. N. Ashy H 2C 186 (in two parts)
Ashley Dri. S. Ashy H 3C 186
Ashley Dri. W. Ashy H 3C 186
Ashley Drove. Oxen & Butt 5C 6
Ashley Gdns. Chan F 7C 132
Ashley Gdns. Wal C 8A 164
Ashley Heath 2B 186
Ashley Ho. Roms 6L 129
Ashley La. L'ton 3E 234
Ashley La. New M & Hord 3E 232
Ashley Lodge. Bas 8B 42 (off Frescade Cres)
Ashley Meadows. New M 2E 232
Ashley Meadows. Roms 4N 129
Ashley Pk. Ashy H 2D 186
Ashley Rd. Bentw 6L 79
Ashley Rd. Bourn 8B 228
Ashley Rd. Farn 8M 29
Ashley Rd. New M 4C 232
Ashley Rd. Poole 9A 226
Ashley Wlk. Ame 6A 66
Ashley Wlk. Ports 1H 215
Ashling Clo. Bourn 6N 227
Ashling Clo. Water 6G 180
Ashling Cres. Bourn 6M 227
Ashling Gdns. Water 5G 181
Ashling La. Ports 7E 214
Ashling Pk. Rd. Water 5G 180
Ashlyn Clo. Fare 8M 197
Ashmansworth 7M 7
Ashmead. Bord 4J 101
Ashmead Rd. Sotn 8E 158
Ashmede. Bourn 3G 245
Ashmoor La. Old B 5L 43
Ashmore Av. Bart S 6C 232
Ashmore Clo. W'ish 5H 121 (off Green, The)
Ashmore Gro. Christ 5G 230
Ashmore La. W'ish 5H 121
Ashmore Rd. Win 5G 105
Ash Path. Mid W 4B 72
Ashridge. Farn 5H 29
Ashridge Av. Bourn 1H 227
Ashridge Clo. Sotn 2L 173
Ashridge Gdns. Bourn 1H 227
Ashridge Pde. Bourn 1H 227
Ash Rd. A'sht 1L 65
Ash Rd. Asht 8H 171
Ash Rd. Bish G 1G 9
Ashtead Clo. Fare 9J 199
Ashton 1L 163
Ashton Clo. Bish W 2K 163
Ashton Ct. Poole 3E 244
Ashton Cross. E Wel 1A 156
Ashton Ho. Sotn 9D 174
Ashton La. Bish W 2K 163
Ashton Pl. Chan F 3N 131
Ashton Rd. Bourn 4K 227
Ashton Way. Fare 8N 211
Ash Tree Clo. Farn 9E 28
Ashtree Clo. New M 4E 232
Ash Tree Clo. Okly 2C 58
Ashtree Ct. Chan F 9A 132
Ash Tree Rd. And 1J 69
Ash Tree Rd. Sotn 1C 174
Ashurst 8H 171
Ashurst Bridge 4J 171
Ashurst Bri. Rd. Tot 4J 171
Ashurst Campsite. Asht 1G 190
Ashurst Clo. Asht 8H 171
Ashurst Clo. Sotn 9E 174
Ashurst Clo. T'ley 5G 11
Ashurst Clo. Win 3H 105
Ashurst Ct. Gos 4F 238
Ashurst Rd. Bourn 3A 228
Ashurst Rd. Ports 9F 200
Ash Wlk. Alr 1F 108
Ashwell Av. Cam 7N 19
Ashwood. Chine 1F 42
Ashwood. L Hth 7F 196
Ashwood. White 4H 197
Ashwood Clo. Hav 5B 202
Ashwood Clo. Hay I 4G 242
Ashwood Gdns. Sotn 8K 159
Ashwood Gdns. Tot 4J 171
Ashwood Lodge. Fare 7D 198 (off Northwood Sq.)
Ashwood Way. Bas 4M 41
Ashwood Way Roundabout. Bas 4M 41
Aspen Av. Wars 9A 196
Aspen Clo. Col C 4L 133
Aspen Clo. H End 3A 176
Aspen Clo. W'hill 6J 101
Aspen Gdns. Hook 1H 45
Aspen Gdns. Poole 6D 226
Aspengrove. Gos 7G 212
Aspen Holt. Sotn 6M 159
Aspen Pl. New M 5C 232
Aspen Rd. Poole 7D 226
Aspen Wlk. Tot 2H 171
Aspen Way. Poole 7D 226
Aspen Way. Water 5A 182
Aspex Art Gallery. 3D 240 (6N 5)
Aspin Way. B'wtr 8D 18
Asquith Clo. Christ 9N 229
Assheton Ct. Fare 1M 213
Astbury Av. Poole 6D 226
Aster Rd. Bas 3J 59
Aster Rd. Sotn 7A 160
Astley St. S'sea 3D 240 (6M 5)
Aston Mead. Christ 2H 229
Aston Rd. S'sea 4G 241
Aston Rd. Water 9L 181
Astor Cres. Lud 1C 30
Astra Ct. Hythe 4M 193
Astral Gdns. Hamb 6K 195
Astra Wlk. Gos 3M 239
Astrid Clo. Hay I 4J 243
Asturias Way. Sotn 7A 174
Asylum Rd. Sotn 4M 173 (2D 4)
Atalanta Clo. S'sea 2K 241
Atbara Rd. Chu C 7M 47
Atheling Rd. Hythe 5M 193
Athelstan Rd. Bourn 9H 229
Athelstan Rd. Sotn 3C 174
Athelston Ct. L'ton 3D 234
Athena Av. Water 6N 201
Athena Clo. F Oak 9L 133
Atherfield Rd. Sotn 8D 158
Atherley Ct. Sotn 2K 173
Atherley Rd. Hay I 3E 242
Atherley Rd. Sotn 4J 173
Atherstone Wlk. S'sea 3D 240 (6N 5)
Athlone Clo. Enh A 2A 52
Atholl Ct. And 7N 51
Atholl Rd. W'hill 5J 101
Atkinson Clo. Gos 5J 239
Atkins Pl. Fare 6M 197
Atlantic Clo. Sotn 8N 173
Atlantic Pk. Vw. W End 8E 160
Atlantis Av. Water 7M 201
Atrebatti Rd. S'hrst 4E 18
Attenborough Clo. Fle 9N 27
Attlee Gdns. Chu C 7L 47
Attwood Clo. A'hlt 5C 152
Attwood Clo. Bas 7A 42
Attwood Clo. Mobile Home Pk. Bas 7A 42
Attwoods Drove. Comp 5G 127
Aubrey Clo. Hay I 3E 242
Aubrey Clo. Mil S 8M 235
Auburn Mans. Poole 1F 244
Auchinleck Way. A'sht 9G 49
Auckland Av. Broc 7D 148
Auckland Clo. Tidw 8E 30
Auckland Pl. Broc 7C 148
Auckland Rd. Christ 7E 230
Auckland Rd. Sotn 3E 172
Auckland Rd. E. S'sea 5D 240
Auckland Rd. W. S'sea 5D 240 (9N 5)
Audemer Ct. Ring 9M 185
Audley Pl. Eastl 1K 161
Audret Clo. Fare 2K 213
Augustine Rd. Cosh 8K 201
Augustine Rd. Sotn 4N 173
Augustine Way. Charl 7K 51
Augustus Clo. Chan F 5C 132
Augustus Dri. Bas 4L 41
Augustus Wlk. And 7A 52
Augustus Way. Chan F 5C 132
Auklet Clo. Bas 3H 59
Auriol Dri. Hav 9N 201
Austen Av. Bourn 1H 227
Austen Av. Win 1F 126
Austen Clo. Tot 4K 171
Austen Clo. Win 4L 105
Austen Gdns. White 1F 196
Austen Gro. Bas 9N 41
Austen Rd. Farn 6J 29
Austerberry Way. Gos 8G 212
Auster Clo. Christ 7D 230
Austin Av. Poole 4A 244
Austin Clo. Bourn 9A 228
Austin Ct. Ports 8C 200
Austins Cotts. F'ham 8D 64
Australia Clo. Ports 2E 240
Aust Rd. Fare 9N 197
Autumn Copse. New M 4E 232
Autumn Pl. Sotn 1M 173
Autumn Rd. Bourn 3B 226
Autumn Rd. March 9F 172
Avalon. Poole 5A 244
Avalon Ct. Ems 7M 203
Avebury Av. Bourn 1J 227
Avebury Gdns. Chan F 3M 131
Avenger Clo. Chan F 7N 131
Avens Clo. H Hth 5N 161
Avenue C. Hythe 9C 194
Avenue Clo. And 1L 69
Avenue Clo. Lip 2D 116
Avenue Ct. Gos 5J 239
Avenue Ct. Poole 2E 244
Avenue D. Hythe 9C 194
Avenue De Caen. S'sea 6D 240
Avenue E. Hythe 9C 194
Avenue La. Bourn 2J 245 (7K 247)
Avenue Rd. Bourn 2J 245 (7J 247)
Avenue Rd. Broc 7C 148
Avenue Rd. Christ 7J 229
Avenue Rd. Fare 8B 198
Avenue Rd. Farn 8M 29
Avenue Rd. Fle 1L 47
Avenue Rd. Gos 2L 239
Avenue Rd. Gray 4L 103
Avenue Rd. Hay I 5F 216
Avenue Rd. Lash 3M 79
Avenue Rd. L'ton 2D 234
Avenue Rd. New M 3B 232
Avenue Rd. Sotn 2M 173
Avenue Rd. Walk 5L 231
Avenue Rd. Win 6J 105 (6J 237)
Avenue Shop. Cen., The. Bourn 2J 245 (7K 247)
Avenue Sucy. Cam 9J 19
Avenue, The. A'sht 3L 65
Avenue, The. Alr 1D 108
Avenue, The. And 1L 69
Avenue, The. Bar S 7N 71
Avenue, The. Bas 2F 60
Avenue, The. Bish W 3L 163
Avenue, The. Bourn 4K 227
Avenue, The. Cam 9K 19
Avenue, The. C'then 1D 18
Avenue, The. Fare 9L 197
Avenue, The. Far W 7M 59
Avenue, The. Fle 2K 47
Avenue, The. Frox 7C 138
Avenue, The. Gos 5J 239
Avenue, The. Gray 4M 103
Avenue, The. Hath 9L 33
Avenue, The. Lip 2C 116
Avenue, The. Ptsfld 1M 145
Avenue, The. Poole 5E 244
Avenue, The. Port 9B 66
Avenue, The. Sotn 8L 159 (1D 4)
Avenue, The. Tidw 8G 30
Avenue, The. Twy 7L 127
Avery Ct. A'sht 9K 49 (off Alice Rd.)
Avery La. Gos 9H 213
Aviary Ct. Bas 3F 42
Aviation Pk. Hurn 6C 218
Aviation Pk. W. Hurn 6A 218
Aviemore Dri. Okly 1C 58
Avington Clo. Eastl 7H 133
Avington Ct. Sotn 7L 159
Avington Grn. Hav 3H 203
Avington Pk. 1H 107
Avlan Ct. Win 9K 105
Avocet Clo. S'sea 2J 241
Avocet Cres. Coll T 5F 18
Avocet Ho. S'sea 2J 241
Avocet Quay. Ems 1N 217
Avocet Wlk. Gos 6C 212
Avocet Way. Water 3A 182
Avon 5J 219
Avon Av. Ring 5G 186
Avonborne Way. Chan F 4N 131
Avon Bldgs. Christ 7L 229
Avon Castle Dri. Ring 4G 186
Avon Causeway. Hurn 8E 218
Avoncliffe Rd. Bourn 2H 247
Avon Clo. Bourn 8A 228
Avon Clo. Farn 5G 29
Avon Clo. Lee S 2B 238
Avon Clo. L'ton 3C 234
Avon Clo. Ptsfld 3L 145
Avon Ct. And 8B 52
Avon Ct. F'ham 9E 64
Avon Ct. F'bri 9J 151
Avon Ct. Net A 4F 194
Avon Ct. Poole 1E 244
Avon Cres. Roms 5B 130
Avondale Ct. Sotn 9N 159
Avondale Mobile Home Pk. Col C 3L 133
Avondale Rd. A'sht 2K 65
Avondale Rd. Fle 1M 47
Avondale Rd. Ports 1G 240
Avondale Rd. Water 1N 201
Avon Dyke. D'ton 3K 119
Avon Gdns. Brans 6D 220
Avon Grn. Chan F 7B 132
Avon Heath Country Pk. & Vis. Cen. 6D 186
Avon Ho. Bourn 3J 245 (9J 247)
Avon Ho. Sotn 4A 174
Avon Meade. F'bri 9H 151
Avon Mdw. D'ton 2K 119
Avon M. Bourn 8N 227
Avon Pk. Ring 2G 186
Avon Rd. Bourn 8N 227
Avon Rd. Bulf B 3B 66
Avon Rd. F'ham 9E 64
Avon Rd. Okly 1D 58
Avon Rd. Sotn 1D 174
Avon Rd. Tidw 9C 30
Avon Rd. E. Christ 6K 229
Avon Rd. W. Christ 6J 229
Avon Run Clo. Christ 9D 230
Avon Run Rd. Christ 9D 230
Avon Trad. Pk. Christ 7K 229
Avon Vw. Gods 1N 153
Avon Vw. Pde. Burt 3M 229
Avon Vw. Rd. Burt 3M 229
Avon Wlk. Bas 6E 42
Avon Wlk. Fare 9J 199
Avon Way. W End 9J 161
Avon Wharf. Christ 8M 229
Award Rd. Chu C 6L 47 (in two parts)
Awbridge 9F 122
Awbridge Hill 9G 123
Awbridge Rd. Hav 5C 202
Axford 3F 78
Axford Clo. Bourn 3B 228
Axford Rd. Ellis 2H 79
Axmansford 6C 10
Ayesgarth. Chu C 6N 47
Ayjay Clo. A'sht 3K 65
Aylen Rd. Ports 6H 215
Aylesbury Rd. Bourn 1A 246
Aylesbury Rd. Ports 8G 214
Aylesham Way. Yate 7L 17
Ayliffe Ho. Bas 7M 41
Ayling Clo. Gos 9E 212
Ayling Ct. F'ham 3H 65
Ayling Hill. A'sht 1H 65
Ayling La. A'sht 2H 65
Aylings Clo. Bas 6K 41
Aylward's Dri. Lwr F 4C 98
Aylward St. Ports 2B 240 (3K 5)
Aylwards Way. Neth W 1N 87
Aylwin Clo. Bas 9B 42
Aynsley Ct. Sotn 3J 173
Ayres La. Burgh 3D 8
Ayrshire Gdns. Fle 8N 27
Aysgarth Rd. Water 1M 201
Aysha Clo. New M 5C 232
Azalea Av. Lind 2M 101
Azalea Clo. Hav 5J 203
Azalea Clo. St I 3D 186
Azalea Ct. And 3K 69
Azalea Gdns. Chu C 6N 47

B

Babbs Mead. F'ham 9C 64
Babs Fields. Bent 7K 63
Bach Clo. Bas 3M 59
Back Dri. C'then 3A 18
Back Drove. W'slw 5F 86
Back La. Brim C 2B 10
Back La. Bucks H 10M 63
Back La. H'rd & Lash 2M 79
Back La. Mort W 1B 12
Back La. Mott 9B 88
Back La. S'wick 3N 199
Back La. Sway 5K 223
Back La. App 3C 50
Back La. Ver D 8D 6
Bk. of the Walls. Sotn 8M 173 (9D 4) (in two parts)
Back St. Win 1K 127
Bacon Clo. Coll T 6F 18
Bacon Clo. Sotn 9D 174
Bacon La. Churt 4E 84
Bacon La. Hay I 4D 242
Badajos Rd. A'sht 8H 49
Baddesley 8G 131
Baddesley Clo. N Bad 7E 130
Baddesley Gdns. Hav 2D 202
Baddesley Pk. Ind. Est. N Bad 8G 130
Baddesley Rd. N Bad 4M 131
Baden Clo. New M 5C 232
Baden Powell Ho. Roms 5M 129 (off Winchester Rd.)
Baden Powell Rd. Lngmr 4J 115
Baden Powell Way. Roms 5M 129
Bader Clo. H End 2N 175
Bader Ct. Farn 4H 29
Bader Way. White 4H 197
Badger Brow. Water 3A 202
Badger Clo. Eastl 1K 161
Badger Clo. Fare 7N 197
Badger Clo. Four M 4K 97
Badger Ct. Eastl 1K 161
Badger Farm 1G 127
Badger Farm Rd. Win 9F 104 (in two parts)
Badger Rd. Fare 3B 212
Badgers Bank. Lych 3G 42
Badgers Clo. Ashy H 3C 186
Badgers Clo. Fle 3L 47
Badgers Clo. Sway 5K 223
Badgers Copse. Cam 1N 29
Badgers Copse. New M 9D 222
Badgers Holt. Yate 8L 17
Badgers Ri. N'bry 1C 8
Badgers, The. Net A 3G 195
Badgers Wlk. Dib P 7L 193
Badger Way. Ews 2N 63
Badgerwood Dri. Frim 2M 29
Badger Wood Pl. Sotn 1D 174
Badminston Drove. Fawl 8G 209
Badminston La. Fawl 7G 208
Badshear La. Cher 7F 108
Badshot Farm La. Bad L 5J 65
Badshot Lea 4K 65
Badshot Lea Rd. Bad L 6H 65
Badshot Pk. Bad L 4J 65
Baffins 9H 215
Baffins Rd. Ports 1H 241
Bagber Rd. Tot 3M 171
Bagmore 2L 79
Bagmore La. H'rd 3J 79
Bagnum La. Crow 6N 187
Bagot Ho. Gos 9H 213
Bagshot M. Sotn 7D 174
Bagwell La. Odi & W'fld 6N 45
Baigent Clo. Win 6N 105
Bailey Clo. Bot 4D 176
Bailey Clo. Frim 4M 29
Bailey Clo. New M 2E 232
Bailey Clo. Win 8H 105
Bailey Dri. Christ 7J 229
Bailey Green 2K 137
Bailey Grn. Sotn 9E 160
Baileys Clo. B'wtr 9E 18

Bailey's Down—Beaconsfield Rd.

Bailey's Down. 1D 124
Baileys Hill. Wim G 8F 148
Bailey's Rd. S'sea 3E 240
Bain Av. Cam 2K 29
Baird Av. Bas 9N 41
Baird Rd. Farn. 6L 29
Bakehouse M. A'sht. 9J 49
Baker Rd. Bourn. 1D 226
Bakers Drove. Rown. 6D 158
Bakers Fld. Gthm 4E 114
Baker St. Ports 9E 214
Bakers Wharf. Sotn 5A 174
Balaclava Rd. Sotn 3E 174
Balchin Ho. Ports 3K 5
Balcombe Rd. Poole 2E 244
Balderton Clo. Ports 4G 214
Baldwin Clo. Christ. 8N 229
Balfour Clo. Christ. 6F 230
Balfour Clo. Gos 1F 238
Balfour Dri. Liss 1E 140
Balfour Rd. Bourn. 5K 227
Balfour Rd. Ports 7F 214
Balfour Rd. Sotn. 5G 174
Balintore Ct. Coll T 5F 18
Balksbury Hill. Up Cl. 3K 69
Balksbury Hill Ind. Est. Up Cl 4L 69
Balksbury Rd. Up Cl 4L 69
Ball & Wicket La. F'ham 3E 64
Ballantyne Rd. Farn. 6J 29
Ballard Clo. Bas 8L 41
Ballard Clo. New M. 2C 232
Ballard Clo. Sotn. 1C 172
Ballard Ct. Gos 3K 239
Ball Hill. 1N 7
Balliol Clo. Fare. 8F 196
Balliol Rd. Ports 8F 214
Balliol Way. Owl 4G 19
Ball's La. Cher 2H 135
Balmerlawn. 5D 148
Balmer Lawn Rd. Broc 5D 148
Balmoral Av. Bourn. 5B 228
Balmoral Clo. Alt 5D 80
Balmoral Clo. Chan F 4N 131
Balmoral Clo. Gos 6F 212
Balmoral Clo. Sotn. 6H 159
Balmoral Ct. Bas. 8L 41
Balmoral Ct. Sotn 4F 172
Balmoral Cres. F'ham 4D 64
Balmoral Dri. Frim 4N 29
Balmoral Dri. Water 5K 201
Balmoral Ho. Bourn 2H 245 (6G 247)
Balmoral Rd. And. 1N 69
Balmoral Rd. Fare. 6A 198
Balmoral Rd. Poole. 2A 244
Balmoral Wlk. New M. 3A 232
Balmoral Way. Bas 4J 59
Balmoral Way. Ptsfld 9M 139
Balmoral Way. Rown 5C 158
Balsan Clo. Bas 3M 41
Baltic Rd. W End. 9J 161
Banbury Av. Sotn 6G 174
Band Hall Pl. Hook 2H 45
Bangor Rd. Sotn. 4G 173
Banister Gdns. Sotn 3L 173
Banister Grange. Sotn. 3L 173
Banister M. Sotn. 3L 173
Banister Park. 3L 173
Banister Pk. Bowling Club. 4A 160
Banister Rd. Sotn 3L 173
Bank. 3M 189
Bank Chambers. Poole 1C 244 (off Penn Hill Av.)
Bank Clo. Christ 8L 229
Bankhill Dri. L'ton. 1D 234
Bank Rd. A'sht. 6M 49
Bankside. F'ham 3H 65
Bankside. Gos 5H 239
Bankside. L'ton. 9D 224
Bank Side. Sotn 7C 160
Bankside Ho. Win 6J 105 (6J 237)
Bankside Rd. Bourn 3L 227
Banks Rd. Poole 9A 244
Banks, The. Sher E. 8A 122
Bank St. Bish W. 3M 163
Bankview. L'ton 9D 224
Bannerman Rd. Ptsfld 9M 139
Banning St. Roms. 6L 129
Bannister Ct. Tot. 3N 171
Bannister Gdns. E'sly 5H 17
Bannister Gdns. Yate 8B 18
Bapaume Rd. Ports 3G 214
Baptist Hill. St M. 9L 35
Barbara Clo. Chu C. 5N 47
Barbe Baker Av. W End 9G 161
Barbel Av. Bas. 6F 42
Barberry Clo. Fle 4M 47
Barberry Dri. Tot. 1H 171
Barberry Way. B'wtr 2H 29
Barbour Clo. Odi. 2E 62 (off Woolridge Cres.)
Barcelona Clo. And. 9A 52
Barclay Ho. Gos 3N 239 (off Trinity Grn., in two parts)
Barclay M. Hythe 9M 193
Bardon Way. Fare 9N 197
Bardwell Clo. Bas 7L 41
Baredown, The. Nat S 4D 44
Bar End Ind. Est. Win 9M 105
Bar End Rd. Win 8M 105 (9P 237) (in two parts)
Barfield Clo. Win 8M 105
Barfields. L'ton 2E 234
Barfields Ct. L'ton 2E 234
Barfleur Clo. Fare 7N 197
Barfleur Rd. Fare 3C 212
Barford. 8G 85
Barford Clo. Chan F 4N 131
Barford Clo. Fle 3B 48
Barford La. Churt 7G 85
Barford La. D'ton 1L 119
Bargates. Christ 7K 229
Bargate Shop. Cen. Sotn 6M 173 (6D 4)
Bargate St. Sotn 6L 173 (6C 4)
Bargate, The. 6D 4
Barge Clo. A'sht 6N 49
Barge La. S'fld 2D 14
Barham Clo. Gos 1K 239
Barham Rd. Ptsfld 1M 145
Barham Way. Ports 4E 214
Baring Clo. E Stra 7M 77
Baring Clo. It Ab. 8K 93
Baring Dri. Cowes 5N 237 (off Baring Rd.)
Baring Rd. Bourn 1K 247
Baring Rd. Cowes. 5N 237
Baring Rd. Win 7M 105
Barker Mill Clo. Rown 5D 158
Barkis Ho. Ports 9E 214
Barkis Mead. Owl 3G 18
Bark Mill M. Roms 6L 129
Barlands Clo. Burt 4M 229
Barle Clo. W End 9F 160
Barleycorn Wlk. Cad. 6N 155 (off Romsey Rd.)
Barley Down Dri. Win. 1H 127
Barley Hill. Dun. 4E 122
Barley Mow Clo. W'fld 3E 46
Barley Mow Hill. Head 1B 102
Barley Way. Fle. 7N 27
Barlow Clo. Fare 6L 211
Barlows La. And 4M 69
Barlows Rd. T'ley 6H 11
Barnaby Clo. D'ton 2J 119
Barnard Way. A'sht. 8H 49
Barnbrook Rd. Sar G 5B 196
Barn Clo. Cam 7N 19
Barn Clo. Ems. 9K 203
Barn Clo. La. A'wrth. 7M 7
Barncroft. App 5A 50
Barncroft. F'ham 9E 64 (in two parts)
Barncroft Way. Hav 5D 202
Barnes Clo. Bourn 3H 227
Barnes Clo. Farn 8M 29
Barnes Clo. Sar G. 5A 196
Barnes Clo. Sotn 4G 174
Barnes Clo. W Wel. 9N 121
Barnes Clo. Win 9J 105
Barnes Cres. Bourn 3H 227
Barnes La. Hord. 5H 233 (in two parts)
Barnes La. Sar G 3B 196
Barnes Rd. Bourn. 3H 227
Barnes Rd. Frim. 4N 29
Barnes Rd. Ports. 1F 240
Barnes Rd. Sotn. 4G 174
Barnes Wallis Ct. Ame 5A 66 (off Rayleigh Cres.)
Barnes Wallis Rd. Fare 5G 196
Barnes Way. Hav 6D 202
Barnet Side. 8E 112
Barnet Side La. Frox. 1D 138
Barnetts Wood La. Bigh 6A 96
Barney Evans Cres. Water 7L 181
Barney Hayes La. Cad. 3A 170
Barnfield. Christ 6F 230
Barn Fld. Yate. 8N 17
Barnfield Clo. Lwr Fr 7G 63
Barnfield Clo. Sotn 9C 174
Barnfield Ct. Fare 9A 198
Barnfield Ct. Sotn. 9D 174
Barnfield Flats. Sotn 9D 174
Barnfield Heath. 3E 218
Barnfield Ri. And. 3L 69
Barnfield Rd. Ptsfld 1B 146
Barnfield Rd. Sotn 9D 174
Barnfield Way. Sotn 9D 174
Barn Fold. Water. 9B 182
Barn Grn. Clo. Water 6G 180
Barn La. Four M 6G 96
Barn La. Okly 2C 58
Barn Mdw. Clo. Chu C 8K 47
Barn Piece. Chan F 6L 131
Barnsfield Cres. Tot. 3J 171
Barnsfield Rd. St L 6D 186
Barnside Way. Liss 2E 140
Barnsland. W End. 8G 160
Barns, The. Dum 1C 78
Barnwood Rd. Fare. 8N 197
Baroda Rd. Tidw 8F 30
Baron Rd. Hamb. 6K 195
Barons Ct. Poole 1F 244
Barons Mead. Sotn. 8D 158
Baronsmere Ct. Gos 3J 239
Barons Rd. Bourn. 1B 226
Barossa Rd. Cam. 6M 19
Barracane Dri. C'then 1C 18
Barrack La. Crow. 4M 187
Barrack Rd. A'sht 9J 49
Barrack Rd. Christ 6G 228
Barracks Rd. Green 1G 9
Barracks Rd. S'sea 5K 241
Barra Clo. Okly 9C 40
Barratt Ind. Pk. White 4F 196
Barrett Ct. Bas 9D 42
Barrie Clo. White. 1F 196
Barrie Rd. Bourn. 3K 227
Barrie Rd. F'ham. 3C 64
Barrington Clo. Eastl 7D 132
Barrington Ct. Bourn 7H 227
Barrington Ho. Ports. 9E 214
Barrington Ter. S'sea 7N 5
Barron Pl. Bas 3K 41
Barrow Down Gdns. Sotn 7J 175
Barrow Dri. Bourn 4C 228
Barrowgate Rd. Bourn 3N 227
Barrowgate Way. Bourn 3A 228
Barrow Hill. 9M 69
Barrow Hill. Good C 1K 73
Barrow Hill Rd. Copy 8C 156
Barrow Rd. Bourn. 4C 228
Barrows La. Land. 8H 121
Barrows La. Sway. 8J 223
Barrow Way. Bourn 4C 228
Barrs Av. New M. 2B 232
Barrs Wood Dri. New M 2C 232
Barrs Wood Rd. New M 2C 232
Barry Rd. Sotn 4F 174
Barry Way. Bas 3M 59
Bars Hill. Cowes. 5P 237
Barters Clo. Sotn 1E 172
Bartholomew Clo. Win 5L 105
Bartlett Clo. Fare. 6A 198
Bartlett Dri. Bourn. 6E 228
Bartletts, The. Hamb. 7L 195
Bartley. 4B 170
Bartley Av. Tot. 4L 171
Bartley Rd. W'lnds 6C 170
Bartley Way. Hook. 3J 45
Bartley Wood Bus. Pk. E. Hook 3J 45
Bartley Wood Bus. Pk. W. Hook 3H 45
Bartok Clo. Bas. 1N 59
Barton Chase. Bart S 7A 232
Barton Clo. A'sht. 1G 64
Barton Clo. Charl 7K 51
Barton Clo. Roms. 4A 130
Barton Comn. La. New M 6C 232
Barton Comn. Rd. New M 7C 232
Barton Ct. Av. Bart S. 7A 232
Barton Ct. Rd. New M 5B 232
Barton Cres. Sotn. 1D 174
Barton Cft. Bart S 7B 232
Barton Cross. Water. 3B 182
Barton Dri. Bart S. 6A 232
Barton Dri. Hamb 6K 195
Barton Dri. H End. 3A 176
Barton Drove. Bar S & Sut S 5A 76
Barton End. Alt. 5E 80
Barton Grn. Bart S 7C 232
Barton Gro. Ports 5J 215
Barton Ho. Bart S. 7N 231
Barton La. Bart S. 6M 231
Barton Lodge. Poole. 9A 226
Barton on Sea. 7A 232
Barton-on-Sea Golf Course. 8C 232
Barton Pk. Ind. Est. Eastl 1F 160
Barton Rd. Eastl. 9G 132
Barton's Ct. Odi 8K 45
Bartons Dri. Yate 9N 17
Bartonside Rd. New M 6L 231
Barton's La. Old B 4G 43 (in three parts)
Bartons Rd. F'bri. 1J 153
Bartons Rd. Hav. 4G 202
Barton Stacey. 5A 76
Bartons, The. F'bri 1J 153
Bartons, The. H End 4L 175
Bartons Way. Farn 5E 28
Barton Way. Bart S. 6A 232
Barton Wood Rd. Bart S 7N 231
Bartram Rd. Tot 4N 171 (in two parts)
Barwell Clo. C'then 1B 18
Barwell Gro. Ems 6L 203
Barwell Ter. H End 4A 176
Bascott Clo. Bourn 5E 226
Bascott Rd. Bourn 5D 226
Bashley. 8B 222
Bashley Comn. Rd. New M 8B 222
Bashley Cross Rd. New M 1M 231
Bashley Dri. New M 9C 222
Bashley Rd. New M 8B 222
Basingbourne Clo. Fle 5M 47
Basingbourne Rd. Fle 6L 47
Basing Dean. Priv 9M 111
Basing Dri. A'sht. 3K 65
Basingfield Clo. Old B 7J 43
Basing House. 5H 43
Basing M. Bish W 4M 163 (off Basingwell St.)
Basing Park. 9L 111
Basing Rd. Hav. 4E 202
Basing Rd. Old B. 5F 42
Basingstoke. 6A 42
Basingstoke Bus. Cen. Bas 9N 41
Basingstoke Cricket Club. 7B 42
Basingstoke Enterprise Cen. Bas 7K 41
Basingstoke Golf Club. 5H 59
Basingstoke Ice Rink. 6L 41
Basingstoke Rd. Alt 5B 80
Basingstoke Rd. Heck. 8C 14 (in two parts)
Basingstoke Rd. K're 2B 6
Basingstoke Rd. King W & Abb W 9A 92
Basingstoke Rd. Old Al. 6F 94
Basingstoke Rd. R'dll 5G 20
Basingstoke Rd. Rise 1G 14
Basing Vw. Bas 6D 42
Basing Way. Chan F. 8M 131
Basingwell St. Bish W 4M 163
Basin St. Ports 8E 214
Bassenthwaite Rd. Bord 2J 101
Basset Clo. Frim. 4N 29
Bassett. 5L 159
Bassett Av. Sotn 8L 159
Bassett Clo. Sotn 7L 159
Bassett Ct. Sotn 7L 159
Bassett Cres. E. Sotn 7L 159
Bassett Cres. W. Sotn. 8L 159
Bassett Dale. Sotn 5L 159
Bassett Gdns. Sotn. 7L 159
Bassett Green. 6N 159
Bassett Grn. Sotn. 6N 159
Bassett Grn. Clo. Sotn 6M 159
Bassett Grn. Ct. Sotn 6N 159
Bassett Grn. Dri. Sotn 5M 159
Bassett Grn. Rd. Sotn 4M 159
Bassett Heath Av. Sotn 4L 159
Bassett Lodge. Sotn 7L 159
Bassett Mdw. Sotn 7L 159
Bassett M. Sotn 6L 159
Bassett Rd. Poole. 8A 226
Bassett Row. Sotn 5L 159
Bassett Wlk. Hav 3D 202
Bassett Wood Dri. Sotn 5L 159
Bassett Wood M. Sotn 7L 159
Bassett Wood Rd. Sotn 5L 159
Bass Manor Pk. Brewery 5G 80
Batchelor Cres. Bourn 3D 226
Batchelor Dri. Old B 6K 43
Batchelor Grn. Burs 1L 195
Batchelor Rd. Bourn. 3D 226
Batchelor's Barn Rd. And 1B 70
Batcombe Clo. Bourn 3C 226
Bath & Wells Ct. Gos 1E 238
Bath Clo. Sotn. 4F 174
Bath Hill Ct. Bourn 2L 245 (7N 247)
Bath Hill Roundabout. Bourn 3L 245 (8N 247)
Bathing La. Ports 4A 240 (6H 5)
Bath La. Fare. 8E 198
Bath La. Cotts. Fare 9E 198
Bath La. Lwr. Fare. 8E 198
Bath Rd. Bourn 3K 245 (8M 247)
Bath Rd. Cam 7M 19
Bath Rd. Cowes 5P 237
Bath Rd. Ems. 1M 217
Bath Rd. L'ton 3F 234
Bath Rd. Sotn 4F 174
Bath Rd. S'sea 4G 240
Bath Sq. Ports. 3A 240 (6H 5)
Bath St. Sotn 3M 173 (1E 4)
Bathurst Clo. Hay I 4E 242
Bathurst Way. Ports 6C 214
Battenburg Av. Ports 6F 214
Battenburg Rd. Gos 2L 239
Batten Clo. Christ 7N 229
Batten Rd. D'ton 1J 119
Battens Av. Over 2E 56
Battens Way. Hav 5F 202
Batten Way. Sotn 7C 160
Batterley Drove. Cran. 8M 149
Battery Clo. Gos 8H 213
Battery Hill. Bish W. 3L 163
Battery Hill. Win 8G 104
Battery Promenade. Ports 4A 240 (7H 5)
Battery Rd. Cowes 5N 237
Battery Row. Ports 4B 240 (8J 5)
Battle Clo. Sar G. 5C 196
Battledown Cotts. Okly 1G 58
Battramsley. 5B 224
Battramsley Cross. 6C 224
Batt's Corner. 2N 83
Baughurst Common. 4E 10
Baughurst Rd. Baug 5E 10
Baughurst Rd. R'dll. 4F 20
B Avenue. Hythe 4C 208 (Eighth St., in two parts)
B Avenue. Hythe 3A 208 (Fourteenth St.)
Baverstock Rd. Poole 6F 226
Baverstocks. Alt. 2G 80
Bawdsey Rd. Ame 6A 66
Baxter Rd. Sotn. 5J 175
Baybridge. 5D 134
Baybridge La. Ows 5D 134
Baybridge Rd. Hav 4H 203
Bay Clo. Sotn 7E 174
Bayfield Av. Frim 2M 29
Bayfields. S'sea 9N 5
Bayford Clo. B'wtr. 3J 29
Bay House Sports Hall 4F 238
Bayly Av. Fare 2M 213
Baynard Clo. Bas 4D 42
Bay Rd. Gos. 4H 239
Bay Rd. Sotn. 7E 174
Bays Ct. L'ton 2C 234
Bays Rd. Penn 2B 234
Bayswater Ho. S'sea 4E 240
Baythorn Clo. Ports 9E 214
Bay Tree Gdns. March 9E 172
Bay Tree Lodge. Fare 6N 211
Bay Trees. Sotn. 4J 175
Baytree Way. Christ. 5F 230
Bay Vw. New M 7L 231
Bayview Ct. Hay I 5D 242
Baywood Clo. Farn 7E 28
Bazaar Rd. Tidw 9A 30
Beach Av. Bart S. 7A 232
Beach Dri. Ports. 9A 200
Beach La. Net A 3E 194
Beach Piece Way. Bas 3K 59
Beach Rd. Ems 9L 203
Beach Rd. Hay I 5E 242 (in two parts)
Beach Rd. Lee S. 2A 238
Beach Rd. Poole. 5E 244
Beach Rd. S'sea 6E 240
Beach's Cres. Lit L 1N 21
Beachway. Fare 2M 213
Beacon Bottom. 3D 196
Beacon Bottom. Park G 3D 196
Beacon Clo. Evtn. 5L 233
Beacon Clo. Park G 3D 196
Beacon Clo. Rown 5C 158
Beacon Ct. F'bri 8H 151
Beacon Dri. Highc 7H 231
Beacon Gdns. Fle 2K 47
Beacon Hill. 1N 103
Beacon Hill & Nature Reserve. 8D 8
Beacon Hill Ct. Hind. 1M 103
Beaconhill La. Ext. 6N 135
Beacon Hill La. Ext. 8M 135
Beacon Hill Pk. Hind. 1K 103
Beacon Hill Rd. Chu C & Ews 6N 47
Beacon Hill Rd. Hind. 1L 103
Beacon M. W End. 2H 175
Beacon Mt. Park G 3D 196
Beacon Rd. Bourn 3J 245 (8K 247)
Beacon Rd. W End 1H 175
Beaconsfield Av. Ports 1H 215
Beaconsfield Rd. Bas 7C 42
Beaconsfield Rd. Christ 7L 229

Beaconsfield Rd. Fare 9D 198
Beaconsfield Rd. Poole 9B 226
Beaconsfield Rd. Water 1M 201
Beacon Sq. Ems 9L 203
Beacon Way. Park G 3D 196
Beales Clo. And 1A 70
Beale's Ct. W Tyth 7L 87
Bealeswood La. Dock 2A 84
Bealing Clo. Sotn 7N 159
Beal's Pightle. Char A 5H 21
Beam Hollow. F'ham 3E 64
Beamond Ct. Ports 1H 215
Bear Ct. Bas 4G 42
Bear Cross Roundabout. Bourn 1D 226
Bear Hill. K're 3A 6
Bear La. F'ham 7D 64
Bearslane Clo. Tot 1K 171
Bearwood 1B 226
Bearwood Gdns. Fle 2M 47
Beatrice Rd. Sotn 3H 173
Beatrice Rd. S'sea 5F 240
Beattie Ri. H End 9N 161
Beatty Clo. L Hth 5E 196
Beatty Clo. Ring 9M 185
Beatty Ct. And 1C 70
Beatty Ct. Sotn 5G 175
Beatty Dri. Gos 5H 239
Beatty Ho. Ports 1E 240 (off Fyning St.)
Beatty Rd. Bourn 5M 227
Beauchamp Av. Gos 6E 212
Beauchamps Gdns. Bourn 6D 228
Beauclerk Grn. W'fld 2B 46
Beau Ct. New M 3B 232
Beaucroft Rd. Wal C 8A 164
Beaufort Av. Fare 6B 198
Beaufort Clo. Christ 7D 230
Beaufort Dri. Bish W 3M 163
Beaufort Rd. Bord 2J 101
Beaufort Rd. Bourn 9F 228
Beaufort Rd. Chu C 4N 47
Beaufort Rd. F'ham 7E 64
Beaufort Rd. Hav 7D 202
Beaufort Rd. S'sea 6E 240
Beaufort Rd. Win 8K 105 (9K 237)
Beaulieu 7E 206
Beaulieu Abbey 6E 206
Beaulieu Av. Christ 7H 229
Beaulieu Av. Fare 9J 199
Beaulieu Av. Hav 3D 202
Beaulieu Clo. New M 3N 231
Beaulieu Clo. Sotn 6G 159
Beaulieu Clo. Win 2H 105
Beaulieu Ct. Bas 6E 42 (off Loddon Dri.)
Beaulieu Ct. Sotn 1M 173
Beaulieu Gdns. B'wtr 8E 18
Beaulieu Gdns. Cvn. Pk. Christ 7H 229
Beaulieu Pl. Gos 6E 212
Beaulieu Rd. Beau 6F 206
Beaulieu Rd. Bourn 4F 244
Beaulieu Rd. Christ 7H 229
Beaulieu Rd. Dib P & Hythe 9K 193
Beaulieu Rd. Eastl 8E 132
Beaulieu Rd. Hamb 6K 195
Beaulieu Rd. Lyn & Beau 2C 148
Beaulieu Rd. March 3C 192
Beaulieu Rd. Ports 7F 214
Beaumaris Clo. And 3L 69
Beaumaris Clo. Chan F 8M 131
Beaumaris Gdns. Hythe 4L 193
Beaumond Grn. Win 8L 237
Beaumont Clo. Fare 6N 197
Beaumont Clo. Sotn 8K 159
Beaumont Ct. Gos 8J 213
Beaumont Gro. A'sht 9G 49
Beaumont Ri. Fare 5N 197
Beaumont Rd. Poole 6C 244
Beaumont Rd. Tot 3N 171
Beaumont Way. Ame 5A 66 (off Porton Rd.)
Beaurepaire Clo. Braml 1E 22
Beauworth 2J 135
Beauworth Av. Sotn 2G 175
Beaver Dri. Eastl 1L 161
Beaver Ind. Est. Christ 8C 230
Beaver La. Yate 8A 18
Beavers Clo. Alt 4E 80
Beavers Clo. F'ham 8C 64
Beavers Clo. T'ley 4G 10
Beavers Hill. F'ham 8B 64
Beavers M. Bord 3K 101
Beavers Rd. F'ham 8C 64
Becher Rd. Poole 1C 244
Bechin Clo. Chu C 8J 47
Beck Clo. Sar G 6B 196
Beckett Clo. Bas 6J 41
Beckett Ct. Wort 7J 41
Beckett Rd. And 1L 69
Beckford La. S'wick 9N 179
Beck Gdns. F'ham 4D 64
Beckham La. Ptsfld 9K 139
Beckley 1L 231
Beckley Copse. Walk 4J 231
Beck St. Ports 2C 240 (3L 5)
Becton La. Bart S 5C 232
Becton Mead. Bart S 5C 232
Beddington Ct. Lych 3H 43
Bede Dri. Charl 7K 51
Bedenham 5F 212
Bedenham La. Gos 5F 212 (in three parts)
Bedfield La. Win 1M 105
Bedford Av. Frim G 7N 29
Bedford Av. Sotn 8C 174
Bedford Clo. F'bri 8J 151
Bedford Clo. Hav 9H 203
Bedford Clo. H End 4A 176
Bedford Clo. W'hill 5J 101
Bedford Cres. Bourn 7F 228
Bedford Cres. Frim G 6N 29
Bedford La. Frim G 6N 29
Bedford Place 4L 173
Bedford Pl. Sotn 4L 173 (1C 4)
Bedford Rd. Ptsfld 9K 139
Bedford Rd. N. Poole 4A 226
Bedford Rd. S. Poole 4A 226
Bedford St. Gos 1J 239
Bedford St. S'sea 3D 240 (5N 5)
Bedford Wlk. Bas 6C 42
Bedhampton 7C 202
Bedhampton Hill. Hav 8A 202 (in two parts)
Bedhampton Hill Rd. Hav 8B 202
Bedhampton Ho. Ports 1E 240 (off Crasswell St.)
Bedhampton Rd. Hav 7C 202
Bedhampton Rd. Ports 8G 214
Bedhampton Way. Hav 5F 202
Bedser Sq. And 7A 52
Bedwell Clo. Rown 5E 158
Beech 6A 80
Beecham Berry. Bas 3M 59
Beecham Rd. Ports 9F 214
Beech Av. Bourn 1F 246
Beech Av. Cam 9M 19
Beech Av. Christ 6G 228
Beech Av. Sotn 3C 174
Beechbrook Av. Yate 8A 18
Beech Clo. A'hlt 5D 152
Beech Clo. Braml 2H 23
Beech Clo. Chan F 3B 132
Beech Clo. Evtn 6L 233
Beech Clo. Hamb 7J 195
Beech Clo. Mid W 4B 72
Beech Clo. Over 9E 38
Beech Clo. P Cnr 9G 50
Beech Clo. Port 9B 66
Beech Clo. Roms 6B 130
Beech Clo. Thru 1N 67
Beech Clo. Water 8N 181
Beech Clo. Win 2F 126
Beech Copse. Win 5F 104
Beech Ct. Sotn 7D 174
Beech Ct. Whitc 4G 54
Beech Cres. Hythe 9M 193
Beechcrest Vw. Hook 1H 45
Beechcroft Clo. And 9N 51
Beechcroft Clo. Chan F 7B 132
Beechcroft Clo. Fare 8L 197
Beechcroft Clo. Lip 3N 115
Beechcroft Cotts. Bro'tn 2A 86
Beechcroft La. Ring 9L 185
Beechcroft M. Ring 9L 185 (off Beechcroft La.)
Beechcroft Rd. Gos 4J 239
Beechcroft Way. Chan F 6B 132
Beechdale Clo. Cal 9J 157
Beechdale Wlk. Cal 9J 157
Beechdown Ho. Bas 1L 59
Beech Dri. B'wtr 9F 18
Beech Dri. Chine 9H 23
Beechen La. Lyn 4C 148
Beeches Clo. Pitt 6E 86
Beeches Hill. Bish W 9G 134
Beeches, The. And 1L 69
Beeches, The. Awb 8E 122
Beeches, The. Bourn 6D 228
Beeches, The. Coom B 3G 119
Beeches, The. F Oak 2A 162
Beeches, The. Hat W 4L 59
Beeches, The. W Wel 1A 120
Beechey Rd. Bourn 9L 227
Beechfield. Newt T 6E 66
Beechfield Ct. Sotn 2G 172
Beech Gdns. Hamb 7J 195
Beech Grange. Land 1J 155
Beech Gro. Gos 4J 239
Beech Gro. Hay I 3H 243
Beech Gro. Ows 5C 134
Beech Gro. Wher 1E 74
Beech Hanger. Chol 4F 66
Beech Hanger End. Gray 4K 103
Beech Hanger Rd. Gray 4K 103
Beech Hangers La. Alt 8D 62
Beech Hill 1C 102 (Bordon)
Beech Hill 1B 14 (Reading)
Beech Hill. Head D 3C 102
Beech Hill Rd. B Hill & Spen W 1A 14
Beech Hill Rd. Head 1B 102
Beechlands Rd. Meds 3J 97
Beech La. Gray 3K 103
Beech La. St L 6B 186
Beechmount Rd. Sotn 6L 159
Beechnut Dri. B'wtr 7D 18
Beechnut Ind. Est. A'sht 1K 65
Beechnut Rd. A'sht 1K 65
Beech Ride. Fle 4L 47
Beech Ride. S'hrst 5D 18
Beech Rd. Alr 1F 108
Beech Rd. Asht 8H 171
Beech Rd. Bish G 1H 9
Beech Rd. Chan F 4B 132
Beech Rd. Fare 7A 198
Beech Rd. Farn 5J 29
Beech Rd. H End 3A 176
Beech Rd. Sotn 4G 173
Beech Rd. Tidw 7E 30
Beech Rd. Water 6C 168
Beech Tree Clo. Okly 2C 58
Beech Tree Dri. Bad L 5J 65
Beech Tree Wlk. Mott & Bro'tn 6B 88
Beech Wlk. And 2K 69
Beech Way. Bas 4L 41
Beech Way. Water 5B 182
Beechwood. Chine 9F 22
Beechwood. F'bri 1G 153
Beechwood Av. Bourn 1C 246
Beechwood Av. New M 2N 231
Beechwood Av. Water 3M 201
Beechwood Clo. Bas 4L 59
Beechwood Clo. Chan F 3M 131
Beechwood Clo. Chu C 5K 47
Beechwood Clo. Wars 9A 196
Beechwood Ct. Bourn 2J 245 (8K 247)
Beechwood Ct. Liss 8F 114
Beechwood Cres. Chan F 3M 131
Beechwood Gdns. Bourn 1D 246
Beechwood Gdns. Sotn 2D 174
Beechwood La. Burl 7E 188
Beechwood Lodge. Fare 7D 198
Beechwood Ri. W End 1G 174
Beechwood Rd. Alt 6D 80
Beechwood Rd. Bart 7N 155
Beechwood Rd. Holb 5A 208
Beechwood Rd. Ports 4F 214
Beechwood Way. Dib P 7H 193
Beechworth Rd. Hav 8F 202
Beehive Wlk. Ports 3B 240 (6K 5)
Beeston Ct. Ports 9F 214
Beethoven Rd. Bas 2N 59
Beggars Drove. Sut S 7D 76
Beggars La. Win 6M 105
Begonia Clo. Bas 3J 59
Begonia Rd. Sotn 7N 159
Behrendt Clo. Gos 1J 239
Belaga Clo. Mid W 3A 72
Belben Clo. Poole 4B 226
Belben Rd. Poole 4A 226
Belbins. Roms 9M 123
Belbins Bus. Pk. Roms 1N 129
Belfield Rd. Bourn 1K 247
Belfry Sq. Hat W 5J 59
Belfry Wlk. Fare 7F 196 (in two parts)
Belgrave Ct. B'wtr 1F 28
Belgrave Ind. Est. Sotn 4B 174
Belgrave M. H Win 6C 26
Belgrave Rd. Poole 3E 244
Belgrave Rd. Sotn 9A 160
Belgrave Rd. Ind. Est. Sotn 9A 160
Belgravia Rd. Ports 7G 214
Bellair Ho. Hav 8G 202
Bellair Rd. Hav 8G 202
Bellamy Ct. Sotn 2B 174
Belland Dri. A'sht 1G 65
Bell Clo. Farn 6L 29
Bell Clo. Fawl 6D 208
Bell Cres. Water 3M 201
Bell Davies Rd. Fare 7L 211
Bellemoor Rd. Sotn 1H 173
Bellever Hill. Cam 8N 19
Belle Vw. Mans. Bourn 2H 247
Bellevue 4M 173
Bellevue. Whitc 5G 54
Belle Vue Clo. A'sht 9M 49
Belle Vue Clo. Bourn 1G 246
Belle Vue Cres. Bourn 1J 247
Belle Vue Enterprise Cen. A'sht 9N 49
Belle Vue Gdns. Bourn 1J 247
Bellevue La. Ems 7M 203
Belle Vue Rd. A'sht 9M 49
Bellevue Rd. And 3A 70
Belle Vue Rd. Bourn 1G 246
Bellevue Rd. Eastl 9E 132
Belle Vue Rd. Old B 5J 43
Belle Vue Rd. Poole 2A 244
Bellevue Rd. Sotn 4M 173 (2D 4)
Bellevue Ter. Sotn 4M 173 (1E 4)
Bellevue Ter. S'sea 4C 240 (8M 5)
Bellfield 1J 211
Bellfield. Fare 1J 211
Bellflower Clo. Christ 6D 230
Bellflower Way. Chan F 5L 131
Bellflower Way. Fare 6J 197
Bell Hill 8L 139
Bell Hill. Ptsfld 7L 139
Bell Hill Ridge. Ptsfld 8L 139
Bell Holt. N'bry 1C 8 (off Conifer Crest)
Bell Ho. Alr 2F 108
Bell La. B'wtr 8E 18
Bell La. Ellis 1J 79
Bell La. Ink 1G 7
Bell Mdw. Rd. Hook 2H 45
Bell Rd. And 1B 70
Bell Rd. Bas 4F 42
Bell Rd. Ports 9E 200
Bells La. Fare 6M 211
Bell St. Lud 1E 30
Bell St. Roms 5L 129
Bell St. Sotn 7M 173 (7E 4)
Bell St. Whitc 5G 54
Bell Yd. Whitc 5G 54
Belmont Av. Bourn 4N 227
Belmont Clo. And 3A 70
Belmont Clo. Dib P 7M 193
Belmont Clo. Fare 5N 211
Belmont Clo. Farn 5H 29
Belmont Clo. Water 8C 168
Belmont Gro. Hav 7C 202
Belmont Heights. Hat W 5L 59
Belmont M. Cam 1L 29
Belmont M. Head 2A 102
Belmont Pl. S'sea 4D 240
Belmont Rd. And 3A 70
Belmont Rd. Cam 9L 19
Belmont Rd. Chan F 9A 132
Belmont Rd. New M 2D 232
Belmont Rd. Poole 9A 226
Belmont Rd. Sotn 2N 173
Belmont St. S'sea 4D 240 (7N 5)
Belmore Clo. Ports 9F 214
Belmore La. L'ton 3D 234
Belmore La. Ows & Uphm 4D 134
Belmore Rd. L'ton 3D 234
Belney La. S'wick 2E 200
Belstone M. Farn 5J 29
Belstone Rd. Tot 3L 171
Belton Rd. Cam 8N 19
Belton Rd. Sotn 7F 174
Belt, The. Dam 4A 150
Belvedere Clo. Fle 2H 47
Belvedere Clo. Ptsfld 9M 139
Belvedere Ct. B'wtr 1F 28
Belvedere Gdns. Chine 8H 23
Belvedere Rd. Bourn 8L 227
Belvedere Rd. Christ 7K 229
Belvedere Rd. Dib P 7M 193
Belvedere Rd. Farn 1L 49
Belvidere 5A 174
Belvidere Ho. Sotn 4A 174
Belvidere Rd. Sotn 6A 174
Belvidere Ter. Sotn 5A 174 (in two parts)
Belvoir Clo. Fare 8C 198
Belvoir Pk. Poole 2F 244
Bembridge. Net A 3G 195
Bembridge Clo. Sotn 6A 160
Bembridge Ct. C'then 1A 18
Bembridge Ct. Hay I 6J 243
Bembridge Cres. S'sea 6F 240
Bembridge Dri. Hay I 6J 243
Bembridge Lodge. Lee S 2A 238
Bemister Rd. Bourn 6L 227
Bemister's La. Gos 3N 239
Benbow Clo. Water 3C 182
Benbow Ct. And 1C 70
Benbow Cres. Poole 4C 226
Benbow Gdns. Cal 9J 157
Benbow Ho. Ports 3J 5
Benbow Pl. Ports 2B 240 (3J 5)
Benbridge Av. Bourn 1D 226
Bench, The 3D 148
Bencroft Ct. Sotn 6N 159
Bendigo Rd. Christ 6H 229
Benedict Clo. Roms 5B 130
Benedict Way. Fare 8N 199
Beneficial St. Ports 2B 240 (3J 5)
Benellen Av. Bourn 1G 245
Benellen Gdns. Bourn 1G 245
Benellen Rd. Bourn 9G 227
Benellen Towers. Bourn 1G 245
Benenden Grn. Alr 2F 108
Benford Ct. Odi 9L 45 (off Buryfields)
Bengal Rd. Bourn 5J 227
Bengal Rd. Bulf B 3B 66
Benger's La. Mott 3D 122
Benham Dri. Ports 4G 215
Benham Drove. Neth W 1M 87
Benham Gro. Fare 2M 213
Benham La. Rise 2H 15
Benhams Farm Clo. Sotn 1E 174
Benham's La. Gthm 2E 114
Benhams Rd. Sotn 9E 160
Benin Rd. Per D 5B 30
Ben La. F'ley 8F 86
Benmore Clo. New M 4D 232
Ben More Gdns. Chan F 4N 131
Benmore Rd. Bourn 5L 227
Bennet Clo. Alt 4E 80
Bennet Clo. Bas 4D 42
Bennet Ct. Cam 8L 19
Bennett Ho. Bourn 1G 244 (off Westbourne Clo.)
Bennett Rd. Bourn 8M 227
Bennetts La. Burl 7F 188
Bennett Wlk. Black 6D 208
Bennion Rd. Bourn 3G 226
Bensgreen La. Frox 2E 138
Benson Clo. Brans 6D 220
Benson Rd. C'then 1B 18
Benson Rd. Sotn 2G 173
Benta Clo. Mid W 3A 72
Bentham Ct. Sotn 7M 159
Bentham Rd. Gos 4K 239
Bentham Way. Swanw 1A 196
Bentley 7K 63
Bentley Clo. King W 9M 91
Bentley Clo. Water 2C 182
Bentley Ct. Hav 4H 203
Bentley Ct. Sotn 1M 173
Bentley Cres. Fare 7B 198
Bentley Dri. Elve 9J 27
Bentley Grn. Sotn 2G 175
Bentley Rd. Bourn 3K 227
Bentley Way. W'slw 5H 87
Bent St. Neth W 1N 87
Bentworth 6L 79
Bentworth Clo. Hav 5D 202
Benwell Clo. Odi 2E 62 (off Kersley Cres.)
Bepton Down. Ptsfld 1N 145
Berber Clo. White 3F 196
Bercote Clo. Win 1F 104
Bere Clo. Chan F 4M 131
Bere Clo. Win 4H 105
Bere Farm La. N Boar 2H 199
Bere Hill 3A 70 (Andover)
Bere Hill 4H 55 (Whitchurch)
Bere Hill. Whitc 4H 55
Berehill Cvn. Pk. Whitc 4H 55
Bere Hill Clo. Whitc 4H 55
Bere Hill Cres. And 2B 70
Berehurst. Alt 6E 80
Bere Rd. Water 6G 181
Beresford Cen., The. Bas 3F 42
Beresford Clo. And 4N 69
Beresford Clo. Chan F 7C 132
Beresford Clo. Poole 8B 226
Beresford Clo. Water 3M 201
Beresford Gdns. Chan F 7C 132
Beresford Gdns. Christ 8A 230
Beresford Ga. And 9D 52
Beresford Rd. Bourn 1E 246
Beresford Rd. Chan F 7C 132
Beresford Rd. Fare 5N 211
Beresford Rd. L'ton 2C 234
Beresford Rd. Poole 8B 226
Beresford Rd. Ports 7F 214
Bereweeke Av. Win 3J 105
Bereweeke Clo. Win 5J 105
Bereweeke Rd. Win 5J 105
Bereweeke Way. Win 4J 105
Berewyk Clo. Bas 3J 59

Bergen Cres. H End 5N 175
Berkeley Av. Poole 6A 226
Berkeley Clo. Fare 6L 211
Berkeley Clo. Fle. 2N 47
Berkeley Clo. Sotn 3K 173 (1A 4)
Berkeley Ct. Lee S 2B 238
Berkeley Dri. Bas 2A 60
Berkeley Gdns. H End 5N 175
Berkeley Rd. Bourn 7J 227
Berkeley Rd. Sotn 4L 173 (1B 4)
Berkeley Sq. Hav 8H 203
Berk Ho. Bas 5E 42
Berkshire Clo. Ports 2E 240
Bermuda Clo. Bas 1C 42
Bermuda Ct. Highc 7J 231
Bernard Av. Four M 5J 97
Bernard Av. Ports 9H 201
Bernard Ct. Cam 9K 19
Bernard Powell Ho. Hav 8G 202
Bernards Clo. Christ 6G 229
Bernard St. Sotn 7M 173 (7D 4)
Berne Ct. Bourn 2L 245 (7N 247)
Bernersh Clo. S'hrst 4E 18
Berney Rd. S'sea 3K 241
Bernina Av. Water 8K 181
Bernina Clo. Water 8K 181
Bernstein Rd. Bas 3L 59
Bernwood Gro. Black 9C 208
Berrybank. Coll T 7G 18
Berry Clo. H End 4A 176
Berry Ct. Hook 3G 45
Berry Ct. Lit L 2N 21
Berry Down 2G 124
Berrydown La. Over 3F 56
Berrydown La. P Can 3F 78
Berrydown Rd. Hav 2C 202
Berryfield Rd. Hord 4H 233
Berry Hill. Ropl 1B 110
Berrylands. Liss 7F 114
Berry La. Fare 6K 211
Berry La. Twy 6K 127
Berry Mdw. Cotts. S'wick 3N 199
Berrywood Gdns. H End 3M 175
Berrywood La. Bentw & Lwr Wd 5H 79
Berthon Ho. Roms 6L 129
Bertie Rd. S'sea 3J 241
Bertram Rd. New M 2D 232
Berwick Rd. Bourn 8J 227
Berwyn Clo. Bas 8J 41
Berwyn Wlk. Fare 9A 198
Beryl Av. Gos 8H 213
Beryton Clo. Gos 1J 239
Beryton Rd. Gos 1J 239
Besomer Drove. Lover 9D 120
Bessborough Rd. Poole 6C 244
Bessemer Clo. Ver 5A 184
Bessemer Rd. Bas 9A 42
Beswick Av. Bourn 5H 227
Beta Ho. Sotn 2H 159
Beta Rd. Farn 7H 29
Bethany Ct. Poole 7E 226
Bethany Ho. Bourn 9A 228
Bethel Clo. F'ham 4F 64
Bethel La. F'ham 3E 64
Bethia Clo. Bourn 8A 228
Bethia Rd. Bourn 7A 228
Betjeman Wlk. Yate 9L 17
Betsy Clo. Brans 6D 220
Betsy La. Brans 6D 220
Betteridge Dri. Rown 5C 158
Bettesworth Rd. Ports 9F 214
Betula Clo. Water 3A 202
Beulah Rd. Sotn 1F 172
Bevan Clo. Sotn 9C 174
Bevan Rd. Water 5N 181
Beveren Clo. Fle 8N 27
Beverley Clo. Bas 1C 60
Beverley Clo. Park G 5F 196
Beverley Cres. Farn 1H 49
Beverley Gdns. Bourn 3H 227
Beverley Gdns. Burs 9J 175
Beverley Gdns. Roms 3B 130
Beverley Gdns. Swanm 6D 164
Beverley Gro. Ports 8N 201
Beverley Heights. Sotn 8D 160
Beverley Rd. Dib P 9L 193
Beverley Rd. Fare 7M 211
Beverly Clo. Gos 6F 212
Beverston Rd. Ports 8B 200
Bevis Clo. Fawl 6D 208
Bevis Clo. Wars 9A 196
Bevis Rd. Gos 2K 239
Bevis Rd. Ports 7E 214
Bevis Rd. N. Ports 7E 214
Bevois Gdns. Sotn 3M 173
Bevois Hill. Sotn 2N 173
Bevois M. Sotn 3M 173
Bevois Mount 2M 173
Bevois Town 3M 173
Bevois Valley 3N 173
Bevois Valley Rd. Sotn 3N 173
Bexington Clo. Bourn 3C 226
Bexmoor. Old B 5H 43
Bexmoor Way. Old B 5H 43
Beyne Rd. Win 2F 126
Bible Fields. Dum 1C 78
Bicester Clo. Whitc 5G 54
Bickerley Gdns. Ring 2J 187
Bickerley Grn. Ring 2J 187
Bickerley Rd. Ring 1J 187
Bickerley Ter. Ring 1J 187
Bicknell Ho. Bourn 2G 244 (off Westbourne Clo.)
Bicknell Rd. Frim 2N 29
Bickton 4J 153
Bickton Wlk. Hav 3D 202
Bicton Rd. Bourn 3F 226
Bidbury La. Hav 8C 202
Bidden 2B 62
Biddenfield La. Wick & Shed 6N 177
Bidden Rd. Upt G & Odi 3A 62
Biddesden La. Lud 1F 30
Biddlecombe Clo. Gos 8E 212
Biddlesgate Ct. Sotn 7L 173 (7C 4)
Bideford Clo. Farn 5J 29
Bideford Clo. Sotn 1D 172
Bietigheim Way. Cam 7L 19
Biggin Wlk. Fare 9A 198
Bighton Dean La. Bigh & Meds 6M 95
Bighton Hill. Ropl 8B 96
Bighton La. Bigh & Bish S 6L 95
Bighton Rd. Meds 2C 96
Big Tree Cotts. Sob 5L 165
Bilbao Ct. And 9C 52
Bilberry Clo. L Hth 7C 196
Bilberry Ct. Win 6K 105 (7L 237)
Bilberry Dri. March 8D 172
Billett Av. Water 9N 181
Billing Clo. S'sea 4J 241
Billington Gdns. H End 9A 162
Billington Pl. Penn 4D 234
Bill Stillwell Ct. Ports 6D 214
Billy Lawn Av. Hav 4F 202
Bilton Bus. Pk. Ports 5K 215
Bilton Cen., The. Ports 9D 200
Bilton Ind. Est. Bas 2F 42
Bilton Rd. Bas 2F 42
Bilton Way. Ports 6K 215
Bindon Clo. Poole 7C 226
Bindon Clo. Sotn 9F 158
Bindon Rd. Sotn 9F 158
Binfields Clo. Lych 2G 43
Binfields Roundabout. Lych 1G 42
Bingham Av. Poole 6A 244
Bingham Clo. Christ 7A 230
Bingham Dri. L'ton 3E 234
Bingham Rd. Bourn 6L 227
Bingham Rd. Christ 7A 230
Bingley Clo. Alt 4E 80
Bingley Clo. Bas 4D 42
Binley 4M 35
Binley Bottom. St M 7J 35
Binley Ct. T'ley 5J 11
Binnacle Way. Ports 9C 200
Binness Path. Ports 1M 215
Binness Way. Ports 1M 215
Binnie Rd. Poole 9C 226
Binsey Clo. Sotn 2D 172
Binstead Clo. Sotn 6A 160
Binstead Copse. Fle 4L 47
Binstead Rd. Bucks H 10L 63
Binstead Rd. Holyb & B'std 1M 81
Binsted 2D 82
Binsted Dri. B'wtr 8F 18
Binsteed Rd. Ports 8F 214
Binswood Nature Reserve 9C 82
Binton La. Seale 8N 65
Birch Av. Burt 3M 229
Birch Av. Fle 2L 47
Birch Av. Mid W 4B 72
Birch Av. New M 9N 221
Birch Clo. Bord 5K 101
Birch Clo. Cam 5N 19
Birch Clo. Col C 4K 133
Birch Clo. Liss 1F 140
Birch Clo. Poole 2C 244
Birch Clo. Roms 6C 130
Birch Clo. St L 5A 186
Birch Clo. Sotn 9F 158
Birch Clo. Water 7M 181
Birch Ct. Win 8G 105
Birch Dale. Hythe 7N 193
Birchdale Clo. Wars 9A 196
Birch Dri. B'wtr 1F 28
Birch Dri. Bourn 4D 228
Birch Dri. Gos 4E 212
Birchen Clo. Park G 5F 196
Birchen Rd. Park G 5F 196
Birches Clo., The. N Bad 7E 130
Birches Crest. Hat W 4M 59
Birches, The. B'wtr 8D 18
Birches, The. Farn 8F 28
Birches, The. Sotn 2F 174
Birchett Rd. A'sht 9J 49
Birchett Rd. Farn 7G 29
Birchfields. Cam 9L 19
Birchglade. Cal 9J 157
Birch Gro. Chlbn 6G 75
Birch Gro. Eastl 6E 132
Birch Gro. Hook 1H 45
Birch Gro. New M 5B 232
Birch Gro. W'hill 6J 101
Birchlands. Tot 5K 171
Birchlands Ct. S'hrst 3G 18
Birchmore Clo. Gos 6E 212
Bircholt Rd. Lip 2N 115
Birch Pde. Fle 2L 47
Birch Rd. Chilw 3L 159
Birch Rd. Head D 1C 102
Birch Rd. H End 3A 176
Birch Rd. St I 4E 186
Birch Rd. Sotn 8F 158
Birch Rd. T'ley 3E 10
Birch Tree Clo. Ems 5M 203
Birch Tree Dri. Ems 5M 203
Birchview Clo. Yate 9M 17
Birchwood. Chine 9G 22
Birch Wood. Sotn 5J 175
Birchwood Clo. Christ 6G 230
Birchwood Dri. A'hlt 5D 152
Birchwood Gdns. H End 2N 175
Birchwood Lodge. Fare 7D 198 (off Northwood Sq.)
Birchwood M. Poole 2B 244
Birchwood Rd. Park 2B 244
Birchy Hill. Sway 6K 223
Birdfield. Chan F 5K 131
Birdham Rd. Hay I 5L 243
Birdlip Clo. Water 4A 182
Birdlip Rd. Ports 8C 200
Birdwood Gro. Fare 9H 199
Birdwood Rd. Coll T 6H 19
Bird World 8N 63
Birdworld & Underwaterworld 8N 63
Birinus Rd. Win 5L 105
Birkbeck Pl. Owl 4G 19
Birkdale Av. Ports 8K 201
Birkenholme Clo. Head D 3E 102
Birmingham Ct. Gos 2F 238
Biscay Clo. Fare 5L 211
Bishearne Gdns. Liss 9D 114
Bishop Clo. Poole 7G 226
Bishop Ct. Ring 1K 187
Bishop Rd. Bourn 6L 227
Bishops Clo. Bourn 7C 228
Bishops Clo. Fle 5M 47
Bishops Clo. T'ley 4G 11
Bishops Clo. Tidw 8G 31
Bishops Clo. Tot 2L 171
Bishops Ct. Eastl 7H 133
Bishops Cres. Sotn 6D 174
Bishopsfield Rd. Fare 1A 212
Bishops Ga. Fare 6F 196
Bishop's Green 1H 9
Bishop's La. Bish W 4M 163
Bishops La. Shir H 1D 178
Bishops Mead. F'ham 8D 64
Bishops Rd. F'ham 4D 64
Bishops Rd. Sotn 7C 174
Bishops Sutton Rd. Alr 9G 94
Bishopstoke 9H 133
Bishopstoke La. Bram 6J 133
Bishopstoke Mnr. Eastl 9G 133
Bishopstoke Rd. Eastl 9F 132
Bishopstoke Rd. Hav 4E 202
Bishopstone 3C 118
Bishopstone Hollow. B'stne 4B 118
Bishop St. Ports 2B 240 (3K 5)
Bishop Sumner Dri. F'ham 4E 64
Bishop's Vw. Four M 5G 97
Bishop's Waltham 4M 163
Bishop's Waltham Palace 4M 163
Bishop's Way. And 1M 69
Bishopswood Ct. Baug 4F 10
Bishopswood Golf Course 6F 10
Bishopswood La. Baug & T'ley 4E 10
Bishop's Wood Rd. Swanm & Mis 8D 164
Bishopswood Rd. T'ley 4F 10
Bisley Ct. Sotn 7F 174
Bissingen Way. Cam 7M 19
Bisterne 9J 187
Bisterne Close 8F 188
Bisterne Clo. Burl 7F 188
Bitham La. Hung & Ink 1E 6
Bittern Clo. Bas 2H 59
Bittern Clo. Coll T 5F 18
Bittern Clo. Gos 9K 213
Bitterne 3E 174
Bitterne Clo. Hav 3F 202
Bitterne Cres. Sotn 4E 174
Bitterne Mnr. Ho. Sotn 3A 174
Bitterne Park 1B 174
Bitterne Rd. Sotn 4D 174 (in three parts)
Bitterne Rd. E. Sotn 3E 174
Bitterne Rd. W. Sotn 3A 174
Bitterne Village. Sotn 3E 174
Bitterne Way. L'ton 4D 234
Bitterne Way. Sotn 4C 174
Blackbarn Rd. Port D 1D 86
Blackberry Clo. Four M 4K 97
Blackberry Clo. Water 7D 168
Blackberry Dri. F Oak 2M 161
Blackberry La. Christ 8B 230
Blackberry La. Four M 6J 97
Blackberry Ter. Sotn 3N 173 (1F 4)
Blackberry Wlk. Lych 4F 42
Blackbird Clo. Bas 2H 59
Blackbird Clo. Coll T 5F 18
Blackbird Clo. Water 6N 181
Blackbird Ct. And 7A 52
Blackbird La. Bish G 1H 9
Blackbird Rd. Eastl 2B 160
Blackbird Way. Brans 7E 220
Blackbird Way. Lee S 9B 212
Blackbrook Bus. Pk. Fare 8A 198
Blackbrook Ho. Dri. Fare 8A 198
Blackbrook Pk. Av. Fare 8A 198
Blackbrook Rd. Fare 7M 197
Blackburn Ct. Gos 2F 238
Blackbushe Airport. B'wtr 1L 27
Blackbushe Bus. Pk. Yat 9M 17
Blackbushe Clo. Sotn 6E 158
Blackbushe Pk. Yate 8M 17
Blackbushes Rd. E'sly 3G 27
Blackbush Rd. Mil S 8J 233
Blackcap Clo. Row C 9G 183
Blackcap Pl. Coll T 5G 18
Black Cottage La. Wick 8E 178
Black Dam 8E 42
Black Dam Cen. Bas 8E 42
Blackdam Nature Reserve 7G 42
Black Dam Roundabout. Bas 7F 42
Black Dam Way. Bas 8E 42
Blackdown Clo. Bas 8K 41
Blackdown Clo. Dib P 7J 193
Blackdown Cres. Hav 5E 202
Blackfield 7C 208
Blackfield Rd. Black & Fawl 7C 208
Blackfield Rd. Bourn 3A 228
Blackfriars Clo. S'sea 3E 240
Blackfriars Rd. S'sea 2E 240
Blackheath Rd. F'ham 3C 64
Blackhill 2A 156
Black Hill Rd. W Wel 3M 155
Blackhorse La. Shed 1A 178
Black Horse La. Wint E 4A 86
Blackhouse La. N Boar 9J 179
Black La. Lover 8E 120
Black La. Pitt 6E 86
Blackman Gdns. A'sht 2K 65
Blackmoor Golf Course 6G 100
Blackmoor Rd. Blkmr 8F 100
Black Moor Rd. Ver 4A 184
Blackmoor Wlk. Hav 4H 203
Blackmore La. Frox 1E 138
Blacknest 10L 63
Blacknest Golf Course 2J 83
Blacknest Rd. Bent & B'std 9K 63
Blacksmiths Roundabout. And 9A 52
Blackstocks La. Nat S 6B 44
Blackstone Clo. Farn 6F 28
Black Swan Bldgs. Win 7L 237
Black Swan Yd. And 1A 70
Blackthorn Clo. Penn 4B 234
Blackthorn Clo. Sotn 5D 174
Blackthorn Clo. S Won 3G 91
Blackthorn Cres. Farn 4H 29
Blackthorn Dri. Gos 7J 213
Blackthorn Dri. Hay I 4J 243
Blackthorne Clo. Bord 4K 101
Blackthorn Grn. Col C 4L 133
Blackthorn Rd. Hay I 4J 243
Blackthorn Rd. Sotn 5D 174
Blackthorn Rd. Water 9C 168
Blackthorn Ter. Ports 1C 240 (2K 5)
Blackthorn Wlk. Water 9B 182 (off Barn Fold)
Blackthorn Way. Bas 5L 41
Blackthorn Way. New M 2E 232
Blackwater 9G 18 (Camberley)
Blackwater 2G 228 (Christchurch)
Blackwater. Lyn 1N 189
Blackwater Clo. Bas 6D 42
Blackwater Clo. Okly 1D 58
Blackwater Clo. Ports 9E 200
Blackwater Dri. Tot 1K 171
Blackwater Gro. A'hlt 5B 152
Blackwater Ind. Est. B'wtr 8G 18
Blackwater M. Tot 1K 171
Blackwater Pk. A'sht 1N 65
Blackwater Trad. Est. A'sht 2N 65
Blackwater Valley Golf Club 5M 17
Blackwater Valley Rd. Cam 9H 19
Blackwater Valley Route. A'sht 4N 65
Blackwater Valley Route. Farn 5M 29
Blackwater Vw. Finch 3L 17
Blackwater Way. A'sht 2M 65
Blackwell Rd. Wor D 4G 90
Blackwood Ho. Ports 9E 214
Bladon Clo. Hav 6J 203
Bladon Rd. Sotn 9H 159
Blaegrove La. Up N 7B 44
Blair Atholl Ri. Fare 7B 198
Blair Av. Poole 1A 244
Blair Clo. New M 3N 231
Blaire Pk. Yate 5L 17
Blair Rd. Bas 8B 42
Blaise Clo. Farn 9M 29
Blake Clo. C'then 1E 18
Blake Clo. Nurs 6C 158
Blake Clo. Odi 2E 62 (off Woolridge Cres.)
Blake Ct. Gos 3N 239
Blake Dene Rd. Poole 4A 244
Blake Hill Av. Poole 4B 244
Blake Hill Cres. Poole 5G 244
Blakemere Cres. Ports 8D 200
Blakeney Rd. Sotn 9C 158
Blake Rd. Gos 2L 239
Blake Rd. Ports 8L 201
Blakes Ct. And 9N 51
Blake's La. T'ley 4H 11
Blakesley La. Ports 4K 215
Blakes Ride. Yate 7L 17
Blanchard Rd. Bish W 3L 163
Blandford Ct. Mil S 7K 235
Blandford Rd. Coom B 6D 118
Blandford Row. Stockb 3F 88
Blanket St. E Wor 8M 81
Blankney Clo. Fare 6L 211
Blann Clo. Nurs 6B 158
Blashford 7J 185
Blaven Wlk. Fare 9A 198
Bleak Hill 7F 152
Bleaklow Clo. Sotn 2E 172
Blechynden 5K 173
Blechynden Ter. Sotn 5K 173 (4A 4)
Bledlow Clo. N'bry 1C 8
Blencowe Dri. Chan F 7K 131
Blendon Dri. And 9K 51
Blendworth 3D 182
Blendworth Cres. Hav 6E 202
Blendworth Ho. Ports 1E 240 (off Lake Rd.)
Blendworth La. Horn 3D 182
Blendworth La. Sotn 3G 174
Blendworth Rd. S'sea 2J 241
Blenheim. Poole 2E 244
Blenheim Av. Sotn 1M 173
Blenheim Clo. Alt 5G 80
Blenheim Clo. Chan F 8L 131
Blenheim Clo. Four M 4J 97
Blenheim Clo. Tong 3N 65
Blenheim Clo. Tot 4K 171
Blenheim Ct. Christ 6J 229
Blenheim Ct. Farn 1M 49
Blenheim Ct. Sotn 1M 173
Blenheim Ct. S'sea 4H 241
Blenheim Cres. F'ham 5C 64

Blenheim Cres.—Bramble La.

Blenheim Cres. Hord. 2F 232
Blenheim Dri. Christ. 7D 230
Blenheim Gdns. Dib P. 7J 193
Blenheim Gdns. Gos. 8K 213
Blenheim Gdns. Hav. 7H 203
Blenheim Gdns. Sotn 9N 159
Blenheim Ho. Eastl 1F 160
Blenheim Ho. Roms 5A 130 (off Chambers Av.)
Blenheim Pk. A'sht 4L 49
Blenheim Rd. A'sht. 4K 49
Blenheim Rd. Eastl 1E 160
Blenheim Rd. Old B 6K 43
Blenheim Rd. Water 5A 182
Bleriot Cres. White 4H 197
Blighmont Av. Sotn 4G 172
Blighmont Cres. Sotn 4G 172
Blighton La. F'ham 6M 65
Blind La. Curd 9H 163
Blind La. W End 6N 161
Blind La. Wick 5B 178
Bliss Clo. Bas 1N 59
Bliss Clo. Water 4M 201
Blissford 6A 154
Blissford Clo. Hav. 4H 203
Blissford Cross. Bliss 6A 154
Blissford Hill. Frog & Bliss 7A 154
Blissford Rd. Bliss 1N 153
Blissmore La. W'hll 8D 50
Bloomfield Av. Bourn 4K 227
Bloomfield Pl. Bourn 4K 227
Bloomsbury Wlk. Sotn 8C 174
Bloomsbury Way. B'wtr 1E 28
Blossom Clo. Bot 4B 176
Blossom Sq. Ports 1B 240 (2K 5)
Bloswood Dri. Whitc 5F 54
Bloswood La. Whitc 2D 54
Blount Rd. Ports 4C 240 (7L 5)
Bloxworth Rd. Poole 6D 226
Blue Anchor La. Sotn 7L 173 (7C 4)
Blue Ball Corner. Win 7P 237
Blue Ball Hill. Win 6M 105 (7P 237)
Bluebell Clo. Christ. 6D 230
Bluebell Clo. Water 3N 201
Bluebell Copse. L Hth 7C 196
Bluebell Rd. Lind 2M 101
Bluebell Rd. Sotn 7N 159
Bluebell Wlk. Fle 1L 47
Bluehaven Wlk. Hook 2F 44
Blue Hayes Clo. And. 2N 69
Blueprint Portfield Rd. Ports 6H 215
Blue Pryor Ct. Chu C 8K 47
Bluestar Gdns. H End 9N 161
Bluethroat Clo. Coll T 5G 18
Blue Timbers Clo. Bord 5J 101
Bluff Cove. A'sht 8L 49
Bluff, The. Bourn 2K 227
Blundell La. Burs 8M 175
Blunden Clo. Bas 1B 60
Blunden Rd. Farn 8H 29
Blyth Clo. Christ. 2G 229
Blyth Clo. Sotn 9C 158
Blythswood Ct. New M 7A 232
Blythwood Dri. Frim 2M 29
Boakes Pl. Asht. 8J 171
Boames La. Enb 1A 8
Boardwalk Shop. Cen., The. Port S 2B 214
Boardwalk, The. Port S 1C 214
Boarhunt 4J 199
Boarhunt Clo. Ports 2E 240
Boarhunt Rd. Fare 6G 198
Boatyard Ind. Est., The. Fare 9D 198
Bob Hann Clo. Poole 9B 226
Bockhampton Rd. Bock 1N 229
Bodley Rd. Poole 6C 244
Bodmin Clo. Bas 8K 41
Bodmin Rd. Eastl 9J 133
Bodmin Rd. Ports 9B 200
Bodorgan Rd. Bourn 1K 245 (5L 247)
Bodowen Clo. Burt 4N 229
Bodowen Rd. Burt 4N 229
Bodycoats Rd. Chan F 6B 132
Bogmoor Clo. Four M 5J 97
Bohemia 9E 120
Bohemia La. Redl 9D 120
Bohunt 3C 116 (Bird Garden)
Boiler Rd. Fawl 7J 209
Boiler Rd. Ports 9A 214 (1H 5)
Bolde Clo. Ports 5J 215
Boldens Rd. Gos 6K 239
Bolderwood Clo. Eastl 1K 161
Boldre 6D 224
Boldre Clo. Hav 5C 202
Boldre Clo. New M 6M 231
Boldre Clo. Poole 7B 226
Boldre La. Bold 8D 224
Boldrewood Rd. Sotn 7K 159
Boleyn Cres. Bourn 2N 227
Bolhinton Av. March 9C 172
Bolle Rd. Alt 6D 80
Bolley Av. Bord 1G 100
Bolton Clo. Bourn 2H 247
Bolton Cres. Bas 7N 41
Bolton Rd. Bourn 2H 247
Bolton's Bench 2C 148
Boltons, The. Mil S 8K 235
Boltons, The. Water 6M 201
Bonchurch Clo. Sotn 6A 160
Bonchurch Rd. S'sea 2H 241
Bond Clo. Bas 3F 42
Bond Clo. Sway 4J 223
Bondfields Cres. Hav 3E 202
Bond Rd. Sotn 1C 174
Bond St. Bulf B 3B 66
Bond St. Sotn 4A 174
Bones La. Bton 7K 145
Bonfire Corner. Ports 1B 240 (2J 5)
Bonham Rd. Bourn 7K 227
Bonhams Clo. Holyb 1L 81
Boniface Clo. Tot 2K 171
Boniface Cres. Sotn 8C 158
Bonington Clo. Christ 6A 230
Bonners Fld. Bent 7K 63
Boon Way. Okly 9C 40
Boorley Green 1D 176
Boothby Clo. Tot 4N 171
Bordean La. Frox 8C 138
Borden Gates. And 2N 69
Borden Trad. Est. Bord 2F 100
Border End. Hasl 9M 103
Border Rd. Hasl 9M 103
Borderside. Yate 7K 17
Bordon Clo. T'ley 5G 11
Bordon Rd. Hav 4F 202
Boreen, The. Head 2D 102
Boreham Rd. Bourn 9G 228
Borelli M. F'ham 8E 64
Borelli Yd. F'ham 8E 64
Borkum Clo. And 7M 51
Borman Way. S Won 3J 91
Borodin Clo. Bas 2A 60
Borough Ct. Rd. H Win 9L 25
Borough Gro. Ptsfld 2L 145
Borough Hill. Ptsfld 1L 145
Borough Rd. Ptsfld 2K 145
Borough, The. Cron 3L 63
Borough, The. D'ton 2J 119
Borough, The. F'ham 8D 64
Borovere Clo. Alt 6E 80
Borovere Gdns. Alt 6E 80
Borovere La. Alt 6E 80
Borrowdale Rd. Sotn 1D 172
Borsberry Clo. And 1A 70
Borthwick Rd. Bourn 9B 228
Boscobel Rd. Win 5K 105
Boscombe 2C 246 (Bournemouth)
Boscombe 8D 66 (Salisbury)
Boscombe Cliff Rd. Bourn 2B 246
Boscombe Cres. Bourn 1B 246
Boscombe Gro. Rd. Bourn 9A 228
Boscombe Overcliff Dri. Bourn 2C 246
Boscombe Promenade. Bosc 2B 246
Boscombe Rd. Ame 6A 66
Boscombe Spa Rd. Bourn 1A 246
Boscowen Clo. And 1C 70 (off London Rd.)
Bosenhill La. W'frd 3N 135
Bosham Rd. Ports 8G 215
Bosham Wlk. Gos 6D 212
Bosley Clo. Christ 4H 229
Bosley Way. Christ 4H 229
Bosmere Gdns. Ems 8L 203
Bosmere Rd. Hay I 5L 243
Bossington 7D 88
Bossington Clo. Rown 6D 158
Bostock Clo. Spar 3B 104
Boston Ct. Chan F 5B 132
Boston Rd. Ports 8F 200
Bosuns Clo. Fare 2D 212
Bosville. Eastl 6D 132
Boswell Clo. Bot 3D 176
Boswell Clo. Sotn 4G 175
Bosworth M. Bourn 2M 227
Botany Bay 8E 174
Botany Bay Rd. Sotn 7F 174
Botany Hill. F'ham & Seale 9M 65
Botisdone Clo. Ver D 8E 6
Botley 3D 176
Botley Dri. Hav 3D 202
Botley Gdns. Sotn 7J 175
Botley Hill. Bot 4E 176
Botley Ind. Est. Bot 3E 176
Botley Mills Craft and Bus. Cen. Bot 3D 176
Botley Pk. Country Club & Golf Course 9C 162
Botley Rd. Curd & Bish W 3F 176
Botley Rd. Curd & Shed 3J 177
Botley Rd. F Oak & Durl 2A 162
Botley Rd. N Bad & Chilw 7F 130
Botley Rd. Roms & N Bad 5N 129
Botley Rd. N Bad & Chilw 6C 130
Botley Rd. Sotn 8G 174 (in three parts)
Botley Rd. Swanw & Park G 1D 196
Botley Rd. W End & H End 1J 175
Bottings Ind. Est. Curd 3F 176
Bottlebrush La. Wim G 7F 148
Bottle La. Matt 3G 24
Bottom La. W Wel 9M 121 (in two parts)
Bottom Rd. Neth W 1M 87
Boughton Ct. Ports 4K 215
Boulnois Av. Poole 2C 244
Boulter La. S'wick 2B 200
Boulter's Rd. A'sht 9K 49
Boulton Rd. S'sea 4F 240
Boundary Clo. Sotn 3E 172
Boundary La. St L 7A 186
Boundary Rd. Bourn 6H 227 (in two parts)
Boundary Rd. Burs 1K 195 (in two parts)
Boundary Rd. Dock & Row 2N 83
Boundary Rd. Farn 1L 49
Boundary Rd. Gray 4M 103
Boundary Roundabout. Poole 6H 227
Boundary Vs. B'wtr 9G 19
Boundary Way. Hav 8E 202
Boundary Way. Ports 7J 201
Bound La. Hay I 5G 243
Boundstone. Hythe 6L 193
Boundway. Sway 6F 222
Bounty Ri. Bas 7B 42
Bounty Rd. Bas 7B 42
Bounty's La. Poole 9C 226
Bourley La. Ews 9B 48
Bourley Rd. A'sht 9D 48
Bourley Rd. Chu C & Ews 7A 48
Bourne Av. Bourn 2J 245 (5J 247)
Bourne Av. Sotn 1H 173
Bourne Clo. Bourn 2H 245 (6G 247)
Bourne Clo. Ott 9G 126
Bourne Clo. Port 9B 66
Bourne Clo. Water 4B 182
Bourne Clo. W Wel 1A 120
Bourne Ct. A'sht 2J 65
Bourne Ct. And 8B 52 (off River Way)
Bourne Ct. Bas 6E 42
Bourne Ct. Bourn 2K 245 (6L 247)
Bourne Fld. Sher 8N 21
Bournefields. Twy 6M 127
Bourne Gdns. Port 9B 66
Bourne La. Ship B 2C 66
Bourne La. Twy 6L 127
Bourne La. W'lnds 4D 170
Bourne Mdw. St M 1M 53
Bourne Mill Ind. Est. F'ham 7G 64
Bournemouth 2K 245
Bournemouth A.F.C. 8B 228
Bournemouth Av. Gos 9J 213
Bournemouth Central Bus. Pk. Bourn 9N 227
Bournemouth Ho. Bourn 2M 245
Bournemouth Ho. Hav 4G 202
Bournemouth Info. & Vis. Bureau. 2K 245 (7M 247)
Bournemouth International Airport. Hurn 7B 218
Bournemouth International Cen. Roundabout. Bourn 8L 247
Bournemouth International Conference Cen. 3K 245 (8L 247)
Bournemouth Memorial Homes. Bourn 5C 228
Bournemouth Pier. 3K 245 (9M 247)
Bournemouth Rd. Chan F 1N 159
Bournemouth Rd. Lyn 2A 148
Bournemouth Rd. Pale 6K 67
Bournemouth Rd. Poole 1A 244
Bournemouth Sta. Roundabout. Bourn 1M 245
Bournemouth W. Roundabout. Bourn 1H 245 (6H 247)
Bourne Pines. Bourn 1K 245 (off Dean Pk. Rd.)
Bourne Ri. Coll D 1H 31
Bourne River Ct. Bourn 1H 245 (5G 247)
Bourne Rd. Ports 9C 200
Bourne Rd. Sotn 5J 173
Bourne Rd. Tidw 8D 30
Bourne Rd. W'lnds 5C 170
Bourne, The. Fle 5M 47
Bourne Valley 8F 226
Bourne Valley Clo. Port 1C 86
Bourne Valley Rd. Poole 1E 244
Bourne Vw. All 8D 66
Bournewood Dri. Bourn 1G 244
Bourton Gdns. Bourn 6E 228
Bouverie Clo. Bart S 5A 232
Boveridge 5K 149
Boveridge Gdns. Bourn 2M 227
Bowater Clo. Cal 1J 171
Bowater Way. Cal 1J 171
Bowcombe. Net A 2G 194
Bowcott Hill. Head 2B 102
Bowden La. Sotn 9A 160
Bowden Rd. Poole 4A 226
Bow Dri. Sher L 4L 23
Bowenhurst Gdns. Chu C 7M 47
Bowenhurst La. Cron 1K 63
Bowenhurst Rd. Chu C 6M 47
Bowen La. Ptsfld 1M 145
Bower Clo. Holb 5A 208
Bower Clo. Sotn 9D 174
Bower Rd. Bourn 6A 228
Bowers Clo. Water 6A 182
Bowers Gro. La. Ropl 8B 96
Bowers Hill. Redl 1M 119
Bowers La. Ver D 7D 6
Bowerwood Cotts. F'bri 2F 152
Bowerwood Rd. F'bri 2F 152
Bowes Hill. Row C 7J 183
Bowes Lyon Ct. Water 3B 182
Bow Fld. Hook 2J 45
Bow Gdns. Sher L 4L 23
Bow Gro. Sher L 3L 23
Bowland Ri. Chan F 5M 131
Bowland Ri. New M 4D 232
Bowland Way. Black 9C 208
Bowler Av. Ports 1G 241
Bowler Ct. Ports 1G 241
Bowling All. Cron 1L 63
Bowling Grn. Ct. Frim G 5N 29
Bowling Grn. Dri. Hook 2F 44
Bowling Grn. La. Pent 1F 148
Bowlings, The. Cam 7L 19
Bowman Ct. Sotn 7F 174 (Butts Rd.)
Bowman Ct. Sotn 7B 174 (Florence Rd.)
Bowman Ct. Well C 1B 18
Bowman Rd. Chine 8G 23
Bowmonts Rd. T'ley 5J 11
Bow St. Alt 6E 80
Bowyer Clo. Bas 7B 42
Boxall's Gro. A'sht 3J 65
Boxall's La. A'sht 3J 65
Boxgrove Ho. Ports 1E 240
Boxwood Clo. Fare 8K 199
Boxwood Clo. Water 3M 201
Boyatt Cres. Eastl 4E 132
Boyatt La. Ott & Eastl 3E 132 (in three parts)
Boyatt Shop. Cen. Eastl 7D 132
Boyatt Wood 7D 132
Boyce Clo. Bas 2L 59
Boyd Clo. Fare 7L 211
Boyd Rd. Gos 5D 212
Boyd Rd. Poole 8D 226
Boyes La. Col C 3L 133
Boyle Cres. Water 4L 201
Boyne Mead Rd. King W 8M 91
Boyne Ri. King W 7M 91
Boyneswood Clo. Meds 3K 97
Boyneswood La. Meds 3J 97
Boyneswood Rd. Meds 3K 97
Boynton Clo. Chan F 4N 131
Brabant Clo. White 2E 196
Brabazon Dri. Christ 7D 230
Brabazon Rd. Fare 4G 197
Brabon Rd. Farn 7H 29
Bracebridge. Cam 8J 19
Bracher Clo. And 1A 70
Bracken Bank. Lych 3G 43
Brackenbury. And 9K 51
Bracken Clo. Ashy H 4A 186
Bracken Clo. N Bad 9F 130
Bracken Cres. Eastl 1K 161
Brackendale Clo. Cam 1N 29
Brackendale Rd. Bourn 6N 227
Brackendale Rd. Cam 8M 19
Bracken Heath. Water 9B 182
Brackenhill. Poole 4E 244
Bracken La. Sotn 1F 172
Bracken La. W'hill 7F 100
Bracken La. Yate 7K 17
Bracken Pl. Chilw 4M 159
Bracken Rd. Bourn 1F 246
Bracken Rd. N Bad 9F 130
Bracken Rd. Ptsfld 2B 146
Brackens, The. Bas 4L 59
Brackens, The. Dib P 6J 193
Brackens, The. L Hth 7E 196
Brackens Way. L'ton 4F 234
Brackens Way. Poole 5D 244
Bracken Way. Walk 5K 231
Brackenway Rd. Chan F 4A 132
Brackenwood Dri. T'ley 4G 11
Bracklesham Clo. Farn 5J 29
Bracklesham Clo. Sotn 7D 174
Bracklesham Pl. Bart S 7A 232
Bracklesham Rd. Gos 8F 212
Bracklesham Rd. Hay I 6M 243
Brackley Av. F Oak 9M 133
Brackley Av. H Win 6A 26
Brackley Clo. Hurn 7D 218
Brackley Way. Bas 1L 59
Brackley Way. Tot 2K 171
Bracknell La. H Win 4A 26
Bradburne Rd. Bourn 2J 245 (6J 247)
Bradbury Clo. Whitc 5F 54
Bradford Ct. Gos 1E 238
Bradford Junct. S'sea 3F 240
Bradford Rd. Bourn 2N 227
Bradford Rd. S'sea 3E 240
Brading Av. Gos 6E 212
Brading Av. S'sea 5H 241
Brading Clo. Sotn 6A 160
Bradley 5H 79
Bradley Ct. Hav 3H 203
Bradley Grn. Sotn 7G 159
Bradley Peak. Win 5G 104
Bradley Rd. Win 3G 105
Bradly Rd. Fare 7M 197
Bradman Sq. And 7A 52 (off Cricketers Way)
Bradpole Rd. Bourn 4B 228
Bradshaw Clo. F Oak 1B 162
Bradstock Clo. Poole 6D 226
Bradwell Clo. Charl 7K 51
Braehead. Hythe 7L 193
Braemar Av. Bourn 1K 247
Braemar Av. Ports 1J 215
Braemar Clo. Bourn 1K 247
Braemar Clo. Fare 6A 198
Braemar Clo. Gos 6F 212
Braemar Dri. Highc 5G 231
Braemar Dri. Okly 9C 40
Braemar Rd. Gos 5F 212
Braemore Rd. D'ton 2J 119
Braeside Clo. Sotn 5C 174
Braeside Clo. Win 1F 126
Braeside Cres. Sotn 5C 174
Braeside Rd. St L 4B 186
Braeside Rd. Sotn 5C 174
Braggers La. Brans 4C 220
Brahms Rd. Bas 2N 59
Braidley Rd. Bourn 2J 245 (6K 247)
Braine L'Alleud Rd. Bas 5C 42
Braintree Rd. Ports 8E 200
Braishfield 5B 124
Braishfield Clo. Sotn 1E 172
Braishfield Gdns. Bourn 4A 228
Braishfield Rd. Brfld 5B 124
Braishfield Rd. Hav 5G 202
Bramber Rd. Gos 9J 213
Bramble Clo. A'hlt 5D 152
Bramble Clo. Eastl 7F 132
Bramble Clo. Fare 7K 211
Bramble Clo. Hav 6J 203
Bramble Clo. Holb 5A 208
Bramble Dri. Roms 3B 130
Bramblegate. F Oak 2A 162
Bramble Hill. Alr 1F 108
Bramble Hill. Chan F 6N 131
Bramble La. Highc 5K 231
Bramble La. Sar G 4B 196

Bramble La. Water 4B 168
Bramble M. Sotn. 2E 174
Bramble Rd. Ptsfld 1B 146
Bramble Rd. S'sea 3F 240
Brambles Bus. Cen., The. Water 9K 181
Brambles Clo. Col C 4L 133
Brambles Clo. Four M 5J 97
Brambles Enterprise Cen., The. Water 9K 181
Brambles Farm Ind. Est. Water 1L 201
Brambles La. Cowes 5N 237
Brambles Rd. Lee S 9N 211
Bramble Wlk. L'ton 1C 234
Bramble Way. Brans 6D 220
Bramble Way. Gos 6C 212
Bramble Way. Old B 5K 43
Bramblewood Pl. Fle. 2K 47
Brambling Clo. Bas. 3H 59
Brambling Clo. Sotn 5G 158
Brambling Rd. Row C 9H 183
Bramblings, The. Tot 3J 171
Bramblys Clo. Bas 7B 42
Bramblys Dri. Bas 7B 42
Brambridge 4J 133
Brambridge. Bram 4J 133
Brambridge Pk. Garden Cen. 3H 133
Brambridge Pk. Miniature Railway 3H 133
Bramdean 1M 135
Bramdean Clo. T'ley 6H 11
Bramdean Dri. Hav 4D 202
Bramdean La. Bish S 6H 109
Bramdean M. Sotn 5C 174
Bramdean Rd. Sotn 2H 175
Bramdown Heights. Bas 4K 59
Bramham Moor. Fare 6L 211
Bramley 1G 22
Bramley Clo. Alt 5G 80
Bramley Clo. L'ton 4E 234
Bramley Clo. Water 1N 201
Bramley Corner 1C 22
Bramley Ct. C'then 1A 18
Bramley Cres. Sotn 8F 174
Bramley Gdns. Gos 6J 239
Bramley Gdns. H Hth 4N 161
Bramley Green 2H 23
Bramley Grn. Rd. Braml 2H 23
Bramley Ho. H End 4M 175
Bramley Ho. S'sea 3D 240
Bramley La. B'wtr 8D 18
Bramley La. Braml 9G 12
Bramley Rd. Bourn 1G 226
Bramley Rd. Braml 4D 22
Bramley Rd. Cam 2K 29
Bramley Rd. Lit L 3L 21
Bramley Rd. Sher L 3L 23
Bramley Rd. Sil 4A 12
Bramleys, The. W'ish 5H 121
Bramley Wlk. W'hill 5G 100
Bramling Av. Yate 7L 17
Brampton Ct. Bourn 2J 245 (6K 247)
Brampton Ct. Chan F 6A 132
Brampton Gdns. Hat W 5L 59
Brampton La. Ports 4K 215
Brampton Mnr. Sotn 6L 159
Brampton Tower. Sotn 6L 159
Bramshaw 4L 155
Bramshaw. New M 7L 231
Bramshaw Clo. Win 3G 105
Bramshaw Ct. Hav 4H 203
Bramshaw Gdns. Bourn 3A 228
Bramshaw Golf Course 6K 155
Bramshaw Way. New M 6M 231
Bramshill 6M 15
Bramshill Council Houses. Brams 6L 15
Bramshill Park 9N 15
Bramshill Rd. Brams & E'sly 7J 15
Bramshot 9E 102
Bramshot Dri. Fle. 1M 47
Bramshot La. Farn 6E 28
Bramshot La. Fle 8C 28
Bramshot Rd. Farn 1C 48
Bramshott Chase 7K 103
Bramshott Dri. Hook 2H 45
Bramshott Hill. Dib 4G 192
Bramshott Rd. Pass 6B 102
Bramshott Rd. Sotn 1D 194
Bramshott Rd. S'sea 3G 241
Bramston Rd. Sotn 2H 173
Brancaster Av. Charl 7K 51
Branches La. Sher E 6N 121
Branders Clo. Bourn 1K 247
Branders La. Bourn 9K 229
Brandon Clo. Alt 4E 80
Brandon Ct. Poole 1F 244 (off Poole Rd.)
Brandon Ct. S'sea 4F 240
Brandon Ho. S'sea 5F 240
Brandon Rd. Chu C 6K 47
Brandon Rd. S'sea 5E 240
Brandy Mt. Alr 9F 94
Branksome 8C 226
Branksome Av. Chlbn 5F 74
Branksome Av. Sotn 1H 173
Branksome Bldgs. Bourn 7J 247
Branksome Bus. Pk. Poole 7D 226
Branksome Clo. Cam 7N 19
Branksome Clo. Chlbn 5F 74
Branksome Clo. New M 4C 232
Branksome Clo. Win 8F 104
Branksome Ct. Fle. 2L 47
Branksome Ct. Poole 5D 244
Branksome Dene Rd. Bourn 3F 244
Branksome Hill Rd. Bourn 8F 226
Branksome Hill Rd. Coll T & Owl 6G 18
Branksome Park 3D 244
Branksome Pk. Rd. Cam 7N 19
Branksome Towers. Poole 5F 244
Branksome Wood Gdns. Bourn 1H 245
Branksomewood Rd. Fle. 1K 47
Branksome Wood Rd. Poole & Bourn 9F 226 (5H 247)
Bransbury 8M 71
Bransbury Clo. Sotn 7H 159
Bransbury Rd. S'sea 4J 241
Bransgore 7D 220
Bransgore Av. Hav 5C 202
Bransgore Gdns. Brans 6D 220
Bransley Clo. Roms 3A 130
Branson Rd. Bord 4K 101
Branton Clo. Bas 8L 41
Branwell Clo. Christ 5K 229
Branwood Clo. Evtn 5M 233
Brasenose Clo. Fare 8F 196
Brasher Clo. Eastl 1L 161
Brassey Clo. Bourn 5L 227
Brassey Rd. Bourn 5K 227
Brassey Rd. Win 5K 105
Brassey Ter. Bourn 5K 227
Brasted Ct. S'sea 2K 241
Braunstone Clo. Ports 8B 200
Braxell Lawn. Hav 3D 202
Braxton Courtyard. Mil S 7M 233
Braxton Ho. Win 5N 105
Braye Clo. S'hrst 4E 18
Brazenhead La. Wolv 4A 20
Breachfield. Burgh 3D 8
Breach La. Chut S 3B 32
Breach La. Poul 5A 188
Breach La. Sher L 4M 23
Breamore 3L 151
Breamore Clo. Eastl 6E 132
Breamore Clo. New M 3N 231
Breamore Rd. Sotn 3H 175
Brean Clo. Sotn 9D 158
Brecon Av. Ports 8J 201
Brecon Clo. Chan F 9N 131
Brecon Clo. Dib P 6K 193
Brecon Clo. Fare 9A 198
Brecon Clo. Farn 5F 28
Brecon Clo. New M 4D 232
Brecon Clo. Roms 4A 130 (off Viney Av.)
Brecon Rd. Sotn 5G 174
Bredenbury Cres. Ports 8D 200
Bredon Wlk. Fare 9A 198
Breech Clo. Ports 4G 215
Breech, The. Coll T 6G 19
Bremble Clo. Poole 4A 226
Bremen Gdns. And 7M 51
Brenchley Clo. Fare 1K 213
Brendon Clo. Bourn 4B 228
Brendon Clo. Dib P 7J 193
Brendon Grn. Sotn 2E 172
Brendon Rd. Fare 9N 197
Brendon Rd. Farn 5F 28
Brent Ct. Ems 9L 203
Brentwood Cres. Sotn 1E 174
Bresler Ho. Ports 8C 200
Brethart Rd. Frim 3N 29
Breton Clo. White 2E 196
Brewells La. Liss & Rake 8K 115
Brewer Clo. Bas 8L 41
Brewer Clo. L Hth 5E 196
Brewers Clo. Farn 7J 29
Brewers La. Gos 6E 212
Brewers La. Twy 8K 127
Brewers La. W Tis 8J 111
Brewer St. Ports 1D 240 (2N 5)
Brewhouse La. H Win 6C 26
Brewhouse Sq. Gos 1M 239
Brewster Clo. Water 7A 182
Briar Clo. Christ 8B 230
Briar Clo. Gos 4G 239
Briar Clo. Water 5B 182
Briardene Ct. Tot 3L 171
Briarfield Gdns. Water 4B 182
Briar La. Four M 4K 97
Briarleas Ct. Farn 3M 49
Briars Clo. Farn 9F 28
Briars, The. Water 1K 201
Briarswood. Sotn 1G 173
Briarswood Ri. Dib P 7J 193
Briar Way. Roms 3B 130
Briar Way. T'ley 5J 11
Briar Wood. Liss 7F 114
Briarwood Clo. Fare 9D 198
Briarwood Gdns. Hay I 4F 242
Briarwood Rd. Tot 4J 171
Brickenswood. New M 7L 231
Brickfield Cotts. A'sht 2F 64
Brickfield Cotts. C'then 2B 18
Brickfield La. Chan F 7N 131
Brickfield La. Wal 1F 234
Brickfield Rd. Sotn 9A 160
Brickfields Clo. Lych 3G 43
Brickfield Trad. Est. Chan F 7A 132
Brickhouse Hill. E'sly 7F 16
Brickiln Ind. Est. T'ley 4J 11
Brickiln La. Four M 1N 97
Brick Kiln La. Shald & Alt 3C 80
Brick Kiln La. W Tis 7G 111
Brick La. Brans 3G 220
Brick La. Fle 1L 47
Brickmakers Rd. Col C 4K 133
Bricksbury Hill. F'ham 3E 64
Brickwoods Clo. Roms 4A 130
Brickworth La. W'ish 5F 120
Brickworth Rd. W'ish 5F 120
Brickyard Rd. Swanm 8B 164
Brickyard, The. Wins 2B 170
Bricky Lake La. Ower 4C 156
Bridefield Clo. Water 7L 181
Bridefield Cres. Water 7L 181
Bridge Clo. Burs 9M 175
Bridge Cotts. Liss 7D 114
Bridge Ct. Roms 6L 129
Bridge Ct. T'ley 5J 11
Bridge End. Cam 9K 19
Bridgefield. F'ham 8F 64
Bridgefoot Dri. Fare 8E 198
Bridgefoot Hill. Fare 8F 198
Bridgefoot Path. Ems 9M 203
Bridge Ho. Gos 4E 212
Bridge Industries. Fare 6E 198
Bridgemary 5E 212
Bridgemary Av. Gos 5F 212
Bridgemary Gro. Gos 3E 212
Bridgemary Rd. Gos 3E 212
Bridgemary Way. Gos 3E 212
Bridgemead. Frim 4L 29 (off Frimley High St.)
Bridge Mead. Meon 8N 135
Bridge Meadows. Liss 1E 140
Bridge M. Tong 3N 65
Bridge Rd. A'sht 2J 65
Bridge Rd. Alr 1D 108
Bridge Rd. B'stne 3C 118
Bridge Rd. Burs & Swanw 9M 175
Bridge Rd. Cam 1K 29
Bridge Rd. Ems 8M 203
Bridge Rd. Farn 8H 29
Bridge Rd. L'ton 2F 234
Bridge Rd. Roms 5N 129
Bridge Rd. Sar G & Park G 3B 196
Bridge Rd. Sotn 7B 174
Bridgers Clo. Rown 6D 158
Bridges Av. Ports 8A 200
Bridges Clo. Eastl 9D 132
Bridges Cotts. W Wel 9N 121
Bridge Shop. Cen., The. Ports 2F 240
Bridgeside Clo. Ports 2E 240
Bridge Sq. F'ham 8E 64
Bridges, The. Mort W 1B 12
Bridges, The. Ring 1H 187
Bridge St. And 2N 69
Bridge St. Christ 8M 229
Bridge St. F'bri 1J 153
Bridge St. Over 2D 56
Bridge St. S'wick 3M 199
Bridge St. Titch 9K 197
Bridge St. Wick 6C 178
Bridge St. Win 7M 105 (8P 237)
Bridget Clo. Water 3C 182
Bridge Ter. Shaw 7J 127
Bridge Ter. Sotn 7N 173
Bridgetts La. Mart W 5C 92
Bridge Wlk. Yate 6N 17
Bridgewater Rd. Poole 8B 226
Bridge Yd. L'ton 2F 234
Bridgwater Ct. Sotn 4H 173
Bridle Clo. E Tis 1D 112
Bridle Clo. Gray 4J 103
Bridle Ct. A'sht 9G 49
Bridle Cres. Bourn 6F 228
Bridle Path. Water 2B 182
Bridlington Av. Sotn 2J 173
Bridport Ct. Sotn 5H 173
Bridport Rd. Poole 6D 226
Bridport St. Ports 2D 240
Brierley Clo. Bourn 1J 227
Brierley Rd. Bourn 2H 227
Brigantine Rd. Wars 8B 196
Brigham Clo. Ports 5F 214
Brighstone Clo. Sotn 6A 160
Brighstone Rd. Ports 1F 214
Brightlands Av. Bourn 1J 247
Brighton Av. Gos 8H 213
Brighton Hill 2L 59
Brighton Hill Cen. Bas 2M 59
Brighton Hill Pde. Bas 2M 59
Brighton Hill Retail Pk. Bas 9N 41
Brighton Hill Roundabout. Bas 9N 41
Brighton Rd. A'sht 2L 65
Brighton Rd. Sotn 3L 173
Brighton Rd. Sway 3H 223
Brighton Way. Bas 2M 59
Brightside. Water 3L 201
Brightside Rd. Sotn 9E 158
Brights La. Hay I 2F 242
Brightstone La. Four M & Lwr F 5N 97
Brightwells Rd. F'ham 8E 64
Brimley Hill Ct. K're 2B 6 (off St Mary's Rd.)
Brimpton Common 2B 10
Brimpton La. Brim C 3B 10
Brimpton Rd. Brim & Brim C 1A 10
Brimpton Rd. Brim C & Baug 3C 10
Brindle Clo. A'sht 3K 65
Brindle Clo. Sotn 6M 159
Brinksway. Fle 2M 47
Brinn's La. B'wtr 8E 18
Brinsons Clo. Burt 3M 229
Brinton La. Hythe 4M 193
Brinton's Rd. Sotn 5M 173 (3E 4)
Brinton's Ter. Sotn 4M 173 (2E 4)
Brisbane Clo. Per D 4B 30
Brisbane Gdns. Bulf B 3C 66
Brisbane Ho. Ports 9E 214
Brisbane Rd. Christ 5H 229
Brislands La. Ropl & Four M 8D 96
Bristol Ct. Gos 2E 238
Bristol Rd. S'sea 5G 241
Bristow Rd. Cam 1K 29
Britain St. Ports 2B 240 (4K 5)
Britannia Clo. Bord 4K 101
Britannia Ct. Sotn 5A 174
Britannia Gdns. H End 8M 161
Britannia Rd. Sotn 5N 173
Britannia Rd. S'sea 3E 240
Britannia Rd. N. S'sea 3E 240
Britannia Way. Christ 7D 230
Britannia Way. Gos 9L 213
Britannia Wharf. Sotn 6A 174
Britannic Ho. Sotn 5A 174 (off Kent St.)
Britnell Ho. Ptsfld 9M 139
Briton St. Sotn 7M 173 (8D 4)
Brittain Ct. S'hrst 6E 18
Britten Rd. Bas 1N 59
Britten Rd. Lee S 1A 238
Britten Way. Water 5M 201
Brixey Clo. Poole 7A 226
Brixey Rd. Poole 7A 226
Brixworth Clo. Ports 8B 200
Broadacres. Fle 3J 47
Broad Av. Bourn 5A 228
Broadbent Clo. Sotn 5C 158
Broad Chalke 3A 118
Broad Chalke Down. Win 1G 127
Broad Cft. Row C 7J 183
Broadcut. Fare 7E 198
Broadfields Clo. Mil S 7K 235
Broad Gdns. Ports 9M 201
Broad Grn. Sotn 6M 173 (5E 4)
Broadhalfpenny La. T'ley 4J 11
Broadhill La. Bliss 2N 153
Broadhurst. Farn 8E 28
Broadhurst Av. Bourn 2J 227
Broadhurst Gro. Lych 4G 42
Broadlands 7L 129
Broadlands. Farn 1N 49
Broadlands Av. Bourn 1J 247
Broadlands Av. Eastl 6E 132
Broadlands Av. Water 3M 201
Broadlands Clo. Bent 7K 63
Broadlands Clo. Bourn 3A 228
Broadlands Clo. Walk 4K 231
Broadlands Rd. Broc 6B 148
Broadlands Rd. Sotn 7N 159
Broad La. Cher 7G 109
Broad La. Hmbdn 4C 180
Broad La. L'ton 3F 234
Broad La. N Bad 7D 130
Broad La. Swanm 6C 164
Broadlaw Wlk. Shop. Precinct. Fare 1A 212
Broad Layings 2A 8
Broad Leaze. Hook 1G 45
Broadley Clo. Holb 4A 208
Broadly Clo. Penn 4B 234
Broadmayne Rd. Poole 7D 226
Broadmead 2L 233
Broadmead. Farn 9F 28
Broadmead Clo. L'ton 4F 234
Broadmeadow Clo. Tot 3L 171
Broadmeadows La. Water 2A 202
Broadmead Rd. Nurs 5C 158
Broadmere 6A 60
Broadmere. Far W 7N 59
Broadmere Av. Hav 4F 202
Broadmoor Est. C'then 1F 18
Broad Oak 7N 45 (Hook)
Broadoak 3B 176 (Southampton)
Broad Oak. Bot 3B 176
Broad Oak. T'ley 5K 11
Broadoak Clo. Holb 5A 208
Broad Oak La. Odi 8N 45
Broad Oak Works. Ports 4J 215
Broad Rd. Monx 6B 68
Broadsands Dri. Gos 4F 238
Broadsands Wlk. Gos 4G 238
Broadshard Ct. Ring 8K 185
Broadshard La. Ring 8K 185
Broad St. Alr 9F 94
Broad St. Ports 3A 240 (6H 5)
Broadview Clo. B'std 1E 82
Broad Vw. La. Win 2E 126
Broad Wlk. Bas 2E 60
Broad Wlk. Frim 2N 29
Broad Wlk. Ids 5E 182
Broadwater Av. Poole 3A 244
Broadwater Rd. Roms 6L 129
Broadwater Rd. Sotn 8D 160
Broad Way. Frox 5C 138
Broadway. Hamb 4J 195
Broadway. South 1J 247
Broadway. Whitc 6H 55
Broadway Gables. Poole 1B 244
Broadway La. Bourn 3N 227
Broadway La. Love 4L 181
Broadway Pk. Ptsfld 3M 145
Broadway, The. And 2N 69 (off Western Rd.)
Broadway, The. N'brne 1H 227
Broadway, The. S'hrst 6D 18
Broadway, The. Sotn 1N 173 (SO17)
Broadway, The. Sotn 3H 175 (SO18)
Broadway, The. Win 7L 105 (8N 237)
Broad Woods La. W Wel 7N 121
Brocas Dri. Bas 4D 42
Brockbridge 1L 165
Brockbridge Rd. Drox 1L 165
Brockenhurst 7C 148
Brockenhurst Av. Hav 3D 202
Brockenhurst Dri. Yate 9N 17
Brockenhurst Manor Golf Course 1M 223
Brockenhurst Rd. A'sht 2K 65
Brockenhurst Rd. Bourn 4M 227
Brockenhurst Rd. New M 6B 222
Brockham Hill La. Froy 8D 62
Brockhampton 8C 202
Brockhampton La. Hav 8E 202
Brockhampton Rd. Hav 9D 202 (in two parts)
Brockhills La. New M 1D 232
Brockhurst 1J 239
Brockhurst Ind. Est. Gos 7H 213
Brockhurst Rd. Gos 8H 213
Brockishill Rd. Bart 8N 155
Brocklands. Hav 8D 202

Brocklands. Yate 9L 17
Brockle Clo. Chu C 7K 47
Brockley Rd. Bourn. 2J 227
Brocks Clo. Dib P 7J 193
Brocks Pine. St L 5C 186
Brodrick Av. Gos 4J 239
Brokenford. 3K 171
Brokenford Av. Tot 3N 171
Brokenford Bus. Cen. Tot 3M 171
Brokenford La. Tot 3M 171
Broken Way. New 2F 8 (in two parts)
Bromelia Clo. Braml 9G 12
Bromley Rd. Sotn 1D 174
Brompton Pas. Ports 9E 214
Brompton Rd. S'sea 5G 241
Bromyard Cres. Ports 8D 200
Bronte Av. Christ 5K 229
Bronte Clo. Tot 4K 171
Bronte Gdns. White 1F 196
Bronte Way. Sotn 4C 174
Bronze Clo. Hat W 6J 59
Brook. 9E 88 (King's Somborne)
Brook. 5L 155 (Lyndhurst)
Brook Av. F'ham 3H 65
Brook Av. New M 2B 232
Brook Av. Wars 6N 195
Brook Av. N. New M 1C 232
Brook Clo. Bourn 2G 226
Brook Clo. Fle 3M 47
Brook Clo. N Bad 9F 130
Brook Clo. Owl 4G 18
Brook Clo. Sar G 6A 196
Brook Cotts. Yate 7M 17
Brook Ct. Sotn 5J 173
Brookdale Clo. Water 1N 201
Brooke Clo. King W 7M 91
Brookers La. Gos 5C 212 (in two parts)
Brooke's Hill. 7H 157
Brookes Hill Ind. Est. Cal 7H 157
Brook Farm Av. Fare 8B 198
Brookfield Clo. Chine 9H 23
Brookfield Clo. Hav 7E 202
Brookfield Gdns. Sar G 5C 196
Brookfield Pl. Sotn 9N 159
Brookfield Rd. A'sht 8N 49
Brookfield Rd. F Oak 1M 161
Brookfield Rd. Ports 1F 240
Brookfields. W Wel 1A 120
Brook Gdns. Ems 9K 203
Brook Gdns. Farn 1H 49
Brook Grn. T'ley 5K 11
Brook Hill. 6H 47 (Fleet)
Brook Hill. 5L 155 (Lyndhurst)
Brook Ho. F'ham 4F 64 (off Fairview Gdns.)
Brook Ho. Sotn 7E 174
Brookhouse Rd. Farn 9H 29
Brookland Clo. Penn 3C 234
Brooklands. A'sht 1G 65
Brooklands Clo. F'ham 3F 64
Brooklands Rd. Bish W 3M 163
Brooklands Rd. F'ham 3G 64
Brooklands Rd. Hav 7B 202
Brooklands Way. F'ham 3G 64
Brook La. Bot 3C 176
Brook La. Hmbdn 5C 166
Brook La. Nea 8D 220
Brook La. Wars 8N 195
Brook La. W'grn 2A 154
Brookley Clo. F'ham 7L 65
Brookley Rd. Broc 7C 148
Brookly Gdns. Fle 1N 47
Brooklyn Clo. Ott 1G 132
Brooklyn Ct. New M 3A 232
Brooklyn Dri. Water 1N 201
Brooklynn Clo. Wal C 9A 164
Brookmead Ct. F'ham 9D 64
Brookmeadow. Fare 8B 198
Brookmead Way. Hav 9F 202
Brook Rd. Bourn 2G 226
Brook Rd. Cam 9K 19
Brook Rd. F Oak 1N 161
Brook Rd. L'ton 4F 234
Brook Rd. Poole 9A 226
Brook Rd. Sotn 3E 174
Brooksby Clo. B'wtr 8D 18
Brooks Clo. Ring 2L 187
Brooks Clo. Whitc 6H 55
Brooks Experience, The. 7N 237
Brookside. F'ham 4E 64
Brookside. Gos 3D 212
Brookside. Land 9J 121
Brookside. S'hrst 6E 18
Brookside. S G'ly 8M 153
Brookside. Tot 5M 171
Brookside Av. Sotn 3E 172
Brookside Cen. Sotn 3D 172
Brookside Clo. Brans 6C 220
Brookside Clo. Water 6G 181
Brookside Dri. Sar G 6A 196
Brookside Residential Pk. Homes. Farn 3J 29
Brookside Rd. Brans 6C 220
Brookside Rd. Broc 6C 148
Brookside Rd. Hav 9D 202 (Harts Farm Way)
Brookside Rd. Hav 7C 202 (Lower Rd.)
Brookside Wlk. T'ley 5J 11
Brookside Way. Highc 5G 231
Brookside Way. Sotn 7C 160
Brookside Way. W End 9J 161
Brooks Ri. And 9L 51
Brooks Shop. Cen., The. Win 6L 105 (7N 237)
Brook St. Bish W 4M 163
Brooks Way. Win 9N 125
Brook Ter. F'bri 2J 153
Brook, The. Old Al 7F 94
Brook Trad. Est., The. A'sht 9N 49
Brookvale Clo. Bas 6B 42
Brookvale Ct. Sotn 1M 173
Brookvale Rd. Sotn 1M 173
Brook Valley. Sotn 9F 158
Brook Wlk. Cal 1J 171
Brookway. Anna V 5J 69
Brook Way. Christ 7E 230
Brook Way. Roms 3N 129
Brookwood Av. Eastl 9D 132
Brookwood Ind. Est. Eastl 9E 132
Brookwood Rd. Farn 8M 29
Brookwood Rd. Sotn 2C 172
Broom Acres. Fle 5L 47
Broom Acres. S'hrst 5D 18
Broom Clo. S'sea 2L 241
Broom Clo. Water 4A 202
Broome Clo. Yate 6M 17
Broomfield Cres. Gos 9D 212
Broomfield La. L'ton 2E 234
Broomfield Rd. W'hill 5G 100
Broomfiled Dri. A'hlt 5D 152
Broom Hill. E End 4A 236
Broom Hill. Ews 2N 63
Broomhill. Land 1J 155
Broomhill Clo. Penn 4B 234
Broomhill Rd. Farn 7F 28
Broom Hill Way. Eastl 5E 132
Broomleaf Corner. F'ham 8F 64
Broomleaf Rd. F'ham 8F 64
Broomrigg Rd. Fle 1J 47
Broom Rd. Ptsfld 2B 146
Broom Rd. Poole 5A 226
Brooms Gro. Sotn 7H 175
Broom Sq. S'sea 2L 241
Broom Way. B'wtr 9F 18
Broom Way. Lee S 9B 212
Broomy Clo. Dib 5H 193
Brougham La. Gos 1J 239
Brougham Pl. F'ham 3D 64
Brougham Rd. S'sea 3D 240 (6N 5)
Brougham St. Gos 1J 239
Broughton. 2A 86
Broughton Av. Bourn 2J 227
Broughton Clo. Bourn 3J 227
Broughton Clo. Sotn 1F 172
Broughton Drove. Bro'tn & Chat 5B 88 (in two parts)
Broughton M. Frim 3N 29
Broughton Rd. Chat 3C 88
Broughton Rd. Lyn 1B 148
Brown Candover. 7B 78
Brown Cft. Hook 2F 44
Browndown Rd. Lee S 4E 238
Brownen Rd. Bourn 6M 227
Brownhill Clo. Chan F 5A 132
Brownhill Ct. Sotn 8D 158
Brownhill Gdns. Chan F 5A 132
Brownhill Ho. Sotn 8D 158
Brownhill Rd. Chan F 5A 132
Brownhill Rd. New M 4M 221
Brownhill Rd. N Bad 8F 130 (in two parts)
Brownhill Way. Sotn 8B 158
Browning Av. Bourn 1C 246
Browning Av. Ports 8N 199
Browning Av. Sotn 4H 175
Browning Clo. Bas 3D 42
Browning Clo. Eastl 9D 132
Browning Clo. Tot 3K 171
Browning Clo. White 9F 176
Browning Dri. Win 6H 105
Browning Rd. Chu C 7K 47
Browning Rd. Poole 8B 226
Brownings Clo. Penn 2A 234
Brownlow Av. Sotn 4D 174
Brownlow Clo. Ports 9E 214
Brownlow Gdns. Sotn 4E 174
Browns Clo. Braml 9G 12
Brownsea Clo. New M 3N 231
Brownsea Ct. Poole 5A 244
Brownsea Vw. Av. Poole 4A 244
Brownsea Vw. Clo. Poole 4A 244
Browns La. Dam 3N 149
Browns La. E End 5B 236
Browns La. Ports 4J 215
Brownsover Rd. Farn 8E 28
Brownwich La. Fare 4F 210 (in two parts)
Brow Path. Water 7K 201
Browsholme Clo. Eastl 6E 132
Brow, The. Gos 3N 239
Brow, The. Water 7J 201
Broxburn Clo. Chan F 3C 132
Broxhead Common Nature Reserve. 9L 83
Broxhead Farm Rd. Lind 8K 83
Broxhead Rd. Hav 3G 203
Broxhead Trad. Est. Lind 1L 101
Bruce Clo. Fare 6C 198
Bruce Rd. S'sea 5G 241
Brudenell Av. Poole 6B 244
Brudenell Rd. Poole 6B 244
Brue Clo. Chan F 5N 131
Brune La. Lee S & Gos 7C 212 (in two parts)
Brunel Clo. H End 1A 176
Brunel Clo. Mich 4J 77
Brunel Clo. Ver 5A 184
Brunel Ga. And 8H 51
Brunel Rd. Bas 5N 41
Brunel Rd. Ports 5F 214
Brunel Rd. Sotn 2B 172
Brunel Rd. Tot 8K 157
Brunel Way. Fare 4G 196
Brunstead Pl. Poole 1F 244
Brunstead Rd. Poole 1E 244
Brunswick Clo. F Oak 9M 133
Brunswick Gdns. Hav 7D 202
Brunswick Pl. Bas 1A 60
Brunswick Pl. L'ton 2E 234
Brunswick Pl. Sotn 4L 173 (2C 4)
Brunswick Rd. F Oak 9M 133
Brunswick Sq. Sotn 7M 173 (8D 4)
Brunswick St. S'sea 3D 240 (6N 5)
Bruntile Clo. Farn 2M 49
Brushers. Brans 3G 220
Bruyn Ct. F'bri 9K 151
Bruyn Rd. F'bri 9K 151
Bryanstone Clo. Chu C 5M 47
Bryanstone Rd. Bourn 7J 227
Bryanston Rd. Sotn 5B 174
Bryant Rd. Poole 6E 226
Bryce Gdns. A'sht 3L 65
Bryces La. Bro C 7B 78
Brydges Rd. Lud 1D 30
Bryher Bri. Port S 1C 214
Bryher Island. Port S 1B 214
Brympton Clo. F'bri 9G 150
Bryony Clo. L Hth 7C 196
Bryony Gdns. H Hth 5N 161
Bryony Way. Water 2A 202
Bryson Rd. Ports 9E 200
Bubb La. W End 8L 161
Bub La. Christ 8A 230
Buccaneers Clo. Christ 8N 229
Buccleuch Rd. Poole 4E 244
Bucehayes Clo. Highc 6J 231
Buchanan Av. Bourn 8B 228
Buchanan Rd. Sotn 6E 158
Buchan Av. White 1F 196
Buchan Ct. Dib P 7H 193
Buckby La. Bas 6E 42
Buckby La. Ports 4K 215
Bucket Corner. 5H 131
Bucketts Farm Clo. Swanm 6D 164
Buckfast Clo. Bas 2B 42
Buckholt Rd. Bro'tn 5A 88
Buckingham Building. Ports 2C 240 (3L 5)
Buckingham Clo. Alt 5D 80
Buckingham Ct. Bas 2J 59
Buckingham Ct. Fare 6N 197
Buckingham Grn. Ports 9F 214
Buckingham Mans. Bourn 2L 245
Buckingham Pde. Bas 1J 59
Buckingham Rd. Ptsfld 1K 145
Buckingham Rd. Poole 7B 226
Buckingham St. Ports 1D 240
Buckingham Wlk. New M 3N 231
Buckingham Way. Frim 3N 29
Buckland. 1D 234 (Lymington)
Buckland. 8F 214 (Portsmouth)
Buckland Av. Bas 1M 59
Buckland Clo. Eastl 6E 132
Buckland Clo. Farn 5L 29
Buckland Clo. Water 7L 181
Buckland Dene. L'ton 1D 234
Buckland Gdns. Cal 9J 157
Buckland Gro. Christ 4G 230
Buckland Pde. Bas 9M 41
Buckland Path. Ports 9E 214
Buckland Rd. Poole 9A 226
Buckland St. Ports 9F 214 (in two parts)
Buckland Ter. Poole 9A 226
Buckland Vw. L'ton 1D 234
Bucklers Ct. Hav 2D 202
Bucklers Ct. L'ton 3D 234
Bucklers Ct. Ports 7E 214
Bucklers Hard. 1E 236
Buckler's Hard Maritime Mus. 1E 236
Bucklers Hard Rd. Beau 8E 206
Bucklers M. L'ton 3D 234
Bucklers Rd. Gos 8L 213
Bucklers, The. Mil S 9H 233
Bucklers Way. Bourn 3A 228
Buckley Ct. Sotn 1G 172
Buckmore Av. Ptsfld 8K 139
Bucksey Rd. Gos 8E 212
Bucks Head Hill. Meon 8N 135
Bucks Horn Oak. 10N 63
Buckskin. 8L 41
Buckskin La. Bas 9J 41
Buckstone Clo. Evtn 5M 233
Buckthorn Clo. Tot 2H 171
Budden's La. Mis 2G 178
Buddens Rd. Wick 6C 178
Buddle Hill. N Gor 6M 153
Buddlesgate. Sut S 7D 76
Budd's Clo. Bas 7B 42
Budds La. Bord 2H 101
Budds La. Roms 3L 129
Budds La. Ind. Est. Roms 3L 129
Bude Clo. Ports 8A 200
Buffbeards La. Hasl 8N 103
Buffins Corner. Odi 9J 45
Buffins Rd. Odi 9J 45
Bugle St. Sotn 7L 173 (8C 4)
Bulbarrow Wlk. Fare 9A 198
Bulbeck Rd. Hav 8F 202
Bulbery. Abb A 6F 68
Bulldowne Wlk. Sway 4J 223
Bulford. 3A 66
Bulford Camp. 3B 66
Bulford Droveway. Bulf 3A 66
Bulford Kiwi, The. 3C 66
Bulford Rd. Durr 3A 66
Bulford Rd. Ship B & Tidw 1E 66 (in two parts)
Bullar Rd. Sotn 3C 174
Bullar St. Sotn 4N 173 (2F 4)
Buller Ct. Farn 2L 49
Bullers Rd. F'ham 4G 64
Bullfield La. Bentw 6J 79
Bullfinch Clo. Coll T 5G 18
Bullfinch Clo. Tot 3J 171
Bullfinch Ct. Lee S 9B 212
Bull Hill. 6H 225
Bull Hill. Pill 6H 225
Bull Hill. Rake 1K 141
Bullington La. Bar S 5A 76
Bullington La. Sut S 5D 76
Bull La. Min 8M 155
Bull La. Rise 2D 14 (in two parts)
Bull La. Wal C 8N 163
Bullrush Clo. Dib P 8L 193
Bulls Copse La. Water 4A 182
Bullsdown Clo. Sher L 3K 23
Bulls Drove. Lud 4M 31
Bulls Drove. W Tyth 9L 87
Bulls La. Bro Ch 3A 118
Bulpitts Hill. Ver D 8E 6
Bulser Ancient Farm 6F 168
Bunkers Hill. 6E 180
Bunkers Hill. Water 7E 180
Bunnian Pl. Bas 5C 42
Bunns La. Den 7N 179
Bunny La. Roms 8L 123
Bunny La. W'ish 5L 121
Bunstead. 7B 126
Bunstead La. Hurs 7B 126
Bunting Gdns. Water 6N 181
Bunting M. Bas 3H 59
Buntings. Alt 2F 80
Burbidge Gro. S'sea 5H 241
Burbury Woods. Cam 7N 19
Burbush Clo. Holb 5A 208
Burcombe La. Hang 4A 188
Burcombe Rd. Bourn 1G 226
Burcote Dri. Ports 4J 215
Burdale Dri. Hay I 4K 243
Burdock Clo. Christ 5D 230
Burdock Clo. Good C 9M 69
Bure Clo. Christ 8D 230
Bure Ct. Christ 8D 230
Bure Haven Dri. Christ 8C 230
Bure Homage Gdns. Christ 8D 230
Bure Homage La. Christ 8C 230
Bure La. Christ 9D 230
Bure Pk. Christ 8D 230
Bure Rd. Christ 8D 230
Burfield. High 4A 8
Burford Clo. Christ 5G 228
Burford Ct. Bourn 2M 245
Burford La. Broc 6D 148
Burford Rd. Cam 9K 19
Burgate Clo. Hav 6D 202
Burgate Ct. Burg 7K 151
Burgate Fields. F'bri 8J 151
Burgates. 8D 114
Burgesmede Ho. Ptsfld 1M 145
Burgess Clo. Bourn 2D 226
Burgess Clo. Hay I 6K 243
Burgess Clo. Odi 9J 45
Burgess Ct. Sotn 7N 159
Burgess Gdns. Sotn 8K 159
Burgess La. Kint H 1K 7
Burgess Rd. Bas 5B 42
Burgess Rd. Sotn 8J 159 (in two parts)
Burghclere. 3E 8
Burghclere Rd. Hav 3H 203
Burghclere Rd. Sotn 1D 194
Burghead Clo. Coll T 6F 18
Burgh Hill Rd. Pass 8B 102
Burgoyne Rd. Sotn 6J 175
Burgoyne Rd. S'sea 6E 240
Burgundy Clo. L Hth 7C 196
Burgundy Ter. Ports 5F 214
Buriton. 7K 145
Buriton Clo. Fare 8M 199
Buriton Ho. Ports 2E 240 (off Buriton St.)
Buriton Rd. Win 2H 105
Buriton St. Ports 1E 240
Burkal Dri. And 6N 51
Burke Dri. Sotn 4G 175
Burleigh Rd. Bourn 8G 228
Burleigh Rd. Frim 4M 29
Burleigh Rd. Ports 9G 214
Burley. 7E 188
Burley Clo. Chan F 8N 131
Burley Clo. Hav 3H 203
Burley Clo. New M 6M 231
Burley Down. Chan F 8N 131
Burley Golf Club 8E 188
Burley La. Ashe 5H 57
Burley Lawn. 7E 188
Burley Rd. Brans 8C 220
Burley Rd. Broc 1E 222
Burley Rd. Poole 8A 226
Burley Rd. Win 2H 105
Burley Rd. Wink & Bock 1M 229
Burley Street. 6D 188
Burley Way. B'wtr 7E 18
Burling Ter. Poole 1E 244
Burlington Arc. Bourn 2K 245 (6M 247)
Burlington Ct. A'sht 1J 65
Burlington Ct. B'wtr 1F 28
Burlington Ct. Sotn 5F 174
Burlington Mans. Sotn 3H 173
Burlington Rd. Ports 7F 214
Burlington Rd. Sotn 4K 173 (1A 4)
Burma Ho. Sotn 7C 160
Burma Rd. Roms 6M 129
Burma Rd. N. Hythe 3F 208
Burma Rd. S. Hythe 3F 208
Burma Way. March 9E 172
Burmese Clo. White 2E 196
Burnaby Building. Ports 2C 240 (4L 5)
Burnaby Clo. Bas 8L 41
Burnaby Ct. Bourn 4F 244
Burnaby Rd. Bourn 4G 244
Burnaby Rd. Ports 2C 240 (4L 5)
Burnbank Gdns. Tot 3L 171
Burne Clo. Wor D 5H 91
Burne-Jones Dri. Coll T 7F 18
Burnett Av. Christ 6H 229
Burnett Clo. Hythe 7N 193
Burnett Clo. Sotn 1C 174
Burnett Clo. Win 4G 105
Burnett Rd. Christ 7J 229
Burnett Rd. Gos 1H 239

Burnetts Fields—Captains Row

Burnetts Fields. *H Hth* 4N **161**
Burnetts Gdns. *H Hth*. 4N **161**
Burnetts La. *W End & H Hth* 8L **161**
Burney Bit. *P Hth* 5L **11**
*Burney Ho. Gos . . . . 3M **239** (off South St.)*
Burney Rd. *Gos* 4G **239**
Burnham Beeches. *Chan F* 6N **131**
Burnham Chase. *Sotn*. 3F **174**
Burnham Dri. *Bourn*. 7N **227**
Burnham Rd. *Burt* 4M **229**
Burnham Rd. *F'bri*. 8J **151**
Burnham Rd. *Ports*. 8L **201**
Burnham Rd. *T'ley* 3F **10**
Burnhams Clo. *And* 6N **51**
Burnham's Wlk. *Gos* 3M **239**
Burnham Wood. *Fare* 6C **198**
Burnleigh Gdns. *New M* 2D **232**
Burnley Clo. *T'ley*. 6H **11**
Burnmoor Mdw. *Finch* 3H **17**
Burnsall Clo. *Farn*. 6K **29**
Burns Av. *Chu C*. 5N **47**
Burns Clo. *Bas* 3D **42**
Burns Clo. *Eastl* 2C **160**
Burns Clo. *Farn* 6H **29**
Burns Clo. *S Won*. 3J **91**
Burnside. *Christ* 6F **230**
Burnside. *Fle* 2M **47**
Burnside. *Gos*. 3D **212**
Burnside. *Water* 9A **182**
Burns Pl. *Sotn*. 9F **158**
Burns Rd. *Bourn* 7G **229**
Burns Rd. *Eastl* 2D **160**
Burns Rd. *Sotn*. 4H **175**
Burnt Ho. La. *Brans* 6C **220**
Burnt Ho. La. *Fare* 3N **211**
Burnt Ho. La. *Pill* 6F **224**
Burrard Gro. *L'ton*. 4F **234**
Burr Clo. *Col C* 4K **133**
Burrell Ho. *S'sea* 8M **5**
Burrell Rd. *Frim* 4L **29**
Burrfields Retail Pk. *Ports* 7J **215**
Burrfields Rd. *Ports* 7H **215**
Burridge. **9E 176**
Burridge Rd. *Bot*. 4F **176**
Burridge Rd. *Bur* 8D **176**
Burrill Av. *Ports* 9H **201**
Burrowfields. *Bas*. 5K **59**
Burrows Clo. *Hav*. 6G **203**
Burrows La. *Ver*. 9M **149**
Bursledon. **2M 195**
Bursledon Heights. *Burs* 9M **175**
Bursledon Pl. *Water* 4L **201**
Bursledon Rd. *H End*. 6M **175**
Bursledon Rd. *Sotn & Burs* 4E **174**
Bursledon Rd. *Water* 4L **201**
Bursledon Towermill. 8L **175**
Burtley Rd. *Bourn*. 2H **247**
Burton. **3M 229**
Burton Clo. *Ashy H*. 3A **186**
Burton Clo. *Burt*. 5M **229**
Burtoncroft. *Burt* 3M **229**
Burton Hall Pl. *Burt* 3M **229**
Burton Rd. *Christ* 7A **230**
Burton Rd. *Poole* 2E **244**
Burton Rd. *Sotn* . . . 4K **173** (1A **4**)
Burton's Gdns. *Old B* 4J **43**
*Burwood Clo. Ame. . . . . 5A **66** (off Rayleigh Cres.)*
Burwood Gro. *Hay I*. 2G **243**
Bury Brickfield Pk. Cvn. Site. *Tot* 6B **172**
Bury Clo. *Gos*. 3K **239**
Bury Cres. *Gos*. 3K **239**
Bury Cross. *Gos* 3J **239**
Burydown Mead. *N Wal* 9B **58**
Buryfields. *Odi* 9L **45**
Bury Hall La. *Gos*. 4H **239**
Bury Hill Clo. *Anna V* 5K **69**
Bury La. *Bro Ch* 3A **118**
Bury La. *Tot* 5A **172**
Bury Rd. *Bas*. 5M **41**
Bury Rd. *Gos* 3J **239**
Bury Rd. *March* 7C **172**
Bury Rd. *Poole*. 4C **244**
Bury, The. **9L 45**
Bury, The. *Odi*. 8L **45**
Bus Drove. *Cals* 8J **209**
Bushells Farm. *F'bri* 2H **153**
Bushey Rd. *Bourn* 5N **227**
Bush Ho. *S'sea* 4D **240** (7N **5**)
Bushmead Dri. *Ashy H*. . . . 3B **186**
Bushnells Dri. *K're*. 2A **6**
Bush St. E. *S'sea* 4D **240** (7N **5**)
Bush St. W. *S'sea* 4D **240** (7N **5**)
Bushy Mead. *Water* 6K **201**
Bushywarren La. *H'rd*. 9E **60**
Busigny Barracks. *Per D*. . . . 3B **30**
Busk Cres. *Farn* 9H **29**
Busket La. *Win* 7L **105** (8N **237**)
Busketts Way. *Asht* 8G **170**
Bustards Corner. *Neth W* 1N **87**
Buster Wlk. *Ptsfld*. 9A **140**
Butcher St. *Ports* . . . 2B **240** (4J **5**)
Bute Dri. *Highc*. 6K **231**
Butler Clo. *Bas* 7L **41**
Butlers Clo. *Lcky* 2N **121**
Butlers La. *Ring*. 8M **185**
Butlocks Heath. **3H 195**
Butser Ct. *Water*. 8D **168**
Butser Wlk. *Fare*. 9A **198**
Butt Clo. *Lud* 4K **31**
Buttercup Clo. *H End* 4L **175**
Buttercup Clo. *Hythe* 8M **193**
Buttercup Clo. *Lind* 2M **101**
Buttercup Dri. *Christ* 5D **230**
Buttercup Wlk. *Tot* 5K **171**
Buttercup Way. *L Hth* 6B **196**
Butterfield Dri. *Ame* 5A **66**
Butterfield Rd. *Sotn* 8K **159**
Butterfields. *Cam* 9K **19**
Butterfly Dri. *Ports*. 8B **200**
Butter Furlong Rd. *W Gri* 1D **120**
Buttermere. **3E 6**
Buttermere Clo. *Bord* 2J **101**
Buttermere Clo. *Farn* 8G **29**
Buttermere Clo. *Sotn* 9D **158**
*Buttermere Ct. Ash V . . . . . . 7N **49** (off Lakeside Clo.)*
Buttermere Dri. *Bas* 1J **59**
Buttermere Gdns. *Alr* 2F **108**
Buttery, The. *Christ* 7N **229**
Butt La. *B'stne* 3C **118**
Button's La. *Selb* 4H **113**
Button's La. *W Wel*. 1B **120**
Buttsash. **9N 193**
Butts Ash Av. *Hythe*. 9M **193**
Butts Ash Gdns. *Hythe* . . . 8M **193**
Butts Ash La. *Hythe* 9L **193**
Butts Bri. Hill. *Hythe* 7M **193**
Buttsbridge Rd. *Hythe* 8M **193**
Butt's Clo. *Sotn* 6H **175**
Butts Clo. *Wim G* 8G **148**
Butts Clo. *Win* 5H **105**
Butt's Cres. *Sotn* 6G **175**
Butts Farm La. *Bish W*. 3N **163**
Butts Green. **4A 122**
Butts Grn. *Lcky*. 4A **122**
Butts Hill. *Up Ch*. 2N **31**
Butts Lawn. *Broc* 6C **148**
Butts Mdw. *Hook* 2G **44**
Butts M. *Alt*. 6E **80**
Butts Paddock. *Broc*. 6C **148**
Butts Rd. *Alt*. 6E **80**
Butt's Rd. *Sotn* 8F **174**
Butt's Sq. *Sotn*. 6G **175**
Butts, The. **6E 80**
Butts, The. *Alt*. 6E **80**
Butts, The. *Meon* 8N **135**
Butts, The. *Sil*. 5A **12**
Butt St. *Lud* 1C **30**
Butt St. *Lud* 4K **31**
Butty, The. *Bas* 6E **42**
Byam's La. *March* 8F **172**
Byerley Rd. *Ports*. . . . . 2G **240** (in two parts)
Bye Rd. *Swanw* 1A **196**
Byes La. *Sil*. 7A **12**
Byeways. *High* 4A **8**
Byeways. *Hythe* 7L **193**
Byfields Rd. *K're*. 2A **6**
Byfleet Av. *Old B*. 5J **43**
Byngs Bus. Pk. *Water*. 7J **181**
Byng Wlk. *And* 1C **70**
By-Pass Rd. *Sut S* 7C **76**
Byrd Clo. *Water*. 4M **201**
Byrd Gdns. *Bas*. 3L **59**
Byres, The. *Fare*. 5M **211**
Byron Av. *Win* 6H **105**
Byron Clo. *Bas* 2D **42**
Byron Clo. *Bish W* 3A **164**
Byron Clo. *Fare*. 7C **198**
Byron Clo. *Fle* 3M **47**
Byron Clo. *Lud*. 1D **30**
Byron Clo. *Yate*. 9L **17**
Byron Ct. *Sotn*. 4K **173** (2A **4**)
Byron Dri. *C'then* 2D **18**
Byron Ho. *New M*. 4B **232**
Byron Rd. *Bart S* 6N **231**
Byron Rd. *Bourn*. 1C **246**
Byron Rd. *Eastl*. 8F **132**
Byron Rd. *Ports* 8G **214**
Byron Rd. *Sotn*. 4G **175**
By-the-Wood. *Cal*. 9K **157**
Byways. *Yate*. 8L **17**
Byworth Clo. *F'ham* 8B **64**
Byworth Rd. *F'ham*. 8B **64**

C

Cable St. *Sotn*. 5A **174**
Cabot Dri. *Dib*. 6H **193**
Cabot Way. *New M*. 3A **232**
Cabrol Rd. *Farn*. 7J **29**
Cabul Rd. *Tidw*. 9B **30**
Cadet Way. *Chu C*. 7N **47**
Cadgwith Pl. *Port S* 1C **214**
Cadhay Clo. *New M* 3A **232**
Cadland Ct. *Ocn V* 7A **174**
Cadland Pk. Est. *Hythe*. . . . 3A **208**
Cadland Rd. *Hythe* . . . . 3F **208** (Burma Rd. S.)
Cadland Rd. *Hythe* . . . . 2N **207** (Forest La.)
Cadley. **1H 31**
Cadley Rd. *Coll D*. 1H **31**
Cadnam. **6N 155**
Cadnam Clo. *A'sht*. 4L **65**
Cadnam Clo. *Okly*. 9D **40**
Cadnam Ct. *Gos* 4F **238**
Cadnam Cres. *Ame*. 6A **66**
Cadnam Green. **5N 155**
Cadnam La. *Cad*. 5N **155**
Cadnam Lawn. *Hav* 2D **202**
Cadnam Rd. *S'sea*. 4J **241**
Cadnam Way. *Bourn*. 3A **228**
Cadogan Rd. *A'sht*. 4M **49**
Cadogan Rd. *Ring*. 1L **187**
Cador Dri. *Fare*. 2K **213**
Caen Ho. *Fare*. 9A **198**
Caerleon Av. *Sotn*. 4G **174**
Caerleon Clo. *Hind* 1L **103**
Caerleon Dri. *And*. 6N **51**
Caerleon Dri. *Sotn*. 4F **174**
Caernarvon Clo. *Bas*. 6L **41**
Caernarvon Gdns. *Chan F* 8M **131**
Caernarvon Ho. *Bourn* 6J **247**
Caesar Clo. *Bas*. 4L **41**
Caesar Ct. *A'sht* 9G **49**
Caesar Rd. *And*. 7A **52**
Caesars Ct. *F'ham*. 4E **64**
Caesar's Way. *Whitc* 4F **54**
Cafaude. **5E 22**
Cains Clo. *Fare*. 5M **211**
Caird Av. *New M*. 4D **232**
Cairngorm Clo. *Bas* 7K **41**
Cairngorm Pl. *Farn*. 5G **28**
Cairns Clo. *Christ* 6J **229**
Cairo Ter. *Ports*. 9E **214**
Caistor Clo. *Sotn*. 7F **158**
Caithness Clo. *Okly*. 1C **58**
Caker La. *E Wor* 6J **81**
Caker Stream Rd. *Alt* 4H **81**
Calabrese. *Swanw*. 2E **196**
Calbourne. *Net A* 2G **195**
Calcot Hill. *Curd*. 8H **163**
Calcot La. *Curd*. 8G **163**
Caldecote Wlk. *S'sea* 3D **240** (5M **5**)
Calder Clo. *Sotn*. 2D **172**
Calder Ct. *And* 8B **52**
Calder Ho. *Ports* 3J **5**
Calderwood Dri. *Sotn* 6E **174**
Caledonia Dri. *Dib*. 6J **193**
Caledonian Clo. *Christ* 7D **230**
Caledon Rd. *Poole* 2B **244**
Calender Clo. *Alt*. 6F **80**
California Clo. *Tot*. 1H **171**
Calkin Clo. *Christ* 5K **229**
Calleva Clo. *Bas* 3K **59**
Calleva Ind. Pk. *A'mstn*. 3E **10**
Calleva Mus. 4A **12**
Calleva Roman Town. 4C **12**
Calmore. **9H 157**
Calmore Clo. *Bourn* 3A **228**
Calmore Cres. *Cal*. 9H **157**
Calmore Dri. *Cal* 9J **157**
Calmore Gdns. *Tot* 3J **171**
Calmore Ind. Est. *Tot* . . . . . 9L **157** (in two parts)
Calmore Rd. *Cal & Tot*. . . . 9H **157**
Calpe Av. *Lyn* 1B **148**
Calshot. **8K 209**
Calshot Beach. *Cals* 9L **209**
Calshot Castle. 7M **209**
Calshot Clo. *Cals* 8K **209**
Calshot Ct. *Ocn V*. 8A **174**
Calshot Dri. *Chan F* 9M **131**
Calshot Foreshore Country Pk. 1M **237**
Calshot Marshes Bird Sanctuary. 6L **209**
Calshot Rd. *Fawl*. 5F **208**
Calshot Rd. *Hav* 2C **202**
Calshot Way. *Gos*. 7D **212**
Calthorpe Houses. *Elve*. 4E **26**
Calthorpe Rd. *Fle* 1K **47**
Calton Gdns. *A'sht* 3L **65**
Calvecroft. *Lip*. 2E **116**
Calvert Cen., The. *W'cott* . . . 4N **77**
Calvert Clo. *A'sht*. 1M **65**
Calvin Rd. *Bourn* 6K **227**
Camargue Clo. *White* 1E **196**
Camberley. **7M 19**
Camber Pl. *Ports* 4B **240** (7J **5**)
Camberry Clo. *Bas* 8D **42**
Cambrai Barracks. *Per D* . . . 4B **30**
Cambria Dri. *Dib* 6J **193**
Cambrian Clo. *Burs*. 8L **175**
Cambrian Clo. *Cam*. 8K **19**
Cambrian Rd. *Farn* 5F **28**
Cambrian Ter. *S'sea* 4E **240**
Cambrian Wlk. *Fare* 1B **212**
Cambrian Way. *Bas* 8K **41**
Cambridge Building. *Ports* 3C **240** (5L **5**)
Cambridge Dri. *Chan F*. . . . 9A **132** (in two parts)
Cambridge Gdns. *Christ* . . . 4J **229**
Cambridge Grn. *Chan F* . . . 9A **132**
Cambridge Grn. *Fare*. 7F **196**
Cambridge Ho. *Ports* 3C **240** (6L **5**)
Cambridge Junct. *Ports* 3C **240** (6L **5**)
Cambridge Meadows. *F'ham* 9B **64**
Cambridge Pl. *F'ham* 8E **64**
Cambridge Rd. *A'sht*. 9H **49**
Cambridge Rd. *Bourn* 2H **245** (6H **247**)
Cambridge Rd. *C'then*. 1E **18**
Cambridge Rd. *Gos* 1G **239**
Cambridge Rd. *Lee S* 2B **238**
Cambridge Rd. *Owl* 4G **18**
Cambridge Rd. *Ports* 3C **240** (6L **5**)
Cambridge Rd. *Sotn* 2M **173**
Cambridge Rd. E. *Farn* . . . . . 2L **49** (in two parts)
Cambridge Rd. W. *Farn*. . . . . 2L **49** (in two parts)
*Cambridge Sq. Cam . . . . 7L **19** (off Cambridge Wlk.)*
Cambridge Wlk. *Cam* 7L **19**
Camcross Clo. *Ports*. 8C **200**
Camden Clo. *Bourn* 5M **227**
Camden Hurst. *Mil S* 8H **235**
Camden St. *Gos* 1J **239**
Camdentown. **2J 239**
Camden Wlk. *Fle*. 2A **48**
Camel Green. **4E 152**
Camel Grn. Rd. *A'hlt*. 4D **152**
Camelia Clo. *Hav*. 6J **203**
Camelia Gdns. *Sotn* 9E **160**
Camelia Gro. *F Oak*. 1B **162**
Camellia Clo. *N Bad* 7F **130**
Camellia Gdns. *New M*. 4C **232**
Camelot Clo. *And*. 8N **51**
Camelot Cres. *Fare* 8K **199**
Camelsdale. **2N 117**
Camelsdale Rd. *Hasl* 1N **117**
Cameron Clo. *Gos*. 5E **212**
Cameron Ct. *Sotn*. 6E **158**
Cameron Rd. *A'sht*. 4M **49**
Cameron Rd. *Christ* 7N **229**
Camfield Clo. *Bas*. 8D **42**
Camford Clo. *Hat W* 6J **59**
Camilla Clo. *Bulf*. 3A **66**
Camlea Clo. *Bas*. 8D **42**
Camley Clo. *Sotn* 9C **174**
Camomile Dri. *Lud*. 1D **30**
Campbell Clo. *A'sht*. 3L **65**
Campbell Clo. *Fle* 2K **47**
Campbell Clo. *Grat* 5K **67**
Campbell Clo. *Yate* 7B **18**
Campbell Ct. Bus. Pk. *Braml* 2J **23**
Campbell Cres. *Water*. 4K **201**
Campbell Mans. *S'sea*. 4F **240**
Campbell Rd. *A'sht* 8J **49**
Campbell Rd. *Bourn*. 9B **228**
Campbell Rd. *Braml* 2J **23**
Campbell Rd. *Burt*. 3M **229**
Campbell Rd. *Eastl* 2F **160**
Campbell Rd. *S'sea*. 4E **240**
Campbell St. *Sotn*. 4A **174**
Campbell Way. *F Oak* 1N **161**
Camp Farm Rd. *A'sht*. 6M **49**
Camp Hill. *F'ham* 9L **65**
Campion Clo. *B'wtr* 1H **29**
Campion Clo. *H Hth* 5A **162**
Campion Clo. *Lind*. 3M **101**
Campion Clo. *Wars*. 8B **196**
Campion Clo. *Water* 3A **202**
Campion Dri. *Roms* 3B **130**
Campion Gro. *Christ*. 8B **230**
Campion Rd. *Sotn* 5H **175**
Campion Way. *H Win* 5C **26**
Campion Way. *King W*. 9N **91**
Campion Way. *L'ton* 1E **234**
Camp Rd. *Bord*. 3J **101**
Camp Rd. *Farn* 3L **49**
Camp Rd. *Gos*. 5F **212**
Campsie Clo. *Bas* 7K **41**
Camrose Way. *Bas*. 9D **42**
Cams Bay Clo. *Fare* 8H **199**
Cams Hall Golf Course 9F **198**
Cams Hill. *Fare* . . . . 8F **198** (in two parts)
Cams Hill. *Hmbdn* 9C **166**
Camus Clo. *Chu C*. 6J **47**
Cam Wlk. *Bas*. 6E **42**
Camwood Clo. *Bas*. 8D **42**
Canada. **2M 155**
Canada Pl. *Sotn* 7K **159**
Canada Rd. *Sotn*. 8C **174**
Canada Rd. *W Wel* 2B **120**
Canada Way. *Bord*. 3J **101**
Canada Way. *Lip*. 3E **116**
Canal Clo. *A'sht* 6M **49**
Canal Clo. *N War*. 7J **45**
Canal Clo. *Roms*. 3N **129**
Canal Wlk. *Ports*. 2E **240**
Canal Wlk. *Sotn* . . . 7M **173** (7D **4**)
Canberra Clo. *Gos* 3H **239**
Canberra Clo. *Yate* 5K **17**
Canberra Ct. *Gos* 3H **239**
Canberra Dri. *Bulf B* 3C **66**
Canberra Ho. *Ports*. 2D **240**
Canberra Rd. *Christ* 6H **229**
Canberra Rd. *Ems* 5N **217**
Canberra Rd. *Nurs* 7A **158**
Canberra Towers. *Sotn*. . . . 1D **194**
Candleford Ga. *Lip* 2D **116**
Candlemas Pl. *Sotn*. 2M **173**
Candover Clo. *T'ley* 6H **11**
Candover Ct. *Sotn*. 1E **194**
Candy La. *Sotn* 3J **175**
Canes La. *Lind* 2L **101**
Canford Av. *Bourn* 5D **226**
Canford Cliffs. **5D 244**
Canford Cliffs Av. *Poole* . . . 3B **244**
Canford Cliffs Rd. *Poole*. . . 4C **244**
Canford Clo. *Shed* 3A **178**
Canford Clo. *Sotn*. 9C **158**
Canford Ct. *Poole* 7C **244**
Canford Cres. *Poole* 6C **244**
Canford Gdns. *Bourn* 5E **226**
Canford Rd. *Bourn* 5E **226**
Canford Way. *Poole* 4A **226**
Canhouse La. *Rake & Rog* 1K **141**
Canning Rd. *A'sht* 9M **49**
Cannock Wlk. *Fare* 1A **212**
Cannon Clo. *Coll T*. 5H **19**
Cannon Ho. *L'ton* 2E **234**
Cannon St. *L'ton* 2E **234**
Cannon St. *Sotn*. 2H **173**
Canoe Clo. *Wars*. 8C **196**
Canon Ct. *Eastl*. 1N **161**
Canons Barn Clo. *Fare* 8L **199**
*Canons Clo. Tidw . . . . 8G **31** (off Church La.)*
Canon's Ct. *K're* 2A **6**
Canon St. *Win* . . . 7K **105** (9L **237**)
Canons Wlk. *Mil S* 7K **235**
Canterbury Av. *Sotn*. 7G **174**
*Canterbury Clo. Ame . . . . . . 5A **66** (off Rayleigh Cres.)*
Canterbury Clo. *Bas* 2K **59**
Canterbury Clo. *Lee S* 3D **238**
Canterbury Dri. *Dib* 6H **193**
Canterbury Rd. *Fare* 5M **211**
Canterbury Rd. *Farn* 1M **49**
Canterbury Rd. *S'sea* 4G **241**
Canterton La. *Brook* 6L **155**
Canton St. *Sotn*. . . . 4L **173** (1B **4**)
Canute Dri. *Brans*. 6D **220**
Canute Ho. *Sotn* 7E **4**
Canute Rd. *Sotn* . . . 7N **173** (8F **4**)
Canute Rd. *Win*. 8M **105**
Canute's Pavilion. *Ocn V* 8N **173** (9G **4**)
Canvey Ct. *Sotn* 9D **158**
Capella Ct. *Bourn* 3K **245** (8M **247**)
Capella Gdns. *Dib* 6J **193**
Capel Ley. *Water* 5M **201**
Capers End La. *Curd* 1H **177**
Capesthorne. *Christ* 9D **230**
Capital Ho. *Win*. 6L **237**
Capon Clo. *Sotn* 7C **160**
Capstan Gdns. *L Hth*. 6F **196**
Capstone Pl. *Bourn*. 8A **228**
Capstone Rd. *Bourn* 8M **227**
Captain's Pl. *Sotn* . . . 7N **173** (8F **4**)
Captain's Row. *L'ton* 2F **234**
Captains Row. *Ports* 4B **240** (7J **5**)

Caravan Pk. Hay I. 8G 217
Caraway. White. 2G 197
Carberry Dri. Fare 1K 213
Carbery Av. Bourn 1G 246
Carbery Ct. Hav 2D 202
Carbery Gdns. Bourn 9H 229
Carbery La. Bourn. 1F 246
Carbery Row. Bourn 1F 246 (off Carbery La.)
Carbis Clo. Port S. 1B 214
Carbonel Clo. Bas 6J 41
Cardew Rd. Liss 2F 140
Cardiff Rd. Ports 6E 214
Cardigan Rd. Bourn 6K 227
Cardigan Rd. Poole 9D 226
Cardinal Dri. Water 9B 182
Cardinal M. And 1M 69
Cardinal Way. L Hth 6E 196
Cardington Ct. Sotn 7E 158
Carey Rd. Bourn 4K 227
Carey Rd. Sotn 5G 175
Careys Cotts. Broc 6C 148
Careys Rd. Bourn 2A 228
Carfax Av. Tong 2N 65
Cargate Av. A'sht 1J 65
Cargate Gro. A'sht 1J 65
Cargate Hill. A'sht 1H 65
Cargate Ter. A'sht 1H 65
Carisbrooke. Net A 2G 194
Carisbrooke Av. Fare 6K 211
Carisbrooke Clo. Alr 2F 108
Carisbrooke Clo. Bas 5L 41
Carisbrooke Clo. Hav 7H 203
Carisbrooke Ct. New M 3A 232
Carisbrooke Ct. Roms 3N 129
Carisbrooke Cres. Chan F 7C 132
Carisbrooke Dri. Sotn 4D 174
Carisbrooke Rd. Gos 5D 212
Carisbrooke Rd. S'sea 3H 241
Carisbrooke Way. Christ 5G 231
Carless Clo. Gos 9F 212
Carleton Clo. Hook 2F 44
Carlinford. Bourn 2C 246
Carlings. Alt 6E 80
Carlin Pl. Cam 9L 19
Carlisle Clo. Bas 5L 41
Carlisle Rd. Sotn 2G 172
Carlisle Rd. S'sea 2E 240
Carlisle Rd. Tilf 1K 85
Carlton Av. Bart S 6M 231
Carlton Commerce Cen., The. Sotn 3N 173
Carlton Ct. Sotn 2L 173
Carlton Cres. Chu C 5N 47
Carlton Cres. Sotn 4L 173 (1C 4)
Carlton Gro. Poole 9B 226
Carlton Ho. L'ton 2E 234
Carlton Mt. Bourn 2J 245 (8K 247)
Carlton Pl. Sotn 4L 173 (2C 4)
Carlton Rd. Bourn 1N 245
Carlton Rd. Fare 8M 199
Carlton Rd. Gos 2L 239
Carlton Rd. Head D 3E 102
Carlton Rd. Sotn 3L 173 (1C 4)
Carlton Way. Gos 2L 239
Carlyle Ct. C'then 1E 18
Carlyle Rd. Bourn 8G 228
Carlyle Rd. Gos 2K 239
Carlyn Dri. Chan F 5B 132
Carlyon Clo. Farn 8L 29
Carlyon Clo. Myt 8N 29
Carmans La. Comp 5H 127
Carmarthen Av. Ports 8J 201
Carmarthen Clo. Farn 5H 29
Carmichael Way. Bas 2L 59
Carmine Ct. Gos 1E 238
Carnarvon Rd. Bourn 1B 246
Carnarvon Rd. Gos 3J 239
Carnarvon Rd. Ports 8G 214
Carnation Rd. Sotn 6A 160
Carne Clo. Chan F 4A 132
Carnegie Clo. Poole 9B 226
Carne Pl. Port S 1B 214
Carnival Sq. Fle 2L 47
Caroline Av. Christ 8A 230
Caroline Ct. Sotn 2G 173
Caroline Gdns. Fare 7M 197
Caroline Ho. Ports 2K 5
Caroline Pl. Gos 1K 239
Caroline Rd. Bourn 3F 226
Carolyn Clo. Sotn 8C 174
Carpathia Clo. W End 9E 160
Carpenter Clo. Hythe 5M 193
Carpenter Clo. L'ton 1D 234
Carpenter Clo. S'sea 4H 241
Carpenter Rd. Bar S 4A 76 (off Thuillier Rd.)
Carpenters. Alr 1F 108
Carpenters Clo. Holyb 2K 81
Carpenters Clo. Sher L 3L 23
Carpenters Ct. Bas 9M 41
Carpenter's Down. Bas 2C 42
Carpenter Wlk. Black 6D 208
Carran Wlk. Fare 1A 212
Carrbridge Clo. Bourn 7H 227
Carrbridge Gdns. Bourn 7H 227
Carrbridge Rd. Bourn 7G 227
Carrick La. Yate 7A 18
Carrick Way. New M 4D 232
Carrington Cvn. Pk. Mil S 9M 235
Carrington Clo. Mil S 7L 235
Carrington Cres. T'ley 5H 11
Carrington Ho. Sotn 1M 173
Carrington La. Mil S 7L 235
Carrol Clo. F Oak 2A 162
Carroll Clo. Poole 8E 226
Carronades, The. Sotn 5M 173 (4E 4)
Carronade Wlk. Ports 3G 215
Carshalton Av. Ports 9J 201
Cartel Units. Bas 3F 42
Carter Ho. Gos 3D 212 (off Woodside)
Carter Ho. Ports 2B 240 (3K 5)
Carter's Clay 7B 122
Carter's Clay Rd. Lcky 7B 122
Carter's Clo. Hale 9C 120
Carter's La. March 4D 192
Carters Mdw. Charl 8K 51
Carters Wlk. F'ham 2F 64
Carthage Clo. Chan F 5D 132
Carthagena. Sut S 7D 76
Carthona Dri. Fle 4L 47
Cartwright Clo. Bourn 2G 226
Cartwright Dri. Fare 7H 197
Carvel La. Cowes 5P 237
Carvers Ind. Est. Ring 1J 187
Carvers La. Ring 1K 187
Carysfort Rd. Bourn 1A 246
Casbrook Common 6M 123
Cascades App. Ports 1D 240 (2N 5)
Cascades Cen. Ports 1D 240 (2N 5)
Cashmoor Pl. Poole 7D 226
Cask St. Ports 1N 5
Caslake Clo. New M 5A 232
Caspar John Clo. Fare 7L 211
Caspian Clo. White 2E 196
Cassel Av. Poole & Bourn 4F 244
Cassino Clo. A'sht 9K 49
Casterbridge La. W'hll 8D 50
Castle Av. Hav 8H 203
Castle Av. Highc 6G 231
Castle Av. Win 6K 105 (7L 237)
Castle Bottom Nature Reserve. 9J 17
Castle Clo. Cam 9N 19
Castle Clo. Cran 6J 149
Castle Clo. Mil S 9L 235
Castle Clo. S'sea 4D 240 (7N 5)
Castle Ct. F'ham 7D 64
Castle Ct. Lud 4K 31
Castle Ct. Sotn 4F 172
Castlecraig Ct. Coll T 6F 18
Castle Esplanade. S'sea 7D 240
Castle Farm La. Wick 8D 178
Castle Fld. F'ham 7D 64
Castle Ga. Clo. Bourn 4N 227
Castle Gro. Fare 1M 213
Castle Hill. Cowes 5P 237
Castle Hill. F'ham 7D 64
Castle Hill. Poole 1A 244
Castle Hill. Win 6K 105 (7L 237)
Castle Hill La. Burl 6C 188
Castle Hill La. Cran 7J 149
Castle La. Cals 9K 209
Castle La. Chan F 8M 131
Castle La. Hav 6K 183
Castle La. N Bad 8G 131
Castle La. Ows 7A 134
Castle La. Sotn 7L 173 (7C 4) (in two parts)
Castle La. E. Bourn 5D 228
Castle La. W. Bourn 2L 227
Castlemain Av. Bourn 9F 228
Castlemans La. Hay I 7G 216
Castleman Way. Ring 2K 187
Castle Marina. Lee S 3B 238
Castle Mdw. D'ton 2K 119
Castle M. Ring 3F 186
Castle Pde. Bourn 7G 228
Castlepoint Cen. Bourn 4B 228
Castle Ri. King W 6N 91
Castle Ri. N War 7J 45
Castle Rd. A'sht 7G 48
Castle Rd. Bas 8C 42
Castle Rd. Bourn 5K 227
Castle Rd. Cam 9N 19
Castle Rd. Cowes 5P 237
Castle Rd. Net A 3F 194
Castle Rd. Row C 8G 183
Castle Rd. Sotn 9C 160
Castle Rd. S'sea 4C 240 (8M 5)
Castle Rd. S'wick 3A 200
Castleshaw Clo. Sotn 3E 172
Castle Sq. Bas 6C 42
Castle Sq. Sotn 7L 173 (7C 4)
Castle St. Christ 8L 229
Castle St. Cran 6J 149
Castle St. F'ham 7D 64
Castle St. Fle 4L 47
Castle St. Lud 4K 31
Castle St. Meds 9K 79
Castle St. Portc 9M 199
Castle St. Sotn 3M 173 (1E 4)
Castle St. Titch 9K 197
Castleton Ct. S'sea 8M 5
Castle Trad. Est. Fare 9N 199 & 1A 214
Castle Vw. Gos 8K 213
Castle Vw. Rd. Fare 2M 213
Castleway. Hav 8H 203
Castle Way. Sotn 6L 173 (6C 4)
Castlewood. Ring 3G 186
Castlewood La. Chan F 8N 131
Castle Woods. Redl 2M 119
Caston's Wlk. Bas 7C 42
Caston's Yd. Bas 7C 42
Castor Ct. Chu C 6N 47
Castor Ct. Yate 6L 17
Caswall Ride. Yate 8A 18
Caswell Clo. Farn 6H 29
Catalina Clo. Christ 8C 230
Catamaran Clo. Wars 8C 196
Cateran Clo. Sotn 2E 172
Catesby Gdns. Yate 8K 17
Cathay Gdns. Dib 6H 193
Cathedral Ho. Ports 7J 5
Cathedral Vw. Win 8M 105
Catherine Clo. W End 9J 161
Catherine Cres. D'ton 2H 119
Catherine Gdns. W End 9J 161
Catherington 9B 168
Catherington Down Nature Reserve. 1A 182
Catherington Hill. Cath 8B 168
Catherington La. Water 2A 182
Catherington Way. Hav 5F 202
Catisfield 8L 197
Catisfield Ho. Ports 1E 240 (off Lake Rd.)
Catisfield La. Fare 8L 197
Catisfield Rd. Fare 8M 197
Catisfield Rd. S'sea 2J 241
Catkin Clo. Chine 9G 23
Catmint Clo. Chan F 5L 131
Caton Clo. Poole 6F 226
Cattistock Rd. Bourn 4B 228
Cattle La. Abb A 3E 68
Causeway 2L 145
Causeway. Roms 6K 129
Causeway Cotts. H Win 6D 26
Causeway Cres. Tot 2N 171
Causeway Farm. Water 4B 182
Causeway, The. Bro Ch 3A 118
Causeway, The. Fare 8G 198
Causeway, The. Heck 5F 14
Causeway, The. Ptsfld 4K 145
Causeway, The. W'slw 4H 87
Cavalier Clo. Dib 6J 193
Cavalier Clo. Old B 5K 43
Cavalier Rd. Old B 5K 43
Cavalier Way. Alt 6D 80
Cavalry Ct. A'sht 9G 49
Cavanna Clo. Gos 5D 212
Cavan's Rd. A'sht 5L 49
Cavel Ct. Bas 3H 43
Cavell Dri. Ports 8F 200
Cavendish Clo. Roms 2A 130
Cavendish Clo. Water 1N 201
Cavendish Corner Mobile Home Pk. Ring 9L 185
Cavendish Ct. B'wtr 1F 28
Cavendish Dri. Water 2N 201
Cavendish Gdns. Chu C 6K 47
Cavendish Gro. Sotn 2L 173
Cavendish Gro. Win 3M 105
Cavendish M. A'sht 1J 65
Cavendish M. Sotn 2L 173
Cavendish Pk. Cvn. Site. S'hrst 7G 19
Cavendish Pl. Bourn 9L 227
Cavendish Rd. A'sht 1J 65
Cavendish Rd. Bourn 9K 227
Cavendish Rd. Chu C 7L 47
Cavendish Rd. S'sea 4E 240
C Avenue. Hythe 2A 208
Caversham Clo. Sotn 6E 174
Caversham Clo. W End 2H 175
Caves Farm Clo. S'hrst 5C 18
Cawdor Rd. Bourn 7H 227
Cawte Rd. Sotn 4H 173
Cawte's Pl. Fare 8E 198
Caxton Av. Sotn 4F 174
Caxton Clo. And 9J 51
Caxton Clo. Christ 7B 230
Cayman Clo. Bas 2E 42
Cecil Av. A'sht 8J 171
Cecil Av. Bourn 7M 227
Cecil Av. Sotn 1G 172
Cecil Ct. Bourn 6M 227
Cecil Ct. Cran 6J 149 (off Water St.)
Cecil Gro. S'sea 4C 240 (8M 5)
Cecil Hill. Bourn 6M 227
Cecil Pl. S'sea 4C 240 (8M 5)
Cecil Rd. Bourn 1B 246
Cecil Rd. Poole 8B 226
Cecil Rd. Sotn 7D 174
Cedar Av. B'wtr 8F 18
Cedar Av. Bourn 1H 227
Cedar Av. Christ 6G 228
Cedar Av. St L 5B 186
Cedar Av. Sotn 2H 173
Cedar Clo. A'sht 2N 65
Cedar Clo. Burs 1K 195
Cedar Clo. Gos 7J 213
Cedar Clo. H End 3N 175
Cedar Clo. King W 7M 91
Cedar Clo. T'ley 7K 11
Cedar Clo. Water 3M 201
Cedar Ct. Fare 8E 198
Cedar Ct. S'sea 4E 240
Cedar Cres. Horn 5C 182
Cedar Cres. N Bad 7E 130
Cedar Dri. Evtn 6L 233
Cedar Dri. Fle 2A 48
Cedar Dri. K're 2A 6
Cedar Gdns. Hav 7G 202
Cedar Gdns. New M 5N 231
Cedar Gdns. Sotn 2M 173
Cedar Grange. Poole 1E 244
Cedar Gro. Ports 9J 215
Cedar La. Frim 4M 29
Cedar Lawn. Roms 3B 130
Cedar Mnr. Bourn 2G 245
Cedarmount. Lyn 3B 148
Cedar Pl. Brans 6D 220
Cedar Rd. Eastl 2C 160
Cedar Rd. Farn 9L 29
Cedar Rd. Hythe 9M 193
Cedar Rd. Sotn 2M 173
Cedars Clo. S'hrst 5B 18
Cedars, The. Bourn 1G 245
Cedars, The. Fare 5B 198
Cedars, The. Fle 3N 47
Cedars Vw. E Tyth 8N 87
Cedar Ter. H Win 7A 26
Cedar Tree Clo. Okly 2C 58
Cedar Wlk. And 2K 69
Cedar Wlk. Win 7J 105 (8J 237)
Cedar Way. Bas 4M 41
Cedar Way. Fare 9A 198
Cedarwood. Chine 9E 22
Cedarwood. King W 8N 91
Cedarwood Clo. Cal 2J 171
Cedarwood Clo. F Oak 1B 162
Cedarwood Lodge. Fare 7D 198 (off Northwood Sq.)
Cedric Clo. Black 8D 208
Celandine Av. L Hth 7C 196
Celandine Av. Water 7B 182
Celandine Clo. Chan F 7L 131
Celandine Clo. Christ 6D 230
Celandine Ct. Yate 6K 17
Celia Clo. Water 1B 202
Cellar La. Langr 1A 144
Cellars Farm Rd. Bourn 2K 247
Celtic Dri. And 3L 69
Cement Ter. Sotn 7L 173 (7C 4)
Cemetery Hill. Odi 9L 45
Cemetery La. Water 5G 181
Cemetery Rd. Fle 4K 47
Cemetery Rd. Sotn 2K 173
Centaur St. Ports 8E 214
Centaury Gdns. H Hth 4N 161
Centenary Clo. Sway 5K 223
Centenary Ho. Christ 7L 229
Centenary Way. Bourn 9B 228
Central Av. Poole 8C 226
Central Bri. Sotn 7N 173 (7F 4)
Central Dri. Bourn (BH2) 1J 245 (5K 247)
Central Dri. Bourn (BH7) 8C 228
Central Precinct, The. Chan F 6B 132
Central Rd. Bord 1J 101
Central Rd. Fare 1K 213
Central Rd. Ports 1K 215
Central Rd. Sotn 8M 173 (9E 4)
Central Sta. Bri. Sotn 5K 173 (4A 4)
Central St. Lud 1D 30
Central St. Ports 1E 240
Central Trad. Est. Sotn 6N 173 (5G 4)
Central Way. And 9D 52
Central Way N. Fawl 6J 209
Centre Ct. Sotn 2G 172
Centre Dri. Chine 2G 43
Centre La. Evtn 5M 233
Centre Pl. Ring 1J 187
Centre 27 Retail Pk. H End 1L 175
Centre Way. L Hth 6C 196
Centurion Clo. Coll T 5F 18
Centurion Ind. Pk. Sotn 3A 174
Centurion Way. Bas 3K 59 (in two parts)
Cerdic M. Hamb 5L 195
Cerne Abbas. Poole 4E 244
Cerne Clo. Bourn 2M 227
Cerne Clo. N Bad 8E 130
Cerne Clo. W End 1F 174
Cessac Ho. Gos 6L 239
Chadderton Gdns. Ports 4C 240 (7L 5)
Chaddesley Glen. Poole 7B 244
Chaddesley Pines. Poole 7C 244
Chaddesley Wood Rd. Poole 8C 244
Chadswell Mdw. Hav 8D 202
Chadwell Av. Sotn 6F 174
Chadwick Rd. Eastl 1D 160
Chafen Rd. Sotn 2B 174
Chaffers Clo. Long S 5E 62
Chaffey Clo. Ring 9M 185
Chaffinch Clo. Bas 2J 59
Chaffinch Clo. Coll T 5F 18
Chaffinch Clo. New M 4A 232
Chaffinch Clo. Tot 2J 171
Chaffinch Grn. Water 6M 181
Chaffinch Way. Fare 9H 199
Chaffinch Way. Lee S 9B 212
Chalcraft Clo. Lip 2C 116
Chalcrafts. Alt 3G 81
Chalcroft Distribution Pk. W End 6M 161
Chaldecott Gdns. Bourn 2G 226
Chaldon Grn. Lych 3H 43
Chale Clo. Gos 6E 212
Chalet Ct. Bord 4J 101 (off Chalet Hill)
Chalet Hill. Bord 4J 101
Chalewood Rd. Black 9C 208
Chalfont Av. Christ 3G 229
Chalfont Ct. Sotn 1F 172
Chalfont Dri. Farn 1L 49
Chalice Ct. H End 4L 175
Chalk Clo. Four M 5J 97
Chalkcroft La. Pen M 7G 50
Chalk Hill. Lit Som 5J 89
Chalk Hill. Sob 6L 165
Chalk Hill. W End 2G 174
Chalk Hill Rd. Water 2C 182
Chalk La. Fare (PO15) 8L 197
Chalk La. Fare (PO17) 2D 198
Chalkpit La. Monx 4D 68
Chalk Pit La. W Tyth 7L 87
Chalk Pit Rd. Ports 8C 200
Chalk Pyt Rd. Bro Ch 3A 118
Chalk Ridge. Cath 8D 168
Chalk Ridge. Win 7N 105
Chalkridge Rd. Ports 8H 201
Chalk's Clo. Redl 1M 119
Chalk Va. King S & Spar 6H 89
Chalk Va. Old B 6K 43
Chalky Copse. Hook 1G 44
Chalky La. Bish W 3N 163
Chalky La. Dogm 9D 46
Chalky Wlk. Fare 1L 213
Challenge Enterprise Cen., The. Ports 5J 215
Challenger Dri. Gos 9L 213
Challenger Way. Dib 5J 193
Challis Clo. Bas 9L 41
Challis Ct. Lud 1E 30
Challis Ct. Sotn 7M 173 (7E 4)
Challoner Clo. Bas 8L 41
Chalmers Way. Hamb 6J 195
Chaloner Cres. Dib P 8M 193
Chalton 7J 169
Chalton Cres. Hav 4D 202
Chalton Ho. Ports 1D 240
Chalton La. Water 5B 168 (in two parts)
Chalvington Rd. Chan F 7A 132
Chalybeate Clo. Sotn 9G 159
Chamberlain Gro. Fare 9C 198
Chamberlain Rd. Sotn 8M 159
Chamberlains Mdw. Heck 7H 15
Chamber La. F'ham 6N 63

Chamberlayne Ct. N Bad 7G 130
Chamberlayne Leisure Cen. 9E 174
Chamberlayne Rd. Burs 1K 195
Chamberlayne Rd. Eastl 2E 160
Chamberlayne Rd. Net A 3F 194
Chambers Av. Roms 5A 130
Chambers Clo. Nurs 6B 158
Chamomile Gdns. Farn 7E 28
Champion Clo. Mil S 8M 235
Champion Way. Chu C 6M 47
Champney Clo. W'hill 6H 101 (in two parts)
Chancellors La. Durl 7B 162
Chancel Rd. L Hth 6E 196
Chanctonbury Ho. S'sea 4D 240
Chandler Rd. Bas 9B 42
Chandlers Clo. Bourn 6E 228
Chandlers Clo. Hay I 5J 243
Chandler's Ford 7A 132
Chandlers Ford Ind. Est. Chan F 7N 131
Chandler's Green 2D 24
Chandler's Grn. Matt 2D 24
Chandlers La. Yate 6M 17
Chandlers Way. Park G 3E 196
Chandos Av. Poole 6E 226
Chandos Ho. Sotn 7M 173 (7D 4)
Chandos St. Sotn 7M 173 (7E 4)
Channel Ct. New M 7N 231
Channel Mouth Rd. Fawl 7K 209
Channels Farm Rd. Sotn 6B 160
Channel Way. Ocn V 7N 173
Chant Clo. Christ 7N 229
Chant Clo. Wher 2E 74
Chantrell Wlk. Fare 6N 197
Chantreys. Fle 3J 47
Chantry Cen., The. And 1N 69
Chantry Clo. Highc 5H 231
Chantry Clo. Hook 3G 45
Chantry Ct. Frim 3M 29 (off Church Rd.)
Chantry La. Up Ch 1M 31
Chantry M. Bas 3K 59
Chantry Rd. Gos 9H 213
Chantry Rd. Sotn 7N 173 (7G 4)
Chantry Rd. Water 2B 182
Chantrys Ct. F'ham 8C 64 (off Chantrys, The)
Chantrys, The. F'ham 8B 64
Chantry St. And 1N 69
Chantry, The. Bourn 1L 245 (5N 247)
Chantry, The. Fare 6F 196
Chapel Av. Mich 7K 77
Chapel Clo. A'prt 3B 68
Chapel Clo. Brfld 7B 124
Chapel Clo. Dum 9F 58
Chapel Clo. Houtn 6E 88 (off Horsebridge Rd.)
Chapel Clo. Old B 4J 43
Chapel Clo. W End 9H 161
Chapel Ct. Bro'tn 1A 86
Chapel Ct. Wher 2F 74
Chapel Cres. Sotn 6E 174
Chapel Drove. H End 4M 175 (in two parts)
Chapel Drove. H Hth 4N 161
Chapel Gdns. Lind 2L 101
Chapel Hill. Bas 5B 42
Chapel Hill. W Gri 2D 120
Chapel La. Ash H 2N 9
Chapel La. B'stne 3C 118
Chapel La. Black 8C 208
Chapel La. Brans 7C 220
Chapel La. Bro'tn 1A 86
Chapel La. Burl 7E 188
Chapel La. Charl A 4A 120
Chapel La. Curd 1H 177
Chapel La. E Bol 1B 236
Chapel La. Estn & Win 2D 106
Chapel La. Enh A 4A 52
Chapel La. Farn & B'wtr 4H 29
Chapel La. Fawl 5E 208
Chapel La. Grat 5L 67
Chapel La. Lud 1C 30
Chapel La. Lyn 2A 148
Chapel La. Nom 2J 155
Chapel La. Ott 3F 132
Chapel La. Pad C 1M 11
Chapel La. Redl 2N 119
Chapel La. Rise 2G 14
Chapel La. Stoke 7H 35
Chapel La. Sway 6L 223
Chapel La. Tims 5K 123
Chapel La. Lcky 4N 121
Chapel La. Tot 5L 171
Chapel La. Water 2M 201
Chapel La. Wolv 5N 9 (off Woolverton Rd.)
Chapel La. Wolv C 9A 10
Chapel Mead. E'sly 5H 17
Chapel Pond Dri. N War 8J 45
Chapel Ri. Ring 6G 186
Chapelriver Clo. And 2L 69
Chapel Rd. Cam 8K 19
Chapel Rd. Meon 9N 135
Chapel Rd. Sar G 3B 196
Chapel Rd. Sob 9K 165
Chapel Rd. Sotn 6N 173 (6F 4)
Chapel Rd. Swanm 6D 164
Chapel Rd. W End 9H 161
Chapel Row. H Win 5C 26 (in two parts)
Chapelside. Fare 9K 197
Chapel Sq. Coll T 7H 19
Chapel Sq. Gos 9H 213
Chapel St. E Meon 3L 143
Chapel St. Farn 6M 29
Chapel St. Gos 8K 213
Chapel St. N Wal 9A 58
Chapel St. Ptsfld 9M 139
Chapel St. Ports 8F 214
Chapel St. Sotn 6M 173 (6E 4)
Chapel St. S'sea 4D 240 (7M 5)
Chaplains Av. Water 7L 181
Chaplains Clo. Water 7L 181
Chaplain's Hill. C'then 1F 18
Chappell Clo. Lip 2E 116
Chapter Ter. H Win 5C 26
Charden Ct. Sotn 3F 174
Charden Rd. Eastl 1L 161
Charden Rd. Gos 8F 212
Charfield Clo. Fare 9N 197
Charfield Clo. Win 9J 105
Charing Clo. Ring 2K 187
Charing Cross 5B 152
Chark La. Lee S 8B 212
Charlcot Clo. Whitc 7G 55
Charlcot Farm. Whitc 7G 55
Charlcott Lawn. Hav 3D 202
Charlecote Clo. Farn 9M 29
Charlecote Dri. Chan F 4M 131
Charlecote Ho. Sotn 5J 173 (off Millbrook Rd. E.)
Charledown Clo. Over 3D 56
Charledown Rd. Over 3D 56
Charlemont Dri. Fare 8F 198
Charlesbury Av. Gos 3H 239
Charles Clark Ho. S'sea 3H 241
Charles Clo. Hook 2G 45
Charles Clo. Water 3L 201
Charles Clo. Win 4M 105
Charles Cres. New M 1C 232
Charles Dalton Ct. And 2N 69
Charles Dickens Birthplace Mus. 9D 214
Charles Dickens St. Ports 2D 240 (4N 5)
Charles Gdns. Bourn 4G 227
Charles Knott Gdns. Sotn 3L 173
Charles La. Crow 8A 188
Charles Ley Ct. Fawl 5F 208
Charles Norton-Thomas Ct. Ports 2C 240 (4K 5) (off St George's Way)
Charles Richards Clo. Bas 8B 42
Charles Rd. Christ 6B 230
Charles St. Bas 7M 41
Charles St. Ptsfld 1L 145
Charles St. Ports 1E 240
Charles St. Sotn 7M 173 (7E 4)
Charleston Clo. Hay I 3E 242
Charleston Rd. Hythe 9B 194
Charles Watts Way. H End 3J 175
Charlesworth Dri. Water 8L 181
Charlesworth Gdns. Water 9L 181
Charles Wyatt Ho. Sotn 3M 173
Charleton-All-Saints 4A 120
Charliejoy Gdns. Sotn 4N 173
Charlotte Clo. And 1C 70
Charlotte Clo. Christ 8C 230
Charlotte Clo. F'ham 2F 64
Charlotte Clo. Poole 6G 226
Charlotte Ct. Chan F 5C 132
Charlotte Ct. New M 4B 232
Charlotte Ct. Sotn 8D 174
Charlotte Ct. S'sea 4D 240 (8N 5)
Charlotte M. Gos 5J 239
Charlotte M. Win 7L 237
Charlotte Pl. Sotn 4M 173 (2D 4)
Charlotte St. Ports 1D 240 (2N 5)
Charlton 7L 51
Charlton Clo. Bourn 2N 227
Charlton Clo. Hord 3G 233
Charlton Ct. Owl 4F 18
Charlton Rd. And 8L 51
Charlton Rd. Sotn 2J 173
Charlton Roundabout. And 8L 51
Charltons, The. Bourn 9K 227
Charlwood 2K 111
Charlwood La. Mnkwd 1L 111
Charminster 5M 227
Charminster. S'sea 5F 240 (off Craneswater Pk.)
Charminster Av. Bourn 5M 227
Charminster Clo. Bourn 4M 227
Charminster Clo. Water 1M 201
Charminster Pl. Bourn 4M 227
Charminster Rd. Bourn 8L 227
Charmus Rd. Cal 9H 157
Charmwen Cres. W End 9G 160
Charnock Clo. Hord 3G 233
Charnwood. Gos 6F 212
Charnwood Av. Bourn 3M 227
Charnwood Clo. And 3A 70
Charnwood Clo. Bas 8K 41
Charnwood Clo. Chan F 2A 132
Charnwood Clo. Tot 1K 171
Charnwood Cres. Chan F 2A 132
Charnwood Dri. F'bri 8H 151
Charnwood Gdns. Chan F 2A 132
Charnwood Ho. Bourn 2J 247
Charnwood Way. Black 9C 208
Charter Alley 4H 21
Charter Ho. S'sea 5M 5
Charterhouse Way. H End 1N 175
Charter Rd. Bourn 1B 226
Chartwell. Frim G 7N 29
Chartwell. Poole 2F 244
Chartwell Clo. Eastl 6F 132
Chartwell Clo. Fare 8F 196
Chartwell Dri. Hav 6J 203
Chartwell Gdns. A'sht 4L 49
Chase Bird Sanctuary, The. 2B 8
Chase Clo. Liss 1F 140
Chase Cotts. Gray 6L 103
Chase Farm Clo. Wal C 8A 164
Chase Fld. Lwr F 4D 98
Chase Gro. Wal C 8A 164
Chase N.T. Area, The. 2B 8
Chase Rd. Lind 3K 101
Chase Rd. Liss 1F 140
Chaseside. Bourn 6D 228
Chase, The. Fare 7G 196
Chase, The. Farn 6M 29
Chase, The. Gos 3H 239
Chase, The. Ring 3G 186
Chase, The. Ver 4A 184
Chase Vw. Lwr F 4D 98
Chasewater Av. Ports 9H 215
Chasewater Ct. A'sht 1J 65
Chatburn Av. Water 7M 181
Chatfield Av. Ports 7B 214
Chatfield Clo. Farn 1L 49
Chatfield Ho. Ports 1E 240 (off Fyning St.)
Chatfield Rd. Gos 4E 212
Chatham Clo. Gos 9L 213
Chatham Dri. Ports 4C 240 (8L 5)
Chatham Rd. Win 9G 105
Chatsworth Av. Ports 2G 215
Chatsworth Clo. Fare 8M 197
Chatsworth Ct. S'sea 4E 240
Chatsworth Dri. And 2L 69
Chatsworth Grn. Hat W 4L 59
Chatsworth Gro. F'ham 4D 64
Chatsworth Rd. Bourn 8M 227
Chatsworth Rd. Eastl 6F 132
Chatsworth Rd. Farn 9N 29
Chatsworth Rd. Sotn 4E 174
Chatsworth Way. New M 3N 231
Chatter Alley 4F 46
Chatter All. Dogm 3E 46
Chatter La. Whitc 5G 55
Chattis Hill Stables. Chat 2C 88
Chaucer Av. And 9K 51
Chaucer Av. Ports 8N 199
Chaucer Clo. Bas 2D 42
Chaucer Clo. Fare 7B 198
Chaucer Clo. S Won 2J 91
Chaucer Clo. Water 8M 181
Chaucer Dri. Mil S 7K 235
Chaucer Gro. Cam 8M 19
Chaucer Ho. Ports 2D 240 (4N 5)
Chaucer Rd. C'then 2D 18
Chaucer Rd. Farn 6H 29
Chaucer Rd. Poole 5D 244
Chaucer Rd. Sotn 4H 175
Chaundler Rd. Win 4L 105
Chaundlers Cft. Cron 3L 63
Chauntsingers Rd. Alt 4F 80
Chaveney Clo. Dib P 8L 193
Chawton 8D 80
Chawton Clo. Elve 9H 27
Chawton Clo. Sotn 2H 175
Chawton Clo. Win 2H 105
Chawton End Clo. Four M 3K 97
Chawton Pk. Rd. Chaw & Alt 8B 80
Cheam Way. Tot 1K 171
Cheater's La. Bull H 6P 149
Cheavley Clo. And 1J 69
Cheddar Clo. Sotn 7C 174
Cheddington Rd. Bourn 2L 227
Chedworth Cres. Ports 8B 200
Cheeryble Ho. Ports 9E 214
Chelmer Ct. Bas 6E 42 (off Loddon Dri.)
Chelmsford Rd. Ports 6G 214
Chelsea Ho. Bas 6C 42
Chelsea Rd. S'sea 4E 240
Cheltenham Cres. Lee S 9B 212
Cheltenham Gdns. H End 8N 161
Cheltenham Rd. Poole 9A 226
Cheltenham Rd. Ports 9D 200
Chelveston Cres. Sotn 7F 158
Chelwood Dri. S'hrst 4B 18
Chelwood Ga. Sotn 6L 159
Cheping Gdns. Bot 4D 176
Chepstow Clo. Chan F 6N 131
Chepstow Clo. Tot 2J 171
Chepstow Ct. Water 9B 182
Chequer La. Str S 3B 14
Chequers Clo. Penn 3B 234
Chequers La. E'sly 7H 17
Chequers Rd. Bas 6D 42
Cherberry Clo. Fle 8N 27
Cherbourg Rd. Eastl 2D 160
Cherford Rd. Bourn 4F 226
Cheriton 8E 108
Cheriton Av. Bourn 6F 228
Cheriton Av. Sotn 3G 175
Cheriton Battle Site (1644). 7H 109
Cheriton Clo. Hav 4D 202
Cheriton Clo. T'ley 6H 11
Cheriton Clo. Water 3B 182
Cheriton Clo. Win 5H 105
Cheriton La. Bish S 5H 109
Cheriton La. Cher 9H 109
Cheriton Rd. Eastl 2D 160
Cheriton Rd. Gos 3H 239
Cheriton Rd. Win 5H 105
Cheriton Way. B'wtr 8F 18
Cherque La. Lee S 8C 212
Cherrett Clo. Bourn 2D 226
Cherries Dri. Bourn 4J 227
Cherrimans Orchard. Hasl 9N 103
Cherry Blossom Ct. Ports 9E 214
Cherry Clo. Hook 1H 45
Cherry Clo. Lee S 2C 238
Cherry Clo. S Won 3H 91
Cherry Drove. H Hth 5N 161
Cherry Gdns. Bish W 4N 163
Cherrygarth Rd. Fare 8M 197
Cherryhill Gro. A'sht 1H 65
Cherry Lodge. A'sht 1K 65
Cherryton Gdns. Holb 5N 207
Cherry Tree Av. Fare 9N 197
Cherry Tree Av. Hasl 8N 103
Cherry Tree Av. Tidw 7E 30
Cherry Tree Av. Water 7B 182
Cherry Tree Clo. Evtn 6L 233
Cherry Tree Clo. Farn 7E 28
Cherry Tree Clo. F'ham 7E 64
Cherry Tree Clo. Owl 4F 18
Cherry Tree Clo. St L 5A 186
Cherry Tree Ct. New M 5C 232
Cherry Tree Ct. Wars 8N 195
Cherry Tree Dri. New M 1N 231
Cherry Tree Rd. And 9L 51
Cherry Tree Rd. Row 8N 63
Cherry Tree Wlk. Bourn 3H 245 (9G 247)
Cherry Wlk. Mid W 4B 72 (off Willow Way)
Cherry Wlk. Sotn 2H 173
Cherry Wlk. Wars 9N 195
Cherry Way. Alt 3E 80
Cherrywood. Chine 9F 22
Cherrywood. H End 4M 175
Cherrywood Gdns. Hay I 3G 242
Cherrywood Gdns. Tot 3J 171
Cherrywood Rd. Farn 5J 29
Chervil Clo. Water 1C 182
Cherville Ct. Roms 5L 129
Cherville St. Roms 5L 129
Cherwell Cres. Sotn 2D 172
Cherwell Gdns. Chan F 7B 132
Cherwell Ho. Sotn 1D 172
Cheshire Clo. White 4J 197
Cheshire Dri. Bourn 5D 228
Chesildene Av. Bourn 3A 228 (in two parts)
Chesildene Dri. Bourn 3N 227
Chesil St. Win 7M 105 (9P 237)
Chesil Ter. Win 7M 105 (9P 237)
Chesilton Cres. Chu C 6M 47
Cheslyn Rd. Ports 1J 241
Chessel Av. Bourn 9C 228
Chessel Av. Sotn 3C 174
Chessel Cres. Sotn 3C 174
Chester Courts. Gos 3L 239
Chester Cres. Lee S 3D 238
Chesterfield Clo. Ame 5A 66
Chesterfield Clo. Poole 5D 244
Chesterfield Ct. Bourn 2N 245
Chesterfield Rd. Bas 8D 42
Chesterfield Rd. Ports 8H 215
Chester Pl. Bas 7B 42
Chester Pl. S'sea 5E 240
Chester Rd. Poole 3E 244
Chester Rd. Sotn 1E 174
Chester Rd. Win 6M 105 (7P 237)
Chesterton Gdns. Water 7M 181
Chesterton Pl. White 1F 196
Chester Way. Tong 4N 65
Chestnut Av. A'sht 3N 65
Chestnut Av. And 4M 69
Chestnut Av. Asht 7J 171
Chestnut Av. Bart S 6B 232
Chestnut Av. Blash 3E 184
Chestnut Av. Bourn 1F 246
Chestnut Av. Chan F & Eastl 9A 132
Chestnut Av. Christ 6G 229
Chestnut Av. Col C 3K 133
Chestnut Av. Hav 6B 202
Chestnut Av. S'sea 3G 240
Chestnut Av. Tidw 7D 30
Chestnut Av. Water 5C 182
Chestnut Av. Win 2F 104
Chestnut Bank. Old B 4J 43
Chestnut Clo. Alt 3E 80
Chestnut Clo. B'wtr 9G 18
Chestnut Clo. Chan F 9A 132
Chestnut Clo. Fle 8A 28
Chestnut Clo. Gray 4L 103
Chestnut Clo. Lip 3F 116
Chestnut Clo. Roms 6C 130
Chestnut Clo. Water 6G 181
Chestnut Clo. W End 8H 161
Chestnut Ct. A'sht 9M 49
Chestnut Ct. Bord 5K 101
Chestnut Ct. Row C 1H 203
Chestnut Cres. Mid W 4B 72
Chestnut Dri. Asht 7J 171
Chestnut Dri. Ptsfld 3M 145
Chestnut End. Head 3C 102
Chestnut Gro. Fle 1N 47
Chestnut Lodge. Sotn 8K 159
Chestnut Mead. Win 9K 105
Chestnut Ri. Drox 2K 165
Chestnut Ri. Eastl 2B 160
Chestnut Rd. Broc 7D 148
Chestnut Rd. Farn 7J 29
Chestnut Rd. Sotn 9F 158
Chestnuts, The. L Hth 7D 196
Chestnut Wlk. Alr 1F 108
Chestnut Wlk. Bot 3C 176
Chestnut Wlk. Gos 7J 213
Chestnut Way. Burt 3M 229
Chestnut Way. Fare 8F 196
Cheswell Gdns. Chu C 5K 47
Chettle Rd. Sotn 5J 175
Chetwode Pl. A'sht 3L 65
Chetwode Ter. A'sht 1G 64
Chetwynd Dri. Sotn 7L 159
Chetwynd Rd. Sotn 7L 159
Chetwynd Rd. S'sea 4F 240
Chevening Ct. S'sea 2J 241
Cheviot Clo. Bas 8K 41
Cheviot Clo. Farn 5G 29
Cheviot Clo. N'bry 1C 8
Cheviot Ct. Flats. Christ 6A 230
Cheviot Cres. Sotn 2D 172
Cheviot Dri. Dib 6J 193
Cheviot Dri. Fle 8N 27
Cheviot Grn. Wars 9A 196
Cheviot Rd. S'hrst 4B 18
Cheviot Rd. Sotn 2D 172
Cheviots, The. Poole 2A 244
Cheviot Wlk. Fare 1B 212
Chevron Bus. Pk. Holb 2N 207
Chewter Clo. S'sea 6F 240
Chewton Comn. Rd. Highc 5J 231

Chewton Farm Est. Christ 6L 231
Chewton Farm Rd. Walk 5L 231
Chewton Lodge. Highc 6K 231
Chewton Way. Walk 5K 231
Cheyne Ct. Win 9M 237
Cheyne Gdns. Bourn 3G 245
Cheyne Way. Farn 5H 29
Cheyne Way. Lee S 2B 238
Chichester Av. Hay I 5F 242
Chichester Clo. And 1K 69
Chichester Clo. E Wel 1B 156
Chichester Clo. Gos 6D 212
Chichester Clo. H End 1N 175
Chichester Clo. Sar G 6B 196
Chichester Ho. Hav 6G 202
Chichester Pl. Bas 9N 41
Chichester Rd. Hay I 7J 217
Chichester Rd. Ports 8E 214
Chichester Rd. Ring 8M 185
Chichester Rd. Sotn 3E 174
Chichester Way. Christ 9C 230
Chickenhall La. Eastl 9G 132
Chickerell Clo. Bourn 2M 227
Chicks La. Coll D 2G 31
Chidden 3G 166
Chidden Clo. E Meon 3L 143
Chidden Holt. Chan F 7M 131
Chideock Clo. Poole 8C 226
Chideock Ct. Poole 8C 226
Chidham Clo. Hav 7E 202
Chidham Dri. Hav 7E 202
Chidham Rd. Ports 8H 201
Chidham Sq. Hav 7E 202
Chidham Wlk. Hav 7E 202
Chigwell Rd. Bourn 5M 227
Chilbolton 4F 74
Chilbolton Av. Win 6H 105
Chilbolton Ct. Hav 3H 203
Chilbolton Ct. Win 7G 105
Chilcomb 1B 134
Chilcomb Clo. Lee S 1B 238
Chilcombe Clo. Hav 6F 202
Chilcombe Heights. Win 7M 105 (off Quarry Rd.)
Chilcombe Rd. Bourn 9E 228
Chilcomb La. Win & Chilc 9M 105 (in two parts)
Chilcomb Rd. Sotn 2G 174
Chilcote Rd. Ports 9H 215
Childerstone Clo. Lip 2D 116
Childe Sq. Ports 6D 214
Chilgrove Rd. Ports 9K 201
Chilham Clo. Eastl 5E 132
Chillandham La. It Ab 2F 92 (in two parts)
Chilland La. Mart W 9F 92
Chillenden Ct. Tot 4J 171
Chillerton. Net A 2G 195
Chillingham Way. Cam 9L 19
Chilling La. Wars 3B 210
Chillington Gdns. Chan F 3N 131
Chilmark Ct. Liss 1E 140
Chilsdown Way. Water 5M 201
Chiltern Av. Farn 8F 28
Chiltern Clo. Bart S 5A 232
Chiltern Clo. Bourn 9F 226
Chiltern Clo. Chu C 5N 47
Chiltern Clo. Farn 8E 28
Chiltern Clo. N'bry 1C 8
Chiltern Clo. Tot 5K 171
Chiltern Ct. Alr 1F 108
Chiltern Ct. Gos 2K 239
Chiltern Dri. Bart S 6N 231
Chiltern Grn. Sotn 2D 172
Chiltern Rd. S'hrst 4B 18
Chiltern Wlk. Fare 1B 212
Chiltern Way. Bas 8J 41
Chiltlee Clo. Lip 2E 116
Chiltlee Ct. Lip 2E 116
Chiltlee Mnr. Lip 3E 116
Chiltley La. Lip 4F 116
Chiltley Way. Lip 3E 116
Chilton Candover 6D 78
Chilton Farm Pk. Farn 8E 28
Chilton Ridge. Hat W 5K 59
Chilworth Clo. Chilw 2J 159
Chilworth Drove. Chilw 5G 159 (in two parts)
Chilworth Drove. Sotn 6G 158
Chilworth Gdns. Water 7C 168
Chilworth Golf Course 9G 131
Chilworth Gro. Gos 2J 239
Chilworth Rd. Chilw 2K 159
Chine Av. Sotn 5C 174 (in two parts)
Chine Clo. L Hth 5D 196
Chine Cres. Bourn 3H 245 (8H 247)
Chine Cres. Rd. Bourn 3H 245 (9G 247)
Chineham 1G 43
Chineham Bus. Pk. Chine 8F 22
Chineham Clo. Elve 9J 27
Chineham District Cen. Chine 2G 42
Chineham La. Bas 3D 42
Chineham La. Sher 1A 42
Chineham Pk. Ct. Bas 3E 42
Chine, The. Gos 7G 212
Chingford Av. Farn 7L 29
Chinham Rd. Bart 4B 170
Chinnock Clo. Fle 4L 47
Chippendale Clo. Baug 4E 10
Chippendale Clo. B'wtr 9G 18
Chipstead Ho. Ports 9G 200
Chipstead Rd. Ports 9G 200
Chisels La. Brans 9D 220
Chisholm Clo. Sotn 6E 158
Chislehurst Flats. Bourn 2G 244
Chitty Rd. S'sea 5H 241
Chive Ct. Farn 8E 28
Chivers Clo. Bas 8K 41
Chivers Clo. S'sea 4D 240
Chobham Rd. Frim 3N 29
Cholderton 4F 66
Cholderton Rare Breeds Farm Pk. 4E 66
Cholderton Rd. Chol 4G 66
Cholderton Rd. Newt T 5E 66
Chopin Rd. Bas 2M 59
Chrismas Av. A'sht 1L 65
Chrismas Pl. A'sht 1L 65
Christchurch 8L 229
Christchurch Bay Rd. Bart S 7A 232
Christchurch By-Pass. Christ 7L 229
Christchurch Castle 8L 229
Christchurch Clo. Chu C 7L 47
Christchurch Dri. B'wtr 7E 18
Christchurch Gdns. Water 7J 201
Christchurch Gdns. Win 9K 105
Christchurch Norman House. (Historic Building) 8M 229
Christchurch Priory 8M 229
Christchurch Rd. Bourn 2M 245
Christchurch Rd. Evtn 6L 233
Christchurch Rd. Hurn 9E 218
Christchurch Rd. New M 6M 231
Christchurch Rd. Ring 1J 187
Christchurch Rd. Win 9J 105 (9K 237) (in two parts)
Christchurch Ski Cen. 4E 218
Christie Av. White 1F 196
Christie Wlk. Yate 9M 17
Christine Clo. Ash 1N 65
Christmas Hill. S Won 9D 76
Christopher Way. Ems 7M 203
Christy Ct. T'ley 6J 11
Christy Ind. Est. A'sht 9M 49
Christyne Ct. Water 4L 201
Chudleigh Ct. Farn 8K 29
Church Av. Farn 8L 29
Church Bank Rd. Mich 7L 77
Church Brook. T'ley 7G 10
Church Circ. Farn 1L 49
Church Clo. And 1A 70 (off East St.)
Church Clo. Clan 5B 168
Church Clo. Eastl 8H 133
Church Clo. L Hth 6E 196
Church Clo. Min 9M 155
Church Clo. N Bad 8F 130
Church Common 6L 139
Church Cotts. Bad L 4J 65
Church Cotts. Blkmr 8E 100
Church Ct. Fle 2K 47 (Branksomewood Rd.)
Church Ct. Fle 2L 47 (Church Rd.)
Church Crookham 6M 47
Church End 6K 23
Church End. Sotn 2H 173
Churcher Clo. Gos 4F 238
Churcher Wlk. Gos 4F 238
Church Farm. F'bri 2J 153
Church Farm Cvn. Site. Dib 3G 192
Church Farm Clo. Dib 3G 192
Church Farm Clo. N Wal 8A 58
Churchfield Ct. Lip 3D 116
Church Fld. Rd. Ptsfld 9A 140
Churchfields. Fawl 5F 208
Church Fields. Head 2N 101
Churchfields. Kingsl 7G 83
Churchfields. Twy 7L 127
Churchfields La. Harb 7H 153
Churchfields Rd. Twy 7K 127
Church Gro. Fle 2K 47
Church Hatch. D'ton 1L 119
Church Hill. A'sht 2K 65
Church Hill. Cam 8N 19
Church Hill. Mil S 7L 235
Church Hill. Neth W 1A 88
Church Hill. Redl 2N 119
Church Hill. W End 9G 160
Churchill Av. A'sht 2L 65
Churchill Av. Bish W 2K 163
Churchill Av. Bulf 3A 66
Churchill Av. Odi 1E 62
Churchill Clo. A'hlt 5B 152
Churchill Clo. Alt 6F 80
Churchill Clo. Fare 8F 196
Churchill Clo. Farn 4K 29
Churchill Clo. Four M 4J 97
Churchill Clo. H Win 5A 26
Churchill Clo. King W 6M 91
Churchill Clo. Odi 2E 62 (off Churchill Av.)
Churchill Clo. T'ley 6K 11
Churchill Clo. Tidw 6B 30
Churchill Ct. Bourn 1B 246
Churchill Ct. New M 4A 232
Churchill Ct. Ports 9M 201
Churchill Ct. Water 4A 182
Churchill Cres. Farn 4K 29
Churchill Cres. Head 3B 102
Churchill Cres. Poole 8A 226
Churchill Cres. Yate 8N 17
Churchill Dri. Ems 5M 203
Churchill Gdns. Poole 9A 226
Churchill Ho. Sotn 2G 175
Churchill M. Gos 1J 239 (off Forton Rd.)
Churchill Plaza. Bas 6C 42
Churchill Rd. Bourn 9A 228
Churchill Rd. Poole 9A 226
Churchill Sq. S'sea 5J 241
Churchill Way. And 9A 52
Churchill Way. Bas 6C 42
Churchill Way E. Bas 6D 42
Churchill Way W. And 9J 51
Churchill Way W. Bas 6M 41
Churchill Yd. Ind. Est. Water 9L 181
Church Lands. Braml 1E 22
Church La. Abb A 5F 68
Church La. Awb 9D 122
Church La. Bas 6C 42
Church La. Baug 9E 10
Church La. Bent 7K 63
Church La. Bish S 2K 109
Church La. B'stne 2E 118
Church La. Bold & Pill 4D 224
Church La. Bot 5D 176
Church La. Brfld 6B 124
Church La. Bramd 1N 135
Church La. B'shtt 9D 102
Church La. Broc 8D 148
Church La. Burgh 3E 8
Church La. Burl 7E 188
Church La. Burs 1M 195
Church La. Butt 3E 6
Church La. Charl A 4A 120
Church La. Christ 8L 229
Church La. Clid 3B 60
Church La. Col C 4K 133
Church La. Curd 2G 176
Church La. Dogm 7E 46
Church La. Durl 5C 162
Church La. E Bol 1B 236
Church La. Estn 1C 106
Church La. Ellis 9C 60
Church La. Ews 1N 63
Church La. Farn 8G 28
Church La. Fawl 5E 208
Church La. Finch 1H 17
Church La. Good C 8N 69
Church La. Gray 4L 103
Church La. Gthm 3C 114
Church La. Hmbdn 7D 166
Church La. H Win 8C 26
Church La. Hav 1H 217
Church La. Hay I 5J 217
Church La. Head 1N 101
Church La. Heck 7G 15
Church La. H End 5M 175
Church La. Holyb 1J 81
Church La. Houtn 5E 88
Church La. Hung 4G 7
Church La. King W 9N 91
Church La. Lud 1C 30
Church La. L'ton 3E 234
Church La. Lyn 2B 148
Church La. M'tin 7A 150
Church La. Mart W 9E 92
Church La. Meds 9K 79
Church La. Mott 4F 122
Church La. Neth W 1A 88
Church La. New M 5A 232
Church La. Nurs 5M 157
Church La. Old B 5J 43
Church La. Ows & Beau 3G 134
Church La. Pitt 6E 86 (off Black La.)
Church La. Plait 8L 121
Church La. Priv 2K 137
Church La. Roms 5L 129
Church La. Ropl 2D 110
Church La. Row 8N 63
Church La. Sher E 5M 121
Church La. Sil 6C 12
Church La. Sotn (SO14) 7L 173 (7C 4)
Church La. Sotn (SO17) 9N 159
Church La. Spar 3A 104
Church La. Swanm 5E 164
Church La. Sway 6J 223
Church La. Tidw 8G 31
Church La. Twy 6L 127
Church La. Up Cl 6M 69
Church La. Ver D 7D 6 (in two parts)
Church La. W Meon 8C 136
Church La. Win 9E 90
Church La. Wolv 6M 9
Church La. Wool H 3N 7
Church La. Wort 7J 41
Church La. Corner. Pill 6F 224
Church La. E. A'sht 1J 65
Church La. W. A'sht 1H 65
Church Mead. L'ton 4E 234
Church Pas. F'ham 8D 64
Church Path. Ems 9M 203
Church Path. Fare 8E 198
Church Path. Farn 8G 28 (Minley Rd.)
Church Path. Farn 3L 49 (Queen's Rd.)
Church Path. Farn 8L 29 (Rectory Rd.)
Church Path. Gos 3M 239
Church Path. Hav 1H 217
Church Path. Hook 3F 44
Church Path. Horn 4D 182
Church Path. Newn 2C 44
Church Path. Sher 8N 21
Church Path. Sotn 9N 159 (SO17)
Church Path. Sotn 7E 174 (SO19)
Church Path. Titch 9K 197
Church Path N. Ports 1E 240
Church Pl. Fare 7E 198
Church Pl. Roms 5L 129
Church Rd. A'sht 3L 65
Church Rd. Bourn 2J 247
Church Rd. B'shtt 9E 102
Church Rd. Cowes 5P 237
Church Rd. Eastl 9H 133
Church Rd. E'sly 7E 16
Church Rd. Fare 2N 213
Church Rd. F'ley 8F 86
Church Rd. Fle 1K 47
Church Rd. Frim 3M 29
Church Rd. Gos 5J 239
Church Rd. Hay I 3G 242
Church Rd. Idm 9C 66
Church Rd. King S 9B 86
Church Rd. L Hth 6E 196
Church Rd. Michm 3K 123
Church Rd. Mort W 1B 12
Church Rd. Neth W 8H 73
Church Rd. Newt 2K 179
Church Rd. N Wal 9A 58
Church Rd. Over 2D 56
Church Rd. Owl 4G 18
Church Rd. P Hth 4L 11
Church Rd. Ports 1E 240 (in two parts)
Church Rd. Roms 5L 129
Church Rd. S'hrst 4B 18
Church Rd. Shed 3N 177
Church Rd. Sotn 9B 174
Church Rd. Steep 6K 139
Church Rd. Swanm 5C 164
Church Rd. T'ley 6H 11
Church Rd. Up Farr 4E 98
Church Rd. Wars 8A 196
Church Rd. Westb 6N 203
Church Rd. E. C'then 1D 18
Church Rd. E. Farn 2M 49
Church Rd. W. C'then 1D 18
Church Rd. W. Farn 2L 49
Church Sq. Bas 6C 42
Church St. A'sht 9H 49
Church St. Alt 4F 80
Church St. Bas 6C 42 (in two parts)
Church St. Bentw 6L 79
Church St. Christ 8L 229
Church St. Coll D 2H 31
Church St. Cran 6J 149 (off Square, The)
Church St. Cron 3L 63
Church St. C'then 1D 18
Church St. E Meon 3M 143
Church St. F'bri 2H 153
Church St. Hur T 4D 34
Church St. Liss 8D 114
Church St. Mich 7J 77
Church St. Odi 8K 45 (in two parts)
Church St. Ports 9D 214
Church St. Roms 5L 129
Church St. Ropl 2D 110
Church St. St M 1M 53
Church St. Sotn 2G 173
Church St. Titch 9K 197
Church St. Uphm 8E 134
Church St. Upt G 3A 62
Church St. W Gri 2E 120
Church St. Wher 2F 74
Church St. Whitc 6F 54
Church Vw. H Win 8B 26
Church Vw. Hook 2H 45
Church Vw. Shed 3B 178
Churchview. Sotn 7E 174
Church Vw. S'sea 3H 241
Church Vw. S Warn 4C 62
Church Vw. Westb 6N 203
Church Vw. Yate 6N 17
Church Vw. Clo. Sotn 7E 174
Church Wlk. Lover 8E 120
Churchward Gdns. H End 9N 161
Churchyard Cotts. Alr 9F 94
Churn Clo. Old B 4J 43
Chur St. Bulf B 3B 66
Churt 7H 85
Churt Rd. Churt & Hind 1J 103
Churt Rd. Head & Churt 1C 102
Churt Wynde. Hind 9M 85
Chute Causeway. Up Ch 1N 31 & 9A 6
Chute Ho. Bas 6C 42 (off Church St.)
Cibbons Rd. Chine 9G 23
Cinderford Clo. Ports 8D 200
Cinnamon Ct. Sotn 4K 173 (1A 4)
Circle, The. Bourn 2L 227
Circle, The. Poole 6D 244
Circle, The. S'sea 5E 240 (6E 4)
Circle, The. Wick 6B 178
Circular Rd. Ports 9C 214 (2L 5)
Cirrus Gdns. Hamb 7K 195
City Bus. Cen. Win 6L 105 (6M 237)
City Commerce Cen. Sotn 7N 173 (7F 4)
City Ind. Pk. Sotn 6K 173 (5A 4)
City Mus. 7L 105 (8M 237)
City Mus. & Art Gallery. 4C 240 (7L 5)
City Quay. Ports 3B 240 (5J 5)
City Rd. Win 6K 105 (6L 237)
City Wall Ho. Bas 5E 42
Civic Cen. Rd. Hav 7F 202
Civic Cen. Rd. Sotn 5L 173 (4B 4)
Civic Way. Fare 8E 198
Clack La. F'bri 4D 150
Clacton Rd. Ports 9E 200
Claire Ct. Highc 7J 231
Claire Gdns. Water 9C 168
Clamp Grn. Col C 4K 133
Clandon Ct. Farn 9M 29
Clandon Dri. Eastl 6D 132
Clanfield 5B 168
Clanfield Clo. Chan F 6B 132
Clanfield Dri. Chan F 6B 132
Clanfield Ho. Ports 1E 240
Clanfield Ride. B'wtr 8F 18
Clanfield Rd. Sotn 3G 175
Clanfield Way. Chan F 6B 132
Clanville 3D 50
Clanwilliam Rd. Lee S 1B 238
Clappers Farm Rd. Sil 4E 12
Clapps Ga. Rd. P Hth 4L 11
Clare Clo. Fare 7F 196
Clare Ct. Fle 2M 47
Clare Gdns. Black 9D 208
Clare Gdns. Ptsfld 1B 146
Clare Ho. Gos 9H 213
Clare Lodge Clo. Brans 6C 220
Claremont Av. Bourn 4M 227

Claremont Clo. *Eastl* 6E 132
Claremont Cres. *Sotn* 3F 172
Claremont Gdns. *Water* 5M 201
Claremont Rd. *Bourn* 4M 227
Claremont Rd. *Ports* 2F 240
Claremont Rd. *Sotn* 3F 172
Clarence Clo. *A'sht* 9L 49
Clarence Clo. *Lud* 1C 30
Clarence Esplanade. *S'sea* 5C 240 (9L 5)
Clarence Ho. *Sotn* 4A 174
Clarence Pde. *S'sea* 5C 240 (9M 5)
Clarence Pk. Rd. *Bourn* 8D 228
Clarence Pl. *Christ* 6K 229
Clarence Rd. *Fle* 3L 47
Clarence Rd. *Gos* 2M 239
Clarence Rd. *Lyn* 2B 148
Clarence Rd. *S'sea* 5E 240
Clarence St. *Ports* 1D 240 (1N 5)
Clarendon Av. *And* 3L 69
Clarendon Clo. *Roms* 3A 130
Clarendon Ct. *B'wtr* 1F 28
Clarendon Ct. *Fle* 2L 47
Clarendon Ct. S'sea *6E 240* *(off Clarendon Rd.)*
Clarendon Cres. *Fare* 8E 196
Clarendon Pk. *L'ton* 4D 234
Clarendon Pl. *Ports* 2D 240 (Arundel St.)
Clarendon Pl. *Ports* 1E 240 (Clarendon St.)
Clarendon Rd. *Bourn* 3H 245
Clarendon Rd. *Christ* 7K 229
Clarendon Rd. *Hav* 8E 202
Clarendon Rd. *Sotn* 2F 172
Clarendon Rd. *S'sea* 5D 240
Clarendon Rd. *W Gri* 9C 86
Clarendon St. *Ports* 1E 240
Clarendon Ter. Tidw *8F 30* *(off Grand Trunk Rd.)*
Clarewood Dri. *Cam* 7N 19
Clarke Cres. *Cam* 6G 19
Clarken Green. **9A 40**
Clarke's La. *Tang* 5F 32
Clarke's Rd. *Ports* 1G 240
Clark M. Whitc *5G 54* *(off Church St.)*
Clark Rd. *Farn* 7K 29
Clarks Clo. *Ring* 1K 187
Clarks Hill. *Dipp* 5N 63
Clatford Mnr. *Up Cl* 5L 69
Clatford Oakcuts. **4G 73**
Claude Ashby Clo. *Sotn* 7C 160
Claudeen Clo. *Sotn* 6C 160
Claudia Ct. *Gos* 1H 239
Claudius Clo. *And* 6A 52
Claudius Clo. *Chan F* 5D 132
Claudius Dri. *Bas* 4L 41
Claudius Gdns. *Chan F* 5D 132
Clausentum Clo. *Chan F* 5C 132
Clausentum Rd. *Sotn* 3M 173
Clausentum Rd. *Win* 9K 105
Clausen Way. *Penn* 5C 234
Claxton St. *Ports* 2E 240
Claybank Rd. *Ports* 7H 215
Claybank Spur. *Ports* 7H 215
Claycart Rd. *A'sht* 7F 48 (in two parts)
Claydon Av. *S'sea* 3H 241
Claydon Gdns. *B'wtr* 3J 29
Clayfields Sports Cen. 5J 193
Clayhall. **6L 239**
Clayhall Rd. *Gos* 5J 239
Clayhill. **4C 148**
Clayhill Clo. *Wal C* 7N 163
Claylands Ct. *Bish W* 3L 163
Claylands Rd. *Bish W* 3L 163
Claylands Rd. Ind. Est. *Bish W* 3L 163
Claypits. **9M 175**
Claypits La. *Dib* 6H 193
Claypitt La. *Frox* 8C 112
Clay's La. *Holyb* 1N 81
Clay's La. *E Wor* 7L 81
Clay St. *W'ish* 5H 121
Claythorpe Rd. *Bas* 8L 41
Clayton Clo. *H Win* 7B 26
Clayton Rd. *Bulf* 3A 66
Clayton Rd. *Farn* 3H 29
Cleasby Clo. *Sotn* 3D 172
Clease Way. *Comp* 6G 127
Cleaver Rd. *Bas* 8L 41
Clee Av. *Fare* 9N 197
Cleethorpes Rd. *Sotn* 6F 174
Cleeve Clo. *Ports* 8C 200
Cleeves Clo. *Poole* 4B 226
Cleeves, The. *Tot* 4J 171
Clegg Rd. *S'sea* 4H 241
Clematis Clo. *Christ* 6E 230
Clemence Gdns. *Whitc* 5G 54
Clement Attlee Way. *Ports* 9C 200
Clement M. *Bourn* 2F 244
Clements Clo. *B'std* 1D 82
Clems Way. *Lcky* 4A 122
Clere Gdns. *Chine* 1G 43
Cleric Ct. *Fare* 6G 196
Clevedge Way. *N War* 7J 45
Clevedon Ct. *Farn* 9M 29
Cleveland Clo. *Bart S* 7M 231
Cleveland Clo. *Bas* 8K 41
Cleveland Ct. *Bourn* 3H 245 (8H 247)
Cleveland Ct. *Sotn* 1E 174
Cleveland Dri. *Dib P* 7J 193
Cleveland Dri. *Fare* 9N 197
Cleveland Gdns. *Bourn* 9N 227
Cleveland Rd. *Bourn* 9A 228
Cleveland Rd. *Gos* 4K 239
Cleveland Rd. *Sotn* 9D 160
Cleveland Rd. *S'sea* 3F 240
Clevelands Clo. *Chan F* 3N 131
Cleverley Ho. *Ports* 4J 5
Cleves La. *Upt G* 3A 62
Clewers Hill. **7N 163**
Clewers Hill. *Wal C* 7N 163
Clewers La. *Wal C* 7N 163
Cliddesden. **3B 60**
Cliddesden Ct. *Bas* 9C 42
Cliddesden La. *Bas* 5K 59
Cliddesden Rd. *Bas* 9C 42
Cliddesden Rd. *Clid* 3B 60
Cliff Cres. *New M* 7A 232
Cliffdale Gdns. *Cosh* 8H 201
Cliff Dri. *Christ* 8E 230
Cliff Dri. *Poole* 6D 244
Cliffe Av. *Hamb* 6J 195
Cliffe Rd. *Bart S* 7N 231
Clifford Dibben M. *Sotn* 2M 173
Clifford Pl. *F Oak* 1N 161
Clifford Rd. *Bourn* 5L 227
Clifford St. *Sotn* 5N 173 (4F 4)
Cliff Rd. *Cowes* 5N 237
Cliff Rd. *Fare* 7H 211
Cliff Rd. *Mil S* 9G 233
Cliff Rd. *Sotn* 5J 173
Cliff Ter. *New M* 8A 232
Cliff, The. Sotn *7B 174* *(off Jackman's Clo.)*
Cliff Way. *Comp* 7H 127
Clifton Cres. *Water* 6J 181
Clifton Gdns. *Sotn* 2F 172
Clifton Gdns. *W End* 1G 174
Clifton Hill. *Win* 6K 105 (7K 237)
Clifton Rd. *Bourn* 2G 246
Clifton Rd. *Lee S* 3C 238
Clifton Rd. *Poole* 3B 244
Clifton Rd. *Sotn* 2F 172
Clifton Rd. *S'sea* 5D 240 (9N 5)
Clifton Rd. *Win* 6J 105 (6J 237)
Clifton St. *Gos* 1H 239
Clifton St. *Ports* 1F 240
Clifton Ter. *Bas* 5C 42
Clifton Ter. *S'sea* 5D 240
Clifton Ter. *Win* 6K 105 (7K 237)
Clifton Wlk. *Bas* 6C 42
Climaur Ct. *S'sea* 5E 240
Clingan Rd. *Bourn* 8G 228
Clinkley Rd. *W Tis* 7D 110
Clinton Clo. *Walk* 4K 231
Clinton Rd. *L'ton* 1E 234
Clinton Rd. *Water* 7K 181
Clipper Clo. *Wars* 8B 196
Clive Gro. *Fare* 1L 213
Clive Rd. *A'sht* 1M 65
Clive Rd. *Bourn* 5K 227
Clive Rd. *Christ* 4F 230
Clive Rd. *Ports* 1F 240
Clockhouse Rd. *Farn* 8K 29
Clockhouse Roundabout. *Farn* 8K 29
Clock St. *Ports* 2B 240 (4J 5)
Clocktower Dri. *S'sea* 5J 241
Cloisters, The. *Alt* 4E 80
Cloisters, The. *And* 1N 69
Cloisters, The. *Fare* 7M 197
Cloisters, The. *Frim* 3M 29
Cloisters, The. *L'ton* 3D 234
Cloisters, The. *Ring* 2M 187
Cloisters, The. *Roms* 3L 129
Cloisters, The. *Sotn* 8M 159
Close, The. *Ashy* 4G 186
Close, The. *Bas* 4M 41
Close, The. *Bram* 3H 133
Close, The. *Coll T* 5G 19
Close, The. *Fare* 9L 199
Close, The. *F'ham* 9F 64
Close, The. *Frim* 4L 29
Close, The. *Hamb* 5L 195
Close, The. *Hath* 9J 33
Close, The. *H End* 4M 175
Close, The. *Holb* 5B 208
Close, The. *Langr* 1C 144
Close, The. *Lip* 4E 116
Close, The. *Monk S* 6K 21
Close, The. *New M* 6C 232
Close, The. *Odi* 9K 45
Close, The. *Ports* 1H 215
Close, The. *Redl* 1M 119
Close, The. *Ring* 1J 187
Close, The. *St I* 4D 186
Close, The. *Sotn* 3H 175
Close, The. *S'sea* 4D 240
Close, The. *Sway* 5H 223
Close, The. *Titch* 1J 211
Close, The. *W'bry* 9J 119
Closewood Rd. *Water* 9H 181
Closeworth Rd. *Farn* 3N 49
Clough La. *Burl* 7D 188
Clough La. *W'slw* 4G 87
Clough's Rd. *Ring* 1L 187
Clouston Rd. *Farn* 7H 29
Clovelly Dri. *Hind* 9L 85
Clovelly Pk. *Hind* 9L 85
Clovelly Rd. *Ems* 9L 203
Clovelly Rd. *Hay I* 4J 217
Clovelly Rd. *Hind* 1L 103
Clovelly Rd. *Sotn* 4M 173 (2E 4)
Clovelly Rd. *S'sea* 3H 241
Cloverbank. *King W* 5M 91
Clover Clo. *Christ* 6D 230
Clover Clo. *Gos* 6E 212
Clover Clo. *Lind* 2M 101
Clover Clo. *L Hth* 7B 196
Clover Ct. *New M* 2E 232
Clover Ct. *Water* 3A 202
Clover Fld. *Lych* 4G 42
Clover Gdns. *Lud* 1D 30
Clover La. *Yate* 7K 17
Clover Leaf Way. *Old B* 7J 43
Clover Nooke. *Sotn* 2B 172
Clovers, The. *Poole* 6E 226
Clover Way. *H End* 4L 175
Clover Way. *Roms* 4B 130
Clowes Av. *Bourn* 2L 247
Club Ho. La. *Wal C* 8N 163
Clubhouse Rd. *A'sht* 6H 49
Club La. *Tidw* 8G 30
Cluster Ind. Est. *S'sea* 2G 241
Clydebank Rd. *Ports* 8E 214
Clyde Ct. *And* 8B 52
Clyde Ct. *Gos* 1H 239
Clyde Ho. *Sotn* 5A 174
Clyde Rd. *Gos* 1H 239
Clydesdale Rd. *White* 2E 196
Clydesdale Way. *Tot* 2H 171
Coach Hill. *Fare* 9J 197
Coach Hill Clo. *Chan F* 5N 131
Coach Hill La. *Burl* 6D 188
Coach Ho. *S'sea* 3K 241
Coach Ho. Clo. *Frim* 1N 29
Coach Ho. Gdns. *Fle* 9M 27
Coach Ho. Pl. *Bourn* 9L 227
Coachmans Copse. *Sotn* 9E 160
Coachmans Gro. *S'hrst* 6D 18
Coachmans Halt. *Hmbdn* 9D 166
Coach Rd. *Hamb* 7J 195
Coach Rd. *Wim G* 7E 148
Coach Rd., The. *W Tyth* 8L 87
Coachways. *And* 3N 69
Coal Pk. La. *Swanw* 1A 196
Coalville Rd. *Sotn* 6F 174
Coal Yd. Rd. *S'sea* 2G 240
Coastguard Clo. *Gos* 5H 239
Coastguard Cotts. *Bart S* 6N 231
Coastguard Cotts. *Hav* 2F 216
Coastguard Way. *Christ* 9B 230
Coate Dri. *Wor D* 5G 91
Coates Clo. *Bas* 1A 60
Coates Rd. *Sotn* 6H 175
Coates Way. *Water* 4M 201
Coat Gdns. *Hythe* 6M 193
Cobalt Ct. *Gos* 1E 238
Cobbets Ridge. *F'ham* 9L 65
Cobbett Clo. *Win* 9G 105
Cobbett Ct. *Sotn* 3C 174
Cobbett Grn. *Bas* 9N 41
Cobbett Rd. *Sotn* 3C 174
Cobbett's La. *Yate & B'wtr* 8B 18
Cobbetts M. *F'ham* 8D 64
Cobbett Way. *Bot* 3C 176
Cobblewood. *Ems* 6M 203
Cobden Av. *Ports* 8H 215
Cobden Av. *Sotn* 1B 174
Cobden Bri. *Sotn* 1B 174
Cobden Ct. *Sotn* 2C 174
Cobden Cres. *Sotn* 2D 174
Cobden Gdns. *Sotn* 1C 174
Cobden Heights. *Sotn* 1C 174
Cobden Ri. *Sotn* 1C 174
Cobden St. *Gos* 2K 239
Cobham Gro. *White* 4H 197
Cobham Rd. *Bourn* 3L 227
Coblands Av. *Tot* 3K 171
Cob La. *W'slw* 4F 86
Cobley Clo. *E Woody* 1F 148
Cob M. *A'prt* 3B 68
Coburg Ho. *Sotn* 4A 174
Coburg St. *Ports* 2E 240
Coburg St. *Sotn* 4A 174
Cochrane Clo. *Gos* 1F 238
Cochrane Ho. *Ports* 2B 240 (4J 5)
Cock-A-Dobby. *S'hrst* 4C 18
Cockerell Clo. *Fare* 4F 196
Cockleshell Clo. *Wars* 8B 196
Cockleshell Gdns. *S'sea* 4K 241
Cocklydown La. *Tot* 6K 171
Cockshott La. *Frox* 3H 139
Codrington Ho. *Ports* 3J 5
Cody Rd. *Farn* 9H 29
Coe Clo. *A'sht* 1J 65
Coghlan Clo. *Fare* 7D 198
Coker Clo. *Win* 6K 105 (6J 237)
Colbeck. *Chu C* 7N 47
Colborne Clo. *L'ton* 1E 234
Colbourne Clo. *Brans* 7C 220
Colbourne Ct. *Win* 4L 105
Colbred Corner. *Fle* 8A 28
Colburn Clo. *Sotn* 9C 158
Colbury. **8K 171**
Colbury Gro. *Hav* 4C 202
Colchester Av. *Eastl* 8J 133
Colchester Rd. *Ports* 8E 200
Coldeast Clo. *Sar G* 4B 196
Coldeast Way. *Sar G* 4C 196
Colden La. *Old Al* 6G 94
Coldharbour. *N Wal* 9A 58
Cold Harbour Clo. *Wick* 7B 178
Cold Harbour Cotts. *Clid* 3A 60
Coldharbour Farm Rd. *Ems* 8M 203
Cold Harbour La. *Farn* 4G 29 (in two parts)
Coldharbour La. *Nurs* 3N 157
Coldhill La. *Water* 3M 181 (in two parts)
Cole Av. *A'sht* 8H 49
Colebrook Av. *Ports* 8J 215
Colebrook Av. *Sotn* 1H 173
Colebrook Pl. *Win* 7M 105 (9P 237)
Colebrook St. *Win* 7L 105 (8N 237)
Colebrook Way. *And* 2K 69
Cole Clo. *And* 6N 51
Coleford Bri. Rd. *Myt* 8M 29
Cole Henley. **8H 37**
Cole Hill. *Sob* 6K 165
Colehill Cres. *Bourn* 3M 227
Coleman Clo. *Bas* 4D 42
Coleman Rd. *A'sht* 1M 65
Coleman Rd. *Bourn* 3E 226
Coleman St. *Sotn* 6N 173 (5F 4)
Colemere Gdns. *Highc* 5H 231
Colemore. **4D 112**
Colemore La. *Colem* 6E 112
Colemore Rd. *Bourn* 7F 228
Colemore Sq. *Hav* 5F 202
Colenso Rd. *Fare* 8C 198
Colenzo Dri. *And* 9A 52
Coleridge Av. *Yate* 8A 18
Coleridge Clo. *C'then* 1E 18
Coleridge Clo. *Wars* 8A 196
Coleridge Ct. *Sotn* 5H 175
Coleridge Gdns. *Water* 6N 181
Coleridge Grn. *Christ* 6B 230
Coleridge Rd. *Ports* 8A 200
Colesbourne Rd. *Ports* 8C 200
Coles Clo. *Twy* 6L 127
Cole's La. *Land* 8G 120
Coles Mede. *Ott* 1F 132 (in two parts)
Coleson Rd. *Sotn* 2C 174
Coleville Av. *Fawl* 5F 208
Coleville Rd. *Farn* 7H 29
Coley La. *Chlbn* 5D 74
Colinton Av. *Fare* 8M 199
Coliseum Bus. Cen. *Cam* 1J 29
Collard Way. *Liss* 1E 140
College Clo. *Cam* 5M 19
College Clo. *Hamb* 7K 195
College Clo. *Row C* 8J 183
College Cres. *Coll T* 5G 19
College Gdns. *F'ham* 8D 64
College La. *Ellis* 2H 79
College La. *Ports* 2B 240 (4J 5)
College Pl. *Sotn* 4M 173 (1D 4)
College Ride. *Cam* 6M 19
College Rd. *Bas* 6A 42
College Rd. *Bourn* 1D 246
College Rd. *Coll T* 6G 18
College Rd. *Navy* 2B 240 (2J 5)
College Rd. *Pur* 7M 201
College Rd. *Ring* 1K 187
College Rd. *Sotn* 8B 174
College St. *Ptsfld* 1M 145
College St. *Ports* 2B 240 (4J 5)
College St. *Sotn* 7M 173 (7E 4)
College St. *Win* 7L 105 (9M 237)
College Town. **7G 18**
College Wlk. *Win* 8L 105 (9N 237)
Collett Clo. *H End* 9M 161
Colley Clo. *Win* 3L 105
Colleywater La. *Frox* 3B 138
Collier Clo. *Farn* 7F 28
Collier Clo. *Sotn* 2A 174
Collingbourne Av. *Bourn* 8G 229
Collingbourne Dri. *Chan F* 6M 131
Collingbourne Ducis. **2H 31**
Collington Cres. *Ports* 8C 200
Collingwood. *Farn* 1N 49
Collingwood Ho. *Fare* 7N 197
Collingwood Retail Pk. *Fare* 2C 212
Collingwood Rd. *S'sea* 5E 240
Collingwood Wlk. *And* 1C 70
Collingworth Ri. *Park G* 3E 196
Collins Clo. *Chan F* 6L 131
Collins Clo. *Charl* 7L 51
Collins Ct. *Tidw* 6C 30
Collins Ho. *Chan F* 6B 132
Collins La. *Hurs* 6N 125
Collins La. *Ring* 1K 187
Collins La. *W Har* 5E 146
Collins Rd. *S'sea* 5H 241
Collis Rd. *Ports* 8H 215
Collis Ter. *Lud* 1D 30
Collyers Cres. *Lip* 2G 116
Collyers Rd. *Broc* 9C 148
Colman Ct. *Bourn* 2N 245
Colne Av. *Sotn* 8C 158
Colne Ct. *Sotn* 9D 158
Colne Way. *Bas* 6E 42
Colonnade Rd. *Bourn* 9D 228
Colonnade Rd. W. *Bourn* 9D 228
Colonnade, The. *Sotn* 7B 174
Colpoy St. *S'sea* 3C 240 (6M 5)
Colson Clo. *Win* 6M 105
Colson Rd. *Win* 6M 105
Colt Clo. *Rown* 6E 158
Colt Hill. **7M 45**
Colton Copse. *Chan F* 6L 131
Coltsfoot Clo. *H End* 3M 175
Coltsfoot Dri. *L Hth* 7B 196
Coltsfoot Dri. *Water* 4N 201
Coltsfoot Pl. *Hook* 1J 45
Coltsfoot Rd. *Lind* 2M 101
Coltsfoot Wlk. *Roms* 3B 130
Coltsmead. *Ports* 9A 200
Colts Rd. *Rown* 4D 158
Columbian Way. *Bourn* 4G 227
Columbia Rd. *Bourn* 4F 226
Columbia Trees La. *Bourn* 5G 226
Columbine Clo. *Christ* 5D 230
Columbine Rd. *Bas* 3J 59
Columbine Wlk. *Tot* 5K 171
Columbus Dri. *S'wd B* 8E 28
Columbus Way. *And* 9D 52
Colvedene Clo. *Col C* 3K 133
Colville Clo. *Bourn* 9D 228
Colville Dri. *Bish W* 3N 163
Colville Rd. *Bourn* 9D 228
Colville Rd. *Ports* 9H 201
Colwell Clo. *Sotn* 2C 172
Colwell Rd. *Ports* 1G 214
Colwyn Clo. *Yate* 7M 17
Colyer Clo. *Bas* 8L 41
Combe. **4G 7**
Combe Hill. **4J 7**
Combe La. *Farn* 6J 29
Comber Rd. *Bourn* 3K 227
Comet Way. *Christ* 7C 230
Comfrey Clo. *Farn* 7E 28
Comfrey Clo. *Roms* 3B 130
Comfrey Clo. *Water* 1C 182
Comines Way. *H End* 4J 175
Comley Hill. *Hav* 3J 203
Comley Rd. *Bourn* 4K 227
Commercial Pl. *Ports* 1D 240
Commercial Rd. *A'sht* 2L 65
Commercial Rd. *Bourn* 2J 245 (7J 247)
Commercial Rd. *Ports* 2D 240 (3N 5) (in two parts)

Commercial Rd. Sotn 5K 173 (3A 4)
Commercial Rd. Tot 3N 171
Commercial St. Sotn 3E 174
Commodore Ct. Farn 3L 49
Commodore Ct. Sotn 7N 173 (8F 4)
Commom, The. W'grn 2A 154
Comn. Barn La. Lee S 9B 212 (in two parts)
Common Clo. Chan F 4A 132
Common Fields. H End 4K 175
Common Gdns. Chan F 4A 132
Common Hill. Meds 1E 96
Comn. Hill Rd. Brfld 7C 124
Common La. Selb 1K 113
Common La. S'wick 9N 179
Common La. Titch 9G 197
Common Rd. Chan F 4N 131
Common Rd. H'ly 3K 9
Common Rd. W'ish 5H 121
Common St. Ports 1E 240
Common, The. 8A 150
Common, The. Char A 3F 20
Common, The. Sotn 1K 173
Common, The. W'slw 5H 87
Communication Rd. Green 1G 9
Compass Clo. Gos 1F 238
Compass Clo. Sotn 6E 174
Compass Fld. Hook 2H 45
Compass Point. Fare 9D 198
Compass Rd. Ports 1C 214
Complins. Holyb 2J 81
Compton 8G 65 (Farnham)
Compton 8E 88 (King's Somborne)
Compton 5H 127 (Twyford)
Compton Acres 5C 244 (Garden)
Compton Av. Poole 3B 244
Compton Beeches. St I 3D 186
Compton Clo. Chu C 6N 47
Compton Clo. Eastl 6D 132
Compton Clo. Hav 6F 202
Compton Clo. Hook 2H 45
Compton Clo. Lee S 1B 238
Compton Clo. S'hrst 4E 18
Compton Clo. Win 2F 126
Compton Ct. Hav 7E 202
Compton Dri. Poole 3A 244
Compton Gdns. Poole 3A 244
Compton Ho. Sotn 2G 173
Compton Ho. Tot 1K 171
Compton Pl. Bus. Cen. Cam 9J 19 (off Surrey Av.)
Compton Rd. Chu C 6N 47
Compton Rd. New M 4B 232
Compton Rd. Ports 5F 214
Compton Rd. Tot 2N 171
Compton Rd. Win 7K 105 (9K 237)
Compton's Dri. Plait 7K 121
Compton Sq. And 7B 52
Compton St. Comp 5G 127
Compton Wlk. Sotn 5M 173 (3E 4)
Compton Way. F'ham 8J 65
Compton Way. Win 2F 126
Conan Rd. Ports 4F 214
Concorde Way. Fare 4G 196
Conde Way. Bord 5J 101
Condor Av. Fare 9H 199
Condor Clo. Sotn 7B 174
Coney Grn. Win 4L 105
Conference Dri. L Hth 6E 196
Conference Pl. L'ton 4F 234
Conford Ct. Hav 3D 202
Congleton Clo. Min 8M 155
Conholt Hill. C'hlt 9C 6
Conholt La. C'hlt 9C 6
Conholt Rd. And 4N 69
Conifer Av. Poole 3A 244
Conifer Clo. Baug 3E 10
Conifer Clo. Christ 3G 228
Conifer Clo. Chu C 6L 47
Conifer Clo. Hythe 6K 193
Conifer Clo. St L 4A 186
Conifer Clo. Water 8A 182
Conifer Clo. W'hill 6H 101
Conifer Clo. Win 5J 105
Conifer Cres. Penn 3B 234
Conifer Crest. N'bry 1C 8
Conifer Gro. Gos 4D 212
Conifer M. Fare 8M 199
Conifer Rd. Sotn 7F 158
Conifers. Bourn 2F 244
Conigar Rd. Ems 6M 203
Coniston Av. Bourn 1C 226
Coniston Av. Ports 8H 215
Coniston Clo. Ame 5A 66
Coniston Clo. Farn 9G 29
Coniston Ct. Ash V 7N 49 (off Lakeside Clo.)
Coniston Dri. F'ham 4C 64
Coniston Gdns. H End 5M 175
Coniston Gro. Alr 2F 108
Coniston Rd. Bas 1K 59
Coniston Rd. Bord 2J 101
Coniston Rd. Eastl 1D 160
Coniston Rd. Ring 2L 187
Coniston Rd. Sotn 2B 172
Coniston Wlk. Fare 1A 212
Coniston Way. Chu C 6K 47
Connaught Barracks. A'sht 5M 49
Connaught Clo. Bord 5J 101
Connaught Clo. C'then 2B 18
Connaught Clo. New M 5N 231
Connaught Clo. Yate 7L 17
Connaught Cres. Poole 8C 226
Connaught La. Ports 8A 200
Connaught Rd. A'sht 9L 49
Connaught Rd. Bourn 9E 228
Connaught Rd. Fle 3L 47
Connaught Rd. Hav 8G 202
Connaught Rd. Ports 6E 214
Connaught Rd. Wor D 5G 90
Connemara Cres. White 2E 196
Connigar Clo. Gos 9E 212
Connors Keep. Water 6L 181
Conqueror Way. Fare 7N 211
Conrad Gdns. White 1F 196
Conservatory, The. Win 7M 105
Consort Clo. Eastl 7F 132
Consort Clo. Poole 9A 226
Consort Ct. Fare 8E 198
Consort Ho. Ports 9E 214 (off Princes St.)
Consort Rd. Eastl 7F 132
Constable Clo. Bas 8E 42
Constable Clo. Gos 6L 239
Constable Clo. Sotn 8G 174
Constable Ct. And 9N 51
Constables Ga. Win 8K 237
Constable Way. Coll T 7G 18
Constantine Av. Chan F 6C 132
Constantine Clo. Chan F 6D 132
Constantine Sq. And 7B 52 (off Cricketers Way)
Constantine Way. Bas 4J 59
Constantius Ct. Chu C 7K 47 (off Brandon Rd.)
Constant Rd. Farn 1C 48
Consulate Ho. Sotn 7N 173
Convent Ct. Ems 8L 203
Convent La. Ems 9M 203
Convent Meadows Cvn. Pk. Christ 9M 229
Convent Wlk. Christ 8M 229
Conway Clo. Chan F 9N 131
Conway Clo. Frim 3N 29
Conway Clo. New M 3C 232
Conway Ct. New M 3C 232
Conway Dri. Farn 8F 28
Cook Clo. Ring 9M 185
Cooke Gdns. Poole 8D 226
Cooke Rd. Poole 8D 226
Cookham Clo. S'hrst 4E 18
Cooks La. Awb 9G 123
Cook's La. Cal 9H 157
Cooks La. Lcky 3M 121
Cook St. Sotn 6M 173 (6E 4)
Coolers Farm. Bro'tn 2B 86
Cooley Ho. Gos 4D 212
Coombe 6H 143
Coombe Av. Bourn 4J 227
Coombe Bissett 2G 119
Coombe Clo. Frim 4M 29
Coombedale. L Hth 7E 196
Coombe Dri. Fle 2A 48
Coombe Farm Av. Fare 9C 198
Coombe Gdns. Bourn 4H 227
Coombe Hill Clo. Hill B 4G 141
Coombehurst Dri. Bas 9C 42
Coombe La. Awb 1F 128
Coombe La. Sway 6L 223
Coombe Rd Ter. E Meon 4L 143 (off Coombe Rd.)
Coombe Rd. E Meon 4K 143
Coombe Rd. Gos 9K 213
Coombe Rd. Hill B 4H 141
Coombe Rd. Yate 6L 17
Coombs Clo. Water 1C 182
Cooperage, The. Alt 5E 80
Cooper Dean Dri. Bourn 5C 228
Cooper Gro. Fare 2M 213
Cooper Rd. Asht 7J 171
Cooper Rd. Ports 8J 215
Coopers Clo. A'hlt 4D 152
Coopers Clo. E Wel 1B 156
Cooper's Clo. W End 1G 174
Coopers Clo. Wor D 5H 91
Coopers Ct. Braml 1G 22
Cooper's Hill. E'sly 1G 27
Coopers La. Braml 1F 22
Cooper's La. Sotn 7B 174
Coopers La. Ver 9M 149
Cooper's Lane. W Wel 3N 155 (in two parts)
Coopers Ter. F'ham 7E 64
Coop La. And 5A 44
Copeland Rd. Sotn 1C 172
Copenhagen Towers. Sotn 1C 194
Copenhagen Wlk. C'then 1D 18
Copes La. Brams 6L 15
Copinger Clo. Tot 4J 171
Copland Clo. Bas 2L 59
Copnor 7H 215
Copnor Clo. Wool H 3N 7
Copnor Rd. Ports 3G 214
Copper Beech Clo. Poole 1E 244
Copper Beech Clo. Ports 9M 201
Copper Beeches. Bourn 9K 227
Copper Beech Gdns. Bourn 4H 227
Copperfield Av. Owl 3G 18
Copperfield Ho. Ports 9E 214
Copperfield Rd. Sotn 6M 159
Copperfields. Tot 3H 171
Copper St. S'sea 4C 240 (7M 5)
Coppice Clo. Baug 5D 10
Coppice Clo. F'ham 4G 65
Coppice Clo. New M 2E 232
Coppice Clo. St I 4C 186
Coppice Clo. Win 5G 104
Coppice Gdns. C'then 1B 18
Coppice Gdns. Yate 8M 17
Coppice Hill. Bish W 4M 163
Coppice M. Bas 5L 41
Coppice Rd. Cal 9J 157
Coppice Rd. K're 2C 6
Coppice, The. Broc 6A 148
Coppice, The. Christ 8D 230
Coppice, The. Gos 6F 212
Coppice, The. Water 4A 182
Coppice Vw. Bourn 3J 227
Coppice Way. Fare 6N 197
Coppins Gro. Fare 2L 213
Copse Av. F'ham 3G 64
Copse Av. New M 4C 232
Copse Cvn. Pk., The. W'lnds 5D 170
Copse Cvn. Site, The. Dum 7F 58
Copse Clo. Liss 1F 140
Copse Clo. N Bad 8E 130
Copse Clo. Ott 9G 126
Copse Clo. Ptsfld 9B 140
Copse Clo. Tot 4M 171
Copse Clo. Water 7L 201
Copse End. Fle 3J 47
Copse Fld. Lych 3H 43
Copse La. Bro C 7A 78
Copse La. Chilw 2L 159
Copse La. Chu C 6K 47
Copse La. E'sly 5K 17
Copse La. Gos 7F 212
Copse La. Hamb 7K 195
Copse La. Hay I 8G 217
Copse Rd. Burl 8D 188
Copse Rd. Hasl 1M 117
Copse Rd. New M 4C 232
Copse Rd. Over 9E 38
Copse Rd. Sotn 9D 160
Copse, The. Chan F 7C 132
Copse, The. Fare 5N 197
Copse, The. Farn 9F 28
Copse, The. Roms 3B 130
Copse, The. T'ley 5G 11
Copse Vw. Sotn 5J 175
Copse Vw. Clo. Chine 9G 23
Copse Way. Christ 6G 230
Copsewood Av. Bourn 5B 228
Copsewood Rd. Asht 7J 171
Copsewood Rd. Hythe 6L 193
Copsewood Rd. Sotn 9C 160
Copsey Clo. Ports 9L 201
Copsey Gro. Ports 1L 215
Copsey Path. Ports 9L 201
Copthorne La. Fawl 5F 208
Copythorne 8C 156
Copythorne Clo. Bourn 4A 228
Copythorne Cres. Copy 8C 156
Copythorn Rd. Ports 7G 214
Coracle Clo. Wars 8C 196
Coral Clo. Fare 2L 213
Coral Ct. Gos 1E 238
Coralin Gro. Water 9B 182
Coram Clo. Win 4L 105
Corbar Rd. Christ 6H 229
Corbett Rd. Water 3L 201
Corbiere Av. Poole 5B 226
Corbiere Clo. Sotn 8D 158
Corbin Ct. Penn 4B 234
Corbin Rd. Penn 3B 234
Corbould Rd. Dib P 8L 193
Corby Cres. Ports 4J 215
Cordale Rd. Bas 8B 42
Cordelia Clo. Dib 6J 193
Corelli Rd. Bas 2A 60
Corfe Clo. Alr 2E 108
Corfe Clo. Fare 6K 211
Corfe Vw. Rd. Poole 2A 244
Corfe Wlk. Bas 5L 41
Corfe Way. Farn 2N 49
Corfield Clo. Finch 2H 17
Corhampton 8M 135
Corhampton Cres. Hav 5D 202
Corhampton Golf Course 9L 135
Corhampton Ho. Ports 1E 240 (off Church Rd.)
Corhampton La. Bish W 8K 135
Corhampton Rd. Bourn 8F 228
Coriander Clo. Farn 7E 28
Coriander Dri. Tot 3J 171
Coriander Way. White 1G 197
Corinna Gdns. Dib 6J 193
Corinthian Clo. And 6A 52
Corinthian Clo. Bas 3K 59
Corinthian Rd. Chan F 5C 132
Cork La. March 8E 172
Cormorant Clo. Bas 2H 59
Cormorant Clo. Fare 9H 199
Cormorant Dri. Hythe 7A 194
Cormorant Pl. Coll T 6F 18
Cormorant Wlk. Gos 6D 212
Cornaway La. Fare 1K 213
Cornbrook Gro. Water 9C 182
Cornbunting Clo. Coll T 5F 18
Cornelia Clo. Farn 9F 28
Cornelia Cres. Poole 8E 226
Cornelius Dri. Water 9A 182
Cornel Rd. Sotn 5D 174
Corner Mead. Water 6G 180
Cornerways. E Bol 1B 236
Cornerways. King W 9M 91
Cornes Clo. Win 7H 105
Cornfield. Fare 5D 198
Cornfield Clo. Chan F 6L 131
Cornfield Rd. Lee S 1B 238
Cornfields. And 3B 70
Cornfields. Yate 9L 17
Cornfields, The. Hat W 3L 59
Cornflower Clo. L Hth 6B 196
Cornflower Dri. Christ 5E 230
Cornflower Way. Lud 2D 30
Cornford Way. Christ 6F 230
Cornforth Rd. Cal 1J 171
Cornilla Ct. Poole 3F 244
Cornish Clo. Bas 8L 41
Cornish Gdns. Bourn 5H 227
Corn Mkt. Roms 5L 129
Cornpits La. Dam 4N 149
Corn Store Cotts. N Gor 7L 153
Cornwall Clo. Sotn 9E 160
Cornwall Cres. Sotn 9D 160
Cornwallis Cres. Ports 1E 240
Cornwallis Ho. Ports 1E 240 (off Cornwallis Cres.)
Cornwallis Rd. Mil S 8H 235
Cornwall Rd. Chan F 9A 132
Cornwall Rd. Ports 2F 240
Cornwall Rd. Sotn 9D 160
Cornwall Rd. W'hill 6J 101
Cornwell Clo. Gos 9F 212
Cornwell Clo. Ports 6C 214
Cornwell Gdns. Alt 4F 80
Coronado Rd. Gos 9K 213
Coronation Av. Bourn 4K 227
Coronation Av. Sotn 8K 159
Coronation Clo. Burgh 3D 8
Coronation Clo. Odi 8L 45
Coronation Cotts. Woot L 4G 40
Coronation Eventide Homes. Ports 4F 214
Coronation Homes. Sotn 2H 175
Coronation Pde. Hamb 6J 195
Coronation Rd. A'sht 3K 65
Coronation Rd. Bas 5D 42
Coronation Rd. Hay I 6L 243
Coronation Rd. Lud 1E 30
Coronation Rd. Swanm 6D 164
Coronation Rd. Tidw 6C 30
Coronation Rd. Water 1M 201
Coronation Rd. Yate 6A 18
Coronation Ter. S'thth 9D 150
Corporation Rd. Bourn 9M 227
Corringway. Chu C 5N 47
Corry Rd. Hind 1L 103
Corsair Dri. Dib 6J 193
Cortina Way. H End 5A 176
Cortry Clo. Poole 7E 226
Cort Way. Fare 5M 197
Corunna Main. And 1A 70
Corvette Av. Wars 8C 196
Cosford Clo. Eastl 1L 161
Cosham 9G 201
Cosham Pk. Av. Ports 1G 215
Cossack Grn. Sotn 6M 173 (5E 4)
Cossack La. Win 6L 105 (7N 237)
Cossack La. Ho. Win 7N 237
Cosworth Dri. Dib 6J 193
Cotlands Rd. Bourn 1M 245
Cotsalls. F Oak 2N 161
Cotswold Clo. Bas 7K 41
Cotswold Clo. Dib P 6J 193
Cotswold Clo. Farn 5G 29
Cotswold Clo. Hav 3E 202
Cotswold Ct. Fle 2L 47
Cotswold Rd. S'hrst 4B 18
Cotswold Rd. Sotn 2E 172
Cotswold Wlk. Fare 1B 212
Cottage Clo. Water 7G 180
Cottage Gdns. Farn 8H 29
Cottage Gdns. Poole 9A 226
Cottage Grn. Good C 9M 69
Cottage Grn. H Win 7C 26
Cottage Gro. Gos 2K 239
Cottage Gro. S'sea 3D 240
Cottage La. Liss 1M 139
Cottage M. F'bri 9H 151
Cottage Rd. Mid W 9M 67
Cottagers La. Hord 3H 233
Cottage Vw. Ports 2E 240
Cotterell Ct. Chu C 7L 47
Cotteridge Ho. S'sea 2E 240
Cottesloe Ct. S'sea 5D 240
Cottes Way. Fare 7K 211
Cottesway E. Fare 7L 211
Cottington Clo. K're 2B 6
Cottington's Hill 8K 9
Cott La. Burl 8E 188
Cottle Clo. Bas 9B 42
Cotton Clo. A'sht 8H 49
Cotton Clo. Eastl 9J 133
Cotton Dri. Ems 5L 203 (in two parts)
Cottonworth 4D 74
Cottrell Flats. Farn 3M 49
Cott St. Swanm 6E 164
Cott St. La. Swanm 7G 165 (in two parts)
Cotwell Av. Water 6B 182
Couch Grn. Mart W 8F 92
Coulmere Rd. Gos 1J 239
Coulsdon Rd. H End 4N 175
Coultas Rd. Chan F 2C 132
Council Rd. Bas 7C 42
Countess Gdns. Bourn 6C 228
Country Vw. Fare 4L 211
Country Vw. W Wel 1B 120
County Gdns. Fare 9M 197
Course Park 7F 196
Course Pk. Cres. Fare 7F 196
Ct. Barn Clo. Lee S 9B 212
Ct. Barn La. Lee S 9B 212
Court Clo. Cal 9K 157
Court Clo. Christ 7A 230
Court Clo. Lip 3D 116
Court Clo. L'ton 4D 234
Court Clo. Ports 1J 215
Court Clo. Sotn 4E 174
Court Corner 1K 21
Court Dri. Fle 5M 47
Court Drove. Over 8C 38
Courtenay Clo. Fare 6G 197
Courtenay Pl. L'ton 3E 234
Courtenay Rd. F'ham 3G 64
Courtenay Rd. Win 4L 105
Court Gdns. Cam 8L 19
Court Hill. Dam 7A 150
Courthill Rd. Poole 1A 244
Court Ho. Clo. Hythe 5M 193
Courtier Clo. Dib 6H 193
Courtland Gdns. Sotn 6N 159
Courtlands. L'ton 2E 234
Courtlands Ter. Water 6A 182
Court La. Ports 1J 215
Court La. Ropl 8E 96
Court La. Up Som 5K 89
Courtleigh Mnr. Bourn 1A 246
Court Lodge. L'ton 4D 234
Court Mead. Ports 9J 201
Courtmoor Av. Fle 4M 47
Courtmount Gro. Ports 9H 201
Courtmount Path. Ports 8H 201
Court Rd. A'sht 9J 49

Court Rd. Bourn 5M 227
Court Rd. King W. 1N 105
Court Rd. Lee S 9A 212
Court Rd. Sotn 3L 173
Ct. Royal M. Sotn 2L 173
Courtyard, The. Bourn 5G 247
Courtyard, The. Ptsfld 1M 145
Courtyard, The. Poole 5A 226
Cousins Gro. S'sea 5H 241
Cove 7F 28
Covena Rd. Bourn 8G 229
Coventry Clo. Bas 2K 59
Coventry Ct. Gos 1F 238
Coventry Ct. Win 4L 105
Coventry Rd. Sotn 4L 173 (1B 4)
Coverack Way. Port S 1C 214
Cove Rd. Bourn 4G 226
Cove Rd. Farn 8H 29
Cove Rd. Fle 8N 27
Covert Gro. Water 4A 202
Coverts Clo. F'ham 6G 64
Coverts, The. T'ley 7H 11
Covert, The. Farn 4G 29
Covert, The. Roms 6A 130
Covey Clo. Farn 4J 29
Covey Way. Alr 2D 108
Covindale Ho. S'sea 4H 241
Cowan Rd. Water 4L 201
Coward Rd. Gos 5H 239
Cowdery Heights. Old B 5F 42
Cow Down 5E 70
Cowdown La. Good C 6A 70
Cowdown La. Ids 8N 169
Cowdray Clo. Eastl 1K 161
Cowdray Clo. Sotn 7G 159
Cowdray Ho. Ports 2E 240 (off Arundel St.)
Cowdray Pk. Alt 6F 80
Cowdray Pk. Fare 6K 211
Cowdrey Clo. Bas 3D 42
Cowdrey Gdns. Bourn 4C 228
Cowdrey Sq. And 7A 52
Cow Drove Hill. King S 8B 86
Cowell Dri. Bourn 6D 228
Cowes 5P 237
Cowes Ct. Fare 9M 197
Cowesfield Green 5J 121
Cowes La. Wars 3A 210
Cowfold La. Roth 6G 24
Cow La. Kimp 5D 30
Cow La. Portc 1M 213
Cow La. Ports 1E 214
Cow La. S Hart 8F 146
Cowleas Clo. Awb 8E 122
Cowleas Cotts. Awb 8E 122
Cowley Clo. Sotn 9D 158
Cowley Dri. Wor D 5H 91
Cowley Rd. L'ton 2C 234
Cowleys La. Beau 8K 207
Cowleys Rd. Burt 4M 229
Cowper Av. New M 5B 232
Cowper Rd. Bourn 4K 227
Cowper Rd. Ports 1F 240
Cowper Rd. Sotn 4H 175
Cowpitts La. Ring 7M 185
Cowplain 7A 182
Cowslip Bank. Lych 4G 42
Cowslip Clo. Gos 6E 212
Cowslip Clo. Lind 3M 101
Cowslip Clo. L Hth 7B 196
Cowslip Wlk. Tot 5K 171 (in two parts)
Cowslip Way. Roms 3B 130
Cox Av. Bourn 2M 227
Coxbridge Meadows. F'ham 9B 64
Cox Clo. Bourn 2M 227
Cox Dale. Fare 8F 196
Coxes Mdw. Ptsfld 8L 139
Coxford 9F 158
Coxford Clo. Sotn 9F 158
Coxford Drove. Sotn 8F 158
Coxford Rd. Sotn 9E 158
Cox Grn. Coll T 7F 18
Coxheath Rd. Chu C 5K 47
Coxmoor Clo. Chu C 6A 48
Cox Row. Chan F 9A 132
Cox's Dri. Sotn 8F 174
Cox's Hill. Twy 5L 127
Cox's La. Sotn 8B 174
Coxstone La. Ring 2K 187
Coy Pond Rd. Poole 9E 226
Cozens Clo. Sotn 9C 174
Crabapple Clo. Tot 3J 171
Crabbe Ct. S'sea 3D 240
Crabbe La. Sotn 6M 159 (in two parts)
Crabbs Way. Tot 3H 171
Crabbswood La. Sway 7F 222
Crabden La. Horn 2E 182
Crableck La. Sar G 4N 195
Crabs Hill. Wolv 6M 9
Crabthorn 6L 211
Crabthorne Farm La. Fare 5L 211
Crabton Clo. Rd. Bourn 1C 246
Crabtree. Sotn 1E 172
Crabtree Clo. Burt 4M 229
Crabtree Gdns. Head 2A 102
Crabtree La. Churt 6J 85
Crabtree La. Head 2A 102
Crabtree La. Stoke 7H 35
Crabtree Rd. Cam 2K 29
Crabtree Way. Old B 7J 43
Crabwood Clo. Sotn 9E 158
Crabwood Ct. Hav 2D 202
Crabwood Dri. W End 1J 175
Crab Wood Nature Reserve 6B 104
Crabwood Rd. Sotn 9D 158
Cracknorehard La. March 8F 172
Cracknore Rd. Sotn 5J 173
Craddock Ho. Ports 3J 5
Craddock Ho. Win 5N 105
Cradle La. Bord 4M 83
Craig Ho. S'sea 5E 240 (off Marmion Av.)
Craigmoor Av. Bourn 4B 228
Craigmoor Clo. Bourn 5C 228
Craigmoor Way. Bourn 4B 228
Craigside Rd. St L 5A 186
Craig's Wood 4N 103
Craigwell Rd. Water 5M 201
Crake Pl. Coll T 5F 18
Crampmoor 3D 130
Crampmoor La. Cram 3C 130
Cramptons. Bch 6A 80
Cranberry Clo. March 9E 172
Cranberry Wlk. B'wtr 1H 29
Cranborne 6J 149
Cranborne Common Nature Reserve 7A 152
Cranborne Cres. Poole 6C 226
Cranborne Gdns. Chan F 3N 131
Cranborne Pl. New M 3N 231
Cranborne Rd. Bourn 3J 245 (8K 247)
Cranborne Rd. Crip 7N 149
Cranborne Rd. Ports 8H 201
Cranborne Wlk. Fare 1A 212
Cranbourne 9B 42
Cranbourne Clo. Sotn 1J 173
Cranbourne Ct. Bas 9B 42
Cranbourne Dri. Ott 1F 132
Cranbourne La. Bas 1A 60
Cranbourne Pk. H End 6N 175
Cranbourne Rd. Gos 4L 239
Cranbrook Ct. Fle 9M 27
Cranbrook Rd. Poole 8A 226
Cranbury Av. Sotn 4M 173 (1E 4)
Cranbury Clo. D'ton 3K 119
Cranbury Clo. Ott 1F 132
Cranbury Ct. Sotn 7D 174
Cranbury Gdns. Burs 9K 175
Cranbury Pl. Sotn 4M 173 (1D 4)
Cranbury Rd. Eastl 2E 160 (in two parts)
Cranbury Rd. Sotn 7D 174
Cranbury Ter. Sotn 4M 173 (1E 4)
Cranbury, The. Sotn 1D 4
Cranbury Towers. Sotn 1E 4
Crane Ct. Coll T 5F 18
Cranemoor Av. Christ 4G 231
Cranemoor Clo. Christ 4G 231
Cranemoor Gdns. Highc 4H 231
Cranesfield. Sher 8M 21
Cranes Rd. Sher 8M 21
Crane St. Cran 6J 149
Craneswater Av. S'sea 6F 240
Craneswater Ga. S'sea 6F 240
Craneswater M. S'sea 5F 240 (off Craneswater Pk.)
Craneswater Pk. S'sea 5F 240
Cranford Av. Chu C 6K 47
Cranford Dri. Holyb 2J 81
Cranford Gdns. Chan F 4N 131
Cranford Ho. Sotn 9M 159
Cranford Pk. Dri. Yate 7N 17
Cranford Rd. Ptsfld 2K 145
Cranford Way. Sotn 9M 159
Cranleigh Av. Ports 1F 240
Cranleigh Clo. Ame 5A 66 (off Rayleigh Cres.)
Cranleigh Clo. Bourn 9H 229
Cranleigh Ct. Bourn 9H 229
Cranleigh Ct. Farn 8H 29
Cranleigh Ct. Sotn 2M 173
Cranleigh Gdns. Bourn 9H 229
Cranleigh Paddock. Lyn 1B 148
Cranleigh Rd. Bourn 8G 228
Cranleigh Rd. Fare 1J 213
Cranleigh Rd. H End 4N 175
Cranleigh Rd. Ports 1F 240
Cranmer Dri. Nurs 6B 158
Cranmer Rd. Bourn 6K 227
Cranmore. Net A 2G 194
Cranmore Clo. A'sht 1G 64
Cranmore Gdns. A'sht 1F 64
Cranmore La. A'sht 2F 64
Crantock Gro. Bourn 4C 228
Cranwell Clo. Bourn 2C 226
Cranwell Clo. Brans 6D 220
Cranwell Ct. Sotn 6E 158
Cranwell Cres. Sotn 6F 158
Cranworth Rd. Win 5K 105
Crasswell St. Ports 1D 240 (2N 5) (in two parts)
Craven Ct. Fare 6A 198
Craven Rd. Chan F 6B 132
Craven Rd. Ink 1F 6
Craven St. Sotn 5M 173 (4E 4)
Craven Wlk. Sotn 5M 173 (4D 4)
Crawford Clo. Nurs 6C 158
Crawford Dri. Fare 6B 198
Crawford Gdns. Cam 8K 19
Crawlboys Rd. Lud 1D 30
Crawley 3N 89
Crawley Av. Hav 3G 203
Crawley Dri. Cam 7N 19
Crawley Hill 8M 19
Crawley Hill. Cam 8N 19
Crawley Hill. W Wel 2B 120
Crawley Ridge. Cam 7N 19
Crawshaw Rd. Poole 3A 244
Crawte Av. Holb 6B 208
Crawts Rd. Over 3D 56
Craydown La. Ovr W 7M 67
Creasey Rd. Bourn 1E 226
Credenhill Rd. Ports 8D 200
Credon Clo. Farn 7H 29
Creech Rd. Poole 9A 226
Creech Vw. Den 6F 180
Creedy Gdns. W End 8E 160
Creedy Path. Christ 8L 229
Creek End. Ems 1M 217
Creek Rd. Gos 3M 239
Creek Rd. Hay I 5K 243
Creek Vw. Cvn. Est. Hay I 5L 243
Creighton Rd. Sotn 4E 172
Cremorne Pl. Ptsfld 9M 139
Cremyll Clo. Fare 6M 211
Crendell 6M 149
Crerar Clo. Farn 9F 28
Crescent Clo. Win 1F 126
Crescent Ct. Bart S 7A 232 (off Crescent Dri.)
Crescent Ct. Bourn 3H 245 (8H 247)
Crescent Dri. Bart S 7A 232
Crescent Gdns. Fare 8C 198
Crescent Rd. Bourn 2J 245 (6J 247)
Crescent Rd. Bulf 3A 66
Crescent Rd. Fare 8C 198
Crescent Rd. Gos 6J 239
Crescent Rd. L Hth 6C 196
Crescent Rd. N Bad 7E 130
Crescent Rd. Poole 1C 244
Crescent, The. And 1J 69
Crescent, The. B'wtr 9F 18
Crescent, The. Braml 1F 22 (off Oakmead)
Crescent, The. Crook V 5H 47
Crescent, The. Eastl 8E 132
Crescent, The. Farn 9L 29
Crescent, The. F'ham 2F 64
Crescent, The. Good C 8M 69
Crescent, The. Hur T 4D 34
Crescent, The. March 9D 172
Crescent, The. Meds 3J 97
Crescent, The. Net A 3G 194
Crescent, The. New M 6M 231
Crescent, The. Roms 4A 130
Crescent, The. Sotn 8E 174
Crescent, The. Twy 7L 127
Crescent, The. Uphm 1F 162
Crescent, The. Up Cl 5L 69
Crescent, The. Water 5K 201
Crescent, The. W'lnds 7E 170
Crescent, The. Yate 6N 17
Cressey Rd. Roms 5M 129
Cress Gdns. And 3M 69
Cressy Rd. Ports 9E 214
Crest Clo. Fare 8F 198
Crestland Clo. Water 7A 182
Crest Rd. Poole 8A 226
Crest, The. Water 7K 201
Crest Way. Sotn 6G 175
Crete Cotts. Dib P 9K 193
Crete La. Dib P 8L 193
Crete Rd. Dib P 9L 193
Crichel Mt. Rd. Poole 6A 244
Crichel Rd. Bourn 6L 227
Cricket Chambers. Bourn 1L 245
Cricket Clo. Christ 9B 230
Cricket Clo. Craw 3N 89
Cricket Clo. Hind 1M 103
Cricket Dri. Water 4A 182
Cricketers Way. And 7A 52
Cricket Fld. Gro. C'then 1F 18
Cricket Grn. H Win 6C 26
Cricket Grn. La. H Win 6C 26
Cricket Hill 8A 18
Cricket Hill. Finch 3J 17
Cricket Hill. Yate 1A 28
Cricket Hill La. Yate 1N 27
Cricket Lea. Lind 2L 101
Cricklemede. Bish W 4N 163
Cricklewood Clo. Bish W 4N 163
Criddlestyle 1M 153
Crigdon Clo. Sotn 2D 172
Crimea Rd. A'sht 9K 49 (in two parts)
Crimea Rd. Bourn 7K 227
Cringle Av. Bourn 1K 247
Crinoline Gdns. S'sea 5H 241
Cripley Rd. Farn 6F 28
Cripplegate La. E Bol 1B 236
Cripplestyle 7N 149
Cripstead La. Win 9K 105
Crispin Clo. Highc 6H 231
Crispin Clo. H Hth 5N 161
Crispin Clo. L Hth 5E 196
Crisspyn Clo. Water 4B 182
Criswick Clo. Abb A 7F 68
Critchell's Green 2N 121
Critchmere 8N 103
Critchmere Hill. Hasl 8N 103
Critchmere La. Hasl 9N 103
Critchmere Va. Hasl 9N 103
Criterion Arc. Bourn 2K 245 (7L 247)
Crittall Clo. Sway 5K 223
Croad Ct. Fare 8E 198
Crockerhill 1D 198
Crockford Clo. New M 1C 232
Crockford La. Chine 2E 42
Crockford Rd. W Gri 2D 120
Croft Av. And 3N 69
Crofters Clo. S'hrst 5C 18
Crofters Mdw. Lych 3G 42
Croft Gdns. Alt 4E 80
Croft Gdns. And 3N 69
Croft Heights. W'ish 5H 121
Croftlands Av. Fare 5M 211
Croft La. Cron 3L 63
Croft La. Hay I 7G 216
Croft La. Yate 6M 17
Crofton Av. Lee S 8M 211
Crofton Clo. Christ 5H 229
Crofton Clo. Sotn 1M 173
Crofton Clo. Water 4K 201
Crofton Ct. Fare 6M 211
Crofton La. Fare 7L 211
Crofton Rd. Ports 6F 214
Crofton Rd. S'sea 2J 241
Crofton Way. Swanm 6C 164
Crofton Way. Wars 8N 195
Croft Rd. A'sht 2K 65
Croft Rd. Bourn 4K 227
Croft Rd. Christ 7B 230
Croft Rd. H Win 8A 26
Croft Rd. Nea 9D 220
Croft Rd. Okly 9C 40
Croft Rd. Ports 7E 214 (in two parts)
Croft Rd. Ring 8M 185
Crofts, The. Hat W 4L 59
Croft, The. B'stne 3C 118
Croft, The. Cal 9J 157
Croft, The. Chan F 9A 132
Croft, The. Fare 4M 211
Croft, The. Fle 3J 47
Croft, The. Newt T 6E 66
Croft, The. Yate 6N 17
Cromalt Clo. Dib P 7J 193
Cromarty Av. S'sea 3J 241
Cromarty Clo. Fare 5L 211
Cromarty Rd. Sotn 6D 158
Crombie Clo. Water 6N 181 (in two parts)
Cromer Gdns. Poole 9D 226
Cromer Rd. Bourn 7A 228
Cromer Rd. Poole 1D 244
Cromer Rd. Ports 8F 200
Cromer Rd. Sotn 1C 172
Cromhall Clo. Fare 9M 197
Crompton Way. Fare 4F 196
Cromwell Clo. Old B 5J 43
Cromwell Pl. Bourn 9E 228
Cromwell Rd. Bas 5B 42
Cromwell Rd. Bourn 9E 228
Cromwell Rd. Cam 6M 19
Cromwell Rd. Poole 9B 226
Cromwell Rd. Sotn 3L 173 (1B 4)
Cromwell Rd. S'sea 5J 241
Cromwell Rd. Win 9H 105
Cromwell Way. Farn 5K 29
Crondall 3L 63
Crondall Av. Hav 3E 202
Crondall Ct. Cam 9K 19
Crondall End. Yate 6M 17
Crondall La. Dipp 5N 63
Crondall Rd. Bent 6M 63
Crondall Rd. Crook V 6H 47
Crooked Hays Clo. March 9E 172
Crooked La. New M 6D 232
Crooked Wlk. La. S'wick 6N 199
Crookham 1M 9
Crookham Clo. Hav 4C 202
Crookham Clo. T'ley 7H 11
Crookham Common 1K 9
Crookham Reach. Chu C 6K 47
Crookham Rd. Chu C & Fle 6K 47
Crookham Rd. Sotn 1D 194
Crookham Village 6J 47
Crook Hill 8B 124
Crookhorn 6M 201
Crookhorn La. Drox 3L 165
Crookhorn La. Water 8M 201
Crooksbury La. Seale 9N 65
Crooksbury Rd. F'ham 7K 65
Cropmark Way. Bas 3K 59
Crosby Gdns. Yate 6K 17
Crosby Rd. Bourn 4G 244
Crosby Way. F'ham 9C 64
Crosfield Clo. E Wel 1B 156
Cross & Pillory La. Alt 5F 80
Crossbill Clo. Water 3A 182
Crossborough Gdns. Bas 7D 42
Crossborough Hill. Bas 7D 42
Crossfell Wlk. Fare 1A 212
Crossfield Av. Cowes 5P 237
Cross Gdns. Frim G 6N 29
Crosshouse 7A 174
Cross Ho. Cen. Sotn 7A 174
Crosshouse Rd. Sotn 7A 174
Cross Keys Pas. Win 8N 237
Crossland Clo. Gos 4L 239
Crossland Dri. Hav 6F 202
Cross La. And 1M 69
Cross La. A'wrth 7M 7
Cross La. Bish W 9E 134
Cross La. Frim G 6N 29
Cross La. Water 5A 182
Crossley Ct. Sotn 4H 173
Crossmead Av. New M 4B 232
Cross Rd. Lee S 3C 238
Cross Rd. Sotn 3C 174
Cross St. A'sht 9J 49
Cross St. Bas 7C 42
Cross St. Bish W 3M 163
Cross St. Cowes 5P 237
Cross St. Farn 3L 49
Cross St. Ports 2B 240 (3C 5)
Cross St. S'sea 3E 240
Cross St. Win 6K 105 (7L 237)
Cross, The. B'stne 3C 118
Cross, The. Burl 7E 188
Cross, The. E Meon 3L 143
Cross, The. King S 8B 86
Crosstrees. Sar G 3C 196
Crosswater 4G 85
Crosswater Farm 4H 85
Crosswater La. Churt 4G 85
Cross Way. Christ 5G 228
Cross Way. Hav 7E 202
Crossways. A'sht 1L 65
Crossways. Crook V 5H 47
Crossways. Evtn 5L 233
Crossways. Shaw 8H 127
Crossways Clo. Churt 7H 85
Crossways Clo. D'ton 2H 119
Crossways Rd. Gray & Hind 4L 103
Crossways, The. And 9M 51
Crossways, The. Gos 1K 239
Crossway, The. Fare 9K 199
Crosswell Clo. Sotn 5G 174
Croucher's Cft. Win 4G 104
Croucheston 3C 118
Croucheston Drove. B'stne 3C 118
Croucheston Hollow. B'stne 3C 118
Crouch La. Water 3A 182 (in two parts)
Crow 4M 187

Crow Arch La.—Deepdene La.

Crow Arch La. *Ring* 2L **187**
Crow Arch La. Ind. Est. *Ring* 3L **187**
Crowders Grn. *Col C* 4K **133**
Crowder Ter. *Win* 7K **105** (8K **237**)
Crowdhill. 8N 133
Crow Hill. 6A 188
Crow La. *Crow* 2M **187**
Crowley Dri. *Alt* 5G **80**
Crown Clo. *Poole* 9A **226**
Crown Clo. *Water* 6M **201**
Crown Clo. M. *Alt* 5F **80**
Crown Ct. *Ports* 7K **5** (High St.)
Crown Ct. *Ports* 1E **240** (King Albert St.)
Crown Cres. *Old B* 5H **43**
Crown Dri. *Bad L* 5J **65**
Crownfields. *Odi* 9K **45**
Crown Gdns. *Fle* 3N **47**
Crown Ho. *Lud* 1D **30**
Crown La. *Bad L* 5H **65**
Crown La. *Lud* 1C **30**
Crown La. *Newn* 4B **44**
Crown La. *Old B* 5H **43**
Crown M. *Gos* 3M **239**
Crown Pl. *Owl* 4G **18**
Crown St. *Ports* 1E **240**
Crown St. *Sotn* 2G **173**
Crown Wlk. *Bourn* 1B **246**
Crown Way. *And* 9C **52**
Crowsbury Clo. *Ems* 6L **203**
Crows La. *Up Farr* 4E **98**
Crowsnest La. *Bot* 1C **176**
Crowsport. 6L 195
Crowsport. *Hamb* 6L **195**
Crowther Clo. *Sotn* 6G **175**
Crowthorne. 1E 18
Crowthorne Rd. *S'hrst* 5C **18**
Croyde Clo. *Farn* 6J **29**
Croydon Clo. *Sotn* 7F **158**
Croye Clo. *And* 1M **69**
Cruikshank Lea. *Coll T* 7G **18**
Crummock Rd. *Chan F* 4M **131**
Crundles. *Ptsfld* 1N **145**
Crundwell Ct. *F'ham* 7F **64**
Crusader Ct. *Bourn* 1F **244**
Crusader Ct. *Gos* 9L **213**
Crusader Rd. *Bourn* 2B **226**
Crusader Rd. *H End* 5A **176**
Crusaders Way. *Chan F* 6L **131**
Cruse Clo. *Sway* 5J **223**
Crux Easton. 8N 7
Crystal Way. *Water* 1A **202**
Cucklington Gdns. *Bourn* 2M **227**
Cuckmere La. *Sotn* 2B **172**
Cuckoo Bushes La. *Chan F* 4N **131**
Cuckoo Clo. *N Wal* 9A **58** (in two parts)
Cuckoo Hill Railway. 9M 153 (Miniature Railway)
Cuckoo Hill Way. *Brans* 6E **220**
Cuckoo La. *Fare* 5L **211**
Cuckoo La. *Sotn* 7L **173** (8C **4**)
Cuckoo's Corner. 1L 81
Cudworth Mead. *H End* 1A **176**
Cufaude La. *Braml* 3E **22**
Cufaude La. *Chine* 8G **23**
Cuffelle Clo. *Chine* 9H **23**
Cuffnells Clo. *Mock* 1L **185**
Cul-de-Sac. *New M* 6L **231**
Culford Av. *Tot* 4M **171**
Culford Clo. *Bourn* 4C **228**
Culford Way. *Tot* 4M **171**
Cull Clo. *Poole* 6G **226**
Cullen Clo. *Yate* 8M **17**
Cullens M. *A'sht* 1J **65**
Culley Vw. *Alr* 2F **108**
Cull La. *New M* 9C **222** (in two parts)
Culloden Clo. *Fare* 7A **198**
Culloden Rd. *Fare* 2B **212**
Cullwood La. *New M* 1D **232**
Culver. *Net A* 2G **195**
Culver Clo. *Sotn* 9C **158**
Culver Dri. *Hay I* 6J **243**
Culverin Sq. Ind. Est. *Ports* 4H **215**
Culverlands Clo. *Shed* 4A **178**
Culverley Clo. *Broc* 7C **148**
Culver M. *Win* 7L **105** (9M **237**)
Culver Rd. *Bas* 8B **42**
Culver Rd. *New M* 4A **232**
Culver Rd. *Owl* 4F **18**
Culver Rd. *S'sea* 5H **241**
Culver Rd. *Win* 8K **105**
Culvers. *S Hart* 9G **146** (in two parts)
Culverwell Gdns. *Win* 7K **105** (9L **237**)
Culvery Gdns. *W End* 1E **174**
Cumberland Av. *Bas* 1N **59**
Cumberland Av. *Chan F* 6C **132**
Cumberland Av. *Ems* 5L **203**
Cumberland Bus. Cen. *S'sea* 2E **240**
Cumberland Clo. *Chan F* 6C **132**
Cumberland Ho. *Ports* 1B **240** (2K **5**)
Cumberland House Natural History Mus. & Aquarium. 6G 240
Cumberland Pl. *Sotn* 5L **173** (3B **4**)
Cumberland Rd. *S'sea* 2E **240**
Cumberland St. *Ports* 1B **240** (2K **5**)
Cumberland St. *Sotn* 6N **173** (5F **4**)
Cumberland Way. *Dib* 6H **193**
Cumber Rd. *L Hth* 6B **196**
Cumber's La. *E Meon* 4B **144**
Cumbria Ct. *Farn* 2N **49**
Cumbrian Way. *Sotn* 2D **172**
Cummins Grn. *Burs* 9L **175**
Cumnor Rd. *Bourn* 2L **245** (6N **247**)
Cunard Av. *Sotn* 2H **173**
Cunard Rd. *Sotn* 8M **173** (9E **4**)
Cundell Way. *King W* 6M **91**
Cunningham Av. *Bish W* 3K **163**
Cunningham Clo. *Bourn* 3E **226**
Cunningham Clo. *Christ* 8C **230**
Cunningham Clo. *Ports* 4E **214**
Cunningham Clo. *Ring* 9M **185**
Cunningham Ct. S'sea 5E **240** *(off Collingwood Rd.)*
Cunningham Cres. *Bourn* 3E **226**
Cunningham Cres. *Sotn* 6E **174**
Cunningham Dri. *Gos* 5F **212**
Cunningham Dri. *L Hth* 5E **196**
Cunningham Gdns. *Burs* 1K **195**
Cunningham Ho. *Bish W* 3L **163**
Cunningham Pl. *Bourn* 3E **226**
Cunningham Rd. *Horn* 3C **182**
Cunningham Rd. *Water* 4L **201**
Cunnington Rd. *Farn* 1N **49**
Cupernham. 3A 130
Cupernham Clo. *Roms* 3N **129**
Cupernham La. *Roms* 1N **129**
Curbridge Nature Reserve. 6F 176
Curdridge Clo. *Hav* 4G **203**
Curdridge La. *Curd* 9J **163**
Curie Rd. *Ports* 8F **200**
Curlew Clo. *Bas* 1J **59**
Curlew Clo. *Ems* 9L **203**
Curlew Clo. *Hythe* 7N **193**
Curlew Clo. *Sotn* 6G **159**
Curlew Dri. *Fare* 9H **199**
Curlew Dri. *Hythe* 7N **193**
Curlew Gdns. *Water* 6N **181**
Curlew Path. *S'sea* 2J **241**
Curlew Rd. *Bourn* 4A **228**
Curlew Rd. *Christ* 8C **230**
Curlews. *Alt* 2F **80**
Curlew Sq. *Eastl* 1C **160**
Curlew Wlk. *Gos* 5C **212**
Curlew Wlk. *Hythe* 7N **193**
Curly Bri. Clo. *Farn* 4H **29**
Curtis Clo. *Head* 1A **102**
Curtis Ct. *Chu C* 6M **47**
Curtis La. *Head* 1N **101**
Curtis Mead. *Ports* 4G **214**
Curtis Mus. 5F 80
Curtis Rd. *Alt* 6G **81**
Curtis Rd. *Poole* 9A **226**
Curtiss Gdns. *Gos* 3H **239**
Curve, The. *Gos* 5D **212**
Curve, The. *Water* 4N **181**
Curzon Ct. *Sotn* 7J **159**
Curzon Dri. *Chu C* 6N **47**
Curzon Howe Rd. *Ports* 2B **240** (3K **5**)
Curzon Pl. *Penn* 4D **234**
Curzon Rd. *Bourn* 8A **228**
Curzon Rd. *Water* 2M **201** (in two parts)
Curzon Way. *Christ* 6F **230**
Cusden Dri. *And* 8N **51**
Custards. 1C 148
Custards, The. *Lyn* 1C **148**
Cutbush La. *Sotn & W End* 9E **160** (in two parts)
Cuthbert Rd. *Ports* 1G **240**
Cutler Clo. *New M* 3D **232**
Cutler Clo. *Poole* 7G **227**
Cutlers La. *Fare* 5M **211**
Cutter Av. *Wars* 8B **196**
Cut Throat La. *Drox* 1K **165**
Cut Throat La. *Swanm* 5E **164**
Cutts Arch. *Drox* 4K **165**
Cutts Rd. *A'sht* 4M **49**
Cuxhaven Way. *And* 7M **51**
Cygnet Ct. *Fare* 9H **199**
Cygnet Ct. *Fle* 9N **27**
Cygnet Ho. *Gos* 9K **213**
Cygnet Rd. *Ports* 1N **215**
Cygnus Gdns. *Dib* 6H **193**
Cynthia Rd. *Poole* 7A **226**
Cypress Av. *Sotn* 5D **174**
Cypress Cres. *Water* 5A **182**
Cypress Dri. *Fle* 2B **48**
Cypress Gdns. *Bot* 3D **176**
Cypress Gdns. *Tot* 3J **171**
Cypress Gro. *And* 2J **69**
Cypress Gro. *Evtn* 5L **233**
Cypress Hill Ct. *Farn* 3H **29**
Cypress Rd. *W'hill* 5F **100**
Cypress Way. *B'wtr* 8D **18**
Cypress Way. *Hind* 5M **103**
Cyprus Rd. *Fare* 8F **196**
Cyprus Rd. *Hat W* 5L **59**
Cyprus Rd. *Ports* 8F **214**
Cyril Rd. *Bourn* 8N **227**

D

Dacre Clo. *Charl* 7K **51**
Dacres Wlk. *Mil S* 7K **235**
Daffodil Clo. *Bas* 2J **59**
Daffodil Rd. *Sotn* 7A **160**
Daggons. 7P 149
Daggons Rd. *A'hlt* 7P **149**
Dahlia Clo. *Bas* 2K **59**
Dahlia Rd. *Sotn* 7M **159**
Daintree Clo. *Sotn* 7H **175**
Dairy Clo. *Christ* 7N **229**
Dairy La. *Sotn* 7N **157**
Dairymoor. *Wick* 6C **178**
Dairy Wlk. *H Win* 6C **26**
Daisy La. *Gos* 3J **239**
Daisy La. *L Hth* 6E **196**
Daisy Mead. *Water* 3A **202**
Daisy Rd. *Sotn* 7N **159**
Dakota Clo. *Christ* 7D **230**
Dale Clo. *Win* 1E **104**
Dale Dri. *Gos* 3D **212**
Dale Gdns. *S'hrst* 5C **18**
Dale Grn. *Chan F* 3N **131**
Dale Pk. Ho. *Ports* 2D **240**
Dale Rd. *Fare* 5N **211**
Dale Rd. *Hythe* 6L **193**
Dale Rd. *Sotn* 9H **159**
Dales La. *Hurn* 8B **218**
Dales Way. *Tot* 2H **171**
Dale, The. *Water* 7K **201**
Dale Valley Clo. *Sotn* 9H **159**
Dale Valley Gdns. *Sotn* 9H **159**
Dale Valley Rd. *Sotn* 9H **159**
Dalewood. *Bas* 9J **41**
Dalewood Av. *Bourn* 1C **226**
Dalewood Rd. *Fare* 8N **197**
Dalkeith Arc. *Bourn* 2K **245** (6M **247**)
Dalkeith La. *Bourn* 2K **245** (6M **247**)
Dalkeith Rd. *Poole* 4E **244** (in two parts)
Dalkeith Steps. *Bourn* 6M **247**
Dalley Ct. *S'hrst* 6F **18**
Dalling Rd. *Poole* 9E **226**
Dallington Clo. *Fare* 7M **211**
Dalmally Gdns. *Sotn* 2D **174**
Dalmeny Rd. *Bourn* 2K **247**
Damask Gdns. *Water* 9B **182**
Damen Clo. *H End* 5M **175**
Damerham. 3P 149
Damerham Rd. *Bourn* 3A **228**
Damerham Rd. *Cran* 6J **149**
Dampier Clo. *Gos* 9E **212**
Damsel La. *P Can* 4F **78**
Damsel Path. *Bas* 6E **42**
Damson Cres. *F Oak* 2L **161**
Damson Hill. *Swanm* 2D **164**
Danbury Ct. *Ems* 7N **203**
Dancers Mdw. *Sher* 9A **22**
Dances Clo. *And* 9A **52**
Dance's La. *Whitc* 4H **55**
Dances Way. *Hay I* 3E **242**
Dandelion Clo. *Gos* 6D **212**
Dando Rd. *Water* 6H **181**
Dandy's Ford La. *Sher E* 7N **121**
Danebury. 1B 88
Danebury Clo. *Hav* 3E **202**
Danebury Gdns. *Chan F* 8M **131**
Danebury Ring. 8E 72
Danebury Rd. *Hat W* 4K **59**
Danebury Wlk. *Frim* 4N **29**
Danebury Way. *Nurs* 8C **158**
Dane Clo. *Black* 7D **208**
Danecrest Rd. *Hord* 3G **232**
Danegeld Clo. *And* 6A **52**
Danehurst. *Mil S* 8G **233**
Danehurst New Rd. *Tip* 7D **222** (in two parts)
Danehurst Pl. *And* 1J **69**
Danemark Ct. *Win* 6L **105** (6N **237**)
Dane Rd. *Mil S* 8H **233**
Danesbrook La. *Water* 2A **202**
Danesbury Av. *Bourn* 1J **247**
Danes Clo. *Bart S* 7B **232**
Daneshill. 3F 42
Daneshill Ct. *Chine* 2G **43**
Daneshill Dri. *Lych* 3G **43**
Daneshill E. Ind. Est. *Bas* 4F **42**
Daneshill Ho. *Chine* 3G **42**
Daneshill Ind. Est. *Bas* 4F **42**
Daneshill Roundabout. *Bas* 4F **42**
Danes Rd. *Awb & Shoot* 1D **128**
Danes Rd. *Fare* 8K **199**
Danes Rd. *Win* 5L **105**
Danes, The. *Bas* 6D **42**
Danestream Clo. *Mil S* 8K **235**
Danestream Ct. *Mil S* 8L **235**
Daneswood Rd. *New M* 3D **232**
Daniells Clo. *L'ton* 3E **234**
Daniell's Wlk. *L'ton* 4E **234**
Daniel Rd. *Whitc* 6H **55**
Daniel's Ct. *Ring* 1H **187**
Daniels Wlk. *Cal* 1H **171**
Dankworth Rd. *Bas* 2L **59** (in three parts)
Danley La. *L'mre* 3J **117**
Danvers Dri. *Chu C* 7K **47**
Daphne Dri. *Chu C* 8K **47**
Dapple Pl. *March* 9F **172**
Darby Green. 8C 18
Darby Grn. La. *B'wtr* 8D **18**
Darby Grn. Rd. *B'wtr* 8C **18**
Darcy Clo. *Bas* 4D **42**
D'arcy Ho. *Bas* 8L **41**
Darent Ct. Bas 6E **42** *(off Loddon Dri.)*
Dare's La. *Ews* 1M **63**
Dark Hollow. *Ptsfld* 9L **139**
Dark La. *Bish S* 4H **109**
Dark La. *Black* 7C **208** (in two parts)
Dark La. *Hint* 2J **231**
Dark La. *New M* 2A **232**
Dark La. *Sher* 9N **21**
Dark La. *W'frd* 6A **136**
Darleydale Clo. *Owl* 3F **18**
Darlington Gdns. *Sotn* 1J **173**
Darlington Rd. *Bas* 4B **42**
Darlington Rd. *S'sea* 4F **240**
Darracott Rd. *Bourn* 1D **246**
Darren Clo. *Fare* 4N **211**
Darren Ct. *Fare* 7D **198**
Darset Av. *Fle* 1M **47**
Dart Ho. *Sotn* 2D **174**
Dartington Rd. *Eastl* 7H **133**
Dartmouth M. *S'sea* 4C **240** (8M **5**)
Dartmouth Rd. *Ports* 6H **215**
Dartmouth Wlk. *Bas* 8L **41**
Dartmouth Way. *Bas* 8L **41**
Dart Rd. *Farn* 6F **28**
Dart Rd. *W End* 8F **160**
Darvill Rd. *Ropl* 1B **110**
Darvills La. *F'ham* 8E **64**
Darwin Av. *Christ* 5H **229**
Darwin Clo. *Bulf B* 3C **66**
Darwin Ct. *Poole* 1E **244**
Darwin Gro. *A'sht* 8L **49**
Darwin Ho. Ports 2E **240** *(off Australia Clo.)*
Darwin Rd. *Eastl* 8F **132**
Darwin Rd. *Sotn* 3J **173**
Darwin Way. *Gos* 1F **238**
Dashwood Clo. *Alt* 6D **80**
Dasna Rd. *Tidw* 9B **30**
Daubney Gdns. *Hav* 3D **202**
Daulston Rd. *Ports* 9G **214**
Daunch Clo. *Tidw* 7B **30**
Dauntsey Drove. *W'hll* 8A **50**
Dauntsey La. *W'hll* 9A **50**
Davenport Clo. *Gos* 1E **238**
Daventry La. *Ports* 4K **215**
D Avenue. *Hythe* 2B **208**
David Ct. *Roms* 6N **129**
Davidia Ct. *Water* 3A **202**
David's Garden. Pitt 6E **86** *(off Black La.)*
David's La. *Ring* 3F **186**
Davidson Ct. *Ports* 4K **5**
Davies Ct. *Poole* 9C **226**
Davis Clo. *Gos* 8E **212**
Davis Fld. *New M* 4A **232**
Davis Gdns. *Coll T* 6G **18**
Davis Rd. *Poole* 9C **226**
Davis Way. *Fare* 2C **212**
Davy Clo. *Bas* 7N **41**
Dawkins Way. *New M* 4B **232**
Daw La. *Hay I* 8F **216**
Dawlish Av. *Sotn* 2J **173**
Dawnay Clo. *Sotn* 6B **160**
Dawnay Rd. *Cam* 5K **19** (in two parts)
Dawn Clo. *Bourn* 4G **227**
Dawn Gdns. *Win* 8G **105**
Daws Av. *Bourn* 5E **226**
Dawson Lodge. *W End* 1K **175**
Dawson Rd. *Sotn* 8G **174**
Dawtrey Ct. *Sotn* 9A **160**
Day La. *Water* 3L **181**
Dayrell Clo. *Cal* 1H **171**
Dayshes Clo. *Gos* 5D **212**
Dayslondon Rd. *Water* 4L **201**
D-Day Mus. & Overlord Embroidery. 6D 240
Deacon Clo. *Sotn* 5E **174**
Deacon Cres. *Sotn* 5E **174**
Deacon Gdns. *Bourn* 1E **226**
Deacon Rd. *Bourn* 1E **226**
Deacon Rd. *Kimp* 7M **31**
Deacon Rd. *L Hth* 7E **196**
Deacon Rd. *Sotn* 5E **174**
Deacon Trad. Est. *Eastl* 1G **160**
Deadbrook La. *A'sht* 8M **49**
Deadman's Plack Monument. 3H 71
Deadmoor La. *Burgh* 2D **8**
Deadwater. 3M 101
Deal Clo. *Fare* 4M **211**
Deal Rd. *Ports* 8F **200**
Dean. 9H 135 (Corhampton)
Dean. 3C 104 (Sparsholt)
Dean Clo. *Win* 4G **104**
Dean Ct. *H End* 3M **175**
Dean Ct. *Horn* 3C **182**
Dean Ct. *Sotn* 2C **174**
Deane. 1L 57
Deane Ct. *Hav* 4H **203**
Deane Down Drove. *Win* 2F **104**
Deane Gdns. *Lee S* 1B **238**
Deanery. 7L 105 (9M 237)
Deanery, The. *Chan F* 3N **131**
Deanes Clo. *Bas* 5D **42**
Deane's Pk. Rd. *Fare* 8F **198**
Dean Farm Est. *Fare* 4C **198**
Deanfield Clo. *Hamb* 7K **195**
Dean La. *Bish W* 8H **135**
Dean La. *Hav* 4K **183**
Dean La. *Spar & Win* 3B **104**
Dean La. *W'ish* 5H **121**
Deanlane End. 5L 183
Dean Pk. Cres. *Bourn* 1K **245** (5M **247**)
Dean Pk. Rd. *Bourn* 1K **245** (5M **247**)
Dean Rd. *E Grim & W Dean* 1F **120**
Dean Rd. *F Oak* 2M **161**
Dean Rd. *Ports* 9H **201**
Dean Rd. *Sotn* 2E **174**
Dean Rd. *W Dean* 1J **121**
Deans Clo. *Tidw* 8G **31**
Deans Ct. *Mil S* 7K **235**
Deanscroft Rd. *Bourn* 2J **227**
Deans Dell. *Frox* 4E **138**
Deansfield Clo. *Roms* 4A **130**
Deans Ga. *Fare* 7M **211**
Deansleigh Rd. *Bourn* 5E **228**
Deans Rd. *Bourn* 9E **228**
Deans, The. *Bourn* 1K **245**
Dean St. *Ports* 2B **240** (4K **5**)
Dean Swift Cres. *Poole* 5A **244**
Deanswood Dri. *Water* 9M **181**
Deanswood Rd. *T'ley* 5G **10**
Dean, The. *Alr* 9E **94**
Dean Vs. *Know* 2N **197**
Dearing Clo. *Lyn* 2B **148**
Dearly Cft. *W'grn* 2A **154**
Decies Rd. *Poole* 9A **226**
De Courtenai Clo. *Bourn* 1B **226**
Decouttere Clo. *Chu C* 6K **47**
Dee Clo. *Chan F* 7N **131**
Deep Dell. *Water* 5B **182**
Deepdene. *Hasl* 9N **103**
Deepdene La. *Bourn* 1C **226**

Deepdene, The. Sotn 2C 174
Deeping Clo. Sotn 9D 174
Deeping Ga. Water 2A 202
Deep La. Bas 6A 42
Deep Well Dri. Cam 8N 19
Deerhurst Clo. Tot 4K 171
Deerhurst Cres. Ports 8B 200
Deer La. L'ton 8D 224
Deer Leap. Fare 4N 197
Deerleap Clo. Hythe 6M 193
Deerleap La. Tot 7K 171
Deerleap Way. Hythe 6M 193
Deerleap Way. New M 9C 222
Deer Pk. Clo. New M 2A 232
Deer Pk. Farm Ind. Est. F Oak 2B 162
Deer Pk. Vw. Odi 8L 45
Deer Rock Rd. Cam 6N 19
Defender Rd. Sotn 7B 174
Defender Wlk. Sotn 7B 174
Defoe Clo. White 1F 196
De Grouchy La. Sotn 1M 173
De Havilland Way. Christ 9B 230
Delamere Gdns. Bourn 3J 227
Delamere Rd. S'sea 4F 240
De La Rue Ho. Bas 5E 42
Delaval Ho. Ports 3K 5
De La Warr Rd. Mil S 8J 235
Delft Clo. L Hth 6C 196
Delft Gdns. Water 8M 181
Delft M. Christ 8N 229
Delhi Barracks. Tidw 9B 30
Delhi Clo. Poole 2B 244
Delhi Rd. Bourn 4J 227
Delibes Rd. Bas 2A 60
De Lisle Clo. Ports 4G 214
De Lisle Rd. Bourn 7K 227
Delius Av. Sotn 7H 175
Delius Clo. Bas 1N 59
Delius Wlk. Water 4M 201
Dellands. Over 3D 56
Dellands La. Over 3C 56
Dell Clo. F Oak 2N 161
Dell Clo. Water 7J 201
Dellcrest Path. Ports 8J 201 (in two parts)
Dellfield. Frox 3E 138
Dellfield. Okly 8D 40
Dellfield Clo. Ports 8B 200
Dell Piece E. Horn 5D 182
Dell Piece W. Horn 4B 182
Dell Quay Clo. Gos 6D 212
Dell Rd. And 9L 51
Dell Rd. Finch 2K 17
Dell Rd. Sotn 9D 160
Dell Rd. Win 8N 105
Dell, The. Fare 8F 198
Dell, The. F'ham 3F 64
Dell, The. Grat 4L 67
Dell, The. Hav 7B 202
Dell, The. K're 2B 6
Dell, The. New M 6L 231
Dell, The. Old B 6K 43
Dell, The. Ver D 8E 6
Dell, The. Yate 8M 17
Delme Ct. Fare 8C 198
Delme Dri. Fare 7F 198
Delme Sq. Fare 8D 198
Delphi Way. Water 7N 201
Delta Bus. Pk. Fare 1D 212
Delta Clo. Christ 7C 230
Delta Ho. Sotn 2H 159
De-Lucy Av. Alr 1D 108
De Lunn Bldgs. Win 6M 237
Delville Clo. Farn 9F 28
De Mauley Rd. Poole 5C 244
De Mowbray Way. L'ton 4D 234
Dempsey Clo. Sotn 6F 174
Denbigh Clo. Eastl 7D 132
Denbigh Clo. Tot 5K 171
Denbigh Dri. Fare 7B 198
Denbigh Gdns. Sotn 7L 159
Dene Clo. Bord 5J 101
Dene Clo. Chilw 4L 159
Dene Clo. Ring 8M 185
Dene Clo. Ropl 1B 110
Dene Clo. Sar G 5B 196
Dene Ct. And 2A 70
Dene Hollow. Ports 9L 201
Dene Path. And 2A 70
Dene Ri. Hur T 4E 34
Dene Rd. And 2A 70
Dene Rd. Asht 8J 171
Dene Rd. Farn 9H 29
Deneside Copse. Penn 4B 234
Dene, The 3E 34
Dene, The. Hur T 4D 34
Dene, The. Ropl 1B 110
Dene Way. Asht 7J 171
Denewood Rd. Bourn 2F 244
Denewulf Clo. Bish W 3M 163
Denham Clo. Fare 6L 211
Denham Clo. Win 4K 105
Denham Ct. Win 4L 105
Denham Dri. Bas 9L 41
Denham Dri. Highc 5H 231
Denham Dri. Yate 8N 17
Denham Fields. Eastl 9N 133
Denham Gdns. Net A 4F 194
Denhill Clo. Hay I 2E 242
Denholm Clo. Ring 8N 185
Denman Clo. Fle 2A 48
Denmark Rd. Bourn 5K 227
Denmark Sq. A'sht 9M 49
Denmark St. A'sht 9M 49
Denmead 5G 181
Denmead. New M 2E 232
Denmead Cvn. Pk. Water 6H 181
Denmead Ho. Ports 1E 240
Denmead La. Den 4J 181
Denmead Rd. Bourn 7G 229
Denmead Rd. Sotn 2G 174
Denmead Rd. T'ley 5H 11
Dennett Ho. Win 5A 106
Denning Clo. Fle 4K 47
Denning M. S'sea 2D 240
Dennison Ct. Sotn 2G 172
Dennistoun Av. Christ 7B 230
Dennistoun Clo. Cam 8M 19
Dennis Way. Liss 2F 140
Denny Clo. Fawl 5F 208
Denton Way. Frim 2M 29
Denville Av. Fare 2M 213
Denville Clo. Ports 9N 201
Denville Clo. Path. Ports 9N 201
Denvilles 6J 203
Denvilles Clo. Hav 7H 203
Denzil Av. Net A 3G 194
Denzil Av. Sotn 4M 173 (1E 4)
Depedene Clo. Holb 4N 207
Deports Heights. Meon 8N 135
Deptford La. Grey 8F 44
Derby Ct. Gos 1E 238
Derbyfields. N War 5J 45
Derby Ho. Eastl 2E 160
Derby Rd. Bourn 1N 245
Derby Rd. Eastl 1C 160
Derby Rd. Ports 7E 214
Derby Rd. Sotn 5N 173 (3F 4)
De Redvers Rd. Poole 3A 244
Dereham Way. Poole 8D 226
Derek Horn Ct. Cam 7K 19
Deridene Ct. Tot 4K 171
Derlyn Rd. Fare 8C 198
Derritt La. Brans 9L 219
Derry Brian Gdns. New M 4B 232
Derry Down 2M 53
Derry Rd. Farn 4H 29
Dersingham Clo. Ports 8F 200
Derwent Clo. Bord 2J 101
Derwent Clo. Bourn 4L 227
Derwent Clo. Fare 4N 211
Derwent Clo. Farn 8G 28
Derwent Clo. F'ham 4C 64
Derwent Clo. Water 9C 168
Derwent Clo. W End 1F 174
Derwent Dri. Tot 2H 171
Derwent Gdns. Alr 2F 108
Derwent Rd. Bas 1J 59
Derwent Rd. Lee S 2B 238
Derwent Rd. New M 1C 232
Derwent Rd. Sotn 1D 172
Desborough Clo. Ports 8B 200
Desborough Rd. Eastl 2E 160
Devenish Rd. Win 3H 105
Dever Clo. Mich 7J 77
Deverel Clo. Christ 6K 229
Deverell Pl. Water 6K 201
Dever Way. Okly 1D 58
Devil's Highway, The. C'then 1A 18
Devils Highway, The. Rise 2J 15
Devil's Jumps, The 4K 85
Devils La. Lip 3G 116
Devine Gdns. Eastl 1H 161
Devon Clo. Chan F 9A 132
Devon Clo. Coll T 6F 18
Devon Clo. Fle 8N 27
Devon Dri. Chan F 9A 132
Devon Rd. Bord 4J 101
Devon Rd. Christ 6H 229
Devon Rd. Ports 5H 215
Devonshire Av. S'sea 3G 241
Devonshire Gdns. Burs 8L 175
Devonshire Gdns. Hythe 9M 193
Devonshire Mans. Sotn 2B 4
Devonshire Pl. A'sht 1H 65
Devonshire Pl. Bas 7B 42
Devonshire Rd. Sotn 4L 173 (1B 4)
Devonshire Sq. S'sea 3G 240
Devonshire Way. Fare 9M 197
Dewar Clo. Fare 4F 196
Deweys La. Lud 1D 30
Deweys La. Ring 1J 187
Dew La. Eastl 9D 132
Dewpond Wlk. Lych 3G 42
Dewsbury Ct. Sotn 9E 160
Dexter Sq. And 7B 52
Dexter Way. Fle 8N 27
Dhekelia Ct. Ports 1E 240
Dial Clo. Brans 5F 220
Diamond Clo. F'bri 2H 153
Diamond Ct. F'bri 2H 153
Diamond Hill. Cam 6N 19
Diamond Ridge. Cam 6M 19
Diamond St. S'sea 4C 240 (7M 5)
Diana Clo. Bas 8N 41
Diana Clo. Ems 5L 203
Diana Clo. Gos 3G 239
Diana Ct. Highc 7J 231
Dibben Wlk. Roms 3B 130
Dibble Dri. N Bad 9E 130
Dibden 4H 193
Dibden Clo. Bourn 3A 228
Dibden Clo. Hav 5C 202
Dibden Golf Course 4H 193
Dibden Lodge Clo. Hythe 4L 193
Dibden Purlieu 8K 193
Dibles Pk. Cvn. Site. Wars 8B 196
Dibles Rd. Wars 8A 196
Dibles Wharf. Sotn 5A 174
Dibley Clo. Bas 8L 41
Dickens Clo. Ports 9E 214
Dickens Dell. Tot 3H 171
Dickens Dri. White 9F 176
Dicken's La. Bas & Old B 9G 43 (in two parts)
Dickens Mus. 9D 214
Dickenson Wlk. Alr 2F 108
Dickens Rd. Bourn 7H 229
Dickens Way. Yate 8M 17
Dicker's La. Alt 4G 81
Dickson Pk. Wick 6C 178
Dickson Rd. And 2G 68
Didcot Rd. Sotn 1H 173
Dieppe Cres. Ports 4F 214
Dieppe Gdns. Gos 3H 239
Dight Rd. Gos 5L 239
Diligence Clo. Burs 9L 175
Dilly La. Bart S 6B 232
Dilly La. H Win 8B 26
Dilton 9F 204
Dimond Clo. Sotn 1C 174
Dimond Hill. Sotn 1C 174
Dimond Rd. Sotn 9C 160
Dines Clo. Hur T 4D 34
Dingle Rd. Bourn 1E 246
Dingle Way. L Hth 5D 196
Dinham Ct. New M 2E 232
Dinham Rd. New M 2E 232
Dinorben Av. Fle 4K 47
Dinorben Beeches. Fle 4K 47
Dinorben Clo. Fle 4K 47
Dipley 5L 25
Dipley Rd. H Win 4J 25
Dippenhall 5N 63
Dippenhall Rd. Dipp 5N 63
Dippenhall St. Cron 3L 63
Dirty Dri. N Bad 7J 131
Dirty La. Bentw 7J 79
Disa Ho. Sotn 2A 4
Discovery Clo. Fare 3M 211
Disraeli Rd. Christ 8N 229
Ditcham Cres. Hav 5E 202
Ditchbury. L'ton 9D 224
Ditton Clo. Fare 5M 211
Divers Clo. Alt 2F 80
Dix Hill. P Grn 7K 11
Dixon Rd. Braml 3H 23
Dixons La. Bro'tn 1A 86
Dockenfield 2A 84
Dockenfield Clo. Hav 5C 202
Dockenfield St. Bucks H 10M 63
Dock La. Beau 7F 206
Dock Mill Cotts. S'sea 5E 240
Dock Rd. Gos 3L 239
Dockyard Apprentice Exhibition Mus. 2A 240 (3H 5)
Doctors Drove. Hur T 4C 34
Doctor's Hill 1A 128
Doctor's Hill. Sher E 5N 121
Doctors La. W Meon 8D 136
Dodds La. Swanm 6D 164
Dodgson Clo. W'grn 2A 154
Dodwell La. Burs 9M 175
Dodwell Ter. Burs 9M 175
Doe Copse Way. New M 2N 231
Dogflud Way. F'ham 7E 64
Dogkennel La. Hmbdn 7G 166
Dogmersfield 5F 46
Dogwood Dell. Water 4N 201
Doiley Bottom. Hur T 4J 35
Doiley Hill. Hur T 2F 34
Dolbery Rd. N. Poole 4B 226
Dolbery Rd. S. Poole 5A 226
Dollis Dri. F'ham 7F 64
Dollis Grn. Braml 1G 23
Dolly's Hill 9H 49
Dolman Rd. Gos 4L 239
Dolomans La. Hur T 4B 34
Dolphin Av. Bourn 1J 227
Dolphin Clo. Eastl 1K 161
Dolphin Clo. Hasl 9N 103
Dolphin Ct. Fare 4L 211
Dolphin Ct. Lee S 1A 238
Dolphin Ct. Poole 3F 244
Dolphin Ct. S'sea 6G 240
Dolphin Cres. Gos 4L 239
Dolphin Hill. Twy 7L 127
Dolphin Pl. Bart S 7B 232
Dolphin Quay. Ems 9N 203
Dolphin Way. Gos 6M 239
Dolton Rd. Sotn 8E 158
Doman Rd. Cam 9H 19
Dome All. Win 7L 105 (9M 237)
Dominica Clo. Bas 1D 42
Dominie Wlk. Lee S 1B 238
Dominion Cen. Bourn 3C 226
Dominion Rd. Bourn 3C 226
Dominy Clo. Hythe 5N 193
Domitian Gdns. Bas 3L 41
Domum Rd. Ports 6G 215
Domum Rd. Win 8M 105
Domvilles App. Ports 7C 214
Donaldson Rd. Ports 2G 214
Doncaster Drove. Eastl 4C 160
Doncaster Rd. Eastl 3E 160
Donigers Clo. Swanm 5C 164
Donigers Dell. Swanm 5C 164
Donkey La. Bot 3D 176
Donlan Dri. Farn 2E 48
Donnelly Rd. Bourn 9J 229
Donnelly St. Gos 1J 239
Donnington Clo. Cam 9K 19
Donnington Ct. Win 5L 105
Donnington Dri. Chan F 9M 131
Donnington Dri. Christ 7D 230
Donnington Gro. Sotn 9N 159
Donoughmore Rd. Bourn 1A 246
Dora's Green 3N 63
Dora's Grn. La. Dipp & Ews 4N 63
Dora's Grn. Rd. Dipp 5M 63
Dorcas Clo. Water 9A 182
Dorcas Ct. Cam 1K 29
Dorchester Clo. Bas 6K 41
Dorchester Ct. Sotn 2L 173
Dorchester Rd. Hook 2G 44
Dorchester Way. Grey 7G 44
Dore Av. Fare 9K 199
Doreen Clo. Farn 5G 28
Dores La. Brfld 6D 124
Dorian Gro. Alr 2D 108
Doric Clo. Chan F 5D 132
Dorking Cres. Ports 1G 215
Dorland Gdns. Tot 4K 171
Dormer Clo. C'then 1C 18
Dormington Rd. Ports 8D 200
Dormy Clo. Sar G 6A 196
Dormy Way. Gos 7D 212
Dornan Ho. Sotn 3M 173 (1D 4)
Dorney Ct. Ports 1H 215
Dornie Rd. Poole 6C 244
Dornmere La. Water 2A 202
Dorothy Ct. S'sea 4E 240
Dorothy Dymond St. Ports 2D 240 (4N 5)
Dorrel Clo. Bas 4K 59
Dorrick Ct. Sotn 3L 173
Dorrien Rd. Gos 9K 213
Dorrita Av. Water 6A 182
Dorrita Clo. S'sea 5G 240
Dorrits, The. Tot 3H 171
Dorset Clo. Bulf 3A 66
Dorset Clo. Water 4B 182
Dorset Ho. Poole 3E 244
Dorset Lake Av. Poole 5A 244
Dorset Rd. Bourn 9G 226
Dorset Rd. Chan F 9A 132
Dorset Rd. Christ 6B 230
Dorset St. Sotn 4M 173 (1D 4)
Dorstone Rd. Ports 8D 200
Dorval Ho. Sotn 3K 173
Dorval Mnr. Sotn 3K 173
Doswell Way. Bas 5D 42
Douai Clo. Farn 8L 29
Double Hedges. Bulf 3A 66
Doughty Way. And 9D 52
Douglas Av. Christ 8J 229
Douglas Ct. Christ 8J 229
Douglas Cres. Sotn 4G 175
Douglas Gdns. Hav 5G 203
Douglas Gdns. Poole 9C 226
Douglas Keep. Water 6M 181
Douglas M. Bourn 9F 228
Douglas Pl. Farn 7J 29
Douglas Ride. Wool H 3A 8
Douglas Rd. And 1H 69
Douglas Rd. Bourn 1H 247
Douglas Rd. Poole 9C 226
Douglas Rd. Ports 9H 215
Douglas Way. Hythe 5L 193
Douro Clo. Baug 4D 10
Dove Clo. And 8A 52
Dove Clo. Bas 1H 59
Dove Clo. Water 6N 181
Dove Ct. Alt 2G 80
Dove Dale. Eastl 1B 160
Dovedale Clo. Owl 3F 18
Dove Gdns. Park G 4E 196
Dove La. Brfld 6G 125
Dover Clo. Alr 2F 108
Dover Clo. Bas 5M 41
Dover Clo. Fare 5L 211
Dover Clo. Poole 2E 244
Dover Ct. Hay I 2E 242
Dovercourt Rd. Ports 2H 215
Dover Rd. Poole 2E 244
Dover Rd. Ports 8H 215
Dover St. Sotn 3M 173 (1E 4)
Doveshill Cres. Bourn 3H 227
Doveshill Gdns. Bourn 3H 227
Doveshill Mobile Home Pk. Bourn 3H 227
Doveys Clo. Burl 7E 188
(off Ringwood Rd.)
Dowden Gro. Alt 3F 80
Dowds Clo. H End 2M 175
Dowlands Clo. Bourn 2H 227
Dowlands Rd. Bourn 2H 227
Dowley Ct. Titch 9J 197
Downend 8G 199
Down End. Ports 8K 201
Downend Rd. Fare 8H 199
Down End Rd. Ports 8K 201
Downey Clo. Bourn 4D 226
Down Farm La. Win 7G 91
Down Farm Pl. Water 1C 182
Down Ga. Alr 2E 108
Downham Clo. Water 7N 181
Downhouse Rd. Water 7A 168
Downing Ct. Titch 8F 196
Downing St. F'ham 8D 64
Downland Clo. Bot 3C 176
Downland Clo. L Hth 5D 196
Downland Pl. H End 5M 175
Downlands Clo. D'ton 3K 119
Downlands Rd. Win 1F 126
Downlands Way. S Won 3G 91 (in two parts)
Down La. Map 8N 43
Down La. P Can 5G 78
Down La. Roms 4A 130
Downley Rd. Hav 5H 203
Down Lodge Clo. A'hlt 4D 152
Down Rd. Horn 1C 182 (in three parts)
Down Rd. Kimp 8K 31
Downs Clo. Water 6N 201
Downscroft Gdns. H End 3M 175
Downside. Gos 6F 212
Downside. Hind 9M 85
Downside Av. Sotn 4E 174
Downside Rd. Water 6K 201
Downside Rd. Win 4F 104
Downsland Ct. Bas 7A 42
(off Downsland Pde.)
Downsland Pde. Bas 7A 42
Downsland Rd. Bas 7A 42
Downs Pk. Av. Tot 4N 171
Downs Pk. Cres. Tot 4N 171
Downs Pk. Rd. Tot 4N 171
Downs Rd. Ovr W 7M 67
Downs Rd. S Won 3G 90
Down St. Dum 9F 58
Downs Vw. Holyb 1L 81
Downsview Rd. Head D 2E 102
Downsview Way. Per D 5B 30
Downs Way. Alt 6D 80
Downsway, The. Fare 9L 199 (in two parts)
Downton 8G 233
(Lymington)
Downton 2L 119
(Salisbury)
Downton Clo. Bourn 3N 227
Downton La. Down 8G 233
Downton Rd. Sotn 9D 160
Downtown Hill. Redl 7C 120
Downview Clo. Hind 1M 103

Downview Rd. *M'tin* 9C **118**
Downwood Clo. *Dib P* 7H **193**
Downwood Clo. *F'bri* 9G **150**
Downwood Way. *Horn* 1C **182**
Doyle Av. *Ports* 4F **214**
Doyle Clo. *Ports* 4F **214**
Doyle Ct. *Ports* 5F **214**
Doyle Ct. *Sotn* 9D **174**
Doyle Gdns. *Yate* 9M **17**
Doyle Ho. *Hav* 6B **202**
Doyne Rd. *Poole* 1C **244**
Dradfield La. *Sob* 2K **179**
Dragon Est. *Ports* 1M **215**
Dragonfly Dri. *Lych* 3G **43**
Dragon La. *Ring* 8K **187**
Dragon St. *Ptsfld* 1M **145**
Dragoon Clo. *Sotn* 6G **174**
Dragoon Ct. *A'sht* 9G **49**
Dragoon Way. *Christ* 7J **229**
Drake Clo. *Christ* 8B **230**
Drake Clo. *L Hth* 4E **196**
Drake Clo. *March* 8F **172**
Drake Clo. *New M* 3A **232**
Drake Clo. *Ring* 8N **185**
Drake Ct. *And* 9C **52**
Drake Ho. *Ports* 2B **240** (3J **5**)
Drake Rd. *Eastl* 8J **133**
Drake Rd. *Lee S* 9N **211**
Drakes Clo. *Hythe* 7L **193**
Drakes Ct. *March* 7E **172**
Draper Rd. *Bourn* 2E **226**
Draper Rd. *Christ* 7A **230**
Drapers Copse Mobile Home Pk. *Dib* 5J **193**
Draycote Rd. *Water* 8C **168**
Draycott Rd. *Bourn* 4H **227**
Draymans Way. *Alt* 5F **80**
Drayton 1K **143** (Petersfield)
Drayton 1K **215** (Portsmouth)
Drayton 6N **71** (Winchester)
Drayton Clo. *Sotn* 1D **194**
Drayton La. *Ports* 8J **201**
Drayton Pl. *Tot* 3K **171**
Drayton Rd. *Ports* 7F **214**
Drayton St. *Win* 8G **104**
Dreadnought Rd. *Fare* 3B **212**
Dresden Dri. *Water* 8M **181**
Dreswick Clo. *Christ* 2G **229**
Drew Clo. *Poole* 7G **226**
Drift Rd. *Chlbn* 6L **75**
Drift Rd. *Fare* 7F **198**
Drift Rd. *Water* 6B **168**
Drift Rd. *W'hill* 8F **100**
Drift, The. *Row C* 9H **183**
Driftway Rd. *Hook* 2J **45**
Driftway, The. *Drox* 3M **165**
Driftwood Gdns. *S'sea* 5K **241**
Driftwood Gdns. *Tot* 4J **171**
Drill Shed Rd. *Ports* 7C **214**
Drinkwater Clo. *Eastl* 9D **132**
Drive, The. *Dib* 6J **193**
Drive, The. *E Wel* 1A **156**
Drive, The. *Fare* 8C **198**
Drive, The. *Gos* 6C **212**
Drive, The. *Hav* 6F **202**
Drive, The. *Okly* 1D **58**
Drive, The. *Poole* (BH12) 9B **226**
Drive, The. *Poole* (BH13) 6B **244**
Drive, The. *Sher E* 6L **121**
Drive, The. *Tot* 5M **171**
Drive, The. *W End* 8F **160**
Droffatts Ho. *Sotn* 3J **173**
Droke, The. *Ports* 1G **215** (in two parts)
Drove Clo. *Coom B* 2G **119**
Drove Clo. *Twy* 8K **127**
Drove Cotts. *E Wor* 8M **81**
Drove Hill. *Chlbn* 5F **74**
Drove La. *Alr* 9C **94**
Drove La. *Coom B* 1G **118**
Drove Rd. *Chlbn* 4F **74**
Drove Rd. *Sotn* 5F **174**
Drove Rd. *S'wick* 5B **200**
Drovers End. *Fle* 8A **28**
Drovers Way. *F'ham* 4C **64**
Drove, The. *And* 1K **69**
Drove, The. *Black* 7C **208**
Drove, The. *Cal* 1H **171**
Drove, The. *Durl* 3G **163**
Drove, The. *H'ly* 2L **9**
Drove, The. *H Hth* 5A **162**
Drove, The. *Ink* 1F **6**
Drove, The. *Sil* 3C **12**
Drove, The. *Sotn* 3E **174**
Drove, The. *Twy* 8K **127**
Drove, The. *W End* 8K **161**
Drove, The. *W Wel* 1B **120**
Droxford 2K **165**
Droxford Clo. *Gos* 3H **239**
Droxford Cres. *T'ley* 6G **11**
Droxford Rd. *Bourn* 8E **228**
Droxford Rd. *Swanm* 7E **164**
Druitt Rd. *Christ* 6B **230**
Drum La. *Ptsfld* 9M **139**
Drum Mead. *Ptsfld* 1L **145**
Drummond Clo. *Four M* 5G **97**
Drummond Clo. *Win* 9J **105**
Drummond Ct. *Eastl* 7F **132**
Drummond Ct. *Sotn* 7C **174**
Drummond Dri. *Sotn* 2A **174**
Drummond Rd. *Bourn* 1A **246**
Drummond Rd. *H End* 1N **175**
Drummond Rd. *Hythe* 5M **193**
Drummond Rd. *Ports* 1E **240**
Drummond Way. *Chan F* 4N **131**
Drury Clo. *Hur P* 1A **76**
Drury La. *Bentw* 6L **79**
Drury La. *Mort* 1F **12**
Drury Rd. *Bourn* 3F **244**
Dryden Av. *Ports* 8N **199**
Dryden Clo. *Ashy H* 3B **186**
Dryden Clo. *Bas* 2D **42**
Dryden Clo. *Fare* 7B **198**
Dryden Clo. *Water* 8M **181**
Dryden Pl. *Mil S* 7K **235**
Dryden Rd. *Farn* 6H **29**
Dryden Rd. *Sotn* 5J **175**
Dryden Way. *Lip* 1C **116**
Drysdale M. *S'sea* 5J **241**
Duart Ct. *New M* 3D **232**
Duchess Clo. *Alt* 5E **80**
Ducking Stool La. *Christ* 8L **229**
Duck Island La. *Ring* 2J **187**
Ducklands. *Bord* 5K **101**
Duck La. *Bourn* 1D **226**
Duckmead La. *Liss* 9G **115**
Duckpond La. *Water* 2E **182**
Ducks La. *Neth W* 1N **87**
Duckworth Ho. *Ports* 2B **240** (4K **5**)
Duddon Clo. *W End* 1F **174**
Duddon Way. *Bas* 6E **42**
Dudleston Heath Dri. *Water* 8B **182**
Dudley Av. *Hord* 3G **233**
Dudley Clo. *Bas* 6K **41**
Dudley Clo. *W'hill* 6H **101**
Dudley Ct. *Chu C* 5M **47**
Dudley Gdns. *Bourn* 1H **227**
Dudley Pl. *New M* 5B **232**
Dudley Rd. *Bourn* 1H **227**
Dudley Rd. *Ports* 9H **215**
Dudley Vw. *F'bri* 8J **151**
Dudmoor Farm Rd. *Christ* 2J **229**
Dudmoor La. *Christ* 8G **218** (Avon Causeway)
Dudmoor La. *Christ* 2J **229** (Dudmoor Farm Rd.)
Dugald Drummond St. *Ports* 2D **240** (4N **5**)
Duisburg Way. *S'sea* 4C **240** (8L **5**)
Duke Clo. *And* 9C **52**
Duke Cres. *Ports* 9E **214**
Duke of Cornwall Av. *Cam* 4M **19**
Duke of Edinburgh Ho. *Ports* 2L **5**
Duke Rd. *H End* 5A **176**
Dukes Clo. *Alt* 6D **80**
Dukes Clo. *F'ham* 4K **64**
Dukes Clo. *Ptsfld* 9K **139**
Dukes Ct. Bish W *3M 163* *(off St Bonnet Dri.)*
Dukes Dri. *Bourn* 1C **226**
Duke's Dri. *Estn* 3G **106**
Dukesfield. *Christ* 4G **228**
Dukes Keeps. *Sotn* 7F **4**
Dukes Mead. *Fle* 2J **47**
Dukes Mill Cen. *Roms* 5L **129**
Dukes Pk. *A'sht* 5M **49**
Duke's Ride. *C'then* 1A **18**
Dukes Ride. *Sil* 5N **11**
Dukes Rd. *Gos* 1J **239**
Dukes Rd. *Sotn* 2N **173**
Dukes Ter. *A'sht* 8K **49**
Duke St. *Mich* 7J **77**
Duke St. *Sotn* 7N **173** (7F **4**)
Dukes Wlk. *F'ham* 4C **64**
Dukes Wlk. *Water* 2M **201**
Duke's Way. Bulf *3A 66* *(off John French Way)*
Dukeswood Dri. *Dib P* 8L **193**
Dulsie Rd. *Bourn* 8G **227**
Dumas Clo. *Yate* 8M **17**
Du Maurier Clo. *Chu C* 8K **47**
Dumbarton Clo. *Ports* 8E **214**
Dumbleton Clo. *Sotn* 5K **175**
Dumbleton's Towers. *Sotn* 6J **175**
Dummer 9F **58**
Dummer Clump 9H **59**
Dummer Ct. *Hav* 3D **202**
Dummer Down La. *Dum* 1B **78**
Dummer Golf Club 8G **58**
Dummer La. *Chut S* 1A **32**
Dummer La. *Up Ch* 9A **6**
Dummer M. *Win* 7K **105** (9L **237**)
Dummers Rd. *Brfld* 6C **124**
Dumpers Drove. *H Hth* 4A **162**
Dumpford La. *Nye* 4L **147**
Dunbar Clo. *Sotn* 6E **158**
Dunbar Cres. *Walk* 4H **231**
Dunbar Rd. *Bourn* 8J **227**
Dunbar Rd. *S'sea* 3J **241**
Dunbridge 4D **122**
Dunbridge La. *Dun & Awb* 4D **122**
Dunbridge Rd. *Lcky* 4A **122**
Duncan Clo. *Sotn* 9C **174**
Duncan Cooper Ho. *Water* 2L **201**
Duncan Ct. *And* 1C **70**
Duncan Ct. *Sotn* 5G **175**
Duncan Rd. *New M* 2E **232**
Duncan Rd. *Park G* 3E **196**
Duncan Rd. *S'sea* 5E **240**
Duncan's Clo. *Fy'd* 9N **31**
Duncans Dri. *Fare* 9L **197**
Duncliff Rd. *Bourn* 1K **247**
Duncombe Dri. *Blash* 7E **184**
Duncombe Rd. *E Meon* 4L **143**
Duncton Rd. *Water* 6D **168**
Duncton Way. *Gos* 5E **212**
Dundas Clo. *Ports* 6J **215**
Dundas La. *Ports* 7J **215**
Dundas Spur. *Ports* 6J **215**
Dundee Clo. *Fare* 6A **198**
Dundee Rd. *Sotn* 1A **174**
Dundonald Clo. *Hay I* 2G **243**
Dundonald Clo. *Sotn* 9B **174**
Dundridge 2D **164**
Dundridge La. *Bish W* 2N **163**
Dundridge La. *Bro C* 6C **78**
Dundry Way. *H End* 3N **175**
Dune Crest. *Poole* 9A **244**
Dunedin Clo. *Tidw* 8E **30**
Dunedin Gro. *Christ* 7E **230**
Dunford Clo. *New M* 5N **231**
Dunford Rd. *Poole* 9B **226**
Dungells Farm Clo. *Yate* 9N **17**
Dungells La. *Yate* 9M **17**
Dunhills La. *Enh A* 3A **52**
Dunhurst Clo. *Hav* 6G **202**
Dunkeld Rd. *Bourn* 8H **227**
Dunkeld Rd. *Gos* 9H **213**
Dunketts La. *Baug* 8B **10** (in two parts)
Dunkirk Clo. *Sotn* 7J **159**
Dunkirk Rd. *Sotn* 7H **159**
Dunkirt La. *Abb A* 8D **68** (in two parts)
Dunley 3E **36**
Dunley Dri. *Elve* 9H **27**
Dunley's Hill. *N War & Odi* 8J **45**
Dunlin Clo. *Christ* 9D **230**
Dunlin Clo. *S'sea* 2L **241**
Dunmow Hill. *Fle* 1M **47**
Dunmow Rd. *And* 3A **70**
Dunn Clo. *S'sea* 4J **241**
Dunnings La. *N Bad* 7D **130**
Dunnock Clo. *Row C* 9H **183**
Dunsbury Way. *Hav* 3E **202**
Dunsells Clo. *Ropl* 1E **110**
Dunsell's La. *Ropl* 1E **110**
Dunsford Cres. *Bas* 4L **41**
Dunsmore Clo. *S'sea* 3D **240** (6N **5**)
Dunsmore Gdns. *Yate* 8K **17**
Dunstable Wlk. *Fare* 9N **197**
Dunstall Pk. *Farn* 5J **29**
Dunstan's Drove. *Ibt* 2A **34**
Dunster Clo. *Sotn* 6H **159**
Dunvegan Dri. *Sotn* 6H **159**
Dunwood Hill 3D **128**
Dunwood Manor Golf Club 1D **128**
Durban Clo. *Roms* 3N **129**
Durban Homes. *Ports* 1E **240**
Durban Rd. *Ports* 9G **214**
Durbridges. *H'ly* 3K **9**
Durdells Av. *Bourn* 1E **226**
Durdells Gdns. *Bourn* 1E **226**
Durford Ct. *Hav* 3D **202**
Durford Rd. *Ptsfld* 1A **146**
Durham Gdns. *Water* 4N **201**
Durham Rd. *Owl* 3G **18**
Durham St. *Gos* 1J **239**
Durham St. *Ports* 2D **240**
Durham Way. *Bas* 2K **59**
Durland Clo. *New M* 5B **232**
Durland Rd. *Water* 2C **182**
Durleighmarsh 9F **140**
Durley 5E **162**
Durley Av. *Water* 7M **181**
Durley Brook Rd. *Durl* 5C **162**
Durley Chine. *Bourn* 3H **245** (9H **247**)
Durley Chine Ct. *Bourn* 3H **245** (9H **247**)
Durley Chine Rd. *Bourn* 2H **245** (7H **247**)
Durley Chine Rd. S. *Bourn* 3H **245** (8H **247**)
Durley Clo. *And* 2L **69**
Durley Cres. *Tot* 5K **171**
Durley Gdns. *Bourn* 3H **245** (9H **247**)
Durley Hall Rd. *Durl* 2E **162**
Durley Rd. *Bourn* 3J **245** (8J **247**)
Durley Rd. *Gos* 1H **239**
Durley Rd. *H Hth* 3A **162**
Durley Rd. S. *Bourn* 3H **245** (8J **247**)
Durley Street 3G **162**
Durley St. *Durl* 5E **162**
Durlston Cres. *Christ* 2G **229**
Durlston Rd. *Poole* 3A **244**
Durlston Rd. *Sotn* 1C **172**
Durnford Clo. *Chlbn* 4F **74**
Durnford Rd. *Sotn* 4N **173** (2F **4**)
Durngate Pl. *Win* 6M **105** (7P **237**)
Durngate Ter. *Win* 6M **105** (7P **237**)
Durnsford Av. *Fle* 4M **47**
Durns Town 5K **223**
Durnstown. *Sway* 5K **223**
Durrant Rd. *Bourn* 1J **245** (5K **247**)
Durrant Rd. *Poole* 2A **244**
Durrants 1H **203**
Durrants Gdns. *Row C* 1H **203**
Durrants Rd. *Row C* 2H **203**
Durrant Way. *Sway* 5J **223**
Durrington Pl. *Bourn* 8E **228**
Durrington Rd. *Bourn* 8E **228**
Dursley Cres. *Ports* 9D **200**
Durweston Clo. *Bourn* 3M **227**
Dutton La. *Eastl* 8F **132**
Dutton's Rd. *Roms* 4L **129** (in two parts)
Dyer Rd. *Sotn* 3H **173**
Dymchurch Ho. *Ports* 9F **200**
Dymoke St. *Ems* 5L **203**
Dymott Clo. *Sotn* 5J **173**
Dyneley Grn. *Sotn* 1E **174**
Dyram Clo. *Eastl* 7D **132**
Dysart Av. *Ports* 1J **215**
Dyserth Clo. *Sotn* 9F **174**
Dyson Dri. *Win* 4L **105**

E

Eadens La. *Bart* 2D **170**
Eagle Av. *Water* 6L **181**
Eagle Clo. *Alt* 2F **80**
Eagle Clo. *Bas* 2H **59**
Eagle Clo. *Chan F* 8N **131**
Eagle Clo. *Fare* 9H **199**
Eagle Ct. *Bas* 5G **42**
Eaglehurst. Poole *1E 244* *(off Poole Rd.)*
Eagle Rd. *Bish G* 2H **9**
Eagle Rd. *Lee S* 9N **211**
Eagle Rd. *Poole* 1E **244**
Eagles Nest. *S'hrst* 4C **18**
Eames La. *Hawk* 6M **113**
Eardley Av. *And* 9J **51**
Earle Ho. *Win* 6A **106**
Earle Rd. *Bourn* 4G **244**
Earlham Dri. *Poole* 1A **244**
Earlsbourne. *Chu C* 7N **47**
Earls Clo. *Ame* 6A **66**
Earls Clo. *Eastl* 1L **161**
Earlsdon St. *S'sea* 3D **240** (5N **5**)
Earlsdon Way. *Highc* 6H **231**
Earls Gro. *Cam* 7N **19**
Earl's Ri. *Wint E* 3A **86**
Earls Rd. *Fare* 1D **212**
Earl's Rd. *Sotn* 2M **173**
Earlswood Dri. *A'hlt* 5C **152**
Earnley Rd. *Hay I* 5M **243**
Earthpits La. *Pent* 2G **148**
Eastacre. *Win* 5J **105**
East Anton 6B **52**
East Aston 1A **76**
East Av. *Bourn* 8G **226**
East Av. *F'ham* 4F **64**
East Av. *New M* 7L **231**
East Av. Roundabout. *Bourn* 8J **227**
E. Bank Rd. *Broc* 8D **148**
East Bargate. *Sotn* 6M **173** (6D **4**)
East Boldre 1B **236**
E. Boldre Rd. *E Bol* 9A **206**
Eastbourne Av. *Gos* 8H **213**
Eastbourne Av. *Sotn* 2J **173**
Eastbourne Rd. *Ports* 8H **215**
Eastbrook Clo. *Gos* 8H **213**
Eastbrook Clo. *Park G* 4D **196**
Eastbrooke Rd. *Alt* 4G **80**
E. Cams Clo. *Fare* 8H **199**
East Cholderton 2A **68**
Eastchurch Clo. *Sotn* 7E **158**
East Cliff 2M **245** (8N **247**)
Eastcliff Clo. *Lee S* 9B **212**
E. Cliff Promenade. *Bourn* 3L **245** (8M **247**)
E. Cliff Way. *Christ* 7E **230**
East Clo. *Bart S* 6M **231**
E. Copsey Path. *Ports* 9L **201**
E. Cosham Rd. *Ports* 8J **201**
Eastcot Clo. *Holb* 5A **208**
Eastcott Clo. *Bourn* 6D **228**
East Ct. *Cosh* 9J **201**
East Ct. *Ports* 9F **214**
Eastcroft Rd. *Gos* 2H **239**
East Dean 2L **121**
E. Dean Rd. *E Dean & Lcky* 2M **121**
East Dri. *Eastl* 8H **133**
East End 6A **150** (Damerham)
East End 4A **236** (Lymington)
East End 3M **7** (Newbury)
East End 8E **136** (Petersfield)
Eastern Av. *And* 2A **70**
Eastern Av. *S'sea* 1J **241**
Eastern Ind. Est. *Ports* 2K **215**
Eastern La. *C'then* 1G **19**
Eastern Pde. *Fare* 1D **212**
Eastern Pde. *S'sea* 6G **240**
Eastern Rd. *A'sht* 9M **49**
Eastern Rd. *Bord* 1J **101**
Eastern Rd. *Fawl* 6J **209**
Eastern Rd. *Hav* 7F **202**
Eastern Rd. *L'ton* 2D **234**
Eastern Rd. *Ports* 6C **214** (PO2)
Eastern Rd. *Ports* 3K **215** (PO6 & PO3)
Eastern Rd. *W End* 1H **175**
Eastern Vs. Rd. *S'sea* 6E **240**
Eastern Way. *Fare* 8E **198**
Eastern Way. *Mil S* 8M **235**
Easter Rd. *Bourn* 4L **227**
Eastfield Av. *Bas* 6D **42**
Eastfield Av. *Fare* 1B **212**
Eastfield Clo. *And* 1B **70**
Eastfield Ct. *Ring* 1M **187**
Eastfield La. *E Har* 8K **147**
Eastfield La. *Ring* 1M **187**
Eastfield Rd. *And* 1A **70**
Eastfield Rd. *Sotn* 2A **174**
Eastfield Rd. *S'sea* 4H **241**
Eastfield Rd. *S'wick* 7C **200**
East Ga. *Ports* 9D **214**
Eastgate St. *Sotn* 7M **173** (7D **4**)
Eastgate St. *Win* 7M **105** (8P **237**)
E. Gomeldon Rd. *Gom* 2C **86**
East Grn. *B'wtr* 9E **18**
East Grimstead 1F **120**
East Harting 9J **147**
E. Harting St. *E Har* 9J **147**
East Hill. *L'ton* 2E **234**
East Hill. *Win* 8M **105**
E. Hill Clo. *Fare* 7F **198**
E. Hill Dri. *Liss* 2F **140**
E. Hoe Rd. *Hmbdn* 9B **166**
East Ho. Av. *Fare* 6N **211**
East Howe 3G **226**
E. Howe La. *Bourn* 3G **226**
Eastlake Av. *Poole* 8A **226**
Eastlake Clo. *Ptsfld* 1B **146**
Eastlake Heights. *S'sea* 4L **241**
Eastland Gate 5L **181**
Eastland Ga. Cotts. *Love* 4L **181**
Eastlands. *New M* 5C **232**
East La. *Alr* 2A **108**
East La. *Evtn* 5M **233**
Eastleigh 1F **160**
Eastleigh Lakeside Railway 3D **160**
Eastleigh Mus. 1E **160**

Eastleigh Rd. F Oak 2N 161
Eastleigh Rd. Hav 6J 203
East Liss 1F 140
East Lodge. Fare 8M 197
East Lodge. Lee S. 1A 238
E. Lodge Pk. Ports 9N 201
Eastlyn Rd. P Hth 4L 11
Eastman's Fld. Chlbn. 5F 74
East Martin 9D 118
Eastmead. Farn. 8K 29
Eastmeare Ct. Tot 4J 171
East Meon 3L 143
E. Meon Rd. Water 4A 168
Eastney 4K 241
Eastney Esplanade. S'sea 5H 241
Eastney Farm Rd. S'sea 4K 241
Eastney Pumping Station Mus. 4K 241
Eastney Rd. S'sea 3J 241
Eastney St. S'sea. 5J 241
East Oakley 1E 58
Eastoke 5J 243
Eastoke Av. Hay I 6K 243
Easton Comn. Hill. W'slw . . . 5J 87
Easton La. Estn 9D 92
Easton La. Win 6M 105
Easton La. Bus. Cen. Win 6M 105
E. Overcliff Dri. Bourn 3L 245 (8N 247)
Eastover Ct. Hav. 3D 202
East Pallant. Hav. 8F 202
East Pk. Ter. Sotn 5M 173 (3D 4)
East Parley 7A 218
East Portway. And. 1J 69
East Rd. Bar S 5B 76
East Rd. Hythe 9B 194
East Rd. S'wick. 3B 200
Eastrop 6E 42
Eastrop La. Bas 6D 42
Eastrop Roundabout. Bas 6D 42
Eastrop Way. Bas 6D 42
East Sta. Rd. A'sht 1K 65
East Stratton 7M 77
East St. Alr 9F 94
East St. And . . . . 1A 70 (in two parts)
East St. Fare 8E 198
East St. F'ham. 7E 64
East St. Hmbdn. 8E 166
East St. Hav 8F 202
East St. Portc. 9M 199
East St. Ports 4A 240 (6H 5)
East St. Rog 9L 141
East St. Sotn 6M 173 (6D 4)
East St. Titch. 9J 197
East St. Cen. Sotn 6M 173 (6E 4)
E. Surrey St. Ports 2D 240
East Tisted 1D 112
East Tytherley 8N 87
Eastview Gdns. Up Farr 4E 98
E. View Rd. Ring. 1L 187
Eastville Rd. Eastl. 2N 161
East Way. Bourn 5M 227
Eastways. Bish W 4M 163
East Wellow 7A 128
East Winterslow 4H 87
Eastwood. Sher E 6M 121
Eastwood Clo. Hay I. 3H 243
Eastwood Ct. Roms 5L 129
East Woodhay 3L 7
E. Woodhay Rd. Win 2H 105
Eastwood Rd. Ports 4F 214
East Worldham 7N 81
Eaton Rd. Cam 9K 19
Eaton Rd. Poole 3E 244
E Avenue. Hythe 3C 208
Ebblake 5A 184
Ebblake Ind. Est. Ver 5A 184
Ebble Clo. Tidw 7D 30
Ebden Rd. Win. 6M 105
Ebenezer La. Ring. 1J 187
Ebery Gro. Ports 1J 241
Ebor Rd. Poole 8B 226
Ecchinswell 5H 9
Ecchinswell Rd. K're. 5G 9
Echo Barn La. Wrec 7N 63
Ecton La. Ports. 5K 215
Eddeys Clo. Head D 1D 102
Eddeys La. Head D. 1D 102
Eddy Rd. A'sht 1L 65
Eddystone Ct. Churt 7H 85
Eddystone Rd. Tot 9K 157
Edelvale Rd. Sotn 1F 174
Edelweiss Clo. Lud. 2D 30
Edenbridge Rd. S'sea 2J 241
Eden Path. Ports. 8K 201
Eden Ri. Fare 9D 198
Eden Rd. W End 9F 160
Eden St. Ports. 1D 240 (2N 5)
Eden Wlk. Chan F. 7N 131
Edgar Clo. And 6A 52
Edgar Cres. Fare 2M 213
Edgar Rd. Win 8K 105
Edgar Vs. Win . . 7K 105 (9K 237)
Edgbarrow Ct. C'then 2C 18
Edgbarrow Ri. S'hrst 3C 18
Edgbarrow Sports Cen. . . . 2E 18
Edgbaston Ho. S'sea 3D 240
Edgcumbe Pk. Dri. C'then . . . 1C 18
Edgbarrow Woods Nature Reserve 3D 18
Edgecombe Cres. Gos 8E 212
Edgedale Clo. C'then 1D 18
Edgefield Gro. Water 9C 182
Edgehill Clo. Bas. 8K 41
Edgehill Rd. Bourn 6J 227
Edge Hill Rd. Sotn 1D 174
Edgerly Gdns. Ports 2G 215
Edgeware Rd. S'sea 2H 241
Edifred Rd. Bourn. 2L 227
Edinburgh Ct. A'sht. . . . . 9H 49 (off Queen Elizabeth Dri.)
Edinburgh Ct. Sotn . . . . 4F 172 (off Regents Pk. Rd.)
Edinburgh Rd. King W. 6M 91
Edinburgh Rd. Ports 2C 240 (3M 5)
Edington Clo. Bish W 3L 163
Edington Rd. Win. 4L 105
Edison Rd. Bas. 4N 41
Edith Haisman Clo. Sotn. . . 5J 173
Edmondsham 8K 149
Edmondsham Ho. Bourn 2J 245 (7K 247)
Edmondsham Rd. Ver 9M 149
Edmund Rd. S'sea. 4F 240
Edmunds Clo. Bart S 5A 232
Edmunds Clo. Bot. 5A 176
Edney Clo. Chu C 5N 47
Edney Path. Sar G 3A 196
Edneys La. Water 6J 181
Edrich Sq. And 8A 52
Edric's Grn. Chol. 4F 66
Education Path. Ports 1F 214
Edward Av. Cam 8J 19
Edward Av. Eastl. 8H 133
Edward Clo. Black. 7C 208
Edward Gdns. Hav 8C 202
Edward Gro. Fare 8N 199
Edward May Ct. Bourn 2E 226
Edward Rd. Alt 3F 80
Edward Rd. Bourn. . . . . 3F 226 (in two parts)
Edward Rd. Christ 6B 230
Edward Rd. Hythe 5M 193
Edward Rd. Poole. 9A 226
Edward Rd. Sotn 3H 173
Edward Rd. Win 9J 105
Edwards Clo. L'ton 3B 234
Edwards Clo. Ports. 8C 200
Edwards Clo. Water 8N 181
Edward St. A'sht. 9H 49
Edward Ter. Alr 1F 108
Edwina Clo. N Bad 8G 130
Edwina Clo. Ring 8M 185
Edwina Clo. Sotn 4D 174
Edwina Ho. Sotn. 7C 160
Edwina Mountbatten Ho. Roms . . . . 5L 129 (off Palmerston St.)
Edwin Jones Grn. Sotn. . . . 2K 173
Eelmoor Plain Rd. A'sht 7F 48
Eelmoor Rd. A'sht. 6F 48
Eelmoor Rd. Farn. 1H 49
Effingham Gdns. Sotn 6G 174
Efford Ct. Penn. 4B 234
Efford Way. Penn 4B 234
Egan Clo. Ports 5G 215
Egbert Rd. Win. 5L 105
Egbury 5B 36
Egbury Rd. St M 1M 53
Egerton Gdns. Bourn 8A 228
Egerton Rd. Bourn 8A 228
Egerton Rd. Cam 7H 19
Eggars Clo. Alt 4H 81
Eggars Ct. A'sht 1K 65
Eggars Fld. Bent. 7K 63
Eggar's Hill. A'sht 2J 65
Eggleton Clo. Chu C 6K 47
Eglantine Clo. Water. 6B 182
Eglantine Wlk. Water 6B 182
Eglinton Rd. Tilf 2K 85
Egmont Clo. Ring 6F 186
Egmont Dri. Ring 6G 186
Egmont Gdns. Ring 6G 186
Egypt 6D 76
Egypt Esplanade. Cowes . . . 5N 237
Egypt Hill. Cowes 5N 237
Eight Acres. Hind 9L 85
Eight Acres. Roms 5N 129
Eighth St. Hythe 4C 208
Eights, The. A'prt 3B 68
Eileen Beard Ho. Hav 4G 203
Elaine Gdns. Water. 5N 181
Elan Clo. W End 1F 174
Eland Rd. A'sht 1M 65
Elbe Way. And 7M 51
Elbow Corner. Bas 6C 42
Elcombes Clo. Lyn 2B 148
Elderberry Bank. Lych 3G 42
Elderberry Clo. Clan 7D 168
Elderberry Clo. F Oak 1L 161
Elderberry La. Christ 8B 230
Elderberry Rd. Lind 3M 101
Elderberry Way. Water 6B 182
Elder Clo. L Hth 7C 196
Elder Clo. March 9F 172
Elder Clo. Win 1G 126
Elder Ct. Win 1G 126
Elderfield Clo. Ems. 6N 203
Elderfield Rd. Hav 2D 202
Elder Grn. Col C 4L 133
Eldergrove. Farn. 2N 49
Elder Rd. Hav. 6H 203
Elderwood. Chine 9F 22
Eldon Av. Bart S 6N 231
Eldon Building. S'sea 3D 240 (5N 5)
Eldon Clo. Bart S 6N 231
Eldon Clo. King S 9B 86
Eldon Ct. S'sea 3D 240 (6N 5)
Eldon Ho. Sotn 7M 173 (7E 4)
Eldon Pl. Bourn. 2F 244
Eldon Rd. Bourn 5J 227
Eldon Rd. King S 8G 88
Eldon St. S'sea 3D 240 (6N 5)
Eldridge Gdns. Roms. 4M 129
Eleanor Clo. Pass 7N 101
Eleanor Ct. Lud. 1C 30
Eleanor Dri. Bourn 1B 226
Eleanor Gdns. Christ 6H 229
Electron Way. Chan F. 6A 132
Elettra Av. Water. 1K 201
Eleventh St. Hythe . . . . 3B 208 (in two parts)
Elgar Clo. Bas. 2N 59
Elgar Clo. Gos. 5J 239
Elgar Clo. Ports 9N 199
Elgar Clo. Sotn. 7G 175
Elgar Rd. Bourn 2H 227
Elgar Rd. Sotn 7G 175
Elgar Wlk. Water 4M 201
Elgin Clo. Fare 7B 198
Elgin Clo. Hythe. 6M 193
Elgin Rd. Bourn 7H 227
Elgin Rd. Poole. . . . . 3A 244 (in two parts)
Elgin Rd. Ports. 2G 215
Elgin Rd. Sotn. 5J 173
Eling 5A 172
Eling Clo. Win. 3H 105
Eling Ct. Hav. 3D 202
Elingfield Ct. Tot. 3N 171
Eling Hill. Tot 5A 172
Eling La. Tot. 3N 171
Eling Vw. Sotn 3C 172
Eling Wharf. Tot 3A 172
Eliot Dri. Hasl 9N 103
Eliot Ho. New M 4B 232
Elise Clo. Bourn 6E 228
Elizabethan Ri. N Wal 8A 58
Elizabeth Av. Christ 6J 229
Elizabeth Clo. D'ton 2H 119
Elizabeth Clo. King W 6M 91
Elizabeth Clo. W End 1H 175
Elizabeth Clo. Wick. 6B 178
Elizabeth Ct. A'sht. . . . . 9H 49 (off Queen Elizabeth Dri.)
Elizabeth Ct. Bourn. 2L 245
Elizabeth Ct. Fare 1B 212
Elizabeth Ct. Gos. 1J 239
Elizabeth Ct. Ports 9G 201
Elizabeth Ct. Sotn. 1A 174
Elizabeth Ct. W End 1H 175
Elizabeth Cres. Hord 4J 233
Elizabeth Dri. Chu C. 6M 47
Elizabeth Gdns. Christ. 7F 230
Elizabeth Gdns. Dib P 8M 193
Elizabeth Gdns. S'sea. 5G 241
Elizabeth Ho. Cal. 9J 157
Elizabeth Rd. Bas 8N 41
Elizabeth Rd. Stub 6N 211
Elizabeth Rd. Water. 4M 201
Elizabeth Rd. Wick 6C 178
Elizabeth Way. Bish W 4L 163
Elizabeth Way. Eastl 7F 132
Eliza Pl. Gos 2L 239
Elkhams Clo. Evtn. 5L 233
Elkins Gro. F'ham. 8B 64
Elkstone Rd. Ports 8C 200
Ellachie Gdns. Gos 6K 239
Ellachie M. Gos. 6K 239
Ellachie Rd. Gos 6K 239
Elland Clo. F Oak 2N 161
Elldene Ct. Tot. 5L 171
Ellen Dri. Fle 8A 28
Ellen Gdns. Braml 1F 22
Ellen Gdns. Chan F 7M 131
Ellerslie Chambers. Bourn 2K 245 (7M 247)
Ellerslie Clo. Fare 7K 211
Ellery Gro. L'ton 1E 234
Elles Clo. Farn. 9K 29
Elles Rd. Farn. 1G 49
Ellingham 4J 185
Ellingham Clo. Alr. 1F 108
Ellingham Dri. Blash 5F 184
Ellingham Drove. Blash. . . . 4J 185
Ellingham Rd. New M 6M 231
Ellington Clo. And. 2H 69
Ellington Dri. Bas 3L 59
Elliot Clo. Tot 3K 171
Elliot Ri. H End 9N 161
Elliots Cvn. Est. Hay I 5L 243
Elliott Pk. Ind. Est. A'sht . . . 9N 49
Elliott Rd. Bourn 3C 226
Ellisfield 1H 79
Ellisfield Rd. Hav. 5E 202
Ellison Way. Tong. 3N 65
Ellis Rd. Sotn 5J 175
Ellwood Av. Sotn. 5J 175
Ellwood Clo. Sotn 4J 175
Elm Av. Christ. 5H 229
Elm Av. New M. 4B 232
Elm Av. Penn 5C 234
Elm Bank. Yate. 6M 17
Elm Bank Rd. And 3N 69
Elm Clo. Bord 4K 101
Elm Clo. Lud 1F 30
Elm Clo. Mid W 4B 72
Elm Clo. Pitt 6E 86
Elm Clo. Sotn 7L 159
Elm Clo. Thru. 1M 67
Elm Clo. Est. Hay I 4F 242
Elm Clo. Wars 8A 196
Elm Ct. New M 4B 232
Elm Ct. S'hrst. 3G 18
Elm Ct. Sotn. 7D 174
Elm Ct. Win 6J 105 (6J 237)
Elm Cres. F'ham 3F 64
Elm Cres. Hythe. 1M 207
Elm Cres. Uphm 8E 134
Elmcroft Clo. Frim G. 5N 29
Elmdale. Ptsfld 9N 139
Elmdale Clo. Wars 8A 196
Elmdale Gro. E Wel. 2B 156
Elm Dri. Ptsfld 3L 145
Elmers Marsh 9J 117
Elmers Way. Brans. 6D 220
Elmes Dri. Sotn. 3E 172
Elmes Rd. Bourn. 4J 227
Elmeswelle Rd. Water. 4A 182
Elm Farm Gro. K're. 2B 6
Elmfield Clo. W'flls 3M 119
Elmfield La. Cals 9J 209
Elmfield N. Block. Sotn. . . . 5J 173
Elmfield W. Block. Sotn. . . . 5J 173
Elm Gdns. Bourn 9G 226
Elm Gdns. W End. 8H 161
Elmgate Dri. Bourn. 7D 228
Elm Gro. Eastl 1D 160
Elm Gro. F'ham. 3E 64
Elm Gro. Gos 2K 239
Elm Gro. Hay I 4G 242
Elm Gro. K're 2B 6
Elm Gro. S'sea 4D 240 (7N 5)
Elmgrove Rd. Farn 8K 29
Elmhurst. T'ley. 5H 11
Elmhurst Rd. Bourn 1E 226
Elmhurst Rd. Fare 9D 198
Elmhurst Rd. Gos. 3L 239
Elm La. Hav. 8F 202
Elm La. Tong 2N 65
Elmleigh Rd. Hav 7F 202
Elm Lodge. S'sea . . . . 4E 240 (off St Peters Gro.)
Elm M. Gray 4L 103
Elmore Av. Lee S 2B 238
Elmore Clo. Lee S. 2B 238
Elmore Dri. Ashy H. 2B 186
Elmore Rd. Lee S 3B 238
Elm Pk. Rd. Hav 7F 202
Elm Pl. A'sht 2L 65
Elm Rd. Alr 1F 108
Elm Rd. Bish W 3A 164
Elm Rd. F'ham 3F 64
Elm Rd. Hav. 9G 203
Elm Rd. Over 9E 38
Elm Rd. Sher. 1M 41
Elm Rd. Win. 6J 105 (6J 237)
Elms Clo. S'hth. 9D 150
Elmsdown Ct. Ring 1J 187
Elmsleigh Ct. Sotn. 7M 159
Elmsleigh Gdns. Sotn 7M 159
Elmsleigh Rd. Farn. 8H 29
Elmslie Gdns. Burs. 9K 175
Elms Rd. A'sht. 1J 65
Elms Rd. Fare. 1D 212
Elms Rd. Fle 2A 48
Elms Rd. Hook 1G 44
Elmstead Rd. Poole 5D 244
Elms, The. And 2M 69
Elms, The. B'wtr. 9G 18
Elm St. Sotn 6N 173
Elm St. S'sea 4D 240 (7M 5)
Elmsway. Bourn 1H 247
Elm Ter. Sotn 7N 173
Elm Tree Clo. Asht 8H 171
Elmtree Gdns. Eastl 1E 160
Elmtree Gdns. Roms 6B 130
Elmtree Rd. Ports 9M 201
Elmwood. Chine 8E 22
Elmwood Av. F'bri. 9F 150
Elmwood Av. Water. 3M 201
Elmwood Clo. Alt 6D 80
Elmwood Ct. Sotn 9G 159
Elmwood Lodge. Fare. 7D 198
Elmwood Pde. Bas 4L 41
Elmwood Rd. Ports. 4F 214
Elmwood Way. Bas. 4L 41
Elmwood Way. Highc. 7H 231
Elphinstone Rd. Highc 6K 231
Elphinstone Rd. S'sea 5D 240 (9N 5)
Elsfred Rd. Fare 7K 211
Elsie Fudge Ho. Water 6N 201
Elsley Clo. Frim G. 6N 29
Elson 8J 213
Elson La. Gos 8J 213
Elson Rd. Gos 8H 213
Elstead Gdns. Water. 5K 201
Elsted 8N 147
Elsted Rd. E'std 8N 147
Elston Pl. A'sht 2L 65
Elston Rd. A'sht 2L 65
Elstree Rd. Sotn 5C 174
Eltham Clo. Bourn. 6E 228
Elver Ct. Tot 4N 171
Elvetham 7G 27
Elvetham Clo. Fle. 9M 27
Elvetham Cres. Elve 9J 27
Elvetham Heath Way. Elve & Fle 9J 27
Elvetham La. Elve 4E 26
Elvetham Pl. Fle 9K 27
Elvetham Rd. Fle. 1J 47
Elvin Clo. Hord. 2G 232
Elwell Grn. Hay I 4F 242
Elwyn Rd. Bourn 9N 227
Ely Ct. Gos 2F 238
Emanuel St. Ports. 9E 214
Embankment Way. Ring 2L 187
Embassy Ct. S'sea. 3F 240
Embleton Rd. Head D. 1D 102
Embley Clo. Cal 9K 157
Embley La. E Wel 6D 128
Embley Pk. Ind. Est. E Wel 5E 128
Embsay Rd. Swanw 1A 196
Emden Rd. And 7M 51
Emerald Clo. Ashy H. 2B 186
Emerald Clo. Sotn. 4F 174
Emerald Clo. Water. 2A 202
Emer Clo. N Bad 7F 130
Emerson Ct. C'then 1D 18
Emery Down 2M 189
Emery Down Dri. Elve 9H 27
Emily Clo. Christ. 5J 229
Emily Ct. Poole. 9C 226
Emily Davies Halls. Sotn. 4B 4
Emmanuel Clo. Fare 7F 196
Emmett Rd. Rown 6E 158
Emmons Clo. Hamb 8L 195
Empress Av. Farn 7K 29
Empress Pk. Ind. Est. Sotn 3N 173
Empress Rd. Lyn 2B 148
Empress Rd. Sotn . . . . 9M 173 (Central Rd.)
Empress Rd. Sotn . . . . 3N 173 (1F 4) (Imperial Rd.)
Empress Way. Lud 1C 30
Empshott Rd. S'sea 3G 241
Empson Wlk. Lee S 9B 212
Emsbrook Dri. Ems 7M 203
Emsworth 8M 203
Emsworth By-Pass. Ems 8J 203
Emsworth Cen., The. Ems 9M 203
Emsworth Comn. Rd. Hav & Ems 4K 203
Emsworth Ho. Ems. 8K 203
Emsworth Ho. Clo. Ems 8L 203
Emsworth Rd. Hav. 8G 202
Emsworth Rd. L'ton 2E 234
Emsworth Rd. Ports. 7F 214
Emsworth Rd. Sotn 2G 173

Emsworth Rd. Thor I . . . . . 5N 217 (in two parts)
Enborne Row. 1B 8
Enborne St. Enb . . . . 1A 8 (in two parts)
Encombe Clo. Poole 6D 226
Endeavour Clo. Gos 3M 239
Endeavour Clo. Sotn. 3G 172
Endeavour Pk. Ring 2L 187
Endeavour Way. Hythe 4L 193
Enderleigh Ho. Hav 8E 202
Enderwood Clo. Tot 2H 171
Endfield Clo. Christ 5J 229
Endfield Rd. Bourn 4L 227
Endfield Rd. Christ 5H 229
Endle St. Sotn. 7A 174
Endofield Clo. Fare 2B 212
Enfield Gro. Sotn 7C 174
Engineers Rd. Green 1H 9
Englands Way. Bourn 2B 226
Englefield Rd. Sotn. 3B 174
English Rd. Sotn 3G 172
English Wood. Bas 4L 41
Enham Alamein. 3A 52
Enham Arch Roundabout. And 8A 52
Enham La. And. 5N 51
Enham La. Charl 7L 51
Enmill La. Win 8A 104
Ennel Copse. N Bad 8F 130
Ennerdale Clo. Bas 9K 41
Ennerdale Clo. Water 9C 168
Ennerdale Gdns. Alr 2F 108
Ennerdale Gdns. W End 1F 174
Ennerdale Gro. F'ham 4C 64
Ennerdale Rd. Bord. 2J 101
Ennerdale Rd. Fare. 4N 211
Ennerdale Rd. Sotn 9D 158
Ensbury. 1J 227
Ensbury Av. Bourn 5H 227
Ensbury Clo. Bourn 5H 227
Ensbury Ct. Bourn 4J 227
Ensbury Park. 4H 227
Ensbury Pk. Rd. Bourn 4J 227
Ensign Dri. Gos. 1F 238
Ensign Pk. Hamb 7J 195
Ensign Way. Hamb 7J 195
Enterprise Clo. Wars. 8B 196
Enterprise Ct. Bas. 4E 42
Enterprise Ho. Ports. 4N 5
Enterprise Ind. Est. Water 2C 182
Enterprise Rd. Chilw. 2H 159
Enterprise Rd. Water 2C 182
Enterprise Way. Hurn 6A 218
Enterprise Way. Sotn 8N 173 (9F 4)
Enyon M. Ring 2J 187
Eperston Rd. Water 4A 182
Epping Clo. Sotn. 1F 174
Epsilon Ho. Sotn. 2J 159
Epsom Clo. Cam. 5L 19
Epsom Clo. H Hth. 4A 162
Epsom Ct. White. . . . . 1F 196 (off Timor Clo.)
Epsom Down. Alt 6F 80
Epworth Rd. Ports 7G 215
Erasmus Pk. Win 5N 105
Erica Clo. L Hth 6C 196
Erica Clo. Water 7B 182
Erica Way. Water 6B 182
Ericksen Rd. Bourn 3G 226
Eric Rd. Fare 6M 211
Eric Taplin Ct. S'sea 4F 240
Erinbank Mans. Bourn 2N 245
Erles Rd. Lip. 2E 116
Ernest Clo. Ems 8M 203
Ernest Rd. Hav 6C 202
Ernest Rd. Ports 9F 214
Erpingham Rd. Poole 1E 244
Erskine Clo. P Hth 4M 11
Erskine Ct. Sotn 6F 158
Erskine Rd. Win 7J 105 (9J 237)
Escombe Rd. Eastl 9H 133
Escur Clo. Ports 4G 214
Esdaile La. Burl . . . . 7D 188 (off Ringwood Rd.)
Esher Clo. Bas 1M 59
Esher Gro. Water 8K 181
Eskdale Clo. Water 9C 168
Eskdale Ct. Ash V. . . . . 6N 49 (off Lakeside Clo.)
Esmond Clo. Ems 9M 203
Esmonde Clo. Lee S 1B 238
Esplanade. Can C 6D 244
Esplanade. Cowes. 5P 237
Esplanade. Lee S 2A 238
Esplanade Gdns. S'sea 5K 241
Esplanade, The. Gos. 3N 239
Essex Av. Christ 5J 229
Essex Clo. Bord. 3J 101
Essex Grn. Chan F 1A 160
Essex Rd. Bas. 6B 42
Essex Rd. Bord 3J 101
Essex Rd. S'sea 3H 241
Esslemont Rd. S'sea. 4G 240
Estella Rd. Ports 8E 214
Estridge Clo. Burs. 9L 175
Ethelbert Dri. Charl. 7K 51
Ethelburt Av. Sotn. 6A 160
Ethelred Gdns. Tot 4J 171
Ethel Rd. Ports 1F 240
Eton Clo. Bas 4J 59
Eton Gdns. Bourn. 1G 244
Eton Pl. F'ham 3D 64
Eton Rd. S'sea. 3F 240
Ettrick Rd. Poole. 4E 244
Etwall. Quar 3L 67
Eucalyptus Av. St L 6D 186
Europa Clo. Braml 1G 22
European Way. Sotn 8N 173 (9E 4)
Euryalus Rd. Fare. 2B 212
Euskirchen Way. Bas 6L 41
Euston Gro. Ring 2K 187
Euston Rd. S'sea. 2J 241
Eva Allaway Ct. Ports 4K 5
Evans Clo. Ashy H 2B 186
Evans Clo. Bourn 5D 226
Evans Clo. Ovr W 8L 67
Evans Clo. Ports. 6C 214
Evans Ho. Bas 4N 41
Evans Rd. S'sea 3H 241
Evans St. Sotn 6M 173 (6E 4)
Evelegh Rd. Ports. 9L 201
Eveley Clo. W'hill 6G 100
Eveley La. W'hill 7E 100
Evelyn Av. A'sht 2K 65
Evelyn Clo. Wal C 7A 164
Evelyn Cres. Sotn 2J 173
Evelyn M. Alr. 9F 94
Evelyn M. Bourn 5K 227
Evelyn Rd. Bourn 5K 227
Evelyn Woods Rd. A'sht 4L 49
Evenlode Rd. Sotn 1D 172
Evenlode Way. S'hrst 5E 18
Eventide Homes. Bourn 4B 228
Everdene Ho. Bourn 5E 228
Everdon La. Ports. 4K 215
Everell Ct. S'sea 6E 240
Everest Rd. Cam 5M 19
Everest Rd. Christ. 6A 230
Everglades Av. Water 7N 181
Evergreen Clo. March 9E 172
Evergreen Clo. Water 2L 201
Evergreens. Ashy H 3B 186
Evergreens. Tot 4N 171
Evering Av. Poole 5A 226
Evering Gdns. Poole. 5A 226
Everlea Clo. Evtn. 5L 233
Everleigh Rd. Coll D. 2G 31
Everon Gdns. New M 4C 232
Eversfield Clo. And 1M 69
Evershot Rd. Bourn 4B 228
Eversley. 4D 16
Eversley Centre. 5G 17
Eversley Cres. Hav 5E 202
Eversley Cross. 6H 17
Eversley Dri. Elve 9H 27
Eversley Pl. Win. 9H 105
Eversley Rd. Yate 6K 17
Eversley St. E'sly 4D 16
Everton. 5M 233
Everton Rd. Hord & Evtn 2G 233
Evesham Clo. Bourn. 6E 228
Evesham Clo. Sotn. 6N 159
Evesham Ct. Poole 3E 244
Evesham Wlk. Bas 2C 42
Evesham Wlk. Owl 4F 18
Evingar Gdns. Whitc. 4G 54
Evingar Rd. Whitc 5G 54
Ewart Ct. Hythe 4M 193
Ewart Rd. Ports. 9F 214
Ewell Way. Tot 1K 171
Ewhurst Clo. Hav 5D 202
Ewhurst Rd. R'dll 8C 20
Ewshot. 2N 63
Ewshot La. Chu C & Ews 8L 47
Exbury. 1G 236
Exbury Clo. Eastl 1K 161
Exbury Dri. Bourn 1D 226
Exbury Gardens. 1G 236
Exbury Rd. Beau 5H 207
Exbury Rd. Black 7C 208
Exbury Rd. Hav 4G 202
Exbury Way. And 2L 69
Excellent Rd. Fare. 3B 212
Excelsior Rd. Poole 2A 244
Exchange Rd. Ports 2C 240 (4M 5)
Exeter Clo. Bas 3K 59
Exeter Clo. Eastl 7D 132
Exeter Clo. Ems 6M 203
Exeter Clo. L Hth 6C 196
Exeter Clo. Sotn 1E 174
Exeter Ct. Gos. 1E 238
Exeter Ct. Highc 7K 231
Exeter Cres. Bourn 3K 245 (7L 247)
Exeter Gdns. Yate 6L 17
Exeter Grange. Bourn 8L 247
Exeter La. Bourn 2K 245 (7L 247)
Exeter Pk. Mans. Bourn . . . 8L 247
Exeter Pk. Rd. Bourn 3K 245 (8L 247)
Exeter Rd. Bourn 2K 245 (7L 247)
Exeter Rd. Sotn. 2E 174
Exeter Rd. S'sea 5G 240
Exford Av. Sotn 3G 174
Exford Dri. Sotn. 3G 174
Exleigh Clo. Sotn. 4F 174
Exmoor Clo. Bas. 8K 41
Exmoor Clo. Tot. 3H 171
Exmoor Clo. White 2E 196
Exmoor Rd. Sotn 4N 173 (2E 4)
Exmouth Gdns. H Hth 4N 161
Exmouth Rd. Gos 8J 213
Exmouth Rd. S'sea 5E 240
Exmouth St. Sotn 5M 173 (4D 4)
Exton. 7N 135
Exton Gdns. Fare 7L 199
Exton Rd. Bourn. 7F 228
Exton Rd. Hav 4H 203
Eyebright Clo. H Hth. 5N 161
Eyeworth Wlk. Dib 5H 193
Eynham Av. Sotn 4G 174
Eynham Clo. Sotn. 4G 174
Eyre Clo. Tot. 4K 171

F

Faber Clo. Hav 5G 203
Faber M. Roms. 4A 130
Faberstown. 2F 30
Fabers Yd. Win. . . 6K 105 (7L 237)
Fabian Clo. Bas. 7B 42
Fabian Clo. Water 1A 202
Faccombe. 6K 7
Factory Rd. Eastl 1E 160
Fairacre. Wool H. . . . . 3A 8 (off Aird Clo.)
Fairacre Ri. Fare 9L 197
Fairacre Wlk. Fare. 1L 211
Fairbairn Wlk. Chan F 6L 131
Fairbourne Clo. Water 8M 181
Fair Clo. Whitc . . . . 6F 54 (in two parts)
Fairclose Dri. Win 1F 104
Fair Cross. 3B 14
Faircross Clo. Holb 5A 208
Fairdown Clo. Win 7N 105
Fairfax Clo. Win 9F 104
Fairfax Ct. Sotn. 4J 175
Fairfax Ind. Est. A'sht 9N 49
Fairfax M. Farn 1M 49
Fairfax M. Sotn. 4J 175
Fairfax Rd. Farn 5K 29
Fairfield. Christ 7L 229
Fairfield. Roms. 3N 129
Fairfield. Whitc. 4G 55
Fairfield Av. Fare. 1A 212
Fairfield Clo. Christ. 7L 229
Fairfield Clo. Ems 7M 203
Fairfield Clo. Hythe 5L 193
Fairfield Clo. L'ton. 3E 234
Fairfield Dri. Frim 1N 29
Fairfield Grn. Four M 4K 97
Fairfield Lodge. Sotn 7H 159
Fairfield Rd. Bart S. 7N 231
Fairfield Rd. Hav. 8F 202
Fairfield Rd. Shaw 8H 127
Fairfield Rd. Win. 5J 105
Fairfields Arts Cen. 7C 42
Fairfield Sq. Ports 9F 200
Fairfields Rd. Bas 8C 42
Fairfield, The. F'ham . . . . 8E 64 (in two parts)
Fairgate Cen., The. Burg . . . 7K 151
Fair Grn. Sotn 5F 174
Fairground Ind. Pk. W'hll . . . 8C 50
Fairhaven Ct. Bourn 1B 246
Fairholme Gdns. F'ham. 9E 64
Fairholme Pde. Hook 2G 45
Fairhome Clo. Gos 9J 213
Fairings, The. F'bri . . . . 1J 153 (off Market Pl.)
Fair Isle Clo. Fare 5L 211
Fairisle Rd. Sotn. 7D 158
Fairland Clo. Fle 3N 47
Fair La. Win 6C 106
Fairlawn Clo. Rown 5E 158
Fairlawn Ho. Win 7K 105 (9K 237)
Fairlawn Rd. T'ley 6K 11
Fair Lea. Bourn 3J 245 (9J 247)
Fairlead Dri. Gos 1F 238
Fairlea Grange. Sotn 7L 159
Fairlea Rd. Ems. 6M 203
Fairlea Rd. L'ton. 2E 234
Fairlie. Ring. 8M 185
Fairlie Clo. H End. 8N 161
Fairlie Pk. Ring. 8L 185
Fairlight Gdns. Four M. 4K 97
Fairmead Clo. Coll T 6G 19
Fairmead Ct. Hay I 4E 242
Fair Mdw. Way. Ems 9K 203
Fairmead Wlk. Water 7A 182
Fairmead Way. Tot 5L 171
Fairmile. 6K 229
Fairmile. Fle 5L 47
Fairmile Ho. Christ 6J 229
Fairmile Rd. Christ. 4H 229
Fair Oak. . . . . 1N 161 (Eastleigh)
Fair Oak. . . . . 3N 9 (Thatcham)
Fair Oak Ct. F Oak 1N 161
Fair Oak Ct. Gos. 4F 238
Fair Oak Dri. Hav 6F 202
Fair Oak Green. 7J 13
Fair Oak La. Str S. 7J 13
Fair Oak Rd. Eastl 9H 133
Fairoak Way. Baug. 4D 10
Fair Piece. Wher. 2E 74
Fairthorn Ct. Bourn 1K 245
Fairthorne Gdns. Gos. 3J 239
Fairthorne Ho. Bas. 8N 41
Fairthorne Ri. Old B. 6K 43
Fairview. Alr. 2E 108
Fairview Clo. Hythe. 6M 193
Fairview Clo. Roms 3A 130
Fairview Ct. Gos 3G 238
Fairview Dri. Hythe. 7L 193
Fairview Dri. Roms 3A 130
Fair Vw. Gdns. F'ham 4F 64
Fairview Mdw. Okly 2D 58
Fairview Pde. Hythe 7M 193
Fairview Pk. Poole 2A 244
Fairview Rd. Head D 2D 102
Fairview Ter. Head 1C 102
Fairwater Clo. Gos 7D 212
Fairway Bus. Cen. Ports 6J 215
Fairway Clo. Lip. 3N 115
Fairway Dri. Christ 8J 229
Fairway Est. Bourn. 2B 226
Fairway Gdns. Rown 6D 158
Fairway Rd. Hythe 5L 193
Fairway Rd. Poole 5A 244
Fairways. 8B 50
Fairways. Hind. 1K 103
Fairways. W'hll 8B 50
Fairway, The. Fare 9L 199
Fairway, The. Farn 2C 48
Fairway, The. F'ham 3F 64
Fairway, The. Gos. 7E 212
Fairway, The. New M 7C 232
Fairway, The. Row C. 8J 183
Fairway, The. Wars 8C 196
Fairway, The. W'hill 6G 100
Fairy Cross Way. Water . . . 7B 182
Fakenham Way. Owl 4F 18
Falaise Clo. A'sht 9K 49
Falaise Clo. Sotn 7H 159
Falaise Rd. Mid W 4A 72
Falcon Clo. Bas 1H 59
Falcon Clo. Fare. 9H 199
Falcon Clo. Tidw 7D 30
Falcon Coppice. Wool H. 3A 8
Falcon Ct. Alt 2F 80
Falcon Ct. Frim 3M 29
Falcon Dri. Christ. 9C 230
Falconer Ct. Holb. 2A 208
Falcon Fields. Fawl. 5F 208
Falcon Fields. T'ley 3H 11
Falcon Grn. Ports 1N 215
Falcon Ho. Gdns. Wool H . . . 3A 8
Falcon Rd. Water. 3A 182
Falcon Sq. Eastl. 2B 160
Falcon Vw. Win 1G 127
Falcon Way. Bot. 1C 176
Falcon Way. Yate 7L 17
Falconwood Clo. F'bri 1G 152
Falkland Ct. Chan F . . . . . . 9A 132 (off Falkland Rd.)
Falkland Ct. Farn 3N 49
Falkland Rd. Bas 1D 42
Falkland Rd. Chan F. 1A 160
Falkland Rd. Sotn. 2F 172
Falklands Clo. Lee S 9B 212
Falklands Rd. Ports. 4F 214
Falkner Ct. F'ham 8E 64
Falkner Rd. F'ham 8D 64
Falkners Clo. Fle. 8A 28
Fallowfield. Fle 8A 28
Fallow Fld. Win. 1G 127
Fallowfield. Yate 6L 17
Fallows, The. New M 1C 232
Falmouth Rd. Ports 8A 200
Falstaff Way. Tot. 5K 171
Fanshawe St. Sotn 4M 173 (1E 4)
Fantails. Alt. 2F 80
Fanum Ho. Bas. 5E 42
Faraday Ct. Bas. 3E 42
Faraday Pk. And. 9H 51
Faraday Rd. Bas 3E 42
Faraday Rd. Farn 6L 29
Farcroft Rd. Poole 9A 226
Farcrosse Clo. S'hrst 5E 18
Fareham. 8D 198
Fareham Dri. Yate. 6L 17
Fareham Enterprise Cen. Fare 2C 212
Fareham Heights. Fare 6F 198
Fareham Ind. Pk. Fare. 6F 198
Fareham Pk. Rd. Fare 5M 197
Fareham Rd. Gos. 3D 212
Fareham Rd. S'wick 4N 199
Fareham Rd. Wick 7C 178
Fareham Shop. Cen. Fare 8D 198
Faringdon Clo. S'hrst 4E 18
Faringdon Ct. Win. . . . . 4L 105 (off Northlands Dri.)
Faringdon Rd. Sotn 3H 175
Farleigh Clo. Hav 4D 202
Farleigh La. Dum 9H 59
Farleigh Ri. Bas 9D 42
Farleigh Rd. Clid 7M 59
Farleigh Wallop. 8N 59
Farleigh Wallop Dri. Elve . . . 9H 27
Farley. 8F 86
Farley Clo. F Oak 2A 162
Farley Clo. Win 1F 126
Farley Ct. Farn. 1M 49
Farley Ct. Sotn 9J 159
Farley La. Brfld. 4C 124
Farley Mount Country Pk. 8N 89
Farley Mt. Rd. Spar 8M 89
Farley St. Neth W. 9N 67
Farlington. 9M 201
Farlington Av. Cosh 8K 201
Farlington Marshes Nature Reserve. 3M 215
Farlington Rd. Ports. 7G 214
Farm Clo. Hamb 7L 195
Farm Clo. Ring 9K 185
Farm Clo. Yate 8N 17
Farm Cotts. Bas. 3M 41
Farmdene Clo. Christ 6F 230
Farm Dri. Fle 8N 27
Farm Edge Rd. Fare. 7M 211
Farmers Wlk. Evtn 6L 233
Farmery Clo. Sotn 7B 160
Farm Ground Clo. Hook 2J 45
Farm Ho. Clo. Fare 3M 211
Farmhouse Way. Water 5A 182
Farm La. Asht. 8H 171
Farm La. Christ. 9C 230
Farm La. Cron. 3L 63
Farm La. Mort W 1C 12
Farm La. Clo. Water 3L 201
Farm La. N. Bart S 6B 232
Farm La. S. Bart S 7B 232
Farmlea Rd. Ports 9B 200
Farm Rd. A'sht 8N 49
Farm Rd. Fare 7H 197
Farm Rd. Frim 2N 29
Farm Rd. L Pk. 3F 68
Farmside Gdns. Ports 4G 215
Farm Vw. Ems. 6M 203
Farm Vw. Yate 8N 17
Farm Vw. Av. Water 6B 168
Farm Vw. Dri. Chine 9H 23
Farnborough. 9K 29
Farnborough Aerospace Pk. Farn 3H 49
Farnborough Airfield. Farn 3G 49
Farnborough Bus. Cen. Farn 1H 49
Farnborough Ga. Retail Pk. Farn 5L 29
Farnborough Green. 6L 29
Farnborough Park. 9L 29
Farnborough Rd. A'sht. 9G 49
Farnborough Rd. Farn 3K 49
Farnborough Rd. F'ham & A'sht 2F 64
Farnborough Street. 8M 29

Farnborough St. Farn. 6M 29
Farnham. 8E 64
Farnham Bus. Cen. F'ham 7E 64
Farnham Bus. Pk. F'ham 9D 64
Farnham By-Pass. F'ham 9B 64
Farnham Castle. 7D 64
Farnham Castle Keep. 7D 64
Farnham Maltings. 8E 64 (off Bridge Sq.)
Farnham Mus. 8D 64
Farnham Pk. Clo. F'ham 4D 64
Farnham Pk. Dri. F'ham 4D 64
Farnham Pk. Golf Course. 6D 64
Farnham Retail Pk. F'ham 7G 64
Farnham Rd. Bord. 1J 101
Farnham Rd. Fle 2B 48
Farnham Rd. Liss 2C 140
Farnham Rd. Odi. 8L 45
Farnham Rd. Ptsfld. 6A 140
Farnham Rd. Poole 7E 226
Farnham Rd. Row 9M 63
Farnham Trad. Est. F'ham 6H 65
Farnleys Mead. L'ton. 4E 234
Faroe Clo. Bas. 2E 42
Faroes Clo. Fare 5L 211
Farrell Clo. Cam 1L 29
Farriers Clo. Braml 1G 23
Farriers Ct. S'sea. 5E 240
Farriers Fld. Ellis. 1H 79
Farriers Wlk. Gos 2M 239 (off Clarence Rd.)
Farriers Way. Water 9C 182
Farrier Way. Fare 2D 212
Farringdon. 4E 98
Farringdon Bus. Pk. Lwr F 4C 98
Farringdon Rd. Hav 5G 203
Farringdon Way. T'ley. 6H 11
Farringford Rd. Sotn 4H 175
Farrington. Bourn. 3G 245
Farrs Av. And 3A 70
Farthingale Ter. Ports 4B 240 (7K 5) (off Peacock La., in two parts)
Farthing Fields. Head 2A 102
Farthing La. Ports 4B 240 (7K 5)
Farthings Ga. Water. 6M 201
Farthings, The. Highc 6J 231
Farwell Clo. Burt 3M 229
Farwell Rd. Poole 4A 226
Fastnet Clo. Sotn 6D 158
Fastnet Ho. S'sea 6E 240
Fastnet Way. Fare 5L 211
Fathersfield. Broc 6C 148
Fathoms Reach. Hay I. 3E 242
Faulston. 3D 118
Faulston Cotts. B'stne. 3D 118
Faulston Drove. B'stne 4E 118
Faulston Mill La. B'stne 3D 118
F Avenue. Hythe 2C 208
Faversham Rd. Owl. 4F 18
Fawcett Rd. New M 4A 232
Fawcett Rd. S'sea 3F 240
Fawconer Rd. K're 2B 6
Fawley. 5F 208
Fawley Bus. Cen. Black. 5E 208
Fawley By-Pass. Fawl 5F 208
Fawley Ct. Hav 4H 203
Fawley Grn. Bourn 3A 228
Fawley La. Ows. 3B 134 (in two parts)
Fawley La. Priv 9J 111
Fawley Rd. Holb 5C 208
Fawley Rd. Hythe. 7M 193
Fawley Rd. Ports. 3F 214
Fawley Rd. Sotn 4F 172
Fawn Gdns. New M 2A 232
Fay Clo. Fare 6M 211
Fayre Rd. Fare 1C 212
Fayrewood Chase. Bas 3K 59
Fearon Rd. Ports. 6F 214
Feathers La. Bas. 7C 42
Feathers Yd. Bas. 7C 42
Feld Way. Lych 3H 43
Felix Rd. Gos 9K 213
Fell Clo. L Hth. 5D 196
Fell Dri. Lee S. 9B 212
Fellows Rd. Farn 2M 49
Felmer Dri. King W. 8N 91
Feltham Clo. Roms. 4B 130
Felton Cres. Highc 6H 231
Feltons Pl. Ports. 3G 215
Fen Av. Fare 1D 212
Fencott Pl. Bas 5C 42
Fenleigh Clo. Bart S 5C 232
Fenn Bank. Bourn 2K 245 (6L 247)
Fennel Clo. Chine 8H 23
Fennel Clo. Farn 8D 28
Fennel Gdns. L'ton 1D 234
Fennell Clo. Water. 9L 181
Fenn's Yd. F'ham 8D 64
Fenton Rd. Bourn 8F 228
Fenwick Ct. Bourn 9M 227
Ferbies. Fle 5M 47
Ferguson Clo. Bas 9C 42
Fermor Dri. A'sht 8H 49
Fern Barrow. Poole 6F 226
Fern Clo. A'hlt. 5D 152
Fern Clo. Burt 4M 229
Fern Clo. Ptsfld. 1B 146
Ferncote Rd. Bord 4K 101
Ferncroft Clo. Fare. 7M 211
Ferncroft Gdns. Bourn 1H 227
Ferncroft Rd. Bourn 1H 227
Ferndale. H End 5A 176
Ferndale. Water 2N 201
Ferndale Gdns. Hook 1G 45
Ferndale M. Gos. 4D 212
Ferndale Rd. And 9L 51
Ferndale Rd. Chu C. 7L 47
Ferndale Rd. March 9E 172
Ferndale Rd. New M. 1C 232
Ferndene Way. Sotn 2D 174
Ferndown Ct. Alt. 4G 81
Ferndown Ct. F'bri 1G 153
Ferndown Gdns. Farn. 8G 28
Fern Dri. Chu C. 5K 47
Fern Dri. Hav 7G 202
Ferneham Rd. Fare 7M 197
Ferney Clo. Chaw 9D 80
Ferney La. Old Al & Meds 9G 79
Fernglade. New M. 3B 232
Fernheath Clo. Bourn 4E 226
Fernheath Rd. Bourn. 3E 226
Fernhill Clo. B'wtr. 3H 29
Fernhill Clo. F'ham 4D 64
Fernhill Dri. F'ham 4D 64
Fernhill Fields. New M 1B 232
Fernhill Flats. Bourn 2K 245 (6L 247)
Fernhill La. B'wtr 3G 29
Fern Hill La. Brfld. 4D 124
Fernhill La. F'ham. 4D 64
Fernhill La. New M 1B 232
Fernhill Rd. B'wtr & Farn 2G 28
Fernhill Rd. New M. 3B 232
Fernhills Rd. Hythe. 8N 193
Fernhill Wlk. B'wtr 3H 29
Fernhurst Clo. Hay I 4D 242
Fernhurst Rd. S'sea 3G 241
Fernie Clo. Fare. 6L 211
Fernlea. W'hill. 6G 100
Fernlea Clo. Ashy H 4B 186
Fernlea Gdns. Sotn. 8K 159
Fernlea Way. Dib P 6J 193
Fernmount Cen., The. New M 1B 232
Fern Rd. Hythe 6L 193
Fern Rd. Sotn. 8D 174
Fernside Clo. Holb 5A 208
Fernside Clo. Sotn 2E 172
Fernside Ct. Sotn 7K 159
Fernside Rd. Bourn 6H 227
Fernside Wlk. F Oak 1A 162
Fernside Way. Eastl 1A 162
Ferns Mead. F'ham. 9C 64
Ferns, The. F'ham. 3E 64
Fern Way. Fare 6G 197
Fernwood Clo. St I 3E 186
Fernwood Cres. Sotn 2D 174
Fernwood Ho. Cowp. 8A 182
Fernyhurst Av. Rown 6E 158
Ferrell Fld. Hook 2F 44
Ferris Av. Bourn 4N 227
Ferris Clo. Bourn 4A 228
Ferris Pl. Bourn 4A 228
Ferrol Rd. Gos 1L 239
Ferrybridge Grn. H End 4N 175
Ferry Gdns. Gos 3N 239
Ferrymans Quay. Net A 4F 194
Ferry Rd. Bourn 2J 247
Ferry Rd. Hay I. 3N 241
Ferry Rd. Hythe 6L 193
Ferry Rd. S'sea. 4L 241 (in two parts)
Festing Gro. S'sea 5G 240
Festing Rd. S'sea 5G 240
Feversham Av. Bourn 5B 228
Fibbards Rd. Broc. 7C 148
Fiddlers Fld. Shald 10A 62
Field Clo. Comp 7G 126
Field Clo. Gos. 3D 212
Field Clo. L Hth. 7D 196
Field Clo. Roms 5N 129
Field Clo. Sotn 6A 160
Fielden Clo. N Bad 8E 130
Fielden Ct. K're. 3A 6
Field End. F'ham. 6H 65
Field End. King W. 8N 91
Fielder Dri. Fare 2D 212
Fielders Ct. Alt. 5F 80
Fielders Ct. Water. 5K 201
Fielders, The. E'sly 5H 17
Fielders Way. E Wel 1B 156
Fieldfare Av. Yate 7L 17
Fieldfare Clo. Water 7C 168
Fieldfare Ct. Tot. 2J 171
Field Ga. Dri. K're. 2A 6
Field Ga. Dri. Wool H 2A 8 (off Greenlands)
Fieldhouse Dri. Lee S 8B 212
Fielding Gdns. C'then 1D 18
Fielding Rd. Coll T 7G 19
Field La. Frim. 3M 29 (in three parts)
Fieldmore Rd. Gos 9K 213
Field Path. Farn 3H 29
Field Pl. Lip. 3E 116
Field Pl. New M 6M 231
Field Rd. Farn. 3H 29
Fields Clo. Black. 7C 208
Field Stores App. A'sht 8L 49
Field Vw. Chan F. 6L 131
Field Wlk. L'ton. 1D 234
Field Way. A'sht 8N 49
Fieldway. Christ. 5F 230
Field Way. Comp 7G 127
Fieldway. Fle 3J 47
Fieldway. Gods 9N 151
Fieldway. Gods 5A 154 (off Southampton Rd.)
Fieldway. Ring. 9L 185
Field Way. Water 6G 181
Fifth Av. Hav. 7H 203
Fifth Av. Ports 9F 200
Fifth St. Green 1G 9
Fifth St. Hythe 3D 208 (D Avenue, in two parts)
Fifth St. Hythe. 5C 208 (South Av.)
Fifth St. Ports. 9G 214
Figsbury Ridge. Wint G 3B 86
Figsbury Rd. Wint D. 3A 86
Filmer Clo. Gos. 8F 212
Filmore Hill. 2H 137
Filmorehill La. Priv. 2G 137
Filton Clo. Cal 1J 171
Filton Rd. L'ton. 2D 234
Fincham End Dri. C'then 1B 18
Finchampstead. 2H 17
Finchampstead Ridges. 2L 17
Finch Clo. T'ley 6J 11
Finchdean. 4K 183
Finchdean Rd. Hav. 5D 202
Finchdean Rd. Row C 8J 183
Finches Grn. Alt 2F 80
Finches, The. Sotn 2G 172 (SO16)
Finches, The. Sotn 9N 159 (SO17)
Finchfield Av. Bourn 1D 226
Finchmead La. Ptsfld 9H 139
Finch Rd. S'sea. 4L 241
Finch's La. Twy. 7K 127
Finchwood Farm Ind. Units. Hay I 7H 217
Findhorn Clo. Coll T 6F 18
Findings, The. Farn. 4G 28
Findon Rd. Gos. 8K 213
Fingle Dri. And 1L 69
Finisterre Clo. Fare 4L 211
Finkley Down Farm Pk. & Mus. 7D 52
Finkley Rd. Mid Wy 4G 52
Finlay Clo. Sotn 6G 175
Fintry Pl. Farn. 5G 28
Fintry Wlk. Farn 5G 28
Finzi Clo. Sotn 7G 175
Fiona Clo. Win 6N 105
Fir Av. New M. 4C 232
Firbank Rd. Bourn 6M 227
Fir Clo. Fle. 3L 47
Fir Clo. Lyn. 3B 148
Fir Copse Rd. Water 6L 201
Fircroft. Fle 2L 47
Fircroft Dri. Chan F. 7B 132
Fir Dri. B'wtr 1F 28
Firecrest Clo. Sotn 6G 158
Firecrest Rd. Bas 4H 59
Fire Sta. Rd. A'sht. 8K 49
Fire Thorn Clo. Fle. 4M 47
Firglen Dri. Yate 6N 17
Firgo La. Longp & Tuft. 1C 76
Fir Gro. W'hill. 6G 101
Firgrove Clo. N Bad. 8E 130
Firgrove Ct. Farn. 8K 29
Firgrove Ct. F'ham 9D 64
Firgrove Ct. Sotn 3H 173
Firgrove Cres. Ports. 3G 214
Firgrove Hill. F'ham. 9E 64
Firgrove La. N Boar 8H 179
Firgrove Pde. Farn 8K 29
Firgrove Rd. E'sly & Yate 7J 17
Firgrove Rd. Farn 8K 29
Firgrove Rd. N Bad 8E 130
Firgrove Rd. Sotn. 3H 173
Firgrove Rd. W'hill 6G 100
Firlands Av. Cam 8M 19
Firlands Ri. Hav 8A 202
Firmain Rd. Poole. 5B 226
Firmount Clo. Evtn. 5M 233
Firmstone Rd. Win. 6M 105
Fir Rd. Asht 8H 171
Firs Av. Water. 8N 181
Firs Clo. Farn 1L 49
Firs Clo. Firs 4E 86
Firs Cres. King W. 7M 91
Firsdown. 4E 86
Firs Dri. H End 5L 175
Firs Glen Rd. Bourn 6H 227
Firshill. Christ. 5G 231
Firs La. Odi. 9J 45
Firs La. Poole 5A 244
Firs Pk. Ptsfld 1B 146
Firs Rd. Firs 4D 86
First Av. Cath 8C 168
First Av. Cosh. 9G 200
First Av. Farl 9L 201
First Av. Hav. 7H 203
First Av. Sotn 3C 172
Firs, The. And. 1L 69
Firs, The. Bourn 1L 245 (5N 247)
Firs, The. Gos 7F 212
Firs, The. Ink 1H 7
Firs, The. Lip 3D 116
Firs, The. Sotn 7L 159
First Marine Av. Bart S 7A 232
First St. Green 1H 9
First St. Hythe. 5E 208 (A Avenue)
First St. Hythe. 9C 194 (Avenue D)
Firs Way. Bas 4K 41
Firs Way. Whitc 5G 55
Firth Clo. Sil 5A 12
Fir Tree All. A'sht. 9J 49 (off Victoria Rd.)
Fir Tree Av. Hasl. 9M 103
Fir Tree Clo. H Hth 4N 161
Fir Tree Clo. St L. 6A 186
Firtree Clo. S'hrst 4B 18
Fir Tree Corner. Baug 3E 10
Fir Tree Ct. Sotn 2F 174
Firtree Cres. Hord. 3G 232
Fir Tree Gdns. Water. 5C 182
Firtree Gro. Hythe 9M 193
Fir Tree Hill. A'hlt 4D 152
Fir Tree La. Christ 5F 230
Firtree La. H Hth. 3L 161
Fir Tree Rd. Cad 3A 170
Fir Tree Rd. Hay I. 4G 242
Fir Tree Way. Fle. 3N 47
Firtree Way. Sotn 5F 174
Fir Va. Rd. Bourn 2K 245 (6M 247)
Firview. Lip. 3D 116
Firway. Gray 2G 102
Firwood Cvn. Pk. Chan F 4A 132
Firwood Clo. Chan F. 4A 132
Firwood Dri. Cam 8L 19
Fisgard Rd. Gos 9K 213
Fisher Clo. And. 1C 70
Fisher Clo. Fare. 5L 211
Fisher Ho. Chine. 3G 42
Fishermans Av. Bourn. 1E 246
Fishermans Bank. Christ 9A 230
Fishermans Quay. L'ton. 2F 234
Fishermans, The. Ems 9N 203
Fishermans Wlk. Bourn. 2F 246
Fisherman's Wlk. Fare 1M 213
Fisherman's Wlk. Hay I 5L 243
Fishermen's Clo. A'sht 6N 49
Fisher Rd. Gos 5E 212
Fishers Fld. St M. 9L 35
Fishers Gro. Ports 1M 215
Fishers Hill. Fare. 7K 197
Fisher's Rd. Tot 4N 171
Fishery Creek Cvn. Pk. Hay I 5K 243
Fishery La. Hay I. 5J 243
Fishlake Meadows. Roms 3L 129
Fiske Clo. Bas. 7L 41
Fiske Ct. Yate 7A 18
Fitzgerald Clo. White. 1F 196
Fitzharris Av. Bourn 7L 227
Fitzherbert Rd. Ports. 1L 215
Fitzherbert Spur. Farl 1M 215
Fitzherbert St. Ports 1D 240
Fitzhugh. 3L 173
Fitzhugh Pl. Sotn 3L 173 (1B 4)
Fitzhugh St. Sotn 5L 173 (4B 4)
Fitzmaurice Rd. Christ 6H 229
Fitzpatrick Ct. Ports 8E 200
Fitzroy Clo. Sotn. 4L 159
Fitzroy Rd. Fle. 1J 47
Fitzroy Wlk. Ports 1E 240
Fitzwilliam Av. Fare. 6K 211
Fitzwilliam Clo. Bourn. 1C 226
Fitzwygram Cres. Hav. 6F 202
Five Acres Clo. Lind 2L 101
Five Ash Rd. Meds. 3H 97
Five Bells La. Neth W 1N 87
Five Bridges Rd. Win 2J 127
Five Elms Dri. Roms. 6A 130
Fivefields Clo. Win 7N 105
Fivefields Rd. Win 7N 105
Five Heads Rd. Water. 2A 182
Five Lanes. St M. 1K 53
Five Post La. Gos 1K 239
Flag Farm. Poole. 6B 244
Flag Head Chine. Poole. 7C 244
Flaghead Rd. Poole. 6C 244
Flag Staff Grn. Gos 1M 239
Flag Wlk. Water 5N 181
Flambard Av. Christ. 5J 229
Flambard Rd. Poole 3A 244
Flamborough Clo. Sotn. 8C 158
Flamingo Ct. Fare 9H 199
Flamstone St. B'stne. 3C 118
Flanders Ho. Fare 9A 198
Flanders Ind. Pk. H End. 2M 175
Flanders Rd. H End 2M 175
Flashett, The. W'slw 5H 87
Flathouse Quay. Ports 9D 214
Flathouse Rd. Ports 1C 240 (2L 5) (Anchor Ga. Rd.)
Flathouse Rd. Ports 9D 214 (1N 5) (Victory Retail Pk.)
Flats, The. B'wtr 9D 18
Flaxfield Ct. Bas 6B 42
Flaxfield Rd. Bas. 6B 42
Flaxfields End. F'bri 1H 153
Flazen Clo. Bourn 3B 226
Fleet. 2L 47 (Fleet)
Fleet. 8G 216 (Hayling Island)
Fleet Bus. Pk. Chu C. 7N 47
Fleet Clo. Gos 7F 212
Fleetend. 9C 196
Fleet End Bottom. Wars 9C 196
Fleetend Clo. Hav 3E 202
Fleet End Rd. Wars. 8C 196
Fleet Farm Camping & Caravan Site. Hay I 8G 217
Fleet Hill. Finch 3E 16
Fleetlands. 3F 212
Fleetlands Golf Course. 3F 212
Fleet La. Finch. 3E 16
Fleet Pond Nature Reserve. 9A 28
Fleet Rd. A'sht. 4C 48
Fleet Rd. Fle & Farn 9B 28 (Cove Rd.)
Fleet Rd. Fle 3L 47 (Reading Rd. N.)
Fleet Rd. H Win 6C 26
Fleming Av. N Bad 8G 130
Fleming Clo. Fare 5G 197
Fleming Clo. Farn. 6M 29
Fleming Clo. Lud 1D 30
Fleming Ct. N Bad 8G 130
Fleming Pk. Golf Course. 1C 160
Fleming Pl. Col C 2K 133
Fleming Pl. Roms 4M 129
Fleming Rd. Sotn 7B 160
Fleming Rd. Win. 3G 105
Flensburg Clo. And 7M 51
Fletcher Clo. Bas. 7A 42
Fletcher Clo. Bourn. 3H 227
Fletcher Clo. Dib 6J 193
Fletcher Rd. Bourn 3H 227
Fletchers Fld. Lip 3E 116
Fletchers Ho. Lip 3D 116
Fletchwood La. Asht 8F 170 (in two parts)
Fletchwood Rd. Tot 4H 171
Fleur De Lys Pk. Pill 6F 224
Fleuret Clo. Hythe 8M 193
Flexford Clo. Chan F 3M 131
Flexford Clo. High. 4A 8
Flexford Gdns. Hav. 6G 203

Flexford La. Sway . . . 9K 223
Flexford Nature Reserve. . . . 4M 131
Flexford Rd. N Bad . . . 6H 131
Flinders Clo. And . . . 9E 52
Flinders Ct. S'sea . . . 5J 241
Flint Clo. And . . . 3L 69
Flint Clo. Sotn . . . 6J 175
Flint Ho. Path. Ports . . . 2K 215
Flint La. Cla . . . 2E 50
Flint St. S'sea . . . 4C 240 (7M 5)
Floating Bri. Rd. Sotn . . . 7A 174
Flood Street. . . . 4K 151
Flood, The. W'slw . . . 4G 87
Floral Way. And . . . 3K 69
Flora Twort Gallery. . . . 1M 145
Florence Clo. E Wel . . . 1B 156
Florence Clo. Yate . . . 7M 17
Florence Ct. And . . . 7A 52
(in two parts)
Florence Portal Clo. Lave . . . 5N 55
Florence Rd. Bourn . . . 1B 246
Florence Rd. Coll T . . . 6F 18
Florence Rd. Fle . . . 5M 47
Florence Rd. Poole . . . 1A 244
Florence Rd. Sotn . . . 8B 174
Florence Rd. S'sea . . . 6E 240
Florence Way. Bas . . . 3L 41
Florentine Way. Water . . . 1A 202
Florin Mall. Bourn . . . 1B 246
(off Royal Arc.)
Florins, The. Fare . . . 8D 196
Florins, The. Water . . . 6M 201
Floriston Gdns. New M . . . 3E 232
Florrie Pl. Lwr F . . . 4D 98
Floud La. W Meon . . . 8C 136
Flowerdew Ct. And . . . 3A 70
Flowerdown Barrows. . . . 2G 104
Flowerdown Cvn. Pk. Win . . . 1G 104
Flowerdown Clo. Cal . . . 2J 171
Flowers Clo. Hamb . . . 6J 195
Flowers La. Plait . . . 7M 121
Flume Rd. Hythe . . . 4G 209
Flushards. L'ton . . . 3F 234
Flying Bull Clo. Ports . . . 8E 214
(off Flying Bull La.)
Flying Bull La. Ports . . . 8E 214
Focus 303 Bus. Cen. And . . . 9D 52
Focus Way. And . . . 9C 52
Foden Rd. A'sht . . . 1J 65
Foldsgate Clo. Lyn . . . 1B 148
Foley Ho. Ports . . . 1E 240
Folkestone Rd. Ports . . . 9H 215
Folly Clo. Fle . . . 4M 47
Folly Drove. Hale . . . 1B 154
Folly Farm La. Ashy . . . 2F 186
Folly Fld. Bish W . . . 4N 163
Folly Hill. F'ham . . . 4C 64
Folly La. Braml & Str . . . 1J 23
Folly La. Hann . . . 9N 9
Folly La. Ptsfld . . . 1M 145
Folly La. N. F'ham . . . 3D 64
Folly La. S. F'ham . . . 4C 64
Folly Roundabout, The. And . . . 9N 51
Font Clo. Fare . . . 6F 196
Fontley La. L Hth . . . 6K 197
Fontley Rd. Titch . . . 5K 197
(in two parts)
Fontwell Clo. A'sht . . . 9M 49
Fontwell Clo. Cal . . . 1J 171
(in two parts)
Fontwell Dri. Alt . . . 6F 80
Fontwell Gdns. H Hth . . . 4A 162
Fontwell M. Water . . . 9B 182
Fontwell Rd. S'sea . . . 5E 240
Foord Rd. H End . . . 5L 175
Football Grn. Min . . . 8M 155
Footner Clo. Roms . . . 2B 130
Footners La. Burt . . . 4M 229
Forbes Chase. Coll T . . . 6F 18
Forbes Clo. Sotn . . . 5E 158
Forbes Rd. King W . . . 7M 91
Forbury Rd. S'sea . . . 3E 240
Ford Av. Chan F . . . 8B 132
Fordingbridge. . . . 1J 153
Fordingbridge Rd. A'hlt . . . 3D 152
Fordingbridge Rd. S'sea . . . 4J 241
Fordington Av. Win . . . 6H 105 (6H 237)
Fordington Rd. Win . . . 6J 105 (6H 237)
Fordington Vs. Chan F . . . 6A 132
Ford La. Far H & Brams . . . 1L 15
Ford La. Upt G & S Warn . . . 2C 62
Ford Rd. Gos . . . 1H 239
Forehead, The. Mort . . . 1L 13
Foreland Clo. Christ . . . 2G 228
Foreland Ct. Hay I . . . 5J 243
Forelle Cen., The. Ver . . . 5A 184
Foremans Cotts. Gos . . . 5M 239
Foreshore N. Hythe . . . 2F 208
Foreshore S. Hythe . . . 3F 208
Forest Av. Water . . . 7N 181
Forest Cen., The. Bord . . . 4K 101
Forest Clo. Baug . . . 3E 10
Forest Clo. Chan F . . . 4A 132
Forest Clo. Christ . . . 5F 230
Forest Clo. N Bad . . . 7D 130
Forest Clo. Ver . . . 5A 184
Forest Clo. Wal C . . . 8A 164
Forest Clo. Water . . . 7N 181
Forest Corner. Liss . . . 7F 114
Forest Ct. New M . . . 4C 232
Forestdale. Hind . . . 4M 103
Forest Dean. Fle . . . 8A 28
Forest Dri. Chine . . . 8G 23
Forest Dri. Tidw . . . 8E 30
Forest Edge. Fawl . . . 5E 208
Forest Edge Clo. Ashy H . . . 3A 186
Forest Edge Dri. Ashy H . . . 3A 186
Forest Edge Rd. Crow . . . 6A 188
Forest End. Fle . . . 5L 47
Forest End. S'hrst . . . 4B 18
Forest End. Water . . . 2L 201
Forest End Rd. S'hrst . . . 4B 18
Forester Rd. Sob . . . 1J 179
Foresters Ga. Black . . . 9C 208
Foresters Rd. Fawl . . . 6D 208
Foresters Way. C'then . . . 2H 19
Forest Front. Hythe . . . 9L 193
(in two parts)
Forest Gdns. Lyn . . . 2B 148
Forest Gdns. Wal C . . . 8A 164
Forest Ga. Black . . . 9D 208
Forest Ga. Gdns. L'ton . . . 5D 234
Forest Glade. Row . . . 8N 63
Forest Glade Clo. Broc . . . 7A 148
Forest Hall. Broc . . . 7D 148
Forest Hills. Cam . . . 9K 19
Foresthills Ct. Ring . . . 2N 187
Forest Hills Dri. Sotn . . . 8C 160
Forest Hill Way. Dib P . . . 7L 193
Forest Ho. Bourn . . . 3L 245 (7N 247)
Forestlake Av. Ring . . . 2N 187
Forest La. Fare . . . 1D 198
Forest La. Hythe . . . 2N 207
Forest La. Lind . . . 1M 101
Forest La. P Twen . . . 3E 70
Forest La. Poul . . . 6A 188
Forest La. T'ley . . . 7K 11
Forest La. Up Ch . . . 2N 31
Forest La. Clo. Lip . . . 2C 116
Forest Mead. Water . . . 7G 181
Forest Mdw. Dib P . . . 9M 193
Forest Mere. . . . 6N 115
Forest Oak Dri. New M . . . 1B 232
Forest Park. . . . 7B 148
Forest Pk. Rd. Broc . . . 6B 148
Forest Pines. New M . . . 2B 232
Forest Ri. Christ . . . 4F 230
Forest Ri. Liss . . . 8F 114
Forest Rd. Brans . . . 2G 220
Forest Rd. Burl . . . 6D 188
Forest Rd. Chan F . . . 4B 132
Forest Rd. C'then . . . 1E 18
Forest Rd. Den . . . 6A 180
Forest Rd. Gthm & Liss . . . 5D 114
Forest Rd. Hale . . . 9C 120
Forest Rd. Liss . . . 7F 114
Forest Rd. Nom . . . 4H 155
Forest Rd. Poole . . . 4E 244
Forest Rd. Wal C . . . 8A 164
Forest Rd. W'hill & Bord . . . 6J 101
(in two parts)
Forestside. . . . 4N 183
Forestside Av. Hav . . . 4G 203
Forestside Gdns. Ring . . . 8M 185
Forestside, The. Ver . . . 4A 184
Forest Vw. Broc . . . 7A 148
Forest Vw. New M . . . 9M 221
Forest Vw. Sotn . . . 6L 173 (7C 4)
Forest Vw. Clo. Bourn . . . 4L 227
Forest Vw. Rd. Bourn . . . 3L 227
Forest Way. Christ . . . 4F 230
Forest Way. Evtn . . . 5L 233
Forest Way. Gos . . . 6F 212
Forge Clo. Braml . . . 2H 23
Forge Clo. Burs . . . 9L 175
Forge Clo. F'ham . . . 7F 64
Forge Fld. And . . . 9A 52
Forge La. A'sht . . . 5H 49
Forge La. Fawl . . . 5F 208
Forge Rd. Black . . . 9D 208
Forge Rd. Kingsl . . . 8E 82
Forge Rd. Slea . . . 7K 83
Forges La. E'sly . . . 2A 16
Forneth Gdns. Fare . . . 9L 197
Forster Rd. Sotn . . . 3M 173
Forsyth Gdns. Bourn . . . 5G 227
Forsythia Clo. Hav . . . 5H 203
Forsythia Clo. H End . . . 2M 175
Forsythia Pl. Sotn . . . 5D 174
Fort Brockhurst. . . . 7H 213
Fort Cumberland Rd. S'sea . . . 4L 241
Fortescue Rd. Bourn . . . 8L 227
Fortescue Rd. Poole . . . 7B 226
Fort Fareham Ind. Site. Fare . . . 2C 212
Fort Fareham Rd. Fare . . . 2B 212
Forth Clo. Chan F . . . 7N 131
Forth Clo. Fare . . . 5L 211
Forth Clo. Farn . . . 6F 28
Forth Ho. Sotn . . . 4A 174
Fort Hill Dri. Bas . . . 5L 41
Forties Clo. Fare . . . 4L 211
Fort Narrien. Coll T . . . 6G 19
Fort Nelson. . . . 6K 199
Forton. . . . 2K 239
(Gosport)
Forton. . . . 5L 71
(Winchester)
Forton Rd. Gos . . . 1J 239
Forton Rd. Ports . . . 1F 240
Fort Rd. Gos . . . 6J 239
Fort Rd. Sotn . . . 7C 174
Fortrose Clo. Coll T . . . 6F 18
Fortune Ct. Chan F . . . 6A 132
Fortune Ho. Gos . . . 2J 239
Fortunes Way. Hav . . . 8N 201
Fort Wallington Ind. Est. Fare . . . 7F 198
Fort Widley. . . . 7G 200
Forty Acre La. Bton . . . 9A 146
Forum Clo. Bas . . . 6K 41
Forum, The. Hav . . . 7E 202
Forward Dri. Penn . . . 4C 234
Fosbury. . . . 6C 6
Fosseway. C'then . . . 1B 18
Fossewood Dri. Cam . . . 5M 19
Foster Clo. Fare . . . 4M 211
Foster Rd. Gos . . . 4J 239
Foster Rd. Ports . . . 1E 240
Fosters Bus. Pk. Hook . . . 3E 44
Foul La. Meds . . . 9K 79
Founders Way. Gos . . . 6F 212
Foundry Ct. Ports . . . 2B 240 (3K 5)
Foundry Cres. Burs . . . 1K 195
Foundry La. Sotn . . . 2G 173
Foundry Rd. Anna V . . . 5J 69
Foundry Rd. Redl . . . 1M 119
Fountain Ct. Col C . . . 3L 133
Fountain Ct. H End . . . 4M 175
Fountain Ct. Poole . . . 3F 244
Fountain Rd. Selb . . . 8L 99
Fountains Clo. Bas . . . 2B 42
Fountain's Mall. Odi . . . 8L 45
Fountain St. Ports . . . 2D 240 (3N 5)
Fountain Way. Christ . . . 8L 229
Four Acre Coppice. Hook . . . 1J 45
Four Acres. Bot . . . 4D 176
Four Lanes Clo. Chine . . . 9H 23
Four Marks. . . . 4K 97
Four Marks Grn. Hav . . . 3H 203
Four Oaks. High . . . 4A 8
Fourposts. . . . 5K 173
Fourposts Hill. Sotn . . . 5K 173 (3A 4)
Fourshells Clo. Fawl . . . 6D 208
Fourteenth St. Hythe . . . 3A 208
Fourth Av. Hav . . . 7H 203
Fourth Av. Ports . . . 9F 200
Fourth St. Green . . . 1G 9
(off Warehouse Rd.)
Fourth St. Hythe . . . 5D 208
(in two parts)
Fourth St. Ports . . . 1G 240
Fowey Clo. Chan F . . . 5N 131
Fowey, The. Black . . . 6C 208
Fowler Rd. Farn . . . 9H 29
Fowler's Rd. A'sht . . . 5L 49
Fowlers Rd. H End . . . 2M 175
Fowlers Wlk. Chilw . . . 1J 159
Foxbury. Gos . . . 4F 212
Foxbury Clo. Hythe . . . 7M 193
Foxbury Gro. Fare . . . 1K 213
Foxbury La. Gos . . . 4F 212
(in two parts)
Foxbury Rd. St L . . . 7C 186
(in two parts)
Fox Clo. Eastl . . . 1K 161
Foxcombe Clo. Swanm . . . 5C 164
Foxcote Gdns. New M . . . 3A 232
Foxcott Clo. Sotn . . . 1D 194
Foxcotte. . . . 7J 51
Foxcotte Clo. Charl . . . 8K 51
Foxcotte La. Charl . . . 7J 51
Foxcotte Rd. Charl . . . 7J 51
Foxcott Gro. Hav . . . 4F 202
Foxcroft. Chu C . . . 6M 47
Foxcroft Dri. Holb . . . 5N 207
Foxdown. . . . 9E 38
Foxdown. Over . . . 9E 38
Foxdown Clo. Cam . . . 8L 19
Fox Dri. Yate . . . 6N 17
Foxes Clo. Water . . . 3M 201
Foxes La. W Wel . . . 7N 121
Fox Fld. Evtn . . . 5L 233
Foxglade. Black . . . 9D 208
Foxglove Clo. Bas . . . 3J 59
Foxglove Clo. Christ . . . 6E 230
Foxglove Dri. Bord . . . 5K 101
Foxglove Pl. New M . . . 2E 232
Foxgloves. Fare . . . 6E 198
Foxgloves, The. H End . . . 5A 176
Foxhall. . . . 8L 59
Foxhayes La. Black . . . 9D 208
Fox Heath. Farn . . . 9E 28
Foxhills. . . . 6J 171
Foxhills. Asht . . . 6J 171
Foxhills Clo. Asht . . . 7J 171
Foxholes Rd. Bourn . . . 1J 247
Foxlands. Black . . . 9D 208
Fox Lane. . . . 4G 29
Fox La. Bramd . . . 1N 135
Fox La. E'sly C . . . 5J 17
Fox La. Okly . . . 9E 40
Fox La. Win . . . 9G 104
Foxlea Gdns. Gos . . . 9K 213
Foxley Clo. B'wtr . . . 8E 18
Foxley Dri. Ports . . . 4J 215
Foxmoor Clo. Okly . . . 8D 40
Fox Pond La. Penn . . . 4C 234
Fox Rd. Hasl . . . 9N 103
Fox's Furlong. Chine . . . 8J 23
Fox's La. K're . . . 3A 6
Fox's Wlk. Black . . . 9D 208
Foxtail Dri. Dib P . . . 8L 193
Fox Way. Ews . . . 2N 63
Foxwold Ho. Bourn . . . 1J 247
Foxwood. Fle . . . 9A 28
Foxwood Av. Christ . . . 9B 230
Fox Yd. F'ham . . . 8D 64
Foxy Paddock. Black . . . 9D 208
Foye La. Chu C . . . 6N 47
Foyes Ct. Sotn . . . 3J 173
Foy Gdns. Wars . . . 8N 195
Foyle Pk. Bas . . . 9B 42
Foyle Rd. Chan F . . . 6N 131
Frampton Clo. Col C . . . 3K 133
Frampton Clo. New M . . . 1D 232
Frampton Pl. Ring . . . 1J 187
Frampton Rd. Bourn . . . 6L 227
Frampton Way. King W . . . 8N 91
Frampton Way. Tot . . . 4M 171
France Hill Dri. Cam . . . 8L 19
Francesca Ct. Christ . . . 7A 230
Frances Rd. Bas . . . 7B 42
Frances Rd. Bourn . . . 1M 245
Frances Rd. Pur . . . 6L 201
Francis Av. Bourn . . . 3B 226
Francis Av. S'sea . . . 4G 240
Francis Clo. Lee S . . . 2C 238
Francis Gdns. Win . . . 4M 105
Francis Pl. Fare . . . 6N 211
Francis Rd. Horn . . . 8C 168
Francis Rd. Poole . . . 9C 226
Franconia Dri. Nurs . . . 8A 158
Frank Judd Ct. Ports . . . 4K 5
Frankland Cres. Poole . . . 2C 244
Frankland Ter. Ems . . . 9N 203
Franklin Av. H Win . . . 5B 26
Franklin Av. T'ley . . . 4F 10
Franklin La. Bish W . . . 8H 135
Franklin Rd. Bourn . . . 3L 227
Franklin Rd. Gos . . . 9E 212
Franklin Rd. New M . . . 2D 232
Franklin Rd. Twy . . . 6L 127
Franklyn Av. Sotn . . . 6E 174
Frank Miles Ho. S'sea . . . 3D 240
(off Somers Rd.)
Frankston Rd. Bourn . . . 1F 246
Fraser Clo. Old B . . . 5J 43
Fraser Clo. Sotn . . . 5E 158
Fraser Mead. Coll T . . . 7G 18
Fraser Rd. Gos . . . 4E 212
Fraser Rd. Hav . . . 7D 202
Fraser Rd. King W . . . 7M 91
Fraser Rd. Poole . . . 5D 226
Fraser Rd. Ports . . . 6C 214
Fraser Rd. S'sea . . . 3E 240
Frater. . . . 6G 212
Frater La. Gos . . . 7J 213
Fratton. . . . 3F 240
Fratton Ct. Ports . . . 2F 240
(off Penhale Rd.)
Fratton Ind. Est. S'sea . . . 2G 241
Fratton Rd. Ports . . . 2F 240
Fratton Way. F Oak . . . 2N 161
Frayslea. Dib P . . . 7M 193
Freda Rd. Christ . . . 8J 229
Freda Routh Gdns. F Oak . . . 1A 162
Frederica Rd. Bourn . . . 6J 227
Frederick St. A'sht . . . 9J 49
Frederick St. Ports . . . 1D 240 (1N 5)
Frederick St. Sotn . . . 4N 173 (1F 4)
Freefolk. . . . 4L 55
Freefolk Grn. Hav . . . 3H 203
Freefolk Priors. Free . . . 4L 55
Freegrounds Clo. H End . . . 4N 175
Freegrounds Rd. H End . . . 4N 175
Freelands Dri. Chu C . . . 6K 47
Freemantle. . . . 4H 173
Freemantle Bus. Cen. Sotn . . . 5H 173
Freemantle Clo. Bas . . . 4E 42
Freemantle Clo. Sotn . . . 5D 174
Freemantle Comn. Rd. Sotn . . . 5D 174
Freemantle Rd. Gos . . . 9K 213
Freestone Rd. S'sea . . . 5E 240
Free St. Bish W . . . 3N 163
Fremington Ct. New M . . . 3C 232
Frenches La. Roms . . . 4B 128
Frenches, The. . . . 3B 128
French Gdns. B'wtr . . . 9F 18
Frenchies Vw. Water . . . 6F 180
Frenchmans Creek. Chu C . . . 7K 47
Frenchman's Rd. Ptsfld . . . 9L 139
Frenchmoor. . . . 9L 87
Frenchmoor La. E Dean . . . 1K 121
French Rd. Lngmr . . . 3J 115
French St. Ports . . . 4B 240 (7J 5)
French St. Sotn . . . 7L 173 (8C 4)
Frendstaple Rd. Water . . . 2N 201
Frensham. . . . 1E 84
Frensham Av. Fle . . . 2A 48
Frensham Clo. Bourn . . . 3J 227
Frensham Clo. H End . . . 4N 175
Frensham Clo. Yate . . . 7L 17
Frensham Common. . . . 2G 84
Frensham Common Country Pk. . . . 3G 85
Frensham Country Pk. Interpretative Cen. . . . 2E 84
Frensham Ct. H End . . . 4N 175
Frensham Ct. S'sea . . . 3G 241
Frensham La. Head D & Churt . . . 8A 84
Frensham La. Lind & Head . . . 1M 101
Frensham Rd. S'sea . . . 3G 241
Frere Av. Fle . . . 4K 47
Frescade Cres. Bas . . . 8B 42
Freshfield Gdns. Water . . . 1M 201
Freshfield Rd. Sotn . . . 3G 173
Freshfield Sq. Sotn . . . 3G 173
Freshwater Ct. Chan F . . . 3C 132
Freshwater Ct. Lee S . . . 1A 238
Freshwater Ho. Fare . . . 9M 197
Freshwater Rd. Christ . . . 8E 230
Freshwater Rd. Ports . . . 1F 214
Freshwood Dri. Yate . . . 9N 17
Friars Cliff. . . . 8E 230
Friars Cft. Cal . . . 9J 157
Friars Cft. Net A . . . 2F 194
Friars Fld. F'ham . . . 7D 64
Friarsgate. Win . . . 6L 105 (7N 237)
Friars Pond Rd. Fare . . . 8M 197
Friars Rd. Christ . . . 8D 230
Friars Rd. Eastl . . . 2D 160
Friars Wlk. Bart S . . . 6B 232
(in two parts)
Friars Way. Sotn . . . 7B 160
Friary Clo. S'sea . . . 5E 240
Friary, The. S'sea . . . 5D 240
Friday's Heron. Cran . . . 6J 149
(off Penny's La.)
Friend Av. A'sht . . . 1M 65
Friesian Clo. Fle . . . 8N 27
Frimley. . . . 3M 29
Frimley Bus. Pk. Frim . . . 4L 29
Frimley By-Pass. Frim . . . 4L 29
Frimley Green. . . . 5N 29
Frimley Grn. Rd. Frim & Frim G . . . 3M 29
Frimley Gro. Gdns. Frim . . . 3M 29
Frimley High St. Frim . . . 4L 29
Frimley Rd. Cam & Frim . . . 8J 19
Fritham. . . . 6G 154
Fritham Clo. Tot . . . 3J 171
Fritham Gdns. Bourn . . . 3A 228
Fritham Rd. Sotn . . . 2H 175
Frith Common. . . . 5M 9
Frithend. . . . 4M 83
Frith End Rd. Bord . . . 3K 83
Frith La. Wick . . . 4C 178
Frithmead Clo. Bas . . . 9B 42

Frobisher Av.—Gladys Av.

Frobisher Av. Poole 5D 226
Frobisher Clo. Christ. 8B 230
Frobisher Clo. Gos 1E 238
Frobisher Clo. Ring 9M 185
Frobisher Ct. March 7F 172
Frobisher Gdns. Ems 9M 203
Frobisher Gdns. Sotn 6G 175
Frobisher Gro. Fare 1L 213
Frobisher Ho. Ports 2B 240 (3J 5)
Frobisher Ind. Cen. Roms 3L 129
Froddington Rd. S'sea 3E 240
Frodsham Way. Owl 3G 18
Froghall. Dib P. 8M 193
Frogham 7A 154
Frogham Grn. Hav 3C 202
Frogham Hill. Frog 3M 153
Froghole La. King S 8A 86
Frog La. F'bri 3H 153
Frog La. Lit L 8N 11
Frog La. Map 6N 43
Frog La. Roth 5D 24
Frogmore 8E 18 (Camberley)
Frogmore 3N 143 (Petersfield)
Frogmore. Fare 9M 197
Frogmore Ct. B'wtr 9E 18
Frogmore Gro. B'wtr 9E 18
Frogmore La. Nurs 8C 158
Frogmore La. Water 5N 181
Frogmore Pk. Dri. B'wtr 9E 18
Frogmore Rd. B'wtr 8D 18
Frogmore Rd. S'sea 3H 241
Frogs Hole. K're 2A 6
Frome Clo. Bas 6E 42
Frome Clo. Farn 6F 28
Frome Clo. March 9F 172
Frome Clo. Okly 1E 58
Frome Rd. W End 8E 160
Fromond Clo. L'ton 1E 234
Fromond Rd. Win 3G 105
Frosthole Clo. Fare 6A 198
Frosthole Cres. Fare 6A 198
Frostlane 8A 194
Frost La. Hythe 8M 193
Frost Rd. Bourn 2D 226
Froude Av. Gos 5L 239
Froude Rd. Gos 5L 239
Frouds Clo. Hook 3F 44
Froxfield Clo. Win 2H 105
Froxfield Gdns. Fare 8L 199
Froxfield Green 5C 138
Froxfield Ho. Ports 1E 240 (off Buriton St.)
Froxfield Rd. Hav 4H 203
Froyle Ct. Hav 4H 203
Froyle La. S Warn 4D 62
Fry Clo. Fawl 6D 208
Fry Clo. Hamb 5L 195
Fryer Clo. Bourn 1F 226
Fryern Arc. Chan F 5B 132
Fryern Clo. Chan F 6C 132
Fryern Ct. Rd. Burg 7H 151
Fryern Hill 6C 132
Fry Rd. Gos 2L 239
Frys La. Evtn 5L 233
Fry's La. Meon 9N 135
Fry's La. Yate 6A 18
Fry Sq. And 8A 52 (off Cricketers Way)
Fuchsia Gdns. Sotn 9J 159
Fugelmere Rd. Fle 1A 48
Fugelmere Wlk. Fle 1A 48
Fulbrook Way. Odi 2E 62
Fulflood 6K 105
Fulflood Ct. Win 6J 105 (6H 237)
Fulflood Rd. Hav 4E 202
Fulham Ho. Bas 6C 42
Fullers La. Wool H 3M 7
Fullers Rd. Row 8N 63
Fullers Va. Head 2B 102
Fullerton 5C 74
Fullerton Clo. Elve 9H 27
Fullerton Clo. Hav 4H 203
Fullerton Clo. Sotn 1D 194
Fullerton Rd. L'ton 2C 234
Fullerton Rd. Up Cl & Good C 7G 68
Fullerton Rd. Wher 4D 74
Fullerton Way. T'ley 6J 11
Fulmar Clo. Bas 3H 59
Fulmar Clo. Sotn 6G 158
Fulmar Dri. Hythe 7N 193
Fulmar Rd. Christ 9C 230
Fulmar Wlk. Gos 5C 212
Fulmer Wlk. Water 6M 181
Fulwood Av. Bourn 1C 226
Funtington Rd. Ports 8G 215
Funtley 4A 198
Funtley Ct. Fare 5A 198
Funtley Hill. Fare 5A 198
Funtley La. Fare 4A 198
Funtley Rd. Fare 3N 197
Furdies. Water 6F 180
Furley Clo. Win 6M 105
Furlonge Ho. Ems 8L 203
Furlong M. Ring 1J 187
Furlong Shop. Cen., The. Ring 1J 187
Furlong, The. Ring 1J 187
Furneaux Gdns. Fare 6D 198
Furness Rd. S'sea 6E 240
Furniss Way. Hay I 3D 242
Further Vell-Mead. Chu C 7K 47
Fury Way. Fare 5L 211
Furze Bank La. Bourn 4G 226
Furze Clo. Sotn 5E 174
Furze Cft. New M 5B 232
Furzedale Gdns. Hythe 8N 193
Furzedale Pk. Hythe 8N 193
Furzedown Cres. Hav 4G 203
Furzedown La. A'prt 2N 67
Furzedown M. Hythe 8N 193
Furzedown Rd. King S 9B 86
Furzedown Rd. Sotn 9M 159
Furze Dri. Per D 5B 30
Furze Hall. Fare 5D 198
Furzehall Av. Fare 6D 198
Furze Hill 8A 154
Furze Hill. F'ham 7M 65
Furze Hill Cres. C'then 1E 18
Furze Hill Dri. Poole 4A 244
Furze Hill Rd. Head D 3D 102 (in two parts)
Furze Hill Rd. Tidw 9D 30
Furze La. S'sea 3L 241
Furzeley Corner 8G 180
Furzeley Golf Course 8G 181
Furzeley Rd. Water 8G 180
Furze Mdw. Nye 4K 147
Furzen La. Ellis 2H 79
Furze Rd. Sotn 5E 174
Furze Rd. T'ley 3F 10
Furze Va. Rd. Head D 3D 102
Furze Way. Water 6B 182
Furzey Av. Hythe 7N 193
Furzey Clo. Fawl 7D 208
Furzey Gardens 8L 155
Furzey La. Beau 6A 206
Furzey Lodge 6A 206
Furzley 3M 155
Furzley Ct. Hav 3C 202
Furzley La. W Wel 3M 155
Furzley Rd. W Wel 3M 155
Furzy Whistlers Clo. Brans 6D 220
Fushia Clo. Hav 5J 203
Fuzzy Drove. Bas 2H 59
Fyeford Clo. Rown 5E 158
Fyfield 9N 31
Fyfield Clo. B'wtr 8F 18
Fyfield Clo. White 1F 196
Fyfield La. Fy'd 9N 31
Fyfield Rd. Fy'd 9N 31
Fyfield Way. Per D 5B 30
Fyfield Way. Win 1F 104
Fylingdales Clo. Bas 7J 41
Fyning 8M 141
Fyning La. Rog 8M 141
Fyning St. Ports 1E 240

G

Gable End. Farn 8K 29
Gable Head 2G 242
Gable M. Hay I 3G 243
Gables. Gray 4M 103
Gables Clo. Farn 8J 29
Gables Ct. Sotn 6L 159
Gables Rd. Chu C 7L 47
Gaffney Clo. A'sht 4M 49
Gage Clo. Lych 4G 43
Gage Clo. March 8F 172
Gainsborough Av. New M 1C 232
Gainsborough Clo. Cam 6N 19
Gainsborough Clo. Farn 1M 49
Gainsborough Clo. Sotn 8G 174
Gainsborough Ct. And 9M 51
Gainsborough Ct. Bourn 9E 228
Gainsborough Ct. Fle 2M 47
Gainsborough Ct. N Bad 8G 130
Gainsborough Ho. S'sea 5F 240
Gainsborough M. Fare 9J 197
Gainsborough Rd. Ashy H 3B 186
Gainsborough Rd. Bas 9D 42
Gainsborough Rd. Bourn 7C 228
Gainsford Rd. Sotn 5B 174
Gains Rd. S'sea 5F 240
Galahad Clo. And 8N 51
Galaxie Rd. Water 6B 182
Gale Moor Av. Gos 4F 238
Gales Ct. And 1N 69
Galileo Pk. And 9J 51
Gallaghers Mead. And 1J 69
Galleon Clo. Wars 8C 196
Galleries, The. A'sht 9J 49 (off High St.)
Galley La. H'ly 2J 9
Gallipoli Rd. Bulf B 3C 66
Gallops, The. Fare 7G 196
Gallop, The. Yate 6N 17
Gallop Way. Poole 7G 226
Galloway Clo. Bas 8K 41
Galloway Clo. Fle 8A 28
Gallwey Rd. A'sht 8K 49
Gally Hill Rd. Chu C 6K 47
Galsworthy Rd. Tot 3K 171
Galton Av. Christ 8J 229
Galt Rd. Ports 9M 201
Galway Rd. Yate 9M 17
Gamble Clo. Sotn 6D 174
Gambledown La. Sher E 4N 121
Gamble Rd. Ports 8E 214 (6E 4)
Gamblins La. Shir H 2B 178
Gamma Ho. Sotn 2H 159
Gander Dri. Bas 3L 41
Ganders Bus. Pk. Kingsl. 6H 83
Ganders Clo. Selb 7L 99
Gangbridge La. St M 8J 35
Ganger Farm La. Roms 2B 130
Ganger Rd. Roms. 2B 130
Gannet Clo. Bas 2H 59
Gannet Clo. Hythe 7N 193
Gannet Clo. Sotn 6G 158
Gannets, The. Fare 5L 211
Gantry, The 5L 173
Garbett Rd. Win 6N 105
Garbetts Way. Tong 4N 65
Garbitts La. Rog 1L 147
Garden City. Dib 3F 192
Garden Clo. And 1A 70
Garden Clo. Farn 9G 28
Garden Clo. Hay I 4F 242
Garden Clo. Hook 2F 44
Garden Clo. K're 2B 6
Garden Clo. Lyn 2A 148
Garden Clo. New M 5B 232
Garden Clo. La. N'bry 1C 8
Garden Ct. Bourn 8A 228
Garden Ct. Fare 9M 199
Gardeners Grn. Ship B 2A 66
Gardeners La. E Wel 6F 128
Garden Hill La. Meon 7P 135 (in two parts)
Garden Ho. Bourn 2L 245
Gardenia Dri. Fare 6H 197
Garden La. St L 5B 186
Garden La. S'sea 4D 240 (8N 5)
Garden La. Win 6L 105 (7N 237)
Garden M. Wars 8N 195
Garden Rd. Burl 7D 188
Gardens Cres. Poole 5A 244
Gardens Rd. Poole 5A 244
Gardens, The. Bro'tn 1A 86
Gardens, The. Hmbdn 8E 166
Gardens, The. Hav 8H 203
Garden Ter. S'sea 5E 240
Gardiner Clo. March 8F 172
Gardner Rd. Christ 6H 229
Gardner Rd. Fare 1J 211
Gardner Rd. Ring 2L 187
Garendon Ct. F'bri 9H 151
Garfield Av. Bourn 9A 228
Garfield Clo. Bish W 3M 163
Garfield Rd. Bish W 3M 163
Garfield Rd. Cam 8L 19
Garfield Rd. Net A 3E 194
Garfield Rd. Ports 8E 214
Garfield Rd. Sotn 3C 174
Garland Av. Ems 6M 203
Garland Ct. Gos 2K 239
Garland Way. Tot 2H 171
Garnet Fld. Yate 8K 17
Garnet Rd. Bord 5K 101
Garnett Clo. Fare 4M 211
Garnier Pk. Wick 6C 178
Garnier Rd. Win 9K 105
Garnier St. Ports 2E 240
Garnock Rd. Sotn 8B 174
Garratt Clo. H End 9N 161
Garrett Clo. K're 1A 6
Garretts Clo. Sotn 9E 174
Garrick Gdns. Sotn 8E 174
Garrick Ho. Ports 4G 214
Garrick Way. Frim G 5N 29
Garrison Hill. Drox 1K 165
Garrow Dri. L'ton 1E 234
Garsdale Clo. Bourn 1E 226
Garston Clo. E Meon 4L 143
Garston Mede. Chlbn 4F 74
Garstons Clo. Fare 9J 197
Garstons Rd. Fare 9J 197
Gar St. Win 7K 105 (8L 237)
Garth Clo. Bord 3J 101
Garth Clo. St L 4A 186
Garth Rd. Bourn 5L 227
Garth, The. Alt 4G 80
Garth, The. Ash 1N 65
Garth, The. Farn 8M 29
Garton Rd. Sotn 7C 174
Gascoigne La. Ropl 1C 110
Gashouse Hill. Net A 4G 194
Gaskell Clo. Holyb 2J 81
Gason Hill Rd. Tidw 6C 30
Gaston Gdns. Roms 4M 129
Gaston La. S Warn 2C 62
Gaston La. Up Farr 4E 98
Gaston's Wood Ind. Est. Bas 2E 42
Gatcombe. Net A 2G 195
Gatcombe Av. Ports 6G 215
Gatcombe Dri. Ports 5G 214
Gatcombe Gdns. Fare 9L 197
Gatcombe Gdns. W End 9E 160
Gate Ho. Rd. Fare 1J 213
Gatehouse, The. W End 9G 160
Gatekeeper Clo. Win 6N 105
Gaters Hill. Sotn 7E 160
Gaters La. Wint D 3A 86
Gateway Ho. Bas 5E 42
Gateway, The. Poole 1D 244
Gatwick Clo. Sotn 7F 158
Gauldy La. Baug 3E 20
Gaulter Clo. Hav 6G 202
Gauvain Clo. Alt 6G 80
Gavan St. Sotn 5H 175
G Avenue. Hythe 2D 208
Gawaine Clo. And 6N 51
Gawn Pl. Gos 5L 239
Gaydon Ri. Bourn 2C 226
Gaylyn Way. Fare 9L 197
Gaza Av. E Bol 1B 236
Gaza Ho. Fare 6M 197
Gazelle Clo. Gos 2F 238
Gazing La. W Wel 1B 120
Gazings, The. W Wel 1B 120
Geale's Ct. Alt 3G 81
Geale's Cres. Alt 3G 80
Geddes Way. Ptsfld 9B 140
Geffery's Fields. Bas 7D 42
Geffery's Ho. Hook 1H 45
Gemini Clo. Sotn 7E 158
General Johnson Ct. Win 8G 105
Geneva Av. Bourn 9G 229
Genoa Clo. Penn 5C 234
Genoa Ct. And 6A 52 (in two parts)
Genoa Ho. Port S 1B 214
Gentles La. Pass & Head 6C 102
Gento Clo. Bot 4B 176
Geoffrey Av. Water 7J 201
Geoffrey Cres. Fare 1D 212
George Byng Way. Ports 8D 214
George Ct., The. Ports 7K 5
George Curl Way. Sotn I 5D 160
George Eyston Dri. Win 8H 105
George Gdns. A'sht 3L 65
Georgeham Rd. Owl 3F 18
George Perrett Way. Chan F 8L 131
George Rd. Fle 2N 47
George Rd. Mil S 7J 235
George VI Rd. Tidw 6C 30
George St. Bas 6A 42
George St. Eastl 9F 132
George St. Gos 2L 239
George St. K're 2B 6
George St. Ports 9F 214
George Yd. And 2A 70
George Yd., The. Alr 9F 94
Georgia Clo. And 3K 69
Georgia Clo. Lee S 9B 212
Georgia La. A'prt & Mid W 3N 67
Georgia La. Grat 5L 67 (off St Monxton Rd.)
Georgian Clo. Cam 6N 19
Georgian Clo. Ring 9K 185
Georgian Way. Bourn 2K 227
Georgina Clo. Poole 6G 226
Georgina Ct. Fle 2M 47
Georgina Gdns. P Hth 5L 11
Georgina Talbot Ho. Poole 6F 226
Gerald Rd. Bourn 8L 227
Gerald Sq. Alt 2G 80
Gerard Cres. Sotn 4H 175
Gerard Ho. Ports 4F 214
Germaine Clo. Highc 6H 231
German Rd. Braml 2H 23
Gershwin Ct. Bas 2M 59
Gershwin Rd. Bas 2L 59
Gervis Pl. Bourn 2K 245 (7L 247)
Gervis Rd. Bourn 2L 245 (7N 247)
Gibbons Clo. S'hrst 6E 18
Gibb's La. Bord 1F 100
Gibbs Rd. Sotn 5L 173 (4C 4)
Gibbs Way. Yate 9L 17
Gibraltar Clo. Fare 7N 197
Gibraltar Rd. Fare 2B 212
Gibraltar Rd. S'sea 4L 241
Gibson Clo. Lee S 9B 212 (in two parts)
Gibson Clo. White 3H 197
Gid La. Up Fro 8G 63
Giffard Dri. Farn 7H 29
Giffards Mdw. F'ham 9G 64
Gifford Clo. Fare 7A 198
Gilbard Ct. Chine 9H 23
Gilbert Clo. A'hlt 4E 152
Gilbert Clo. Bas 2D 42
Gilbert Clo. Gos 8F 212
Gilbert Clo. L'ton 4D 234
Gilbert Mead. Hay I 3E 242
Gilbert Rd. Bourn 8A 228
Gilbert Rd. Cam 3L 29
Gilbert's Grn. Ship B 2B 66
Gilberts Mead Clo. Anna V 5J 69
Gilberts Piece. Coll D 1H 31
Gilbert Street 9F 96
Gilbert Way. Water 4M 201
Gilbert White's Ho. 7L 99
Gilbert White Way. Alt 3F 80
Gilbury Clo. Sotn 7C 160
Gilchrist Gdns. Wars 1N 209
Giles Clo. Fare 6D 198
Giles Clo. Gos 1J 239
Giles Clo. H End 1A 176
Giles Ct. T'ley 5J 11
Giles La. Land 9L 121
Giles Rd. T'ley 5J 11
Gilkicker Rd. Gos 6L 239
Gillam Rd. Bourn 1H 227
Gillcrest. Fare 5F 196
Gillett Rd. Poole 7G 226
Gillham's La. Hasl 2H 117
Gillian Av. A'sht 2L 65
Gillian Clo. A'sht 2M 65
Gillies Dri. Bas 3L 41
Gillies, The. Fare 8C 198 (in two parts)
Gillingham Clo. Bourn 3N 227
Gillingham Clo. King W 8N 91
Gillingham Rd. Mil S 8K 235
Gillman Rd. Ports 8M 201
Gilmour Gdns. Alt 2G 80
Gilpin Clo. Pill 6F 224
Gilpin Clo. Sotn 5J 175
Gilpin Hill. Sway 5J 223
Gilpin Pl. Sway 4H 223
Gins La. Beau 3E 236
Gipsy Gro. Sotn 3H 173
Gipsy La. Ring 9L 185
Girton Clo. Fare 8F 196
Girton Clo. Owl 4G 19
Gisborne Clo. Tidw 8E 30
Gitsham Gdns. Water 6K 201
Gladdis Rd. Bourn 2D 226
Glade Clo. Chine 1G 42
Glades, The. L Hth 5D 196
Glade, The. Ashy H 3B 186
Glade, The. Black 9C 208
Glade, The. Bucks H 10M 63
Glade, The. Chan F 3D 132
Glade, The. Fare 5N 197
Glade, The. F'ham 3F 64
Glade, The. Hay I 6J 243
Glade, The. Water 1A 202
Gladiator Way. Farn 3J 49
Gladstone Clo. Christ 8N 229
Gladstone Gdns. Fare 1L 213
Gladstone Pl. Ports 8E 214
Gladstone Rd. Bourn 9C 228
Gladstone Rd. Gos 9J 213
Gladstone Rd. Poole 9A 226
Gladstone Rd. Sotn 5F 174
Gladstone Rd. E. Bourn 9C 228
Gladstone Rd. W. Bourn 9B 228
Gladstone St. Win 6K 105 (6L 237)
Gladys Av. Cowp 6A 182

Gladys Av. *Ports* 6E **214**
Glamis Av. *Bourn* 1J **227**
Glamis Clo. *Okly.* 9D **40**
Glamis Clo. *Water.* 1A **202**
Glamis Ct. *Fare* 5M **211**
Glamorgan Rd. *Water.* 9B **168**
Glasgow Rd. *S'sea* 4J **241**
Glasslaw Rd. *Sotn* 2E **174**
Glasspool. *Water.* 5F **180**
Glastonbury Clo. *Bas* 3B **42**
Glaston Hill Rd. *E'sly.* 5F **16**
Glayshers Hill. *Head D* 1C **102**
Gleadowe Av. *Christ* 8J **229**
Glebe. **7M 163**
Glebe Clo. *Bentw* 6L **79**
Glebe Clo. *Dum.* 9F **58**
Glebe Clo. *Hay I* 2E **242**
Glebe Clo. *Pitt.* 6E **86**
Glebe Clo. *T'ley.* 6J **11**
Glebe Corner. *Wick.* 7D **178**
Glebe Ct. *Bot* 2D **176**
Glebe Ct. *F Oak.* 1A **162**
Glebe Ct. *Fle* 2L **47**
Glebe Ct. *Sotn.* 9M **159**
Glebe Dri. *Gos* 7E **212**
Glebefield Gdns. *Ports* . . . 9F **200**
Glebe Fields. *Bentw* 6L **79**
Glebefields. *Mil S* 7K **235**
Glebeland Rd. *Cam.* 9H **19**
Glebelands. *Good C* 7A **70**
Glebe La. *H Win* 7C **26**
Glebe La. *Land* 9J **121**
Glebe La. *Tilf.* 3L **85**
Glebe La. *Wort* 7J **41**
Glebe Mdw. *E Dean* 2L **121**
Glebe Mdw. *Over* 2D **56**
Glebe Pk. Av. *Hav.* 8A **202**
Glebe Rd. *Bton.* 7K **145**
Glebe Rd. *Cron.* 3L **63**
Glebe Rd. *Farn.* 7H **29**
Glebe Rd. *Head.* 2A **102**
Glebe, The. *B'wtr* 9G **18**
Glebe, The. *Fare.* 7M **211**
Glenavon. *New M.* 4D **232**
Glenavon Gdns. *Yate* 9N **17**
Glenavon Rd. *Highc* 5H **231**
Glenbrook Wlk. *Fare* 9M **197**
Glencarron Way. *Sotn.* 8K **159**
Glen Clo. *And* 1L **69**
Glen Clo. *Bart S* 6M **231**
Glen Clo. *Hind.* 1L **103**
Glencoe Rd. *Bourn.* 7C **228**
Glencoe Rd. *Poole* 9B **226**
Glencoe Rd. *Ports* 9G **214**
Glen Ct. *Hind* 1L **103**
Glencoyne Gdns. *Sotn* 9E **158**
Glenda Clo. *Wars* 9A **196**
Glendale. *L Hth.* 7D **196**
Glen Dale. *Row C* 8J **183**
Glendale. *Swanm* 7D **164**
Glendale Av. *N'bry* 1C **8**
Glendale Clo. *Christ* 3G **229**
Glendale Ct. *Christ* 3G **229**
Glendale Pk. *Fle* 1J **47**
Glendale Rd. *Bourn* 1K **247**
Glendale Rd. *T'ley* 4G **11**
Glendales. *Bart S* 6M **231**
Glendene Pk. *New M* 9N **221**
Glendowan Rd. *Chan F* . . . 5M **131**
Glen Dri. *New M.* 6L **231**
Gleneagles. *Christ.* 8J **229**
Gleneagles Av. *Poole* 3B **244**
Gleneagles Clo. *Hat W* 5J **59**
Gleneagles Dri. *Farn* 9E **28**
Gleneagles Dri. *Water.* 8B **182**
Glenelg. *Fare.* 7B **198**
Glenesha Gdns. *Fare* 7N **197**
Glen Eyre Clo. *Sotn* 7M **159**
Glen Eyre Dri. *Sotn* 6M **159**
Glen Eyre Rd. *Sotn.* 6L **159**
Glen Eyre Way. *Sotn* 7M **159**
Glenferness Av. *Bourn.* . . . 1G **245**
Glen Fern Rd. *Bourn*
. . . . 2L **245** (6N **247**)
Glenfield Av. *Sotn.* 3D **174**
Glenfield Clo. *W'slw* 5H **87**
Glenfield Cres. *Sotn* 3D **174**
Glenfield Way. *Sotn* 3D **174**
Glengariff Rd. *Poole* 3A **244**
Glengarry. *New M* 4D **232**
Glengarry Way. *Christ.* 8E **230**
Glenhurst Clo. *B'wtr* 9G **19**
Gleninnes. *Coll T* 4G **19**
Glenives Clo. *St I* 4C **186**
Glenlea. *Gray* 6N **103**
Glenlea Clo. *W End.* 1H **175**
Glenlea Dri. *W End.* 1H **175**
Glenlea Hollow. *Gray* 7N **103**
Glenleigh Av. *Ports.* 1G **215**
Glenleigh Pk. *Hav.* 7H **203**
Glenmeadows Dri. *Bourn*
. . . . 1F **226**

Glenmoor Clo. *Bourn* 5H **227**
Glenmoor Rd. *Bourn* 6H **227**
Glenmore Ct. *Sotn.* 2M **173**
Glenn Rd. *W End* 9H **161**
Glen Pk. *Col C* 3M **133**
Glen Rd. *Bourn.* 1B **246**
Glen Rd. *Fle* 3L **47**
Glen Rd. *Gray* 4M **103**
Glen Rd. *Hind* 1M **103**
Glen Rd. *Sotn.* 9B **174**
Glen Rd. *Swanw.* 2C **196**
(in two parts)
Glenroyd Gdns. *Bourn* 1H **247**
Glenside. *Hythe.* 6L **193**
Glenside. *New M* 7K **231**
Glenside. *W End.* 1H **175**
Glenside Av. *Sotn.* 6H **175**
Glen Spey. *New M* 4E **232**
Glen, The. *Gos* 7G **212**
Glen, The. *P Hth* 4L **11**
Glen, The. *Poole.* 8B **226**
Glenthorne Clo. *Fare.* 7N **211**
Glenthorne Mdw. *E Meon*
. . . . 4M **143**
Glenthorne Rd. *Ports.* 7H **215**
Glenville Clo. *Walk.* 4K **231**
Glenville Gdns. *Bourn.* 4G **227**
Glenville Gdns. *Hind.* 3N **103**
Glenville Rd. *Bourn* 4G **226**
Glenville Rd. *Walk.* 4J **231**
Glenwood Av. *Sotn* 6M **159**
Glenwood Ct. *F Oak* 1B **162**
Glenwood Gdns. *Water*
. . . . 7N **181**
Glidden Clo. *Ports.* 2E **240**
Glidden La. *Hmbdn.* 8F **166**
Globe Farm La. *B'wtr* 8D **18**
Glorney Mead. *Bad L* 4J **65**
Gloster Ct. *Seg W* 4F **196**
Gloucester Clo. *Four M* . . . 5H **97**
Gloucester Clo. *Frim G* 6N **29**
Gloucester Clo. *Ptsfld.* 1K **145**
Gloucester Ct. *Ptsfld* 9M **139**
Gloucester Dri. *Bas.* 2K **59**
Gloucester Ho. Gos. *3L **239***
(off Holly St.)
Gloucester M. *S'sea*
. . . . 3D **240** (6N **5**)
Gloucester Pl. *S'sea*
. . . . 4D **240** (7N **5**)
Gloucester Rd. *A'sht.* 3L **65**
Gloucester Rd. *Bourn.* 8C **228**
Gloucester Rd. *Poole* 9C **226**
Gloucester Rd. *Ports*
. . . . 1B **240** (1J **5**)
Gloucester Rd. *Water.* 3N **201**
Gloucester Sq. *Sotn.* 8D **4**
Gloucester Ter. *S'sea*
. . . . 4D **240** (7N **5**)
Gloucester Vw. *S'sea*
. . . . 4D **240** (6N **5**)
Glovers Fld. *Hasl* 9N **103**
Glyn Dri. *Fare.* 6M **211**
Glyn Jones Clo. *Fawl* 6D **208**
Glynswood. *Cam* 1N **29**
Glyn Way. *Fare.* 6M **211**
Goatacre Rd. *Meds.* 2E **96**
Goat La. *Bas.* 6D **42**
Goch Way. *Charl.* 8L **51**
Goddard Clo. *W Wel.* 1B **120**
Goddards Clo. *Sher L* 4L **23**
Goddards Firs. *Okly.* 2E **58**
Goddards La. *Cam* 1K **29**
Goddards La. *Sher L* 4K **23**
Goddards Mead. *And* 2L **69**
Goddard Sq. And *8B **52***
(off Cricketers Way)
Godfrey Olson Ho. *Eastl* . . . 9F **132**
Godfrey Pink Way. *Bish W*
. . . . 4N **163**
Godfrey Way. *S'hrst* 5F **18**
Godiva Lawn. *S'sea* 4K **241**
Godshill. 5A **154**
Godshill Clo. *Bourn* 3A **228**
Godson Ho. *Win.* 7N **237**
Godwin Clo. *Ems* 6L **203**
Godwin Clo. *Win* 3G **104**
Godwin Cres. *Water* 7C **168**
Godwinscroft. 9E **220**
Godwins Fld. *Comp* 5G **127**
Godwit Clo. *Gos* 8K **213**
Godwit Rd. *S'sea* 1K **241**
Gofton Av. *Ports* 1J **215**
Goggs La. *Redl.* 8D **120**
Goldcrest Clo. *Fare.* 9G **199**
Goldcrest Clo. *Yate* 7L **17**
Goldcrest Gdns. *Sotn* 6F **158**
Goldcrest La. *Tot.* 2J **171**
Golden Ct. *W End.* 8K **161**
Golden Cres. *Evtn.* 5L **233**
Goldenfields. *Lip.* 3F **116**

Goldenfields Clo. *Lip.* 3F **116**
Golden Gro. *Sotn.* . . . 5N **173** (4F **4**)
Golden Hill. **2F 232**
Golden Hind Pk. *Hythe* 7L **193**
Goldenleas Dri. *Bourn* 3B **226**
Golden Lion Roundabout. *Bas*
. . . . 9C **42**
Golden Pot. **8B 62**
Goldfinch Bottom. **1H 9**
Goldfinch Clo. *A'sht* 2H **65**
Goldfinch Clo. *New M.* 4A **232**
Goldfinch Gdns. *Bas.* 4H **59**
Goldfinch La. Bish G *1G **9***
(off Linden Rd.)
Goldfinch La. *Lee S* 9B **212**
Goldfinch Way. *S Won* 2J **91**
Gold Hill. *Kingsl* 7H **83**
Gold La. *A'sht.* 7N **49**
Gold Mead Clo. *L'ton* 4E **234**
Goldring Clo. *Hay I* 4G **243**
Goldsmith Av. *S'sea* 3F **240**
Goldsmith Clo. *Tot* 3K **171**
Goldsmith Rd. *Eastl* 2D **160**
Goldsmith Way. *C'then* 1D **18**
Gold St. *S'sea* 4C **240** (7M **5**)
Goldwire Dri. *Chan F.* 7L **131**
Golf Course Rd. *Sotn.* 6K **159**
Golf La. *W'hill* 5F **100**
Golf Links Av. *Hind.* 1K **103**
Gomer Ct. *Gos* 4G **238**
Gomer La. *Gos.* 3G **238**
Gondreville Gdns. *Chu C* . . 7K **47**
Goodacre Dri. *Chan F* 7L **131**
Goodden Cres. *Farn* 9H **29**
Goodens, The. *Cher* 9E **108**
Goodhalls La. *H End* 3L **175**
(in two parts)
Goodison Clo. *F Oak* 2M **161**
Goodlands Va. *H End* 3L **175**
Goodman Clo. *Bas* 7A **42**
Good Rd. *Poole* 7A **226**
Goodsell Clo. *Fare.* 6L **211**
Goodwin Clo. *Sotn.* 9C **158**
Goodwood Clo. *Alt* 6F **80**
Goodwood Clo. *Cam.* 5L **19**
Goodwood Clo. *Fare.* 7G **196**
Goodwood Clo. *Gos* 8K **213**
Goodwood Clo. *Water* 9B **182**
Goodwood Ct. *H Hth* 4A **162**
Goodwood Gdns. *Tot* 2J **171**
Goodwood Pl. *Farn.* 9N **29**
Goodwood Rd. *Eastl.* 7D **132**
Goodwood Rd. *Gos* 8K **213**
Goodwood Rd. *S'sea.* 4F **240**
Goodworth Clatford. **8N 69**
Goodworth Vw. *Good C* . . . 8N **69**
Goodwyns Clo. *Ship B* 2A **66**
Goodwyns Grn. *Alt.* 2G **80**
Goodyers. *Alt.* 5G **81**
Gooseberry La. *Ring.* 1J **187**
Goose Green. **4C 146**
Goose Grn. *Hook* 1F **44**
Goose Grn. *Lyn* 3B **148**
Goose Hill. **2L 9**
Goose Rye Ct. *Lip* 3D **116**
Gordleton Ind. Est. *Penn*
. . . . 1N **233**
Gordon Av. *Cam.* 9K **19**
Gordon Av. *Chu C.* 5N **47**
Gordon Av. *Sotn.* 2M **173**
Gordon Av. *Win* 8N **105**
Gordon Clo. *Bas.* 5D **42**
Gordon Ct. *Cam.* 8L **19**
Gordon Cres. *Cam.* 9L **19**
Gordon Mt. *Christ.* 5K **231**
Gordon Mt. Flats. *Christ* . . . 6J **231**
Gordon Rd. *A'sht.* 1J **65**
(in two parts)
Gordon Rd. *Bourn* 1A **246**
Gordon Rd. *Cam.* 9L **19**
Gordon Rd. *Chan F.* 3B **132**
Gordon Rd. *C'then* 2F **18**
Gordon Rd. *Curd.* 1J **177**
Gordon Rd. *Fare.* 8C **198**
Gordon Rd. *Farn* 3M **49**
(in two parts)
Gordon Rd. *Gos* 3J **239**
Gordon Rd. *Highc* 6J **231**
Gordon Rd. *Penn* 3C **234**
Gordon Rd. *Poole.* 9E **226**
Gordon Rd. *Ports*
. . . . 4C **240** (8L **5**)
Gordon Rd. *Water.* 3L **201**
Gordon Rd. *Win*
. . . . 6L **105** (6N **237**)
Gordon Rd. S. *Poole.* 9E **226**
Gordon Ter. *Sotn* 8E **174**
Gordon Wlk. *Yate* 8A **18**
Gordon Way. *Burt* 5M **229**
Gore End. **1M 7**
Gore End Rd. *Ball* 1M **7**

Gore Grange. *New M* 4A **232**
Gore Rd. *New M* 4M **231**
Gore Rd. Ind. Est. *New M*
. . . . 4N **231**
Gorey Rd. *Poole* 5B **226**
Goring Av. *Water.* 6D **168**
(in three parts)
Goring Fld. *Win* 5G **104**
Gorleston Rd. *Poole* 9D **226**
Gorley Ct. *Hav.* 3D **202**
Gorley Lynch. *Gor L* 5N **153**
Gorley Rd. *Ring* 9M **185**
Gorran Av. *Gos.* 7E **212**
Gorrings, The. *King S* 9B **86**
Gorsecliff Ct. *Bourn.* 1A **246**
Gorsecliff Rd. *Bourn.* 5H **227**
Gorse Clo. *L Hth* 7C **196**
Gorse Clo. *New M.* 2E **232**
Gorse Clo. *St L* 4A **186**
Gorsedown Clo. *W'hill.* 6G **100**
Gorsefield Rd. *New M.* 1C **232**
Gorselands. *F'ham* 3E **64**
Gorselands. *T'ley.* 5H **11**
Gorselands. *Yate* 9M **17**
Gorselands Clo. *Head D* . . . 3E **102**
Gorselands Rd. *Sotn* 1F **174**
Gorselands Way. *Gos.* 8F **212**
Gorse Rd. *Frim* 2N **29**
Gorse Rd. *Ptsfld.* 1B **146**
Gorse Way. *Fle* 4M **47**
Gorseway, The. *Hay I* 4D **242**
Gort Clo. *A'sht* 4N **49**
Gort Cres. *Sotn* 6F **174**
Gort Rd. *Bourn.* 3F **226**
Goscombe La. *Gund.* 8M **95**
Goslings Cft. *Selb* 6L **99**
Gosport. **3M 239**
Gosport & Stokes Bay Golf
Course. 6L **239**
Gosport Ho. *Hav* 4H **203**
Gosport La. *Lyn* 2C **148**
Gosport Mus. **3M 239**
Gosport Rd. *Chaw.* 1D **98**
Gosport Rd. *Fare.* 1D **212**
Gosport Rd. *Lee S* 2B **238**
Gosport Rd. *Stub* 6N **211**
Gosport St. *L'ton* 2F **234**
Gotham. **8M 149**
Gothic Bldgs. *S'sea* 4E **240**
Gough Rd. *Fle* 1K **47**
Gough's Mdw. *S'hrst.* 6D **18**
Gould Clo. *Lud.* 1C **30**
Government Ho. Rd. *A'sht*
. . . . 3J **49**
Government Rd. *A'sht.* 7M **49**
Governor's Rd. *Coll T* 7H **19**
Gover Rd. *Sotn* 1B **172**
Gower Clo. *Bas* 4C **42**
Gower Cres. *Hook* 2H **45**
Gower Pk. *Coll T* 6F **18**
Goyda Ho. *Gos* 1H **239**
Grace Bennett Clo. *Farn* . . . 5J **29**
Grace Dieu Gdns. *Burs* 9K **175**
Grace La. *W'grn.* 2A **154**
Gracemere Cres. *Bas.* 3H **59**
Grace Reynolds Wlk. *Cam*
. . . . 7L **19**
Grace Sq. *And* 8B **52**
Gracious St. *Selb.* 7K **99**
Graddidge Way. *Tot* 3K **171**
Gradwell La. *Four M* 7H **97**
Graemar La. *Sher E* 6M **121**
Grafton Clo. *Bourn.* 7L **227**
Grafton Clo. *Christ.* 8N **229**
Grafton Clo. *W'hill* 5J **101**
Grafton Gdns. *Penn.* 5C **234**
Grafton Gdns. *Sotn* 6H **159**
Grafton Rd. *Bourn* 8L **227**
Grafton Rd. *Win.* 8K **105**
Grafton St. *Ports.* 9D **214**
Grafton Way. *Bas* 7M **41**
Graham Ct. *Sotn* 4E **174**
Graham Ho. *Sotn.* 4A **174**
Graham Rd. *Gos* 1J **239**
Graham Rd. *Sotn*
. . . . 4M **173** (2E **4**)
Graham Rd. *S'sea* 4F **240**
Graham St. *Sotn.* 4A **174**
Grainger Clo. *Bas* 1N **59**
Grainger Gdns. *Sotn* 7G **175**
Grammarsham La. *Far W*
. . . . 8A **60**
Grampian Rd. *S'hrst* 3B **18**
Grampian Way. *Bas.* 8K **41**
Granada Clo. *Water* 6A **182**
Granada Pl. *And* 9B **52**
Granada Rd. *H End* 5L **175**
Granada Rd. *S'sea* 6F **240**
Granby Gro. *Sotn* 8N **159**
Granby Rd. *Bourn* 2L **227**
Grand Av. *Bourn.* 1F **246**
Grand Av. *Cam.* 7L **19**

Grand Division Row. *S'sea*
. . . . 4K **241**
Grand Pde. *Bourn* 1G **226**
Grand Pde. *Hay I* 5G **243**
Grand Pde. *Ports*
. . . . 4B **240** (8J **5**)
Grand Trunk Rd. *Tidw.* 8F **30**
Grange Clo. *Alr.* 1E **108**
Grange Clo. *Evtn.* 6M **233**
Grange Clo. *Fy'd.* 9N **31**
Grange Clo. *Gos.* 1H **239**
Grange Clo. *Hav.* 7H **203**
Grange Clo. *Sotn* 7C **160**
Grange Clo. *Win* 1J **127**
Grange Ct. *Bourn.* 2M **245**
Grange Ct. *Net A.* 3F **194**
Grange Ct. *Sotn.* 6C **160**
Grange Cres. *Gos.* 1H **239**
Grange Dri. *H End* 2A **176**
Grange Estate. **8C 186**
Grange Est. *Chu C* 6L **47**
Grange Gdns. *Poole.* 7C **226**
Grange La. *Gos* 8E **212** (6E **4**)
(in two parts)
Grange La. *H Win* 6A **26**
Grange M. *Roms* 3B **130**
Grange Pk. *H End.* 1N **175**
Grange Rd. *Alr* 1E **108**
Grange Rd. *Bourn* 2G **246**
Grange Rd. *Cam.* 8N **19**
Grange Rd. *Christ* 7D **230**
Grange Rd. *Chu C.* 6L **47**
Grange Rd. *Farn.* 5K **29**
Grange Rd. *Gos* 3F **238**
Grange Rd. *H End* 2N **175**
Grange Rd. *Net A.* 3E **194**
Grange Rd. *Ptsfld.* 2L **145**
Grange Rd. *Ports* 7E **214**
Grange Rd. *St L* 6A **186**
Grange Rd. *Sotn.* 1G **172**
Grange Rd. *Tilf.* 1K **85**
Grange Rd. *Tong* 4N **65**
Grange Rd. *Win* 2J **127**
Grange Rd. Bus Cen. *Christ*
. . . . 7C **230**
Grange, The. **2A 94**
Grange, The. *Evtn* 6M **233**
Grange, The. *Fren* 1F **84**
Grangewood Ct. *F Oak.* . . . 1M **161**
Grangewood Gdns. *F Oak*
. . . . 1M **161**
Grantham Av. *Hamb* 6J **195**
Grantham Clo. *Owl.* 4G **18**
Grantham Ct. *Eastl* 1E **160**
Grantham Rd. *Bourn* 9B **228**
Grantham Rd. *Eastl* 1D **160**
(in two parts)
Grantham Rd. *Sotn* 4D **174**
Grantley Dri. *Fle* 4L **47**
Grantley Rd. *Bourn.* 1C **246**
Grant Rd. *C'then* 2E **18**
Grant Rd. *Ports* 9L **201**
Grants Av. *Bourn* 8A **228**
Grants Clo. *Bourn.* 8A **228**
Granville Clo. *Hav.* 8G **203**
Granville Pl. *Bourn* 6M **247**
Granville Pl. *Win* 8M **105**
Granville Rd. *Bourn* 9D **228**
Granville Rd. *Poole.* 9A **226**
Granville St. *Sotn.* 6N **173**
Grasdean Clo. *Sotn.* 1E **174**
Grasmere. *Eastl* 1D **160**
Grasmere Clo. *Bord.* 2J **101**
Grasmere Clo. *Christ.* 3G **229**
Grasmere Clo. *W End* 1F **174**
Grasmere Ct. *Sotn.* 9D **158**
Grasmere Gdns. *New M*
. . . . 1C **232**
Grasmere Ho. *Ports* 8C **200**
Grasmere Rd. *Bourn.* 1D **246**
Grasmere Rd. *Farn.* 9G **28**
Grasmere Rd. *F'ham* 4C **64**
Grasmere Rd. *Poole* 9A **244**
Grasmere Way. *Fare.* 4N **211**
Graspan Rd. *Lud.* 2F **30**
Grassmere Way. *Water.* 8B **182**
Grassymead. *Fare.* 5F **196**
Grateley. **4L 67**
Grateley Clo. *Sotn* 1D **194**
Grateley Cres. *Hav.* 5C **202**
Grateley Drove. *Grat.* 5K **67**
(in two parts)
Grateley Rd. *Chol* 4F **66**
Graton Clo. *Gos* 9L **213**
Gratton Clo. *Sut S* 7D **76**
Gravel Clo. *Bro C* 7C **78**
Gravel Clo. *D'ton.* 1J **119**
Gravel Hill. **2E 168**
Gravel Hill. *Shir H & Swanm*
. . . . 1C **178**
Gravel Hill Rd. *Bent* 8L **63**
Gravel La. *Bar S* 6A **76**

Gravel La.—Gull Clo.

Gravel La. *E Meon* 3N **143**
Gravel La. *Four M* 6F **96**
Gravel La. *Ring* 1J **187**
(in two parts)
Gravelly Clo. *N End* 1M **7**
Gravelly Clo. *T'ley* 7J **11**
Gravel Rd. *Chu C* 5N **47**
Gravel Rd. *Farn* 3M **49**
Gravel Rd. *F'ham* 3D **64**
Gravel Wlk. *Black* 6D **208**
Graveney Sq. And. *8A 52*
(off Cricketers Way)
Gray Clo. *Wars* 7C **196**
Graycot Clo. *Bourn.* 1G **227**
Grayland Clo. *Hay I.* 3E **242**
Grayling Mead. *Roms* 3M **129**
Graylings. *Sotn* 2F **172**
Grays Av. *Hythe* 6N **193**
Grays Clo. *Col C* 4K **133**
Grays Clo. *Gos* 4G **238**
Grays Clo. *Roms* 5N **129**
Grays Ct. *Ports* 3B **240** (6K **5**)
Grayshot Dri. *B'wtr* 8E **18**
Grayshott. **4L 103**
Grayshott. *Gray* 4M **103**
Grayshott Clo. *Win* 2H **105**
Grayshott Laurels. *Lind* . . . 2M **101**
Grayshott Rd. *Gos* 3H **239**
Grayshott Rd. *Head D* 1D **102**
Grayshott Rd. *S'sea* 3G **241**
Great Austins. *F'ham* 9F **64**
Gt. Austins Ho. *F'ham* 9F **64**
Gt. Binfields Cres. *Lych* 3G **43**
Gt. Binfields Rd. *Lych* 2G **42**
Greatbridge Rd. *Roms* 1L **129**
Gt. Copse Dri. *Hav* 3E **202**
Great Croft. *Firs* 4E **86**
Gt. Elms Clo. *Holb* 5N **207**
Greatfield Clo. *Farn* 4K **29**
Greatfield Rd. *Farn* 4J **29**
Gt. Field Rd. *Win* 3H **105**
Greatfield Way. *Row C* 7H **183**
Great Gays. *Fare* 7K **211**
Great Hanger. *Ptsfld* 1A **146**
Greatmead. *Lyn* 3B **148**
Great Mead. *Water* 7H **181**
Gt. Minster St. *Win*
. . . . 7L **105** (8M **237**)
Gt. Oaks Chase. *Chine* 1F **42**
Great Posbrook. **2H 211**
Great Salterns Golf Course.
. . . . **6K 215**
Gt. Sheldons Coppice. *Hook*
. . . . 2F **44**
Great Shoddesden. **5F 30**
Gt. Southsea St. *S'sea*
. . . . 4D **240** (7N **5**)
Great Weir. *Alr* 8F **94**
Gt. Well Dri. *Roms* 4N **129**
Gt. Western Cotts. *Bas* 5C **42**
Greatwood Clo. *Hythe* 7M **193**
Greaves Clo. *Bourn* 3G **227**
Grebe Clo. *Alt* 2E **80**
Grebe Clo. *Bas* 3H **59**
Grebe Clo. *Christ* 8C **230**
Grebe Clo. *Fare* 9H **199**
Grebe Clo. *Mil S* 8L **235**
Grebe Clo. *Water* 6M **181**
Green Acre. *A'sht* 1H **65**
Green Acre. *Bart S* 6B **232**
Greenacre. *Bro'tn* 2A **86**
Green Acre. *K're* 2B **6**
Grn. Acre Cvn. Site. *Christ*
. . . . 7B **230**
Greenacre Gdns. *Water* 5L **201**
Greenacres. *Bord* 3L **101**
Green Acres. *D'ton* 2H **119**
Greenacres. *Poole* 2E **244**
Green Acres. *R'fld* 8L **65**
Greenacres. *Wool H* 3A **8**
Grn. Acres Clo. *Ring* 3G **186**
Greenacres Dri. *Ott* 1G **133**
Greenaway La. *Wars* 7A **196**
Greenaways, The. *Okly* 9D **40**
Greenbank Cres. *Sotn* 6L **159**
Greenbanks Clo. *Mil S* 7K **235**
Greenbanks Gdns. *Fare*
. . . . 7F **198**
Greenbank Way. *Cam* 2M **29**
Greenbirch Clo. *Bas* 3H **59**
Greenbury Clo. *Bas* 6L **41**
Green Clo. *Hythe* 5M **193**
Green Clo. *Old Al* 6F **94**
Green Clo. *S Won* 3J **91**
Green Clo. *W'ish* 5H **121**
Green Clo. *Win* 1L **105**
Green Clo. *W'lnds* 6F **170**
Green Cres. *Gos* 7E **212**
Greencroft. *Farn* 8K **29**
Green Cross. **7J 85**
Grn. Cross La. *Churt* 7J **85**
Greendale Clo. *Chan F* 6C **132**
Greendale Clo. *Fare* 5N **197**
Greendale, The. *Fare* 5N **197**
Green Dri. *A'hlt* 4E **152**
Green Drove. *W Gri* 1D **120**
Green End. *Yate* 6N **17**
Grn. Farm Gdns. *Ports* 4G **215**
Green Fld. Clo. *H End* 6M **175**
Greenfield Clo. *Lip* 1E **116**
Greenfield Cres. *Water* 5C **182**
Greenfield Gdns. *Bart S*
. . . . 6C **232**
Greenfield Ri. *Water* 7B **182**
Greenfields. *Hawk* 6M **113**
Greenfields. *Liss* 1F **140**
Greenfields. *Nye* 5K **147**
Greenfields. *Poole* 6D **226**
Greenfields. *W Gri* 2E **120**
Greenfields Av. *Alt* 4D **80**
Greenfields Av. *Tot* 1L **171**
Greenfields Clo. *Nye* 4K **147**
Greenfields Clo. *Tot* 1L **171**
Greenfinch Clo. *Eastl* 2B **160**
Greenfinch Wlk. *Hight* 2M **187**
Green Glades. *Chu C* 6L **47**
Greenham Common. **1G 9**
Greenhanger. *Churt* 8J **85**
Greenhaven. *Yate* 8L **17**
Greenhaven Cvn. Pk. *Hay I*
. . . . 6L **243**
Greenhaven Clo. *And* 2B **70**
Greenhill Av. *Win*
. . . . 6J **105** (7H **237**)
Greenhill Clo. *Win*
. . . . 6H **105** (7H **237**)
Greenhill La. *Rown* 3D **158**
Greenhill La. *Uphm* 7D **134**
(in two parts)
Greenhill Rd. *F'ham* 9G **64**
Greenhill Rd. *Win*
. . . . 7H **105** (7H **237**)
Greenhills. *F'ham* 9G **64**
Greenhill Ter. *Roms* 6K **129**
Greenhill Ter. *Win*
. . . . 6J **105** (7H **237**)
Greenhill Vw. *Roms* 6K **129**
Grn. Hollow Clo. *Fare* 5B **198**
Grn. Jacket Clo. *Win* 9J **105**
Greenlands. *Wool H* 2A **8**
Greenlands Rd. *Cam* 3K **29**
Greenlands Rd. *K're* 2B **6**
Green La. *Amp* 4D **130**
Green La. *Bad L* 4H **65**
Green La. *Bart S* 6C **232**
Green La. *Bish S* 1L **109**
Green La. *Bish W* 4N **163**
Green La. *Black* 8D **208**
Green La. *B'wtr* 9G **18**
Green La. *Bourn* 2G **227**
Green La. *Bur* 9E **176**
Green La. *Burs* 8K **175**
Green La. *Cal* 7H **157**
Green La. *Chilw* 2L **159**
Green La. *Christ* 1J **231**
Green La. *Churt* 8H **85**
Green La. *Crow* 5L **187**
Green La. *Dock* 2A **84**
Green La. *D'ton* 1K **119**
Green La. *Ellis* 2H **79**
Green La. *Fac* 7J **7**
Green La. *F'bri* 3F **150**
(Clack La.)
Green La. *F'bri* 9J **151**
(Salisbury Rd.)
Green La. *F'mre* 9D **18**
Green La. *Gos* 5J **239**
(Anglesey Rd., in three parts)
Green La. *Gos* 9K **213**
(Grove Rd.)
Green La. *Hamb* 7L **195**
Green La. *Hmbdn* 6C **166**
Green La. *H Win* 7B **26**
Green La. *Hay I* 4E **242**
Green La. *Holb* 6N **207**
Green La. *Lwr S* 1A **196**
Green La. *Mnkwd* 2K **111**
Green La. *Monx* 4B **68**
Green La. *Newt V* 1H **113**
Green La. *Oss* 6M **221**
Green La. *P Grn* 9L **11**
Green La. *Ports* 5G **215**
Green La. *Ring* 1K **187**
Green La. *Roth* 8E **24**
Green La. *S'hrst* 6E **18**
Green La. *Sotn* 9D **158**
Green La. *Stoke* 6G **35**
Green La. *Str S* 5J **13**
Green La. *Swanm* 6J **165**
(Cott St. La.)
Green La. *Swanm* 4E **164**
(Jervis Ct. La.)
Green La. *W'frd* 3N **135**
Green La. *Wars* 8C **196**
Green La. *Water* 4N **167**
(Hinton Mnr. La.)
Green La. *Water* 5F **180**
(Southwick Rd.)
Green La. *Water* 7C **168**
(White Dirt La.)
Green La. *W Tis* 7E **110**
Green La. *Yate* 7L **17**
Green La. Clo. *Cam* 6L **19**
Green La. Cotts. *Churt* 7H **85**
Green La. Cotts. *F'ham* 5H **65**
Greenlea Clo. *Water* 7J **201**
Greenlea Cres. *Sotn* 6B **160**
Greenlea Gro. *Gos* 9H **213**
Greenleas. *Frim* 2N **29**
Greenleas Clo. *Yate* 6M **17**
Green Leys. *Chu C* 7L **47**
Green Link. *Lee S* 2B **238**
Green Loaning. *Christ* 9B **230**
Greenmead Av. *Evtn* 5L **233**
Grn. Meadows La. *Good C*
. . . . 7N **69**
Green Pk. *Bourn* 2A **246**
Green Pk. Clo. *Win* 4M **105**
Green Pk. Rd. *Sotn* 3D **172**
Grn. Pond Corner. *Hav* 8H **203**
Grn. Pond La. *Amp* 1H **131**
Grn. Ride Clo. *Haz H* 2M **25**
Green Rd. *Bourn* 6L **227**
Green Rd. *Fare* 4M **211**
Green Rd. *Gos* 5J **239**
Green Rd. *S'sea* . . . 4D **240** (7N **5**)
Greens Clo. *Bish W* 3L **163**
Greens Clo. *Eastl* 2L **161**
Greensey. *Rag A* 4B **50**
Greenside Ct. *Bart S* 8B **232**
Greens Meade. *W'flls* 2M **119**
Green Springs. *Cron* 2L **63**
Green's School La. *Farn* 8J **29**
Green Stile. *Meds* 1F **96**
Grn. Stile. *Meds* 9K **79**
Green St. *E Wor* 7B **82**
Green, The. **8L 87**
Green, The. *Bad L* 5J **65**
Green, The. *Bar S* 5B **76**
Green, The. *B'wtr* 9E **18**
Green, The. *Bourn* 9G **227**
Green, The. *Charl* 8L **51**
Green, The. *F'ham* 4E **64**
Green, The. *Liss* 9D **114**
Green, The. *N War* 6H **45**
Green, The. *Over* 2E **56**
Green, The. *Pitt* 6E **86**
Green, The. *Ports*
. . . . 2B **240** (3J **5**)
Green, The. *Roms* 3B **130**
Green, The. *Row C* 8J **183**
Green, The. *Sar G* 3B **196**
Green, The. *Seale* 9N **65**
Green, The. *T'ley* 7J **11**
Green, The. *Water* 5F **180**
Green, The. *Whitc* 5H **55**
Green, The. *W'ish* 5H **121**
Green, The. *Yate* 7L **17**
Green Wlk. *Fare* 6A **198**
Green Way. *A'sht* 8N **49**
Green Way. *Bas* 6L **41**
Greenway. *E Meon* 4N **143**
Greenway. *Sher L* 4L **23**
Greenway. *Wool H* 2A **8**
Greenway Clo. *L'ton* 3C **234**
Greenway La. *Bton* 6J **145**
Greenway Rd. *Gos* 1K **239**
Greenways. *Chan F* 6C **132**
Greenways. *Fle* 5L **47**
Greenways. *Highc* 6H **231**
Greenways. *Mil S* 7J **235**
Greenways. *S'hrst* 4D **18**
Greenways. *Sotn* 6B **160**
Greenways. *Swanm* 6D **164**
Greenways Av. *Bourn* 3N **227**
Greenways Rd. *Broc* 7D **148**
Greenway, The. *Ems* 6M **203**
Greenwich, The. *Black* 6C **208**
Greenwich Way. *And* 8N **51**
Greenwood Av. *Poole* 4A **244**
Greenwood Av. *Ports* 9E **200**
Greenwood Av. *Rown* 5C **158**
Greenwood Clo. *Eastl* 2D **160**
Greenwood Clo. *Fare* 5C **198**
Greenwood Clo. *Roms* 4N **129**
Greenwood Copse. *St I* 4C **186**
Greenwood Dri. *Chine* 8G **23**
Greenwood La. *Durl* 4C **162**
Greenwood Rd. *Bourn* 5J **227**
Greenwoods. *New M* 5C **232**
Greenwoods. *Whitc* 4G **55**
Greenwood Way. *St I* 4D **186**
Greetham St. *S'sea*
. . . . 2D **240** (4N **5**)
Gregory Clo. *Bas* 4D **42**
Gregory Gdns. *Cal* 1J **171**
Gregory Ho. *Hook* 2G **44**
Gregory La. *Durl* 6E **162**
Gregson Av. *Gos* 5E **212**
Gregson Clo. *Gos* 5E **212**
Grenadier Clo. *L Hth* 7E **196**
Grenadiers Way. *Farn* 9E **28**
Grendon Clo. *Sotn* 6N **159**
Grenehurst Way. *Ptsfld* . . . 1M **145**
Grenfell Rd. *Bourn* 3K **227**
Grenfield Ct. *Ems* 6M **203**
Grensell Clo. *E'sly* 5H **17**
Grenville Clo. *Lip* 2E **116**
Grenville Clo. *Ring* 8N **185**
Grenville Ct. *Bourn*
. . . . 1H **245** (5G **247**)
Grenville Ct. *Sotn* 3K **173**
Grenville Dri. *Chu C* 5K **47**
Grenville Gdns. *Dib P* 8M **193**
Grenville Gdns. *Frim G* 6N **29**
Grenville Ho. *Ports* 4K **5**
Grenville Rd. *S'sea* 4F **240**
Gresham Ind. Est. *A'sht* 9N **49**
Gresham Rd. *Bourn* 5L **227**
Gresham Way. *Frim G* 6N **29**
Gresley Gdns. *H End* 9N **161**
Gresley Rd. *Bas* 5D **42**
Grevillea Av. *Fare* 6H **197**
Greville Clo. *A'sht* 8J **49**
Greville Grn. *Ems* 5L **203**
Greville Rd. *Sotn* 3J **173**
Greyfriars. *Win* 7P **237**
Greyfriars Ct. *S'sea* 4D **240**
Greyfriars Rd. *Fare* 7M **197**
Greyhound Clo. *H End* 8M **161**
Greyhound La. *Over* 3D **56**
Greys Ct. *A'sht* 9G **48**
Greys Farm Clo. *Cher* 1K **135**
Greyshott Av. *Fare* 9M **197**
Greystoke Av. *Bourn* 1D **226**
Greystoke Ct. *C'then* 1C **18**
Greywell. **9F 44**
Greywell Av. *Sotn* 7H **159**
Greywell Clo. *T'ley* 5G **11**
Greywell Ct. *Sotn* 7H **159**
Greywell Rd. *Hav* 4F **202**
Greywell Rd. *Old B & Map*
. . . . 6L **43**
Greywell Rd. *Up N & Grey*
. . . . 6B **44**
Greywell Shop. Cen. *Hav*
. . . . 4F **202**
Greywell Sq. *Hav* 4F **202**
Grieg Clo. *Bas* 1N **59**
Grieve Clo. *Tong* 3N **65**
Griffen Clo. *Eastl* 1J **161**
Griffen Clo. *Yate* 9M **17**
Griffin Ct. *Sotn* 2A **174**
Griffin Ind. Pk. *Tot* 8L **157**
Griffin Wlk. *Gos* 1E **238**
Griffin Way N. *Hook* 9H **25**
Griffin Way S. *Hook* 1J **45**
Griffiths Gdns. *Bourn* 1F **226**
Griffon Clo. *Burs* 9L **175**
Griffon Clo. *Farn* 9F **28**
Grigg La. *Broc* 7C **148**
Grimstead Rd. *F'ley & E Grim*
. . . . 8E **86**
Grimstead Rd. *W Gri* 2D **120**
Grindle Clo. *Fare* 8L **199**
Gritanwood Rd. *S'sea* 4J **241**
Grosvenor Clo. *Ashy H* 3A **186**
Grosvenor Clo. *Hat W* 5K **59**
Grosvenor Clo. *Sotn* 9A **160**
Grosvenor Ct. *B'wtr* 1F **28**
Grosvenor Ct. *Bourn* 1A **246**
Grosvenor Ct. *Fare* 6N **211**
Grosvenor Ct. *Roms* 5B **130**
Grosvenor Ct. Sotn *1A 174*
(off Grosvenor Rd.)
Grosvenor Dri. *Win* 4M **105**
Grosvenor Gdns. *Bourn* 1B **246**
Grosvenor Gdns. *Sotn* 9A **160**
Grosvenor Gdns. *W End*
. . . . 2H **175**
Grosvenor Ho. *Bas* 6D **42**
Grosvenor Ho. *S'sea* 3D **240**
Grosvenor Mans. *Sotn* 2B **4**
Grosvenor M. *Gos* 2L **239**
Grosvenor M. *L'ton* 1D **234**
Grosvenor M. *Sotn* 9A **160**
Grosvenor Rd. *A'sht* 9J **49**
Grosvenor Rd. *Bourn* 2G **244**
Grosvenor Rd. *Chan F* 3C **132**
Grosvenor Rd. *Meds* 4F **96**
Grosvenor Rd. *Sotn* 9A **160**
Grosvenor Sq. *Sotn*
. . . . 4L **173** (2C **4**)
Grosvenor St. *S'sea* 3D **240**
Grouse Green. **7K 15**
Grove Av. *Fare* 2L **213**
Grove Av. *Gos* 2L **239**
Grove Bldgs. *Gos* 3L **239**
Grovebury. *L Hth* 7D **196**
Grove Clo. *Bas* 8D **42**
Grove Copse. *Sotn* 9G **174**
Gro. Cross Rd. *Frim* 3M **29**
Gro. Farm Mdw. Cvn. Pk. *Christ*
. . . . 4G **228**
Grovefields Av. *Frim* 3M **29**
Grove Gdns. *Sotn* 9F **174**
Grove Ho. *S'sea* 4E **240**
Grovelands Rd. *Win* 5F **104**
Grove La. *Redl* 1N **119**
Groveley Bus. Cen. *Christ*
. . . . 8A **230**
Groveley Rd. *Bourn* 3F **244**
Groveley Rd. *Christ* 8A **230**
Grovely Av. *Bourn* 1C **246**
Grovely Way. *Cram* 3D **130**
Grove M. *Sotn* 8F **174**
Grove Pk. Ind. Est. *Alt* 4H **81**
Grove Pastures. *L'ton* 3E **234**
Grove Pl. *L'ton* 3E **234**
Grove Pl. *Sotn* 8F **174**
Grove Rd. *Alt* 6F **80**
Grove Rd. *Bart S* 7A **232**
Grove Rd. *Bas* 9C **42**
Grove Rd. *Bourn*
. . . . 2L **245** (7N **247**)
Grove Rd. *Cam* 8N **19**
Grove Rd. *Chu C* 6N **47**
Grove Rd. *Cosh* 1K **215**
Grove Rd. *Enh A* 9N **33**
Grove Rd. *Fare* 8C **198**
Grove Rd. *Gos* 1K **239**
Grove Rd. *Hav* 8F **202**
Grove Rd. *Hind* 1K **103**
Grove Rd. *Lee S* 1A **238**
Grove Rd. *L'ton* 3F **234**
Grove Rd. *Shaw* 8G **127**
Grove Rd. *Sotn* 3H **173**
Grove Rd. E. *Christ* 6K **229**
Grove Rd. N. *S'sea* 4E **240**
Grove Rd. S. *S'sea* 5D **240**
Grove Rd. W. *Christ* 6J **229**
Grovers Gdns. *Hind* 1M **103**
Groves Clo. *S Won* 3G **91**
Groves Down. *W Wel* 9N **121**
Grove St. *Sotn* 6N **173** (6F **4**)
Grove, The. *A'sht* 1J **65**
Grove, The. *Bourn* 3K **227**
Grove, The. *Burs* 9L **175**
Grove, The. *Christ* 5H **229**
Grove, The. *Cowes* 5P **237**
Grove, The. *Fare* 6L **211**
Grove, The. *Farn* 2M **49**
Grove, The. *Frim* 3M **29**
Grove, The. *Lip* 2D **116**
Grove, The. *Min* 9L **155**
Grove, The. *Net A* 2H **195**
Grove, The. *Pen M* 6F **50**
Grove, The. *Sotn* 9F **174**
Grove, The. *Westb* 6N **203**
Grower Gdns. *Bourn* 2E **226**
Grugs La. *Cran* 6J **149**
Gruneisen Rd. *Ports* 6D **214**
Guardhouse Rd. *Ports*
. . . . 9C **214** (1M **5**)
Guardian Ct. *Sotn* 1M **173**
Guardroom Rd. *Ports* 7C **214**
Gudge Heath La. *Fare* 6N **197**
Guelders, The. *Water* 6M **201**
Guernsey Clo. *Bas* 1D **42**
Guernsey Clo. *Sotn* 8D **158**
Guernsey Dri. *Fle* 8N **27**
Guernsey Rd. *Poole* 5B **226**
Guessens La. *Titch* 9J **197**
Guessens Path. *Titch* 9J **197**
Guest Av. *Poole* 8D **226**
Guest Clo. *Poole* 8E **226**
Guest Rd. *Eastl* 9H **133**
Guildford Ct. *Gos* 2F **238**
Guildford Dri. *Chan F* 9N **131**
Guildford Rd. *A'sht* 3M **65**
Guildford Rd. *F'ham* 7F **64**
Guildford Rd. *Fle* 3A **48**
Guildford Rd. *Ports* 1F **240**
(in three parts)
Guildford Rd. *R'fld* 6J **65**
Guildford Rd. E. *Farn* 2L **49**
Guildford Rd. W. *Farn* 2L **49**
Guildford St. *Sotn* 5N **173**
Guildhall Gallery.
. . . . **7L 105 (8N 237)**
Guildhall Sq. *Ports*
. . . . 2D **240** (4N **5**)
Guildhall Wlk. *Ports*
. . . . 3D **240** (5M **5**)
Guildhill Rd. *Bourn* 1H **247**
Guillemont Fields. *Farn* 7F **28**
Guillemot Clo. *Hythe* 6N **193**
Guillemot Gdns. *Gos* 5D **212**
Guinea Ct. *Chine* 8H **23**
Gull Clo. *Gos* 6D **212**

Gull Coppice. White 2F 196
Gullet La. Meds & Four M 6B 96
Gulliver Clo. Poole 5A 244
Gulls, The. March 8E 172
Gullycroft Mead. H End . . . 3M 175
Gun Hill. A'sht. 8K 49
Gun Ho. Ports. 3C 240 (5M 5)
Gunners Bldgs. Ind. Est. Ports 4G 215
Gunners La. Bro C 6B 78
Gunners Pk. Bish W. 4A 164
Gunners Row. S'sea 5J 241
Gunner St. Bulf B 3B 66
Gunners Way. Gos 8H 213
Gunns Farm. Lip. 4E 116
Gunstore Rd. Ports 4H 215
Gunville. 6M 153
Gunville Cres. Bourn 3M 227
Gunville Hill. W'slw. 5H 87
Gunville Rd. W'slw. 5H 87
Gunwharf Quays. Ports 3B 240 (5J 5)
Gunwharf Rd. Ports 3B 240 (6J 5)
Gurdons. Alt. 7D 80
Gurkha Mus., The. 7K 105 (8K 237)
Gurnard Rd. Ports. 1F 214
Gurnays Mead. W Wel 1A 120
Gurney Ct. Odi 9K 45
Gurney Rd. Sotn. 2H 173
Gurney Rd. S'sea 3J 241
Gussage Rd. Poole. 6C 226
Gutner La. Hay I 7J 217
Guttridge La. T'ley 5G 11
Guy's Clo. Ring. 1L 187
Gwatkin Clo. Hav 6C 202
Gwynne Rd. Poole 9C 226
Gymnastic Cen. 1D 240
Gypsy La. Chilc. 9E 106
Gypsy La. Coom B 3G 119
Gypsy La. Water. 5N 181

H

Haarlem M. Christ 7N 229
Habens La. Hmbdn. 2B 180
Habin. 2L 147
Habin Hill. Rog 9L 141
Hack Dri. Col C. 4K 133
Hacketts La. Drox 9L 135
Hackett Way. Fare. . . . . 2C 212 (off Sharlands Rd.)
Hackleys La. E Wel 7A 128
Hacks La. Craw 3N 89
Hackupps La. Michm 4K 123
Hackwood Clo. And 2K 69
Hackwood Cotts. Bas 9D 42
Hackwood La. Clid 4B 60
Hackwood Rd. Bas. 7C 42
Hackwood Rd. Roundabout. Bas 8D 42
Hackworth Gdns. H End. . . . 8N 161
Hadden Rd. Bourn 6A 228
Haddon Clo. Fare 8A 198
Haddon Dri. Eastl 7E 132
Haddon Hill. 5B 228
Hadleigh Gdns. Eastl. 7E 132
Hadleigh Gdns. Frim G 6N 29
Hadleigh Pl. Bas. 6B 42
Hadleigh Rd. Ports 9E 200
Hadley Fld. Holb. 3N 207
Hadow Rd. Bourn. 3G 226
Hadrian Rd. And. 7A 52
Hadrians. F'ham. 6G 64
Hadrians Clo. Chan F 5C 132
Hadrians Way. Bas 4L 41
Hadrian Way. Chilw 4K 159
Haflinger Dri. White 1E 196
Haglane Copse. Penn 4C 234
Hagley Rd. Fle 1K 47
Hahnemann Rd. Bourn 3J 245 (8J 247)
Haig Av. Poole 4C 244
Haig Ct. Ports 5F 214
Haig La. Chu C. 6N 47
Haig Rd. A'sht. 1L 65
Haig Rd. Alr 9F 94
Haig Rd. And 1L 69
Haig Rd. Bulf B. 3B 66
Haig Rd. Cam. 7H 19
Haig Rd. Eastl. 1L 161
Haileybury Gdns. H End. . . . 1N 175
Hailsham Clo. Owl. 4F 18
Hailstone Rd. Bas. 3C 42
Haking Rd. Christ. 7N 229
Halcyon Dri. Thru. 1N 67
Halden Clo. Roms. 3A 130
Hale. . . . . 5F 64 (Farnham)
Hale. . . . . 9C 120 (Fordingbridge)
Hale Av. New M 4C 232
Halebrose Ct. Bourn. 2H 247
Halecommon. 8K 141
Hale Ct. Ports 9F 214
Hale Gdns. New M 4C 232
Hale Ho. Clo. Churt 7H 85
Hale Ho. La. Churt 7H 85
Hale La. Hale 1A 154
Hale Pl. F'ham 5G 64
Hale Reeds. F'ham 4F 64
Hale Rd. F'ham 5F 64
Hale Rd. W'grn. 2A 154
Hales Dri. H End 5L 175
Halesowen Ho. S'sea 6N 5
Hale St. N. Ports. 1E 240
Hale St. S. Ports. 1E 240
Hale Way. Frim 4M 29
Halewood Way. Christ. 6J 229
Haley La. Bentw 5L 79
Half Moon St. Ports 2B 240 (3J 5)
Halfpenny La. Ports 4B 240 (7K 5)
Halfway Rd. Fawl 7J 209
Halifax Clo. And. 9M 51
Halifax Clo. Farn. 9H 29
Halifax Ct. W End 9G 160
Halifax Ri. Water 2N 201
Halifax Way. Christ. 7D 230
Halimote Rd. A'sht 1J 65
Hall Clo. Bish W. 3N 163
Hall Clo. Cam 7N 19
Hallett Clo. Sotn 9E 160
Hallett Rd. Hav 7H 203
Halletts Clo. Fare 5M 211
Hall Farm Cres. Yate. 8N 17
Halliards, The. Fare 1D 212
Halliday Clo. Bas. 9B 42
Halliday Clo. Gos 2K 239
Halliday Cres. S'sea 4K 241
Hall Lands La. F Oak. 1A 162
Hall La. Up Farr & Selb. 5F 98
Hall La. Yate. 8M 17
Hallmark Clo. Coll T. 5G 18
Hallowell Ho. Ports. 1D 240
Hall Rd. Alt. 2G 81
Hall Rd. Bourn 3D 226
Halls Farm Clo. Win 3J 105
Hall's La. Roth 4E 24
Hall Way, The. Win 1F 104
Halnaker La. E Meon. 3J 143
Halsey Clo. Gos 4H 239
Halstead Ho. Baug 4F 10
Halstead Rd. Ports 9E 200
Halstead Rd. Sotn 9D 160
Halters End. Gray 4J 103
Halterworth. 5B 130
Halterworth Clo. Roms. . . . 5A 130
Halterworth La. Roms 5B 130
Halton Clo. Brans 7D 220
Halton Rd. Per D 4B 30
Haltons Clo. Tot 1K 171
Halyard Clo. Gos. 9F 212
Halyards. Hamb 5L 195
Hambert Way. Tot. 5L 171
Hamble Av. B'wtr 8F 18
Hamble Cliff. 6H 195
Hamblecliff Ho. Hamb 6H 195
Hamble Cliff Stables. Hamb 6H 195
Hamble Clo. Okly 1D 58
Hamble Clo. Wars 8N 195
Hamble Ct. Bas. 6E 42
Hamble Ct. Chan F 7B 132
Hamble Ct. Fare 5L 211
Hambledon. 8D 166
Hambledon Clo. Win 2H 105
Hambledon Gdns. Bourn 8F 228
Hambledon La. Sob 9L 165
Hambledon Pde. Water. 8K 181
Hambledon Rd. Bourn 7E 228
Hambledon Rd. Clan. 5A 168
Hambledon Rd. Den. 5G 180
Hambledon Rd. Hmbdn 1D 180
Hambledon Rd. Water . . . . . 8K 181 (in three parts)
Hamble Dri. T'ley 5K 11
Hamble Ho. Fare. 1C 212
Hamble Ho. Gdns. Hamb 7L 195
Hamble La. Burs. 1K 195
Hamble La. Hamb. 6J 195
Hamble La. Water 4M 201
Hamble-le-Rice. 7L 195
Hamble Mnr. Ct. Hamb. 7L 195
Hamble Pk. Cvn. Site. Wars 8C 196
Hamble Rd. Gos. 3H 239
Hambleside Ct. Hamb. 7K 195
Hamble Springs. Bish W 4N 163
Hamble Wood. Bot. 4D 176
Hamblewood Ct. Bot. 4E 176
Hambrook Rd. Gos 1J 239
Hambrook St. S'sea 4C 240 (8M 5)
Hamburg Clo. And. 7M 51
Ham Down. 1B 156
Hamdown Cres. E Wel 1B 156
Hameldon Clo. Sotn 3E 172
Hamelyn Clo. Bas. 7B 42
Hamelyn Rd. Bas 7B 42
Hamesmoor Rd. Myt 8N 29
Hamesmoor Way. Myt 8N 29
Hamfield Dri. Hay I 3E 242
Hamilton Clo. Ame . . . . 5A 66 (off Rayleigh Cres.)
Hamilton Clo. Bas. 4N 41
Hamilton Clo. Bord 3L 101
Hamilton Clo. Bourn. 9A 228
Hamilton Clo. Christ. 9B 230
Hamilton Clo. Hav. 9F 202
Hamilton Ct. Bourn 9M 227
Hamilton Ct. Mil S. 8J 235
Hamilton Ct. S'sea 5D 240 (9N 5)
Hamilton Enterprise Cen. Ports 1M 215
Hamilton Gro. Gos 6D 212
Hamilton Ho. Ports . . . . 1F 240 (off Clive Rd.)
Hamilton M. Hythe 8N 193
Hamilton Pk. D'ton 1L 119
Hamilton Pl. A'sht. 1H 65
Hamilton Rd. Bourn 9A 228
Hamilton Rd. Chu C 5N 47
Hamilton Rd. Cosh. 9N 199
Hamilton Rd. Eastl 9H 133
Hamilton Rd. Hythe 9N 193
Hamilton Rd. Lngmr. 4J 115
Hamilton Rd. S'sea 5E 240
Hamilton Way. New M 4N 231
Ham La. Baug. 7B 10
Ham La. Cath 2N 181
Ham La. Gos. 8J 213
Hamlet Ct. Fawl. 5F 208
Hamlet Way. Gos 7H 213
Hammer. 1M 117
Hammer Bottom. 9L 103
Hammer Hill. Hasl. 2L 117
Hammer La. B'shtt C. 7L 103
Hammer La. Churt & Gray 8G 84
Hammer La. Hasl 1J 117
Hammersley Rd. A'sht 4K 49
Hammer Va. Hasl 9L 103
Hammerwood Copse. Hasl 1M 117
Hammond Ct. Gos 3N 239
Hammond Ind. Pk. Fare 7N 211
Hammond Rd. Bas. 8B 42
Hammond Rd. Fare 7N 197
Hammonds Clo. Tot 2L 171
Hammond's Green. 2K 171
Hammond's Grn. Tot 2K 171
Hammond's La. Ropl 2D 110
Hammonds La. Tot. 2L 171
Hammond's Pas. Win. 8L 237
Hammonds Way. Tot 2L 171
Hampage Grn. Hav. 2D 202
Hampden La. Bourn 9E 228
Hampshire Clo. A'sht 3M 65
Hampshire Clo. Bas 8J 41
Hampshire Clo. Bulf . . . . 3A 66 (off Churchill Av.)
Hampshire Clo. Christ. 4J 229
Hampshire Corporate Pk. Chan F 9N 131
Hampshire County Golf Club, The. 2K 175
Hampshire Ct. Bourn 2J 245 (6L 247)
Hampshire Ct. Chan F. 9A 132
Hampshire Hatches La. Ring 4K 187
Hampshire Ho. Bourn. 6L 247
Hampshire International Bus. Pk. Chine 8F 22
Hampshire Rd. Bord 3J 101
Hampshire Rose Bowl, The. 1K 175
Hampshire St. Ports 9F 214
Hampshire Tennis and Health Club. 1K 175
Hampshire Ter. Ports 3C 240 (6M 5)
Hampstead Ho. Bas . . . . 6C 42 (off Church St.)
Hampton Clo. Black 8C 208
Hampton Clo. Chu C 7M 47
Hampton Clo. Water. 2A 202
Hampton Ct. Bas. 5M 41
Hampton Ct. Bourn 1H 245 (5H 247)
Hampton Dri. Ring 8L 185
Hampton Gdns. Black 8C 208
Hampton Gro. Fare 9L 197
Hampton Hill. Swanm 5C 164
Hampton La. Black 6C 208
Hampton La. Win 5G 105
Hampton Park. 8N 159
Hampton Rd. F'ham. 4C 64
Hampton Towers. Sotn. 1C 194
Hamptworth. 9H 121
Hamptworth Golf Course. 8G 121
Hamptworth Rd. Land 8E 120
Hamtun Cres. Tot. 1L 171
Hamtun Gdns. Tot 1L 171
Hamtun Rd. Sotn. 7G 174
Hamtun St. Sotn . . . 7L 173 (7C 4)
Hanbidge Cres. Gos 4F 212
Hanbidge Wlk. Gos 4F 212
Hanbury Way. Cam 1L 29
Hancombe Rd. S'hrst 4C 18
Handcroft Clo. Cron 2L 63
Handel Clo. Bas 1N 59
Handel Rd. Sotn . . . 4L 173 (3B 4)
Handel Ter. Sotn . . . 5K 173 (3A 4)
Handford La. Yate 8N 17
Handford Pl. Sotn 4L 173 (1C 4)
Handley Ct. Ring 1J 187
Handley Rd. Gos 1H 239
Handsworth Ho. S'sea 3E 240
Hangerfield Clo. Yate 8M 17
Hanger Rd. T'ley 4F 10
Hangersley. 4A 188
Hangersley Hill. 4A 188
Hangers, The. Bish W 2N 163
Hanger, The. Head 9A 84
Hanger Way. Ptsfld 1A 146
Hanging Bushes La. W'hll 8F 50
Hankinson Rd. Bourn. 6L 227
Hanley Rd. Sotn. 2J 173
Hanlon Ct. Bourn 2E 226
Hanmore Rd. Chine 1F 42
Hannah Gdns. Water. 1N 201
Hannah Way. Penn 9N 223
Hannam's Farm. Cron 3L 63
Hannay Ri. Sotn 5H 175
Hannington. 9L 9
Hannington Pl. Bourn 9D 228
Hannington Rd. Bourn. . . . 9D 228
Hannington Rd. Hav 2D 202
Hann Rd. Rown. 5D 158
Hanns Way. Eastl. 9E 132
Hanover Bldgs. Sotn 6M 173 (6D 4)
Hanover Clo. And. 3K 69
Hanover Clo. Frim 3N 29
Hanover Clo. Roms 5L 129
Hanover Clo. Yate 6N 17
Hanover Ct. Hythe. 5M 193
Hanover Ct. Lip 1D 116
Hanover Ct. Ports 4B 240 (6K 5)
Hanover Dri. Fle. 8A 28
Hanover Gdns. Bas 9B 42
Hanover Gdns. Fare. 6D 198
Hanover Gdns. Farn. 6G 29
Hanover Ho. And . . . . 2A 70 (off London St.)
Hanover Ho. Gos 3D 212
Hanover Ho. Tot. 2N 171
Hanoverian Way. White . . . 2F 196
Hanover Lodge. Win 8K 105
Hanover St. Ports 2B 240 (3J 5)
Hanson Rd. And. 9L 51
Hanway Rd. Ports 8F 214
Ha'penny Dell. Water 6M 201
Happersnapper Hangers Nature Reserve. 9J 113
Harbeck Rd. Bourn 3N 227
Harborough Rd. Sotn 4L 173 (1B 4)
Harbour Clo. Farn. 4J 29
Harbour Clo. Poole 7B 244
Harbour Ct. Bart S. 7N 231
Harbour Cres. Christ 9A 230
Harbourne Gdns. W End 9F 160
Harbour Pde. Sotn 6K 173 (5A 4)
Harbour Prospect. Poole 5A 244
Harbour Rd. Bourn 2K 247
Harbour Rd. Gos. 2M 239
Harbour Rd. Hay I 3C 242
Harbourside. Hav. 2F 216
Harbour Side Cvn. & Camping Site. Ports 7L 215
Harbour Tower. Gos 3N 239
Harbour Vw. Fare 2L 213
Harbour Vw. Ct. Christ . . . 9L 229
Harbour Watch. Poole 6A 244
Harbour Way. Ems 9N 203
Harbour Way. Ports 6D 214
Harbridge. 9H 153
Harbridge Ct. Hav. 2D 202
Harbridge Green. 8H 153
Harcourt Clo. Water 6A 182
Harcourt Rd. Bourn 9D 228
Harcourt Rd. Cam. 8J 19
Harcourt Rd. Fare. 1L 211
Harcourt Rd. Gos 2J 239
Harcourt Rd. Ports 9F 214
Harcourt Rd. Sotn 2B 174
Harding La. F Oak . . . . 9M 133 (in two parts)
Harding Rd. Gos 1H 239
Hardings La. H Win 6C 26
Hardings Rd. Bucks H & Fren 10M 63
Hard Interchange, The. Ports 2B 240 (4J 5)
Hardley. 2N 207
Hardley Ind. Est. Hythe . . . 2M 207
Hardley La. Hythe. 1N 207
Hard, The. Ports. 2B 240 (3J 5)
Hardwicke Clo. Sotn. 9E 158
Hardwicke Way. Hamb. . . . 7H 195
Hardwick Rd. Chan F 6B 132
Hardy Av. Yate. 9M 17
Hardy Clo. L Hth. 5E 196
Hardy Clo. New M 3A 232
Hardy Clo. Sotn 4G 173
Hardy Dri. Hythe 7N 193
Hardyfair Clo. W'hll 8E 50
Hardy Grn. C'then 1D 18
Hardy La. Bas. 7B 42
Hardy Rd. Eastl. 2E 160
Hardy Rd. Poole. 1B 244
Hardy Rd. Ports. 9M 201
Hardy's Fld. K're. 1A 6
Harebell Clo. Fare. 6E 198
Harebell Clo. H Win 5C 26
Harebell Gdns. H Win. 5C 26
Harefield. . . . . 4A 130 (Romsey)
Harefield. . . . . 3G 174 (Southampton)
Harefield Ct. Roms. 4A 130
Harefield Rd. Sotn 7A 160
Hare La. Cran 7L 149
Hare La. Twy. 9L 127
Hare Rd. New M & Hord 3E 232
Hares Grn. Bourn. 6D 228
Hare's La. H Win 4D 26
Harestock. 2G 105
Harestock Clo. Win 1H 105
Harestock Rd. Hav 6D 202
Harestock Rd. Win. 3G 104
Harewood Av. Bourn 7C 228
Harewood Clo. Eastl 6E 132
Harewood Cres. Bourn. . . . 7C 228
Harewood Forest Ind. Est. Longp 6J 71
Harewood Gdns. Bourn . . . 7C 228
Hare Wood Grn. Key 9N 235
Harewood Mobile Home Pk. And 9E 52
Harewood Pl. Bourn 8E 228
Harfield Clo. Hook 2G 44
Harford Clo. Penn 5B 234
Harford Rd. Poole 6A 226
Harkness Dri. Water. 1B 202
Harland Cres. Sotn 1J 173
Harland Rd. Bourn 1K 247
Harlaxton Clo. Eastl 7D 132
Harlech Clo. Bas. 6L 41
Harlech Dri. Chan F. 8M 131
Harlech Rd. B'wtr 9F 18
Harlequin Gro. Fare 8B 198
Harleston Rd. Ports 8E 200
Harley Ct. Wars 8A 196
Harley La. W Wel 3L 155
Harley Wlk. Ports 1E 240
Harlington Way. Fle 2L 47
Harlyn Rd. Sotn 1E 172
Harmsworth Rd. T'ley 5H 11
Harold Clo. Tot. 4K 171
Harold Gdns. Alt. 3G 80
Harold Jackson Ter. Bas. . . . 7D 42
Harold Rd. Fare 5N 211
Harold Rd. Hay I 5H 243
Harold Rd. Sotn. 3H 173
Harold Rd. S'sea 4F 240
Harpton Clo. Yate. 6N 17
Harpton Pde. Yate 6N 17

Harpway La.—Heatherbrae Gdns.

Harpway La. Brans 8M 219
Harrage, The. Roms 5M 129
Harrier Clo. Lee S 1B 238
Harrier Clo. Sotn 5G 158
Harrier Clo. Water 3A 182
Harriers Clo. Christ 6F 230
Harrier Way. Hythe 2N 207
Harrier Way. Ptsfld 2B 146
Harriet Clo. Fare 6L 211
Harrington Dri. Bulf B 3B 66
Harris Av. H End 2N 175
Harris Ct. Lip 4D 116
Harris Hill. Bas 3K 59
Harris La. Ids 6K 169
Harrison Av. Bourn 8A 228
Harrison Clo. Burt 3M 229
Harrison Ho. Ports 6E 214
Harrison Rd. Fare 7D 198
Harrison Rd. Sotn 8A 160
Harrison's Cut. Sotn (SO14) 6N 173 (6E 4)
Harrison's Cut. Sotn (SO15) 1G 173
Harris Rd. Gos 5F 212
Harris Way. New M 9D 222
Harroway. Hur P & Whitc 5M 53
Harroway. Whitc & Free 2H 55
Harroway La. Pen H & And 7G 50
Harrow Clo. Nea 8D 220
Harrow Down. Win 1H 127
Harrowgate La. Water 2H 181
Harrow La. Ptsfld 7M 139
Harrow Rd. Brans & Nea 8C 220
Harrow Rd. S'sea 3F 240
Harrow Way. And 8G 50 (Hopkinson Way)
Harrow Way. And 9K 51 (Upper Dro.)
Harrow Way. Okly 8M 39
Harrow Way. Over 6F 38
Harrow Way, The. Bas 1N 59
Harry Barrows Clo. Ring 2K 187
Harry Sotnick Ho. Ports 1G 240
Hart Cen., The. Fle 2L 47
Hart Clo. Farn 4G 28
Hart Clo. New M 2A 232
Hart Ct. Sotn 7D 174
Hartfordbridge 4E 26
Hartford Ct. H Win 6C 26
Hartford Ho. Ports 4C 240 (7M 5)
Hartford Ri. Cam 7M 19
Hartford Rd. H Win 6B 26
Hartford Ter. H Win 6C 26
Hart Hill. Hythe 8A 194
Harthill Drove. Redl 3N 119
Harting Clo. Water 7D 168
Harting Down. Ptsfld 1A 146
Harting Gdns. Fare 8L 199
Harting Rd. Bourn 7G 229
Hartington Rd. Gos 1H 239
Hartington Rd. Sotn 5N 173 (3G 4)
Hartland Pl. Farn 6J 29
Hartland's Rd. Fare 8D 198
Hartley Av. Sotn 9N 159
Hartley Clo. B'wtr 8D 18
Hartley Clo. Dib P 8M 193
Hartley Clo. Eastl 2L 161
Hartley Gdns. T'ley 6H 11
Hartley La. H Wes 2N 23
Hartley Mauditt 1L 99
Hartley Mdw. Whitc 5F 54
Hartley M. H Win 5C 26 (off High St.)
Hartley Rd. Eastl 2L 161
Hartley Rd. Ports 5E 214
Hartleys. Sil 5A 12
Hartley Wlk. Dib P 8M 193
Hartley Wintney 6B 26
Hartley Wintney Golf Course 5D 26
Hart Plain Av. Water 6L 181 (in two parts)
Hartsbourne Dri. Bourn 6E 228
Harts Farm Way. Hav 9B 202
Hartsgrove Av. Black 8C 208
Hartsgrove Clo. Black 7C 208
Hartshill Rd. T'ley 5F 10
Harts La. Burgh 4D 8
Hartsleaf Clo. Fle 3L 47
Harts Leap Clo. S'hrst 4D 18
Harts Leap Rd. S'hrst 5C 18
Harts Way. Evtn 5L 233
Hartswood. Chine 1F 42
Harts Yd. F'ham 8D 64
Hart, The. F'ham 8D 64
Hartwell Rd. Ports 5J 215
Hartwood Gdns. Water 8M 181
Harvard Rd. Owl 4G 19
Harvest Clo. Win 1H 127
Harvest Clo. Yate 9L 17
Harvest Cres. Fle 7N 27
Harvester Dri. Fare 8L 197
Harvester Way. L'ton 9D 224
Harvestgate Wlk. Hav 3D 202
Harvesting La. E Meon 5A 144
Harvest La. B'stne 3D 118
Harvest Rd. Chan F 6L 131
Harvest Rd. Water 5F 180
Harvest Way. Lych 4G 42
Harvey Brown Ho. Hay I 2G 243
Harvey Ct. Black 6C 208
Harvey Cres. Wars 8C 196
Harvey Gdns. Hythe 6N 193
Harvey Rd. Bourn 9D 228
Harvey Rd. Eastl 9J 133
Harvey Rd. Farn 7E 28
Harvey Rd. Ports 8F 200
Harveys Fld. Over 2D 56
Harwich Rd. Ports 8E 200
Harwood Clo. Gos 4E 212
Harwood Clo. Tot 2L 171
Harwood Pl. King W 7N 91
Harwood Ri. Wool H 2A 8 (in two parts)
Harwood Rd. Gos 4E 212
Haselbury Rd. Tot 3M 171
Haselfoot Gdns. Sotn 3J 175
Haselworth Dri. Gos 6K 239
Haskells Clo. Lyn 3A 148
Haslar Cres. Water 8K 181
Haslar Jetty Rd. Gos 5M 239
Haslar Rd. Gos 3N 239 (in three parts)
Haslar Sea Wall. Gos 6M 239
Haslar Ter. Gos 5M 239
Haslemere Av. Highc 6H 231
Haslemere Gdns. Hay I 5M 243
Haslemere Pl. Christ 5J 231
Haslemere Rd. Lip 2E 116
Haslemere Rd. S'sea 4G 241
Hassocks, The. Water 2A 202
Hassocks Workshops. Bas 4F 42
Hastards La. Selb 7L 99
Hasted Dri. Alr 2E 108
Hastings Av. Gos 8H 213
Hastings Clo. Bas 6K 41
Hastings Ho. Ports 6D 214
Hastings Rd. Bourn 4C 228
Hatch 6L 43
Hatchberry La. Ver D 8E 6
Hatch Bottom 9H 161
Hatch Cvn. Pk. Old B 7K 43
Hatch Ct. Hav 2C 202
Hatchers La. Ows 4B 134
Hatches, The. Frim G 6M 29 (in two parts)
Hatchet Clo. Hale 9C 120
Hatchet Green 9C 120
Hatchet La. Beau 8B 206
Hatchet La. Hath 9J 33
Hatchett Hill. Lwr C 5A 32
Hatchetts Dri. Hasl 9L 103
Hatch La. Liss 1G 140
Hatch La. Old B 5J 43
Hatch La. Ver D 7E 6
Hatchley La. Uphm 8C 134 (in two parts)
Hatch Mead. W End 9G 161
Hatch Warren 4K 59
Hatch Warren Cotts. Hat W 3L 59
Hatchwarren Gdns. Bas 3N 59
Hatchwarren La. Bas 3N 59
Hatch Warren La. Hat W 3K 59 (in three parts)
Hatch Warren Retail Pk. Bas 4J 59
Hatfield Ct. New M 3N 231
Hatfield Gdns. Bourn 6E 228
Hatfield Gdns. Farn 9N 29
Hatfield Rd. S'sea 4H 241
Hathaway Clo. Eastl 8F 132
Hathaway Gdns. Bas 3E 42
Hathaway Gdns. Water 9B 182
Hathaway Rd. Bourn 1G 247
Hatherden 1J 51
Hatherell Clo. W End 1H 175
Hatherley Cres. Fare 9J 199
Hatherley Dri. Fare 9K 199
Hatherley Mans. Sotn 3H 173
Hatherley Rd. Ports 8B 200
Hatherley Rd. Win 5J 105
Hatherwood. Yate 8B 18
Hatley Rd. Sotn 2E 174
Hattem Pl. And 8M 51
Hatt Hill 3D 122
Hattingley Rd. Meds 9H 79
Hatt La. Mott 3D 122
Haughurst Hill 4C 10
Haughurst Hill. Baug 5B 10
Havant 6F 202
Havant and Waterlooville F.C. 4G 203
Havant Bus. Cen. Hav 9D 202
Havant By-Pass. Hav 9C 202
Havant By-Pass. Ports & Hav 2H 215
Havant Farm Clo. Hav 6F 202
Havant Mus. & Art Gallery 8G 202
Havant Retail Pk. Hav 8B 202
Havant Rd. Cosh & Hav 9G 201
Havant Rd. Ems 8J 203
Havant Rd. Hay I 5F 216
Havant Rd. Horn & Row C 3D 182
Havant Rd. Ports 7F 214
Havant St. Ports 2B 240 (3J 5)
Havelock Ct. Wars 8N 195
Havelock Mans. S'sea 3F 240
Havelock Rd. Poole 9E 226
Havelock Rd. Sotn 5L 173 (3B 4)
Havelock Rd. S'sea 3E 240
Havelock Rd. Wars 8N 195
Havelock Way. Christ 4F 230
Haven Ct. Mil S 8J 235
Haven Cres. Fare 7J 211
Havendale. H End 5A 176 (in two parts)
Haven Gdns. New M 4C 232
Haven Rd. Hay I 6L 243
Haven Rd. Poole 7B 244
Havenstone Way. Sotn 7C 160
Haven, The. Eastl 6F 132
Haven, The. Gos 5K 239
Haven, The. H End 6M 175
Haven, The. L Hth 5F 196
Haven, The. S'sea 2J 241
H Avenue. Hythe 2D 208
Haven Way. F'ham 6F 64
Haverstock Rd. Bourn 4M 227
Haviland Ct. Bourn 9C 228
Haviland Rd. Bourn 1C 246
Haviland Rd. E. Bourn 9C 228
Havisham Rd. Ports 9E 214
Havre Towers. Sotn 1C 194
Hawden Rd. Bourn 5E 226
Haweswater Clo. Bord 2J 101
Haweswater Clo. Sotn 1E 172
Haweswater Ct. Ash V 6N 49 (off Lakeside Clo.)
Hawfinch Clo. Sotn 5G 158
Hawk Clo. Bas 2H 59
Hawk Clo. Fare 6L 211
Hawk Conservancy, The 1B 68
Hawke Clo. And 9C 52
Hawkes Clo. H Win 5B 26
Hawke St. Ports 2B 240 (3J 5)
Hawkeswood Rd. Sotn 3A 174
Hawkewood Av. Water 8L 181
Hawkfield La. Bas 7B 42
Hawkhill. Dib 6H 193
Hawkhurst Clo. Sotn 9E 174
Hawkins Clo. Ring 8M 185
Hawkins Ct. March 7E 172
Hawkins Gro. Chu C 5J 47
Hawkins Rd. Gos 6F 212
Hawkins Rd. Poole 5D 226
Hawkins Way. Fle 3A 48
Hawkley 7M 113
Hawkley Clo. Hav 3E 202
Hawkley Dri. T'ley 6J 11
Hawkley Grn. Sotn 9D 174
Hawkley Rd. Hawk 7M 113
Hawkshaw Clo. Lip 2F 116
Hawks Mead. Liss 9D 114
Hawkswood Av. Frim 2N 29
Hawkwell. Chu C 7N 47
Hawkwell. Fare 8H 199
Hawkwood Rd. Bourn 1B 246
Hawley 1G 29
Hawley Ct. Farn 4G 29
Hawley Grn. B'wtr 1G 28
Hawley Lane 4K 29
Hawley La. Farn 3J 29 (in three parts)
Hawley La. Ind. Est. Farn 4K 29
Hawley Rd. B'wtr 9F 18
Haworth Clo. Christ 5K 229
Hawstead Grn. Hav 3D 202
Hawthorn 7K 97
Hawthorn Clo. A'sht 2N 65
Hawthorn Clo. Alr 1F 108
Hawthorn Clo. Col C 4L 133
Hawthorn Clo. F Oak 1N 161
Hawthorn Clo. Fare 8K 199
Hawthorn Clo. H End 4A 176
Hawthorn Clo. Mich 8J 77
Hawthorn Clo. New M 2D 232
Hawthorn Ct. Ptsfld 1B 146
Hawthorn Cres. Cosh 2G 215
Hawthorn Dri. Sway 5J 223
Hawthorne Clo. Grat 4L 67
Hawthorne Cres. B'wtr 9G 19
Hawthorne Gro. Hay I 3G 243
Hawthorne Rd. Tot 2K 171
Hawthorn Hill. Mid W 4B 72 (off Willow Way)
Hawthorn La. Four M 7L 97
Hawthorn La. Sar G 4B 196
Hawthorn Ri. Hook 1H 45
Hawthorn Rd. Bock & Christ 8A 220
Hawthorn Rd. Bourn 6K 227
Hawthorn Rd. Den 6F 180
Hawthorn Rd. Four M 7J 97
Hawthorn Rd. Horn 9C 168
Hawthorn Rd. Hythe 6L 193
Hawthorn Rd. Sotn 9M 159
Hawthorn Rd. Tidw 7E 30
Hawthorns. Alt 3E 80
Hawthorns, The. Baug 5E 10
Hawthorns, The. Bish W 2K 163
Hawthorns, The. Christ 8B 230
Hawthorns, The. Eastl 2C 160
Hawthorns, The. March 9F 172 (Limes, The)
Hawthorns, The. March 9E 172 (Main Rd.)
Hawthorns Urban Wildlife Cen., The 2L 173
Hawthorn Wlk. Lee S 1B 238
Hawthorn Way. Bas 5L 41
Hayburn Rd. Sotn 9C 158
Haydn Clo. King W 7M 91
Haydn Rd. Bas 2M 59
Haydock Clo. Alt 6F 80
Haydock Clo. Tot 2J 171
Haydock M. Water 9B 182
Haydon Pl. Yate 7A 18
Haydon Rd. Poole 4F 244
Hay Down La. A'prt 2N 67
Haydown Leas. Ver D 8E 6
Hayes Av. Bourn 8B 228
Hayes Clo. Fare 6N 197
Hayes Clo. King S 9A 86
Hayes Ct. S'sea 4E 240
Hayes Mead. Holb 3N 207
Hayle Rd. W End 9F 160
Hayley Clo. Hythe 9L 193
Hayley La. S Warn & Long S 3D 62
Hayling Av. Ports 9H 215
Hayling Billy Bus. Cen. Hay I 3D 242
Hayling Clo. Fare 9N 197
Hayling Golf Course 4C 242
Hayling Island 4G 242
Haymarket Theatre 7C 42
Haynes Way. Dib P 8K 193
Hays Cotts. Steep 6K 139
Haysoms Clo. New M 5C 232
Hayter Gdns. Roms 4N 129
Hayters Way. A'hlt 4D 152
Hayward Clo. Tot 3K 171
Hayward Ct. Holb 4A 208
Haywarden Pl. H Win 5C 26
Haywards Bus. Cen. Hav 6H 203
Haywards Ct. Ports 3B 240 (6K 5)
Haywood Dri. Fle 4M 47
Hazel Av. Farn 9H 29 (in three parts)
Hazelbank Clo. Lip 2F 116
Hazel Bank Clo. Ptsfld 9A 140
Hazelbank M. Lip 2F 116
Hazel Clo. A'hlt 5D 152
Hazel Clo. And 3K 69
Hazel Clo. Chan F 2A 132
Hazel Clo. Christ 5E 230
Hazel Clo. Col C 3L 133
Hazel Clo. Okly 1D 58
Hazelcombe. Over 3E 56
Hazel Coppice. Hook 1H 45
Hazel Ct. New M 5C 232
Hazel Ct. S'sea 3G 241
Hazeldean Ct. Row C 9H 183
Hazeldean Dri. Row C 9H 183
Hazeldene. Chine 1G 43
Hazeldene Gdns. It Ab 8H 93
Hazeldene Rd. Lip 2N 115
Hazeldown Rd. Rown 6D 158
Hazel Dri. Elve 9H 27
Hazeleigh Av. Sotn 8C 174
Hazeley 1L 25
Hazeley Bottom 4N 25
Hazeley Clo. H Win 5B 26
Hazeley Down 3B 134
Hazeley Grn. Hav 4H 203
Hazeley Heath 2M 25
Hazeley Lea 9M 15
Hazeley Lea. H Win 9M 15
Hazeley Rd. Twy 7L 127
Hazel Farm Rd. Tot 3J 171
Hazel Grn. Baug 4D 10
Hazel Gro. Asht 7F 170
Hazel Gro. Hind 5N 103
Hazel Gro. L Hth 7E 196
Hazel Gro. Water 6C 168
Hazel Gro. Win 9H 105
Hazelholt Dri. Hav 6D 202
Hazell Av. Bourn 4F 226
Hazell Rd. F'ham 8B 64
Hazel Rd. Four M 4K 97
Hazel Rd. Penn 2A 234
Hazel Rd. Sotn 6B 174
Hazel Rd. Water 6C 168
Hazelton Clo. Bourn 6D 228
Hazel Wlk. Ptsfld 3M 145
Hazelwood. Chine 8F 22
Hazelwood. Fare 3L 211
Hazelwood Av. Hav 6B 202
Hazelwood Av. New M 2N 231
Hazelwood Clo. Bas 4M 41
Hazelwood Dri. Bas 4M 41
Hazelwood Rd. Sotn 1E 174
Hazlemere Dri. St L 5B 186
Hazleton Ind. Est. Horn 4C 182
Hazleton Way. Water 5B 182
Headbourne Worthy Ho. Win 1M 105
Head Down. Ptsfld 1A 146
Headington Clo. Bas 2M 59
Headland Dri. L Hth 5D 196
Headlands Bus. Pk. Blash 7K 185
Headlands, The. D'ton 2J 119
Headley 2A 102 (Bordon)
Headley 2J 9 (Thatcham)
Headley Clo. Lee S 1B 238
Headley Down 3E 102
Headley Fields. Head 2A 102
Headley Hill Rd. Head 2B 102
Headley La. Pass 6A 102
Headley Pk. Cotts. Head 7M 83
Headley Rd. Gray & Hind 3G 102
Headley Rd. Lind 2M 101
Headley Rd. Lip 1D 116
Headmore La. Four M 6M 97
Headon Ct. F'ham 9F 64
Headon Vw. W Meon 8D 136
Headquarters Rd. Bulf B 3C 66
Heads Farm Clo. Bourn 1J 227
Head's Hill 1H 9
Heads La. Bourn 1J 227
Head's La. Ink C 1J 7
Headswell Av. Bourn 2J 227
Headswell Cres. Bourn 2J 227
Headswell Gdns. Bourn 1J 227
Heanor Clo. Bourn 4G 226
Hearmon Clo. Yate 7A 18
Hearn 9D 84
Hearne Gdns. Shir H 1C 178
Hearn Va. Head D 9C 84
Hearsey Gdns. B'wtr 7D 18 (in two parts)
Hearts of Oak M. L'ton 2D 234
Heath Clo. F Oak 2A 162
Heath Clo. F'ham 3E 64
Heath Clo. Hind 9L 85
Heath Clo. Water 3B 182
Heathcote Pl. Hurs 6N 125
Heathcote Rd. Bord 4J 101
Heathcote Rd. Bourn 1C 246
Heathcote Rd. Cam 8M 19
Heathcote Rd. Chan F 6B 132
Heathcote Rd. Ports 7G 215
Heath Cotts. Hind 1L 103
Heath Ct. Baug 3E 10
Heath Ct. Ptsfld 2M 145
Heath End 3E 64 (Farnham)
Heath End 2M 7 (Newbury)
Heath End 4F 10 (Thatcham)
Heath End Rd. Baug 5D 10
Heathen St. Durl 7D 162
Heatherbank Rd. Bourn 2G 244
Heatherbrae Gdns. N Bad 8E 130

Heather Chase. Eastl. 1L 161
Heather Clo. A'sht. 1G 64
Heather Clo. Bourn 2A 228
Heather Clo. Gos 6D 212
Heather Clo. Hord. 3H 233
Heather Clo. St L 5B 186
Heather Clo. Tot 3L 171
Heather Clo. Walk 5J 231
Heather Clo. Water 3N 201
Heather Clo. W'hill 6G 101
Heather Cotts. Hind 8M 85
Heather Ct. Sotn. 3G 175
Heatherdale Rd. Cam 9L 19
Heatherdeane Rd. Sotn 9M 159
Heatherdene Av. C'then 1A 18
Heatherdene Rd. Chan F 3C 132
Heather Dri. And 9M 51
Heather Dri. Chu C 6L 47
Heather Dri. Lind 2L 101
Heather Dri. T'ley 3F 10
Heatherfield. Bton. 7K 145
Heather Gdns. Fare. 6N 197
Heather Gdns. Farn. 1F 48
Heather Gro. H Win 5B 26
Heatherlands Ri. Poole 9B 226
Heatherlands Rd. Chilw 3L 159
Heather La. Up N 6C 44
Heatherlea Rd. Bourn. 1G 247
Heatherley Clo. Cam 8K 19
Heatherley Ct. S'sea 4E 240
Heatherley Rd. Cam 8K 19
Heather Lodge. New M 3B 232
Heather Rd. Bourn 3H 227
Heather Rd. Fawl 6D 208
Heather Rd. Ptsfld 1B 146
Heather Row La. Up N & Nat S 4E 44 (in two parts)
Heatherstone Av. Dib P 9L 193
Heatherton M. Ems 6M 203
Heatherview Clo. N Bad 7E 130
Heather Vw. Rd. Poole 7D 226
Heather Way. Kemp 3J 59
Heathfield. 6H 221 (Christchurch)
Heathfield. 8N 197 (Fareham)
Heathfield. Hythe 7L 193
Heathfield Av. Fare 8N 197
Heathfield Av. Poole 6E 226
Heathfield Clo. Chan F 2A 132
Heathfield Clo. Sotn 7G 174
Heathfield Ct. Fle 4K 47
Heathfield Rd. Bas 3M 59
Heathfield Rd. Chan F 2A 132
Heathfield Rd. Ptsfld 1B 146
Heathfield Rd. Ports 8E 214
Heathfield Rd. Sotn 7F 174
Heath Gdns. Net A 2H 195
Heath Green. 9H 79
Heath Grn. La. Meds 9H 79
Heath Hill. Dock 5A 84
Heath Hill Rd. N. C'then 1D 18
Heath Hill Rd. S. C'then 1D 18
Heath Ho. Clo. H End 6M 175
Heath Ho. Gdns. H End 6M 175
Heath Ho. La. H End 6M 175
Heathlands. Baug 4E 10
Heathlands. Burgh 3B 8
Heathlands. Shed 3A 178
Heathlands Clo. Burt 3M 229
Heathlands Clo. Chan F 4A 132
Heathlands Ct. Yate 9A 18
Heathlands Rd. Chan F 4A 132
Heathland St. A'sht 9J 49
Heath La. Butt 4E 6
Heath La. Cron & Ews 3L 63
Heath La. E Bol 9B 206
Heath La. F'ham 3E 64
Heath La. Titch 1H 211
Heath Lawns. Fare 8N 197
Heathman St. Neth W 1A 88
Heath Ride. Finch & C'then 1M 17
Heath Ri. Cam 8M 19
Heath Rd. Hasl 1M 117
Heath Rd. Hord 3G 232
Heath Rd. L Hth 6C 196
Heath Rd. N Bad 9F 130
Heath Rd. P Hth 4L 11
Heath Rd. Ptsfld 1M 145
Heath Rd. St L 4A 186
Heath Rd. Sotn 5E 174
Heath Rd. Walk 5K 231
Heath Rd. Wick & Sob 2H 179
Heath Rd. E. Hurn 3C 218
Heath Rd. E. Ptsfld 3A 146
Heath Rd. N. L Hth 5C 196
Heath Rd. S. L Hth 6C 196
Heath Rd. W. Hurn 1B 218
Heath Rd. W. Ptsfld 2N 145
Heathrow Copse. Baug 5D 10
Heathside La. Hind 1M 103
Heathside Way. H Win 5B 26
Heath, The. Den 6H 181
Heath Va. And 2A 70
Heathview. Hook 1J 45
Heathway. Cam 8M 19
Heathway Clo. Cam 8M 19
Heathwood Av. Bart S 6N 231
Heathwood Clo. Yate 6N 17
Heathwood Rd. Bourn 6J 227
Heathy Clo. Bart S 6A 232
Heathyfields Rd. F'ham 4B 64
Heaton Rd. Bourn 4F 226
Heaton Rd. Gos 9H 213
Heavytree Rd. Poole 1A 244
Hebrides Clo. Fare 5L 211
Heckfield. 7H 15
Heckfield Clo. Hav 4H 203
Heckfield Dri. Elve 9H 27
Hector Clo. Water 7M 201
Hector Rd. Fare 2C 212
Heddon Wlk. Farn 5J 29
Hedera Rd. L Hth 6C 196
Hedge Cft. Yate 7L 17
Hedge End. 4N 175
Hedge End Bus. Cen. H End 1M 175
Hedge End Retail Pk. H End 3L 175 (in two parts)
Hedge End Rd. And 3A 70
Hedge End Wlk. Hav 3J 203
Hedgerley. New M 6C 232
Hedgerow Clo. Rown 4D 158
Hedgerow Dri. Sotn 1F 174
Hedgerow Gdns. Ems 6M 203
Hedgerows, The. Lych 3H 43
Hedges Clo. Ship B 2A 66
Hedley Clo. Fawl 7D 208
Hedley Gdns. H End 9M 161
Hedley Wlk. Black 7D 208
Heenan Clo. Frim G 5N 29
Heidelberg Rd. S'sea 3G 240
Heights, The. Fare 7F 198
Heights, The. H End 4L 175
Heilin Way. Lud 1C 30
Hele Clo. Bas 9B 42
Helena Rd. S'sea 5G 240
Helen Ct. Farn 8K 29
Helford Ct. And 8B 52
Helford Gdns. W End 9F 160
Helix Bus. Pk. Cam 1K 29
Hell Corner. 1J 7
Hellyer Rd. S'sea 4H 241
Helm Clo. Gos 1F 238
Helsby Clo. Fare 9A 198
Helsted Clo. Gos 3G 238
Helston Dri. Ems 6L 203
Helston Rd. Ports 8A 200
Helvellyn Rd. Sotn 2E 172
Helyar Rd. Bourn 4C 228
Hemdean Gdns. W End 1H 175
Hemlock Rd. Water 6M 181
Hemlock Way. Chan F 7L 131
Hemming Clo. Tot 4L 171
Hemmingway Gdns. White 1F 196
Hempland La. Holyb 1K 137
Hempsted Path. Ports 8C 200
Hempsted Rd. Ports 8C 200
Hemsley Wlk. Water 6A 182
Henderson Pk. Mobile Homes. S'sea 4K 241
Henderson Rd. S'sea 4J 241
Hendford Gdns. Bourn 4H 227
Hendford Rd. Bourn 4H 227
Hendon Rd. Bord 5J 101
Hendren Sq. And 8B 52
Hendy Clo. S'sea 4D 240
Hengest Clo. Charl 7K 51
Hengistbury Rd. Bart S 6N 231
Hengistbury Rd. Bourn 1J 247
Hengist Pk. Bourn 1L 247
Hengist Rd. Bourn 1A 246
Henley. 5C 6
Henley Clo. Farn 4G 28
Henley Dri. Frim G 5N 29
Henley Gdns. Bourn 7D 228
Henley Gdns. Fare 5N 197
Henley Gdns. Yate 8N 17
Henley Rd. S'sea 5G 240
Henry Clo. Holb 2N 207
Henry Cort Dri. Fare 6M 197
Henry Rd. Eastl 8H 133
Henry Rd. Sotn 3G 173
Henry St. Gos 3L 239
Henry St. Sotn 4L 173 (1B 4)
Henstead Ct. Sotn 4L 173 (2B 4)
Henstead Rd. Sotn 4L 173 (2B 4)
Hensting. 6A 134
Hensting La. Fish P & Ows 5M 133
Henty Rd. Sotn 2G 172
Henville Clo. Gos 8F 212
Henville Rd. Bourn 9N 227
Henwood Down. Ptsfld 1N 145
Hepplewhite Clo. Baug 4E 10
Hepplewhite Dri. Bas 3J 59
Hepworth Clo. And 9N 51
Hepworth Clo. Sotn 8G 174
Hepworth Cft. Coll T 7G 18
Herald Ct. A'sht 1K 65
Herald Ind. Est. H End 1M 175
Herald Rd. H End 1M 175
Herbert Av. Poole 6A 226
Herbert Ct. Poole 6B 226
Herberton Rd. Bourn 9F 228
Herbert Rd. Bourn 3F 244
Herbert Rd. Fle 2K 47
Herbert Rd. Gos 2H 239
Herbert Rd. New M 3C 232
Herbert Rd. S'sea 5F 240
Herbert Rd. W'fls 2M 119
Herbert St. Ports 9D 214
Herbert Walker Av. Sotn 5F 172 (7A 4) (in two parts)
Herbs End. Farn 7E 28
Hercules St. Ports 8E 214
Hereford Clo. Odi 9J 45
Hereford Ct. Gos 1E 238
Hereford Ct. S'sea 4E 240 (off Hereford Rd.)
Hereford La. F'ham 4D 64
Hereford Mead. Fle 8N 27
Hereford Rd. Bas 6L 41
Hereford Rd. S'sea 4E 240
Hereward Clo. Roms 5A 130
Heritage Ct. Win 7N 237
Heritage Gdns. Fare 1J 213
Heritage Pk. Bas 5K 59
Heritage Vw. Hat W 5K 59
Hermes Clo. Fle 2A 48
Hermes Rd. Lee S 9N 211
Hermitage. 9N 203
Hermitage Clo. Bish W 3K 163
Hermitage Clo. Farn 2M 49
Hermitage Clo. Hav 5E 202
Hermitage Gdns. Water 1N 201
Herm Rd. Poole 5B 226
Herne Rd. Ptsfld 1N 145 (in two parts)
Herne Rd. Ports 9F 200
Hern La. Hyde 4K 153
Heron Clo. Alt 2F 80
Heron Clo. Chu C 5A 48
Heron Clo. S'sea 2J 241
Heron Clo. Sway 6J 223
Heron Ct. Rd. Bourn 7L 227
Herondale. Hasl 9N 103
Heron La. Tims 7K 123
Heron Pk. Lych 2G 43
Heron Quay. Ems 1N 217
Heron Ri. And 3A 70
Herons Clo. Fare 4M 211
Herons Ct. Hay I 2H 243
Herons Mead. Bourn 1A 228
Heron Sq. Eastl 1C 160
Herons Wood. Cal 9K 157
Heron Way. Bas 2H 59
Heron Way. Gos 5D 212
Heron Wood Rd. A'sht 2M 65
Herretts Gdns. A'sht 1M 65
Herrett St. A'sht 2M 65
Herriard. 9H 61
Herriard Way. T'ley 6J 11
Herrick Clo. Sotn 6H 175
Herriot Ct. Yate 9M 17
Herriot Ho. Water 7A 182
Herriott Clo. Water 5A 182
Hertford Clo. F'bri 8J 151
Hertford Pl. Ports 9E 214
Hertsfield. Fare 6F 196
Hesketh Clo. St I 3D 186
Hesketh Ho. Sotn 4H 173
Hestan Clo. Christ 2G 229
Hester Rd. S'sea 3J 241
Hesters Vw. Long S 5E 62
Hestia Clo. Roms 4B 130
Heston Wlk. Gos 4G 238
Hewett Clo. Fare 1J 211
Hewett Ho. Titch 1J 211
Hewett Rd. Fare 1J 211
Hewett Rd. Ports 6F 214
Hewetts Ri. Wars 9N 195
Hewitt Clo. Gos 1J 239
Hewitt's Rd. Sotn 5J 173
Hewlett Ct. Fare 8E 198
Hewshott Gro. Lip 1G 117
Hewshott La. Lip 1E 116
Hexagon Cen., The. Chan F 1A 160
Hexagon, The. And 3K 69
Hexham Clo. Owl 3F 18
Heye's Dri. Sotn 7G 174
Heyford Clo. Ame 5A 66 (off Rayleigh Cres.)
Heysham Rd. Sotn 2G 173
Heyshott Gdns. Water 7D 168
Heyshott Rd. S'sea 3G 241
Heytesbury Rd. Bourn 8G 229
Heyward Rd. S'sea 4F 240
Heywood Gdns. Hav 3D 202
Heywood Grn. Sotn 5J 175
Hibberds Fld. Cran 6J 149
Hibberd Way. Bourn 5H 227
Hibiscus Gro. Bord 5K 101
Hickes Clo. Bourn 2D 226
Hickley Path. Fare 7E 198
Hickory Dri. Win 2H 105
Hickory Gdns. W End 8G 161
Hicks Clo. T'ley 5J 11
Hicks La. B'wtr 8D 18
Hides Clo. Whitc 6G 55
Hides Hill La. Beau 4D 206
Highams Clo. K're 2C 6
Highbank Av. Water 6J 201
Highbank Gdns. F'bri 1J 153
High Beeches. Frim 2M 29
Highbridge. 5H 133
Highbridge Rd. Highb & Col C 5G 132
Highbridge Rd. Poole 2A 244
Highbury Bldgs. Ports 2G 214
Highbury Clo. F Oak 2N 161
Highbury Clo. New M 3C 232
Highbury Gro. Ports 2G 215
Highbury Rd. Anna V 5K 69
Highbury St. Ports 3B 240 (6K 5)
Highbury Way. Ports 2G 214
Highclere. 4A 8
Highclere Av. Hav 5D 202
Highclere Castle. 6B 8
Highclere Rd. A'sht 2M 65
Highclere Rd. Sotn 8J 159
Highclere Way. Chan F 9M 131
Highcliff Av. Sotn 2M 173
Highcliffe. 6J 231
Highcliffe Castle Golf Course. 7F 230
Highcliffe Corner. Christ 6K 231
Highcliffe Dri. Eastl 5E 132
Highcliffe Rd. Christ 6C 230
Highcliffe Rd. Gos 3H 239
Highcliffe Rd. Win 8M 105
High Copse. F'ham 4C 64
High Ct. S'sea 4H 241
Highcroft. Win 7H 105
Highcroft Ind. Est. Water 2C 182
Highcroft La. Water 2C 182
High Cross. 3E 138
High Cross. Frox 3E 138
High Cross La. Frox 5B 138
Highcrown M. Sotn 9M 159
Highcrown St. Sotn 9M 159
Highdown. Fle 1M 47
Highdowns. Hat W 4L 59
High Dri. Bas 9L 41
High Dri. Gos 7E 212
Higher Mead. Lych 3G 43
Highfield. 9M 159
Highfield. L'ton 3D 234
Highfield. Twy 8L 127
Highfield Av. A'sht 3J 65
Highfield Av. Fare 9B 198
Highfield Av. L'ton 3C 234
Highfield Av. Ring 9K 185
Highfield Av. Sotn 8L 159
Highfield Av. Twy 8L 127
Highfield Av. Water 9N 181
Highfield Chase. Bas 6A 42
Highfield Clo. A'sht 2K 65
Highfield Clo. Chan F 6C 132
Highfield Clo. Farn 8H 29
Highfield Clo. Sotn 9M 159
Highfield Clo. Sway 5J 223
Highfield Clo. Water 9N 181
Highfield Cres. Hind 3N 103
Highfield Cres. Sotn 9N 159
Highfield Cres. W'slw 5G 87
Highfield Dri. Ring 8K 185
Highfield Gdns. A'sht 2J 65
Highfield Gdns. Liss 1G 140
Highfield Gdns. Sway 5J 223
Highfield La. Lip 4F 116
Highfield La. Sotn 9M 159
Highfield La. W'flls 3M 119
Highfield Pde. Water 9A 182
Highfield Path. Farn 8H 29
Highfield Rd. Bourn 4J 227
Highfield Rd. Chan F 6C 132
Highfield Rd. Farn 8H 29
Highfield Rd. Gos 1H 239
Highfield Rd. L'ton 2C 234
Highfield Rd. Ptsfld 9M 139
Highfield Rd. Ports 2E 240
Highfield Rd. Ring 9K 185
Highfield Rd. Sotn 1L 173
Highfields. Over 3E 56
Highfields. Wars 8C 196
Highfield Ter. Win 7J 105 (8K 237)
High Firs Gdns. Roms 5B 130
High Firs Rd. Roms 4B 130
High Firs Rd. Sotn 5F 174
Highgate La. Farn 7L 29
Highgate Rd. Ports 7H 215
Highgrove. Farn 5K 29
Highgrove Clo. Tot 5K 171
Highgrove Ind. Pk. Ports 5J 215
Highgrove Rd. Ports 8J 215
High Howe Clo. Bourn 2C 226
High Howe Gdns. Bourn 2C 226
High Howe La. Bourn 2C 226
Highland Av. Christ 5K 231
Hi ghland Clo. Ems 9L 203
Highland Dri. Fle 8N 27
Highland Dri. Okly 9C 40
Highland Rd. A'sht 9M 49
Highland Rd. Cam 5N 19
Highland Rd. Ems 8L 203
Highland Rd. Poole 9A 226
Highland Rd. S'sea 5G 240
Highlands Clo. Dib P 7M 193
Highlands Clo. N Bad 7D 130
Highlands Cres. Bourn 2G 226
Highlands Ho. Sotn 7B 174
Highlands Pk. Fare 6A 198
Highlands Rd. And 2B 70
Highlands Rd. Bart S 6B 232
Highlands Rd. Bas 8J 41
Highlands Rd. Cosh 9L 201
Highlands Rd. Fare 9L 197
Highlands Rd. F'ham 3E 64
Highland St. S'sea 5H 241
Highlands Way. Dib P 7L 193
Highlands Way. W'ish 5H 121
Highland Ter. S'sea 4G 241
High La. Bro Ch 3A 118
High Lawn Way. Hav 4E 202
High Marryats. Bart S 7B 232
High Mead. Fare 6A 198
Highmeadow. Sotn 4G 174
Highmoor Clo. Poole 2A 244
Highmoor Rd. Bourn 5E 226
Highmoor Rd. Poole 2A 244
Highmoors. Chine 9G 22
Highmount Clo. Win 7M 105
Highnam Gdns. Sar G 5C 196
High Oaks Clo. L Hth 6D 196
High Oaks Gdns. Bourn 2C 226
High Pk. Rd. F'ham 7D 64
Highpath Way. Bas 3L 41
High Pines. Christ 7F 230
High Pitfold. Gray 6M 103
Highridge. Alt 5D 80
High Ridge Cres. New M 3D 232
High Rd. Bro Ch & B'stne 3A 118
High Rd. Sotn 8B 160
High St. A'sht 9J 49
High St. Alt 5F 80
High St. And 2N 69
High St. Ashy H 2B 186
High St. Beau 8E 206
High St. Bish W 4M 163
High St. Bord 5J 101
High St. Bot 3C 176
High St. Bro'tn 1A 86
High St. Bulf 3A 66
High St. Bton 7K 145
High St. Burs 2L 195
High St. Cam 7M 19
High St. Christ 8L 229
High St. Coll D 1H 31
High St. Cosh 1G 214
High St. Cowes 5P 237
High St. Cran 6J 149
High St. C'then 1E 18
High St. Dam 3P 149
High St. D'ton 1L 119
High St. Drox 2K 165
High St. Eastl 2E 160
High St. E Meon 3L 143
High St. Ems 9M 203
High St. Fare 8E 198
High St. Farn 3M 49
High St. F'bri 1J 153
High St. Gos 3M 239

High St.—Holmbrook Gdns.

High St. *Grat.* 4L 67
High St. *Hamb* 7L 195
High St. *Hmbdn* 8E 166
High St. *H Win* 6C 26
High St. *Head* 2A 102
High St. *Hythe* 4M 193
High St. *Lee S* 1A 238
High St. *Lit S* 4B 18
High St. *Lud* 1C 30
High St. *L'ton* 3E 234
High St. *Lyn* 2B 148
High St. *Meds* 9K 79
High St. *Meon* 8N 135
High St. *Mil S* 8K 235
High St. *Monx* 4C 68
High St. *Neth W* 1A 88
High St. *Odi* 8K 45
High St. *Over* 2D 56
High St. *Ptsfld* 1M 145
High St. *Pitt* 6E 86
High St. *Ports* 4B 240 (7J 5)
High St. *Ring* 1J 187
High St. *Row* 8N 63
High St. *S'hrst* 4B 18
High St. *Selb* 7L 99
High St. *Ship B* 1B 66
High St. *Shir H* 3B 178
High St. *Sob* 8K 165
High St. *Sotn* 6M 173 (6C 4)
High St. *S'wick* 3A 200
High St. *Stockb* 2F 88
High St. *Titch* 9J 197
High St. *Tot* 3N 171
High St. *Twy* 8L 127
High St. *W End* 9G 161
High St. *Wher* 2E 74
High St. *Win* 6K 105 (7L 237) (in three parts)
High St. *W'grn* 2A 154
High Thicket Rd. *Dock* 4N 83
Hightown 2N 187 **(Ringwood)**
Hightown 6J 175 **(Southampton)**
Hightown Gdns. *Ring* 2L 187
Hightown Hill. *Ring* 2N 187
Hightown Rd. *Ring* 2K 187
Hightown Towers. *Sotn* 6J 175
Hightown Trad. Est. *Ring* 2L 187
High Trees. *F Oak* 1B 162
High Trees. *Poole* 5E 244
Hightrees. *Water* 1N 201
Hightrees Av. *Bourn* 5B 228
High Trees Dri. *Win* 4J 105
High Vw. *Fare* 8L 199
High Vw. *Ptsfld* 9M 139
Highview Clo. *Christ* 3H 229
High Vw. Clo. *Farn* 8J 29
Highview Gdns. *Poole* 7A 226
High Vw. Lodge. *A'sht* 9J 49
High Vw. Rd. *Farn* 8J 29
High Vw. Way. *Sotn* 2D 174
High Wlk. *Fare* 6A 198
Highways Rd. *Comp* 8G 127
Highway, The. *Charl A* 4N 119
Highwood 3A 188
Highwood Clo. *A'hlt* 4A 152
Highwood Clo. *Yate* 9M 17
Highwood La. *Roms* 4B 130
Highwood Lawn. *Hav* 2D 202
Highwood Ridge. *Bas* 4K 59
Highwood Rd. *Broc* 8C 148
Highwood Rd. *Gos* 9E 212
Highwood Rd. *Poole* 1C 244
Highworth Cotts. *Baug* 4C 10
Higworth Cvn. Pk. *Hay I* 2F 242
Higworth La. *Hay I* 2F 242
Hilary Av. *Ports* 1H 215
Hilary Ct. *Gos* 1F 238
Hilda Gdns. *Water* 6H 181
Hilda Pl. Sotn 5A 174 *(off Kent St.)*
Hilda Rd. *Poole* 8C 226
Hilden Way. *Win* 1E 104
Hilder Gdns. *Farn* 9M 29
Hilfield. *Yate* 8B 18
Hill 4K 173
Hilland Ri. *Head* 3B 102
Hillary Clo. *Fare* 7B 198
Hillary Clo. *Lyn* 4C 148
Hillary Rd. *Bas* 4A 42
Hillary Rd. *Christ* 6A 230
Hillborough Ct. *S'sea* 4E 240
Hillborough Cres. *S'sea* 4E 240
Hillbrook Ri. *F'ham* 4D 64
Hill Brow 3G 141
Hillbrow Clo. *Fare* 6N 197
Hill Brow Clo. *Row C* 9H 183
Hillbrow Rd. *Bourn* 8E 228
Hill Brow Rd. *Liss & Hill B* 1E 140
Hillbury Av. *And* 3L 69
Hillbury Pk. *A'hlt* 5D 152
Hillbury Rd. *A'hlt* 4D 152
Hill Clo. *Brans* 7C 220
Hill Clo. *F Oak* 7N 133
Hill Clo. *W'grn* 2A 154
Hill Corner Farm Cvn. Pk. *Farn* 5F 28
Hillcrest. *F'ham* 2F 64
Hillcrest. *Fle* 9M 27
Hillcrest. *T'ley* 4H 11
Hillcrest Av. *Chan F* 6B 132
Hillcrest Clo. *Bourn* 3L 227
Hillcrest Clo. *N Bad* 7E 130
Hillcrest Ct. *Bas* 5K 41
Hillcrest Dri. *Chan F* 6B 132
Hillcrest Gdns. *Wal C* 7N 163
Hillcrest Rd. *Bourn* 3L 227
Hillcrest Wlk. *Bas* 6K 41
Hill Cft. *Fare* 6G 197
Hilldene Way. *W End* 1H 175
Hillditch. *L'ton* 9D 224
Hilldown Rd. *Sotn* 9N 159
Hilldowns Av. *Ports* 6D 214
Hill Dri. *Fare* 6N 197
Hill End Rd. *Monk S* 4M 21
Hiller Wlk. *Lee S* 1B 238
Hill Farm La. *Sut S* 6C 76
Hill Farm Rd. *Mnkwd* 5J 111
Hill Farm Rd. *Sotn* 4K 173
Hillgarth. *Hind* 2M 103
Hill Grove 6E 164
Hill Gro. La. *Swanm* 6E 164
Hillgrove Rd. *Sotn* 8D 160
Hill Head 8L 211 **(Fareham)**
Hillhead 9K 209 **(Southampton)**
Hill Head Rd. *Fare* 7K 211
Hill Ho. Hill. *Lip* 8B 102
Hillhouse La. *H'ly* 3K 9
Hill Houses 9D 108
Hillhouses La. *Cher* 9D 108
Hillier Way. *Win* 4L 105
Hill La. *Brans* 7C 220
Hill La. *Christ* 4A 230
Hill La. *Col C* 3K 133
Hill La. *E Har* 9H 147
Hill La. *Sotn* 1A 4
Hillman Rd. *Poole* 9B 226
Hillmead Gdns. *Hav* 7B 202
Hill Mdw. *Over* 9D 38
Hill Park 6N 197
Hill Pk. Rd. *Fare* 5N 197
Hill Pk. Rd. *Gos* 1H 239
Hill Pl. *Burs* 1M 195
Hillpound 7E 164
Hill Ri. *Meon* 8N 135
Hill Ri. *Twy* 7L 127
Hill Rd. *Bar S* 7N 71
Hill Rd. *Fare* 8M 199
Hill Rd. *F'ham* 3E 64
Hill Rd. *Gray* 4L 103
Hill Rd. *Hind* 1L 103
Hill Rd. *Hurn* 1D 218
Hill Rd. *Okly* 1C 58
Hillsborough Ct. *Farn* 4G 29
Hill Side 9N 45
Hillside. *Abb A* 5F 68
Hillside. *Baug* 9D 10
Hillside. *Cam* 6H 19
Hillside. *Curd* 2J 177
Hillside. *Whitc* 5J 55
Hillside. *Win* 1F 104
Hillside Av. *Roms* 5N 129
Hillside Av. *Sotn* 1C 174
Hillside Av. *Water* 7J 201
Hillside Clo. *Alt* 3F 80
Hillside Clo. *Chan F* 6B 132
Hillside Clo. *Crook V* 5H 47
Hillside Clo. *Head D* 1C 102
Hillside Clo. *Water* 8C 168
Hillside Clo. *W Dean* 2J 121
Hillside Clo. *Win* 4G 105
Hillside Cres. *Frim* 5N 29
Hillside Cres. *Ports* 8A 200
Hillside Dri. *Christ* 2G 228
Hillside Ind. Est. *Horn* 2C 182
Hillside La. *F'ham* 2F 64
Hillside Rd. *A'sht* 2H 65
Hillside Rd. *F'ham* 3G 65
Hillside Rd. *Hasl* 1N 117
Hillside Rd. *L'ton* 3C 234
Hillside Rd. *Odi* 1F 62
Hillside Rd. *Poole* 5D 226
Hillside Rd. *Win* 5G 104
Hillside Vs. *Charl* 8L 51
Hillsley Rd. *Ports* 7A 200
Hillson Dri. *Fare* 6M 197
Hillson Ho. *Fare* 6N 197
Hillsons Rd. *Bot* 3E 176
Hill Sq. *Lych* 2H 43
Hillstead Ct. *Bas* 7C 42
Hillstreet 6J 157
Hill St. *Cal* 5J 157
Hill Ter. *Alr* 9F 94
Hill Ter. *Eastl* 7N 133
Hill Top 5H 207
Hilltop. *Win* 1G 104
Hill Top Av. *Tidw* 6C 30
Hilltop Cres. *Ports* 7K 201
Hilltop Dri. *Sotn* 6H 175
Hilltop Gdns. *Horn* 8D 168
Hilltop Rd. *Beau* 5G 206
Hilltop Rd. *Over* 9E 38
Hilltop Rd. *S'wick* 7B 200
Hilltop Vw. *Yate* 8L 17
Hill Vw. *E Meon* 3L 143
Hill Vw. *E'std* 8N 147
Hillview. *Water* 5C 182
Hill Vw. Cvn Pk. *F Oak* 7M 133
Hill Vw. Rd. *Bas* 8N 41
Hillview Rd. *Bourn* 2H 227
Hill Vw. Rd. *Brfld* 7B 124
Hill Vw. Rd. *Fare* 8L 199
Hill Vw. Rd. *F'ham* 8B 64
Hillview Rd. *Hythe* 6L 193
Hill Vw. Rd. *Michm* 5H 123
Hill Wlk. *Fare* 6N 197
Hill Way. *Ashy H* 3C 186
Hillway, The. *Chan F* 5B 132
Hillway, The. *Fare* 9L 199
Hilly Clo. *Ows* 5C 134
Hillyfields 7C 158
Hillyfields. *Nurs* 7C 158
Hilsea 5F 214
Hilsea Cres. *Ports* 3F 214
Hilsea Mkt. *Ports* 3F 214
Hiltingbury 3A 132
Hiltingbury Clo. *Chan F* 3B 132
Hiltingbury Ct. *Chan F* 3N 131
Hiltingbury Rd. *Chan F* 3N 131
Hiltingbury Rd. *Hav* 4G 203
Hiltom Rd. *Ring* 1L 187
Hilton Rd. *Gos* 4L 239
Hilton Rd. *H End* 3N 175
Hilton Rd. *New M* 2C 232
Hindell Clo. *Farn* 4J 29
Hindhead 3N 103
Hindhead Rd. *Hasl* 8N 103
Hinkler Ct. *Sotn* 6H 175
Hinkler Rd. *Sotn* 4J 175
Hinstock Clo. *Farn* 9J 29
Hinton 3H 231
Hinton Ampner 1L 135
Hinton Ampner House & Gardens 1L 135
Hinton Clo. *Hav* 5C 202
Hinton Clo. *T'ley* 6H 11
Hinton Cres. *Sotn* 5J 175
Hinton Fields. *King W* 9N 91
Hinton Hill. *Hint A* 1L 135
Hinton La. *Tichb* 5E 108
Hinton Mnr. La. *Love & Clan* 2N 181
Hinton Mnr. Rd. *Water* 6A 168
Hinton Rd. *Bourn* 2K 245 (6M 247)
Hinton Wood. *Bourn* 3L 245 (8N 247)
Hinton Wood Av. *Christ* 4G 231
Hinton Wood La. *Hint* 4G 230
Hinwood Clo. *Bro'tn* 1A 86
Hipley 6N 179
Hipley Rd. *Hav* 6G 202
Hippenscombe 8B 6
Hipple La. *A'wrth* 7M 7
Hirst Copse. *St M* 9M 35
Hirst Rd. *Hythe* 6N 193
Hispano Av. *White* 2F 196
Hitches La. *Crook V & Fle* 5H 47
Hitherwood Clo. *Water* 9B 182
Hive Gdns. *Poole* 7B 244
Hives Way. *L'ton* 9D 224
H. Jones Cres. *A'sht* 8L 49
H.M.S. Alliance 4N 239
H.M.S. Daedalus Cvn. Pk. *Gos* 2E 238
H.M. Submarine Holland 1. 4N 239
H.M.S. Victory 1A 240 (2H 5)
H.M.S. Warrior 2A 240 (4H 5)
Hoadlands. *Ptsfld* 9N 139
Hoads Hill. *Wick* 8C 178
Hobart Dri. *Hythe* 6M 193
Hobart Rd. *New M* 4A 232
Hobb La. *H End* 5A 176
Hobbs Clo. *Bish S* 2L 109
Hobbs Pk. *St L* 4C 186
Hobbs Pas. *Gos* 3N 239
Hobbs Rd. *Poole* 6A 226
Hobbs Sq. And 8B 52 *(off Cricketers Way)*
Hobby Clo. *Ports* 4H 215
Hobley La. *Wool H* 2N 7
Hobson Way. *Holb* 5B 208
Hoburne Cvn. Pk. *Christ* 6E 230
Hoburne Gdns. *Christ* 5E 230
Hoburne La. *Christ* 5E 230
Hockford La. *Brim C* 1N 9
Hockham Ct. *Hav* 2C 202
Hockley Clo. *Ports* 9E 200
Hockley Cotts. *Cher* 1H 135
Hockley Golf Course 3L 127
Hockley Link. *Comp* 3J 127
Hockley Path. *Ports* 9F 200
Hocombe 2N 131
Hocombe Dri. *Chan F* 2N 131
Hocombe Pk. Clo. *Chan F* 2N 131
Hocombe Rd. *Chan F* 2N 131
Hocombe Wood Rd. *Chan F* 2M 131
Hodder Clo. *Chan F* 7N 131
Hodges Clo. *Hav* 6G 202
Hoe 3B 164
Hoeford Clo. *Fare* 2D 212
Hoe Gate 3N 179
Hoe La. *N Bad* 1A 158
Hoe Rd. *Bish W* 3N 163
Hoe St. *Hmbdn* 4A 180
Hoe, The. *Gos* 7G 212
Hogarth Clo. *Bas* 7F 42
Hogarth Clo. *Coll T* 7G 19
Hogarth Clo. *Roms* 3A 130
Hogarth Clo. *Sotn* 8G 174
Hogarth Ct. *And* 8M 51
Hoggarth Clo. *Ptsfld* 9N 139
Hog Hatch 4C 64
Hoghatch La. *F'ham* 4C 64
Hogmoor Rd. *W'hill* 6G 100
Hog's Back. *Seale* 6M 65
Hog's Back Brewery 5N 65
Hogs Lodge La. *Clan* 9D 144
Hogue Av. *Bourn* 1H 227
Hogwood La. *W End* 5J 161
Holbeach Clo. *Ports* 8F 200
Holbeche Clo. *Yate* 8K 17
Holbein Clo. *Bas* 8E 42
Holborne Clo. *N'bry* 1C 8
Holbrook Clo. *F'ham* 2H 65
Holbrook Recreation Cen. 7G 212
Holbrook Rd. *Fare* 9D 198
Holbrook Rd. *Ports* 1E 240
Holbrook Way. *A'sht* 3K 65
Holbury 4B 208
Holbury Clo. *Bourn* 3B 228
Holbury Ct. *Hav* 4H 203
Holbury Drove. *Holb* 5N 207
Holbury La. *E Dean & Lcky* 1M 121
Holcot La. *Ports* 4K 215
Holcroft Ho. *Sotn* 4J 175
Holcroft Rd. *Sotn* 5J 175
Holdaway Clo. *King W* 8N 91
Holdenby Ct. *Ports* 3K 215
Holdenhurst 3D 228
Holdenhurst Av. *Bourn* 8F 228
Holdenhurst Clo. *Water* 1C 182
Holdenhurst Rd. *Bourn* 2M 245 (Landsdowne Cres.)
Holdenhurst Rd. *Bourn* 3C 228 (Throop Rd.)
Holden La. *Cher* 2H 135
Holder Rd. *A'sht* 1N 65
Hole La. *Bent* 7K 63
Hole La. *Curd* 1J 177
Hole La. *Hmbdn* 2A 180
Holes Clo. *Hord* 2G 232
Holfleet 1N 229
Holiday Hills Reptillery 3L 189
Holkham Clo. *Sotn* 8D 158
Hollam Clo. *Fare* 9L 197
Hollam Cres. *Fare* 9L 197
Hollam Dri. *Fare* 9L 197
Hollam Rd. *S'sea* 2J 241
Holland Clo. *Chan F* 9A 132
Holland Clo. *F'ham* 9G 64
Holland Dri. *And* 7M 51
Holland Gdns. *Fle* 3M 47
Holland Pk. *Sar G* 6C 196
Holland Pl. *Gos* 6F 212
Holland Pl. *Sotn* 1G 172
Holland Rd. *Sotn* 8B 174
Holland Rd. *S'sea* 3F 240
Holland Rd. *Tot* 3J 171
Hollands Clo. *Win* 1F 104
Hollands Wood Dri. *New M* 1B 232
Hollenden. *Poole* 1E 244
Hollies Clo. *Sway* 6J 223
Hollies, The. *B'wtr* 3J 29
Hollies, The. *N'bry* 1C 8
Hollies, The. *W Wel* 1B 120
Hollingbourne Clo. *Sotn* 2B 174
Hollington 4N 7
Hollington Cross 6N 7
Hollington La. *High* 4N 7
Hollin's Wlk. *Bas* 6C 42
Hollist La. *E Har* 8J 147
Hollman Dri. *Roms* 4K 129
Holloway Av. *Bourn* 1D 226
Hollow La. *Hay I* 4F 242
Hollow La. *Head* 1A 102
Hollowshot La. *K're* 3A 6
Hollow, The. *Bro'tn* 5B 88
Hollow, The. *Ews* 2M 63
Hollow Way. *Gray* 3L 103
Holly Acre. *Yate* 8N 17
Hollybank. *Lee S* 2B 238
Hollybank Clo. *Hythe* 6M 193
Hollybank Clo. *Water* 5C 182
Hollybank Cres. *Hythe* 5L 193
Hollybank La. *Ems* 5M 203
Hollybank Rd. *Hythe* 5L 193
Hollybrook Av. *Sotn* 8H 159
Hollybrook Clo. *Sotn* 9G 159
Hollybrook Gdns. *L Hth* 4D 196
Hollybrook Pk. *Bord* 4K 101
Hollybrook Rd. *Sotn* 9H 159
Hollybush Ind. Est. *A'sht* 6N 49
Hollybush La. *A'sht* 6N 49
Hollybush La. *Baug* 2F 20
Hollybush La. *E'sly* 5H 17
Hollybush Ride. *Finch* 1M 17 (in two parts)
Holly Clo. *A'sht* 9L 49
Holly Clo. *Braml* 2H 23
Holly Clo. *E'sly* 6H 17
Holly Clo. *Farn* 8J 29
Holly Clo. *Head* 2E 102
Holly Clo. *Hythe* 1M 207
Holly Clo. *St L* 4A 186
Holly Clo. *Sar G* 6B 196
Hollycombe Clo. *Lip* 4E 116
Hollycombe Gardens 7G 116
Hollycombe Quarry Railway 7G 117
Hollycombe Steam Collection 6G 116
Holly Ct. *Bourn* 2H 245
Holly Ct. *C'then* 1A 18
Holly Cross 8G 13
Holly Dell. *Sotn* 6K 159
Holly Dri. *Old B* 5K 43
Holly Dri. *Water* 3A 202
Hollyfields Clo. *Cam* 8K 19
Holly Gdns. *Burt* 5N 229
Holly Gdns. *Mil S* 7J 235
Holly Gdns. *W End* 8H 161
Holly Grn. Ri. *Bourn* 2C 226
Holly Gro. *Fare* 5A 198
Holly Hatch Rd. *Tot* 4L 171
Holly Hedge Clo. *Frim* 2N 29
Holly Hedge Rd. *Frim* 2N 29
Holly Hill. *Sotn* 6K 159
Holly Hill Clo. *Sotn* 6K 159
Holly Hill La. *Sar G* 5N 195
Holly Hill Mans. *L Hth* 5B 196
Holly Hill Woodland Pk. 5A 196
Hollyhock Clo. *Bas* 2J 59
Holly La. *New M* 2D 232
Holly La. *Pill* 6H 225
Holly La. *Sil* 5A 12
Holly La. *Walk* 4L 231
Holly Lodge. *Chan F* 9A 132
Holly Lodge. *Poole* 1E 244
Holly Lodge. *Sotn* 1N 173
Holly M. *Sotn* 7L 159
Holly Oak Ct. *Sotn* 7F 158
Holly Oak Rd. *Sotn* 8F 158 (in two parts)
Holly Rd. *A'sht* 9L 49
Holly Rd. *Asht* 8H 171
Holly Rd. *Black* 8C 208
Holly Rd. *Farn* 8H 29
Holly St. *Gos* 3L 239
Hollytree Gdns. *Frim* 4M 29
Hollytrees. *Chu C* 5K 47
Holly Wlk. *And* 3K 69
Holly Wlk. *Mid W* 4B 72
Hollywater Rd. *Bord & Pass* 6L 101
Holly Way. *B'wtr* 9F 18
Hollywell Dri. *Port S* 1C 214
Hollywood Clo. *N Bad* 8E 130
Hollywood La. *L'ton* 1D 234
Holman Clo. *Water* 8A 182
Holmbrook Clo. *Farn* 8E 28
Holmbrook Gdns. *Farn* 8E 28

Holmbush Ct.—Hurstbourne Av.

Holmbush Ct. S'sea 4D 240
Holm Clo. Ring 8M 185
Holmdale Rd. Gos 9H 213
Holmefield Av. Fare 2B 212
Holme Rd. Highc 6K 231
Holmes Clo. Bas 4L 59
Holmes Clo. Net A 3F 194
Holmes Ct. And 2L 69
Holmesland Dri. Bot 3C 176
Holmesland La. Bot 3C 176
Holmesland Wlk. Bot 3C 176
Holmfield Av. Bourn 7F 228
Holmgrove. Fare 6F 196
Holm Hill La. Christ 8K 221
Holmhurst Av. Highc 5G 231
Holm Oak Clo. Win 1E 104
Holmsley Clo. Penn 4B 234
Holmsley Clo. Sotn 3G 175
Holmsley Ct. Tot 2H 171
Holmsley Rd. New M 4M 221
Holmwood Gth. Hight 2N 187
Holne Ct. S'sea 4K 241
Holst Clo. Bas 3N 59
Holst Way. Water 4M 201
Holt Clo. Farn 5L 29
Holt Clo. Wick 6B 178
Holt Cotts. Ash H 3N 9
Holt Ct. Sotn 1C 194
Holt Down. Ptsfld 1A 146
Holt End La. Bentw 8K 79
Holt Gdns. Row C 7H 183
Holtham La. Selb 2G 113
Holt La. Hook 4J 45
Holt La. Tang 5H 33
Holt La. Wolv 5N 9
Holt Pound 8N 63
Holt Pound La. Holt P 7N 63
Holt Rd. Poole 8D 226
Holt Rd. Sotn 3L 173 (1B 4)
Holt Vw. Eastl 1K 161
Holt Way. Hook 1J 45
Holtwood 1M 7
Holworth Clo. Bourn 3C 226
Holy Barn Clo. Bas 1J 59
Holyborne Rd. Roms 5A 130
Holybourne 1K 81
Holybourne Rd. Hav 6F 202
Holyrood Av. Sotn 9N 159
Holyrood Clo. Water 2A 202
Holyrood Ct. Bas 8K 41
Holyrood Ho. Sotn 7M 173 (7D 4)
Holyrood Pl. Sotn 7M 173 (7D 4)
Holywell Clo. Farn 5J 29
Holywell Rd. Swanm 1F 178
Homeborough Ho. Hythe 4M 193
Homebridge Ho. F'bri 9J 151
Homedale Ho. Bourn 9K 227
Home Farm Bus. Pk. Lcky 9N 87
Home Farm Clo. Farn 6M 29
Home Farm Clo. Hythe 6N 193
Home Farm Gdns. Charl 7K 51
Home Farm Rd. Elve 5G 26
Homefayre Ho. Fare 8D 198
Homefield. Roms 3N 129
Home Fld. Dri. Nurs 6B 158
Homefield Ho. New M 4B 232
Homefield Path. Ports 1K 215
Homefield Rd. Ports 1K 215
Homefield Way. Bas 2L 41
Homefield Way. Water 5B 168
Homeforde Ho. Broc 7D 148
Homefort Ho. Gos 3K 239 (off Stoke Rd.)
Homegrove Ho. S'sea 4E 240
Homeheights. S'sea 5D 240 (9N 5)
Homelands Est. Christ 8J 229
Home La. Spar 3A 104
Homelea Clo. Farn 4K 29
Homeleigh Ho. Bourn 9L 227
Home Mead. N Wal 9B 58
Home Mead. Water 7G 180
Homemead Ho. Roms 6L 129
Homeoaks Ho. Bourn 9K 227
Homepark Ho. F'ham 8E 64
Home Pk. Rd. Yate 7N 17
Homepoint Ho. Sotn 3E 174
Homer Clo. Gos 8D 212
Homer Clo. Water 8M 181
Homer Farm La. Black 1J 237
Homerise Ho. Win 6M 237
Home Rd. Bourn 1F 226
Homerose Ho. S'sea 3D 240
Home Rule Rd. L Hth 5E 196
Homeryde Ho. Lee S 2A 238
Homesea Ho. S'sea 4D 240 (6N 5)
Homeside Rd. Bourn 4L 227
Homespinney Ho. Sotn 9B 160
Homestead Rd. Meds 2E 96
Homesteads Rd. Bas 1J 59
Home Way. Ptsfld 1B 146
Homewell. Hav 8F 202
Homewood Clo. New M 3D 232
Homington Rd. Coom B 2G 119
Homington Rd. Hom 4J 119
Hone Hill. S'hrst 5D 18
Hones Yd. Bus. Pk. F'ham 8F 64
Honeybottom Rd. T'ley 4H 11
Honeybourne Cres. Bourn 1K 247
Honeycritch La. Frox 2H 139
Honey La. Burl 8D 188
Honey La. Cher 1H 135
Honey La. Fare 4N 197
Honey La. Selb 8M 99
Honeyman La. Ows 4D 134
Honeysuckle Clo. Bas 2J 59
Honeysuckle Clo. Gos 5D 212
Honeysuckle Clo. L Hth 4D 196
Honeysuckle Clo. Win 1H 127
Honeysuckle Clo. Yate 7K 17
Honeysuckle Cotts. Sotn 7A 160
Honeysuckle Ct. Water 4N 201
Honeysuckle La. Head D 2D 102
Honeysuckle Rd. Sotn 7M 159
Honeysuckle Way. Chan F 6M 131
Honeysuckle Way. Christ 6D 230
Honeywood Clo. Ports 4G 215
Honeywood Clo. Tot 1K 171
Honister Clo. Sotn 2D 172
Honister Gdns. Fle 1A 48
Hood Clo. And 1C 70
Hood Clo. Bourn 5F 226
Hood Clo. L Hth 5E 196
Hood Cres. Bourn 5F 226
Hood Rd. Sotn 2E 174
Hook 2H 45 (Hook)
Hook 1C 210 (Southampton)
Hook Bird Sanctuary 1M 209
Hook Clo. Amp 2M 131
Hook Common 4F 44
Hook Cres. Amp 2M 131
Hook La. Baug 7B 10
Hook La. Monx 6B 68
Hook La. Okly & Up Wn 5A 40
Hook La. Ropl 2A 110
Hook La. Wars & Fare 1D 210
Hook Park 2N 209
Hook Pk. Rd. Wars 1N 209
Hookpit Farm La. King W 7M 91
Hook Rd. Amp 1K 131
Hook Rd. Grey 7F 44
Hook Rd. Hook 4G 45
Hook Rd. K're 2C 6
Hook Rd. N War 6J 45
Hook Rd. Roth 7F 24
Hook's Farm Way. Hav 6D 202
Hook's La. Hav 6C 202 (in two parts)
Hookstile La. F'ham 9E 64
Hook Water Clo. Chan F 2N 131
Hook Water Rd. Chan F 2M 131
Hookwood La. Amp 2L 131
Hookwood La. Up Ch 4A 32
Hoopersmead. Clid 3B 60
Hoopers Way. Okly 1D 58
Hope Grant's Rd. A'sht 7J 49 (in two parts)
Hope La. F'ham 4D 64
Hopeman Clo. Coll T 5F 18
Hope Rd. W End 9J 161
Hope St. Ports 1D 240 (1N 5)
Hopeswood. Gthm 3F 114
Hope Way. A'sht 8H 49
Hopfield Clo. Water 2M 201
Hopfield M. Water 3M 201
Hopfield Rd. H Win 7B 26
Hop Garden. Chu C 7K 47
Hop Garden Rd. Hook 2F 44
Hop Gdns. W'ish 5H 121
Hop Garden, The. S Hart 9G 146
Hopkins Clo. Bourn 4D 228
Hopkins Clo. Ports 9N 199
Hopkins Ct. S'sea 5J 241
Hopkinson Way. And 9H 51
Hopton Gth. Lych 2H 43
Horace Rd. Bourn 1B 246
Hordle 2G 233
Hordle La. Hord 6G 233
Hordle Rd. Hav 5B 202
Horlock Rd. Broc 6D 148
Hormer Clo. Owl 4F 18
Hornbeam Clo. Farn 7E 28
Hornbeam Clo. H End 4A 176
Hornbeam Clo. Owl 4F 18
Hornbeam Clo. S Won 3J 91
Hornbeam Gdns. W End 8H 161
Hornbeam Pl. Hook 1H 45
Hornbeam Rd. Chan F 6K 131
Hornbeam Rd. Hav 6H 203
Hornby Clo. Wars 9A 196
Hornchurch Rd. Sotn 7E 158
Horndean 4C 182
Horndean Cvn. Site. Horn 1C 182
Horndean Ho. Ports 1E 240
Horndean Precinct. Horn 3D 182
Horndean Rd. Ems 4K 203
Horne Rd. Bulf 3B 66
Hornes Fld. Ct. Chu C 7K 47 (off Brandon Rd.)
Hornet Clo. Fare 7N 197
Hornet Clo. Gos 4L 239
Hornetide Ho. Lee S 2A 238
Hornet Rd. Ems 5N 217
Hornet Rd. Fare 3B 212
Horning Rd. Poole 9D 226
Horn Rd. Farn 7G 29
Horns Drove. Rown 6C 158
Horns Hill. Sob 9K 165
Horns Hill. Sotn 5C 158
Horris Hill 1D 8
Horsa Clo. Bourn 1H 247
Horsa Ct. Bourn 1H 247
Horsa Rd. Bourn 1H 247
Horsea La. Ports 4E 214
Horsea Rd. Ports 4F 214
Horsebridge 7E 88
Horsebridge Rd. Bro'tn 2B 86
Horsebridge Rd. Houtn & King S 6D 88
Horsebridge Way. Rown 6D 158
Horsecroft. Roms 4M 129
Horsefair Ct. Roms 5L 129
Horsefair M. Roms 5L 129
Horsefair, The. Roms 5L 129
Horse La. Ropl 7E 96
Horseport 1K 153
Horsepost La. Hmbdn 8H 167
Horse Sands Clo. S'sea 4L 241
Horseshoe Bend. Gray 4J 103
Horseshoe Bri. Sotn 2N 173
Horseshoe Clo. Fare 7G 196
Horseshoe Comn. Roundabout. Bourn 6M 247
Horseshoe Ct. Bourn 1K 245 (5M 247)
Horseshoe Cres. Bord 4K 101
Horseshoe Dri. Roms 2A 130
Horseshoe La. Ibt 3C 34
Horseshoe Lodge. Wars 8B 196
Horseshoe, The. Poole 9A 244
Horsham Av. Bourn 1G 227
Horsham Rd. Owl 4F 18
Horshells Drove. Ovr W 8B 67
Horton Clo. Bourn 3N 227
Horton Heath 4A 162
Horton Rd. Ashy H 2A 186
Horton Rd. Gos 4E 212
Horton Rd. Wood 9H 149
Horton Way. Eastl 1K 161
Horwood Gdns. Bas 9A 42
Hosker Rd. Bourn 9E 228
Hosketts La. Neth W 1N 87
Hoskins Ho. Ports 2L 5
Hospital Hill. A'sht 8J 49
Hospital La. Fare 2N 213
Hospital of St Cross, The. 1K 127
Hospital Rd. A'sht 8J 49
Hospital Rd. Shir H 1C 178
Hostel Rd. Farn 3K 49
Hotspur Clo. Hythe 4L 193
Houchin St. Bish W 4M 163
Houghton 5E 88
Houghton Clo. Hav 3H 203
Houghton Drayton 6E 88
Houghton Lodge & Gardens. 4E 88
Hound 3J 195
Hound Clo. Net A 4H 195
Hound Green 1H 25
Hound Grn. Clo. Hnd G 1H 25
Houndmills 5N 41
Houndmills Rd. Bas 5N 41
Houndmills Roundabout. Bas 4A 42
Hound Rd. Net A 4G 195
Hound Rd. Gdns. Net A 3H 195
Hound Way. Net A 3G 195
Houndwell Pl. Sotn 6M 173 (6E 4)
Hounsdown 6M 171
Hounsdown Av. Tot 5M 171
Hounsdown Clo. Tot 5M 171
Ho. Farm Rd. Gos 3G 238
Houseman Rd. Farn 6H 29
Houseplat Ct. Chu C 7K 47 (off Annettes Cft.)
Hove Ct. Lee S 1A 238
Hoveton Gro. Chan F 4N 131
Howard Clo. Burl 7E 188 (off Ringwood Rd.)
Howard Clo. Chan F 8B 132
Howard Clo. Christ 8B 230
Howard Clo. F Oak 1N 161
Howard Clo. Fle 2A 48
Howard Clo. Sotn 7C 160
Howard Cole Way. A'sht 9G 49
Howard Dri. Farn 8D 28
Howard Lodge. S'sea 5D 240
Howard Oliver Ho. Hythe 6N 193
Howard Rd. Bas 8D 42
Howard Rd. Bourn 7N 227
Howard Rd. Ports 4F 214
Howard Rd. Sotn 4J 173
Howard's Gro. Sotn 2H 173
Howards La. Holyb 10D 62
Howards Mead. Penn 4B 234
Howard Vw. Bas 8M 41
Howe Clo. Christ 9B 230
Howe Clo. New M 3A 232
Howe Rd. Gos 1E 238
Howerts Clo. Wars 1A 210
Howes Gdns. Chu C 5K 47
Howeth Clo. Bourn 3H 227
Howe, The. Farn 2C 48
Howeth Rd. Bourn 4G 227
Howgare Rd. Bro Ch 4A 118
Howlett Clo. L'ton 2C 234
Howton Clo. Bourn 1G 227
Howton Rd. Bourn 1G 227
Hoxley Rd. Bourn 2H 227
Hoylake Clo. Gos 7E 212
Hoylake Rd. Ports 8K 201
Hoyle Clo. Uphm 9D 134
Hoylecroft Clo. Fare 6A 198
Hubbard Rd. Bas 4A 42
Hubert Hamilton Rd. Bulf B 3B 66
Hubert Rd. Win 1J 127
Huckers La. Selb 7L 99
Huckswood La. Ids 7L 169
Huddington Glade. Yate 8K 17
Hudson Clo. Gos 1E 238
Hudson Clo. Poole 4A 226
Hudson Clo. Ring 9M 185
Hudson Ct. Tot 4K 171
Hudson Davies Clo. Pill 6F 224
Hudson Rd. S'sea 3E 240
Hudsons Mdw. Hnd G 1H 25
Hughes Clo. Black 7C 208
Hughs Bus. Cen. Christ 7C 230
Hugo Platt. Rog 9K 141
Huish La. Old B 7J 43
Hulbert Rd. Water & Hav 1M 201 (in three parts)
Hulbert Way. Bas 9L 41
Hulfords La. H Win 3C 26
Hullam La. Newt V 9G 99
Hull Cres. Bourn 2B 226
Hulles Way. N Bad 8E 130
Hull Rd. Bourn 2B 226
Hull Way. Bourn 2B 226
Hulse Lodge. Sotn 2L 173
Hulse Rd. Sotn 2L 173
Hulton Clo. Sotn 9B 174
Humber Clo. Fare 5L 211
Humber Clo. S'hrst 5F 18
Humber Gdns. Burs 9L 175
Humber La. Tidw 8F 30
Humberstone Rd. And 3N 69
Humbers Vw. King S 7G 88
Humber Way. S'hrst 5F 18
Humbly Grove 6B 62
Hummicks, The. Beau 8H 207
Humphrey Pk. Chu C 8L 47 (in two parts)
Humphrey's Bri. Christ 7E 230
Hundred Acre Roundabout. And 1J 69
Hundred Acres 6H 179
Hundred Acres Rd. Wick 8G 178
Hundred La. P'mre 8F 224
Hundred, The. F'bri 1J 153
Hundred, The. Roms 5L 129
Hundred, The. Water 9L 181
Hungerfield Clo. Brans 6C 220
Hungerford 5N 153
Hungerford. Burs 2K 195
Hungerford Clo. S'hrst 5E 18
Hungerford Hill. Hun 5N 153
Hungerford La. C'hlt 9C 6
Hungerford La. Hath & Char D 9K 33
Hungerford La. Tang 4G 32
Hungerford Rd. Bourn 3A 228
Hungerford Rd. E Graf 4D 6
Hunnels Clo. Chu C 8K 47
Hunt Av. Net A 3G 194
Hunt Clo. S Won 3J 91
Hunter Clo. Christ 7C 230
Hunter Clo. Gos 9F 212
Hunter Clo. Holb 2N 207
Hunter Ct. Sotn 1G 172
Hunter Rd. Ems 5N 217
Hunter Rd. Farn 9H 29
Hunter Rd. Ports 8G 200
Hunter Rd. S'sea 4G 241
Hunters Chase. Lip 1D 116
Hunters Chase. Swanm 8E 164
Hunters Clo. Okly 8D 40
Hunters Clo. Ver 4A 184
Hunters Ct. Burs 6M 175
Hunters Cres. Roms 2B 130
Hunters Cres. Tot 4H 171
Hunters Hill. Tot 7K 171
Hunters Lodge. Fare 8L 197
Hunters Ride. Water 3M 201
Hunter's Ride. Win 9K 125
Hunters Rd. Lngmr 4J 115
Hunters Way. Eastl 1L 161
Huntfield Rd. Bourn 3M 227
Huntingdon Clo. Fare 8F 196
Huntingdon Clo. Tot 1L 171
Huntingdon Gdns. Christ 4J 229
Huntingdon Gdns. H Hth 5A 162
Huntingford Clo. Hind 9L 85
Hunting Ga. And 1J 69
Huntley Clo. Ports 8C 200
Huntly Rd. Bourn 8H 227
Huntly Way. Sotn 3D 174
Hunton 7F 76
Hunton Clo. Sotn 8J 159
Hunton Down La. Sut S 7F 76
Hunton La. Sut S 7E 76
Hunt Rd. Christ 6A 230
Huntsbottom La. Liss & Hill B 1F 140
Hunts Clo. Hook 2J 45
Hunts Comn. H Win 5C 26
Hunts Cotts. H Win 5C 26
Hunts La. Cam 1K 29
Hunt's La. E Chol 3A 68
Huntsman Clo. Water 5N 181
Huntsman's M. Myt 9N 29
Huntsmead. Alt 5G 81
Huntsmoor Rd. T'ley 5F 10
Hunts Pond Rd. Park G & Fare 4E 196
Huntvale Rd. Bourn 3M 227
Hurdcott 4A 86
Hurdcott La. Wint E 4A 86
Hurdles Mead. L'ton 2F 234 (off Gosport St.)
Hurdles Mead. Mil S 9K 235
Hurdles, The. Christ 6H 229
Hurdles, The. Fare 7G 196
Hurdle Way. Comp 5G 126
Hurland La. Head 3B 102
Hurlands Bus. Cen. F'ham 6H 65
Hurlands Clo. F'ham 6H 65
Hurlands Pl. F'ham 6J 65
Hurley Clo. Ame 5A 66
Hurlingham Gdns. Sotn 6M 159
Hurn 8E 218
Hurn Bridge Sports Club. 8E 218
Hurn Clo. Ring 2G 186
Hurn Ct. Hav 3H 203
Hurn Ct. La. Hurn 9C 218
Hurne Ct. Bas 6E 42 (off Lytton Rd.)
Hurn La. Ring 2G 187
Hurn Rd. Christ 2G 228
Hurn Rd. Ring 2G 186
Hurn Way. Christ 5G 229
Huron Dri. Lip 3E 116
Hurricane Dri. Rown 5D 158
Hursley 6N 125
Hursley Clo. Bourn 6F 228
Hursley Ct. Chan F 3N 131
Hursley Dri. Black 9C 208
Hursley Rd. Chan F 1N 131
Hursley Rd. Hav 4D 202
Hurstbourne Av. Christ 5G 231

Hurstbourne Clo. Hav. 3D 202
Hurstbourne Pl. Sotn 1D 194
Hurstbourne Priors. 8B 54
Hurstbourne Tarrant. 4D 34
Hurst Clo. Chan F 8M 131
Hurst Clo. Fare 7K 211
Hurst Clo. Lip 1C 116
Hurst Clo. Tot 2M 171
Hurst Clo. Walk. 4L 231
Hurst Ct. Mil S 8J 235
Hurstdene Rd. Bourn 4N 227
Hurst Grn. Gos 6D 212
Hurst Grn. Clo. Sotn 9E 174
Hurst Grn. Clo. Water. 8B 182
Hurst Hill. Poole 5A 244
Hurst La. Ows. 8C 134
Hurst La. Priv 2A 138
Hurstly La. Bold 3B 224
Hurstmere Clo. Gray 4M 103
Hurst Rd. A'sht 7L 49
Hurst Rd. Farn 4K 29
Hurst Rd. Mil S. 9K 235
Hurst Rd. Ring 8K 185
Hurst, The. W'fld 2E 46
Hurstville Dri. Water. 3N 201
(in two parts)
Hussar Clo. Christ. 7J 229
Hussar Ct. A'sht 9G 48
Hussar Ct. Water 9K 181
Hussell La. Meds 9K 79
Hussey Clo. Win 4L 105
Husseys La. Lwr Fr 7H 63
(in two parts)
Hutfield Ct. Gos 2K 239
(off Lees La.)
Hutton Sq. And. 8B 52
Hutwood Rd. Chilw 3M 159
Huxley Clo. L Hth 7F 196
Huxley Ct. Dib P. 7H 193
Hyacinth Clo. Bas 2J 59
Hyde. 4M 153
Hyde Abbey Rd. Win
. . . . 6L 105 (6M 237)
Hyde Church La. Win 5L 105
Hyde Church Path. Win . . . 5L 105
(off Hyde St.)
Hyde Clo. Sotn 1H 173
Hyde Clo. Sway. 5J 223
Hyde Clo. Tot 3H 171
Hyde Clo. Win. 5K 105
Hyde End. 1N 9
Hyde End La. Brim. 1M 9
Hyde Ga. Win 5L 105
Hyde Ho. Gdns. Win 5L 105
Hyde La. Cron. 2K 63
Hyde La. Churt & Thur 7M 85
Hyde La. Ecc 2H 9
Hyde La. Hyde 5M 153
Hyde Lodge. Win 5K 105
Hyden Farm La. Clan & E Meon
. . . . 5L 167
Hyde Pk. Ho. S'sea. 3D 240
Hyde Pk. Rd. S'sea. 3D 240
Hyde Rd. Bourn 1G 226
Hydes Platt. Sil. 5A 12
Hyde St. S'sea. . . . 4D 240 (7N 5)
Hyde St. Win
. . . . 6L 105 (6M 237)
Hyde, The. New M 2N 231
Hylton Ct. T'ley 5J 11
Hylton Rd. Ptsfld 1M 145
Hymans Way. Tot. 3M 171
Hynesbury Rd. Christ 8E 230
Hyson Cres. Lud. 1F 30
Hyssop Clo. White 2G 196
Hythe. 4M 193
Hythe By-Pass. Dib 4G 192
Hythe Clo. T'ley 6H 11
Hythe Rd. March 1D 192
Hythe Rd. Ports 8F 200

I

Ian Gibson Ct. S'sea. 2E 240
(off Carlisle Rd.)
Ibbertson Clo. Bourn 4C 228
Ibbertson Rd. Bourn. 5C 228
Ibbertson Way. Bourn. 4C 228
Ibbett Rd. Bourn. 4G 226
Ibbotson Way. Tot 5K 171
Ibsen Clo. White 1F 196
Ibsley. 2K 185
Ibsley Clo. Bourn 8N 227
Ibsley Gro. Hav. 6D 202
Ibthorpe. 3C 34
Ibworth La. Hann. 9M 9
Icarus Pl. Water 7N 201
Icknield Way. And. 5A 52
Ida Ct. Sotn 8D 174
Iddesleigh Rd. Bourn
. . . . 8K 227 (5F 4)
Ideal Pk. Homes Cvn. Site. Bram
. . . . 6K 133
Idminston Rd. Port. 1C 86
Idmiston. 9C 66
Idsworth Clo. Horn. 4E 182
Idsworth Ho. Ports 1D 240
(off Crasswell St.)
Idsworth Rd. Cowp. 8B 182
Idsworth Rd. Ports. 8H 215
Iford. 7F 228
Iford Clo. Bourn 8H 229
Iford Ct. Hav. 3H 203
Iford Gdns. Bourn 7F 228
Iford La. Bourn. 7G 228
Iford Roundabout. Bourn
. . . . 7F 228
Ilex Clo. King W. 7M 91
Ilex Clo. P Hth. 4L 11
Ilex Clo. Yate. 7L 17
Ilex Cres. L Hth. 6C 196
Ilex Wlk. Hay I. 4J 243
Iley La. Mil S 9C 234
Ilford Bridge Golf Course.
. . . . 4F 228
Ilford Bri. Home Pk. Bourn
. . . . 7G 229
Ilynton Av. Firs 4E 86
Imadene Clo. Lind. 3L 101
Imadene Cres. Lind. 3L 101
Imber Av. Ame 6A 66
Imber Dri. Highc. 6H 231
Imber Rd. Win 6N 105
Imber Way. Sotn 6G 174
Imbre Ct. Poole 6C 244
Imjin Clo. A'sht 8K 49
Imperial Av. Sotn 2G 173
Imperial Pk. Ind. Est. Sotn
. . . . 3N 173
Imperial Rd. Sotn
. . . . 3N 173 (1G 4)
Imperial Way. W Dock 5H 173
Implacable Rd. Lee S 9N 211
Impstone Rd. P Hth. 4M 11
Imran Ct. A'sht 1L 65
Inchmery La. Exby 2G 236
Ingersley Ri. W End 1J 175
Ingle Dell. Cam 9M 19
Ingledene Clo. Gos 3K 239
Ingledene Clo. Hav. 7D 202
Ingle Glen. Dib P 8M 193
Ingle Grn. Cal 1H 171
Inglegreen Clo. New M. . . . 5A 232
Ingleside. Net A 2G 195
Ingleside Clo. Fare 9L 197
Ingleton Rd. Sotn 1C 172
Inglewood. F Oak 9N 133
Inglewood Av. Bourn 5C 228
Inglewood Dri. Bas. 4K 59
Inglewood Dri. New M 4C 232
Inglis Rd. S'sea 4F 240
Ingoldfield La. Sob & Newt
. . . . 9L 165
Ingram Ct. Sotn 2A 174
Ings Clo. Alt 6F 80
Ingworth Rd. Poole. 9E 226
Inhams La. Water. 6E 180
Inhams Rd. Holyb. 2K 81
Inhams Way. Sil. 5N 11
Inhurst. 5C 10
Inhurst Av. Water 9A 182
Inhurst La. Baug. 4C 10
Inhurst Rd. Ports 6F 214
Inhurst Way. T'ley. 4F 10
Inkerman Rd. Sotn. 7B 174
Inkpen. 1H 7
Inkpen Common Nature Reserve.
. . . . 1J 7
Inkpen Gdns. Lych 3H 43
Inkpen Wlk. Hav. 2D 202
Ink, The. Yate. 6M 17
Inmans La. Ptsfld 8A 140
Innisfail Gdns. A'sht 2H 65
Institute Rd. A'sht
(GU11). 4L 49
Institute Rd. A'sht
(GU12) 1M 65
Instow Gdns. Farn. 5J 29
Intec Bus. Cen. Bas. 3F 42
International Way. Sotn . . . 1C 194
Inveravon. Christ 9B 230
Inverclyde Rd. Poole 1A 244
Invergordon Av. Ports. 1J 215
Inverkip Clo. Lee S 9A 212
Inverleigh Rd. Bourn. 8F 228
Inverness Av. Fare 6A 198
Inverness Rd. Gos 1J 239
Inverness Rd. Poole. 6C 244
Inverness Rd. Ports 9F 214
Inverness Way. Coll T. 6F 18
Invincible Rd. Farn 1J 49
Inwood Rd. Liss 2F 140
Ionic Clo. Chan F 5D 132
Iping Av. Hav 4E 202
Ipley Way. Hythe 7M 193
Ipoh Clo. Mid W. 3A 72
Ipswich Rd. Poole & Bourn
. . . . 1F 244
Ireland Way. Water 4M 201
Iris Clo. Bas 3J 59
Iris Rd. Bourn. 5K 227
Iris Rd. Sotn. 7N 159
Ironbridge Cres. Park G
. . . . 3D 196
Ironbridge La. S'sea 3K 241
Iron Mill Clo. Fare. 6N 197
Ironmill La. Titch 4L 197
Ironside Ct. Sotn 7C 4
Irvine Clo. Fare 6C 198
Irvine Dri. Farn. 4G 28
Irvine Way. Christ. 6A 230
Irving Rd. Bourn. 1F 246
Irving Rd. Sotn 1E 172
Irwell Clo. Bas 6E 42
Irwell Clo. Chan F 7M 131
Irwin Heights. Gos 8J 213
Isaacs Clo. Poole 7F 226
Isambard Brunel Rd. Ports
. . . . 2D 240 (4N 5)
Isbley Drove. Ibly 9K 153
Isington. 9J 63
Isington La. Is'ton. 8J 63
Isington Rd. B'std. 1D 82
Isis Clo. Sotn 2D 172
Isis Way. S'hrst. 5F 18
Island Clo. Hay I 5F 216
Island Farm La. Steep. 5K 139
Island Vw. New M. 7L 231
Island Vw. Av. Christ 8D 230
Island Vw. Clo. Mil S 9L 235
Island Vw. Ct. New M 7A 232
Island Vw. Rd. New M. . . . 7M 231
Island Vw. Ter. Ports 7D 214
Island Vw. Wlk. Fare 8L 199
Islay Gdns. Ports 8G 201
Isle of Wight Model Railways
Exhibition. 5P 237
(off Parade, The)
Itchel La. Cron 2K 63
Itchen. 7B 174
Itchen Av. Eastl. 1K 161
Itchen Bri., The. Sotn 7A 174
Itchen Clo. Okly 1D 58
Itchen Clo. Ptsfld 2L 145
Itchen Clo. W Wel. 1A 120
Itchen Ct. And. 8B 52
Itchen Ct. Win. 8P 237
Itchen Grange. Eastl 9H 133
Itchenor Rd. Hay I 5M 243
Itchen Rd. Hav 3H 203
Itchenside Clo. Sotn. 7D 160
Itchen Valley Country Pk. &
Vis. Cen. 6G 160
Itchen Vw. It Sto 1N 107
Itchen Vw. Sotn 7D 160
Itchin Clo. Tot. 4K 171
Ithica Clo. Hay I 3G 243
Ivamy Pl. Bourn 4D 226
Ivanhoe Rd. Sotn 1J 173
Ivar Gdns. Lych 3H 43
Ively Rd. Farn. 9G 28
(in two parts)
Ives Clo. Yate 6L 17
Ivor Clo. Holb 4A 208
Ivy Clo. St L 4A 186
Ivy Clo. Tot 9L 157
Ivy Clo. Win 9J 105
Ivy Ct. Water. 5L 201
Ivy Dene. Sotn 6H 175
Ivydene Gdns. Water 6A 182
Ivy Down La. Okly 7A 40
Ivyhole Hill. Elve. 5G 26
Ivy Ho. Bourn. 2H 245
Ivy Ho. Gos. 3L 239
Ivyhouse La. Frox. 3D 138
Ivy La. Blash. 6K 185
Ivy La. F'ham 8D 64
Ivy La. Navy. 1B 240 (1J 5)
Ivy La. W End 9F 160
Ivy Orchard. Water. 5B 168
Ivy Rd. A'sht 9M 49
Ivy Rd. Sotn 2A 174
Ivy Ter. H End 4M 175
Iwerne Clo. Bourn 2M 227

J

Jacaranda Clo. Fare. 5H 197
Jacaranda Rd. Bord 4J 101
Jack Clo. Chan F. 6K 131
Jack Cockerill Way. S'sea
. . . . 6E 240
Jackdaw Clo. Bas. 2H 59
Jackdaw Clo. Cowp 6M 181
Jackdaw Ri. Eastl 2B 160
Jackie Wigg Gdns. Tot 3N 171
Jacklyns Clo. Alr. 2E 108
Jacklyns La. Alr 2E 108
Jackman's Clo. Sotn. 7B 174
Jackman's Hill. Ows 3C 134
Jackson Clo. Ports 1K 215
Jackson Gdns. Poole 8A 226
Jackson Rd. Poole 8A 226
Jacobean Clo. Walk 5K 231
Jacob Rd. Coll T 6J 19
Jacob's All. Bas 7C 42
Jacobs Clo. Roms 5N 129
Jacobs Clo. Water 6C 168
Jacob's Gutter La. Tot 5M 171
(in two parts)
Jacob's St. Ports 1D 240
Jacob's Wlk. Tot. 6L 171
Jacob's Yd. Bas 7C 42
Jacomb Pl. Gos. 6F 212
Jacqueline Av. Water 5L 201
Jacqueline Rd. Poole 7A 226
Jade Ct. Gos 1E 238
Jagdalik Rd. Tidw. 8G 30
Jago Rd. Ports 1A 240 (2H 5)
Jamaica Pl. Gos 3L 239
Jamaica Rd. Gos 2M 239
James Butcher Ct. S'sea
. . . . 6E 240
(off Eastern Villas Rd.)
James Callaghan Dri. Fare
. . . . 7A 200
James Clo. Bas. 4D 42
James Clo. Gos. 4E 212
James Clo. Hay I. 3E 242
James Copse Rd. Water. . . 5N 181
James Ct. Roms. 6N 129
James Grieve Av. L Hth . . . 7D 196
James Hockey Gallery. . . . 8D 64
James Howell Ct. Water. . . 6G 181
Jameson Rd. Bourn 5J 227
Jameson Rd. Sotn 7D 174
James Rd. A'sht. 4M 49
James Rd. Cam 2K 29
James Rd. Gos 4E 212
James Rd. Hav. 7E 202
James Rd. Poole. 9E 226
James St. Sotn 6N 173 (5F 4)
James Way. Cam 2K 29
Jamrud Rd. Tidw 9B 30
Janaway Gdns. Sotn. 2B 174
Jane Austen's House. 8D 80
Janes Clo. Black 8C 208
Janred Ct. Bart S 7N 231
Jan Smuts Clo. Lngmr 5J 115
Janson Rd. Sotn. 3H 173
Japonica Way. Hav 6J 203
Jardine Sq. And 8B 52
(off Cricketers Way)
Jarndyce Wlk. Ports 9E 214
Jarvis Clo. E Cen 5H 17
Jarvis Fields. Burs 1M 195
Jasmine Ct. Gos 1E 238
Jasmine Ct. L'ton 2D 234
Jasmine Gro. Water 3A 202
Jasmine Rd. Bas. 2K 59
Jasmine Rd. H End 2M 175
Jasmine Wlk. Fare 9A 198
Jasmine Way. Bord. 5K 101
Jasmine Way. Water. 6C 168
Jasmond Rd. Ports 2G 215
Jason Pl. Water 7M 201
Jason Way. Gos 8H 213
Jaundrells Clo. New M 3D 232
Java Dri. White 2F 196
Javelin Clo. Ame 5A 66
(off Porton Rd.)
Javelin Rd. Ems 5N 217
J Avenue. Hythe 2D 208
Jay Clo. Ews 2N 63
Jay Clo. Fare. 3L 211
Jay Clo. Water 3A 182
Jays Clo. Bas 1B 60
Jays Ct. Christ 6K 231
Jays Nest Clo. B'wtr 9F 18
Jealous La. L'ton 5A 224
Jean Orr Ct. Chu C. 6M 47
Jefferson Av. Bourn 8A 228
Jefferson Rd. Bas. 4C 42
Jeffries Clo. Rown 6D 158
Jellalabad Barracks. Tidw
. . . . 9C 30
Jellicoe Av. Gos 5H 239
Jellicoe Ct. And. 9C 52
(off Admirals Way)
Jellicoe Dri. Christ 8B 230
Jellicoe Ho. H End 2A 176
Jellicoe Ho. Ports 1E 240
(off Fyning St.)
Jellicoe Way. Ports. 7C 214
Jenkins Gro. Ports 9J 215
Jenkins Pl. Farn. 3M 49
Jenkyn Place Gardens. . . . 7K 63
Jenkyns Clo. Bot 3D 176
Jenner Rd. Ports 8G 200
Jenner Way. Alt 2G 80
Jenner Way. Roms 4B 130
Jennie Grn. La. Lwr Wld & Bentw
. . . . 7J 79
Jennings Rd. Poole 3A 244
Jennings Rd. Tot 2N 171
Jennys Wlk. Yate 7A 18
Jenson Gdns. And 2L 69
Jephcote Rd. Bourn 2D 226
Jermyns La. Amp. 1B 130
Jerome Corner. C'then 2E 18
Jerome Ct. Sotn 4H 175
Jerram Clo. Gos 4H 239
Jerrett's La. Nurs 8C 158
Jersey Clo. Bas. 1D 42
Jersey Clo. Fare 7N 211
Jersey Clo. Fle 8N 27
Jersey Clo. Poole 5B 226
Jersey Clo. Sotn. 8D 158
Jersey Rd. Poole 5B 226
Jersey Rd. Ports 8F 214
Jervis Ct. And. 9C 52
Jervis Ct. La. Swanm 3B 164
Jervis Dri. Gos 1K 239
Jervis Rd. Ports 6D 214
Jesmond Av. Highc 6H 231
Jesmond Gro. L Hth 8D 196
Jessamine Rd. Sotn 9G 158
Jesse Clo. Yate. 8B 18
Jessett Dri. Chu C. 7K 47
Jessica Clo. Water 9B 182
Jessie Rd. Gos 3J 239
Jessie Rd. Hav 6C 202
Jessie Rd. S'sea 3F 240
Jessie Ter. Sotn. . . . 7M 173 (8E 4)
Jessop Clo. Hythe. 4L 193
Jessopp Clo. Bourn 2K 227
Jessop Wlk. Hythe 4L 193
(off Jessop Clo.)
Jesty Rd. Alr. 2D 108
Jetty Rd. Hythe. 3F 208
Jewell Rd. Bourn 5C 228
Jewry St. Win 6L 105 (7L 237)
Jex Blake Clo. Sotn 7G 159
Jibbs Mdw. Braml 1G 22
Jinny La. Roms. 8L 123
Joanna Clo. D'ton. 2H 119
Job's Corner. 2E 162
Jobson Clo. Whitc 5G 55
Jockey La. Eastl 7J 133
Jodrell Clo. Water. 3C 182
John Bunyan Clo. White . . . 1F 196
John Clo. A'sht. 2G 64
John Darling Mall. Eastl . . . 8E 132
John Eddie Ct. Bas 8L 41
John French Way. Bulf 3A 66
John Hansard Art Gallery.
. . . . 8M 159
John Marshall Ct. Ports . . . 8E 214
John Morgan Clo. Hook. . . . 1G 45
John Pounds Cen. Ports
. . . . 2C 240 (3L 5)
Johnson St. Sotn
. . . . 6M 173 (5E 4)
(in two parts)
Johnson Vw. White 3H 197
Johnson Way. Chu C 6M 47
Johns Rd. Fare. 1D 212
John's Rd. Sotn 8B 174
Johnstone Rd. Christ 8A 230
John St. Sotn 7M 173 (8E 4)
Joices Yd. Bas 7C 42
Jonas Nichols Sq. Sotn. 5F 4
Jonathan Clo. L'ton 1E 234
Jonathan Hill. New C 1E 8
Jonathan Rd. Fare 8A 198
Jones La. Hythe 5L 193
Jopps Corner. Burt 2M 229
Jordan Ho. Sotn. 5H 173
Jordans La. Pill 5H 225
Jordans La. Sway. 4K 223
Joseph Nye Ct. Ports 4K 5
Joseph St. Gos 3L 239
Josian Wlk. Sotn . . . 5N 173 (4F 4)
Jouldings La. Far H 1N 15
Joule Rd. And. 9H 51
Joule Rd. Bas 4A 42
Jowitt Dri. New M. 4A 232
Joyce Dickson Clo. Ring. . . . 2L 187
Joy's La. Chlbn 4E 74
Joys La. Nor W. 7L 225
Jubilee Av. Ows 7B 134
Jubilee Av. Ports 8N 199
Jubilee Bus. Cen. Water . . . 1L 201
Jubilee Clo. Eastl 2D 160
Jubilee Clo. Farn. 8F 28
Jubilee Clo. F'bri 1F 152
Jubilee Clo. N Lit 2G 36
Jubilee Clo. P Hth. 4L 11

Jubilee Clo.—Kings Clo.

Jubilee Clo. Ring 9M 185
Jubilee Ct. Fare 1C 212
Jubilee Ct. H End 5M 175
Jubilee Ct. Sway 6J 223
Jubilee Cres. Poole 9B 226
Jubilee Gdns. Bourn 4H 227
Jubilee Gdns. Sotn 3F 174
Jubilee Hall Rd. Farn 8L 29
Jubilee Ho. Ems 8K 203
Jubilee La. Gray 4L 103
Jubilee M. Net A 3E 194
Jubilee Path. Hav 8D 202
Jubilee Rd. A'sht 3K 65
Jubilee Rd. Bas 7C 42
Jubilee Rd. Fare 9M 199
Jubilee Rd. Finch 1J 17
Jubilee Rd. F'bri 1F 152
Jubilee Rd. Gos 2K 239
Jubilee Rd. Poole 9B 226
Jubilee Rd. Roms 4L 129
Jubilee Rd. S'sea 4G 240
Jubilee Rd. Water 9L 181
Jubilee Ter. S'se 4C 240 (7M 5)
Julia Clo. Highc 6H 231
Julian Clo. Chilw 5K 159
Julian Ct. Sotn 9C 160
Julian Rd. Sotn 7F 174
Julie Av. Fare 8A 198
Juliet Ct. Water 1A 202
Julius Clo. Bas 3L 41
Julius Clo. Chan F 6C 132
Julyan Av. Poole 6E 226
Jumar Clo. Wars 1A 210
Jumpers Av. Christ 6H 229
Jumpers Common 6J 229
Jumpers Rd. Christ 6J 229
Jumps Rd. Churt 5G 84
Junction Rd. And 9M 51
Junction Rd. Bourn 6K 227
Junction Rd. Tot 3N 171
June Dri. Bas 6K 41
Juniper Cen., The. Christ 6J 229
Juniper Clo. Chine 8H 23
Juniper Clo. N Bad 7E 130
Juniper Clo. Penn 4B 234
Juniper Clo. W'hill 5F 100
Juniper Clo. Win 9H 105
Juniper Ct. Sotn 3C 174
Juniper Rd. Farn 7E 28
Juniper Rd. Firs 4E 86
Juniper Rd. Sotn 3D 174
Juniper Rd. Water 1C 182
Juniper Sq. Hav 9F 202
Jupiter Clo. Sotn 8E 158
Jura Clo. Ports 8H 201
Jurds Lake Way. Sotn 9B 174
Jurd Way. Burs 9K 175
Justin Clo. Fare 9A 198
Justin Gdns. Bourn 2J 227
Justinian Clo. Chan F 5D 132
Jute Clo. Fare 8K 199
Jutland Clo. White 2E 196
Jutland Cres. And 6M 51
Juventu Clo. Hav 5G 202

K

Kamptee Copse. New M 9C 222
Kandy Rd. Bulf B 3B 66
Kanes Hill. Sotn 4J 175
Kanes Hill Cvn. Site. Sotn 6K 175
Karachi Clo. Tidw 7C 30
Karen Av. Ports 2K 215
Kashmir Ct. Farn 2L 49
Kassassin St. S'sea 5H 241
Kassel Clo. Water 1B 202
Katherine Chance Clo. Burt 3M 229
Kathleen Clo. Bas 9B 42
Kathleen Rd. Sotn 7E 174
Katrina Gdns. Hay I 2G 242
Katrine Cres. Chan F 4M 131
Katterns Clo. Christ 4H 229
Kayak Clo. Wars 8B 196
Kay Cres. Head D 1C 102
Kayleigh Clo. Tot 4K 171
Kealy Rd. Gos 1J 239
Kearsney Av. Ports 5F 214
Keast Wlk. Gos 4F 212
Keats Av. Mil S 7K 235
Keats Av. Ports 8N 199
Keats Clo. Bas 2D 42
Keats Clo. S Won 3H 91
Keats Clo. Water 6N 181
Keats Clo. White 9E 176
Keats Clo. Win 1G 126
Keats Gdns. Fle 2N 47
Keats Ho. Hav 5E 202
Keats Ho. New M 4B 232
Keats Rd. Sotn 4G 174
Keats Way. Yate 9L 17
Keble Clo. Chan F 7A 132
Keble Clo. Hurs 6N 125
Keble Rd. Chan F 8A 132
Keble St. Win 8G 105
Keble Way. Owl 3G 19
Keeble Clo. Bourn 1H 227
Keeble Cres. Bourn 1H 227
Keeble Rd. Bourn 1H 227
Keelan Ct. S'sea 5E 240
Keel Clo. Gos 9F 212
Keel Clo. Ports 5K 215
Keepers Clo. Chan F 6N 131
Keeper's Hill. A'prt 4A 68
Keeper's La. Mott 3C 122
Keeping 1E 236
Keeps Mead. K're 1A 6
Keep, The. Fare 9M 199
Kefford Clo. Water 4B 182
Keith Clo. Gos 1K 239
Keith Ho. Ports 3K 5
Keith Lucas Rd. Farn 1H 49
Keith Rd. Bourn 8G 227
Kelburn Clo. Chan F 5N 131
Kellett Rd. Sotn 2K 173
Kelly Ct. Fare 7D 198
Kelly Ct. S'sea 4F 240
Kelly Ho. Sotn 7C 160
Kellynch Clo. Alt 4E 80
Kelly Rd. Water 4M 201
Kellys Wlk. And 2L 69
Kelmscott Gdns. Chan F 3M 131
Kelsall Gdns. New M 3B 232
Kelsey Clo. Fare 8E 196
Kelsey Clo. Liss 9F 114
Kelsey Gro. Yate 8A 18
Kelsey Head. Port S 1B 214
Kelston Clo. Sotn 3F 172
Kelvin Clo. Hythe 6M 193
Kelvin Gro. Fare 9M 199
Kelvin Gro. Net A 3G 194
Kelvin Hill. Bas 8N 41
Kelvin Rd. Eastl 1D 160
Kemmel Rd. Per D 4A 30
Kemmitt Way. And 3L 69
Kempenfelt Ho. Ports 3K 5
Kemp Rd. Bourn 6K 227
Kempshott 2K 59
Kempshott Gdns. Bas 2J 59
Kempshott Gro. Bas 7J 41
Kempshott La. Bas 3J 59
Kempshott Pk. Ind. Est. Kemp 6H 59
Kempshott Roundabout. Kemp 3K 59
Kemps Quay Ind. Pk. Sotn 3B 174
Kempton Clo. Alt 6F 80
Kempton Ct. Farn 1H 49
Kempton Ct. White 1F 196 (off Timor Clo.)
Kempton Pk. Water 9B 182
Kemp Welch Leisure Cen. 6B 226
Kemshott Ct. Hav 3D 202
Ken Berry Ct. Hav 3H 203
Kench, The. Hay I 3N 241
Kendal Av. Ports 7H 215
Kendal Av. Sotn 1C 172
Kendal Clo. Chan F 5C 132
Kendal Clo. Farn 8G 28
Kendal Clo. Water 6A 182
Kendal Ct. Sotn 1C 172
Kendal Gdns. Bas 9K 41
Kendrick Rd. N'bry 1C 8
Kenilworth Clo. Lee S 9B 212
Kenilworth Clo. New M 3C 232
Kenilworth Ct. Christ 7K 229
Kenilworth Ct. Poole 5D 244
Kenilworth Ct. Win 4L 105 (off Northlands Dri.)
Kenilworth Cres. Fle 1A 48
Kenilworth Dri. Eastl 6E 132
Kenilworth Gdns. W End 1J 175
Kenilworth Ho. Sotn 4A 174 (off Kent St.)
Kenilworth Rd. Bas 5K 41
Kenilworth Rd. Farn 7E 28
Kenilworth Rd. Fle 2N 47
Kenilworth Rd. Sotn 4L 173 (2B 4)
Kenilworth Rd. S'sea 6E 240
Kenley Rd. Head D 2D 102
Kenmore Clo. Chu C 6N 47
Kenmore Clo. Frim 4M 29
Kenmore Clo. Tot 6L 171
Kennard Ct. New M 3A 232
Kennard Rd. New M 2A 232
Kennedy Av. Fare 6A 198
Kennedy Clo. Water 5L 201
Kennedy Cres. Gos 5G 239
Kennedy Rd. Sotn 8E 158
Kennel La. Win 2F 104
Kennels La. Farn 9D 28
Kennet Clo. Bas 6E 42
Kennet Clo. Farn 6G 28
Kennet Clo. Gos 6K 239
Kennet Clo. W End 8F 160
Kenneth Ct. Christ 7K 231
Kennet Rd. Ptsfld 2L 145
Kennet Rd. Tidw 7D 30
Kennett Clo. Roms 4B 130
Kennett Rd. Roms 4B 130
Kennet Way. Okly 1D 58
Kennington La. Cad 3B 170
Ken Rd. Bourn 1H 247
Kensington Clo. Eastl 7H 133
Kensington Ct. Elve 8J 27
Kensington Dri. Bourn 1H 245 (5H 247)
Kensington Fields. Dib P 7J 193
Kensington Gdns. Fare 7F 196
Kensington Ho. Bas 6C 42 (off Timberlake Rd.)
Kensington Pk. Mil S 8J 235
Kensington Rd. Gos 4L 239
Kensington Rd. Ports 6G 215
Kenson Gdns. Sotn 6E 174
Kent Gdns. Tot 5K 171
Kent Gro. Fare 2L 213
Kent Ho. Sotn 4A 174
Kentidge Rd. Water 4L 201
Kentigern Dri. C'then 1F 18
Kentish Rd. Sotn 3H 173
Kent La. Harb 8F 152
Kent Rd. Chan F 9A 132
Kent Rd. Fle 2N 47
Kent Rd. Gos 4D 212
Kent Rd. Poole 8C 226
Kent Rd. Sotn 1A 174
Kent Rd. S'sea 4C 240 (8M 5)
Kent Rd. W'hill 5J 101
Kentsboro 3A 72
Kent's Oak 8D 122
Kent St. Ports 2B 240 (4K 5)
Kent St. Sotn 5A 174
Kenwith Av. Fle 2A 48
Kenwood Rd. Fare 2M 213
Kenwyn Clo. W End 9F 160
Kenya Rd. Fare 1K 213
Kenyon Rd. Ports 6G 214
Kenyons Yd. And 1L 69
Keppel Clo. Ring 1L 187
Kerchers Fld. Over 3D 56
Kerfield Way. Hook 2H 45
Kerley Rd. Bourn 3J 245 (8K 247)
Kern Clo. Sotn 8E 158
Kerrfield. Win 7H 105 (in two parts)
Kerrfield M. Win 7H 105
Kerrigan Ct. Sotn 2M 173
Kerry Clo. Chan F 6A 132
Kerry Clo. Fle 8N 27
Kerry Clo. Penn 3C 234
Kersley Cres. Odi 2E 62
Kesteven Way. Sotn 2E 174
Kestrel Clo. Bish W 3K 163
Kestrel Clo. Bot 1C 176
Kestrel Clo. Ews 2N 63 (off Fox Way)
Kestrel Clo. Fare 4L 211
Kestrel Clo. March 9D 172
Kestrel Clo. Sotn 6G 158
Kestrel Clo. Tidw 7E 30
Kestrel Clo. Water 7C 168
Kestrel Clo. Win 1H 127
Kestrel Ct. Alt 2F 80
Kestrel Ct. Ring 9K 185
Kestrel Dri. Christ 8C 230
Kestrel Pl. Ports 1N 215
Kestrel Rd. Bas 1H 59
Kestrel Rd. Eastl 1B 160
Kestrels, The. Burs 1K 195
Kestrel Way. A'hlt 5E 152
Keswick Av. Ports 8H 215
Keswick Ct. New M 1C 232
Keswick Rd. Bourn 1C 246
Keswick Rd. New M 1C 232
Keswick Rd. Sotn 7B 174
Ketchers Fld. Selb 9M 99
Ketelbey Ri. Bas 3A 60
Kettering Ter. Ports 8D 214
Keverstone Ct. Bourn 2A 246
Kevin Clo. K're 2D 6
Kevin Clo. Wool H 2A 8 (off Douglas Ride)
Kevins Dri. Yate 6A 18
Kevins Gro. Fle 2N 47
Kevlyn Cres. Burs 9J 175
Kewlake La. Cad 5M 155
Kew La. Burs 2L 195
Kew Wlk. And 2L 69
Keydell Av. Water 5A 182
Keydell Clo. Water 5A 182
Keyes Clo. Christ 8B 230
Keyes Clo. Gos 5E 212
Keyes Clo. Poole 5D 226
Keyes Ct. S'sea 5E 240 (off Albert Rd.)
Keyes Rd. Gos 5E 212
Keyhaven 10N 235
Keyhaven Clo. Gos 6C 212
Keyhaven Dri. Hav 4C 202
Keyhaven Rd. Mil S 8L 235
Keynes Clo. Chu C 7N 47
Keynsham Rd. Sotn 4F 174
Keynsham Way. Owl 3F 18
Keysworth Av. Bart S 6A 232
Keytech Cen. Bas 4M 41
Khandala Gdns. Water 5N 201
Khartoum Rd. Sotn 9M 159
Khyber Rd. Poole 9B 226
Kidmore La. Water 3G 181
Kielder Clo. Chan F 5M 131
Kielder Gro. Gos 6F 212
Kiel Dri. And 7M 51
Kilbride. Poole 1E 244
Kilbride Path. Ports 8E 214
Kildare Clo. Bord 3J 101
Kildare Rd. Bord 3J 101
Kilford Ct. Bot 4D 176
Kilham La. Win 7E 104
Killarney Clo. Sotn 7J 175
Kilmarnock Rd. Bourn 5K 227
Kilmeston 2L 135
Kilmeston Clo. Hav 3F 202
Kilmeston Rd. Kilm 1K 135
Kilmington Way. Highc 6G 231
Kilmiston Clo. Ports 9F 214
Kilmiston Dri. Fare 8L 199
Kilmuir Clo. Coll T 6F 18
Kiln Acre Ind. Site. Fare 6D 198
Kiln Clo. Dib P 6K 193
Kiln Fld. Liss 9D 114
Kiln Gdns. H Win 6B 26
Kiln Grn. Col C 4L 133
Kiln Hill. Sob 2K 179
Kiln La. Brfld 7A 124
Kiln La. Bton 8J 145
Kiln La. Monk S 7J 21
Kiln La. Mort 1H 13
Kiln La. Old Al 6F 94 (in two parts)
Kiln La. Ott & Bram 2F 132 (in two parts)
Kiln La. Redl 1N 119
Kiln Rd. Fare 5B 198
Kiln Rd. Ports 7H 215
Kiln Rd. Sher 9N 21
Kilnside. Water 7G 180
Kilns, The. Alt 5H 81
Kiln Way. A'sht 3K 65
Kiln Way. Gray 2G 103
Kilnyard Clo. Tot 1K 171
Kilpatrick Clo. Ports 8E 214
Kilwich Way. Fare 2K 213
Kimbell Rd. Bas 9A 42
Kimber Clo. Chine 1G 42
Kimberley. Chu C 7N 47
Kimberley Clo. Charl 8L 51
Kimberley Clo. Christ 6J 229
Kimberley Clo. F Oak 1A 162
Kimberley Ct. Sotn 8C 174
Kimberley Rd. Bas 8N 41
Kimberley Rd. Bourn 8F 228
Kimberley Rd. Lngmr 4H 115
Kimberley Rd. Poole 2A 244
Kimberley Rd. S'sea 5H 241
Kimber Rd. Bourn 3D 226
Kimbers. Ptsfld 9L 139
Kimbers La. F'ham 7F 64
Kimbolton Rd. Ports 1H 241
Kimbridge 6F 122
Kimbridge Clo. Sotn 6D 158
Kimbridge Cres. Hav 3G 203
Kimbridge La. Kim 6F 122
Kimmeridge Av. Poole 6A 226
Kimpton 9M 31
Kimpton Clo. Lee S 1B 238
Kimpton Ct. Hav 3H 203
Kimpton Dri. Elve 9H 27
Kindersley Pk. Homes. Abb A 6G 69
Kineton Rd. Sotn 1K 173
King Albert Ct. Ports 1F 240
King Albert St. Ports 1E 240
King Alfred Pl. Win 5L 105
King Alfred's Statue 8N 237
King Alfred Ter. Win 5L 105
King Arthur's Ct. Ports 9L 201
King Arthur's Way. And 7N 51
King Arthur's Way Roundabout. And 6A 52
King Charles St. Ports 3B 240 (6J 5)
King Clo. St I 4C 186
King Cup Av. L Hth 6C 196
Kingdom Clo. Fare 4G 196
Kingdom's M. Alt 5F 80
King Edward Av. Bourn 4K 227
King Edward Av. Sotn 2F 172
King Edward Pk. Cvn. Pk. Chan F 3L 131
King Edward's Cres. Ports 6E 214
Kingfisher Cvn. Pk. Gos 4E 238
Kingfisher Clo. Bas 1H 59
Kingfisher Clo. Bord 5K 101
Kingfisher Clo. Bourn 8H 229
Kingfisher Clo. Chu C 6M 47
Kingfisher Clo. Farn 6E 28
Kingfisher Clo. Hamb 5L 195
Kingfisher Clo. Hay I 5J 243
Kingfisher Clo. Row C 9H 183
Kingfisher Clo. Water 6M 181
Kingfisher Clo. Whitc 5G 55
Kingfisher Copse. L Hth 6E 196
Kingfisher Ct. Alt 2F 80
Kingfisher Ct. Bas 5B 42
Kingfisher Ct. Hav 6H 203
Kingfisher Dri. Yate 7L 17
Kingfisher Rd. Eastl 1B 160
Kingfishers. Fare 9H 199
Kingfishers. Ship B 2B 66
Kingfisher Way. Christ 9C 230
Kingfisher Way. March 9D 172
Kingfisher Way. Ring 7L 185
Kingfisher Way. Roms 4M 129
King George Av. Bourn 4K 227
King George Av. Ptsfld 9M 139
King George Mobile Home Pk. New M 5A 232
King George Rd. And 1K 69
King George Rd. Fare 1L 213
King George's Av. Sotn 4E 172
King Harold Ct. Win 8J 105
King Henry Building. Ports 2C 240 (4M 5)
King Henry I St. Ports 2C 240 (4M 5)
King James Ter. Ports 7J 5
King John Av. Bourn 1B 226
King John Av. Fare 1K 213
King John Clo. Bourn 1B 226
King John Rd. K're 2B 6
King John's House 5L 129
King Johns Rd. N War 7J 45
Kingland Mkt. Sotn 6M 173 (5E 4)
King La. Frox 5F 138
King La. Grat & Ovr W 6L 67
King La. Cotts. Ovr W 8M 67
King Richard Clo. Ports 9E 200
King Richard Dri. Bourn 1A 226
King Richard I Rd. Ports 2C 240 (4M 5)
King's Arms La. Ring 1J 187
Kings Arms Row. Ring 1J 187
King's Av. Christ 8J 229
Kings Av. Hamb 6J 195
Kings Av. Poole 3B 244
Kings Av. Tong 2N 65
Kings Av. Win 9J 105
Kings Bench All. Ports 2B 240 (3K 5)
Kingsbere Av. Bourn 4F 226
Kingsbourne Clo. Wint D 3A 86
Kingsbridge Copse. Newn 3E 44
Kingsbridge La. Sotn 5L 173 (4B 4)
Kingsbridge Rd. Poole 2A 244
Kingsbury Rd. Sotn 3N 173
Kingsbury's La. Ring 1J 187
Kingsclear Pk. Cam 9M 19
Kingsclere 2B 6
Kingsclere Av. Hav 3D 202
Kingsclere Av. Sotn 9D 174
Kingsclere Clo. Sotn 9D 174
Kingsclere Pk. K're 1A 6
Kingsclere Rd. Bas 4A 42
Kingsclere Rd. Over 7D 38
Kingsclere Rd. R'dll & Bas 7B 20 (in two parts)
Kings Clo. Chan F 5B 132
Kings Clo. King W 6M 91
Kings Clo. L'ton 2D 234
Kings Clo. Lyn 2B 148
Kings Clo. Row C 8G 183
Kings Clo. Twy 6L 127

Kings Copse Av.—Landguard Rd.

Kings Copse Av. H End 6A 176
King's Copse Rd. Black. 8A 208
Kings Copse Rd. H End 6A 176
Kingscote Rd. Cosh 7A 200
Kingscote Rd. Cowp. 7L 181
Kings Ct. Tong 2N 65
King's Cres. Cam 5L 19
Kings Cres. L'ton 2D 234
Kings Cres. Poole 3C 244
Kingscroft. Fle 3M 47
Kingscroft Ct. Hav 8D 202
Kings Cft. La. Hav. 8C 202
Kingsdale Ct. Win 6K 105 (6L 237)
Kingsdown Pl. Ports 2F 240
Kingsdown Rd. Water. 8K 181
Kingsdown Way. Sotn 9D 160
King's Elms. Bar S 5A 76
Kingsey Av. Ems 9L 203
Kings Farm La. Hord. 4J 233
Kingsfernsden La. Ptsfld 8N 139
Kings Fld. Burs 9L 175
Kingsfield. L'ton 4G 234
Kingsfield. Ring 2K 187
Kings Fld. Gdns. Burs. 8L 175
Kingsfold Av. Sotn 8D 160
Kingsford Clo. W'flls 3M 119
King's Furlong 8B 42
Kings Furlong Cen. Bas 8B 42
King's Furlong Dri. Bas. 8A 42
Kingsgate. Poole 2F 244
Kingsgate Rd. Win 9K 105
Kingsgate St. Win 8L 105 (9M 237)
Kingsgrove Ind. Est. Farn 9J 29
Kings Head Yd. Win 7L 105 (8M 237)
King's Hill. Bch 9M 79
Kings Ho. Sotn 7M 173 (7E 4)
Kings Keep. Fle 5M 47
King's Keep. S'hrst 4D 18
Kingsland Clo. Ports 8D 200
Kingsland Ct. Sotn 6M 173 (5E 4)
Kingsland Ho. Sotn 4D 4
Kingsland Ind. Pk. Bas 2F 42
Kingsland Mkt. Sotn 6M 173 (5E 4)
Kingsland Rd. Alt 5E 80
Kingsland Sq. Sotn 6M 173 (5E 4)
King's La. Frox 3C 138
Kings La. Sway 8L 223
Kings La. Win 7B 106
Kingsley 7H 83
Kingsley Av. Bourn 1K 247
Kingsley Av. Cam 9L 19
Kingsley Bungalows. Alr 2D 108
Kingsley Bus. Pk. Kingsl 7H 83
Kingsley Clo. Bourn 1K 247
Kingsley Clo. C'then 2D 18
Kingsley Gdns. Tot 3H 171
Kingsley Grn. Hav. 3E 202
Kingsley Ho. Bourn. 5K 227
Kingsley Ho. Ems 9L 203
Kingsley Pk. Whitc 4G 54
Kingsley Pl. Win 9J 105
Kingsley Rd. E'sly 6F 16
Kingsley Rd. Farn 6H 29
Kingsley Rd. Gos 9H 213
Kingsley Rd. Sotn. 3G 172
Kingsley Rd. S'sea 4J 241
Kings Mead 2E 178
Kingsmead. Alt 5G 80
Kingsmead. Anna V 5J 69
Kingsmead. Farn 8K 29
Kingsmead. Frim G 5N 29
Kingsmead. W Wel 1B 120
Kingsmead. Wick 2E 178
Kingsmead Av. Fare 7N 211
Kingsmead Ct. Sotn 1G 172
Kings Mdw. And 2A 70
King's Mdw. Over 2D 56
Kingsmead Shop. Cen. Farn 8K 29
Kings Mede. Water 5A 182
Kingsmill Clo. Gos 4H 239
Kingsmill Rd. Bas 9B 42
Kings Orchard. Okly 2D 58
Kings Paddock. W'slw 5G 86
Kings Pde. Fle 1M 47
Kings Pk. Bourn 8B 228
Kings Pk. Dri. Bourn 8D 228 (Central Dri.)
Kings Pk. Dri. Bourn. 8B 228 (Holdenhurst Rd.)
Kings Pk. Rd. Bourn. 8B 228
King's Pk. Rd. Sotn 4M 173 (2D 4)
Kings Peace, The. Gray. 4L 103
Kings Pightle. Chine 9G 23
King's Pond Nature Reserve. 4G 81
Kings Ride. Black 9C 208
King's Ride. Cam 4M 19 (in two parts)
King's Rd. A'sht 1G 65
Kings Rd. Alt 6D 80
King's Rd. Bas 8N 41
King's Rd. Bourn. 7L 227
King's Rd. Chan F. 6A 132
King's Rd. Cowp. 7N 181
King's Rd. C'then 1D 18
King's Rd. Ems. 9L 203
Kings Rd. Enh A 3A 52
King's Rd. Fare 8D 198
Kings Rd. Fle 1M 47
King's Rd. Gos 3K 239
King's Rd. Hay I 1G 243
King's Rd. Lee S. 9A 212
Kings Rd. L'ton. 2D 234
Kings Rd. New M 2D 232
Kings Rd. Ptsfld 9K 139
Kings Rd. Sil 4N 11
King's Rd. S'sea 4C 240 (7M 5)
Kings Rd. Win 8G 104
King's Royal Hussar's Mus., The. 7K 105 (8K 237)
King's Saltern Rd. L'ton 4F 234
King's Somborne 9B 86
King's Ter. Ems 9M 203
King's Ter. S'sea 4C 240 (7M 5)
Kingston 1F 240 (Portsmouth)
Kingston 6J 187 (Ringwood)
Kingston. Net A 2G 195
Kingston Cres. Ports. 8E 214
Kingstone Clo. And. 3L 69
Kingston Gdns. Fare. 5N 197
Kingston Pk. Penn 4D 234
Kingston Rd. Gos 2H 239
Kingston Rd. Ports. 8E 214
Kingston Rd. Sotn. 4J 173
Kingstons Ind. Est. A'sht 9N 49
King St. Ems 9N 203
King St. Gos 2M 239
King St. Odi 8L 45 (in two parts)
King St. Sotn 7M 173 (7E 4)
King St. S'sea 3C 240 (6M 5) (in two parts)
King St. Westb 6N 203
Kingsvale Ct. Bas 7A 42
King's Wlk. Coll T. 7H 19
Kings Wlk. Whitc 5G 55
Kings Wlk. Win. 8N 237
Kingsway. A'sht 1G 65
Kingsway. And 8D 52
Kingsway. B'wtr 8F 18
Kingsway. Chan F 5B 132
Kingsway. Hay I 5G 216
Kings Way. Row C 9G 183
Kingsway. Sotn. 5M 173 (4E 4)
Kings Way. Swanm 6H 165
Kings Way. Uphm 7E 134
Kingsway Clo. Christ. 5J 229
Kingsway Ct. Chan F 4C 132
Kingsway Gdns. And 7N 51
Kingsway Gdns. Chan F 4C 132
Kingsway, The. Fare 9L 199
Kingswell Clo. Bourn 4H 227
Kingswell Gdns. Bourn 4F 226
Kingswell Gro. Bourn 4F 226
Kingswell Path. Ports 1D 240 (2N 5)
Kingswell Rd. Bourn 4F 226
Kingswell St. Ports 2D 240 (3N 5)
Kingswood. March 9F 172
Kingswood Firs. Gray 5K 103
Kingswood La. Hind 5L 103
Kingswood Ri. Four M 5G 97
Kingsworthy Ct. King W 1N 105
Kingsworthy Rd. Hav 6F 202
Kings Yd. And. 1A 70
King William St. Ports 1B 240 (2K 5)
Kinloss Ct. Sotn 6F 158
Kinnell Clo. Ems 9M 203
Kinross Cres. Ports 1J 215
Kinross Rd. Bourn 8J 227
Kinross Rd. Tot 3M 171
Kinsbourne Av. Bourn 4H 227
Kinsbourne Clo. Sotn 4J 175
Kinsbourne Ri. Sotn 4K 175
Kinsbourne Way. Sotn 4J 175
Kinson 2F 226
Kinson Gro. Bourn 1G 227
Kinson Rd. Bourn 5E 226
Kintyre Clo. Okly 9C 40
Kintyre Rd. Ports 8G 201
Kinver Clo. Roms 3A 130
Kipling Clo. White 9E 176
Kipling Clo. Yate 9M 17
Kipling Ct. Sotn 9D 174
Kipling Rd. Eastl 9D 132
Kipling Rd. Ports 5F 214
Kipling Wlk. Bas 8N 41
Kirby Rd. Ports 6F 214
Kirby Way. Bourn 1G 247
Kirkee Rd. Tidw 9C 30
Kirk Gdns. Tot 5M 171
Kirkham Av. Burt 3M 229
Kirkham Clo. Owl 3F 18
Kirk Knoll. Head 2B 102
Kirkstall Rd. S'sea 6F 240
Kirtley Clo. Ports 2K 215
Kirton Rd. Ports 1K 215
Kitchener Rd. A'sht 5M 49
Kitchener Rd. Lngmr 4H 115
Kitchener Rd. Sotn 8A 160
Kitchers Clo. Sway 4J 223
Kitcombe La. Four M 6N 97
Kite Clo. Water 6M 181
Kite Hill Cotts. Bas 8J 41
Kites Cft. Clo. Fare 8F 196
Kit La. Ellis 2J 79
Kitnocks Hill. Curd 2H 177
Kitscroft Rd. Bourn 1G 226
Kittiwake Clo. Bourn 8G 229
Kittiwake Clo. Gos 6D 212
Kitt's La. Bramd 3C 136
Kitts La. Churt 7G 85
Kitwalls La. Mil S 7K 233
Kitwood 8H 97
Kitwood Grn. Hav 4H 203
Kitwood La. Ropl 8J 97
Kitwood Rd. Four M 8J 97
Kivernell Pl. Mil S 7J 235
Kivernell Rd. Mil S 8J 235
Kleves Ct. Sotn 4F 174
Knapp Hill 9J 125
Knapp 9H 125
Knapp Clo. Christ 6K 229
Knapp Clo., The. Coll D 2G 31
Knapp La. Amp 9H 125
Knapp La. T'ley 7K 11
Knapp Mill Av. Christ 6K 229
Knapps Hard. W Meon 8C 136
Knatchbull Clo. Roms 5M 129
Kneller Ct. Fare 5B 198
Knellers La. Tot 6K 171
Knight Clo. Crook V 5H 47
Knight Clo. Win 4L 105
Knightcrest Pk. Evtn 5M 233
Knighton Heath Clo. Bourn 2C 226
Knighton Heath Golf Course. 2B 226
Knighton Heath Ind. Est. Bourn 4C 226
Knighton Heath Rd. Bourn 2C 226
Knighton Pk. New M 6N 231
Knighton Rd. Bro Ch 3A 118
Knighton Rd. Sotn 6D 174
Knights Bank Rd. Fare 7J 211
Knightsbridge Ct. Bourn 8K 247
Knightsbridge Dri. H'ly 1J 9
Knightsbridge Gro. Cam. 6N 19
Knightsbridge Rd. Cam 6N 19
Knightsbridge Rd. Enh A 3B 52
Knights Clo. Wars 8B 196
Knight's Clo. W'slw 4G 87 (off Middleton Rd.)
Knights Enham 5N 51
Knights Enham Roundabout. And 5N 51
Knights La. Ball 1N 7
Knights Pk. Bas 4A 42
Knights Pk. Rd. Bas 4A 42
Knights Rd. Bourn 1B 226
Knights Rd. F'ham 3G 64
Knightstone Ct. Ports 4G 214
Knightstone Grange. Hythe 7M 193
Knight St. Bas. 7A 42
Knights Way. Alt. 5D 80
Knights Yd. Hur T 4D 34
Knightwood. New M 7L 231
Knightwood Av. Hav. 4G 202
Knightwood Av. Lyn 2B 148
Knightwood Clo. Asht. 8H 171
Knightwood Clo. Christ. 6F 230
Knightwood Clo. Lyn 2B 148
Knightwood Oak 4K 189
Knightwood Rd. Chan F 4L 131
Knightwood Rd. Hythe 7N 193
Knightwood Vw. Chan F 6A 132
Knockhundred La. B'shtt C 7K 103
Knockwood La. Neth W 9N 67
Knole Gdns. Bourn 1A 246
Knole Rd. Bourn 9A 228
Knoll Clo. Fle 1M 47
Knoll Ct. Fle 9M 27
Knoll Gdns. St I 4C 186
Knoll Rd. Cam 7M 19
Knoll Rd. Fle 1M 47
Knoll Wlk. Cam 7M 19
Knollys Ho. Ports 1F 240
Knollys Rd. A'sht 8H 49
Knollys Rd. P Hth 4M 11
Knook, The. Coll T 6F 18
Knotgrass Rd. L Hth 7B 196
Knowland Dri. Mil S 7K 235
Knowle Cres. K're 2B 6
Knowle Hill. Eastl 5F 132
Knowle La. H Hth 4A 162
Knowle Rd. Broc 6B 148
Knowles Av. C'then 1B 18
Knowles Clo. Bord 5J 101
Knowles Clo. Christ 7A 230
Knowles Mdw. Hill B 4G 141
Knowlings, The. Whitc 6H 55
Knowlton 9F 148
Knowlton Gdns. Bourn 2M 227
Knowsley Cres. Ports 1H 215
Knowsley Rd. Ports 1G 215
Knox Clo. Chu C 6J 47
Knox Rd. Hav 8D 202
Knox Rd. Ports 7D 214
Knyght Clo. Roms 6N 129
Knyveton Rd. Bourn 1M 245
Kohat Clo. Tidw 7B 30
Kohat Ct. A'sht 9H 49
Kohat Rd. Tidw 9C 30
Kohima Clo. A'sht 8K 49
Kootenay Av. Sotn 3J 175
Kooyong Clo. E Wel 1B 156
Krooner Rd. Cam 1K 29
Kynegils Rd. Win 4H 105
Kynon Clo. Gos 8L 213
Kytes La. Durl 6E 162

L

Laburnum Av. Cosh 1K 215
Laburnum Clo. A'sht 1J 65
Laburnum Clo. N Bad 7F 130
Laburnum Ct. Sotn 7B 174
Laburnum Cres. Hythe 1M 207
Laburnum Dri. Evtn 6M 233
Laburnum Dri. King W 7M 91
Laburnum Gdns. Chu C 6N 47
Laburnum Gro. Eastl 9E 132
Laburnum Gro. Hay I 3H 243
Laburnum Gro. Ports 7F 214
Laburnum Ho. Bourn 2K 227
Laburnum Ho. H End 4A 176
Laburnum Pas. A'sht 9J 49
Laburnum Path. Ports 9K 201
Laburnum Rd. A'sht 1J 65
Laburnum Rd. Fare 1D 212
Laburnum Rd. F'ham 3G 64
Laburnum Rd. H End 4A 176
Laburnum Rd. Sotn 7A 160
Laburnum Rd. Water 3L 201
Laburnums, The. B'wtr 8D 18
Laburnum Way. Bas 5M 41
Lackford Av. Tot 4L 171
Lackford Way. Tot 4M 171
Lacon Clo. Sotn 2C 174
Ladies Wlk. And 3A 70
Ladram Rd. Gos 3G 239
Ladwell 9N 125
Ladwell Clo. N'bry 1C 8
Lady Betty's Dri. Fare 3H 197
Ladybridge Rd. Water 5K 201
Ladycroft. Alr 2C 108
Ladycross Rd. Hythe 7M 193
Lady Diana Ct. Lud 1D 30
Ladygate Dri. Gray 4J 103
Lady Godley Clo. Tidw 9C 30
Lady Jane Wlk. Lud 1D 30
Lady Pl. Ct. Alt 5F 80
Ladysmith Clo. Christ 7A 230
Ladysmith Pl. Bord 2H 101
Ladyway. Idm 9C 66
Lady Well La. Alr 8F 94
Ladywood. Eastl 6D 132
Ladywood Av. Farn 8E 28
Ladywood Ho. S'sea 3D 240
Laffan's Rd. A'sht 5E 48
Laffans Rd. Odi 2F 62
Lagado Clo. Poole 5A 244
Lagoon Clo. Poole 5A 244
Lahore Clo. Tidw 7C 30
Lahore Rd. Tidw 9C 30
Laidlaw Clo. Poole 6F 226
Lainston Clo. Win 4G 105
Lake Ct. Hurs 1L 131
Lake Dri. Bord 4K 101
Lake End Way. C'then 1C 18
Lake Farm Clo. H End 2N 175
Lake Gro. Rd. New M 2A 232
Lake Ho. Sotn 4H 173
Lakeland Dri. Frim 3N 29
Lakeland Gdns. March 9D 172
Lakelands. Baug 4D 10
Lakelands Dri. Sotn 4H 173
Lake La. Dock 2A 84
Lake Rd. Bourn 1F 226
Lake Rd. Chan F 4C 132
Lake Rd. Curd 2J 177
Lake Rd. Ports 1D 240
Lake Rd. Sotn 8B 174
Laker Sq. And 8B 52
Lakeside. Fare 4A 198
Lakeside. Hight 2M 187
Lakeside. Lee S 3B 238
Lakeside Av. Ports 9J 215
Lakeside Av. Rown 6D 158
Lakeside Bus. Pk. S'hrst 6C 18
Lakeside Clo. Ash V 7N 49
Lakeside Clo. Charl 8K 51
Lakeside Country Pk. 3D 160
Lakeside Ct. Fle 9N 27
Lakeside Ct. S'sea 5G 240
Lakeside Dri. Brams 8A 16
Lakeside Gdns. Farn 5F 28
Lakeside Gdns. Hav 7F 202
Lakeside Holiday Village. Hay I 5K 243
Lakeside Pines. New M 2C 232
Lakeside Rd. Ash V 7N 49
Lakeside Rd. Farn 4J 49
Lakeside Rd. Poole 4E 244
Lakeside, The. B'wtr 9F 18
Lakesmere Rd. Horn 4C 182
Lakes, The. Swanm 7C 164
Lake Vw. H Win 5C 26
Lakeview Dri. Hight 2N 187
Lakewood Clo. Chan F 4B 132
Lakewood Rd. Asht 7J 171
Lakewood Rd. Chan F 5B 132
Lakewood Rd. Highc 5G 231
Lamb Clo. And 2B 70
Lambdens Wlk. T'ley 5H 11
Lambdown App. Per D 5A 30
Lambdown Ter. Per D 7H 31
Lamberhurst Clo. Sotn 1E 194
Lambert Clo. Water 4M 201
Lambert Cres. B'wtr 9E 18
Lamborne Clo. S'hrst 4C 18
Lamborough La. Cher 9F 108
Lambourn Clo. Fare 9N 197
Lambourne Clo. Dib P 8L 193
Lambourne Clo. Spar 3A 104
Lambourne Clo. Thru 1N 67
Lambourne Dri. L Hth 6D 196
Lambourne Ho. H End 4M 175
Lambourne Rd. W End 9F 160
Lambourne's Hill 5N 31
Lambourne Way. Thru 1N 67
Lambourne Way. Tong 3N 65
Lambourn Sq. Chan F 6N 131
Lamb Roundabout, The. And 2N 69
Lambs Clo. Over 2E 56
Lambs Lease. Liss 2G 140
Lambs Row. Lych 4G 42
Lamerton Clo. Bord 3J 101
Lamerton Rd. Bord 3J 101
Lammas Clo. Cowes 5N 237
Lammas Rd. Hythe 7M 193
Lampard La. Churt 6F 84
Lampards Clo. Roth 6F 24
Lampeter Av. Ports 9J 201
Lampton Gdns. Bourn 5K 227
Lanark Clo. Frim 2N 29
Lancaster Av. F'ham 9E 64
Lancaster Clo. And 9M 51
Lancaster Clo. Burs 9L 175
Lancaster Clo. Christ 7E 230
Lancaster Clo. Fare 8K 199
Lancaster Clo. Lee S 3D 238
Lancaster Ct. W End 9G 160
Lancaster Dri. Cam 7M 19
Lancaster Rd. Bas 5B 42
Lancaster Rd. Sotn 8E 158
Lancaster Way. Farn 5L 29
Lancaster Way. Water 3N 201
Lancelot Clo. Chan F 6L 131
Lancer Clo. Christ 7J 229
Lancer Ct. A'sht 9G 48
Lance's Hill. Sotn 3D 174
Landale Clo. Enh A 3A 52
Landford 1J 155
Landford Gdns. Bourn 4A 228
Landford Way. Bourn 4A 228
Landfordwood 7J 121
Landguard Rd. Sotn 4J 173
Landguard Rd. S'sea 4H 241

Landon Ct. Gos. 5J 239
Landon Rd. Gos 8F 212
Landport. 9E 214
Landport St. Ports 1E 240
Landport St. S'sea 3C 240 (6M 5)
Landport Ter. Ports 3C 240 (6M 5)
Landport Vw. Ports 1D 240 (2N 5)
Landseer Clo. Bas. 8E 42
Landseer Clo. Coll T. 7G 18
Landseer Ct. And. 9M 51
Landseer Rd. Bourn 2G 244
Landseer Rd. Sotn 7G 174
Lands End Rd. Burs. 2M 195
Lane End. 6K 111 (Alresford)
Lane End. 3G 134 (Winchester)
Lane End. Braml. 2G 23
Lane End Dri. Ems. 9M 203
Lanehays Rd. Hythe 6L 193
Lanesbridge Clo. W'Inds 5F 170
Lanes End. Fare 6M 211
Lanes, The. New M. 1B 232
Lane, The. Bourn 9N 227
Lane, The. Cad 6N 155
Lane, The. Fawl. 5F 208
Lane, The. Gos 6J 239
Lane, The. S'sea 5G 240
Lane, The. T'ley. 5J 11
Langbar Clo. Sotn. 4C 174
Langbrook Clo. Hav 9F 202
Langdale Av. Ports 1J 215
Langdale Clo. Farn 8G 28
Langdale Clo. Sotn 2E 172
Langdale Ct. Ash V. 6N 49 (off Lakeside Clo.)
Langdon Ct. Poole 1B 244
Langdon Rd. Poole 1A 244
Langdown. 6N 193
Langdown Firs. Hythe 6M 193
Langdown Lawn. Hythe 7M 193
Langdown Lawn Clo. Hythe 7M 193
Langdown Rd. Hythe 6M 193
Langford La. Redl. 5D 120
Langford Rd. Ports. 9G 214
Langham Clo. N Bad. 8E 130
Langham Rd. Alt. 5E 80
Langhorn Rd. Sotn. 7A 160
Langley. 7L 115 (Liphook)
Langley. 9D 208 (Southampton)
Langley Chase. Ring. 3D 186
Langley Clo. Chu C 7L 47
Langley Dri. A'sht 2J 65
Langley Dri. Cam 7N 19
Langley Garden. F'bri 8K 151
Langley Lodge Gdns. Black 9D 208
Langley Rd. Christ 5G 230
Langley Rd. Poole 1C 244
Langley Rd. Ports. 8F 214
Langley Rd. Sotn 4F 172
Langrish. 9C 138
Langrish Clo. Hav. 3G 203
Langrish Rd. Sotn 7G 159
Langside Av. Poole 6E 226
Langstone. 1F 216
Langstone Av. Hav 2F 216
Langstone Bri. Hav & Hay I 3G 216
Langstone High St. Hav 2F 216
Langstone Ho. Fare 1C 212
Langstone Ho. Hav. 6G 202
Langstone Marina Heights. S'sea 4L 241
Langstone Rd. Hav. 9F 202
Langstone Rd. Ports 1H 241
Langstone Wlk. Fare. 9N 197
Langstone Wlk. Gos. 6D 212
Langton Clo. Bart S 6C 232
Langton Clo. Win 5J 105
Langton Dri. Head 9C 84
Langton Rd. Bish W. 3L 163
Langton Rd. Bourn. 9C 228
Langtons Ct. Alr. 1G 108
Langtry Pl. Cowes 5P 237
Lanham La. Win 7B 104 (in three parts)
Lankhills Rd. Win. 4K 105
Lansdowne Av. And 3L 69
Lansdowne Av. Fare. 2M 213
Lansdowne Av. Water 6J 201
Lansdowne Av. Win 9K 105
Lansdowne Clo. Roms 4L 129
Lansdowne Ct. Bourn. 2N 245
Lansdowne Ct. Roms 4L 129
Lansdowne Ct. Win 9K 105
Lansdowne Cres. Bourn 2L 245
Lansdowne Gdns. Bourn 1L 245
Lansdowne Gdns. Roms 4L 129
Lansdowne Hill. Sotn 7L 173 (7C 4)
Lansdowne Ho. Gos 1J 239
Lansdowne Rd. A'sht 1J 65
Lansdowne Rd. Alt. 3G 80
Lansdowne Rd. Bourn 9L 227
Lansdowne Rd. Sotn. 3F 172
Lansdowne St. S'sea 3C 240 (6M 5)
Lansdown Roundabout, The. Bourn. 2L 245
Lansley Rd. Bas 3C 42
Lantana Clo. Water. 3N 201
Lantern Ct. Win. 8J 105
Lanyard Dri. Gos. 1F 238
Lapin La. Bas 5K 59
Lapthorn Clo. Gos 4D 212
Lapwing Clo. Gos 9K 213
Lapwing Clo. Water 3B 182
Lapwing Dri. Tot 2J 171
Lapwing Gro. Fare 9H 199
Lapwing Ri. Whitc. 5F 54
Lapwing Rd. S'sea 2K 241
Lara Clo. Bourn 3A 228
Larch Av. Holb 3A 208
Larch Clo. Cam. 4N 19
Larch Clo. Hord 3G 232
Larch Clo. King W 6M 91
Larch Clo. Lee S 2C 238
Larch Clo. Lip. 3D 116
Larch Clo. Mid W 4B 72
Larch Clo. St I 4D 186
Larch Clo. W End 8H 161
Larch Ct. Ports 1E 240
Larchdale Clo. Wars 9A 196
Larch Dri. And. 2J 69
Larch Dri. K're 2B 6
Larches Gdns. Fare 8M 197
Larches Way. B'wtr 8D 18
Larchfield Rd. Fle. 4M 47
Larchfield Way. Water. 5C 182
Larch Rd. Head D. 1D 102
Larch Rd. Sotn 8F 158
Larch Row. Gods 9N 151
Larch Vw. Gods 9N 151
Larch Way. Burs 1K 195
Larch Way. Farn 9E 28
Larchwood. Chine 8E 22 (Crockford La.)
Larchwood. Chine 9G 22 (Hanmore Rd.)
Larchwood Av. Hav. 5B 202
Larchwood Ct. Sotn 5J 173
Larchwood Rd. Tot 4J 171
Larchwood Rd. Ptsfld. 3K 145
Larg Dri. Win 2G 105
Lark Clo. And 8A 52
Lark Clo. Bas 2H 59
Lark Clo. Tidw. 7E 30
Larkfield. Chine 9G 22
Larkfield Clo. F'ham 7B 64
Larkfield Rd. F'ham 8B 64
Lark Hill Ri. Win. 1H 127
Larkhill Rd. Ports 4G 215
Larkin Clo. Lud 1E 30
Lark Ri. Lip. 1C 116
Lark Rd. Christ 8C 230
Lark Rd. Eastl. 2B 160
Larks Barrow Hill. Whitc 8G 37
Larksfield Av. Bourn 3N 227
Larkshill Clo. New M 2C 232
Larkspur Chase. Sotn 5J 175
Larkspur Clo. A'sht 3J 65
Larkspur Clo. L Hth 7B 196
Larkspur Clo. Swanm. 6C 164
Larkspur Dri. Chan F. 6L 131
Larkspur Dri. March 1D 192
Larkspur Gdns. H End 4N 175
Larkspur Gdns. Holb 4N 207
Larkswood Clo. S'hrst 4C 18
Larkwhistle Farm Rd. Mich S 4K 77
Larkwhistle Wlk. Hav 2C 202
Larmer Clo. Fle. 4J 47
Larwood Sq. And 8B 52 (off Cricketers Way)
Lascelles Ct. Bourn. 8E 228
Lascelles Rd. Bourn 8E 228
Laser Clo. Wars 8B 196
Lasham. 4M 79
Lasham Grn. Hav 4H 203 (off Newnham Ct.)
Lasham Wlk. Fare. 9N 197
Lashly Mdw. Hmbdn 8D 166
Latch Farm Av. Christ. 6K 229
Latchmere Green. 8B 12
Latchmoor Drove. W'ish 9H 121
Latchmore Dri. Dib. 5H 193
Latchmore Forest Gro. Water 7A 182
Latchmore Gdns. Water 7M 181
Latelie Clo. Net A 4G 194
Latham Av. Frim. 2N 29
Latham Clo. F Oak. 1M 161
Latham Ct. Sotn 3G 172
Latham Rd. F Oak 1M 161
Latham Rd. Roms 4M 129
Latimer Ct. Ports. 4J 215
Latimer Ga. Sotn. 8E 4
Latimer Rd. Bourn 6K 227
Latimers Clo. Highc 5H 231
Latimer St. Roms 5L 129
Latimer St. Sotn 7M 173 (8E 4)
Lauder Clo. Frim. 2N 29
Lauderdale. Farn 1F 48
Launcelot Clo. And. 7N 51
Launcelyn Clo. N Bad 9E 130
Launceston Clo. Gos. 9L 213
Launceston Dri. Eastl 7D 132
Laundry La. Heck. 9H 15
Laundry La. Mil S. 8L 235
Laundry La. S'hrst 7G 18
Laundry Rd. Sotn 8F 158
Laundry Yd. Whitc 5G 54
Laurel Clo. Cam. 9M 19
Laurel Clo. Christ 5F 230
Laurel Clo. Farn 9E 28
Laurel Clo. Gos. 9L 213
Laurel Clo. Hord 2F 232
Laurel Clo. Hythe 6L 193
Laurel Clo. L Hth. 5E 196
Laurel Clo. N War 8J 45
Laurel Clo. St L. 4B 186
Laurel Clo. Sotn 7B 174
Laurel Gdns. A'sht. 3J 65
Laurel Gdns. L Hth 5E 196
Laurel La. St L 5B 186
Laurel Pl. Mid W. 4B 72
Laurel Rd. L Hth 5E 196
Laurel Rd. Water 6C 182
Laurels, The. Bas 5D 42
Laurels, The. F'ham 3H 65
Laurels, The. Fle 2M 47
Laurence Ct. F Oak. 1N 161
Laurence Ct. Lud 1D 30
Laurence Grn. Ems 5M 203
Laurie Wlk. Black 7D 208
Lauriston Dri. Chan F. 3N 131
Laurus Clo. Water. 4A 202
Laurus Wlk. Lee S 1B 238
Lavant Clo. Water. 9B 182
Lavant Ct. Ptsfld 9L 139
Lavant Dri. Hav. 6G 202
Lavant Fld. Chaw 8E 80
Lavant St. Ptsfld 9L 139
Lavell's La. Str S 5H 13
Lavender Clo. Sotn. 5D 174
Lavender Gdns. Bord 5J 101
Lavender Rd. Bas 3J 59
Lavender Rd. Bourn 2A 228
Lavender Rd. Hord 3F 232
Lavender Rd. Water 3A 202
Lavender Wlk. Bourn 2A 228
Laverock Lea. Fare 8L 199
Laverstoke. 5N 55
Laverstoke Clo. Rown 6D 158
Laverstoke La. Lave. 6M 55
Lavey's La. Fare 3K 197
Lavington Cotts. Bas. 3J 43
Lavington Gdns. N Bad. 9E 130
Lavinia Rd. Gos 2K 239
Lavinia Rd. Poole 7A 226
Lawday Link. F'ham 3C 64
Lawday Pl. F'ham 3C 64
Lawday Pl. La. F'ham 3C 64
Lawford Cres. Yate. 7N 17
Lawford Ri. Bourn 3L 227
Lawford Rd. Bourn. 2L 227
Lawford Way. Tot 3L 171
Lawn Clo. Gos. 8F 212
Lawn Clo. Mil S 9L 235
Lawn Ct. Bourn 1H 245 (5H 247)
Lawn Dri. L Hth 7D 196
Lawn Ho. Win. 7N 237
Lawn Rd. Eastl 8F 132
Lawn Rd. Mil S. 9L 235
Lawn Rd. Penn. 3B 234
Lawn Rd. Sotn 2N 173
Lawn Rd. Win. 1F 104
Lawnside Rd. Sotn 2F 172
Lawns, The. Christ. 6K 231
Lawns, The. Farn 9G 28
Lawn St. Win. 6L 105 (7N 237)
Lawnswood. F Oak. 2A 162
Lawnswood Clo. Water 8N 181
Lawn Vw. New M. 1M 231
Lawrence Av. Water 8M 181
Lawrence Clo. And 8M 51
Lawrence Clo. Bas. 2D 42
Lawrence Ct. Bourn. 8N 227
Lawrence Ct. Sotn 8D 174
Lawrencedale Ct. Bas 7A 42
Lawrence Dri. Poole 4C 244
Lawrence Gro. Sotn. 8D 174
Lawrence Ho. Hythe 5N 193
Lawrence Houses. Grat 4L 67
Lawrence La. N Gor. 6L 153
Lawrence Mans. S'sea 4F 240
Lawrence Rd. Fare. 7B 198
Lawrence Rd. Fle. 3L 47
Lawrence Rd. Ring 7M 185
Lawrence Rd. S'sea 4F 240
Lawrence Sq. Gos. 3M 239 (off Walpole Rd.)
Lawrence Wlk. Gos 1F 238
Lawrence Way. Cam 9H 19
Lawrence Way. Win 4L 105 (off Worthy Rd.)
Lawson Clo. Swanw 1A 196
Lawson Rd. Poole 8A 226
Lawson Rd. S'sea. 3F 240
Laws Ter. A'sht. 8L 49
Laxton Clo. L Hth. 6E 196
Laxton Clo. Sotn 8E 174
Lay Fld. Hook 2F 44
Layton Ct. Poole 9B 226
Layton Rd. Gos 5E 212
Layton Rd. Poole. 9B 226
Leabrook. Sar G 4D 196
Lea Clo. Bad L 4J 65
Lea Clo. Bas. 6E 42
Leacock Clo. Swanm. 6D 164
Lea Ct. F'ham 3H 65
Leaden Vere. Long S 4E 62
Leafey La. Gray 1G 103
Leafy La. White 3H 197
Leagreen. 6J 233
Lealand Gro. Ports. 9L 201
Lealand Rd. Ports 1L 215
Lea La. Fle 4K 47
Leamington Cres. Lee S 9B 212
Leamington Ho. S'sea 3D 240 (5N 5)
Leamington Rd. Bourn. 7L 227
Leander Clo. Eastl 7E 132
Leander Dri. Gos 9L 213
Lea-Oak Gdns. Fare 6N 197
Leap Hill Rd. Bourn. 8D 228
Lea Rd. Black. 9C 208
Lea Rd. Cam 2K 29
Lear Rd. Gos 2K 239
Leaside Way. Sotn. 6A 160
Lea Springs. Fle 4J 47
Lea, The. Fle. 4J 47
Leatherhead Gdns. H End 9A 162
Lea Way. A'sht. 8N 49
Leaway. Bad L 5J 65
Leaway, The. Fare. 9M 199
Leawood Rd. Fle 4J 47
Leaze, The. Bulf 3A 66 (off John French Way)
Lebanon Rd. Sotn 3C 172
Le Borowe. Chu C 7K 47
Lechlade Gdns. Bourn. 6D 228
Lechlade Gdns. Fare 5A 198
Leckford. 8B 74
Leckford Clo. Fare 7L 199
Leckford Clo. Sotn. 2H 175
Leckford Golf Course. 1H 89
Leckford La. Stockb 2G 88
Leckford Rd. Hav. 3G 203
Ledbury Rd. Christ 9B 230
Ledbury Rd. Ports. 8D 200
Lederle La. Gos 3E 212
Ledgard Clo. Poole 1A 244
Ledger Hill Clo. Bulf. 3A 66 (off Orchard End)
Lee Church La. Lee. 2M 157
Lee Ct. A'sht. 2L 65
Leedam Rd. Bourn 2H 227
Lee Drove. Roms. 2N 157
Lee Ground. 4J 197
Leelands. Penn 5D 234
Lee La. Roms & Nurs 8N 129
Lee-on-the-Solent. 1A 238
Lee-on-the-Solent Golf Course. 7C 212
Leep La. Gos 5K 239
Lee Rd. A'sht 9G 48
Lee Rd. Gos 1J 239
Lees Clo. Christ. 2G 229
Lees Hill. S Warn. 4C 62
Leesland Rd. Gos. 2J 239
Lees La. Gos 2K 239
Lees La. N. Gos 2K 239
Lees Mdw. Hook 2J 45
Leeson Rd. Bourn 7B 228
Lefroy Av. Bas 4D 42
Lefroy Ho. Bas. 4D 42
Lefroy Pk. Fle 2L 47
Lefroy's Fld. Cron 2L 63
Leger Clo. Chu C 6K 47
Legge Cres. A'sht 1G 64
Legion Clo. Sotn. 7A 160
Legion La. King W. 8M 91
Legion Rd. Hay I 3G 242
Lehar Clo. Bas. 2M 59
Leicester Ct. Gos 2F 238
Leicester Pl. And 2N 69
Leicester Rd. Poole 1C 244
Leicester Rd. Sotn 9J 159
Leicester Way. Win 5N 105
Leigham Va. Rd. Bourn 1G 246
Leigh Clo. And 2B 70
Leigh Ct. F Oak. 9C 132
Leigh Gdns. And. 2B 70
Leigh Park. 3E 202
Leigh Pk. L'ton 2C 234
Leigh Pk. Gardens. 3G 202
Leigh Pk. Shop. Cen. Hav 4F 202 (off Greywell Sq.)
Leigh Rd. And 2A 70
Leigh Rd. Chan F & Eastl 8A 132
Leigh Rd. Fare 7C 198
Leigh Rd. Hav. 7F 202
Leigh Rd. New M 3B 232
Leigh Rd. Sotn 1M 173
Leighton Av. Sotn. 2G 173
Leighton Lodge. Bourn 1H 245 (5H 247)
Leighton Rd. Sotn 7C 174
Leipzig Rd. Chu C 8N 47
Leisure, The. Gos 4F 212
Leisure World. 6K 173
Leith Av. Fare. 8M 199
Leith Dri. A'sht 8H 49
Lemon Gro. W'hill 6H 101
Lemon Rd. Sotn. 3G 172
Lena Clo. Lud. 1D 30
Lendorber Av. Ports. 9H 201
Lendore Rd. Frim 4M 29
Lennel Gdns. Chu C 5A 48
Lennon Way. Bas 2L 59
Lennox Clo. Chan F 4C 132
Lennox Clo. Gos. 6L 239
Lennox Clo. Sotn 6E 158
Lennox Ct. S'sea. 5E 240 (off Lennox Rd. N.)
Lennox Rd. Bas 9N 41
Lennox Rd. N. S'sea. 5E 240
Lennox Rd. S. S'sea 5E 240
Lennox Row. Ports 1B 240 (2K 5)
Len Smart Ct. Bas 3D 42
Lensyd Gdns. Water. 4N 181
Lenten St. Alt 5E 80
Lent Hill Ct. Win. 8H 105
Lentune Way. L'ton. 4D 234
Leofric Ct. S'sea 4K 241
Leominster Rd. Ports. 8C 200
Leonard Cheshire Clo. Ame 6A 66 (off McKie Rd.)
Leonard Clo. Frim 4M 29
Leonard Rd. Gos 2L 239
Leonards Ct. Sotn 2B 172
Leopold Av. Farn 7K 29
Leopold Dri. Bish W. 3L 163
Leopold St. S'sea 5F 240
Le Patourel Clo. Christ. 7N 229
Lepe. 3K 237
Lepe Country Pk. 3K 237
Lepe Rd. Black. 9C 208
Lerryn Rd. Gos 6F 212
Leslie Loader Ct. Eastl 7E 132
Leslie Loader M. Sotn 5C 174
Leslie Rd. Bourn. 6K 227
Lester Av. Hav 7C 202
Lester Rd. Gos. 2H 239
Lestock Way. Fle 2A 48
Levell Ct. Lud. 1D 30
Leven Av. Bourn. 9H 227
Leven Clo. Bourn 1H 245
Leven Clo. Chan F. 4M 131
Leventhorpe Ct. Gos. 3L 239
Levern Dri. F'ham. 4E 64
Leveson Clo. Gos. 4H 239
Leviathan Clo. Fare. 6N 211
Levignen Clo. Chu C. 6J 47
Lewes Clo. Eastl 6E 132
Lewin Clo. Col C. 4K 133
Lewins Wlk. Burs 9K 175
Lewis Clo. Bas 4D 42
Lewis Clo. Dib P. 7H 193
Lewisham Way. Owl 4F 18
Lewis Ho. Sotn. 5M 173 (4E 4)

Lewis Rd. Ems 6N 203
Lewis Silkin Way. Sotn 7F 158
Lewry Clo. H End 3N 175
Lexby Rd. Tot 4N 171
Lexden Gdns. Hay I 3E 242
Leybourne Av. Bourn 1G 227
(in two parts)
Leybourne Av. Sotn 2D 174
Leybourne Clo. Bourn 1G 227
Leybrook Common. 6G 186
Leydene Av. Bourn 5C 228
Leydene Clo. Bourn 5C 228
Leydene Pk. E Meon 1M 167
Leyland Clo. Gos 4K 239
Leyland Rd. Poole 4C 226
Ley Rd. Farn 4J 29
Leyside. Christ 7B 230
Leyside. C'then 1C 18
Leyton Rd. Sotn 4A 174
Leyton Way. And 3K 69
Liam Clo. Hav 5G 202
Liberties, The. Sob 9K 165
Liberty Ct. Christ 7J 229
Liberty Rd. Newt 2J 179
Liberty Row. Hamb 7L 195
(off Meadow La.)
Liberty, The. Water 7F 180
Library Rd. Bourn 5K 227
Library Rd. Fern 5E 4
Library Rd. Poole 9C 226
Library Rd. Tot 3N 171
Lichen Way. March 8E 172
Lichfield Ct. Gos 2F 238
(off Gazelle Clo.)
Lichfield Dri. Gos 9L 213
Lichfield Rd. Fare 6F 196
Lichfield Rd. Ports 1H 241
Lickfolds Rd. Row 9N 63
Liddell Clo. Finch 2H 17
Liddel Way. Chan F 7N 131
Liddiards Way. Pur 6M 201
Lidiard Gdns. S'sea 5J 241
Lightfoot Gro. Bas 9C 42
Lightfoot Lawn. S'sea 4K 241
Light Infantry Mus., The. 6K 105 (7K 237)
Lightning Clo. Fawl 6D 208
Lightning Rd. Ame 5A 66
(off Boscombe Rd.)
Lightsfield. Okly 9D 40
Lilac Clo. Bord 5J 101
Lilac Clo. Hav 6J 203
Lilac Clo. Ring 9L 185
Lilac Rd. Sotn 7N 159
Lilac Way. Bas 5M 41
Lilian Pl. Lwr F 4D 98
Lille Barracks. A'sht 4M 49
Lilley Clo. March 8E 172
Lilley Ct. C'then 1D 18
Lillies, The. H Hth 4N 161
Lilliput. 5A 244
Lilliput Rd. Poole 5A 244
Lillywhite Cres. And 6A 52
Lily Av. Water 7J 201
Lily Clo. Bas 2J 59
Limberline Rd. Ports 4H 215
Limberline Spur. Ports 3H 215
Limbrey Hill. Upt G 3A 62
Lime Av. Alt 4E 80
Lime Av. Sotn 5E 174
Lime Clo. Col C 4L 133
Lime Clo. Dib P 7K 193
Lime Clo. Sotn 5E 174
Limecroft. Yate 8M 17
Lime Dri. Fle 8A 28
Lime Gdns. Bas 6E 42
Lime Gdns. W End 8H 161
Lime Gro. Alt 3E 80
Lime Gro. Evtn 6L 233
Lime Gro. Hay I 3C 242
Lime Gro. Ports 8C 200
Limekiln La. Bish W 9H 135
Limekiln La. E Meon 4C 144
(in two parts)
Limekiln La. Holb 3N 207
(in two parts)
Lime Kiln La. Est. Holb 3N 207
Limekiln Rd. Chut F 6B 32
Lime Rd. Alr 1F 108
Limes Av. Burgh 3E 8
Limes Clo. B'shtt 8E 102
Limes Clo. Liss 1E 140
Limes Rd. Farn 7E 28
Limes, The. Bas 2J 59
Limes, The. Braml 2J 23
Limes, The. Gos 7F 212
Limes, The. Hav 9F 202
Limes, The. March 9F 172
Limes, The. Port 1C 86
Lime St. A'sht 9H 49
Lime St. Sotn 7M 173 (7E 4)
Lime Tree Clo. A'hlt 4C 152
Lime Tree Ho. L'ton 2E 234
Limetree Wlk. Win 6A 106
Lime Tree Way. Chine 9F 22
Lime Wlk. And 3K 69
Lime Wlk. Bot 3C 176
Lime Wlk. Dib P 7K 193
Limited Rd. Bourn 5L 227
Linacre Rd. Sotn 5H 175
Linbrook Almshouses. Ring 7M 185
Linbrook Ct. Ring 8K 185
Lin Brook Dri. Ring 7M 185
Linchmere. 3K 117
Linchmere Rd. Hasl 3K 117
Lincoln Av. Bourn 8A 228
Lincoln Av. Christ 4J 229
Lincoln Clo. Bas 3K 59
Lincoln Clo. Fare 6F 196
Lincoln Clo. Roms 3A 130
Lincoln Ct. Gos 2F 238
Lincoln Ct. Lip 2E 116
Lincoln Ct. Sotn 9K 159
Lincoln Ct. W End 9G 160
Lincoln Grn. Alt 6E 80
Lincoln Ri. Water 6A 182
Lincoln Rd. Poole 7B 226
Lincoln Rd. Ports 2F 240
Lincolns Ri. Eastl 3F 132
Linda Gro. Water 7N 181
Linda Rd. Fawl 5F 208
Lindbergh Clo. Gos 2F 238
Lindbergh Ri. White 3H 197
Lind Clo. Water 6N 201
Linden Av. Odi 7M 45
Linden Av. Old B 6J 43
Linden Clo. Lud 1E 30
Linden Clo. Wal C 8A 164
Linden Ct. Old B 6J 43
Linden Ct. Park G 5E 196
Linden Ct. Ring 9J 185
Linden Ct. Roms 5L 129
Linden Ct. Sotn 8F 160
Linden Dri. Liss 1E 140
Linden Gdns. H End 5A 176
Linden Gdns. Ring 9J 185
Linden Gro. Chan F 4A 132
Linden Gro. Gos 4K 239
Linden Gro. Hay I 4G 242
Linden Lea. Fare 8K 199
Linden Rd. Bish G 1G 9
Linden Rd. Bourn 3L 227
Linden Rd. Head D 2D 102
Linden Rd. Poole 8A 226
Linden Rd. Roms 5M 129
Linden Rd. Sotn 7F 158
Lindens Clo. Ems 7M 203
Lindens, The. Burt 3N 229
Lindens, The. F'ham 9F 64
Linden Wlk. N Bad 7E 130
Linden Way. Hav 6F 202
Linden Way. L'ton 2C 234
Linden Way. Water 5C 182
Lindford. 2M 101
Lindford Chase. Lind 2L 101
Lindford Rd. Bord 1K 101
Lindford Wey. Lind 2L 101
Lindisfarne Clo. Ports 9H 201
Lindley Av. S'sea 5H 241
Lindley Gdns. Alr 2F 108
Lindon Ct. S'sea 3G 241
Lind Rd. Gos 6L 239
Lindsay Gdns. Poole 1E 244
Lindsay Mnr. Poole 1E 244
Lindsay Pk. Poole 1E 244
Lindsay Rd. Poole 1D 244
Lindsay Rd. Sotn 4J 175
Lindsey Ho. S'sea 5E 240
(off Richmond Rd.)
Lindum Clo. A'sht 1J 65
Lindum Dene. A'sht 1J 65
Lindurn Ct. Poole 1E 244
Lindway. Park G 3D 196
Liners Ind. Est. Sotn 4H 173
Lineside. Burt 6M 229
Lines, The. K're 1A 6
Linford. 4B 188
Linford Clo. New M 2B 232
Linford Ct. F Oak 1N 161
Linford Ct. Hav 2D 202
Linford Cres. Sotn 8J 159
Linford Rd. Ring 8M 185
Ling Cres. Head D 1D 102
Ling Dale. Sotn 4L 159
Lingdale Pl. Sotn 2M 173
Lingdale Rd. Bourn 8G 228
Lingen Clo. And 7N 51
Lingfield Clo. Alt 6F 80
Lingfield Clo. Old B 6K 43
Lingfield Ct. Ports 4C 240 (7L 5)
Lingfield Gdns. Sotn 9D 160
Lingfield Grange. Poole 2F 244
Lingmala Gro. Chu C 6N 47
Lingwood Av. Christ 8A 230
Lingwood Clo. Sotn 4L 159
Lingwood Wlk. Sotn 4L 159
Linhorns La. New M 1B 232
Linkenholt. 6G 6
Linkenholt Way. Hav 4C 202
Linklater Path. Ports 9E 214
Linklater Rd. Ports 9E 214
Link Rd. Alt 2G 81
Link Rd. K're 2C 6
Link Rd. Ring 8M 185
Link Rd. Sotn 8E 158
Link Rd. S'wick 7C 200
Links Clo. Row C 9H 183
Links Dri. Christ 5G 228
Linkside. 1L 103
Linkside Av. Bourn 6B 228
Linkside E. Hind 9L 85
Linkside N. Hind 9K 85
Linkside S. Hind 1L 103
Linkside W. Hind 9K 85
Links La. Hay I 4C 242
Links La. Row C 8H 183
Links Rd. Poole 3B 244
Links Rd. Win 5H 105
Links, The. Gos 7E 212
Links, The. W'hill 6G 100
Links Vw. Av. Poole 4B 244
Links Vw. Way. Sotn 5L 159
Links Way. Farn 9E 28
Link, The. And 1J 69
Link, The. Water 9A 182
Linkway. Cam 9L 19
Linkway. C'then 1B 18
Link Way. Fare 7M 211
Linkway. Fle 5L 47
Link Way. Okly 1D 58
Linkway Pde. Fle 5L 47
Linnet Clo. Bas 9J 41
Linnet Clo. Hight 2M 187
Linnet Clo. Ptsfld 2B 146
Linnet Clo. Water 6M 181
Linnet Ct. Gos 1H 239
Linnet Ct. New M 4A 232
Linnet La. Bish G 1G 9
(off Ash Rd.)
Linnet Sq. Eastl 2B 160
Linnets Rd. Alr 2E 108
Linnets, The. Fare 9H 199
Linnets, The. Tot 2J 171
Linnets Way. Alt 3F 80
Linnies La. Sway 8H 223
Linsford Bus. Pk. Myt 9N 29
Linstead Rd. Farn 4G 28
Linsted La. Head 9N 83
Linton Clo. T'ley 6J 11
Linton Dri. And 9M 51
Linwood. 1B 188
Linwood Clo. Hythe 7M 193
Linwood Rd. Bourn 7M 227
Lion & Lamb Way. F'ham 8D 64
Lion & Lamb Yd. F'ham 8D 64
Lion Clo. Over 3D 56
Lion Ct. Bas 5G 42
Lion Ga. Building. Ports 2C 240 (3L 5)
Lionheart Clo. Bourn 1B 226
Lionheart Way. Burs 9K 175
Lions Fld. Oakh 3C 100
Lions Hall. Win 7K 105 (9L 237)
Lions Hill Way. Ashy H 4A 186
Lions La. Ashy H 3A 186
Lion St. Ports 2C 240 (3L 5)
(in two parts)
Lions Wood. St L 4B 186
Lion Ter. Ports 2C 240 (4L 5)
(in three parts)
Lion Way. Chu C 6N 47
Liphook. 2G 117
Liphook Golf Course. 5C 116
Liphook Ho. Hav 4H 203
Liphook Rd. Hasl 9N 103
Liphook Rd. Head & Pass 4A 102
Liphook Rd. Lind 2L 101
Liphook Rd. Pass & Hasl 3H 117
Liphook Rd. W'hill 7H 101
Lipizzaner Fields. White 1E 196
Lippen La. W'frd 5P 135
Lipscombe Ri. Alt 3F 80
Lisa Ct. Bas 7B 42
Lisbon Rd. Sotn 4J 173
Liskeard Dri. Farn 6J 29
Lisle Clo. L'ton 3D 234
Lisle Clo. Win 2E 126
Lisle Court. 3J 235
Lisle Ct. Win 8J 105
Lisle Ct. Rd. L'ton 2H 235
Lisle Way. Ems 6L 203
Lismoyne Clo. Fle 1L 47
Liss. 1E 140
Liss Dri. Elve 9H 27
Liss Forest. 8F 114
Liss Rd. S'sea 3G 241
Lister Rd. Bas 9A 42
Lister Rd. Ports 9G 200
Litchfield. 2G 36
Litchfield Clo. Charl 7K 51
Litchfield Cres. Sotn 1D 174
Litchfield Dri. Elve 8H 27
Litchfield Ho. T'ley 5H 11
Litchfield Rd. Sotn 1D 174
Litchfield Rd. Win 2H 105
Litchford Rd. New M 2D 232
Lith Av. Horn 2C 182
Lith Cres. Horn 1C 182
Lith La. Horn 2A 182
(Catherington La.)
Lith La. Horn 1B 182
(Lith Cres.)
Lit. Abshot Rd. Fare 9E 196
Lit. Aldershot La. Baug 3B 10
Lit. Anglesey. Gos 5K 239
Lit. Anglesey Rd. Gos 5J 239
Lit. Arthur St. Ports 9F 214
Lit. Ashton La. Bish W 9G 134
Lit. Austins Rd. F'ham 9F 64
Lit. Barn Pl. Liss 1G 140
Lit. Barrs Dri. New M 2C 232
Lit. Basing. Old B 4G 43
Little Bullington. 4C 76
Lit. Bull La. Wal C 9N 163
Lit. Burn. Sway 5J 223
Little Clo. Gos 4E 212
Lit. Coburg St. Ports 2E 240
Lit. Copse. And 3L 69
Lit. Copse. Fle 4L 47
Lit. Copse. Yate 6N 17
Lit. Copse Chase. Chine 1F 42
Lit. Corner. Water 7G 181
Little Ct. Poole (BH13) 5D 244
Little Ct. Poole (BH14) 6A 244
Little Cft. Yate 8N 17
Littlecroft Av. Bourn 3M 227
Lit. Dean Ct. Stockb 2G 88
Lit. Dean La. Upt G 4B 62
Lit. Dene Copse. Penn 4B 234
Littledown. 6F 6
(Andover)
Littledown. 6D 228
(Bournemouth)
Littledown Av. Bourn 7B 228
Littledown Dri. Bourn 7B 228
Littledown Leisure Cen. 6D 228
Little Drove. W'grn 2A 154
(off Brook La.)
Lit. Drove Rd. Chlbn 5F 74
Lit. Fallow. Lych 3G 43
Littlefield Cres. Chan F 6K 131
Littlefield Rd. Alt 4G 80
Lit. Forest Mans. Bourn 2L 245 (7N 247)
Lit. Forest Rd. Bourn 9H 227
Lit. Fosters. Poole 7C 244
Little Gays. Fare 6K 211
Lit. George St. Ports 9F 214
Little Grn. Gos 5J 239
Littlegreen Av. Hav 5G 203
Lit. Grn. Orchard. Gos 4J 239
Lit. Hambrook St. S'sea 4C 240 (7M 5)
Lit. Hayes La. It Ab 9J 93
Lit. Hoddington. Upt G 3B 62
Lit. Hoddington Clo. Upt G 3B 62
Little Holbury. 3N 207
Lit. Holbury Pk. Homes. Holb 3N 207
Lit. Hyden La. Clan 3B 168
Lit. Kimble Wlk. H End 4N 175
Lit. Knowle Hill. K're 1D 6
Lit. Lance's Hill. Sotn 3D 174
Little La. Gos 5J 239
Little London. 2C 52
(Andover)
Little London. 1A 86
(Stockbridge)
Little London. 1N 21
(Tadley)
Lit. London Rd. Sil 6A 12
Little Mead. Water 7H 181
Little Meads. Roms 5K 129
Littlemill La. Dam 3P 149
Lit. Minster St. Win 7L 105 (8M 237)
Little Moor. S'hrst 4E 18
Littlemoor Av. Bourn 2B 226
Lit. Oak Rd. Sotn 7L 159
Little Park. 4F 68
Littlepark Av. Hav 6B 202
Lit. Park Clo. H End 4M 175
Lit. Park Farm Rd. Fare 4F 196
Littlepark Ho. Hav 6A 202
Little Posbrook. 3J 211
Lit. Quob La. W End 9J 161
Lit. Reynolds. Tot 5K 171
Little Sandhurst. 4C 18
Little Shoddesden. 7M 31
Lit. Shore La. Bish W 4N 163
Little Somborne. 5J 89
Lit. Southsea St. S'sea 4C 240 (7M 5)
Littleton. 2F 104
Littleton Gro. Hav 5F 202
Littleton La. Spar & Win 2E 104
Littleton Rd. Win 2F 104
Little Vigo. Yate 9L 17
Lit. Wellington St. A'sht 9J 49
Lit. Woodfalls Dri. W'flls 9C 120
Littlewood Gdns. L Hth 6B 196
Littlewood Gdns. W End 1H 175
Lit. Woodham La. Gos 2E 238
Littleworth Rd. Seale 9N 65
Litton Gdns. Okly 1D 58
Liverpool Ct. Gos 2F 238
Liverpool Rd. Fare 2B 212
Liverpool Rd. Ports 2B 240
Liverpool St. Sotn 3M 173 (1E 4)
Livery Rd. W'slw 5G 86
Livesay Gdns. Ports 1G 241
Livia Clo. And 6A 52
Livingstone Ct. Gos 1F 238
Livingstone Rd. And 9D 52
Livingstone Rd. Bourn 1E 246
Livingstone Rd. Christ 7N 229
Livingstone Rd. Poole 8A 226
Livingstone Rd. Sotn 2M 173
Livingstone Rd. S'sea 4E 240
Llangar Gro. C'then 1C 18
Lloyd Av. March 9D 172
Loader Clo. King W 8N 91
Loane Rd. Sotn 7D 174
Lobelia Ct. Water 3A 202
Lobelia Rd. Sotn 7A 160
Locarno Rd. Ports 6H 215
Loch Rd. Poole 9C 226
Lock App. Port S 1B 214
Locke Clo. Grat 5K 67
(off Streetway Rd.)
Lockerley. 4A 122
Lockerley Clo. L'ton 4E 234
Lockerley Cres. Sotn 1E 172
Lockerley Rd. Dun 5B 122
Lockerley Rd. Hav 6G 202
Locke Rd. H End 2N 175
Locke Rd. Lip 2F 116
Locke's Drove. Tang & Ibt 3L 33
Lockhams Rd. Curd 2H 177
Lock Rd. A'sht 6M 49
Locksbridge La. Braml 2E 22
Locks Heath. 6D 196
Locks Heath Cen. L Hth 6D 196
Locksheath Clo. Hav 3D 202
Locks Heath Pk. Rd. L Hth 8E 196
Lock's La. Spar 3A 104
Locksley Ct. Sotn 3L 173
Locksley Rd. Eastl 2C 160
Locksmead. Bas 6E 42
Locks Rd. L Hth 7D 196
Locksway Rd. S'sea 3J 241
Lockswood Keep. L Hth 5D 196
Lockswood Rd. L Hth 6C 196
Lock Vw. Port S 1B 214
Lockwood Clo. Farn 4G 29
Loddon Bus. Cen. Bas 4F 42
Loddon Cen., The. Bas 3F 42
Loddon Ct. Bas 9C 42
Loddon Dri. Bas 6D 42
Loddon Ho. Bas 5D 42
Loddon Mall. Bas 6C 42
Loddon Rd. Farn 6F 28
Lode Hill. D'ton 1L 119
Lodge Av. Ports 9H 201
Lodge Clo. A'sht 2L 65
Lodge Clo. And 1L 69
Lodge Clo. Poole 1C 244
Lodge Ct. Poole 1C 244
Lodge Dri. Dib P 8L 193
Lodge Dri. W'hll 8D 50
Lodge Drove. W'flls 9C 120
Lodge Gdns. Gos 4J 239
Lodge Gro. Yate 7B 18
Lodge Hill. Newt 4K 179
Lodge La. Beau 1C 236
Lodge La. Chut F 7B 32
Lodge Rd. Christ 6H 229
Lodge Rd. Hav 8B 202

Lodge Rd. L Hth 6E 196
Lodge Rd. Penn 3B 234
Lodge Rd. Sotn 3M 173
Lodge, The. Sotn 3L 173
Lodge, The. Water 3A 202
Lodge Va. E Wel 1B 156
Lodsworth. Farn 9F 28
Lodsworth Clo. Water 7D 168
Lodsworth Ho. Ports 1E 240
Loewy Cres. Poole 4B 226
Lofting Clo. Eastl 1J 161
Logan Clo. Sotn 6E 158
Loggon Rd. Bas 9B 42
Lomax Clo. H End 1N 175
Lombard Av. Bourn 9G 229
Lombard Ct. Ports 7K 5
Lombard St. Ports 4B 240 (7J 5)
Lombardy Clo. Gos 6G 212
Lombardy Ri. Water 4N 201
Lomond Clo. Okly 9C 40
Lomond Clo. Ports 8E 214
Londesborough Rd. S'sea 4F 240
Londlandes. Chu C 7K 47
London Av. Ports 6E 214
London La. Avon 5J 219
London La. Fac 7K 7
London Mall. Ports 6F 214
London Minstead 8M 155
London Rd. And & And D 2A 70
London Rd. Bas 7D 42
London Rd. B'wtr & Cam 8H 19
London Rd. Cosh & Water 9G 201
London Rd. E'sly & B'wtr 3F 26
London Rd. H Win 5D 26
London Rd. Holyb 2J 81
London Rd. Hook & H Win 1J 45
London Rd. Lip 2E 116
London Rd. Newn & Hook 5N 43
London Rd. Odi 8L 45 (in two parts)
London Rd. Old B 7F 42
London Rd. Over 2D 56
London Rd. Ptsfld & Hill B 8A 140
London Rd. Ports 3F 214
London Rd. Sotn 4L 173 (2C 4)
London Rd. Stockb 2G 88
London Rd. Water 1D 182 (in two parts)
London Rd. Whitc & Lave 5H 55
London Rd. Win & King W 2M 105
London St. And 2A 70
London St. Bas 7C 42
London St. Whitc 5G 55
London Tavern Cvn. Pk., The. Ring 9M 185
Lone Barn La. Bish W 7K 135
Lone Valley. Water 6K 201
Longacre Clo. Liss 1F 140
Long Acre Ct. Ports 9F 214
Longacre Ri. Chine 1F 42
Longacres. Fare 5F 196
Long & Short Lythes, The. 6L 99
Longbarrow Clo. Bourn 5C 228
Longbarrow Clo. S Won 3J 91
Long Beech Dri. Farn 9E 28
Long Beech Dri. Tot 4K 171
Long Bri. F'ham 8E 64
Longbridge Clo. Cal 9K 157
Longbridge Clo. Sher L 3M 23
Longbridge Ct. Cal 9K 157
Longbridge Ho. S'sea 5M 5
Longbridge Ind. Pk. Sotn 7A 174
Longbridge Rd. Braml 1G 22
Long Clo. D'ton 1J 119 (in two parts)
Longclose Rd. H End 3A 176
Long Common 9C 162
Long Copse. Holb 5B 208
Long Copse Chase. Chine 1F 42
Long Copse La. Ems 5M 203
Longcroft. Bent 7K 63
Longcroft Clo. Bas 7B 42
Longcroft Rd. K're 1A 6
Long Cross Hill. Head 2A 102
Long Cross La. Hat W 4J 59
Long Curtain Rd. S'sea 5B 240 (9K 5)
Longdean Clo. Ports 8B 200
Long Down 2N 191
Longdown. Fle 5L 47
Longdown Lodge. S'hrst 5D 18
Longdown Rd. S'hrst 4C 18
Long Dri. Gos 7E 212
Long Dri. W End 9J 161
Long Drove. E Grim 9F 86
Long Drove. W Gri 1D 120
Longfellow Pde. Bas 3D 42
Longfield. Okly 8D 40
Longfield Av. Fare 1N 211
Longfield Clo. Farn 4J 29
Longfield Clo. N Wal 9A 58
Longfield Clo. S'sea 2K 241
Longfield Dri. Bourn 1E 226
Longfield Rd. Ems 6L 203 (in two parts)
Longfield Rd. F Oak 2A 162
Longfield Rd. Hord 4J 233
Longfield Rd. Win 6N 105
Longford Clo. Cam 9M 19
Longford Pl. Penn 5D 234
Long Garden M. F'ham 8D 64 (off Long Garden Wlk.)
Long Garden Pl. F'ham 7D 64
Long Garden Wlk. F'ham 8D 64
Long Garden Wlk. E. F'ham 7D 64
Long Garden Wlk. W. F'ham 7D 64
Long Garden Way. F'ham 8D 64
Long Gro. Baug 3D 10
Long Hedge Drove. St M 8K 35
Long Hill. Seale 9N 65
Longhouse Grn. Win 6N 105
Long La. Burs 1L 195
Long La. Chine 1H 43
Long La. Holb 2N 207
Long La. March 9C 172
Long La. Odi 1F 62
Long La. Ring 4L 187
Long La. Upt G 5A 62
Long La. Clo. Holb 5B 208
Longleat Gdns. New M 3N 231
Longleat Gdns. Sotn 7G 158
Longleat Sq. Farn 9N 29
Longleaze. Stoke 7H 35
Longley Rd. F'ham 9F 64
Longmead. Fle 5M 47
Longmead. Liss 1E 140
Longmead. Wool H 2A 8
Longmead Av. Eastl 8H 133
Longmead Gdns. Hav 1F 216
Longmeadow. Frim 1N 29
Longmeadow Gdns. Hythe 5M 193
Longmead Rd. Burl 7D 188
Longmead Rd. Sotn 9E 160
Long Mickle. S'hrst 4C 18
Longmoor Dri. Lip 2N 115
Longmoor Rd. Bas 7B 42
Longmoor Rd. Gthm 4E 114
Longmoor Rd. Lip 2M 115
Longmore Av. Sotn 8B 174
Longmore Cres. Sotn 8B 174
Longmynd Dri. Fare 9N 197
Longparish 2A 76
Longparish Ct. And 2A 70 (off London Rd.)
Longparish Rd. Fort & Longp 6L 71
Longparish Rd. Hur P 9B 54
Longparish Rd. Wher 1F 74 (in two parts)
Long Park 8C 90
Long Priors. W Meon 8C 136
Longridge Rd. H End 4N 175
Long Rd. Bourn 2G 226
Long Rd. Ptsfld 8N 139
Long Rd. Sob 5L 165
Longroden La. Tun 4J 61
Longs Ct. Whitc 5G 54 (in two parts)
Longshore Way. S'sea 3L 241
Longs La. Fare 5N 211
Longstaff Gdns. Fare 6B 198
Long Steeple La. W'bry 8K 119
Longstock 9M 73
Longstock Clo. And 2L 69
Longstock Clo. Chine 8J 23
Longstock Clo. Sotn 1E 194
Longstock Ct. And 2A 70 (off London Rd.)
Longstock Cres. Tot 3K 171
Longstock Rd. Good C 5M 73
Longstock Rd. Hav 3H 203
Long Sutton 4E 62
Longs Wlk. Ports 9E 214
Long Wlk. F'ham 7D 64
Long Wlk. Mich 8L 77
Long Wlk. Win 3B 106
Long Water Dri. Gos 6L 239
Longwater La. E'sly 5H 17
Longwater La. Finch 2J 17
Longwater Rd. Finch & E'sly 4H 17
Longwood Av. Water 7N 181
Longwood Dean La. Ows 5F 134
Longwood Rd. Ows 5D 134
Lonsdale Av. Fare 2M 213
Lonsdale Av. Ports 1H 215
Lonsdale Rd. Bourn 7K 227
Loose Hanger. Redl 9D 120
Loperwood. Cal 9F 156
Loperwood La. Cal 7G 156 (in two parts)
Loraine Av. Highc 6L 231
Lordington Clo. Ports 9J 201
Lord Montgomery Way. Ports 3C 240 (5M 5)
Lord Mountbatten Clo. Sotn 7C 160
Lords Ct. Ports 1E 240
Lordsfield Gdns. Over 2C 56
Lord's Hill 7E 158
Lords Hill Cen. E. Sotn 7E 158
Lords Hill Cen. W. Sotn 7E 158
Lord's Hill District Cen. Sotn 7E 158
Lords Hill Way. Sotn 7D 158
Lord's St. Ports 1E 240
Lord's Wood 5J 133
Lordswood. Highb 5J 133
Lordswood. Sil 5N 11
Lordswood Clo. Sotn 7J 159
Lordswood Ct. Sotn 7H 159
Lordswood Gdns. Sotn 7J 159
Lordswood La. Chilw 3J 159
Lordswood Rd. Sotn 7H 159
Loreille Gdns. Rown 4D 158
Loring Ho. Ports 4F 214
Lorne Pk. Rd. Bourn 2L 245 (6N 247)
Lorne Pl. Sotn 3E 174
Lorne Rd. S'sea 4F 240
Lortemore Pl. Roms 5L 129
Loughwood Clo. Eastl 6E 132
Louisburg Rd. Bord 1J 101
Louise Margaret Rd. A'sht 8L 49
Louis Flagg Ho. S'sea 3D 240
Lovage Gdns. Tot 3J 171
Lovage Rd. White 2G 196
Lovage Way. Water 1C 182
Lovatt Gro. Fare 6N 197
Lovedean 4N 181
Lovedean La. Water 2N 181
Lovedon La. King W 6M 91
Lovegroves. Chine 9H 23
Love La. And 2A 70
Love La. K're 2B 6 (in two parts)
Love La. Mil S 8K 235
Love La. Odi 2E 62
Love La. Ptsfld 9N 139 (in two parts)
Love La. Roms 5L 129
Love La. Twy 8M 127
Love La. Uphm 5J 135
Love La. W'grn 2A 154 (off High St.)
Love La. Yate 7K 17
Lovell Clo. S Won 3J 91
Lovell Clo. Thru 1M 67
Lovells Wlk. Alr 1E 108
Lover 8E 120
Loveridge Clo. And 6A 52
Loveridge Clo. Bas 9B 42
Lovers La. Fren 1E 84
Lovett Rd. Ports 5G 215
Lovett Wlk. Win 3G 104
Lovington La. Avtn & Alr 1L 107
Lowa Clo. Tidw 8C 30
Lowa Rd. Tidw 8C 30
Lowcay Rd. S'sea 5F 240
Lowden Clo. Win 1H 127
Lowe Clo. A'sht 8H 49
Lwr. Alfred St. Sotn 4N 173 (1G 4)
Lwr. Ashley Rd. New M 3E 232
Lwr. Banister St. Sotn 4L 173 (2C 4)
Lower Bartons. F'bri 1J 153
Lwr. Baybridge La. Ows 7C 134
Lower Bellfield. Titch 1J 211
Lwr. Bere Wood. Water 2N 201
Lwr. Broadmoor Rd. C'then 1E 18
Lower Brook 1J 123
Lwr. Brookfield Rd. Ports 1F 240
Lwr. Brook St. Bas 6A 42
Lwr. Brook St. Win 6L 105 (7N 237)
Lwr. Brownhill Rd. Sotn 9B 158
Lower Buckland 1E 234
Lwr. Buckland Rd. L'ton 1D 234
Lower Bullington 5C 76
Lower Burgate 7K 151
Lwr. Canal Wlk. Sotn 8M 173 (9D 4)
Lower Canes. Yate 7K 17
Lwr. Charles St. Cam 7L 19
Lwr. Chase Rd. Wal C & Swanm 7A 164
Lwr. Chestnut Dri. Bas 8A 42
Lwr. Church La. F'ham 8D 64
Lwr. Church Path. Ports 2D 240
Lwr. Church Rd. Fare 6F 196
Lwr. Church Rd. S'hrst 4A 18
Lwr. Church St. Bas 6C 42
Lower Common 4C 16
Lower Comn. E'sly 4C 16
Lwr. Common Rd. W Wel 2B 120
Lwr. Crabbick La. Water 6C 180
Lower Daggons 6N 149
Lwr. Densome Wood. W'grn 2A 154
Lwr. Derby Rd. Ports 7D 214
Lwr. Drayton La. Ports 1K 215 (in two parts)
Lwr. Duncan Rd. Park G 4E 196
Lwr. Evingar Rd. Whitc 5G 54
Lower Exbury 3G 236
Lwr. Farlington Rd. Ports 9M 201
Lwr. Farnham Rd. A'sht 3K 65
Lower Farringdon 4C 98
Lwr. Forbury Rd. S'sea 3E 240
Lower Froyle 7H 63
Lower Green 7G 82 (Bordon)
Lower Green 6M 113 (Liss)
Lower Green 1F 6 (Hungerford)
Lower Gro. W'bry 1E 150
Lwr. Grove Rd. Hav 8G 202
Lower Hanger. Hasl 9L 103
Lwr. Heyshott. Ptsfld 1N 145
Lwr. Lamborough La. Cher 9F 108
Lower La. Bish W 3M 163
Lower La. Harb 7F 152
Lower Mead. Liss 1E 140
Lower Mead. Ptsfld 1A 146
Lwr. Mead End Rd. Sway 6G 222
Lower Moor. Yate 8N 17
Lwr. Moors Rd. Col C 3K 133
Lwr. Mortimer Rd. Sotn 7B 174
Lwr. Mount St. Elve 9J 27
Lwr. Mullins La. Hythe 6K 193
Lwr. Neatham Mill La. Holyb 1K 81 (in two parts)
Lwr. Nelson St. A'sht 9J 49
Lwr. Newport Rd. A'sht 2M 65
Lwr. New Rd. W End 1H 175
Lwr. Northam Rd. H End 4N 175
Lwr. Paice La. Meds 4C 96
Lower Pennington 6D 234
Lwr. Pennington La. Penn 4D 234
Lwr. Pool Rd. Brams 9A 16
Lwr. Preshaw La. Uphm 7H 135
Lower Quay. Fare 9D 198
Lwr. Quay Clo. Fare 9D 198
Lwr. Quay Rd. Fare 9D 198
Lower Ratley 1F 128
Lower Rd. Charl A 5A 120
Lower Rd. Hav 8B 202
Lower Rd. S Won 3G 91
Lwr. St Helens Rd. H End 5N 175
Lwr. Sandhurst Rd. Finch & S'hrst 3J 17
Lwr. Sandy Down. Bold 4B 224
Lower Slackstead 6F 124
Lwr. South Vw. F'ham 7E 64
Lwr. Spinney. Wars 1N 209
Lwr. Stanmore La. Win 9J 105
Lower St. Brfld 6A 124
Lower Swanwick 1A 196
Lwr. Swanwick Rd. Swanw 1A 196
Lower Test Marshes Nature Reserve 1N 171
Lwr. Turk St. Alt 5F 80
Lower Turmer 2G 184
Lwr. Tye Farm Cvn. Pk. Hay I 7J 217
Lower Upham 9D 134
Lwr. Vicarage Rd. Sotn 7B 174
Lwr. Wardown. Ptsfld 9A 140 (in two parts)
Lwr. Weybourne La. F'ham & Bad L 4H 65
Lower Wield 6H 79
Lwr. William St. Sotn 4B 174
Lwr. Wingfield St. Ports 1E 240
Lwr. Wokingham Rd. Finch & C'then 1N 17
Lwr. Woodside. L'ton 6E 234
Lwr. Wote St. Bas 6C 42
Lwr. York St. Sotn 4B 174
Lowestoft Rd. Ports 8E 200
Loweswater Gdns. Bord 2J 101
Lowford 8K 175
Lowford Hill. Burs 9K 175
Lowicks Rd. Tilf 2K 85
Lowland Rd. Water 6F 180
Lowlands Rd. Bas 8J 41
Lowlands Rd. B'wtr 9E 18
Low La. Bad L 4K 65
Lowndes Bldgs. F'ham 7D 64
Lowry Clo. Coll T 7F 18
Lowry Ct. And 9M 51
Lowry Gdns. Sotn 8G 175
Lowther Gdns. Bourn 9N 227
Lowther Rd. Bourn 8L 227
Loxwood Av. Chu C 4K 47
Loxwood Rd. Water 4N 181
Loyalty La. Old B 5J 43
Luard Ct. Hav 8H 203
Lubeck Dri. And 7M 51
Lucas Clo. Rown 6E 158
Lucas Clo. Yate 8N 17
Lucas Dri. Yate 8N 17
Lucas Fld. Hasl 9N 103
Lucas Rd. Poole 8A 226
Luccombe Pl. Sotn 9J 159
Luccombe Rd. Sotn 9J 159
Lucerne Av. Bourn 9G 229
Lucerne Av. Water 8K 181
Lucerne Gdns. H End 3L 175
Lucerne Rd. Mil S 8K 235
Lucewood La. F'ley 8E 86
Luckham Clo. Bourn 4M 227
Luckham Gdns. Bourn 4N 227
Luckham Pl. Bourn 4M 227
Luckham Rd. Bourn 4M 227
Luckham Rd. E. Bourn 4M 227
Lucknow Barracks. Tidw 8C 30
Lucknow St. Ports 2F 240
Lucky La. Pill 6G 224
Ludcombe. Water 5G 181
Ludgershall 1D 30
Ludgershall Bus. Pk. Ver D 2C 30
Ludgershall Castle 4K 31
Ludgershall Rd. Coll D 2H 31
Ludgershall Rd. Tidw 7D 30
Ludlow Clo. Bas 6L 41
Ludlow Gdns. Bas 6M 41
Ludlow Rd. Ports 8C 200
Ludlow Rd. Sotn 6C 174
Ludshott Common 4F 102
Ludshott Common & Waggoners Wells 4F 102
Ludshott Gro. Head D 2D 102
Ludwells La. Wal C 7B 164
Lugano Clo. Water 8L 181
Luke Rd. A'sht 2G 65
Luke Rd. E. A'sht 2G 65
Lukes Clo. Hamb 7L 195
Lukin Dri. Nurs 5B 158
Lulworth Bus. Cen. Tot 9L 157
Lulworth Clo. Chan F 9N 131
Lulworth Clo. Farn 5J 29
Lulworth Clo. Hay I 2G 242
Lulworth Clo. Sotn 9D 158
Lulworth Grn. Sotn 9D 158
Lulworth Rd. Lee S 2A 238
Lumber La. B'ton 9E 148
Lumby Dri. Ring 9L 185
Lumby Dri. Cvn. Pk. Ring 9L 185
Lumley 8N 203
Lumley Gdns. Ems 8N 203
Lumley Path. Ems 8N 203
Lumley Rd. Ems 8N 203
Lumsden Av. Sotn 3H 173
Lumsden Mans. Sotn 3H 173
Lumsden Rd. S'sea 4L 241
Lundy Clo. Bas 2E 42
Lundy Clo. Sotn 6D 158
Lundy Wlk. Fare 5L 211
Lune Clo. Bas 6E 42
Lunedale Rd. Dib P 9K 193
Lupin Clo. Bas 2J 59
Lupin Rd. Sotn 6A 160

Luscombe Rd.—Manor Rd.

Luscombe Rd. *Poole* 3A **244**
Luther Rd. *Bourn* 6K **227**
Lutman St. *Ems* 5L **203**
Luton Rd. *Sotn* 6F **174**
Lutyens Clo. *Lych.* 2G **42**
Luxton Clo. *Bot.* 2C **176**
Luzborough La. *Roms* 8A **130**
Lyall Pl. *F'ham* 3D **64**
Lyburn Clo. *Sotn* 7H **159**
Lyburn Ct. *Sotn* 7H **159**
Lyburn Rd. *Land & Nom* 1G **155** (in two parts)
Lych Ga. Clo. *S'hrst* 5B **18**
Lych Ga. Ct. *Ring.* 2M **187**
Lychgate Dri. *Water* 2B **182**
Lychgate Grn. *Fare* 3M **211**
Lyde Clo. *Okly* 1D **58**
Lydford Clo. *Farn* 5J **29**
Lydford Gdns. *Bourn* 4E **226**
Lydford Rd. *Bourn* 4E **226**
Lydgate. *Mil S* 9H **233**
Lydgate. *Tot* 3K **171**
Lydgate Clo. *Sotn* 6H **175**
Lydgate Grn. *Sotn* 6H **175**
Lydgate Rd. *Sotn* 6H **175**
Lydiard Clo. *Eastl* 7E **132**
Lydlynch Rd. *Tot.* 3L **171**
Lydney Clo. *Ports* 9D **200**
Lydney Rd. *L Hth* 6C **196**
Lydwell Clo. *Bourn* 1D **226**
Lye Copse Av. *Farn* 4K **29**
Lye Heath. 3E 200
Lyell Rd. *Poole* 8A **226**
Lyeway La. *Ropl* 2E **110**
Lyeway Rd. *Ropl* 1H **111**
Lyford Rd. *Bas* 5C **42**
Lymbourn Rd. *Hav* 8G **202**
Lyme Clo. *Eastl* 7D **132**
Lyme Cres. *Highc* 6H **231**
Lymefields. *Mil S* 8M **233**
Lymer La. *Sotn* 5B **158**
Lymer Vs. *Nurs* 5B **158**
Lymington. 3E 234
Lymington Av. *Yate* 8L **17**
Lymington Bottom. *Four M* 5J **97**
Lymington Bottom Rd. *Meds & Four M.* 3H **97**
Lymington Clo. *Bas* 3K **59**
Lymington Clo. *Four M* 5J **97**
Lymington Ri. *Four M* 5J **97**
Lymington Rd. *Broc* 9D **148**
Lymington Rd. *Christ & Highc* 7E **230**
Lymington Rd. *E End* 9N **225**
Lymington Rd. *Evtn & Mil S* 6M **233**
Lymington Rd. *New M & Evtn* 5B **232** (in two parts)
Lymington Vineyard. 4B 234
Lymore. 7M 233
Lymore La. *Evtn & Mil S* 6M **233**
Lymore Valley. *Mil S* 7M **233**
Lymore Valley Herb Garden. 6M 233
Lynams. *Chu C* 8K **47**
Lynch. 2B 56
Lynchborough Rd. *Pass* 7N **101**
Lynch Clo. *Win* 4J **105**
Lynchford La. *Farn* 3N **49**
Lynchford Rd. *Farn* 4K **49** (in two parts)
Lynch Hill. 5H 55
Lynch Hill. *Whitc* 5G **55**
Lynch Hill Pk. *Whitc.* 4H **55**
Lynch La. *W Meon* 9D **136**
Lynch Rd. *F'ham* 8F **64**
Lynch, The. *Over* 2B **56**
Lynch, The. *Whitc* 5H **55**
Lyn Ct. *Bas* 6E **42**
Lyndale Clo. *Mil S.* 7L **235**
Lyndale Dri. *Fle.* 2B **48**
Lyndale Rd. *Park G* 5E **196**
Lynden Clo. *Fare.* 9L **197**
Lynden Ga. *Sotn* 7E **174**
Lyndford Ter. *Fle.* 4L **47**
Lyndhurst. 2C 148
Lyndhurst Av. *A'sht* 4L **65**
Lyndhurst Av. *B'wtr* 7E **18**
Lyndhurst Clo. *Hay I* 5G **242**
Lyndhurst Clo. *Win* 2H **105**
Lyndhurst Dri. *Bas* 4L **59**
Lyndhurst Ho. *Hav* 3E **202**
Lyndhurst Rd. *Asht.* 1F **190**
Lyndhurst Rd. *Beau* 7E **206**
Lyndhurst Rd. *Bock* 2B **230**
Lyndhurst Rd. *Broc* 7D **148**
Lyndhurst Rd. *Burl* 6E **188**
Lyndhurst Rd. *Christ & Hint* 6C **230**
Lyndhurst Rd. *Gos* 3J **239**
Lyndhurst Rd. *Land* 8J **121** (in two parts)
Lyndhurst Rd. *Ports.* 6G **214**
Lyndock Clo. *Sotn* 8C **174**
Lyndock Pl. *Sotn* 8C **174**
Lyndsey Clo. *Farn.* 8D **28**
Lyndum Clo. *Ptsfld* 9M **139**
Lyndum Pl. *Lind.* 2L **101**
Lyne Pl. *Water* 4B **182**
Lyne's La. *Ring* 1J **187**
Lynford Av. *Win* 4J **105**
Lynford Way. *Win* 4J **105**
Lynn Clo. *W End* 8F **160**
Lynn Rd. *Ports* 8G **214**
Lynn Way. *Farn.* 5H **29**
Lynn Way. *King W* 9N **91**
Lynric Clo. *Bart S* 7B **232**
Lynton Ct. *Tot* 4L **171**
Lynton Cres. *Christ* 3G **229**
Lynton Gdns. *Fare* 6B **198**
Lynton Ga. *S'sea* 5D **240** (9N **5**)
Lynton Gro. *Ports.* 8H **215**
Lynton Mdw. *Chlbn.* 4F **74**
Lynton Rd. *Bord* 4J **101**
Lynton Rd. *H End.* 3N **175**
Lynton Rd. *Ptsfld* 9L **139**
Lynwood Av. *Water.* 7L **181**
Lynwood Clo. *Lind.* 2M **101**
Lynwood Ct. *L'ton* 3D **234**
Lynwood Ct. *Win* 4K **105**
Lynwood Dri. *And.* 1L **69**
Lynwood Gdns. *Hook.* 2G **45**
Lynx Clo. *Eastl* 1K **161**
Lyon Av. *New M* 3C **232**
Lyon Rd. *Poole.* 4C **226**
Lyon St. *Sotn* 4M **173** (1E **4**)
Lyon Way. *Frim.* 3L **29**
Lyon Way Ind. Est. *Frim* 3L **29**
Lysander Clo. *Christ.* 7D **230**
Lysander Way. *Water* 1A **202**
Lyson's Rd. *A'sht* 1J **65**
Lysses Ct. *Fare* 8E **198**
Lysses Path. *Fare* 8E **198**
Lyster Rd. *F'bri* 9K **151**
Lystra Rd. *Bourn* 3L **227**
Lyteltane Rd. *L'ton* 4D **234**
Lytham Clo. *W'hill* 5G **100**
Lytham Rd. *Sotn.* 1E **174**
Lythe La. *Strd* 7G **139**
Lyton Path. *Baug* 8E **10**
Lytton Rd. *Bas* 6D **42**
Lytton Rd. *Bourn* 9N **227**
Lytton Rd. *Hythe* 7N **193**
Lyvers La. *E Grim* 9F **86**

M

Mabbs La. *H Win* 8B **26**
Mabey Av. *Bourn* 4H **227**
Mabey Clo. *Gos* 5L **239**
Mablethorpe Rd. *Ports* 8F **200**
Macadam Way. *And* 9H **51**
MacAndrew Rd. *Poole* 6D **244**
MacArthur Cres. *Sotn.* 2E **174**
Macaulay Av. *Ports.* 8A **200**
MacCallum Rd. *Enh A.* 2A **52**
McCartney Wlk. *Bas* 3L **59**
MacDonald Rd. *F'ham* 3D **64**
McDonalds Almshouses. *F'ham* 9C **64**
McFauld Way. *Whitc.* 6G **55**
McIntyre Rd. *Hurn* 7C **218**
McKay Clo. *A'sht.* 8L **49**
MacKenzie Gdns. Bulf B *3A* ***66*** *(off Bulford Rd.)*
McKernan Ct. *S'hrst* 5B **18**
McKinley Rd. *Bourn* 3G **244**
MacKlin Ho. *Win.* 8J **237**
Maclaren Rd. *Bourn* 3K **227**
Maclean Rd. *Bourn.* 3D **226**
MacNaghten Rd. *Sotn* 3B **174**
MacNaghten Woods. *Cam* 7N **19**
McNaughton Clo. *Farn* 9E **28**
Macpennys Woodland Garden. 6E 220
Macrae Rd. *Yate* 7M **17**
McWilliam Clo. *Poole* 6G **226**
McWilliam Rd. *Bourn* 4L **227**
Madden Clo. *Gos* 4H **239**
Maddison St. *Sotn* 6L **173** (6C **4**)
Maddocks Hill. *Ropl.* 2C **110**
Maddoxford La. *Bot* 9C **162**
Maddoxford Way. *Bot.* 1C **176**
Madeira Clo. *Bas.* 2E **42**
Madeira Rd. *Bourn* 2L **245**
Madeira Rd. *Poole* 9B **226**
Madeira Rd. *Ports* 5F **214** (5E **4**)
Madeira Wlk. *Hay I* 4F **242**
Madeira Wlk. *L'ton* 3F **234**
Madeley Rd. *Chu C.* 5N **47**
Madeline Rd. *Ptsfld* 9M **139**
Madison Av. *Bourn.* 8A **228**
Madison Clo. *Gos.* 8G **212**
Madison Ct. *Fare.* 8E **198**
Madox Brown End. *Coll T* 6G **18**
Madrid Rd. *And* 9B **52**
Madrisa Ct. *L'ton* 2E **234**
Mafeking Rd. *S'sea.* 4G **241**
Maffey Ct. *Bot* 3D **176**
Magazine La. *March* 8E **172**
Magdala Rd. *Cosh* 1G **215**
Magdala Rd. *Hay I* 4E **242**
Magdalen Ct. *Ports* 5F **214**
Magdalene Rd. *Owl* 3H **19**
Magdalene Way. *Fare* 7F **196**
Magdalen Hill. *Win* 7M **105**
Magdalen La. *Christ.* 8K **229**
Magdalen M. *Win.* 8P **237**
Magdalen Rd. *Ports* 5E **214**
Magdalen Row. *Ptsfld.* 1L **145**
Magellan Clo. *And* 9D **52**
Magennis Clo. *Gos* 9F **212**
Magenta Ct. *Gos.* 1E **238**
Magna Rd. *Wim & Bourn* 1C **226**
Magnolia Clo. *And* 2L **69**
Magnolia Clo. *Bourn.* 9K **229**
Magnolia Clo. *Dib.* 5H **193**
Magnolia Clo. *Fare* 9A **198**
Magnolia Clo. *Owl.* 4F **18**
Magnolia Ct. *Bas* 2B **42**
Magnolia Ct. *Bourn* 2H **245**
Magnolia Gro. *F Oak.* 1B **162**
Magnolia Ho. *Bourn* 2K **227**
Magnolia Rd. *Sotn* 5D **174**
Magnolia Way. *Fle* 4M **47**
Magnolia Way. *Water* 6C **182**
Magnus Dri. *Bas.* 3K **59**
Magpie Clo. *Bas* 2H **59**
Magpie Clo. *Bord* 5K **101**
Magpie Clo. *Bourn* 3N **227**
Magpie Clo. Ews. *2N* ***63*** *(off Badger Way)*
Magpie Clo. *Fare* 9G **199**
Magpie Dri. *Tot* 3J **171**
Magpie Gdns. *Sotn.* 6G **174**
Magpie Gro. *New M* 4A **232**
Magpie La. *Eastl.* 1C **160**
Magpie La. *Lee S* 9B **212**
Magpie Rd. *Hav* 5J **183**
Magpie Wlk. *Hav* 6G **183**
Magpie Wlk. *Water.* 6L **181**
Mahler Clo. *Bas* 2A **60**
Maida Rd. *A'sht* 7K **49**
Maiden La. *L'ton.* 5E **234**
Maidenthorn La. *N Wal.* 9B **58**
Maidford Gro. *Ports* 4K **215**
Maidment Clo. *Bourn* 2C **226**
Maidstone Cres. *Ports* 8F **200**
Main Dri. *S'wick* 3B **200**
Main Rd. *Ame.* 2L **66**
Main Rd. *Col C & Fish P* 3L **133**
Main Rd. *Dib* 4H **193**
Main Rd. *E End.* 4A **236**
Main Rd. *Ems.* 9N **203**
Main Rd. *Gos* 4F **212**
Main Rd. *Navy.* 1A **240** (2H **5**)
Main Rd. *Holyb.* 2A **208**
Main Rd. *Kingsl* 7G **82**
Main Rd. *March* 9E **172**
Main Rd. *Ott & Comp* 2F **132**
Main Rd. *T'ley.* 7J **11**
Main Rd. *Tot.* 6L **171**
Main Rd. *Wal* 9G **224**
Main Rd. *Win* 9E **90**
Main Rd. *Wint E.* 4A **86**
Mainsail Dri. *Fare.* 9D **198**
Mainstone. *Roms* 7K **129**
Mainstream Ct. *Eastl* 9H **133**
Main St. *Green* 1G **9**
Main St. *Yate* 6N **17**
Maisemore Gdns. *Ems* 1K **217**
Maitland Rd. *Farn.* 3K **49**
Maitlands Clo. *Tong* 4N **65**
Maitlands, The. *Bourn* 3H **245** (8G **247**)
Maitland St. *Ports.* 9E **214**
Maizemore Wlk. *Lee S* 1B **238**
Majestic Rd. *Bas.* 4J **59**
Majestic Rd. *Nurs.* 8A **158**
Majorca Av. *And.* 9B **52**
Majorca Mans. *Bourn* 2J **245** (6J **247**)
Makins Ct. *Alr.* 1E **108**
Malcolm Clo. *Chan F* 3C **132**
Malcolm Clo. *L Hth.* 6E **196**
Malcolm Ho. *Ports* 4G **214**
Malcolm Rd. *Chan F.* 3C **132**
Malcomb Clo. *Bourn.* 2K **247**
Malcroft M. *March* 9F **172**
Maldive Rd. *Bas* 2E **42**
Maldon Clo. *Eastl.* 9H **133**
Maldon Rd. *Ports* 9E **200**
Maldon Rd. *Sotn* 5C **174**
Malham Gdns. *Bas* 5K **59**
Malibres Rd. *Chan F.* 4D **132**
Malin Clo. *Fare* 5L **211**
Malin Clo. *Sotn.* 7D **158**
Malins Rd. *Ports.* 9E **214**
Mallard Clo. *Alr.* 9F **94**
Mallard Clo. *And.* 8A **52**
Mallard Clo. *Bas.* 3H **59**
Mallard Clo. *Bish W* 3K **163**
Mallard Clo. *Bourn* 5N **227**
Mallard Clo. *Christ* 8C **230**
Mallard Clo. *Hasl* 9N **103**
Mallard Clo. *Hord.* 3H **233**
Mallard Clo. *Roms.* 4M **129**
Mallard Gdns. *Gos* 6D **212**
Mallard Gdns. *H End* 9N **161**
Mallard Rd. *Bourn* 5A **228**
Mallard Rd. *Row C.* 9H **183**
Mallard Rd. *S'sea* 2J **241**
Mallards. *Alt* 3F **80**
Mallards Rd. *Burs.* 2K **195**
Mallards, The. *Fare.* 6C **198**
Mallards, The. *Hav* 1E **216**
Mallard Way. *Yate.* 7L **17**
Mallett Clo. *H End.* 9B **162**
Mallory Clo. *Christ* 6B **230**
Mallory Cres. *Fare* 6C **198**
Mallow Clo. *Christ* 6E **230**
Mallow Clo. *Lind* 2M **101**
Mallow Clo. *L Hth.* 7C **196**
Mallow Clo. *Ports.* 9G **201**
Mallow Clo. *Water* 3N **201**
Mallow Rd. *H End.* 4L **175**
Mallows, The. *New M.* 2E **232**
Malls Shop. Cen., The. *Bas* 6C **42**
Mall, The. And *2N* ***69*** *(off Bridge St.)*
Mall, The. *Chan F* 5C **132**
Mall, The. *Ports* 7E **214**
Mall, The. *Tidw* 8F **30**
Malmesbury Clo. *F Oak* 1N **161**
Malmesbury Ct. *Bourn* 8N **227**
Malmesbury Ct. *Net A* 4E **194**
Malmesbury Fields. *Bas.* 2M **59**
Malmesbury Gdns. *Win* 4H **105**
Malmesbury Lawn. *Hav* 3C **202**
Malmesbury Pk. Pl. *Bourn* 9N **227**
Malmesbury Pk. Rd. *Bourn* 8L **227**
Malmesbury Pl. *Sotn* 3J **173**
Malmesbury Rd. *Roms.* 4L **129**
Malmesbury Rd. *St L* 5B **186**
Malmesbury Rd. *Sotn.* 3J **173**
Malmsbury Rd. *W'hill.* 5J **101**
Malory Clo. *Sotn* 4H **175**
Malpass Rd. *Wor D* 5G **90**
Malshanger La. *Okly.* 7A **40**
Malta Clo. *Bas* 2C **42**
Malta Rd. *Ports.* 8F **214**
Maltby's. *Selb* 7L **99**
Malthouse Clo. *Chu C.* 6K **47**
Malthouse Clo. *Estn* 1C **106**
Malthouse Clo. *Roms* 4L **129**
Malthouse Ct. *Lip* 2E **116**
Malthouse Gdns. *March* 9E **172**
Malthouse La. *Bigh.* 6L **95**
Malthouse La. *Fare.* 8D **198**
Malthouse La. *Sman.* 2B **52**
Malthouse La. *T'ley* 7K **11**
Malthouse La. *Up Ch* 2N **31**
Malthouse Meadows. *Lip* 2E **116**
Malthouse M. *Holyb* 2J **81**
Malthouse Rd. *Ports.* 8E **214**
Maltings Clo. *Alt.* 5F **80**
Maltings, The. *Braml* 2G **22**
Maltings, The. *Fare* 7F **198**
Maltings, The. *Lip.* 2F **116**
Maltings, The. *Ptsfld* 1M **145**
Malt La. *Bish W.* 3M **163**
Malus Clo. *Fare.* 1B **212**
Malvern Av. *Fare.* 1A **212**
Malvern Clo. *Bas.* 8J **41**
Malvern Clo. *Bish W.* 4N **163**
Malvern Clo. *Bourn.* 3L **227**
Malvern Dri. *Dib P* 6J **193**
Malvern Gdns. *H End* 9A **162**
Malvern M. *Ems* 8M **203**
Malvern Rd. *Bourn* 3L **227**
Malvern Rd. *Farn* 5F **28**
Malvern Rd. *Gos* 2H **239**
Malvern Rd. *Hill B* 3G **141**
Malvern Rd. *Sotn* 9H **159**
Malvern Rd. *S'sea.* 6E **240**
Malvern Way. Port *9B* ***66*** *(off Southbourne Way)*
Malwood. 8L 155
Malwood Av. *Sotn.* 8J **159**
Malwood Clo. *Hav* 3G **203**
Malwood Gdns. *Tot.* 2J **171**
Malwood Rd. *Hythe* 5L **193**
Malwood Rd. W. *Hythe* 5L **193**
Manaton Way. *H End.* 1M **175**
Manawey Bus. Units. *A'sht* 1N **65**
Manchester Ct. *Gos* 2F **238**
Manchester Rd. *Net A* 4E **194**
Manchester Rd. *Ports.* 2F **240**
Manchester Rd. *Sway* 4H **223**
Mancroft Av. *Fare* 6M **211**
Mandale Clo. *Bourn* 2E **226**
Mandale Rd. *Bourn* 3D **226**
Mandarin Way. *Gos* 1E **238**
Mandela Way. *Sotn* 5K **173** (3A **4**)
Manderley. *Mil S.* 9L **235**
Mandora Rd. *A'sht* 7K **49**
Manica Clo. *Bord* 4J **101**
Manley James Clo. *Odi* 8L **45**
Manley Rd. *Burs.* 9K **175**
Mann Clo. *Whitc.* 6H **55**
Manners La. *S'sea.* 3F **240**
Manners Rd. *S'sea* 3F **240**
Manning Av. *Christ.* 5E **230**
Manningford Clo. *Win.* 3L **105**
Mannings Heath Rd. *Poole* 5A **226**
Mannington Pl. *Bourn.* 7J **247**
Manns Clo. *W End* 9G **160**
Mannyngham Way. *Tims* 6K **123**
Manor Av. *Poole* 6A **226**
Manor Bri Ct. *Tidw* 7D **30**
Manor Clo. *Abb A* 6F **68**
Manor Clo. *Alt* 2G **81**
Manor Clo. *Bas* 4J **59**
Manor Clo. *Burs* 9K **175**
Manor Clo. *F'bri* 1J **153**
Manor Clo. *Hasl* 9N **103**
Manor Clo. *Hav* 8F **202**
Manor Clo. *Mil S* 8L **233**
Manor Clo. *Ship B* 2B **66**
Manor Clo. *Tong* 3N **65**
Manor Clo. *Tot* 4L **171**
Manor Clo. *Wick* 8C **178**
Manor Clo. *Win* 6M **105**
Manor Copse. *And* 5A **52**
Manor Ct. *Chu C* 7M **47**
Manor Ct. *Fare* 5G **196**
Manor Ct. *Ring* 9J **185**
Manor Cres. *Burs* 9K **175**
Manor Cres. *Hasl* 9N **103**
Manor Cres. *Ports.* 1J **215**
Manor Farm. *B'stne* 2E **118**
Mnr. Farm Clo. *Bro Ch* 3A **118**
Mnr. Farm Clo. *Eastl* 1J **161**
Mnr. Farm Clo. *New M* 5A **232**
Manor Farm Country Pk. 7A 176
Mnr. Farm Grn. *Twy* 8K **127**
Mnr. Farm Gro. *Eastl.* 1J **161**
Mnr. Farm La. *Michm.* 4K **123**
Manor Farm Mus. 6D 176
Mnr. Farm Rd. *F'bri.* 9F **150**
Mnr. Farm Rd. *Sotn* 1B **174**
Manor Farmyard. *Bourn* 3E **228**
Manor Fields. *Lip* 2F **116**
Manor Gdns. *Ring.* 9J **185**
Manor Ho. Av. *Sotn* 4D **172**
Manor Ho. Flats. *Tong* 4N **65**
Manor La. *Old B* 5J **43**
Manor Lea. *Hasl.* 9N **103**
Mnr. Lodge Rd. *Row C.* 8G **182**
Manor M. *Ports* 9K **201**
Manor Park. 9M 155
Mnr. Park Av. *Ports* 8H **215**
Mnr. Park Dri. *Yate.* 8N **17**
Manor Pk. Ind. Est. *A'sht* 1L **65**
Manor Ri. *Anna V* 5L **69**
Manor Rd. *A'sht.* 2H **65**
Manor Rd. *Alt.* 2G **80**
Manor Rd. *And* 9M **51**
Manor Rd. *Bourn.* 2M **245**
Manor Rd. *Chilw.* 3J **159**
Manor Rd. *Christ* 8K **229**
Manor Rd. *Dib* 4F **192**
Manor Rd. *Durl* 3G **163**
Manor Rd. *Eastl* 1J **161**
Manor Rd. *E Tyth* 8N **87**
Manor Rd. *Farn* 8M **29**
Manor Rd. *F'ham* 6G **64**
Manor Rd. *Hay I* 3E **242**
Manor Rd. *Holb* 4A **208**

Manor Rd.—Mayhill La.

Manor Rd. Mil S. 8L 233
Manor Rd. New M 3B 232
Manor Rd. Ports 9F 214
Manor Rd. Ring 1K 187
Manor Rd. Sher 9N 21
Manor Rd. Twy. 8K 127
Manor Rd. N. Sotn 6C 174
Manor Rd. S. Sotn 7C 174
Manor Ter. Burs 9J 175
Manor Vs. Wick 7C 178
Manor Wlk. A'sht 1K 65
(in two parts)
Manor Way. Hay I. 5G 242
Manor Way. Lee S 1A 238
Mansbridge Cotts. Sotn . . . 7D 160
Mansbridge Rd. Eastl 2E 160
Mansbridge Rd. Sotn & W End
. . . . 7C 160
Manse La. T'ley 7K 11
Mansel Clo. Poole 7G 227
Mansel Ct. Sotn 9D 158
Mansell Clo. Dib P 8K 193
Mansel Rd. E. Sotn 1D 172
Mansel Rd. W. Sotn 9C 158
Mansergh Wlk. Tot. 2H 171
Mansfield Av. Poole 1A 244
Mansfield Clo. Poole. 1A 244
Mansfield La. Wick 6L 177
Mansfield Rd. Bas 9N 41
Mansfield Rd. Bourn. 5J 227
Mansfield Rd. Gos 8E 212
Mansfield Rd. Poole 1A 244
Mansfield Rd. Ring 1J 187
Mansion Ct. S'sea 6F 240
Mansion Dri. Brams 9A 16
Mansion Rd. Sotn 4H 173
Mansion Rd. S'sea 6F 240
Manston Ct. Sotn 7E 158
Mansvid Av. Ports. 1J 215
Mantle Clo. Gos 9F 212
Mantle Sq. Ports. 6C 214
Mant's La. Win
. . . . 7M 105 (9P 237)
Maple Clo. Alr. 2E 108
Maple Clo. Alt. 3F 80
Maple Clo. Bart S 7C 232
Maple Clo. B'wtr. 8E 18
Maple Clo. Burs 1K 195
Maple Clo. Ems 7M 203
Maple Clo. Fare 8M 197
Maple Clo. Highc 7H 231
Maple Clo. Lee S 2C 238
Maple Clo. Mid W. 4B 72
Maple Clo. Roms 6B 130
Maple Clo. S'hrst 4B 18
Maple Ct. Bas 7K 41
Maple Cres. Bas 4C 42
Maple Cres. Lud 1F 30
Maple Cres. Water 5C 168
Maple Dri. Firs 4E 86
Maple Dri. King W. 7M 91
Maple Dri. Water 6H 181
Mapledurwell. 7M 43
Maple Gdns. Tot 4J 171
Maple Gdns. Yate 8N 17
Maple Gro. T'ley. 5H 11
Maplehurst Chase. Bas. 4K 59
Maple Leaf Clo. Farn 9H 29
Maple Leaf Dri. Bord. 3J 101
Maple Leaf Gdns. Eastl. . . . 1E 160
Maple Rd. Bourn 6K 227
Maple Rd. Hythe. 9N 193
Maple Rd. Sotn. 3C 174
Maple Rd. S'sea 5E 240
Maple Sq. Eastl. 2C 160
Maples, The. Chan F. 4A 132
Mapleton Rd. H End. 4N 175
Mapletree Av. Water 5C 182
Maple Wlk. A'sht 2M 65
Maple Wlk. And 3K 69
Maple Wlk. Ptsfld 3M 145
Maple Way. Head D 1D 102
Maplewood. Chine 9F 22
Maple Wood. Hav. 8B 202
Maplewood Clo. Tot 4J 171
Maplin Rd. Sotn. 9C 158
Marabout Clo. Christ 7A 230
Maralyn Av. Water 3M 201
Marathon Pl. Eastl 9M 133
Marbream Clo. F'bri 9F 150
Marchant Rd. And. 2L 69
March Clo. And. 9A 52
Marchesi Ct. Fare. 4M 211
Marchwood. 9E 172
Marchwood By-Pass. March
. . . . 4M 171
Marchwood Ct. Gos 4F 238
(off Broadsands Dri.)
Marchwood Ind. Est. March
. . . . 7F 172
Marchwood Rd. Bourn. . . . 3G 227
Marchwood Rd. Hav. 3E 202
Marchwood Rd. Sotn 4G 173
Marchwood Rd. Tot 6A 172
Marchwood Ter. March 8E 172
(off Main Rd.)
Marcus Clo. Eastl. 1M 161
Mardale Rd. Sotn 2C 172
Mardale Wlk. Sotn 2C 172
Marden Paddock. Broc. . . . 7C 148
Marden Way. Ptsfld 1N 145
Mardon Clo. Sotn 6C 160
Mares La. Ows 3B 134
Mareth Clo. A'sht 9K 49
Margam Av. Sotn 5D 174
Margaret Clo. Water 9L 181
Margaret Rd. Bas. 7M 41
Margarita Rd. Fare 7A 198
Margate Rd. S'sea. 3E 240
Margery's Ct. Ports
. . . . 2B 240 (4K 5)
Margha Rd. Tidw 8C 30
Marguerite Clo. Braml 1G 22
Marianne Clo. Sotn. 4E 172
Marianne Rd. Poole 6G 226
Marie Av. D'ton. 2H 119
Marie Clo. Poole 7B 226
Marie Rd. Sotn. 7G 175
Marigold Clo. Bas 2J 59
Marigold Clo. Fare 7A 198
Marina Bldgs. Gos 3K 239
(off Stoke Rd.)
Marina Clo. Ems. 1N 217
Marina Clo. Hamb. 7L 195
Marina Ct. Bourn 2B 246
Marina Gro. Fare. 1L 213
Marina Gro. Ports 9J 215
Marina Keep. Port S 2B 214
Marina, The. Bourn. 2B 246
Marina Towers. Bosc 2B 246
Marina Vw. Christ 9J 229
Marine Cotts. Gos. 2K 239
Marine Ct. S'sea. 5H 241
Marine Dri. Bart S 7N 231
Marine Dri. E. Bart S 8A 232
Marine Dri. W. Bart S. 7M 231
Marine Pde. Sotn 6N 173
Marine Pde. E. Lee S 2A 238
Marine Pde. W. Lee S. 9N 211
Marine Point. Bart S. 7A 232
Marine Prospect. Bart S . . . 7A 232
Marine Rd. Bourn. 2G 247
Mariners Clo. Hamb 5L 195
Mariners Clo. T'ley. 7K 11
Mariners Ct. L'ton 4F 234
Mariners Dri. Farn. 6L 29
Mariners M. Hythe. 5M 193
Mariners Wlk. S'sea 2J 241
Mariners Way. Gos 4M 239
Mariners Way. Wars. 8N 195
Marine Wlk. Hay I 4J 243
Marion Rd. S'sea. 6F 240
Maritime Av. March. 7F 172
Maritime Wlk. Sotn
. . . . 8N 173 (9F 4)
Maritime Way. E Dock
. . . . 8M 173 (9E 4)
(in two parts)
Marjoram Clo. Farn 8D 28
Marjoram Cres. Water 7B 182
Marjoram Way. White. 2G 197
Markall Clo. Cher 9F 108
Markan Rd. Idm 9C 66
Mark Anthony Ct. Hay I . . . 4E 242
Mark Clo. Ports 4G 215
Mark Clo. Sotn 3G 172
Mark Ct. Water 1M 201
Marken Clo. L Hth 6C 196
Market Bldgs. Sotn. 7B 160
Market Chambers. Bas 7C 42
(off Church St.)
Market Hill. Cowes 5P 237
Market La. Win
. . . . 7L 105 (8M 237)
Market Pde. Hav 8F 202
Market Pl. Bas 7C 42
Market Pl. F'bri 1J 153
Market Pl. Ring. 1J 187
Market Pl. Roms. 5L 129
Market Pl. Sotn . . . 7M 173 (7D 4)
Market Pl. Whitc. 5G 54
Market Sq. Alt 5F 80
Market St. Alt 5F 80
Market St. Eastl. 2F 160
(in two parts)
Market St. Win
. . . . 7L 105 (8M 237)
Marketway. Ports
. . . . 1D 240 (2N 5)
Markham Ct. Cam 7M 19
Markham Rd. Bourn 6L 227
Mark La. Bas 7C 42
(off London Rd.)
Mark La. P Cnr & And 9G 51
Mark's La. New M. 9B 222
Markson Rd. S Won. 3G 90
Marks Rd. Bourn 3K 227
Mark's Rd. Fare 6A 212
Marks Tey Rd. Fare 3M 211
Mark Way. Lcky 1M 121
Markway Clo. Ems 8K 203
Marland Ho. Sotn
. . . . 5L 173 (4C 4)
Marlands Lawn. Hav. 3C 202
Marlands Shop. Cen. Sotn
. . . . 6L 173 (4C 4)
Marlborough Clo. Fle 3B 48
Marlborough Clo. Water . . . 4L 201
Marlborough Ct. Chan F
. . . . 8M 131
Marlborough Ct. Dib P 7K 193
Marlborough Ct. Poole 1F 244
(off Poole Rd.)
Marlborough Gdns. H End
. . . . 8N 161
Marlborough Gdns. Okly . . . 9D 40
Marlborough Gro. Fare 1L 213
Marlborough Ho. Sotn 2L 173
Marlborough Mans. Bourn
. . . . 8E 228
Marlborough Park. 4N 49
Marlborough Pk. Hav 6H 203
Marlborough Pl. L'ton 1D 234
Marlborough Ri. Cam. 7N 19
Marlborough Rd. Bourn
. . . . 2G 244 (7G 247)
Marlborough Rd. Bulf B 4B 66
Marlborough Rd. Chan F
. . . . 3C 132
Marlborough Rd. Coll D 1H 31
Marlborough Rd. Gos. 1H 239
Marlborough Rd. Poole 1A 244
Marlborough Rd. Sotn 2G 173
Marlborough Row. Ports
. . . . 1B 240 (1J 5)
Marlborough St. And 1N 69
Marlborough Trad. M. Chine
. . . . 1E 42
Marlborough Vw. Farn 7E 28
Marldell Clo. Hav 4G 203
Marles Clo. Gos 8F 212
Marley Av. Hasl 3N 117
Marley Av. New M 2N 231
Marley Clo. New M. 3A 232
Marley La. Hasl 1N 117
Marley Mt. Sway. 6F 222
Marlhill Clo. Sotn. 9D 160
Marlin Clo. Gos. 1F 238
Marline Rd. Poole 8B 226
Marl La. F'bri. 8F 150
Marlow Clo. Fare 5A 198
Marlow Dri. Christ 3G 229
Marlowe Clo. Bas. 3D 42
Marlowe Ct. Sotn. 9D 174
Marlowe Ct. Water 9L 181
Marlow Rd. Bish W 3K 163
Marlpit Dri. Walk. 4J 231
Marlpit La. New M 7B 222
Marl's La. Bas. 7C 22
Marls Rd. Bot 3B 176
Marmion Av. S'sea 5E 240
Marmion Grn. Christ. 7B 230
Marmion Rd. S'sea. 5D 240
Marne Ho. Fare. 9A 198
Marne Rd. Bulf B 3B 66
Marne Rd. Sotn 3E 174
Marpet Clo. Bourn 1D 226
Marples Way. Hav 8D 202
Marquis Way. Bourn. 1A 226
Marram Clo. L'ton. 9E 224
Marrels Wood Gdns. Pur
. . . . 5K 201
Marrowbrook Clo. Farn. 9J 29
Marrowbrook La. Farn 1H 49
Marryat Ct. Christ. 7K 231
Marryat Ct. New M. 3A 232
Marryat Rd. New M 3A 232
Marsden Ct. Lave 4N 55
Marsden Rd. Ports 9C 200
Marshall Clo. Farn 5H 29
Marshall Gdns. Bas 4C 42
Marshall Rd. Coll T. 6F 18
Marshall Rd. Hay I 5J 243
Marshall Sq. And 8B 52
(off Cricketers Way)
Marsh Clo. Bord 4L 101
Marsh Clo. Ports 2K 215
Marshcourt. Lych 3G 43
Marshfield Clo. March 9C 172
Marshfield Ho. Ports. 1L 215
Marsh Gdns. H End 9N 161
Marsh Ho. Sotn . . . 7M 173 (7E 4)
Marshlands Rd. Ports. 1L 215
Marshlands Spur. Ports. . . 1M 215
Marsh La. Bent. 7L 63
Marsh La. Brea. 4K 151
Marsh La. Christ 4J 229
(Fairmile Rd., in two parts)
Marsh La. Christ 8N 229
(Purewell, in two parts)
Marsh La. Coom B 2G 119
Marsh La. E'sly. 6J 17
Marsh La. Fare. 6K 211
Marsh La. Fawl. 4F 208
Marsh La. L'ton 9D 224
Marsh La. Sotn. . . . 6M 173 (7F 4)
Marsh Pde. Hythe. 5M 193
(off Marsh, The)
Marsh, The. Brea 3L 151
Marsh, The. Hythe 4M 193
Marshwood Av. Water 2A 202
Marston Clo. New M 1C 232
Marston Dri. Farn 5K 29
Marston Ga. Win
. . . . 6L 105 (6M 237)
Marston Gro. Christ. 5G 230
Marston La. Ports 4J 215
Marston Rd. F'ham 8B 64
Marston Rd. New M 1C 232
Marston Rd. Sotn 5H 175
Marsum Clo. And 6N 51
Martello Clo. Gos 4F 238
Martello Pk. Poole 6D 244
Martello Rd. Poole. 4C 244
Martello Rd. S. Poole 4D 244
Martells Ct. Ports
. . . . 3B 240 (6K 5)
Martells, The. New M. 7C 232
Martin. 9C 118
Martin Av. Fare 6N 211
Martin Av. Water 6H 181
Martin Clo. Bas 4D 42
Martin Clo. Lee S. 9B 212
Martin Clo. Swanm 7D 164
Martin Clo. Tidw. 8E 30
Martindale Ter. Sotn 2D 172
(off Kendal Av.)
Martin Drove End. 8B 118
Martin Drove End. M'tin
. . . . 8B 118
Martingale Ct. A'sht 9G 49
Martin Rd. Fare 6N 211
Martin Rd. Hav 5G 202
Martin Rd. Ports 8H 215
Martins Clo. Alt 3G 80
Martins Clo. B'wtr 9F 18
Martins Fields. Comp 5G 127
Martin's Hill Clo. Burt 5M 229
Martins Hill La. Burt 5M 229
Martins La. Chlbn 4G 74
Martins Pk. Cvn. Pk. Farn
. . . . 5F 28
Martins Ri. W'ish. 5H 121
Martin's Rd. Broc 6D 148
Martins, The. F Oak 2A 162
Martin St. Bish W 4L 163
Martins Wood. Chine. 9G 22
Martin Way. And 8A 52
Martin Way. Frim. 3N 29
Martlesham Rd. Ame. 6A 66
Martley Gdns. H End 9N 161
Marvic Ct. Hav. 3E 202
Marvin Clo. Bot 3B 176
Marvin Way. Bot 3B 176
Marvin Way. Sotn 4G 175
Marwell Clo. Bourn 7D 228
Marwell Dri. Ows 7B 134
Marwell Zoological Pk.
. . . . 7B 134
Marybridge Clo. Tot 4L 171
Maryfield. Sotn . . . 6N 173 (6F 4)
Maryland Clo. Sotn 8D 160
Maryland Ct. Mil S. 8H 235
Maryland Gdns. Mil S 8H 235
Mary La. Newt V 7N 97
Mary La. N Wal 8A 58
Mary Mitchell Clo. Ring . . . 1J 187
(off Bickerley Rd.)
Mary Rose Clo. Fare 6A 198
Mary Rose Ct. Bas. 7A 42
Mary Rose M. Alt 3G 81
Mary Rose Mus.
. . . . 2B 240 (3J 5)
Mary Rose Ship Hall.
. . . . 1A 240 (2H 5)
Mary Rose St., The. Ports
. . . . 2D 240 (4N 5)
Masefield Av. Ports 8A 200
Masefield Clo. Eastl. 9D 132
Masefield Cres. Water 7N 181
Masefield Gdns. C'then 2D 18
Masefield Grn. Sotn. 4H 175
Maskell Way. Farn 9E 28
Mason Clo. Yate. 8A 18
Mason Pl. S'hrst 5B 18
Mason Rd. Farn. 6G 29
Mason Way. A'sht 3K 65
Masseys La. E Bol 9B 206
Masten Cres. Gos 8E 212
Masters Ct. Bourn
. . . . 2H 245 (6G 247)
Masterson Clo. Christ 7N 229
Matapan Rd. Ports 4E 214
Matcham La. Hurn 8E 218
Matheson Rd. Sotn. 5E 158
Mathew Ter. A'sht 9L 49
Mathias Wlk. Bas. 4M 59
Matilda Dri. Bas 3K 59
Matilda Pl. Win
. . . . 6L 105 (6M 237)
Matley Gdns. Tot 3H 171
Matthew Rd. A'sht 2G 64
Matthews Clo. Farn 3N 49
Matthews Clo. Hav 6C 202
Matthews La. E Bol 1B 236
Matthews Rd. Cam. 5L 19
Matthews Way. Fle 1L 47
Matthews Way. Okly. 1E 58
Mattingley. 3K 25
Mattingley Dri. Elve 8H 27
Mattock Way. Chine 9F 22
Maturin Clo. L'ton 3D 234
Maundeville Cres. Christ
. . . . 6G 229
Maundeville Rd. Christ. . . . 6H 229
Maunsell Way. H End 8M 161
Maureen Clo. Poole 7A 226
Maurepas Way. Water 2L 201
Mauretania Ho. Sotn 4A 174
Mauretania Rd. Nurs 7A 158
Maurice Rd. Bourn. 6A 228
Maurice Rd. S'sea 3K 241
Maury's La. W Wel. 1A 120
Mavins Rd. F'ham. 9F 64
Mavis Cres. Hav 7F 202
Mavis Rd. Bourn 5M 227
Maw Clo. Bas. 2A 60
Maxine Clo. S'hrst 4D 18
Maxstoke Clo. S'sea 2E 240
Maxwell Rd. Bourn. 7L 227
Maxwell Rd. Poole. 6D 244
Maxwell Rd. Sotn. 7E 174
Maxwell Rd. S'sea 4H 241
May Av. L'ton 1D 234
Maybray King Way. Sotn
. . . . 3D 174
Maybrick Clo. S'hrst. 4B 18
Maybrook. Chine 8G 22
Maybury Clo. Frim. 4M 29
Maybush. 9D 158
Maybush Ct. Sotn. 1F 172
May Bush La. Sob 2K 179
Maybush Rd. Sotn. 9D 158
May Clo. Head 3A 102
May Clo. Holb. 5B 208
May Clo. Old B. 5K 43
May Clo. Owl 5F 18
May Copse. Holb 5B 208
May Cres. Ash 1N 65
May Cres. Holb. 5B 208
Maycroft Ct. Sotn 2L 173
Maydman Sq. Ports 1H 241
Mayfair Ct. Bot. 3D 176
Mayfair Ct. Bourn. 3G 244
Mayfair Ct. Elve 8K 27
Mayfair Gdns. Bourn 2E 226
Mayfair Gdns. Sotn. 3L 173
Mayfair Ho. Bas 6C 42
(off Timberlake Rd.)
Mayfield Av. Poole 2C 244
Mayfield Av. Tot 2L 171
Mayfield Clo. Bad L 3K 65
Mayfield Clo. Fare 5N 211
Mayfield Clo. Ship B. 2A 66
Mayfield Ct. E'sly 5G 17
Mayfield Ridge. Hat W 5L 59
Mayfield Rd. Bourn 4K 227
Mayfield Rd. Cam. 3K 29
Mayfield Rd. Farn. 5H 29
Mayfield Rd. F'bri 9F 150
Mayfield Rd. Gos 4L 239
Mayfield Rd. Ports 6F 214
Mayfield Rd. Sotn 8N 159
May Firs. Hale 1D 154
Mayflower Clo. Chan F. . . . 7N 131
Mayflower Clo. Chine 1F 42
Mayflower Clo. Fare. 7M 211
Mayflower Clo. L'ton 3G 234
Mayflower Dri. S'sea 2K 241
Mayflower Dri. Yate 6K 17
Mayflower Rd. Sotn. 2G 173
Mayflower Rd. W'hill 6H 101
Mayflowers, The. Sotn . . . 7M 159
Mayflower Theatre. 5L 173
Mayfly Clo. F'bri 9J 151
Mayford Rd. Poole 8F 226
May Gdns. Bourn 3C 226
May Gdns. Walk. 4K 231
Mayhall Rd. Ports 7H 215
Mayhill La. Swanm. 5E 164

Maylands Av.—Middleton Wlk.

Maylands Av. S'sea 2H 241
Maylands Rd. Hav 7B 202
May La. Pill 6G 224
Mayles Clo. Wick 7C 178
Mayles La. Wick 9A 178
Mayles Rd. S'sea 2J 241
Maylings Farm Rd. Fare
. . . . 6B 198
Maynard Clo. Gos 4E 212
Maynard Pl. Water 3B 182
Maynard Rd. Tot 3M 171
Maynard's Wood. Chine 1F 42
Mayo Clo. Ports 9E 214
May Pl. Bas 7C 42
Maypole Vs. Eastl 4F 132
Mayridge. Fare 6F 196
May Rd. Sotn 3H 173
May's La. Fare 5M 211
May St. Bas 6A 42
Maytree Clo. F Oak 1A 162
Maytree Clo. L Hth 6D 196
May Tree Clo. Win 1G 126
Maytree Gdns. Water 7M 181
May Tree Rd. And 9K 51
Maytree Rd. Chan F 2A 132
Maytree Rd. Cowp 7M 181
Maytree Rd. Fare 8C 198
Maytree Rd. Sotn 4E 174
Mayvale Clo. March 9E 172
Meacher Clo. Tot 2L 171
Meadbrook Gdns. Chan F
. . . . 6A 132
Mead Clo. And 2M 69
Mead Clo. Roms 5A 130
Mead Ct. Chan F 6A 132
Mead Cres. Sotn 8B 160
Meadcroft Clo. Wars 9A 196
Mead End 6G 223
(Lymington)
Mead End 7H 181
(Waterlooville)
Meadend Clo. Hav 4H 203
Mead End Rd. Sway 6G 222
Mead End Rd. Water 7H 181
Meade Rd. Lud 1E 30
Meadham La. Hann 9K 9
Mead Hatchgate. Hook 1G 44
Mead Hedges. And 3L 69
Mead Hedges Footpath. And
. . . . 2M 69
Mead La. Bton 8L 145
Mead La. F'ham 8D 64
Meadow Av. F'bri 9H 151
Meadow Av. L Hth 5D 196
Meadow Bank. F'ham 8D 64
Meadowbank Rd. Fare 8N 197
Meadow Cvn. Site. Sher L
. . . . 3L 23
Meadow Clo. Alr 1F 108
Meadow Clo. B'wtr 9F 18
Meadow Clo. Brans 8L 219
(Ringwood Rd.)
Meadow Clo. Brans 7C 220
(West Rd.)
Meadow Clo. Burl 8D 188
Meadow Clo. F'bri 9H 151
Meadow Clo. Hay I 5F 216
Meadow Clo. Lip 2E 116
Meadow Clo. N Bad 9F 130
Meadow Clo. Ring 8L 185
Meadow Clo. Tot 5M 171
Meadow Clo. Wal C 7N 163
Meadow Clo. W End 9J 161
Meadow Ct. Bourn 3L 227
Meadow Ct. Ems 9M 203
Meadow Ct. Farn 8H 29
Meadow Ct. Fle 2L 47
Meadow Ct. F'bri 9H 151
Meadow Ct. W'ish 5J 121
Meadow Ct. Clo. Bourn 3L 227
Mdw. Crest Wood. Broc
. . . . 6A 148
Meadowcroft Clo. Ott 1G 132
Meadow Dri. Good C 9M 69
Meadow Edge. Water 7J 201
Meadow End. Lip 1E 116
Meadow Gdns. Wal C 7A 164
Meadow Gro. Chan F 8A 132
Meadowhead Rd. Sotn 8L 159
Meadowland. Chine 9F 22
Meadow Land. Christ 8B 230
Meadowland. King W 8M 91
Meadowlands. Hav 8G 203
Meadowlands. L'ton 2B 234
Meadowlands. Ring 4K 187
Meadowlands. Row C 7J 183
Meadow La. Burt 4M 229
(in two parts)
Meadow La. Hamb 7L 195
Meadow La. H Win 6B 26
Meadowmead Av. Sotn 3F 172
Meadowridge. Hat W 5L 59
Meadow Ri. N Wal 9B 58
Meadow Ri. Water 7B 182
Meadow Rd. Bas 9B 42
Meadow Rd. Bulf 3A 66
Meadow Rd. Farn 5K 29
Meadow Rd. New M 2C 232
Meadow Rd. Penn 4C 234
Meadow Rd. Ring 9L 185
Meadows Cvn. Site, The. New M
. . . . 5A 232
Meadowside Clo. Sotn 7C 160
Meadows, The. Cam 8G 19
Meadows, The. Churt 7H 85
Meadows, The. Fare 6E 198
Meadows, The. Sar G 4D 196
Meadows, The. Sher L 3L 23
Meadows, The. Water 1K 201
Meadow St. S'sea
. . . . 4C 240 (7M 5)
Meadowsweet. Water 9B 182
Meadowsweet Way. H Hth
. . . . 4N 161
Meadowsweet Way. Ports
. . . . 8E 200
Meadow, The. Lyn 3B 148
Meadow, The. New M 6L 231
Meadow, The. Roms 3M 129
Meadow, The. Water 6G 180
Meadow Vw. B'stne 2D 118
Meadow Vw. Bord 4K 101
Meadow Vw. Chu C 6K 47
Meadow Vw. Ropl 1D 110
Meadow Vw. Whitc 5F 54
Meadowview Clo. Per D 5B 30
Mdw. View Rd. Bourn 2C 226
Meadow Wlk. Fle 4J 47
Meadow Wlk. Gos 3D 212
Meadow Wlk. Liss 1F 140
Meadow Wlk. Ports
. . . . 1D 240 (2N 5)
Meadow Way. A'sht 8N 49
Meadow Way. And 1K 69
Meadow Way. Bart S 7B 232
Meadow Way. B'wtr 8E 18
Meadow Way. Fawl 5E 208
Meadow Way. Lip 1E 116
Meadow Way. Ring 9L 185
Meadow Way. Win 1G 126
Mead Rd. And 2M 69
Mead Rd. Chan F 6A 132
Mead Rd. Penn 4B 234
Mead Rd. Win 1J 127
Meads, The. Chan F 7M 131
Meads, The. Roms 5K 129
Meads, The. S Hart 8G 146
Mead, The. Farn 9K 29
Mead, The. Gos 5D 212
Mead, The. Hythe 6K 193
Mead, The. Lip 1D 116
Mead, The. Liss 1E 140
Mead, The. Old B 5J 43
Mead, The. Ptsfld 2K 145
Mead Vw. Good C 8N 69
Mead Way. Fare 6D 198
Meadway. Frim 2N 29
Meadway. Water 9A 182
Meadway, The. Christ 4F 230
Mears Rd. F Oak 1A 162
Meath Clo. Hay I 6J 243
Mede Clo. Over 3E 56
Medieval Merchant's House.
. . . . 8C 4
Medina Chambers. Sotn
. . . . 8L 173 (9C 4)
Medina Clo. Chan F 7C 132
Medina Ct. Lee S 9N 211
Medina Gdns. Okly 1D 58
Medina Ho. Fare 1C 212
Medina Rd. Ports 9E 200
Medina Rd. Sotn 1G 173
Medina Way. Christ 8E 230
Medlar Clo. Burt 5N 229
Medlar Clo. H End 4A 176
Medlar Dri. B'wtr 1H 29
Medley Pl. Sotn 3F 172
Medlicott Way. Swanm 7D 164
Medonte Clo. Fle 3N 47
Medstead 9K 79
Medstead & Four Marks Station
Railway Exhibition 4J 97
Medstead Dri. Elve 8J 27
Medstead Rd. Bch 8N 79
Medstead Rd. Hav 6F 202
Medwall Grn. Sotn 5H 175
Medway Av. Okly 9D 40
Medway Ct. Bas 6E 42
Medway Dri. Chan F 4M 131
Medway Dri. Farn 6G 28
Meerut Rd. Broc 6C 148
Meerut Rd. Tidw 8C 30
Meeting Ho. La. Ring 1J 187
Megana Way. Brfld 8B 124
Megan Ct. Ports 1G 215
Megan Rd. W End 9H 161
Meggeson Av. Sotn 9D 160
Meitner Clo. Braml 9G 13
Melbourne Gdns. Bulf B 3C 66
Melbourne Gdns. H End . . . 4N 175
Melbourne Ho. Ports 1D 240
Melbourne Pl. S'sea
. . . . 3C 240 (5M 5)
Melbourne Rd. Bourn 8N 227
Melbourne Rd. Christ 5H 229
Melbourne Rd. H End 4N 175
Melbourne St. Sotn
. . . . 6N 173 (6G 4)
Melbury Av. Poole 7B 226
Melbury Clo. L'ton 3D 234
Melbury Ct. Sotn 1L 173
Melchet Clo. Sher E 6L 121
(off Drive, The)
Melchet Rd. Sotn 2G 174
Melford Gdns. Bas 9J 41
Melick Clo. March 8E 172
Meliot Ri. And 6N 51
Melksham Clo. Owl 4F 18
Mellersh Clo. Chu C 7K 47
Mellishes Bottom 8G 178
Mellor Clo. Ports 9E 200
Melrose Av. Farn 7E 28
Melrose Clo. Bord 5J 101
Melrose Clo. S'sea 3J 241
Melrose Ct. Cal 1J 171
(in two parts)
Melrose Ct. New M 3D 232
Melrose Ct. Win 8K 105
Melrose Gdns. Gos 9H 213
Melrose Rd. Sotn 9J 159
Melrose Wlk. Bas 3A 42
Melton Ct. Poole 1E 244
Melville Clo. Sotn 6H 159
Melville Gdns. Bourn 6J 227
Melville Rd. Bourn 6J 227
Melville Rd. Gos 9J 213
Melville Rd. S'sea 5L 241
Melville Ter. F'ham 8D 64
Melvin Jones Ho. Fare 4M 211
Memorial Bungalows. Lave
. . . . 5N 55
Memorial Rd. Hook 3G 44
Memorial Sq. Ports
. . . . 2D 240 (4N 5)
Mendip Clo. Bas 8J 41
Mendip Clo. New M 4C 232
Mendip Gdns. Dib P 7J 193
Mendip Rd. Farn 5G 28
Mendip Rd. Sotn 2E 172
Mendips Rd. Fare 9A 198
Mendips Wlk. Fare 9N 197
Mengham 4H 243
Mengham Av. Hay I 5G 243
Mengham Ct. Hay I 4H 243
Mengham La. Hay I 4G 243
Mengham Rd. Hay I 4G 242
Menin Ho. Fare 7M 197
Menin Way. F'ham 9F 64
Menslands La. Hmbdn 2A 180
Menzies Clo. Sotn 6E 158
Meon 4G 211
Meon Clo. Farn 6F 28
Meon Clo. Gos 6D 212
Meon Clo. Ptsfld 9L 139
Meon Clo. Roms 5B 130
Meon Clo. T'ley 4G 11
Meon Clo. Water 7D 168
Meon Ct. Sotn 2H 175
Meon Cres. Chan F 7B 132
Meon Gdns. Swanm 6D 164
Meon Ho. Fare 1C 212
Meon Rd. Bourn 8E 228
Meon Rd. Fare 4G 211
Meon Rd. Okly 1D 58
Meon Rd. Roms 5B 130
Meon Rd. S'sea 3H 241
Meonside Ct. Wick 7C 178
Meonstoke 8N 135
Meon Valley Golf Course.
. . . . 2N 177
Meon Valley Vineyard 7E 164
Meon Wlk. Bas 6D 42
Meonwara Cres. W Meon
. . . . 8E 136
Mercer Clo. Bas 7L 41
Mercer Way. Roms 4N 129
Merchants Pl. Win
. . . . 6L 105 (7N 237)
Merchants Row. Ports
. . . . 4B 240 (7J 5)
(off White Hart Rd.)
Merchants Wlk. Sotn 8C 4
Merchistoun Rd. Water . . . 3B 182
Mercia Av. Charl 7K 51
Mercury Clo. Bord 4K 101
Mercury Clo. Sotn 7E 158
Mercury Gdns. Hamb 5L 195
Mercury Pl. Water 7M 201
Merdon Av. Chan F 4A 132
Merdon Clo. Chan F 4B 132
Mere Cft. Fare 6G 197
Meredith Clo. Christ 7A 230
Meredith Gdns. Tot 4K 171
Meredith Rd. Ports 5F 214
Meredith Towers. Sotn 6J 175
Meredun Clo. Hurs 6N 125
Merepond La. Priv 2L 137
Merganser Clo. Gos 9K 213
Meriden Clo. Poole 6D 244
Meriden Ct. Win 4L 105
(off Northlands Dri.)
Meriden Rd. S'sea
. . . . 3C 240 (5M 5)
Meridian Cen. Hav 8F 202
Meridian Point. Sotn 2D 4
Meridians Cross. Sotn
. . . . 8N 173 (9F 4)
Meridians, The. Christ 8J 229
Merivale. Fle 3J 47
Merlewood Clo. Bourn 1K 245
Merley Dri. Highc 6J 231
Merlin Clo. Bish W 3L 163
Merlin Clo. Hight 2M 187
Merlin Ct. Frim 3M 29
Merlin Dri. Ports 4H 215
Merlin Gdns. Fare 8K 199
Merlin Gdns. H End 3M 175
Merlin Lodge. Sotn 7B 174
Merlin Mead. Bas 4H 59
Merlin Quay. Sotn 6A 174
Merlin Rd. Four M 5J 97
Merlins Clo. F'ham 9E 64
Merlin Way. Chan F 5L 131
Merlin Way. Christ 9C 230
Merlin Way. Farn 9F 28
Mermaid Ct. Bosc 2B 246
Mermaid Rd. Fare 3B 212
Mermaid Way. Sotn
. . . . 8N 173 (9F 4)
Merriatt Clo. Bas 9C 42
Merrick Way. Chan F 4M 131
Merridale Rd. Sotn 6C 174
Merrie Gdns. W'grn 2A 154
Merrieleas Clo. Chan F 5A 132
Merrieleas Dri. Chan F 5A 132
Merriemeade Clo. Dib P . . . 8K 193
Merriemeade Pde. Dib P
. . . . 8K 193
Merrileas Gdns. Bas 2J 59
Merritown 8B 218
Merritown La. Hurn 8A 218
Merritt Ct. Chan F 9B 132
Merrivale Av. Bourn 9H 229
Merrivale Clo. Hythe 6K 193
Merrivale Rd. Ports 5F 214
Merron Clo. Yate 8M 17
Merrow Av. Poole 7F 226
Merrow Clo. Fare 9J 199
Merrydown La. Chine 1H 43
Merryfield. Chine 9F 22
Merryfield. Fare 5F 196
Merryfield Av. Hav 4D 202
Merryfield Clo. Brans 7C 220
Merryfield La. Bourn 2G 226
Merryfield Rd. Ptsfld 9A 140
Merry Gdns. N Bad 7F 130
Merry Oak 5D 174
Merryoak Grn. Sotn 5D 174
Merryoak Rd. Sotn 6D 174
Merrytree Clo. W Wel 1B 120
Merryweather Est. Ring
. . . . 9M 185
Mersea Gdns. Sotn 6E 174
Mersey Ct. And 8B 52
Mersham Gdns. Sotn 3E 174
Merstone Rd. Gos 6E 212
Merthyr Av. Ports 8J 201
Merton Av. Fare 2M 213
Merton Clo. F'bri 8J 151
Merton Clo. Owl 3H 19
Merton Ct. S'sea 4E 240
Merton Cres. Fare 2L 213
Merton Gro. Ring 9J 185
Merton Rd. Bas 5B 42
Merton Rd. Sotn 8N 159
Merton Rd. S'sea 4D 240
Meryl Rd. S'sea 3K 241
Meryon Rd. Alr 2E 108
Mesh Pond. D'ton 1H 119
Mesh Rd. Michm 3H 123
Meteor Rd. Ems 5N 217
Methuen Clo. Bourn 9N 227
Methuen Rd. Bourn 9M 227
Methuen Rd. Lngmr 3H 115
Methuen Rd. S'sea 4H 241
Methuen St. Sotn
. . . . 3M 173 (1D 4)
Metuchen Way. H End 6N 175
Meudon Av. Farn 9K 29
Mews Ct. Ott 1F 132
Mewsey Ct. Hav 2D 202
Mews La. Win 7J 105 (8J 237)
Mews, The. Black 9D 208
Mews, The. Bourn
. . . . 2H 245 (7H 247)
Mews, The. Braml 2J 23
Mews, The. Chan F 9A 132
Mews, The. Gos 3N 239
Mews, The. Hav 5E 202
Mews, The. Ptsfld 9M 139
Mews, The. Ports 1F 240
(off Clive Rd.)
Mews, The. Rown 5E 158
Mews, The. S'sea 5E 240
(off Collingwood Rd.)
Mey Clo. Water 2A 202
Meynell Clo. Eastl 9D 132
Meyrick Clo. Brans 8C 220
Meyrick Dri. N'bry 1C 8
Meyrick Pk. Cres. Bourn
. . . . 8K 227
Meyrick Pk. Golf Course.
. . . . 1J 245
Meyrick Pk. Mans. Bourn
. . . . 1K 245 (5L 247)
Meyrick Rd. Bourn 2M 245
Meyrick Rd. Hav 8D 202
Meyrick Rd. Ports 7D 214
Micawber Ho. Ports 9E 214
Michael Crook Clo. Hav . . . 6C 202
Michaelmas Clo. Yate 9N 17
Michaelmas Drove. W'hll
. . . . 9B 50
Michaels Way. F Oak 1A 162
Michael's Way. Hythe 5L 193
Micheldever 8J 77
Micheldever Clo. Whitc 7H 55
Micheldever Dri. Elve 9H 27
Micheldever Rd. And 2A 70
Micheldever Rd. Whitc 6G 55
Michelgrove Rd. Bourn 2B 246
Michelmersh 4K 123
Michelmersh Clo. Rown 6D 158
Michelmersh Grn. Bourn
. . . . 4A 228
Michigan Way. Tot 2H 171
Mickleham Clo. Poole 6F 226
Mickle Hill. S'hrst 4C 18
Midanbury 1D 174
Midanbury B'way. Sotn . . . 1D 174
Midanbury Ct. Sotn 2C 174
Midanbury Cres. Sotn 1D 174
Midanbury La. Sotn 3C 174
Midanbury Wlk. Sotn 2D 174
Midas Clo. Water 5N 201
Middle Bockhampton 9A 220
Middlebridge St. Roms
. . . . 6L 129
Middlebrook. Bish W 3M 163
Middle Brook St. Win
. . . . 7L 105 (8N 237)
(in two parts)
Middle Church La. F'ham . . . 8D 64
Middle Comn. Rd. Penn . . . 3A 234
Middle Ct. Ports 9F 214
(off Inverness Rd.)
Middlecroft La. Gos 1H 239
Middle Gordon Rd. Cam 8L 19
Middle Hill. A'sht 8J 49
Middle La. Ring 1K 187
Middle Mead. Fare 9L 197
Middle Mead. Hook 2G 44
Middle Mdw. Liss 1F 140
Middlemoor Rd. Frim 3N 29
Middle Old Pk. F'ham 6B 64
Middle Pk. Way. Hav 5D 202
Middle Rd. Bourn 1G 226
Middle Rd. L'ton 3D 234
Middle Rd. N Bad 7F 130
Middle Rd. Park G 4E 196
Middle Rd. Sotn 7E 174
Middle Rd. Sway 5J 223
Middle Rd. Tip 7E 222
Middle Rd. Win
. . . . 6J 105 (6J 237)
Middlesex Rd. S'sea 4J 241
Middle St. Sotn 3M 173
Middle St. S'sea . . . 3D 240 (5N 5)
Middleton 5N 71
Middleton. W'slw 5G 87
Middleton Clo. Fare 1A 212
Middleton Clo. Sotn 9E 160
Middleton Gdns. Bas 4C 42
Middleton Gdns. Farn 6G 28
Middleton Ri. Water 7D 168
Middleton Rd. Bourn 4J 227
Middleton Rd. Cam 7N 19
Middleton Rd. Ring 9K 185
Middleton Rd. W'slw 4G 87
Middleton Wlk. Fare 1A 212

Middle Wallop 9N 67
Middleway, The. *And D & Longp* 9G 52
Middle Winterslow 5H 87
Midfield Clo. *Fare* 1B 212
Midgham Rd. *F'bri* 3F 152
Mid-Hants Railway 4J 97 (Watercress Line)
Midhurst Ho. *Ports* 1E 240
Midhurst Rd. *Lip* 3E 116
Midland Rd. *Bourn* 5K 227
Midlands Est. *W End* 9G 161
Midlane Clo. *Bas* 9B 42
Midlington Hill. *Drox* 4H 165
Midlington Rd. *Drox* 4K 165
Midway. *Hythe* 6L 193
Midway Rd. *Ports* 3F 214
Midways. *Fare* 7M 211
Midwood Av. *Bourn* 5C 228
Mike Hawthorn Dri. *F'ham* 7E 64
Milbeck Clo. *Water* 7A 182
Milborne Cres. *Poole* 7C 226
Milburn Clo. *Bourn* 1G 244
Milburn Rd. *Bourn* 1F 244
Milbury Cres. *Sotn* 4E 174
Mildenhall. *Bourn* 3H 245
Mildmay Ct. *Odi* 9L 45
Mildmay Ct. *Win* 8P 237
Mildmay St. *Win* 9H 105
Mildmay Ter. *H Win* 6C 26
Milebush Rd. *S'sea* 2K 241
Mile End La. *Meon* 7A 142
Mile End Rd. *Ports* 9D 214
Miles La. *W'ish* 3J 121
Milestones Mus. 6N 41
Milford Clo. *Hav* 6D 202
Milford Ct. *Gos* 4F 238
Milford Ct. *Mil S* 8L 235
Milford Ct. *S'sea* 3J 241
Milford Cres. *Mil S* 8L 235
Milford Dri. *Bourn* 1D 226
Milford Gdns. *Chan F* 6C 132
Milford on Sea 9L 235
Milford Pl. *Mil S* 10L 235
Milford Rd. *Evtn & Penn* 6M 233
Milford Rd. *L'ton* 4D 234
Milford Rd. *New M* 5C 232
Milford Rd. *Ports* 2E 240
Milford Trad. Est. *Mil S* 8L 235
Military Rd. *Fare* 7F 198
Military Rd. *Lee S* 4E 238
Military Rd. *Gos* 6J 239 (Fort Rd., in three parts)
Military Rd. *Gos* 6J 213 (Gunners Way)
Military Rd. *Gos* 3G 238 (Privett Rd.)
Military Rd. *Hils* 3G 214
Military Rd. *Navy* 1C 240 (1M 5)
Military Rd. *Ports* 8K 201
Milkingpen La. *Old B* 5J 43
Milk La. *Water* 3K 201
Milkwood Ct. *Tot* 3J 171
Milky Way. *Bton* 8M 145
Millais Rd. *Sotn* 7C 174
Millam Ct. *Hay I* 3E 242
Milland La. *Lip* 7C 116
Milland Rd. *Win* 8M 105
Millard Clo. *Bas* 4A 42
Millbank 5A 174
Millbank Ho. *Sotn* 4A 174
Millbank St. *Sotn* 5A 174
Millbank Wharf. *Sotn* 5A 174
Millbridge Gdns. *Sotn* 6F 174
Mill Bri. Rd. *Yate* 5L 17
Millbrook 3D 172
Millbrook Clo. *Chan F* 7N 131
Millbrook Clo. *Liss* 1F 140
Millbrook Dri. *Hav* 3G 203
Millbrook Flyover. *Sotn* 3D 172
Millbrook Point Rd. *Sotn* 5E 172 (in two parts)
Millbrook Rd. *Sotn* 3D 172
Millbrook Rd. E. *Sotn* 4H 173
Millbrook Rd. W. *Sotn* 4G 172
Millbrook Towers. *Sotn* 9D 158
Millbrook Trad. Est. *Sotn* 4E 172 (Tanner's Brook Way)
Millbrook Trad. Est. *Sotn* 3D 172 (Third Av.)
Millburns, The. *Tims* 6K 123
Mill Chase Rd. *Bord* 3L 101
Mill Clo. *Hasl* 9N 103
Mill Clo. *Hay I* 6F 216
Mill Clo. *Nurs* 6C 158
Mill Clo. *Sher L* 3M 23
Mill Clo. *Water* 6J 181
Mill Clo. *Wher* 2E 74
Mill Corner. *Fle* 8A 28
Millcourt. *F Oak* 1A 162
Mill Ct. *F'bri* 1H 153
Milldam. *Ports* 2C 240 (4L 5)
Mill Drove. *Coll K* 1G 30
Mill End. *Dam* 7A 150
Mill End. *Ems* 9N 203
Millennium Clo. *Water* 4M 201
Millennium Ct. *Bas* 6A 42
Millennium Ct. *Water* 4M 201
Millennium Ho. *F'ham* 9C 64
Millennium Spinnaker Tower 3A 240 (5H 5)
Miller Clo. *New M* 2D 232
Miller Dri. *Fare* 6B 198 (in two parts)
Miller Rd. *Christ* 7N 229
Millers La. *Win* 2C 126
Millers Rd. *T'ley* 5H 11
Millers Way. *Dib P* 7L 193
Mill Est. Yd. *Sotn* 6B 158
Millgate Ct. *F'ham* 7F 64
Mill Ga. Ho. Ports 2B 240 (4K 5) *(off St George's Sq.)*
Mill Green 2K 9
Millgreen La. *H'ly* 2K 9
Millhams St. *Christ* 8L 229
Millhams St. N. *Christ* 8L 229
Mill Hill. *Alr* 9F 94
Mill Hill. *Bot* 4D 176
Mill Hill Av. *Tidw* 6C 30
Mill Ho. Bus. Cen. *Sotn* 6A 174
Mill Ho. Cen. *Tot* 3N 171
Milliken Clo. *Fawl* 6D 208
Millins Clo. *Owl* 4G 18
Mill Lane 1K 63
Mill La. *Abb W* 9A 92
Mill La. *Alt* 4H 81
Mill La. *Bish S* 1J 109
Mill La. *Broc* 7D 148
Mill La. *Burl* 6F 188
Mill La. *Cron* 1D 84
Mill La. *Curd* 8G 162
Mill La. *Drox* 2K 165 (in two parts)
Mill La. *E End* 1M 235
Mill La. *Ecc* 5G 9
Mill La. *Ems* 8N 203 (in two parts)
Mill La. *Gos* 1K 239
Mill La. *H Wes* 4B 24
Mill La. *Hav* 8C 202
Mill La. *Hawk* 6M 113
Mill La. *Highc* 6K 231
Mill La. *Hurn* 9E 218
Mill La. *Lang* 1E 216
Mill La. *Lind* 3M 101
Mill La. *Longp* 2A 76
Mill La. *L'ton* 2F 234
Mill La. *Min* 9N 155
Mill La. *N War* 7H 45
Mill La. *Nurs* 7L 157
Mill La. *Penn* 8L 223
Mill La. *Ptsfld* 7A 140
Mill La. *Ports* 9D 214
Mill La. *Roms* 5K 129
Mill La. *S Hart* 9G 147
Mill La. *Steep* 5L 139
Mill La. *Str S* 7J 13
Mill La. *Titch* 8K 197
Mill La. *Water* 7F 200
Mill La. *W Wel* 7N 121
Mill La. *Wick* 5C 178
Mill La. *Wim* 7J 149
Mill La. *W'slw* 4H 87
Mill La. *Yate* 5N 17
Mill La. Ind. Est. *Alt* 4H 81
Mill Mdw. *Mil S* 7J 235
Millmere. *Yate* 6N 17
Mill Path. *Tidw* 6B 30
Mill Pond Rd. *Gos* 1K 239
Mill Pond, The. *Holb* 2N 207
Mill Quay. *Ems* 1N 217
Mill Ri. *Dun* 4D 122
Mill Rd. *Bas* 3L 41
Mill Rd. *Christ* 6K 229
Mill Rd. *Den* 6H 181
Mill Rd. *Fare* 9C 198
Mill Rd. *Gos* 1J 239
Mill Rd. *Liss* 1E 140
Mill Rd. *Rise* 2J 15
Mill Rd. *Sotn* 3E 172
Mill Rd. *Tot* 3N 171
Mill Rd. *Water* 3L 201
Mill Rd. N. *Bourn* 3A 228
Mill Rd. S. *Bourn* 4A 228
Mill Rythe Holiday Village. *Hay I* 1J 243
Mill Rythe La. *Hay I* 9G 217
Mills Rd. *Ports* 7E 214
Mills, The. *Poole* 8C 226
Mill Stream. *F'ham* 4G 65
Millstream Clo. *And* 3M 69
Millstream Ri. *Roms* 5K 129
Millstream, The. *Hasl* 1N 117
Millstream Trad. Est. *Ring* 3K 187
Mill St. *Eastl* 8F 132
Mill St. *Titch* 9K 197
Mill Vw. *Grey* 9F 44
Millvina Clo. *W'lnds* 6F 170
Millway. *Durl* 6E 162
Mill Way. *Tot* 5L 171
Millway Clo. *And* 2L 69
Millway Rd. *And* 2L 69
Millyford Clo. *New M* 6M 231
Milne Clo. *Dib P* 7H 193
Milner Ct. *Sotn* 2H 173
Milne Rd. *Bulf B* 3B 66
Milner Pl. *Win* 8J 105
Milner Rd. *Bourn* 3G 245
Milnthorpe La. *Win* 7J 105 (9H 237)
Milsons, The. *Stockb* 3F 88
Milton 3J 241
Milton Av. *And* 9K 51
Milton Clo. *Bas* 3D 42
Milton Clo. *Poole* 2B 244
Milton Ct. *S'sea* 2H 241
Milton Gro. *L Hth* 7E 196
Milton Gro. *New M* 4C 232
Milton La. *S'sea* 2G 240
Milton Locks. *S'sea* 3L 241
Milton Mead. *New M* 4A 232
Milton Pde. *Water* 8M 181
Milton Pk. Av. *S'sea* 3J 241
Milton Rd. *Ame* 6A 66
Milton Rd. *Bourn* 9L 227
Milton Rd. *Eastl* 7F 132
Milton Rd. *Poole* 2B 244
Milton Rd. *Ports & S'sea* 1H 241
Milton Rd. *Sotn* 4K 173 (1A 4)
Milton Rd. *Water* 9L 181
Milverton Clo. *Christ* 5G 231
Milverton Clo. *Tot* 5N 171
Milverton Ct. *Sotn* 3F 174
Milverton Ho. *S'sea* 3D 240
Milverton Rd. *Tot* 4N 171
Milverton Rd. *Win* 6H 105 (6H 237)
Milvil Ct. *Lee S* 1A 238
Milvil Rd. *Lee S* 1A 238
Mimosa Clo. *Fare* 6H 197
Mimosa Clo. *Lind* 2M 101
Mimosa Ct. *And* 3K 69
Mimosa Dri. *F Oak* 1B 162
Minchens La. *Braml* 1F 22
Mincingfield La. *Durl* 6G 162
Minden Clo. *And* 7N 51
Minden Clo. *Chine* 1F 42
Minden Ho. *Fare* 9B 198
Minden Ho. Roms 5N 129 (off Chambers Av.)
Minden Way. *Win* 9G 104
Minehurst Rd. *Myt* 8N 29
Minerva Clo. *Water* 7M 201
Minerva Dri. *Gos* 9L 213
Ministry Rd. *Green* 1H 9
Minley 2N 27
Minley Clo. *Farn* 8G 28
Minley Ct. *Hav* 4H 203
Minley Gro. *Fle* 9N 27
Minley La. *Yate* 2N 27
Minley Link Rd. *Farn* 8D 28
Minley Rd. *B'wtr & Farn* 4B 28 (in two parts)
Minley Rd. *Fle & B'wtr* 5M 27
Minnitt Rd. *Gos* 3N 239
Minstead 9M 155
Minstead Av. *Sotn* 2G 175
Minstead Clo. *T'ley* 7H 11
Minstead Clo. *Win* 2H 105
Minstead Dri. *Yate* 8M 17
Minstead Rd. *Bourn* 3G 226
Minstead Rd. *S'sea* 4J 241
Minster Clo. *Fare* 7M 197
Minster Ct. *Cam* 9H 19
Minster Ct. *Sotn* 4H 173
Minster La. *Win* 7L 105 (8M 237)
Mintern Clo. *Eastl* 7H 133
Minterne Grange. *Poole* 6A 244
Minterne Rd. *Bourn* 4L 227
Minterne Rd. *Christ* 8A 230
Minterne Rd. *Poole* 6A 244
Minter's Lepe. *Water* 6M 201
Mint Rd. *Liss* 9F 114
Mint, The 8G 115
Mint Yd. *Win* 8M 237
Mintys Hill. *Rockb* 2C 150
Mirror Clo. *Wars* 8C 196
Mislingford 1F 178
Mislingford Rd. *Swanm* 7E 164
Misselbrook La. *N Bad* 8J 131
Missenden Acres. *H End* 2N 175
Mission La. *Water* 7A 182
Mistletoe Gdns. *Sar G* 4B 196
Mistletoe Rd. *Yate* 9N 17
Mitchell Av. *H Win* 7B 26
Mitchell Clo. *And* 9H 51
Mitchell Clo. *Bart S* 7B 232
Mitchell Clo. *Fare* 4G 196
Mitchell Dri. *F Oak* 9N 133
Mitchell Gdns. *Bas* 3L 59
Mitchell Point. *Hamb* 7J 195
Mitchell Rd. *Eastl* 1F 160
Mitchell Rd. *Hav* 6B 202
Mitchells Clo. *Roms* 5M 129
Mitchells Clo. *W'flls* 2M 119
Mitchell Way. *Ports* 5J 215
Mitchell Way. *Sotn* 5D 160
Mitford Rd. *Alr* 1D 108
Mitre Copse. *Eastl* 1K 161
Mizen Way. *Gos* 1F 238
Mizzen Ho. *Port S* 1B 214
Moat Clo. *Braml* 9G 12
Moat Clo. *Holb* 5N 207
Moat Ct. *Bourn* 9F 226
Moat Ct. *Gos* 4F 238
Moat Dri. *Gos* 4F 238
Moat Hill. *Sotn* 8D 160
Moat La. *Bart S* 5A 232 (in two parts)
Moat Wlk. *Gos* 4F 238
Mobile Home Pk. *Water* 8D 168
Mockbeggar 1M 185
Mockbeggar La. *Ibly & Mock* 2J 185
Moffat Rd. *Christ* 7N 229
Moffats Clo. *S'hrst* 5C 18
Moggs Mead. *Ptsfld* 1N 145 & 9A 140
Moir Ho. *Dib P* 8K 193
Mole Clo. *Farn* 6F 28
Molefields. *Mil S* 7L 235
Mole Hill. *Water* 4N 201
Molesworth Rd. *Gos* 3L 239 (in two parts)
Molyneaux Rd. *New M* 3E 232
Momford Rd. *Win* 2F 126
Monachus La. *H Win* 5C 26
Monarch Clo. *Bas* 4J 59
Monarch Clo. *L Hth* 7D 196
Monarch Clo. *Water* 2A 202
Monarch Way. *W End* 9K 161
Monarch Way. *Win* 8G 104
Monastery Rd. *Sotn* 3C 174
Monckton Rd. *Gos* 6K 239
Monckton Rd. *Ports* 6H 215
Mon Cres. *Sotn* 3G 174
Moneyer Rd. *And* 7M 51
Moneyfield Av. *Ports* 8H 215
Moneyfield La. *Ports* 8H 215
Moneyfield Path. *Ports* 7J 215
Mongers Piece. *Chine* 8H 23
Monier Williams Rd. *Bar S* 6N 71
Moniton Est. *Bas* 7K 41
Monks Brook Clo. *Eastl* 2C 160
Monks Brook Ind. Pk. *Chan F* 7N 131
Monks Clo. *Farn* 8L 29
Monks Clo. *Tidw* 7C 30
Monks Ct. *L'ton* 4F 234
Monkshanger. *F'ham* 8G 65
Monk Sherborne 8K 21
Monk Sherborne Ho. *Monk S* 7K 21
Monk Sherborne Rd. *R'dll & Char A* 5F 20
Monks Hill. *Ems* 3N 203
Monks Hill. *Fare* 8M 211
Monkshood Clo. *Christ* 5D 230
Monks Orchard. *Ptsfld* 8M 139
Monks Path. *Farn* 7M 29
Monks Path. *Sotn* 8C 160
Monks Pl. *Tot* 4K 171
Monks Ri. *Fle* 2J 47
Monks Rd. *Net A* 3F 194
Monks Rd. *Win* 5L 105
Monks Wlk. *Dib P* 9K 193
Monk's Wlk. *F'ham* 9H 65
Monks Way. *Bourn* 1A 226
Monks Way. *Eastl* 2C 160
Monks Way. *Fare* 7L 211
Monks Way. *Sotn* 7C 160
Monks Well. *F'ham* 9K 65
Monkswell Grn. *Christ* 8N 229
Monks Wood. *Ptsfld* 8M 139
Monks Wood Clo. *Sotn* 5N 159
Monkswood Cres. *T'ley* 6H 11
Monkton 6E 148
Monkton Cres. *Poole* 6C 226
Monkton Drove. *Wim G* 6E 148
Monkton La. *F'ham* 5G 64
Monkton La. *Tot* 4J 171
Monkton Pk. *F'ham* 6H 65
Monkwood 4J 111
Monkwood Clo. *Hav* 4D 202
Monkworthy Dri. *Ashy H* 3C 186
Monmouth Clo. *Chan F* 6N 131
Monmouth Ct. *Ring* 1J 187
Monmouth Gdns. *Tot* 5K 171
Monmouth Rd. *Ports* 6E 214
Monmouth Sq. *Win* 8F 104
Monnow Gdns. *W End* 1F 174
Monroe Clo. *Gos* 4G 238
Monsanto Ho. *Bas* 2G 42
Mons Av. *Bulf B* 3B 66
Mons Barracks. *A'sht* 6L 49
Mons Clo. *A'sht* 4N 49
Monson Ho. *Ports* 1F 240
Montacute Clo. *Farn* 8M 29
Montague Av. *Sotn* 7H 175
Montague Clo. *Cam* 8K 19
Montague Clo. *Sotn* 7H 175
Montague Ct. *Dib P* 9K 193
Montague Gdns. *Ptsfld* 1B 146
Montague Pl. *Bas* 8C 42
Montague Rd. *Bourn* 1E 246
Montague Rd. *Eastl* 9H 133
Montague Rd. *Ports* 7F 214
Montague Wallis Ct. *Ports* 2B 240 (4K 5)
Montagu Pk. *Christ* 7J 231
Montagu Rd. *Highc* 7K 231
Montana Ct. *Water* 3N 201
Monteagle La. *Yate* 8L 17
Monteray Dri. *Hord* 2G 233
Monterey Dri. *Hav* 5G 203
Monterey Dri. *L Hth* 7D 196
Montfort Clo. *Roms* 5B 130
Montfort Heights. *Roms* 5B 130
Montfort Rd. *Roms* 6B 130
Montgomerie Rd. *S'sea* 3E 240
Montgomery Av. *Bourn* 3F 226
Montgomery Av. *Tot* 2K 171
Montgomery Clo. *S'hrst* 5D 18
Montgomery Clo. *Win* 9G 105
Montgomery Path. *Farn* 9H 29
Montgomery Rd. *Farn* 9H 29
Montgomery Rd. *Gos* 4E 212
Montgomery Rd. *Hav* 8G 202
Montgomery Rd. *Sotn* 3E 174
Montgomery Wlk. *Water* 4L 201
Montgomery Way. *Chan F* 9N 131
Montpelier Clo. *Park G* 6F 196
Montreal Ct. *A'sht* 1H 65
Montreal Wlk. *Lip* 3E 116
Montrose Av. *Fare* 8N 199
Montrose Clo. *Bot* 4B 176
Montrose Clo. *Fle* 3N 47
Montrose Clo. *Frim* 2N 29
Montrose Clo. *W'hill* 6K 101
Montrose Dri. *Bourn* 4F 226
Montserrat Pl. *Bas* 1D 42
Montserrat Rd. *Bas* 1D 42
Montserrat Rd. *Lee S* 1A 238
Monument Chase. *W'hill* 6K 101
Monument Ct. *Sotn* 9D 4
Monument La. *Fare* 4K 199
Monument La. *L'ton* 1G 234
Monxton 4D 68
Monxton Grn. *Hav* 3H 203
Monxton La. *W'hll* 8C 50 (in two parts)
Monxton Rd. *And* 2F 68 (in two parts)
Monxton Rd. *Grat* 4L 67
Monxton Rd. Roundabout. *And* 1H 69
Moody Rd. *Fare* 7L 211
Moody's Hill. *W Dean* 2J 121
Moonhills La. *Beau* 6G 206
Moonrakers Way. *Christ* 5G 230
Moonscross Av. *Tot* 6M 171
Moor Clo. *Owl* 4G 19
Moor Clo. *W'hill* 4G 100
Moor Ct. La. *Spar* 6N 89
Moorcroft Av. *Burt* 3M 229
Moorcroft Clo. *Sut S* 7D 76
Moordown 4L 227
Moordown Clo. *Bourn* 3L 227
Moore Av. *Bourn* 3E 226
Moore Clo. *And* 9N 51
Moore Clo. *Chu C* 6M 47

Moore Clo. New M 5A 232
Moore Cres. Net A 3G 194
Moore Gdns. Gos 3H 239
Moore Rd. Chu C 6M 47
Moorfield Gro. Bourn 4K 227
Moorfields Rd. Poole 5D 244
Moorfoot Gdns. Bas 8K 41
Moorgreen 9K 161
Moorgreen Pk. Cvn. Site. W End 9K 161
Moorgreen Rd. Hav 4G 203
Moorgreen Rd. W End 1J 175
Moorhams Av. Bas 4J 59
Moorhead Ct. Ocn V 8A 174
Moorhill Gdns. Sotn 3J 175
Moorhill Rd. Burl 8D 188
Moorhill Rd. W End 2H 175
Moorings, The. Bas 6E 42
Moorings, The. Bourn 7H 227
Moorings, The. Christ 9J 229
Moorings, The. Fare 1D 212
Moorings, The. Hind 4N 103
Moorings Way. S'sea 2J 241
Moorland Av. Bart S 6A 232
Moorland Clo. Dib P 6J 193
Moorland Clo. L Hth 5D 196
Moorland Ga. Ring 3K 187
Moorland Rd. Bourn 1A 246
Moorland Rd. Ports 1F 240
Moorlands Clo. Broc 7A 148
Moorlands Clo. Fle 3N 47
Moorlands Clo. Hind 3N 103
Moorlands Cres. Sotn 2F 174
Moorlands Pl. Cam 8J 19
Moorlands Rd. Cam 9J 19
Moorlands Rd. Swanm 4C 164
Moor La. W'ish 7F 120
Moorlea. Bourn 9M 227
Moor Pk. Water 8B 182
Moor Pk. La. F'ham 7G 65 (in two parts)
Moor Pk. Way. F'ham 8H 65
Moor Rd. Farn 4J 29
Moor Rd. Frim 4N 29
Moor Rd. Hasl 1L 117
Moor Rd. Lngmr 5G 115
Moors Clo. Col C 3K 133 (in two parts)
Moors Clo. Hurn 8E 218
Moorside. Win 7P 237
Moorside Clo. Bourn 3F 226
Moorside Clo. Farn 3J 29
Moorside Rd. Bourn 3E 226
Moorside Rd. Win 5N 105
Moors Nature Reserve, The. 5A 164
Moors, The. Tong 3N 65
Moors Valley Country Pk. & Vis. Cen. 9A 184
Moors Valley Golf Course. 8A 184
Moors Valley Railway. 9A 184
Moortown 3K 187
Moortown Av. Ports 8K 201
Moortown La. Ring 4K 187
Moorvale Rd. Bourn 4L 227
Moor Vw. Old B 4J 43
Moot Clo. And 6A 52
Moot Clo. D'ton 3L 119
Moot Gdns. D'ton 3K 119
Moot La. Hale 1A 154
Mopley. Black 9D 208
Mopley Clo. Black 9D 208
Morant Ct. New M 3C 232
Morant Rd. Ring 8L 185
Moraunt Clo. Gos 8L 213
Moraunt Dri. Fare 1K 213
Moray Av. Coll T 5F 18 (in two parts)
Mordaunt Dri. Well C 2D 18
Mordaunt Rd. Sotn 3M 173
Morden Rd. Bourn 5J 227
Morecombe Ct. S'sea 3E 240
Moreland Clo. Alt 6G 80
Moreland Rd. Gos 2K 239
Morelands Ct. Water 5N 201
Morelands Rd. Water 5M 201
Moresby Ct. Fare 8D 198
Morestead 3B 134
Morestead Rd. Win 9M 105 (in two parts)
Moreton Clo. Chu C 7L 47
Moreton Clo. Churt 7G 85
Moreton Rd. Bourn 2M 227
Morgan Le Fay Dri. N Bad 5L 131
Morgan Rd. H End 5N 175
Morgan Rd. S'sea 3K 241
Morgan's Dri. Fare 3M 211
Morgan's La. Pent 1G 148
Morgan's La. Wint D 3A 86
Morgans Ri. Rd. Redl 1M 119
Morgan's Vale 2M 119
Morgans Va. Rd. Redl 2M 119
Morgaston Rd. Bram 6M 21
Morland Rd. A'sht 3K 65
Morland Rd. Sotn 1H 173
Morland's Rd. A'sht 6M 49
Morley Clo. Bourn 9D 228
Morley Clo. Burt 3M 229
Morley Clo. Sotn 4D 174
Morley Clo. Yate 8L 17
Morley Cres. Water 7A 182
Morley Dri. Bish W 3M 163
Morley Rd. Bas 1B 60
Morley Rd. Bourn 9D 228
Morley Rd. F'ham 9E 64
Morley Rd. S'sea 5H 241
Morningside Av. Fare 8N 199
Mornington Clo. And 4N 69
Mornington Clo. Baug 4D 10
Mornington Dri. Win 4G 104
Mornington Rd. Cowes 5N 237 (off Queen's Rd.)
Mornington Rd. W'hill 4F 100
Mornish Rd. Poole 3D 244
Morpeth Av. Tot 2M 171
Morris Clo. Dib 5J 193
Morris Clo. Gos 3D 212
Morrison Av. Poole 7D 226
Morris Rd. Farn 3M 49
Morris Rd. Sotn 5K 173 (3A 4)
Morris St. Hook 3E 44
Morse Ct. Net A 3E 194
Morse Rd. Bas 7N 41
Morshead Cres. Fare 6B 198
Mortimer Clo. Christ 8C 230
Mortimer Clo. H Win 8A 26
Mortimer Clo. King W 9M 91
Mortimer Clo. Net A 3F 194
Mortimer Clo. Tot 1K 171
Mortimer Gdns. T'ley 6J 11
Mortimer La. Strat S 4J 13
Mortimer La. Bas 6B 42
Mortimer Lawn. Hav 2D 202
Mortimer Rd. Bot 4D 176
Mortimer Rd. Bourn 5M 227
Mortimer Rd. Ports 8D 200
Mortimer Rd. Sotn 6C 174
Mortimers Dri. F Oak 1A 162
Mortimers Ind. Units. Ower 5E 156
Mortimers La. F Oak 1N 161
Mortimer Way. N Bad 9E 130
Mortimer West End 1C 12
Mortimore Rd. Gos 1H 239
Morval Clo. Farn 8G 28
Mosaic Clo. Sotn 6K 175
Moscrop Ct. Bas 7B 42
Mosedale Wlk. Sotn 2D 172
Moselle Clo. Farn 7F 28
Moselle Ct. Sotn 5H 173
Moss Clo. Liss 1F 140
Moss Dri. March 8E 172
Mossleigh Av. Rown 6E 158
Mossley Av. Poole 5D 226
Moss Rd. Win 6M 105
Mottcombe Rd. Poole 3E 244
Mottisfont 3E 122
Mottisfont Abbey & Gardens. 3F 122
Mottisfont Clo. Sotn 4F 172
Mottisfont Rd. Eastl 8E 132
Moulin Av. S'sea 5F 240
Moulsham Copse La. Yate 6L 17
Moulsham Grn. Yate 6L 17
Moulsham La. Yate 6L 17
Moulshay La. Sher L 7K 23
Mound Clo. Gos 4J 239
Mountain Ash Clo. Sotn 3G 175
Mount Av. New M 5B 232
Mountbatten Av. Cowes 5N 237
Mountbatten Av. Roms 5M 129
Mountbatten Bus. Cen. Sotn 5J 173
Mountbatten Clo. Christ 8C 230
Mountbatten Clo. Gos 4E 212
Mountbatten Ct. A'sht 9J 49 (off Birchett Rd.)
Mountbatten Ct. Win 3J 105
Mountbatten Dri. Water 3K 201
Mountbatten Gdns. Bourn 4C 228
Mountbatten Ho. Navy 1B 240 (2J 5)
Mountbatten Ho. Sotn 2C 4
Mountbatten Pl. King W 7N 91
Mountbatten Retail Pk. Sotn 6K 173 (4A 4)
Mountbatten Ri. S'hrst 4B 18
Mountbatten Rd. Eastl 7E 132
Mountbatten Rd. Poole & Bourn 4F 244
Mountbatten Rd. Tot 3K 171
Mountbatten Sports Cen. 5E 214
Mountbatten Sq. S'sea 5J 241
Mountbatten Way. Sotn 5H 173
Mt. Carmel Rd. Pale 6J 67
Mount Clo. High 3A 8
Mount Clo. New M 5B 232
Mount Clo. Win 3J 105
Mount Dri. Chan F 8C 132
Mount Dri. Fare 9L 197
Mounters La. Chaw 7D 80
Mountfield. Hythe 5K 193
Mt. Grace Dri. Poole 6A 244
Mt. Heatherbank. Bourn 6L 247
Mt. Hermon Rd. Pale 6K 67
Mounthouse Clo. Hythe 4M 193
Mountjoy Ct. Ports 4B 240 (7J 5)
Mount La. Lcky 3N 121
Mount Pleasant 5F 80 (Alton)
Mount Pleasant 7N 223 (Lymington)
Mt. Pleasant. A'prt 3B 68
Mt. Pleasant. F'ham 9C 64
Mt. Pleasant. Free 4L 55
Mt. Pleasant. H Win 6C 26
Mt. Pleasant. King W 9M 91
Mt. Pleasant. Ring 1K 187
Mt. Pleasant. Roms 6L 129
Mt. Pleasant. S'hrst 4C 18
Mt. Pleasant. T'ley 5G 11
Mt. Pleasant Camping Pk. Hurn 6F 218
Mt. Pleasant Dri. Bourn 5C 228
Mt. Pleasant Dri. Brans 6E 220
Mt. Pleasant Dri. T'ley 5G 11
Mt. Pleasant Ind. Est. Sotn 3N 173
Mt. Pleasant La. L'ton 7N 223
Mt. Pleasant Rd. A'sht 9L 49
Mt. Pleasant Rd. Alt 5F 80
Mt. Pleasant Rd. Gos 5K 239
Mt. Pleasant Rd. Lind 2L 101
Mt. Pleasant Rd. Sotn 3N 173 (1F 4)
Mount Rd. Bourn 2E 226
Mountsom's La. Up Farr 3F 98
Mounts Way. Elve 9H 27
Mt. Temple. Roms 5N 129
Mount, The 3A 8
Mount, The. Fle 1M 47
Mount, The. Gos 7G 212
Mount, The. Head 1C 102
Mount, The. Ring 9M 185
Mount, The. Sotn 1F 172 (Romsey Rd.)
Mount, The. Sotn 7L 159 (Winchester Rd.)
Mount Vw. A'sht 1J 65
Mount Vw. Eastl 8F 132
Mountview Av. Fare 8N 199
Mt. View Rd. Win 1F 126
Mourne Clo. Bas 7K 41
Mousehole La. Hythe 6M 193
Mousehole La. Sotn 2D 174
Mousehole Rd. Ports 8A 200
Mowatt Rd. Gray 5M 103
Mowbray Rd. Sotn 6F 174
Moxhams. F'bri 1J 153
Moyles Ct. Rock 3M 185
Mozart Clo. Bas 2N 59
Muccleshell Clo. Hav 5G 202
Mucklands La. Bentw 7K 79
Muddyford Rd. Redl 7C 120
Mudeford 9B 230
Mudeford. Christ 9B 230
Mudeford Grn. Clo. Christ 9B 230
Mudeford La. Christ 8A 230 (in two parts)
Mude Gdns. Christ 9C 230
Mud La. E'sly 4C 16
Mugs La. King S 8B 86
Mulberries, The. F'ham 6H 65
Mulberry Av. Fare 7M 211
Mulberry Av. Ports 9H 201
Mulberry Clo. Bourn 5E 226
Mulberry Clo. C'then 1E 18
Mulberry Clo. Gos 3K 239
Mulberry Clo. Owl 5F 18
Mulberry Corner. Chan F 8M 131
Mulberry Ct. Four M 4K 97
Mulberry Gdns. F'bri 2H 153
Mulberry Gro. Evtn 6L 233
Mulberry La. Ports 1H 215
Mulberry La. Sar G 4B 196
Mulberry Mead. Whitc 5H 55
Mulberry Path. Ports 1H 215
Mulberry Rd. March 9E 172
Mulberry Wlk. Sotn 2H 173
Mulberry Way. Chine 9G 22
Mulfords Hill. T'ley 4H 11
Mull Clo. Okly 9C 40
Mullen Clo. Sotn 6C 174
Mullenscote Pk. Cvn. Pk. W'hll 9A 50
Mullenspond 1N 67
Mullins Clo. Bas 3C 42
Mullins Clo. Poole 6G 226
Mullion Clo. Port S 1C 214
Mumby Rd. Gos 2L 239
Mundays Row. Water 1C 182
Munnings Clo. Bas 8E 42
Munnings Ct. And 9M 51
Munnings Dri. Coll T 7F 18
Munro Cres. Sotn 3E 172
Munster Rd. Poole 2B 244
Munster Rd. Ports 6E 214
Murefield Rd. Ports 2E 240
Muria Est. Sotn 5A 174
Muriel Rd. Water 1M 201
Murley Rd. Bourn 6L 227
Murray Clo. And 4M 69
Murray Clo. Fare 7A 198
Murray Clo. Sotn 4J 175
Murray Rd. Farn 9H 29
Murray Rd. Water 4B 182
Murray's La. Ports 1A 240 (1H 5)
Murrell Green 9L 25
Murrell Grn. Hav 4H 203
Murrell Grn. Bus. Pk. Hook 1L 45
Murrell Grn. Rd. H Win 7L 25
Murrells La. Cam 1K 29
Murrills Est. Fare 9N 199
Muscliff 2L 227
Muscliffe Ct. Hav 4H 203
Muscliffe La. Bourn 2L 227
Muscliffe Rd. Bourn 5K 227
Muscott Clo. Ship B 2A 66
Museum of Archaeology. 8M 173 (9D 4)
Museum of Army Flying. 5A 72
Museum of Electricity. 7L 229
Museum of the Iron Age, The. 1A 70
Museum Rd. Ports 3C 240 (6L 5)
Musgrave Clo. Bas 2M 59
Musgrove Gdns. Alt 4E 80
Musket Copse. Old B 5H 43
Mussett Clo. Tot 3L 171
Mustang Av. White 2E 196
Myers Clo. Swanm 6D 164
Myland Clo. Bas 3D 42
Mylen Bus. Cen. And 1L 69
Mylen Rd. And 1L 69
My Lord's La. Hay I 4H 243
Myrtle Av. Fare 1M 213
Myrtle Av. Tot 4K 171
Myrtle Clo. Gos 5E 212
Myrtle Clo. Hord 2G 233
Myrtle Dri. B'wtr 8F 18
Myrtle Gro. Ports 9J 215
Myrtle Rd. Bourn 8N 227
Myrtle Rd. Sotn 7G 158
Mytchett 9N 29
Myvern Clo. Holb 5B 208

N

Naafi Roundabout. A'sht 9K 49
Nada Rd. Christ 5F 230
Nadder Rd. Tidw 8D 30
Nailsworth Rd. Ports 8C 200
Naini Tal Rd. Tidw 7C 30
Nairn Clo. Frim 2N 29
Nairn Ct. Bourn 7J 227
Nairn Rd. Bourn 8J 227
Nairn Rd. Poole 6C 244
Naish Ct. Hav 2C 202
Naish Dri. Gos 7J 213
Naish Holiday Village. New M 6L 231
Naish Rd. Bart S 7M 231
Namu Rd. Bourn 5J 227
Nancy Rd. Ports 2F 240
Napier Clo. A'sht 4N 49
Napier Clo. C'then 1E 18
Napier Clo. Gos 2F 238
Napier Clo. Tidw 8E 30
Napier Cres. Fare 8M 197
Napier Rd. C'then 1E 18
Napier Rd. Sotn 5J 175
Napier Rd. S'sea 5E 240
Napier Rd. Water 4C 182
Napier Wlk. And 9C 52
Napoleon Av. Farn 6K 29
Napoleon Dri. Bas 4L 41
Narrow La. Ring 9N 185
Narrow La. Roms 5L 129
Narvik Rd. Ports 4E 214
Naseby Clo. Ports 8B 200
Naseby Rd. Bourn 5L 227
Nash Clo. Bas 4C 42
Nash Clo. Dib P 8J 193
Nash Clo. Farn 8H 29
Nashe Clo. Fare 6N 197
Nashe Ho. Fare 6M 197
Nashes Green 1M 79
Nashe Way. Fare 6M 197
Nash Meadows. S Warn 4D 62
Nash Rd. Dib P 8J 193
Nasmith Clo. Gos 3G 238
Nately Rd. Grey 8D 44
Nat Gonella Sq. Gos 3M 239 (off Walpole Rd.)
National Diary Mus. 3H 15
National Motor Mus. 6E 206
Nations Hill. King W 8M 91
Navigators Way. H End 1N 175
Navy Rd. Ports 1B 240 (1J 5)
Nea Clo. Christ 6F 230
Neacroft 9D 220
Neacroft Clo. New M 6M 231
Nea Dri. Blash 3D 184
Nea Rd. Christ 6G 230
Neatham 2L 81
Neath Rd. Bas 6E 42
Neath Way. Chan F 6M 131
Needles Ho. Fare 1C 212
Needles Point. Mil S 8K 235
Needles Vw. Bourn 2H 247
Neelands Gro. Ports 9N 199
Neilson Clo. Chan F 5A 132
Nelson Av. Fare 1K 213
Nelson Av. Ports 6E 214
Nelson Clo. A'sht 1L 65
Nelson Clo. F'ham 2F 64
Nelson Clo. Holb 5A 208
Nelson Clo. New M 3A 232
Nelson Clo. Roms 4M 129
Nelson Clo. Stockb 3F 88
Nelson Ct. Fare 2B 212
Nelson Ct. Hythe 8N 193
Nelson Cres. Water 3C 182
Nelson Dri. Christ 8B 230
Nelson Ga. Sotn 5K 173 (3A 4)
Nelson Hill. Sotn 5K 173
Nelson Ho. Gos 3N 239 (off South St.)
Nelson Ind. Pk. H End 1M 175
Nelson La. Fare 6L 199
Nelson Lodge. Bas 4N 41
Nelson Pl. L'ton 3F 234
Nelson Rd. Eastl 8H 133
Nelson Rd. F'ham 2F 64
Nelson Rd. Gos 3K 239
Nelson Rd. Poole & Bourn 1E 244
Nelson Rd. Ports 9E 214
Nelson Rd. Sotn 4H 173
Nelson Rd. S'sea 4D 240
Nelson Rd. Win 7N 105
Nelsons Gdns. H End 8N 161
Nelson's Monument. 6L 199
Nelson St. A'sht 9J 49
Nelson Wlk. And 9C 52
Nelson Way. Cam 9H 19
Nepaul Rd. Tidw 7C 30
Nepean Clo. Gos 6K 239
Neptune Ct. Gos 6F 212
Neptune Ct. Sotn 7E 158
Neptune Rd. Bord 5K 101
Neptune Rd. Fare (PO14) 3B 212
Neptune Rd. Fare (PO15) 7M 197
Neptune Way. Sotn 8N 173 (9F 4)
Nerissa Clo. Water 1A 202
Nerquis Clo. Roms 4A 130
Nesbitt Clo. Gos 5D 212
Nessus St. Ports 8E 214
Nest Bus. Pk. Hav 5H 203
Nestor Clo. And 9M 51
Netherfield Clo. Alt 4E 80
Netherfield Clo. Hav 8G 203
Netherhall Gdns. Bourn 2G 245
Netherhill La. Bot 1E 176
Netherhouse Ct. Chu C 5J 47
Netherhouse Moor. Chu C 4J 47
Netherton 7H 7
Netherton Rd. Gos 9H 213
Nether Vell-Mead. Chu C 7K 47
Nether Wallop 1A 88
Netley 4F 194
Netley Abbey. 3E 194

Netley Cliff. *Net A* 4F **194**
Netley Clo. *Chan F* 9N **131**
Netley Firs Clo. *Sotn* 6K **175**
Netley Firs Rd. *H End* 5L **175**
Netley Hill Est. *Sotn* 6K **175**
Netley Lodge Clo. *Net A* 4G **194**
Netley Marsh 4G **170**
Netley Pl. *S'sea* 9N **5**
Netley Rd. *Fare* 8F **196**
Netley Rd. *S'sea* 5D **240** (9N **5**)
Netley St. *Farn* 3K **49**
Netley Ter. *S'sea* 5D **240** (9N **5**)
Nettlebeds La. *Old Al* 4J **95**
Nettlecombe Av. *S'sea* 6F **240**
Nettlestone. *Net A* 2G **194**
Nettlestone Rd. *S'sea* 5H **241**
Netton Clo. *B'stne* 3C **118**
Netton St. *B'stne* 3C **118**
Neuvic Way. *Whitc* 6H **55**
Nevada Clo. *Farn* 9F **28**
Neva Rd. *Sotn* 2D **174**
Neville Av. *Fare* 2M **213**
Neville Clo. *And* 3A **70**
Neville Clo. *Bas* 9C **42**
Neville Ct. *Bas* 4F **42**
Neville Ct. *Gos* 2K **239**
Neville Dri. *Roms* 3M **129**
Neville Duke Rd. *Farn* 4H **29**
Neville Gdns. *Ems* 6L **203**
Neville Rd. *Ports* 9H **215**
Nevil Shute Rd. *Ports* 5H **215**
Newall Rd. *And* 2G **68**
New Ashgate Gallery 8D 64
New Barn Clo. *Fle* 4J **47**
New Barn Cotts. *Spar* 4C **90**
New Barn La. *Alt* 6F **80**
New Barn La. *Wher* 9E **70**
New Barn Rd. *Bton* 2J **169**
Newbarn Rd. *Hav* 6B **202**
Newbolt Clo. *Water* 7M **181**
Newbolt Rd. *Ports* 8N **199**
Newbridge 4N **155**
Newbridge. *Net A* 3G **195**
New Bri. La. *Bas* 6F **42**
Newbridge Rd. *Cad* 4N **155**
Newbridge Way. *Penn* 5C **234**
New Brighton 7M **203**
New Brighton Rd. *Ems* 8M **203**
Newbroke Rd. *Gos* 8F **212**
New Bldgs. *Chut C* 4D **32**
Newburgh St. *Win* 6K **105** (6K **237**)
Newbury By-Pass. *Wash W & Burgh* 1B **8**
Newbury Clo. *F Oak* 1M **161**
Newbury Dri. *Bourn* 5H **227**
Newbury La. *Pen M* 7G **50**
Newbury Pl. *Wars* 7C **196**
Newbury Rd. *And* 6N **51**
Newbury Rd. *K're* 2A **6** (Fox's La.)
Newbury Rd. *K're* 1A **6** (Union La.)
Newbury Rd. *Sotn* 1H **173**
Newbury Rd. *Whitc* 5G **55**
Newbury Rd. Junct. *Bas* 4M **41**
Newbury St. *And* 1A **70**
Newbury St. *Whitc* 5G **55**
New Cheriton 1K **135**
Newchurch Rd. *T'ley* 4G **10**
Newcliffe Gdns. *H End* 5M **175**
New Cliff Ho. *Sotn* 9C **174**
Newcomb Clo. *And* 4M **69**
Newcombe Rd. *Bourn* 9H **229**
Newcombe Rd. *Ports* 1F **240**
Newcombe Rd. *Sotn* 4K **173** (1A **4**)
Newcomen Ct. *Ports* 6D **214**
Newcomen Rd. *Ports* 6D **214**
Newcome Pl. *A'sht* 3M **65**
Newcome Rd. *F'ham* 4G **64**
New Cotts. *Sotn* 9B **158**
New Ct. *Fare* 4G **196**
New Ct. *Ring* 1H **187**
New Cres. *Lud* 2C **30**
Newcroft Gdns. *Christ* 6K **229**
New Cut. *Hay I* 5F **216**
New Dawn Clo. *Farn* 9F **28**
New Down La. *Pur* 7H **201**
New Drove. *Lud* 2C **30**
Newenham Rd. *L'ton* 4E **234**
New Farm Ind. Est. *Alr* 2D **108**
New Farm Rd. *Alr* 1D **108**
New Farm Rd. *Mich* 7L **77**
Newfield Av. *Farn* 6G **28**
Newfield Rd. *Liss* 8F **114**
New Forest Dri. *Broc* 6A **148**
New Forest Enterprise Cen. *Tot* 5L **171**
New Forest Golf Course 1D 148
New Forest Mus. 2C 148
New Forest Owl Sanctuary 3M 187
Newfound 7E **40**
Newgate La. *Fare* 5C **212**
Newgate La. Ind. Est. *Fare* 2D **212** (in two parts)
Newgrounds 5A **154**
New Haig Rd. *Bulf B* 3B **66**
New Ho. La. *App* 3A **50**
New Inn La. *Bart* 4B **170**
New Inn La. *E Bol* 1B **236**
New Inn Rd. *Bart* 4B **170**
Newlands. *Fare* 8M **197**
Newlands. *Fle* 5M **47**
Newlands Av. *Gos* 3J **239**
Newlands Av. *Sotn* 3H **173**
Newlands Clo. *Black* 7C **208**
Newlands Clo. *Chan F* 7K **131**
Newlands Clo. *Yate* 8N **17**
Newlands Copse. *Black* 7D **208**
Newlands La. *Water* 8G **180**
Newlands Mnr. *Evtn* 7L **233**
Newlands Rd. *Bourn* 8D **228**
Newlands Rd. *Cam* 3K **29**
Newlands Rd. *Christ* 7B **230**
Newlands Rd. *Fawl* 6C **208**
Newlands Rd. *New M* 5C **232**
Newlands Rd. *Water* 4L **201**
New La. *Hav* 7G **202**
New La. *Holyb* 10E **62**
New La. *King S* 6G **88**
New La. *Mil S* 8M **235**
New La. *New M* 9A **222**
New La. *S Hart* 9G **147**
Newlease Rd. *Water* 4N **201**
Newlyn Wlk. *Roms* 3N **129**
Newlyn Way. *Poole* 7C **226**
Newlyn Way. *Port S* 1B **214**
Newman Bassett Ho. *Bas* 5L **41**
Newman La. *Alt* 4H **81**
Newmans Ct. *F'ham* 3C **64**
Newmans Hill. *Wick* 2D **178**
Newman St. *Sotn* 2G **172**
Newmans Way. *Bulf* 3A **66**
Newmarket Clo. *H Hth* 4A **162**
New Mkt. Sq. *Bas* 6C **42**
Newmer Ct. *Hav* 3C **202**
New Mill Cotts. *Hasl* 9M **103**
New Mill La. *E'sly* 3B **16**
New Mill Rd. *E'sly* 3B **16**
New Milton 4B **232**
New Milton Recreation Cen. 4A 232
Newmorton Rd. *Bourn* 2L **227**
Newney Clo. *Ports* 4G **214**
Newnham Ct. *Hav* 4H **203**
Newnham La. *Old B & Newn* 3J **43**
Newnham Pk. *Hook* 3F **44**
Newnham Rd. *Newn & Hook* 3D **44**
New North Dri. *Sher L* 5M **23**
New Paddock Clo. *Holyb* 1J **81**
New Pde. *Bourn* 3J **227**
New Pde. *Fare* 9M **199**
New Pk. Rd. *Bourn* 1F **246**
Newport Clo. *Chan F* 8M **131**
Newport La. *Brfld* 7A **124**
Newport Rd. *A'sht* 1L **65**
Newport Rd. *Gos* 2H **239**
New Rd. *Asht* 7H **171**
New Rd. *Bas* 6C **42**
New Rd. *Bish W* 1N **163**
New Rd. *Black* 7C **208**
New Rd. *B'wtr* 9G **18**
New Rd. *Bourn* 1J **227** (in two parts)
New Rd. *Braml* 4A **22**
New Rd. *Chu C* 5N **47**
New Rd. *Clan* 7C **168**
New Rd. *Col C* 3K **133**
New Rd. *Eastl* 1M **161**
New Rd. *E'sly* 6J **17**
New Rd. *Fare* 8C **198**
New Rd. *H Win* 6B **26**
New Rd. *Hasl* 1N **117**
New Rd. *Hav* 7D **202**
New Rd. *Hook* 3G **44**
New Rd. *Hythe* 9N **193** (Hardley La., in two parts)
New Rd. *Hythe* 5M **193** (Marsh, The)
New Rd. *Key* 9N **235**
New Rd. *Land* 1K **155**
New Rd. *Love* 4M **181**
New Rd. *Meon* 9N **135**
New Rd. *Mich S* 4J **77**
New Rd. *Mid W* 9M **67**
New Rd. *Mock* 1L **185**
New Rd. *Net A* 3E **194**
New Rd. *N War* 7J **45**
New Rd. *P Grn & Lit L* 9K **11**
New Rd. *Poole* 8B **226**
New Rd. *Ports* 9F **214**
New Rd. *Ring* 4K **187**
New Rd. *Rockb* 2B **150**
New Rd. *Roms* 4N **129**
New Rd. *S'hrst* 5C **18**
New Rd. *Sotn* 5M **173** (4D **4**)
New Rd. *Swanm* 8B **164**
New Rd. *Swanw* 1C **196**
New Rd. *T'ley* 6F **10**
New Rd. *Tims & Michm* 6K **123**
New Rd. *Wars* 9A **196** (in two parts)
New Rd. *W'hill* 6H **101**
New Rd. *Win* 9F **90**
New Rd. Cotts. Selb 7L **99** (off Selborne Rd.)
New Rd. E. *Ports* 8G **215**
Newstead Rd. *Bourn* 1G **247**
New St. *And* 8A **52**
New St. *Bas* 7C **42**
New St. *L'ton* 2E **234**
New St. *Ring* 2K **187**
New St. Stockb 2F **88** (off High St.)
New St. *Str S* 5M **13**
New St. M. *L'ton* 2E **234**
New Theatre Royal 2D 240 (4M 5)
Newton 6G **121**
Newton Clo. *Fare* 4M **211**
Newton Clo. *W'ish* 5H **121**
Newton Common 7N **97**
Newton La. *Newt V* 7D **98**
Newton La. *Roms* 5L **129**
Newton La. *W'ish* 6G **121**
Newton Morrell. *Poole* 2B **244**
Newton Pl. *Lee S* 9A **212**
Newton Rd. *Bart S* 6C **232**
Newton Rd. *Farn* 6M **29**
Newton Rd. *Poole* 5C **244**
Newton Rd. *Sotn* 1C **174**
Newton Rd. *Twy* 6L **127**
Newton Stacey 2K **75**
Newton Toney 6E **66**
Newton Toney. *Bulf B* 6E **66**
Newton Valence 9G **99**
Newton Way. *Tong* 3N **65**
Newtown 5E **80** (Alton)
Newtown 3K **163** (Bishops Waltham)
Newtown 3E **242** (Hayling Island)
Newtown 9L **155** (Lyndhurst)
Newtown 1E **8** (Newbury)
Newtown 4N **173** (Northam)
Newtown 7A **226** (Poole)
Newtown 9B **122** (Romsey)
Newtown 9A **196** (Warash)
Newtown 4L **179** (Waterlooville)
Newtown 9E **174** (Woolston)
Newtown. *Bro Ch* 3A **118**
New Town. *Portc* 9M **199**
Newtown. *T'ley* 4G **11**
Newtown Clo. *And* 2L **69**
Newtown Ct. *Wars* 8N **195**
Newtown La. *Hay I* 3E **242**
Newtown Rd. *Eastl* 8E **132**
Newtown Rd. *Lip* 3E **116**
Newtown Rd. *New* 1E **8**
Newtown Rd. *S'hrst* 5D **18**
Newtown Rd. *Sher E & Awb* 2A **128**
Newtown Rd. *Sotn* 8E **174**
Newtown Rd. *Wars* 1N **209**
Newtown Vs. *Lud* 2F **30**
New Valley Rd. *Mil S* 8J **235**
New Wokingham Rd. *Wok & C'then* 1C **18**
Nicholas Clo. *Walk* 4K **231**
Nicholas Ct. *Hay I* 4E **242**
Nicholas Ct. *Lee S* 2A **238**
Nicholas Cres. *Fare* 7B **198**
Nicholas Gdns. *Bourn* 4G **226**
Nicholas Rd. *Black* 9C **208**
Nicholl Pl. *Gos* 6E **212**
Nichol Rd. *Chan F* 3B **132**
Nicholson Gdns. Ports 2E **240** (off Boarhunt Clo.)
Nicholson Pl. *Alr* 1D **108**
Nicholson Wlk. *Rown* 5C **158**
Nicholson Way. *Hav* 6E **202**
Nichols Rd. *Sotn* 5N **173** (3F **4**)
Nichols Town 5M **173**
Nickel Clo. *Win* 6M **105**
Nickel St. *S'sea* 4C **240** (7M **5**)
Nickleby Gdns. *Tot* 3H **171**
Nickleby Ho. *Ports* 9E **214**
Nickleby Rd. *Water* 5B **168**
Nickson Clo. *Chan F* 4N **131**
Nicolson Clo. *Ame* 5A **66**
Nicotiania Ct. Chu C 7K **47** (off Annettes Cft.)
Nightingale Av. *Eastl* 2A **160**
Nightingale Clo. *Burs* 1K **195**
Nightingale Clo. *Farn* 6E **28**
Nightingale Clo. *Gos* 1H **239**
Nightingale Clo. *Roms* 5N **129**
Nightingale Clo. *Row C* 9G **183**
Nightingale Clo. *W Wel* 1A **120**
Nightingale Clo. *Win* 8F **104**
Nightingale Ct. *Sotn* 4H **173**
Nightingale Cres. *Shir H* 2B **178**
Nightingale Dri. *Tot* 2J **171**
Nightingale Gdns. *Bas* 3L **41**
Nightingale Gdns. *Hook* 2G **45**
Nightingale Gdns. *S'hrst* 5D **18**
Nightingale Gro. *Sotn* 3H **173**
Nightingale Ho. *Net A* 5G **195**
Nightingale Ho. *Roms* 4N **129**
Nightingale M. *L Hth* 6E **196**
Nightingale M. *Net A* 5G **195**
Nightingale Pk. *Hav* 8H **203**
Nightingale Ri. *Over* 3E **56**
Nightingale Rd. *Bord* 5K **101**
Nightingale Rd. *Ptsfld* 2K **145**
Nightingale Rd. *Ports* 8G **200**
Nightingale Rd. *Sotn* 3H **173**
Nightingale Rd. *S'sea* 5C **240** (9M **5**)
Nightingale Wlk. *Net A* 5G **194**
Nightjar Clo. *Ews* 2N **63**
Nightjar Clo. *Water* 3A **182**
Nile Rd. *Sotn* 9M **159**
Nile St. *Ems* 9M **203**
Nimrod Dri. *Gos* 1F **238** (in two parts)
Nine Acres. *Steep M* 4A **140**
Nine Elms La. *Fare* 5F **198**
Ninian Clo. *F Oak* 2N **161**
Ninian Pk. Rd. *Ports* 6H **215**
Ninian Path. *Ports* 6H **215**
Ninth St. *Hythe* 4B **208**
Niton Clo. *Gos* 6E **212**
Noads Clo. *Dib P* 7L **193**
Noads Way. *Dib P* 8K **193**
Nobbs La. *Ports* 3B **240** (6K **5**)
Nobes Av. *Gos* 5E **212**
Nobes Clo. *Gos* 6F **212**
Noble Clo. *Bourn* 5D **226**
Noble Rd. *H End* 4A **176**
Nob's Crook. *Col C* 4L **133**
Noel Clo. *Broc* 7D **148**
Noel Rd. *Bourn* 5F **226**
Nomad Clo. *Sotn* 1F **174**
Nomansland 2J **155**
Nook, The. *Eastl* 7F **132**
Nook, The. *Gos* 7G **212**
Nook, The. *S'hrst* 5C **18**
Norbury Clo. *Chan F* 5N **131**
Norbury Gdns. *Hamb* 7J **195**
Norcliffe Clo. *Bourn* 3F **226**
Norcliffe Rd. *Sotn* 2M **173**
Norcroft Ct. *Sotn* 9H **159**
Norden Clo. *Bas* 5C **42**
Norden Ho. *Bas* 5D **42**
Nordik Gdns. *H End* 5N **175**
Nore Cres. *Ems* 8K **203**
Nore Farm Av. *Ems* 8K **203**
Noreuil Rd. *Ptsfld* 1K **145**
Norfolk Av. *Christ* 4J **229**
Norfolk Ct. *Chan F* 9A **132**
Norfolk Cres. *Hay I* 5D **242**
Norfolk Ho. *Hav* 8G **202**
Norfolk M. *Hay I* 4E **242**
Norfolk Rd. *Gos* 9H **213**
Norfolk Rd. *Sotn* 2J **173**
Norfolk St. *S'sea* 4D **240** (7N **5**)
Norgett Way. *Fare* 2K **213**
Norham Av. *Sotn* 9H **159**
Norham Clo. *Sotn* 9H **159**
Norland Rd. *S'sea* 4F **240**
Norlands Dri. *Ott* 9G **126**
Norley Clo. *Hav* 4E **202**
Norleywood 7M **225**
Norleywood. *Highc* 6H **231**
Norleywood Rd. *E End* 6K **225**
Norman Av. *Poole* 8D **226**
Norman Clo. *Bord* 4K **101**
Norman Clo. *Fare* 2M **213**
Norman Ct. *F'ham* 9E **64**
Norman Ct. *S'sea* 5F **240**
Norman Ct. La. *Up Cl* 4M **69**
Normandy 5F **234**
Normandy Clo. *Rown* 5D **158**
Normandy Clo. *Sway* 5H **223**
Normandy Ct. *Wars* 8N **195**
Normandy Ct. *Wick* 6D **178**
Normandy Dri. *Christ* 7N **229**
Normandy Gdns. *Gos* 3H **239**
Normandy Ho. Roms 5N **129** (off Chambers Av.)
Normandy La. *L'ton* 4F **234**
Normandy M. *Alt* 4F **80**
Normandy Rd. *Ports* 4E **214**
Normandy St. *Alt* 4F **80**
Normandy Way. *F'bri* 9H **151**
Normandy Way. *March* 7E **172**
Norman Gdns. *H End* 5L **175**
Norman Gdns. *Poole* 8E **226**
Norman Ho. *Sotn* 4A **174**
Normanhurst Av. *Bourn* 5A **228**
Norman Rd. *Black* 8D **208**
Norman Rd. *Gos* 2J **239**
Norman Rd. *Hay I* 5H **243**
Norman Rd. *Sotn* 5J **173**
Norman Rd. *S'sea* 4F **240**
Norman Rd. *Win* 8K **105**
Normans Flats. *Win* 8K **105**
Normanton Clo. *Christ* 5J **229**
Normanton Rd. *Bas* 4C **42**
Norman Way. *Hav* 7C **202**
Normay Ri. *N'bry* 1C **8**
Norn Hill. *Bas* 5D **42**
Norn Hill Clo. *Bas* 5D **42**
Norris Clo. *Ashy H* 4B **186**
Norris Clo. *Roms* 2B **130**
Norris Clo. *W'hill* 6G **100**
Norris Gdns. *Hav* 9G **203**
Norris Gdns. *New M* 5B **232**
Norris Hill. *Sotn* 1C **174**
Norris Hill Rd. *Fle* 3A **48**
Norrish Rd. *Poole* 9A **226**
Norset Rd. *Fare* 7M **197**
North Acre. *Longp* 2A **76**
Northam 4A **174**
Northam Bri. *Sotn* 4A **174**
Northam Bus. Cen. *Sotn* 4A **174**
Northam Cen. Sotn 5A **174** (off Kent St.)
Northam M. *Ports* 2E **240**
Northampton La. *Black* 8C **208**
Northam Rd. *Sotn* 5N **173** (4E **4**)
Northam St. *Ports* 1E **240**
Northanger Clo. *Alt* 4E **80**
Northarbour Rd. *Ports* 9D **200**
Northarbour Spur. *Ports* 9E **200**
North Av. *F'ham* 3F **64**
North Av. *Ports* 3F **214**
North Baddesley 8G **130**
N. Battery Rd. *Ports* 6C **214**
North Bay. *Ems* 5N **217**
North Boarhunt 8J **179**
North Bockhampton 8B **220**
Northbourne 1H **227**
Northbourne Av. *Bourn* 1H **227**
Northbourne Clo. *Dib P* 8M **193**
Northbourne Gdns. *Bourn* 1J **227**
Northbourne Pl. *Bourn* 1H **227**
Northbourne Roundabout. *Bourn* 1J **227**
Northbrook 2M **163** (Southampton)
Northbrook 7J **77** (Winchester)
Northbrook Av. *Win* 7M **105**
Northbrook Clo. *Ports* 9E **214**
Northbrook Clo. *Win* 7N **105**
Northbrook Ct. *Win* 7N **105**
Northbrook Ind. Est. *Sotn* 9H **159**
Northbrook Rd. *A'sht* 2K **65**
Northbrook Rd. *Sotn* 5N **173** (3F **4**)
North Camp 4L **49**
N. Camp Sta. Roundabout. *Farn* 3N **49**
North Charford 9C **120**
N. Charford Drove. *W'bry* 8L **119**
North Clo. *A'sht* 1N **65**
North Clo. *Farn* 4J **29**
North Clo. *Gos* 3H **239**
North Clo. *Hav* 9G **202**
North Clo. *L'ton* 2E **234**
North Clo. *Roms* 3B **130**
North Common 9A **122**
N. Common La. *Land* 8H **121**

N. Common La.—Oak Tree Rd.

N. Common La. L'ton . . . 8N 223
Northcote Rd. Bourn . . . 1M 245
Northcote Rd. Farn. . . . 6H 29
Northcote Rd. Sotn. . . . 9A 160
Northcote Rd. S'sea . . . 4F 240
Northcott Clo. Gos . . . 4H 239
North Ct. Ports . . . 9F 214
North Ct. Sotn . . . 2G 172
North Cres. Hay I . . . 4H 243
Northcroft Rd. Gos. . . . 1H 239
N. Cross St. Gos . . . 3M 239
Northdene Rd. Chan F . . . 7A 132
North Dri. Oss . . . 8M 221
North Dri. S'wick . . . 3A 200
North Dri. Win. . . . 1F 104
N. East Clo. Sotn . . . 5G 174
N. E. Ind. Area. Hurn . . . 6B 218
N. East Rd. Sotn. . . . 6E 174
North End. . . . 7E 108 (Alresford)
North End. . . . 3P 149 (Fordingbridge)
North End. . . . 2L 7 (Newbury)
North End. . . . 6F 214 (Portsmouth)
North End. Bro'tn . . . 1A 86
N. End Av. Ports . . . 6E 214
N. End Clo. Chan F. . . . 8A 132
N. End Gro. Ports . . . 6E 214
Northend La. Drox . . . 1J 165
North End La. Harb . . . 6G 152
Northern Access Rd. Fawl . . . 6G 209 (in two parts)
Northern Anchorage. Sotn . . . 7B 174
Northern Av. And . . . 9N 51
Northern Pde. Ports . . . 5E 214
Northern Rd. Fawl. . . . 6J 209
Northern Rd. Ports. . . . 2G 214
Northerwood Av. Lyn . . . 2A 148
Northerwood Clo. N Bad . . . 8E 130
Northesk Ho. Ports. . . . 1E 240
Northey Rd. Bourn . . . 8H 229
North Fareham. . . . 5D 198
N. Farm Rd. Farn . . . 4H 29
North Farnborough. . . . 8K 29
Northfield Av. Fare . . . 1B 212
Northfield Cvn. Pk. Fare . . . 7K 199
Northfield Clo. A'sht. . . . 1M 65
Northfield Clo. Bish W . . . 2K 163
Northfield Clo. Chu C . . . 5A 48
Northfield Clo. Water . . . 9C 168
Northfield La. Chaw . . . 8C 80
Northfield Pk. Fare . . . 8K 199
Northfield Rd. Chu C . . . 5N 47
Northfield Rd. Mil S. . . . 8M 235
Northfield Rd. Ring. . . . 8K 185
Northfield Rd. Sher L . . . 3L 23
Northfield Rd. Sotn . . . 8D 160
North Fields. Twy . . . 6L 127
Northfields Farm La. Wick . . . 5D 178
North Front. Sotn . . . 5M 173 (4D 4) (in two parts)
N. Fryerne. Yate . . . 5N 17
Northgate Av. Ports . . . 8G 215
Northgate La. Ellis . . . 9C 60
N. Gate Rd. Farn. . . . 1L 49
Northgate Way. Bas . . . 4J 59
North Gorley. . . . 6L 153
N. Greenlands. Penn. . . . 4C 234
N. Grove Ho. S'sea . . . 4E 240
North Hants Golf Course. . . . 8N 27
North Harbour. . . . 2C 214
N. Harbour Bus. Pk. Ports . . . 1D 214
North Hayling. . . . 5J 217
North Head. Mil S. . . . 9H 233
North Hill. Fare. . . . 6D 198
North Hill. S'wick . . . 7C 200
N. Hill Clo. Win. . . . 4K 105
N. Hill Ct. Win. . . . 5K 105
North Houghton. . . . 4E 88
Northington. . . . 9A 78
Northington Rd. It Ab . . . 8J 93
Northington Rd. N'ton D . . . 1M 93
North Kingston. . . . 6M 187
Northlands. . . . 7H 121
Northlands Clo. Tot. . . . 2K 171
Northlands Dri. Win . . . 4L 105
Northlands Gdns. Sotn. . . . 3K 173
Northlands Rd. Eastl. . . . 9E 132
Northlands Rd. Roms. . . . 6B 130
Northlands Rd. Sotn. . . . 3K 173
Northlands Rd. Tot . . . 2L 171
North La. A'sht. . . . 8M 49
North La. Beau . . . 4D 206
North La. Bton . . . 7K 145
North La. Chal. . . . 6J 169
North La. Nom . . . 2J 155
North La. S Hart. . . . 8G 146
North La. Water . . . 5B 168
North La. W Tyth . . . 6L 87
Northleigh Corner. Sotn . . . 6C 160
N. Lodge Rd. Poole . . . 1C 244
North Mall. Fle . . . 2L 47
Northmead. Farn. . . . 8K 29
Northmere Dri. Poole . . . 7D 226
Northmere Rd. Poole . . . 8C 226
N. Millers Dale. Chan F . . . 3M 131
Northmore Clo. L Hth. . . . 4E 196
Northmore Rd. L Hth . . . 4E 196
Northney. . . . 4J 217
Northney La. Hay I . . . 4J 217
Northney Rd. Hay I. . . . 3G 216
North Oakley. . . . 2H 39
Northolt Gdns. Sotn . . . 6F 158
Northover Ct. Bourn . . . 7H 227
Northover La. Tip . . . 8F 222
Northover Rd. Penn . . . 2A 234
Northover Rd. Ports . . . 8J 215
North Pde. Bord . . . 1H 101
N. Park Bus. Cen. Know . . . 1N 197
Northpark Ironworks. . . . 9N 117
North Poulner. . . . 7M 185
N. Poulner Rd. Ring . . . 8L 185
North Ripley. . . . 3N 219
North Rd. A'sht . . . 4M 49 (in two parts)
North Rd. Ame . . . 6A 66 (in two parts)
North Rd. Bourn . . . 9B 228
North Rd. Broc . . . 7D 148
North Rd. Dib P . . . 7J 193
North Rd. King W . . . 6M 91
North Rd. Ptsfld. . . . 9M 139
North Rd. Sotn . . . 1A 174
North Rd. S'wick . . . 7B 200
North Rd. Water . . . 9C 168
North Rd. E. S'wick . . . 3B 200
North Rd. W. S'wick . . . 3B 200
North Row. Braml . . . 9G 12
N. Shore Rd. Hay I . . . 3D 242
Northside La. Gund & Bish S . . . 8M 95
North Street. . . . 8D 96 (Alresford)
North Street. . . . 1L 151 (Fordingbridge)
North St. Bed . . . 7D 202
North St. Bish S . . . 1K 109
North St. Bro Ch. . . . 3A 118
North St. Ems . . . 8M 203
North St. Gos. . . . 3M 239 (in two parts)
North St. Hav . . . 8F 202
North St. K're. . . . 2B 6
North St. Penn . . . 4C 234
North St. Ports . . . 1E 240 (Cornwallis Cres.)
North St. Ports . . . 2B 240 (3K 5) (Queen St.)
North St. Rog . . . 9L 141
North St. Westb . . . 4N 203
North St. Arc. Hav. . . . 8F 202
N. Stroud La. Ptsfld . . . 3D 144
North Sydmonton. . . . 2H 9
North Tidworth. . . . 7B 30
North Town. . . . 9M 49
Northtown Trad. Est. Ald . . . 9N 49
N. Trestle Rd. Hythe . . . 2F 208
Northumberland Ct. Ring . . . 1J 187
Northumberland Rd. Sotn . . . 5N 173 (3G 4)
Northumberland Rd. S'sea . . . 3F 240
Northumberland Rd. W'hill . . . 6J 101
North Vw. Win . . . 6J 105 (6J 237)
N. View. Rd. T'ley. . . . 6K 11
North Wallington. . . . 7E 198
North Wallington. Fare . . . 7E 198
North Walls. Win . . . 6L 105 (6M 237)
North Waltham. . . . 9A 58
N. Waltham Rd. Okly . . . 3B 58
North Warnborough. . . . 8J 45
North Way. And . . . 8C 52
North Way. Gos . . . 4E 212
North Way. Hav. . . . 8E 202
Northway. Port D . . . 9D 66
Northway. Titch . . . 6H 197
Northways. Stub. . . . 6N 211
North Weirs. . . . 7A 148
N. Weirs. Broc. . . . 8M 189
N. W. Ind. Area. Hurn . . . 6A 218 (in two parts)
North Wood. New M. . . . 7L 231
Northwood Clo. Sotn. . . . 5M 159
Northwood La. Hay I . . . 7G 216
Northwood Rd. Ports . . . 4F 214
Northwood Sq. Fare . . . 7D 198
Nortoft Rd. Bourn . . . 8M 227
Norton Clo. Christ . . . 7N 229
Norton Clo. Sotn. . . . 7C 174
Norton Clo. S'wick . . . 3A 200
Norton Clo. Water. . . . 2L 201
Norton Dri. Fare . . . 6C 198
Norton Ho. Bas. . . . 8L 41
Norton Ride. Lych . . . 4G 43
Norton Rd. Bourn. . . . 6J 227
Norton Rd. Rise . . . 2G 14
Norton Rd. S'wick . . . 3A 200
Norton Welch Clo. N Bad . . . 8G 130
Norway Clo. Bourn. . . . 5K 227
Norway Rd. Ports. . . . 4G 215
Norwich Av. Bourn . . . 2H 245 (6H 247)
Norwich Av. Cam . . . 1N 29
Norwich Av. W. Bourn . . . 2H 245 (6G 247)
Norwich Clo. Bas . . . 3K 59
Norwich Clo. Sar G. . . . 5B 196
Norwich Ct. Bourn . . . 7J 247
Norwich Mans. Bourn . . . 2H 245 (6H 247)
Norwich Pl. Lee S. . . . 9A 212
Norwich Rd. Bourn . . . 2J 245 (7J 247)
Norwich Rd. Ports . . . 8E 200
Norwich Rd. Sotn. . . . 9D 160
Norwood Pl. Bourn. . . . 9E 228
Nottingham Pl. Lee S . . . 9A 212
Nouale La. Poul . . . 1N 187
Novello Clo. Bas . . . 3M 59
Novello Gdns. Water . . . 3M 201
Noyce Dri. F Oak. . . . 2A 162
Noyce Gdns. Bourn. . . . 4E 228
Nuffield Cen. Ports . . . 3C 240 (5L 5)
Nuffield Dri. Owl. . . . 4H 19
Nuffield Theatre. . . . 8M 159
Nugent Rd. Bourn. . . . 1J 247
Nunns Pk. W'ish. . . . 5H 121
Nuns Rd. Win . . . 5L 105
Nuns Wlk. Win . . . 5L 105 (in two parts)
Nunton Drove. Nun. . . . 5J 119 (in two parts)
Nursery Clo. Chine. . . . 9H 23
Nursery Clo. Ems . . . 6M 203
Nursery Clo. Fle . . . 3B 48
Nursery Clo. Gos . . . 5D 212
Nursery Clo. Hook . . . 1G 44
Nursery Fld. Liss . . . 2D 140
Nursery Gdns. Chan F . . . 9A 132
Nursery Gdns. Roms . . . 5N 129
Nursery Gdns. Sotn . . . 4F 174
Nursery Gdns. Water . . . 5A 182
Nursery Gdns. Win . . . 6H 105 (7H 237)
Nursery Gro. H End . . . 5N 175
Nursery La. Fare . . . 6M 211
Nursery Rd. Alr. . . . 1F 108
Nursery Rd. Alt . . . 3G 80
Nursery Rd. Bourn . . . 3L 227
Nursery Rd. Hav. . . . 7C 202
Nursery Rd. Ring . . . 2K 187
Nursery Rd. Sotn . . . 1B 174
Nursery Ter. N War. . . . 7J 45
Nurse's Path. Twy. . . . 7L 127
Nursling. . . . 6C 158
Nursling Cres. Hav. . . . 4G 203
Nursling Grn. Bourn. . . . 4A 228
Nursling Ind. Est. Nurs. . . . 7A 158
Nursling St. Nurs . . . 6B 158
Nursted. . . . 5A 146
Nutash. Fare . . . 5F 196
Nutbane. . . . 2E 50
Nutbane Clo. And . . . 2L 69
Nutbane La. Cla. . . . 3F 50
Nutbean La. S'fld . . . 1K 15
Nutbeem Rd. Eastl . . . 1E 160
Nutbourne. F'ham. . . . 3G 65
Nutbourne Ho. Ports. . . . 1L 215
Nutbourne Rd. Hay I . . . 5L 243
Nutbourne Rd. Ports. . . . 1L 215
Nutburn. . . . 7G 130
Nutburn Rd. N Bad. . . . 7G 130
Nutchers Drove. King S . . . 8B 86
Nutcombe. . . . 5N 103
Nutcombe Down. . . . 4N 103
Nutcombe Down, Tyndall Wood & Craigs. . . . 4N 103
Nutcombe La. Hind . . . 7N 103
Nutfield Ct. Sotn. . . . 8D 158
Nutfield Pl. Ports . . . 1E 240
Nutfield Rd. Rown . . . 5C 158
Nuthatch Clo. Ews . . . 2N 63 (off Badger Way)
Nuthatch Clo. Row C . . . 9H 183
Nutley Clo. Bord . . . 5J 101
Nutley Clo. Bourn. . . . 2D 226
Nutley Clo. Yate . . . 8N 17
Nutley Dri. Elve. . . . 9J 27
Nutley La. Dum . . . 9H 59
Nutley Rd. Hav. . . . 4D 202
Nutley Way. Bourn . . . 3D 226
Nutmeg Ct. Farn . . . 7E 28
Nutsey Av. Tot . . . 9K 157
Nutsey Clo. Tot. . . . 8L 157
Nutsey La. Tot. . . . 9L 157
Nutshalling Av. Rown . . . 6C 158
Nutshalling Clo. Cal. . . . 9J 157
Nutshell La. F'ham . . . 4E 64
Nutwick Rd. Hav. . . . 6H 203
Nutwood Way. Tot . . . 9L 157
Nyewood. . . . 4K 147
Nyewood Av. Fare . . . 8M 199
Nyewood Industries. Nye . . . 4K 147
Nyria Way. Gos . . . 3M 239

O

Oakapple Gdns. Ports . . . 9M 201
Oak Av. Christ. . . . 6G 229
Oak Av. Owl. . . . 4F 18
Oak Bank. And . . . 3N 69
Oakbank Rd. Eastl . . . 8G 133
Oakbank Rd. Sotn. . . . 7B 174
Oak Clo. Bas. . . . 6E 42
Oak Clo. Baug. . . . 5D 10
Oak Clo. Dib P . . . 8K 193
Oak Clo. F'ley . . . 8F 86
Oak Clo. K're. . . . 2C 6
Oak Clo. Lyn. . . . 3B 148
Oak Clo. Mid W . . . 4B 72
Oak Clo. Okly . . . 1D 58
Oak Clo. Over. . . . 3D 56
Oak Clo. Sotn . . . 2B 172
Oak Clo. Tidw . . . 7E 30
Oak Clo. Uphm . . . 8E 134
Oak Clo. Water. . . . 8M 181
Oak Coppice Clo. Eastl . . . 1L 161
Oak Cotts. Hasl. . . . 9N 103 (in two parts)
Oak Ct. Fare. . . . 7M 197
Oak Ct. Farn . . . 2N 49
Oak Ct. F'ham. . . . 9D 64
Oakcroft La. Fare . . . 3M 211
Oakdene. Alt . . . 3E 80
Oakdene. Gos . . . 7F 212
Oakdene. Sotn . . . 9N 159
Oakdene. Tot. . . . 3J 171
Oakdene Ct. F Oak . . . 1N 161
Oakdown Rd. Fare . . . 5N 211
Oak Dri. F Oak . . . 1N 161
Oak Dri. Ptsfld . . . 3L 145
Oakenbrow. Dib P. . . . 7J 193
Oakenbrow. Sway. . . . 4H 223
Oaken Copse. Chu C. . . . 7N 47
Oaken Copse Cres. Farn . . . 5K 29
Oakes, The. Fare. . . . 4L 211
Oak Farm Clo. B'wtr . . . 8E 18
Oakfield Ct. Hav . . . 4H 203
Oakfield Rd. Bart . . . 3B 170
Oakfield Rd. B'wtr . . . 9G 19
Oakfield Rd. P Hth . . . 4L 11
Oakfield Rd. Tot. . . . 3M 171
Oakfields. Cam . . . 8K 19
Oakfields. Eastl . . . 5E 132
Oakfields. Lych. . . . 3G 43
Oakfields Clo. Ecc. . . . 5G 9
Oakford Ct. Bourn. . . . 3A 228
Oak Gdns. Evtn. . . . 6L 233
Oak Grn. Pde. Four M. . . . 4K 97
Oak Grn. Way. Sotn . . . 2E 174
Oak Grove. . . . 7G 19
Oak Gro. Cres. Coll T . . . 7G 19
Oakgrove Gdns. Eastl . . . 1J 161
Oakgrove Rd. Eastl . . . 1J 161
Oak Hanger Clo. Hook . . . 2H 45
Oakhanger Rd. Bord . . . 3F 100
Oak Hill. Alr. . . . 2F 108
Oakhill. Burs . . . 9M 175
Oakhill Clo. Burs . . . 9M 175
Oakhill Clo. Chan F. . . . 7C 132
Oakhill Ct. Chan F. . . . 7C 132
Oakhill Rd. Head D. . . . 2D 102
Oak Hill Rd. P Can . . . 4F 78
Oakhill Ter. Burs . . . 9M 175
Oakhurst. Gray. . . . 4M 103
Oakhurst Clo. Net A . . . 3G 195
Oakhurst Dri. Water . . . 1A 202
Oakhurst Gdns. Water. . . . 7J 201
Oakhurst Rd. Sotn. . . . 8M 159
Oakhurst Way. Net A . . . 3G 195
Oakland Av. F'ham . . . 3G 64
Oakland Dri. March . . . 9D 172
Oakland Rd. Whitc . . . 5G 54
Oaklands. H Win. . . . 7B 26
Oaklands. L'ton . . . 4F 234
Oaklands. S Won . . . 3H 91
Oaklands. Yate . . . 7N 17
Oaklands Av. Tot . . . 3M 171
Oaklands Clo. F'bri. . . . 9H 151
Oaklands Clo. Win. . . . 8F 104
Oaklands Gdns. Fare. . . . 8F 196
Oaklands Gro. Water. . . . 7L 181
Oaklands Pk. Hook C . . . 4E 44
Oaklands Rd. Hav. . . . 8G 202
Oaklands Rd. Ptsfld . . . 9L 139
Oaklands, The. Chan F . . . 9A 132
Oaklands Way. Bas . . . 5L 41
Oaklands Way. Dib P . . . 7H 193
Oaklands Way. Fare. . . . 8F 196
Oaklands Way. Sotn . . . 7L 159
Oakland Ter. H Win. . . . 6C 26
Oak La. Ring. . . . 9L 185
Oaklea Clo. Water . . . 7J 201
Oaklea Dri. E'sly . . . 3B 16
Oak Leaf Clo. March. . . . 1D 192
Oaklea Gdns. Braml . . . 2J 23
Oakleigh Clo. Highc . . . 7H 231
Oakleigh Cres. Tot. . . . 4L 171
Oakleigh Dri. Land . . . 1J 155
Oakleigh Gdns. Roms. . . . 5N 129
Oakley. . . . 1C 58
Oakley Clo. Holb. . . . 4A 208
Oakley Dri. Fle . . . 3M 47
Oakley Ho. Sotn . . . 3L 173
Oakley Ho. S'sea . . . 4D 240 (7N 5)
Oakley John Wlk. Sotn. . . . 4D 174
Oakley La. Mott. . . . 1F 122
Oakley La. Okly. . . . 1C 58
Oakley Pl. H Win. . . . 6C 26 (off High St.)
Oakley Rd. Bord . . . 2J 101
Oakley Rd. Cam . . . 9K 19
Oakley Rd. Hann. . . . 9L 9
Oakley Rd. Hav. . . . 4D 202
Oakley Rd. Mott . . . 2E 122
Oakley Rd. Sotn . . . 1E 172
Oak Lodge. Bord. . . . 5J 101
Oakmead. Braml . . . 9F 12
Oakmead Gdns. Bourn. . . . 2C 226
Oak Mdw. Clo. Ems . . . 6N 203
Oakmont Dri. Water . . . 8N 181
Oakmount Av. Chan F. . . . 8B 132
Oakmount Av. Sotn . . . 1M 173
Oakmount Av. Tot . . . 2M 171
Oakmount Rd. Chan F . . . 5C 132
Oak Pk. Dri. Hav. . . . 6G 202
Oak Pk. Golf Complex. . . . 3M 63
Oakridge. . . . 4D 42
Oakridge Cen. Bas . . . 4D 42
Oakridge Ho. Bas . . . 4D 42
Oakridge Rd. Bas . . . 4A 42
Oakridge Rd. Sotn . . . 2C 172
Oakridge Towers. Bas. . . . 4D 42
Oak Rd. A'hlt. . . . 5C 152
Oak Rd. Bish W . . . 3N 163
Oak Rd. Bourn . . . 8N 227
Oak Rd. Burs . . . 1K 195
Oak Rd. Dib P. . . . 8J 193
Oak Rd. Fare. . . . 7N 197
Oak Rd. Farn. . . . 9L 29
Oak Rd. New M . . . 3D 232
Oak Rd. Sotn . . . 8B 174
Oak Rd. Water . . . 6C 168
Oaks Coppice. Water . . . 4A 182
Oaks Dri. St L. . . . 5A 186
Oakshott. . . . 9K 113
Oakshott Dri. Hav. . . . 4G 203
Oaks, The. Burs . . . 1K 195
Oaks, The. Farn. . . . 9F 28
Oaks, The. Fle . . . 2J 47
Oaks, The. Sotn . . . 5D 174
Oaks, The. T'ley . . . 5G 11
Oaks, The. Yate . . . 8N 17
Oak St. Gos. . . . 3L 239
Oak Thorn Clo. Gos . . . 1E 238
Oaktree. Sotn . . . 8K 159
Oaktree Cvn. Pk. W End . . . 7H 161
Oak Tree Clo. A'sht. . . . 2N 65
Oak Tree Clo. Chlbn . . . 5F 74
Oak Tree Clo. Col C. . . . 4K 133
Oak Tree Clo. Head. . . . 3B 102
Oak Tree Clo. T'ley . . . 4H 11
Oaktree Ct. Mil S. . . . 8J 235
Oak Tree Dri. Ems. . . . 5L 203
Oak Tree Dri. Hook. . . . 1H 45
Oak Tree Dri. Liss . . . 1F 140
Oaktree Gdns. H End . . . 4M 175
Oak Tree La. Hasl. . . . 9M 103
Oaktree Pde. Brans. . . . 6D 220 (in two parts)
Oak Tree Rd. Sotn . . . 1B 174

Oak Tree Rd.—Ormsby Rd.

Oak Tree Rd. W'hill. 6H 101
Oaktrees. F'ham 4D 64
Oak Tree Vw. F'ham 4G 64
Oak Tree Way. Eastl 7E 132
Oaktree Way. S'hrst 4C 18
Oakum Ho. Ports 1H 241
Oak Va. W End 8F 160
Oakville Mans. Sotn 3B 4
Oak Wlk. F Oak 1N 161
Oakway. A'sht 2N 65
Oakway. Bent 7K 63
Oakway Dri. Frim 3N 29
Oakwood. Bourn 7J 227
Oakwood. Chine 9F 22 (Crockford La.)
Oakwood. Chine 9G 22 (Hanmore Rd.)
Oakwood. Chu C 7M 47
Oakwood Av. Hav 6B 202
Oakwood Av. New M 2C 232
Oakwood Av. Ott. 1G 132
Oakwood Cen., The. Hav 5H 203
Oakwood Clo. Bourn 4M 227
Oakwood Clo. Chan F 3B 132
Oakwood Clo. Ott 9G 127
Oakwood Clo. Roms 3A 130
Oakwood Clo. Wars 9A 196
Oakwood Ct. Chan F 3B 132
Oakwood Ct. W End 8J 161
Oakwood Dri. Sotn 6H 159
Oakwood Rd. Bourn 4L 227
Oakwood Rd. Chan F 4B 132
Oakwood Rd. Hay I 4F 242
Oakwood Rd. Highc 5G 231
Oakwood Rd. Ports 4F 214
Oakwood Way. Hamb 6L 195
Oakwoood Ct. New M 3C 232
Oasis, The. Poole 1E 244
Oast Ho. Cres. F'ham 4E 64
Oast Ho. Dri. Fle 8A 28
Oast Ho. La. F'ham 5F 64
Oast La. A'sht 3K 65
Oates Memorial Mus. 7L 99
Oates Rd. Bourn 5J 227
Oatfield Gdns. Cal 1J 171
Oatlands. Roms 4M 129
Oatlands Clo. Bot 1C 176
Oatlands Rd. Bot 1C 176
Oatley Wlk. Black 6D 208
Oatsheaf Pde. Fle 3L 47
Oban Clo. Okly 9C 40
Oban Rd. Bourn 7J 227
O'Bee Gdns. Baug 4E 10
Obelisk Rd. Sotn 8B 174
Obelisk Way. Cam 7L 19 (in two parts)
Oberfield Rd. Broc 6A 148
Oberon Clo. Water 1A 202
Ober Rd. Broc 6B 148
Oberursel Way. A'sht 9H 49
Occupation La. Fare 9H 197
Oceanarium. 3K 245 (9M 247)
Ocean Clo. Fare 7N 197
Ocean Ct. Hay I 5E 242
Ocean Heights. Bourn 2C 246
Ocean Pk. Ports 7J 215
Ocean Quay. Sotn 5A 174
Ocean Rd. E Dock 9M 173
Ocean Rd. Fare 3B 212
Ocean Village. 8N 173
Ocean Way. Sotn 8N 173 (9F 4)
Ochil Clo. Bas 8K 41
Ockendon Clo. S'sea 3D 240 (6N 5)
Ocknell Gro. Dib 6H 193
O'Connell Rd. Eastl 1C 160
O'Connor Rd. A'sht 4N 49
Octavia Gdns. Chan F 5D 132
Octavia Hill. Win 8H 105
Octavian Clo. Bas 3K 59
Octavia Rd. Sotn 7C 160
Octavius Ct. Water 9B 182
Odd La. Mort 4F 12
Odell Clo. Fare 6B 198
Odette Gdns. T'ley 4J 11
Odiham. 8L 45
Odiham Castle. 7H 45
Odiham Clo. Chan F 9N 131
Odiham Clo. Sotn 7E 158
Odiham Rd. F'ham 3B 64
Odiham Rd. H Win & W'fld 8A 26
Odiham Rd. Odi & W'fld 5M 45
Odiham Rd. Rise & Heck 2G 14
Odway La. Bton 8L 145
Officers Row. Braml 3J 23
Oglander Rd. Win 4L 105
Ogle Rd. Sotn 6L 173 (5C 4)
O'Jays Ind. Pk. Ports 6H 215
Okement Clo. W End 9F 160
Okingham Clo. Owl 3F 18
O.K. Mobile Home Pk. Christ 6D 230
Olaf Clo. And 6A 52
Olave Clo. Lee S 1A 238
Old Acre Rd. Alt 6E 80
Old Barn Clo. Cal 9J 157
Old Barn Clo. Christ 4G 229
Old Barn Clo. N Wal 9A 58
Old Barn Clo. Ring 1M 187
Old Barn Cres. Hmbdn 9D 166
Old Barn Gdns. Water 4N 181
Old Barn La. Churt 6K 85
Old Barn Rd. Christ 4G 229
Old Basing. 4J 43
Old Basing Mall. Bas 6C 42
Old Beggarwood La. Hat W 5H 59 (in two parts)
Oldberg Gdns. Bas 2A 60
Old Bitumen Rd. Hythe 4F 208
Old Blandford Rd. Coom B 3G 118
Old Brickfield Rd. A'sht 3K 65
Old Brick Kiln Trad. Est., The. R'dll 5G 20
Old Brickyard Rd. S'thh 9E 150
Old Brickyard, The. Nye 4J 147
Old Bri. Clo. Burs 9M 175
Old Bri. Ho. Rd. Burs 9M 175
Old Bri. Rd. Bourn 6G 228
Old Bri. Rd. S'sea 5F 240
Oldbury Ct. Sotn 9C 158
Oldbury Ho. S'sea 6N 5
Oldbury Way. Fare 9M 197
Old Canal. S'sea 3J 241
Old Canal Pl. Bas 6E 42
Old Canal, The. S'sea 3J 241
Old Christchurch La. Bourn 2K 245 (6M 247)
Old Christchurch Rd. Bourn 2K 245 (7L 247) (in two parts)
Old Christchurch Rd. Evtn 5L 233
Old Coach Rd. Bulf 3A 66
Old Coach Rd. Ship B & Kimp D 1C 66
Old Coach Rd., The. Abb A 7G 68
Old Commercial Rd. Ports 9D 214
Old Comn. L Hth 5D 196
Old Comn. Gdns. L Hth 5D 196
Old Comn. Rd. Bas 7E 42
Old Comn. Way. Lud 1D 30
Old Compton La. F'ham 8G 65
Old Copse Rd. Hav 7G 202
Oldcorne Hollow. Yate 8K 17
Old Cottage Clo. W Wel 1B 120
Old Cove Rd. Fle 9N 27
Old Cracknore Clo. March 8E 172
Old Dean Rd. Cam 6M 19
Old Ditcham. 7A 146
Old Down Clo. Bas 2J 59
Old Down La. Ows 3C 134 (in two parts)
Old Down Rd. And 9M 51
Olde Farm Dri. B'wtr 7D 18
Oldenburg. White 1E 196
Oldenburg Clo. And 7M 51
Old English Dri. And 6M 51
Old Farm Clo. Poul 7M 185
Old Farm Copse. W Wel 1C 120
Old Farm Dri. Sotn 8D 160
Old Farmhouse M. L'ton 1E 234 (off Lwr. Buckland Rd.)
Old Farmhouse M. L'ton 2E 234 (off New St.)
Old Farm La. Fare 7M 211
Old Farm Wlk. L'ton 3D 234
Old Farm Way. Ports 1M 215
Old Farnham La. F'ham 9E 64
Oldfield Vw. H Win 7B 26
Old Flour Mill, The. Ems 9N 203
Old Forge Clo. A'hlt 4B 152
Old Forge End. S'hrst 6D 18
Old Forge Garden. Bro'tn 1A 86
Old Forge, The. Baug 4E 10
Old Forge, The. Shed 3N 177
Old Garden Clo. L Hth 7F 196
Old Gdns. Win 4K 105
Oldgate Gdns. Ports 4G 214
Old Gosport Rd. Fare 9D 198
Old Grn. La. Cam 6L 19
Old Heath Way. F'ham 3E 64
Old Hillside Rd. Win 5G 104
Old Hill, The. Wher 1E 74
Old Ivy La. W End 9F 160
Old Kempshott La. Bas 9J 41
Old Kennels Clo. Win 2E 126
Old Kennels La. Win 2E 126
Old Kiln Clo. Churt 6H 85
Old Kiln La. Churt 5H 85
Old La. A'sht 3J 65 (GU11)
Old La. A'sht 8N 49 (GU12)
Old La. Ash H 2N 9
Old La. Dock 3C 84
Old La. Water 9B 168
Old Litten La. Frox 2J 139
Old London Rd. Ports 4G 214
Old London Rd. Stockb 2G 88
Old Lyndhurst Rd. Cad 6N 155
Old Magazine Clo. March 8E 172
Old Malthouse La. Fordb 4A 86
Old Maltings, The. L'ton 2D 234
Old Mnr. Farm. Hav 8B 202
Old Mnr. Way. Ports 1J 215
Old Micheldever Rd. And 4F 70
Old Mill Flats. Ring 2J 187
Old Mill La. Ptsfld 8A 140
Old Mill La. Water & Hmbdn 3J 181
Old Mill Way. Sotn 1F 172
Old Milton. 5A 232
Old Milton Grn. New M 5A 232
Old Milton Rd. New M 5A 232
Old Monteagle La. Yate 7K 17
Old Netley. 9J 175
Old Odiham Rd. Alt 8B 62
Old Orchards. L'ton 4F 234
Old Orchard Shop. Cen. Poole 1E 244 (off Princess Rd.)
Old Orchard, The. S Warn 4C 62
Old Palace Farm. King S 9B 86
Old Pk. Clo. F'ham 4C 64
Old Pk. La. F'ham 3B 64 (in two parts)
Old Pk. Rd. Bish S 2N 109
Old Parsonage Ct. Ott 1G 132
Old Pharmacy Ct. C'then 1D 18
Old Pond Clo. Cam 3L 29
Old Portsmouth. 3B 240
Old Potbridge Rd. W'fld 2N 45
Old Priory Clo. Hamb 7L 195
Old Priory Rd. Bourn 1J 247
Old Pump Ho. Clo. Fle 1A 48
Old Reading Rd. Bas 5D 42
Old Rectory Clo. Ems 6N 203
Old Rectory Ct. Tot 5A 172
Old Rectory Gdns. Abb W 9A 92
Old Rectory Gdns. Farn 8M 29
Old Rectory La. Twy 6L 127
Old Rectory Rd. Ports 9M 201
Old Rectory, The. S Warn 4D 62 (off Alton Rd.)
Old Redbridge Rd. Sotn 2B 172
Old Reservoir Rd. Ports 1L 215
Old River. Water 7G 181
Old Rd. Gos 4L 239
Old Rd. Roms 3N 129
Old Rd., The. Ports 2G 214
Old Romsey Rd. Cad 6N 155
Old St Johns M. Bourn 3K 227
Old Salisbury La. Roms 2C 128 (in two parts)
Old Salisbury Rd. Abb A 6H 69
Old Salisbury Rd. Ower 4E 156
Old School Clo. Fle 2M 47
Old School Clo. H Win 6C 26
Old School Clo. Holb 2N 207
Old School Clo. Net A 2G 195
Old School Dri. Hay I 5H 243
Old School Gdns. W End 9J 161
Old School La. Yate 7M 17
Old School Rd. Hook 3E 44
Old School Rd. Liss 1E 140
Old School Ter. Fle 2M 47 (off Old School Clo.)
Old School, The. Bish W 4L 163
Old School Theatre, The. 5F 132
Old Shamblehurst La. H End 9N 161
Old Shirley. 9F 158
Old Spring La. Swanm 6D 164
Old Stable M. Win 9E 90
Old Stacks Gdns. Ring 2M 187
Old Star Pl. Ports 2B 240 (3J 5)
Old Station App. Win 7M 105 (8P 237)
Old Station Rd. It Ab 9H 93
Old Station Way. Bord 2F 100
Old Stockbridge Rd. Grat & Mid W 5K 67
Old Stoke Rd. Sto C 2L 91
Old St. Fare 7K 211 (in two parts)
Old Swanwick La. Lwr S 1A 196
Old Thorns Golf Course & Country Club. 3N 115
Old Timbers. Hay I 4F 242
Old Turnpike. Fare 6D 198
Old Turnpike Bus. Pk. Fare 7D 198
Old Van Diemans Rd. Water 4K 201
Old Vicarage Clo. Bourn 1J 227
Old Vicarage La. King S 8B 86
Old Vicarage La. Sway 6K 223
Old Vineries, The. F'bri 1G 152
Old Vyne La. Baug 3F 20
Old Ward Rd. Bulf B 3B 66
Old Well Clo., The. Sotn 7G 174
Old Welmore. Yate 8A 18
Old Winchester Hill Fort. 6D 142
Old Winchester Hill La. W'frd & W Meon 1A 142 (in two parts)
Old Winchester Hill Nature Reserve. 6E 142
Old Winton Rd. And 2A 70
Oldwood Chase. Farn 9D 28
Old Worting Rd. Bas 7L 41
Old Wymering La. Ports 9F 200
Oleander Clo. L Hth 4D 196
Oleander Dri. Tot 2H 171
Olinda St. Ports 1F 240
Olive Cres. Fare 2M 213
Olive Rd. Sotn 7F 158
Oliver Ri. Alt 4F 80
Oliver Rd. Penn 3C 234
Oliver Rd. Sotn 8B 160
Oliver Rd. S'sea 4H 241
Oliver's Battery. 1F 126
Oliver's Battery Cres. Win 1F 126
Oliver's Battery Gdns. Win 2F 126
Oliver's Battery Rd. N. Win 9F 104
Oliver's Battery Rd. S. Win 2F 126
Olivers Clo. Braml 2H 23
Olivers Clo. Tot 3H 171
Oliver's La. Braml 9H 13
Oliver's Wlk. Lych 4G 43
Olivia Clo. Water 9A 182
Olympic Way. Eastl 9L 133
Omdurman Rd. Sotn 9M 159
Omega Cen. S'sea 2E 240
Omega Enterprise Pk. Chan F 6A 132
Omega Ho. S'sea 2E 240
Omega Pk. Alt 5H 81
Omega St. S'sea 2E 240
Omni Bus. Cen. Alt 5H 81
Onibury Clo. Sotn 1E 174
Onibury Rd. Sotn 1E 174
Onslow Clo. Bas 2F 42
Onslow Rd. Sotn 4M 173 (1E 4)
Onslow Rd. S'sea 6E 240
Ontario Gdns. Bulf B 3A 66
Ontario Way. Lip 3E 116
Openfields. Head 2A 102
Ophir Gdns. Bourn 9M 227
Ophir Rd. Bourn 9M 227
Ophir Rd. Ports 6E 214
Oracle Dri. Water 6M 201
Orange Gro. Gos 7F 212
Orange Gro. Pale 6K 67
Orange La. Ovr W 8M 67
Orange Row. Ems 9M 203
Oratory Gdns. Poole 5D 244
Orchard Av. Eastl 2K 161
Orchard Cvn. Pk., The. W'lnds 5D 170
Orchard Clo. Alr 2F 108
Orchard Clo. Bad L 4K 65
Orchard Clo. B'wtr 3H 29
Orchard Clo. Christ 8K 229
Orchard Clo. Col C 3K 133
Orchard Clo. Edm 8K 149
Orchard Clo. E'std 8N 147
Orchard Clo. Fawl 5F 208
Orchard Clo. F'bri 9J 151
Orchard Clo. Gos 7J 213
Orchard Clo. Hay I 5F 242
Orchard Clo. N Bad 7E 130
Orchard Clo. Ring 9K 185
Orchard Clo. S Won 3G 90
Orchard Clo. Tot 5M 171
Orchard Clo. Water 4C 182
Orchard Ct. Bot 3B 176
Orchard Ct. Cron 3L 63
Orchard Ct. New M 3C 232
Orchard End. Bulf 3A 66
Orchard Gdns. A'sht 2L 65
Orchard Gdns. F'bri 1J 153
Orchard Ga. S'hrst 5D 18
Orchard Gro. Fare 1J 213
Orchard Gro. New M 5B 232
Orchard Gro. Water 7N 181
Orchard Ho. Alt 5G 80 (off Orchard La.)
Orchard Ho. Sotn 7M 173 (7D 4)
Orchard Ho. Tong 3N 65
Orchard La. Alt 4G 80
Orchard La. Ems 9N 203
Orchard La. Roms 5L 129
Orchard La. Sotn 7M 173 (7E 4)
Orchard Lea. Sher L 4L 23
Orchard Lea. Swanm 8D 164
Orchard Leigh. New M 4C 232
Orchard Pl. Sotn 7M 173 (8D 4)
Orchard Pl. Whitc 5G 54 (off Church St.)
Orchard Rd. And 9L 51
Orchard Rd. Bad L 4J 65
Orchard Rd. Bas 7L 41
Orchard Rd. F Oak 1N 161
Orchard Rd. Farn 8J 29
Orchard Rd. Gos 1M 239
Orchard Rd. Hav 9F 202
Orchard Rd. Hay I 5G 243
Orchard Rd. L Hth 7C 196
Orchard Rd. Redl 1M 119
Orchard Rd. S'sea 3F 240
Orchard Rd. S Won 3G 90
Orchard St. Bourn 2J 245 (7K 247)
Orchards Way. Sotn 9M 159
Orchards Way. W End 1H 175
Orchard Ter. Alt 4G 80 (off Orchard La.)
Orchard, The. Brans 7E 220
Orchard, The. Chilw 2K 159
Orchard, The. Hook 1G 45
Orchard, The. Mil S 8K 235
Orchard, The. Over 3D 56
Orchard, The. Ports 1G 215
Orchard, The. Sotn 6N 159
Orchard, The. T'ley 5K 11
Orchard, The. Water 6G 180
Orchard Wlk. Bourn 2J 245 (7K 247)
Orchard Wlk. Win 6M 237 (Jewry St.)
Orchard Wlk. Win 4H 105 (Stoney La.)
Orchard Way. A'sht 2L 65
Orchard Way. Cam 2K 29
Orchard Way. Dib P 7K 193
Orcheston Rd. Bourn 8M 227
Orchid Dri. Lud 2D 30
Orchid Way. Christ 7M 229
Ordnance Ct. Ind. Est. Ports 3H 215
Ordnance Rd. A'sht 9K 49
Ordnance Rd. Gos 3M 239
Ordnance Rd. Sotn 4M 173 (1D 4)
Ordnance Rd. Tidw 8D 30
Ordnance Roundabout. A'sht 9K 49
Ordnance Row. Ports 2B 240 (4J 5)
Ordnance Way. March 7F 172
Oregon Clo. Sotn 6E 174
Orford Clo. Christ 2G 229
Orford Ct. Ports 1G 215
Orford Rd. Ame 6A 66
Oriana Way. Nurs 7A 158
Oriel Bus. Pk. Alt 4H 81
Oriel Dri. Fare 8F 196
Oriel Hill. Cam 9M 19
Oriel Rd. Ports 6E 214
Oriental Ter. Sotn 7M 173 (8D 4)
Orient Dri. Win 3G 104
Orion Clo. Fare 6N 211
Orion Clo. Sotn 7E 158
Orion Ind. Cen. Sotn 6D 160
Orkney Clo. Bas 2E 42
Orkney Clo. Sotn 7D 158
Orkney Rd. Ports 8G 201
Ormesby Dri. Chan F 3N 131
Ormond Clo. F Oak 9M 133
Ormonde Rd. Poole 3E 244
Ormsby Rd. S'sea 4D 240

Orpen Rd. Sotn 7G 175
Orpine Clo. Fare 6J 197
Orsmond Clo. Water 3N 201
Orwell Clo. Farn 6G 29
Orwell Clo. Sotn 1D 172
Orwell Cres. Fare 7F 196
Orwell Rd. Ptsfld 2L 145
Osborn Cres. Gos 4D 212
Osborne Clo. Alt 5D 80
Osborne Clo. Bas 4B 42
Osborne Clo. Net A 4H 195
Osborne Clo. Water 2A 202
Osborne Ct. Farn 3L 49
Osborne Ct. Mil S 8J 235
Osborne Dri. Chan F 7C 132
Osborne Dri. Fle 4N 47
Osborne Gdns. F Oak 2A 162
Osborne Gdns. Sotn 1A 174
Osborne Rd. And 2M 69
Osborne Rd. Bourn 6J 227
Osborne Rd. Farn 2L 49
Osborne Rd. Gos 2M 239
Osborne Rd. Lee S 1A 238
Osborne Rd. New M 3B 232
Osborne Rd. Ptsfld 9M 139
Osborne Rd. Poole 2A 244
Osborne Rd. S'sea 5D 240 (9N 5)
Osborne Rd. Tot 3N 171
Osborne Rd. Wars 9N 195
Osborne Rd. N. Sotn 1A 174
Osborne Rd. S. Sotn 2N 173
Osborne Vw. Rd. Fare 7K 211
Osborn Ind. Est. Hook 3H 45
Osborn Mall. Fare 8E 198
Osborn Rd. Fare 8D 198
Osborn Rd. F'ham 6F 64
Osborn Rd. S. Fare 8D 198
Osborn Sq. Fare 8E 198
Osborn Way. Hook 3H 45
Osbourne Ho. W Wel 1B 120
Osier Clo. Ports 6D 214
Oslands La. Swanw 2A 196
Osler Clo. Braml 9G 13
Oslo Towers. Sotn 1C 194
Osnaburgh Hill. Cam 8K 19
Osprey Clo. Christ 9C 230
Osprey Clo. March 9D 172
Osprey Clo. Ports 1N 215
Osprey Clo. Sotn 6G 158
Osprey Ct. Fare 9H 199
Osprey Dri. Hay I 4H 243
Osprey Gdns. Lee S 1B 238
Osprey Quay. Ems 1N 217
Osprey Rd. Bas 1H 59
Ossemsley. 7N 221
Ossemsley S. Dri. New M 7N 221
Osterley Clo. Bot 4B 176
Osterley Rd. Sotn 5C 174
Oswald Clo. Bourn 4J 227
Oswald Rd. Bourn 4J 227
Othello Dri. Water 1A 202
Otterbourne. 2F 132
Otterbourne. Bourn 1H 245 (5H 247)
Otterbourne Cres. Hav 4D 202
Otterbourne Cres. T'ley 7H 11
Otterbourne Golf Cen. 8D 126
Otterbourne Hill. Ott 3E 132
Otterbourne Ho. Ott 2F 132
Otterbourne Ho. Gdns. Ott 2F 132
Otterbourne Pk. Wood & Nature Reserve. 3F 132
Otterbourne Rd. Comp 5H 127
Otterbourne Rd. Shaw 7H 127
Otter Clo. Eastl 1K 161
Otter Clo. Gos 2F 238
Otters Wlk. New M 9C 222
Ouse Clo. Chan F 4M 131
Outer Circ. Sotn 7F 158
Outlands La. Curd 4G 176
Outram Rd. S'sea 4E 240
Outwick. 3J 151
Oval Gdns. Gos 3H 239
Oval Rd. Lcky 2N 121 (off Cooks La.)
Oval, The. And 7B 52
Oval, The. Liss 1E 140
Overbrook. Hythe 7L 193
Overbrook Way. N Bad 7D 130
Overbury Rd. Poole 2A 244
Overcliffe Mans. Bourn 2N 245
Overcliff Ri. Sotn 7K 159
Overdale Pl. W'hill 6J 101
Overdale Ri. Frim 1N 29
Overdale Wlk. W'hill 6J 101
Overdell Ct. Sotn 3K 173 (1A 4)
Over Links Dri. Poole 3B 244
Overlord Clo. Cam 5L 19
Overstrand Cres. Mil S 9K 235
Overton. 2E 56
Overton Clo. A'sht 4L 65
Overton Cres. Hav 4D 202
Overton Rd. Mich S 4J 77
Over Wallop. 8M 67
Oviat Clo. Tot 3H 171
Ovington Av. Bourn 7F 228
Ovington Ct. Sotn 2H 175
Ovington Dri. Elve 9J 27
Ovington Gdns. Bourn 7F 228
Ovington Rd. Eastl 2E 160
Owen Clo. Gos 9E 212
Owen Ho. Ports 1G 241 (off Whitcombe Gdns.)
Owen Rd. Eastl 1D 160
Owens Rd. Win 5K 105
Owen St. S'sea 5H 241
Ower. 5F 156 (Romsey)
Ower. 8J 209 (Southampton)
Ower La. Cals 8J 209
Owlsmoor. 3F 18
Owlsmoor Rd. Owl 5F 18 (in two parts)
Owls Rd. Bourn 2A 246
Owl Wlk. Ows 7B 134
Owslebury. 5C 134
Owslebury Bottom. Ows 4C 134
Owslebury Gro. Hav 4F 202
Oxburgh Clo. Eastl 7D 132
Ox Drove. And & Pic P 9E 52
Ox Drove. Bro Ch 6A 118 (in two parts)
Ox Drove. Burgh 3D 8
Ox Drove. Ows 2C 134
Ox Drove. Pic P 9K 31
Ox Drove. S Won 3K 91
Ox Drove. Stockb & Craw 2L 89
Ox Drove Ri. Pic P 7G 52
Ox Drove, The. Bro C 8D 78
Ox Drove Way. Old Al 9G 79 (Ferney La.)
Ox Drove Way. Old Al 6G 94 (Kiln La.)
Oxenbourne Nature Reserve. 1E 168
Oxenden Ct. Tong 2N 65
Oxenden Rd. Tong 2N 65
Oxenwood. 6B 6
Oxenwood Grn. Hav 3D 202
Oxey Clo. New M 5B 232
Oxford Av. Bourn 9E 228
Oxford Av. Sotn 4M 173 (3E 4)
Oxford Clo. Fare 7B 198
Oxford La. Bourn 1F 226
Oxford La. Drox 3G 165
Oxford M. Sotn 7M 173 (8E 4)
Oxford Rd. Bourn 1M 245
Oxford Rd. Farn 2L 49
Oxford Rd. Gos 2H 239
Oxford Rd. Owl 3G 19
Oxford Rd. Sotn 3M 173
Oxford Rd. S'sea 4F 240
Oxford Rd. Sut S 7D 76
Oxford St. Sotn 7M 173 (8E 4)
Oxford Ter. Sway 5J 223
Oxlease Clo. Roms 3N 129
Oxlease La. H'rd 9F 60
Oxleys Clo. Fare 9L 197
Oxted Ct. S'sea 2J 241
Oyster Clo. Bas 3K 59
Oyster Ind. Est. Ports 1K 215
Oyster M. Ports 4B 240 (7J 5)
Oyster Quay. Port S 1C 214
Oyster St. Ports 4B 240 (7J 5)
Oyster Vw. Lee S 9N 211
Ozier Rd. Sotn 9E 160

P

Pacific Clo. Sotn 8N 173
Packenham Rd. Bas 8A 42
Pack La. Okly & Bas 8D 40
Packridge La. Roms 2D 158
Padbury Clo. Ports 4G 215
Paddington Clo. Bourn 2B 226
Paddington Gro. Bourn 3B 226
Paddington Ho. Bas 6C 42 (off Hollin's Wlk.)
Paddington Rd. Ports 7G 214
Paddock. New M 7L 231
Paddock Clo. St I 4C 186
Paddock Clo. S Won 3J 91
Paddock Clo. Wint D 3A 86
Paddock Ct. H Win 7B 26
Paddock End. Water 7G 181
Paddock Fld. Chlbn 3G 74
Paddockfields. Old B 4J 43
Paddock Gdns. L'ton 1D 234
Paddock Rd. Bas 8M 41
Paddocks, The. Bourn 2H 227
Paddocks, The. Fawl 5F 208
Paddock, The. Broc 7C 148
Paddock, The. Cal 9J 157
Paddock, The. Eastl 6F 132
Paddock, The. Fare 4M 211
Paddock, The. Frog 7A 154
Paddock, The. Gos 4J 239
Paddock, The. Gray 3J 103
Paddock, The. H Win 5C 26
Paddock, The. Head 2A 102
Paddock, The. K're 2A 6
Paddock, The. King W 9N 91
Paddock Wlk. Bas 8M 41
Paddock Wlk. Ports 9B 200
Paddock Way. Alr 2E 108
Paddock Way. Lip 1D 116
Paddock Way. Ptsfld 2K 145
Padfield Clo. Bourn 8H 229
Padget Rd. Ring 8M 185
Padnell Av. Water 7A 182
Padnell Pl. Water 8B 182
Padnell Rd. Water 7A 182
Padstow Pl. F'bri 2H 153
Padwell Rd. Sotn 3M 173
Padwick Av. Ports 9H 201
Padwick Clo. Bas 7B 42
Padwick Ct. Hay I 4E 242
Paffard Clo. Gos 9E 212
Page Clo. Holb 6B 208
Pages Bungalows. Bas 6D 42
Pages La. E Bol 1B 236
Pages Yd. Whitc 6G 54 (off Winchester St. W.)
Paget Clo. Tidw 6B 30
Paget Rd. Bourn 2E 226
Paget Rd. Gos 5J 239
Paget St. Sotn 7N 173 (7G 4)
Pagham Clo. Ems 9N 203
Pagham Gdns. Hay I 5M 243
Paice La. Meds 3E 96
Paices Hill. A'mstn 2F 10
Paignton Av. Ports 8H 215
Paignton Rd. Sotn 1E 172
Paimpol Pl. Roms 6L 129
Pain's Rd. S'sea 3E 240
Painswick Clo. Ports 9D 200
Painswick Clo. Sar G 3C 196
Painter Clo. Ports 5K 215
Painters Fld. Win 1J 127
Painters Pightle. Hook 2F 44
Paisley Rd. Bourn 9F 228
Pakenham Dri. A'sht 8H 49
Palace Clo. King S 9A 86
Palace Ga. Odi 8K 45
Palace Ga. Farm. Odi 8K 45
Palace House. 7E 206
Palace La. Beau 7E 206
Palace M. Bish W 4M 163 (off Winchester Rd.)
Pale La. Elve 8G 27
Pale La. H Win & Elve 3E 46 (in two parts)
Palestine. 6K 67
Palestine Rd. Pale 6J 67
Palfrey Rd. Bourn 2H 227
Paling Bus. Pk. H End 6M 175
Palk Rd. Hav 7D 202
Pallant Gdns. Fare 7F 198
Pallant, The. Hav 8F 202
Pallet Clo. Col C 4K 133
Pallot Clo. Burs 9K 175
Palma Apartments. New M 7L 231
Palm Ct. S'sea 5D 240
Palmer Clo. Bas 3D 42
Palmer Dri. And 1C 70
Palmer Pl. New M 2B 232
Palmers Clo. F Oak 1A 162
Palmer's Rd. Ems 8M 203
Palmers Rd. Ind. Est. Ems 8M 203
Palmerston Av. Christ 8N 229
Palmerston Av. Fare 8D 198
Palmerston Bus. Pk. Fare 1C 212
Palmerston Clo. Farn 9F 28
Palmerston Ct. Win 9K 105
Palmerston Dri. Fare 1C 212
Palmerston Ho. Sotn 7D 4
Palmerston Mans. S'sea 5D 240 (off Palmerston Rd.)
Palmerston M. Bourn 9B 228
Palmerston Rd. Bourn 9B 228
Palmerston Rd. Hay I 3G 242
Palmerston Rd. Poole 1B 244
Palmerston Rd. Sotn 5M 173 (4D 4)
Palmerston Rd. S'sea 5D 240
Palmerston St. Roms 5L 129
Palmerston Way. Gos 5G 239
Palm Hall Clo. Win 7N 105
Palm Rd. Sotn 8F 158
Palmyra Rd. Gos 9J 213
Palomino Dri. White 2E 196
Pamber Dri. Elve 9J 27
Pamber End. 3K 21
Pamber Forest Nature Reserve. 7M 11
Pamber Green. 9L 11
Pamber Heath. 4L 11
Pamber Heath Rd. P Hth 5K 11
Pamber Rd. Char A 4H 21
Pamber Rd. Sil 4N 11
Pamela Av. Ports 8A 200
Pamplyn Clo. L'ton 2C 234
Pangbourne Av. Ports 1J 215
Pangbourne Clo. Sotn 6E 174
Pankridge St. Cron 3L 63
Pannall Rd. Gos 9J 213
Panorama Rd. Poole 9A 244
Pan St. Ports 1D 240 (1N 5)
Pansy Rd. Sotn 7M 159
Pantheon Rd. Chan F 5D 132
Pantile Dri. Hook 2J 45
Pantiles, The. F'bri 1G 153
Pantings La. High 4A 8
Panton Clo. Ems 6L 203
Panwell Rd. Sotn 3E 174
Papermakers. Over 3E 56
Paper Mill La. Alt 4G 80
Parade Ct. Ports 3F 214
Parade, The. Bas 5D 42
Parade, The. Bourn 2H 247
Parade, The. Cowes 5P 237
Parade, The. Fare 5M 211
Parade, The. Frim 4M 29
Parade, The. Gos 5D 212
Parade, The. Navy 1B 240 (2J 5)
Parade, The. New M 3E 232 (Lwr. Ashley Rd.)
Parade, The. New M 5A 232 (Southern La.)
Parade, The. T'ley 4H 11
Parade, The. Yate 7A 18
Paradise La. Ems 5N 203
Paradise La. Fare 8G 198 (in two parts)
Paradise La. Wal C 5A 164
Paradise La. W'lnds 4D 170
Paradise St. Ports 1D 240 (2N 5)
Parchment St. Win 7L 105 (8M 237) (in two parts)
Parchment, The. Hav 8F 202
Pardoe Clo. H End 5N 175
Pardown. 3D 58
Pardown. Okly 3E 58
Parfitts Clo. F'ham 8C 64
Parham Clo. New M 3N 231
Parham Dri. Eastl 8D 132
Parham Rd. Bourn 4G 226
Parham Rd. Gos 1L 239
Parish Clo. F'ham 4C 64
Parish Ct. L'ton 2E 234
Parish Rd. Farn 3L 49
Park Av. Cam 9L 19
Park Av. L'ton 2D 234
Park Av. Old B 6J 43
Park Av. Water 7K 201
Park Av. Win 6L 105 (6N 237)
Park Building. Ports 2C 240 (4M 5)
Park Clo. Broc 6D 148
Park Clo. Burt 3M 229
Park Clo. Gos 1H 239
Park Clo. Hythe 5N 193
Park Clo. Kingsl 7H 83
Park Clo. March 9C 172
Park Clo. Mil S 8L 235
Park Clo. New M 1D 232
Park Clo. Okly 9C 40
Park Clo. Win 4L 105
Park Clo. Wrec 9M 63
Park Clo. Rd. Alt 3G 80
Pk. Corner Rd. H Win 5C 26
Park Ct. Cowes 5P 237
Park Ct. F'ham 7F 64
Park Ct. Mil S 8J 235
Park Ct. Poole 2F 244
Park Ct. Roms 7B 130
Park Ct. S'sea 4D 240 (7N 5)
Park Ct. Win 4L 105
Park Cres. Ems 8K 203
Park Drove. Ovr W 7N 67
Parker Clo. Gos 7J 213
Parker Gdns. Water 7K 201
Parker Rd. Bourn 7K 227
Pk. Farm Av. Fare 5M 197
Pk. Farm Clo. Fare 6N 197
Pk. Farm Ind. Est. Cam 3L 29
Pk. Farm Rd. Water 5L 201
Parkfields. Yate 8N 17
Park Gdns. Bas 8D 42
Park Gdns. Christ 7A 230
Park Gate. 4E 196
Park Ga. Bus. Cen. Swanw 3E 196
Park Ga. M. Bourn 7J 247
Park Glen. Park G 5F 196
Park Gro. Ports 1G 215
Park Hill. Chu C 6L 47
Park Hill. Old B 5H 43
Parkhill Clo. B'wtr 9F 18
Pk. Hill Clo. Holb 5A 208
Parkhill Rd. B'wtr 9F 18
Park Ho. S'sea 5D 240 (9N 5)
Park Ho. Win 6N 237
Park Ho. Farm Way. Hav 5B 202
Parkhouse Rd. Ship B 2A 66
Parkhurst Fields. Churt 7H 85
Parkland Clo. Ver 5A 184
Parkland Dri. Bart S 6A 232
Parkland Gro. F'ham 2H 65
Parklands. Den 7G 180
Parklands. Sar G 5D 196
Parklands. Sotn 1C 174
Parklands. Tot 2M 171
Parklands Av. Water 5A 182
Parklands Bus. Pk. Den 7G 180
Parklands Clo. Chan F 5A 132
Parklands Clo. Gos 1K 239
Parklands Way. Port 9B 66
Park La. Abb W 9A 92
Park La. A'hlt 4C 152
Park La. Bed 7C 202
Park La. Bourn 2K 227
Park La. Brit 8G 87
Park La. Cam 8L 19
Park La. Churt 7D 84
Park La. Cosh 9H 201
Park La. Cowp 8A 182
Park La. Drox 2K 165
Park La. Fare 6D 198
Park La. Finch 2C 16
Park La. H'ly 2L 9
Park La. Holb 4N 207
Park La. Lwr Fr 8H 63
Park La. March 8B 172
Park La. Mil S 9J 235 (De La Warr Rd.)
Park La. Mil S 4D 236 (Thorns La.)
Park La. Mort 3J 13
Park La. Old B 6J 43
Park La. Ott & Eastl 3F 132 (in two parts)
Park La. Quar 3L 67
Park La. Ropl 5B 110
Park La. Sotn 5L 173 (3B 4)
Park La. Stub 5M 211 (in three parts)
Park La. Swanm 3D 164
Park La. Twy 8L 127
Park La. Water 9B 182
Park La. Wim G 7G 148
Park Mans. Bourn 7N 227
Park Mans. Ports 1H 215
Park Mt. Alr 9E 94
Park Pde. Hav 5E 202 (in two parts)
Park Pl. Chu C 6L 47
Pk. Prewett Rd. Bas 3L 41
Park Rd. A'sht 2K 65
Park Rd. Bish W 3K 163
Park Rd. Bourn 1L 245
Park Rd. Cam 1K 29
Park Rd. Chan F 4A 132
Park Rd. Den 5G 180
Park Rd. Farn 2N 49
Park Rd. F'ham 6F 64
Park Rd. F'bri 9J 151
Park Rd. Gos 5K 239
Park Rd. Hay I 3C 242
Park Rd. L'ton 2D 234
Park Rd. Mil S 8L 235
Park Rd. New M 1D 232 (Ashley Comn. Rd.)
Park Rd. New M 5A 232 (Christchurch Rd.)
Park Rd. Ptsfld 1M 145
Park Rd. Ports 3B 240 (5K 5)
Park Rd. S'hrst 6E 18
Park Rd. Sotn 4H 173
Park Rd. S Hart 9F 146
Park Rd. Tidw 8D 30
Park Rd. Water 5K 201

Park Rd. *Win* 4K **105**
Park Rd. N. *Hav* 7E **202**
Park Rd. Roundabout. *Farn* 3N **49**
Park Rd. S. *Hav* 8F **202**
Park Row. *F'ham* 7D **64**
Park Royal. *Ports* 5F **214**
Parkside. *Christ.* 5F **230**
Parkside. *F'ham* 4E **64**
Parkside. *Hav* 7C **202**
Parkside. *Ring* 2K **187**
Parkside. *Tot* 5M **171**
Parkside Av. *Sotn* 2C **172**
Parkside Gdns. *Bourn* 4J **227**
Parkside Gdns. *Win* 4G **105**
Parkside La. *Ropl* 4B **110**
Parkside Rd. *Bas* 8D **42**
Parkside Rd. *Poole* 1A **244**
Parkstone. 1A **244**
Parkstone Av. *Poole* 1A **244**
Parkstone Av. *S'sea* 6F **240**
Parkstone Dri. *Cam.* 9L **19**
Parkstone Golf Course. 5C 244
Parkstone La. *S'sea* 5F **240**
Parkstone Rd. *Ropl* 4D **110**
Park St. *Bord* 4J **101**
Park St. *Cam.* 7L **19**
Park St. *Gos* 2K **239**
Park St. *Sotn* 2G **173**
Park St. *S'sea* 3C **240** (6M **5**)
Park Terraces. *Gos* 3L **239**
Park, The. *Drox* 2J **165**
Park, The. *New M* 7L **231**
Park Vw. *B Hill* 1B **14**
Park Vw. *Bot* 3D **176**
Parkview. *Bourn* 1J **245** (5K **247**)
Park Vw. *H End* 3M **175**
Park Vw. *New M* 4B **232**
Park Vw. *Row C* 1H **203**
Park Vw. *Shaw* 7J **127**
Parkview Clo. *And.* 8L **51**
Pk. View Ct. *Bourn* 7N **227**
Pk. View Ho. *Fare* 5D **198**
Park Vs. *B'wtr* 2H **29**
Parkville Rd. *Sotn* 7B **160**
Park Vista. *E Meon* 3L **143**
Park Wlk. *Fare* 6N **197**
Park Wlk. *Sotn* 5M **173** (4D **4**)
Parkwater Rd. *W'ish* 5K **121**
Parkway. *Cam* 1L **29**
Parkway. *C'then* 1C **18**
Park Way. *F Oak* 1B **162**
Parkway. *Fare* 6D **198**
Park Way. *Hav* 8E **202**
Parkway. *White* 2H **197**
Parkway Ct. *Chan F* 5B **132**
Parkway Dri. *Bourn* 6A **228**
Parkway Gdns. *Chan F* 5A **132**
Parkway Retail Pk. *Bourn* 1N **245**
Parkway, The. *Gos* 6D **212**
Parkway, The. *Sotn* 6M **159**
Parkwood Cen. *Water* 1M **201**
Parkwood Clo. *Chine* 8G **23**
Pk. Wood Clo. *H End* 3A **176**
Parkwood La. Bourn *9E 228* *(off Hosker Rd.)*
Parkwood Rd. *Bourn* 9D **228**
Parley La. *Parl* 8A **218**
Parley Rd. *Bourn* 4L **227**
Parliament Pl. *Win* 1G **126**
Parmiter Ho. Win. *6M 105* *(off Wales St.)*
Parnell La. *Michm.* 3L **123**
Parnell Rd. *Eastl.* 1D **160**
Parnholt Lane. *Brfld* 3C **124**
Parr Rd. *Ports.* 9E **200**
Parry Clo. *Ports* 9N **199**
Parry Rd. *Sotn* 6H **175**
Parsonage Barn La. *Ring* 9K **185**
Parsonage Clo. *F'bri* 1J **153**
Parsonage Clo. *Ptsfld.* 8A **140**
Parsonage Clo. *Up Farr.* 4E **98**
Parsonage Est. *Rog* 9L **141**
Parsonage Hill. *F'ley* 8E **86**
Parsonage La. *Durl.* 5E **162**
Parsonage Pk. Dri. *F'bri* 9H **151**
Parsonage Rd. *Bourn* 2L **245** (7N **247**)
Parsonage Rd. *Sotn* 4N **173**
Parsonage Way. *Frim* 3N **29**
Parsons Clo. *Chu C.* 6L **47**
Parsons Clo. *Ports.* 4G **215**
Parsons Fld. *S'hrst.* 5D **18**
Parsons La. *Hind* 1L **103**
Part La. *Rise.* 2G **15**
Part La. *S'fld.* 1J **15**
Partridge Av. *Yate* 7L **17**
Partridge Clo. *Bar S* 5A **76**
Partridge Clo. *Christ.* 9C **230**
Partridge Clo. Ews *2N 63* *(off Badger Way)*
Partridge Clo. *Fare* 9G **199**
Partridge Clo. *Frim.* 3N **29**
Partridge Down. *Win.* 2F **126**
Partridge Dri. *Poole* 4A **244**
Partridge Gdns. *Water* 6L **181**
Partridge Grn. *Alt* 3F **80**
Partridge Grn. *New M.* 9C **222**
Partridge Rd. *Broc* 8C **148**
Partridge Rd. *Dib P.* 8L **193**
Partridge Wlk. *Poole.* 4A **244**
Partry Clo. *Chan F* 4M **131**
Passage La. *Wars* 8M **195**
Passfield Av. *Eastl* 2C **160**
Passfield Clo. *Eastl.* 1C **160**
Passfield Common. 7N 101
Passfield Common & Comford Moor. 7N 101
Passfield Enterprise Cen. *Pass* 7N **101**
Passfield Mill Bus. Pk. *Pass* 6N **101**
Passfield Rd. *Pass* 7A **102**
Passfield Wlk. *Hav* 4H **203**
Passford Hill. *L'ton* 8D **224**
Passingham Wlk. *Water* 6A **182**
Pasteur Rd. *Ports* 9F **200**
Pastures, The. *Cher* 8E **108**
Pastures, The. *Fare* 5F **196**
Pastures, The. *King W.* 6M **91**
Pastures, The. *Water.* 7F **180**
Pat Bear Clo. *Sotn* 2B **172**
Patchway Dri. *Fare.* 9M **197**
Paternoster Ho. *Win.* 8N **237**
Paternoster Row. *Win* 7L **105** (8N **237**)
Paterson Clo. *Bas* 3L **59**
Pathfinders, The. *Farn* 9E **28**
Patricia Clo. *W End* 9H **161**
Patricia Dri. *H End* 3A **176**
Patrick Howard Dobson Ct. *Water* 6N **181**
Patrick's Clo. *Liss* 1F **140**
Patrick's Copse Rd. *Liss* 1F **140**
Patten Av. *Yate.* 8M **17**
Patterdale Ho. *Ports* 8C **200**
Pattinson Cres. *And* 2G **69**
Paul Clo. *A'sht* 2G **65**
Paulet Clo. *Sotn* 1E **174**
Paulet Lacave Av. *Sotn.* 5C **158**
Paulet Pl. *Old B.* 5J **43**
Paulet Pl. *Win.* 9J **105**
Pauletts La. *Cal* 9H **157**
Paul's Fld. *E Cen.* 5G **17**
Paulsgrove. 9C **200**
Paulsgrove Enterprise Cen. *Ports* 9C **200**
Paulsgrove Ind. Cen. *Ports* 9C **200**
Paulsgrove Rd. *Ports* 8G **214**
Pauls La. *Sway* 7L **223**
Paulson Clo. *Chan F.* 4A **132**
Paultons Golf Centre & Course. 4C 156
Paultons Pk. 5J 157
Paultons Pk. Watermill. 5E 156
Pauncefoot Hill. *Roms* 1H **157**
Pauncefote Rd. *Bourn* 9D **228**
Pauntley Rd. *Christ.* 8A **230**
Pavan Gdns. *Bourn* 4G **226**
Pavilion Clo. *F Oak* 3N **161**
Pavilion Ct. *Sotn.* 3K **173**
Pavilion La. *A'sht* 8G **48**
Pavilion Rd. *A'sht* 1G **64**
Pavilion Rd. *H End* 2B **176**
Pavilions End, The. *Cam* 1M **29**
Pavilion, The. 3K 245 (8M 247)
Paviours. *F'ham* 7D **64**
Pawmers Mead. *Chu C.* 8K **47**
Pax Hill. *Bent* 7J **63**
Paxton Clo. *Bas* 3K **59**
Paxton Clo. *H End* 5A **176**
Paxton Rd. *Fare* 8B **198**
Paynes Clo. *Bro'tn* 1A **86**
Paynes Clo. *H'ly* 3K **9**
Paynes Hay Rd. *Brfld* 5A **124**
Paynes La. *Bro'tn* 1A **86**
Paynes La. *F Oak* 9N **133**
Paynes Mdw. *Lych* 3H **43**
Payne's Rd. *Sotn* 4H **173**
Paynes Rd. *Sotn.* 4H **173**
Peabody Rd. *Farn* 2M **49**
Peace Clo. *Brans* 7C **220**
Peach Gro. *Pale* 6K **67**
Peach Rd. *Sotn.* 7F **158**
Peach Tree Clo. *Farn.* 5J **29**
Peacock Clo. *Fare.* 9G **199**
Peacock La. *Ports* 4B **240** (7K **5**)
Peacock Pl. *Win.* 6N **105**
Peak Clo. *Sotn* 2E **172**
Peak Dri. *Fare.* 9N **197**
Peake Clo. *Lych* 4G **43**
Peaked Hill. 8L **49**
Peake New Rd. *Meon.* 6P **135**
Peakfield. *Fren* 1E **84**
Peakfield. *Water* 6F **180**
Peak La. *Fare* 9N **197**
Peak La. *Uphm* 8F **134**
Peak Rd. *Water.* 6A **168**
Peak, The. *Row C* 7J **183** (in two parts)
Pealsham Gdns. *F'bri* 9H **151**
Pearce Ct. *Gos* 2L **239**
Pearcesmith Ct. *Bart S* 7N **231**
Pearces Pl. *K're* 2B **6**
Pear Clo. *Poole* 1F **244**
Pearl Gdns. *Bourn* 2G **227**
Pearl Rd. *Bourn* 2G **227**
Pearman Ct. *Penn.* 4C **234**
Pearman Dri. *And.* 1C **70**
Pearman Dri. *L'ton* 4F **234**
Pearson Av. *Poole* 9A **226**
Pearson Gdns. *Bourn* 1H **227**
Pear Tree Av. *Fle.* 1L **47**
Peartree Av. *Sotn* 6C **174**
Pear Tree Clo. *A'hlt.* 4C **152**
Pear Tree Clo. *Bot.* 9C **162**
Pear Tree Clo. *Brans.* 7D **220**
Peartree Clo. *Fare.* 5N **211**
Pear Tree Clo. *Lind* 3L **101**
Peartree Clo. *Sotn* 6B **174**
Pear Tree Clo. *W Wel* 1A **120**
Peartree Ct. *L'ton* 4E **234**
Pear Tree Dri. *Land.* 2J **155**
Peartree Gdns. *Sotn.* 4E **174**
Peartree Green. 6C **174**
Peartree Rd. *Dib P* 7K **193**
Pear Tree Rd. *Lind* 3L **101**
Peartree Rd. *Sotn.* 6B **174**
Pease Cft. *S Hart* 9G **146**
Peatmoor Clo. *Fle.* 1K **47**
Pebble Clo. *Hay I* 5H **243**
Pebble Ct. *March* 8E **172**
Pebmarsh Rd. *Ports.* 9E **200**
Peckham Av. *New M.* 4B **232**
Pedam Clo. *S'sea* 4H **241**
Peddlars Gro. *Yate* 7A **18**
Peddlars Wlk. *Ring* 1J **187**
Peel Clo. *Poole.* 9A **226**
Peel Clo. *Roms.* 3B **130**
Peel Common. 6C **212**
Peel Ct. *Christ.* 8J **229**
Peel Ct. *Farn.* 3L **49**
Peel Ct. *H Win* 6B **26**
Peel Gdns. *K're.* 1A **6**
Peel Pl. *S'sea* 3D **240** (6N **5**)
Peel Rd. *Gos.* 2L **239**
Peel St. *Sotn.* 5A **174**
Peewit Hill. *Burs.* 7L **175** (in two parts)
Peewit Hill Clo. *Burs.* 7L **175**
Pegasus Av. *A'sht* 8N **49**
Pegasus Av. *Hord.* 4H **233**
Pegasus Clo. *Gos* 2F **238**
Pegasus Clo. *Hamb* 7K **195**
Pegasus Clo. *Hasl* 1M **117**
Pegasus Clo. *Sotn* 7E **158**
Pegasus Ct. *Bourn* 9L **227**
Pegasus Ct. *Fle.* 1L **47**
Pegasus Ct. *New M* 3B **232**
Pegasus Ct. *Whitc* 4G **54**
Pegasus Rd. *Farn.* 5H **29**
Peggotty Ho. *Ports* 9E **214**
Peggotty Pl. *Owl.* 3G **19**
Pegham Ind. Est. *Fare* 3M **197**
Pelham. *Poole.* 1E **244**
Pelham Clo. *Christ* 8N **229**
Pelham Clo. *Old B.* 6J **43**
Pelham Clo. *W'hill.* 6J **101**
Pelham Rd. *Gos* 2K **239**
Pelham Rd. *S'sea* 4D **240** (8N **5**)
Pelham Rd. Pas. *S'sea* 4D **240** (7N **5**)
Pelham Ter. *Ems* 9N **203**
Pelican Clo. *Fare.* 7N **197**
Pelican Ct. *Hurs* 6N **125**
Pelican Mead. *Hight.* 2M **187**
Pelican Rd. *Fare* 3B **212**
Pelican Rd. *P Hth* 3L **11**
Pelton Rd. *Bas* 5A **42**
Pembers Clo. *F Oak* 1A **162**
Pemberton Rd. *Lyn* 2C **148**
Pembrey Clo. *Sotn* 6E **158**
Pembridge Rd. *F'bri* 8K **151**
Pembroke B'way. *Cam* 8L **19**
Pembroke Chambers. *Ports* 7K **5**
Pembroke Clo. *Eastl* 7D **132**
Pembroke Clo. *Ports* 4B **240** (7K **5**)
Pembroke Clo. *Roms* 5M **129**
Pembroke Clo. *Tot.* 2N **171**
Pembroke Ct. *And* 1A **70**
Pembroke Ct. *Gos* 7E **212**
Pembroke Ct. *Sotn* 1M **173**
Pembroke Cres. *Fare* 6K **211**
Pembroke Pde. *Yate* 6A **18**
Pembroke Rd. *Bas.* 6K **41**
Pembroke Rd. *Bourn* 3F **244**
Pembroke Rd. *Poole* 7B **226**
Pembroke Rd. *Ports* 4B **240** (7K **5**) (in two parts)
Pembroke Rd. *Sotn* 6F **174**
Pembury Pl. *A'sht* 1L **65**
Pembury Rd. *Fare* 4N **211**
Pembury Rd. *Hav* 9G **203**
Pemerton Rd. *Bas.* 4D **42**
Pemerton Rd. *Win.* 3H **105**
Penarth Av. *Ports.* 9J **201**
Pen Clo. *And* 1B **70**
Pen Craig. *Poole* 2F **244**
Pendarvis Ct. *Gray.* 4L **103**
Pendennis Clo. *Bas* 5K **41**
Pendennis Rd. *Ports* 8A **200**
Pendle Clo. *Sotn* 2E **172**
Pendle Grn. *Lcky* 2N **121**
Pendleton Gdns. *Black.* 7C **208**
Pendula Way. *Eastl.* 7J **133**
Penelope Ct. *Christ* 7K **231**
Penelope Gdns. *Burs* 9K **175**
Penfold Cft. *F'ham.* 6H **65** (in two parts)
Penford Paddock. *Bish W* 4N **163**
Pengelly Av. *Bourn.* 1J **227**
Pengilly Rd. *F'ham* 9D **64**
Penhale Gdns. *Fare* 8E **196**
Penhale Rd. *Ports* 2F **240**
Penhale Way. *Tot.* 5L **171**
Penhurst Rd. *Hav* 7B **202**
Peninsula Rd. *Win* 7J **105** (9J **237**)
Peninsula Sq. *Win* 7K **105** (8K **237**)
Penistone Clo. *Sotn.* 8E **174**
Penjar Av. *Water* 5K **201**
Penk Ridge. *Hav* 9N **201**
Pennant Hills. *Hav.* 7B **202**
Pennant Pk. *Fare* 6E **198**
Pennant Way. *Christ* 7B **230**
Pennard Way. *Chan F* 8M **131**
Penn Clo. *Bart S* 5N **231**
Pennefather's Rd. *A'sht.* 8H **49**
Pennerly Ct. *Hav* 2D **202**
Penner Rd. *Hav* 1E **216**
Penn Hill Av. *Poole* 2B **244**
Pennine Clo. *Bas* 8K **41**
Pennine Gdns. *Dib P* 7J **193**
Pennine Ho. *Sotn.* 3E **172**
Pennine Rd. *Sotn* 3D **172**
Pennine Wlk. *Fare* 1A **212**
Pennine Way. *Bas* 8K **41**
Pennine Way. *Chan F.* 8B **132**
Pennine Way. *Farn* 5F **28**
Pennine Way. *Lee S.* 3C **238**
Pennings Rd. *Tidw.* 6C **30**
Pennington. 3C 234
Pennington Clo. *Col C* 4K **133**
Pennington Clo. *Penn* 4C **234**
Pennington Oval. *Penn* 4B **234**
Pennington Way. *Fare* 6N **197**
Penns Rd. *Ptsfld* 9L **139**
Penns Wood. *Farn* 2M **49**
Penn Way. *Gos* 4G **239**
Pennycress. *L Hth.* 7B **196**
Penny Hedge. *New M* 6C **232**
Penny Hill. *Coll D* 2H **31**
Penny Hill Cvn. Pk. *B'wtr* 2M **27**
Penny La. *Bourn* 1B **246**
Penny La. *Stockb* 3G **88**
Penny Pl. *Water* 6M **201**
Pennys Clo. *F'bri* 8J **151**
Pennys Cres. *F'bri* 8J **151**
Penny's Hatch. *K're* 2C **6**
Penny's La. *Cran* 6J **149**
Penny's La. *F'ley* 8F **86**
Pennys La. *F'bri.* 9J **151**
Penny's Mead. Cran. *6J 149* *(off Penny's La.)*
Penny St. *Ports* 4B **240** (8J **5**)
Penny Way. *Christ* 8E **230**
Pennywell Gdns. *New M* 2E **232**
Penrhyn Av. *Ports* 9J **201**
Penrhyn Clo. *A'sht.* 1K **65**
Penrhyn Clo. *Eastl* 7D **132**
Penrith Rd. *Bas* 7B **42**
Penrith Rd. *Bourn* 1D **246**
Penrose Clo. *Ports* 6E **214**
Penryn Dri. *Head D.* 2E **102**
Pensdell Farm Cotts. *Bas* 1C **60**
Penshurst Way. *Eastl* 6E **132**
Pentagon, The. *Black* 6E **208**
Pentere Rd. *Water* 4A **182**
Pentice, The. *Win* 8M **237**
Pentire Av. *Sotn* 1J **173**
Pentire Way. *Sotn.* 9J **159**
Pentland Clo. *Bas.* 8K **41**
Pentland Clo. *Dib P.* 7J **193**
Pentland Pl. *Farn* 5G **28**
Pentland Ri. *Fare.* 8M **199**
Penton Corner. 9G **50**
Penton Ct. *Hav.* 3H **203**
Penton Grafton. 7F **50**
Penton La. *Cla* 2E **50**
Penton Mewsey. 6G **50**
Penton Pl. *Win* 8M **105**
Penton Rd. *Twy* 6L **127**
Pentons Hill. *Frog* 4N **153**
Pentridge. 2G **148**
Pentridge Way. *Tot.* 5K **171**
Penwith Dri. *Hasl.* 2M **117**
Penwood. 3B **8**
Penwood Grn. *Hav.* 4H **203**
Penwood Heights. *Burgh* 3B **8**
Penwood Rd. *Wash W* 1C **8**
Peper Harow. *Water* 4B **182**
Peppard Clo. *Sotn* 3E **174**
Peppercorn Way. *H End* 8M **161**
Pepys Av. *Sotn.* 5H **175**
Pepys Clo. *Gos.* 6K **239**
Pepys Clo. *S'sea.* 4G **240**
Percivale Rd. *Chan F* 8L **131**
Percival Rd. *Ports* 8G **215**
Percy Chandler St. *Ports* 1E **240**
Percy Clo. *Hythe.* 4L **193**
Percy Rd. *Bourn.* 1B **246**
Percy Rd. *Gos* 3L **239**
Percy Rd. *Sotn* 2F **172**
Percy Rd. *S'sea.* 3F **240**
Peregrine Clo. *Tot.* 4J **171**
Peregrine Rd. *Christ.* 8C **230**
Peregrines, The. *Fare.* 9H **199**
Perham Cres. *Lud.* 1E **30**
Perham Down. 4B **30**
Perins Clo. *Alr* 2D **108**
Periwinkle Clo. *Lind.* 2M **101**
Perkins Ho. *Ports* 3L **5**
Pern Dri. *Bot* 3D **176**
Peronne Clo. *Ports.* 3G **214**
Peronne Rd. *Ports* 3G **214**
Perowne St. *A'sht.* 9H **49**
Perran Rd. *Sotn* 1C **172**
Perring Av. *Farn.* 4G **29**
Perry Dri. *Fle* 2J **47**
Perryfield Gdns. *Bourn.* 6E **228**
Perryhill Dri. *S'hrst* 4B **18**
Perry Way. *F'ham.* 3D **64**
Perry Way. *Head.* 3B **102**
Perrywood Clo. *Holb* 5A **208**
Perrywood Gdns. *Tot* 2J **171**
Perseus Pl. *Water* 6M **201**
Pershore Clo. *L Hth* 6D **196**
Pershore Rd. *Bas.* 2C **42** (in two parts)
Persian Dri. *White* 2E **196**
Persley Rd. *Bourn* 2H **227**
Perth Clo. *Christ.* 5H **229**
Perth Clo. *Per D* 4B **30**
Perth Ho. *Ports.* 2E **240**
Perth Rd. *Gos.* 5F **212**
Perth Rd. *S'sea.* 3J **241**
Pervin Rd. *Ports* 9G **201**
Peshawar Clo. *Tidw* 7B **30**
Pesthouse La. *Whitc* 4G **54**
Peststead La. *Sob.* 7L **165**
Peter Ashley La. *Ports* 8L **201**
Peterborough Ct. Gos. *2F 238* *(off Anson Clo.)*
Peterborough Rd. *Ports* 8F **200**
Peterborough Rd. *Sotn* 3M **173**
Peterhouse Clo. *Owl.* 3H **19**
Peters Clo. *L Hth* 6B **196**
Peterscroft Av. *Asht.* 9G **171**
Petersfield. 1M 145
Petersfield. *Okly* 2D **58**
Petersfield Bus. Pk. *Ptsfld* 1K **145**
Petersfield Clo. *Chine.* 8H **23**
Petersfield Golf Course. 1A 146 (Sussex Rd.)
Petersfield Ho. Ports *1E 240* *(off St Faith's Rd.)*
Petersfield Mus. 1M 145
Petersfield Pl. *Bourn.* 7E **228**

Petersfield Rd. *Bourn* 8D **228**
(in two parts)
Petersfield Rd. *Bton* 7K **145**
Petersfield Rd. *Cher & Bramd*
. . . . 1J **135**
Petersfield Rd. *Clan* 5C **168**
Petersfield Rd. *Gthm & W'hill*
. . . . 5D **114**
Petersfield Rd. *Hav* 7E **202**
Petersfield Rd. *Ropl* 2A **110**
Petersfield Rd. *Win* 7M **105**
(in two parts)
Petersham Clo. *Water* 9L **181**
Petersham Ho. *S'sea* 6E **240**
(off Clarendon Rd.)
Peterson's Tower. 9J **223**
Peters Rd. *L Hth* 6B **196**
Petit Rd. *Bourn* 3L **227**
Petrel Cft. *Bas* 2H **59**
Petrel Wlk. *Gos* 6D **212**
Petrie Rd. *Lee S* 1B **238**
Petticoat La. *Redl* 1N **119**
Pettinger Gdns. *Sotn* 2B **174**
Petty Clo. *Roms* 6N **129**
Pettycot Cres. *Gos* 5D **212**
Petty's Brook Rd. *Chine* 8H **23**
Petunia Clo. *Bas* 2J **59**
Petworth Clo. *Bas* 4K **59**
Petworth Gdns. *Eastl* 7E **132**
Petworth Gdns. *Sotn* 6G **159**
Petworth Rd. *Ports* 1J **241**
Pevensey Clo. *Sotn.* 1C **172**
Peveral Wlk. *Bas* 8M **41**
Peveral Way. *Bas* 8M **41**
Peverells Rd. *Chan F* 5C **132**
Peverells Wood Av. *Chan F*
. . . . 5C **132**
Peverells Wood Clo. *Chan F*
. . . . 5D **132**
Peveril Clo. *Ashy H.* 2C **186**
Peveril Rd. *Sotn* 6C **174**
Pewsey Pl. *Sotn* 9J **159**
Pheaben's Fld. *Braml* 1F **22**
Pheasant Clo. *Bar S* 5B **76**
Pheasant Clo. *Bas* 2H **59**
Pheasant Clo. *Tidw.* 8D **30**
Pheasant Copse. *Fle* 1J **47**
Pheasant La. *Bish G.* 1G **9**
Pheby Rd. *Bas.* 9M **41**
Phi Ho. *Sotn.* 2H **159**
Philip Rd. *Water.* 4N **201**
Phillimore Rd. *Sotn* 7B **160**
Phillips Clo. *Head.* 2B **102**
Phillips Clo. *Rown.* 5D **158**
Phillips Clo. *Tong.* 2N **65**
Phillips Cres. *Head.* 2B **102**
Philpott Dri. *March.* 9E **172**
Phoenix Bldgs. *Ports* 6H **215**
Phoenix Clo. *Burs.* 9L **175**
Phoenix Ct. *A'sht.* 1J **65**
Phoenix Ct. *H Win* 8A **26**
Phoenix Ct. *K're* 2B **6**
Phoenix Green. 8A **26**
Phoenix Grn. *H Win* 8A **26**
Phoenix Ind. Pk. *Eastl* 1G **160**
Phoenix Pk. Ter. *Bas.* 5C **42**
Phoenix Sq. *Ports.* 4F **214**
Phoenix Ter. *H Win.* 8A **26**
Phoenix Way. *Gos.* 7F **212**
Phyldon Clo. *Poole.* 9A **226**
Phyldon Rd. *Poole* 8A **226**
Physic Garden, The. 1M **145**
Pickaxe La. *S Warn & Alt*
. . . . 5C **62**
Picket Clo. *F'bri.* 9J **151**
Picket Hill. 5B **188**
Picket Piece. 7F **52**
Picket Post. 5C **188**
Picketts Hill. *Slea* 7K **83**
Picket Twenty. *And & P Twen*
. . . . 1D **70**
Pickford Rd. *Bourn.* 5J **227**
Pickford St. *A'sht* 9K **49**
Pickwick Clo. *Tot* 3H **171**
Pickwick Ho. *Ports* 9E **214**
Picton Ho. *S'sea* . . . 3D **240** (5N **5**)
Picton Rd. *And* 4M **69**
Pidham La. *E Meon* 3B **144**
Pier App. *Bourn*
. . . . . . 3K **245** (8M **247**)
Pier Head Rd. *Ports* 8B **214**
Pierrefonde's Av. *Farn.* 7J **29**
Pier Rd. *S'sea* 5C **240** (9L **5**)
Pier St. *Lee S* 1A **238**
Pier Theatre.
. . . . . . 3K **245** (8M **247**)
(off Pier App.)
Pigeonhouse Fld. *Sut S* . . . 7D **76**
(off Stockbridge Rd.)
Pigeonhouse La. *Far W* . . . 8N **59**
Pigeonhouse La. *Pur* 3E **200**
Pigeons Clo. *Braml.* 2H **23**

Pig Shoot La. *Hurn* 2C **228**
Pike Clo. *A'sht.* 9L **49**
Pikeshill. 1B **148**
Pikes Hill Av. *Lyn* 1A **148**
Pilands Wood Rd. *Burs* . . . 1K **195**
Pilbrow Ct. *Gos* 3H **239**
Pilchards Av. *F Oak* 9M **133**
Pilcot. 5G **46**
Pilcot Rd. *Crook V* 5G **46**
Pilgrim Pk. Homes. *Ring*
. . . . 9M **185**
Pilgrim Pl. *Sotn* 7C **160**
Pilgrims Clo. *Chan F* 7L **131**
Pilgrim's Clo. *New M* 2D **232**
Pilgrims Ga. *Win.* 5J **105**
Pilgrims Ho. *Win.* 5J **105**
Pilgrims Way. *And* 9B **52**
Pilgrims Way. *Fare* 7L **211**
Pilgrims Way. *Head* 2A **102**
Pilley. 6G **225**
Pilley Bailey. 5G **225**
Pilley Bailey. *Pill* 5G **225**
Pilley Hill. *Pill* 6E **224**
Pilley St. *Pill* 6F **224**
Pill Hill. *W'ish* 5H **121**
Pilwing Clo. *Fare* 9M **197**
Pilot Hight Rd. *Bourn* 2E **226**
Pilots Vw. *Ame.* 5A **66**
(off Porton Rd.)
Pimpernel Clo. *L Hth* 7B **196**
Pimpernel Way. *Lych* 4G **42**
Pine Av. *Bourn* 1F **246**
Pine Av. *Cam* 9M **19**
Pine Av. *Poole* 7D **226**
Pine Bank. *Hind* 3N **103**
Pinebeach Ct. *Poole* 5E **244**
Pinecliffe Av. *Bourn.* 1F **246**
Pinecliffe Rd. *New M* 7L **231**
Pinecliff Rd. *Poole* 5E **244**
Pine Clo. *Asht.* 7J **171**
Pine Clo. *Bart S* 6N **231**
Pine Clo. *Bord* 5K **101**
Pine Clo. *Coll T.* 6G **19**
Pine Clo. *Dib P* 7L **193**
Pine Clo. *Land.* 1J **155**
Pine Clo. *Mid W* 4B **72**
Pine Clo. *N Bad.* 7E **130**
Pine Clo. *S Won* 3J **91**
Pine Clo. *Win* 2F **126**
Pine Ct. *A'sht.* 9J **49**
Pine Ct. *Ems* 5M **203**
Pine Cres. *Chan F* 3A **132**
Pine Cres. *Highc.* 7G **230**
Pine Dri. *B'wtr* 1G **29**
Pine Dri. *Poole* 2D **244**
(in two parts)
Pine Dri. *St I* 4C **186**
Pine Dri. *Sotn.* 3H **175**
Pine Dri. *Water.* 6C **168**
Pine Dri. E. *Poole* 3E **244**
Pine Dri. E. *Sotn* 3J **175**
Pinefield Rd. *Sotn* 9D **160**
Pinefields Clo. *C'then* 1D **18**
Pine Grange. *Bourn* 2L **245**
Pine Gro. *Chu C* 6N **47**
(in two parts)
Pine Gro. *Hav.* 8G **203**
Pinegrove Rd. *Sotn* 7D **174**
Pinehill Ri. *S'hrst* 5E **18**
Pinehill Rd. *Bord.* 5J **101**
Pinehill Rd. *C'then* 1D **18**
Pineholt Clo. *St I* 3D **186**
Pinehurst. *Mil S* 8J **235**
Pinehurst. *T'ley* 6H **11**
Pinehurst Av. *Christ* 9B **230**
Pinehurst Av. *Farn* 1K **49**
Pinehurst Clo. *Water* 8C **182**
Pinehurst Cotts. *Farn* 1K **49**
Pinehurst Rd. *Sotn* 4L **159**
Pinehurst Roundabout. *Farn*
. . . . 9K **29**
Pinelands Ct. *Bourn* 7N **227**
Pinelands Ct. *Sotn* 7H **159**
Pinelands Mobile Home Pk.
Pad C 1L **11**
Pinelands Rd. *Chilw* 3L **159**
Pine Mnr. Rd. *Ashy H.* 3A **186**
Pine Mt. Rd. *Cam* 9M **19**
Pine Pk. Mans. *Poole* 1E **244**
Pine Rd. *A'hlt* 5C **152**
Pine Rd. *Bish W* 3N **163**
Pine Rd. *Bourn.* 5K **227**
Pine Rd. *Chan F* 3N **131**
Pine Rd. *Four M.* 4K **97**
Pine Rd. *Roms* 6B **130**
Pines Rd. *Fle.* 1L **47**
Pines Rd. *Lip* 2A **116**
Pines, The. *And* 1M **69**
Pines, The. *Fare* 8J **199**
Pines, The. *Gods* 5A **154**
(off Southampton Rd.)
Pines, The. *Poole* 3E **244**

Pines, The. *Sotn* 8G **159**
Pinetops Clo. *Penn.* 3B **234**
Pine Tree Clo. *Cowes* 5N **237**
Pine Tree Gdns. *Water* 8A **182**
Pine Tree Glen. *Bourn* 2G **244**
Pine Trees Clo. *Fare* 9N **197**
Pine Va. Cres. *Bourn.* 3J **227**
Pine Vw. *Head D.* 1E **102**
Pine Vw. Clo. *Bad L* 5J **65**
Pineview Clo. *Bourn* 9L **175**
Pine Vw. Clo. *W'fls* 9C **120**
Pine Wlk. *And.* 3K **69**
Pine Wlk. *Chilw* 4K **159**
(in two parts)
Pine Wlk. *Liss.* 8F **114**
Pine Wlk. *Sar G* 4D **196**
Pine Way. *Sotn.* 4L **159**
Pinewood. *Chine.* 9E **22**
Pinewood. *Gos.* 7G **212**
Pinewood. *Sotn* 5L **159**
Pinewood Av. *Bourn.* 1H **227**
Pinewood Av. *Hav.* 6B **202**
Pinewood Clo. *Baug.* 4D **10**
Pinewood Clo. *Bourn.* 1H **227**
Pinewood Clo. *Fare* 4N **211**
Pinewood Clo. *Roms* 3B **130**
Pinewood Clo. *S'hrst* 5B **18**
Pinewood Clo. *Walk* 4J **231**
Pinewood Ct. *Fle* 1M **47**
Pinewood Cres. *Farn.* 7E **28**
Pinewood Cres. *Hythe* 7N **193**
Pinewood Dri. *Hythe* 8N **193**
Pinewood Dri. *New.* 2E **8**
Pinewood Hill. *Fle* 1M **47**
Pinewood Lodge. *Fare* 7D **198**
(off Northwood Rd.)
Pinewood Pk. *Farn* 5E **28**
Pinewood Pk. *Sotn.* 5K **175**
Pinewood Rd. *Brnk P* 4F **244**
Pinewood Rd. *Highc.* 5H **231**
Pinewood Rd. *Hord.* 3F **232**
Pinewood Rd. *St I* 4C **186**
Pinkerton Rd. *Bas.* 9L **41**
Pinkney La. *Lyn.* 4M **189**
Pink Rd. *Ports.* 8F **214**
Pinks Hill. *Fare* 7F **198**
Pinks La. *Baug.* 4E **10**
Pinnell Clo. *Bas.* 4J **59**
Pinsley Dri. *S'wick* 3A **200**
Pintail Clo. *Bas.* 3H **59**
Pinto Clo. *White.* 2F **196**
Pipers Ash. *Ring* 9M **185**
Pipers Clo. *Tot* 4K **171**
Pipers Cft. *Chu C.* 7M **47**
Pipers Dri. *Christ.* 7C **230**
Pipers Mead. *Water* 6A **168**
Pipers Patch. *Farn* 8K **29**
Pipers Wood Ind. Est. *Water*
. . . . 1K **201**
Piping Clo. *Col C* 4K **133**
Piping Grn. *Col C* 4K **133**
Piping Rd. *Col C.* 4K **133**
Pipit Clo. *Gos.* 9K **213**
Pipit Clo. *Water.* 4A **182**
Pippin Clo. *Christ* 4H **229**
Pippin Clo. *L'ton* 4E **234**
Pipson La. *Yate* 8N **17**
Pipsons Clo. *Yate.* 7N **17**
Pirbright Rd. *Farn* 9L **29**
Pirelli St. *Sotn* . . . 6L **173** (5B **4**)
Pirrie Clo. *Sotn.* 1J **173**
Pitcairn Clo. *Bas.* 1D **42**
Pitcairn M. *S'sea* 5J **241**
Pitchponds Rd. *Wars* 9N **195**
Pitcot La. *Ows* 5C **134**
Pitcroft Av. *Bton* 7M **145**
Pitcroft La. *Ports* 8E **214**
(in two parts)
Pitcroft Rd. *Ports* 7E **214**
Pitfield La. *Mort* 1H **13**
Pitfold Av. *Hasl.* 9M **103**
Pitfold Clo. *Hasl.* 9N **103**
Pither Rd. *Odi.* 2E **62**
Pithouse La. *Christ.* 6G **218**
Pitman Clo. *Bas.* 9K **41**
Pitmore Clo. *Eastl* 4F **132**
Pitmore La. *Penn.* 6M **223**
Pitmore La. *Sway.* 5K **223**
Pitmore Rd. *Eastl* 4F **132**
Pitreavie Rd. *Ports.* 2G **215**
Pitt. 9E **104**
Pittard Rd. *Bas.* 8A **42**
Pitter Clo. *Win.* 1F **104**
Pitt Hill La. *Hmbdn* 9F **166**
Pittmore Rd. *Burt.* 4M **229**
Pitt Rd. *Sotn.* 4H **173**
Pitts Deep La. *E End.* 5B **236**
Pitts La. *And.* 3N **69**
Pitts La. *B'stne.* 3D **118**
Pitts Pl. *New M.* 4E **232**

Pitts Rd. *A'sht* 7K **49**
Pitt Way. *Farn.* 7H **29**
Pit Wlk. *Newt T.* 5F **66**
Pitymoor La. *S'wick* 5C **200**
Place Ct. *A'sht.* 3L **65**
Place Ho. Clo. *Fare* 8M **197**
Place La. *Comp* 5H **127**
Place Mill. 9L **229**
Plaitford Green. 7M **121**
Plaitford Gro. *Hav.* 5B **202**
Plaitford Wlk. *Sotn* 1E **172**
Plantaganet Cres. *Bourn*
. . . . 1B **226**
Plantation. *Evtn.* 6M **233**
Plantation Ct. *L'ton.* 2D **234**
Plantation Dri. *March.* 9D **172**
Plantation Dri. *Walk* 4J **231**
Plantation Hill. 7M **9**
Plantation Rd. *And.* 2L **69**
Plantation Rd. *Hill B.* 4G **141**
Plantation Rd. *T'ley.* 3F **10**
Plantation Rd. *Tidw.* 9D **30**
Plantation Rd. *W Wel* 2M **155**
Plantation Row. *Cam* 8K **19**
Plantation, The. *Curd* 1H **177**
Plantation, The. *Sher L* 4L **43**
Plantation, The. *W'slw* 5G **86**
Plantation Way. *W'hill.* 6F **100**
Plant Pk. Rd. *Ring* 5F **186**
Plants Clo. *E Wel* 1B **156**
Plassey Cres. *Bourn.* 1G **226**
Plassey Rd. *Tidw.* 7C **30**
Plastow Green. 3L **9**
Platform Rd. *Sotn*
. . . . . . 8M **173** (9D **4**)
Platoff Rd. *L'ton.* 6E **234**
Player Ct. *F'bri* 9J **151**
Players Cres. *Tot.* 5L **171**
Playfair Rd. *S'sea* 3E **240**
Playfields Dri. *Poole* 8C **226**
Plaza Pde. *Roms* 5M **129**
Pleasance Way. *New M* 3A **232**
Pleasant Hill. *T'ley* 5H **11**
Pleasant Rd. *S'sea* 3J **241**
Pleasant View. 7F **174**
Plemont Clo. *Poole.* 5C **226**
Pless Rd. *Mil S.* 8H **233**
Plestor, The. *Selb* 7L **99**
Plough Gdns. *Bro'tn.* 2A **86**
Plough La. *Brams.* 1L **25**
Plough La. *Sob.* 9L **165**
Plough Rd. *Yate.* 6A **18**
Plough Way. *Win* 1H **127**
Plover Clo. *And.* 8A **52**
Plover Clo. *Bas.* 1J **59**
Plover Clo. *Fare* 6L **211**
Plover Clo. *Sotn.* 6G **158**
Plover Clo. *Mil S* 8M **235**
Ploverfield. *Burs.* 1M **195**
Plover La. *E'sly.* 4B **16**
Plover Reach. *S'sea* 2J **241**
Plover Rd. *Tot.* 3J **171**
Plovers Down. *Win.* 2F **126**
Plovers Rd. *Water.* 3A **182**
Plovers Way. *Alt.* 2G **80**
P.L.P.H. Rd. *Hythe.* 3E **208**
Plumer Rd. *Lngmr.* 3H **115**
Plum Fell La. *Selb.* 8L **99**
Plumley Wlk. *Hav.* 2D **202**
Plumpton Gdns. *Ports* 5K **215**
Plumpton Gro. *Water.* 9B **182**
Plumpton Way. *Alt.* 6F **80**
Plymouth Dri. *Fare* 6K **211**
Plymouth St. *S'sea* 3D **240**
Poachers Fld. *S Warn* 4D **62**
Pococks La. *Hawk* 7M **113**
Poets Way. *Win* 6H **105**
Poinsettia Clo. *Fare* 6H **197**
Pointout Clo. *Sotn* 8K **159**
Pointout Rd. *Sotn.* 8K **159**
Pokesdown. 9D **228**
Poland La. *Odi* 5L **45**
Polden Clo. *Farn.* 5G **28**
Polecat. 6N **103**
Polecat Copse. 7N **103**
Polecat Corner. 1J **61**
Polecat Hill. *Hind* 6N **103**
Polesden Clo. *Chan F* 4N **131**
Poles La. *L'ton* 5E **234**
Poles La. *Ott.* 7N **125**
Polhampton. 9G **38**
Police Sta. La. *Drox* 2K **165**
Polkerris Way. *Chu C* 7N **47**
Pollards Moor. 1A **170**
Pollards Moor Rd. *Copy*
. . . . 1A **170**
Pollocks Path. 5M **103**
Pollocks Path. *Gray.* 5M **103**
Polmear Clo. *Chu C* 7N **47**
Polygon. 5K **173**

Polygon, The. *Sotn*
. . . . . . 5K **173** (3A **4**)
Pond Clo. *March.* 8E **172**
Pond Clo. *New M* 3B **232**
Pond Clo. *Over.* 4D **56**
Pond Cotts. *Clid.* 3B **60**
Pond Cft. *Yate.* 7A **18**
Pondhead Clo. *Holb* 5A **208**
Pond La. *Churt.* 4E **84**
Pond La. *Water.* 5B **168**
Pond Piece. *Water* 7G **180**
Pond Rd. *Braml.* 2H **23**
Pond Rd. *Head D* 3C **102**
Pond Rd. *Sar G* 3C **196**
Pondside La. *Bish W* 3L **163**
(in two parts)
Pondtail. 2N **47**
Pondtail Clo. *Fle* 3A **48**
Pondtail Gdns. *Fle* 3A **48**
Pondtail Rd. *Fle* 3A **48**
Pond Vw. Clo. *Fle.* 1N **47**
Ponsonby Ho. *S'sea*
. . . . . . 3D **240** (5N **5**)
Ponsonby Rd. *Poole.* 1B **244**
Pook La. *Fare.* 5D **198**
Pook La. *Hav* 1G **217**
(in three parts)
Pookles La. *E Wor* 6N **81**
Pooksgreen. 8C **172**
Pooksgreen. *March* 8B **172**
Poole Commerce Cen. *Poole*
. . . . 9D **226**
Poole Hill. *Bourn*
. . . . . . 2H **245** (7H **247**)
Poole La. *Bourn.* 2D **226**
Poole La. Roundabout. *Bourn*
. . . . 2C **226**
Poole Rd. *Bourn*
. . . . . . 1F **244** (6G **247**)
Poole Rd. *Brnk.* 1D **244**
Poole Rd. *H Win.* 5B **26**
Poors Farm Rd. *Bas* 3M **43**
Pope's Hill. *K're* 2A **6**
Popes La. *Tot.* 3M **171**
Popes La. *Uphm.* 8D **134**
Popham. 3A **78**
Popham Ct. *Hav.* 3C **202**
Popham La. *N Wal* 9A **58**
Poplar Clo. *Baug.* 5D **10**
Poplar Clo. *Brans* 7E **220**
Poplar Clo. *Farn* 7E **28**
Poplar Clo. *Highc* 6K **231**
Poplar Clo. *Sher L* 3L **23**
Poplar Cres. *Ring* 1L **187**
Poplar Dri. *Fare* 9A **198**
Poplar Dri. *March.* 9C **172**
Poplar Gro. *Hay I* 3G **243**
Poplar La. *Brans.* 6E **220**
Poplar Path. *Mid W* 4B **72**
(off Willow Path)
Poplar Rd. *New M* 2E **232**
Poplar Rd. *Sotn.* 4D **174**
Poplars, The. *Wal C* 8A **164**
Poplar Wlk. *F'ham.* 3F **64**
Poplar Wlk. *Ptsfld.* 3L **145**
Poplar Way. *H End* 3A **176**
Poplar Way. *N Bad* 7E **130**
Poplar Way. *Ring* 1L **187**
Popley. 2C **42**
Popley Way. *Bas.* 3A **42**
Poppy Clo. *Christ.* 6D **230**
Poppy Clo. *L Hth* 7C **196**
Poppy Fld. *Lych* 3H **43**
Poppyfields. *Chan F.* 6M **131**
Poppyhills Rd. *Cam* 5N **19**
Poppy Rd. *Sotn* 6A **160**
Porchester Clo. *Charl* 7K **51**
Porchester Rd. *Sotn.* 7C **174**
Porchester Sq. *Bas.* 6C **42**
Porlock Rd. *Sotn* 9C **158**
Portacre Ri. *Bas.* 8A **42**
Portal Clo. *And.* 2H **69**
Portal Rd. *Eastl* 9H **133**
Portal Rd. *Gos* 5E **212**
Portal Rd. *Sotn.* 6F **174**
Portal Rd. *Tot.* 3K **171**
Portal Rd. *Win.* 8M **105**
Portarlington Clo. *Bourn*
. . . . 9F **102**
Portarlington Rd.
Bourn 2G **244** (7G **247**)
Portchester. 9M **199**
Portchester Castle. 2N **213**
Portchester Ct. *Bourn* 9M **227**
Portchester La. *S'wick.* 6M **199**
Portchester Pl. *Bourn* 9M **227**
Portchester Ri. *Eastl* 5E **132**
Portchester Rd. *Bourn* 8L **227**
Portchester Rd. *Fare.* 8H **199**
Portchester Rd. *Ports* 8F **214**

Portchester Roman Fortress.
. . . . .2N 213
Portcreek Cotts. Ports 3J 215
Portcullis Ho. Sotn 9E 4
Portelet Clo. Poole 5B 226
Portelet Ho. Sotn 8C 158
Portelet Pl. H End 5N 175
Porteous Cres. Chan F 6D 132
Porter Clo. Odi 2E 62
(off Woolridge Cres.)
Porter Rd. Bas 1A 60
Portersbridge M. Roms . . .5L 129
Portersbridge St. Roms . . .5L 129
Porters Clo. And 9K 51
Porters Clo. Dum 9F 58
Porter's La. Sotn . .7L 173 (8C 4)
Portesbery Hill Dri. Cam . . .7N 19
Portesbery Rd. Cam 7M 19
Portesham Gdns.
Bourn 2M 227
Portfield Clo. Christ 6K 229
Portfield Ind. Est. Ports . . .5H 215
Portfield Rd. B'stne 1E 118
Portfield Rd. Christ 7J 229
Portfield Rd. Ports 5H 215
Port Hamble. Hamb 6L 195
Portland Building. Ports
. . . . .2C 240 (3L 5)
Portland Bldgs. Sotn 3L 239
Portland Dri. Chu C 7L 47
Portland Dri. Gos 4F 238
Portland Gro. And 1N 69
Portland Ho. Gos 3M 239
Portland Pl. Bourn 1K 245
Portland Rd. Bourn 5L 227
Portland Rd.S'sea
. . . . .5D 240 (9N 5)
Portland Rd. Water 2M 201
Portland's Clo. Ptsfld 8A 140
Portland Sq. Liss 1E 140
Portland St. Fare 8D 198
Portland St. Ports
. . . . .2C 240 (4L 5)
Portland St. Sotn . .6L 173 (5C 4)
Portland Ter. Sotn
. . . . .6L 173 (4C 4)
Portland Ter. S'sea
. . . . .5D 240 (9N 5)
Port La. Hurs 6N 125
Portman Cres. Bourn 1E 246
Portman Rd. Bourn 9C 228
Portman Ter. Bourn 1E 246
Portmore. 8G 225
Portobello Gro. Fare 8M 199
Porton Rd. Ame 4A 66
Port Royal St. S'sea 2E 240
Port Royal St. Ind. Est. S'sea
. . . . .2E 240
Portsbridge Roundabout. Ports
. . . . .2F 214
Portsdown Av. Ports 9K 201
Portsdown Hill Rd. Fare . .6K 199
Portsdown Hill Rd. Ports & Hav
. . . . .7E 200
Portsdown Rd. Fare & Ports
. . . . .8N 199
Portsea. 2B 240
Portside Clo. March 7F 172
Portsmouth. 2B 240
Portsmouth Cathedral.
. . . . .4B 240 (7J 5)
(St Thomas of Canterbury)
Portsmouth Cres. Bas . . .9M 41
Portsmouth Enterprise Cen.
Ports 5J 215
Portsmouth F.C. 3H 241
Portsmouth Golf Course.
. . . . .7M 201
Portsmouth Harbour. . . .2A 240
Portsmouth R.C. Cathedral.
. . . . .2C 240 (3M 5)
Portsmouth Rd. Burs 9L 175
Portsmouth Rd. Cosh 2G 214
Portsmouth Rd. Fish P . . .6M 133
Portsmouth Rd. Frim & Cam
. . . . .3M 29
Portsmouth Rd. Horn 5B 182
Portsmouth Rd. Lee S . . .3B 238
Portsmouth Rd. Lip 5D 116
(Haslemere Rd.)
Portsmouth Rd. Lip & Hind
. . . . .9F 102
(Hewshott La.)
Portsmouth Rd. Sotn & Burs
. . . . .7B 174
Portsmouth Wlk. Bas. . . .9M 41
Portsmouth Way. Bas . . .9M 41
Port Solent. 1B 214
Portsview Av. Fare 8M 199
Portsview Gdns. Fare. 8M 199
Portswood. 1N 173
Portswood Av. Sotn 2N 173

Portswood Cen. Sotn 1N 173
Portswood Clo. T'ley 5K 11
Portswood Dri. Bourn. 2L 227
Portswood Park. 2N 173
Portswood Pk. Sotn 2N 173
Portswood Rd. Hav 3D 202
Portswood Rd. Ports 3F 214
Portswood Rd. Sotn. 2N 173
Portuguese Fireplace. . . .3K 189
Portvw. Cvn. Pk. Hurn. . . .5E 218
Portview Rd. Sotn 9D 160
Portway. Baug 4D 10
Port Way. Port S. 9B 200
Portway. Rise 3G 14
Portway Clo. And 1K 69
Portway Clo. Sotn. 3F 174
Portway Ind. Est. And. 9J 51
(East Portway)
Portway Ind. Est. And 9H 51
(Hopkinson Way)
Portway Pl. Bas 6K 41
Portway Roundabout. And
. . . . .8J 51
Posbrooke Rd. S'sea 3H 241
Posbrook La. Fare 3H 211
Postern Clo. Fare. 9M 199
Postern Ct. Sotn . .7L 173 (7C 4)
Post Horn La. Roth. 7E 24
Post Office La. Dum 9F 58
Post Office La. St I 3D 186
Post Office Rd. Bourn
. . . . .2K 245 (6L 247)
Post Office Rd. Ink. 1H 7
Post Office Rd. Water. 4K 201
Potash Ter. Hav. 7E 202
Potbridge. 3N 45
Pot La. Old B 4N 43
Potley Hill Rd. Yate. 7B 18
Potteries, The. Fare 6D 198
Potteries, The. Farn. 6F 28
Potters Av. Fare 5C 198
Potters Fld. Liss 1F 140
Potters Ga. F'ham. 8C 64
Potters Heron Clo. Amp. . .1K 131
Potters Heron La. Amp. . . .1K 131
Potters Ind. Pk. Chu C . . .6A 48
Potters La. Str T. 1N 23
Potters Wlk. Bas. 6C 42
Potters Way. Poole 3A 244
Pottery La. Ink 1G 7
Poulner. 9M 185
Poulner Clo. Sotn. 9E 174
Poulner Ct. Hav 3C 202
Poulner Mobile Home Pk. Ring
. . . . .7M 185
Poulner Pk. Ring 8M 185
Poultons Clo. Over 4D 56
Poultons Rd. Over 3D 56
Pound Clo. Braml. 1F 22
Pound Clo. Gos. 8F 212
Pound Clo. Head. 2B 102
Pound Clo. Ovr W 8M 67
Pound Clo. Ring. 9K 185
Pound Clo. Up Wld. 8H 79
Pound Cotts. Meon 8N 135
Pound Ga. Alt. 3G 80
Pound Ga. Dri. Fare 8F 196
Pound La. Amp 1G 131
Pound La. Burgh 3D 8
Pound La. Burl. 8D 188
Pound La. Christ. 8L 229
Pound La. Copy 9C 156
Pound La. Dam 3N 149
Pound La. Meon. 8N 135
Pound La. Plait 8M 121
Pound La. Sher E. 6N 121
Pound La. Tot 7L 171
Pound Lea. Hay I 2G 243
Pound Mdw. Sher L. 4M 23
Pound Mdw. Whitc. 5H 55
Pound Rd. A'sht 1L 65
Pound Rd. Burs 9J 175
Pound Rd. King W 7N 91
Pound Rd. Over 3E 56
Pound Rd. Ovr W 8M 67
Pound Rd. Penn. 4B 234
Pound Rd. S'wick. 7C 200
Pounds Ter. Ports
. . . . .1B 240 (2K 5)
Pound Street. 3C 8
Pound St. Sotn. 3E 174
Pound, The. Bro'tn 2A 86
Pound Tree Rd. Sotn
. . . . .6M 173 (5D 4)
Poveys Mead. K're 3C 6
Powell Cres. Tot. 5M 171
Powell Rd. Poole 2A 244
Powerscourt Rd. Bart S. . .7M 231
Powerscourt Rd. Ports . . .8F 214

Powis Clo. New M 3C 232
Powlett Rd. L'ton 3E 234
Poyner Clo. Fare. 7D 198
Poynings Cres. Bas 9D 42
Poynings Pl. Ports
. . . . .4C 240 (7K 5)
Poynters Clo. And 8M 51
Poyntz Rd. Over. 2D 56
Precinct, The. Gos 3M 239
Precinct, The. Hay I 4G 243
Precinct, The. H End 4N 175
Precinct, The. Holb. 4A 208
Precinct, The. Water 2M 201
Precosa Rd. Bot. 5B 176
Predale Way. Titch 7F 196
Premier Bus. Pk. Fare 2D 212
Premier Cen., The. Roms
. . . . .6C 130
Premier Pde. Sotn 8D 160
Premier Way. Roms 7C 130
Prentice Clo. Farn. 4K 29
Prescelly Clo. Bas. 7K 41
Preshaw Clo. Sotn. 7H 159
Preston Candover. 5E 78
Preston La. Burt. 4N 229
Preston Rd. Ports. 8G 214
Preston Way. Christ 6F 230
Prestwood Clo. Bart S 5A 232
Prestwood Rd. H End. 4N 175
Pretoria Clo. Lngmr. 4H 115
Pretoria Rd. H End. 5M 175
Pretoria Rd. Lud. 2F 30
Pretoria Rd. S'sea. 4G 241
Preymead Ind. Est. Bad L
. . . . .3K 65
Pricketts Hill. Shed. 3B 178
Prideaux-Brune Av. Gos . .4E 212
Priest Cft. Black 6C 208
Priestcroft Dri. Black 6C 208
Priestfields. Fare. 7F 196
Priestlands. Roms 4L 129
Priestlands Clo. W'lnds . . .4G 170
Priestlands La. Penn. 3C 234
Priestlands Pl. L'ton 3D 234
Priestlands Rd. Penn 3C 234
Priest La. Brans 8L 219
Priestley Clo. Tot 3K 171
Priestley Rd. Bas 3N 41
Priestley Rd. Bourn. 5F 226
Priestwood Clo. Sotn. 3H 175
Primate Rd. Fare 6G 196
Primrose Clo. Chan F 8L 131
Primrose Clo. Gos 3E 212
Primrose Clo. H End. 5N 175
Primrose Ct. Water 3A 202
Primrose Dri. H Win. 5C 26
Primrose Gdns. Farn 9G 28
Primrose Gdns. Hat W 4K 59
Primrose La. Liss & Rake
. . . . .9J 115
Primrose La. W'flls. 8C 120
Primrose Rd. Lud. 1D 30
Primrose Rd. Sotn. 7M 159
Primrose Wlk. Fle 1L 47
Primrose Wlk. Yate. 7L 17
Primrose Way. Christ 5D 230
Primrose Way. L Hth 7C 196
Primrose Way. Roms 4B 130
Primrose Way. S'hrst 4D 18
Prince Albert Gdns. And. . . .2N 69
(off Western Rd.)
Prince Albert Rd. S'sea. . . .4H 241
Prince Alfred St. Gos 4K 239
Prince Charles Clo. Lud . . .4K 31
Prince Charles Cres. Farn. .4K 29
Prince Clo. And. 8C 52
Prince Dri. S'hrst 4C 18
Prince George's St. Hav . . .8F 202
Prince George St. Ports
. . . . .2B 240 (3K 5)
Prince of Wales Av. Sotn
. . . . .3F 172
Prince of Wales Clo. Water
. . . . .2A 202
Prince of Wales Ct. A'sht . .9H 49
(off Queen Elizabeth Dri.)
Prince of Wales Rd. Bourn
. . . . .1F 244
Prince of Wales Rd. Gos
. . . . .3L 239
Prince of Wales Wlk. Cam
. . . . .7L 19
Prince Regent Ct. S'sea . . .6N 5
Prince Rd. Fare. 2B 212
Prince Rd. Rown 5D 158
Prince's Av. A'sht 6K 49
Prince's Bldgs. Win 7N 237
Princes Clo. Bish W 3L 163
Princes Clo. Redl 1N 119
Princes Clo. W'hill 6H 101
Princes Cotts. E Meon 4L 143
Princes Ct. Ports. 9E 214

Princes Ct. Sotn. 4A 174
Princes Cres. Bas 8N 41
Princes Cres. Lyn 2D 148
Princes Dri. Water. 9A 182
Prince's Esplanade. Cowes
. . . . .5M 237
(in two parts)
Princes Hall. 4A 174
Princes Hill. Redl. 1N 119
Princes Ho. Sotn 4A 174
(off Graham St.)
Princes Ho. S'sea
. . . . .4C 240 (7M 5)
(off King's Ter.)
Prince's Marsh. 3D 140
Princes Mead (Shop. Cen.) Farn
. . . . .8K 29
Princes Pl. New M. 2D 232
Prince's Pl. Ports. 9D 214
Prince's Pl. Win 9J 105
Princes Rd. Ptsfld 9K 139
Prince's Rd. Roms 4L 129
Princes Rd. Sotn 4J 173
Princess Av. Christ. 8L 229
Princess Clo. W End 9J 161
Princess Ct. Win
. . . . .6L 105 (6M 237)
Princess Dri. Alt 5D 80
Princess Gdns. Water 3B 182
Princess Mary Gdns. Lud
. . . . .1D 30
Princess Rd. Asht 8H 171
Princess Rd. Poole & Bourn
. . . . .1E 244
(in two parts)
Prince's St. Ports 9E 214
Princes St. Sotn. 4A 174
Princess Way. Cam 7L 19
Princes Way. A'sht 9H 49
Prince William Ct. Eastl. . . .1K 161
Prinstead Clo. Win 8M 105
Prinsted Cres. Ports. 1L 215
Prinsted Wlk. Fare. 9N 197
Printers Row. Win 7L 237
Priors Barton. Win. 9K 105
Priors Clo. Christ 7E 230
Priors Clo. Farn 4J 29
Priors Clo. K're 2B 6
Priors Ct. Ash 1N 65
Priorsdean Av. Ports 1H 241
Priorsdean Cres. Hav 5D 202
Priors Dean Rd. Win 2H 105
Priors Hill La. Burs. 1J 195
Priors Keep. Fle 3N 47
Prior's La. B'wtr. 8C 18
Priors Rd. T'ley 3G 10
Priors Row. N War. 7J 45
Priors Way. Win. 2F 126
Priors Way, The. Mnkwd
. . . . .5J 111
Priors Wood. C'then 1N 17
Priory Av. Sotn 1B 174
Priory Clo. Bish W 3L 163
Priory Clo. Fle 3J 47
Priory Clo. Sotn 1B 174
Priory Ct. Bish W 3L 163
Priory Ct. Cam. 8H 19
Priory Ct. S'sea 3F 240
Priory Cres. S'sea 3H 241
Priory Gdns. Fare. 1L 213
Priory Gdns. Old B 4J 43
Priory Gdns. Water. 9M 181
Priory Ho. Sotn . . .5M 173 (4E 4)
Priory Ind. Pk. Christ. 7D 230
Priory La. Free 4L 55
Priory La. Fren. 1K 85
Priory La. H Win. 8A 26
Priory Pk. Fle 2L 47
Priory Quay. Christ 9M 229
Priory Rd. Bourn
. . . . .3J 245 (8K 247)
Priory Rd. Eastl. 2D 160
Priory Rd. Fare 7N 197
Priory Rd. Gos. 8K 213
Priory Rd. Net A. 3F 194
Priory Rd. Sotn 1A 174
Priory Rd. S'sea. 5H 241
Priory Rd. S'wick. 3B 200
Priory St. Farn 8M 29
Priory, The. Bish W 4L 163
Priory Vw. Pl. Bourn 3L 227
Priory Vw. Rd. Bourn. 3L 227
Priory Vw. Rd. Burt. 3M 229
Prite La. Tichb 6E 108
Privet La. App & Fy'd 7N 31
Privet Rd. Bourn 6J 227
Privet Rd. Lind 2M 101
Privett. 3L 137
(Alton)
Privett. 3G 238
(Gosport)
Privett Clo. Lych 3H 43

Privett Ho. Ports . . .1B 240 (2K 5)
Privett Pl. Gos 3G 239
Privett Rd. Fare 7M 197
Privett Rd. Frox 3D 138
Privett Rd. Gos. 4E 238
Privett Rd. Water 6L 201
Prochurch Rd. Water 6B 182
Proctor Clo. Sotn 5H 175
Proctor Dri. N Bad 9E 130
Proctor La. Ports 2G 240
Promenade. Christ. 9D 230
Promenade. Lee S 9N 211
Promenade. Poole 9B 244
(in two parts)
Promenade. Ports & S'sea
. . . . .4B 240 (8J 5)
Promenade Ct. Lee S 1A 238
Promenade, The. Hythe. . . .4M 193
Promenade, The. Ports. . . .7E 214
Prospect Av. Farn. 6K 29
Prospect Hill. Head. 8A 84
Prospect Ho. Sotn 5D 174
Prospect La. Hav 4H 203
Prospect Pl. Chan F 6A 132
Prospect Pl. Hythe. 4M 193
Prospect Rd. Alr. 2D 108
Prospect Rd. Farn. 8J 29
Prospect Rd. Ports. 9D 214
Prospect Rd. Row 8N 63
Prospect Vs. Bas 9A 42
Protea Gdns. Titch 8K 197
Provene Clo. Wal C 7A 164
Provene Gdns. Wal C 7N 163
Providence Hill. Burs 8L 175
Provost St. F'bri 1J 153
Pruetts La. Liss & Ptsfld
. . . . .4E 140
Prunus Clo. Sotn 6H 159
Przewalski Wlk. Ows 7B 134
Pucknall. 6E 124
Puckridge Hill Rd. A'sht . . .5G 48
Pudbrooke Gdns. H End
. . . . .2M 175
Pudbrook Ho. Bot. 4C 176
Pudding La. Win 1M 105
Puddle Slosh La. S'hth. . . .9G 150
Puffin Clo. Bas. 4H 59
Puffin Clo. Sotn. 6G 159
Puffin Cres. Fare. 4L 211
Puffin Gdns. Gos 5D 212
Puffin Wlk. Water. 6L 181
Pug's Hole. W Tyth. 8L 87
Pulens Cres. Ptsfld. 9B 140
Pulens La. Ptsfld. 8A 140
Pullman Way. Ring. 2K 187
Pump La. Gos. 7E 212
Pump La. Water. 5A 182
Pundle Grn. Bart. 4B 170
Punsholt La. W Tis 7F 110
Purbeck Dri. Fare. 9N 197
Purbeck La. Cran 8L 149
Purbeck Rd. Bart S 7M 231
Purbeck Rd. Bourn
. . . . .2J 245 (7J 247)
Purbeck St. Ports
. . . . .2C 240 (4L 5)
Purbeck Wlk. Fare 9N 197
Purbrook. 5M 201
Purbrook Chase Precinct. Water
. . . . .6M 201
Purbrook Clo. Sotn 7H 159
Purbrook Gdns. Water 4K 201
Purbrook Heath Rd. Water
. . . . .4G 200
Purbrook Rd. Ports. 2F 240
Purbrook Rd. T'ley. 5G 11
Purbrook Way. Pur & Hav
. . . . .5N 201
Purcell Clo. Bas 1A 60
Purcell Clo. Water 4M 201
Purcell Rd. Sotn. 7H 175
Purchase Rd. Poole 7F 226
Purewell. 8A 230
Purewell. Christ 8N 229
Purewell Clo. Christ 8A 230
Purewell Ct. Christ 7A 230
Purewell Cross. Christ 8A 230
Purewell Cross Rd. Christ
. . . . .7M 229
Purewell M. Christ 8N 229
Purkess Clo. Chan F 5B 132
Purkiss Clo. W'lnds 5C 170
Purley Way. Frim 4N 29
Purley Way. Plait 9M 121
Purlieu Dri. Dib P 7J 193
Purmerend Clo. Farn 7E 28
Purrocks, The. Ptsfld. 8M 139
Purser's La. Bramd. 2E 136
Purslane Gdns. Fare. 6H 197
Purvis Clo. Ame 5A 66
Purvis Gdns. Sotn 8F 174
Pussex La. Hurn. 7D 218

Putmans La.—Redcar St.

Putmans La. *W Har* 6E **146**
Puttenham Rd. *Chine* 9H **23**
Puttock Clo. *Hasl.* 1M **117**
Pycroft Clo. *Hay I* 5J **217**
Pycroft Clo. *Sotn* 5E **174**
Pye La. *Cran* 6M **149**
Pyestock **2D 48**
Pyestock Cres. *Farn* 8E **28**
Pye St. *Ports.* 1D **240** (2N **5**)
Pyland's La. *Burs.* 7M **175**
Pyle Clo. *Water.* 6A **182**
Pyle La. *Horn* 5E **182**
Pylewell Rd. *Hythe.* 4M **193**
Pyotts Copse. *Old B* 2H **43**
Pyotts Ct. *Old B* 2H **43**
Pyott's Hill. **3H 43**
Pyott's Hill. *Old B* 2H **43**
Pyramid Cen. *Ports.* 5J **215**
Pyramids Leisure Cen., The. 6E 240
Pyrford Clo. *Gos* 4G **239**
Pyrford Clo. *Water.* 8M **181**
Pyrford Gdns. *L'ton* 4E **234**
Pyrford M. *L'ton* 4E **234**
Pytchley Clo. *Fare.* 6K **211**

Q

Quadrangle, The. *Eastl* 8E **132**
Quadrangle, The. *Roms* 6C **130**
Quadrant. *F'bri* 2J **153**
Quail Way. *Water* 4A **182**
Quaker Ct. *Ring.* 2J **187**
Quantock Clo. *Bas* 8K **41**
Quantock Rd. *Sotn* 2D **172**
Quantocks, The. *Dib P* 7J **193**
Quarely Rd. *Hav* 3C **202**
Quarley **2L 67**
Quarr Ho. *Sway.* 4J **223**
Quarry La. *Yate.* 8A **18**
Quarry Rd. *Redl* 2N **119**
Quarry Rd. *Win* 7M **105**
Quarterdeck Av. *Ports.* 7C **214**
Quarters Rd. *Farn.* 1K **49**
Quartremaine Rd. *Ports* 5J **215**
Quartremaine Rd. Ind. Est. *Ports* 6J **215**
Quay Haven. *Swanw.* 2A **196**
Quay Hill. *L'ton* 2F **234**
Quay La. *Gos* 7K **213**
Quay La. *H'way* 3N **239**
Quay La. *Lwr S.* 2A **196**
Quayle Dri. *Bourn.* 1D **226**
Quay Rd. *Christ* 8L **229**
Quay Rd. *L'ton* 2F **234**
Quayside. *Bot.* 4D **176**
Quay Side Commerce Cen. *Fare* 9D **198**
Quayside Rd. *Fawl* 7K **209**
Quayside Rd. *Sotn* 3A **174**
Quayside Wlk. *March* 7E **172**
Quays Swimming Complex, The. 7L 173
Quay St. *Fare* 9E **198** (in two parts)
Quay St. *L'ton* 2F **234**
Quay, The. *Christ.* 9M **229**
Quay, The. *Hamb* 7L **195**
Quebec **5E 146**
Quebec Gdns. *B'wtr* 9F **18**
Quebec Gdns. Bulf B *3B* ***66*** *(off Vimy Cres.)*
Quebec Gdns. *Burs.* 9K **175**
Queen Alexandra's Royal Army Nursing 9F 48
Queen Anne's Dri. *Hav* 7C **202**
Queen Anne's Ga. *F'ham.* 3F **64**
Queen Anne's Wlk. *Bas.* 6C **42**
Queen Elizabeth Av. *L'ton* 2D **234**
Queen Elizabeth Country Pk. & Info. Cen. 2F 168
Queen Elizabeth Ct. *Sotn* 8A **160**
Queen Elizabeth Dri. *A'sht* 9H **49**
Queen Elizabeth Rd. *Cam* 4M **19**
Queen Katherine Rd. *L'ton* 3F **234**
Queen Mary Av. *Bas* 5C **42**
Queen Mary Av. *Bourn* 4K **227**
Queen Mary Av. *Cam* 8J **19**
Queen Mary Clo. *Fle* 9L **27**
Queen Mary Rd. *Fare.* 1M **213**
Queen Rd. *Fare.* 2B **212**
Queen's Av. *A'sht.* 8J **49**
Queens Av. *And.* 1M **69**
Queens Av. *Christ.* 9L **229**
Queens Bldgs. *Sotn* 6M **173** (6E **4**)
Queensbury Mans. *Bourn* 2L **245** (7N **247**)
Queensbury Pl. *B'wtr* 1E **28**
Queens Clo. *Farn* 3K **49**
Queens Clo. *Hythe* 6N **193**
Queens Clo. *Lee S* 1A **238**
Queens Clo. *Lud.* 1D **30**
Queen's Clo. *Roms.* 5N **129**
Queens Ct. *Bourn* 6M **227**
Queen's Ct. *Bourn* 5G **247**
Queen's Ct. *Farn* 3L **49**
Queens Ct. *Gos.* 3L **239**
Queens Ct. *New M* 3E **232**
Queen's Ct. *Sotn* 5K **173** (3A **4**)
Queens Cres. *Fare* 5N **211**
Queens Cres. *Horn.* 3B **182**
Queen's Cres. *S'sea* 4D **240** (8N **5**)
Queensdale Ct. Bas. *8B* ***42*** *(off Pittard Rd.)*
Queensfield. *Dum* 9F **58**
Queens Gdns. *Bourn* 1H **245** (5G **247**)
Queens Gdns. *F'bri* 9J **151**
Queens Ga. *S'sea.* 9M **5**
Queen's Ga. Rd. *Farn* 3K **49**
Queens Gro. *New M.* 2D **232**
Queen's Gro. *S'sea.* 5D **240**
Queens Gro. *Water.* 4L **201**
Queens Ho. *Sotn* 7M **173** (7D **4**)
Queens Keep. *S'sea* 5D **240**
Queensland Rd. *Bourn.* 9D **228**
Queens La. *F'ham.* 3E **64**
Queen's Mall, The. *Ports* 2D **240** (4N **5**)
Queensmead. *Farn* 8K **29**
Queens Mead. *Win.* 8G **104**
Queensmount. *Bourn.* 7N **227**
Queen's Pde. *Bas* 6C **42**
Queen's Pde. *Gos.* 3G **239**
Queen's Pde. *Lyn* 2B **148**
Queen's Pde. *Water* 2M **201**
Queen's Pde. Path. *A'sht.* 5K **49**
Queen's Pk. Av. *Bourn.* 6M **227**
Queens Pk. Gdns. *Bourn* 7N **227**
Queens Pk. Golf Course. 6B 228
Queens Pk. Rd. *Bourn* 7A **228**
Queens Pk. S. Dri. *Bourn* 7A **228**
Queens Pk. W. Dri. *Bourn* 7N **227**
Queen's Pl. *S'sea* 4D **240**
Queens Ride. *N Bad* 8D **130**
Queen's Rd. *A'sht* 1H **65**
Queen's Rd. *Alt.* 5E **80**
Queen's Rd. *Bas.* 6A **42**
Queens Rd. *Bourn* 2H **245** (6G **247**)
Queens Rd. *Cam.* 9K **19**
Queens Rd. *Chan F.* 3B **132**
Queen's Rd. *Christ* 8A **230**
Queen's Rd. *Cowes* 5N **237**
Queen's Rd. *Fare* 8D **198**
Queen's Rd. *Farn* 3L **49**
Queens Rd. *F'ham* 4E **64**
Queen's Rd. *Fle* 4M **47**
Queen's Rd. *Gos.* 2L **239**
Queen's Rd. *Navy* 1A **240** (1H **5**)
Queens Rd. *K're* 3C **6**
Queens Rd. *Lee S.* 3B **238**
Queens Rd. *Lip* 3M **115**
Queens Rd. *Lyn* 2C **148**
Queens Rd. *N War* 8J **45**
Queens Rd. *Ptsfld.* 9K **139**
Queens Rd. *Poole.* 1B **244**
Queen's Rd. *Ports.* 8F **214**
Queen's Rd. *Sotn* 9H **159**
Queens Rd. *Wars* 9N **195**
Queen's Rd. *Water.* 8M **181**
Queens Rd. *Whitc* 7H **55**
Queen's Rd. *Win.* 7H **105**
Queen's Roundabout. *Farn* 4K **49**
Queens Ter. *Sotn* 7M **173** (8E **4**)
Queen's Ter. *S'sea* 4D **240** (8N **5**)
Queenstown Rd. *Sotn.* 4J **173**
Queen St. *A'sht* 9M **49**
Queen St. *Ems* 9N **203**
Queen St. *Hale* 1B **154**
Queen St. *L'ton.* 3D **234**
Queen St. *Ports* 2B **240** (3J **5**)
Queen St. *Twy* 7K **127**
Queens Vw. *Net A* 3F **194**
Queensway. *And.* 8C **52**
Queensway. *Hay I.* 5G **216**
Queensway. *New M* 3N **231**
Queens Way. *Ring* 1L **187**
Queen's Way. *Sotn* 7M **173** (8D **4**)
Queen's Way. *S'sea* 4D **240** (8N **5**)
Queensway, The. *Fare.* 9K **199**
Queenswood Av. *Bourn* 5B **228**
Queen Victoria Ct. *Farn.* 7K **29**
Queen Victoria's Wlk. *Coll T* 7H **19**
Queenwood Ri. *Bro'tn* 2A **86**
Queenwood Rd. *Bro'tn* 2A **86**
Querida Clo. *Lwr S.* 1A **196**
Quetta Pk. *Chu C* 9N **47**
Quidhampton **1E 56**
Quilter Clo. *Sotn.* 6H **175**
Quilter Rd. *Bas* 1L **59**
Quince Tree Way. *Hook* 2H **45**
Quinney's. *Farn.* 2L **49**
Quintin Clo. *Christ* 6H **231**
Quinton Clo. *S'sea* 3E **240**
Quintrell Av. *Fare.* 9J **199**
Quob Farm Clo. *W End* 8J **161**
Quob La. *W End* 7J **161**
Quomp. *Ring* 1K **187**

R

Racecourse La. *Ports* 9C **200**
Racecourse Vw. *Lyn.* 1B **148**
Racedown **2K 67**
Rachel Clo. *Eastl* 1M **161**
Rack Clo. *And.* 1A **70**
Rack Clo. Rd. *Alt* 5E **80**
Rackfield. *Hasl.* 8M **103**
Rackstraw Rd. *S'hrst* 4E **18**
Racton Av. *Ports.* 9J **201**
Racton Rd. *Ems.* 6M **203**
Radcliffe Ct. *Sotn* 4N **173**
Radcliffe Rd. *Sotn* 5N **173**
Radclyffe Rd. *Fare* 7E **198**
Radford Clo. *F'ham* 5G **64**
Radford Gdns. *Bas.* 9A **42**
Radleigh Gdns. *Tot.* 2H **171**
Radley Clo. *H End* 1N **175**
Radnor St. *S'sea.* 3D **240**
Radstock Rd. *Sotn.* 7B **174**
Radway Cres. *Sotn* 2J **173**
Radway Rd. *Sotn* 2J **173**
Raebarn Clo. *Cher.* 9F **108**
Raeburn Dri. *H End* 3N **175**
Raeburn Way. *Coll T.* 7F **18**
Rafborough **9H 29**
Rafborough Footpath. *Farn* 9J **29**
Ragged Appleshaw **4C 50**
Raghill. *A'mstn* 1K **11**
Raglan Clo. *A'sht.* 1L **65**
Raglan Clo. *Chan F.* 8L **131**
Raglan Ct. *Bas* 2L **59**
Raglan Ct. *Eastl* 6E **132**
Raglan Ct. *Park G.* 4D **196**
Raglan Gdns. *Bourn* 4E **226**
Raglan St. *S'sea* 2E **240**
Ragmore La. *Frox.* 9D **112**
Rails La. *Hay I* 4H **243**
Railway Cotts. *Bas* 7H **41**
Railway Cotts. *Bord* 2F **100**
Railway Cotts. *Old B.* 5G **43**
Railway Cotts. *Sotn* 2B **172** (in two parts)
Railway Flats. *Ports* 2F **240**
Railway Rd. *Lngmr.* 3J **115**
Railway Ter. *Hint* 4G **230**
Railway Triangle Ind. Est. *Cosh* 2J **215**
Railway Vw. *Ports.* 2E **240**
Railway Vw. Rd. *Sotn.* 2A **174**
Rainbow Clo. *Old B* 6K **43**
Rainbow Pl. *Sotn* 4H **173**
Rainham Clo. *Bas.* 3H **59**
Rake **1K 141**
Rake Bus. Pk. *Rake* 1K **141**
Rake Industries. *Rog* 3M **141**
Rakemakers. *Holyb.* 1K **81**
Rake Rd. *Liss* 1E **140**
Raleigh Clo. *Christ* 9B **230**
Raleigh Clo. *New M* 3A **232**
Raleigh Clo. *Ring.* 9M **185**
Raleigh Ho. *Ports* 4K **5**
Raleigh Rd. *Poole.* 4C **226**
Raleigh Wlk. *Gos* 1F **238**
Raleigh Way. *Frim* 1N **29**
Raley Rd. *L Hth* 7D **196**
Ralph Jessop Ct. *Poole* 7C **226**
Ralph La. *Roms* 3N **129**
Ramalley **4N 131**
Ramalley La. *Chan F.* 4N **131** (in two parts)
Rambler Dri. *Gos* 1E **238**
Ramblers Way. *Water.* 9B **182**
Ramillies Clo. *A'sht.* 4N **49**
Ramillies Ho. *Fare* 1A **212**
Ramillies Ho. Gos. *3L* ***239*** *(off Anchorage, The)*
Ramillies Park **5M 49**
Ramley Rd. *Penn* 9N **223**
Rampart Gdns. *Ports* 3G **214**
Rampart Rd. *Sotn.* 3B **174**
Rampart Row. *Gos.* 4N **239** (in two parts)
Ramparts, The. *And* 3L **69**
Rampart, The. *L'ton.* 1D **234**
Rampton Rd. *Whitc* 6H **55**
Ramptons Mdw. *T'ley.* 6K **11**
Ramsay Pl. *Gos* 6E **212**
Ramsay Rd. *King W.* 8N **91**
Ramsdale Av. *Hav.* 4C **202**
Ramsdean **3D 144**
Ramsdean Rd. *Ptsfld* 3D **144**
Ramsdell **5F 20**
Ramsdell Clo. *T'ley.* 6H **11**
Ramsdell Rd. *Elve.* 8J **27**
Ramsdell Rd. *P End* 2K **21**
Ramsdell Rd. *Wolv.* 6N **9**
Ramsey Ct. *Christ.* 8J **229**
Ramsey Rd. *Hay I* 4G **242**
Ramshill. *Ptsfld* 9M **139**
Ramshot Clo. *N Wal.* 8A **58**
Rams Wlk. *Ptsfld.* 1M **145**
Rances Way. *Win* 9J **105**
Randall Clo. *Cal.* 9J **157**
Randall Rd. *Chan F.* 2B **132**
Randalls La. *Burl* 6C **188**
Randell Clo. *B'wtr.* 3G **29**
Randell Ho. *B'wtr* 3G **29**
Randolph Dri. *Farn* 9E **28**
Randolph Rd. *Bourn.* 1B **246**
Randolph Rd. *Poole* 9A **226**
Randolph Rd. *Ports* 5F **214**
Randolph St. *Sotn* 3H **173** (in two parts)
Ranelagh Gdns. *Sotn* 3K **173**
Ranelagh Rd. *Hav.* 8D **202**
Ranelagh Rd. *Highc* 7H **231**
Ranelagh Rd. *Ports* 7D **214**
Ranelagh Rd. *Win.* 8K **105**
Ranfurly Gdns. *Dib P* 8K **193**
Range Gdns. *Sotn.* 7F **174**
Range Grn. *Ports* 5D **214**
Range Ride. *Cam* 6H **19**
Range Vw. *Coll T* 5G **19**
Rankine Clo. *Bad L* 4J **65**
Rankine Rd. *Bas* 4E **42**
Rank, The. *St M* 9K **35**
Rank, The. *W'hll.* 8D **50**
Ranmore Ct. Dib. *6H* ***193*** *(off Hawkhill)*
Rannoch Clo. *Fare* 6A **198**
Ransome Clo. *Fare* 1J **211**
Ranvilles La. *Fare* 9L **197**
Rapallo Clo. *Farn* 8L **29**
Raphael Clo. *Bas.* 8E **42**
Rapley Clo. *Cam.* 5N **19**
Rapson Clo. *Ports* 8D **200**
Rareridge La. *Bish W* 3N **163**
Rashleigh Ct. *Chu C* 7N **47**
Rashmere Ga. *Hmbdn* 9D **166**
Rassett Mead. *Chu C* 8K **47**
Ratcliffe Rd. *Dib P* 8L **193**
Ratcliffe Rd. *Farn* 4H **29**
Ratcliffe Rd. *H End.* 3N **175**
Ratlake **9L 125**
Ratlake La. *Win.* 9L **125**
Ratsey La. *Ports* 1F **240**
Rattigan Gdns. *White* 1F **196**
Ravel Clo. *Bas* 1N **59**
Ravelin Clo. *Cron* 3L **63**
Ravelin Ho. *Ports* 3C **240** (6M **5**)
Raven Clo. *Gos.* 1E **238**
Raven Clo. *Tidw* 8D **30**
Raven Clo. *Yate.* 7L **17**
Raven Cft. *S'sea* 4D **240** (7N **5**)
Raven Rd. *Hook* 2G **45**
Raven Rd. *Sotn* 4N **173** (2F **4**)
Ravens Clo. *Fare* 6N **211**
Ravenscourt Rd. *Bourn.* 9F **228**
Ravenscourt Rd. *L'ton* 3D **234**
Ravenscroft. *Hook* 1H **45**
Ravenscroft Clo. *Burs.* 9K **175**
Ravenscroft Way. *Bot.* 1C **176**
Ravensdale Clo. *Poole* 8A **226**
Ravensdale Cotts. *B'shtt C* 7L **103**
Ravenshall. *Bourn* 3H **245** (9G **247**)
Raven Sq. *Alt* 2F **80** (in two parts)
Raven Sq. *Eastl* 1B **160**
Ravens Way. *Mil S* 8K **235**
Ravenswood. *Fare.* 6F **196**
Ravenswood Av. *C'then* 1A **18**
Ravenswood Gdns. *S'sea* 5E **240**
Raven Way. *Christ* 9C **230**
Ravine Rd. *Bourn* 1E **246**
Ravine Rd. *Poole* 5D **244**
Rawlings Rd. *Hook.* 3H **45**
Rawlinson Rd. *Bulf B* 3B **66**
Rawlinson Rd. *Cam* 7H **19**
Rawlinson Ter. *Ports* 1B **240** (2K **5**)
Rayleigh Cres. *Ame* 5A **66**
Rayleigh Rd. *Bas* 6B **42**
Raymond Clo. *Holb* 5B **208**
Raymond Clo. *W End.* 8K **161**
Raymond Rd. *Ports* 8N **199**
Raymond Rd. *Sotn* 2J **173**
Rayners Dri. *Poole* 9B **226**
Rayners Gdns. *Sotn* 7B **160**
Raynes Rd. *Lee S.* 3B **238**
Rayngolds. *Chu C.* 8K **47**
Rays Clo. *T'ley* 5J **11**
Reading Rd. *Chine* 3E **42** (in two parts)
Reading Rd. *E'sly* 5E **16**
Reading Rd. *Farn* 2L **49**
Reading Rd. *Finch* 1B **16**
Reading Rd. *Hnd G & Roth* 1J **25**
Reading Rd. *Roth & Hook* 8H **25**
Reading Rd. *Sher L* 4L **23**
Reading Rd. *Yate & B'wtr* 6L **17**
Reading Rd. N. *Brams* 9A **16**
Reading Rd. N. *Fle* 1J **47**
Reading Rd. Roundabout. *Bas* 3E **42**
Reading Rd. S. *Fle & Chu C* 3L **47**
Reading Room La. *Curd.* 2G **176**
Readon Clo. *Ptsfld* 9N **139**
Read's Fld. *Four M* 5J **97**
Rebbeck Rd. *Bourn* 8D **228**
Rebecca Clo. *Chu C* 8K **47**
Recess, The. *Eastl.* 7F **132**
Record Rd. *Ems* 8L **203**
Recreation Clo. *Farn.* 3H **29**
Recreation Flats. *W Wel.* 1B **120**
Recreation Rd. *And* 1A **70**
Recreation Rd. *Lud* 1D **30**
Recreation Rd. *Odi* 9K **45**
Recreation Rd. *Poole* 8B **226**
Recreation Rd. *Row.* 8N **63**
Rectory Av. *Ports* 8N **201**
Rectory Clo. *Fare.* 5M **211**
Rectory Clo. *Gos.* 5J **239**
Rectory Clo. *S'hrst* 5B **18**
Rectory Clo. *T'ley* 7J **11**
Rectory Ct. *Bot.* 3C **176**
Rectory Hill. *W Dean.* 1J **121**
Rectory Hill. *W Tyth* 7L **87**
Rectory La. *Bent.* 7K **63**
Rectory La. *B'shtt.* 8E **102**
Rectory La. *Brea.* 2L **151**
Rectory La. *Bro'tn* 1A **86**
Rectory La. *It Ab* 7K **93**
Rectory La. *Meon.* 8N **135**
Rectory La. *Wolv* 7M **9**
Rectory Pl. *W'hll* 8D **50**
Rectory Rd. *Farn* 8L **29**
Rectory Rd. *Hav* 9F **202** (in two parts)
Rectory Rd. *Hook.* 3G **44**
Rectory Rd. *Okly* 9A **40**
Reculver Way. *Charl* 7K **51**
Redan Clo. *Highc.* 7H **231**
Redan Gdns. *A'sht* 9L **49**
Redan Hill **9M 49**
Redan Hill Ind. Est. *A'sht* 9L **49**
Redan Rd. *A'sht* 9L **49**
Redan, The. *Gos.* 6L **239**
Red Barn Av. *Fare* 8L **199**
Red Barn La. *Fare.* 5A **198**
Redbreast Rd. *Bourn* 3L **227**
Redbreast Rd. N. *Bourn* 3L **227**
Redbridge Causeway. *Sotn* 2A **172**
Redbridge Dri. *And* 2M **69**
Redbridge Flyover. *Sotn* 2B **172**
Redbridge Gro. *Hav* 6D **202**
Redbridge Hill. *Sotn* 1E **172**
Redbridge La. *Old B* 6F **42**
Redbridge La. *Ropl* 2H **111**
Redbridge La. *Sotn & Nurs* 9B **158**
Redbridge Rd. *Sotn* 2B **172**
Redbridge Towers. *Sotn* 2B **172**
Redbrook **3K 153**
Redbrook Cotts. *F'bri* 3K **153**
Redcar Av. *Ports* 7H **215**
Redcar St. *Sotn* 2G **173**

Redcliffe Clo. Burt 4M 229
Redcliffe Gdns. S'sea 6F 240
Redcote Clo. Sotn 3F 174
Redcourt. Sotn 7L 159
Redcrest Gdns. Cam 8N 19
Redcroft La. Burs 9L 175
Rede Ct. Farn 2L 49
Redenham 2A 50
Redenham Drove. R'hm 2A 50
Redfields La. Chu C 1M 63
Redfields Pk. Chu C 8L 47
Redfords, The. Tot 1L 171
Redhearn Fields. Churt 6G 85
Redhearn Grn. Churt 6G 85
Red Hill. 8H 49
(Aldershot)
Red Hill. 2K 227
(Bournemouth)
Red Hill. 1N 7
(Newbury)
Red Hill.. . . . . 8J 183
(Rowlands Castle)
Red Hill. Haz H 2L 25
Red Hill. Meds 3J 97
Redhill. Sotn. 7K 159
Redhill Av. Bourn 4J 227
Redhill Clo. Bourn. 3J 227
Redhill Clo. Sotn. 7K 159
Redhill Ct. Bourn 2K 227
Redhill Cres. Bourn 3K 227
Redhill Cres. Sotn. 7K 159
Redhill Dri. Bourn. 4J 227
Redhill Ho. Ports 1E 240
Redhill Pk. Homes. Bourn
. . . . 1K 227
Redhill Rd. Row C 1H 203
Redhill Roundabout. Bourn
. . . . 2K 227
Redhill Way. Sotn. 7K 159
Red Ho. Cvn. Site. W'hill
. . . . 4F 100
Red Ho. Ct. Rog 9L 141
Redhouse M. Lip 4E 116
Red House Mus. 8L 229
Redhouse Pk. Gdns. Gos
. . . . 1G 239
Redlands. 2M 63
Redlands. Poole 9D 226
Redlands Dri. Sotn. 4D 174
Redlands Gro. S'sea 3K 241
Redlands La. Cron & Ews
. . . . 2L 63
Redlands La. Ems 5M 203
(in two parts)
Redlands La. Fare. 8B 198
Red La. A'mstn. 1K 11
Red La. Ellis 3J 79
Red La. Head 9D 84
Red La. Uphm 6C 134
Red La. W Tyth. 8K 87
Red La. W'slw 4H 87
Red Leaves. Wal C 9A 164
Red Lion La. Bas 7C 42
Red Lion La. F'ham 9D 64
Red Lion La. Over 2D 56
Red Lodge. Chan F. 9N 131
Redlynch. 1N 119
Redlynch Clo. Hav 5H 203
Redmoor Clo. Sotn. 4D 174
Rednal Ho. S'sea. 2E 240
Red Oaks. Row. 8N 63
Red Oaks Dri. Park G 4F 196
Redon Way. And. 8L 51
Redoubt Ct. Fare. 2B 212
Red Post La. And 2F 68
Red Post La. W'hll 9D 50
Redrice. 8H 69
Red Rice Rd. Up Cl 8H 69
Redrise Clo. Holb 5N 207
Redshank Rd. Water. 3A 182
Redvers Buller Rd. A'sht. . . . 4L 49
Redvers Clo. L'ton 4E 234
Redvers Rd. Christ 7A 230
Redward Rd. Rown. 6E 158
Redwing Ct. S'sea. 2K 241
Redwing Gdns. Tot 2J 171
Redwing Rd. Bas 3H 59
Redwing Rd. Water 7C 168
Redwood. Chine 8F 22
Redwood Clo. Dib P. 6H 193
Redwood Clo. L'ton 1C 234
Redwood Clo. Ring. 1L 187
Redwood Clo. W End. 9G 161
Redwood Ct. Water 1M 201
Redwood Dri. Fare 9K 199
Redwood Gdns. Tot 4J 171
Redwood Gro. Hav. 5G 202
Redwood La. Meds. 9L 79
Redwood Lodge. Fare 7D 198
Redwoods Way. Chu C. 6N 47
Redwood Way. Sotn 5M 159
Reed Clo. A'sht 5M 49
Reed Dri. March 8E 172
Reedling Dri. S'sea. 2K 241
Reedmace Clo. Water. 3A 202
Reeds La. Liss 8J 115
Reed's Pl. Gos. 2J 239
Reeds Rd. Gos 9K 213
Rees Rd. Wor D 5G 90
Reeves Clo. W Wel. 1B 120
Reeves Rd. A'sht. 1L 65
Reeves Way. Burs. 9K 175
Regal Clo. Ports 9G 201
Regency Ct. Ports
. . . . 3B 240 (6J 5)
Regency Cres. Christ 6J 229
Regency Gdns. Water. 3L 201
Regency Pl. Fare. 8A 198
Regency Pl. Ring 9K 185
Regent Clo. Fle 3M 47
Regent Clo. Ott. 9G 127
Regent Ct. Bas 5D 42
Regent Ct. Ports 9E 214
Regent Ct. Sotn. 1M 173
Regent Ct. Win 4L 105
(off Northlands Dri.)
Regent Dri. Bourn. 6C 228
Regent Ho. H End. 8N 161
Regent Pl. S'sea . . . 4C 240 (8M 5)
Regent Rd. Chan F 6B 132
Regents Ct. And 9D 52
Regents Ct. Hav 9F 202
Regents Ct. Sotn 2G 172
Regents Ga. Sar G 4B 196
Regents Gro. Sotn 1G 173
Regents M. Ptsfld. 9K 139
Regent's Pk. Gdns. Sotn
. . . . 3G 172
Regent's Pk. Rd. Sotn. 4F 172
Regents Pl. S'hrst 5E 18
Regent St. Fle 3M 47
Regent St. Ports. 9D 214
Regent St. Sotn 6L 173 (5C 4)
Regent Way. Christ. 8L 229
Regiment Clo. Farn. 9E 28
Reginald Mitchell Ct. Eastl
. . . . 8D 132
Reginald Rd. S'sea. 4H 241
Reid St. Christ 7K 229
Reigate Ho. Ports 1E 240
Reith Way. And. 9H 51
Relay Rd. Water 1L 201
Reldas, The. Ports
. . . . 4B 240 (7J 5)
(off Oyster St.)
Reliant Clo. Chan F. 7N 131
Rembrandt Clo. Bas 8E 42
Remembrance Gdns. Chine
. . . . 1F 42
Renda Rd. Holb 4A 208
Renny Rd. Ports 2F 240
Renoir Clo. Bas. 8E 42
Renouf Clo. Penn 3C 234
Renown Clo. Chan F. 7N 131
Renown Gdns. Water. 5N 181
Renown Ho. Gos. 3L 239
(off Anchorage, The)
Renown Way. Chine 8G 22
Repton Clo. Gos. 3G 238
Repton Gdns. H End. 9A 162
(in two parts)
Reservoir La. H End 4L 175
Reservoir La. Ptsfld. 7M 139
Resolution Ho. Gos. 3L 239
(off Anchorage, The)
Rest-a-Wyle Av. Hay I 2G 243
Restharrow. Bourn 1L 245
Reston Roundhill. 9J 113
Restormel Clo. Bas. 5K 41
Retreat, The. Eastl. 8F 132
Retreat, The. Fle. 5K 47
Retreat, The. S'sea 4D 240
Retreat, The. Tot. 5N 171
Reubens Cres. T'ley 6H 11
Revelstoke Av. Farn 7K 29
Revenge Clo. S'sea. 1K 241
Revenge Ho. Gos 3L 239
Rewlands Dri. Win 3G 105
Rex Est. Chan F 7B 132
Reynards Clo. T'ley 5H 11
Reynolds Clo. Bas. 7F 42
Reynolds Ct. And. 8M 51
Reynolds Ct. Roms 6N 129
Reynolds Dale. Asht. 5K 171
Reynolds Grn. Coll T. 7F 18
Reynolds Ho. Bas. 9L 41
Reynolds Rd. F Oak 2A 162
Reynolds Rd. Gos. 5L 239
Reynolds Rd. Sotn. 2H 173
Reyntiens Vw. Odi 9L 45
Rhine Banks. Farn. 7F 28
Rhinefield Arboretum. 6K 189
Rhinefield Clo. Broc 6B 148
Rhinefield Clo. Eastl 1K 161
Rhinefield Clo. Hav. 5C 202
Rhinefield Ornamental Drive.
. . . . 5K 189
Rhinefield Rd. Broc 6K 189
Rhinefield Rd. New M 5N 221
Rhiners Clo. Sway. 4J 223
Rhodes Sq. And 7B 52
Rhyme Hall M. Fawl 5F 208
Rhys Ct. S'sea 3H 241
Ribble Clo. Chan F 7B 132
Ribble Ct. Sotn. 1D 172
Ribble Pl. Farn 6G 28
Ribble Way. Bas 6E 42
Ricardo Cres. Christ 8C 230
Richard Clo. Fle 4K 47
Richard Gro. Gos 7J 213
Richard Moss Ho. Win
. . . . 6M 237
Richards Clo. Black 6D 208
Richards Clo. L Hth 6D 196
Richards Ct. Sotn. 1G 172
Richards Ct. W End 9G 160
Richard Taunton Pl. Sotn
. . . . 9M 159
Richborough Dri. Charl. 7J 51
Richlans Rd. H End 4N 175
Richmond Clo. Cal 1H 171
Richmond Clo. Chan F 3A 132
Richmond Clo. Farn 9F 28
Richmond Clo. Fle 5L 47
Richmond Clo. Hay I 3D 242
Richmond Clo. W'hill 5J 101
Richmond Ct. Bourn. 7N 227
Richmond Ct. Mil S. 8J 235
Richmond Ct. New M 3B 232
Richmond Dri. Hay I. 3D 242
Richmond Gdns. Bourn
. . . . 2K 245 (6L 247)
Richmond Gdns. Sotn 1N 173
Richmond Hill. Bourn
. . . . 2K 245 (7L 247)
Richmond Hill Dri. Bourn
. . . . 2K 245 (6L 247)
Richmond Ho. Bourn
. . . . 2K 245 (6L 247)
Richmond Ho. Ports. 4L 5
Richmond Ho. S'hrst 6G 19
Richmond La. Roms 3N 129
Richmond Pk. Ott. 9H 127
Richmond Pk. Av. Bourn
. . . . 7M 227
Richmond Pk. Clo. Bourn
. . . . 8A 228
Richmond Pk. Cres. Bourn
. . . . 7N 227
Richmond Pk. Rd. Bourn
. . . . 7M 227
Richmond Pl. Ports
. . . . 2C 240 (4L 5)
Richmond Pl. S'sea 5D 240
Richmond Ri. Fare 8L 199
Richmond Rd. Bas 5B 42
Richmond Rd. Coll T 5G 19
Richmond Rd. Gos 3J 239
Richmond Rd. Lee S 9N 211
Richmond Rd. Poole 9A 226
Richmond Rd. Sotn 4H 173
Richmond Rd. S'sea. 5E 240
Richmond St. Sotn
. . . . 7M 173 (7E 4)
Richmond Ter. S'sea. 9N 5
Richmond Wood Rd. Bourn
. . . . 7M 227
Richville Rd. Sotn. 2F 172
Rickett La. Roth 4D 24
Ridding Clo. Sotn. 1G 173
Riddings La. H'ly 2M 9
Riders La. Hav 5E 202
(in two parts)
Rideway Clo. Cam 9K 19
Ridge. 2J 157
Ridge Clo. Hat W 5L 59
Ridge Clo. Water 7C 168
Ridge Common. 7J 139
Ridge Comn. La. Strd & Steep
. . . . 8H 139
Ridgefield Gdns. Christ. . . . 6F 230
Ridge La. Bot 7G 176
Ridge La. Newn & Roth 2D 44
Ridge La. Roms 2H 157
Ridgemoor Clo. Hind 2N 103
Ridgemount Av. Sotn 6L 159
Ridgemount La. Sotn 6L 159
Ridges, The. 1K 17
Ridge, The. W'flls & Redl
. . . . 9C 120
Ridge Top La. Frox. 7D 138
Ridgeway. Win 9G 104
Ridgeway Clo. Chan F. 7C 132
Ridgeway Clo. F Oak 9N 133
Ridgeway Clo. Ports. 8A 200
Ridgeway La. L'ton. 4D 234
Ridgeway Pde. Chu C 6M 47
Ridgeway, The. Alt 6F 80
Ridgeway, The. Fare 8G 198
Ridgeway Wlk. Chan F. 7C 132
Ridgewood Clo. Dib. 5H 193
Ridgway. Hav. 8D 202
Ridings, The. Eastl 1L 161
Ridings, The. Liss 1G 140
Ridings, The. Ports 4G 214
Ridings, The. Wal C 7A 164
Ridley Clo. Fle 4L 47
Ridley Clo. Holb. 4A 208
Ridley Rd. Bourn 6K 227
Ridleys Piece. S Warn 4D 62
Ridout Clo. Bourn 5F 226
Rifle Way. Farn. 9E 28
Rigby Rd. Sotn 2N 173
Riggs Gdns. Bourn 4D 226
Riley La. Old B 4J 43
Riley Rd. Wor D 5J 91
Rimbault Clo. A'sht 4M 49
Rimbury Way. Christ 6K 229
Rimes's La. Baug 7F 10
Rimington Gdns. Roms . . . 2A 130
Rimington Rd. Water 7M 181
Ringbury. L'ton 9D 224
Ringlet Way. Win. 6N 105
Ringsgreen La. Frox 3G 139
Ringshall Gdns. Braml 1F 22
Ring, The. Chilw 4K 159
Ringway Cen., The. Bas. . . . 4N 41
Ringway E. Bas 4E 42
Ringway Ho. Bas 4E 42
Ringway N. Bas 4L 41
Ringway S. Bas 9B 42
Ringway W. Bas. 4N 41
Ringwood. 1J 187
Ringwood Dri. N Bad. 7D 130
Ringwood Ho. Hav. 4F 202
Ringwood La. Wim G 7G 148
Ringwood Recreation Cen.
. . . . 1K 187
Ringwood Rd. A'hlt 5C 152
Ringwood Rd. Avon. 7K 219
Ringwood Rd. B'wtr. 7E 18
Ringwood Rd. Brans 6C 220
(in two parts)
Ringwood Rd. Burl 6C 188
Ringwood Rd. Farn 5L 29
Ringwood Rd. Fern & St L
. . . . 7A 186
Ringwood Rd. F'bri 2K 153
Ringwood Rd. Ibly & N Gor
. . . . 9K 153
Ringwood Rd. Nea & Walk
. . . . 9E 220
Ringwood Rd. N Gor 6M 153
Ringwood Rd. Poole & Bourn
. . . . 6A 226
Ringwood Rd. S'sea. 4J 241
Ringwood Rd. Ston C 8K 155
Ringwood Rd. Tot 4D 170
Ringwood Rd. Ver 4A 184
Ringwood Rd. Retail Pk. Bourn
. . . . 3C 226
Ringwood Rd. Service Rd. Ashy H
. . . . 5C 186
Ringwood Trad. Est. Ring
. . . . 2K 187
(in two parts)
Ripley. 5M 219
Ripley Gro. Ports. 8H 215
Ripon Ct. Gos. 2F 238
Ripon Ct. H Hth 4A 162
Ripon Gdns. Water 9B 182
Ripon Rd. Bourn 6L 227
Ripplesmore Clo. S'hrst . . . 5D 18
Ripplewood. March 9F 172
Ripstone Gdns. Sotn. 8N 159
Riseley. 2G 14
Rise, The. Broc 7C 148
Rise, The. C'then 1B 18
Rise, The. Finch. 3D 16
Rise, The. Water 7L 201
Ritchie Clo. Hay I. 4G 242
Ritchie Ct. Sotn 6F 174
Ritchie Rd. Bourn. 2F 226
Rival Moor Rd. Ptsfld 1B 146
River Clo. Four M. 5J 97
River Ct. Hurn 7D 218
Riverdale Av. Water 2A 202
Riverdale Clo. F'bri. 9J 151
Riverdale La. Christ. 8K 229
Riverdene Pl. Sotn. 2B 174
River Gdns. Mil S. 8L 235
River Grn. Hamb 7L 195
Riverhead. Bish S 2L 109
Riverhead Clo. S'sea 2J 241
River La. Fare 3M 197
River La. F'ham 6N 63
Riverlea Rd. Christ. 8K 229
Rivermead. Idm 9C 66
Rivermead Clo. Roms 5K 129
Rivermead Ct. Ems 6N 203
Rivermead Gdns. Christ
. . . . 4H 229
Rivermead Ho. Roms. 5K 129
Rivermead Rd. Cam 2K 29
Rivermede. Bord 3K 101
River M. Eastl. 9H 133
River Pk. Leisure Cen.
. . . . 5L 105
River Rd. Yate. 5L 17
Rivers Clo. Farn 2N 49
Riversdale Clo. Sotn. 1C 194
Riversdale Rd. Bourn 1K 247
Riverside. Bourn. 2K 227
Riverside. Eastl 9H 133
Riverside. Good C 7N 69
Riverside. Ring. 2J 187
Riverside Av. Bourn 4E 228
Riverside Av. Fare 6F 198
Riverside Bus. Pk. F'ham . . . 7F 64
Riverside Bus. Pk. L'ton . . . 2F 234
Riverside Cvn. Pk. Hamb
. . . . 4L 195
Riverside Clo. Bart 4C 170
Riverside Clo. Farn. 7H 29
Riverside Clo. Liss 1E 140
Riverside Clo. Old B 3J 43
Riverside Clo. Over. 2E 56
Riverside Ct. F'ham 7E 64
Riverside Ct. Sotn 2B 174
Riverside Gdns. Hav. 7F 202
Riverside Gdns. Roms 6K 129
Riverside Grn. King S. 8B 86
Riverside Ho. Win 7P 237
Riverside Indoor Bowl Club.
. . . . 5L 105
Riverside Ind. Pk. F'ham. . . . 7F 64
Riverside La. Bourn 9J 229
Riverside M. Wick 7C 178
Riverside Pk. Cam 1J 29
Riverside Pk. Christ 9K 229
Riverside Pk. F'ham 7F 64
Riverside Pl. F'bri 1J 153
Riverside Rd. Bourn 9J 229
Riverside Ter. Ems 9N 203
Riverside Wlk. Ptsfld 1N 145
Riverside Way. Cam 1J 29
Riversmeet Golf Course.
. . . . 9N 229
Rivers Reach. L'ton. 3F 234
River's St. S'sea 3E 240
River Vw. Tot. 5M 171
Riverview Clo. Chlbn 4E 74
River Vw. Ho. Sotn. 7B 174
River Vw. Rd. Sotn. 9B 160
Riverview Ter. Swanw 1A 196
River Wlk. Sotn 8C 160
River Way. And. 8A 52
River Way. Christ 5G 228
River Way. Hav. 6G 202
Riverwey Ind. Est. Alt. 4H 81
Rives Av. Yate. 8K 17
Riviera. Bourn 2M 245
Riviera Ct. Bourn
. . . . 2H 245 (6H 247)
Riviera Ct. Poole 6D 244
R. J. Mitchell Cen., The. Sotn
. . . . 6A 174
R. L. Stevenson Av. Bourn
. . . . 2F 244
Roads Hill. Water. 1N 181
Road Vw. Ports 8D 214
Robard Ho. Burs 9K 175
Robere Ho. Sotn. 7C 174
Robert Cecil Av. Sotn 7C 160
Robert Ho. Roms 4M 129
Robert Mack Ct. Ports
. . . . 2C 240 (4K 5)
Robert Mays Rd. Odi 9J 45
Roberts Clo. Evtn 5M 233
Roberts Clo. King W 6M 91
Roberts Clo. Wick 6C 178
Robertshaw Ho. Lyn. 1B 148
Robertson Rd. Alr. 2E 108
Roberts Rd. A'sht 1L 65
Roberts Rd. Bar S 5A 76
Roberts Rd. Bourn. 8D 228
Roberts Rd. Cam 7J 19
Roberts Rd. Gos 1H 239
Roberts Rd. Hythe 5L 193
Roberts Rd. Lngmr 4H 115
Roberts Rd. Lud. 2C 30
Roberts Rd. Sotn 5J 173
Roberts Rd. Tot. 4M 171
Robert Whitworth Dri. Roms
. . . . 3M 129
Robina Clo. Water 2A 202
Robin Clo. Alt. 2G 80
Robin Clo. Bas 2J 59
Robin Cres. New M 1M 231
Robin Gdns. Tot 2J 171

Robin Gdns.—Royal Ct.

Robin Gdns. *Water* 6L **181**
Robin Gro. *New M* 4A **232**
Robin Hood Clo. *Farn* 5J **29**
Robinia Grn. *Sotn.* 6H **159**
Robin La. *Bish G* 1G **9**
Robin La. *S'hrst* 5D **18**
Robin's Bow. *Cam* 9K **19**
Robins Clo. *Fare* 5M **211**
Robins Gro. Cres. *Yate* 7L **17**
Robin's Mdw. *Fare* 8F **196**
Robinson Ct. *Fare* 8L **199**
Robinson Rd. *Fare* 7L **211**
Robinson Way. *Bord.* 5K **101**
Robinson Way. *Ports* 6K **215**
Robin Sq. *Eastl.* 1A **160**
Robins Way. *Christ.* 9D **230**
Robin Way. *And* 8A **52**
Robsall Clo. *Poole* 7C **226**
Roche Court & Art Sculpture Pk. 3J 87
Rocheford Clo. *W'slw.* 4H **87**
Rochester Clo. *Bas* 2K **59**
Rochester Ct. *Gos.* 2F **238**
Rochester Gro. *Fle* 3L **47**
Rochester Rd. *Bourn* 2F **226**
Rochester Rd. *S'sea* 4G **241**
Rochester St. *Sotn* 5A **174**
Rochford Rd. *Bas* 6B **42**
Rochford Rd. *Ports.* 9E **200**
Rockall Clo. *Sotn* 6D **158**
Rockbourne. **2C 150**
Rockbourne Clo. *Hav* 5C **202**
Rockbourne Gdns. *New M* 6M **231**
Rockbourne La. *Dam* 3P **149**
Rockbourne Rd. *W'bry & Coom B* 7F **118**
Rockbourne Rd. *Rockb & S'hth* 3C **150**
Rockbourne Rd. *Win* 2H **105**
Rockdale Dri. *Gray.* 4M **103**
Rockery Clo. *Dib* 5H **193**
Rockery, The. *Farn* 9F **28**
Rockfield Way. *Coll T* 5F **18**
Rockford. **5M 185**
Rockford Clo. *Bourn* 2J **247**
Rock Gdns. *A'sht* 1H **65**
Rockingham Way. *Fare.* 9K **199**
Rockleigh Dri. *Tot.* 6K **171**
Rockleigh Rd. *Sotn.* 8J **159**
Rockmoor La. *Ver D* 6E **6**
Rockram Clo. *Bart* 3B **170**
Rockram Gdns. *Dib* 6H **193**
Rockrose Way. *Ports* 7B **200**
Rockstone Ct. *Sotn* 4M **173** (1E **4**)
Rockstone La. *Sotn* 4M **173** (1D **4**)
Rockstone Pl. *Sotn* 4L **173** (1C **4**)
Rockville Dri. *Water.* 2M **201**
Rodbourne Clo. *Evtn.* 6L **233**
Rodfield La. *Mich S & Alr* 8M **107**
Rodfield La. *Ows & Cher* 1F **134**
Roding Clo. *Bas* 6E **42**
Rodlease La. *Bold.* 4E **224**
Rodmel Ct. *Farn.* 2N **49**
Rodney Clo. *Gos.* 9E **212**
Rodney Clo. *Poole* 6E **226**
Rodney Ct. *And* 9C **52**
Rodney Ct. *Sotn.* 6G **175**
Rodney Dri. *Christ* 8B **230**
Rodney Ho. *Gos* 3M **239**
Rodney Rd. *S'sea.* 2G **241**
Rodney Way. *Water* 4B **182**
Rodwell Clo. *Bourn* 1G **227**
Roebuck Av. *Fare* 3N **197**
Roebuck Clo. *New M* 3C **232**
Roebuck Clo. *Ports* 1G **214**
Roedeer Copse. *Hasl* 9N **103**
Roe Downs Rd. *Meds* 1G **97**
Roentgen Rd. *Bas.* 4F **42**
Roeshot Cres. *Christ.* 5F **230**
Roeshot Hill. *Christ.* 5E **230**
Roewood Clo. *Holb.* 5A **208**
Roewood Rd. *Holb* 5A **208**
Rogate. **9L 141**
Rogate Gdns. *Fare* 8L **199**
Rogate Ho. *Ports* 1E **240**
Roger Penny Way. *Gods* 5A **154**
Rogers Clo. *Eastl* 8J **133**
Rogers Clo. *Gos.* 1K **239**
Rogers Ct. *Alt* 5F **80**
Rogers Ho. *Lee S.* 2B **238**
Rogers Mead. *Hay I* 5F **216**
Rogers Rd. *Eastl.* 8J **133**
Roi-Mar Home Pk. *Bourn* 2A **228**
Roker Way. *F Oak* 2M **161**
Rokes Pl. *Yate* 7K **17**
Roland Clo. *Water* 4B **182**
Roller Skating Rink. 3F 214
Rollestone Rd. *Holb* 5N **207**
Rolls Dri. *Bourn* 1L **247**
Roman Clo. *Chan F.* 5C **132**
Roman Dri. *Chilw* 4K **159**
Roman Gdns. *Dib P* 8J **193**
Roman Gro. *Fare* 2M **213**
Roman Ho. *Wort* 6K **41**
Roman Mdw. *D'ton* 2K **119**
Roman Quay. *F'bri* 1J **153**
Roman Ride. *C'then* 1N **17**
Roman Rd. *Bas.* 7J **41**
Roman Rd. *Chilw* 3L **159**
Roman Rd. *Dib P.* 6H **193**
Roman Rd. *Hythe* 2N **207**
Roman Rd. *Twy* 7L **127**
Roman Rd. *W'slw.* 4G **87**
Roman Row. *Bish W* 3N **163**
Romans Bus. Pk. *F'ham* 7F **64**
Romans Fld. *Sil* 4A **12**
Romans Ga. *P Hth.* 4M **11**
Roman's Rd. *Win* 8K **105** (9L **237**)
Roman Way. *And* 6A **52**
Roman Way. *Bar S* 5B **76**
Roman Way. *Dib P* 8J **193**
Roman Way. *F'ham* 6G **64**
Roman Way. *Hav* 7C **202**
Roman Way. *Stockb* 2E **88**
Roman Way. *Wort.* 7J **41**
Romany, The. *Farn* 2C **48**
Romayne Clo. *Farn* 7J **29**
Romford Rd. *Wars* 9A **196**
Romill Clo. *W End.* 8F **160**
Romley Ct. *F'ham* 9F **64**
Romney Clo. *Bourn.* 3J **227**
Romney Rd. *Bourn* 2J **227**
Romsey. **5L 129**
Romsey Av. *Fare* 9J **199**
Romsey Av. *Ports* 1J **241**
Romsey By-Pass. *Roms* 6K **129**
Romsey Clo. *A'sht.* 4L **65**
Romsey Clo. *Bas* 2B **42**
Romsey Clo. *B'wtr* 7E **18**
Romsey Clo. *Eastl.* 9E **132**
Romsey Ct. *Sotn.* 4J **173**
Romsey Golf Course. 4B 158
Romsey Ind. Est. *Roms* 4L **129**
Romsey Rd. *Ame* 6A **66**
Romsey Rd. *Bro'tn.* 2A **86**
Romsey Rd. *Cad* 6N **155**
Romsey Rd. *Eastl* 9E **132**
Romsey Rd. *Good C & Cot* 8B **70**
Romsey Rd. *King S* 8E **88**
Romsey Rd. *Lcky* 4A **122**
Romsey Rd. *Lyn.* 1B **148**
Romsey Rd. *Mid W & Neth W* 9M **67**
Romsey Rd. *Nurs & Sotn* 4B **158**
Romsey Rd. *Ower & Roms* 5F **156**
Romsey Rd. *Water* 9C **168**
Romsey Rd. *W Wel* 9N **121**
Romsey Rd. *W'ish* 5H **121**
Romsey Rd. *Win* 1C **126** (8H **237**) (in three parts)
Romyns Ct. *Fare.* 8B **198**
Ronald Bowker Ct. *Win.* 6J **105**
Ronald Pugh Ct. *Sotn.* 7C **160**
Rookcliff. *Mil S.* 8J **235**
Rookcliff Way. *Mil S* 8J **235**
Rooke Ho. *Ports* 3K **5**
Rookery Av. *White* 2E **196**
Rookery La. *Brea* 2J **151**
Rookery La. *Bro'tn* 2B **86**
Rookery, The. *Ems* 8N **203**
Rookery, The. *Whitc.* 5G **55**
Rookesbury Pk. Cvn. Site. *Wick* 5F **178**
Rookes Clo. *Water* 4B **182**
Rookes La. *L'ton* 4D **234**
Rookes M. *Ptsfld* 9N **139**
Rook Hill Rd. *Christ* 8D **230**
Rook La. *Mich.* 7J **77**
Rookley. *Net A* 2G **195**
Rooksbridge. *Dib* 6H **193**
Rooksbury Cft. *Hav* 4G **202**
Rooksbury Rd. *And* 3L **69**
Rooksdown Av. *Bas* 3L **41**
Rooksdown La. *Bas* 3K **41** (in two parts)
Rooks Down Rd. *Win.* 9H **105**
Rooksfield. *Bish G* 2G **9**
Rooksway Gro. *Fare.* 9H **199**
Rookswood. *Alt.* 3F **80**
Rookswood Clo. *Hook* 2H **45**
Rookwood Av. *Owl.* 3G **18**
Rookwood Clo. *Eastl.* 6F **132**
Rookwood Gdns. *F'bri* 1G **152**
Rookwood La. *Meds* 4D **96**
Rookwood Vw. *Water.* 5G **180**
Rope Hill. *Bold* 6C **224**
Rope Wlk. *Hamb.* 7L **195**
Ropewalk, The. *Fare.* 9D **198**
Rope Yarn La. *Stoke* 6J **35**
Ropley. **2E 110**
Ropley Clo. *Sotn.* 1E **194**
Ropley Clo. *T'ley* 6G **11**
Ropley Dean. **1B 110**
Ropley Rd. *Bourn* 7F **228**
Ropley Rd. *Colem* 1N **111**
Ropley Rd. *Hav* 4H **203**
Ropley Soke. **7F 96**
Rosary Gdns. *Yate* 7N **17**
Roscrea Clo. *Bourn.* 1L **247**
Roscrea Dri. *Bourn* 1L **247**
Rosebank Clo. *Rown* 6D **158**
Rosebank Clo. *T'ley* 5H **11**
Rosebank Lodge. *Rown* 6D **158**
Rosebay Clo. *H Hth* 5N **161**
Rosebay Ct. *Water* 4N **201**
Rosebay Gdns. *Hook* 1J **45**
Roseberry Clo. *Bas.* 5K **59**
Rosebery Av. *Hythe* 7M **193**
Rosebery Av. *Ports.* 1H **215**
Rosebery Clo. *Ver.* 4A **184**
Rosebery Cres. *Eastl.* 6F **132**
Rosebery Rd. *Alr* 1E **108**
Rosebery Rd. *Bourn.* 9D **228**
Rosebrook Ct. *Sotn* 3C **174**
Rosebud Av. *Bourn* 4L **227**
Rose Clo. *Bas.* 2K **59**
Rose Clo. *H End* 2N **175**
Rose Clo. *Hythe.* 7M **193**
Rosecott. *Horn* 3D **182**
Rosecrae Clo. *New M.* 2A **232**
Rosedale. *A'sht* 9L **49**
Rosedale Av. *Roms* 5N **129**
Rosedale Clo. *Christ.* 8A **230**
Rosedale Clo. *Fare* 9J **197**
Rosedene Gdns. *Fle* 1L **47**
Rosedene La. *Coll T* 7F **18**
Rose Est., The. *Hook* 3H **45**
Rosefield Ct. H Win *5C 26* *(off Monachus La.)*
Rose Gdns. *Bourn* 4K **227**
Rose Gdns. *Farn.* 9G **28**
Rosehill. *Water* 4A **182**
Rosehill Clo. *Brans* 6D **220**
Rosehill Dri. *Brans* 6C **220**
Rosehip Clo. *F Oak* 2L **161**
Rosehip Way. *Lych.* 4G **42**
Rose Hodson Ct. *K're* 1A **6**
Rose Hodson Pl. *Bas* 4L **41**
Roselands. *Sotn* 2H **175**
Roselands. *Water* 5A **182**
Roselands Clo. *F Oak.* 9M **133**
Roselands Gdns. *Sotn.* 9M **159**
Roseleigh Dri. *Tot.* 4L **171**
Rosemary Clo. *Farn* 7F **28**
Rosemary Clo. *Win* 6M **105** (7P **237**)
Rosemary Ct. *Tot* 3H **171**
Rosemary Dri. *T'ley* 7H **11**
Rosemary Gdns. *B'wtr* 8E **18**
Rosemary Gdns. *H End* 5N **175**
Rosemary Gdns. *Poole.* 7A **226**
Rosemary Gdns. *White* 1G **197**
Rosemary La. *B'wtr* 7E **18**
Rosemary La. *Ports* 2B **240** (4J **5**)
Rosemary La. *Row.* 8N **63**
Rosemary Price Ct. *H End* 2N **175**
Rosemary Rd. *Poole* 7A **226**
Rosemary Wlk. *Lee S.* 1B **238**
Rosemary Way. *Cowp* 6B **182**
Rosemoor Gro. *Chan F.* 3N **131**
Rosemount Rd. *Bourn* 3F **244**
Rosendale Rd. *Chan F* 8B **132**
Rose Rd. *Sotn.* 2M **173**
Rose Rd. *Tot* 4N **171**
Rosery, The. *Gos* 6K **239**
Rosetta Rd. *S'sea* 3J **241**
Rose Wlk. *Fle* 1L **47**
Rosewall Rd. *Sotn* 8E **158**
Rosewarne Ct. *Win.* 5L **105**
Rosewood. *Chine* 9F **22**
Rosewood. *Gos* 7G **212**
Rosewood Gdns. *March* 9F **172**
Rosewood Gdns. *New M* 2A **232**
Rosewood Gdns. *Water* 6C **168**
Rosewood Rd. *Lind.* 2M **101**
Rosina Clo. *Water.* 1B **202**
Roslin Rd. *Bourn* 7J **227**
Roslin Rd. S. *Bourn.* 7H **227** (in two parts)
Roslyn Ho. *S'sea* 4D **240** (7N **5**)
Rosoman Ct. *Sotn* 6D **174**
Rosoman Rd. *Sotn.* 6D **174**
Rossan Av. *Wars* 9A **196**
Ross Clo. *Bas.* 9B **42**
Ross Gdns. *Bourn* 1A **226**
Ross Gdns. *Sotn.* 9F **158**
Ross Glades. *Bourn* 8J **227**
Rossington Av. *Sotn.* 3D **174**
Rossington Way. *Sotn* 3D **174**
Rossini Clo. *Bas.* 2N **59**
Rossiters La. *W'lnds* 5D **170** (in two parts)
Rossiters Quay. *Christ.* 8M **229**
Rossley Clo. *Christ.* 4G **230**
Rosslyn Clo. *N Bad.* 8F **130**
Ross M. *Net A* 4E **194**
Rossmore. **7B 226**
Rossmore Gdns. *A'sht* 1G **65**
Rossmore Pde. *Poole.* 6A **226**
Rossmore Rd. *Poole* 6A **226**
Ross Rd. *Ring* 7M **185**
Ross Way. *Lee S* 9B **212**
Roston Clo. *Sotn* 8E **160**
Rostrevor La. *S'sea.* 6F **240**
Rosyth Rd. *Sotn.* 3D **174**
Rotary Ct. *Net A* 3F **194**
Rotary Ho. *Sotn* 1J **173**
Rothay Ct. *Bas* 6E **42**
Rothbury Clo. *Sotn.* 6E **174**
Rothbury Clo. *Tot.* 1K **171**
Rothbury Pk. *New M* 4C **232**
Rotherbank Farm La. *Liss* 8E **114**
Rother Clo. *Ptsfld.* 9B **140**
Rother Clo. *S'hrst.* 5E **18**
Rother Clo. *W End* 1F **174**
Rothercombe La. *Ptsfld* 9G **138**
Rother Dale. *Sotn.* 7J **175**
Rotherfield Pk. 1B 112
Rotherfield Rd. *Bourn.* 2E **246**
Rotherfield Rd. *Highc* 5J **231**
Rother Rd. *Farn* 6G **29**
Rotherwick. **7E 24**
Rotherwick Clo. *Hav.* 4H **203**
Rotherwick Ct. *Farn* 3L **49**
Rotherwick La. *H Wes* 4B **24**
Rotherwick Rd. *T'ley* 6H **11**
Rothesay Dri. *Highc* 7G **230**
Rothesay Rd. *Bourn.* 8G **227**
Rothesay Rd. *Gos.* 9J **213**
Rothsbury Dri. *Chan F* 6N **131**
Rothschild Clo. *Sotn.* 9C **174**
Rothville Pl. *Chan F* 2N **131**
Rothwell Clo. *Ports.* 8B **200**
Rothwell Ho. *C'then* 1E **18**
Rotten Green. **7J 27**
Rotten Grn. La. *Bas* 7K **27**
Rotten Hill. *Lave & Over.* 4N **55**
Rotterdam Dri. *Christ.* 7N **229**
Rotterdam Towers. *Sotn* 1D **194**
Rotunda Est. *A'sht* 9K **49**
Roughdown. **7A 208**
Roughdown La. *Holb* 7A **208**
Roumelia La. *Bourn* 1B **246**
Roundabouts, The. *Liss* 9F **114**
Roundaway La. *Cla.* 9E **32**
Round Clo. *Yate* 8B **18**
Round Copse. *Dib* 6H **193**
Roundhaye Rd. *Bourn* 1D **226**
Round Hill. **8G 49**
Round Hill. *F'bri* 1J **153**
Roundhill Clo. *Sotn.* 1E **174**
Roundhouse Ct. *Hay I* 5H **243**
Roundhouse Dri. *Tot* 4H **171**
Roundhouse Mdw. *Ems* 1N **217**
Roundhuts Ri. *Win.* 6N **105**
Roundmead Rd. *Bas.* 7B **42**
Round Tower, The. 4A 240 (7H 5)
Roundtown. *Tun* 2J **61**
Roundway. *Water.* 1N **201**
Roundway Ct. *And* 1L **69**
Roundways. *Bourn.* 3C **226**
Rounton Rd. *Chu C* 5M **47**
Routs Way. *Rown.* 4D **158**
Rowallan Av. *Gos* 8E **212**
Rowan Av. *Water* 8B **182**
Rowan Clo. *Burs.* 1K **195**
Rowan Clo. *Cam.* 5N **19**
Rowan Clo. *Christ.* 6F **230**
Rowan Clo. *Fle* 2A **48**
Rowan Clo. *Lee S.* 2B **238**
Rowan Clo. *Roms.* 6B **130**
Rowan Clo. *St L* 4A **186**
Rowan Clo. *Sotn.* 8F **158**
Rowan Clo. *S Won* 3J **91**
Rowan Clo. *Swanm* 7D **164**
Rowan Clo. *Sway* 6J **223**
Rowan Clo. *T'ley* 5J **11**
Rowan Clo. *Tot* 4K **171**
Rowan Ct. *Sotn* (SO16) 9H **159**
Rowan Ct. *Sotn* (SO19) 7D **174**
Rowan Ct. *S'sea* 3G **241**
Rowan Dale. *Chu C* 6L **47**
Rowan Dri. *Christ* 6F **230**
Rowan Gdns. *H End* 4A **176**
Rowan Rd. *Hav* 6H **203**
Rowan Rd. *T'ley* 6J **11**
Rowans Clo. *Farn.* 3G **28**
Rowanside Clo. *Head D* 3E **102**
Rowans Pk. *L'ton* 3D **234**
Rowans, The. *Hind* 5M **103**
Rowans, The. *March.* 9E **172**
Rowan Tree Clo. *Liss* 1F **140**
Rowan Way. *Fare* 9L **197**
Row Ash. **3K 177**
Rowbarrow Droke. *Broc* 3L **205**
Rowborough Rd. *Sotn* 2D **174**
Rowbury Rd. *Hav.* 3D **202**
Rowdell Cotts. *Ropl* 1D **110**
Rowden Clo. *W Wel* 2B **120**
Rowe Asheway. *L Hth.* 6C **196**
Rowena Ct. S'sea *4E 240* *(off Outram Rd.)*
Rowena Rd. *Bourn* 9J **229**
Rowes All. *Ports* 3A **240** (6H **5**)
Rowes La. *E End* 4A **236**
Rowhay La. *Uphm* 8D **134** (in two parts)
Rowhill Av. *A'sht.* 1H **65**
Rowhill Cres. *A'sht* 2H **65**
Rowhill Dri. *Dib* 6H **193**
Rowhills. *F'ham* 2F **64**
Rowhills Clo. *F'ham* 3H **65**
Rowin Clo. *Hay I.* 5K **243**
Rowland Rd. *Fare.* 7B **198**
Rowland Rd. *Ports.* 8N **199**
Rowlands Av. *Water* 9M **181**
Rowlands Castle Golf Course. 8G 183
Rowlands Castle Rd. *Horn & Ids* 4D **182**
Rowlands Clo. *Chan F* 8M **131**
Rowland's Clo. *Mort W* 1B **12**
Rowlands Wlk. *Sotn.* 9E **160**
Rowledge. **8N 63**
Rowley Clo. *Bot* 2C **176**
Rowley Ct. *Bot* 2C **176**
Rowley Dri. *Bot* 2C **176**
Rowlings Rd. *Win* 3H **105**
Rowner. **7E 212**
Rowner Clo. *Gos.* 7E **212**
Rowner La. *Gos* 6E **212**
Rowner Rd. *Gos.* 6C **212** (in two parts)
Rowner Wlk. *Gos* 8E **212** (in two parts)
Rownhams. **4D 158**
Rownhams Clo. *Rown* 5D **158**
Rownhams Ct. *Sotn* 8E **158**
Rownhams Ho. *Sotn* 5D **158**
Rownhams La. *N Bad & Rown* 7E **130**
Rownhams La. *Rown.* 6E **158** (in two parts)
Rownhams Pk. *Rown.* 3D **158**
Rownhams Rd. *Bourn* 3N **227**
Rownhams Rd. *Hav.* 4D **202**
Rownhams Rd. *N Bad.* 9F **130**
Rownhams Rd. *Sotn.* 9E **158**
Rownhams Rd. N. *Sotn* 5E **158**
Rownhams Way. *Rown* 5D **158**
Rowse Clo. *Roms* 3M **129**
Row, The. H Win *6C 26* *(off High St.)*
Row, The. *Redl* 1M **119**
Row Wood La. *Gos* 7D **212**
Roxbee Cox Ct. *Farn.* 1B **48**
Roxburghe Clo. *W'hill* 5J **101**
Roxburgh Ho. *L Hth.* 6D **196**
Royal Aerospace Establishment. *Farn.* 1K **49**
Royal Aerospace Establishment Rd. *Farn.* 2K **49**
Royal Albert Wlk. *S'sea* 5F **240**
Royal Arc. *Bourn* 1B **246**
Royal Armouries Museum of Artillery, The. 6K 199
Royal Army Dental Corps Mus. *4L 49* *(off Evelyn Woods Rd.)*
Royal Chapel Mus. 5G 195
Royal Clo. *Bas.* 5J **59**
Royal Clo. *Christ.* 6J **229**
Royal Ct. *Sotn* 9N **159**

Royal Cres. Rd. *Sotn*
. . . . 7N **173** (8F **4**)
Royale Clo. *A'sht*. 2L **65**
Royal Gdns. *Row C* 9G **183**
Royal Garrison Church.
. . . . 4B **240** (8K **5**)
Royal Ga. *S'sea*. 5J **241**
Royal Green Jackets Mus., The.
. . . . 6K **105** (7K **237**)
Royal Hampshire
   Regiment Mus., The.
. . . . 7K **105** (8L **237**)
Royal London Pk. *H End*
. . . . 2M **175**
Royal Marines Mus. 5K **241**
Royal Naval Cotts. *S'wick*
. . . . 3A **200**
Royal Naval Mus.
. . . . 1A **240** (2H **5**)
Royal Naval War Memorial.
. . . . 6C **240**
Royal Navy Submarine Mus.
. . . . 4N **239**
Royal Oak Clo. *Yate* 7A **18**
Royal Oak Pas. *Win*. 7M **237**
Royal Oak Rd. *Bourn* 1G **226**
Royal Sovereign Av. *Fare*
. . . . 3C **212**
Royal Victoria Country Pk.
. . . . 5H **195**
Royal Way. *Water*. 2A **202**
Royal Winchester Golf Course.
. . . . 7E **104**
Royce Clo. *And*. 9H **51**
Royden La. *Bold*. 3D **224**
Roydon Clo. *Win*. 9J **105**
Roy's Copse. *Dib* 5H **193**
Roy's La. *Sob*. 9L **165**
Royston Av. *Eastl* 7E **132**
Royston Cen., The. *Ash V*
. . . . 3N **49**
Royston Clo. *Sotn*. 9N **159**
Royston Ct. *Tot*. 1L **171**
Royston Pl. *Bart S* 6C **232**
Rozel Ct. *Sotn*. 8D **158**
Rozeldene. *Hind*. 4N **103**
Rozelle Clo. *Win*. 1E **104**
Rozelle Rd. *Poole*. 1A **244**
Rozel Mnr. *Poole*. 3F **244**
Rubens Clo. *Bas*. 9E **42**
Rubens Clo. *New M* 3C **232**
Ruby Rd. *Sotn*. 4E **174**
Rudd Hall Ri. *Cam*. 1M **29**
Rudd La. *Michm*. 5K **123**
Rudgwick Clo. *Fare*. 9K **199**
Rudmore Ct. *Ports*. 7D **214**
Rudmore Rd. *Ports* 8D **214**
Rudmore Roundabout. *Ports*
. . . . 8E **214**
Rudmore Sq. *Ports* 8D **214**
Ruffield Clo. *Win* 4G **105**
Rufford Clo. *Eastl*. 6E **132**
Rufford Clo. *Fle* 5M **47**
Rufford Gdns. *Bourn* . . . 9H **229**
Rufus Clo. *Chan F*. 4C **132**
Rufus Clo. *Rown* 5C **158**
Rufus Ct. *Lyn* 2C **148**
Rufus Gdns. *Tot* 3J **171**
Rufus Stone. 7L **155**
Rugby Rd. *Owl* 4G **18**
Rugby Rd. *S'sea* 3F **240**
Rumbridge Gdns. *Tot*. . . . 4N **171**
Rumbridge St. *Tot* 4M **171**
Rune Dri. *And* 6M **51**
Runfold. 6L **65**
Runfold St George. *Bad L* . . 5K **65**
Runnymede. *Fare* 5N **197**
Runnymede. *W End* 1H **175**
Runnymede Ct. *Farn*. 5J **29**
Runnymede Ct. *W End*. . . 1H **175**
Runton Rd. *Poole*. 9D **226**
Runway, The. *Christ*. . . . 7D **230**
Runwick La. *F'ham* 6M **63**
Rushden Way. *F'ham* 3F **64**
Rushes Farm. *Ptsfld*. . . . 9L **139**
Rushes Rd. *Ptsfld*. 9L **139**
Rushes, The. *Bas* 6E **42**
Rushes, The. *March*. . . . 8E **172**
Rushfield Rd. *Liss* 2E **140**
Rushford Warren. *Christ*
. . . . 9B **230**
Rushington Av. *Tot* 4M **171**
Rushington Bus. Pk. *Tot*
. . . . 5L **171**
Rushington La. *Tot*. 5L **171**
Rushmere. 9F **166**
Rushmere La. *Den* 3F **180**
Rushmere Rd. *Bourn* . . . 7F **228**
Rushmere Wlk. *Hav* 3D **202**
Rushmoor. 2L **85**
Rushmoor Clo. *Fle*. 4M **47**
Rushmoor Ct. *Farn*. 3L **49**

Rushmoor La. *Lwr Wd & Bentw*
. . . . 6H **79**
Rushmoor Rd. *A'sht* 6F **48**
Rushpole Ct. *Dib* 6H **193**
Rushton Cres. *Bourn* . . . 8K **227**
Ruskin Av. *Bourn*. 3M **227**
Ruskin Clo. *Bas*. 8F **42**
Ruskin Ct. *C'then* 1A **18**
Ruskin Rd. *Eastl*. 8E **132**
Ruskin Rd. *S'sea*. 3H **241**
Ruskin Way. *Water*. 6N **181**
Rusland Clo. *Chan F*. . . . 5N **131**
Russel Ct. *New M*. 3B **232**
Russell Churcher Ct. *Gos*
. . . . 9H **213**
Russell Clo. *Lee S* 1B **238**
Russell-Cotes Art Gallery & Mus.
. . . . 3L **245** (8N **247**)
Russell Cotes Rd. *Bourn*
. . . . 3L **245** (8N **247**)
Russell Ct. *B'wtr* 8F **18**
Russell Ct. *March* 8E **172**
Russell Dri. *Christ* 8N **229**
Russell Dri. *Dun* 4D **122**
Russell Gdns. *St I*. 3E **186**
Russell Pl. *Fare* 8D **198**
Russell Pl. *Sotn* 1N **173**
Russell Rd. *Bas* 8C **42**
Russell Rd. *Hav* 6F **202**
Russell Rd. *Lee S* 2B **238**
Russell Rd. *Win* 4L **105**
Russell St. *Gos* 1J **239**
Russell St. *Sotn* . . . 7M **173** (7E **4**)
Russell Way. *Ptsfld*. 2N **145**
Russell Rd. *Bourn*. 1H **227**
Russet Clo. *Alr* 2E **108**
Russet Clo. *Swanm* 7D **164**
Russet Clo. *Tong* 3N **65**
Russet Gdns. *Cam*. 1M **29**
Russet Glade. *A'sht*. 2F **64**
Russet Ho. *H End* 4M **175**
Russett Clo. *L'ton*. 4F **234**
Russett Clo. *Rise* 2G **14**
Russett Rd. *Alt*. 5G **80**
Russetts Dri. *Fle* 3M **47**
Rustan Clo. *F Oak*. 1A **162**
Rustan Clo. *H End* 4N **175**
Rustic Glen. *Chu C* 6L **47**
Rustington Ho. *Ports* 2D **240**
   (off Up. Arundel St.)
Ruth Clo. *Farn*. 7E **28**
Rutherford Cen., The. *Bas*
. . . . 3E **42**
Rutherford Rd. *Bas*. 3E **42**
Rutland Clo. *A'sht*. 8J **49**
Rutland Ct. *Sotn*. 3E **174**
Rutland Gdns. *Burs* 9L **175**
Rutland Mnr. *Poole*. 1E **244**
Rutland Rd. *Bourn*. 6M **227**
Rutland Rd. *Christ* 5J **229**
Rutland Ter. *A'sht* 8J **49**
Rutland Way. *Sotn* 1E **174**
Ruxley Clo. *Holb*. 4A **208**
Ryan Gdns. *Bourn*. 1F **226**
Ryan Mt. *S'hrst* 5C **18**
Rydal Clo. *Bas*. 9J **41**
Rydal Clo. *Bord*. 2J **101**
Rydal Clo. *Christ* 2G **229**
Rydal Clo. *Farn* 9F **28**
Rydal Clo. *Ports* 8C **200**
Rydal Dri. *Chu C* 6K **47**
Rydal Ho. *Ports* 8C **200**
Rydal Rd. *Gos*. 8J **213**
Ryde Ct. *A'sht*. 1L **65**
Ryde Gdns. *Yate* 7L **17**
Ryde Pl. *Lee S* 3C **238**
Ryde Ter. *Sotn* 7N **173**
Ryebeck Rd. *Chu C* 6M **47**
Rye Clo. *Chan F* 6L **131**
Rye Clo. *Farn* 6G **29**
Rye Clo. *Fle* 7A **28**
Rye Common. 1J **63**
Rye Cft. *Chu C* 7K **47**
Ryecroft. *Fare*. 7F **196**
Ryecroft. *Hav*. 8H **203**
Ryecroft Av. *Bourn* 1C **226**
Ryecroft Gdns. *B'wtr* 9G **18**
Rye Dale. *Asht* 7J **171**
Ryedown La. *E Wel*. 8C **128**
Ryefield Clo. *Ptsfld*. 1B **146**
Ryeland Clo. *Fle* 8A **28**
Ryelaw Rd. *Chu C* 6M **47**
Rye Paddock La. *Fawl*. . . 4F **208**
Rylandes Ct. *Sotn*. 8E **158**
Ryle Rd. *F'ham* 9D **64**
Ryon Clo. *And* 6N **51**

S

Sabre Ct. *A'sht* 9G **49**
Sabre Rd. *Ems* 5N **217**

Sackville St. *S'sea*
. . . . 3D **240** (6N **5**)
   (in two parts)
Saddleback Rd. *Cam* 5N **19**
Saddleback Way. *Fle*. . . . 8N **27**
Saddler Corner. *S'hrst* . . . 6D **18**
Saddlers Clo. *Eastl* 6E **132**
Saddlers Clo. *Sut S* 7D **76**
Saddlers Scarp. *Gray* . . . 3J **103**
Saddlewood. *Cam*. 9L **19**
Sadlers La. *Dib P*. 8M **193**
Sadlers Rd. *Ink*. 1E **6**
Sadlers Wlk. *Ems*. 9N **203**
Saffron Clo. *Chine* 8H **23**
Saffron Ct. *Farn* 8E **28**
Saffron Ct. *L Hth* 7B **196**
Saffron Dri. *Christ* 6D **230**
Saffron Way. *Bourn* 3B **226**
Saffron Way. *White* 1G **196**
Sage Clo. *Water* 3A **202**
Sages La. *Priv* 8K **111**
Sainfoin La. *Okly* 2D **58**
   (in three parts)
Sainsbury Clo. *And* 3M **69**
Sainsbury Lodge. Ports . . . 2F **240**
   (off Lucknow St.)
St Agathas Rd. *Hamb*. . . . 5L **195**
St Agathas Way. *Ports*
. . . . 1D **240** (2N **5**)
St Albans Av. *Bourn*. . . . 7M **227**
St Albans Ct. *Gos* 2F **238**
St Albans Cres. *Bourn* . . 7M **227**
St Albans Rd. *Bourn* . . . 7M **227**
St Alban's Rd. *Hav* 5G **202**
St Alban's Rd. *Sotn*
. . . . 5N **173** (3F **4**)
St Albans Rd. *S'sea* 4G **241**
St Albans Roundabout. *Farn*
. . . . 3L **49**
St Aldhelms. *Poole*. 1D **244**
St Aldhelm's Clo. *Poole* . 2D **244**
St Aldhelm's Rd. *Poole*. . 1D **244**
St Andrew Clo. *Water*. . . . 9C **168**
St Andrews. *Christ* 8K **229**
St Andrews Bldgs. *Hamb*
. . . . 7K **195**
St Andrews Clo. *N Bad*. . . 7D **130**
St Andrews Clo. *Tims*. . . 7K **123**
St Andrews Ct. *Ports*
. . . . 3C **240** (5M **5**)
St Andrews Grn. *Meon*. . 8N **135**
St Andrews Pk. *H Hth*. . . 5N **161**
St Andrew's Rd. *Bas* . . . 8M **41**
St Andrew's Rd. *Farl*. . . . 9N **201**
St Andrew's Rd. *Gos* . . . 3K **239**
St Andrew's Rd. *Hay I* . . 5H **243**
St Andrew's Rd. *Sotn*
. . . . 5M **173** (3D **4**)
St Andrew's Rd. *S'sea* . . 4E **240**
St Andrews Rd. *Tidw*. . . . 8C **30**
St Andrews Rd. *W'hill* . . 5G **100**
St Andrew's Way. *Frim*. . . 5N **29**
St Anne's Av. *Bourn* 9H **229**
St Annes Clo. *Good C* . . 9M **69**
St Annes Clo. *Win* 9G **105**
St Annes Gdns. *L'ton* . . . 3D **234**
St Anne's Gdns. *Sotn*. . . 8C **174**
St Anne's Gro. *Fare*. 1B **212**
St Annes Ho. *Roms* 6L **129**
St Annes La. *Shed*. 3N **177**
St Annes M. *Sotn*. 2M **173**
St Ann's Clo. *And*. 2M **69**
   (in two parts)
St Ann's Ct. *Bourn* 9B **228**
St Ann's Cres. *Gos* 1J **239**
St Ann's Rd. *Horn*. 3C **182**
St Ann's Rd. *S'sea* 4G **241**
St Anthony's Rd. *Bourn* . . 9K **227**
St Antony's. *Bourn*
. . . . 3H **245** (8G **247**)
St Aubin's Av. *Sotn*. 5E **174**
St Aubins Clo. *Four M*. . . 5J **97**
St Aubin's Pk. *Hay I*. . . . 4D **242**
St Aubyns La. *Hang* 4A **188**
St Augustine Gdns. *Sotn*. . 1B **174**
St Augustine Rd. *S'sea*. . 5G **240**
St Augustine's Clo. *A'sht* . . 1M **65**
St Augustin's Rd. *Bourn*. . 9K **227**
St Austell Clo. *Eastl*. . . . 9J **133**
St Austins. *Gray*. 4M **103**
St Barbara's Clo. *Braml*. . . 2J **23**
St Barbara Way. *Ports* . . 4G **215**
St Barbe Clo. *Roms* 6N **129**
St Barbe Mus. 2E **234**
St Bartholomew's Gdns. *S'sea*
. . . . 4E **240**
St Bede's Ct. *Win* 5L **105**
St Benedicts Clo. *A'sht* . . . 1J **65**
St Bernard Ho. *Sotn* 7E **4**
St Bernard's Cen. *Bas*. . . 5D **42**
St Birinus Rd. *W'flls* . . . 2M **119**

St Blaize Rd. *Roms*. 4A **130**
St Boniface Ct. *N Bad*. . . 9F **130**
St Bonnet Dri. *Bish W*. . . 3M **163**
St Brelade Pl. *Sotn*. 8C **158**
St Brelades. *Poole* 4A **244**
St Brelades Av. *Poole*. . . 4B **226**
St Catherine's Hill. 3H **229**
St Catherine's Hill Fort.
. . . . 1L **127**
St Catherine's Hill La. *Christ*
. . . . 4J **229**
St Catherine's Hill Nature
   Reserve. 1L **127**
St Catherine's Pde. *Christ*
. . . . 5J **229**
St Catherine's Path. *Bourn*
. . . . 2H **247**
St Catherine's Rd. *Bourn*
. . . . 2H **247**
St Catherine's Rd. *Eastl*. . 7E **132**
St Catherine's Rd. *Hay I*. . 4C **242**
St Catherine's Rd. *Sotn* . . 1B **174**
St Catherine's Rd. *Win* . . 8M **105**
St Catherine St. *S'sea* . . . 6E **240**
St Catherines Vw. *H End*
. . . . 4L **175**
St Catherine's Vw. *Win* . . 9M **105**
St Catherines Way. *Chilc*
. . . . 9N **105**
St Catherine's Way. *Christ*
. . . . 3G **229**
St Catherine's Way. *Fare*. . 8G **199**
St Chad's Av. *Ports*. 6F **214**
St Christopher Av. *Fare* . . 6D **198**
St Christophers Clo. *A'sht*
. . . . 9M **49**
St Christophers Clo. *Bas* . . 8L **41**
St Christophers Clo. *N Bad*
. . . . 8E **130**
St Christophers Gdns. *Gos*
. . . . 6E **212**
St Christopher's Pl. *Farn* . . 9H **29**
St Christopher's Rd. *Farn* . . 9J **29**
St Christophers Rd. *Hav*
. . . . 5C **202**
St Clair Rd. *Poole* 7C **244**
St Clares Av. *Hav* 2D **202**
St Clares Ct. *Hav*. 3D **202**
St Clements Clo. *Roms*. . 4L **129**
St Clements Ct. *Farn* 5K **29**
St Clements Gdns. *Bourn*
. . . . 9A **228**
St Clements Rd. *Bourn* . . 9A **228**
St Clement St. *Win*
. . . . 7K **105** (8L **237**)
St Clements Yd. *Win*. . . . 8L **237**
St Colman's Av. *Ports*. . . 9N **201**
St Cross Ct. *Win* 9K **105**
St Cross Mede. *Win*. 1J **127**
St Cross Rd. *Cron* 3L **63**
St Cross Rd. *F'ham* 7E **64**
St Cross Rd. *Win*
. . . . 2J **127** (9L **237**)
St Cuthbert's Clo. *L Hth* . . 5E **196**
St Cuthbert's La. *L Hth* . . 5E **196**
St Davids Clo. *Cal* 1J **171**
St David's Clo. *Farn*. 4H **29**
St David's Clo. *F'ham* . . . 3G **65**
St Davids Clo. *Odi* 9J **45**
St David's Ct. *Bourn* 9B **228**
St Davids Ct. *Gos*. 1E **238**
St David's Ct. *N Bad* 9F **130**
St David's Dri. *Bas*. 8N **41**
St Davids Rd. *Clan* 6C **168**
St Davids Rd. *L Hth* 6C **196**
St David's Rd. *S'sea*. . . . 3E **240**
St Denys. 2A **174**
St Denys. *New M* 5C **232**
St Denys Rd. *Sotn*. 1N **173**
St Denys Wlk. *Hav*. 3D **202**
St Edmondsbury Ct. Gos
. . . . 2F **238**
   (off Anson Clo.)
St Edmund Clo. *Fare* 8E **196**
St Edmunds Rd. *Sotn*. . . 2G **172**
   (in two parts)
St Edward's Rd. *Gos* 3K **239**
St Edwards Rd. *Net A* . . . 2F **194**
St Edwards Rd. *S'sea*
. . . . 4D **240** (8N **5**)
St Edwards Ter. *Gos*. . . . 1J **239**
St Elizabeths Av. *Sotn* . . 3F **174**
St Evox Clo. *Rown* 6E **158**
St Faith Clo. *Four M*. . . . 5H **97**
St Faith's Clo. *Gos* 2J **239**
St Faith's Rd. *Ports* 1E **240**
St Faith's Rd. *Win* 9K **105**
St Francis Av. *Sotn*. 2F **174**
St Francis Clo. *Black* . . . 9C **208**
St Francis Clo. *Ports* . . . 4F **214**
St Francis Pl. *Hav* 6E **202**
St Francis Rd. *Black* 9C **208**

St Francis Rd. *Gos* 6L **239**
St Gabriels Lea. *Chine* . . . 9H **23**
St Gabriel's Rd. *Sotn* . . . 3F **174**
St George Clo. *Burs*. 8K **175**
St George's Av. *Bourn* . . . 6N **227**
St Georges Av. *Hav* 8H **203**
St George's Bus. Cen. *Ports*
. . . . 2B **240** (4K **5**)
St George's Clo. *Bad L*. . . 5K **65**
St Georges Clo. *Bourn*. . . 6N **227**
St Georges Clo. *Christ*. . . 7F **230**
St Georges Cotts. *W'grn*
. . . . 3N **151**
St George's Ct. *Bourn*. . . . 9B **228**
St George's Ct. *Fare*. 9D **198**
St George's Ct. *N Bad*. . . . 9F **130**
St Georges Ct. *Owl*. 3G **18**
St George's Ct. *S'sea*
. . . . 4C **240** (8M **5**)
St George's Cres. *F'bri* . . . 9J **151**
St Georges Dri. *Brans*. . . 7D **220**
St George's Ind. Cen. *S'sea*
. . . . 2H **241**
St George's Ind. Est. *Cam*
. . . . 1K **29**
St George's M. F'ham 7D **64**
   (off Bear La.)
St George's Rd. *A'sht*. . . . 1K **65**
St George's Rd. *Bad L & F'ham*
. . . . 4K **65**
   (in two parts)
St George's Rd. *Cam*. . . . 7M **19**
St George's Rd. *Cosh*. . . . 9G **201**
St George's Rd. *F'ham* . . . 9F **64**
St George's Rd. *F'bri*. 9J **151**
St George's Rd. *Hay I* . . . 4D **242**
St George's Rd. *L Hth* . . . 6C **196**
St George's Rd. *Ports*
. . . . 3B **240** (5K **5**)
St George's Rd. *S'sea*. . . 5H **241**
St Georges Rd. *Tidw* 8C **30**
St George's Rd. E. *A'sht*. . 1K **65**
St George's Sq. *Bish W*
. . . . 4M **163**
St George's Sq. *Ports*
. . . . 2B **240** (4K **5**)
St George's St. *Sotn*
. . . . 6M **173** (6E **4**)
St George's St. *Win*
. . . . 6L **105** (7M **237**)
   (in two parts)
St George's Wlk. Water . . 2M **201**
   (off Hambledon Rd.)
St George's Way. *Ports*
. . . . 2B **240** (4K **5**)
St George's Yd. F'ham 8D **64**
   (off Castle St.)
St Giles Clo. *Win*. 7M **105**
St Giles Hill. *Win*. 7M **105**
St Giles Way. *Water* 9C **168**
St Helena Gdns. *Sotn*. . . 8D **160**
St Helena Way. *Fare* 9L **199**
St Helen's Clo. *S'sea* . . . 5G **240**
St Helen's Ct. S'sea. 6F **240**
   (off St Helen's Pde.)
St Helens Cres. *S'hrst*. . . 5D **18**
St Helens Ho. *Fare*. 9M **197**
St Helens M. Eastl 1A **162**
   (off Stubbington Way)
St Helier Pl. *Sotn*. 8D **158**
St Helier Rd. *Poole*. 5B **226**
St Hellen's Rd. *Ports* . . . 9L **201**
St Herman's Cvn. Est. *Hay I*
. . . . 5J **243**
St Herman's Rd. *Hay I* . . . 5J **243**
St Hilda Av. *Water* 9C **168**
St Hubert Rd. *And* 2L **69**
St Hubert Rd. *Water*. 9C **168**
St Ives. 3D **186**
St Ives End La. *St I* 4D **186**
St Ives Gdns. *Bourn*. . . . 9K **227**
St Ives Pk. *Ashy H*. 3D **186**
St Ives Wood. *St I* 3E **186**
St James. *Bourn*. 2B **246**
St James' Av. *F'ham* 6F **64**
St James Clo. *Braml* 2J **23**
St James Clo. *F'ham* 7E **64**
St James' Clo. *Water* . . . 7C **168**
St James Clo. *Sotn* 1H **173**
St James Ho. *Sotn*
. . . . 7M **173** (7E **4**)
St James' La. *Win*
. . . . 7J **105** (8H **237**)
St James Pk. Cvn. Pk. *Chan F*
. . . . 3M **131**
St James' Rd. *Ems*. 9M **203**
St James Rd. *Fle* 3L **47**
St James Rd. *Sway* 5K **223**
St James Rd. *W End*. . . . 1J **175**
St James's Clo. *Sotn*. . . . 1H **173**
St James's Pk. Rd. *Sotn*
. . . . 9H **159**
St James Sq. *Bourn*. . . . 9D **228**

St James's Rd.—Sandringham Clo.

St James's Rd. *Sotn* 1H **173**
St James's Rd. *S'sea* 3D **240** (6N **5**)
St James's St. *Ports* 2C **240** (3L **5**)
St James St. *Lud* 1C **30**
St James' Ter. *F'ham* 7E **64**
St James' Ter. *Win* 7K **105** (8K **237**)
St James' Vs. *Win* 7K **105** (9K **237**)
St James Way. *Fare* 9L **199**
St John Clo. *Braml* 2H **23**
St John's Av. *Water* 5M **201**
St John's Cen. *H End* 4M **175**
St John's Cen. *N Bad* 7F **130**
St John's Clo. *Gos* 2K **239**
St Johns Clo. *Hay I* 5E **242**
St John's Clo. *Hook* 2H **45**
St Johns Clo. *Rown* 4D **158**
St John's Cotts. *Hook* 3E **44**
St John's Ct. Bourn *9B* ***228***
(off Palmerston M.)
St John's Ct. *Farn* 7F **28**
St Johns Ct. *March* 9E **172**
St John's Ct. *N Bad* 9G **130**
St John's Ct. *Ports* 7D **214**
St Johns Dri. *March* 9D **172**
St Johns Gdns. *Bourn* 5K **227**
St Johns Gdns. *Roms* 4M **129**
St John's Glebe. *Rown* 5D **158**
St Johns La. *Shed* 3A **178**
St Johns M. *L Hth* 6F **196**
St Johns M. *S'sea* 4E **240**
St John's Piece. *Okly* 2D **58**
St John's Rd. *And* 1A **70**
St Johns Rd. *Bourn* 1B **246**
St John's Rd. *Christ* 8J **229**
St John's Rd. *Cosh* 9G **201**
St John's Rd. *Eastl* 8F **132**
St John's Rd. *Farn* 8F **28**
St Johns Rd. *H Win* 7C **26**
St John's Rd. *Hav* 5C **202**
St John's Rd. *H End* 6L **175**
St John's Rd. *L Hth* 7E **196**
St Johns Rd. *New M* 8B **222**
St John's Rd. *Okly* 9D **40**
St John's Rd. *S'hrst* 6D **18**
St John's Rd. *Win* 6M **105**
St John's Sq. *Gos* 2K **239**
St Johns St. *Hythe* 5M **193**
St John's St. *Win* 7M **105** (8P **237**)
St Johns Wlk. *Bas* 6C **42**
St Joseph Clo. *L Hth* 6E **196**
St Joseph's Cres. *Chine* 1G **43**
St Joseph's Rd. *A'sht* 1J **65**
St Julien's Hospital Almshouses. *Sotn* 8D **4**
St Just Clo. *Newt T* 6E **66**
St Lawrence Clo. *H End* 9A **162**
St Lawrence Rd. *Alt* 4F **80**
St Lawrence Rd. *Eastl* 8E **132**
St Lawrence Rd. *Sotn* 7N **173** (8F **4**)
St Ledger's Pl. *Bourn* 8A **228**
St Ledger's Rd. *Bourn* 8A **228**
St Leonards 6B **186**
St Leonards. Grat *4L* ***67***
(off Lawrence Houses)
St Leonards Av. *Chine* 9H **23**
St Leonard's Av. *Hay I* 3G **242**
St Leonards Clo. *Bulf* 3A **66**
St Leonards Clo. *Fare* 6H **197**
St Leonards Clo. *S Won* 3H **91**
St Leonard's Rd. *Bourn* 8M **227**
St Leonards Rd. *E End* 4A **236**
St Leonard's Rd. *Win* 8N **105**
St Leonards Vw. *W'bry* 1E **150**
St Leonards Way. *Ashy H* 3A **186**
St Lucia Pk. *Bord* 2K **101**
St Lukes Clo. *Bas* 8L **41**
St Lukes Clo. *H End* 1N **175**
St Luke's Rd. *Bourn* 7K **227**
St Luke's Rd. *Gos* 1J **239**
St Margaret's Av. *Christ* 8K **229**
St Margarets Clo. *Sotn* 3F **174**
St Margarets Ho. Sotn *2L* ***173***
(off Hulse Rd.)
St Margarets La. *Fare* 8H **197**
St Margaret's Rd. *Bourn* 4F **226**
St Margaret's Rd. *Eastl* 8G **133**
St Margaret's Rd. *Hay I* 4G **243**
St Marks Clo. *Braml* 2H **23**
St Marks Clo. *Chan F* 3D **132**
St Mark's Clo. *Farn* 2L **49**
St Mark's Clo. *Gos* 6K **239**
St Marks Ct. *Gos* 2H **239**
St Mark's Pl. *F'ham* 3D **64**
St Mark's Pl. *Gos* 5K **239**
St Marks Rd. *Bourn* 3F **226**
St Mark's Rd. *Gos* 6J **239**
St Marks Rd. *Penn* 3B **234**
St Mark's Rd. *Ports* 7E **214**
St Martins Clo. *Eastl* 8H **133**
St Martins Clo. *Sotn* 8D **158**
St Martin's Clo. *Win* 6M **105**
St Martin's Ho. *S'sea* 6E **240**
St Martins Trade Pk. *Win* 5M **105**
St Mary Bourne 1M **53**
St Mary Gro. *Hord* 4J **233**
St Mary Magdalen Almshouses. *Win* 7M **105** (9P **237**)
St Mary's 4M **173**
St Mary's. Roms *6L* ***129***
(off Banning St.)
St Mary's Av. *Braml* 2J **23**
St Mary's Av. *Gos* 5J **239**
St Mary's Church Clo. *Sotn* 7B **160**
St Marys Clo. *Alt* 6F **80**
St Mary's Clo. *Brans* 7E **220**
St Mary's Clo. *Drox* 2K **165**
St Mary's Clo. *King W* 1N **105**
St Mary's Clo. *Lover* 8D **120**
St Mary's Clo. *Old B* 5J **43**
St Mary's Clo. *S'hrst* 5E **18**
St Mary's Ct. *Bas* 6D **42**
St Mary's Ct. *Bourn* 2H **247**
St Mary's Ct. *Braml* 2J **23**
St Mary's Ho. *Ports* 1G **241**
St Mary's Mdw. *Abb A* 5G **69**
St Marys Pl. *F'ham* 7E **64**
St Mary's Pl. *Sotn* 6M **173** (6E **4**)
St Mary's Rd. *Bourn* 8A **228**
St Mary's Rd. *Cam* 7L **19**
St Mary's Rd. *Eastl* 8H **133**
St Mary's Rd. *Fare* 4M **211**
St Mary's Rd. *H Win* 7B **26**
St Mary's Rd. *Hay I* 4F **242**
St Mary's Rd. *K're* 2B **6**
St Mary's Rd. *Liss* 1E **140**
St Mary's Rd. *Net A* 3G **195**
St Mary's Rd. *Ports* 1F **240**
St Mary's Rd. *Sotn* 4M **173** (2E **4**)
St Marys Ter. *Twy* 7L **127**
St Mary St. *Sotn* 5N **173** (4F **4**)
St Mary St. *Win* 9H **105**
St Matthews Clo. *Sotn* 5N **173** (3E **4**)
St Matthew's Ct. *Gos* 2M **239**
St Matthew's Rd. *Ports* 9G **201**
St Matthew's Rd. *Win* 4H **105**
St Merrin's Clo. *Bourn* 2G **226**
St Michael's. *Bourn* 7H **247**
St Michael's Building. *Ports* 2C **240** (4M **5**)
St Michaels Clo. *Black* 7D **208**
St Michaels Clo. *Fle* 3N **47**
St Michael's Clo. *N Wal* 9N **57**
St Michaels Clo. *Tidw* 9C **30**
St Michaels Ct. *Bourn* 7H **247**
St Michaels Ct. *Ports* 8C **200**
St Michael's Gdns. *Win* 7K **105** (9L **237**)
St Michael's Gro. *Fare* 1B **212**
St Michael's Ho. *Fare* 9B **198**
St Michael's La. *Bourn* 2J **245** (7J **247**)
St Michael's M. *Bourn* 7J **247**
St Michael's Pas. *Win* 8L **105** (9M **237**)
St Michael's Pl. *Bourn* 7J **247**
St Michael's Rd. *A'sht* 1K **65**
St Michael's Rd. *Bas* 8L **41**
St Michael's Rd. *Bourn* 2J **245** (7J **247**)
St Michael's Rd. *Cam* 8K **19**
St Michael's Rd. *Farn* 6K **29**
St Michael's Rd. *Hav* 5C **202**
St Michael's Rd. *L Hth* 7C **196**
St Michael's Rd. *Ports* 3C **240** (5M **5**)
St Michael's Rd. *S'hrst* 5B **18**
St Michaels Rd. *Tot* 2M **171**
St Michael's Rd. *Win* 8K **105** (9L **237**)
St Michael's Roundabout. *Bourn* 2H **245** (7H **247**)
St Michael's Sq. *Sotn* 7C **4**
St Michael's St. *Sotn* 7L **173** (7C **4**)
St Michaels Way. *Water* 9C **168**
St Monica Rd. *Sotn* 7E **174**
St Neot's Rd. *E'sly* 5C **16**
St Nicholas Av. *Gos* 8D **212**
St Nicholas Clo. *Fle* 2L **47**
St Nicholas Clo. *Lud* 1F **30**
St Nicholas Ct. *Bas* 7M **41**
St Nicholas Ri. *King W* 9M **91**
St Nicholas Rd. *Hav* 6C **202**
St Nicholas Row. *Wick* 7C **178**
St Nicholas St. *Ports* 4B **240** (7K **5**)
St Osmunds Rd. *Poole* 1A **244**
St Patricks Av. *Tidw* 9B **30**
St Patrick's Ct. *N Bad* 9F **130**
St Patrick's La. *Liss* 9H **115**
St Patrick's Rd. *Bas* 8N **41**
St Paul's Ct. *Win* 7L **237**
St Paul's Hill. *Win* 6K **105** (6K **237**)
St Paul's La. *Bourn* 1M **245**
St Paul's Pl. *Bourn* 1L **245**
St Paul's Pl. *Win* 6K **105**
St Paul's Rd. *Bas* 8N **41**
St Paul's Rd. *Bourn* 1L **245**
St Pauls Rd. *Sar G* 3B **196**
St Paul's Rd. *S'sea* 3C **240** (6M **5**)
St Paul's Sq. *S'sea* 3C **240** (6M **5**)
St Peter's Av. *Hay I* 6J **217**
St Peters Clo. *Curd* 2G **177**
St Peter's Clo. *Good C* 7A **70**
St Peters Clo. *H'ly* 2J **9**
St Peter's Clo. *Ship B* 2B **66**
St Peters Clo. *T'ley* 6H **11**
St Peter's Ct. *Bourn* 2L **245** (6N **247**)
St Peter's Cres. *Bourn* 2K **245** (6N **247**)
St Peter's Gdns. *Yate* 7N **17**
St Peters Gro. *S'sea* 4E **240**
St Peters Pk. *A'sht* 2G **64**
St Peter's Rd. *Bas* 7L **41**
St Peter's Rd. *Bourn* 2K **245** (7M **247**)
St Peter's Rd. *Hay I* 4J **217**
St Peter's Rd. *Ptsfld* 1M **145**
St Peter's Roundabout. *Bourn* 2L **245** (7N **247**)
St Peter's Sq. *Ems* 9M **203**
St Peter's St. *Bish W* 3M **163**
St Peter St. *Win* 6L **105** (7M **237**)
(in two parts)
St Peter's Wlk. *Bourn* 7L **247**
St Peter's Way. *Frim* 5N **29**
St Phillips Ct. *Fle* 2M **47**
St Phillip's Way. *Sotn* 3F **174**
St Piran's Av. *Ports* 9H **215**
St Quentin Ho. Fare *1A* ***212***
(off Bishopsfield Rd.)
St Ronan's Av. *S'sea* 5F **240**
St Ronan's Rd. *S'sea* 6F **240**
St Saviours Clo. *Bourn* 7F **228**
St Sebastian Cres. *Fare* 6D **198**
St Simon Clo. *L Hth* 6E **196**
St Simon's Rd. *S'sea* 5E **240**
St Stephen's Clo. *Up N* 6B **44**
St Stephen's Ct. *Bourn* 5K **247**
St Stephen's Rd. *Bourn* 1J **245** (5J **247**)
St Stephen's Rd. *Ports* 8F **214**
St Stephen's Rd. *Win* 4H **105**
St Stephen's Way. *Bourn* 2K **245** (6L **247**)
St Swithun Clo. *Bish W* 3L **163**
St Swithuns Clo. *Cram* 3C **130**
St Swithuns Ct. *Sotn* 1E **4**
St Swithun's Rd. *Bourn* 1M **245**
St Swithun's Rd. *Ports* 6G **215**
St Swithun's Rd. S. *Bourn* 1M **245**
St Swithun's Roundabout. *Bourn* 2M **245**
St Swithuns Ter. *Win* 7K **105** (9L **237**)
St Swithun St. *Win* 7K **105** (9L **237**)
St Swithuns Vs. *Win* 7L **105** (9M **237**)
St Theresa's Clo. *Hav* 6C **202**
St Thomas Av. *Hay I* 4D **242**
St Thomas Clo. *Bas* 4B **42**
St Thomas Clo. *Bourn* 4H **227**
St Thomas Clo. *Charl* 7L **51**
St Thomas Clo. *Fare* 6E **198**
St Thomas Ct. *Eastl* 1A **162**
St Thomas Pk. *L'ton* 3D **234**
St Thomas' Pas. *Win* 7K **105** (8L **237**)
St Thomas's Ct. *Ports* 3B **240** (6K **5**)
St Thomas's Rd. *Gos* 8K **213**
St Thomas's St. *Ports* 4B **240** (7J **5**)
St Thomas St. *L'ton* 3D **234**
St Thomas St. *Win* 7K **105** (9L **237**)
St Tristan Clo. *L Hth* 7E **196**
St Ursula Gro. *S'sea* 4E **240**
St Valerie Rd. *Bourn* 9K **227**
St Valerie Rd. *Gos* 4K **239**
St Vigor Way. *Col C* 3K **133**
(in two parts)
St Vincent Cres. *Water* 4B **182**
St Vincent Leisure Cen. 1K **239**
St Vincent Rd. *Gos* 1K **239**
St Vincent Rd. *S'sea* 5E **240**
St Vincent St. *S'sea* 3D **240** (5M **5**)
St Winifred's Rd. *Bourn* 9K **227**
St Winifred's Rd. *Sotn* 9H **159**
Salamanca. *C'then* 1A **18**
Salamanca Pk. *A'sht* 8H **49**
Salcombe Av. *Ports* 7H **215**
Salcombe Clo. *Chan F* 8N **131**
Salcombe Cres. *Tot* 4L **171**
Salcombe Rd. *Sotn* 3H **173**
Salcombe Rd. *Tot* 4L **171**
Salcot Rd. *Win* 4L **105**
Salem St. *Sotn* 1H **173**
Salerno Clo. *A'sht* 8J **49**
Salerno Dri. *Gos* 3H **239**
Salerno Ho. *Fare* 1B **212**
Salerno Ho. Roms *5A* ***130***
(off Chambers Av.)
Salerno Rd. *Ports* 4E **214**
Salerno Rd. *Sotn* 7H **159**
Sales Ct. *A'sht* 1H **65**
Salesian Vw. *Farn* 3N **49**
Salet Way. *Water* 9B **182**
Salisbury Clo. *Alt* 6G **80**
Salisbury Clo. *Eastl* 8F **132**
Salisbury Clo. *Odi* 9J **45**
Salisbury Ct. *Eastl* 8F **132**
Salisbury Gdns. *Bas* 7L **41**
Salisbury La. *Ovr W & Mid W* 8M **67**
Salisbury Rd. *Abb A* 3B **72**
Salisbury Rd. *Alr* 1E **108**
Salisbury Rd. *And* 3K **69**
Salisbury Rd. *Anna V* 4J **69**
Salisbury Rd. *B'wtr* 8E **18**
Salisbury Rd. *Blash & Ibly* 4J **185**
Salisbury Rd. *Bourn* 1B **246**
Salisbury Rd. *Brea* 4L **151**
Salisbury Rd. *Bro'tn* 3N **87**
Salisbury Rd. *Bulf* 3A **66**
Salisbury Rd. *Burt & Christ* 2M **229**
Salisbury Rd. *Charl A & D'ton* 5A **120**
Salisbury Rd. *Coom B* 2G **119**
Salisbury Rd. *Cosh* 1H **215**
Salisbury Rd. *E Wel & Ower* 2A **156**
Salisbury Rd. *Farn* 8L **29**
Salisbury Rd. *F'bri* 9J **151**
Salisbury Rd. *Grat & Pale* 5K **67**
Salisbury Rd. *Land & Plait* 9K **121**
Salisbury Rd. *Ower* 6F **156**
Salisbury Rd. *Poole* 9A **226**
Salisbury Rd. *Ring & Blash* 9J **185**
Salisbury Rd. *Ship B & Tidw* 3G **66**
Salisbury Rd. *Shoot & Roms* 3D **128**
Salisbury Rd. *Sotn* 8M **159**
Salisbury Rd. *S'sea* 5G **240**
Salisbury Rd. *W'ish & Land* 6G **121**
Salisbury Rd. *Wink* 9L **219**
Salisbury Rd. Arc. *Tot* 3M **171**
Salisbury St. *Cran* 6J **149**
Salisbury St. *F'bri* 1J **153**
Salisbury St. *Sotn* 4L **173** (2C **4**)
Salisbury Ter. *Lee S* 2B **238**
Salmon Dri. *Eastl* 1K **161**
Salmond Rd. *And* 1H **69**
Salmons Rd. *Odi* 9J **45**
Salona Clo. *Chan F* 5D **132**
Salterns Av. *S'sea* 2J **241**
Salterns Clo. *Hay I* 4J **243**
Salterns Ct. *Poole* 5A **244**
Salterns Est. *Fare* 1D **212**
Salterns La. *Burs* 3L **195**
Salterns La. *Fare* 1D **212**
Salterns La. *Fawl* 4F **208**
Salterns La. *Hay I* 4H **243**
Saltern's Rd. *Fare & Lee S* 8L **211**
Salterns Way. *Poole* 5A **244**
Salter Rd. *Poole* 9A **244**
Salters Acres. *Win* 3G **104**
Salters Heath 4M **21**
Salters Heath Rd. *Monk S* 6K **21**
Salters La. *Win* 4F **104**
Saltgrass La. *Key* 10N **235**
Saltings, The. *Hav* 2F **216**
Saltings, The. *Ports* 1M **215**
Salt La. *Uphm* 6G **134**
Saltmarsh La. *Hay I* 2E **242**
Saltmarsh Rd. *Sotn* 7N **173** (8G **4**)
Salt Mead. *Sotn* 9A **160**
Saltmeat La. *Gos* 1M **239**
Saltram Rd. *Farn* 1N **49**
Salvia Clo. *Water* 3A **202**
Salwey Rd. *Bot* 5A **176**
Samber Clo. *L'ton* 2C **234**
Sammy Miller Motorcycle Mus. 4N **231**
Sampan Clo. *Wars* 8B **196**
Samphire Clo. *L'ton* 1D **234**
Sampson Rd. *Fare* 2B **212**
Sampson Rd. *Ports* 1A **240** (2H **5**)
Sampson's Almshouses. *F'ham* 9B **64**
Samson Clo. *Gos* 9F **212**
Samuel Rd. *Ports* 1G **240**
Sam Whites Hill. *Up Cl* 5L **69**
San Carlos App. *A'sht* 9L **49**
Sancreed Rd. *Poole* 7C **226**
Sandbanks 9A **244**
Sandbanks Dri. *Bas* 3K **59**
Sandbanks Rd. *Poole* 5A **244**
Sandbourne Rd. *Bourn* 4G **244**
Sand Clo. *W Wel* 1B **120**
Sandcroft Clo. *Gos* 4G **238**
Sandecotes Rd. *Poole* 1A **244**
Sandell Ct. *Sotn* 6N **159**
Sanderling Rd. *S'sea* 2K **241**
Sanderlings. *Hight* 2M **187**
Sanderlings, The. *Hay I* 5G **243**
Sanderson Cen., The. *Gos* 2K **239**
Sandford 8N **187**
Sandford Av. *Gos* 3F **238**
Sandford Clo. *Bourn* 3N **227**
Sandford Clo. *K're* 2D **6**
Sandford Ct. *A'sht* 1H **65**
Sandford Rd. *A'sht* 1H **65**
Sandford Rd. *F'ham* 3D **64**
Sandford Rd. *T'ley* 5G **10**
Sandford Springs Golf Course 6M **9**
Sandheath Rd. *Hind* 9L **85**
Sand Hill. *Farn* 5K **29**
Sand Hill Ct. *Farn* 5K **29**
Sandhill La. *Lee S* 8C **212**
(in two parts)
Sandhills Cvn. Pk. *Christ* 9D **230**
Sandhurst 6D **18**
Sandhurst Ct. *S'sea* 4E **240**
Sandhurst La. *B'wtr* 7D **18**
Sandhurst Rd. *C'then* 2D **18**
Sandhurst Rd. *Sotn* 4K **173** (2A **4**)
Sandhurst Rd. *Yate* 6B **18**
Sandhurst Sports Cen. 5F **18**
San Diego Rd. *Gos* 1K **239**
Sandilands Way. *Hythe* 8M **193**
Sandisplatt. *Fare* 9M **197**
Sandle Copse. *F'bri* 9E **150**
Sandleford Rd. *Hav* 2D **202**
Sandleheath 9D **150**
Sandleheath Ind. Est. *S'hth* 9E **150**
Sandle Mnr. Dri. *F'bri* 9F **150**
Sandlewood Clo. *Cal* 2J **171**
Sandlewood Clo. *Water* 6C **168**
Sandmartin Clo. *Bart S* 7A **232**
Sandon Ct. *Bourn* 7N **227**
Sandown Clo. *Alt* 6G **80**
Sandown Clo. *B'wtr* 8F **18**
Sandown Clo. *Gos* 4F **238**
Sandown Cres. *A'sht* 3K **65**
Sandown Dri. *Frim* 2M **29**
Sandown Heights. *Fare* 9M **197**
Sandown Rd. *Christ* 8A **230**
Sandown Rd. *Ports* 1F **214**
Sandown Rd. *Sotn* 1G **172**
Sandpiper Clo. *March* 9D **172**
Sandpiper Clo. *Water* 3A **182**
Sandpiper Rd. *Sotn* 6F **158**
Sandpipers. *Ports* 1M **215**
Sandpiper Way. *Bas* 3H **59**
Sandpit Hill. *Wash W & N'bry* 1C **8**
Sandpit La. *E End* 5B **236**
Sandpit La. *S'fld* 1L **15**
Sandport Gro. *Fare* 1K **213**
Sandringham Clo. *Alt* 5D **80**

Sandringham Clo.—Seymour Rd.

Sandringham Clo. *Bourn* 2M 227
Sandringham Clo. *Chan F* 8L 131
Sandringham Ct. *Bas.* 8M 41
Sandringham Ct. *Bourn* (BH2) 3K 245 (8L 247)
Sandringham Ct. *Bourn* (BH8) 8N 227
Sandringham Ct. Sotn. 4F 172 (off Regents Pk. Rd.)
Sandringham Gdns. *Bourn* 2M 227
Sandringham Ho. And 7N 51 (off Atholl Ct.)
Sandringham La. *Ports* 2F 240
Sandringham Rd. *Fare* 9L 197
Sandringham Rd. *Ptsfld* 9M 139
Sandringham Rd. *Poole* 2A 244
Sandringham Rd. *Ports* 2F 240
Sandringham Rd. *Sotn.* 1C 174
Sandsbury La. *Steep* 8J 139
Sands Clo. *Seale* 8M 65
Sands Drove. *Ink* 1F 6
Sands Rd. *F'ham & Seale* 7L 65
Sands, The. 9N 65
Sands, The. *W'hill* 5F 100
Sandy Balls Holiday Cen. *Gods* 9N 151
Sandy Beach Est. *Hay I* 6M 243
Sandy Brow. *Water* 5L 201
Sandy Clo. *Ptsfld* 1B 146
Sandycroft. *Wars* 8A 196
Sandy Cross. 6N 65
Sandy Down. 3B 224
Sandy Down. *Bold* 3B 224
Sandyfield Cres. *Water* 7M 181
Sandy Hill Rd. *F'ham* 3C 64
Sandy La. *Bourn* 9E 228
Sandy La. *Cam* 7N 19
Sandy La. *Christ.* 4H 229
Sandy La. *Chu C* 7M 47
Sandy La. *F Oak* 1M 161
Sandy La. *Fare* 9J 197
Sandy La. *Farn* 6E 28
Sandy La. *H Win* 7C 26
Sandy La. *Hasl* 8L 103
Sandy La. *Kingsl* 7G 83
Sandy La. *Lyn* 3B 148
Sandy La. *N Bad* 7G 131
Sandy La. *P Hth* 6K 11
Sandy La. *Rake* 2K 141
Sandy La. *Redl* 1N 119
Sandy La. *Roms* 1N 129
Sandy La. *St I* 4C 186
Sandy La. *S'hrst* 4B 18
Sandy La. *Shed & Wal C* 2M 177
Sandy La. *Steep M* 5A 140
Sandy La. *Tilf* 2J 85
Sandy Mead Rd. *Bourn* 5C 228
Sandy Plot. *Burt* 5M 229
Sandy Point. *Hay I* 4M 243
Sandy Point Nature Reserve. 6M 243
Sandy Point Rd. *Hay I* 6L 243
Sandys Clo. *Bas* 8N 41
Sandys Rd. *Bas* 7N 41
Sandys Rd. Roundabout. *Bas* 7N 41
Sandy Way. *Bourn* 3J 227 (in two parts)
Sankey La. *Fle* 8B 28
San Remo Towers. *Bosc* 2B 246
Sanross Clo. *Fare* 7K 211
Santina Clo. *F'ham* 2F 64
Saor M. *And* 1M 69
Sapley La. *Over* 3D 56
Sapphire Ridge. *Water* 2A 202
Saracen Clo. *Penn* 5C 234
Saracens Rd. *Chan F* 5D 132
Sarah Clo. *Bourn* 6E 228
Sarah Robinson Ho. *Ports* 2B 240 (3K 5)
Sarah Sands Clo. *Christ* 6N 229
Sarah Way. *Farn* 8K 29
Sarisbury. 3B 196
Sarisbury Clo. *T'ley* 5G 11
Sarisbury Ct. *L Hth* 5N 195
Sarisbury Ga. *Park G* 4E 196
Sark Rd. *Poole* 6B 226
Sarnia Ct. *Sotn* 7D 158
Sarson. 3B 68
Sarson Clo. *A'prt* 3B 68
Sarson La. *A'prt* 3B 68
Sarson La. *W'hll* 9B 50
Sarum Clo. Mid W 9M 67 (off Cottage Rd.)
Sarum Clo. *Ship B* 2A 66
Sarum Clo. *Win* 7G 105
Sarum Ct. *Poole* 1A 244
Sarum Hill. *Bas* 7B 42
Sarum Ho. *Tot* 1K 171
Sarum Rd. *Chan F* 6C 132
Sarum Rd. *T'ley* 4G 10
Sarum Rd. *Win* 7B 104
Sarum Vw. *Win* 7F 104
Sarum Wlk. *L'ton* 9D 224
Satchell La. *Hamb* 3J 195
Saturn Clo. *Sotn* 7D 158
Saulfland Dri. *Christ* 6F 230
Saulfland Pl. *Christ* 6F 230
Saunders Gdns. *T'ley* 5H 11
Saunders La. *Awb* 8E 122
Saunders M. *S'sea* 5J 241
Saunton Gdns. *Farn* 6J 29
Savernake Clo. *Gos* 6F 212
Savernake Clo. *Roms* 3A 130
Savile Cres. *Bord* 4J 101
Saville Clo. *Eastl* 7H 133
Saville Clo. *Gos* 4H 239
Saville Gdns. *Fare* 6C 198
Savoy Clo. *And* 2A 70
Savoy Ct. *S'sea* 6F 240
Savoy Gro. *B'wtr* 1F 28
Sawyer Clo. *Win* 5F 104
Sawyer's Hill. *Water* 2H 181
Saxholm Clo. *Sotn* 5L 159
Saxholm Dale. *Sotn* 5L 159
Saxholm Way. *Sotn* 5L 159
Saxley Ct. *Hav* 3C 202
Saxonbury Rd. *Bourn* 8H 229
Saxon Cen., The. *Christ* 7L 229
Saxon Clo. *Fare* 8K 199
Saxon Clo. *Wars* 8B 196
Saxon Clo. *Water* 8C 168
Saxon Ct. *And* 7N 51
Saxon Cft. *F'ham* 9E 64
Saxonford Rd. *Christ* 7E 230
Saxon Gdns. *H End* 5L 175
Saxon Ho. *Sotn* 4A 174
Saxonhurst. *D'ton* 2L 119
Saxonhurst Clo. *Bourn* 1J 227
Saxonhurst Gdns. *Bourn* 2J 227
Saxonhurst Rd. *Bourn* 2H 227
Saxon King Gdns. *Bourn* 1L 247
Saxon Leas. *W'slw* 5H 87
Saxon Mdw. *D'ton* 2L 119
Saxon Pl. *L'ton* 9D 224
Saxon Ri. *Coll D* 1H 31
Saxon Rd. *Black* 7D 208
Saxon Rd. *Sotn.* 5J 173
Saxon Rd. *Win* 5L 105
Saxon Sq. *Christ.* 8L 229
Saxon Wlk. *Chan F.* 7C 132
Saxon Way. *A'hlt* 5D 152
Saxon Way. *And* 7M 51
Saxon Way. *Lych* 4G 42
Saxon Way. *Roms* 5A 130
Saxony Way. *Yate* 9M 17
Sayers Clo. *Frim G* 5N 29
Sayers Rd. *Eastl.* 1H 161
Scafell Av. *Fare.* 9N 197
Scallows La. *W Wel* 8N 121
Scamblers Mead. *Pen G* 7F 50
Scantabout Av. *Chan F* 5C 132
Scarlatti Rd. *Bas.* 2A 60
Scarlet Oaks. *Cam* 1N 29
Scarlett's Rd. *A'sht* 8J 49
Sceptre Ct. *Wal I* 9D 52
Scholars' Wlk. *Ports.* 1K 215
School Clo. *Chan F.* 7N 131
School Clo. *L'ton* 3C 234
School Fields. *Kingsl* 7G 82
School Hill. *C'then* 1F 18
School Hill. *S'hrst.* 4C 18
School Hill. *Sob* 5L 165
School La. *Bent* 7K 63
School La. *Bish S* 1K 109
School La. *Bourn* 1F 226
School La. *Brans* 3G 220
School La. *Bro'tn* 4A 88
School La. *Chan F* 8M 131
School La. *Den.* 5D 180
School La. *Ems* 4N 203 (Long Copse La.)
School La. *Ems* 9M 203 (West St.)
School La. *Ews* 2N 63
School La. *Gods* 5A 154
School La. *Hamb* 8L 195
School La. *It Ab* 8J 93
School La. *Liss* 1E 140
School La. *L'ton* 2E 234
School La. *Mil S* 8M 233
School La. *Min* 8L 155
School La. *Neth W* 9N 67
School La. *Ptsfld* 7A 140
School La. *Pill.* 6F 224
School La. *Ports* 9E 214
School La. *Ring* 1K 187
School La. *Rise* 2J 15
School La. *Ropl* 2D 110
School La. *St I* 3D 186
School La. *St M* 9L 35
School La. *Sil* 4A 12
School La. *Ver D* 8E 6
School La. *Win* 1L 105
School La. *Yate* 7L 17
School Pl. *Sotn* 6C 174
School Rd. *Bord* 3J 101
School Rd. *Brans* 3F 220
School Rd. *Burs* 9L 175
School Rd. *Fawl* 5E 208
School Rd. *Gos* 7H 213
School Rd. *Gray* 4K 103
School Rd. *Hasl* 1N 117
School Rd. *Hav* 8E 202
School Rd. *Hythe* 5M 193
School Rd. *Lover* 9D 120
School Rd. *Nom* 2J 155
School Rd. *Rise* 1J 15
School Rd. *Roms* 3B 130
School Rd. *Row* 8N 63
School Rd. *Tot* 4N 171
School Rd. *Twy* 7K 127
School Rd. *W Wel* 2C 120
School Rd. *Wick* 7C 178
Schooners Clo. *Lee S* 1B 238
Schooner Way. *S'sea* 1K 241
Schooner Way. *Wars* 8B 196
Schubert Rd. *Bas* 2N 59
Scimitars, The. *Fare* 5L 211
Scivier's La. *Uphm* 1F 162
Scotland Clo. *F Oak* 1B 162
Scotland Hill. *S'hrst* 4C 18
Scotney Ct. *Hav* 3H 203
Scotney Rd. *Bas* 4C 42
Scots Ct. *Hook* 1J 45
Scott Clo. *And* 9D 52
Scott Clo. *Col C* 4L 133
Scott Clo. *Fare* 4M 211
Scott Clo. *King S* 9B 86
Scott Clo. *Poole* 5D 226
Scotter Rd. *Bourn* 8E 228
Scotter Rd. *Eastl* 9H 133
Scotter Sq. *Eastl* 9H 133
Scott Ho. *Bas* 5D 42
Scott Ho. *Ports* 6D 214
Scott Rd. *Eastl* 1D 160
Scott Rd. *Hils* 3G 215
Scott Rd. *Navy* 1A 240 (2H 5)
Scott Rd. *Poole* 5D 226
Scott Rd. *Sotn* 9D 174
Scott's Ct. *Farn* 5K 29
Scott's Grn. *Christ* 6B 230
Scotts Hills La. *Christ.* 7N 229 (in two parts)
Scrag Hill. 6E 130
Scratchface La. *Hav* 7B 202
Scratchface La. *H'rd* 2K 79
Scratchface La. *Water* 5N 201 (in three parts)
Scrubbs La. *Bish S* 5H 109
Scullards La. *Sotn* 6L 173 (5C 4)
Scures Rd. *Hook* 2F 44
Seabird Way. *Fare* 1D 212
Seabourne Pl. *Bourn* 9E 228
Seabourne Rd. *Bourn* 9D 228
Seabreeze Way. *Mil S* 8H 233
Seacliff Ct. *Bourn* 2G 246
Seacombe Grn. *Sotn* 1C 172
Seacombe Rd. *Poole* 9A 244
Sea Crest Rd. *Lee S* 2B 238
Seacroft Av. *Bart S* 6N 231
Seafarers Wlk. *Hay I* 6M 243
Seafield. 4L 239
Seafield Clo. *Bart S* 7A 232
Seafield Dri. *Bourn* 9H 229
Seafield Pk. Rd. *Fare* 7L 211
Seafield Rd. *Bart S* 6N 231
Seafield Rd. *Bourn* 1G 247
Seafield Rd. *Christ* 8E 230
Seafield Rd. *Fare* 1K 213
Seafield Rd. *Ports* 7H 215
Seafield Rd. *Sotn* 9C 158
Seafields. *Ems* 9L 203
Seafield Ter. *Gos* 4L 239
Seaford Clo. *Burs* 9K 175
Sea Front. *Hay I* 4C 242
Sea Front Est. *Hay I* 5H 243
Seagarth Clo. *Sotn* 8J 159
Seagarth La. *Sotn* 8J 159
Seager's Ct. *Ports* 4A 240 (7H 5)
Sea Gro. Av. *Hay I* 5G 242
Seagrove Rd. *Ports* 7E 214
Seagull Clo. *Bas* 2H 59
Seagull Clo. *S'sea* 1K 241
Seagull La. *Ems* 8M 203 (in two parts)
Seagull Rd. *Bourn* 5N 227
Seagulls, The. *Lee S* 3C 238
Seahorse Wlk. *Gos* 2M 239
Sea Kings. *Fare* 5L 211 (in two parts)
Sea La. *Fare* 8M 211
Seale La. *Seale* 6M 65 (in two parts)
Sea Life Cen. 6D 240 (Southsea)
Seal Rd. *Bas* 6C 42
Seaman's Corner. 8L 155
Seamans La. *Min* 8L 155
Seamead. *Fare* 8M 211
Sea Mill Gdns. *Ports* 2B 240 (4K 5)
Seamoor La. *Bourn* 2F 244
Seamoor Rd. *Bourn* 2F 244
Sea Pines. *Mil S* 9J 235
Searing Way. *T'ley* 4G 11
Searle Rd. *F'ham* 9E 64
Searles Clo. *Alr* 1F 108
Searl's La. *Roth & Hook* 8H 25 (in two parts)
Sea Rd. *Bart S* 6N 231
Sea Rd. *Bosc* 2B 246
Sea Rd. *Mil S* 8L 235
Sea Rd. *Sotn* 7B 174
Sea Rd. *South* 2J 247
Seathrift Clo. *Lee S* 1A 238
Seathwaite Ho. *Ports* 8C 200
Seaton Av. *Ports* 8H 215
Seaton Clo. *Fare* 6M 211
Seaton Clo. *Highc* 6K 231
Seaton Clo. *L'ton* 1E 234
Seaton Clo. *W End* 1G 174
Seaton Rd. *Cam* 8K 19
Seaton Rd. *Highc* 6K 231
Sea View. 5G 243
Seaview Av. *Fare* 8N 199
Seaview Ct. *Gos* 4F 238
Seaview Ct. *Lee S* 2B 238
Sea Vw. Est. *Net A* 4F 194
Sea Vw. Rd. *Hay I* 4J 243
Sea Vw. Rd. *New M* 7L 231
Sea Vw. Rd. *Ports* 8K 201
Sea Vw. Rd. *Walk* 5L 231
Sea Vixen Ind. Est. *Christ* 7C 230
Seaward Av. *Bart S* 7N 231
Seaward Av. *Bourn* 1E 246
Seaward Gdns. *Sotn* 6C 174
Seaward Path. *Poole* 5E 244
Seaward Rd. *Sotn* 6C 174
Seaward Tower. *Gos* 3N 239
Seaway. *New M* 6C 232
Seaway Av. *Christ* 7E 230
Seaway Cres. *S'sea* 3L 241
Seaway Gro. *Fare* 2L 213
Seawinds. *Mil S* 9H 233
Sebastian Gro. *Water* 1A 202
Sebastopol Rd. *A'sht* 9K 49
Second Av. *Farl* 1L 215
Second Av. *Hav* 7H 203
Second Av. *Ports* 9F 200
Second Av. *Sotn* 2C 172
Second Marine Av. *Bart S* 8B 232
Second St. *Hythe* 9C 194 (Avenue E.)
Second St. *Hythe* 5D 208 (South Av.)
Second St. E. *Green* 1H 9
Second St. W. *Green* 1H 9
Sedbergh Ho. *Sotn* 1C 172
Sedbergh Rd. *Sotn* 1C 172
Sedgefield Clo. *Ports* 9A 200
Sedgefield Clo. *Tot* 2J 171
Sedgeley Gro. *Gos* 8J 213
Sedge Mead. *Net A* 4F 194
Sedgemead Ct. *Net A* 4F 194
Sedgemoor. *Farn* 5K 29
Sedgewick Clo. *Gos* 8E 212
Sedgewick Ct. *Eastl* 9H 133
Sedgewick Rd. *Eastl* 9H 133
Sedgewick Rd. *Sotn* 5G 174
Sedgley Clo. *S'sea* 3E 240
Sedgley Rd. *Bourn* 6J 227
Seebys Oak. *Coll T* 7F 18
Seeviours Ct. Whitc 5F 54 (off Well's La.)
Segars La. *Twy* 8K 127
Segensworth E. Ind. Est. *Fare* 4G 197 (in two parts)
Segensworth N. Ind. Est. *Fare* 4H 197
Segensworth Rd. *Fare* 5G 196
Segensworth W. Ind. Est. *Seg W* 4F 196
Sekkong Clo. *Mid W* 4A 72
Selangor Av. *Ems* 8J 203
Selborne. 7L 99
Selborne Av. *A'sht* 3K 65
Selborne Av. *Hav* 4D 202
Selborne Av. *Sotn* 2G 174
Selborne Clo. *B'wtr* 7E 18
Selborne Clo. *Hook* 2H 45
Selborne Ct. *Roms* 3B 130
Selborne Dri. *Eastl* 8E 132
Selborne Gdns. *Gos* 3H 239
Selborne Pl. *Win* 9H 105
Selborne Rd. *Alt & Selb* 7E 80
Selborne Rd. *Tot* 1K 171
Selborne Wlk. *Sotn* 2G 174
Selborne Wlk. *T'ley* 5H 11
Selborne Way. *W'hill* 5F 100
Selbourne Clo. *Ptsfld* 8M 139
Selbourne Rd. *Hav* 8E 202
Selbourne Ter. *Ports* 2F 240
Selby Wlk. *Bas* 2C 42
Seldon Clo. *Win* 1F 126
Selfridge Av. *Bourn* 2L 247
Selfridge Clo. *Bourn* 2L 247
Selhurst Ho. *Ports* 1E 240
Selhurst Way. *F Oak* 2N 161
Sellwood Rd. *Net A* 3G 194
Sellwood Way. *New M* 6M 231
Selma Ct. *S'sea* 5E 240
Selsdon Av. *Roms* 4A 130
Selsey Av. *Gos* 8J 213
Selsey Av. *S'sea* 5H 241
Selsey Clo. *Hay I* 5M 243
Selsey Clo. *Sotn* 8D 158
Selsmore. 5J 243
Selsmore Av. *Hay I* 5J 243
Selsmore Rd. *Hay I* 4G 243
Selworth La. *Sob* 8K 165
Selwyn Dri. *Yate* 7L 17
Selwyn Gdns. *Eastl* 7E 132
Sembal Ho. *Sotn* 2A 4
Sengana Clo. *Bot* 4B 176
Senlac Rd. *Roms* 5A 130
Sennen Pl. *Port S* 1B 214
Sentinel Clo. *Water* 9B 182
Sepen Meade. *Chu C* 7K 47
Seps 4 Rd. *Hythe* 4G 209
September Clo. *W End* 1H 175
Seremban Clo. *Mid W* 3A 72
Serle Clo. *Tot* 3H 171
Serle Gdns. *Tot* 4K 171
Sermon Rd. *Win* 5F 104
Serpentine Rd. *Fare* 6D 198
Serpentine Rd. *S'sea* 5D 240 (Clarence Pde.)
Serpentine Rd. *S'sea* 5D 240 (9N 5) (Osborne Rd.)
Serpentine Rd. *Wid* 6K 201
Service Rd. *Ports* 9E 200
Setley. 2A 224
Setley Gdns. *Bourn* 3B 228
Seton Dri. *Hook* 3F 44
Setters Clo. *Col C* 4K 133
Set Thorns Rd. *Sway* 5K 223
Settle Clo. *Sotn* 2G 172
Settlers Clo. *Ports* 1E 240
Sett, The. *Yate* 8L 17
Sevenoaks Dri. *Bourn* 7D 228
Sevenoaks Rd. *Ports* 9F 200
Seventh St. Green 1G 9 (off Warehouse Rd.)
Seventh St. *Hythe* 3C 208 (D Avenue, in two parts)
Seventh St. *Hythe* 5C 208 (South Av., in three parts)
Seventon Rd. *N Wal* 9A 58
Severals, The. *Sher* 9M 21
Severn Clo. *Fare* 9J 199
Severn Clo. *Ports* 8C 200 (in two parts)
Severn Clo. *S'hrst* 5E 18
Severn Gdns. *Okly* 1D 58
Severn Rd. *Farn* 6G 28
Severn Rd. *Sotn* 2D 172
Severn Way. *Bas* 6E 42
Severn Way. *W End* 9H 161
Seville Cres. *And* 9B 52 (in two parts)
Seward Ri. *Roms* 4B 130
Seward Rd. *Hythe* 6N 193
Seymour Clo. *Cal* 1J 171
Seymour Clo. *Chan F* 7C 132
Seymour Clo. *Ports* 9E 214
Seymour Clo. *Sotn* 8H 159
Seymour Ct. *C'then* 1A 18
Seymour Ct. *Fle* 1M 47
Seymour Ct. Odi 8L 45 (off Seymour Pl.)
Seymour Ho. *Sotn* 8J 159
Seymour La. *N Bad* 8E 130
Seymour Pl. *Odi* 8L 45
Seymour Rd. *Bas* 9L 41

Seymour Rd.—Sirius Ct.

Seymour Rd. Head D 3E 102
Seymour Rd. Lee S 3B 238
Seymour Rd. Ring 8L 185
Seymour Rd. Sotn 8H 159
Shackleton Ho. Ports 6F 214
Shackleton Rd. Gos 8F 212
Shackleton Sq. And . . . . . . 7B 52 (off Cricketers Way)
Shackleton Sq. Brans 6D 220
Shadwell Ct. Ports 6D 214
Shadwell Rd. Ports 6E 214
Shady Nook. F'ham 4D 64
Shaftesbury Av. Chan F 8A 132
Shaftesbury Av. Sotn 1N 173
Shaftesbury Av. Water 5L 201
Shaftesbury Ct. Farn 3L 49
Shaftesbury Mt. B'wtr 2F 28
Shaftesbury Rd. Bourn 8N 227
Shaftesbury Rd. Gos . . . . . 3L 239 (in two parts)
Shaftesbury Rd. S'sea 5D 240 (9N 5)
Shaftesbury St. F'bri 1H 153
Shags Mdw. Lyn 2B 148
Shakespeare Av. And 9K 51
Shakespeare Av. Sotn 2N 173
Shakespeare Bus. Cen. Eastl 8F 132
Shakespeare Dri. Tot 9K 157
Shakespeare Gdns. Farn 7F 28
Shakespeare Gdns. Water 7M 181
Shakespeare M. Titch . . . . . 9K 197 (off East St.)
Shakespeare Rd. Bas 3D 42
Shakespeare Rd. Bourn 7G 229
Shakespeare Rd. Eastl 7D 132
Shakespeare Rd. Ports 1F 240
Shakespeare Ter. Ports 7K 5
Shalbourne Ri. Cam 8M 19
Shalbourne Rd. Gos 9J 213
Shalcombe. Net A 2G 194
Shalden. 10A 62
Shalden Clo. Sotn 7H 159
Shalden Green. 8B 62
Shalden La. Shald 5N 79
Shalden Rd. A'sht 2M 65
Shaldon Rd. Hav 3H 203
Shaldon Way. Fle 3J 47
Shales Rd. Sotn 3F 174
Shallows La. Bold 7D 224
Shallows, The. Brea 4M 151
Shamblehurst La. H End 9N 161
Shamblehurst La. N. H End 9A 162
Shamblehurst La. S. H End 2N 175
Shamrock Clo. Frim 4M 29
Shamrock Clo. Gos 3M 239
Shamrock Enterprise Cen. Gos 7H 213
Shamrock Quay. Sotn 5B 174
Shamrock Rd. Sotn 7B 174
Shamrock Vs. Sotn 1A 174
Shamrock Way. Hythe 3M 193
Shanklin Ct. A'sht 1L 65
Shanklin Cres. Sotn 1K 173
Shanklin Pl. Fare 9M 197
Shanklin Rd. Sotn 9J 159
Shanklin Rd. S'sea 3F 240
Shannon Clo. Fare 7N 197
Shannon Ho. Sotn . . . . 5A 174 (off Kent St.)
Shannon Rd. Fare . . . . 4L 211 (Old St.)
Shannon Rd. Fare . . . . 3C 212 (Royal Sovereign Av.)
Shannon Way. Chan F 6M 131
Shapland Av. Bourn 1C 226
Shapley Heath. W'fld 1A 46
Shappen Hill La. Burl 8D 188
Shapton Clo. Holb 4N 207
Sharlands Rd. Fare 2C 212
Sharon Ct. Gos 2L 239
Sharon Rd. W End . . . . 9G 160 (in two parts)
Sharpley Clo. F'bri 8H 151
Sharpness Clo. Fare 9M 197
Sharp Rd. Poole 7E 226
Sharps Clo. Ports 5J 215
Sharps Rd. Hav 4H 203
Sharvells Rd. Mil S 7J 235
Shavard La. Meon 8N 135
Shaves La. New M 1B 232
Shaw Clo. And 1J 69
Shaw Clo. Tot 3K 171
Shaw Clo. W End 9E 160
Shawcross Ind. Pk. Ports 3H 215
Shawfield Rd. Hav 8G 203
Shawford. 6H 127
Shawford Clo. Sotn 7K 159
Shawford Clo. Tot 3H 171
Shawford Gdns. Bourn 4A 228
Shawford Gro. Hav 4C 202
Shawford Rd. Bourn 3A 228
Shawford Rd. Shaw 7J 127
Shaw La. Baug 7E 10
Shaw Pk. C'then 2D 18
Shaw Pightle. Hook 2F 44
Shaw Rd. Ring 7M 185
Shayer Rd. Sotn 1H 173
Sheardley La. Drox 3A 166
Shearer Rd. Ports 9F 214
Shear Hill. Ptsfld 8A 140
Shears Brook Clo. Brans 6D 220
Shears Rd. Eastl 9J 133
Shearwater Av. Fare 8G 199
Shearwater Clo. Gos 6D 212
Shearwater Dri. Ports 1N 215
Sheddon Pl. Spar 4B 104
Shedfield. 3B 178
Sheep Drove. Neth W 2M 87
Sheep Fair. And 1B 70
Sheep Fair Clo. And 1B 70
Sheep Ho. F'ham 9E 64
Sheep Pond La. Drox 9L 135
Sheep St. Ptsfld 1M 145
Sheepwash. Burgh 2D 8
Sheepwash La. Burgh 2D 8
Sheepwash La. R'dll 6F 20
Sheepwash La. Water 9F 180
Sheepwash Rd. Horn . . . . . . 7C 182 (in two parts)
Sheet. 7A 140
Sheffield Clo. Eastl 7H 133
Sheffield Clo. Farn 8H 29
Sheffield Ct. Gos 1E 238
Sheffield Rd. Ports 2F 240
Shelbourne Clo. Bourn 8N 227
Shelbourne Rd. Bourn 8M 227
Sheldon's La. Hook 2F 44
Sheldons Rd. Hook 2G 44
Sheldrake Gdns. Hord 3J 233
Sheldrake Gdns. Sotn 6G 159
Sheldrake Rd. Christ 9C 230
Shelford Rd. S'sea 2J 241
Shell Ct. March 8E 172
Shellcroft. Wars 9A 196
Shelley Av. Ports 8N 199
Shelley Clo. Ashy H 3A 186
Shelley Clo. Bas 3D 42
Shelley Clo. Bourn 9B 228
Shelley Clo. Christ 7E 230
Shelley Clo. Fle 3M 47
Shelley Clo. It Ab 9H 93
Shelley Clo. Win 6H 105
Shelley Ct. Cam 8L 19
Shelley Ct. Sotn 5K 173 (3A 4)
Shelley Gdns. Bourn 9B 228
Shelley Gdns. Water 7M 181
Shelley Hamlets. Christ 7F 230
Shelley Hill. Christ 7F 230
Shelley Ho. New M 4B 232
Shelley La. Ower 1D 156
Shelley Ri. Farn 6H 29
Shelley Rd. Bourn 9B 228
Shelley Rd. Eastl 2D 160
Shelley Rd. Poole 9B 226
Shelley Rd. Sotn 4H 175
Shelley Rd. Tot 9K 157
Shelley Rd. E. Bourn 9B 228
Shelleys La. E Wor 7M 81
Shelley Wlk. Yate 8L 17
Shelley Way. Mil S 7K 235
Shell La. Colem 3B 112
Shelton Rd. Bourn 8F 228
Shenley Clo. Fare 7M 197
Shepards Clo. Fare 9M 197
Sheppeard's Way. Gos 5L 239
Shepherd & Flock Roundabout. F'ham 7G 65
Shepherd Clo. Highc 5H 231 (6F 4)
Shepherds Clo. Bart 4B 170
Shepherds Clo. Win 1F 126
Shepherds Down. Alr 2E 108
Shepherdshey Rd. Cal 1H 171
Shepherds Hill. Blash 3E 184
Shepherds La. Blash 3D 184
Shepherds La. Comp 7D 126
Shepherds Purse Clo. L Hth 7B 196
Shepherds Ri. Ver D 8E 6
Shepherds Rd. Bart 4B 170
Shepherds Rd. Win 6N 105
Shepherds Row. And 2B 70
Shepherds Spring La. And 1N 69
Shepherds Wlk. Farn 5G 28
Shepherds Way. Bourn 7D 228
Shepherds Way. C'then 1A 18
Shepherds Way. Lip 4E 116
Shepherds Way. Nurs 6B 158
Sheppard Clo. Water 4A 182
Sheppard Clo. Whitc 6G 55
Sheppard Rd. Bas 9B 42
Sheppard Sq. And . . . . 8B 52 (off Cricketers Way)
Sheraton Av. Bas 3K 59
Sheraton Clo. B'wtr 9G 18
Sherborne Ct. Eastl 6D 132
Sherborne Rd. Bas 4B 42
Sherborne Rd. Farn 2M 49
Sherborne Rd. Sher 9N 21
Sherborne Rd. Sotn 9N 159
Sherborne St. John. 8N 21
Sherborne Way. H End 4N 175
Sherbrooke Clo. King W 7N 91
Sherecroft Gdns. Bot 3E 176
Sherfield. Wint D 3A 86
Sherfield Av. Hav 4G 202
Sherfield Clo. Bourn 4A 228
Sherfield English. 6N 121
Sherfield English La. Plait 9L 121
Sherfield Green. 3L 23
Sherfield Ho. Sotn 4K 173 (1A 4)
Sherfield on Loddon. 4L 23
Sherfield Rd. Braml 1G 22
Sheridan Clo. A'sht 2J 65
Sheridan Clo. Sotn 5H 175
Sheridan Clo. Win 9G 104
Sheridan Cres. Baug 4E 10
Sheridan Gdns. Tot 3K 171
Sheridan Gdns. White 1F 196
Sheridan Rd. Frim 4M 29
Sheringham Rd. Poole 9D 226
Sheringham Rd. Ports 8E 200
Sherley Grn. Burs 9L 175
Sherlock Lea. E'sly 6H 17
Sherringham Clo. Fawl 5F 208
Sherrington Way. Bas 9A 42
Sherwin Cres. Farn 4K 29
Sherwin Wlk. Gos 4J 239
Sherwood Av. H End 6N 175
Sherwood Clo. Bas 4L 59
Sherwood Clo. Christ 7J 229
Sherwood Clo. Liss 7F 114
Sherwood Clo. Sotn 8K 159
Sherwood Gdns. Sar G 5B 196
Sherwood Rd. Chan F 3C 132
Sherwood Rd. Gos 3J 239
Sherwood Way. Black 9C 208
Shetland Clo. Ports 8G 201
Shetland Clo. Tot 2H 171
Shetland Ri. White 2E 196
Shetland Rd. Bas 2D 42
Shetland Way. Fle 8N 27
Shieldhall. . . . . . . 8N 173 (9G 4) (Steam Ship)
Shillinglee. Water 5M 201
Shillingstone Dri. Bourn 2M 227
Shillingstone Gdns. Poole 7D 226
Shillito Rd. Poole 9B 226
Shingle Bank Dri. Mil S . . . 8K 235
Shinwell Ct. Sotn 1G 173
Ship All. Farn 6L 29
Shipbuilding Rd. Ports 1A 240 (1H 5)
Shipcote La. Bish W 1M 163
Ship La. Farn 6L 29
Ship Leopard St. Ports 2B 240 (3J 5)
Shipley Clo. Alt 3G 81
Shipley Ct. Lip 3D 116
Shipley Rd. Twy 6L 127
Shipton Bellinger. 2A 66
Shipton Grn. Hav 3D 202
Shipton Way. Bas 9L 41
Shipwrights Wlk. Key 10N 235
Shipyard Est., The. Hythe 5N 193
Shire Av. Fle 8A 28
Shire Clo. Water 9B 182
Shire Clo. White 2E 196
Shire Ct. A'sht 9G 49
Shires Clo. Ring 4K 187
Shires Copse. Bourn 2J 247
Shires, The. H End 4L 175
Shires Wlk. Tot 3H 171
Shires Way. Yate 6N 17
Shirley. . . . . 5B 220 (Christchurch)
Shirley. . . . . 2G 173 (Southampton)
Shirley Av. Sotn 2H 173
Shirley Av. S'sea 3K 241
Shirley Clo. Brans 6D 220
Shirley Common. 3E 220
Shirley High St. Sotn 2G 173
Shirley Holms. L'ton 6M 223
Shirley Pk. Rd. Sotn 2G 172
Shirley Rd. Bourn 5L 227
Shirley Rd. Park 8A 226
Shirley Rd. Sotn 2H 173
Shirley Rd. S'sea 5F 240
Shirley Towers. Sotn 2H 173
Shirley Warren. 9G 158
Shirnall Hill. Lwr F 4D 98
Shirrel Ct. Gos 4F 238
Shirrell Heath. 1B 178
Shoblands Way. Hythe . . . . 8M 193 (off Sandilands Way)
Shobley. 4B 188
Shoddesden La. Gt Shod 4E 30
Shoddesden La. Lit Sh 7M 31
Shoe La. A'sht 5J 49
Shoe La. Ext 8N 135
Shoe La. Uphm 8E 134
Sholing. 7D 174
Sholing Common. 5F 174
Sholing Ct. Hav 3D 202
Sholing Rd. Sotn 6C 174
Shootash. 3D 128
Shooters Hill Clo. Sotn 7F 174
Shooters Way. Bas 4D 42
Shoot Hill. S'wick 6M 179
Shoot La. Lee S 8B 212
Shop La. Burs & Sotn 8H 175
Shore Av. S'sea 1J 241
Shore Clo. Mil S 9K 235
Shore Cres. Bish W 4N 163
Shorefield Cvn. Pk. Mil S 7H 233
Shorefield Cres. Mil S 8J 235
Shorefield Rd. Down 8G 233
Shorefield Rd. March 8E 172
Shorefield Way. Mil S 7J 235
Shorehaven. Ports 9A 200
Shore La. Bish W 4N 163
Shore Rd. Hythe 5N 193
Shore Rd. Poole 7B 244
Shore Rd. Wars 8M 195
Shorewell. Net A 2G 194
Shorewood Clo. Wars 8C 196
Shorley. 2J 135
Short Clo. Poole 6E 226
Shortdale Rd. A'sht 4L 65
Shortheath. 2D 100
Short Hill. Nom 2H 155
Short Hill. Roms 2B 130
Short La. P Cnr 9F 50
Short Rd. Fare 6K 211
Short Row. Navy . . . 1B 240 (2J 5)
Shorts Clo. Burt 5M 229
Short's Rd. F Oak 1M 161
Short St. A'sht 9J 49
Short St. Lud 1D 30
Shot Hanger. Bas 2J 41
Shotterfield. Ter. Liss 1E 140
Shottermill. 8N 103
Shottermill Pk. Hasl 8N 103
Shottermill Pond. Hasl 1N 117
Shottermill Ponds. 1N 117
Shottermill Rd. Hasl 1N 117
Shotters Hill Clo. W End 1H 175
Shotters La. Newt V 1E 112
Shotts La. L'ton 1J 235
Shraveshill Clo. Tot 1K 171
Shrave, The. Four M 3L 97
Shripple La. W'slw 5H 87
Shrivenham Clo. Coll T 5F 18
Shroeder Clo. Bas 9B 42
Shrubbery Clo. Fare 1L 213
Shrubbery, The. Farn 9F 28
Shrubbery, The. Gos 9H 213
Shrubb's Av. L'ton 2E 234
Shrubbs Hill. Lyn 2B 148
Shrubbs Hill Gdns. Lyn 3B 148
Shrubland Clo. Sotn 2F 174
Shulebrede Priory. 6M 117
Shyshack La. Baug 4E 10
Sian Clo. Chu C 6N 47
Sibelius Clo. Bas 3N 59
Sibland Clo. Fare 9N 197
Sickles Rd. Kingsl 5G 82
Sidbury Circular Rd. Tidw 7B 30
Sidbury Hill Av. Tidw 6C 30
Siddal Clo. Sotn 7G 175
Sidings, The. A'sht 8L 49
Sidings, The. D'ton 1L 119
Sidings, The. Net A 4H 195
Sidlaw Clo. Bas 8J 41
Sidlaws Rd. Farn 5F 28
Sidlesham Clo. Hay I 5M 243
Sidmouth Av. Ports 8H 215
Sidmouth Rd. And 1B 70
Sidney Gdns. Bourn 2N 227
Signal St. Bulf B 3B 66
Silchester. 4A 12
Silchester Clo. And 8L 51
Silchester Clo. Bourn 9K 227
Silchester Dri. Elve 9J 27
Silchester Rd. Braml 1C 22
Silchester Rd. Lit L 2N 21
Silchester Rd. Ports 9J 215
Silchester Rd. T'ley & P Hth 4H 11
Silcock Ho. Bas 5D 42
Silkin Gdns. Tot 4K 171
Silk Mill La. Over 2C 56
Silkstead. 8D 126
Silkstead Av. Hav 3F 202
Silkstead La. Ott . . . . 8C 126 (in two parts)
Silkweavers Rd. And 1A 70
Sillen La. M'tin 9B 118
Silver Birch Av. Fare 9A 198
Silver Birch Clo. Chu C 6L 47
Silver Birch Clo. Liss 1F 140
Silverbirch Clo. Poole 1E 244
Silver Birch Clo. Sotn 6G 174
Silver Birch Cotts. Churt . . . 7M 85
Silver Birches. Burs 1K 195
Silverbirch Rd. And 9L 51
Silver Bus. Pk. Christ 7B 230
Silverdale. Bart S 6C 232
Silverdale. Fle 5M 47
Silverdale Ct. Sotn 3K 173
Silverdale Cres. A'hlt 4D 152
Silverdale Dri. Water 8K 181
Silverdale Rd. Sotn 3K 173 (1A 4)
Silverdale Rd. T'ley 4H 11
Silver Glades. Yate 9M 17
Silver Hill. Coll T 5G 18
Silver Hill. Win 7L 105 (8N 237)
Silver Jubilee Ct. Bourn . . . 4E 226
Silverlock Clo. Ports 8E 214
Silver Pk. Clo. Chu C 5N 47
Silver Sands Gdns. Hay I 5H 243
Silvers End. Dib P 8M 193
Silver St. Christ 8L 229
Silver St. Hord 2G 233
Silver St. Lyn 2M 189
Silver St. S'sea 4C 240 (7M 5)
Silvers Wood. Cal 1J 171
Silverthorne Way. Water . . . 1L 201
Silvertrees. Ems 7M 203
Silver Way. Highc 6G 231
Silverways. Highc 6G 231
Silverweed Clo. Chan F 5L 131
Silverweed Ct. L Hth 7B 196
Silverwood Clo. Win 9H 105
Silvester Clo. Bas 4D 42
Silvester Rd. Water 7M 181
Silvester Way. Chu C 6J 47
Silwood Clo. Win 5H 105
Simmondstone La. Churt . . . 6F 84
Simmons Clo. H End 2N 175
Simmons Grn. Hay I 4J 243
Simmons Wlk. Bas 7D 42
Simms Farm La. Mort 1E 12
Simnel St. Sotn 7L 173 (7C 4)
Simonds Ct. Win 4L 105
Simonds Rd. Lud 1C 30
Simons Clo. Chine 1G 42
Simons Rd. Chine 1F 42
Simons Wood. 1M 17
Simon Way. Sotn 3J 175
Simpson Clo. Fare 8L 199
Simpson Rd. Cosh 8G 200
Simpson Rd. Ports 7D 214
Sims Clo. Braml 2J 23
Sinah La. Hay I 4C 242
Sinah Warren. 3C 242
Sinah Warren Holiday Village. Hay I 3B 242
Sinclair Rd. Sotn 6F 158
Sine Clo. Farn 4K 29
Singleton Dri. Bourn 4G 227
Singleton Gdns. Water 7D 168
Singleton Way. Tot 2H 171
Sinhurst Rd. Cam 9K 19
Sir Christopher Clo. Hythe 5N 193
Sirdar Rd. Sotn 8A 160
Sir Galahad Rd. Chan F 6L 131
Sir George's Rd. Sotn 4J 173
Sir George Staunton Country Pk. 2F 202
Sir George Staunton Ornamental Farm. 3G 202
Sir George Staunton Vis. Cen. 3G 202
Sir Harold Hillier Gardens & Arboretum. 9C 124
Sirius Ct. S'sea 3D 240 (6N 5)

Sirius Ho.—Southsea Esplanade

Sirius Ho. S'sea 5E 240
Sir Max Aitken Mus. 5P 237
Sir Richards Ride. E'sly 9D 16
Siskin Clo. Bish W 3K 163
Siskin Clo. Sotn 6F 158
Siskin Gro. Water 3A 202
Siskin Rd. S'sea 2K 241
Sissinghurst Clo. Sotn 9E 174
Sissinghurst Rd. Fare 1J 213
Six Bells Roundabout. F'ham 5G 64
Six Dials. Sotn 5M 173 (4E 4)
Six Oaks Rd. N Bad. 8F 130
Sixpenny Clo. Fare 8D 196
Sixpenny Clo. Poole 7D 226
Sixth Av. Ports 9F 200
Sixth St. Green 1G 9
Sixth St. Hythe 4C 208 (in three parts)
Sizer Way. Dib 6G 193
Skates La. P Grn. 8K 11
Skew Rd. Fare. 7L 199
Skew Rd. Quar 3L 67
Skintle Grn. Col C. 4K 133
Skipper Clo. March 7F 172
Skipper Way. Lee S 1B 238
Skippetts La. E. Bas 9D 42
Skippetts La. W. Bas. 9C 42
Skipton Rd. Chan F. 8B 132
Sky End La. Hord 4H 233
Skylark Ct. S'sea. 2K 241
Skylark Meadows. Fare 4J 197
Skylark Ri. Whitc 4F 54
Skys Wood Rd. Chan F. 6L 131
Slab La. D'ton & W'flls 7B 120
Slab La. W Wel. 1A 120
Slade Clo. Hord 3H 233
Slade La. Rog. 9H 141
Sladen Corner. 3L 35
Sladen Green. 2L 35
Slades Farm Rd. Bourn 5G 227
Slades Hill. Black 6D 208
Slade's La. Bourn. 6G 227
Slater App. Ports 7C 214
Slater Clo. Tot. 2H 171
Slate Way. Pitt 7D 86
Sleaford. 7K 83
Sleepers Delle Gdns. Win 8J 105 (9H 237)
Sleepers Hill. 7G 105
Sleeper's Hill. Win 8G 105
Sleeper's Hill Gdns. Win 8H 105
Sleeper's Hill Ho. Win. 8H 105
Slepe Cres. Poole 6D 226
Slessor Clo. And. 2H 69
Slim Clo. A'sht 4N 49
Slim Rd. Cam 6K 19
Slindon Clo. Water 6D 168
Slindon Gdns. Hav 8F 202
Slindon St. Ports 2D 240 (3N 5)
Slingsby Clo. Ports 4C 240 (7L 5)
Slinn Rd. Christ 7A 230
Slipper Cvn. Pk. Ems 9N 203
Slipper Rd. Ems 9N 203
Slippery Elm M. Rockb. 2B 150
Slipway, The. Port S 1B 214
Sloane Av. Holb 4B 208
Sloane Ct. Holb. 4B 208
Sloane Pk. Shed 3N 177
Sloane Stanley Ct. Gos 1K 239
Slocum Ho. Gos 3L 239
Sloe Tree Clo. L Hth 7F 196
Slowhill Copse. March 7D 172
Smallfield Dri. Hook 2J 45
Smallwood Dri. T'ley 4H 11
Smannell. 4D 52
Smannell Rd. And & Sman 7A 52
Smannell Rd. Roundabout. And 8N 51
Smay Down La. Oxen 5A 6 (in two parts)
Smeaton Rd. And. 8H 51
Smeaton St. Ports 6D 214
Smeeton Rd. Lee S. 1B 238
Smith Clo. Fawl 6D 208
Smithe Clo. Eastl 9E 132
Smithfield La. Head D. 6C 84
Smithfield Pl. Bourn. 5K 227
Smith Gro. H End. 5N 175
Smith's Fld. Over 3E 56
Smiths Fld. Roms. 3N 129
Smiths La. Shir H. 2B 178
Smiths Mead. N Wal. 9B 58
Smithson Clo. Poole 6F 226
Smiths Quay. Sotn 6A 174
Smith St. Gos 3J 239
Smithy Clo. Holyb. 1K 81
Smithy La. Dock. 6N 83
Smithy La. New M 9A 222
Smithy, The. Braml. 1G 23
Smithy, The. Water 6F 180
Smuggler's La. Mnkwd. 3G 111
Smugglers La. N. Christ 4F 230
Smugglers La. S. Christ 6F 230
Smugglers Rd. Burl 6B 188
Smugglers Vw. New M 7L 231
Smugglers Way. Seale 9N 65
Smugglers Wood Rd. Christ 5F 230
Smythe Rd. Sotn 7H 175
Snailing La. Hawk. 7B 114
Snail's La. Blash 7K 185
Snailslynch. F'ham 8F 64
Snakemoor La. Durl 6A 162
Snapdragon Clo. L Hth 7C 196
Snape Clo. Gos 8E 212
Snellgrove Clo. Cal 9J 157
Snellgrove Pl. Cal 9J 157
Snipe La. Bish G. 2G 9 (off Willow Rd.)
Snoddington Rd. Ship B & Thru 2G 67
Snooks La. L'ton 9H 225
Snowberry Cres. Hav 6H 203
Snowdon Dri. Fare 9A 198
Snowdon Rd. Bourn 1G 244
Snowdon Rd. Farn 5G 29
Snowdrop Clo. Bas 2J 59
Snowdrop Clo. L Hth 7C 196
Snowdrop Gdns. Christ 5D 230
Snowdrop Wlk. Fle 1L 47 (off Stockton Av.)
Soake Rd. Water 7J 181
Soalwood La. Frox 4F 138
Soame's La. Ropl 3F 110
Sobers Sq. And 7B 52
Soberton. 5K 165
Soberton Heath. 1K 179
Soberton Ho. Ports 1E 240 (off Church Rd.)
Soberton Rd. Bourn 7A 228
Soberton Rd. Hav 5E 202
Soberton Towers. Sob 5L 165
Soke Hill. Four M 6F 96
Soke Rd. Sil 1L 11
Soke, The. Alr 9F 94
Solartron Rd. Farn 9K 29
Solby's Rd. Bas 6B 42
Soldridge. 5F 96
Soldridge Clo. Hav 3J 203
Soldridge Rd. Meds 4F 96
Solent Av. L'ton 3F 234
Solent Av. Sotn 4J 175
Solent Breezes. 4C 210
Solent Breezes Cvn. Site. Wars 3B 210
Solent Bus. Cen. Sotn 4G 172
Solent Bus. Pk. White 2H 197
Solent Cen. White. 2H 197
Solent Clo. Chan F 6C 132
Solent Clo. L'ton 3F 234
Solent Ct. Mil S 8H 235
Solent Dri. Bart S 7B 232
Solent Dri. Bas 3K 59
Solent Dri. Hay I 5F 242
Solent Dri. Hythe 5L 193
Solent Dri. Wars 2A 210
Solent Flats. Mil S. 8L 235
Solent Heights. Lee S. 2A 238
Solent Heights. S'sea. 4M 241
Solent Homes. Sotn 4J 175
Solent Ho. Fare. 1C 212
Solent Ho. Hav. 6G 202
Solent Ind. Cen. Sotn. 4H 173
Solent Ind. Est. H End 1N 175
Solent Lodge. New M 5A 232
Solent Meadows. Hamb 8L 195
Solent Meads Golf Course. 2M 247
Solent Pines. Mil S. 8H 235
Solent Rd. Bourn 2K 247
Solent Rd. Dib P. 9K 193
Solent Rd. Fare. 7K 211
Solent Rd. Hav. 8D 202
Solent Rd. New M 7M 231
Solent Rd. Ports 9K 201
Solent Rd. Walk 4K 231
Solent Rd. W Dock 6K 173 (7A 4)
Solent 27. Ports 2K 215
Solent Vw. Bourn 2K 247
Solent Vw. Cals 8K 209
Solent Vw. Fare 8K 199
Solent Vw. Ct. Penn 4C 234
Solent Village. White 3H 197
Solent Way. Gos 4G 239
Solent Way. Mil S 8M 235
Solihull Ho. S'sea 3C 240 (5M 5)
Solly Clo. Poole 7C 226
Solomons La. Wal C & Shir H 9A 164
Solway Ho. Sotn. 4A 174 (off Kent St.)
Somborne Dri. Hav 4F 202
Somborne Ho. Sotn 9D 174
Somborne Pk. Rd. Stockb 3H 89
Somerford. 7C 230
Somerford Av. Christ 6D 230
Somerford Bus. Pk. Christ 7C 230
Somerford Clo. Sotn. 4E 174
Somerford Rd. Christ. 8A 230
Somerford Way. Christ. 7A 230
Somerley Park. 4F 184
Somerley Rd. Bourn 7L 227
Somerley Vw. Ring. 9K 185
Somers Clo. Win 9H 105
Somerset Av. Bord 4J 101
Somerset Av. Sotn 3G 174
Somerset Ct. Farn. 2L 49
Somerset Ct. Sotn 4H 173
Somerset Cres. Chan F. 9B 132
Somerset Rd. Bourn. 9C 228
Somerset Rd. Christ. 7H 229
Somerset Rd. Farn 2L 49
Somerset Rd. Sotn. 9A 160
Somerset Rd. S'sea 6E 240
Somerset Ter. Sotn. 4H 173
Somers Rd. S'sea. 3D 240 (in two parts)
Somers Rd. N. Ports 2F 240
Somers Town. 3D 240
Somerton Av. Sotn 3F 174
Somerton Clo. New M 3E 232
Somervell Clo. Gos. 5J 239
Somervell Dri. Fare. 6B 198
Somerville Ct. And 9C 52
Somerville Cres. Yate 7A 18
Somerville Pl. Ports 6D 214
Somerville Rd. Bourn 2H 245 (7H 247)
Somerville Rd. King W. 6N 91
Somerville Rd. Ring 9M 185
Somme Rd. Lud & Per D 2A 30
Sommers Ct. Sotn 7B 174
Sonnet Way. Water. 1B 202
Sonning Clo. Bas 3H 59
Sonninge Clo. Coll T. 5F 18
Sonning Way. Bourn 4M 227
Soper Gro. Bas. 5C 42
Soper's Bottom. Rag A. 3C 50
Soper's La. Christ. 8K 229
Sopers Row. Old B. 5H 43
Sopley. 8L 219
Sopley Clo. New M 6M 231
Sopley Common Nature Reserve. 8F 218
Sopley Ct. Hav 3H 203
Sopley Farm Bldgs. Brans 9L 219
Sopwith Clo. Christ 8D 230
Sopwith Clo. King S 9B 86
Sopwith Pk. And. 9H 51
Sopwith Way. Swanw. 1C 196
Sorrel Clo. Farn. 7E 28
Sorrel Clo. Roms 3B 130
Sorrel Clo. Water 3A 202
Sorrel Dri. White 2G 197
Sorrell Clo. L Hth 7C 196
Sorrell Ct. Christ. 6D 230
Sorrell's Clo. Chine. 9G 23
Sorrell Way. Christ 6D 230
Sotherington La. Selb 9M 99
South Acre. S Hart. 9G 147
Southampton. 7M 173
Southampton City Art Gallery. 5L 173 (3C 4)
Southampton Clo. B'wtr 7E 18
Southampton (Eastleigh) Airport. Sotn. 4E 160
Southampton F.C. (St Mary's Stadium) 5N 173 (4G 4)
Southampton Golf Course. 5K 159
Southampton Hall of Aviation. 7N 173 (8G 4)
Southampton Hill. Fare. 8J 197
Southampton Ho. Hav 4G 202
Southampton Maritime Mus. 7L 173 (8C 4)
Southampton Rd. Bold. 3A 224
Southampton Rd. Cad 6N 155 (in two parts)
Southampton Rd. Eastl. 3E 160
Southampton Rd. Fare. 7D 198
Southampton Rd. F'bri & Gods 1K 153
Southampton Rd. Hythe. 5K 193
Southampton Rd. Lyn 2C 148
Southampton Rd. Park G & Fare 4E 196 (in two parts)
Southampton Rd. Ports. 9N 199
Southampton Rd. Ring 1J 187
Southampton Rd. Roms 5M 129
Southampton Rd. W Gri & W'ish 3D 120
Southampton Row. Ports 2B 240 (3K 5)
Southampton St. Farn 3K 49
Southampton St. Sotn 4L 173 (1C 4)
S. Atlantic Dri. A'sht. 8L 49
South Av. F'ham. 4F 64
South Av. Hythe. 5C 208
South Av. New M. 4C 232
South Av. Ports 4F 214
South Baddesley. 9L 225
S. Baddesley Rd. L'ton. 2G 235
South Bay. Ems. 5N 217
South Bockhampton. 2A 230
Southbourne. 2H 247
Southbourne Av. Holb 4A 208
Southbourne Av. Ports. 9J 201
Southbourne Cliff Dri. Bourn 2J 247
Southbourne Clo. Port. 9B 66 (off Southbourne Way)
Southbourne Coast Rd. Bourn 2H 247
Southbourne Gro. Bourn 1F 246
Southbourne Overcliff Dri. Bourn 2F 246
Southbourne Promenade. Bourn 2F 246
Southbourne Rd. Bourn. 8E 228
Southbourne Rd. L'ton. 3C 234
Southbourne Sands. Bourn 2G 246
Southbourne Way. Port. 9B 66
Southbrook Clo. Hav 9F 202
Southbrook Cotts. Mich. 7J 77
Southbrook Pl. Mich 7J 77 (off Rook La.)
Southbrook Rd. Hav. 1F 216
Southbrook Rd. Sotn 5K 173 (4A 4)
Southby Dri. Fle. 2N 47
South Camp. 7K 49
S. Charford Drove. W'bry 8K 119
Southcliff. Lee S 9A 212
Southcliffe Rd. Christ 8D 230
Southcliffe Rd. New M 7M 231
S. Cliff Rd. Bourn 3K 245 (9L 247)
Southcliff Rd. Sotn 3M 173 (1D 4)
South Clo. Alr 1D 108
South Clo. Gos 5H 239
South Clo. Hav 9G 202
South Clo. Roms 3B 130
Southcote Rd. Bourn 1M 245
South Ct. Hamb 7J 195
South Ct. Sotn. 2G 172
Southcroft Rd. Gos 2H 239
S. Cross St. Gos. 3M 239
Southdale Ct. Chan F. 6A 132
Southdene Rd. Chan F. 7A 132
South Down. 7H 127
S. Down La. Mich 7L 77
Southdown Rd. Cosh 9H 201
Southdown Rd. Shaw 7H 127
Southdown Rd. T'ley 4G 11
Southdown Rd. Water 9C 168 (in three parts)
Southdown Vw. Water 8K 181
South Dri. Roms 1H 129
South Dri. Sher L. 6L 23
South Dri. Tidw 8G 30
South Dri. Win. 2E 104
S. East Cres. Sotn 6E 174
S. East Rd. Sotn. 6E 174
S. E. Sector. Hurn 7D 218
South End. 4P 149 **(Fordingbridge)**
Southend. 2M 179 **(Southampton)**
S. End Clo. Hurs 7N 125
Southend La. Sob. 2M 179
S. End Rd. And 3A 70
Southend Rd. Bas 6B 42
Southern Gdns. Tot 3L 171
Southernhay. Water. 6G 180
Southern Haye. H Win. 7B 26
Southern La. New M 6A 232
Southern Oaks. Bart S. 5A 232
Southern Rd. Bas 7C 42
Southern Rd. Bord 2H 101
Southern Rd. Bourn 1F 246
Southern Rd. Cam 7L 19
Southern Rd. Fawl 7K 209
Southern Rd. L'ton. 3D 234
Southern Rd. Sotn 6K 173 (4A 4)
Southern Rd. W End 2H 175
Southern Way. Farn 9F 28
Southern Way. F'ham 9E 64
Southey Rd. Christ. 6B 230
South Farnborough. 3M 49
Southfield. Ring 2K 187
Southfield La. Burl 8F 188
Southfield M. Ring. 2K 187
Southfields Clo. Bish W 3M 163
Southfield Wlk. Hav 2C 202
South Front. Roms 5M 129
South Front. Sotn 6M 173 (5E 4)
Southgate M. Win 7K 105 (9L 237)
Southgate St. Win 7K 105 (8L 237)
Southgate Vs. Win 9L 237
South Gorley. 8M 153
South Gro. Fle 8A 28
South Gro. L'ton 3F 234
South Ham. 8M 41
S. Ham Ho. Bas 8L 41
S. Hampshire Ind. Pk. Tot 9K 157
S. Ham Rd. Bas 7N 41
South Harting. 8G 146
South Hayling. 5F 242
South Hill. 8C 132
South Hill. Drox 3J 165
South Hill. Upt G 3B 62
South Hurst. W'hill 6J 101
Southill. A'hlt 4D 152
Southill Av. Poole 8A 226
Southill Gdns. Bourn 5L 227
Southill Rd. Bourn 5L 227
Southill Rd. Poole 8A 226
Southington. 2C 56
Southington Clo. Over 3C 56
Southington La. Over. 2C 56
S. Kinson Dri. Bourn 2E 226
Southlands. Chine. 9F 22
Southlands. Penn. 4C 234
Southlands. Ports 9H 201
Southlands Av. Bourn. 1J 247
South La. Bton 8K 145
South La. D'ton. 2J 119
South La. Nom 2J 155
South La. Water 6B 168 (Drift Rd.)
South La. Water. 1G 183 (North La.)
Southlawns Wlk. Bart S 5A 232
Southlea. Clid. 2B 60
Southlea Av. Bourn. 9J 229
Southleigh Gro. Hay I 3F 242
Southleigh Rd. Ems 6L 203
Southleigh Rd. Hav 8H 203
South Lodge. Fare 8L 197
South Mall. Fle 2L 47
South Mdw. C'then 2F 18
Southmead Rd. A'sht 2K 65
Southmead Rd. Fare 8N 197
S. Millers Dale. Chan F. 5N 131
S. Mill Rd. Sotn 3E 172
Southmoor La. Hav 9D 202
South Normandy. Ports 3B 240 (6K 5)
South Pde. S'sea 6E 240
South Pde. Tot. 2M 171
S. Park Rd. Poole 6E 226
South Pl. Lee S 3C 238
South Ridge. Odi 9L 45
South Rd. Alr. 1D 108
South Rd. Bourn 9B 228
South Rd. Bro'tn 5B 88
South Rd. Cosh 1L 215
South Rd. C'then 2G 18
South Rd. Hay I 4F 242
South Rd. Horn 1C 182 (in two parts)
South Rd. K're 2C 6
South Rd. Lip. 5E 116
South Rd. Ows. 7B 134
South Rd. Ports 9F 214
South Rd. Sotn. 2A 174
South Rd. S'wick 7B 200 (Hilltop Rd.)
South Rd. S'wick 3B 200 (Main Dri.)
Southrope. 2M 79
Southrope Grn. H'rd 1M 79
Southsea. 5D 240
Southsea Esplanade. S'sea 6G 240

306 A-Z Hampshire

Southsea Model Village—Stanley Rd.

Southsea Model Village. 6G 240
Southsea Ter. S'sea 4C 240 (8M 5)
Southsea Works Ind. Est. S'sea 2H 241
Southside Cotts. Longs. 2F 88
Southside Rd. Longp 4N 71
South Spur. S'wick 7C 200
South St. And. 3N 69
South St. Bro Ch 3A 118
South St. Eastl 3E 160
South St. Ems 9M 203
South St. Farn 2N 49
South St. F'ham 8E 64
South St. Gos 4K 239
South St. Hav 9F 202
South St. Hythe 6M 193
South St. Penn 4C 234
South St. Ropl 2D 110
South St. S'sea 4D 240 (7M 5)
South St. Titch 9J 197
South Sway. 9L 223
S. Sway La. Sway 7K 223
South Ter. Ports 2B 240 (3J 5)
South Tidworth. 8G 30
South Town. 3G 97
S. Town Rd. Meds 1G 96
S. Trestle Rd. Hythe 3G 209
South View. 5C 42
South Vw. Cowp 6A 182
Southview. Drox 2K 165
South Vw. Win 6J 105 (7J 237)
S. View Clo. Sut S 7D 76
South Vw. Cotts. Hook 2G 44
South Vw. Gdns. And 2A 70
Southview Pk. Homes. Win 2G 126
S. View Pl. Bourn 3J 245 (8J 247)
Southview Ri. Alt 3E 80
S. View Rd. Christ 8K 229
Southview Rd. Head D 2D 102
S. View Rd. Sotn 2J 173
S. View Rd. Win 2F 126
S. View Ter. St M 2N 53
Southville Rd. Bourn 9E 228
South Wlk. A'sht 9M 49
Southwark Clo. Yate 7M 17
South Warnborough. 4D 62
Southwater. Lee S 9N 211
South Way. And 8C 52
Southway. Cam 9K 19
Southway. Gos 5E 212
Southway. Port D 9D 66
Southway. Titch 6H 197
Southways. Stub 6N 211
South Weirs. 8A 148
South Weirs. Broc 8A 148
Southwell Pk. Rd. Cam 8K 19
S. Western Cres. Poole 3A 244
Southwick. 3A 200
Southwick Av. Fare 8N 199
Southwick By-Pass. S'wick 3M 199
Southwick Clo. Win 2H 105
Southwick Ct. Fare 2C 212
Southwick Hill Rd. Cosh 7E 200
Southwick Ho. Ports 1E 240 (off Crasswell St.)
Southwick Pk. Golf Course. 4B 200
Southwick Pl. Bourn 7F 228
Southwick Rd. Bourn 8F 228
Southwick Rd. Den 6F 180
Southwick Rd. S'wick 4A 200
Southwick Rd. Wick & N Boar 7D 178
South Winchester Golf Course. 1E 126
South Wonston. 3H 91
Southwood. 9F 28
Southwood Av. Bourn 1F 246
Southwood Av. Walk 5J 231
Southwood Bus. Cen. Farn 8F 28
Southwood Clo. Walk 5J 231
Southwood Cres. S'wd B 8F 28
Southwood Gdns. L Hth 6C 196
Southwood Golf Course. 1G 49
Southwood La. Farn 9F 28
Southwood La. Fle 9B 28
Southwood Rd. Farn 9F 28
Southwood Rd. Hay I 5J 243
Southwood Rd. Ports 4F 214
Southwood Rd. Shald 2C 80 & 9A 62
Southwood Village Cen. Farn 9F 28
Sovereign Av. Gos 9L 213
Sovereign Cen. Bourn 1B 246
Sovereign Clo. Bourn 6C 228
Sovereign Clo. S'sea 2L 241
Sovereign Clo. Tot 2J 171
Sovereign Cres. Fare 8D 196
Sovereign Dri. H End & Bot 4A 176
Sovereign Dri. S'sea 2K 241
Sovereign Ga. Ports 1D 240 (off Staunton St.)
Sovereign La. Water 6M 201
Sovereign Way. Eastl 6D 132
Sowcroft La. Alt 7D 62
Sowden Clo. H End 3M 175
Sowley La. E End 1N 235
Spain La. Ellis & Bentw. 3J 79
Spain, The. Ptsfld 1L 145
Spalding Rd. Sotn 5J 175
Spaniard's La. Roms 9M 129
Sparkford Clo. Bourn 6E 228
Sparkford Clo. Win 8J 105 (9J 237)
Sparkford Rd. Win 8J 105 (9J 237)
Sparrow Clo. Water 6N 181
Sparrow Ct. Lee S 9B 212
Sparrowgrove. Ott 9G 127
Sparrow Hawk Clo. Ews 2N 63 (off Badger Way, in two parts)
Sparrow Sq. Eastl 1B 160
Sparrow Way. New M 9B 222
Sparsholt. 3B 104
Sparsholt Clo. Hav 4C 202
Sparsholt La. Win & Spar 3N 125
Sparsholt Rd. Sotn 1D 194
Spartan Clo. Ems 5N 217
Spartan Clo. Fare 3N 211
Spartina Dri. L'ton 9E 224
Sparvells. E'sly 5H 17
Sparvell Way. Cam 7L 19
Spats La. Head D 8A 84
Spear Rd. Sotn 2M 173
Spearywell. 1D 122
Speckled Wood Rd. Bas 2C 42
Specks La. S'sea 2H 241
Speedfield Pk. Retail Pk. Fare 3D 212
Speedwell Clo. Chan F 7N 131
Speedwell Clo. L Hth 7C 196
Speedwell Dri. Christ 6D 230
Speggs Wlk. H End 4N 175
Speltham Hill. Hmbdn 9E 166
Spencer Clo. Chu C 6A 48
Spencer Clo. Four M 4J 97
Spencer Clo. Frim G 6N 29
Spencer Clo. Hay I 4G 242
Spencer Clo. P Hth 4L 11
Spencer Ct. Fare 6A 212
Spencer Ct. New M 4B 232
Spencer Ct. S'sea 5E 240
Spencer Dri. Lee S 2B 238
Spencer Gdns. Water 6M 181
Spencer Rd. Bourn 1N 245
Spencer Rd. Eastl 1C 160
Spencer Rd. Ems 5L 203
Spencer Rd. New M 3B 232
Spencer Rd. Poole 5C 244
Spencer Rd. Sotn 4H 175
Spencer Rd. S'sea 5G 241
Spenlow Clo. Ports 9E 214
Spenser Clo. Alt 3G 81
Spenser Clo. Wars 9A 196
Spenser Ct. W'hill 6J 101
Sperrin Clo. Bas 8K 41
Spetisbury Clo. Bourn 3M 227
Spey Ct. And 8B 52
Spice Quay. Ports 4B 240 (7H 5)
Spicer Ct. Bourn 2J 245 (7J 247)
Spicer Ho. Ports 2L 5
Spicer La. Bourn 1C 226 (in two parts)
Spicers. Alt 5G 80
Spicers Ct. Win 6K 105 (6K 237)
Spicer's Hill. Tot 5L 171
Spicer St. Ports 1D 240
Spicer's Way. Tot 4L 171
Spicewood. Fare 7A 198
Spiers Clo. T'ley 5K 11
Spiers La. Bro C 7D 78
Spiers La. Chil C 3G 94
Spinacre. Bart S 6C 232
Spindle Clo. Hav 6J 203
Spindle Warren. Hav 6J 203
Spindlewood. Chine 8F 22
Spindlewood Clo. Bart S 5B 232
Spindlewood Clo. Sotn 5M 159
Spindlewood Way. March 1E 192
Spinnaker Clo. Gos 9F 212
Spinnaker Clo. Hay I 3E 242
Spinnaker Dri. Ports 4E 214
Spinnaker Grange. Hay I 4J 217
Spinnaker Vw. Hav 8A 202
Spinners Gardens. 7E 224
Spinney Cvn. Pk., The. Alr 9E 94
Spinney Clo. St L 4A 186
Spinney Clo. Water 6M 181
Spinney Dale. Hythe 7N 193
Spinney Gdns. Hythe 7N 193
Spinney, The. Ashy H 2C 186
Spinney, The. Bas 4N 41
Spinney, The. Bramd 9L 109
Spinney, The. Cal 1J 171
Spinney, The. Comp 6G 127
Spinney, The. Den 7G 180
Spinney, The. Eastl 1L 161
Spinney, The. Fare 8H 199
Spinney, The. Fle 3J 47
Spinney, The. Gos 7F 212
Spinney, The. Gray 3J 103
Spinney, The. Hook 1G 45
Spinney, The. Shot 1M 117
Spinney, The. Sotn 5L 159
Spinney, The. Water 4A 182
Spinney, The. Yate 6M 17
Spinney Wlk. Sotn 8D 160
Spinney Way. New M 9B 222
Spitalfields Rd. Alt 4F 80
Spitalhatch. 4H 81
Spital Hatch. Alt 4H 81
Spitfire Ct. Sotn 7A 174
Spitfire End. Win 6A 106
Spitfire Link. Win 7A 106
Spitfire Loop. Sotn 4D 160
Spitfire Quay. Sotn 6A 174
Spitfire Way. Hamb 7K 195
Spithead Av. Gos 6L 239
Spithead Heights. S'sea 4M 241
Spithead Ho. Fare 1C 212
Spittlefields. Ring 1L 187
Spokane Clo. A'sht 2H 65
Sprat's Down. 8H 209
Sprat's Hatch La. Dogm 5C 46
Spratt's Down. 6A 54
Spray Leaze. Lud 1F 30
Sprents La. Over 3E 56
Springbank Rd. Bourn 6C 228
Springbourne. 8N 227
Springbourne Ct. Bourn 9A 228
Spring Clo. F Oak 1N 161
Spring Clo. Sher 8N 21
Spring Clo. Sotn 6D 174
Spring Ct. Lee S 2B 238
Spring Ct. Sotn 5K 173
Spring Cres. Sotn 2N 173
Springcroft. Gos 3D 212
Springcross Av. B'wtr 1F 28
Springdale Ct. Tot 3M 171
Springfarm Rd. Hasl 1N 117
Springfield. Okly 9E 40
Springfield Av. Bourn 1K 247
Springfield Av. Christ 4G 229
Springfield Av. H Win 5B 26
Springfield Av. Holb 4B 208
Springfield Clo. And 1C 70
Springfield Clo. Hav 7B 202
Springfield Clo. L'ton 3G 234
Springfield Clo. Wick 6C 178
Springfield Cotts. Liss 1E 140
Springfield Ct. Sotn 8D 174
Springfield Cres. W'flls 3M 119
Springfield Dri. Tot 4L 171
Springfield Gdns. New M 4E 232
Springfield Gro. Holb 4B 208
Springfield La. Fle 2K 47
Springfield Rd. P Hth 4L 11
Springfields. Old B 4J 43
Springfields Clo. Col C 3K 133
Springfield Way. Fare 7M 211
Spring Firs. Sotn 7D 174
Springford Clo. Sotn 7G 159
Springford Cres. Sotn 8G 159
Springford Gdns. Sotn 7G 159
Springford Rd. Sotn 8G 159
Spring Garden La. Gos 2L 239
Spring Gdns. Alr 2D 108
Spring Gdns. Ems 9M 203
Spring Gdns. Farn 5J 29
Spring Gdns. N Bad 7E 130
Spring Gdns. Poole 9B 226
Spring Gdns. Ports 2D 240 (4M 5)
Spring Gro. Burs 9L 175
Springhead. 1N 117
Spring Hill La. St M 9L 35
Springhill Rd. Chan F 6A 132
Spring Hills. Sotn 5G 175
Spring Ho. Clo. Col C 3L 133
Springlakes Ind. Est. A'sht 8N 49
Spring La. Burgh 4D 8
Spring La. Col C 3K 133
Spring La. Eastl 8H 133
Spring La. F'ham 3C 64
Spring La. New M 4E 232
Spring La. Rise 2E 14 (in two parts)
Spring La. Swanm 7D 164
Spring La. W. F'ham 4C 64
Springles La. Fare 4J 197
Springmead Ct. S'hrst 4G 19
Spring Mdw. Coll D 2G 31
Spring M. And 9A 52
Springpark Ho. Bas 5D 42
Spring Pl. Roms 5L 129
Spring Rd. Bourn 9N 227
Spring Rd. Hythe 5M 193
Spring Rd. L'ton 3G 234
Spring Rd. Sar G 3C 196
Spring Rd. Sotn 4D 174
Springs, The. Str S 5J 13
Spring St. Ports 2D 240 (3N 5)
Spring, The. Water 7G 181
Spring Va. Swanm 6C 164
Spring Va. Water 6B 182
Springvale Av. Bourn 6C 228
Springvale Av. King W 8M 91
Springvale Rd. Win 1M 105
Spring Wlk. Ports 1D 240 (2N 5)
Springwater Clo. Bourn 3E 226
Springwater Rd. Bourn 3E 226
Spring Way. Alr 2E 108
Springwell La. H Win 3C 26
Springwood Av. Water 3N 201
Spring Woods. Fle 4L 47
Spring Woods. S'hrst 4E 18
Sprouts La. Plait 8M 121
Spruce Av. Water 2A 202
Spruce Av. W'hill 4F 100
Spruce Clo. And 2J 69
Spruce Clo. S Won 2J 91
Spruce Clo. Wars 9A 196
Spruce Dri. Sotn 5J 175
Spruce Dri. Tot 2H 171
Spruce Wlk. Lee S 1B 238
Spruce Way. Fle 2B 48
Spurgeon Rd. Bourn 8E 228
Spur Hill Av. Poole 2B 244
Spurlings Rd. Fare 5F 198
Spur Rd. Cosh 9G 200
Spur Rd. Poole 2B 244
Spur Rd. Water 2M 201
Spurs Ct. A'sht 9G 49
Spur, The. Gos 5H 239
Spur, The. Wick 6C 178
Spybush La. Bro C 9C 78
Squarefield Gdns. Hook 1J 45
Square, The. Bas 5D 42
Square, The. Bourn 2K 245 (7L 247)
Square, The. Cran 6J 149
Square, The. F Oak 1N 161
Square, The. Fawl 5F 208
Square, The. Gos 8L 213
Square, The. Gray 4M 103
Square, The. Green 1H 9
Square, The. Hamb 7L 195
Square, The. Hur T 4D 34
Square, The. Lip 2D 116
Square, The. Lcky 9B 122
Square, The. L'ton 3B 234
Square, The. Neth W 1A 88
Square, The. Ptsfld 1M 145
Square, The. Titch 9J 197
Square, The. Westb 6N 203
Square, The. Wick 7C 178 (in two parts)
Square, The. Win 7L 105 (8M 237)
Square Tower, The. 4B 240 (8J 5)
Squarey Clo. D'ton 3K 119
Squires Wlk. Sotn 9C 174
Squirrel Clo. Eastl 1K 161
Squirrel Clo. S'hrst 5D 18
Squirrel Dri. Sotn 7E 174
Squirrel La. Farn 7J 29
Squirrels Clo. Christ 4G 228
Squirrels Wlk. Dib P 7L 193
Stable Clo. Fare 7G 196
Stable Clo. Hook 2F 44
Stable La. Ptsfld 1M 145 (off Folly La.)
Stable Rd. Bord 1H 101
Stables Rd. Tidw 8G 30
Stables, The. Braml 2G 22
Stables, The. Christ 7J 229
Stables, The. L Hth 7D 196
Stable Vw. Yate 6N 17
Stacey Clo. Poole 7A 226
Stacey Ct. Hav 2D 202
Stacey Gdns. Bourn 4C 228
Staff College. 7L 19
Staff College Mus., Sandhurst. 7L 19
Staff College Rd. Cam 7J 19
Stafford Rd. Bourn 2L 245
Stafford Rd. Ptsfld 8M 139
Stafford Rd. Sotn 3J 173
Stafford Rd. S'sea 4E 240
Staff Rd. A'sht 9L 49
Staff Rd. Michm 5H 123
Staffwise Bus. Cen. Cosh 1G 214
Stagbrake Clo. Holb 5N 207
Stag Bus. Pk. Ring 3K 187
Stag Clo. Eastl 1K 161
Stag Clo. New M 2N 231
Stag Gates. Black 7C 208
Stag Hill. Bas 9M 41
Stag Oak La. Chine 8F 22
Stagshorn Rd. Water 3C 182
Stag Way. Fare 4N 197
Stainer Clo. Sotn 7H 175
Stainers La. S Won 3G 91 (in two parts)
Staith Clo. Sotn 5G 174
Stake La. Farn 8J 29
Stakes. 4N 201
Stakes Hill Rd. Water 2M 201
Stakes La. Uphm 1H 163
Stake's La. Uphm 6G 134
Stakes Rd. Water 4K 201
Stalham Rd. Poole 8D 226
Stallard Clo. Ems 8L 203
Stallards La. Ring 1J 187
Stalybridge Clo. Park G 3D 196
Stamford Av. Frim 3N 29
Stamford Av. Hay I 4E 242
Stamford Rd. Bourn 9F 228
Stamford St. Ports 1F 240
Stamford Way. F Oak 2N 161
Stampsey Ct. Ports 6D 214
Stamshaw. 7E 214
Stamshaw Promenade. Ports 4E 214
Stamshaw Rd. Ports 6E 214
Stanbridge Earls. 1H 129
Stanbridge La. Roms 9F 122
Stanbridge Rd. Hav 6H 203
Stanbury Clo. Thru 1N 67
Stanbury Rd. Thru 9M 31
Stancomb Broad La. Meds 4A 96 (in two parts)
Stancombe La. Meds 3E 96
Stancombe La. Shald 9A 62 (in two parts)
Standard Way. Fare 6E 198
Standen Rd. Sotn 6B 158
Standfast La. Hawk 5N 113
Standford Hill. S'frd 6M 101
Standford La. Lind 3M 101
Standford La. S'frd & Pass 6M 101
Standford St. Sotn 6N 173 (6G 4)
Standing Hill. W Tyth 8K 87
Standon. 3N 125
Stanfield. T'ley 4H 11
Stanfield Clo. Poole 7B 226 (in two parts)
Stanfield Rd. Bourn 6J 227
Stanfield Rd. Poole 7B 226
Stanford Clo. Ports 9E 200
Stanford Ct. Hav 4H 203
Stanford Ct. Sotn 7H 175
Stanford End. 2D 14
Stanford Hill. L'ton 3D 234
Stanford Ri. Sway 5J 223
Stanford Rd. Bas 2L 59
Stanford Rd. L'ton 3D 234
Stanham Clo. Wor D 5H 91
Stanhope Dri. Cowes 5P 237 (off Queen's Rd.)
Stanhope Ga. S'sea 5D 240 (9N 5)
Stanhope Rd. Cam 9H 19
Stanhope Rd. Ports 2D 240 (3N 5)
Stanier Way. H End 8N 161
Stanley Av. Ports 8J 215
Stanley Clo. B'stne 3C 118
Stanley Clo. Fare 8A 198
Stanley Clo. Gos 7J 213
Stanley Dri. Farn 9E 28
Stanley La. S'sea 5D 240
Stanley Rd. Bourn 9N 227
Stanley Rd. Ems 9N 203
Stanley Rd. Highc 6J 231

Stanley Rd.—Stroud Grn. La.

Stanley Rd. *Holb.* 4B **208**
Stanley Rd. *L'ton.* 4F **234**
Stanley Rd. *Ports* 7D **214**
Stanley Rd. *Sotn.* 1A **174**
Stanley Rd. *Tot.* 1K **171**
Stanley St. *S'sea.* 5D **240**
Stanmore. 9H **105**
Stanmore La. *Win* 8G **104**
Stannington Clo. *New M* 4C **232**
Stannington Cres. *Tot* 2M **171**
Stannington Way. *Tot* 2M **171**
Stanpit. 8A **230**
Stanpit. *Christ.* 8A **230**
Stanpit Marsh Nature Reserve. 9N 229
Stanstead Rd. *Eastl* 8D **132**
Stansted Clo. *Row C* 8J **183**
Stansted Cres. *Hav.* 3H **203**
Stansted Rd. *S'sea* 3E **240**
Stanswood. 1L **237**
Stanswood Rd. *Fawl.* 2K **237**
Stanswood Rd. *Hav* 3D **202**
Stanton Dri. *Fle.* 3K **47**
Stanton Rd. *Bourn* 4G **227**
Stanton Rd. *Ptsfld* 9L **139**
Stanton Rd. *Sotn* 3E **172**
Stanton Rd. Ind. Est. *Sotn* 3F **172**
Staple Ash La. *Frox* 6C **138**
Staple Clo. *Water* 9L **181**
Staplecross La. *Christ* 6N **229**
Stapleford Clo. *Roms* 3A **130**
Stapleford La. *Durl* 6C **162**
Staple Gdns. *Win* 6K **105** (7L **237**)
Staplehurst Clo. *Sotn* 9F **174**
Staplers Reach. *Gos.* 6D **212**
Stapleton Rd. *Ports* 8H **215**
Staplewood La. *March* 2A **192** (in two parts)
Stapley La. *Ropl* 3E **110**
Stares Clo. *Gos.* 9E **212**
Star Hill. *Churt* 6F **84**
Star Hill. *H Win.* 4E **26**
Star Hill Dri. *Churt* 5F **84**
Starina Gdns. *Water* 1B **202**
Star La. *High* 4A **8**
Star La. *Ring* 1J **187**
Starling Clo. *Bas.* 2H **59**
Starling Sq. *Eastl* 1B **160**
Starling Way. *Lee S* 9B **212**
Star Post Rd. *Cam* 5N **19**
Statham Sq. *And* 7B **52**
Station App. *Alr.* 1F **108**
Station App. *And.* 1L **69**
Station App. *Bas.* 5C **42**
Station App. *B'wtr* 9G **19**
Station App. *Broc.* 7D **148**
Station App. *Ems.* 8M **203**
Station App. *Fare* 8C **198**
Station App. *Farn* 7K **29**
Station App. *Fle* 9N **27**
Station App. *Four M.* 4H **97** (in two parts)
Station App. *Frim.* 4M **29**
Station App. *Grat* 5K **67**
Station App. *It Ab.* 8H **93**
Station App. *Lud* 1D **30**
Station App. *New M* 3B **232**
Station App. *Ports* 2B **240** (4J **5**)
Station Clo. *It Ab* 8H **93**
Station Clo. *Wick* 6C **178**
Station Cotts. *Beau* 8L **191**
Station Downside. *W'fld* 2C **46**
Station Hill. *Bas* 5C **42**
Station Hill. *Burs* 2M **195**
Station Hill. *Curd.* 3F **176**
Station Hill. *F'ham* 8E **64**
Station Hill. *It Ab* 9H **93**
Station Hill. *Over.* 9E **38**
Station Hill. *Ropl* 1A **110**
Station Hill. *Win* 6K **105** (6L **237**)
Station Hill. *W'fld* 1B **46**
Station La. *Chan F* 6A **132**
Station Mall. *Bas* 6C **42**
Station M. *Roms* 4M **129**
Station Rd. *A'hlt* 4C **152**
Station Rd. *A'sht.* 9K **49**
Station Rd. *Alr* 9F **94**
Station Rd. *Alt* 4G **80**
Station Rd. *Bent.* 8K **63**
Station Rd. *Bentw.* 6L **79**
Station Rd. *Bish W* 4M **163**
Station Rd. *Bord.* 2H **101**
Station Rd. *Bulf B* 6E **66**
Station Rd. *Burs* 1M **195**
Station Rd. *Chlbn* 5E **74**
Station Rd. *Christ.* 7K **229**
Station Rd. *Clid* 3B **60**
Station Rd. *Dray* 2K **215**
Station Rd. *Farn* 8K **29**
Station Rd. *F'bri* 9F **150**
Station Rd. *Frim* 3L **29**
Station Rd. *Gos* 9H **213**
Station Rd. *Grat* 5K **67**
Station Rd. *Hay I* 3D **242**
Station Rd. *Hint* 3G **231**
Station Rd. *Hook* 2G **45**
Station Rd. *Lip* 4D **116**
Station Rd. *Liss* 9D **114**
Station Rd. *Mort.* 1K **13**
Station Rd. *Net A* 4F **194**
Station Rd. *New M* 3B **232**
Station Rd. *Nurs.* 6N **157**
Station Rd. *Okly* 1B **58**
Station Rd. *Over* 2E **56**
Station Rd. *Ovr W* 8M **67**
Station Rd. *Park G* 4D **196**
Station Rd. *Park* 1A **244**
Station Rd. *Ptsfld* 9L **139**
Station Rd. *Portc* 9M **199**
Station Rd. *Ports* 8H **215**
Station Rd. *Roms* 5L **129**
Station Rd. *Sob* 5L **165**
Station Rd. *Sotn* (SO15) 2B **172**
Station Rd. *Sotn* (SO19) 7D **174**
Station Rd. *Sway* 5J **223**
Station Rd. *Tidw.* 9D **30**
Station Rd. *W Meon.* 9D **136**
Station Rd. *Whitc.* 4G **55**
Station Rd. *Wick.* 6C **178**
Station Rd. *Win* 6K **105** (6K **237**)
Station Rd. *W'fld* 2C **46**
Station Rd. *Wool H.* 2A **8**
Station Rd. N. *Tot.* 3A **172**
Station Rd. S. *Tot.* 3A **172**
Station St. *L'ton* 2F **234**
Station St. *Ports* 2D **240** (3N **5**)
Station Ter. *Shaw* 7J **127**
Station Yd. *A'hlt* 4B **152**
Staunton. *Bourn* 8M **247**
Staunton Av. *Hay I* 4D **242**
Staunton Rd. *Hav* 7E **202**
Staunton St. *Ports* 1D **240**
Stavedown Rd. *S Won* 3G **90**
Stead Clo. *Hay I* 4H **243**
Stedman Rd. *Bourn* 9E **228**
Steeforth Copse. *Owl* 3G **19**
Steele Clo. *Chan F* 8B **132**
Steele's Rd. *A'sht* 7K **49** (in two parts)
Steels Drove. W'grn 2A **154** *(off High St.)*
Steels La. *Dam* 4P **149**
Steel St. *S'sea.* 4C **240** (7M **5**)
Steep. 6L **139**
Steep Clo. *Fare* 8L **199**
Steep Clo. *Sotn* 2G **175**
Steeple Dri. *Alt* 4F **80**
Steeple Way. *Fare.* 6G **196**
Steep Marsh. 4N **139**
Steepways. *Hind.* 1K **103**
Steerforth Clo. *Ports.* 8E **214**
Steinbeck Clo. *White.* 1F **196**
Stella Ct. *Christ.* 7K **231**
Stem La. *New M.* 3N **231**
Stem La. Ind. Est. *New M* 3N **231**
Stem La. Trad. Est. *New M* 3N **231**
Stenbury Dri. *P Can* 5E **78**
Stenbury Way. *Net A* 2G **195**
Stephen Clo. *Water.* 8B **182**
Stephendale Rd. *F'ham* 6F **64**
Stephen Langton Dri. *Bourn* 1B **226**
Stephen Lodge. *S'sea* 4D **240** (8N **5**)
Stephen Martin Gdns. *F'bri* 9H **151**
Stephen Rd. *Fare* 8B **198**
Stephens Ct. Roms. 6L **129** *(off Middlebridge St.)*
Stephenson Clo. *And* 9J **51**
Stephenson Clo. *Gos* 5J **239**
Stephenson Rd. *Bas.* 5N **41**
Stephenson Rd. *Tot* 8K **157**
Stephenson Way. *Fare* 7H **197**
Stephenson Way. *H End* 8M **161**
Stephens Rd. *T'ley* 5J **11**
Stephen's Wlk. Ring 1J **187** *(off Lyne's La.)*
Steplake La. *Sher E* 6M **121**
Step Ter. *Win* 6J **105** (7J **237**)
Sterling Gdns. *Coll T* 5G **19**
Sterling Pk. *And* 9J **51**
Steuart Rd. *Sotn.* 3B **174**
Stevens Drove. *Houtn.* 4C **88** (in two parts)
Stevens Grn. *St M* 1M **53**
Stevens Hill. *Yate* 8A **18**
Stevenson Cres. *Poole* 2B **244**
Stevenson Rd. Bar S 4A **76** *(off Thuillier Rd.)*
Stevenson Rd. *Bourn* 2K **247**
Steventon. 6L **57**
Steventon Rd. *Sotn* 3G **175**
Stewart Clo. *Bourn.* 9N **227**
Stewart Ho. *Chan F.* 3A **132**
Stewart M. *Bourn.* 9N **227**
Stewart Pl. *Ports.* 9F **214**
Stewart Rd. *Bas* 3F **42**
Stewart Rd. *Bourn* 8L **227**
Stewarts Grn. *Hmbdn.* 8D **166**
Stibbs Way. *Brans* 5E **220**
Stiles Dri. *And* 1C **70**
Stillions Clo. *Alt* 5G **80**
Stillmore Rd. *Bourn* 3B **226**
Stilwell Clo. *Yate.* 7A **18**
Stinchar Dri. *Chan F* 7M **131**
Stinsford Clo. *Bourn* 2M **227**
Stirling Av. *Water* 2N **201**
Stirling Clo. *Farn.* 9J **29**
Stirling Clo. *Frim* 2N **29**
Stirling Clo. *New M* 3C **232**
Stirling Clo. *Tot* 2N **171**
Stirling Ct. *Fare.* 6A **198**
Stirling Ct. *New M* 3C **232**
Stirling Cres. *H End* 1N **175**
Stirling Cres. *Tot* 2N **171**
Stirling Rd. *Bourn.* 7J **227**
Stirling St. *Ports.* 8E **214**
Stirling Wlk. *Roms* 5L **129**
Stirling Way. *Christ* 8D **230**
Stockbridge. 2F **88**
Stockbridge Clo. *Chine* 8J **23**
Stockbridge Clo. *Hav* 4H **203**
Stockbridge Down Nature Reserve. 3J 89
Stockbridge Dri. *A'sht* 4L **65**
Stockbridge Rd. *Good C.* 5G **73**
Stockbridge Rd. *King S* 8B **86**
Stockbridge Rd. *Spar* 4M **89**
Stockbridge Rd. *Sut S* 7D **76**
Stockbridge Rd. *Tims* 6J **123**
Stockbridge Rd. *Win* 2E **104** (6J **237**) (in two parts)
Stockbridge Way. *Yate* 9N **17**
Stocker Clo. *Bas.* 9B **42**
Stocker Pl. *Gos.* 7F **212**
Stockers Av. *Win* 4H **105**
Stockheath. 4E **202**
Stockheath La. *Hav.* 7E **202**
Stockheath Rd. *Hav* 5E **202**
Stockheath Way. *Hav* 6F **202**
Stockholm Dri. *H End.* 5N **175**
Stocklands. *Tot.* 9J **157**
Stock La. *Land* 7J **121**
Stockley Clo. *Holb* 5A **208**
Stockport Rd. *Ame.* 7A **66**
Stocks La. *Meon* 8N **135** (in two parts)
Stocks La. *Priv.* 4H **137**
Stockton Av. *Fle* 9L **27**
Stockton Clo. *H End* 3A **176**
Stockton Pk. *Fle* 1L **47**
Stockwell Pl. *Spar* 3B **104**
Stockwood Way. *F'ham* 3H **65**
Stoddart Av. *Sotn.* 4D **174**
Stodham La. *Liss & Ptsfld* 3D **140**
Stoke. 7H **35** **(Andover)**
Stoke. 7G **216** **(Hayling Island)**
Stoke Charity. 7F **76**
Stoke Charity Rd. *S Won & King W.* 2L **91**
Stoke Common. 7J **133**
Stoke Comn. Rd. *Eastl* 7J **133**
Stoke Farthing. 3B **118**
Stoke Gdns. *Gos.* 3L **239**
Stoke Ga. *Stoke.* 7H **35**
Stoke Heights. *F Oak* 9M **133**
Stoke Hill. *Stoke.* 8G **34**
Stoke Hills. *F'ham* 7E **64**
Stoke Ho. *T'ley* 4H **11**
Stoke La. *Baug* 4C **10**
Stoke La. *Stoke.* 5F **34**
Stoken La. *H Win.* 5M **25**
Stoke Park. 2K **161**
Stoke Pk. Dri. *Eastl* 8H **133**
Stoke Pk. Rd. *Eastl.* 8H **133**
Stoke Rd. *Gos* 3K **239**
Stoke Rd. *Hur T* 5E **34**
Stoke Rd. *Sman* 3D **52**
Stoke Rd. *Sotn* 1F **172**
Stoke Rd. *Win.* 3L **105**
Stokesay Clo. *Hythe* 9M **193**
Stokes Bay Mobile Home Pk. *Gos* 5F **238** (in two parts)
Stokes Bay Rd. *Gos* 5F **238**
Stokes La. *Baug.* 9K **21**
Stokeway. *Gos* 3L **239**
Stoke Wood Clo. *F Oak* 1L **161**
Stokewood Rd. *Bourn* 8K **227**
Stone. 2K **237**
Stonechat Clo. *Ptsfld* 2B **146**
Stonechat Ct. *Christ.* 7B **230**
Stonechat Dri. *Tot* 2H **171**
Stonechat Rd. *Water* 4A **182**
Stone Clo. *And.* 3L **69**
Stone Clo. *W'slw.* 5H **87**
Stone Crop Clo. *L Hth* 7C **196**
Stonecross Ho. *Ports.* 8E **214**
Stonedene Clo. *Head D* 3E **102**
Stone Gdns. *Bourn* 4D **228**
Stoneham Cemetery Rd. *Sotn* 7D **160**
Stoneham Clo. *Ptsfld.* 9K **139**
Stoneham Clo. *Sotn.* 6B **160**
Stoneham Gdns. *Burs* 9K **175**
Stoneham Golf Course. 5N 159
Stoneham La. *Eastl & Sotn* 2C **160**
Stoneham Pk. *Ptsfld* 9K **139**
Stoneham Way. *Sotn.* 7B **160**
Stonehill Pk. *Head D* 3D **102**
Stonehill Rd. *Head D* 3E **102**
Stonehills. 5G **208**
Stonehills. *Fawl* 6G **209**
Stonehills. *Stev* 5K **57**
Stonehouse Ri. *Frim* 3N **29**
Stonehouse Rd. *Lip* 2F **116**
Stone La. *Gos* 3K **239** (in two parts)
Stoneleigh. *Poole* 5D **244**
Stoneleigh Av. *Hord* 2G **232**
Stoneleigh Clo. *Fare* 9K **199**
Stonemasons Ct. *Win.* 7M **237**
Stoner Hill. 5H **139**
Stoner Hill Rd. *Frox.* 3H **139**
Stoners Clo. *Gos* 5D **212**
Stone Sq. *Hav* 5F **202**
Stone St. *A'sht* 2M **65**
Stone St. *S'sea* 4C **240** (7M **5**)
Stoney Bottom. *Gray* 4L **103**
Stoney Clo. *Yate* 9N **17**
Stoney Cross. 8K **155**
Stoney Cross. *Lud.* 1D **30**
Stoney Drove. *Ver D.* 7F **6**
Stoneyfields. *F'ham* 9G **64**
Stoney La. *Meds* 3J **97**
Stoney La. *Win* 4H **105**
Stony Batter. 8M **87**
Stonyford. 7E **156**
Stony Heath. 3D **20**
Stony La. *Burt* 3L **229**
Stony La. *Christ* 7M **229**
Stony La. *Dam.* 4N **149**
Stony La. *Frox* 4E **138**
Stony La. *Ports* 1A **240** (2H **5**)
Stony La. S. *Christ* 8M **229**
Stonymarsh. 4G **123**
Stonymoor Clo. *Holb.* 5A **208**
Stookes Way. *Yate* 9L **17**
Stopples La. *Hord* 2G **232**
Storrington Rd. *Water.* 6D **168**
Stourbank Rd. *Christ.* 8K **229**
Stourcliffe Av. *Bourn* 1F **246**
Stour Clo. *Ptsfld* 2L **145**
Stour Clo. *W End* 8F **160**
Stour Clo. *W Wel.* 1A **120**
Stour Ct. Poole 1E **244** *(off Poole Rd.)*
Stourcroft Dri. *Christ.* 4G **229**
Stourfield Rd. *Bourn* 1E **246**
Stourhead Clo. *And* 2L **69**
Stourhead Clo. *Farn* 8M **29**
Stour Rd. *Bourn* 8N **227**
Stour Rd. *Christ.* 9J **229**
Stour Rd. *Okly.* 1D **58**
Stourvale Av. *Christ.* 6G **229**
Stourvale Gdns. *Chan F.* 7B **132**
Stourvale Pl. *Bourn* 9E **228**
Stourvale Rd. *Bourn* 9E **228**
Stour Wlk. *Bourn.* 2A **228**
Stour Way. *Christ* 4G **228**
Stourwood Av. *Bourn.* 2F **246**
Stourwood Rd. *Bourn* 1G **246**
Stouts La. *Brans* 6D **220**
Stovold's Way. *A'sht* 2H **65**
Stow Cres. *Fare.* 7N **197**
Stowe Clo. *H End.* 1A **176**
Stowe Rd. *S'sea.* 3K **241**
Stradbrook. *Gos* 7D **212**
Stragwyne Clo. *N Bad* 7E **130**
Straight Mile, The. *Roms* 3C **130**
Strand. *Sotn.* 6M **173** (6D **4**)
Strand, The. *Hay I.* 6J **243**
Strand, The. *S'sea* 6E **240**
Strategic Pk. *H End* 3K **175**
Stratfield Av. *T'ley* 6H **11**
Stratfield Dri. *Chan F* 3N **131**
Stratfield Gdns. *Hav.* 2D **202**
Stratfield Mortimer. 1J **13**
Stratfield Pk. *Water* 1K **201**
Stratfield Pl. *New M.* 3N **231**
Stratfield Rd. *Bas* 4B **42**
Stratfield Saye. 5M **13**
Stratfield Saye House. 5C 14
Stratfield Saye Rd. *Str S* 8H **13**
Stratford Ct. *F'ham* 9E **64**
Stratford Ct. *Sotn* 6M **159**
Stratford Ct. Win 4L **105** *(off Northlands Dri.)*
Stratford Ho. *S'sea* 3D **240** (6N **5**)
Stratford Pl. *Eastl* 8F **132**
Stratford Pl. *L'ton.* 1D **234**
Stratford Rd. *Water* 1A **202**
Stratford Tony. 2E **118**
Stratford Tony Rd. *Coom B* 2G **118**
Strathfield Rd. *And* 4M **69**
Strathmore Ct. *Cam.* 7M **19**
Strathmore Rd. *Bourn* 2L **227**
Strathmore Rd. *Gos* 3L **239**
Stratton Clo. *E Stra* 7M **77**
Stratton Clo. *Ports* 9D **200**
Stratton La. *E Stra & N'ton D* 7M **77**
Stratton Rd. *Bas.* 9A **42**
Stratton Rd. *Bourn.* 2N **227**
Stratton Rd. *Sotn.* 1H **173**
Stratton Rd. *Win* 7M **105**
Stratton Wlk. *Farn.* 5J **29**
Strauss Rd. *Bas* 2L **59**
Stravinsky Rd. *Bas.* 2A **60**
Strawberry Fields. *Braml* 9G **13**
Strawberry Fields. *E Bol* 1B **236**
Strawberry Fields. *H End* 4L **175**
Strawberry Hill. *L Hth.* 6C **196**
Strawberry Mead. *F Oak* 2M **161**
Stream Cotts. Frim 3M **29** *(off Gro. Cross Rd.)*
Stream Ho. Dri. *Selb* 7L **99**
Streamleaze. *Fare* 7F **196**
Streamside. *Fle* 3M **47**
Street End. 6F **24** **(Hook)**
Street End. 8G **134** **(Southampton)**
Street End. *Elve* 8G **27**
Street End. *N Bad.* 7G **130**
Streets La. *Crow* 4M **187**
Street, The. *B'std* 1D **82**
Street, The. *Braml* 2E **22**
Street, The. *Crook V.* 6H **47**
Street, The. *Dock* 2A **84**
Street, The. *F'ley* 8F **86**
Street, The. *Fren.* 1E **84**
Street, The. *Grey.* 9F **44**
Street, The. *Long S* 4E **62**
Street, The. *N War* 8H **45**
Street, The. *Old B.* 5H **43**
Street, The. *Roth* 7E **24**
Street, The. *S Hart* 9G **146**
Street, The. *Tong* 3N **65**
Street, The. *W'ish* 5H **121**
Street, The. *W'slw* 5F **86**
Streetway Rd. *Pale* 6K **67**
Strete Mt. *Christ.* 7A **230**
Stride Av. *Ports* 1H **241**
Strides La. *Ring* 1J **187**
Strides Way. *Tot.* 3H **171**
String La. *P Hth & Sil* 6M **11**
Strode Gdns. *St I* 3E **186**
Strode Rd. *Ports* 6D **214**
Strokins Rd. *K're* 1B **6**
Strongs Clo. *Roms.* 4A **130**
Stroud. 9G **139**
Stroud Clo. *Chine* 1F **42**
Stroud Clo. *P Hth* 4L **11**
Stroud Common. 1G **145**
Strouden. 5B **228**
Strouden Av. *Bourn* 5M **227**
Strouden Ct. *Hav* 2D **202**
Strouden Ct. Precinct. *Hav* 2D **202**
Stroud End. *Strd* 9H **139**
Strouden Rd. *Bourn* 5L **227**
Stroud Gdns. *Christ.* 8A **230**
Stroud Grn. La. *Fare* 3N **211**

Stroud Grn. La. Roth 8C 24
Stroud La. B'wtr. 9C 18
Stroud La. Christ 8A 230
Stroud La. Crook V. 6H 47
Stroudley Av. Ports. 2K 215
Stroudley Rd. Bas 3F 42
Stroudley Way. H End. . . . 9A 162
Stroud Pk. Av. Christ 8A 230
Stroudwood Rd. Hav. 6F 202
Stroudwood Rd. Uphm. . . . 9C 134
Struan Clo. Ashy H. 2C 186
Struan Ct. Ashy H. 2D 186
Struan Dri. Ashy H 2D 186
Struan Gdns. Ashy H 2C 186
Stuart Bridgewater Ho. Sotn 3E 174
Stuart Clo. Fare 6M 211
Stuart Clo. Farn. 7J 29
Stuart Ct. And. 7N 51
Stuart Ct. Ports 9G 201
Stuart Cres. Win 8J 105
Stuart Rd. Highc. 6K 231
Stubbings Mdw. Cvn. Pk. Ring 1H 187
Stubbington. 5N 211
Stubbington Av. Ports. 7F 214
Stubbington Av. W'hill 6H 101
Stubbington Grn. Fare 5M 211
Stubbington La. Fare 5N 211
Stubbington Way. F Oak 1A 162
Stubb La. Ows 3F 134
Stubbs Ct. And 8M 51
Stubbs Drove. H End 3A 176
Stubbs Folly. Coll T. 6F 18
Stubbs Moor Rd. Farn 7H 29
Stubbs Rd. Bas 9D 42
Stubbs Rd. Sotn. 8G 174
Stuckton. 3L 153
Stuckton Rd. F'bri. 1K 153
Student Village. 6G 227
Studland Clo. Sotn 1C 172
Studland Dri. Mil S 7J 235
Studland Rd. Bourn 4G 244
Studland Rd. Lee S. 1A 238
Studland Rd. Sotn 2C 172
Studley Av. Holb. 4A 208
Studley Clo. Highc 6L 231
Studley Ct. New M. 6M 231
Stukeley Rd. Bas 7A 42
Sturdee Clo. Frim 3N 29
Sturminster Ho. Sotn 1E 172
Sturminster Rd. Bourn . . . 2M 227
Sturt Rd. F'ham 3D 64
Sturt Rd. Hasl. 9N 103
Styles, The. B'stne 3D 118
Sudbury Rd. Ports 9E 200
Suetts La. Bish W. 5B 164
Suffolk Av. Christ 4J 229
Suffolk Av. Sotn 3J 173
Suffolk Clo. Chan F. 1A 160
Suffolk Cotts. Gos 4K 239
Suffolk Dri. Chan F. 9A 132
Suffolk Dri. White. 2E 196
Suffolk Grn. Chan F 1A 160
Suffolk Rd. And 2M 69
Suffolk Rd. Bourn . . . . 2H 245 (6H 247) (in two parts)
Suffolk Rd. S'sea 4H 241
Suffolk Rd. S. Bourn 1H 245 (5G 247)
Sullivan Clo. Farn 8K 29
Sullivan Clo. Ports 9N 199
Sullivan Rd. Bas. 2N 59
Sullivan Rd. Cam 8J 19
Sullivan Rd. Sotn 6H 175
Sullivan Way. Water. 4M 201
Sultan Rd. Ems 8M 203
Sultan Rd. Ports 9E 214
Sumar Clo. Fare 3N 211
Summer Down La. Hann & Okly 5N 39
Summerfield Clo. Burt. . . . 4M 229
Summerfield Gdns. Sotn 6B 160
Summerfields. Bourn. 7C 228
Summerfields. Chine 8H 23
Summerfields. L Hth 8E 196
Summerfield Ter. Liss. 2E 140
Summerhill. Poole 9A 244
Summerhill Rd. Water 7N 181
Summerhouse Ct. Gray. . . 4M 103
Summerlands Rd. F Oak 1N 161
Summerlands Wlk. Hav . . . 4H 203
Summer La. Beau. 7K 207
Summerleigh Wlk. Fare . . . 3N 211
Summerlug. Wint E 3A 86
Summers Av. Bourn 1F 226
Summer's La. Burt. 5N 229
Summers St. Sotn 4A 174
Summertrees Ct. New M 2E 232
Summit Av. Farn. 8D 28
Summit Way. Sotn. 1D 174
Sumner Ct. F'ham. 7E 64
Sumner Rd. Bton 7K 145
Sumner Rd. F'ham 7E 64
Sunbeam Way. Gos 4K 239
Sunbury Clo. Bord 4K 101
Sunbury Clo. Bourn 1E 226
Sunbury Ct. Bourn 6K 247
Sunbury Ct. Fare 5A 198
Sun Ct. S'sea . . . . 3E 240 (off Sedgley Clo.)
Suncourt Vs. Gos 8H 213
Sunderland Dri. Christ 7D 230
Sunderton La. Water 6B 168
Sundew Clo. Christ. 5E 230
Sundew Clo. New M. 2E 232
Sundridge Clo. Ports. 9F 200
Sunflower Clo. Bas 3J 59
Sun Hill. Cowes . . . . 5P 237 (off Union Rd.)
Sun Hill Cres. Alr . . . . 2F 108 (in two parts)
Sun La. Alr 2F 108
Sun La. Rise 3F 14
Sunningdale. Christ. 8J 229
Sunningdale. Hythe. 6L 193
Sunningdale Clo. Eastl 1K 161
Sunningdale Clo. Gos 7E 212
Sunningdale Cres. Bourn 2G 226
Sunningdale Gdns. Sotn . . . 3F 174
Sunningdale Mobile Home Pk. Col C 3K 133
Sunningdale Rd. Fare 1M 213
Sunningdale Rd. Ports 1H 241
Sunnybank. Red P 3E 68
Sunnybank Rd. Farn . . . . 6F 28 (in two parts)
Sunnydown Rd. Win. 2E 126
Sunnyfield Ri. Burs. 9L 175
Sunnyfield Rd. Bart S. 6B 232
Sunnyheath. Hav. 5E 202
Sunnyhill. Coll D. 2G 31
Sunny Hill Ct. Poole 9B 226
Sunny Hill Rd. A'sht 9F 48
Sunnyhill Rd. Bourn 9E 228
Sunny Hill Rd. Poole 9B 226
Sunnylands Av. Bourn. 1J 247
Sunny Mead. Okly 2D 58
Sunnymead Dri. Water. . . . 8K 181
Sunnymoor Rd. Bourn 5E 226
Sunnyside. Fle 1K 47
Sunnyside Clo. Charl 8K 51
Sunnyside Pk. Cvn. Site. St I 3F 186
Sunnyside Rd. Head D 3E 102
Sunnyside Rd. Poole 7B 226
Sunnyside Wlk. Hav. 2D 202
Sunny Vw. Clo. A'sht. 1L 65
Sunny Wlk. Ports 2A 240 (3H 5)
Sunny Way. Tot 3M 171
Sun Ray Est. S'hrst 5C 18
Sunridge Clo. Poole 8E 226
Sunset Av. Tot. 2L 171
Sunset Lodge. Poole. 3E 244
Sunset Rd. Tot 2L 171
Sunshine Av. Hay I 5H 243
Sunshine Cvn. Pk. W'hill 4F 100
Sun St. Ports. 2B 240 (4K 5)
Sunton. 1H 31
Suntrap Gdns. Hay I. 5H 243
Sunvale Av. Hasl 9M 103
Sunvale Clo. Hasl. 9M 103
Sunvale Clo. Sotn 7F 174
Sunwood Rd. Hav 4D 202
Surbiton Rd. Eastl. 7F 132
Surrey Av. Cam 9J 19
Surrey Clo. Christ 4J 229
Surrey Clo. Tot 5K 171
Surrey Ct. Chan F. 9B 132
Surrey Ct. Sotn. 4H 173
Surrey Gdns. Bourn 1G 245
Surrey Heath Mus. 7M 19
Surrey Ho. Chan F 9B 132
Surrey Lodge. Bourn 1H 245 (5G 247)
Surrey Rd. Chan F 9A 132
Surrey Rd. Poole & Bourn 9E 226
Surrey Rd. Sotn 8B 174
Surrey Rd. S. Bourn. 1G 245
Surrey St. Ports . . . 2D 240 (3N 5)
Sussex Clo. Bourn 1N 227
Sussex Ct. S'sea . . . 4D 240 (8N 5)
Sussex Gdns. Fle 8N 27
Sussex Gdns. Ptsfld 2M 145
Sussex Place. 6M 173
Sussex Pl. Ports. 1D 240
Sussex Pl. S'sea . . . 4D 240 (8N 5)
Sussex Rd. Chan F 9B 132
Sussex Rd. Ptsfld 2M 145
Sussex Rd. Sotn 5M 173 (5D 4)
Sussex Rd. S'sea 4D 240 (8N 5)
Sussex St. Win 6K 105 (7L 237)
Sussex Ter. S'sea 4D 240 (8N 5)
Sutcliffe Sq. And. . . . . 7B 52 (off Cricketers Way)
Sutherland Clo. Roms 3A 130
Sutherland Clo. W'hill 6J 101
Sutherland Ct. And. . . . . 9N 51 (off Artists Way)
Sutherland Rd. Sotn. 6E 158
Sutherland Rd. S'sea. 4F 240
Sutherlands Ct. Chan F. . . . 6A 132
Sutherlands Way. Chan F 5N 131
Sutton Clo. Cowp 7L 181
Sutton Clo. Ports 4J 215
Sutton Fld. W'hill 6H 101
Sutton Gdns. Win 6L 105 (7M 237)
Sutton Pl. Broc. 7D 148
Sutton Rd. Bas. 4C 42
Sutton Rd. Bourn. 5M 227
Sutton Rd. Tot 1L 171
Sutton Rd. Water 7L 181
Sutton Scotney. 7D 76
Suttonwood La. Bigh 7N 95
Suvla La. Bulf B . . . . 3B 66 (off Old Ward Rd.)
Swains Clo. T'ley 5H 11
Swains Rd. T'ley. 5H 11
Swaledale Gdns. Fle. 8N 27
Swale Dri. Chan F 5M 131
Swale Rd. Farn. 6G 28
Swallow Clo. Alt. 2G 80
Swallow Clo. Bas 2H 59
Swallow Clo. Hav 6H 203
Swallow Clo. Tidw 8D 30
Swallow Clo. Tot. 4J 171
Swallow Clo. Yate. 7L 17
Swallow Ct. Lee S. 9B 212
Swallow Ct. Water 5B 168
Swallow Dri. Mil S 8L 235
Swallowfields. And. 7A 52
Swallow Sq. Eastl. 1B 160
Swallow Wood. Fare. 5D 198
Swampton. 9L 35
Swanage Clo. Sotn. 6C 174
Swanage Rd. Lee S 1A 238
Swan Cen., The. Eastl 1F 160
Swan Clo. Ems 9N 203
Swan Clo. Swanw. 2A 196
Swancote. Fare. 9H 199
Swan Ct. Gos 4D 212
Swan Ct. H Win 6C 26
Swan La. S'hrst 6D 18
Swan La. Win 6K 105 (6L 237)
Swanley Clo. Eastl 7E 132
Swan Mead. Hight 2M 187
Swan M. N War. 7J 45
Swanmore. 6D 164
Swanmore Av. Sotn 7F 174
Swanmore Bus. Pk. Swanm 6B 164
Swanmore Clo. Bourn. 7E 228
Swanmore Clo. Win 3G 105
Swanmore Rd. Bourn 8E 228
Swanmore Rd. Drox. 5G 164
Swanmore Rd. Hav 2D 202
Swanmore Rd. Swanm. 4B 164
Swan Quay. Fare. 9F 198
Swan Quay. Sotn 2B 174
Swansbury Dri. Bourn 4E 228
Swan St. Cran. . . . . 6J 149 (off High St.)
Swan St. K're 3A 6
Swan St. Ptsfld. 1L 145
Swans Wlk. Hay I 4J 243
Swanton Gdns. Chan F. 5N 131
Swan Way. Chu C 4J 47
Swanwick. 2E 196
Swanwick Bus. Cen. Lwr S 2A 196
Swanwick Hill. 3F 196
Swanwick La. Swanw. 1N 195
Swanwick Shore Rd. Swanw 2A 196
Swanwick Wlk. T'ley. 5H 11
Swarraton. 9A 78
Swarraton Rd. Hav. 6G 202
Swattons Clo. Bulf 3A 66
Sway. 6J 223
Sway Ct. Hav 4H 203
Sway Gdns. Bourn 4A 228
Sway Rd. Broc 1N 223
Sway Rd. New M & Tip . . . 9B 222
Sway Rd. Penn 1M 233
Swaythling. 7B 160
Swaythling Rd. Hav 3D 202
Swaythling Rd. W End 8F 160
Swedish Houses. T'ley 6J 11
Sweep, The. Ring 1J 187
Sweetbriar Gdns. Water . . . 4N 201
Sweethills Cres. White 1E 196
Swelling Hill. Ropl 9G 96
Sweyns Lease. E Bol 1B 236
Swift Clo. And. 8A 52
Swift Clo. Eastl 1B 160
Swift Clo. Lee S 9B 212
Swift Clo. Water 3A 182
Swift Clo. Win 9H 105
Swift Gdns. Sotn 9B 174
Swift Hollow. Sotn 9B 174
Swift Rd. Ems 5N 217
Swift Rd. F'ham 3E 64
Swift Rd. Sotn 9B 174
Swift's Clo. F'ham. 9K 65
Swinburn Gdns. Water. . . . 6N 181
Swincombe Ri. W End 1F 174
Swing Swang La. Bas. . . . . . . 4F 42 (in two parts)
Swiss Rd. Water 2M 201
Switch Ho. Rd. Fawl 6J 209
Swivelton La. Fare. 5J 199
Sword Clo. Gos 5G 239
Sword Clo. Water. 6B 168
Swordfish Dri. Christ 7D 230
Sword Sands Path. Ports 9K 215
Sword Sands Rd. Ports 9K 215
Sycamore Av. Chan F 3A 132
Sycamore Clo. Burs 1K 195
Sycamore Clo. Christ. 6G 229
Sycamore Clo. Clan 6D 168
Sycamore Clo. Fare. 8F 196
Sycamore Clo. Frim 3N 29
Sycamore Clo. Gos. 7G 212
Sycamore Clo. Mil S. 7J 235
Sycamore Clo. N Bad 7E 130
Sycamore Clo. Roms 6B 130
Sycamore Clo. S'hrst 5D 18
Sycamore Clo. Tidw 8E 30
Sycamore Clo. Water. 7M 181
Sycamore Cotts. Cam. . . . . . . 1K 29 (off Frimley Rd.)
Sycamore Ct. Ring. 7M 185
Sycamore Cres. Chu C 5K 47
Sycamore Cres. Mid W. 4B 72
Sycamore Dri. Frim 2N 29
Sycamore Dri. Hay I 3E 242
Sycamore Dri. Holb 3N 207
Sycamore Dri. King W. 7M 91
Sycamore Rd. Bish W 4A 164
Sycamore Rd. Farn. . . . . 1L 49 (in two parts)
Sycamore Rd. Hord 2G 233
Sycamore Rd. Hythe. 6L 193
Sycamore Rd. Sotn. 9F 158
Sycamores, The. B'wtr. 8D 18
Sycamores, The. Farn 9M 29
Sycamores, The. Hythe 5M 193
Sycamore Wlk. And 3K 69
Sycamore Wlk. Bot. 3D 176
Sycamore Wlk. Ptsfld 3L 145
Sycamore Way. Bas. 4M 41
Sydenham Ct. Ports 2E 240
Sydenham Ter. Ports 2E 240
Sydmanton Clo. Roms 6N 129
Sydmonton. 7F 8
Sydmonton Ct. Hav 3H 203
Sydney Av. Hamb 6J 195
Sydney Clo. Per D 4B 30
Sydney Ho. Ports 1D 240
Sydney Rd. Bord. 4J 101
Sydney Rd. Christ 5H 229
Sydney Rd. Eastl 8H 133
Sydney Rd. Gos 3K 239
Sydney Rd. Sotn 1G 172
Syers Clo. Liss 1E 140
Syers Rd. Liss 1E 140
Sylmor Gdns. Bourn. 4L 227
Sylvan Av. Sotn 4G 174
Sylvan Clo. Hord. 4J 233
Sylvan Clo. St L 4A 186
Sylvan Dri. N Bad 8E 130
Sylvaner Ct. Bas 5C 42
Sylvan La. Hamb. 8L 195
Sylvan Ridge. S'hrst. 4C 18
Sylvan Rd. Poole 8A 226
Sylvans, The. Dib P. 6J 193
Sylvan Vw. Water. 3N 201
Sylvan Way. Chu C 6L 47
Sylvia Clo. Bas 8B 42
Sylvia Cres. Tot. 1L 171
Symes Rd. Roms 5A 130
Symonds Clo. Chan F. 8B 132
Symonds St. Win 7L 105 (9M 237)
Sympson Rd. T'ley 5K 11
Syon Pl. Farn. 8M 29
Sywell Cres. Ports. 4J 215

T

Tadburn Clo. Chan F. 7B 132
Tadburn Clo. Roms 5N 129
Tadburn Grn. Roms . . . . . . 6L 129 (off Banning St.)
Tadburn Rd. Roms. 5N 129
Tadfield Cres. Roms. 5N 129
Tadfield Rd. Roms 5N 129
Tadley. 5J 11
Tadley Bottom. 5K 11
Tadley Clo. Elve. 8J 27
Tadley Comn. Rd. T'ley. 4J 11
Tadley Hill. 7J 11
Tadley Hill. T'ley 6J 11
Tadpole La. Ews. 1N 63
Tagdell La. Horn. 2N 181
Taiping Rd. Mid W 3A 72
Tait Pl. Gos 7F 212
Talavera Pk. A'sht 8J 49
Talbot Av. Bourn. 6H 227
Talbot Clo. Hav. 6D 202
Talbot Clo. Sotn 7L 159
Talbot Ct. Bourn 5K 227
Talbot Ct. Sotn 7M 173 (8D 4)
Talbot Dri. Christ 4H 231
Talbot Dri. Poole 6F 226
Talbot Heath. 7G 227
Talbot Hill Rd. Bourn 6H 227
Talbot Meadows. Poole. . . . 6F 226
Talbot M. Bourn 5F 226
Talbot M. S'sea 3F 240
Talbot Ri. Bourn 4G 226
Talbot Rd. Bourn 6H 227
Talbot Rd. Dib P 8J 193
Talbot Rd. Fare. 7H 197
Talbot Rd. F'ham 9D 64
Talbot Rd. Hav 6D 202
Talbot Rd. S'sea 4F 240
Talbot Roundabout. Bourn 7H 227
Talbot Village. 5F 226
Talbot Woods. 7H 227
Talgarth Dri. Farn. 1M 49
Talisman Bus. Cen. Park G 4E 196
Talisman Clo. C'then. 1N 17
Talland Rd. Fare 8E 196
Tallis Gdns. Bas 1N 59
Talmey Clo. Chine 9F 22
Tamar Clo. Fare. 8J 199
Tamar Down. Water 2A 202
Tamar Dri. Okly 9D 40
Tamar Gdns. W End 9F 160
Tamar Gro. Hythe 6K 193
Tamarisk Clo. Fare. 7M 211
Tamarisk Clo. Hat W. 5L 59
Tamarisk Clo. S'sea 4K 241
Tamarisk Clo. Water 4A 202
Tamarisk Gdns. Sotn 2C 174
Tamarisk Rd. H End. 3M 175
Tamella Rd. Bot 4B 176
Tammy's Turn. Fare 9L 197
Tamorisk Dri. Tot 4J 171
Tamworth Ct. Gos. 4K 239
Tamworth Dri. Fle. 8N 27
Tamworth Rd. Bourn 9C 228
Tamworth Rd. Ports. 1H 241
Tanfield La. Wick 7B 178
Tanfield Pk. Wick 7C 178
Tangier Ct. A'sht. 9H 49
Tangier La. Bish W 4J 163
Tangier Rd. Ports 9H 215
Tanglewood. Fare 6C 198
Tanglewood. March. 9F 172
Tanglewood Clo. Water. . . . 5K 201
Tanglewood Ct. New M. . . . 3C 232
Tangley. 6F 32
Tangley Wlk. Hav 4H 203
Tangmere Clo. Christ 8D 230
Tangmere Dri. Sotn. 7E 158
Tangway. Chine 8G 23
Tangyes Clo. Fare. 5N 211
Tanhouse Clo. H End 5A 176
Tanhouse La. Alt. 5F 80
Tanhouse La. Bot 5A 176
Tan Howse Clo. Bourn 6E 228
Tankerdale La. Steep M & Liss 5B 140
Tankerton Clo. Ports 9F 200
Tankerville Rd. Sotn 7B 174
Tank La. Bro Ch 3A 118
Tank Rd. S'hrst. 8H 19
Tanneries Ind. Est., The. Hav 8E 202

Tanneries, The. Titch 9K 197
Tanner La. Fare 2A 212
Tanner's Brook Way. Sotn 4E 172
Tanners Clo. Wint E 3A 86
Tanners La. E End 2N 235
Tanners La. E Wel 5D 128
Tanners La. S'hth 9C 150
Tanner's La. Water 5G 181
Tanner's Ridge. Water 6M 201
Tanners Rd. N Bad 9F 130
Tanners, The. Fare 9F 196
Tanner St. Win 7L 105 (8N 237)
Tanners Way. Okly 9D 40
Tansy Clo. Water 3A 202
Tansy Mdw. Chan F 8L 131
Tanyards, The. Chan F 3N 131
Taplin Dri. H End 2N 175
Taplings Clo. Win 3H 105
Taplings Rd. Win 3H 105
Taplin's Farm La. W'fld 8C 26 (in two parts)
Taranto Rd. Sotn 7H 159
Tarbat Ct. Coll T 5F 18
Tarbery Cres. Water 3C 182
Target Rd. Ports 5D 214
Tarius Clo. Gos 5F 212
Tarleton Rd. Ports 8C 200
Tarn Clo. Farn 1G 48
Tarn Ri. Horn 9C 168
Tarn Rd. Hind 4M 103
Tarragon Clo. Farn 8E 28
Tarrant Gdns. H Win 8B 26
Tarrant Gdns. Hav 6D 202
Tarrant Rd. Bourn 3M 227
Taskers Dri. Anna V 4J 69
Tasman Clo. Christ 6J 229
Tasman Clo. Ocn V 8N 173 (9G 4)
Tasman Ct. Sotn 8N 173 (9G 4)
Tasmania Clo. Bas 1D 42
Taswell Rd. S'sea 5E 240
Tatchbury La. Wins 9E 156
Tate Ct. Sotn 2B 172
Tate M. Sotn 2B 172
Tate Rd. Sotn 2B 172
Tate Sq. And 7B 52
Tates Rd. Hythe 6N 193 (in two parts)
Tattenham Rd. Broc 8C 148
Tattershall Cres. Fare 1K 213
Tatwin Clo. Sotn 5H 175
Tatwin Cres. Sotn 5H 175
Taunton Dri. Sotn 3F 174
Tavell's Clo. March 9D 172
Tavell's La. March 9C 172
Taverner Clo. Bas 4E 42
Taverners Clo. Sotn 7H 175
Tavistock Clo. Roms 3A 130
Tavistock Gdns. Farn 5K 29
Tavistock Gdns. Hav 8H 203
Tavistock Rd. Fle 2J 47
Tavy Clo. Chan F 6N 131
Taw Dri. Chan F 5N 131
Tawny Cft. S'hrst 5G 18
Tawny Gro. Four M 5H 97
Tawny Owl Clo. Fare 4L 211
Tay Clo. Farn 6G 28
Taylor Clo. Sotn 9B 174
Taylor Dri. Bourn 2A 228
Taylor Dri. Braml 2H 23
Taylor Rd. Gos 5L 239
Taylors Clo. Lind 2L 101
Taylors Corner. Win 1M 105
Taylors La. Lind 2L 101
Taylor's La. Rise 1F 14
Taylors La. Sher L 7J 23
Teacher's Ter. Liss 1E 140
Teachers Way. Holb 4N 207
Teak Ho., The. Poole 5F 244
Teal Clo. Fare 9H 199
Teal Clo. Hay I 4H 243
Teal Clo. Tot 3J 171
Teal Clo. Water 3A 182
Teal Cres. Bas 3H 59
Teal Wlk. Gos 5D 212
Teapot Row. S'sea 5J 241
Teasel Clo. Lud 2D 30
Teazle Clo. Ptsfld 2B 146
Tebourba Cotts. Sway 6J 223
Tebourba Dri. Gos 4J 239
Tebourba Ho. Fare 9A 198
Tebourba Way. Curd 3G 176
Tebourba Way. Sotn 3D 172
Technology Cen. & Intech. 7G 104
Tedder Clo. And 2H 69
Tedder Clo. Bourn 3F 226
Tedder Gdns. Bourn 3F 226
Tedder Rd. Bourn 3F 226
Tedder Rd. Gos 5F 212
Tedder Rd. Sotn 2E 174
Tedder Way. Tot 3K 171
Teddington Rd. S'sea 4H 241
Ted Kelly Ct. Ports 2B 240 (4K 5)
Tees Clo. Chan F 5M 131
Tees Clo. Farn 6G 28
Tees Farm Rd. Col C 4K 133
Tees Grn. Col C 4K 133
Tegdown. Ptsfld 9A 140
Teg Down Meads. Win 5F 104
Tegg Down Rd. Bish S 3N 109
Teglease Grn. Hav 2D 202
Teignmouth Rd. Gos 9H 213
Teignmouth Rd. Ports 8H 215
Tekels Av. Cam 8M 19
Tekels Pk. Cam 8N 19
Tekels Way. Cam 1N 29
Telconia Clo. Head D 3E 102
Telegraph La. Four M 4L 97
Telegraph Rd. W End 2J 175
Telephone Rd. S'sea 3F 240
Telford Gdns. H End 9A 162
Telford Ga. And 9H 51
Telford Ho. Bas 4N 41
Telford Rd. Bas 4N 41
Telford Rd. Ports 5F 214
Telford Way. Fare 4F 196
Teme Cres. Sotn 1D 172
Teme Rd. Sotn 2D 172
Tempest Av. Water 2A 202
Tempest Rd. Ame 5A 66 (off Porton Rd.)
Templar Clo. Bourn 5D 226
Templar Clo. S'hrst 5C 18
Templars Mede. Chan F 9N 131
Templars Way. Chan F 8L 131
Templecombe Rd. Eastl 2K 161
Temple Dri. Avtn 1H 107
Temple Gdns. Sotn 8D 174
Temple La. E Meon 4L 143
Templemere. Fare 1L 211
Temple M. Bourn 8A 228
Temple Rd. Liss 8F 114
Temple Rd. Sotn 8D 174
Temple's Clo. F'ham 9L 65
Temple St. Ports 1D 240
Templeton Clo. Ports 5F 214
Temple Towers. Bas 5B 42
Tempus Bus. Cen. Bas 4A 42
Tenby Clo. Sotn 2E 174
Tenby Dri. Chan F 8M 131
Tench Way. Roms 4M 129
Tennyson Clo. Bish W 3A 164
Tennyson Clo. Holb 3N 207
Tennyson Cres. Water 8L 181
Tennyson Gdns. Fare 7C 198
Tennyson Rd. Bourn 4K 227
Tennyson Rd. Eastl 2D 160
Tennyson Rd. Ports 8G 215
Tennyson Rd. Sotn 2N 173
Tennyson Rd. Tot 9K 157
Tennyson Way. Bas 8N 41
Tensing Clo. Fare 6C 198
Tensing Rd. Christ 6A 230
Tenterton Av. Sotn 9F 174
Tenth St. Hythe 4B 208
Terence O'Hara Ct. S'sea 5F 240 (off Albert Rd.)
Terminus Ind. Est. Ports 2D 240
Terminus Rd. Cowes 5P 237
Terminus Ter. Sotn 7N 173 (8E 4)
Tern Clo. Bas 3H 59
Tern Clo. Hythe 7N 193
Tern Ct. Bourn 8G 229
Tern Wlk. Gos 5D 212
Tern Wlk. S'sea 2J 241
Terrace Rd. Bourn 2J 245 (7K 247)
Terraces, The. Chaw 8D 80
Terrace, The. Cam 8H 19
Terrace, The. C'then 1F 18
Terrace, The. Dam 6A 150
Terrace, The. Estn 1D 106
Terrace, The. Farn 9N 29
Terrace, The. Rockb 3C 150
Terrier Clo. H End 8N 161
Terrington Av. Christ 5G 230
Terriote Clo. Chan F 5A 132
Terwick Common. 8N 141
Terwick Ri. Rog 7N 141
Tesimond Dri. Yate 8K 17
Testbourne Av. Tot 3K 171
Testbourne Clo. Tot 3K 171
Testbourne Rd. Tot 3K 171
Test Clo. Ptsfld 2L 145
Testcombe Rd. Gos 4J 239
Testlands Av. Nurs 5C 158
Test La. Sotn 8A 158
Test M. Whitc 5G 55
Test Mills. Roms 4K 129
Test Ri. Chlbn 5F 74
Test Rd. E Dock 9M 173
Test Rd. Whitc 6G 55
Test Valley Bus. Pk. N Bad 6F 130
Test Valley Golf Course. 1J 77
Test Valley Small Bus. Cen. Sotn 9A 158
Test Way. Bas 6E 42
Test Way. St M 8G 34
Test Way. Ver D 6G 6
Testwood. 1L 171
Testwood Av. Tot 1L 171
Testwood Cres. Tot 9K 157
Testwood La. Tot 2M 171
Testwood Pl. Tot 2N 171
Testwood Rd. Hav 4D 202
Testwood Rd. Sotn 4G 173
Tethering Drove. Hale 9C 120
Tetney Clo. Sotn 8D 158
Teviot Ho. Sotn 4A 174 (off York Clo.)
Teviot Rd. Chan F 7M 131
Tewkesbury Av. Fare 6M 197
Tewkesbury Av. Gos 9J 213
Tewkesbury Clo. Bas 2C 42
Tewkesbury Clo. Ports 9E 200
Texas Dri. Win 3F 126
Textile Est. Yate 6N 17
Thackeray Mall. Fare 8D 198 (off Fareham Shop. Cen.)
Thackeray Rd. Sotn 2N 173
Thackeray Sq. Fare 8D 198
Thackham's La. H Win 7M 25
Thacking Grn. Col C 4K 133
Thames Clo. Farn 6G 28
Thames Clo. W End 8F 160
Thames Ct. Bas 6E 42
Thames Dri. Fare 5N 197
Thamesmead Clo. Gos 9H 213
Thatched Cottage Pk. Lyn 1D 148
Thatchers La. Brans 5B 220
Thatchers La. Nor W 7M 225
Theal Clo. Coll T 5F 18
Theatre M. S'sea 5E 240
Theobald Rd. Hurn 7D 218 (off Brackley Clo.)
Theseus Rd. Lee S 9N 211
Thetchers Clo. New M 1C 232
Thetford Gdns. Chan F 4M 131
Thetford Rd. Gos 9H 213
Thetford Rd. Poole 9D 226
Thibet Rd. S'hrst 5E 18
Thicket, The. Fare 8H 199
Thicket, The. Gos 7G 212
Thicket, The. Roms 6B 130
Thicket, The. S'sea 4E 240
Thicket, The. Wid 7L 201
Thieves' La. Clan 3D 168
Third Av. Hav 7G 203
Third Av. Ports 9F 200
Third Av. Sotn 3D 172
Third St. Green 1G 9
Third St. Hythe 5D 208
Thirlmere. Eastl 1D 160
Thirlmere Clo. Bord 2J 101
Thirlmere Clo. Fare 4N 211
Thirlmere Clo. Farn 8G 28
Thirlmere Cres. Chu C 6K 47
Thirlmere Ho. Ports 8C 200
Thirlmere Rd. Sotn 9D 158
Thirlstane Firs. Chan F 8N 131
Thirsk Ct. A'sht 9M 49
Thirteenth St. Hythe 3B 208
Thistlebarrow Rd. Bourn 8B 228
Thistledown. Water 5B 182
Thistledown Clo. And 9L 51
Thistledowne Gdns. Ems 9N 203
Thistle Rd. Chan F 7L 131
Thistle Rd. H End 4M 175
Thomas Clo. Tot 4K 171
Thomas Lewis Way. Sotn (SO14 & SO17) 2N 173
Thomas Lewis Way. Sotn (SO17 & SO16) 1A 174
Thomas Rd. Bar S 4A 76 (off Thuillier Rd.)
Thomas Rd. N Bad 8F 130
Thompson's La. Ows 6A 134 (in two parts)
Thompsons La. Water 5D 180
Thorburn Chase. Coll T 7G 18
Thoresby Ct. New M 3N 231
Thornbrake Rd. Gos 4L 239
Thornbury Av. Black 8C 208
Thornbury Av. Sotn 3K 173
Thornbury Clo. Fare 9M 197
Thornbury Heights. Chan F 3D 132
Thornbury Rd. Bourn 1K 247
Thornbury Wood. Chan F 3D 132
Thornby Ct. Ports 4K 215
Thorncliffe Clo. Ports 4G 214
Thorn Clo. Eastl 7E 132
Thorn Clo. Four M 4K 97
Thorn Clo. Ptsfld 2B 146
Thorncombe Clo. Bourn 2M 227
Thorn Ct. Four M 5J 97
Thorn Cres. Four M 5J 97
Thorncroft Rd. Ports 2F 240
Thorndike Clo. Sotn 9F 158
Thorndike Rd. Sotn 9E 158
Thorn Dri. Four M 5J 97
Thorne Clo. Coom B 2G 119
Thorneley Rd. K're 2B 6
Thorners Ct. Sotn 4L 173 (2B 4)
Thorner's Homes. Sotn 2G 172
Thorness Clo. Sotn 1C 172
Thorneybank Rd. Wint G 3B 86
Thorney Clo. Fare 9N 197
Thorneycroft Ind. Est. Bas 6A 42
Thorney Hill. 3F 220
Thorney Island. 5N 217
Thorney Rd. Ems 9N 203
Thornfield. H'ly 1J 9
Thornfield Clo. Water 9C 168
Thornfield Dri. Highc 5H 231
Thornfield Grn. B'wtr 1H 29
Thornford Rd. H'ly 1H 9 (in two parts)
Thorngate Ct. Gos 2J 239
Thorngate Way. Gos 3M 239
Thornham Rd. New M 3E 232
Thorn Hill. 5H 175
Thornhill Av. Sotn 4H 175
Thornhill Clo. Fawl 6D 208
Thornhill Homes. Sotn 5H 175 (off Tatwin Clo.)
Thornhill Park. 4G 175
Thornhill Pk. Rd. Sotn 3H 175
Thornhill Rd. A'sht 7M 49
Thornhill Rd. Fawl 6D 208
Thornhill Rd. Sotn 7J 159
Thornhill Roundabout. Chine 1H 43
Thornhill Way. Chine 8G 23
Thorni Av. Fare 6M 197
Thorn La. Four M 5J 97
Thornleigh Rd. Sotn 8C 174
Thornley Rd. Bourn 2H 227
Thorns La. E End 4C 236
Thornton Av. Wars 8N 195
Thornton Clo. Water 7J 201
Thornton End. Holyb 2J 81
Thornton Rd. Gos 8K 213
Thornycroft Av. Sotn 8B 174
Thornycroft Roundabout. Bas 6N 41
Thorold Rd. Chan F 3C 132
Thorold Rd. F'ham 7E 64
Thorold Rd. Sotn 2C 174
Thorpe Gdns. Alt 4D 80
Thorrowgood Ho. Ports 8E 214
Threadgill Way. Ship B 2A 66
Three Acre Clo. New M 6N 231
Three Acre Dri. Bart S 6A 232
Three Acres. Water 7H 181
Three Ashes. 6C 12
Three Castles Path. Ellis 1J 79
Three Castles Path. E'sly 2D 26 (in two parts)
Three Castles Path. H Win 4C 26 (Springwell La.)
Three Castles Path. H Win & W'fld 7C 26 (Church La., in two parts)
Three Castles Path. N War 7H 45
Three Castles Path. Tun 5G 60 (in two parts)
Three Castles Path. Wins 7D 60 (in three parts)
Threefield La. Sotn 7M 173 (7E 4)
Three Horse Shoes La. Bramd 3F 136
Three Oaks. Sotn 5J 175
Three Stiles Rd. F'ham 7B 64
Three Tun Clo. Ports 2B 240 (4K 5)
Thresher Clo. Water 9C 182
Threshers Corner. Fle 8A 28
Throgmorton Rd. Yate 8K 17
Throop. 2B 228
Throop Clo. Bourn 4D 228
Throop Rd. Bourn 1A 228
Throopside Av. Bourn 2A 228
Thrush Clo. Bas 1H 59
Thrush Rd. Poole 5A 226
Thrush Wlk. Water 7M 181
Thruxton. 1M 67
Thruxton Airfield Rd. Thru 2L 67
Thruxton Ct. Sotn 5C 174
Thruxton Motor Racing Circuit. 1M 67
Thruxton Rd. Hav 4C 202
Thuiller Rd. Bar S 6N 71
Thumwood. Chine 9G 23
Thundery Hill. Seale 6N 65
Thurbern Rd. Ports 6F 214
Thurlow Clo. Ame 5A 66 (off Rayleigh Cres.)
Thurmell Clo. H End 6N 175
Thurmell Wlk. H End 6N 175
Thurmond Cres. Win 8G 105
Thurmond Rd. Win 8G 104
Thursby Rd. Highc 4H 231
Thursley Rd. Churt & Thur 5L 85
Thurston Clo. Chan F 5B 132
Thurston Ho. Fle 2K 47
Thurston Pl. Bas 1A 60
Thurstons. B'std 1D 82
Thwaite Rd. Poole 9F 226
Thyme Av. White 1G 196
Thyme Clo. Chine 7G 23
Thyme Ct. Farn 7E 28
Tibb's Mdw. Up Ch 2N 31 (off Butts Hill)
Tiberius Clo. Bas 4L 41
Tiberius Rd. And 7A 52
Tichborne Clo. B'wtr 8F 18
Tichborne Down. Alr 2E 108
Tichborne Gro. Hav 4D 202
Tichborne Pl. A'sht 2M 65
Tichborne Rd. Eastl 3D 160
Tichborne Rd. Sotn 2H 175
Tichborne Way. Gos 6F 212
Ticklecorner La. Mort 3H 13
Tickleford Dri. Sotn 9E 174
Tickner Clo. Bot 5B 176
Ticonderoga Gdns. Sotn 9C 174
Tidcombe Grn. Hav 2C 202
Tide Mill. 4A 172
Tidemill Clo. Christ 6K 229
Tides Reach. Sotn 2B 174
Tides Way. March 8E 172
Tideway Gdns. S'sea 3K 241
Tidpit. 9D 118
Tidworth. 8E 30
Tidworth Camp. 9B 30
Tidworth Rd. Coll D 2G 31
Tidworth Rd. Hav 5F 202
Tidworth Rd. Lud 2A 30
Tidworth Rd. Port & All 9B 66
Tiffany Clo. Hord 2G 233
Tiffield Clo. Ports 4K 215
Tigwells Fld. S Warn 4D 62
Tilbrook Rd. Sotn 2F 172
Tilburg Rd. Christ 7N 229
Tilbury's Clo. Bord 4J 101
Tildbury Cotts. Sut S 4C 76
Tilden Rd. Comp 8H 127
Tile Barn Clo. Farn 7J 29
Tilebarn La. Broc 1N 223
Tilford Rd. Churt 5L 85
Tilford Rd. F'ham & Tilf 9F 64
Tilford Rd. Hind 1M 103
Tilford Rd. Water 4N 181
Tillingbourn. Fare 6F 196
Tillington Gdns. Water 7D 168
Tilly Down. 3B 50
Tilmore Gardens. 9M 139
Tilmore Gdns. Ptsfld 8M 139
Tilmore Rd. Ptsfld 9M 139
Tilney Clo. Alt 4E 80
Timber Clo. F'ham 8D 64 (off Hart, The)
Timbercroft Clo. Four M 6H 97
Timberlake Rd. Bas 6B 42
Timberlane. Water 5L 201
Timberley Clo. Holb 4A 208
Timberley Ho. Ports 2E 240 (off Railway Vw.)
Timberley La. Redl 8E 120
Timberley Pl. C'then 1A 18
Timbers, The. Fare 8M 197
Timor Clo. Bas 2D 42
Timor Clo. White 1E 196
Timothy Clo. Bourn 1H 227
Timpson Rd. Ports 1F 240
Timsbury. 7K 123
Timsbury Cres. Hav 6E 202
Timsbury Dri. Sotn 1E 172
Timson Clo. Tot 4J 171
Tincleton Gdns. Bourn 2M 227

Tindal Clo.—Turk St.

Tindal Clo. Yate 7N 17
Tindale Rd. Sotn 9D 158
Tinker All. Sotn 4E 160
Tinkers Cross 7H 151
Tinker's La. Bentw 6L 79
Tinley Gdns. Odi 8L 45
Tinneys Clo. W'flls 9C 120
Tins, The. L'ton 2E 234
Tintagel Clo. And 7N 51
Tintagel Clo. Bas 5L 41
Tintagel Clo. Sotn 5H 159
Tintagel Dri. Frim 3N 29
Tintagel Way. Port S 1C 214
Tintern Clo. Bas 3A 42
Tintern Clo. Ports 8B 200
Tintern Gro. Sotn 5K 173
Tintern Rd. Gos 3J 239
Tin Yd. La. Bock 1N 229
Tipner 5C 214
Tipner Grn. Ports 5D 214
Tipner La. Ports 5C 214
Tipner Rd. Ports 6D 214
Tipper La. S Hart 9G 146
Tippett Gdns. Bas 3A 60
Tiptoe 7E 222
Tiptoe Grn. Hav 3H 203 (off Sopley Ct.)
Tiptoe Rd. New M 6B 222
Tipton Ho. S'sea 3D 240
Tiptree Clo. Eastl 7E 132
Tisted Ct. Hav 4H 203
Titanic Memorial. 5L 173 (3C 4)
Titchbourne Ho. H End 3N 175
Titchfield 9H 197
Titchfield Abbey 7K 197
Titchfield By-Pass. Titch 8J 197
Titchfield Clo. T'ley 6J 11
Titchfield Common 8F 196
Titchfield Haven Bird Sanctuary. 6H 211
Titchfield Haven Nature Reserve Vis. Cen. 7J 211
Titchfield Hill. Fare 9K 197 (in two parts)
Titchfield Industries. Titch 9K 197
Titchfield La. Fare & Wick 9M 177
Titchfield Park 6G 197
Titchfield Pk. Rd. Fare 6G 197
Titchfield Rd. Stub 9K 197
Tithe Barn. L'ton 1E 234
Tithelands La. Bramd 1A 136
Tithe Mdw. Hat W 5L 59
Tithe, The. Water 7G 180
Tithewood Clo. Chan F 2N 131
Tittymouse La. W'hll 8C 50
Titus Gdns. Water 1A 202
Tiverton Ct. Fare 7D 198
Tiverton Rd. Bas 6K 41
Tivoli Clo. Chan F 5D 132
Toad La. B'wtr 9G 19
Tobago Clo. Bas 2C 42
Tobruk Clo. Enh A 3A 52
Tobys Garden. Ptsfld 1M 145
Toby St. Ports 1D 240 (2N 5)
Tockington Ct. Yate 7N 17
Todber Clo. Bourn 3B 226
Todhurst Ho. Ports 2E 240
Todmore. Gthm 3E 114
Tokar St. S'sea 5H 241
Tokio Rd. Ports 7H 215
Toledo Gro. And 9B 52
Tolefrey Gdns. Chan F 6L 131
Tollard Clo. Poole 6C 226
Tollard Ct. Bourn 9K 247
Tollbar Way. H End 2L 175
Tollgate. Chan F 1A 160
Tollgate Clo. Okly 8D 40
Tollgate Estates. Roms 1H 129
Tollgate Rd. And 9K 51
Tollgate Rd. Swanw 1A 196
Tollway. Chine 8H 23
Tolpuddle Gdns. Bourn 2M 227
Tolpuddle Way. Yate 8B 18
Tomkyns Clo. Chan F 6L 131
Tomlins Av. Frim 2N 29
Tomlins Clo. T'ley 6H 11
Toms La. Linw 1B 188
Tonbridge St. S'sea 5D 240
Tonge Rd. Bourn 1F 226
Tongham 4N 65
Tongham Meadows. Tong 3N 65
Tongham Rd. A'sht 2M 65
Tongham Rd. F'ham 5M 65
Tongham Rd. R'fld 6L 65
Tonnant Clo. Fare 6N 211
Toogoods Way. Nurs 6C 158
Toomer Clo. Fawl 6D 208
Toothill Rd. Roms 2B 158
Topaz Gro. Water 1B 202
Topiary Gdns. L Hth 5E 196
Topiary, The. Farn 9G 28
Topiary, The. Lych 3H 43
Toplady Pl. F'ham 3E 64
Top La. Ring 1K 187
Torbay Rd. Poole 2A 244
Torberry Dri. Ptsfld 2A 146
Torch Clo. Eastl 1M 161
Tor Clo. Fare 8G 198
Tor Clo. Water 6N 201
Torcross Clo. Sotn 8C 174
Torfrida Ct. S'sea 4K 241
Tormead. Hythe 6K 193
Tornay Gro. N Bad 8E 130
Toronto Pl. Gos 2K 239
Toronto Rd. Ports 9F 214
Torquay Av. Gos 8J 213
Torquay Av. Sotn 2J 173
Torque Clo. Sotn 6J 175
Torre Clo. Eastl 6E 132
Torridge Gdns. W End 8F 160
Torrington Clo. Lind 2M 101
Torrington Clo. Sotn 6E 174
Torrington Rd. Ports 5F 214
Tor Rd. F'ham 8B 64 (in two parts)
Tortworth Clo. Fare 9N 197
Tor Way. Ptsfld 1M 145
Torwood Gdns. Eastl 1K 161
Tosson Clo. Sotn 2D 172
Tote Hill 8A 122
Totford 8B 78
Tot Hill 3D 8
Totland Clo. Farn 6J 29
Totland Clo. Sotn 2D 172
Totland Ct. Mil S 8J 235
Totland Rd. Gos 6E 212
Totland Rd. Ports 1F 214
Totnes Clo. Eastl 7D 132
Tottehale Clo. N Bad 9E 130
Tottenham Clo. Braml 9G 13
Tottenham Rd. Ports 1F 240
Tottenham Wlk. Owl 4F 18
Totters La. H Win 9M 25
Totton 3N 171
Totton & Eling Bowls Cen. 3H 171
Totton By-Pass. Tot 4M 171
Totton Wlk. Hav 3D 202
Totton Western By-Pass. Ower & Cal 6G 156
Totton Western By-Pass. Tot 2G 171
Tourist Info. Cen. 5L 49 (Aldershot)
Tourist Info. Cen. 5F 80 (Alton)
Tourist Info. Cen. 2N 69 (Andover)
Tourist Info. Cen. 7C 42 (Basingstoke)
Tourist Info. Cen. 8L 229 (Christchurch)
Tourist Info. Cen. 5P 237 (Cowes)
Tourist Info. Cen. 9E 132 (Eastleigh)
Tourist Info. Cen. 8D 198 (Fareham)
Tourist Info. Cen. 8D 64 (Farnham)
Tourist Info. Cen. 2L 47 (Fleet)
Tourist Info. Cen. 1J 153 (Fordingbridge)
Tourist Info. Cen. 3M 239 (Gosport)
Tourist Info. Cen. 8F 202 (Havant)
Tourist Info. Cen. 5H 243 (Hayling Island)
Tourist Info. Cen. 2E 234 (Lymington)
Tourist Info. Cen. 2C 148 (Lyndhurst)
Tourist Info. Cen. 1M 145 (Petersfield)
Tourist Info. Cen. 2D 240 (3N 5) (Portsmouth, Commercial Rd.)
Tourist Info. Cen. 8D 214 (Portsmouth, George Byng Way)
Tourist Info. Cen. 2B 240 (3J 5) (Portsmouth, Hard, The)
Tourist Info. Cen. 1J 187 (Ringwood)
Tourist Info. Cen. 5L 129 (Romsey)
Tourist Info. Cen. 3E 158 (Rownhams)
Tourist Info. Cen. 5L 173 (4C 4) (Southampton)
Tourist Info. Cen. 7L 105 (8N 237) (Winchester)
Tournai Clo. A'sht 4N 49
Tournerbury Golf Course. 2H 243
Tournerbury La. Hay I 3G 243
Tourney Rd. Bourn 1B 226
Tovey Ct. And 9C 52
Tovey Pl. King W 8N 91
Towans, The. Poole 9A 244
Tower Arts Cen., The. 8F 104
Tower Clo. Charl 7K 51
Tower Clo. Gos 4F 238 (in two parts)
Tower Clo. Hind 3N 103
Tower Clo. Lip 2D 116
Tower Ct. Bourn 3J 245 (9J 247)
Tower Ct. Wars 8N 195
Tower Ct. Win 6K 105 (6L 237)
Tower Gdns. Hav 2F 216
Tower Gdns. Sotn 7L 159
Tower Hill. Farn 9J 29
Tower Hill Ct. K're 2A 6
Tower Ho. Sotn 8C 174
Tower Ind. Est., The. Eastl 2G 160
Tower La. Eastl 1G 160
Tower Pl. W End 1H 175
Tower Rd. Bourn 9B 228
Tower Rd. Hind 3N 103
Tower Rd. Lip 2D 116
Tower Rd. Poole 3F 244
Tower Rd. S'sea 4G 241
Tower Rd. Win 6K 105 (6L 237)
Tower Rd. W. Poole 4E 244
Towers Dri. C'then 1D 18
Towers, The. Net A 4E 194
Tower St. Alt 6E 80
Tower St. Ems 9M 203
Tower St. Ports 4A 240 (7H 5)
Tower St. Win 6K 105 (7L 237)
Town Cen. E. Junct. Bas 6F 42
Town Clo. Ropl 1E 110
Town Hall Rd. Hav 8F 202
Townhill District Cen. W End 9F 160
Townhill Park 9E 160
Townhill Way. W End 9E 160
Town La. Ptsfld 8A 140
Town Mill La. Whitc 5H 55
Town Mt. Ports 3C 240 (6M 5)
Town Quay. Cowes 5P 237 (off High St.)
Town Quay. Ports 3B 240 (6H 5)
Town Quay. Sotn 7L 173 (8C 4)
Townsend 4D 228
Towns End 2B 20
Townsend. Pitt 6E 86
Townsend Clo. Bas 7A 42
Townsend Clo. Bourn 1F 226
Townsend La. M'tin 9A 118
Townside Pl. Cam 7M 19
Town Sq. Cam 7L 19
Town Sta. Roundabout. And 2N 69
Townsville Rd. Bourn 4M 227
Town Wall. 7C 4
Towpath Mead. S'sea 3K 241
Toynbee Clo. Eastl 9E 132
Toynbee Rd. Eastl 9E 132
Tozer Clo. Bourn 4D 226
Trade Dri. Owl 3G 18
Trafalgar Clo. Chan F 7N 131
Trafalgar Ct. Christ 9B 230
Trafalgar Ct. Fare 1B 212
Trafalgar Ct. F'ham 9D 64
Trafalgar Ct. S'sea 5E 240 (off Richmond Rd.)
Trafalgar Ho. Hythe 6N 193
Trafalgar Pl. L'ton 2F 234
Trafalgar Pl. Ports 1F 240
Trafalgar Rd. Bourn 7K 227
Trafalgar Rd. Sotn 8M 173 (9E 4) (SO14)
Trafalgar Rd. Sotn 4H 173 (SO15)
Trafalgar Sq. Gos 2K 239
Trafalgar St. Win 7K 105 (8L 237)
Trafalgar Way. Cam 9H 19
Trafalgar Way. Hythe 8N 193
Trafalgar Way. Stockb 3F 88
Trafford Rd. F Oak 2M 161
Trafford Rd. Frim 4M 29
Trajan Wlk. And 7A 52
Trampers La. N Boar 9J 179
Tranby Rd. Sotn 6C 174
Tranmere Clo. L'ton 4F 234
Tranmere Rd. S'sea 3J 241
Trapshill 1H 7
Traveller's End. Win 5H 105
Travis La. S'hrst 6E 18
Treadwheel Rd. Ids 4G 183
Treagore Rd. Cal 1J 171
Trearnan Clo. Sotn 2E 172
Treble Clo. Win 1F 126
Trebor Av. F'ham 9F 64
Tredegar Rd. S'sea 4G 241
Tredenham Clo. Farn 3L 49
Treebys Clo. Burt 5N 229
Treeside. Christ 4E 230
Treeside Av. Tot 3N 171
Treeside Dri. F'ham 3G 64
Treeside Rd. Sotn 2H 173
Treeside Way. Water 9M 181
Trefoil Clo. H Win 5B 26
Trefoil Clo. Water 2N 201
Trefoil Way. Christ 6E 230
Tregaron Av. Ports 9J 201
Tregenn Ho. Lip 2D 116
Tregolls Dri. Farn 9L 29
Tregonwell Rd. Bourn 2J 245 (7K 247)
Trellis Dri. Lych 3H 43
Treloar Rd. Hay I 6M 243
Treloyhan Clo. Chan F 8B 132
Tremona Ct. Sotn 9G 158
Tremona Rd. Sotn 8G 159
Trenchard Av. Wint G 3B 86
Trenchard Pk. Bord 3J 101
Trenchard Rd. And 1H 69
Trenchmead. Bas 3L 41
Trenley Clo. Holb 5A 208
Trent Clo. Farn 6G 29
Trent Clo. Sotn 1D 174
Trentham Av. Bourn 6E 228
Trentham Clo. Bourn 6E 228
Trent Ho. Sotn 5A 174
Trent Rd. Sotn 1D 174
Trent Wlk. Fare 9J 199
Trent Way. Bas 6E 42
Trent Way. Lee S 2B 238
Trent Way. W End 9H 161
Tresham Cres. Yate 7K 17
Tresillian Clo. Walk 4K 231
Tresillian Gdns. W End 9F 160
Tresillian Way. Walk 4K 231
Trevis Rd. S'sea 3K 241
Trevone. New M 3C 232
Trevone Clo. Tot 5L 171
Trevor Rd. S'sea 4F 240
Trevose Clo. Chan F 8B 132
Trevose Clo. Gos 7E 212
Trevose Cres. Chan F 7B 132
Trevose Way. Fare 8E 196
Triangle Gdns. Nurs 8C 158
Triangle La. Fare 4H 211
Triangle, The. Bourn 2J 245 (7J 247)
Triangle, The. New M 6L 231
Triangle, The. Sotn 1B 174
Tribe Rd. Gos 2J 239
Tricorn, The. Ports 1D 240 (2N 5)
Trilakes Country Pk. 5B 18
Trimaran Rd. Wars 8B 196
Trimmers. F'ham 9C 64
Trimmers Clo. F'ham 3D 64
Trimmer's Ct. Ports 4B 240 (6H 5)
Trimmers Fld. F'ham 9G 64
Trimmers Wood. Hind 1M 103
Trimm's Drove. W'grn 2A 154 (off High St.)
Trims Ct. Over 2D 56
Tringham Ho. Bourn 6E 228
Trinidad Clo. Bas 2C 42
Trinidad Cres. Poole 6A 226
Trinidad Ho. Poole 6A 226
Trinity. Bourn 6N 247
Trinity. Owl 3G 19
Trinity Chu. La. Cowes 5P 237
Trinity Clo. Gos 3M 239
Trinity Ct. Chan F 6B 132
Trinity Ct. Col C 4M 133
Trinity Ct. March 8E 172
Trinity Ct. Sotn 4H 173
Trinity Ct. Tot 9L 157
Trinity Fields. F'ham 3C 64
Trinity Gdns. Fare 8C 198
Trinity Grn. Gos 3N 239
Trinity Hill. F'ham 3C 64
Trinity Hill. Meds 9K 79
Trinity Ind. Est. Sotn 3E 172
Trinity Ri. Pen M 6F 50
Trinity Rd. Bourn 1L 245 (5N 247)
Trinity Rd. Meds & Bentw 8K 79
Trinity Rd. Sotn 5M 173 (3E 4)
Trinity St. Fare 7D 198
Tripps End Cvn. Site. H End 3A 176
Tristan Clo. Cals 9J 209
Tristram Clo. Chan F 8L 131
Triton Cen., The. Roms 7C 130
Triumph Clo. Fare 7N 197
Triumph Rd. Fare 3B 212
Troak Clo. Christ 6A 230
Trojan Way. Water 6N 201
Troon Cres. Ports 8K 201
Trosnant Rd. Hav 7E 202
Trotsford Mdw. B'wtr 9E 18
Trotton Marsh 6N 141
Trotts 7B 172
Trotts La. March 6B 172
Trotwood Clo. Owl 3G 19
Trout Rd. Hasl 9N 103
Trowbridge Clo. Rown 6D 158
Trowbridge Ct. Win 7M 237
Trowe's La. B Hill 1B 14
Trowe's La. S'fld 1H 15
Trueman Sq. And 7B 52 (off Cricketers Way)
Truman Rd. Bourn 1F 226
Truncheaunts La. E Wor 8H 81
Trunk Rd. Farn 8E 28
Truro Ct. Gos 1E 238
Truro Ri. Eastl 9J 133
Truro Rd. Ports 8A 200
Truscott Av. Bourn 7L 227
Trussell Clo. Win 3H 105
Trussell Cres. Win 3H 105
Trust Clo. Hook 2F 44
Trypletts. Chu C 8K 47
Tubb's La. Char A 4J 21 (in two parts)
Tubb's La. High 4A 8
Tucks Clo. Brans 6C 220
Tuckton 9J 229
Tuckton Clo. Bourn 1G 247
Tuckton Rd. Bourn 1G 247
Tudor Av. Ems 5L 203
Tudor Clo. A'hlt 5D 152
Tudor Clo. Braml 2D 22
Tudor Clo. Cal 2J 171
Tudor Clo. Fare 8K 199
Tudor Clo. Gos 8F 212
Tudor Clo. Gray 5M 103
Tudor Clo. Hay I 5F 242
Tudor Ct. And 7N 51
Tudor Ct. Fare 1C 212
Tudor Ct. Ports 9G 201
Tudor Ct. S'sea 6E 240
Tudor Ct. T'ley 5H 11
Tudor Cres. Ports 2G 214
Tudor Dri. Yate 9N 17
Tudor Gdns. H End 5L 175
Tudor House Mus. 7L 173 (7C 4)
Tudor Way. Chu C 7M 47
Tudor Way. King W 7M 91
Tudor Wood Clo. Sotn 7L 159
Tuffin Clo. Nurs 6B 158
Tufton 8F 54
Tukes Av. Gos 4D 212
Tulip Clo. Bas 3J 59
Tulip Gdns. Hav 7C 202
Tulip Gdns. L Hth 6C 196
Tulip Rd. Sotn 7A 160
Tulls La. S'frd 5N 101
Tulworth Clo. Elve 8K 27
Tumulus Clo. Sotn 6J 175
Tunball La. F'bry 7B 6
Tunbridge Cres. Lip 1D 116
Tunbridge La. B'shtt 6C 102
Tunbridge La. Lip 9D 102
Tunnel La. N War 7H 45
Tunstall Rd. Ports 8E 200
Tunstall Rd. Sotn 6J 175
Tunworth 5K 61
Tunworth Ct. Hav 4H 203
Tunworth Ct. T'ley 5J 11 (off Tunworth M.)
Tunworth M. T'ley 5J 11
Tunworth Rd. Map 7M 43
Tupman Ho. Ports 9E 214
Turbary Clo. Poole 6B 226
Turbary Gdns. T'ley 4H 11
Turbary Pk. Av. Bourn 3D 226
Turbary Retail Pk. Bourn 3C 226
Turbary Rd. Poole 7B 226
Turin Ct. And 6A 52 (in two parts)
Turkey Island 3B 178
Turk's La. Mort C 1E 12
Turk St. Alt 5F 80 (in two parts)

Turmer. 1G 184
Turnberry Clo. Christ. 8J 229
Turnberry Dri. Hat W. 5J 59
Turner Av. Gos 7F 212
Turner Clo. Bas 7F 42
Turner Ct. And 9M 51
Turner Pl. Coll T 7F 18
Turner Rd. Ports 9E 214
Turners Av. Elve 8J 27
Turners Farm Cres. Hord 4H 233
Turner's Grn. La. Elve 8H 27
(in two parts)
Turners Oak Ct. Sotn 1H 173
Turners Way. Elve & Fle 9J 27
Turnpike Down. Win. 6N 105
Turnpike Way. H End 2M 175
Turnpike Way. Okly. 9C 40
Turnstone End. Yate 7L 17
Turnstone Gdns. Sotn 6G 158
Turtle Clo. Fare 4L 211
Turvy King Ct. Water 6G 181
Tuscam Way. Cam 9H 19
Tuscan Wlk. Chan F 6C 132
Tuscany Way. Water 1B 202
Tuscany Way. Yate 9M 17
Tussocks, The. March 8E 172
Tutland Rd. N Bad 8E 130
Tutor Clo. Hamb 6K 195
Tutts La. W Wel 9N 121
Tweedale Rd. Bourn 3N 227
Tweed Clo. Chan F 5M 131
Tweed Clo. Farn 6G 29
Tweed Ct. Hav 5E 202
Tweed La. Bold 6D 224
Tweedsmuir Clo. Bas 7K 41
Tweedsmuir Clo. Farn 9F 28
Twelfth St. Hythe 3B 208
(in two parts)
Twelve Acre Cres. Farn 7F 28
Tweseldown Rd. Chu C 7N 47
Twiggs End Clo. L Hth 5C 196
Twiggs La. March 3C 192
Twiggs La. End. March 4B 192
Twisell Thorne. Chu C. 7K 47
Twittens Way. Hav 8F 202
Two Ga. La. Over 3E 56
Two Gate Mdw. Over 2E 56
Two Ways Ct. W'hill 6H 101
Twyford Av. Ports 5E 214
(in two parts)
Twyford Av. Sotn 1H 173
Twyford Clo. Bourn 4A 228
Twyford Ct. Win 4L 105
Twyford Dri. Lee S 9B 212
Twyford Rd. Eastl 9F 132
Twynham Av. Christ 7K 229
Twynham Clo. D'ton 3K 119
Twynham Rd. Bourn 2H 247
Twynham Rd. Cam 8L 19
Twynhams Hill. Shir H 2C 178
Tye. 7J 217
Tyfield. Sher 9N 21
Tyler Ct. Hav 4E 202
Tylers Clo. L'ton 1D 234
Tyleshades, The. Roms 6N 129
Tylney La. Newn 2D 44
Tylney Pk. Golf Course 8D 24
Tylston Mdw. Lip 1D 116
Tyndale Cres. Bourn 2N 227
Tyndall Wood 4N 103
Tyne Clo. Chan F 7M 131
Tyne Clo. Farn 6G 28
Tynedale Clo. Gos 8H 213
Tyneham Av. Poole 6A 226
Tyne Way. W End 9J 161
Tyrells La. Burl 6D 188
Tyrrel Lawn. Hav 2D 202
Tyrrell Gdns. Bourn 4D 228
Tyrrells Ct. Brans 6D 220
Tyrrel Rd. Chan F 5A 132
Tyseley Rd. S'sea 2D 240
Tytherley Grn. Bourn 4A 228
Tytherley Grn. Hav 3H 203
Tytherley Rd. Sotn 2G 174
Tytherley Rd. W'slw 5J 87

U

Ugsdell Clo. New M 3B 232
Ullswater. Eastl 2E 160
Ullswater Av. Farn 9G 28
Ullswater Av. W End 1F 174
Ullswater Clo. Bord 2J 101
Ullswater Clo. F'ham 4C 64
Ullswater Gro. Alr 2F 108
Ullswater Ho. Ports 8C 200
Ullswater Rd. Sotn 1D 172
Undercliff Dri. Bourn 3L 245 (9M 247)
Undercliff Gdns. Sotn 7K 159
Undercliff Rd. Bourn 2B 246
Underdown Av. Water 7L 201
Undershore. L'ton 8F 224
Undershore Rd. L'ton 1F 234
Underwater World 8N 63
Underwood Av. Ash 1N 65
Underwood Clo. Sotn 7K 159
Underwood Rd. Eastl 8H 133
Underwood Rd. Sotn 7K 159
Unicorn Ga. Navy 1C 240 (1M 5)
Unicorn Rd. Navy 1C 240 (1M 5)
Unicorn Rd. Lee S 9N 211
Union Clo. Owl 3G 18
Union La. Drox 1J 165
Union La. K're 1A 6
Union Pl. Ports 1E 240
Union Ri. Lngmr 4J 115
Union Rd. Cowes 5P 237
Union Rd. F'ham 8E 64
Union Rd. Hav 8E 202
Union Rd. Sotn 4A 174
Union St. A'sht 9J 49
Union St. And 1A 70
(off East St.)
Union St. Fare 8E 198
Union St. Farn 8J 29
Union St. Ports 2B 240 (3K 5)
Union St. Win 6M 105 (7P 237)
Union Ter. A'sht 9J 49
Universal Marina. Sar G 3N 195
University Cres. Sotn 8N 159
University Parkway. Sotn 2H 159
University Rd. Sotn 7N 159
University Roundabout. Bourn 6G 227
Unwin Clo. Sotn 9B 174
Upfallow. Lych 4H 43
Up Green 7J 17
Up Green. E'sly 7J 17
Upham 8E 134
Upham St. Uphm 9D 134
Uphill Rd. Win 1F 104
Upland La. Hawk 7M 113
Upland Rd. Cam 6M 19
Uplands 6D 198
Uplands Av. Bart S 6B 232
Uplands Clo. S'hrst 5D 18
Uplands Cres. Fare 6D 198
Uplands La. Four M 6H 97
Uplands Rd. Bourn 5M 227
Uplands Rd. Den 4D 180
Uplands Rd. Dray 8K 201
Uplands Rd. F'ham 9G 65
Uplands Rd. Row C 8J 183
Uplands Rd. Win 3J 105
Uplands Way. Sotn 9M 159
Upmill Clo. W End 8F 160
Upnor Clo. Per D 4B 30
Up. Arundel St. Ports 2D 240
Up. Banister St. Sotn 4L 173 (1C 4)
Up. Barn Copse. F Oak 9M 133
Up. Bere Wood. Water 3N 201
Up. Broadmoor Rd. C'then 1E 18
Up. Brook Dri. L Hth 7B 196
(in two parts)
Up. Brook St. Win 7L 105 (8M 237)
(in three parts)
Up. Brownhill Rd. Sotn 8E 158
Up. Bugle St. Sotn 7L 173 (7C 4)
Upper Bullington 5D 76
Upper Burgate 6K 151
Upper Canterton 7K 155
Up. Charles St. Cam 7L 19
Up. Chestnut Dri. Bas 8A 42
Up. Church La. F'ham 8D 64
Up. Church Rd. Shed 3A 178
Upper Chute 1N 31
Upper Clatford 5L 69
Up. College Ride. Cam 5N 19
Up. Common Rd. Penn 2N 233
Up. Cornaway La. Fare 7K 199
(in two parts)
Up. Crabbick La. Water 5D 180
Up. Crescent Rd. N Bad 7E 130
Up. Deacon Rd. Sotn 4F 174
Upper Drove. And 1J 69
Up. Elms Rd. A'sht 1J 65
Up. Farm Rd. Okly 2D 58
Upper Froyle 8G 63
Up. Gordon Rd. Cam 8M 19
Up. Gordon Rd. Highc 5J 231
Upper Green 7G 83
(Bordon)
Upper Green 1H 7
(Hungerford)
Up. Grove Rd. Alt 6F 80
Upper Hale 4E 64
Up. Hale Rd. F'ham 3C 64
Up. Heyshott. Ptsfld 1N 145
Up. High St. Win 6K 105 (6K 237)
Up. Hinton Rd. Bourn 2K 245 (7M 247)
Up. House Ct. Wick 7C 178
Upper Kingston 5L 187
Up. Lamborough La. Cher 8G 108
Up. Lanham La. Old Al 9F 78
Up. Mead Clo. F Oak 1A 162
Up. Moors Rd. Bram 4K 133
Upper Mt. Liss 2D 140
Up. Mount St. Elve 9J 27
Up. Mullins La. Hythe 6K 193
Up. Neatham Mill La. Holyb 2J 81
Up. New Rd. W End 1H 175
Up. Northam Clo. H End 4L 175
Up. Northam Dri. H End 4J 175
Up. Northam Rd. H End 3L 175
Up. Norwich Rd. Bourn 2H 245 (7J 247)
Up. Old Pk. La. F'ham 5B 64
Up. Old St. Fare 4L 211
Up. Park Rd. Cam 8M 19
Upper Parkstone 9A 226
Upper Pennington 3A 234
Upper Piece. Water 7H 181
Upper Ratley 9E 122
Upper Rd. Poole 7A 226
Up. St Helens Rd. H End 6M 175
Up. St Michael's Gro. Fare 9B 198
Up. St Michael's Rd. A'sht 2K 65
Up. Shaftesbury Av. Sotn 9N 159
Up. Sherborne Rd. Bas 4B 42
Upper Shirley 9J 159
Up. Shirley Av. Sotn 1H 173
Upper Slackstead 4G 124
Up. Soldridge Rd. Meds 5E 96
Up. South Vw. F'ham 7E 64
Upper Spinney. Wars 9N 195
Upper Street 2J 151
Upper St. Fle 2L 47
Upper Swanmore 3E 164
Up. Terrace Rd. Bourn 2J 245 (7K 247)
Upper Timsbury 5K 123
Upperton 6G 146
Up. Toothill Rd. Rown 2D 158
Up. Union St. A'sht 9J 49
Up. Union Ter. A'sht 9J 49
Up. Verran Rd. Cam 1M 29
Up. Wardown. Ptsfld 9A 140
Up. Weston La. Sotn 8E 174
Up. Weybourne La. F'ham 2F 64
Upper Wharf. Fare 9E 198
Upper Wield 8G 79
Upper Wootton 1E 40
Upper Wyke 1H 53
Uppleby Rd. Poole 9A 226
(in two parts)
Upron Fld. Clo. Bas 3K 59
Up Somborne 5K 89
Up St. Dum 1C 78
Up St. N Wal 9A 58
Upton 9G 6
(Andover)
Upton 4C 158
(Southampton)
Upton Clo. Farn 9M 29
Upton Clo. Hav 2D 202
Upton Cres. Bas 4B 42
Upton Cres. Nurs 4C 158
Upton Grey 3A 62
Upton Grey Clo. Win 3H 105
Upton Grey Rd. Upt G & Odi 3A 62
Upton La. Nurs 6N 157
Utrecht Ct. Christ 7N 229

V

Vadne Gdns. Gos 1K 239
Vaggs La. Hord 8E 222
Valdean Mobile Home Pk. Alr 9F 94
Vale Clo. Poole 1C 244
Vale Dri. Sotn 1D 174
Vale Gro. Gos 9J 213
Vale Lodge. Bourn 9A 228
Valencia Clo. Christ 2G 229
Valencia Way. And 9A 52
Valentine Av. Sotn 7G 175
Valentine Clo. Fare 6M 197
Valentine Ct. Sotn 7G 175
Valentine Ct. Water 1A 202
Valerian Av. Fare 6J 197
Valerian Clo. H Hth 5N 161
Valerian Rd. H End 4N 175
Vale Rd. Bourn 1N 245
Vale Rd. Cam 9J 19
Vale Rd. Poole 1C 244
Vale Rd. Win 8N 105
Vale Rd. W'flls 2M 119
Vale, The. Hythe 6L 193
Vale, The. L Hth 7E 196
Vale, The. Okly 1D 58
Vale, The. S'sea 5D 240
Vale, The. Water 1C 182
Valetta Pk. Ems 9L 203
Valette Rd. Bourn 2L 227
Valeview. Sway 8G 222
Vale Way. King W 6M 91
Vale Wood La. Gray 3L 103
Valiant Gdns. Ports 4E 214
Valiant Way. Christ 7D 230
Valley Clo. Black 7D 208
Valley Clo. Christ 3H 229
Valley Clo. Col C 4K 133
Valley Clo. Water 6K 201
Valley Clo. W'flls 2M 119
Valley Ct., The. Win 8H 105
Valleydene. Dib P 7L 193
Valley La. Brans 3G 220
Valley Mead. Anna V 4J 69
Valley Pk. Dri. Water 7D 168
Valley Ri. Sar G 5B 196
Valley Ri. Up Cl 5L 69
Valley Rd. Bourn 4B 228
Valley Rd. Chan F 5A 132
Valley Rd. Tot 5M 171
Valley Rd. Win 1F 104
Valley Side. Lip 1D 116
Valley, The. Win 8G 105
Valley Vw. Poole 7F 226
Valley Vw. S'hrst 6C 18
Valley Wlk. Uphm 6G 134
Valley Way. P Hth 4L 11
Valmeade Clo. Hook 2H 45
Valroy Clo. Cam 7M 19
Valsheba Dri. Fare 7L 211
Vanburgh Gdns. Bas 3K 59
Vanburgh Ho. H End 2A 176
Vanburgh Way. Chan F 3N 131
Vancouver Gdns. Bulf B 3A 66
Van Dyck Clo. Bas 7F 42
Vanguard Rd. Bourn 5B 228
Vanguard Rd. Sotn 2E 174
Vanners La. Enb 1N 7
Vanstone Rd. Gos 8F 212
Vardy Clo. Sotn 7H 175
Varna Rd. Bord 4K 101
Varna Rd. Sotn 5H 173
Varney Clo. Farn 7G 29
Varos Clo. Gos 1J 239
Vaudrey Clo. Sotn 1H 173
Vaughan Clo. Sotn 5J 175
Vaughan Rd. Dib 5H 193
Vaughans. Alt 5G 80
Vauxhall Way. Ptsfld 1L 145
Veals La. March 2F 192
Vear's La. Col C 4L 133
Vecta Clo. Christ 8E 230
Vectis Clo. Four M 5H 97
Vectis Ct. Sotn 7L 159
Vectis Rd. Bart S 7M 231
Vectis Rd. Gos 4G 239
Vectis Way. Ports 1G 214
Velder Av. S'sea 2H 241
Vellan Ct. Sotn 1C 172
Velmead Clo. Fle 4N 47
Velmead Rd. Fle 4M 47
Velmore Rd. Chan F 8N 131
Velsheda Ct. Hythe 3M 193
Velvet Lawn Rd. New M 2A 232
Venerable Rd. Fare 3C 212
Vengeance Rd. Lee S 9A 212
Venice Clo. Water 1A 202
Venice Ct. And 7A 52
(in two parts)
Venison Ter. Bro'tn 1A 86
Venning Av. Bourn 1C 226
Ventnor Ct. Sotn 6A 160
Ventnor Rd. Gos 5D 212
Ventnor Rd. S'sea 3F 240
Ventnor Ter. A'sht 1L 65
Ventnor Way. Fare 8G 198
Ventry Clo. Poole 1D 244
Venture Ind. Pk. Gos 5F 212
Venture Ind. Pk. Ports 3H 215
Venture Rd. Chilw 2J 159
Venture Roundabout. Bas 8D 42
Venture Sidings. S'sea 2G 240
Verandah Cotts. H Win 6C 26
(off High St.)
Verbena Cres. Water 6B 182
Verbena Way. H End 4A 176
Verden Way. And 7M 51
Verdi Clo. Bas 2M 59
Verdon Av. Hamb 6J 195
Verger Clo. Fare 6F 196
Verge Wlk. A'sht 3J 65
Verity Sq. And 7B 52
Vermont Clo. Sotn 7L 159
Vernalls Clo. Bourn 1H 227
Vernalls Gdns. Bourn 1H 227
Verner Clo. Head 3A 102
Verne, The. Chu C 6M 47
Verney Clo. Bourn 3F 226
Verney Rd. Bourn 3E 226
Vernham Bank 8D 6
Vernham Dean 8E 6
Vernham Rd. Win 4H 105
Vernham Row 7D 6
Vernham Street 7F 6
Verno La. Christ 5E 230
Vernon Av. S'sea 2H 241
(in two parts)
Vernon Building. Ports 3B 240 (5J 5)
Vernon Clo. Ame 5A 66
Vernon Clo. Bish W 1N 163
Vernon Clo. Gos 2J 239
Vernon Ct. F'ham 8C 64
Vernon Ct. Ports 6F 214
Vernon Hill. Bish W 1M 163
Vernon M. S'sea 2H 241
Vernon Rd. Gos 2J 239
Vernon Rd. Ports 6H 215
Vernon Wlk. Sotn 4L 173 (2C 4)
(in two parts)
Verona Av. Bourn 9G 228
Verona Rd. Chan F 5C 132
Veronica Clo. Bas 3J 59
Veronica Dri. Crook V 6J 47
Verran Rd. Cam 1M 29
Verulam Pl. Bourn 2K 245 (6M 247)
Verulam Rd. Sotn 3N 173
Verwood Cres. Bourn 1K 247
Verwood Rd. Ashy 9E 184
Verwood Rd. Hav 3H 203
Veryan. Fare 8A 198
Vesey Clo. Farn 7J 29
Vespasian Gdns. Bas 3L 41
Vespasian Rd. And 7A 52
Vespasian Rd. Sotn 3B 174
Vespasian Way. Chan F 6C 132
Vesta Way. Chan F 5C 132
Vestry Clo. And 1M 69
Vetch Clo. Christ 6D 230
Vetch Fld. Hook 2J 45
Viables Craft Cen. 1B 60
Viables Ind. Est. Bas 1B 60
Viables La. Bas 1C 60
Viables Roundabout. Bas 1A 60
Vian Clo. Gos 4E 212
Vian Pl. King W 7N 91
Vian Rd. Water 3L 201
Vicarage Dri. H End 5M 175
Vicarage Farm Bus. Pk. F Oak 7N 133
Vicarage Gdns. Chu C 7L 47
Vicarage Gdns. Gray 4L 103
Vicarage Gdns. Hord 3H 233
(in two parts)
Vicarage Hill. Alt 5F 80
Vicarage Hill. H Win 7C 26
Vicarage La. Copy 1B 170
Vicarage La. Curd 3F 176
Vicarage La. Fare 5M 211
Vicarage La. F'ham 8D 64
(Downing St.)
Vicarage La. F'ham 3E 64
(Heath La.)
Vicarage La. Hmbdn 8E 166
Vicarage La. Hasl 9N 103
Vicarage La. Hord 3H 233
Vicarage La. Hnd G 3F 24
Vicarage La. Ropl 2C 110
Vicarage La. Swanm 6D 164
Vicarage La. Yate 6M 17
Vicarage Pk. Redl 2M 119
Vicarage Rd. Alt 6E 80
Vicarage Rd. B'wtr 9G 19
Vicarage Rd. Bourn 4J 227
Vicarage Rd. Lover 8E 120
Vicarage Rd. March 9E 172
Vicarage Rd. Yate 6L 17
Vicarage Ter. Gos 8H 213
Vicarage Way. Burt 4N 229
Vice La. B'shaw 3L 155
Viceroy Rd. Sotn 7E 174
Vickers Bus. Cen. Bas 3N 41
Vickers Clo. Bourn 4E 228

Vickery Way—Warwick Clo.

Vickery Way. Christ 6N 229
Victena Rd. F Oak 1N 161
Victoria Av. Bourn 5J 227
Victoria Av. Cam 8J 19
Victoria Av. Hay I 4F 242
Victoria Av. Water 6J 201
Victoria Bldgs. Bish W 3L 163
Victoria Clo. L Hth 8D 196
Victoria Ct. And 2M 69
Victoria Ct. Durl 4F 162
Victoria Ct. Fle 2L 47
Victoria Cres. Poole 8B 226
Victoria Dri. B'wtr 9E 18
Victoria Gdns. Fle 2L 47
Victoria Gdns. F'bri 1G 153
Victoria Gdns. Ring 2K 187
Victoria Ga. Win 5K 105
Victoria Glade. Net A 4G 195
Victoria Gro. S'sea 4E 240
Victoria Hill Rd. Fle 2K 47
Victoria M. Net A 4F 194
Victoria Pk. Rd. Bourn 5J 227
Victoria Pl. Bas 7K 41
Victoria Pl. Bourn 9N 227
Victoria Pl. Gos 3K 239
Victoria Pl. L'ton 4E 234
Victoria Rd. A'sht 9J 49
Victoria Rd. Alt 4F 80
Victoria Rd. Bish W 3L 163
Victoria Rd. Bourn 9N 227
Victoria Rd. Christ 9A 230
Victoria Rd. Eastl 7F 132
Victoria Rd. Ems 8L 203
Victoria Rd. Farn 8J 29
Victoria Rd. F'ham 8E 64
Victoria Rd. Fle 2K 47
Victoria Rd. F'bri 1G 152
Victoria Rd. Hay I 6F 216
Victoria Rd. Mil S 8H 235
Victoria Rd. Net A 3E 194
Victoria Rd. Owl 4G 18
Victoria Rd. Poole 9A 226
Victoria Rd. Ports 1A 240 (1H 5)
Victoria Rd. Sotn 9B 174
Victoria Rd. Water 2M 201
Victoria Rd. Win 5K 105
Victoria Rd. E. Alt 4G 80
Victoria Rd. N. S'sea 4E 240
Victoria Rd. S. S'sea 5E 240
Victoria Sq. Lee S 1A 238
Victoria St. Bas 7C 42
Victoria St. Gos 2L 239
Victoria St. Ports 9D 214
Victoria St. Sotn 5A 174
Victoria Swimming Cen. 2C 240
Victoria Wlk. W End 9J 161
Victor Rd. Ports 9G 215
Victor St. Sotn 1G 173
Victory Av. Water 4A 182
Victory Clo. Chan F 7N 131
Victory Ct. Gos 7F 212
Victory Cres. Sotn 3G 173
Victory Ga. Ports 2B 240 (3J 5)
Victory Grn. Ports 6D 214
Victory Ho. Port S 1B 214
Victory Retail Pk. Ports 9D 214
Victory Rd. Fare 6N 211
Victory Rd. Ports 2B 240 (4J 5)
Victory Rd. Sotn 4G 173
Victory Roundabout. Bas 6B 42
Victory Sq. Sotn 3G 173
Victory Trad. Est. Ports 6J 215
Victory Way. Rown 4D 158
Vigo La. Yate 8M 17
Vigo Rd. And 1A 70
Vigo Rd. Roundabout. And 1A 70
Viking Clo. Black 8D 208
Viking Clo. Bourn 1K 247
Viking Clo. Fare 5L 211
Viking Clo. Sotn 6D 158
Vikings, The. Roms 5B 130
Viking Way. And 6A 52
Viking Way. Bourn 1K 247
Viking Way. Christ 9C 230
Viking Way. Water 8C 168
Villa Gdns. Water 1M 201
Village Clo. Fare 6M 211
Village Ga. Titch 8J 197
Village Rd. Gos 5H 239
Village St. Bentw 6L 79
Village St. Chlbn 4F 74
Village St. Good C 7N 69
Village St. Ptsfld 7A 140
Village, The. Finch 2H 17
Village, The. N Lit 3G 37
Village Way. Yate 6N 17
Ville De Paris Rd. Fare 3C 212
Villette Clo. Christ 5K 229
Villiers Ct. S'sea 5D 240
Villiers Ct. Win 8L 237
Villiers Rd. Dib P 9L 193
Villiers Rd. Sotn 3H 173
Villiers Rd. S'sea 5D 240 (in two parts)
Vimouters Ct. F'bri 1H 153
Vimy Cres. Bulf B 3B 66
Vimy Ho. Fare 9A 198
Vince Clo. Bourn 1F 226
Vincent Av. Sotn 9H 159
Vincent Clo. New M 4B 232
Vincent Dri. And 2A 70
Vincent Gro. Fare 1L 213
Vincent Rd. New M 3A 232
Vincent Rd. Sotn 2H 173
Vincent's Gro. Sotn 2G 173
Vincent St. Sotn 2H 173
Vincent's Wlk. Sotn 6M 173 (6D 4)
Vindomis Clo. Holyb 1K 81
Vine Bank. Sotn 2F 174
Vine Clo. A'sht 5J 49
Vine Clo. Bourn 7D 228
Vine Clo. Sar G 6A 196
Vine Coppice. Water 5M 201
Vine Farm Clo. Poole 6G 226
Vine Farm Rd. Poole 6F 226
Vinegar Hill. Mil S 7K 235
Vine Rd. Sotn 8F 158
Vinery Clo. Whitc 5G 55
Vinery Gdns. Sotn 9H 159
Vinery Rd. Sotn 9H 159
Vinery, The. New M 3C 232
Vinery Wlk. New M 3C 232
Vineside. Gos 7G 212
Vine St. A'sht 1J 65
Vine Tree Clo. T'ley 6K 11
Vineyard Clo. Sotn 7B 174
Vineyards, The. N Bad 8F 130
Viney Av. Roms 4A 130
Viney Rd. L'ton 5E 234
Vinnells La. W Meon 6E 136
Vinneys Clo. Burt 4M 229
Vinns La. Over 3C 56
Vinson Rd. Liss 1F 140
Violet Av. Fare 6L 211
Violet Clo. Bas 3J 59
Violet Clo. Chan F 6M 131
Violet La. Baug 6C 10
Violet La. New M 2B 232
Violet Rd. Sotn 7M 159
Virginia Clo. Ame 5A 66
Virginia Clo. Poole 7A 226
Virginia Gdns. Farn 1L 49
Virginia Pk. Rd. Gos 1H 239
Viscount Clo. Bourn 1A 226
Viscount Ct. And 9D 52
Viscount Ct. Bourn 1B 226
Viscount Dri. Christ 7D 230
Viscount Wlk. Bourn 1A 226
Vistarama 7L 247
Vita Rd. Ports 5F 214
Vitellius Gdns. Bas 3L 41
Vitre Gdns. L'ton 4E 234
Vivaldi Clo. Bas 3N 59
Vivash Rd. Ports 2F 240
Vivian Clo. Chu C 5N 47
Vivian Rd. Bas 4D 42
Vixen Clo. Fare 6L 211
Vixen Wlk. New M 9C 222
Vockins Clo. Tidw 6C 30
Vokes Clo. Sotn 5F 174
Vulcan Clo. S'hrst 6C 18
Vulcan Clo. Sotn 3E 172
Vulcan Ct. S'hrst 6C 18
Vulcan Rd. Sotn 3E 172
Vulcan Way. Christ 7D 230
Vulcan Way. S'hrst 6C 18
Vyne Clo. Alt 4F 80
Vyne Mdw. Sher 8A 22
Vyne Rd. Bas 5C 42
Vyne Rd. Sher & Braml 8A 22
Vyne, The 6C 22
Vyse La. Sotn 7L 173 (8C 4)

W

Wade Ct. Rd. Hav 9G 202
Wade Hill Drove. Cal 7G 156
Wade La. Hav 1G 216 (in two parts)
Wade Rd. Bas 4F 42
Wadham. Owl 4H 19
Wadham Rd. Ports 6E 214
Wadhurst Gdns. Sotn 1E 194
Wadhurst Rd. H End 4N 175
Wadley's Drove. Cran 6K 149
Wadwick 4N 35
Waggoners Way. Gray 4J 103
Waggoners Wells 6J 103
Waggoners Wells Rd. Gray 4J 103
Wagner Clo. Bas 2N 59
Wagon La. Hook 1H 45
Wagon Yd. F'ham 8D 64
Wagtail Dri. New M 4A 232
Wagtail Rd. Water 3A 182
Wagtail Way. Fare 9H 199
Wainscott Rd. S'sea 5H 241
Wainsford Clo. Penn 3B 234 (in two parts)
Wainsford Rd. Evtn 4M 233
Wainsford Rd. Penn 3A 234
Wainwright Clo. Ports 2K 215
Wainwright Gdns. H End 8N 161
Wait End Rd. Water 3M 201
Wakefield Av. Bourn 1J 227
Wakefield Av. Fare 6B 198
Wakefield Ct. Roms 5M 129
Wakefield Ct. Sotn 1E 174
Wakefield Ct. Water 6N 201
Wakefield Rd. Sotn 1E 174
Wakeford Clo. P Hth 4L 11
Wakeford Ct. P Hth 3L 11
Wakeford Pl. Wars 8D 196
Wakefords Copse. Chu C 8N 47
Wakefords Pk. Chu C 8N 47 (in three parts)
Wakefords Way. Hav 3G 203
Wake Lawn. S'sea 4K 241
Wakely Gdns. Bourn 1E 226
Wakely Rd. Bourn 1F 226
Walberant Bldgs. Ports 4G 214
Walberton Av. Ports 9H 201
Walberton Ct. Ports 9H 201
Walburton Way. Water 7D 168
Walbury Hill 3G 7
Walcott Av. Christ 5J 229
Waldegrave Clo. Sotn 9B 174
Walden Gdns. Water 3B 182
Walden Rd. Ports 6D 214
Waldon Gdns. W End 9F 160
Waldorf Heights. B'wtr 1F 28
Wales St. Win 6M 105 (7P 237)
Walford Rd. Ports 8D 200
Walhampton 1F 234
Walhampton Hill. L'ton 1F 234
Walhampton Obelisk 2G 234
Walker Gdns. H End 1N 175
Walker Pl. Gos 7F 212
Walker Rd. Ports 6D 214
Walkers Clo. F Oak 1A 162
Walker's La. N. Black 7C 208
Walker's La. S. Black 9D 208
Walker's Ridge. Cam 9N 19
Walkford 5K 231
Walkford La. New M 4M 231
Walkford Rd. Walk 5K 231
Walkford Way. Walk 5K 231
Walks Shop. Cen., The. Bas 6C 42
Walk, The. Sher L 5M 23
Walk, The. Win 6K 105 (8K 237)
Walkwood Av. Bourn 6E 228
Wallace La. E Bol 1B 236
Wallace Rd. Ports 8G 214
Wallace Rd. Sotn 9D 174
Wallace Way. A'sht 8H 49
Walldown Rd. W'hill 7J 101
Walled Gdns., The. S Warn 4D 62
Walled Mdw. And 2A 70
Wallington 7F 198
Wallington Ct. Fare 1B 212 (PO14)
Wallington Ct. Fare 6F 198 (PO16)
Wallington Dri. Chan F 4N 131
Wallington Hill. Fare 7E 198
Wallington Orchard. Fare 6F 198
Wallington Rd. Ports 7G 215
Wallington Shore Rd. Fare 7E 198 (in two parts)
Wallington Way. Fare 7E 198
Wallin's Copse. Chine 1G 42
Walliscott Rd. Bourn 5E 226
Wallis Ct. Bas 5M 41
Wallisdean Av. Fare 9B 198
Wallisdean Av. Ports 9J 215
Wallisdown 5D 226
Wallisdown Heights. Bourn 5D 226
Wallisdown Rd. Poole & Bourn 4B 226
Wallisdown Roundabout. Poole 5E 226
Wallis Dri. Braml 2J 23
Wallis Gdns. Water 9M 181
Wallis Rd. Bas 8C 42
Wallis Rd. Bourn 5F 226
Wallis Rd. Water 9M 181
Wall La. Sil 3B 12
Wallop Dri. Bas 4J 59
Wallop Drove. Neth W 2M 87
Wallop Rd. Grat & Mid W 5L 67 (in two parts)
Wallrock Wlk. Ems 5M 203
Walls Cvn. Pk. Hook 1J 45
Walls Ct. Frim 4N 29
Walmer Clo. Eastl 5E 132
Walmer Rd. Ports 2F 240
Walnut Av. Sotn 6C 160
Walnut Clo. A'sht 2J 65
Walnut Clo. Alt 3F 80
Walnut Clo. Chan F 2A 132
Walnut Clo. New M 3A 232
Walnut Clo. Sotn 1E 172
Walnut Clo. Yate 9N 17
Walnut Dri. Fare 6L 211
Walnut Gro. Sotn 2E 172
Walnut Gro. Win 5H 105
Walnut Tree Clo. Hay I 4F 242
Walnut Tree Clo. S Won 3H 91
Walnut Tree Ground. Fy'd 9N 31
Walnut Tree Rd. And 2M 69
Walpole Gdns. H Win 5C 26
Walpole La. Swanw 1B 196
Walpole Rd. Bourn 9A 228
Walpole Rd. Gos 3M 239
Walpole Rd. Win 9G 104
Walpole Ter. Gos 4K 239
Walsall Rd. Ports 1H 241
Walsford Rd. Bourn 9G 227
Walsingham Clo. Ports 8E 200
Walsingham Dene. Bourn 6C 228
Walsingham Gdns. Sotn 8D 160
Waltham Bus. Pk. Swanm 7C 164
Waltham Chase 8A 164
Waltham Clo. Drox 1J 165
Waltham Clo. Fare 7L 199
Waltham Clo. Owl 4F 18
Waltham Ct. Over 2E 56
Waltham Cres. Sotn 7G 159
Waltham La. Ashe 7J 57
Waltham La. Over 4F 56
Waltham Rd. Bourn 7E 228
Waltham Rd. Over 2E 56
Waltham St. S'sea 3C 240 (5M 5)
Walton Clo. Fle 3L 47
Walton Clo. Gos 3J 239
Walton Clo. Water 4M 201
Walton Ct. Fare 5N 197
Walton Ct. Ports 6K 5
Walton Pl. Win 9H 105
Walton Rd. Bourn 4G 227
Walton Rd. Gos 3J 239
Walton Rd. Ports 2J 215
Walton Rd. Sotn 6H 175
Walton Rd. Ind. Est. Ports 2K 215
Waltons Av. Holb 4A 208
Walworth Enterprise Cen. And 9C 52
Walworth Ind. Est. And 8E 52
Walworth Rd. And & Pic P 9C 52
Walworth Roundabout. And 9C 52
Wandesford Pl. Gos 7J 213
Wangfield La. Curd 1F 176
Wansbeck Clo. Chan F 7N 131
Wansdyke, The. Ink 1F 6
Wanstead Clo. Ring 8L 185
Wantage Rd. Coll T 5F 18
Warbler Clo. Sotn 5G 159
Warbler Clo. Water 3A 182
Warbleton Rd. Chine 9H 23
Warblington 1H 217
Warblington Av. Hav 8H 203
Warblington Castle 9H 203
Warblington Clo. Chan F 9M 131
Warblington Clo. Roms 4A 130 (off Selsdon Av.)
Warblington Clo. T'ley 6J 11
Warblington Ct. Ports 3B 240 (6K 5)
Warblington Rd. Ems 1L 217
Warblington St. Ports 3B 240 (6K 5)
Warborne 7F 224
Warborne La. P'mre 6G 224
Warbrook Ct. Hav 4H 203
Warbrook La. E'sly 5D 16
Warburton Clo. Sotn 6J 175
Warburton Rd. Sotn 5H 175
Ward Av. Cowes 5P 237
Ward Clo. And 8N 51
Ward Ct. Hay I 4E 242
Ward Cres. Ems 6N 203
Warden Clo. W End 1H 175
Wardens Clo. Hay I 2F 242
Warders Ct. Gos 2K 239
Ward Ho. Ports 1C 240 (2K 5)
Wardle Rd. Highb 5H 133
Wardley 9E 116
Ward Rd. S'sea 5H 241
Wardroom Rd. Ports 7C 214
Wareham Ct. Bourn 8E 228
Warehouse Rd. Green 1G 9
Warfield Av. Water 2M 201
Warfield Cres. Water 2M 201
Wargrove Dri. Coll T 5F 18
Warlock Clo. Sotn 7H 175
Warmwell Clo. Bourn 3M 227
Warnborough Ct. Hav 3H 203
Warner Ct. Win 4L 105 (off Northlands Dri.)
Warnes La. Burl 8D 188
Warnford 5P 135
Warnford Clo. Gos 3H 239
Warnford Cres. Hav 4D 202
Warnford Rd. Bourn 7E 228
Warnford Rd. Cptn 8N 135
Warren Av. Chan F 7C 132
Warren Av. Christ 9B 230
Warren Av. Sotn 9F 158
Warren Av. S'sea 2H 241
Warren Clo. Chan F 7C 132
Warren Clo. Fle 4N 47
Warren Clo. H Win 7C 26
Warren Clo. Hay I 3C 242
Warren Clo. Ring 3G 187
Warren Clo. S'hrst 5C 18
Warren Clo. Sotn 9F 158
Warren Clo. W'hill 5F 100
Warren Corner 2N 63 (Farnham)
Warren Corner 1G 139 (Petersfield)
Warren Corner. Ews 2N 63
Warren Cres. Sotn 9F 158
Warren Dri. Abb A 6F 68
Warren Dri. Ring 3G 186
Warren Edge Clo. Bourn 2J 247
Warren Edge Rd. Bourn 2J 247
Warren Gdns. Roms 3A 130
Warren La. Beau 3E 236
Warren La. Ows 1E 134
Warren La. Prior D 1H 139 (in two parts)
Warren La. Ring 3G 187
Warren Nature Reserve, The. 8H 113
Warren Park 2D 202
Warren Pk. Mil S 8H 233
Warren Pl. Cal 9J 157
Warren Ri. Frim 2N 29
Warren Rd. Bourn 3F 244
Warren Rd. Liss 7F 114
Warren Rd. Lngmr 4J 115
Warren Rd. Poole 1B 244
Warren Rd. Win 6N 105
Warrenside. S Hart 9G 146
Warrens La. Charl A 5A 120
Warren, The. A'sht 1H 65
Warren, The. F'ham 2G 64
Warren, The. Holb 3N 207
Warren, The. Per D 5B 30
Warren, The. T'ley 5G 11
Warren Way. Bas 8L 41
Warrington M. A'sht 2G 64
Warrior Bus. Cen., The. Ports 1M 215
Warrior Clo. Chan F 8N 131
Warrior Pk. Ind. Est. Chan F 8N 131
Warrys Clo. Hythe 9M 193
Warsash 8A 196
Warsash Clo. Hav 3E 202
Warsash Ct. Wars 8N 195
Warsash Gro. Gos 6D 212
Warsash Rd. Titch 9G 197
Warsash Rd. Wars & Fare 8A 196
Warspite Clo. Ports 4E 214
Warton Clo. E Bol 1B 236 (off Chapel La.)
Warton Rd. Bas 5D 42
Warwick Av. New M 3C 232
Warwick Bottom. St M 8L 35
Warwick Clo. A'sht 2L 65
Warwick Clo. Chan F 8M 131
Warwick Clo. Lee S 3C 238
Warwick Clo. Whitc 5G 54
Warwick Clo. Win 4K 105

Warwick Ct.—W. Cliff Gdns.

Warwick Ct. Bourn. 7M 227
Warwick Ct. Win. 4L 105 (off Northlands Dri.)
Warwick Cres. S'sea 3D 240
Warwick Ho. Sotn. 4A 174 (off Kent St.)
Warwick Pl. Bourn 9D 228
Warwick Pl. W Wel. 1B 120
Warwick Rd. Bas 5L 41
Warwick Rd. Bourn 9D 228
Warwick Rd. Poole 2A 244
Warwick Rd. Sotn 9J 159
Warwick Rd. Tot 2M 171
Warwick Way. Wick 6C 178
Wasdale Clo. Owl 3F 18
Wasdale Clo. Water 9C 168
Wash Brook. Hook 1G 45
Washbrook Rd. Ports 9E 200
Wash Common. 1C 8
Washford Clo. Bord 3L 101
Washford La. Lind & Bord 2L 101
Washington Av. Bourn 8A 228
Washington Rd. Ems. 8M 203
Washington Rd. Ports 8E 214
Wash Water. 1C 8
Wash Water. Wash W. 1A 8
Wasing. 1D 10
Watchetts Dri. Cam. 2L 29
Watchetts Lake Clo. Cam 1M 29
Watchetts Rd. Cam. 9K 19
Watch Ho. La. Cowes 5P 237
Watch La. Free 7L 37
Watchmoor Pk. Cam. 1J 29
Watchmoor Point. Cam. 9J 19
Watchmoor Rd. Cam 1J 29
Watchmoor Trade Cen. Cam 9J 19
Watcombe Rd. Bourn. 1G 246
Waterbeech Dri. H End 2N 175
Waterberry Dri. Water 9K 181
Water Clo. Win 7L 105 (9N 237)
Watercress Mdw. Alr 2D 108
Waterditch. 1D 230
Waterditch Rd. Brans. 1D 230
Water End La. And 4N 43
Water End Pk. And 4A 44
Waterford Clo. L'ton 3F 234
Waterford Gdns. Highc 7J 231
Waterford La. L'ton 3F 234
Waterford Pl. Highc 7J 231
Waterford Rd. Highc. 6K 231
Waterford Rd. New M 3D 232
Waterfront Bus. Pk. Fle 9N 27
Watergate. Gos. 3N 239
Watergate La. Bulf 3A 66
Waterhouse La. Sotn 3G 172
Waterhouse Mead. Coll T 6F 18
Waterhouse Way. Sotn. 3G 172
Wateridge Rd. Bas 3D 42
Water La. Abb W 1A 106
Water La. Alt 6H 81
Water La. Bish S. 2L 109
Water La. Bourn. 7G 228
Water La. Chu C 7J 47
Water La. Dib P 7K 193
Water La. Farn 5J 29
Water La. F'ham 6G 65
Water La. It Sto 1N 107
Water La. Ows 6B 134
Water La. Sotn. 5L 173 (3B 4)
Water La. Tot 2K 171
Water La. Win 7M 105 (8P 237)
Waterlily Clo. Bas 6E 42
Waterlock Gdns. S'sea 3L 241
Waterloo Av. Bas 4L 41
Waterloo Clo. Water 7L 181
Waterloo Ct. And 2N 69
Waterloo Ind. Est. H End 1M 175
Waterloo Park. 8K 49
Waterloo Pl. C'then 1D 18
Waterloo Rd. A'sht 1L 65
Waterloo Rd. Bourn 7K 227
Waterloo Rd. C'then 1C 18
Waterloo Rd. Gos 6L 239
Waterloo Rd. Hav 7F 202
Waterloo Rd. L'ton 2F 234
Waterloo Rd. Sotn 4H 173
Waterloo St. S'sea 3D 240 (5N 5)
Waterloo Ter. Anna V 5K 69
Waterloo Ter. Sotn 4L 173 (2C 4)
Waterlooville. 9K 181
Waterlooville Golf Course. 8B 182
Waterloo Way. Ring 2K 187
Watermain Rd. Hurn 2D 218
Waterman Clo. Bord 5L 101
Watermans La. Dib P 8K 193
Waterman Ter. S'sea 4F 240 (off Boulton Rd.)
Watermead. Christ 9K 229
Watermead Rd. Ports 1M 215
Watermill Rd. Christ 6K 229
Watermills Clo. And 3M 69
Water Rede. Chu C 8K 47
Water Ridges. Okly 2D 58
Waters Edge. H End 4M 175
Water's Edge. Lee S 3B 238
Waters Edge. Poole 7B 244
Watersedge. Wick 6C 178
Watersedge Gdns. Ems 9M 203
Waters Edge Rd. Ports 9B 200
Waters Grn. Broc 6D 148
Waters Grn. Ct. Broc 6D 148
Watership Down. 7G 9
Watership Dri. Ring 2N 187
Waterside. Christ 9B 230
Waterside. Hythe 4L 193
Waterside Clo. Bord 3K 101
Waterside Clo. Ring 8L 185
Waterside Ct. Alt 4G 81
Waterside Ct. Fle 9N 27
Waterside Gdns. Fare 7F 198
Waterside La. Fare 2N 213
Waterside M. Fle 9N 27
Waterside Rd. Roms 3N 129
Waterside Sq. Hythe 4L 193
Watersmeet. Fare 1D 212
Watersmeet. Win 9P 237
Waters, The. Fare 4A 198
Water St. Bulf 3A 66 (off Coach Rd.)
Water St. Cran 6J 149
Water Way. Bas 6E 42
Waterworks Cotts. Bas. 6A 42
Waterworks Rd. Ott 9G 127
Waterworks Rd. Ptsfld 6N 139
Waterworks Rd. Ports 9L 201
Watery La. And 9A 52
Watery La. Christ 5C 230
Watery La. Chu C 8K 47
Watery La. Kint H 1L 7
Watery La. Up Cl. 5L 69
Watkin Rd. Bourn 1C 246
Watkin Rd. H End 9A 162
Watley Clo. Nurs. 6C 158
Watley La. Spar 3B 104
Watley La. Twy 7M 127 (in two parts)
Watling End. Bas 3K 59
Watson Acre. And. 1L 69
Watson Wlk. Tot 3J 171
Watson Way. Bas. 4M 41
Watt Clo. And 9J 51
Watton Clo. Bourn 4D 228
Watton La. Drox 1L 165
Watton Rd. Holb. 4A 208
Watts Clo. Sotn 9D 158
Watts Rd. Farn. 7H 29
Watts Rd. H End. 3N 175
Watts Rd. Ports 9E 214
Wavecrest Clo. March. 7F 172
Wavell Clo. Bas 9N 41
Wavell Rd. Bourn 2F 226
Wavell Rd. Gos 5F 212
Wavell Rd. Sotn 3E 174
Wavell Rd. Tidw 6B 30
Wavell Way. Win 9G 104
Wavendon Av. Bart S 6N 231
Waveney Clo. Lee S 1B 238
Waveney Grn. Sotn 1D 172
Waverley Av. Bas 9B 42
Waverley Av. Fle 9L 27
Waverley Av. Net A 4G 195
Waverley Clo. Bulf B. 3B 66 (off Avon Rd.)
Waverley Clo. F'ham 8F 64
Waverley Clo. F'bri 8J 151
Waverley Clo. Odi 8M 45
Waverley Clo. Roms 3A 130
Waverley Ct. Net A 4G 195
Waverley Dri. Cam 8N 19
Waverley Dri. S Won 3J 91
Waverley Gro. S'sea 5F 240
Waverley Ho. New M 4C 232
Waverley La. F'ham 8F 64
Waverley Path. Gos 4G 238
Waverley Rd. Dray 9K 201
Waverley Rd. Farn 9M 29
Waverley Rd. F'bri 8J 151
Waverley Rd. New M 4C 232
Waverley Rd. Sotn 5J 173
Waverley Rd. S'sea 6E 240
Wayfarer Clo. S'sea 2K 241
Wayfarer Clo. Wars 8C 196
Wayfarers. Gos 9F 212
Wayfarer's Wlk. Dum & Kemp 8G 58
Wayfarer's Wlk. Hann 4K 39
Wayfarers Walk. High 4K 7
Wayfarer's Wlk. Okly 4C 58 (in two parts)
Wayfarer's Wlk. Stev 2L 57
Waylands Pl. H End 6M 175
Wayman Rd. Farn 4G 28
Waynflete Clo. Bish W 3M 163
Waynflete La. F'ham 8B 64
Waynflete Pl. Win 8G 105
Ways End. Cam 9N 19
Wayside. Lwr S 1A 196
Wayside Clo. Mil S 7L 235
Wayside Cotts. Churt 5F 84
Wayside Rd. Bas 6K 41
Wayside Rd. Bourn 1H 247
Wayside Rd. St L 7B 186
Wayte St. Ports 1G 214
Weald Clo. L Hth 5D 196
Weale Ct. Bas 5C 42
Weardale Rd. Chan F 8B 132
Weatherby Gdns. H Win 6C 26
Weathermore La. Four M 4L 97
Weaver Moss. S'hrst 6D 18
Weavers Clo. And 1A 70
Weavers Clo. W'slw 5H 87 (off Youngs Paddock)
Weavers Grn. Hav 6J 203
Weavers La. Ink 1G 6
Weavers Piece. Roth 7E 24
Weavers Pl. Chan F 3N 131
Weavers Yd. F'ham 8D 64
Weavills Rd. Eastl 1L 161
Webb Clo. Chine 1G 42
Webb Clo. Hay I 5G 242
Webbers Way. Gos 5L 239
Webb La. Hay I 5G 242
Webb Rd. Fare 2M 213
Webbs Clo. Ashy H 2A 186
Webbs Farm Clo. Whitc 7G 55
Webbs Grn. Sob 8K 165
Webbs La. Abb A 7E 68
Webbs Way. Ashy H 2B 186
Webbs Way. Bourn 5D 226
Webburn Gdns. W End 8E 160
Webster Rd. Bourn 3L 227
Webster Rd. Win 5F 104
Wedgewood Clo. Fare 6M 211
Wedgewood Clo. Holb 4A 208
Wedgwood Gdns. Brans 6E 220
Wedgwood Way. Water 8M 181
Wedman's La. Roth 6F 24
Wedman's Pl. Roth 6F 24
Wedmore Clo. Win 2E 126
Weeke. 4H 105
Weeke Mnr. Clo. Win 4H 105
Weeks Ct. Bish W 4N 163 (off Shore La.)
Weevil La. Gos 1M 239
Weir Av. Farn 9J 29
Weir Clo. Farn 9J 29
Weir Rd. Farn 1B 48
Weir Rd. H Win 8A 26
Weirs, The. Win 9P 237
Weir, The. Whitc 7G 54
Welbeck Av. Sotn 9N 159
Welbeck Clo. Farn 9H 29
Welch Rd. Gos 9J 213
Welch Rd. S'sea 5F 240
Welch Way. Rown 6E 158
Welchwood Clo. Water 4N 181
Weldon Av. Bourn 1C 226
Weldon Clo. Chu C 6N 47
Well. 5H 63
Welland Gdns. W End 9F 160
Welland Grn. Sotn 2D 172
Wellands Rd. Lyn 2B 148
Wella Path. Bas 9A 42
Wella Rd. Bas 9A 42
Wellbrooke Gdns. Chan F 5N 131
Wellburn Clo. S'hrst 6D 18
Well Clo. Cam 9K 19
Well Clo. New M 4A 232
Well Clo. N Wal 9A 58
Well Clo. Woot L 4G 40
Well Copse Clo. Water 1C 182
Weller Dri. Cam 1L 29
Weller Ho. Ports 9E 214
Wellers Clo. Tot 3H 171
Wellesley Av. Christ 7D 230
Wellesley Clo. Water 2M 201
Wellesley Ct. And 3N 69
Wellesley Dri. C'then 1A 18
Wellesley Garden. F'ham 3E 64
Wellesley Ga. A'sht 1K 65
Wellesley Rd. A'sht 8F 48
Wellesley Rd. And 3N 69
Wellesley Rd. Tilf 2K 85
Welles Rd. Chan F 6B 132
Well Hill. Den 3E 180
Well Ho. Clo. W'bry 9J 119
Well Ho. La. Win 1J 105
Wellhouse Rd. Bch 8N 79
Wellington Av. A'sht 9G 49
Wellington Av. Christ 7E 230
Wellington Av. Fle 1N 47
Wellington Av. Sotn 3F 174
Wellington Av. W'hill 5J 101
Wellington Bus. Pk. C'then 1A 18
Wellington Cen., The. A'sht 9J 49
Wellington Clo. Dib P 8J 193
Wellington Clo. Horn 4D 182
Wellington Clo. S'hrst 5E 18
Wellington Country Pk. 4H 15
Wellington Ct. Bourn 2H 245 (6G 247)
Wellington Ct. Hav 7F 202
Wellington Ct. New M 3B 232
Wellington Ct. Sotn 4J 173
Wellington Ct. W End 9G 160
Wellington Cres. Baug 4D 10
Wellington Gdns. A'sht 1H 65
Wellington Gro. Fare 1L 213
Wellingtonia Av. C'then 1L 17
Wellingtonia Roundabout. C'then 1A 18
Wellington La. F'ham 3F 64
Wellington Monument. 8G 48 (Aldershot)
Wellington Monument. 5F 14 (Hook)
Wellington Pk. H End 1L 175
Wellington Rd. And 9M 51
Wellington Rd. Bourn 8L 227
Wellington Rd. C'then 1E 18
Wellington Rd. Poole 2A 244
Wellington Rd. S'hrst 5D 18
Wellington Rd. Sotn 9B 160
Wellington Rd. Tidw 8E 30
Wellington Roundabout. A'sht 9G 49
Wellington Sports Cen. 1B 18
Wellington St. A'sht 9J 49
Wellington St. S'sea 3D 240 (5N 5)
Wellington Ter. Bas 4L 41
Wellington Ter. S'hrst 5E 18
Wellington Way. Water 2M 201
Well in the Fld. La. Free 4K 55
Well La. Hamb 7L 195
Well La. Lwr Fr & Long S 7G 63
Well La. Swanm 4D 164
Wellmans Mdw. K're 1A 6
Well Mdw. Hav 3E 202
Wellowbrook Clo. Chan F 6M 131
Wellow Clo. Hav 6D 202
Wellow Clo. Sotn 3G 174
Wellow Drove. W Wel 7N 121
Wellow Gdns. Fare 7F 196
Wellow Golf Course. 8E 128
Wellow Wood. 7M 121
Wellow Wood Rd. W Wel 7M 121
Well Rd. Cron 3L 63
Wells Clo. White 1F 196
Well's La. Whitc 6F 54
Wellsmoor. Fare 7F 196
Wells Pl. Eastl 1E 160
Wellspring Ho. Bas 9L 41
Wells Rd. Eastl 1F 160
Well St. Burgh 3E 8
Wellswood Gdns. Row C 7J 183
Wellsworth La. Row C 7J 183
Welsh Dri., The. E'sly 8B 16
Welshers La. Comp 5G 127
Welsh La. Rise 3D 14
Welshman's Rd. Pad C & Mort W 1M 11
Wembley Gro. Ports 2H 215
Wembley Way. F Oak 2N 161
Wendleholme Nature Reserve. 5N 195
Wendover Clo. Bart S 5A 232
Wendover Rd. Hav 7E 202
Wensley Dri. Fle 9M 27
Wensley Gdns. Ems 6M 203
Wentwood Gdns. New M 4E 232
Wentworth Av. Bourn 1D 246
Wentworth Clo. Bourn 2D 246
Wentworth Clo. F'ham 4H 65
Wentworth Clo. Yate 8N 17
Wentworth Cres. Hat W 5J 59
Wentworth Dri. Christ 8J 229
Wentworth Dri. Water 3B 182
Wentworth Gdns. Alt 4E 80
Wentworth Gdns. Holb 6B 208
Wentworth Gdns. Sotn 9F 174
Wentworth Grange. Win 8J 105
Wentworth Gro. Holb 5B 208
Wescott Way. Bourn 2C 226
Wesermarsch Rd. Water 6A 182
Wesley Clo. Bourn 9N 227
Wesley Clo. Sotn 6H 175
Wesley Ct. Ports 2F 240
Wesley Gro. Ports 5G 215
Wesley Rd. King W 8N 91
Wesley Rd. Poole 9A 226
Wesley Wlk. Bas 6C 42
Wessex Av. New M 4B 232
Wessex Av. Odi 1E 62
Wessex Clo. Bas 8B 42
Wessex Clo. Black 8D 208
Wessex Clo. Christ 7E 230
Wessex Ct. Sotn 6E 174
Wessex Cres. Odi 1E 62 (off Wessex Av.)
Wessex Dri. Odi 1E 62
Wessex Dri. Win 4J 105
Wessex Est. Ring 9M 185
Wessex Gdns. And 1M 69
Wessex Gdns. Fare 1K 213
Wessex Gdns. Roms 5A 130
Wessex Ga. Ind. Est. Water 4C 182
Wessex La. Sotn 8B 160
Wessex Pl. F'ham 9E 64
Wessex Rd. Ring 9L 185
Wessex Rd. Water 8C 168
Wessex Rd. W End 8F 160
Wessex Way. Bourn 1F 244 (6G 247)
Wessex Way. Col C 4L 133
West Av. F'ham 4F 64
West Bargate. Sotn 6L 173 (6C 4)
W. Battery Rd. Ports 7C 214
W. Bay Rd. Sotn & W Dock 4F 172
Westbeams Rd. Sway 5J 223
Westborn Rd. Fare 8D 198
Westbourne. 2F 244
Westbourne Arc. Bourn 2F 244
Westbourne Av. Ems 7M 203
Westbourne Av. Holb 4A 208
Westbourne Clo. Bourn 2G 244
Westbourne Clo. Ems 7N 203
Westbourne Ct. Hav 7E 202
Westbourne Cres. Sotn 1M 173
Westbourne Mans. Sotn 1M 173
Westbourne Pk. Rd. Bourn 3F 244
Westbourne Rd. Coll T 6G 19
Westbourne Rd. Ems 6N 203
Westbourne Rd. Ports 8G 215
Westbroke Gdns. Roms 3M 129
Westbrook Cen., The. Water 9B 182
W. Brook Clo. Okly 2D 58
Westbrook Clo. Park G 3D 196
Westbrook Ct. Bas 7J 41
Westbrooke Clo. And 2N 69
Westbrooke Clo. Water 4B 182
Westbrooke Rd. Alt 5E 80
Westbrook Gro. Water 4L 201
Westbrook Rd. Fare 2M 213
Westbrook Wlk. Alt 5F 80 (off Market St.)
Westbrook Way. Sotn 7C 160
Westburn Fields. Lwr Fr 8H 63
Westbury Av. Fle 3B 48
Westbury Clo. Bart S 6B 232
Westbury Clo. Brans 8C 220
Westbury Clo. Christ 5F 230
Westbury Clo. Fle 3A 48
Westbury Clo. Ports 8C 200
Westbury Ct. H End 5M 175
Westbury Gdns. F'ham 6G 64
Westbury Gdns. Fle 3B 48
Westbury Mall. Fare 8D 198
Westbury Manor Mus. 8D 198
Westbury Rd. Fare 8D 198
Westbury Rd. Ring 1L 187
Westbury Rd. Sotn 3E 172
Westbury Sq. Fare 8D 198
Westby Way. A'sht 9M 49
Westby Rd. Bourn 1B 246
West Cliff. 3J 245
Westcliff Clo. Lee S 9B 212
W. Cliff Cotts. Bourn 8J 247
Westcliffe Bldgs. Bart S 7N 231
W. Cliff Gdns. Bourn 3J 245 (9J 247)

W. Cliff M.—Whitebeam Gdns.

W. Cliff M. Bourn 3J 245 (8K 247)
Westcliff M. Sotn 7B 174
W. Cliff Promenade. Bourn 3H 245 (9H 247) (in two parts)
W. Cliff Rd. Bourn 3G 244 (9G 247)
Westcliff Wlk. Hythe 4L 193 (off Waterside Sq.)
W. Cliff Zig-Zag. Bourn 9J 247
West Clo. Bourn 1K 247
West Clo. F'ham 3F 64
West Clo. Penn 4B 234
West Common 1J 237
West Comn. Black 9B 208
Westcot Rd. Holb 5N 207
West Ct. Ports 9F 214
West Ct. Sotn 2G 172
West Ct. S'sea 4H 241
Westcroft Pde. New M 4B 232
Westcroft Rd. Gos 2H 239
West Dean 1J 121
Westdeane Ct. Bas 7A 42
W. Dean Rd. W'slw 5J 87
Westdown Rd. Bourn 1E 226
W. Downs Clo. Fare 5C 198
West Dri. Eastl 8H 133
West End 3C 96 (Alton)
West End 1A 212 (Fareham)
West End 1J 175 (Southampton)
West End. Sher 8M 21
W. End Cen. A'sht 9H 49 (off Queen's Rd.)
W. End Clo. Win 6J 105 (7J 237)
West End Green 5J 13
W. End Gro. F'ham 8C 64
W. End La. Fren 9N 63
W. End La. Meds 2C 96
W. End Rd. Sotn 3E 174 (SO18)
W. End Rd. Sotn & Burs 6K 175 (SO19 & SO31)
W. End Rd. W End 1H 175
W. End Ter. Win 6J 105 (7J 237)
Westerham. Poole 2E 244
Westerham Clo. Ports 9F 200
Westerham Rd. Bourn 2F 244
Westering. Roms 3B 130
Westerley Clo. Wars 8B 196
Western Av. And 1N 69
Western Av. Bart S 6M 231
Western Av. Bourn 1H 227
Western Av. Ems 9K 203
Western Av. Poole 2C 244
Western Av. W Dock 5E 172
Western Clo. Bourn 1H 227
Western Ct. Fare 8C 198
Western Cross. Odi 9K 45
Western District Cut. Sotn 3J 173
Western Esplanade. Sotn 5K 173 (4A 4)
Westerngate. Poole 2F 244
Western La. Odi 8K 45
Western Pde. Ems 1L 217
Western Pde. S'sea 4C 240 (8M 5)
Western Rd. A'sht 1G 65
Western Rd. And 2N 69
Western Rd. Bord 1H 101
Western Rd. Chan F 3C 132
Western Rd. Fare 8D 198
Western Rd. Fawl 6J 209
Western Rd. Hav 7E 202
Western Rd. Liss 1E 140
Western Rd. L'ton 2D 234
Western Rd. Poole 5D 244
Western Rd. Ports 9D 200
Western Rd. W End 1H 175
Western Rd. Win 6J 105 (6J 237)
Western Rd. Ind. Est. Ports 9E 200
Western Ter. Ports 6D 214
Western Way. Bas 9M 41
Western Way. Fare 8C 198
Western Way. Gos 4G 238
West Farm. Coll D 1H 31
Westfield 4G 242
Westfield Av. Fare 9B 198
Westfield Av. Hay I 4F 242
Westfield Clo. Hamb 7J 195
Westfield Clo. H Hth 4A 162
Westfield Clo. T'ley 5K 11
Westfield Comn. Hamb 7H 195
Westfield Corner. Sotn 6C 160
Westfield Ct. Fle 2M 47
Westfield Cres. Chan F 8A 132
Westfield Dri. Swanm 9F 164
Westfield Drove. Bea 3H 135
Westfield Gdns. Christ 5D 230
Westfield Ind. Est. Gos 3J 239
Westfield Ind. Est. Horn 3D 182
Westfield La. Wrec 7N 63
Westfield Lido 1L 21
Westfield Oaks. Hay I 4F 242
Westfield Rd. Bas 8D 42
Westfield Rd. Bourn 1H 247
Westfield Rd. Cam 2K 29
Westfield Rd. Chan F 9A 132
Westfield Rd. Gos 2H 239
W. Field Rd. King W 6N 91
Westfield Rd. L'ton 4F 234
Westfield Rd. Sotn 3F 172
Westfield Rd. S'sea 4H 241
Westfield Rd. Tot 2M 171
Westfield Rd. Win 1F 104
West Fryerne. Yate 5N 17
Westgate. Fare 7M 211
Westgate Clo. Bas 5K 41
Westgate M. W End 1J 175
Westgate Pk. Bourn 2F 244
Westgate St. Sotn 7L 173 (8C 4)
Westgate, The. 6K 105 (7L 237) (off High St.)
West Glade. Farn 8F 28
West Green 7M 25
West Grn. Yate 6L 17
West Green House 7M 25
West Grn. Rd. H Win 5M 25
West Grimstead 2E 120
West Gro. F'bri 1H 153
West Ham 6M 41
W. Ham Clo. Bas 7L 41
W. Ham Est. Bas 7N 41
W. Ham La. Bas 7K 41
W. Ham La. E. Bas 6M 41
W. Ham Leisure Pk. Bas 6M 41
W. Ham Roundabout. Bas 7M 41
West Harting 6F 146
W. Haye Rd. Hay I 6K 243
West Hayes. L'ton 3F 234
West Hayes. Win 7H 105
West Heath 7H 29 (Farnborough)
West Heath 3G 20 (Tadley)
W. Heath Rd. Farn 8H 29
West Hill 7K 105
W. Hill Ct. Sotn 5K 173 (3A 4)
W. Hill Dri. Hythe 4L 193
W. Hill Dri. Win 6J 105 (7H 237)
West Hill Park 9K 197
W. Hill Pk. Win 6H 105
W. Hill Pl. Bourn 2J 245 (7J 247)
W. Hill Rd. Bourn 2H 245 (7H 247)
W. Hill Rd. S Won 2J 91
W. Hill Rd. N. S Won 2J 91
W. Hill Rd. S. S Won 3J 91
W. Hoe La. Bish W 4B 164
W. Horton Clo. Eastl 1K 161
W. Horton La. Eastl 2K 161
West Howe 2C 226
W. Howe Clo. Bourn 2E 226
W. Howe Ind. Est. Bourn 3C 226
West Hurn 9C 218
Westland Clo. Ame 5A 66 (off Rayleigh Cres.)
Westland Ct. Farn 8F 28
Westland Dri. Water 5N 201
Westland Gdns. Gos 4J 239
Westlands. Brans 7C 220
Westlands Gro. Fare 1L 213
West La. Evtn 5M 233
West La. Hay I 3E 242
West La. N Bad 7D 130
West La. N War 6H 45
West Leigh 4G 203
Westley 6N 89
Westley Clo. Win 5H 105
Westley Gro. Fare 9B 198
Westley La. Spar 6N 89
West Liss 1E 140
West Lodge. Lee S 9N 211
Westlyn Rd. P Hth 4L 11
Westman Rd. Win 4H 105
West Mansion. Bourn 2G 244
Westmarch Bus. Cen. And 8A 52
Westmarch Ct. Sotn 9A 160
W. Marlands Rd. Sotn 5L 173 (4C 4)
Westmead. Farn 9K 29
Westmead. F'ham 8D 64
Westmead Clo. Hay I 4D 242
West Meon 8C 136
West Meon Woodlands 2E 136
Westminster Clo. Bas 3K 59
Westminster Clo. Fle 1M 47
Westminster Ct. New M 7A 232
Westminster Gdns. Fare 6F 196
Westminster Ga. Win 9F 104
Westminster Ho. Bas 6C 42 (off Timberlake Rd.)
Westminster Pl. Ports 9E 214
Westminster Rd. Mil S 9H 233
Westminster Rd. Poole 4F 244
Westminster Rd. E. Poole 4F 244
Westmoreland Ct. Hord 3G 233
Westmorland Way. Chan F 7C 132
Weston 4H 145 (Petersfield)
Weston 1D 194 (Southampton)
Weston Av. S'sea 3J 241
Weston Clo. Sotn 9D 174
Weston Clo. Upt G 3A 62
Weston Corbett 7N 61
Weston Ct. Ports 2E 240 (off Canal Wlk.)
Weston Cres. Sotn 3G 174
Weston Down Rd. Mich 7H 77
Weston Dri. Bourn 2M 245
Weston Gro. Rd. Sotn 8B 174
Weston Homes. Sotn 1D 194
Weston Ho. Ptsfld 1L 145
Weston La. Nurs 7N 157
Weston La. Sotn 1C 194
Weston La. West 4H 145
Weston La. W'slw 5G 86
Weston Pde. Sotn 1C 194
Weston Patrick 5A 62
Weston Rd. Eastl 9E 132
Weston Rd. Ptsfld 1N 145
Weston Rd. Upt G 4A 62
W. Overcliff Dri. Bourn 3G 244 (9H 247)
Westover La. Ring 2G 187
Westover Rd. Bourn 2K 245 (7M 247)
Westover Rd. Fle 2N 47
Westover Rd. Mil S 8K 235
Westover Rd. Ports 8J 215
Westover Rd. Sotn 2B 172
West Pk. App 4B 50
W. Park Dri. Dam 6A 150
W. Park La. Dam 3P 149
W. Park Rd. Sotn 5L 173 (4B 4)
West Point. Lee S 1A 238
West Portway. And 8H 51
W. Quay Retail Pk. Sotn 6K 173 (5A 4)
W. Quay Rd. Sotn 6K 173 (5A 4)
W. Quay Shop. Cen. Sotn 6L 173 (5C 4)
Westray Clo. Bas 4E 42
Westridge. High 4A 8
West Ridge. Seale 5N 65
Westridge Ct. Sotn 1N 173
Westridge Rd. Sotn 1N 173
West Rd. Bar S 5A 76
West Rd. Bourn 9D 228
West Rd. Brans 6C 220
West Rd. Cam 8M 19
West Rd. Dib P 8J 193
West Rd. Ems 9K 203
West Rd. Farn 5K 29
West Rd. H End 4K 175
West Rd. Hythe 8B 194
West Rd. Mil S 9H 233
West Rd. Sotn (SO14) 8M 173 (9D 4)
West Rd. Sotn (SO19) 8C 174
West Rd. S'wick 3B 200
Westrow Gdns. Sotn 3K 173
Westrow Rd. Sotn 3K 173
Westside. All 7D 66
Westside Clo. Bas 8M 41
Westside Vw. Water 9K 181
West Southbourne 1F 246
W. Station Ter. Bourn 2H 245 (6G 247) (off Queens Rd.)
West Stratton 7K 77
West St. Alr 9F 94
West St. And 1N 69 (in two parts)
West St. Burgh 4D 8
West St. Ems 9M 203
West St. Fare 8C 198 (in two parts)
West St. F'ham 9B 64
West St. F'bri 1H 153
West St. Hmbdn 9D 166
West St. Hav 7D 202 (in two parts)
West St. Hythe 4L 193
West St. Odi 9J 45
West St. Portc 9K 199 (in two parts)
West St. Ports 4A 240 (7H 5)
West St. Ring 1H 187
West St. Rog 9K 141
West St. Sob 6K 165
West St. Sotn 7L 173 (7C 4)
West St. S'wick 3N 199
West St. T'ley 5J 11 (in two parts)
West St. Titch 9J 197
West Tisted 7F 110
West Town 4E 242
West Tytherley 7L 87
W. Undercliff Promenade. Bourn 4G 244 (9J 247)
West Vw. W'hll 6G 100
West Vw. Wim G 7G 148
West Vw. Dri. Chlbn 5F 74
Westview Rd. Christ 8A 230
W. View Rd. Head D 3E 102
Westview Rd. Win 4E 104
Westward Rd. H End 2N 175
West Way. And 9C 52
West Way. Bourn 4M 227
West Way. Penn 4C 234
Westway. Titch 6H 197
W. Way Clo. Bourn 5M 227
Westways. Hav 9N 201
Westways. Stub 6N 211
Westways Clo. Nurs 6C 158
West Wellow 1B 120
West Wing. Net A 2E 194
West Winterslow 5F 86
Westwood Bus. Pk. Tot 8K 157
Westwood Clo. Ems 7N 203
Westwood Ct. Sotn 2M 173
Westwood Ct. Tot 9L 157
Westwood Ct. W End 1H 175
Westwood Gdns. Chan F 4C 132
West Woodhay 1K 7
Westwood Mans. Sotn 1M 173
Westwood Park 1N 173
Westwood Rd. Lyn 1B 148
Westwood Rd. Net A 2F 194
Westwood Rd. Ports 4F 214
Westwood Rd. Sotn 2L 173
Westwoods Pk. New M 1M 231
Westwood Vw. Kilm 2L 135
West Worldham 9L 81
Wetherby Ct. Tot 2K 171
Wetherby Gdns. Charl 8L 51
Wetherby Gdns. Farn 3L 49
Wetherby Gdns. Tot 2J 171
Wetherdown. Ptsfld 1N 145
Wey Bank. Bent 8L 63
Weybank Clo. F'ham 8E 64
Weybourne 4G 65
Weybourne Rd. F'ham & A'sht 5G 64
Weybridge Mead. Yate 6A 18
Weybrook Ct. Sher 8M 21
Weybrook Pk. Golf Course 2L 41
Wey Clo. Cam 8K 19
Weydon Farm La. F'ham 9D 64
Weydon Hill Clo. F'ham 9D 64
Weydon Hill Rd. F'ham 9D 64
Weydon La. F'ham 9D 64
Weydon Mill La. F'ham 9D 64
Weyhill 8D 50
Weyhill Bottom 7D 50
Weyhill Clo. Fare 8L 199
Weyhill Clo. Hav 4D 202
Weyhill Clo. T'ley 6H 11
Weyhill Gdns. W'hll 9D 50
Weyhill Ind. Est. W'hll 8B 50
Weyhill Rd. And 1J 69
Weyhill Rd. W'hll & And 8D 50
Weyland Clo. Lip 1E 116
Wey Lodge Clo. Lip 2F 116
Weymouth Av. Gos 8H 213
Weymouth Rd. Poole 9A 226
Weymouth Rd. Ports 7E 214
Weyside. F'ham 8E 64
Weyside Pk. Alt 3H 81
Weysprings Clo. Bas 6E 42
Weywood Clo. F'ham 3H 65
Weywood La. F'ham 3G 65
Whaddon Chase. Fare 6L 211
Whaddon Ct. Hav 3C 202
Whaddon La. Ows 5C 134
Whale Island Way. Ports 7D 214
Whalesmead Clo. Eastl 2K 161
Whalesmead Rd. Eastl 1K 161
Whaley Rd. Ports 7C 214
Wharf Clo. Poole 8C 226
Wharfdale Rd. Bourn 1G 245 (5G 247)
Wharfdale Rd. Poole 8B 226
Wharf Hill. Win 8M 105 (9P 237)
Wharf Mill. Win 9P 237
Wharf Rd. Ports 8D 214
Wharf Rd. Sotn 7B 174
Wharf, The. Odi 7M 45
Wharncliffe Gdns. Highc 7J 231
Wharncliffe Ho. Sotn 7B 174
Wharncliffe Rd. Bourn 1A 246
Wharncliffe Rd. Highc 7H 231
Wharncliffe Rd. Sotn 7B 174
Whartons Clo. Asht 7J 171
Whartons La. Asht 6J 171
What Vere La. Holyb 10E 62
Wheat Clo. Chan F 6L 131
Wheatcroft Dri. Sotn 1F 174
Wheatcroft Rd. Lee S 1B 238
Wheatear Dri. Ptsfld 1B 146
Wheatears Dri. W Wel 1B 120
Wheathold 4N 9
Wheatland Clo. Win 9H 105
Wheatlands. Fare 5F 196
Wheatlands Av. Hay I 6L 243
Wheatlands Cres. Hay I 6L 243
Wheatley 4G 82
Wheatley Grn. Hav 3C 202
Wheatley La. B'std & Kingsl 1F 82
Wheatley Rd. A'sht 8H 49
Wheatleys Clo. Stev 6K 57
Wheaton Grange. Bourn 1H 245 (5G 247)
Wheaton Rd. Bourn 9D 228
Wheatplot Pk. Homes. Bourn 1K 227
Wheatsheaf Common 6D 116
Wheatsheaf Ct. H End 4M 175
Wheatsheaf Dri. Water 7L 181
Wheatstone Rd. S'sea 4F 240
Wheeler Clo. Gos 1K 239
Wheeler Clo. Whitc 6H 55
Wheelers Hill. Hook 2J 45
Wheeler's La. Bourn 1A 226 (in two parts)
Wheelers Wlk. Black 8D 208
Wheelhouse Pk. Cvn. Pk. N Bad 3M 131
Wheelwrights La. Gray 3J 103
Whernside Clo. Sotn 2E 172
Wherwell 2F 74
Wherwell Ct. Hav 4H 203
Whetstone Rd. Farn 8E 28
Whichers Clo. Row C 1H 203
Whichers Ga. Rd. Row C & Hav 1H 203
Whimbrel Clo. S'sea 2L 241
Whinchat Clo. Fare 5M 197
Whinchat Clo. H Win 5B 26
Whinchat Clo. Sotn 5G 158
Whinfield Rd. Dib P 8K 193
Whin Holt. Fle 5M 47
Whins Clo. Cam 9K 19
Whins Dri. Cam 9K 19
Whinwhistle Rd. E Wel 2B 156
Whippingham Clo. Ports 9E 200
Whistler Clo. Bas 8E 42
Whistler Clo. Sotn 7G 174
Whistler Gro. Coll T 7F 18
Whistler Rd. Sotn 7G 174
Whistlers La. Sil 4A 12
Whitaker Cres. Penn 3C 234
Whitby Clo. Christ 2G 229
Whitby Clo. Farn 2N 49
Whitby Ct. Mil S 8H 235
Whitby Rd. Mil S 8H 235
Whitchurch 5G 54
Whitchurch Clo. A'sht 4M 65
Whitchurch Silk Mill 6G 54
Whitcombe Clo. Tot 3L 171
Whitcombe Gdns. Ports 1G 241
Whiteacres Clo. Gos 2K 239
White Av. Lngmr 4H 115
White Barn Cres. Hord 3H 233
Whitebeam Clo. Col C 4L 133
Whitebeam Clo. Fare 9A 198
Whitebeam Clo. Water 5C 182
Whitebeam Gdns. Farn 9E 28

White Beam Ri. Clan. 6C 168
Whitebeam Rd. H End 4A 176
Whitebeam Way. N Bad 7F 130
Whitebines. F'ham 8F 64
White City. Wool H 2A 8
Whitecliffe Av. Ports 9H 215
Whitecliffe Ct. Gos 3F 238
White Cloud Pk. S'sea 4G 241
White Cloud Pl. S'sea 4G 241
White Cottage Clo. F'ham 4F 64
Whitecroft. Hythe 7M 193
Whitecross Gdns. Ports 5G 214
Whitedell La. Fare 5F 198
White Dirt La. Water 9B 168
Whitedown. Alt 6E 80
Whitedown La. Alt 6D 80
Whitedown Rd. T'ley 5F 10
White Farm Clo. Bourn 6H 227
White Farm La. Butt 4D 6
Whitefield Lodge. New M 3B 232
Whitefield Rd. Holb 5A 208
Whitefield Rd. New M 3B 232
White Gates. Durl 6E 162
Whitehall. Christ 9L 229
Whitehall La. Lit Som 5J 89
White Harmony Acres Ind. Est. W End 6J 161
White Hart All. Ports 4B 240 (7J 5)
Whitehart Fields. Ring 9M 185
White Hart Ind. Est. B'wtr 9G 18
White Hart La. Bas 7D 42
White Hart La. Cad 6N 155 (off Romsey Rd.)
White Hart La. Char A 4G 21
White Hart La. Fare 1K 213
White Hart Rd. F Oak 2N 161
Whitehart Rd. Gos 3K 239
White Hart Rd. Ports 4B 240 (7J 5)
Whitehaven. Fare 1K 213
Whitehaven. Water 4D 182
Whitehaven Home Pk. Black 8C 208
Whitehayes Clo. Burt 4N 229
Whitehayes Rd. Burt 4M 229
Whitehead Clo. Lych 4G 43
White Heather Ct. Hythe 3M 193
White Hill. Ecc 5G 9
White Hill. Hath 8K 33
White Hill. K're 8J 9
White Hill. Long S 5G 62
White Hill. Pitt 6E 86
Whitehill Clo. Cam 6M 19
Whitehill Clo. Sotn 2G 175
Whitehill La. Alr 2G 108
Whitehill Pk. W'hill 7K 101
Whitehill Rd. S'frd 6L 101
Whitehorn Dri. Land 1J 155
White Horse La. Finch 1G 16
White Horse La. Water 3H 181
White Horses. Bart S 7N 231
White Ho. Clo. Bas 9M 41
Whitehouse Gdns. Ptsfld 8L 139
Whitehouse Gdns. Sotn 4F 172
White Ho. Gdns. Yate 6M 17
White Ho. Wlk. F'ham 3F 64
White Knights. Bart S 7A 232
White Ladies Clo. Hav 8G 202
Whitelands. Brans 3F 220
White La. Hann 6J 39
White La. Twy 5L 127
White La. Wes C 7M 61
White La. Upt G 1A 62
Whiteley Village Shop. Cen. White 1H 197
Whitelaw Rd. Sotn 3G 173
Whiteleaf La. Hmbdn 4C 166
Whitelegg Way. Bourn 1J 227
Whiteley. 1F 196
Whiteley La. Bur 8E 176
Whiteley La. Fare 1H 197
Whiteley Way. White 3G 196
White Lion Courtyard. Ring 1J 187
White Lion Wlk. Gos 2M 239
White Lion Way. Yate 6N 17
White Lodge Gdns. Fare 5A 198
Whitemoor La. Ower 7E 156
Whitemoor Rd. Broc 6A 148
Whitenap. 6B 130
Whitenap Clo. Roms 6A 130
Whitenap La. Roms 6A 130
White Oak Wlk. Hav 4H 203
White Oak Way. Anna V 5J 69
Whiteparish. 5H 121
White Rd. Coll T 7H 19
White Rd. Eastl 8H 133
Whites Clo. Hook 2F 44
Whites Ct. Ports 7E 214
Whites Hill. Ows 5B 134
Whiteshoot. Bro'tn 5A 88
Whiteshoot. Redl 9D 120
Whiteshoot Hill. Redl 9C 120
Whiteshute La. Win 1H 127 (in two parts)
Whites La. Fawl 5F 208
Whites Pl. Gos 2K 239
Whites Rd. Farn 2N 49
White's Rd. Sotn 5E 174
Whitestone Clo. Sotn 2E 172
Whitestones. Bas 4L 59
White Swan Rd. Ports 2C 240 (4M 5)
Whitethorn Rd. Hay I 4H 243
Whitewater Ri. Dib P 7L 193
Whitewater Ri. Hook 1J 45
Whitewater Rd. N War 7J 45
White Way. Ext 6L 135
White Way. Pitt 6D 86
Whiteway M. Wars 8N 195
White Wings Ho. Water 6G 181
Whitewood. Chine 9G 22
Whitfield Pk. Ring 3E 186
Whithedwood Av. Sotn 2J 173
Whithy Clo. Roms 4M 129
Whitlet Clo. F'ham 9D 64
Whitley Rd. Yate 9N 17
Whitley Row. S'sea 2K 241
Whitley Way. New M 1C 232
Whitlock Ri. B'stne 2D 118
Whitmarsh La. Chine 9J 23
Whitmoor Va. Gray 9G 84
Whitmoor Va. Rd. Gray 9H 85
Whitmore Clo. Owl 5F 18
Whitmore Grn. F'ham 4G 64
Whitmore Vale. 2K 103
Whitnal. 8M 37
Whitney Rd. Bas 4F 42
Whitsbury. 9J 119
Whitsbury Clo. Bourn 4A 228
Whitsbury Rd. F'bri 7H 151
Whitsbury Rd. Hav 4G 203
Whitstable Rd. Ports 9F 200
Whittingham Ct. Bourn 9E 228
Whittington Clo. Hythe 7L 193
Whittington Ct. Ems 9M 203
Whittle Av. Fare 4F 196
Whittle Clo. S'hrst 4C 18
Whittle Cres. Farn 5H 29
Whittle Rd. And 9H 51
Whitway. 5C 8
Whitwell. Net A 2G 195
Whitwell Rd. S'sea 6F 240
Whitworth Clo. Gos 3K 239
Whitworth Ct. Sotn 2B 174
Whitworth Cres. Sotn 2B 174
Whitworth Rd. Gos 3J 239
Whitworth Rd. Ports 8G 215
Whitworth Rd. Sotn 2B 174
Whyke Ct. Hav 7E 202
Why Not La. And 1L 69
Whyte Av. A'sht 2M 65
Whyte Clo. Holb 5N 207
Whyteways. Eastl 8E 132
Wick. 1L 247 (Christchurch)
Wick. 1J 119 (Salisbury)
Wick Clo. New M 4N 231
Wick Dri. New M 4N 231
Wicket Rd. Bourn 1G 226
Wicket, The. Hythe 7L 193
Wickfield Av. Christ 8L 229
Wickfield Clo. Christ 8L 229
Wickham. 6C 178
Wickham Clo. Alt 6D 80
Wickham Clo. Chu C 5K 47
Wickham Clo. T'ley 5H 11
Wickham Ct. Chu C 5K 47
Wickham Ct. Gos 4F 238
Wickham Cft. Wick 7C 178
Wickham Ho. Sotn 1M 173
Wickham Pk. Golf Course. 6A 178
Wickham Pl. Chu C 5K 47
Wickham Rd. Bourn 9D 228
Wickham Rd. Cam 5N 19
Wickham Rd. Chu C 5K 47
Wickham Rd. Curd 3F 176
Wickham Rd. Fare 1D 198
Wickham Rd. Sob 8J 165
Wickham St. Ports 2B 240 (3J 5)
Wickham Vineyard. 3L 177
Wick Hill La. Finch 1J 17 (in two parts)
Wick La. Bourn 9J 229
Wick La. Christ 9L 229
Wick La. D'ton 7L 119
Wicklea Rd. Bourn 1L 247
Wicklow Clo. Bas 8K 41
Wicklow Dri. Chan F 7M 131
Wickmeads Rd. Bourn 9K 229
Wick 1 Ind. Est. New M 4N 231
Wickor Clo. Ems 7N 203
Wickor Way. Ems 6N 203
Wick 2 Ind. Est. New M 4N 231
Wicor Mill La. Fare 1K 213
Wicor Path. Fare 2M 213 (Bayly Av.)
Wicor Path. Fare 1J 213 (Cador Dri.)
Widbury Rd. Penn 4C 234
Widden Clo. Sway 5J 223
Widdicombe Av. Poole 3C 244
Widecombe Dri. Hythe 5K 193
Wide La. Sotn & Sotn I 6C 160
Wide La. Clo. Broc 7C 148
Widgeon Clo. Gos 9K 213
Widgeon Clo. Sotn 5G 159
Widgeon Ct. Fare 9H 199
Widgeons. Alt 3F 80
Widget Clo. Bourn 4F 226
Widlers La. Uphm 8E 134 (in two parts)
Widley. 6K 201
Widley Ct. Fare 2C 212
Widley Ct. Dri. Ports 1H 215
Widley Gdns. Water 6L 201
Widley Rd. Cosh 9H 201
Widley Rd. Ports 6D 214
Widley Wlk. Water 7G 201
Widmore Rd. Bas 9L 41
Wield Clo. Hav 5C 202
Wield Rd. Meds 7H 79
Wigan Cres. Hav 7B 202
Wights Wlk. Bas 3K 59
Wight Vw. Lee S 9N 211
Wigley. 5F 156
Wigmoreash Drove. Butt 3F 6
Wigmore Ho. Ports 1E 240
Wigmore Rd. T'ley 4F 10
Wilberforce Clo. Win 8G 105
Wilberforce Rd. Gos 6L 239
Wilberforce Rd. S'sea 4D 240 (8N 5)
Wilby La. Ports 4K 215
Wilcon Ct. F Oak 4A 162
Wilcot Clo. Ame 6A 66
Wild Arum Way. Chan F 7L 131
Wildburn Clo. Cal 9J 157
Wild Cherry Way. Chan F 6M 131
Wilde Clo. Tot 3K 171
Wildern Clo. L Hth 6C 196
Wilderness Heights. W End 1G 175
Wilderness Rd. Frim 2N 29
Wildern La. H End 2N 175
Wilders Clo. Frim 1N 29
Wilderton Rd. Poole 2D 244
Wilderton Rd. W. Poole 1E 244
Wildfell Clo. Christ 5K 229
Wildground La. Hythe 8M 193
Wild Grounds Nature Reserve. 9D 212
Wildhern. 8L 33
Wild Herons. Hook 2J 45
Wildmoor La. Sher L 4M 23 (in two parts)
Wildmoor Wlk. Hav 4H 203
Wildown Gdns. Bourn 2J 247
Wildown Rd. Bourn 2K 247
Wild Ridings. Fare 9L 197
Wild Rose Cres. L Hth 7B 196
Wildwood Dri. Baug 4D 10
Wildwood Gdns. Yate 9M 17
Wilfred Rd. Bourn 1C 246
Wilkins Clo. Water 5B 168
Wilkinson Dri. Bourn 4D 228
Wilks Clo. Nurs 6B 158
Willems Av. A'sht 9H 49
Willems Roundabout. A'sht 9H 49
Willersley Clo. Ports 8D 200
Willesley Warren. 5B 38
Will Hall Clo. Alt 6D 80 (Basingstoke Rd.)
Will Hall Clo. Alt 7C 80 (Chawton Pk. Rd.)
William Booth Ho. Ports 2C 240 (2L 5)
William Clo. Fare 7N 211
William Clo. Walk 4J 231
William Ct. Christ 7K 231
William Farthing Clo. A'sht 9J 49
William George Ct. Lee S 2A 238
William Hitchcock Ho. Farn 5K 29
William Macleod Way. Sotn 1F 172
William Price Gdns. Fare 7D 198
William Rd. Bourn 7C 228
William Rd. L'ton 1E 234
Williams Clo. Gos 9F 212
Williams Clo. Holb 5B 208
Williams Ind. Pk. New M 4N 231
Williamson Clo. Lud 1C 30
Williams Rd. Ports 5J 215
William St. Sotn 5A 174
Williams Way. Fle 2A 48
William Way. Alt 3G 80
Willian Pl. Hind 1N 103
Willington Clo. Cam 7K 19
Willis Av. N Bad 8G 130
Willis La. Four M 7L 97
Willis Mus., The. 7C 42
Willis Rd. Gos 3L 239 (in two parts)
Willis Rd. Ports 2D 240 (3N 5)
Willis Rd. Sotn 6B 160
Willis Waye. King W 9M 91 (in two parts)
Willment Marine & Bus. Pk. Sotn 6B 174
Willments Ind. Est. Sotn 7A 174
Willoughby Clo. Alt 4E 80
Willoughby Way. Bas 5M 41
Willow Av. F'bri 9H 151
Willow Clo. Bord 4K 101
Willow Clo. Bourn 9F 226
Willow Clo. Hav 8G 202
Willow Clo. H End 4A 176
Willow Clo. Lip 3F 116
Willow Clo. Myt 8N 29
Willow Clo. St L 4A 186
Willow Clo. W End 9J 161
Willow Corner. Baug 4E 10
Willow Ct. Alt 5E 80
Willow Ct. Frim 3M 29 (off Gro. Cross Rd.)
Willow Ct. Sotn 8F 158
Willow Cres. Farn 5K 29
Willowdale Clo. Ptsfld 9G 138
Willowdene Clo. Hav 5B 202
Willowdene Clo. New M 3D 232
Willow Dri. Christ 9K 229
Willow Dri. March 1E 192
Willow Dri. Ptsfld 3M 145
Willow Dri. Ring 3K 187
Willowford. Yate 7N 17
Willow Gdns. Lip 3F 116
Willow Gdns. N Bad 7E 130
Willow Grn. Col C 4L 133
Willow Gro. And 2M 69
Willow Gro. F Oak 1A 162
Willow Herb Clo. L Hth 7B 196
Willow La. B'wtr 9F 18
Willow La. Brans 4F 220
Willow Mead. Bourn 2A 228
Willow Mead Clo. Coom B 2G 119
Willowmead Clo. N'bry 1C 8
Willow Pl. Gos 2K 239
Willow Rd. Bish G 2G 9
Willow Rd. Bish W 4A 164
Willow Rd. Liss 1E 140
Willow Rd. T'ley 5H 11
Willows End. S'hrst 5D 18
Willows, The. And 3M 69
Willows, The. Chan F 9A 132
Willows, The. New M 6C 232
Willows, The. N War 7J 45
Willows, The. Ports 6D 214
Willows, The. Water 6F 180
Willows, The. W End 9J 161
Willow Tree Av. Water 8B 182
Willowtree Gdns. Fare 9A 198
Willow Tree Ho. Penn 4C 234
Willow Tree Ri. Bourn 3F 226
Willow Tree Wlk. Sotn 7F 174
Willow Wlk. Bart S 7C 232
Willow Way. A'sht 2N 65
Willow Way. Bas 4M 41
Willow Way. Christ 9K 229
Willow Way. F'ham 4F 64
Willow Way. Mid W 4B 72
Willow Way. S'hrst 4B 18
Willow Way. Sher L 3L 23
Willow Wood Rd. Hay I 4G 242
Wills Rd. Poole 1D 244
Wills Way. Roms 6N 129
Wilmcote Gdns. S'sea 3E 240 (off Tyseley Rd.)
Wilmcote Ho. S'sea 2E 240
Wilmer Rd. Eastl 1E 160
Wilmington Clo. Sotn 8D 160
Wilmot Clo. Eastl 7J 133
Wilmott Clo. Gos 2H 239
Wilmott La. Gos 2H 239
Wilmott Way. Bas 5M 41
Wilsom. 5H 81
Wilsom Clo. Alt 5G 81
Wilsom Rd. Alt 5H 81
Wilson Clo. Fle 4K 47
Wilson Clo. Mid W 4A 72
Wilson Ct. F'bri 1J 153
Wilson Gro. S'sea 4E 240
Wilson Rd. A'sht 1M 65
Wilson Rd. Bourn 9A 228
Wilson Rd. Farn 9H 29
Wilson Rd. Poole 1A 244
Wilson Rd. Ports 6D 214
Wilsons Rd. Head D 2D 102
Wilson St. Sotn 5A 174
Wilton Av. Sotn 4K 173 (1A 4)
Wilton Clo. Christ 5G 229
Wilton Clo. Gos 3H 239
Wilton Ct. Farn 9M 29
Wilton Ct. Sotn 2J 173
Wilton Cres. Sotn 1J 173
Wilton Dri. Water 5A 182
Wilton Gdns. New M 3A 232
Wilton Gdns. Sotn 1J 173
Wilton Mnr. Sotn 1C 4
Wilton Pl. Bas 7A 42
Wilton Pl. S'sea 5E 240
Wilton Rd. Bourn 9C 228
Wilton Rd. Cam 1K 29
Wilton Rd. Sotn 9H 159
Wilton Ter. S'sea 5E 240
Wiltshire Clo. Bulf 3A 66 (off Churchill Av.)
Wiltshire Gdns. Brans 7B 220
Wiltshire Rd. Brans 7B 220
Wiltshire Rd. Chan F 9B 132
Wiltshire St. S'sea 3C 240 (5M 5)
Wilverley Av. Bourn 4C 228
Wilverley Av. Hav 5G 203
Wilverley Clo. Penn 4B 234
Wilverley Pl. Black 7C 208
Wilverley Rd. Broc 7C 148
Wilverley Rd. Christ 7C 230
Wilverley Rd. New M 5A 222
Wimbledon Pk. Rd. S'sea 5E 240
Wimborne Ho. Bourn 8K 227
Wimborne Rd. Bourn 8K 227 (5M 247) (BH3 & BH2)
Wimborne Rd. Bourn (BH10 & BH3) 2K 227
Wimborne Rd. Bourn 1D 226 (BH11 & BH10, in two parts)
Wimborne Rd. S'sea 3H 241
Wimborne St Giles. 7G 148
Wimborne St. Cran 6J 149 (off Square, The)
Wimpole Ct. Ports 1F 240
Wimpole St. Ports 1E 240
Wimpson. 1E 172
Wimpson Gdns. Sotn 1E 172
Wimpson La. Sotn 2D 172
Wincanton Clo. Alt 6G 80
Wincanton Way. Water 9B 182
Winchcombe Clo. Fle 3M 47
Winchcombe Rd. Bas 7B 42
Winchcombe Rd. Ports 8C 200
Winchester. 4J 105
Winchester By-Pass. Win & King W 8K 91
Winchester By-Pass. Wor D & Win 5F 90
Winchester Castle Great Hall. 7K 105 (8L 237)
Winchester Cathedral. 7L 105 (8M 237)
Winchester Cathedral Triforium Gallery. 7L 105 (9M 237)
Winchester City Mill. 7M 105 (8P 237)
Winchester Clo. Ame 6A 66
Winchester Clo. Net A 3F 194
Winchester Clo. Roms 3A 130
Winchester Ct. Gos 2F 238
Winchester Gallery. 6M 105 (6P 237)
Winchester Gdns. And 3A 70
Winchester Heritage Cen. 6L 105 (7N 237) (off Heritage Ct.)
Winchester Hill. Roms 5N 129
Winchester Hill. Sut S 7D 76
Winchester Ho. Hav 4G 202

Winchester Rd.—Woodland Way

Winchester Rd. Alr 1C 108
Winchester Rd. Alt 7E 80
Winchester Rd. And 2A 70
Winchester Rd. Bas 9N 41
Winchester Rd. Bish W & Wal C 4N 163
Winchester Rd. Chan F 6A 132
Winchester Rd. Chaw 9D 80
Winchester Rd. Chilw 3M 159
Winchester Rd. Comp 5H 127
Winchester Rd. Dum & Bas 6G 58
Winchester Rd. Durl & Bot 6A 162
Winchester Rd. F Oak 6M 133
Winchester Rd. Four M 6G 96
Winchester Rd. Good C & Wher 8B 70
Winchester Rd. K're 8J 9
Winchester Rd. King S 8B 86
Winchester Rd. Mich 8J 77
Winchester Rd. New M 1D 232
Winchester Rd. Ptsfld 9D 138
Winchester Rd. Ports 8F 214
Winchester Rd. Roms 5M 129
Winchester Rd. Shed & Wick 4A 178
Winchester Rd. Sotn 1F 172
Winchester Rd. Tilf 1K 85
Winchester Rd. Uphm 8C 134
Winchester Rd. Wher & Chlbn 1F 74 (in two parts)
Winchester Rd. Whitc 6G 55
Winchester Rd. Roundabout. Bas 8A 42
Winchester St. Bas 7C 42
Winchester St. Bot 2C 176
Winchester St. Chlbn 3G 74
Winchester St. Farn 3L 49
Winchester St. Over 2E 56
Winchester St. Sotn 4L 173 (2C 4)
Winchester St. Whitc 5G 55
Winchester Way. B'wtr 7E 18
Winchester Way. Tot 3J 171
Winchfield 1B 46
Winchfield Clo. Sotn 9E 174
Winchfield Ct. W'fld 2F 46
Winchfield Cres. Hav 5B 202
Winchfield Gdns. T'ley 6H 11
Winchfield Ho. Gos 3N 239
Winchfield Hurst 2E 46
Windbury Rd. Sotn 9D 158
Windermere Av. Bas 9J 41
Windermere Av. Fare 4N 211
Windermere Av. Sotn 9C 158
Windermere Clo. Farn 9G 28
Windermere Ct. Ash V 7N 49 (off Lakeside Clo.)
Windermere Gdns. Alr 2F 108
Windermere Gdns. Tot 2L 171
Windermere Ho. Ports 9C 200
Windermere Rd. Bord 2J 101
Windermere Rd. Bourn 7L 227
Windermere Rd. Ports 5G 214
Windermere Rd. W End 1F 174
Windermere Way. F'ham 4C 64
Windfield Dri. Roms 4A 130
Windham M. Bourn 9A 228
Windham Rd. Bourn 9N 227
Windhover Roundabout. Burs 8K 175
Windmill Clo. Mil S 7K 235
Windmill Clo. Ring 4G 187
Windmill Clo. Water 5C 168
Windmill Ct. Dib P 8L 193
Windmill Dri. Head D 1D 102
Windmill Fld. Water 6H 181
Windmill Fields. Four M 4J 97
Windmill Gro. Fare 2K 213
Windmill Hill. A'sht 1L 65
Windmill Hill. Alt 5G 80
Windmill La. Alt 6H 81
Windmill La. Burs 8L 175
Windmill La. Ring 4G 187
Windmill Rd. A'sht 1L 65
Windover Clo. Sotn 4G 175
Windrush Clo. Bas 6E 42
Windrush Gdns. Water 2L 201
Windrush Heights. S'hrst 5C 18
Windrush Rd. Sotn 1D 172
Windrush Way. Hythe 6M 193
Windsor Clo. Alt 5D 80
Windsor Clo. Hord 2F 232
Windsor Clo. St I 4C 186
Windsor Ct. A'sht 9H 49 (off Queen Elizabeth Dri.)
Windsor Ct. Eastl 8H 133
Windsor Ct. Fle 2M 47
Windsor Ct. Poole 2A 244
Windsor Ct. Ports 9G 201
Windsor Ct. Sotn 4F 172 (off Regents Pk. Rd.)
Windsor Ct. Sotn 3C 174 (Bullar Rd.)
Windsor Cres. F'ham 4D 64
Windsor Gdns. Bas 4J 59
Windsor Ga. Eastl 6E 132
Windsor Ho. Ports 2E 240
Windsor Ho. Win 7P 237
Windsor La. S'sea 3E 240
Windsor Pk. Alt 6F 80
Windsor Ride. Cam & C'then 5J 19
Windsor Rd. Alr 2E 108
Windsor Rd. And 1M 69
Windsor Rd. Bourn 1B 246
Windsor Rd. Christ 6H 229
Windsor Rd. Cosh 1G 215
Windsor Rd. Fare 2M 213
Windsor Rd. Farn 2M 49
Windsor Rd. Gos 3J 239
Windsor Rd. Lind 2L 101
Windsor Rd. Meds 3J 97
Windsor Rd. Ptsfld 9M 139
Windsor Rd. Poole 2A 244
Windsor Rd. Tot 4N 171
Windsor Rd. Water 8L 181
Windsor Ter. Sotn 4C 4
Windsor Wlk. Lind 2L 101
Windsor Way. A'hlt 4D 152
Windsor Way. A'sht 9K 49
Windwhistle La. W Gri 3D 120
Windy Gap 1J 103
Winfield Way. Ems 5M 203
Winfrid Ho. Tot 3K 171
Winfrith Cres. Poole 6C 226
Winfrith Way. Nurs 6C 158
Wingate Ct. A'sht 9H 49
Wingate Dri. Sotn 5F 174
Wingate La. Long S 4E 62
Wingate Rd. Gos 7H 213
Wingate Rd. Tot 2K 171
Wingfield Av. Christ 5F 230
Wingfield Ct. Bourn 2N 245
Wingfield St. Ports 9E 214
Wing Rd. Bulf B 3B 66
Wingrove Rd. Asht 7J 171
Wings Clo. F'ham 4D 64
Wings Rd. F'ham 4D 64
Winifred Clo. Eastl 9N 133
Winifred Rd. Water 1M 201
Winkfield Row. Water 5B 182
Winklebury 6L 41
Winklebury Cen. Bas 5L 41
Winklebury Way. Bas 6K 41
Winkle St. Sotn 8M 173 (9D 4)
Winkton 1M 229
Winkton Clo. Burt 3M 229
Winkton Clo. Hav 6D 202
Winkton Common 3L 229
Winkton Grn. Wink 1M 229
Winkworth La. A'mstn 3J 11
Winnall Clo. Win 5N 105
Winnall Ind. Est. Win 4N 105
Winnall Mnr. Rd. Win 6N 105
Winnall Moors Nature Reserve 6M 105
Winnall Trad. Est. Win 5N 105 (Easton La.)
Winnall Trad. Est. Win 6N 105 (Winnall Valley Rd.)
Winnall Valley Rd. Win 6N 105
Winnards Pk. Sar G 5A 196
Winnepeg Gdns. Bulf B 3A 66 (off Bulford Rd.)
Winnham Dri. Fare 8J 199
Winnington. Fare 5N 197
Winnington Clo. Fare 5N 197
Winn Rd. Sotn 2L 173
Winscombe Av. Water 8A 182
Winsford Av. Eastl 2L 161
Winsford Clo. Christ 5F 230
Winsford Clo. Eastl 2L 161
Winsford Gdns. Eastl 2L 161
Winslade 5F 60
Winslade La. Ellis 1J 79
Winslade Rd. Hav 4D 202
Winslade Rd. Win 2G 105
Winsley Av. Bourn 1F 246
Winsor Clo. Hay I 6K 243
Winsor La. Wins 1D 170
Winsor Rd. Bart & Wins 3B 170
Winstanley Rd. Nurs 6B 158
Winstanley Rd. Ports 7D 214
Winston Av. Poole 8D 226
Winston Av. T'ley 6K 11
Winston Churchill Av. Ports & S'sea 3D 240 (5N 5)
Winston Clo. Eastl 8E 132
Winston Clo. Frim G 6N 29
Winston Clo. Hay I 4E 242
Winston Clo. Sotn 9E 158
Winston Ct. Christ 7K 229
Winston Ct. New M 5A 232
Winstone Cres. N Bad 9F 130
Winston Gdns. Poole 8E 226
Winston Pde. New M 5B 232
Winston Pk. Poole 8D 226
Winston Ri. Four M 4H 97
Winston Rd. Bourn 3L 227
Winston Way. Ring 9L 185
Winterbourne Dauntsey 3A 86
Winterbourne Earls 3A 86
Winterbourne Ho. Bas 9L 41
Winterbourne Rd. Ports 8A 200
Winterbourne Rd. Roms 3A 130
Winterdyne M. And 2M 69
Winter Gardens, The. 3J 245 (8K 247)
Winterhill Rd. Ports 9E 200
Winter Rd. S'sea 4H 241
Winters Clo. Holb 5B 208
Wintershill 2J 163
Winters Hill. Durl 3G 163
Winterslow Dri. Hav 3E 202
Winterslow Rd. Port 1C 86
Winters Rd. Shir H 2C 178
Winterthur Way. Bas 6B 42
Winton 6K 227
Winton Chase. And 1B 70
Winton Clo. L'ton 3F 234
Winton Clo. Tidw 8G 31 (off Church La.)
Winton Clo. Win 4K 105
Winton Ct. Ptsfld 1M 145
Winton Ct. W End 1H 175
Winton Cres. Yate 8N 17
Winton Hill. Stockb 2G 88
Winton Rd. A'sht 1J 65
Winton Rd. F'ham 7F 64
Winton Rd. Ptsfld 9M 139
Winton Rd. Ports 6G 215
Winton Sq. Bas 7C 42
Winton St. Sotn 5M 173 (4E 4) (in two parts)
Winton Way. Bourn 5H 227
Winton Way. New M 1C 232
Wiremead La. Thru 1N 67
Wisbech Way. Hord 3G 233
Wisborough Rd. S'sea 5F 240
Wises All. Gos 3N 239
Wises Ct. Gos 3N 239
Wishanger La. Churt 6C 84
Wishart Gdns. Bourn 1M 227
Wishmoor Clo. Cam 5N 19
Wishmoor Rd. Cam 5N 19
Wish Pl. S'sea 4F 240
Wisley Gdns. Farn 9F 28
Wisley Rd. And 2K 69
Wistaria Ho. Bourn 2K 227
Wistaria La. Yate 8M 17
Wisteria Dri. Bord 5J 101
Wisteria Gdns. Hav 5H 203
Wisteria M. Holyb 1K 81 (off London Rd.)
Witan Clo. And 6A 52
Witan Ct. Whitc 4F 54
Witchampton Clo. Hav 4G 203
Witham Clo. Chan F 6M 131
Witherbed La. Fare 5G 197 (in three parts)
Witherington Rd. Alder 3B 120
Withermoor Rd. Bourn 6J 227
Wither Ri. Okly 9C 40
Witherslack Clo. Head D 3D 102
Withers La. E Bol 9B 206
Withes, The. Cron 3L 63
Withewood Mans. Sotn 3H 173
Withies Rd. Gos 8F 212
Withingham Rd. Poole 2D 244
Withington Clo. Ports 8C 200
Witley. Poole 6A 244
Witley Rd. Water 4N 181
Wittcomb Ter. W'hill 6H 101
Wittensford 6M 155
Wittensford La. Brook 6M 155
Wittering Rd. Hay I 5M 243
Wittering Rd. Sotn 6F 158
Witton Hill. Alr 2E 108
Witt Rd. F Oak 1N 161
Witt Rd. W'slw 5H 87
Witts Hill. Sotn 1D 174
Wivelrod Rd. Meds 9M 79
Woburn Av. Farn 8M 29
Woburn Clo. Eastl 6E 132
Woburn Ct. Lee S 3B 238
Woburn Gdns. Bas 8L 41
Woburn Rd. Sotn 6G 159
Wode Clo. Water 8C 168
Wodehouse Rd. Sotn 6C 174
Wokingham Rd. C'then & S'hrst 1A 18
Woking Rd. Poole 1A 244
Wolds, The. Bas 8K 41
Wolfe Clo. Christ 7A 230
Wolfe Clo. Win 9G 104
Wolfe Rd. A'sht 1L 65
Wolfmere La. Gthm 4F 114
Wolf's La. Chaw 8E 80
Wollaston Rd. Bourn 2J 247
Wollstonecraft Rd. Bourn 2C 246
Wolseley Rd. A'sht 1J 65
Wolseley Rd. Poole 8B 226
Wolseley Rd. Sotn 3H 173
Wolsey Way. Mil S 7L 235
Wolterton Rd. Poole 9E 226
Wolverley Ct. Sotn 8J 159
Wolversdene Clo. And 2B 70
Wolversdene Gdns. And 2B 70
Wolversdene Rd. And 2A 70
Wolverton 6N 9
Wolverton Common 9A 10
Wolverton La. Wolv 6N 9
Wolverton Rd. Bourn 9C 228
Wolverton Rd. Hav 4E 202
Wolverton Rd. Sotn 5N 173 (3F 4)
Wolverton Rd. Wolv 6N 9
Wolvesey Castle. 7L 105 (9N 237)
Wolvesey Palace. 7L 105 (9N 237)
Wolvesey Pl. Chan F 8M 131
Wolvesey Ter. Win 8M 105 (9P 237)
Wonderholme Pde. Bourn 4F 226
Wonston 7E 76
Wonston Clo. Sut S 7D 76
Wonston Ct. Hav 3H 203
Wonston La. S Won 1G 90 & 9D 76
Wonston Rd. Sotn 7G 159
Woodbarn, The. F'ham 9E 64
Woodberry La. Row C & Ems 8J 183
Woodbine Clo. Burgh 2D 8
Woodbine Clo. S'hrst 6E 18
Woodbourne. F'ham 3G 65
Woodbourne Clo. Fare 8N 197
Woodbourne Clo. Liss 1F 140
Woodbourne Clo. Yate 7N 17
Woodbridge Dri. Cam 6M 19
Woodbridge La. E Meon 3A 144
Woodbridge Rd. B'wtr 8D 18
Woodbury. Bourn 3L 245 (8N 247)
Woodbury. Broc 7A 148
Woodbury Av. Bourn 4B 228
Woodbury Av. Hav 9F 202
Woodbury Av. Ptsfld 8L 139
Woodbury Clo. Christ 3H 229
Woodbury Gro. Water 5N 181
Woodbury Rd. Hat W 3K 59
Wood Clo. Bas 5K 59
Wood Clo. Sotn 7G 175
Woodcock Bottom 2K 103
Woodcock Clo. Tidw 9D 30
Woodcock La. Hord 3H 233
Woodcocks Cres. Bourn 6D 228
Woodcot 4D 212
Woodcot Cres. Hav 3G 203
Woodcote Grn. Fle 3J 47
Woodcote La. Fare 5C 212
Woodcote La. Uphm 8E 134
Woodcote Rd. Butt 3E 6
Woodcote Rd. Sotn 8A 160
Woodcot Gdns. Farn 8F 28
Woodcott 1A 36
Woodcott Ter. A'sht 2M 65
Woodcroft Gdns. Water 5N 181
Woodcroft La. Water 5N 181
Woodend 2H 179
Wood End. C'then 1B 18
Wood End. Farn 9M 29
Woodend Rd. Bourn 6J 227
Woodend Rd. Crow 6A 188
Wood End Way. Chan F 6M 131
Wooden Ho. La. Pill 5H 225
Wooderson Clo. F Oak 9M 133
Woodfalls 3M 119
Woodfern. Gods 9N 151
Woodfield. Kingsl 7G 83
Woodfield Av. Ports 8M 201
Woodfield Cotts. Frox 2H 139
Woodfield Dri. Win 8F 104
Woodfield Gdns. Christ 5F 230
Woodfield Pk. Rd. Ems 8N 203
Woodfield Rd. Bourn 1E 226
Woodford Clo. Ring 1M 187
Woodford Ct. Bourn 9C 228
Woodford Rd. Bourn 1N 245
Woodgarston Dri. Bas 4J 59
Woodgarston La. Up Wn 3E 40
Woodgason La. Hay I 7J 217
Woodgate. Fle 9A 28
Wood Glade Clo. March 9E 172
Woodgreen 2A 154
Woodgreen Av. Hav 7D 202
Woodgreen Dri. Bourn 2B 226
Woodgreen Rd. Brea & W'grn 4M 151
Woodgreen Rd. Win 2H 105
Woodgreen Wlk. Cal 1H 171
Woodhall Way. Fare 6A 198
Woodhayes Av. Christ 4G 230
Woodhay Wlk. Hav 3H 203
Woodhill La. Fren 10N 63
Wood Hill La. Long S 4E 62
Woodhouse 3B 52
Woodhouse. Poole 2E 244
Woodhouse La. Ash H & Brim 2M 9
Woodhouse La. Bot 3A 176
Woodhouse La. Ids 4G 183
Woodhouse La. Row C & Hav 6H 183
Woodhouse Rd. Horn 2F 182
Woodington 6C 128
Woodington Clo. Hav 3G 203
Woodington Rd. E Wel 6C 128
Woodland Av. Bourn 1D 246
Woodland Clo. E Wel 1B 156
Woodland Clo. Sotn 3H 175
Woodland Ct. Chu C 7K 47 (off Brandon Rd.)
Woodland Ct. Hat W 5H 59
Woodland Dri. Braml 2J 23
Woodland Dri. W'slw 4G 87
Woodland Drove. Col C 1L 133
Woodland M. W End 1H 175
Woodland Pl. Sotn 3K 173
Woodland Ri. Chu C 6L 47
Woodlands 6E 170
Woodlands. Burgh 3B 8
Woodlands. Chine 8H 23
Woodlands. Fare 7F 198
Woodlands. Fle 1L 47
Woodlands. Over 2D 56
Woodlands. Poole 1E 244
Woodlands. Yate 1N 27
Woodlands Av. Ems 6L 203
Woodlands Av. F'ham 3H 65
Woodlands Bus. Village. Bas 5E 42
Woodlands Cvn. Pk. Hord 3H 233
Woodlands Clo. B'wtr 3G 28
Woodlands Clo. Brans 7C 220
Woodlands Clo. Chan F 2B 132
Woodlands Clo. Dib P 8K 193
Woodlands Clo. Gos 1E 238
Woodlands Clo. Sar G 3C 196
Woodlands Ct. Alt 7D 80
Woodlands Ct. Dib P 8K 193
Woodlands Ct. Owl 4H 19
Woodlands Ct. Win 5L 105
Woodlands Dri. Net A 3H 195
Woodlands Dri. W'lnds 6D 170
Woodlands Drove. Asht 7F 170
Woodlands Gdns. Roms 3A 130
Woodlands Gro. Water 4L 201
Woodlands La. Hay I 2E 242
Woodlands La. Liss 3G 140
Woodlands Rd. Bart S 7N 231
Woodlands Rd. Baug 4D 10
Woodlands Rd. Broc 9C 148
Woodlands Rd. Cam 8K 19
Woodlands Rd. Farn 6F 28
Woodlands Rd. Tot 6E 170
Woodlands, The. King W 9N 91
Woodlands, The. W'hill 7J 101
Woodland St. Ports 1F 240
Woodlands Wlk. B'wtr 3G 28
Woodlands Way. And 1B 70
Woodlands Way. Burs 1K 195
Woodlands Way. Hav 5F 202
Woodlands Way. N Bad 8E 130
Woodlands Way. St I 4C 186
Woodlands Way. Sotn 2L 173
Woodland, The. Chan F 3M 131
Woodland Va. Sotn 6F 174
Woodland Vw. Burs 1K 195
Woodland Vw. Mil S 8B 233
Woodland Vw. Water 4N 181
Woodland Wlk. Bourn 1D 246
Woodland Way. Highc 6F 230
Woodland Way. Mil S 8J 235
Woodland Way. New M 9C 222

Wood La. Beau 6B 206
Wood La. B Hill 2B 14
Wood La. Bramd. 9L 109
Wood La. Farn 9J 29
Wood La. Fle 2A 48
Wood La. Mil S. 8J 235
Wood La. S'wick. 3B 200
Wood La. Up N. 6C 44
Woodlane Clo. Bramd 9M 109
Wood Lark Gdns. Ptsfld 1B 146
Wood Lawn Clo. Bart S 6A 232
Woodlea Clo. Win 4J 105
Woodlea Gdns. W End 1J 175
Woodlea Way. Amp 2L 131
Wood Leigh. Fle. 3M 47
Woodleigh Clo. Hav 6J 203
Woodley. 2B 130
Woodley Clo. Roms 2B 130
Woodley Clo. Flats. Roms 2B 130
Woodley Gdns. L'ton 1D 234
Woodley Grange. Roms 3B 130
Woodley La. Roms. 4N 129
Woodley Rd. Gos 3L 239
Woodley Rd. Sotn 7B 174
Woodleys. Ecc 5G 9
Woodley Way. Roms 2B 130
Woodling Cres. Gods 9N 151
Wood Lodge. Cal 1H 171
Woodman Clo. Spar 4B 104
Woodmancote Rd. S'sea 3H 241
Woodmancott. 4A 78
Woodman Ct. Fle 3L 47
Woodmanfield. Upt G 3B 62
Woodman La. Spar 3B 104
Woodmere Cft. Bas 3H 59
Woodmill La. Sotn 8B 160
Wood Moor. Finch 3J 17
Woodmoor Clo. March 9F 172
Wood Pk. Lud 1E 30
Woodpath. S'sea 4D 240
Woodpath Ho. S'sea 4D 240
Woodpecker Clo. Bas 2H 59
Woodpecker Clo. Bord 5J 101
Woodpecker Clo. Ews 2N 63 (off Badger Way)
Woodpecker Clo. Hav 8H 203
Woodpecker Copse. L Hth 6E 196
Woodpecker Dri. March 9D 172
Woodpeckers Dri. Win 4G 105
Woodpecker Way. Eastl 1B 160
Woodrisings, The. Bourn 1H 245 (5H 247)
Wood Rd. Asht 8H 171
Wood Rd. Cam 3K 29
Wood Rd. F'ham 3E 64
Wood Rd. Hind 1M 103
Woodroffe Dri. Bas 1L 59
Woodroffe Wlk. Ems 5M 203
Wood Row. Bourn 2A 228
Woodrow. Water 6F 180
Woodruff Clo. Christ 6E 230
Woodrush Cres. L Hth 7B 196
Woodsedge. Water 3A 202
Woodside. 4E 234 (Lymington)
Woodside. 9L 155 (Southampton)
Woodside. B'wtr 2E 28
Woodside. Cam 6H 19
Woodside. Chilw 1K 159
Woodside. Farn 5K 29
Woodside. Gos 3D 212
Woodside. S'sea 4D 240
Woodside Av. Eastl 9C 132
Woodside Av. L'ton 5E 234
Woodside Clo. Bord 4J 101
Woodside Clo. L'ton 4E 234
Woodside Clo. March 9D 172
Woodside Ct. Sotn 2N 173
Woodside Cres. Bord 4J 101
Woodside Cres. Chilw 1J 159
Woodside Gdns. Asht 7J 171
Woodside Gdns. Chine 8H 23
Woodside Gdns. Fle 2A 48
Woodside La. Farr 3A 98
Woodside La. L'ton 4E 234
Woodside Pk. Bord 4J 101
Woodside Rd. Bourn 1E 246
Woodside Rd. Eastl 8C 132
Woodside Rd. Farn 4H 49
Woodside Rd. F'ham 3G 65
Woodside Rd. N Bad 8E 130
Woodside Rd. Poole 2A 244
Woodside Rd. Sotn 2N 173
Woodside Way. H End 5L 175
Woods La. Clid 3N 59
Woods La. Grey 7F 44
Woodstock Av. Water 5A 182
Woodstock Clo. Fare 8A 198
Woodstock Clo. H End 5A 176
Woodstock Dri. Sotn 1M 173
Woodstock La. Ring 1K 187
Woodstock Mead. Bas 4K 59
Woodstock Rd. Burt 4N 229
Woodstock Rd. Gos 4L 239
Woodstock Rd. Hav 7C 202
Woodstocks. Farn 6L 29
Woods Vw. Rd. Bourn 6H 227
Woodthorpe Gdns. Sar G 3C 196
Woodvale. Fare 7N 197
Woodvale Gdns. New M 2D 232
Woodview Clo. Sotn 5M 159
Woodview Pk. Cvn. Pk. Curd 3F 176
Woodville Clo. B'wtr 8D 18
Woodville Clo. Chine 9G 22
Woodville Dri. Ports 4C 240 (7L 5)
Woodville La. Chine 1G 42
Woodville Ri. Chine 1G 42
Woodville Rd. Fawl 5F 208
Woodville Rd. Hav 7B 202
Wood Wlk. R'dll 7B 20
Woodward Clo. Gos 3H 239
Wood Way. Cam 8K 19
Woodyates. 1F 148
Woofferton Rd. Ports 8B 200
Woolbury Camp. 2J 89
Wooldridge Cres. Odi 2E 62
Woolfield La. Frox 2B 138
Woolford Clo. Win 8G 105
Woolford Way. Bas 5M 41
Wool Gro. And 2B 70
Woolley Ho. Sotn 4E 4
Woolley Sq. And 7B 52
Woolmead Rd. F'ham 7E 64
Woolmead, The. F'ham 7E 64
Woolmead Wlk. F'ham 7E 64 (off Woolmead Rd.)
Woolmer Ct. Hav 4H 203
Woolmer Hill. 8L 103
Woolmer Hill Rd. Hasl 7L 103
Woolmer La. Blash 7K 185
Woolmer La. B'shtt 6C 102 (in two parts)
Woolmer Pond Nature Reserve. 2G 114
Woolmer Rd. Gthm 2F 114
Woolmer St. Ems 5L 203
Woolmer Trad. Est. Bord 4H 101
Woolmer Vw. Gray 4M 103
Woolmer Way. Bord 5H 101
Woolner Av. Ptsfld 9M 139
Woolner Av. Ports 9H 201
Woolsbridge Rd. Ashy H & St L 2C 186
Woolston. 8C 174
Woolston Ct. Gos 4G 238
Woolston Rd. Hav 3C 202
Woolston Rd. Net A 1F 194
Woolton Hill. 2A 8
Woolton Lodge Gdns. Wool H 2A 8
Woolverton. Win 5H 105
Woolwich Clo. Burs 9K 175
Wooteys Way. Alt 3F 80
Wootton. 5B 222
Wootton. Net A 2G 195
Wootton Clo. Woot L 4H 41
Wootton Farm Rd. New M 5N 221
Wootton Gdns. Bourn 2L 245 (6N 247)
Wootton La. Up Wn & Woot L 2E 40
Wootton Mt. Bourn 2L 245 (6N 247)
Wootton Rd. Lee S 3C 238
Wootton Rd. Tip 7D 222
Wootton Rough. New M 7C 222
Wootton St Lawrence. 4G 40
Wootton St. Ports 1G 214
Worbarrow Gdns. Poole 6A 226
Worcester Av. Bas 3K 59
Worcester Clo. Farn 5K 29
Worcester Clo. S'sea 3E 240
Worcester Ct. Gos 1E 238
Worcester Pl. L'ton 4F 234
Worcester Pl. Sotn 8F 174
Wordsworth Av. Bourn 5B 228
Wordsworth Av. Ports 8N 199
Wordsworth Av. Yate 8L 17
Wordsworth Clo. Bas 3D 42
Wordsworth Clo. Bish W 3A 164
Wordsworth Clo. Win 6H 105
Wordsworth Pl. White 9F 176
Wordsworth Rd. Sotn 1H 173
Workhouse La. E Meon 3L 143
Workman's La. Wars 2B 210
Workshop Rd. S'wick 7B 200
Worldham Hill. E Wor 7M 81
Worldham Pk. Golf Course. 6J 81
Worldham Rd. Hav 3H 203
Worlds End. 6B 180
Worrell Dri. Poole 6A 226
Worrell Sq. And 7B 52 (off Cricketers Way)
Worsley Rd. Frim 4N 29
Worsley Rd. S'sea 4D 240 (8N 5)
Worsley St. S'sea 5H 241
Worthing Av. Gos 8H 213
Worthing Rd. S'sea 5E 240
Worthy Ct. Hav 4H 203 (in two parts)
Worthy La. Win 5K 105
Worthy Rd. New M 3B 232
Worthy Rd. Win 5L 105
Worting. 7J 41
Worting Rd. Bas 7M 41
Worting Rd. Okly & Bas 8E 40
Worting Rd. Roundabout. Bas 7L 41
Wortley Rd. Highc 7J 231
Wote St. Bas 7C 42
Wouldham Clo. Per D 4B 30
Wraysbury Pk. Dri. Ems 5M 203
Wrecclesham Hill. Wrec 7N 63
Wrekin Clo. Bas 8K 41
Wrekin, The. Farn 2N 49
Wren Cen., The. Ems 6N 203
Wren Clo. Alt 3G 80
Wren Clo. Christ 9D 230
Wren Clo. Hight 2M 187
Wren Clo. New M 4A 232
Wren Clo. Win 9H 105
Wren Clo. Yate 7L 17
Wren Cres. Poole 9E 226
Wren Gdns. A'hlt 4E 152
Wren Rd. Eastl 2C 160
Wren Way. Fare 9H 199
Wren Way. Farn 5H 29
Wrexham Gro. Water 8B 168
Wright Clo. White 3J 197
Wrights Clo. S Won 3H 91 (in two parts)
Wright's Hill. Sotn 8E 174
Wrights La. Butt & Combe 3G 6
Wrights Wlk. Burs 9K 175
Wrights Way. S Won 3H 91
Wright Way. Fawl 7J 209
Wroxham Rd. Poole 9D 226
Wryneck Clo. Sotn 5F 158
Wulwyn Ct. C'then 1B 18
Wyborn Clo. Hay I 5G 243
Wych La. Gos 4D 212
Wychwood Clo. Bourn 1J 245
Wychwood Dri. Black 1J 237 (off Kings Ride)
Wychwood Dri. Black 9C 208 (West Comn.)
Wychwood Dri. Bourn 9K 227
Wychwood Grange. Bourn 9K 227
Wychwood Gro. Chan F 4C 132
Wyck. 4A 82
Wyck La. E Wor 3N 81 (in two parts)
Wycliffe Rd. Bourn 6K 227
Wycliffe Rd. Sotn 1E 174
Wycote Rd. Gos 4D 212
Wye Ct. And 8B 52
Wyeford Ct. Hav 3H 203
Wykeham Av. Ports 7F 214
Wykeham Clo. Net A 3F 194
Wykeham Clo. Sotn 7K 159
Wykeham Ct. Odi 2E 62
Wykeham Dri. Bas 7J 41
Wykeham Fld. Wick 7C 178
Wykeham Ind. Est., The. Win 4N 105 (in two parts)
Wykeham Pl. L'ton 3E 234
Wykeham Pl. Win 8H 105
Wykeham Rd. F'ham 7E 64
Wykeham Rd. Net A 3F 194
Wykeham Rd. Ports 7F 214
Wykwood. Lip 2F 116
Wyld Grn. La. Liss 9F 114
Wylds La. West 4J 145
Wyllie Rd. Ports 4F 214
Wylye Clo. W End 8F 160
Wylye Rd. Tidw 8D 30
Wymering. 8D 200
Wymering Ct. Farn 9M 29
Wymering La. Ports 9F 200
Wymering Mnr. Clo. Ports 9E 200
Wymering Rd. Ports 8F 214
Wyncombe Rd. Bourn 9E 228
Wyndcliffe Rd. S'sea 4F 240
Wyndham Clo. Walk 4K 231
Wyndham Clo. Water 6B 182
Wyndham Clo. Yate 6N 17
Wyndham Ct. Sotn 5K 173 (3A 4)
Wyndham La. All 7D 66
Wyndham M. Ports 4B 240 (7K 5)
Wyndham Pl. Sotn 5K 173 (3A 4)
Wyndham Rd. And 3L 69
Wyndham Rd. St M 9N 35
Wyndham Rd. Walk 4K 231
Wyndham St. A'sht 1L 65
Wynford Ind. Pk. Roms 9M 123
Wynford Rd. Bourn 2L 227
Wynford Rd. Poole 2A 244
Wynne Gdns. Chu C 6N 47
Wyn Sutcliffe Ct. S'sea 4H 241
Wynter Clo. Bourn 7C 228
Wynter Rd. Sotn 2F 174
Wynton Way. Fare 6M 197
Wynyards Gap. N Bad 8E 130
Wyre Clo. Chan F 6N 131
Wyvern Clo. Chan F 6B 132
Wyvern Clo. Poole 7B 226
Wyvern Rd. Bulf B 3B 66

Y

Yaldhurst Ct. Hav 3H 203
Yaldhurst La. Penn 2B 234
Yale Clo. Owl 3H 19
Yapton St. Ports 2D 240 (3N 5)
Yarborough Rd. S'sea 4D 240 (8N 5)
Yardlea Clo. Row C 9H 183
Yardley Clo. Ports 4K 215
Yardley Rd. H End 5M 175
Yarmley La. W'slw 5G 87
Yarmouth Clo. Poole 9E 226
Yarmouth Gdns. Sotn 1G 172
Yarmouth Rd. Poole 8D 226
Yarnhams Clo. Four M 5J 97
Yarrell Mead. Penn 2B 234
Yarrow Clo. Christ 6D 230
Yarrow Way. L Hth 7B 196
Yateley. 7N 17
Yateley Cen. Yate 7M 17
Yateley Clo. Hav 4C 202
Yateley Common Country Pk. 1N 27
Yateley Dri. E'sly 3H 27
Yateley Rd. S'hrst 5B 18
Yaverland. Net A 3G 195
Yellowhammer Rd. Bas 3H 59
Yellow Hammers. Alt 2F 80
Yelverton Av. Hythe 8M 193
Yelverton Rd. Bourn 2K 245 (6L 247)
Yeo Ct. S'sea 3K 241
Yeoman Ind. Pk. Sotn 9A 158
Yeoman Pk. Sotn 1B 172
Yeomans. E'sly 6H 17
Yeomans Clo. Farn 7J 29
Yeomans Ind. Pk. Bourn 3B 228
Yeomans La. Lip 2C 116
Yeomans La. New 2E 8
Yeomans Pl. Head 2A 102
Yeomans Rd. Bourn 4A 228
Yeomans Way. Bourn 4B 228
Yeomans Way. Cam 8N 19
Yeomans Way. Tot 2M 171
Yeosfield. Rise 2G 14
Yeovil Chase. Sotn 2F 174
Yeovil Clo. Farn 2M 49
Yeovil Rd. Farn 2N 49
Yeovil Rd. Owl 4F 18
Yeovilton Clo. Evtn 5M 233
Yerville Gdns. Hord 3G 233
Yetminster Rd. Farn 2M 49
Yewberry Way. Chan F 6K 131
Yew Clo. K're 2C 6
Yew Hill. 3E 126
Yew La. New M 2D 232
Yew Rd. Sotn 2E 174
Yewside. Gos 6F 212
Yews, The. Horn 3D 182
Yew Tree Av. Cowp 8B 182
Yew Tree Clo. Braml 2H 23
Yew Tree Clo. F Oak 9N 133
Yew Tree Clo. Farn 9E 28
Yew Tree Clo. Good C 8N 69
Yew Tree Clo. H End 4M 175
Yewtree Clo. Hythe 9M 193
Yew Tree Clo. Okly 2D 58
Yew Tree Clo. W'slw 5G 87
Yew Tree Ct. F'bri 2H 153
Yew Tree Ct. New M 5C 232
Yew Tree Ct. Swanw 2E 196
Yew Tree Ct. W End 1J 175
Yew Tree Dri. White 2E 196
Yew Tree Gdns. Den 6F 180
Yewtree La. Nurs 8B 158
Yew Tree Pl. Liss 1F 140
Yew Tree Rd. Hay I 8G 216
Yew Tree Rd. N Wal 9A 58
Yew Tree Wlk. Frim 3N 29
Yoells Cres. Water 4N 181
Yoells La. Water 4N 181
Yokesford Hill. Roms 8L 123
Yokesford Hill Est. Roms 8M 123
Yolland Clo. F'ham 3E 64
Yonge Clo. Eastl 9F 132
York Av. New M 3C 232
York Bldgs. Sotn 6M 173 (6D 4) (in two parts)
York Clo. Bas 2K 59
York Clo. Chan F 8L 131
York Clo. Christ 7J 229
York Clo. H Hth 4A 162
York Clo. Ptsfld 1K 145
York Clo. Sotn 4A 174
York Clo. Tot 2N 171
York Clo. W'hill 5J 101
York Ct. And 7N 51
York Cres. A'sht 1H 65
York Cres. Lee S 3C 238
York Drove. Nom 2J 155
York Drove. Sotn 3F 174
Yorke St. S'sea 3C 240 (6M 5)
Yorke Way. Hamb 6J 195
York Gdns. Fare 2N 213
York Ga. Sotn 6M 173 (6D 4)
York Ho. Bas 8N 41
York Ho. Gos 3M 239
York Ho. Sotn 4A 174
York La. H Win 7B 26
York M. Alt 4G 80
York Pl. Bourn 9D 228
York Pl. New M 3C 232
York Pl. Ports 1C 240 (3L 5)
York Rd. A'sht 1H 65
York Rd. Bourn 1M 245
York Rd. Cam 6M 19
York Rd. Eastl 3E 160
York Rd. Farn 2L 49
York Rd. F'ham 9E 64
York Rd. Net A 3E 194
York Rd. Sotn 3H 173
York Ter. Ports 3G 214
York Ter. La. Cam 8J 19
York Town. 8J 19
York Town Ind. Est. Cam 9J 19
Yorktown Rd. S'hrst & Coll T 5C 18
York Wlk. Sotn 6M 173 (6D 4)
York Way. S'hrst 5D 18
Yorkwood. Liss 1E 140
Youngbridge Ct. Fare 1C 212
Young's Ind. Est. A'mstn 1F 10
Youngs Paddock. W'slw 5H 87 (off Saxon Leas)
Youngs Rd. Alt 4F 80
Youngs Rd. Bourn 1E 226
Yves M. S'sea 5E 240

Z

Zamek Clo. Bourn 1E 226
Zebra Rd. Ows 7B 134
Zetland Ct. Bourn 4F 244
Zetland Path. Ports 1L 215
Zetland Rd. Gos 2K 239
Zetland Rd. Ports 1L 215
Zeus La. Water 6N 201
Zig-Zag Wlk. Bourn 3L 245 (off E. Overcliffe Dri.)
Zinnia Clo. Bas 4J 59
Zinnia Clo. Bourn 4J 227
Zion Rd. Pale 6J 67
Zouch Av. Tidw 7C 30
Zouch Clo. Tidw 7C 30
Zouch Farm Rd. Tidw 7C 30
Zouch Mkt. Tidw 7C 30
Zurich Cen., The. White 2H 197

HOSPITALS and HOSPICES
covered by this atlas.

N.B. Where Hospitals and Hospices are not named on the map, the reference
given is for the road in which they are situated.

ALDERNEY COMMUNITY HOSPITAL —5A **226**
Ringwood Rd.
POOLE
Dorset
BH12 4NB
Tel: 01202 735537

ALTON COMMUNITY HOSPITAL —7D **80**
Chawton Pk. Rd.
ALTON
Hampshire
GU34 1RJ
Tel: 01420 82811

ANDOVER WAR MEMORIAL COMMUNITY HOSPITAL
—9L **51**
Charlton Rd.
ANDOVER
Hampshire
SP10 3LB
Tel: 01264 358811

BLACKBROOK HOUSE MATERNITY HOME —8A **198**
Blackbrook Ho. Dri.
FAREHAM
Hampshire
PO14 1PA
Tel: 01329 232275

BOURNEMOUTH NUFFIELD HOSPITAL, THE —9L **227**
67-71 Lansdowne Rd.
BOURNEMOUTH
BH1 1RW
Tel: 01202 291866

BROADMOOR HOSPITAL —1F **18**
Lwr. Broadmoor Rd.
CROWTHORNE
Berkshire
RG45 7EG
Tel: 01344 773111

CHALYBEATE (BUPA) HOSPITAL —9H **159**
Chalybeate Clo.
SOUTHAMPTON
SO16 6UY
Tel: 023 80 775544

CHASE HOSPITAL —5J **101**
Conde Way
BORDON
Hampshire
GU35 0YZ
Tel: 01420 488801

CHRISTCHURCH HOSPITAL —6J **229**
Fairmile Rd.
CHRISTCHURCH
Dorset
BH23 2JX
Tel: 01202 486361

CLARE PARK BUPA HOSPITAL —4M **63**
Crondall La., Clare Park
FARNHAM
Surrey
GU10 5XX
Tel: 01252 850216

COUNTESS MOUNTBATTEN HOSPICE —9J **161**
Moor Green Hospital, Botley Rd.
SOUTHAMPTON
SO30 3JB
Tel: 023 80 477414

COUNTESS OF BRECKNOCK HOUSE (HOSPICE) —9L **51**
Andover War Memorial Hospital
Charlton Rd.
ANDOVER
Hampshire
SP10 3LB
Tel: 01264 835288

DERWENT HOSPITAL —5E **228**
Castle La. E.
BOURNEMOUTH
BH7 7DR
Tel: 01202 390999

FARNHAM COMMUNITY HOSPITAL —7G **64**
Hale Rd.
FARNHAM
Surrey
GU9 9QL
Tel: 01483 782000

FENWICK HOSPITAL —1A **148**
Pikes Hill
LYNDHURST
Hampshire
SO43 7NG
Tel: 023 80 282782

FLEET COMMUNITY HOSPITAL —1K **47**
Church Rd.
FLEET
Hampshire
GU13 8LD
Tel: 01483 782000

FORDINGBRIDGE HOSPITAL —1J **153**
Bartons Rd.
FORDINGBRIDGE
Hampshire
SP6 1JD
Tel: 014525 652255

FRIMLEY PARK HOSPITAL —2M **29**
Portsmouth Rd.
Frimley
CAMBERLEY
Surrey
GU16 5UJ
Tel: 01276 604604

GOSPORT WAR MEMORIAL HOSPITAL —3J **239**
Bury Rd.
GOSPORT
Hampshire
PO12 3PW
Tel: 0123 92 524611

HAMPSHIRE BMI CLINIC —5F **42**
Basing Rd.
BASINGSTOKE
Hampshire
RG24 7AL
Tel: 01256 357111

HAVANT WAR MEMORIAL HOSPITAL —7E **202**
59 Crossway
HAVANT
Hampshire
PO9 1NG
Tel: 023 92 484256

HERBERT HOSPITAL —3F **244**
Alumhurst Rd.
BOURNEMOUTH
BH4 8EP
Tel: 01202 765323

HOLY CROSS HOSPITAL —8N **103**
Hindhead Rd.
HASLEMERE
Surrey
GU27 1NQ
Tel: 01428 643311

HYTHE HOSPITAL —7M **193**
Beaulieu Rd.
SOUTHAMPTON
SO45 4ZB
Tel: 023 80 846046

KING'S PARK COMMUNITY HOSPITAL —9C **228**
Gloucester Rd.
BOURNEMOUTH
BH7 6JE
Tel: 01202 303757

LEIGH HOUSE HOSPITAL —4A **132**
Cuckoo Bushes La.
EASTLEIGH
Hampshire
SO53 1JY
Tel: 023 80 252418

LEWIS MANNING HOSPICE —6A **244**
1 Crichel Mt. Rd.
POOLE
Dorset
BH14 8LT
Tel: 01202 708470

LYMINGTON HOSPITAL —2D **234**
Southampton Rd.
LYMINGTON
Hampshire
SO41 9ZH
Tel: 01590 677011

LYMINGTON INFIRMARY —2E **234**
East Hill
LYMINGTON
Hampshire
SO41 9ZJ
Tel: 01590 676081

MARCHWOOD PRIORY HOSPITAL —2F **192**
Hythe Rd.
SOUTHAMPTON
SO40 4WU
Tel: 023 80 840044

MEDICAL RECEPTION STATION HOSPITAL —5J **19**
Royal Military Academy, The, Egerton Rd.
CAMBERLEY
Surrey
GU15 4PH
Tel: 01276 412234

MILFORD-ON-SEA WAR MEMORIAL HOSPITAL —8L **235**
Sea Rd., Milford-on-Sea
LYMINGTON
Hampshire
SO41 0PG
Tel: 01590 648100

MOORGREEN HOSPITAL —9K **161**
Botley Rd.
SOUTHAMPTON
SO30 3JB
Tel: 023 80 475400

MOUNT HOSPITAL, THE —7H **133**
Church Rd.
EASTLEIGH
Hampshire
SO50 6ZB
Tel: 023 80 612335

NAOMI HOUSE (WESSEX CHILDREN'S HOSPICE) —7C **76**
Stockbridge Rd., Sutton Scotney
WINCHESTER
Hampshire
SO21 3JE
Tel: 01962 760060

NORTH HAMPSHIRE HOSPITAL —3N **41**
Aldermaston Rd.
BASINGSTOKE
Hampshire
RG24 9NA
Tel: 01256 473202

OAKHAVEN HOSPICE —5D **234**
Lwr. Pennington La.
LYMINGTON
Hampshire
SO41 8ZZ
Tel: 01590 670346

ODIHAM COTTAGE HOSPITAL —9L **45**
Buryfields, Odiham
HOOK
Hampshire
RG29 1NE
Tel: 01256 393600

PARKLANDS HOSPITAL —2M **41**
Aldermaston Rd.
BASINGSTOKE
Hampshire
RG24 9RH
Tel: 01256 817718

PETERSFIELD COMMUNITY HOSPITAL —1L **145**
Swan St.
PETERSFIELD
Hampshire
GU32 3LB
Tel: 023 80 263221

PHYLLIS TUCKWELL HOSPICE —9G **64**
Waverley La.
FARNHAM
Surrey
GU9 8BL
Tel: 01252 729400

PORTSMOUTH BUPA HOSPITAL —4K **203**
Bartons Rd.
HAVANT
Hampshire
PO9 5NP
Tel: 023 92 456000

PRINCESS ANNE HOSPITAL —8G **159**
Coxford Rd.
SOUTHAMPTON
SO16 5YA
Tel: 023 80 777222

QUEEN ALEXANDRA HOSPITAL —9G **200**
Southwick Hill Rd.
Cosham
PORTSMOUTH
PO6 3LY
Tel: 023 92 286000

RAVENSWOOD HOUSE —1A **198**
River La.
FAREHAM
Hampshire
PO17 5NA
Tel: 01329 836000

ROMSEY HOSPITAL —4N **129**
Winchester Hill
ROMSEY
Hampshire
SO51 7ZA
Tel: 01794 512343

ROWANS HOSPICE, THE —5J **201**
Purbrook Heath Rd.
Purbrook
WATERLOOVILLE
Hampshire
PO7 5RU
Tel: 023 92 250001

ROYAL BOURNEMOUTH HOSPITAL —5E **228**
Castle La. E.
BOURNEMOUTH
BH7 7DW
Tel: 01202 303626

ROYAL HAMPSHIRE COUNTY HOSPITAL
—7J **105** (8H **237**)
Romsey Rd.
WINCHESTER
Hampshire
SO22 5DG
Tel: 01962 863535

ROYAL HOSPITAL HASLAR —5M **239**
Haslar Rd.
GOSPORT
Hampshire
PO12 2AA
Tel: 023 92 584255

ROYAL SOUTH HANTS HOSPITAL —4M **173** (1E **4**)
Graham Rd.
SOUTHAMPTON
SO14 0YG
Tel: 023 80 634288

ST ANN'S HOSPITAL —7C **244**
69 Haven Rd.
POOLE
Dorset
BH13 7LN
Tel: 01202 708881

ST CHRISTOPHER'S HOSPITAL —6D **198**
Wickham Rd.
FAREHAM
Hampshire
PO16 7JD
Tel: 01329 286321

ST GEORGE'S HOSPITAL —8J **235**
Whitby Rd., Milford on Sea
LYMINGTON
Hampshire
SO41 0NE
Tel: 01590 643011

ST JAMES HOSPITAL —2K **241**
Locksway Rd.
SOUTHSEA
Hampshire
PO4 8LD
Tel: 023 92 822444

ST MARY'S HOSPITAL —1G **241**
Milton Rd.
PORTSMOUTH
PO3 6AD
Tel: 023 92 286000

ST MICHAEL'S HOSPICE —2N **41**
Park Prewett, Aldermaston Rd.
BASINGSTOKE
Hampshire
RG24 9NB
Tel: 01256 844744

ST WALERIC —4L **105**
Park Rd.
WINCHESTER
Hampshire
SO23 7BE
Tel: 01962 841941

SARUM ROAD B.M.I. HOSPITAL —7G **105**
Sarum Rd.
WINCHESTER
Hampshire
SO22 5HA
Tel: 01962 844555

SOUTHAMPTON GENERAL HOSPITAL —8G **159**
Tremona Rd.
SOUTHAMPTON
SO16 6YD
Tel: 023 80 777222

TATCHBURY MOUNT —9G **157**
Tatchbury Mt.
SOUTHAMPTON
SO40 2RZ
Tel: 023 80 874000

VICTORIA COTTAGE HOSPITAL —9M **203**
North St.
EMSWORTH
Hampshire
PO10 7DD
Tel: 01243 376041

WESSEX NUFFIELD HOSPITAL —3E **132**
Winchester Rd.
EASTLEIGH
Hampshire
SO53 2DW
Tel: 023 80 266377

WESTERN COMMUNITY HOSPITAL —1E **172**
Walnut Gro.
SOUTHAMPTON
SO16 4XE
Tel: 023 80 475401